PENGUIN BOOKS

The New Penguin Guide to the Law

A solicitor, John Pritchard is the best-known commentator on the law in the UK. He is editor in chief of the *Legal 500* (described by *The Times* as 'the bible of the legal profession') and of various other publications from his company Legalease, including the *Practical Lawyer*, the *Property Law Journal*, *European Legal Business* and *Lawyer International*. He also has, in the *International Center for Commercial Law* (www.icclaw.com), one of the largest legal sites on the internet.

The New Penguin Guide to the Law

FIFTH EDITION

Chief Editor John Pritchard
Editor Laura Morrison

With Contributions by
Stuart Baker, Paul Butt, John Cahill, Leslie Carr, Shami
Chakrabarti, Lawrence Davies, Paul Elmhirst, Murray
Fairclough, Philippa Grant, Ashley Holmes, Helen
Howard, Peter Madge, John Moore, Laura Morrison,
Louise Spitz, Stuart Toll, John Wadham (and Liberty
with Doughty Street Chambers).

PENGUIN BOOKS

To Mary, who helped (and to Tom, Sam, Bex and Hil – who didn't)

PENGUIN BOOKS

Published by the Penguin Group
Penguin Books Ltd, 80 Strand, London WC2R ORL, England
Penguin Group (USA) Inc., 375 Hudson Street, New York, New York 10014, USA
Penguin Books Australia Ltd, 250 Camberwell Road, Camberwell, Victoria 3124, Australia
Penguin Books Canada Ltd, 10 Alcorn Avenue, Toronto, Ontario, Canada M4V 3B2
Penguin Books India (P) Ltd, 11 Community Centre, Panchsheel Park, New Delhi – 110 017, India
Penguin Group (NZ), cnr Airborne and Rosedale Roads, Albany, Auckland 1310, New Zealand
Penguin Books (South Africa) (Pty) Ltd, 24 Sturdee Avenue, Rosebank 2196, South Africa

Penguin Books Ltd, Registered Offices: 80 Strand, London WC2R ORL, England

www.penguin.com

First published in Penguin Books 1982
Second edition 1986
Third edition published by Viking 1992
Published in Penguin Books 1993
Fourth edition 2001
Fifth edition 2004
2

Copyright © John Pritchard, 1982, 1986, 1992, 2001, 2005
All rights reserved

The moral right of the editors and contributors has been asserted

Set in in Linotype Minion and The Sans
Typeset by Rowland Phototypesetting Ltd, Bury St Edmunds, Suffolk
Printed in Finland by WS Bookwell

Contents

Part One

THE FAMILY

Part Four

EMPLOYMENT
Murray Fairclough and Lawrence Davies

Part Five

THE CONSUMER
Ashley Holmes

Part Six

INSOLVENCY
Peter Madge and John Moore

Part Seven

BUSINESS
John Moore and Philippa Grant

Business Start-ups

Running the Business

Relationships with Outsiders

Ending the Business

Part Eight

MOTORING
Stuart Baker

The Driver

The Vehicle

Accidents

Prosecution and Penalties

Part Nine

PERSONAL INJURY
John Cahill

The Theory

Practice

Part Ten

CIVIL LIBERTIES AND HUMAN RIGHTS
John Wadham/Liberty,
Doughty Street Chambers and Shami Chakrabarti

Part Eleven

THE ENGLISH LEGAL SYSTEM
Laura Morrison

Part Twelve

LEGAL JARGON

APPENDIX AND INDEXES

Information about the Contributing Authors

The Family

Helen Howard is a family mediator and lawyer based at Richard Howard & Co. in London and Oxford. She writes, trains and broadcasts regularly on family mediation and family law issues.

Louise Spitz is a partner specializing in family law at Manches, a leading firm in the private family law field. She served on the Law Society Family Law Committee for a number of years dealing with pensions and high-value cases. In 2003 she was appointed a Deputy District Judge of the Principal Registry of the Family Division.

Death

Paul Elmhirst has spent 30 years in general practice as a solicitor dealing with the practical issues of wills and probate. He has revised the *Which? Guide to Wills and Probate*.

Housing

Paul Butt is associate professor at the College of Law, Chester, and has over 20 years of experience in lecturing to the profession on conveyancing and landlord and tenant matters.

Welfare Benefits and Tax Credits

Stuart Toll is a social security specialist working for the National Association of Citizens' Advice Bureaux (CABx). He staffs a national telephone consultancy for CABx, providing tactical advice, written follow-up and representation.

Leslie Carr is the Welfare Benefits Law Supervisor at Lambeth Law Centre in Brixton, South London. He has over 20 years' experience of advising and representing his clients at Appeal Tribunals and with appeals to the Social Security Commissioners.

Employment

Murray Fairclough, LLM, PhD, Barrister, is Head of Legal Services for Abbey Legal Protection Ltd. Murray has over 15 years' experience as a specialist employment lawyer, working both in-house and in private practice.

Lawrence Davies has 10 years' experience as a specialist discrimination lawyer and heads up the employment department at Imran Khan & Partners. He is chair of the Employment Law Practitioners' Association.

The Consumer

Ashley Holmes was formerly Head of Legal Affairs at the Consumers' Association. He is a member of the Civil Justice Council, the Community Legal Service Quality Taskforce and the DETR's House Transfer Advisory Group and is the Director of TrustUK (the DTI-backed accreditation body for online codes of practice).

Insolvency

Peter Madge works for the National Association of Citizens' Advice Bureaux at its Specialist Support Unit, providing advice and training on debt and related issues.

Business

John Moore spent eight years as a solicitor in private practice specializing in property law before becoming manager of the Commercial Unit at Abbey Legal Protection Ltd, providing advice on all areas of law to members of trade associations and small and medium-sized businesses.

Philippa Grant is a solicitor and Commercial Legal

Adviser at the Legal Services Centre of Abbey Legal Protection Ltd. Philippa's 11 years of legal experience has mainly been gained in private practice in East Sussex, where she acquired specialist knowledge of banking litigation.

Motoring

Stuart Baker is a barrister who has worked for the Magistrates' Court Service for 27 years. Stuart has contributed to a number of legal textbooks, including *Oakes Magisterial Formulist* and *Stones' Justices' Manual*, and has also collaborated on some of the standard works for the Courts Service, the *Police and Magistrates' Courts Act* and *Endorsement Disqualification* for Bazell.

Personal Injury

John Cahill is a founding partner of Stewarts solicitors based at Lincoln's Inn Fields, London. He heads the personal injury and clinical negligence group at Stewarts and supervises brain and spinal injury claims.

Civil Liberties and Human Rights

John Wadham is a solicitor and the former Director of Liberty (the National Council for Civil Liberties). He has acted for large numbers of applicants in cases before the European Commission and European Court of Human Rights.

The Civil Liberties and Human Rights section of the book was put together with the help of Anna Edmundson and the team of lawyers for Liberty at Doughty Street Chambers – Paul Bogan, Hugh Barton, Nadine Finch, Sadakat Kadri, Robert Latham, Jacky Lule, Anthony Metzer, Nick Paul, Aswini Weereratne, Quincy Whittaker and Ashami Chakrabarti.

Shami Chakrabarti is director of Liberty and a governor of the British Institute of Human Rights. A qualified barrister, Shami worked in the Home Office Legal Adviser's Branch from 1996 on a range of human rights issues relating to asylum, immigration and criminal policy. She became Liberty's in-house counsel in September 2001 and spent much of the next two years writing and speaking about the UK's anti-terror laws. She became Liberty's director in September 2003.

The English Legal System

Solicitor, legal research specialist and journalist, Laura Morrison is the former editor of the *Family Law Journal* and writes for a range of publications for the legal profession including the *In-House Lawyer*, the *Practical Lawyer* and the *UK Legal 500*.

Acknowledgements

Thanks to the Terrence Higgins Trust, and King's College, London for allowing us to reproduce their Living Will and to D. J. Freeman for their assistance in compiling the Legal Jargon section.

Introduction

This book cannot tell you all the law. No one knows all the law, not even the most eminent judge – and certainly not me!

The law is as huge as it is indefinable. Suffice to say that it is impossible to compress more than just a smattering of knowledge into a book of this size. All I can do is to try to extract those parts of the law that seem – to me – to be most relevant and useful to the general reader. So if you see this book as a substitute for the considered advice of a solicitor or barrister, think again.

What a guide of this sort can do is to introduce the reader to the complexities of the law, to remove some of the mysteries that shroud it, and to give an overall view of the law. I hope that information will be sufficient to enable readers to identify the legal element in a problem and to point them in the right direction towards solving that problem.

Finally, two cautionary notes. First, the law changes quickly and any part of this book might be out of date when you read it, so do not treat what is written here as being gospel truth. Secondly, remember that 'a little knowledge can be a dangerous thing'. This book presents a condensed view of the law and it may be that the details which have been omitted are crucial in deciding the answer to your particular legal problem. If in doubt, take legal advice.

The law as described here is up to date to October 2003. It applies only in England and Wales, since Scotland and Northern Ireland have their own laws.

John Pritchard, October 2003

Introduction

As fast as commentators write about family law, both the law and the society within which the law operates change and evolve once again. The following chapters look at law and the family at the beginning of the twenty-first century and are up to date as at the time of going to press. Given the pace of change, it would be wise to check with a family lawyer or the Citizens' Advice Bureaux to see if any other changes have come into being which would affect your own individual position.

Living Together

An increasing number of heterosexual couples are living together without first going up the aisle. Their motives for so doing of course vary. Some couples choose cohabitation as a form of trial marriage, intending to wed if the relationship withstands the test of intimate everyday domesticity; others make a positive long-term commitment to live and bring up children together free from the traditional marital bond.

The law has thus far avoided coming to terms with the consequences of this alternative family form. Even if the couple live together for years, the law does not provide any special protection for a 'common-law' wife if the relationship later fails, although if there are dependent children of the relationship they will be entitled to financial help. Changes and the introduction of greater rights for cohabiting couples whose relationship breaks down have been mooted, but to date no comprehensive laws have made it to the statute books to deal with the financial consequences of relationship breakdown.

THERE IS NO SUCH THING AS A COMMON-LAW MARRIAGE

In England and Wales common-law marriages were legally abolished over 250 years ago, although the term continues to be popularly used. A woman whose cohabitation ends is usually in a much worse position legally than her married sister on divorce. (This is not the case north of the Border, where couples who live together for a long time are treated by Scottish law as if they were married: 'marriage by custom and repute'.)

There are three particular areas where the English cohabitant is seriously disadvantaged:
1 She cannot claim maintenance for herself (although she can of course claim maintenance for any children).
2 She has fewer rights over the family home:
   • unless she is the owner of the home (or joint owner) she can be evicted by her partner;
   • she can only exceptionally claim a share in the value of the home for herself if it is owned solely by the man. She may be able to secure the use of a family home for herself and the children until they complete full-time education, but the home will then revert to the father. By contrast, on divorce, a mother in the same circumstance would have the home or a substantial part of the equity in it transferred to her outright.
3 Unless the man has made any provision for her in his will, she will receive nothing under the rules of intestacy and will be able to claim a share of his estate only if she can prove she was dependent on him.

On the other hand, unmarried fathers are automatically in a much weaker position than unmarried mothers *vis-à-vis* their children. Without any special agreement or court order, unmarried mothers have sole 'parental responsibility' for the child and thus the right, in theory, to take decisions alone about how the child is brought up (but *see* page 80 regarding proposed change in the law). This does not, however, relieve unmarried fathers of the duty to support their children financially (*see further* page 82). The main differences in the law relating to married and unmarried couples are summarized on pages 12–14. The law's comparative non-interference for cohabitants may suit some couples, but they would be wise to consider whether they should take action to avoid some of the legal pitfalls that might otherwise catch them unawares.

HOMOSEXUAL COUPLES

The case law dealing with ownership of a family home has been mostly concerned with ascertaining financial ownership between heterosexual couples whose relationship breaks down. However, the property laws apply to homosexual couples in exactly the same way. A recent case dealt specifically with working out property rights when a homosexual relationship ended (see *Wayling* v *Jones* below). When a gay couple split up, again each should get legal advice as soon as possible to work out the legal consequences. No maintenance will be payable unless there is an enforceable written contract to pay maintenance.

THE FAMILY HOME

When the home is privately owned

The main legal and financial problems that cohabitants usually face are over ownership of the family home. If a couple are married, the law assumes that they are both entitled to a share in the value of the family home. The fact that the house or flat may be legally owned in the name of the husband only is largely irrelevant. The court will regard the home as a family asset to be divided up between husband and wife should the marriage end in divorce. The divorce courts see it as a priority that the wife and children are rehoused and this may even extend to signing over the family home solely to the wife, in addition to maintenance for herself and the children. Much, of course, depends on the circumstances of each family, and the courts also seek to ensure that the husband gets a roof over his head too.

If, however, the couple are unmarried the law does not take such a generous view (from the female cohabitant's viewpoint), for it is primarily concerned with who is the strict legal owner of the property. Since there was no marriage, the courts will *not* presume that the home is family property to be divided up when the relationship ends. So, more often than not, the house or flat will go to the person whose name is on the title deeds. Thus, if the property is in the sole name of the man, it is likely that he alone will be entitled to it. By the same reasoning, if the property is in their joint names then they will probably be regarded as joint owners with both of them entitled to 50 per cent of its value.

So if the couple are unmarried the legal starting-point is to say that the house or flat should go to the person who owns it; the fact that it has been used as a family home is not important. But this presumption is rebuttable. In other words, the person who is not on the title deeds can claim a share of the property if he or she can show that it is, in fact, jointly owned. Often, though, it will be difficult to prove this.

The sort of evidence that must be produced to show that the house is jointly owned would include:

- correspondence between the couple which supports the contention that the property was to be jointly owned even though it was to be put in the sole name of one of them;
- if the deposit for the property was provided by the person whose name is not on the title deeds;
- if the mortgage repayments (capital repayments count more than interest only repayments) were financed by

the person whose name is not on the title deeds, even though the mortgage was taken out in the name of the 'owner';

- if the person whose name is not on the title deeds has done a *great deal* of work to the fabric of the property (furnishings do not count) and so increased its value; and
- if the person whose name is not on the title deeds can show there was an agreement or common intention to share ownership of the property and has acted in reliance on that to her financial detriment (to use legal parlance).

If there is a dispute as to whether the house or flat is jointly owned, the person whose name is not on the title deeds should take legal advice quickly. This area of law is especially complex and a solicitor would need to advise on each individual case, as the case law differs widely. Thus the guidance included here should be seen as brief general statements of the law, which must be amplified by legal advice on any specific case.

TAKING ACTION IN THE COURTS

If it seems that a cohabitant is entitled to a share of the property, the solicitor can start proceedings under the Trusts of Land and Appointment of Trustees Act 1996. This Act provides that a cohabitant who can establish that she is an owner of the property can occupy the property on such terms as the court sees fit. The Act confirmed that cohabitants who can show that they have an interest in the property do indeed have a right to occupy the property (this had been unclear prior to the 1996 Act). The court can make a declaratory order stating the nature or extent of a person's interest in the home, but it does not go so far as being able to make what might be considered to be 'fair' property readjustment orders. Hence the old legal principles still need to be looked at.

Alternatively, one may make a claim under the Family Law Act 1996, which again can establish certainty about occupation of the property (*see* below for a chart comparing some of the factors under each Act). Many legal advisers prefer the Family Law Act 1996 as it has a more welfare-oriented approach; the court can consider the practical implications of different orders for each member of the family. One drawback of choosing to make an application under the Family Law Act 1996 is that the courts tend to be reluctant to make occupation orders under the Act. This is because the remedy of an occupation order in effect 'ousts' one party from the home and, hence, has been seen by the courts as a draconian measure. The courts must weigh up the balance of harm on both sides before making an occupation order – and will consider the children's needs as a priority. The test the courts will apply is: Who will suffer most if an occupation order is not made? The following case illustrates the factors the courts will take into account:

A mother decided to leave her 17-year-old son in the family home in London to move to Somerset. The father, her ex-husband, was living in Kuala Lumpur with his new wife and family, but decided to return to London to look after his son. He sought an occupation order under the Family Law Act 1996 (FLA) in respect of the former family home as he had insufficient funds to pay rent. The mother resisted, saying that her plans to move to Somerset were dependent on releasing capital on the sale of the house. Held: The father's financial position was weaker than the mother's and the well-being of the son and the father's children by his second marriage (who were also relevant children under the terminology of the FLA) required the occupation order to be made. The mother's conduct in abandoning her son and moving without warning the father was taken into account. Balancing these factors, the judge held that he should make an occupation order for six months or until proceedings for financial relief between the parties had been resolved. S v F (Occupation Order) (2000)

The case law which pre-dated the Acts is included in this chapter, as this is likely to remain influential on the courts in determining property rights. Legal proceedings can almost be guaranteed to be expensive and slow – probably taking at least 12 months or so. In the meantime the 'owner' should be prevented from selling the property. This can be done by registering the non-owner's claim as a charge against the property (a solicitor can do this for you), making the property virtually unsellable until the dispute has been resolved. Mediation could also be considered as an alternative means of sorting things out (*see* page 40).

Trusts of Land and Appointment of Trustees Act 1996	Family Law Act 1996
Court can make 'such order as it sees fit'	Court can make occupation order ousting a partner or restricting occupation of the home
Power to exclude depends on consent of beneficiary or approval by court	No consent needed
Uncertainty about what order will be made by court	Court sees ouster order as draconian hence difficult to persuade court to make such an order
Court's powers more restricted	Court's powers more extensive
Long-term remedy can be provided	Orders might be limited to 6 months
Court can order 'rent' to be paid by occupier	Court can order 'rent' to be paid by occupier
Court must consider – intentions of parties – purposes for which the property was held – welfare of any minor – interests of any secured creditor	Court must consider – resources of parties – likely effect of any order on health – safety, well-being of parties/children
No 'balance of hardship' test	Court also must consider the 'balance of hardship' on the parties and children

If the property is in the man's name: establishing a claim for the woman in her own right

The law had often been contradictory about what rights a woman has if the house is in the name of the man alone, but the 1990 case of *Lloyds Bank plc* v *Rosset* helped clear up some (but by no means all!) of the uncertainty. The court said that there were three ways that a woman can show she has a claim on the ownership of the property:
- if there was an agreement between the couple to share;
- if there appeared to be a common intention to share;
- if the man had promised her a permanent home.

The court also said that in addition to proving one of these, the woman must also show:
- that she believed she would have an interest in the property;
- that she acted to her detriment relying on that belief; and
- that the legal owner knew she was acting to her detriment.

An agreement to share

The courts would declare that the woman has an interest in the property where the cohabitants clearly agreed to buy a house together but the legal title to the home was put in the man's name alone. Usually this arose where the man lied to the woman about why she could not be shown as a joint legal owner.

The man told the woman that the only reason why the property was in his name alone was that she was too young to be a legal owner. The woman carried out improvements to the property and was held to have a 25 per cent share in it. Eves v Eves (1975)

A man told his cohabitee that her name should not go on the title deeds to avoid difficulties in her divorce proceedings. She contributed to expenses and was held to have a 50 per cent share in the property. Grant v Edwards (1986)

A common intention to share

If the woman contributed money directly to the purchase or substantial improvement of the home (e.g. for an extension or for the cost of central heating), she would usually be held to have a share in it.

If she had not contributed hard cash, contributions by way of hard labour can give her an interest in the property, although this means more than just carrying out repairs or simple maintenance.

A woman carried out 'an unusual amount of work for a woman', wielding a sledge hammer and helping to build a bungalow. She was given a one-third share of the home.

Cooke *v* Head (1972)

Contributions towards furnishings, decoration or household expenses did not, however, count, even if by so helping out with the finances the man's income could be used to buy property for himself.

The man and woman lived together in a rented flat in the sole name of the man, who was a builder. He purchased a derelict building in his own name, using the building for storage – it was never habitable. The woman contributed to the outgoings of the flat. She argued that by doing so he had been freed to develop his business and so buy the building, so she should have a share of the building. Held: There was no common intention to share at the time of the purchase. The law had to be interpreted strictly and she had acquired no interest in his property. Howard *v* Jones (1989)

Contributions to household expenditure by a woman reflected her natural concern with the well-being of a household and nothing more. They did not give her a share in the value of the family home. Burns *v* Burns (1984)

Contributions by way of keeping the house, and business entertaining, albeit with flair and to a high standard, were insufficient to entitle Miss Windeler to a beneficial interest in the home she had shared with Mr Whitehall.

Windeler *v* Whitehall (1990)

But this area of law is very complex. The law has sometimes had to look to see if the 'trust' which might have been created is a constructive trust or a resulting trust. This sounds like legal jargon, but it has a big direct impact in terms of money.

The issue in this case was quantifying the woman's share in a barn which had been conveyed into her male partner's name. She had made a substantial contribution to the purchase price of the barn and had also contributed in money and labour towards its subsequent conversion into a home for both parties. Was there a constructive or resulting trust? If the former, the court could adopt a broad brushstroke approach in determining the shares but if the latter, the woman would only have an interest equivalent to the

money she had invested. Held: It was a constructive trust, because of the evidence that there was a common intention to share. So the woman got a one third share, instead of the 19.4 per cent share which represented her financial contribution. Drake *v* Whipp (1996)

The promise of a permanent home

The promise of a permanent home (this is also known in legal parlance as the principle of 'proprietary estoppel') can occasionally give a non-legal owner an interest in the property.

In reliance on Mr Pascoe's promise that 'the house and everything in it are yours', Mrs Turner spent a quarter of her capital on the house, which was owned by Mr Pascoe alone. The court held that Mr Pascoe had intended to make a gift of the property and that he could not later renege on his promise. It ordered him to transfer the property to Mrs Turner. Pascoe *v* Turner (1979)

But the courts looked at such cases very strictly. The woman had to show that the man unequivocally intended her to have the house or a share of it. So, in a 1989 case, a man's rather vaguer promise, 'Don't worry – I have told you I will always look after you', did not give the woman either an interest in the value of the home or even a licence to live there.

Two men had lived together in a hotel, owned by the older of the two. The younger man worked for low or no wages for the older man, relying on his belief that the older man would leave him the hotel in his will. The older man died, but the younger man did not inherit the hotel. He successfully brought proceedings. The court held that there had to be a link between the promises relied on and the conduct which constituted the financial detriment and while the promises had to be an inducement to the conduct they did not need to be the sole inducement. Once the claimant proved that promises had been made and that there had been conduct so that the court could infer an inducement, then the burden of proof shifted to the defendant to prove that the plaintiff did not rely on the promises.

Wayling *v* Jones (1995)

This case in itself provides ample illustration of how complicated the law has become.

If the property is in the man's name: establishing a claim for the children or for the woman on behalf of the children

Since 1991, the woman, if she is looking after the children, has been able to make a claim against the man under the Children Act 1989 for a transfer of the home to herself for the benefit of the children or to the children direct.

The court must look at the needs and resources of both ex-partners and the children, any special needs of the children and the way in which the children were being or could have expected to be educated or trained. It is likely that the courts will consider making a transfer only where there are fairly substantial assets involved and if the man is able to rehouse himself adequately. However, the courts will usually only make an order which lasts as long as the children are dependent.

The father of one child of a family of three children was a multi-millionaire. The mother and children were living in a house owned by the father. The mother applied for a transfer of the house outright to the child directly or to her for the benefit of the child. The court rejected this but ordered instead that the house should be settled on the child during her minority or until she completed full-time education. A v A (A Minor: Financial Provision) (1994)

Applications under the Children Act 1989 can also be made where the house is rented and not owner-occupied.

The father of four children was ordered to transfer his interest in the joint tenancy of the council house in which the family were living to the children's mother for the benefit of the children of the family. However, the trial judge failed to take account of the fact that the father had accrued rights to buy under the Housing Act 1980 for nine years. On appeal, the court held a retrial of the case should take place when this, together with his needs, were also taken into account. However, the Court of Appeal also held that such an order was for the benefit of the children and could thus be made under the Children Act 1989.

K v K (Minors: Property Transfer) (1992)

This approach has now been endorsed by the Court of Appeal.

A very wealthy father was ordered to pay a substantial allowance to the mother by way of recognizing her role as the child's primary carer. She had no entitlement to maintenance for herself, but should have control of a budget which reflected her position and the position of the father, socially and financially. A house to the value of £1,000,000 was made available to the mother and child for the duration of the child's full-time education and maintenance of £70,000 a year was ordered. P v T (2003)

If the property is in joint names

Usually the proceeds of the sale will be divided 50/50. If one of the parties thinks he or she is entitled to more than 50 per cent then they can apply to the court under the Trusts of Land and Appointment of Trustees Act 1996.

It sometimes happens that only one of the joint owners wants to sell, while the other wants to keep the property. In these cases, the person who wants to sell can usually insist upon a sale and, if necessary, obtain a court order against their reluctant co-owner. If the property has been a family home, then the court may occasionally decide that it should remain a family home until the youngest child reaches 18 years old. Thus, a sale may be refused until that time – but note that this will apply only if the home was in joint names. If it is in one name only, then almost certainly the court will say that the other partner has no claim on it, and that it would be wrong to prevent the sale (*see* above).

Finally, note that the fact that both of the parties have their names on the title deeds does not *guarantee* that they will both have a share in the property. If the court decides that one of them put their name to the purchase only to help with the mortgage application (but did not, in fact, make any real financial contribution to the mortgage payments), then it may be the case that they are not entitled to a share in the property. But such cases are rare, and the general rule remains that a joint owner can expect a half-share in the property – for, usually, the court will find that there was some home-making contribution (e.g. bringing up the children) that should be taken into account, even if there was no financial contribution.

Avoiding disputes over ownership of the house

Cohabitants can avoid future arguments by clarifying in advance who owns what share of the home and what will happen about the home if the relationship ends, whether by death or by separation. This is usually done by way of a trust deed, which states clearly the proportion in which the couple own the property, whether 50/50 or in unequal shares. The trust deed can also cover other matters. For example:

- granting an option for one party to buy out the other's share;
- setting out the circumstances in which each party could insist on a sale or, alternatively, delay a sale (e.g. until the children leave school);
- agreements as to how the cost of mortgage repayments, repairs, insurance payments and running costs will be divided;
- provisions as to whether cohabitants can assign their shares in the home to someone else.

Trust deeds settle once and for all the division of property between the couple. They are not usually open to challenge by the courts unless there are exceptional circumstances, such as a cohabitant being forced to sign by fraud. The use of trust deeds is not just confined to cohabitants; they can be used by anyone wanting to purchase property together.

When the home is rented

When a marriage ends the courts can often transfer a tenancy from one spouse to another. Thus, it is usually irrelevant whose name is on the rent book or lease, for the court can simply override that and transfer the tenancy as it thinks fit (*see* page 60).

In the past, the courts did not have these powers when the relationship between an unmarried couple ended. The courts could not simply transfer the tenancy as they thought best, but had to allow it to remain with the lawful tenant. All this changed when the Family Law Act 1996 was introduced; the courts now have the power to transfer certain specified tenancies when heterosexual cohabitants separate, whether the tenancy was in the name of the man alone or if it was held jointly. The powers to transfer apply to:

- a protected tenancy/statutory tenancy under the Rent Act 1977;
- a statutory tenancy under the Rent (Agriculture) Act 1976;
- a secure tenancy under s79 of the Housing Act 1985; or
- an assured tenancy or assured agricultural occupancy under Part I of the Housing Act 1988.

When deciding whether or not to order a transfer, the courts will look at all the circumstances of the case, including when and how the tenancy was granted, the housing needs and housing resources of the parties and any relevant children, their financial resources and the likely effect of an order, or the decision not to make an order on the health, safety or well-being of the parties or any relevant children. Where the tenancy had been held in the name of one of them only, the courts will also consider conduct, the nature of the relationship, the length of time they lived together as husband and wife, whether there are any children of them both, and the length of time which has elapsed since they lived together. The court must also consider their suitability as tenants and the landlord has an opportunity to be heard.

On death

If the man is the tenant of the family home and he dies, the woman can claim the tenancy as his 'survivor'. This is because the Rent Acts specifically allow a tenancy to be inherited by a 'member of the family' who was living with the deceased tenant. The courts have held that a mistress, or cohabitant, can be included as a 'member of the family' for this purpose. Similarly, if the woman is the tenant, the man can inherit the tenancy on her death (*see* page 223).

The courts have recently confirmed that the same rules apply where a homosexual couple have lived together and the legal tenant of the property dies when the tenancy was a statutory tenancy under the Rent Acts: *Fitzpatrick v Sterling Housing Association Ltd* (1999). Here the deceased's same-sex partner could succeed to the assured tenancy after death, as the House of Lords (by a majority) held that the survivor was a member of the family too.

The Court of Appeal has decided that a gay partner can also be a successor to a Rent Act 1977 secured tenancy. Paragraph 2 of schedule 1 to the Rent Act 1977 states that 'spouses', and 'persons living with the original tenant as his or her wife or husband' are entitled to succeed to a joint tenancy. The Court of Appeal rejected the argument that, while the deceased's partner could be considered a family member, he did not qualify as a cohabitant. The words 'as his or her wife or husband' should be read as 'as if they were his or her wife or husband': *Mendoza v Ghaidan* (2002).

COHABITANTS AND CHILDREN

If, when children are born, the parents are unmarried, then the mother has sole parental responsibility, giving her alone the right and duty to make decisions about the children's upbringing, such as what names they are given, where they will go to school, what religion they adopt and so on (*see also* page 85). This contrasts with married parents, who are both deemed to have parental responsibility.

Cohabiting parents who intend to live permanently together and share parental care of the children can agree to share parental responsibility. To do so they must sign a special court form, a parental responsibility agreement, available from most county courts, and then register it with the Principal Register of the Family Division. Both parties should, however, seek legal advice, as the sharing of parental responsibility is a permanent step, effective until the child comes of age, even if the relationship does not survive that long.

Unmarried fathers can also acquire parental responsibility by successfully applying to court for a parental responsibility order or a residence order. The Adoption and Children Act 2002 introduced another way by which a natural unmarried father can acquire parental responsibility. The Act provides that an unmarried father acquires parental responsibility where he and the mother register the birth of their child together. However, his name must have been registered on the birth certificate on or after 1 December 2003, when this part of the Act came into force. Unmarried fathers who are already on the child's birth certificate before 1 December 2003 will not automatically acquire parental responsibility under the Act.

MAKING A WILL

Making a will is vitally important for cohabitants as the rules of intestacy give the surviving partner no right to inherit: the estate will automatically be inherited by the deceased's family (*see* Intestacy, page 162).

If the surviving partner was financially dependent on the deceased, he or she may be able to make a claim against the estate (*see* Chapter 14), but the procedure is likely to be lengthy and costly. The Law Commission has recommended that this rule be changed to allow non-dependent cohabitants to claim. Change is long overdue but nothing yet has been done about it.

The only exception to this is an eccentric legal right called *donatio mortis causa* (DMC). Gifts made on the deceased's deathbed can be recognized by the law if they fulfil three requirements:
1 The gift must be made in contemplation of death.
2 The gift must be conditional on death.
3 The gifted object must be handed over in some way (e.g. by the delivery of car keys).

It is, however, far more sensible to make a will rather than rely on the deathbed bounty of a dying partner.

COHABITANTS AND TAX

Sometimes the decision whether or not to marry can be influenced by whether or not a couple will have to pay more tax. Before 1 August 1988 there were tax advantages in living together, as opposed to marrying – the biggest one being double mortgage-interest relief. Towards the end of the 1980s tax treatment of cohabitants and married couples became increasingly similar as tax bonuses for cohabitation were removed. However, by the tax year 2000/01 all of the income tax 'incentives' to marry (principally the married couple's allowance) had been scrapped, so there are no income tax reasons why a couple should decide to marry (hopefully there will be other much more valid if more idealistic reasons!).

There remain a few advantages in choosing marriage over cohabitation on the death of one partner (*see also* Chapter 13) and in respect of pensions. But, by and large, the two states – married and unmarried – are the fiscal equivalents of each other on a day-to-day basis.

Below is a summary of some of the remaining tax *differences*, but as the whole area of tax is complex, further investigation and research will be needed to find out about how the tax laws affect individual couples.

Capital gains tax

Every individual, whether married or not, has an exemption allowance to set off against capital gains tax (CGT) (£7,900 in the tax year 2003/04). But there are two important differences between married couples and cohabitants.

First, a gift from one spouse to another does not give rise to any CGT, but gifts from cohabitants to each other can (*see* below).

A spouse who receives a gift from the other spouse will be treated as having acquired the gift at the same price which the donor paid for it and on the same date when he or she originally acquired it.

So, for example, if a husband bought a painting in 1971 for £500 and then gave it to his wife as a present in 2001 (by which time it was worth £22,000), she will not be liable for CGT when she receives the painting. If she later on sells it, she will be treated as having bought it in 1971 for £500, not having acquired it in 2001 for £22,000. But if she keeps the painting, she will not be liable for CGT.

A gift to a cohabitant, however, will be treated as an immediate chargeable gain. So if the couple above were unmarried but the same circumstances applied, at the date of the gift the woman might have been liable for CGT on £21,500 (although she would be able to set off her personal exemptions and relief for inflation over the period to reduce the amount of tax paid).

Second, a married couple have only one principal private residence exemption from CGT between them, whereas cohabitants each have their own principal private residence exemption if they each own (and usually occupy) separate homes. In practice this can be a considerable tax advantage for cohabitants.

Inheritance tax

Cohabitants are at a particular disadvantage for inheritance tax.

First, the spouse exemption (a spouse who benefits from the deceased partner's will does not have to pay any inheritance tax) does not apply. If inheritance tax is payable, the cohabitant is in no better position than anyone else.

Second, cohabitants (obviously) receive no exemptions for gifts made on their marriage.

COHABITATION CONTRACTS

Cohabitation contracts are by no means a guaranteed way of protecting the cohabitant's position. Historically, contracts between partners have been held to be unenforceable because they were found:
• to be contrary to public policy;

- to be for no consideration (and thus created no proper legal contract);
- to have no intention to create legal relations;
- to have tried to oust the courts' jurisdiction.

Cohabitation (and marriage) contracts are, however, popular in the United States and in Europe, and pressure has been mounting for them to be accepted in this country. As yet no case has decided that cohabitation contracts are legally enforceable. Thus, in law, cohabitation contracts are useful for clarifying agreements between partners but they may well not be worth the paper they are written on in terms of their legal effectiveness. *See also* Marriage contracts, page 25.

MAINTENANCE

Ex-cohabitants cannot claim maintenance for themselves following a breakup, but they can claim maintenance for the children. This can often result in hardship for a woman ex-cohabitant who has spent all her time looking after the family and home and thus has limited work experience and skills to offer in a competitive job market. The law has sometimes implicitly recognized this unfairness by increasing maintenance payments to the children so that they indirectly provide a form of financial support for the woman too, but this approach has been taken only where the man is well off. The mother in *P v T* (2003) (*see* page 9) was awarded maintenance for her child which took into account her needs as the primary carer. In the case of a very wealthy father, the Appeal Court found that it was not necessary to ensure that payments were of direct benefit to the child. It would be sufficient for them to promote the mother's care of the child by allowing her a lifestyle which made her feel comfortable in the society of the parents of the child's friends.

Of course, *both* parents are responsible for financially supporting the children, so claims can be made against the woman too for child support if she deserts the family.

Financial claims for the children are not just limited to income; claims can also be made for lump sums and even for transfers of property.

For claims for child maintenance and other financial relief, *see* page 56.

PERSONAL EFFECTS

The usual rule is that each partner keeps their own belongings (i.e. goods given to them or purchased by one or other individually). Goods bought by the couple intended by them to be jointly owned or out of joint funds should usually be divided 50/50.

If an ex-cohabitant becomes bankrupt, the rule that the things required to satisfy basic domestic needs (e.g. clothes, bedding, furniture and household equipment) do not fall into the hands of the trustee in bankruptcy applies (*see* page 467).

INJUNCTIONS AGAINST COHABITANTS

See page 72.

A List of the Main Differences in the Legal Position of the Married and Unmarried Couple

	Married couple	Unmarried couple
Maintenance	Husband and wife have obligation to maintain one another during the marriage and perhaps afterwards as well.	Neither has a duty to maintain his or her partner, either when they are living together or after they have broken up.
Maintenance for children	Husband has obligation to maintain the children during the marriage and afterwards as well. He is assumed to be the father of all the children born during the marriage. Mother can ask the Child Support Agency to assess and collect maintenance.	The Child Support Agency can assess and collect maintenance. But the mother must prove the father is the father.
Rights over the children	Both husband and wife have an equal say in the child's upbringing. The court can make an order for residence, contact, etc., if it is in the child's best interests.	The father has no automatic rights, as the mother has sole parental responsibility. The father can acquire parental responsibility by agreement with the mother or by court order. Only in an exceptional case will the court grant him a residence order. Under the Adoption and Children Act 2002 an unmarried father

	Married couple	*Unmarried couple*
		will be able to acquire parental responsibility by signing the birth register with the mother.
Income tax	Husband and wives are taxed separately, just as cohabitants are.	
Capital transfer tax	Transfer of property between spouses is exempt.	Transfer between the couple may be taxable.
State pension	A married woman can earn a state pension in her own right, but if she has not made enough contributions she may well be able to claim a pension by virtue of her husband's contributions.	An unmarried woman can claim a state pension only by virtue of her own contributions; she cannot claim a pension by virtue of the man's contributions.
Other state benefits	1. Lump-sum maternity grant can be claimed on the basis of the woman's NI contributions or those of her husband. Weekly maintenance allowance is only payable on the woman's own contributions.	1. Lump-sum maternity grant and weekly maternity allowance can be claimed only on the basis of the woman's NI contributions – not on her partner's contributions.
	2. The married woman is eligible for widow's allowance, widowed mother's allowance and widow's pension.	2. The unmarried woman is not eligible for any of the widows' benefits.
	3. When one spouse applies for public funding the finances of the other spouse will be taken into account, unless the couple are in dispute (e.g. divorce proceedings).	3. A cohabitant's finances are usually taken into account when assessing financial eligibility, unless the couple are in dispute.
Insurance	A married couple can take out insurance against each other's death.	An unmarried couple cannot take out insurance against each other's death; instead they have to insure their own lives and then legally assign the benefit of the insurance policy to their cohabitant.
Inheritance on death	1. If either makes a will that does not provide sufficiently for the other spouse (or the children) the court will alter the will.	1. If either makes a will that does not provide sufficiently for the other cohabitant (or the children) the court can alter the will.
	2. If either dies without a will, most of his/her property will go to the other spouse.	2. If either dies without making a will all his/her property will go to the family (*see* page 163) and not to the other cohabitant. However, it may be possible to get the court to order that part of the estate goes to the cohabitant or the children.
	3. Spouse will inherit funds in joint bank account.	3. Survivor will inherit the funds in joint bank accounts.
Immigration	Either can usually join the spouse who is settled in UK.	Unmarried partner unlikely to be able to join partner who is settled in UK.
Right to occupy the home	Both spouses have equal rights to occupy the matrimonial home, until the marriage is ended by a decree absolute.	Only the owner of the flat/house has a right to occupy it. The other cohabitant can be evicted after due notice – unless he or she has obtained an injunction excluding the owner from the home because of, e.g., domestic violence.

	Married couple	*Unmarried couple*
Rent/mortgage arrears	Other spouse can compel landlord/ mortgagee to accept rent/mortgage payments from him or her.	Other partner cannot compel landlord/ mortgagee to accept payments from him or her (unless he or she is joint tenant or joint borrower).
Inheriting a tenancy of the family home	Will be inherited by surviving spouse (*see* page 223).	Will be inherited by the other partner (*see* page 223).
Right to a share of the family assets	On the breakup of the marriage the wife can claim a share of all the family assets even if they are in the husband's sole name (e.g. the house). Often she will be awarded one-half (or even more) of the assets.	The woman can claim only what is legally hers – she cannot automatically claim a share of her cohabitant's assets (e.g. his house or car). Only if she can show that she has an interest in the property can she claim a share of it. If the property is jointly owned it will usually be divided 50/50.
Domestic violence	The wife can get her violent husband excluded from the home by applying to the court. The question of whose name is on the title deeds or rent book is virtually irrelevant (*see* page 74).	The woman can get her violent cohabitant excluded from the home by applying to the court. The question of whose name is on the title deeds or rent book, while not a major factor, is more relevant than it would be if they were a married couple (*see* page 74). The woman can also get an occupation order or declaratory order under the Family Law Act 1996 or the Trusts of Land and Appointment of Trustees Act 1996.
Ending the relationship	A marriage can be ended only by a court order (i.e. divorce, nullity, etc.). There can be no divorce in the first year of marriage.	The cohabitation agreement can be ended without notice and without any legal formalities at any time either of the couple chooses to terminate it.

Change of Name

CHANGING A SURNAME

An adult in England and Wales can use whatever surname he or she chooses to use. It is the name by which he or she is commonly called that is the correct surname. Thus a person called Brown can simply decide to adopt the name Smith, and the change of surname will be valid. The only restriction on this is that the change of name must not have a fraudulent intent (e.g. to use someone else's cheque book).

It also follows from this that a married woman need not take her husband's surname (*see* page 22). Women are increasingly choosing to keep their own maiden names on marriage. Indeed, after a couple marry, the husband is free to take his wife's name. Or they can hyphenate the two original names if they so choose. This latter option however really only works for one generation, and the couple's offspring won't have the same choice open to them. So if Harriet Harrington and Fred Frederickson become Mr and Mrs Harrington-Frederickson, it would probably be too much of a mouthful for their son Jamie Harrington-Frederickson to add the whole of his surname to his intended Sophie Graham-Jones (assuming her parents had taken a similar route to join their names together). A key reason why people keep their own surnames after marriage is that they are known by that name in their profession or other work and are concerned that they may lose work in future if they switch identity.

An unmarried woman can also take her partner's name as her surname (even if he disagrees) or, again, they can add their surnames together and use the new hyphenated version.

From the law's point of view, anyone can simply change their name as and when they decide to, so long as they then use that name in everyday life.

However, other people may not be prepared to accept such an informal change of name; in particular, banks, the DWP, and other people who pay money to the person will want more formal proof of the new name. On marriage, a copy of the marriage certificate will generally be accepted as sufficient evidence, but otherwise the person may need to produce one of the three following documents.

1 *A note signed by a respected member of the community (e.g. solicitor, JP, doctor, clergyman).* The note should confirm that the new name is the name by which the person is commonly known; however, an unofficial document of this sort is unlikely to impress a bank or other institution (although the passport office will usually accept it).

2 *A statutory declaration.* This is an official way of formalizing the change of name. It is a sworn statement (similar to an affidavit) and a solicitor would probably charge £70 for preparing it. A typical statutory declaration is shown on page 16.

3 *A deed poll.* This is the most formal method of regularizing the change of name and, in practice, is the method most commonly used. A solicitor prepares a formal deed which is signed by the person (i.e. both the old and new names) in front of a solicitor (it must be a solicitor from a different firm of solicitors). The deed might also need to be enrolled with the Supreme Court if the person is a member of one of the professions, so that the deed poll is kept as a permanent record of the change of name. A solicitor would probably charge £70 for preparing and stamping a deed poll.

Changing the name of children

In the past the law did not automatically prevent the change of surname of a child unless a residence order was in force (*see* page 107), when there was a specific prohibition against changing a surname without the other parent's consent or without the court's permission. However, that changed with the 1999 case of *Dawson* v

Wearmouth when the Court of Appeal held that even if the mother alone had parental responsibility (*see* page 85), she cannot unilaterally change her child's surname if the father does not agree to the change. The law is that the surname by which a child is known is profoundly important to the child. If a parent who has parental responsibility wants to change the child's name she should find out if the other parent agrees or not. If the change is agreed the mother is free to call the child by his new name. If the other parent objects, the parent who wants the name change needs to apply to the court to resolve the dilemma by a specific issue order application (*see also* page 108). If the father learns that the mother plans to change a child's surname and again he objects, his course would also be to apply to the court to stop the name change by asking for a specific issue order.

Taking action promptly is important. If the name change occurred a long time ago and the child now knows himself by that name, likewise his family and friends, school and doctor, it will be much harder for the father to get that name change reversed by the courts. (He would also have to explain why he was unaware of the name change for such a long time and if the reason was that he had not kept in touch with the child, then that would count against him.) If the child himself is older, in practice from a mature and articulate 10-year-old upwards, his views will be taken into account by the courts, and the older the child is, the greater weight will be given to his views.

It is not possible to alter the name on a birth certificate. The normal rule is that a birth certificate cannot be altered more than 12 months after registration.

How to change your name

Usually, a statutory declaration is the best method. Prepare a document along the lines of the one below, and then go to a solicitor and 'swear' it in front of him or her (you will be charged a £5.50 fee).

I . . . [*old* name, plus address and occupation] do solemnly and sincerely declare that:

1. I absolutely and entirely renounce, relinquish and abandon the use of my said former surname of . . . and assume, adopt and determine to take and use from the date hereof the surname of . . . in substitution for my former surname of . . .

2. I shall at all times hereafter in all records, deeds and other writings and in all actions and proceedings, as in all dealings and transactions and on all occasions whatsoever, use and subscribe the said name of . . . as my surname in substitution for my former surname of . . . so relinquished as aforesaid to the intent that I may hereafter be called, known or distinguished not by the former surname of . . . but by the surname of . . . only.

3. I authorize and require all persons at all times to designate, describe and address me by the adopted surname of . . .
AND I make this solemn declaration conscientiously believing the same to be true and by virtue of the provisions of the Statutory Declarations Act 1835.

Declared at . . .
this . . . day of . . . 200- . . . [signature] . . .
before me . . .
a solicitor
empowered to administer oaths

Getting Married

BECOMING ENGAGED

The law attaches little significance to engagement; it is only when the couple come to marry that the law lays down detailed requirements as to their status and age. Similarly, the legal effects of an engagement are few, whereas the legal effects of a marriage are many – ranging from the duty to cohabit to the obligation to maintain and provide for the spouse.

Engagement requires no legal formalities; no one's consent needs to be obtained and the couple do not even have to be over the age of 16. This is because the engagement has no legal effect and cannot be enforced by the courts.

Prior to 1970, a contract to marry (i.e. an engagement) was like any other contract, and if it was broken the rejected suitor could sue for breach of contract. But the right to sue has now been abolished and so an agreement to marry (i.e. an engagement) is no longer a legally binding contract. Further, the rejected suitor cannot even sue to recover any losses or expenses incurred in planning and preparing for the marriage. For example, the jilted groom may have booked hotel rooms, or the jilted bride may have spent money on a trousseau, dress, cake, and all the other costs of a reception; none of the expenses can be recovered from the other party unless it was specifically agreed beforehand that he or she would pay them. Similarly, if the father of the rejected bride booked a hall for the reception, he cannot sue the ex-fiancé or even demand that he pay half the booking fee.

Returning the gifts on cancellation

If the couple were sent presents before the wedding was cancelled, then generally those presents ought to be returned to the people who gave them. The law assumes that the gifts were given on the understanding that the couple were to be married, and so if the marriage is called off they are no longer entitled to the presents. If the people who gave the presents do not want them back, the law will usually allow the man to keep the gifts from his friends and relatives and the woman to keep the gifts from her friends and relatives.

The same applies to gifts made by the couple to each other. The law assumes that the gifts were conditional on the marriage taking place, and so should be returned if the marriage is called off. It makes no difference who is to blame for the cancellation of the marriage – the 'guilty' lover is still entitled to have his or her presents returned.

The only exception to this is the engagement ring; the woman can nearly always hold on to this even if she has been the one to call off the wedding. Only in exceptional cases would a court order her to return the ring; for example, when the ring was a family heirloom, and the man had given it to her only on the clear understanding that if she did not become a member of his family then the ring was to be returned.

All these rules are based on a presumption that the gifts were conditional on the marriage taking place. So, if a present was not conditional on the marriage, it would not be returnable. Thus Christmas and birthday presents will not normally have to be returned.

Property bought jointly

Sometimes an engaged couple will buy a house together before their wedding day. If the wedding is cancelled, what happens to the house?

If they cannot agree on what to do with the house or flat, the court will normally order that it be sold. After paying off the mortgage, and the estate agent's and solicitor's fees, the remaining money will be divided between them. The amount that each will receive will depend upon their percentage share in the house, which will partly depend upon how much each put into the purchase. Often, the money will be split 50/50 unless there is clear evidence for dividing it in some other way – for instance, they may have agreed on a one-third/two-thirds ownership when the property was bought.

Warning: complications can arise if the property was not bought in the couple's joint names. *See* page 7 for the principles that apply.

Similar rules apply to furniture and other possessions bought by the couple. If they cannot agree, either can ask the court to order the sale of the items concerned – although it is obviously best to do everything possible to avoid the expense of going to court.

MARRIAGE REQUIREMENTS

Generally, romantic love is the basis of marriage in this country, but this is a relatively recent development. In the past bride seizure, payment and parental arrangement were regarded as the normal methods for deciding on marriage partners.

To be legally valid, a marriage must be:
* voluntary
* between two single people
* who are over 16
* of the opposite sex
* and not closely related.

Voluntary
Both the man and the woman must be acting voluntarily. Force, fear and duress will all invalidate the marriage. But it must be real duress: for instance, social pressure and the desire to please one's parents do not invalidate the marriage.

The marriage will also be invalid if one of the couple does not realize what he or she is doing (e.g. if drink or old age affects their awareness of what is happening).

Similarly, if there was a mistake as to the identity of the other partner the marriage would be invalid. But other mistakes will not invalidate it. For instance, if the man is mistaken as to the financial standing, social status or career prospects of his wife, he cannot argue that he would not otherwise have married her and so claim that the marriage is invalid. Duress can also invalidate the marriage. This can be a particular problem with arranged marriages.

A 19-year-old Hindu girl was forced into an arranged marriage. Had she not agreed, her parents would have thrown her out of the house, leaving her homeless and penniless. The Court of Appeal granted a declaration that the marriage was a nullity – 'the crucial question in these cases . . . is whether the threats, pressure, or whatever it is, is such as to destroy the reality of the consent and overbear the will of the individual'. So, in many ways it was the threat of homelessness and social ostracism that were the key factors in this case, and not so much the mere parental and social pressure. Hirani (1983)

This case should not be taken as showing that all arranged marriages can be set aside, but it is clear evidence of a change of attitude by the courts in being prepared to tackle this difficult problem.

In 2000 the government announced an initiative about the creation of a new team to work with minority communities to put a stop to the practice of forced (as opposed to willingly arranged) marriages. This coincided with news reports about the rescue of a woman who was being forced into marriage unwillingly.

In March 2000, a news story was published about a British student being rescued by Foreign Office officials and Indian police from a forced wedding in India. She was found in the Punjab on the eve of her engagement to a local man she had never met. The student, who is 21 years old, had been flown to Delhi on the pretext of visiting her sick grandmother, and then had her passport taken away by her father and was forced to remain with relatives who were told she must not speak to anyone or telephone.

If the marriage had been entered into under duress, then the wife could have applied for the marriage to be nullified – as if it had never happened. However, the government's initiative is also seeking to resolve the real problems of ostracism by the community in such circumstances. For further information and advice call the Community Liaison Unit at the Foreign and Commonwealth Office on 020 7008 0230.

Between two single people
Neither party can be already married. They must both be either single, widowed or divorced. If one party is divorced, the final decree of divorce must have been obtained (the decree absolute). A divorced person will not usually be allowed to marry for a second time in church, although some clergy in the Churches of England and Wales are more relaxed about divorcees having a church service – the Church will often leave it up to the priest's own conscience. In Scotland, the Church of Scotland does not object to a divorced man or woman remarrying in church – hence Princess Anne's decision to marry her second husband north of the Border.

If either is married at the time of the ceremony the marriage will be void and the offence of bigamy will have been committed (but *see* Polygamous marriages, page 20). In fact, bigamy prosecutions are relatively rare these days because the police do not prosecute if the sole purpose was to allow the couple to live respectably as man and wife. Only 20 per cent or so of bigamy cases are prosecuted. Obviously if the bigamist was acting maliciously or fraudulently then he or she would be prosecuted.

A 'wife' deliberately deceived her 'husband' and concealed the fact that she was already married, when she 'married' for a second time. Because this was a bigamous marriage it was not a true marriage. The Court of Appeal, as well as confirming that she had committed a crime, said that they would not make any financial orders in her favour as it would be 'offensive to the public conscience and contrary to public policy'.   Whiston (1995)

Problems arise when a married person separated from the other spouse many years ago and now wishes to remarry. To avoid the risk of a bigamy prosecution, the court should be asked to grant a decree of presumption of death and divorce, or to grant a divorce based on five years' separation (*see* page 34). Unless such an order is obtained there is always a risk that the second marriage will be bigamous, although there is a special defence for those who have not heard from their spouse for at least seven years and who have no reason to suppose that he or she is still alive. This defence, even if it reduces the risks of a bigamy conviction, may not be enough to save the second marriage. Almost certainly the second, bigamous, marriage will be null and void, so the couple will be in the same position as if they had never been married.

Who are over 16

Since 1929 the minimum age for both parties to a marriage has been 16 years old. Before then, it was 14 for boys and 12 for girls.

If a boy or girl is under 16 years old when married, the marriage will be null and void. In addition, the child will be committing a criminal offence.

A person under the age of 18 needs to obtain parental, or other, consent to the marriage. If the consent is forged, or if the child states that he or she is over 18 years old in order to make consent unnecessary, the marriage will remain valid, but the child will be committing a criminal offence. The marriage will only be invalid if the child is under 16.

Consents. A 16- or 17-year-old will need the signed consent of parents and anyone else with parental responsibility (*see* page 85), but see the table below.

Circumstances	Consent needed from
Married parents	
If the parents were married at the child's birth	Both parents
If the parents have divorced or separated	Both parents
If one of the parents has died	The surviving parent
If both parents have died	The guardian
Where the parents were not married	The mother alone (unless the father has parental responsibility, then he must give consent too)

If the mother has died	The guardian
If there is a residence order for the child	The person in whose favour the residence order was made
If the child is adopted	The adoptive parents
If the child is a ward of court	The court
If the child is in the care of the local authority	The local authority and parents with parental responsibility

If for some reason one of the parents cannot give consent (e.g. because he or she cannot be traced), then special consent will be needed; the registrar of marriages can provide details.

If the parents refuse their consent the child can apply to the court for its consent. Although the application can be to a Family Proceedings Court (a magistrates' court), a county court, or the High Court, it is usually most convenient to apply to the local Family Proceedings Court. The child should go to the court as though he or she wanted to issue an application and explain the position to the warrant officer. Such applications are, however, so rare they are almost unheard of.

Of the opposite sex

Gay (i.e. homosexual or lesbian) marriages currently have no legal validity in England and Wales, although other countries (France, for example) have very recently introduced a form of civil ceremony under which homosexual couples can 'marry'. In 2002, two Private Members' bills were introduced in Parliament, one in the Commons and one in the Lords. Each proposed a system of registration of the status of cohabitants, both same sex and opposite sex. Registration as proposed in these bills would give cohabitants rights similar to the rights conferred on married couples. These have now been shelved while the government considers the whole issue. It is likely to restrict any system of civil registration to same-sex couples. Sex-change marriages likewise are not legal here:

April Ashley was born a man. In 1960 he had undergone a sex-change operation involving removal of the testicles and most of the scrotum, and the formation of an artificial vagina. In September 1963 April Ashley married a man – who was aware of the sex change – and they lived together as man and wife. Three months later the man asked that the marriage be declared null and void because it was a marriage between two men. April Ashley disagreed, saying it was a marriage between a man and a woman. Held: *It was not a valid marriage. April Ashley had been born a man and by all medical criteria he was a male, although psychologically he was transsexual. The sex change had not altered his biological (legal) sex and so the marriage was void. In addition, the marriage could be annulled on the grounds of non-consummation since the artificial vagina did not allow true intercourse.*

Corbet (1970)

The issue of transsexual marriage was considered more recently in the case of Michael and Elizabeth Bellinger. Elizabeth Bellinger underwent a male-to-female sex change operation in 1981 and married Michael Bellinger the same year. The registrar who married the couple did not ask for any evidence of Mrs Bellinger's gender and the couple have lived since then as husband and wife. In July 2002 the European Court of Human Rights ruled the UK's failure to recognize transsexuals in law breached their human rights. But when the House of Lords considered the Bellingers' case in April 2003, they decided that the matter of whether a transsexual person should be treated for all purposes as a member of their chosen sex, including marriage, was a matter for Parliament and not the courts. In December 2002 the Lord Chancellor's Department (now replaced by the Department for Constitutional Affairs) announced proposals for legislative change to allow transsexuals to marry in their adopted sex and to apply for substitute birth certificates showing their new genders. Transsexuals who want to register under their new genders would be able to apply to a new authorizing body. The government has not yet indicated when the law will change.

Elsewhere in the world, a few countries are starting to 'legalize' same-sex marriages. A news report in March 2000 indicated that Vermont was set to be the first American state to pass a law which will in effect recognize a homosexual marriage. A landmark bill there approving same-sex unions and giving gay and lesbian couples the same rights as married heterosexuals was expected to clear the legislative hurdles in its path. The announcement came shortly after the State of California, USA, rejected the idea (*see further* page 5).

And not closely related

Society disapproves of marriages between people from the same family. This is so even when one of the parties is adopted into the family or is now divorced out of the family. So, for example, while a man may marry his female cousin, he cannot marry his son's divorced wife or his brother's adopted daughter.

'The Prohibited Degrees': When Marriage within a Family is Prohibited

A man cannot marry his:	A woman cannot marry her:
mother	father
daughter	son
grandmother	grandfather
granddaughter	grandson
sister	brother
mother-in-law	father-in-law
stepdaughter	stepson
stepmother	stepfather
daughter-in-law	son-in-law
grandfather's wife	grandmother's husband
wife's grandmother	husband's grandfather
wife's granddaughter	husband's grandson
grandson's wife	granddaughter's husband
aunt	uncle
niece	nephew

However, cousins are entitled to marry because the blood-tie link is seen to be sufficiently distant. An adopted child cannot marry his birth relatives, nor (for social and moral reasons) his adoptive parent. Perhaps surprisingly, there is no prohibition on marriage between a child and a brother or sister to whom he or she is related by adoption. The Marriage (Prohibited Degrees of Relationship) Act 1986 also relaxed some of these rules, so for example a man can now, in theory, marry his stepdaughter (i.e. the daughter of his ex-wife, where he was *not* the father of the girl) if, but only if, both parties are under 21 and provided he has never treated her as a child of the family before she reached the age of 18. Should a man wish to marry his mother-in-law nowadays, this is permitted only if his former wife and the father of his former wife are both dead.

The law in this area is complex and anyone in doubt should take legal advice.

Polygamous marriages

No marriage that takes place in this country can be valid if one of the parties is already married. Such a marriage is void and also bigamous (*see* page 18). But some societies allow a man to have more than one wife and the question then arises of whether our courts will recognize all the marriages made by a polygamous foreigner or whether they will recognize only the first marriage and regard the others as bigamous. The position is complicated, but basically our courts will recognize all the marriages if:

1 The marriages complied with the laws of the country where they took place.

A Sikh marriage took place in India. The husband was abroad but was represented at the marriage ceremony by a photograph of himself. Held: This was a valid marriage in India and so it could be recognized in this country.

Birang (1977)

2 The spouses must also have been capable of marrying (i.e. of age, not within the prohibited degrees, etc.) according to the laws of their respective countries of domicile.

However, the law is complex and anyone in doubt should take legal advice.

The formalities of marriage

The Marriage Act 1949 sets out the formalities for a valid marriage. But the Act largely repeats the law that has evolved over the centuries and so the result is bit of a confusing muddle. However, while there are, in theory, an abundance of rules to be observed, failure to observe them very often has no impact on the validity of the marriage. So for example, although the consent of parents is needed where a party to the marriage is under the age of 18, if the couple succeed in getting married and evade this restriction without getting parental consent, the marriage is still a valid marriage. It is impossible to innocently contract to a marriage which is void for lack of formality.

Documents required

A couple who intend to marry will be asked by the registrar or vicar, for example, to prove that they are who they say they are – production of a passport is the simplest method, otherwise two official documents (like a cheque book and driving licence) will be requested. They will also be asked to produce the court stamped seal of decree absolute (if one is remarrying) or the death certificate (if one is widowed) and will need to pay a fee. This varies depending on which location is chosen, where each of the parties lives and how quickly they want to marry. So, for example, the lowest fee for a civil ceremony is a Superintendent Registrar's certificate where both partners live in the same registration district, when the fee is £59 (2000 figures) – this rises to £84 where they live in different registration districts.

Location

There are only certain specified locations in which a valid marriage can take place in England and Wales:

- a District Register Office;
- a church or chapel of the Church of England or Church of Wales;
- an 'approved building' – approved by the local authority under the Marriage Act 1994. You can search websites for approved buildings – for example, www.weddings.co.uk or www.weddingguide.co.uk. Basically, the building must be an immovable structure; tents, marquees, boats and trains are, therefore, not allowed. But there are many beautiful and unusual buildings latterly approved for weddings in this way;
- a naval, military or air force chapel.

There are two basic methods of marrying: first, religious ceremonies by the Church of England or Church of Wales marriages (or military chapels), and second, other religious ceremonies and civil ceremonies.

Church of England and Church of Wales marriages (and military chapels)

Church of England and Church of Wales vicars are licensed to conduct weddings themselves. If you want to get married in church, the first step is to speak to the vicar of the church you would like to marry in. Very often the vicar will be happy to marry as long as one of the couple lives in the parish (or the family has connections there) but the vicar may well insist on attendance at church.

Before the couple can be married they must comply with the formalities. There are three ways in which they can do this.

Banns

The names of the couple are read out in their parish churches on three consecutive Sundays. The marriage must then take place within three months of the last reading of the banns.

Common licence

This is a licence granted by a diocesan bishop and it is valid for three months. It will only be granted if one of the couple has lived for the preceding 15 days in the parish where the marriage is to take place and an affidavit may be required confirming that there is nothing to prevent the marriage. Only one clear day's notice is required.

Special licence

This can only be granted by the Archbishop of Canterbury and it allows the marriage to take place anywhere and at any time. Only about 250 special licences are issued in any one year. They tend to be used for special and urgent reasons: for example, if a person who wishes to marry is too ill to leave hospital.

Other religious ceremonies and civil marriages

Unless the marriage is to be by Church of England ceremony, it can take place only if a Superintendent Registrar's certificate has been issued. There are two alternatives. The certificate can be issued 'with a licence' or 'without a licence'. Contact the Superintendent Registrar of the district where you wish to marry or the approved building manager (to check if the location is free on the date you would prefer).

A certificate without a licence

Allows the marriage to take place 21 days after the notice was given to the registrars for the areas where both parties live. There is a seven-day residence requirement.

A certificate with a licence

Allows the marriage to take place one day after the notice was given. Notice need be given only to one registrar, but one of the parties must have been resident in that area for at least 15 days beforehand.

In both instances the marriage ceremony must take place in the registrar's office, or in a church, chapel, synagogue or meeting-house appropriate to the couple's religion. If the ceremony does not take place in the Register Office, then there will often be an extra fee chargeable by the registrar to attend and officiate over the signing of the Register.

For all marriages

Before the service any necessary certificates or licences must be handed to the registering official. For a marriage to be solemnized, there must be two adult witnesses (who can be complete strangers to the couple) who will also sign their names on the Register.

THE LEGAL EFFECTS OF MARRIAGE

Getting married leads to the creation of new rights and new obligations between the couple. Among other things, they have a duty to maintain one another and to live together, and they impliedly agree to have sex with each other.

The legal consequences for the woman

A new name?

For a woman the most obvious change brought about by the marriage will often be a change of name. However, there is no legal obligation on her to change her name and she can retain her maiden name if she wishes (*see* above). She and her husband may also agree to hyphenate their surnames together.

If she chooses to adopt the husband's name on marriage, she is then entitled to keep her husband's name (and any title) even after he dies or after they divorce and remarry. Alternatively, she can revert to her maiden name if she prefers.

In English law, anybody can call themselves by whatever name they choose, and they can change their names as and when they wish (*see* page 15).

A new nationality?

No. Not automatically. Nationality is a political status of an individual and this is not affected by marriage. A British citizen who marries a foreigner can retain his or her citizenship – but may have dual citizenship (although this depends on the law of the other country involved). The UK law accepts dual citizenship but not every country does (e.g. the USA), so if a woman wants to claim US citizenship she may have to give up her British citizenship.

A new domicile?

A wife need not acquire her husband's domicile, although in practice she will often do so. Domicile should not be confused with nationality, citizenship or residence. *Domicile* is where a person has his or her permanent home or, if he or she is living abroad, where he or she intends to return to permanently. *Residence* is the place where a person happens to be living; a person can be resident in several countries at the same time but can have only one domicile.

How domicile is decided

At birth, a baby will normally acquire its father's domicile, or if the father is dead, its mother's domicile. This is called the 'domicile of origin'.

In practice it is very difficult to change that domicile until the child is 16 years old, but thereafter the child can acquire a 'domicile of choice', depending on the place where he or she is now permanently resident or intends to reside permanently.

Although a wife need not acquire her husband's domicile on marriage, it will usually be the case that she will live with him and that she will plan to spend her life with him in his domicile. Thus, in practice, she will usually acquire that new domicile.

A new passport?

The newly married woman can, if she chooses, have a new passport in her married name. In practice, the bride-to-be who is planning a foreign honeymoon can obtain a passport in her married name before the wedding takes place, although she must agree to surrender it should the marriage be cancelled.

An existing passport can be altered to the woman's new name by sending the passport and the marriage certificate to the Passport Office. They will amend the passport to show her new name.

A newly married wife is not obliged to have a passport in her married name, for she can continue to use her existing passport until it expires. The new passport can then be in her married name – assuming, of course, that she has adopted her husband's name and has not retained her maiden name.

The Passport Office will accept the title 'Ms'.

A new bank account?

If a newly married woman adopts her husband's name she should ensure that her bank changes her account name.

The couple may also consider opening a joint bank account. Generally, this is a good idea but remember that if the marriage breaks down it is quite likely that the money in the account will be divided equally between the couple. As a general guide it can be said that if the wife is dependent on the husband she ought to insist on a joint account; and if he is dependent on her, then he should insist on a joint account (*see* page 48).

A new will?

Marriage automatically revokes a will unless the will was specifically made in contemplation of that marriage. So both new spouses will usually have to make new wills. In the often frantic time preparing for a wedding, this requirement is (understandably) frequently overlooked, but it makes good sense to get around to making a will as soon as possible and join the comparatively few who do (only one in four people get around to making a will), otherwise the intestacy laws will apply and an estate can get divided up in a way that the deceased spouse would not have wanted.

The financial effects of marriage

Marriage may result in:

New tax arrangements

Before April 2000, there used to be an extra tax allowance for married people, but the married couple's allowance was scrapped with effect from 6 April 2000. The tax advantages of getting married are now minimal.

New entitlement to pension benefits

If either spouse has a pension – say a personal pension or an occupational pension – the pension scheme usually allows for a surviving spouse (and dependent children) to receive 'death in service' benefits if the pension scheme member dies while still working or a share of the pension which is paid after retirement if the member dies after retirement. These spouse's pension benefits are however lost on decree absolute – the final stage of divorce proceedings. More recently the law allows a married woman who is divorcing the right to 'earmark' a share of her husband's pension for herself or split her husband's pension so that she will have a pension in her own right and not be dependent on his. *See further* page 64.

New inheritance rights

If a married person dies without having made a will, then most of his or her possessions will pass to the surviving spouse. If there is a will but it leaves little or nothing to the surviving spouse, then the court can intervene to award him or her a fair share of the estate (*see* Chapter 14).

New credit rights

A wife may be able to make her husband liable to pay some of the household bills she incurs (*see* page 48).

New property rights

Both husband and wife will be able to claim a share in their joint assets (*see* page 49).

Maintenance

Both husband and wife are liable to maintain one another financially (*see* page 49).

A new home?

When a couple marry they impliedly agree to live together; this is the 'duty to cohabit'. Married couples are obliged to live together and to give each other the benefit of their company and support; the legal term for this is 'consortium'.

But the courts will not enforce these obligations by making the parties live together or by preventing one spouse from leaving the other or indeed making one spouse have sex with the other. The law regards either spouse as being free to leave if he or she wishes but, by doing so, that spouse will be in desertion and so may be liable to be divorced and be ordered to pay maintenance to the other. In practice, though, many women are not free to leave the marital home when they might otherwise choose to do so; their financial dependence on their husbands, and the need for a home for themselves and the children, prevent them from leaving.

Given that the couple are expected to live together, which one of them can choose where the home is to be? Obviously, the views of both husband and wife should be taken into account, but all things being equal, it is the need to be near the main breadwinner's place of work that often decides the issue. But all the circumstances must be considered, and so the health of the wife or the schooling of the children may be held as sufficient reasons to justify a wife's refusal to move home. Obviously, if both husband and wife are at work, the parties have equal say in the matter and the other circumstances may be decisive.

Sometimes the partners have to accept that, for a temporary period, their homes will be separate. But, overall, such questions are usually of academic interest only. If the couple cannot agree on where to live, it is likely that this is merely a symptom of a deeper problem in their relationship and that the argument over moving is merely a means of expressing their discontent.

Sex within marriage

Sex is part of the duty to cohabit for, by marrying, the couple impliedly agree to have sexual intercourse with each other. Note also that if the marriage is never consummated (i.e. no sex), it may be annulled (*see* page 46).

To use a now very outdated term, 'marital rights' also used to be considered to be part and parcel of the marriage contract – namely that each spouse would agree to have sex with the other.

But, as with so many things legal, the concept of 'reasonableness' prevails and so marriage is taken as an implied consent to a reasonable amount of sex. So, excessive demands for sex or a virtual refusal to have sex will be unreasonable and may justify a petition for divorce on the grounds of 'unreasonable behaviour'. It all depends on the circumstances. For example, a refusal of sex by an invalid may be reasonable, but a refusal of sex by a healthy active person is probably unreasonable. So also will be an insistence on always using contraceptives so that the couple will never have any children. The courts will in any event never force a reluctant spouse to have sex with the other, and such considerations are only taken into account in a divorce.

For a Dark Ages period between 1736 and 1991, it was legally impossible for a man to rape his wife. But a case in the House of Lords on 23 October 1991 ended the exemption of husbands from rape and a man can no longer use marriage as a watertight defence to the charge of rape (although some cases still appear to show he might get a lesser sentence).

Finally, if the woman becomes pregnant the husband cannot stop her having an abortion to destroy the foetus.

A wife asked for an abortion and two doctors certified that continuing the pregnancy could injure her health. She had not consulted her husband, so he sought an injunction forbidding her to have the abortion. Held: No. A husband does not have a legal right to stop his wife having a legal abortion. Paton (1978)

It might be possible, though, for a husband to use his wife's insistence on an abortion as evidence of 'unreasonable behaviour' for a divorce petition.

Contractual obligations between man and wife

Marriage is a contract, but the courts will not enforce the contract between husband and wife. For instance, if the woman was persuaded to marry the man because he said he was wealthy, she cannot sue him for misrepresentation if he lied about his supposed wealth.

The courts will not interfere with a working marriage. So, if a husband arranges to meet his wife at twelve o'clock but she does not keep the appointment, he cannot hold her liable for the losses and expenses he has suffered. This is all part of the wear and tear of marriage. The courts will intervene only if the couple clearly intended a legal relationship to follow on from an agreement, such as when they are discussing a business matter.

Different considerations arise if the marriage is breaking down. If it is no longer a working marriage the courts will intervene in extreme situations. So, if the couple decided to separate and drew up a separation agreement, the courts would probably enforce it if one of the parties did not carry out his or her part of the bargain (although the court could override the terms of the agreement if it was unfair).

Marital confidences and secrets

Most married people tell one another things that they would not tell other people. If necessary, these marital confidences and secrets will be respected by the courts.

So, in a criminal trial the husband or wife of the accused cannot normally be called to give evidence for the prosecution; neither can he or she be forced to give evidence for the defence. Similarly, in a civil case, while the spouse can be called or subpoenaed to give evidence, the judge will excuse the spouse from answering questions if to do so would involve a breach of marital confidences.

If one of the spouses plans to publish the marital secrets the courts may grant an injunction to stop the publication.

The Duke of Argyll divorced the Duchess of Argyll because of her adultery. A year later, the Duke wrote an article for the People in which he disclosed secrets of the Duchess's personal life and conduct, based on what she had told him when they were married. The Duchess applied for an injunction. Held: The injunction would be granted since the articles were a breach of marital confidences. Argyll (1965)

However by the cusp of the twenty-first century, the courts viewed things somewhat differently.

Robin Cook, the then Foreign Secretary, tried to get an injunction stopping his ex-wife publishing her memoirs which included details of his adultery and the end of their marriage. Held: He was not entitled to do so. There was a legitimate public interest in the story to be published (1999).

In any event, the granting of an injunction is a discretionary remedy, and the court will refuse an injunction to someone who has previously been willing to publicize his private life. An older example comes from the rock and roll generation:

John Lennon, the ex-Beatle, applied for an injunction to

stop his former wife, *Cynthia Lennon, writing newspaper articles about their married life.* **Held:** *An injunction would be refused. Both John and Cynthia Lennon had previously made public – in return for payment – intimate details of their relationship. An injunction would not be appropriate.*
Lennon (1978)

Marriage contracts

Marriage contracts have attracted much media interest, not least because, in addition to those once bitten by the divorce bug (and hence being more wary of marrying again), they are more often entered into by stars than by the average man and woman in the street. A 1991 Law Society paper noted:

Current interest in marriage contracts seems to be most marked amongst those who have already experienced the trauma of divorce and wish to protect themselves in the future, the very rich or those who have connections with foreign countries where the use of marriage contracts is common.

Interest in marriage contracts was revived again in 1998, when the then new Labour government indicated that it thought all couples should enter into marriage contracts when they wed. Although this view was popularly received amongst lawyers and financial commentators, it never fired the imagination of the public and at the time of going to press the idea remained that – just an idea.

The term *marriage contract* actually covers two different types of agreement:
● pre-nuptial agreements, made before a couple marry;
● contracts made during marriage, which can include arrangements for division of their property on separation or divorce.

The purpose behind both types is to clarify who will get what in the event of marriage breakdown (whether by separation, death or divorce), often by side-stepping, or trying to override, the court's powers. The formats can, however, be flexible enough to cover agreements about other areas of concern for a couple (e.g. when they want to start trying to conceive). For a suggested list of issues to be covered by a marriage contract see below.

Whether the purpose of circumventing the courts will be successful is in some doubt. Marriage contracts are by no means tried and tested and, in principle, English courts are resistant to the notion that their powers can be overridden. The main case cited in support of the effectiveness of marriage contracts does not give a sure-fire answer and actually related to a marriage in Brazil.

A husband and wife had, as is usual in Brazil, entered into a marriage contract. Could the wife obtain a divorce and claim for financial relief in this country having already

made a marriage contract? **Held:** *Yes, she could claim. The marriage contract would be included as one of the factors which the court would consider in accordance with Matrimonial Causes Act 1973 s25.*
Sabbagh (1975)

The courts have considered the position more recently.

The husband and wife, who were both Canadian, had both been previously married. The husband was the CEO of a mining company in which he had a substantial shareholding. The wife had a background in business and owned a property but her assets were very limited by comparison with the husband's. Soon after they met, the wife became pregnant. She did not want to be an unmarried mother. The husband did not want to marry but did not want her to terminate the pregnancy. He suggested a pre-nuptial agreement and made it clear that he would not marry without one. The marriage took place in 1995 and broke down five years later. The agreement was taken into account in the exercise of the court's discretion as 'one of the more relevant circumstances'. In the judge's view it would have been as unjust to the husband to ignore the existence of the agreement and its terms as it would have been to the wife to hold her strictly to its terms. Although the judge went on to award the wife considerably more than she was entitled to under the terms of the agreement, he said that he bore the agreement in mind, 'as tending to guide the court to a more modest award than might have been made without it'.
M v M (Prenuptial Agreement) (2002)

A pre-nuptial agreement was treated similarly in the case of *K* v *K* (2003). Again, the wife was pregnant at the time of the marriage. The wife's father took an active part in the negotiations leading to the conclusion of a pre-marital agreement under which she accepted a limitation on her entitlement in the event of divorce. The marriage foundered in its second year. The most notable feature of the court order was that the house provided for mother and child was on trust, reverting to the father on the child's adulthood in similar vein to provision for non-marital children. Also, the mother's entitlement to maintenance was limited by her agreement that she would not claim maintenance on divorce.

The position remains currently unclear and the law should be changed to give more certainty. Until that time, entering into a marriage contract is a gamble: it can make your intentions *vis-à-vis* each other as husband and wife clear, but whether the courts will uphold it is another matter. The courts will take the contract into consideration, but may still override it, especially, for example, if the courts take the view that the wife had not had proper disclosure of her husband-to-be's financial position, or if she had been pressured into making the contract or if she did not get independent legal advice.

What Marriage Contracts Can Cover*

The Family Law Committee of the Law Society recommend that Heads of Agreement (so the chief principles of such a contract) would include:

- Ownership of income and assets acquired before the marriage and the possibility of making claims against that property whether on death or divorce.
- Ownership of income or assets acquired in contemplation of or since the marriage:
  - whether assets are to be owned as joint tenants or tenants in common and if so in what proportions;
  - whether assets below a certain value are to be excluded.
- Treatment of gifts or inheritances.
- Ownership of items of personal use: e.g. jewellery.
- Liability for tax and debts.
- Provisions relating to duration, variation, review.
- Which country's law will govern the agreement.
- Liabilities for costs and expenses in relation to drawing up the agreement and any ancillary documentation.
- Methods of resolution of any disputes arising from the document.
- Any other issues of importance to the individual couple concerned.

* Extracted from *Maintenance on Capital Provision on Divorce. Recommendations for Reform of the Law and Procedure Made by the Family Law Committee.* May 1991.

4

Separation and Divorce

In this chapter we are concerned with relationships that are no longer working properly; for some reason the relationship has broken down and either, or both, of the parties now want to separate.

These days the law does not look closely at the conduct of the parties when a marriage is failing. Blame will be relevant only in exceptional cases. The courts are primarily concerned with safeguarding the welfare of any children and also, pragmatically, to ensure that a dead marriage is not perpetuated as an empty shell.

Cohabiting couples

If the pair never married, then there is nothing to stop them separating straight away and there is no legal process which currently (year 2004) needs to be gone through: the relationship can be brought to an immediate end. If, however, a cohabiting couple own property and have children together, then there will be a number of issues to sort out. For an overview of the current law on property for cohabiting couples see page 9 and page 10 for children. Mediation could well provide a useful forum to resolve such issues (*see* page 40).

Married couples

If a couple are married then, in contrast, they will, of course, need to divorce to bring the relationship to a formal end and, again, will need to consider issues involving the children, their home and financial matters.

This section now looks at the legal position on divorce.

Changing patterns of divorce?

Recently published figures from the Office for National Statistics confirm that, in 2002, the number of divorces granted in the UK increased by 1.9 per cent, from 157,000 in 2001 to 160,000. This is the highest number of divorces since 1997. This is the first time that the number of divorces has increased since 1996. In England and Wales, 70 per cent of divorces in 2002 were to couples where both parties were in their first marriage. The corresponding proportion was 80 per cent in 1982. This downward trend largely reflects the fall in the number of first marriages. In 2001, 13 per cent per 1,000 married people were divorced. Over the last ten years the average age at divorce has risen from 39 to 42 years for men and from 36 to 39 years for women, partly reflecting the rise in age at marriage. In 2002, the most frequent fact on which divorce was granted to a woman was the unreasonable behaviour of her husband, while for a man, it was separation for two years with consent.

A bigger picture may yet emerge now that the pension-sharing provisions have been brought into force; anecdotal evidence from family lawyers suggests that many wives were holding back from issuing petitions until their potential pension rights had been strengthened (*see* page 64).

New law on divorce?

At the turn of the last century, a new law, the Family Law Act 1996, was passed which would have radically changed the way couples could divorce. Instead of a *fault*-based system to prove that the marriage was really over, the new law would have switched to a *time*-based system instead – spouses would have had to wait for a period of time (around 18 months for couples with young children) before their marriage could legally end. Future arrangements over the children and money would need to have been sorted out before a divorce order was made by a court. However, in January 2001 the government announced that the proposed divorce reform will not go ahead after all. For the moment, the law will continue to operate on the fault-based system, and divorces will continue to be granted on the basis of adultery, unreasonable behaviour, two years' separation, two years' desertion or five years' separation (*see* page 31).

When a marriage is ending, most people immediately think of divorce as the obvious legal remedy, but there are, in fact, six legal remedies that can be used (*see* below). With all six procedures the courts have wide powers to sort out the couple's financial affairs.

WHICH TO CHOOSE

Each of the six remedies has its uses, its advantages and disadvantages. But the basic decision is to choose between ending the marriage (usually by divorce) or simply separating and keeping the marriage legally alive. Which to choose will obviously depend on individual circumstances and individual emotions. If there is any prospect of a reconciliation then separation is the better choice, since divorce effectively terminates the marriage. If the couple want an amicable divorce, separating for a period beforehand can help reduce the bitterness and make the eventual divorce less emotionally charged. What is commonly known as a 'no fault' divorce is where the couple have lived separately for two years prior to divorcing and both consent to the divorce going ahead.

Legal remedy	See page	Effect
1 Separation by informal agreement	29	These do not legally end the marriage – they just end the obligation to cohabit; the parties cannot remarry
2 Separation under a written deed or formal agreement	29	
3 Occupation order	29	
4 Judicial separation (rare)	29	
5 Divorce	30	These legally end the marriage (i.e. the husband and wife are both single people again)
6 Annulment (rare)	45	

IF A HUSBAND LEAVES HIS WIFE

While the pattern of family life is changing rapidly, it is still the case that many women are financially dependent on their husbands, especially when their children are young. If a man leaves his dependent wife, whichever long-term remedy the woman decides to pursue, she must ensure that she takes steps immediately to protect herself in the short term.

Housing

She should check that her husband is still paying the rent or mortgage. If he is not, she should arrange to do so herself. A landlord or building society cannot refuse to accept payment from her just because the home is in his name (*see* page 60). If she is not registered as a joint owner and the home is in her husband's name alone she should also register her matrimonial home rights against the legal title of the property (*see* page 62).

Financial

She could claim Income Support (or Working Tax Credit) if she has little or no money (income support would be applied for if the wife is not working outside the home, whereas Working Tax Credit may be available if she is in employment already but has not got enough to meet the bills) (*see* Welfare Benefits and Tax Credits, Part Three). She should also consider applying for maintenance for herself and the children. If she has a joint bank account with her husband she should make sure he cannot draw out all the money – perhaps she should even draw half out before the account gets emptied!

Violence

If her husband has been violent, especially if there is danger of further violence, she should see a solicitor. It might be possible to have her husband excluded from the home (*see* page 72).

SEPARATION

If the marriage is in difficulty, the first step need not be divorce. A period of separation can give both parties time to consider whether an end to the marriage is really what they want. If later they do want to go ahead with the divorce, the time spent apart can often pave the way for less heated legal proceedings.

There are four ways of legally separating:
1 a simple agreement to live apart;
2 a formalized agreement to live apart, set out in a deed;
3 an occupation order, which excludes a violent spouse from the home (but this only works where violence has occurred);
4 by judicial separation (relatively rare).

An informal separation agreement

The couple may simply decide to separate, and not reach any formal agreement about maintenance or who looks after the children. Alternatively, they may swap letters and accept those letters as binding. But the trouble is that the law might not regard the agreement as binding. First, the courts do not like to enforce contracts made between husband and wife (*see* page 24) and, second, they may have scant regard for an agreement that was made without the parties having had the benefit of legal advice. Accordingly, it is usually better to consult solicitors, obtain their advice and then have the terms of the agreement set out in a deed.

A couple married in 1954. The wife worked and managed the family finances although the house was bought with equal contributions of capital by both husband and wife, and they both contributed to the mortgage repayments. In 1973, the wife left the husband and went off with another man, taking one of the two children with her. The husband took legal advice and his solicitors drew up a document transferring the house from joint ownership to the husband. The wife did not take legal advice before she signed. In 1975 the wife applied for a share in the family assets. Held: The 1973 transfer should be overruled since it was made at a time of emotional stress. The wife should have a share in the value of the house, on the basis of its 1973 value.

B (1977)

However, if the husband's solicitors had fully explained the effect of the transfer to the wife and urged her to take legal advice, it is likely that the transaction would have been allowed to stand.

A formal separation deed

The courts can vary and alter the terms of a formal separation deed, but they are much less likely to do so than if it was just an informal agreement. This is because a formal deed indicates an intention for the parties to be legally bound and it also usually shows that they took legal advice before signing the agreement. A well-thought-out and considered deed will also reduce the likelihood of future argument as to exactly what was agreed. Once there were tax advantages to be had in formalizing maintenance payments under a deed, but these have now disappeared. Since the tax year 2000/2001, all tax allowances on maintenance payments have been scrapped. Maintenance is paid out of taxed income but is not taxable in the hands of the recipient.

A typical separation deed will contain a maintenance agreement, arrangements for the children and a mutual covenant releasing the other spouse from the marital duty to cohabit. It may also go on to divide up the family assets between the couple.

The terms of the deed can never be totally binding. The court always has the power to alter and vary the terms if it thinks that would be just – for instance, if the husband's income had increased significantly, or if he had deliberately concealed the true size of his wealth and so 'conned' the wife into under-settling. One point to note is that a provision requiring the wife to accept a stated level of maintenance payment for the rest of her life will always be void. The courts recognize that financial circumstances change.

A separation deed can never stop a wife's claims for maintenance – or even a husband's maintenance against his wife if he has been the one looking after the home and children. The only way that a couple can achieve a 'clean break' in financial terms is if they get a court order in divorce confirming this.

From a financially dependent wife's point of view it is important that the deed should entitle her to maintenance. It may be that at the moment she does not need much maintenance from her husband but she can protect her position by inserting an obligation on the husband to pay her even a nominal sum – which could be just 5p a year. As long as a specific sum is stated she can always go to the courts and ask for it to be increased. If no sum is stated, she may find it difficult at a later date to persuade the court to order that she be paid any.

It is usually wise to specify the circumstances that will bring the agreement to an end. These could include the death of either spouse, the commencement of divorce proceedings (in which case the court could make an order for maintenance, etc.) or if the wife should permanently cohabit with another man.

If the agreement releases the spouses from their mutual duty to cohabit then neither can later petition for divorce on the grounds of the other's desertion. If there is no duty to cohabit there can be no desertion.

An occupation order

An occupation order under Part IV of the Family Law Act 1996 can order one spouse to leave the home and/or stop him or her from returning, so it could be viewed as a way of separating formally. However, this remedy is only really available when there is a real danger of violence to the spouse who wants to stay in the home or to the children. These orders are discussed in Chapter 7.

Judicial separation

Judicial separation is a rarely used alternative to divorce proceedings. In 1999, there were 2,282 decrees of judicial separation issued. Of the decrees that are issued each year, over 90 per cent are presented by women. Judicial separation does not end the marriage in the same way that a divorce does. Accordingly, the parties are not free to remarry. But it does end the parties' obligation to live together. If one of the spouses dies intestate (i.e. without a will), the survivor will be able to claim the estate as the surviving spouse.

To obtain a judicial separation, the petitioner has to prove one of the same five grounds as is used to obtain a divorce (*see* below). However, there is no need to show that the marriage has broken down irretrievably. The main procedural difference is that there is no bar on getting a judicial separation in the first year of marriage, as there is on getting a divorce, and so a petitioner can get a judicial separation decree when he or she would not be able to obtain a divorce.

Judicial separation is of limited use these days. It is mainly used by petitioners who have religious scruples about divorcing, but it does not prevent the other spouse from obtaining a divorce if he or she is able to – and don't forget that after five years' separation he or she can get a divorce against the wishes of the other spouse in any event.

DIVORCE

A brief history

Originally, the church courts dealt with all matrimonial matters and those who wanted a divorce had to obtain a special Act of Parliament. The Victorians changed the law to allow a husband to obtain a divorce on the ground of his wife's adultery; later, women were also permitted to obtain a divorce on the ground of adultery. And that was the position until 1937. In that year, A. P. Herbert sponsored an Act which allowed divorce if any one of several 'matrimonial offences' – such as adultery, desertion, and cruelty – could be proved. This was a radical reform and it made divorce more easily obtainable.

Its disadvantage was that it emphasized the 'matrimonial offence' and the need to find the other spouse guilty of misconduct. Thus 'conduct' became very important, for only the 'sinned-against' could start divorce proceedings. The 'sinner' could not initiate the divorce. The concept of the matrimonial offence as the basis of our divorce laws was removed in 1969 when Leo Abse piloted the Divorce Reform Act through Parliament – an Act which aroused bitter controversy and claims that it was a Casanova's charter.

The 1969 changes, together with the Matrimonial Causes Act 1973, form the basis of the current law. Gone is the concept of the matrimonial offence; instead we have the overall question: 'Has the marriage broken down irretrievably?' If so (and this has to be proved by showing one of five facts, such as unreasonable behaviour) then the marriage will be ended, irrespective of who is to blame. 'Sinners' as well as the 'sinned-against' can now petition for divorce, although they will have to wait a sizeable period to do so.

The current divorce law requires the petitioner (the person asking for the divorce) to clear two hurdles before the divorce can be given:

1 Has the marriage lasted a year?
2 Has the marriage broken down irretrievably? This is shown by proving one of five sets of circumstances.

In addition, the petitioner must have lived in (been habitually resident in) this country for the last 12 months or be domiciled here (*see* page 36).

Divorce Hurdle No. 1: Has the marriage lasted a year?

No one can apply for a divorce unless they have been married for at least a year. This is an absolute rule – there are no exceptions. If a married person wants a divorce within the one-year period, all he or she can do is to leave the spouse and wait for the year to expire before filing a divorce petition (*see* page 34 for separation). In practical terms no one can obtain a divorce until about 15 months after marriage. This is because the one-year rule prevents them starting the divorce proceedings for 12 months, and then it generally takes a minimum of three months (often longer than that) for the divorce to go through.

Divorce Hurdle No. 2: Has the marriage broken down irretrievably?

The court wants dead marriages to be ended gracefully. But the law insists that the marriage must be dead. The phrase used is 'that the marriage has irretrievably broken down'. If the marriage has not died – for instance, if it has just temporarily broken down – then divorce is not allowed.

Before the courts will be persuaded that a marriage has irretrievably broken down, the petitioner must first prove that one of five facts, or sets of circumstances, exists. If the petitioner cannot bring his or her case within one of these five facts, then the court cannot say that the marriage has irretrievably broken down, and so no divorce can be granted.

In practice, once the petitioner can show that one of the five facts exists, then the court will more or less presume that the marriage has irretrievably broken down. So, in effect, divorce is now pretty much automatically available on any one of these five bases:

1 The other spouse has committed *adultery* and it is intolerable to live with him/her.
2 The other spouse has *behaved unreasonably*.
3 The other spouse has been in *desertion*, for at least two years.

4 Husband and wife both want a divorce and have been *separated* (living apart) for at least two years.

5 Husband and wife have been *separated* (living apart) for at least five years.

Note, in particular, No. 2, 'the other spouse has behaved unreasonably' – this is a catch-all phrase that covers marital misconduct that does not come within any of the four other factors.

Generally, the courts are not especially demanding in the standard of proof they require. In an undefended case the court will often give the petitioner the benefit of the doubt, even when the evidence is rather weak. The courts will not obstruct the dissolution of dead marriages. This is why it is usually unwise to defend a divorce petition; the mere fact that the couple have got to the divorce court will often be a clear indication that the marriage is not working, and both parties are likely to be advised that there is little point in defending the divorce.

A husband defended his wife's divorce petition on the basis that the wife had committed adultery, that the wife had entered into the marriage purely for financial gain and that she was a bad mother, an unsupportive wife and a drug taker. Held: He could not convincingly argue that the marriage had not broken down irretrievably. The husband had in his defence pulled away every foundation and cornerstone of the matrimonial relationship, and it said much about his attitude to the wife that he could begin to think that a reconciliation might be possible notwithstanding the allegations he had made in the course of defending the divorce. Hadjimilitis (Tsavliris) *v* Tsavliris (2002)

This does not, of course, prevent them from defending claims for maintenance, a share of the family assets, or applying for orders about the children. So, although the divorce may go through straightforwardly, there can still be long and bitter arguments about children and finances – those matters are distinct from the question of whether or not there should be a divorce. The divorce may be undefended, even though everything else is disputed.

GROUNDS FOR DIVORCE

The other spouse has committed adultery

More than mere adultery is needed. The law requires two things:

- that the other spouse has committed adultery;
- that the petitioner finds it intolerable to live with the other spouse, for whatever reason.

Strictly speaking, proving adultery is not enough, for the petitioner must also convince the court that he or she finds it intolerable to live with his or her spouse. In practice, though, the courts will readily assume that if there has been adultery, the petitioner finds it intolerable to live with the other spouse, as long as they have not been living together for a long time since the 'innocent' spouse found out (*see* below).

What is adultery?

Most people have a pretty clear idea what adultery is: it is voluntary sex between two people of different sexes, either or both of them being married. The courts have decided that actual sexual intercourse, involving penetration, but not necessarily orgasm, is necessary for there to be adultery. Sexual familiarity, foreplay or masturbation is not enough. Nor is sexual intercourse with someone else of the same sex – this would have to count as unreasonable behaviour instead. Since adultery must be a voluntary act, sex when drunk or when raped cannot count as adultery. Artificial insemination is not adultery – although it might be grounds for divorce based on 'unreasonable behaviour' if it took place without the consent of the other spouse.

Proving adultery

Fortunately, the courts do not require eyewitness evidence of adultery. They will look at the surrounding circumstances; usually, if the petitioner can show inclination and opportunity, then the court will assume that intercourse took place. Circumstantial evidence will usually suffice: for instance, that the couple have been seen holding hands, kissing, or in a parked car together late at night when they are supposed to be somewhere else; love letters or the contracting of venereal disease may also be sufficient evidence. Similarly, if a wife has a child when it was impossible for the husband to have been the father, that will be proof of her adultery.

Tests can also be used to show that the husband is not the father of his wife's child. Old-fashioned blood tests could not prove who was the father (although they could show if someone was not), but newer and more accurate DNA tests can be proof positive of who the child's father actually is.

If the petitioner thinks his or her spouse is committing adultery but has no evidence, he or she may have to hire an inquiry agent to obtain evidence. He will watch the spouse and keep a record of when and where they met their lover. However, inquiry agents are expensive to hire and it would be unwise for a suspicious husband or wife to hire an agent without first taking advice from a solicitor.

Usually there will be no need for the adultery to be proved by an inquiry agent or by other circumstantial evidence. More often than not, the adulterous spouse will sign a 'confession statement', which is a simple admission setting out when and where the adultery took place and with whom. Before 1991, only rarely would the court allow the name of the other person (the 'co-respondent') to be kept secret. Since then the respondent has been able to conceal the identity of the co-respondent and can simply confess to an act of adultery taking place with an anonymous third party.

Does committing adultery affect rights over children?

Under the old, pre-1969, divorce law, the courts were very concerned with which spouse was the 'guilty party', and in those days an admission of adultery might have seriously affected the rights of that spouse when the court came to decide custody of the children, the division of the family assets and the payment of maintenance. Now, 'guilt' is usually ignored and so the adulterous spouse can sign a confession statement knowing that it will probably make no difference to his or her position when the court decides about who should look after the children and how the money is to be divided.

Carrying on living with the adulterous spouse?

At one time, a petitioner had to show that he or she had stopped living with his or her spouse as soon as they had learnt of the adultery. If she cohabited with him she would probably be held to have forgiven him and so lost the right to petition for divorce. That rule has now been changed so that the petitioner can live with the adulterer for up to six months without it being held against him or her. This is sometimes called the 'kiss-and-make-up rule' – so called, because it allows the couple a chance to try living together and working out their problems without prejudicing their divorce rights.

The six-month period need not be one single period, but can be the total of several short periods of cohabitation. For instance, a husband may commit adultery in January. If the wife continues living with him until March, but then moves out, and returns again in July, she has until September to decide whether to rely on the January adultery as a ground for a divorce. (However, if he is still committing adultery, she can use the latest incident to start off a divorce petition based on adultery.) If the adultery stopped and the six months is exceeded, then that act of adultery cannot be used as a ground for divorce, except as evidence of the other spouse's 'unreasonable behaviour' if that is made the ground for divorce. If a further act of adultery occurs, a new six-month period starts.

Is it intolerable to live with the adulterous spouse?

The law requires the petitioner to prove more than a simple act of adultery; he or she must also show that they find it intolerable to carry on living with their spouse. As explained above, the court will usually accept the act of adultery as being enough to make living together intolerable. The mere fact that the couple lived together for up to six months following the adultery cannot be used to suggest that it is not intolerable for the couple to live together.

The position of the co-respondent

Finally, what of the co-respondent – the person with whom the adultery was committed? Although she is not required to, the petitioning spouse can name the co-respondent in the divorce petition and ask that the legal costs be paid by the adulterous spouse and/or the co-respondent.

The co-respondent can defend the divorce even if the respondent does not. It sometimes happens that the court finds that the respondent did commit adultery but dismisses the case against the co-respondent for lack of evidence.

The other spouse has behaved unreasonably

'Unreasonable behaviour' is a vague and imprecise phrase; deliberately so, for this is the 'catch-all' ground for divorce. Neither Parliament nor the courts have laid down a precise definition of 'unreasonable behaviour' because to do so might narrow the scope of this ground for divorce. Instead, we have an overall test – is the behaviour such that this petitioner cannot reasonably be expected to carry on living with this husband or wife? So it all depends on the facts of the individual case: how serious is the misconduct and what is its effect on the petitioner?

If there is clear physical violence to the petitioner or the children that will undoubtedly be 'unreasonable behaviour'. But few cases are that obvious – usually there is not one single incident but a succession of small, seemingly trivial, events which together combine to make the behaviour unreasonable. So small incidents can, together, add up to unreasonable behaviour, whether the misbehaviour is aimed at the children or the petitioner.

Unreasonable behaviour is the most common ground for divorce, followed by adultery, probably because both of these grounds allow for a divorce to be started straight away, without a waiting period. Both, however, can also lead to much greater friction. Agreeing the contents of the petition in advance with the respondent can pave the way for a less angry divorce.

What is unreasonable behaviour?

Examples are given of the sort of conduct that the courts will look at to see if there has been 'unreasonable behaviour' and, if so, whether the marriage has broken down. Remember that it is impossible to give a simple guide to behaviour that will be regarded as grounds for divorce; it always depends on the circumstances. But examples of conduct that have been held to be 'unreasonable behaviour' include:

- physical assault or ill-treatment, whether or not it causes personal injury, and whether it is aimed at the petitioner or at the children;

- verbal assault (i.e. ill-treatment of a non-physical kind) such as verbal abuse or insults, unkindness, or persistently ignoring the other spouse; threats of assault; boasting of sexual experiences with other people – whether true or not;
- sexual activity with another person which, while improper, is not adultery, such as a lesbian or homosexual relationship, bestiality or petting and kissing;
- adultery followed by over six months' cohabitation as husband and wife;
- unreasonable sexual activity, such as excessive sexual demands on the petitioner, or a complete refusal to have sex or to have sex without using contraceptives, or sodomy and other unnatural sexual activities forced on the petitioner;
- refusal to have children;
- obsessive tidiness; persistent nagging; dirty habits;
- frequent drunkenness – although much will depend upon the effect of the drunkenness; drug-taking;
- financial irresponsibility, such as failure to provide sufficient housekeeping money; failure to look after the home; irresponsible gambling; refusal to work when a reasonable job is available.

A few cases will illustrate how the courts decide whether or not there is 'unreasonable behaviour'. All of these are quite old cases as nowadays both courts and solicitors have a clear idea of what will count and how much evidence will need to be included.

Cases where the behaviour was unreasonable

The husband was retired and decided to renovate the house. He took up floorboards, mixed cement in the living room, and removed the lavatory door for six months. **Held: Unreasonable behaviour.** O'Neill (1975)

The wife suffered from fits and her physical and mental condition deteriorated as a result. She was an in-patient for 18 months and then went home to see if her husband could cope with looking after her. He did everything for her for three weeks but became tense, nervous and irritable. The wife also threw things at the husband's mother, who lived with them. **Held: Unreasonable behaviour, despite the fact that her behaviour was due to a mental condition.** Thurlow (1975)

The Irish wife had been married to the English husband for over 27 years. The wife complained that her husband was very dogmatic and dictatorial, with nationalistic, male chauvinist characteristics, which she had resented for many years. Any item of news or documentary programme about the political situation in Ireland would provoke the husband to make heartless and bigoted remarks about the Irish. He belittled her opinions and she felt unable to speak freely in his company. **Held: Unreasonable behaviour.** Birch v Birch (1991)

Cases where the behaviour was not unreasonable

Attitudes change. In a 1947 case a judge could say: 'It may no doubt be galling – or in some sense of the word humiliating – for the wife to find that the husband prefers the company of his men-friends, his club, his newspapers, his games, his hobbies, or indeed his own society, to association with her . . . But this may be called the reasonable wear and tear of married life.' Over 50 years later, these complaints would be sufficient to justify a divorce petition. Nowadays, the courts do not require serious misbehaviour. Even the case cited below might well be decided differently if it was being judged in the twenty-first century.

The couple had been married for six years and had two children when the husband suddenly lost interest in his wife and was no longer sexually attracted by her. He went out a lot and became absorbed in sports. He refused to visit a marriage guidance counsellor and eventually he left the home. **Held: This was not unreasonable behaviour.** (However, he was in desertion and so his wife would have been able to obtain a divorce on that ground after two years; *see* page 34.) Stringfellow (1976)

The test for unreasonable behaviour

Most of the cases deciding what was and was not unreasonable behaviour came soon after the current divorce laws were introduced. The courts have subsequently taken a common-sense, pragmatic, approach, spelt out in this case:

The correct test for an unreasonable behaviour divorce petition was whether a right-thinking person, knowing the parties and all the circumstances, would consider it reasonable to expect the petitioner to live with the respondent. It was not necessary for the petitioner to prove that the marriage breakdown had actually been caused by the facts she included in her petition. Buffery (1989)

Proving the unreasonable behaviour

Rarely a spouse might have evidence from other people to back up an allegation of unreasonable behaviour, but this is hardly ever necessary. For instance, if a wife has been assaulted by her husband and she received hospital treatment, she should obtain a certificate from the hospital confirming the date, time and nature of the treatment. Similarly, if her GP has been consulted in connection with the marital difficulties, he could write a letter confirming the attendance and his opinion as to the cause. Medical evidence showing that the marriage problems are getting on top of the petitioner can be useful.

Friends, neighbours and relatives may also be able to give evidence as to loss of weight, nervousness, tension, sleeplessness, depression, inability to concentrate at work, lack of interest in hobbies and also of weepiness.

The petitioner should also try to keep a record or diary of the husband's (or wife's) behaviour (i.e. noting, on the day, any way in which he abused or insulted her). Such evidence is usually enough to prove the case, for the court will not expect to be presented with independent eyewitness evidence of assaults or other misbehaviour. Usually four or five incidents of behaviour should be included in a divorce petition, as well as setting out in the divorce petition patterns of behaviour, and that will be sufficient.

Carrying on living with the 'unreasonable' spouse

As with adultery, there is a six-month 'kiss-and-make-up' period for a petitioner relying on unreasonable behaviour. This means that he or she can live with the spouse, and have sexual relations, for a total of up to six months after the last act of misbehaviour. Cohabitation during this kiss-and-make-up period will not be held against him or her. However, once they have lived together for six months then the cohabitation during the kiss-and-make-up period can be taken into account by the court. So the misbehaviour can still be used as the basis of an 'unreasonable behaviour' claim – but their continued living together becomes more relevant.

The other spouse has been in desertion for at least two years

Desertion is now very rarely used as a ground for divorce. However, it was a popular ground before the 1969 reforms and it has evolved into a complex and technical subject. What follows is only an outline, and it is usually wise to take legal advice before petitioning for divorce on the ground of desertion.

There are four elements to desertion:
- living apart;
- with the intention of deserting;
- against the wishes of the other spouse;
- and without justifiable cause.

Living apart

This means that there must be two separate households. It is possible for the couple to live in the same house and yet be living apart (*see* page 35).

With the intention of deserting

Desertion must be a voluntary act. So if a spouse is in prison or in hospital it will usually not be desertion.

Against the wishes of the other spouse

If they both agree to live apart it is 'separation', not desertion.

Without justifiable cause

Obviously if a wife is driven out of the family home by her husband's unreasonable behaviour, she will not be in desertion. But he will be – even though he remains in the family home. This is called 'constructive desertion' and arises where a spouse has behaved in such a way that he or she should have realized that the other spouse would be forced to leave. Constructive desertion cases are rare these days since such behaviour will usually be sufficient to justify a petition on the ground of 'unreasonable behaviour'.

Ending the desertion

The main ways of ending desertion are:
- by a separation agreement – if the couple agree to separate and draw up a separation agreement (*see* page 29), then the living apart will no longer be against the wishes of one of them, so it will become separation, not desertion;
- by a judicial separation order – this ends the marital duty to cohabit and so there can no longer be desertion;
- if the deserter's offer to come home is rejected by the deserted husband or wife – if an honest and genuine offer to return is made, the deserted spouse will become the deserter if the offer is rejected.

The effect of living together again

As with the other grounds of divorce, there is a six-month 'kiss-and-make-up' period in desertion cases. This allows a deserted spouse to resume cohabiting with the other spouse and know that their living together will not end the desertion until they have cohabited for a total of six months. In effect it allows the two-year period to be interrupted for trial periods of reconciliation.

The husband and wife both want a divorce and have been separated (living apart) for at least two years

This is the 'divorce by consent' provision that aroused such controversy when the 1969 reforms were introduced, although nowadays it seems astonishing that such controversy could have arisen. In essence it allows a couple who have been living apart for two years to end the marriage mutually, although one of them will still have to start off the divorce (the petitioner) and one will receive the divorce papers (the respondent) as there is currently no option for applying for a divorce jointly.

If only one of a couple wants a divorce and the other will not consent, there can be no divorce until they have been living apart for five years (*see* page 35).

The main difficulties that arise concern the meaning of 'living apart', for with the housing shortage it is often unrealistic to expect one of the couple to be able to move out and obtain accommodation elsewhere. To meet this situation, the courts have held that a couple can be living in the same house and yet be living apart, if they have 'separate households'. So, although they may share the same kitchen and bathroom, they must not share the same bedroom or living room, nor should they cook for one another nor eat together, nor spend their evenings together or watch TV together. In other words, they should cease living as a couple and act as though they were two strangers sharing the same house.

If the couple have shared the same accommodation and yet claim that they have not been living together, the petitioner will need to produce evidence confirming the current state of affairs and how they have ceased to cohabit.

When the two-year period starts

The two-year period of separation starts either from the date when the couple started living apart *or* from the date when they decided that the marriage was over – whichever is the later. Usually, of course, this will mean the date the couple started living apart, but this need not always be so.

A couple may be arguing and decide that a 'trial separation' would help them sort out their problems. They then separate but both have an intention of resuming cohabitation in the future. However, suppose that soon afterwards the wife decides that the marriage is dead and that there is no point in their resuming cohabitation together; in that case, the two-year period does not run from the date when they started living apart, but from the date when it was decided that the marriage was at an end.

The effect of living together during the two-year period

As with adultery and unreasonable behaviour, there is a six-month 'kiss-and-make-up' period for the two-year separation. This allows the couple to resume cohabitation for up to six months without that ending their separation. If they decide to carry on living apart before the six months are up, then the two-year period of separation carries on as before.

Suppose a couple decide to separate and do so for 12 months. They then resume cohabitation for three months, live apart again for six months, and then cohabit again for two months. So far they have lived 18 months apart and five months together. As long as they do not resume cohabitation for more than a month, they will be able to petition for divorce after a further six months of living apart.

Changing your mind

Before the divorce is made either the husband or wife can change his or her mind and withdraw consent for the divorce. If the decree nisi has been granted, the husband

or wife can still apply to the judge on financial grounds, and the judge will not make the decree absolute unless he is satisfied that:

- the petitioner has made reasonable provision for the other spouse or has promised to do so; or
- the other spouse does not need maintenance.

Husband and wife have been separated (living apart) for at least five years

This allows a blameless spouse to be divorced against his or her will. Subject only to the 'hardship' exception, explained below, there is virtually no way that the petitioner can be prevented from obtaining a divorce.

Living apart

The couple must be living in separate households throughout the five-year period. But it is possible for them to be living in the same house and yet be living in 'separate households' (*see* above).

The effect of living together during the five-year period

As with the other grounds for divorce, the six-month 'kiss-and-make-up' rule applies. So the five-year period can be interrupted by up to six months' resumption of cohabitation, but once they have lived together for more than six months, the five-year period has to start running again.

A couple separated in 1970, but the husband visited the wife regularly, spending weekends and sometimes several weekday nights with her. On three occasions he spent a whole week with her, and between January and March 1975 he lived there continuously. In September 1975 he petitioned for divorce but the wife disputed that they had been living apart for five years. Held: The couple had not been legally 'living together' since they had separated in 1970. They had been keeping separate households since then and his visits had not altered the nature of the relationship. Piper (1978)

However, this was a borderline decision.

The 'hardship' exception

There is a special defence available in separation cases. This allows the respondent (i.e. the defending spouse) to oppose the petition on the grounds that granting the divorce would cause him or her 'grave financial or other hardship, and that in all the circumstances it would be wrong (i.e. unjust) to dissolve the marriage'.

At first glance, this seems to be a defence that could be raised in many cases, especially those in which the respondent is a wife with several children who will be forced to accept a drastic reduction in her living standards. However, the courts have applied it very narrowly, for if the defence were of general application it would undermine the policy of the divorce laws – namely that dead marriages should be ended and not allowed to continue against the wishes of one of the parties.

In 1967, the husband, a Pole, had married his wife, a Sicilian, but the marriage had failed by the end of the year. The wife then went to live in Sicily with the new-born child. In 1972 the husband petitioned for divorce on the ground of five years' separation. The wife said divorce would cause her 'grave hardship' because (a) she was Roman Catholic and divorce was anathema to her, and (b) divorce would result in her and her son being socially ostracized in Sicily to such an extent that they would not be able to continue living there. **Held:** *This was not sufficient hardship. Divorce granted.*   Rukat (1975)

The husband, aged 67, was divorcing his wife aged 63. She pleaded 'other grave hardship' because she was looking after their invalid son and a divorce would cause her great hardship. The trial judge held this was 'grave hardship' and refused the divorce. The husband appealed and, before the appeal was heard, the invalid son died. **Held:** *The divorce would be granted.*   Lee (1973)

The wife opposed the divorce because she and her husband belonged to a backward Hindu caste and divorce would result in a serious social stigma and reduce their daughter's marriage prospects. **Held:** *The divorce would be granted.*
                                                    Balraj (1981)

In fact, the 'grave financial or other hardship' defence has only succeeded in a tiny number of cases. When the defence is raised nowadays, it is often as a tactical strategy to ensure that the respondent wife does get a proper financial settlement.

The husband petitioned for divorce on the basis that he and his wife had lived apart for five years. He was now 47 and she was 50. The wife had only modest earnings and a modest retirement pension. She argued that she would suffer 'grave financial hardship' if the divorce was granted, because she would lose the substantial widow's pension that she would otherwise enjoy if he were to predecease her. **Held:** *The divorce petition should be dismissed unless the husband put forward a proposal acceptable to the court that was sufficient to remove the element of grave financial hardship.*
                                                    K v K (1995)

However, if this case was to be decided again today, it is likely that the husband would have been able to get his divorce because of the ways in which the divorce courts earmark or split pension rights (*see* page 64).

The courts have made it clear that the defence is more likely to protect women than men, and that it is intended to benefit older women, rather than those who are young and healthy and who might remarry. Even so, courts will usually expect such wives to make financial claims in the divorce proceedings to alleviate hardship rather than allow a sham of a marriage to continue.

Financial arrangements

The judge can grant a decree nisi but refuse to make it absolute until he is satisfied that adequate financial provision has been made for the other spouse. This is the same as with the two-year separation by mutual agreement but, in practice, it applies to only a few cases.

DIVORCE: DOMICILE AND RESIDENCE QUALIFICATIONS

In order to claim jurisdiction, it is necessary to comply with Brussels II (a European Regulation dealing with jurisdiction in divorce proceedings). Since May 2000, jurisdiction can be based on the fact that both parties are habitually resident in England and Wales or that they were resident and the petitioner is still resident. If the respondent has not been habitually resident in England and Wales, it is sufficient for the petitioner to be habitually resident here provided she has been here for at least one year ending with the date of the petition or six months if she is also domiciled in England and Wales. Alternatively, if both parties are domiciled in England and Wales, habitual residence is not necessary (*see also* page 22).

THE DEFENCES TO A DIVORCE PETITION

If you are served with a petition for divorce and you do not want to be divorced, are there any defences you can raise to stop the divorce? It will be clear from the above section on the five grounds for divorce that the only possible defences are:

1 That the facts set out in the petition are not true and so the petitioner is not entitled to a divorce (e.g. you have not behaved unreasonably or committed adultery).

2 Although the facts specified in the petition are true, you do not agree that the marriage has broken down irretrievably. It will be remembered that the five grounds for divorce are no more than the permitted ways of showing irretrievable breakdown and that, in theory, one of the grounds can exist without the marriage having broken down. But, in practice, if the petitioner says he or she regards the marriage as having irretrievably broken down, there is usually little that you can do to disprove it. While it takes two to make a marriage, it takes only one to end it.

3 There has been more than the six months' cohabitation allowed under the kiss-and-make-up rule. All the grounds for divorce allow trial reconciliation periods of up to six months without prejudicing the divorce petition (for instance, you can sleep together for up to

six months after adultery; you can cohabit for up to six months during a two-year separation period). If you want to argue that there has been more than six months' cohabitation you will have to produce supporting evidence, such as a diary or the evidence of friends.

4 If you are being divorced against your will under No. 5 (husband and wife have been separated at least five years), then you may be able to raise the special defence that the divorce will cause you 'grave financial or other hardship'. But it is virtually unknown for the defence to succeed and for all practical purposes it might just as well not exist, so limited is its application.

5 If you are being divorced under No. 4 (husband and wife both want a divorce and have been separated for at least two years) or No. 5 (husband and wife have been separated for at least five years) then you can object to the decree nisi being made absolute if the financial arrangements made for you are inadequate (*see* page 35). In practice this defence rarely works in the long term because the courts feel that financial matters are best dealt with separately, and kept distinct from the decision whether or not to grant the divorce. However, as mentioned above, holding up the divorce proceedings in such a way can sometimes happen as a bargaining tactic.

These are the only defences that can be raised to a divorce petition. Generally, therefore, a well-grounded divorce petition cannot be defended. This is reflected in the fact that 99 per cent of petitions are undefended – although this does not mean that the parties are in agreement about the financial arrangements or the future arrangements for the children.

Financial matters – often referred to by lawyers as 'ancillary relief' – are dealt with in a private hearing in the court chambers, and are separate from the question of whether or not there should be a divorce. The point to grasp is that a divorce can be 'undefended' even though the couple are at loggerheads about everything else. The divorce, being undefended, will be simple and straightforward (and hence this aspect at least will be less costly in legal fees) even if there are then long and difficult negotiations (and court hearings) about the children and the finances.

If the divorce is defended – and only about one per cent are – public funding may be available, although the respondent will have to pass means and merits tests. It is not available for undefended divorces although the Legal Help scheme may provide some of the cost of legal advice and assistance (*see* page 38).

GETTING A DIVORCE

How much will it cost?

The cost will vary according to the complexity of the case. The more work involved, the more a solicitor will charge. The basic factor in terms of the divorce itself (remember to keep this separate from issues over children and money) will be whether or not the divorce is defended by the other spouse. If it is defended then the costs will rise dramatically, but only a few divorces are in fact defended. In addition, the costs will increase if there are complicated financial disputes or if there is disagreement over the arrangements for the children. However it is possible to cut the costs dramatically by using a mediator to help resolve issues between you (*see* page 40).

Usually the petitioner will know whether or not the divorce will be defended when the respondent returns the divorce papers to the court, for among the questions is one asking whether or not the respondent is intending to defend the case. If the answer is 'yes' the case is defended and is transferred from the county court to the High Court. If it is defended, legal advice will be necessary, and public funding may be available to help with the cost.

How much will the legal costs be?

It all depends therefore on the extent of the disagreement between the husband and wife. In most cases, the divorce is undefended and one could think in terms of a solicitor charging between £500 and £700 (plus VAT), to which would have to be added court and swearing fees of approximately £220 in total. Generally, solicitors in the south charge more than those in the north! Top notch divorce lawyers in London and other major city centres can charge £300 (plus VAT) an hour or even more – so who you choose as your lawyer will be a major factor in how much you end up paying. It is important, however, to choose a lawyer who knows what he is talking about – i.e. is a family law specialist (*see* below).

If there is a dispute between spouses, and so the case has to go to a trial, one must accept that the legal costs will be high. A defended divorce will probably cost each spouse over £3,500 if they are paying privately and are not entitled to public funding. A dispute over maintenance would probably cost anything from £1,800 upwards and if all the money aspects are bitterly disputed, ending up in a full court hearing, the costs will run into many many thousands of pounds. Children applications probably start at about £1,200, but could go up to £3,000, or even more, if several hearings were needed (although the involvement of 'experts', such as psychiatrists, can result in a bill running into several thousand pounds). In short, therefore, the size of the legal bill will depend upon the extent of the disagreement between the parties.

Remember that public funding may be available, but a husband or wife on public funding usually ends up paying their own legal fees (since the family assets will often be used towards repaying the public funding costs under what is called the 'statutory charge'). This is a most important point that is often overlooked; *see* page 787 for how the rules work. The moral is that there are sound financial reasons for spouses to try to reach some sort of compromise rather than throw away their money on legal costs.

Remember too that you do not have the stark choice of sorting things out directly with your spouse (which you may feel unable to do at present) or sorting things out through solicitors. Nowadays family mediation is much more widely available than it was in the past and if you qualify for publicly funded family mediation (broadly if your disposable income is £707 per month or less (2003 figures) and your capital is under £8,000) then you can get free mediation. Not only are the up-front costs met by the Legal Services Commission (the new term for the Legal Aid Board) but there is no clawback under the statutory charge. Also associated legal costs will be covered under a form of public funding called 'Help with Mediation' and, again, there will be no clawback. These cash incentives to opt for mediation are proffered by the Legal Services Commission as a financial inducement to avoid costly full-blown litigation – so try it and see if it works. (As mediation is always voluntary, you can stop if you find it is not working for you.)

Will public funding pay the costs?

The rules as to financial eligibility for public funding are set out in Chapter 100. Many middle-class wives who, when securely married, were outside the public funding limits may well be eligible when at loggerheads with their husbands and so deprived of their income.

Defended divorces can be very expensive. However, public funding is available to help with all or part of the legal costs – assuming that the applicant comes within the current financial limits.

Public funding is not available for undefended divorces, although it may be available to cover the costs of disputes over the children and/or money matters. This general denial of public funding is, however, subject to three exceptions.

Public funding may be available under 'Legal Help'

Up to April 2000, if you could not get full public funding but wanted some legal help with an undefended divorce, for example, you could apply under what was known as the green-form scheme (or more technically Claim 10).

In April 2000, this scheme was replaced with 'Legal Help' which again is still different from public funding (which covers court proceedings). Broadly, Legal Help covers legal advice and assistance – that is, everything except court proceedings. (See page 789 for how Legal Help works and the financial limits.)

So although a petitioner may not be entitled to full public funding ('Legal Representation') for an undefended divorce, he or she may be able to obtain Legal Help, covering a limited amount of time a solicitor spends on a case (the solicitor can sometimes apply for extensions of this limit). This is supposed to be enough to allow the solicitor to draft the divorce petition, give general advice on the divorce and perhaps write a few letters, although in practice the time allowed is very tight. In short, a solicitor is supposed to be able to do most of the work in the case, except take the actual steps in legal proceedings. These must be done by the petitioner, since the scheme does not cover a solicitor's costs in court proceedings, although it will cover the solicitor's fees in telling the petitioner what to do.

Help with Mediation

Help with Mediation is a new form of legal assistance, introduced again in April 2000. It is designed to give clients going through mediation back-up legal advice in support of the mediation process. So this covers help in drawing up a legally binding document reached in mediation and, where appropriate, help in confirming this agreement in a court order and related conveyancing (property transfer) work. As mentioned beforehand, it is genuinely free legal assistance to those who qualify financially, and the Legal Services Commission will not try to claw back the legal costs from any money received by the publicly funded person.

General Family Help and/or Legal Representation may be granted in more complicated cases

The technical new term for public funding is 'Legal Representation' when there is a proven need to take court-based proceedings, or General Family Help when the dispute can be sorted out through negotiation (or even where proceedings need to be taken to get full financial disclosure from a spouse trying to hide money assets). Before being able to apply for these forms of public funding, in most areas of England and Wales a client must be referred to a family mediator (unless an exemption applies, for example, there has been violence) to find out about family mediation and see if mediation would be a suitable way of sorting things out.

If mediation is not suitable and Legal Representation is granted it will cover the solicitor's fees in conducting the dispute for the petitioner – unlike Legal Help, which covers only advice and assistance from the solicitor.

In an undefended case there is an alternative to paying a solicitor to handle the divorce. Both petitioner and respondent can act for themselves – a summary of the steps to be taken in a do-it-yourself divorce is set out on page 43. However, it is still a good idea to get some legal advice at the outset of divorce proceedings to make sure that you know your legal rights and responsibilities. Although a petitioner, or respondent, is entitled to act for himself or herself in a defended divorce case, this is usually unwise. The complexity of the procedures and the issues involved make it advisable to use a solicitor.

Consulting a solicitor

For how to find a solicitor, see Chapter 98. But remember that solicitors specialize, and the solicitor who handled a friend's conveyance may not be as effective or knowledgeable when conducting a divorce. The Solicitors' Family Law Association has a membership base of around 5,000 solicitors who all specialize in family law. Both the Law Society and the Solicitors' Family Law Association have accreditation schemes for specialist family lawyers. For a list of their local solicitors specializing in family law, send a stamped-addressed envelope to:

The Administrative Secretary, SFLA, PO Box 302, Orpington, Kent BR6 8QX. Tel: 01689 850227 or search on their website (www.sfla.org.uk).

All solicitor members have to sign a code of practice saying that they will promote a constructive and conciliatory rather than an aggressive or angry approach to resolving marriage breakdown problems (which should avoid unnecessary build-up of legal costs).

Many people find it embarrassing to have to tell a complete stranger the full details of their marital affairs, including perhaps, their sexual relationship. However, lawyers will treat their information as strictly confidential and will not tell anyone else about it. They will not be shocked or embarrassed by anything they may be told; in all probability, they will 'have heard it all before' and will treat the matter in as unemotional and professional a manner as would a doctor. It is not for them to become emotionally involved in the case; they are paid to provide objective advice and cannot do that if their judgement is clouded by prejudice in favour of their client.

They will also test the strength of their client's case by asking the sort of questions that the other spouse's solicitor may, in time, ask. Some people are surprised when they are cross-examined by their own solicitor in this way; the reason is that solicitors need to find out the weaknesses in the case so that they can then take steps to strengthen them.

A client who is not happy with his or her choice of solicitor should consider changing to another firm. But this should, however, only be a last resort.

In particular it is important not to blame the solicitor for the law. Just because a solicitor tells a client that the case is hopeless it does not follow that the solicitor is incompetent, or that he or she dislikes the client. If the law does not support the case then it will be pointless to go to another solicitor.

Preparing for the interview with the solicitor

A solicitor's time is money, so to reduce the time spent by the solicitor (and thus reduce costs) it is worthwhile preparing for the interview in advance by providing the solicitor with a summary of the facts of the case. The following is a useful checklist. Of course, not all the information may be readily accessible, but giving as much as you can helps the solicitor to concentrate on the main disputes.

Personal
- Full names and ages of both spouses.
- Telephone numbers (work and home) and addresses (including address where spouses last lived together as husband and wife).
- The date and place of the marriage.
- Occupations of both spouses.
- Details of any previous marriages and relevant court proceedings.

The children
- Full names and dates of birth of natural children and children of the family (like stepchildren).
- Details of schools attended or other training and any special needs (e.g. if a child is disabled).
- Any agreements made about where the children will live, who will look after them and any arrangements for child support.

Finances
- Income (if known) of both spouses.
- Debts, both individual and joint.
- Details of the home:
  – if owned, whether in sole or joint names, its approximate value, and the name and address of the mortgagee;
  – if rented, whether the tenancy is in sole or joint names, and the name and address of the landlord or local authority.
- Details of bank, building society or other accounts and any savings.
- Other assets, for example shares, endowment policies and other life insurances, PEPs, TESSAs and ISAs and, very importantly, pensions.

For the first interview it can be useful to take along (if available):
- the marriage certificate;
- copies of any previous relevant court orders;
- correspondence from solicitors;
- anything else relevant (e.g. letters from creditors).

Can You Get a Divorce?

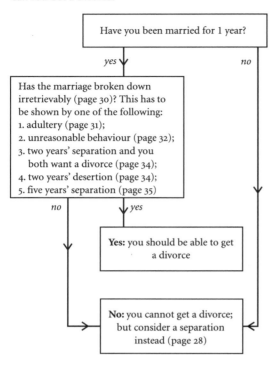

Have you been married for 1 year?

yes ↓   *no*

Has the marriage broken down irretrievably (page 30)? This has to be shown by one of the following:
1. adultery (page 31);
2. unreasonable behaviour (page 32);
3. two years' separation and you both want a divorce (page 34);
4. two years' desertion (page 34);
5. five years' separation (page 35)

no ↓   ↓ *yes*

Yes: you should be able to get a divorce

No: you cannot get a divorce; but consider a separation instead (page 28)

Reconciliation

Divorce is only for dead marriages. If there is any possibility of a reconciliation then the divorce should not go through. There are numerous agencies that will give advice and help to a couple in difficulties: for instance, Relate (formerly Marriage Guidance Council), priests, doctors, therapists and, for more specialized problems, the Family Planning Association, the probation service, child-care officers, etc.

Mediation: definition and purpose

Thankfully the term mediation has, by and large, taken over from the term conciliation, which itself was often confused with 'reconciliation', meaning (of course) getting couples back together again. Mediation is not therapy or counselling and does not look at the past, nor why the relationship has broken down but, instead, it focuses on resolving conflicts for the present and future. In essence, family mediation is a form of alternative dispute resolution (ADR) but differs from ADR in that it not only deals with actual conflicts but also deals with the effects and consequences of marriage breakdown – what happens in the wake of a separation and/or divorce.

Mediators work towards helping ex-partners make decisions over not only their own futures but also those of their children.

Who is family mediation for?

Family mediation can be used for a variety of different family issues. Although mediation is most commonly used by couples (married or unmarried, heterosexual or homosexual) ending their relationship, family mediation can also be used for issues between siblings, family business disputes, inheritance claims and elder mediation, for example. Mediation is hardly ever suitable where there are child protection issues involved and should only be chosen cautiously wherever there has been domestic violence or abuse. In essence, each of the parties who opt for mediation should feel that they will be able to arrive at solutions without fear of any retaliation taking place outside the sessions.

What issues?

It is for the couple who are splitting up to decide what issues they wish to bring to the mediation arena – either individually or jointly. Issues may include the future of the relationship, concerns over their children, disputes over the family home, property, finance, or any other aspect of their affairs. A couple can come at any time to mediation – from a stage when they are just considering splitting up to having divorced years ago but where unresolved conflicts (over the children or maintenance, for example) still remain. If the couple is, as yet, unsure whether they want to separate and want to explore the possibilities for a healthy reconciliation, a referral to marriage guidance or specialist counselling or therapy for couples may be a better way.

What type of mediation? All-issues, property and finance and children-only mediation

Some mediators deal with children-only issues and others deal with the whole spectrum of issues which can come up, for example, whether or not to divorce and on what grounds, dealing with housing, division of capital and debts, maintenance and pensions and, last but by no means least, children issues. Mediation which deals with the whole spectrum is called 'all-issues mediation'. If the couple have no children and want simply to deal with money matters, this type of mediation can be termed 'property and finance'. Some mediators are specialist family lawyers who have trained as mediators while others come from a variety of different backgrounds, often from the mental health sector (such as therapists or counsellors).

The process of mediation

Mediation will usually involve several sessions – four to eight are not uncommon – although how many are needed depends on the number of issues which need sorting out and how complex or tangled the dispute has become already. The first session is very often termed an intake session, when the mediator(s) will explain what mediation is – and is not – and, if both parties want to go ahead, the mediator will ask the clients to sign a mediation agreement which sets out the terms of the mediation and its ground rules. Mediators can give information in an even-handed way but they cannot give advice (which will need to be obtained from a solicitor if necessary).

The agreement will explain the functions of the mediator, that the mediator's role is to be impartial or balanced. The agreement will also help the parties explore the options open to them to help them arrive at solutions appropriate to their circumstances – once there has been a full disclosure of assets, liabilities, income and outgoings. Mediation sessions most often last for an hour and a half, although the initial session can be shorter than this. The mediation agreement should also detail the cost of the mediation – usually fees are worked out on a sessional basis, with extra costs for additional work over and above the sessions, such as time spent in preparing summaries setting out the outcome. Since 1997, the Legal Services Commission has been providing publicly funded family mediation. The income limit (with some allowances for dependants) is £707 per month and a big plus for the scheme is that once publicly funded mediation has been awarded, the Legal Services Commission will pay the mediator's fees and there will be no clawback of these costs under the statutory charge – so mediation will then be genuinely free. If someone wants to apply for public funding, under the mediation scheme, they will first need to go and see a mediator to explore whether mediation will be suitable before being issued with a public funding certificate – the first session with a mediator will in any event be free. Fees for privately paying clients will vary – sometimes assessed on a sliding scale according to income. £75 per person per hour is often quoted – a considerable saving on legal costs.

Mediation – it's always voluntary

Mediation is a voluntary process and will only work if both of the ex-partners are willing to attend. Either can stop the mediation at any time if he or she believes it is no longer helpful.

What mediators can do is to provide information on an even-handed basis, to assist the parties in understanding the principles of the law applicable to their circumstances and the way in which those principles might be applied generally. Information can be provided not only about the law but can also include areas such as finance, welfare benefits, children issues. The purpose is to assist the parties in making informed decisions. The parties will be free to seek their own independent legal advice,

and should indeed be recommended to do so – but this advice should not stem from the mediator.

The mediation will often run most effectively where the parties have already taken legal advice beforehand. The parties will have greater confidence in entering the mediation process and negotiating with each other with the assistance of the mediator in the knowledge of what the parameters of a reasonable settlement might be. Supportive legal advice can continue to help and not hinder the mediation process, and clients may need specific advice on a variety of different issues – pensions for example – for which they can be referred back to their solicitor and/or perhaps an actuary.

Children and family mediation

Mediators can help in many ways over children issues, not only in helping the parents plan workable arrangements for how the children will be spending time with each of their parents but also in helping parents help their children through the usually painful period of separation and/or divorce. Mediators can help parents prepare for telling their children about the separation and arrangements and explain how children might react. Children appreciate clear explanations of what is happening explained in ways appropriate to their age and understanding – but the task of dealing with the children's needs is often very difficult for parents who are having a bad time too. Mediators can help them help their children.

The outcome of mediation

If the mediation is successful in the sense that resolution is achieved over all the disputes brought to the mediation table (this happens in around three in five cases), then the mediator will draw up a Summary or Memorandum of Understanding setting out the proposals reached. The proposals will not yet be binding – each party then has the extra opportunity of getting legal advice before signing anything and their lawyers can translate the terms into a binding document – a Separation Agreement or Consent Order from the courts, for example. However, if the resolution is over children issues, then sometimes the letter setting out the terms of agreement can be shown to the court.

Most couples who opt for mediation find that it is cost-effective – it saves on expensive legal costs of fighting out the disputes through the court – and that there are other less tangible benefits – like improved communication and more co-operation over things to do with the children. However, as with choosing a good solicitor, it is important to choose a good mediator – trained and experienced for the task (anyone can, theoretically, call themselves a mediator without any training whatsoever).

Useful points of contact for finding a family mediator are:

The Solicitors' Family Law Association (Tel: 01689 850 227)

The Family Mediators Association (Tel: 0117 946 7062)

The UK College of Family Mediators (Tel: 0117 904 7223)

National Family Mediation (Tel: 020 7383 5993)

How much publicity for the divorce?

Generally, a divorce will receive no publicity; with around 145,000 divorces each year, the press are likely to be interested only if one of the parties is a public figure.

Undefended divorces are generally arranged by post so there is no court hearing. Defended cases are always heard in open court, however, and the press and public can attend if they wish. But discussion of arrangements for the children and money matters is heard in private, in what are called 'chambers', so these matters are always kept secret.

In addition, the press are subject to strict regulations as to what they can report, namely only:

● the names, addresses and occupations of those involved;

● any charges, defences and counter-charges that are supported by evidence – but not the evidence given;

● any submission on a point of law (and the court's decision);

● the court's judgment and any observations made by the judge when giving judgment and during his summing-up. So the judge can use this indirect route to allow the evidence to be reported.

Is court attendance necessary?

Since the Children Act came into force on 14 October 1991, court appearances in divorces involving children have become much less frequent. It is now possible to get a divorce where all matters are agreed without ever entering the portals of a court. But the broad rule of thumb remains that wherever there is a dispute – over a defended divorce, over the children or over finances – then you will end up in court unless the dispute is resolved through mediation, by the solicitors or by the parties themselves.

The divorce certificate

When the court grants a divorce it will first issue a decree nisi. The decree absolute can be applied for six weeks and one day later, and is usually a formality. It is the certificate of the decree absolute that is needed as a divorce certificate (e.g. if asked for by the tax authorities or by the local authority when applying for rehousing). Copies can be obtained either from the divorce registry or from the county court that granted the divorce.

Solicitors will usually advise not to apply for decree absolute until the money matters are settled. As soon as a decree absolute is made, the marriage is brought to an end, and an ex-spouse who survives the death of the other ex-spouse would not be entitled to any pension benefits, for example (if an ex-husband dies immediately after the divorce and before money matters have been sorted out, this could be very important!).

DIY divorce: the undefended divorce petition

Two factors have made DIY divorce more popular in recent years. First, public funding is no longer available for undefended divorces and, second, the procedure involved has been considerably simplified.

It is not difficult to conduct your own undefended divorce case. But be sure that you are not making a false economy in cutting out solicitors' fees. If there is a considerable amount of money to be argued over or if there are children involved, it is usually wiser to take legal advice than to risk making a mess of your case. Similarly, it is unwise to act for yourself if the case is defended. Defended cases are heard in the High Court, where the procedure is much more formal and legalistic than in a divorce county court, where undefended divorces are heard. If your spouse is likely to be obstructive in any way you would probably be advised to employ a solicitor.

When you start the divorce proceedings (*see* below) you may not know whether your spouse will defend the petition. It is not uncommon for the spouse to say initially that he or she will defend the petition when this is in fact no more than a bargaining tactic in the dispute over the children and/or money. Usually a compromise is worked out and the case ends up as undefended. For instance, a wife may petition for divorce on the grounds of her husband's unreasonable behaviour. He denies this and cross-petitions (i.e. asks for a divorce from her) on the grounds of her adultery. She admits that she has committed adultery. Both sides want a divorce but are raising issues against the other in an attempt to secure more of the family assets or to improve their chances of gaining custody of the children. In the end, the husband proposes that the wife can have her divorce if she accepts only a reduced amount of the value of the matrimonial home, rather than the larger amount she might otherwise have received. If this should happen to you, consult a solicitor before agreeing to anything.

It must be appreciated that the tactics in a divorce case are these days really aimed at the negotiations over money matters and sometimes over the children too, although children should never be used as pawns in a marital battle. The divorce itself is usually regarded as of relatively minor importance, since it is probably a foregone conclusion that the divorce petition will succeed.

For how the courts deal with money matters and children, see Chapters 5, 8 and 9.

A summary of how to obtain your own undefended divorce

1 Obtain a certified copy of your marriage certificate (or the original if you still have it).
2 Draft the divorce papers.
   (**a**) Go to the local divorce county court (or legal stationers) and obtain:
   - three copies (four if it is an adultery case and the co-respondent is named) of the standard divorce petition;
   - if there are children, three copies of the standard Statement of Arrangements for the children (ask for form M4);
   - a copy of the notes for guidance on filling in the forms (usually contained within the petition) and the free booklet on DIY divorce.
   (**b**) Fill in one copy of the Statement of Arrangements form and endeavour to agree the contents with the respondent if possible and get him/her to countersign the form. Also you may wish to try to agree the contents of the petition with the respondent too.

   If the respondent refuses to countersign the Statement of Arrangements and will not co-operate, you can still go ahead with filing the divorce papers (but it would be wise to seek legal advice).

   Use the notes for guidance and the free booklet and the books recommended below for advice on how to fill out the forms.
3 Start the divorce proceedings.
   Take or send to the divorce county court:
   - two copies of the completed and signed divorce petition (three if the divorce is based on adultery and the co-respondent is named) and two copies of the Statement of Arrangements form (if there are any children);
   - the marriage certificate or a certified copy;
   - the fee of £180 (people of limited means are exempted – ask at the court).

   Note: If you are claiming a share in the home and you are not named as a joint owner you may need to register your claim at the Land Registry to protect your position (*see* page 62).
4 The court allocates a reference number and will give the petitioner a slip confirming that number and the day on which the petition was lodged at court. The court sends to the respondent (i.e. your husband or wife):
   - a copy of the divorce petition form and Statement of Arrangements form (if there are children);
   - a Notice of Proceedings form;
   - a form for him or her to acknowledge that he or she has been served with (i.e. received) these documents, called an acknowledgement of service form.
5 The respondent signs the acknowledgement of service form, stating that he or she does not intend to defend the divorce, and sends it back to the court. He or she should do so within three days of receipt. If the respondent fails to do so, the petitioner will have to prove service (i.e. show the court that the respondent has received the divorce papers) by some other means. This can include arranging for the respondent to be served in person with the divorce papers, though the petitioner cannot serve the papers himself or herself. Ask for advice from the court if this problem arises or seek a solicitor's help.
6 The court will then send the petitioner:
   - a copy of the acknowledgement of service form;
   - a standard form to request directions for trial;
   - a standard form of affidavit for you to complete. This will set out the basis of the petition and the evidence in support (if required).
7 Take along the completed affidavit and copy exhibits needed to a solicitor (there will be a fee payable – around £7.50) or a court official to swear. Send these documents back to court, together with the completed form asking for directions for trial.
8 The divorce papers then all go before the District Judge (who used to be called a court registrar). If he thinks the petition is sufficient to entitle the petitioner to a divorce, he will set a date for the decree nisi to be pronounced (but neither party will have to attend court to hear the pronouncement).

   If there are children, the District Judge must also consider whether he or she is satisfied that the court need not make a formal court order about the children (a court order will be made only if it is better for the children that this should be done – *see* Chapter 9).

   If the District Judge is so satisfied, a certificate of satisfaction will be issued to that effect. No court attendance will be required.

   If the District Judge is not so satisfied, then the court can ask for:
   - a welfare report;
   - further evidence;
   - a court hearing when the parties attend.

   After that has been done, the court will again have to consider whether an order is better for the children and either will make no order about the children at all or make a section 8 order (*see* page 108).
9 Once the decree nisi has been pronounced a copy is sent to both spouses, together with the District Judge's certificate or court order about the children.
10 Six weeks and one day after the decree nisi, the petitioner can apply for a decree absolute (the final stage of divorce). Obtain a copy of the standard application

Divorce: Agreed Arrangements for Children

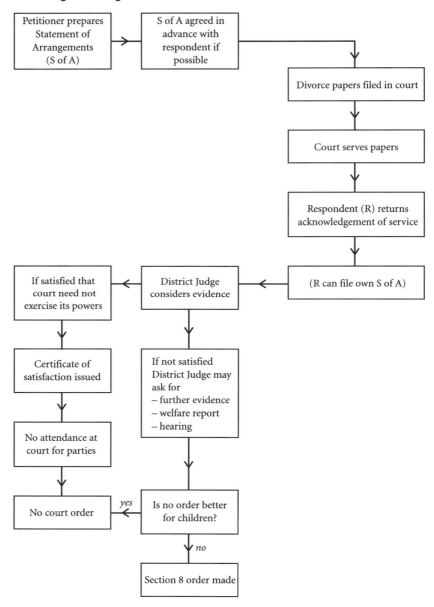

form (ask for form M8) and send a copy of the completed form to the divorce court with the court fee – currently £30. (If the decree absolute is being applied for on notice, i.e. by the respondent, then the court fee rises to £60.)

11 If the petitioner fails to do this the respondent will have to wait for an extra period of three calendar months (i.e. four and a half months since the date of the decree nisi) before making his or her own application for the decree absolute.

12 The District Judge makes the decree absolute and a certificate of decree absolute is sent to both petitioner and respondent.

And that's all there is to it! The whole process usually takes around four or five months, though it is possible to speed things up if there is a special reason (e.g. if the woman is pregnant and wants to get divorced to remarry the father of her unborn child) and if both parties co-operate.

Since the Children Act came into force in 1991, the vast majority of divorce cases, even those involving children, will be dealt with by paperwork only, under the inaptly named special procedure (there is nothing special about it at all). The odd old arrangement of 'section 41 appointments', when parents had to go in front of a judge for an average of four minutes to explain what was happening about the children, has now been scrapped. Now neither party will usually have to attend court about an undefended divorce or about agreed arrangements for the children (although they may have to if there is a problem over finances).

Further information

There are several DIY divorce books on the market. Recommended is *The Which? Guide to Divorce* (Imogen Clout, Which? Ltd). Also there is a useful booklet called *Undefended Divorce*, available from any divorce county court. In a completely straightforward case it will be a sufficient guide, as long as the parties are able to overcome the hurdles of struggling with legal forms.

ALTERNATIVES TO SEPARATION OR DIVORCE

A much less common alternative to separation or divorce is to have the marriage annulled.

ANNULMENT

Annulment is like divorce in that it ends a marriage. But, whereas divorce is granted because the marriage has now broken down irretrievably, an annulment is granted if the marriage was not valid in the first place or if it is

defective in some way. It is, in one sense, as if the marriage never existed. Annulments are relatively rare these days for most eligible couples are able to obtain a divorce instead. Some couples still prefer an annulment, especially if they have religious objections to divorce (e.g. either 'spouse' could remarry in a Church of England church). There are less than 1,000 applications each year (only 658 in 1999) – compared with some 145,000 divorce petitions. One advantage of an annulment claim is that there is no need for the marriage to have lasted a year before the proceedings can be started (*cf.* the rule in divorce cases, page 30). As with divorce, the court can also make orders concerning maintenance, money and the children.

The law distinguishes between two types of annulled marriages – those that are *void* and those that are *voidable.* The distinction is of little practical importance and basically amounts to the fact that (in theory) with the former there was never a marriage, whereas with the latter there was a marriage but it was defective. The children of a voidable marriage will always be legitimate; with a void marriage the children will be illegitimate only if at the time of the conception one of the parents knew that the marriage was probably invalid (which is, of course, extremely rare in practice).

The grounds for annulling a marriage

Void

1 The couple are too closely related.
2 Either was under 16 years of age at the time of marriage.
3 Certain marriage formalities were not followed.
4 The marriage is bigamous.
5 The couple are of the same sex.
6 Invalid polygamous marriage – because, although the marriage was valid abroad, one of the parties was domiciled here at the time of the marriage.

In 1999, rock singer Mick Jagger sought to argue that his Balinese marriage to Jerry Hall had been a sham because certain marriage formalities had not been followed. Jerry Hall was still successful in getting a settlement reputed to be in the region of £5 million.

Voidable

1 No consummation of the marriage because one of the couple was incapable. Consummation is any one act of sexual intercourse involving full penetration and a sustained erection; ejaculation is not necessary. Pre-marital sex does not count as consummation.*

---

* The other spouse can defend the petition if he or she can show both (a) that the petitioner knew of the ground and yet led him/her into believing it would not be used against him/her; and also (b) that it would be unjust to grant the decree. Generally, this covers the situation where the petitioning spouse had accepted the position and treated the marriage as a proper one, but now wants an excuse to end

2 Wilful refusal by the other spouse to consummate the marriage. 'Wilful refusal' means a determined refusal, persisted in over a period of time. It does not cover nervous first-night fears! Only one act of intercourse is necessary for the marriage to have been consummated, but if a spouse then refuses any further sexual advances, he or she is almost certainly guilty of 'unreasonable behaviour', justifying the other spouse in obtaining a divorce (*see* page 32).*

3 Lack of consent at the time of the marriage (e.g. the spouse was drunk, coerced etc.; *see* page 18); or 'mental disorder'.†

4 At the time of the marriage the other spouse was suffering from communicable venereal disease.†

5 At the time of the marriage the woman was pregnant by another man.

Jewish marriages

Jewish spouses require a Jewish divorce (a Get), as well as a civil divorce, in order to be able to remarry within their faith. A Get is granted by mutual consent of both parties. Failure to obtain a Get could be disastrous if either party wishes to remarry and/or if the wife wishes to have more children. The Divorce (Religious Marriages) Act 2002 was passed in order to assist Jewish husbands and wives in obtaining their Get where one of them is not co-operating and wants the civil divorce, but not the Get, or is making heavier financial or other demands than would be sanctioned by the civil courts in exchange for the Get. The Act provides that the Get should have been obtained before the decree nisi will be made absolute. For further information, see www.gettingyour get.co.uk

---

it. Similarly, it would cover the case of a man who advertised for a housekeeper and then proposed marriage to her as a matter of convenience only. If it was clear that there was an implied no-sex agreement then nullity on the ground of wilful refusal to consummate would be refused.

† Proceedings must normally be started within three years of the marriage, otherwise the claim will not be allowed.

5

Money Matters

Married couples are not just legally united; they are also financially united. Both have an obligation to maintain the other and both can claim a share of the joint family assets if the marriage breaks down.

This chapter looks at how the law treats the finances of a married couple. For the law on the finances of an unmarried couple *see* Chapter 1.

TAX AND MARRIAGE

For over 180 years it was a fundamental feature of the UK tax system that the income of a wife was automatically combined with that of her husband. A husband was responsible for dealing with his wife's tax as well as his own and he could even find himself saddled with her tax bill. Wives were treated as tax nonentities.

Husbands and wives could elect for separate taxation but there were disadvantages, tax-wise, in doing so unless both were earning fairly high incomes. Indeed, there were a considerable number of tax disadvantages in being married at all; continuing to cohabit or even to get divorced were sensible decisions from a tax viewpoint.

Such sexist anachronisms were consigned to the past at the beginning of the 1990s. Since 6 April 1990, wives have become fully responsible for their own tax affairs and for paying tax on their own income. Where husbands have to complete a tax return, they nowadays have to provide only details of their own income. Wives have separate tax returns to complete and sign. When corresponding with their tax office, the Inland Revenue again nowadays will deal with wives in their own right and not (as so irritatingly happened in the past) send letters (or even tax refunds) to their husbands.

Husbands and wives, like everyone else, are now each entitled to their own tax-exempt single person's allowance. However in the tax year 2000/01, the married couple's allowance was scrapped – thereby ending at a stroke the slight remaining income tax incentive to get

(and remain!) married. The new Childcare Tax Benefit applies to cohabitants as well as husbands and wives, so no difference there. Husbands and wives do, however, still have some slight advantages on taxes on capital – capital gains tax and inheritance tax.

GIFTS BETWEEN SPOUSES

Usually it is obvious if a gift is intended. For instance, if a woman buys her husband a set of cuff-links they can be presumed to be a present.

It is not, however, always so straightforward. If an item is to be transferred from one spouse to the other then problems can arise. This is because the law is not satisfied with a simple statement, 'You can have my . . . [e.g. car], darling.' The law demands that there should be not only an intention to hand over the item but also either a deed recording the transfer or, at least, a physical delivery of the item from one spouse to the other. In fact, these rules apply to all gifts, whether they be to a spouse, child or friend. But with husband and wife there is more of a risk that the rules will not be complied with. Often, though, they are complied with – but more by luck than design.

For instance, if a husband decides to give his wife his car because he is buying another, it is more likely than not that they will tell the registration authority (DVLA) of the change of ownership and, in addition, he will obviously give her the keys to the car, so the legal requirements are met. Similarly with land, it is usual for the legal formalities to be met, because most people know that transferring land is complicated: the couple will probably instruct a solicitor to do the necessary work and so the legal formalities will be complied with.

However, these rules can cause hardship. Suppose a man owns valuable antique furniture which he decides to give to his wife. He tells her she can have the furniture but the gift is not recorded in writing and clearly there will be no physical transfer of the furniture; it simply stays where it is. Years later, if the husband should become bankrupt and have his assets seized, the wife would lose the furniture. She would be unable to show that it had been given to her by her husband and so it could be seized by the creditors. If the husband had known of the law he could have avoided this by making a signed deed, giving the furniture to his wife – although, obviously, it would have been invalid had it been done just to defraud his creditors.

Tax advantages of separate taxation

Income tax

One advantage of the system of separate taxation is that wives can use their own single person's allowance to set off against investment income from savings or, for example, shares – unlike under the old rules, when they could use tax allowances only to set off against *earned* income. So if a couple have savings which earn interest, it is worthwhile considering transferring some of them to make sure that the tax allowances available to both of the couple are fully used.

The wife has no income or assets of her own, while the husband has a high income, paying higher-rate tax, and also has income-producing assets. By the husband giving some of his investments to his wife to use up fully her tax-free allowance for this year, their combined annual tax bill could be much reduced. Tax savings will increase in following years as the tax allowances are set higher.

The catch is that the gift has to be free from any strings attached. Once the gift is made, the original owning spouse can have no control, influence or benefit from the assets. If both parties trust one another and intend remaining married to one another, there are considerable benefits. But if they later divorce or separate, the original owner cannot stop the other spouse walking off with the gifted asset.

Capital gains tax

Since 6 April 1990, husband and wife have each been entitled to a separate annual exemption from capital gains tax (CGT). Transfers between spouses do not immediately attract CGT: the receiving spouse is treated as having first acquired the asset at the date when the donor spouse first acquired it. Spouses, then, can reduce CGT bills by transferring assets so that both of their CGT allowances are used to maximum advantage.

JOINT BANK ACCOUNT

It is advisable for a couple to have a joint bank account, especially if one of the couple is dependent on the other.

If there is a joint account the court will assume that it is owned equally, unless the contrary can be proved. For instance, if one spouse made *all* the payments into the account and could prove there was no intention to share the money in the account, then he or she may be able to claim all the money in it. But the general rule is that if both husband and wife pay money into the account at various times, they will both be entitled to a half share, even if one spouse contributed more than the other.

Usually, though, if there is a dispute it is likely to be just part of a larger dispute over dividing up the family assets because the marriage has broken down. In that case, the court can make whatever order it thinks fair and the money in the joint account is likely to be dealt with as part of an overall financial settlement (for instance, the money in the joint account may go to the husband, while the wife receives a larger share in the matrimonial home).

SPOUSES' LIABILITIES FOR EACH OTHER'S DEBTS

Husbands and wives are not usually responsible for each other's individual debts. But they are jointly and severally responsible for debts from joint accounts or for joint responsibilities – like mortgage repayments or rent. They are also potentially liable for unpaid council tax bills and other outgoings on the home, even if those are not in their individual names.

What happens if a husband and wife separate and the husband leaves the home, pays the wife maintenance, but is worried that he will end up paying for household bills which are mounting without his having any control over them?

The old law says that it is a defence to a claim by a creditor to show that the husband did, in fact, pay his wife a reasonable amount of maintenance. If the bill arose simply as the result of the woman's bad management, then he should not be held liable. But he must show that the amount was sufficient to cover the expenses.

On the other hand, what happens if the man deserts the woman and fails to pay her anything and she is worried about paying his old household debts? If she contacts the utility and telephone companies, she can ask them to read the meters as soon as possible – the date when they are read then becomes the cut-off date – and transfer the new bills into her own name. While she will be responsible for future bills, it will be up to the utility and telephone companies to chase the man for the old debts.

This applies to the council tax too. Spouses are jointly and severally liable for each other's council tax until the day that the marriage ends or the spouses stop living together. It thus makes good sense to notify the local authority of the day a spouse left home (CCROs will not initiate their own inquiries). After separation, if only one adult is living in the property, then the council tax will be reduced by 25 per cent – so there is an added incentive to let the local authority know.

All debts are potential time-bombs if ignored, but the ones that require immediate action are those secured on the home, such as mortgages. Mortgagees – banks or building societies – must accept payments from a spouse. Contact creditors as soon as possible rather than ignore them; they can agree reduced payments to help tide you over a crisis period.

When dealing with larger debts, it is especially important to look at the overall picture rather than rush frantically around, trying to pay off the creditors who shout loudest for payments. Many Citizens' Advice Bureaux offer a debt counselling service that can advise in greater depth about individuals' rights and responsibilities, and about planning for coping with debt problems (*see* Chapter 52 for more information about managing debts).

MAINTENANCE PAYMENTS AND DIVISION OF THE FAMILY ASSETS WHEN THE MARRIAGE HAS COME TO AN END

There are two fundamental principles:

1 **Every wife has a right to be maintained by her husband and every husband has a right to be maintained by his wife.** This mutual obligation to maintain is one of the legal consequences of marriage and the duty to cohabit together. Even if the couple stop cohabiting, the wife (or husband) may still be able to obtain maintenance for herself and she will certainly be able to obtain maintenance for the children.

2 **When the marriage ends, the courts have a free hand in dividing up the family assets between the couple.** For instance, the house may be in the husband's name, yet the court can order that it be transferred to the wife. One of the most common misapprehensions is that when a marriage ends the husband and wife split everything 50/50. This is not always so. Very often the courts will start off with a 50/50 division of capital as a starting point but they will then make adjustments, so that if the wife does not make claims for maintenance or against pensions (when she would be entitled to do so) then she would gain the greater share of the capital.

Where however there has been a short marriage, and all the assets were in the husband's name initially, the wife is unlikely to get anywhere near a half share. There are an increasing number of cases where the wife has been ordered to pay capital or even maintenance to an impoverished ex-husband. At the heart of it all, the courts will look pragmatically at what the needs and resources are of the husband, the wife and the children (if there are any) and tailor a suitable financial division. The problems with this individually tailored approach are that there is very little certainty in financial issues on divorce and (except in the case of child support) no easy formula which can be applied.

But is a clean break possible?

Courts must now look at whether it will be possible to have a financial 'clean break' between the spouses – usually this is achieved by giving the wife the lion's share of the assets, in return for which she gives up her right to maintenance. But the courts will never order a clean break in respect of children: both parents remain liable financially for children until they are at least 16 years old (and older if they continue their education).

Will the law change?

Family law is always in a state of flux. The key changes are the introduction of pension sharing (or splitting), which adds to the courts' powers to deal with pensions by earmarking them, for example, and changes to the way in which child support is calculated (*see* page 51). Both these new laws have changed the financial aspects of separation and divorce.

How can you get maintenance?

If your husband/wife will voluntarily agree to pay you maintenance there will be no need to go to court. Sometimes, though, a court application is necessary. The procedure to be followed will depend upon whether or not you want a divorce:

If you do want a divorce

Once divorce proceedings have been begun you can apply to the divorce court (i.e. the divorce county court in an undefended divorce; the High Court in a defended case). The court can order maintenance even before the divorce is granted – this is called maintenance pending suit (*see* page 52) which will last as long as the marriage does, i.e. up to decree absolute. Thereafter if you want the maintenance to continue, the maintenance pending suit will technically need to be converted into a 'periodical payments' order.

If you don't want a divorce

Apply to the Family Proceedings Court (a magistrates' court), where the magistrates have been trained to deal with family cases; for maintenance – there is a simple, quick and cheap procedure (*see* page 55). The Family Proceedings Court can make periodical payments orders and lump sum orders not exceeding £1,000.

How can you get a share of the family assets?

Unless your spouse will voluntarily agree to transferring a fair share of the assets, a court application might be necessary, although you should also consider resolving your dispute through mediation (which will be a lot less costly – *see* page 40). The procedure to be followed will depend upon whether or not you want a divorce:

If you do want a divorce

The divorce court can divide up the family assets and property as it thinks fit when the divorce is granted. Often the court will simply be approving (if they think it is fair) an agreement worked out beforehand by the couple through mediation or by the couple with their lawyers.

If you don't want a divorce

The court can divide up the family assets and order that they be sold. But the court will usually look only at the true ownership of the property (although the court can now make an occupation order dealing with who will live in the family home for now). For instance, if the wife is not named on the title deeds she will not receive a share of the matrimonial home unless she contributed money towards its purchase. The court will apply similar rules as with an unmarried couple who are in dispute over property (*see* page 6). Thus a wife will usually be better off if she petitions for a divorce or for judicial separation, for then the court has a wider discretion and will generally give her a larger share.

Guidance for 'older wives' who do not want a divorce

What is the position if the husband is starting off divorce proceedings and the wife not only does not want a divorce but she is very worried about her financial position after divorce? Although the law changed in 1996 enabling a spouse to claim for a future share of her spouse's pension, pension sharing (until recently termed 'pension splitting') has only recently become available. The wife does however have two ways of resisting the divorce until financial matters (at least) are sorted out. She can make an application under section 10 or section 5 of the Matrimonial Causes Act 1973.

- If she makes a section 10 application, the marriage continues for the time being and thus the pension rights are preserved *pro tem*. Solicitors acting for wives who stand to lose out financially by getting divorced and are in their mid-forties, or older, will usually advise submitting a section 10 application unless the wife specially asks them not to take this step.
- As an alternative delaying tactic, the wife could ask her solicitor (it is best for such an application to be made via a solicitor) to file a section 5 application, which in essence says that the divorce should not, on the grounds of grave financial or other hardship, go ahead. Only very rarely will such an application succeed – the courts tend to take the pragmatic view that it takes two to make a go of a marriage and if one wants a divorce then ultimately the marriage should probably be ended. Although a section 5 application should not be made lightly, it will halt the divorce proceedings and give a person more time to negotiate over potential losses of a spouse's financial rights – particularly the pension.

How much maintenance should be paid?

A set of guidelines has emerged over the years and all the courts apply them, although each court will vary slightly in the terms of the orders it will make. Remember that every case is unique, with its own particular facts and its own set of circumstances. So what follows can only be a guide – it does not claim to be a guarantee of what will happen in any particular case. *See* the warning on page 66!

For advice on how to apply to the different courts for the different orders *see* page 54.

There are no fixed rules, but . . .

Starting-points are to work out:
- what the split would be by dividing up the *assets* equally;
- what *child support* would be payable under the Child Support formula; and
- what *maintenance* the wife might otherwise need.
  It is vital to realize that:
- there is no hard and fast rule which says how much each spouse is to get;
- no two cases are ever identical, so it is always impossible to be 100 per cent sure about what a court would order;
- in practice, there is rarely enough money to go around. What might have been a reasonable income for the maintenance of one household will often be totally inadequate for two households. So, usually, both

husband and wife must resign themselves to a drop in their living standards;

- going to court to argue about 'who gets what' is expensive. Even a person on public funding will probably have to put most of his/her share towards the legal costs (*see* page 787), so it is usually better to do everything possible to reach a compromise agreement by negotiation or through mediation. Very often the only people who benefit when a case goes to court are the lawyers!
- the new rules about payment of child support (*see* below) can increase the amounts of maintenance paid to the children, so the wife gets proportionately less if there are dependent children of the family.

So, what follows is no more than a rough guide – each case has its own facts (and its own problems).

What does the court look at?

Each case will be judged on its own merits, but there are a number of considerations which the court must take into account (set out in section 25 of the Matrimonial Causes Act 1973). So it will look at:

- the income, earning capacity, property and other financial resources of both spouses;
- both spouses' financial needs and obligations;
- the standard of living before the marriage broke down;
- both spouses' ages and the length of the marriage;
- any physical or mental disabilities;
- the contributions each has made to the welfare of the family (this includes, e.g., caring for the children);
- in some circumstances, spouses' conduct;
- the value of any benefit, like a pension, which either spouse would lose the chance of acquiring as a result of the divorce.

The approach the court takes is a pragmatic one (it would be foolish to try anything else), looking basically at each party's 'needs and resources'. In practice, if the wife (or whoever is looking after the children) might be able to claim welfare benefits (like income support or Working Tax Credit), this will be looked at too (although the courts do not expect that the state will take over a financial burden which can be shouldered by a husband).

Maintenance for the children (if there are any) is often worked out first and the wife might be 'topped up' in terms of her own maintenance. Or, if there are no children, the wife might receive somewhere between 25 and 35 per cent of the joint gross income for herself. However, husbands are unlikely to be ordered to pay a maintenance bill of more than half of their income to their former wives and children, however great the size of the family.

Changes under the Child Support Acts

New child support rules came into effect on 3 March 2003. The new rules provide a simpler percentage formula so that a non-resident parent pays:

- 15 per cent of his income for one child

- 20 per cent of his income for two children
- 25 per cent of his income for three or more children (the maximum he would have to pay).

It was expected that the new rules would result in lower child maintenance payments for many fathers, although the intention was that more fathers would pay, as the Child Support Agency (CSA) would be able to concentrate more on collecting maintenance instead of spending inordinate time on working out the right figures. *See* page 82 for more details. Check with a solicitor or Citizens' Advice Bureau about how these rules will apply in more detail.

The aim of the court

The court will realize that it cannot hope to put the parties in the same financial position as if there had not been a divorce; there is unlikely to be enough money for that. The court will look at all the circumstances, but it places particular emphasis on the welfare of the children (making sure they have a roof over their heads if possible) and the desirability of the couple becoming financially independent.

Making an agreement with your spouse

What follows is some guidance on how the court will deal with financial disputes between ex-spouses. But that does not mean that ex-spouses have to go to court to work out a division of family money. Most – around 90 per cent – come to an agreement between themselves without ever having to go to the expense of a full court hearing, and thus save more to share between members of the family rather than lining lawyers' pockets.

If there are difficulties in negotiating with a spouse, solicitors can sometimes help, not hinder, as long as the solicitors are specialists in family law (*see* page 39). Mediation services are well worth thinking about (*see also* page 40). *See also* page 59 concerning out-of-court settlements. But before making an agreement, ensure that the terms are fair – this can usually only be done by checking with a solicitor. A useful investment is to spend an hour or so with a solicitor (for which he or she has been fully briefed by you about your family and financial situation) when the solicitor can advise on what the parameters of a reasonable settlement would be. Armed or enlightened with this information, you can then negotiate with your spouse directly or through mediation to sort out something that would work for you both, with the children's interests in mind. Many hundreds if not thousands of pounds can be saved in this way.

MAINTENANCE

Since the Child Support Act 1991 was introduced in 1993, there have been fewer orders for periodical payments (maintenance) made in favour of a wife who is looking after the children than previously – largely because the first call on the non-resident parent's income has been to pay child support. Where there are children the starting-point is to work out what child support would be payable and see if there is anything left to pay spousal maintenance.

The laws as to payment of maintenance apply theoretically equally to men and women, although by far the greater number of applications are made by wives (for the very real reason that usually they are earning less or nothing at all).

Where the wife is able to earn an income in her own right on which she can comfortably support herself, maintenance for her is unlikely to be in issue, although if she is the one looking after the children then of course she will still be entitled to child support for them. The modern trend is to end the financial interdependence of the couple (so that there is a 'clean break', enabling them to start again). So if the wife is financially independent (or could be working), then she may well be denied maintenance.

If she is not working but is capable of so doing (by for example spending two years on a retraining course) then the court might order maintenance for a fixed period only (although the wife could still apply for the maintenance term to be extended as long as she applies before the fixed term expires). However, the wife might be not working at all, looking after small children, or might never have worked throughout her long married life. Or she may have only minimal income or be unable to work through disability, for example. In circumstances like these, the courts will consider maintenance.

Wachtel (1973) was the case that first spelt out the old one-third rule, which is now defunct. The old rule (which was actually not a rule but simply a starting-point for working out how to divide family assets) stated that the wife should get one-third of the family assets and maintenance so that her total income will be one-third of their combined total incomes. But even then it was emphasized that it was no more than a starting-point. As Lord Denning said:

There may be cases where more than one-third is right. There are likely to be many others where less than one-third is the only practicable solution. But one-third as a possible starting-point for the wife's maintenance in her own right might still lead to the correct final result than a starting-point of equality or one-quarter.

In **Wachtel**, *both husband and wife were aged 46. The husband was earning £6,000 p.a. and the wife's earning* capacity was £750 p.a. The only asset was the house, worth some £20,000. The wife received £1,500 p.a. maintenance:

	£
husband's income (gross)	6,000
add *wife's income (gross)*	750
total gross earnings	6,750
divide *by 3*	2,250
deduct *wife's income*	750
maintenance payable	1,500

The wife also received a lump sum of £6,000 (one-third of the family assets would have been £6,666).

It can be interesting to see how a one-third calculation would work although this is no more than a starting-point and certainly cannot be guaranteed to provide the right answer!

However, there is some good news; when working out what figure should be paid (now that the married couple's allowance has been scrapped) there is no need to make complex calculations involving gross and net income and tax. The tax position will be the same after separation or divorce as it was during the marriage, so use the net figures to work out how much needs to be paid. A better approach is to prepare a budget for each new household (basing the figures on existing outgoings and then making adjustments for the changes). How much does this work out to? Can it be trimmed any further? And how much can you afford to pay?

If your case were to go to court, the court would need to have evidence of the net income of both husband and wife (after tax) and the total household budgets would also need to be calculated (in a fairly rough-and-ready way). The earnings of any new boyfriend or girlfriend might be taken into account, but only inasmuch as they free up the income of their partner – they will not be taken into account directly. If, for example, a husband was living with a new partner and not having to pay rent or mortgage payments in a new home, then more of his income would be considered to be 'available' for maintenance payments. You should also consider whether welfare benefits can help (*see* Chapter 29 for further information about what benefits might be available). At the end of this one could see whether both spouses could afford to live on their respective incomes – and how much, if anything, would be left at the end of the week. If there was a wide disparity (e.g. the wife having £50 left to save at the end of each week and the husband having only £15) then the court would probably juggle the figures and partly redress the balance (e.g. by reducing the wife's maintenance by £10 per week, so that she would be left with £40 per week and the husband with £25).

In short, it is a case of juggling the figures to make the best of a bad job.

When there isn't enough money

Often the courts cannot order decent sums of maintenance because the husband's income cannot stretch to
supporting two households. In such a case, all the court
can do is to order the husband to pay as much as it thinks
he can afford. But the court will not order the husband
to pay so much that he will end up with less than the
current social security subsistence levels. The courts will
also take into account obligations to second families too
and how welfare benefits will impact.

*The wife was in receipt of both maintenance and state
benefits. The husband had remarried and had two young
children. He and his second wife had only a small income
and his obligation to pay maintenance to his first wife was
putting him under considerable pressure. If the order to the
first wife were reduced or stopped, the effect would be that
her income would be topped up by state benefits, so she
would not be impoverished. Although the courts normally
do not wish ex-wives to be dependent on public funds,
here the court ordered that the husband should pay no
maintenance at all and that there should be a clean break.*
Ashley v Blackman (1988)

The relevance of conduct

If the wife has been adulterous, can she still expect to
receive maintenance and a share of the family assets? If
the husband has been a terrible husband, never spending
time with the wife and children and having numerous
affairs, is he still entitled to a share in the family assets?
The answer to both questions is basically 'yes'. The same
applies to other types of misconduct, such as cruelty, for
the court is only supposed to take it into account if it is
'gross and obvious'. This is a hopelessly vague phrase but
in practical terms it generally means that the courts will
not ignore bad behaviour if it would be really unfair to
do so. So, in a case where a husband attacked his wife
with an axe, severely disfiguring her, that conduct was
taken into account in her claims for financial relief. That
was an extreme example: in practice the courts tend to
overlook spousal behaviour towards each other.

Short marriages

If the marriage is short-lived the wife may not be entitled
to anything. For instance:

*A wife deserted the husband after a year of marriage. They
were both in their twenties and the wife had a steady job
as a nurse. A magistrates' court ordered the husband to pay
her £8 per week. He appealed. Held: When the marriage
was short and the parties are young and capable of earning*

*a living, only a nominal order should be made. She was
entitled to 10p per week. The judge said, 'In these days of
women's lib, there is no reason why a wife whose marriage
has not lasted long, and has no child, should have a bread
ticket for life.'*
Graves (1973)

However, if the marriage lasts a few years, the wife will
almost certainly be entitled to a third, although, in one
case, a four-year marriage was regarded as 'short' (and
so the wife got no share of the husband's assets). But
there were no children in that case and it is best regarded
as very much an exceptional decision. This is more
typical:

*H and W married when W was 24 and H was 21. They
parted two years later, there being no children. Both had
jobs but he earned more than her (so he was left with about
£25 per week after expenses, and she had only £5 per week).
Held: She was only entitled to nominal maintenance (i.e.
£1 a year). She should not receive normal maintenance
despite the fact that H was much better off than she was.*
Frisby (1984)

Once there is a child of the marriage, the courts tend
to pay little attention to the length of the marriage.

Clean breaks

Since 1984 the courts have had the power to impose a
clean break financially, i.e. ending the wife's right to
maintenance even if she adamantly opposes such a step
(previously the wife always had to consent to a clean
break order). The courts now, potentially, have the power
to order a clean break whenever an application comes up
before them – this can include a later application for a
variation of maintenance payments. They will make a
clean break order where to do otherwise would cause
undue hardship to the husband.

*The husband and wife divorced in 1971 and he was ordered
to pay her periodical payments. She suffered from schizo-
phrenia and was dependent on state benefits. He was a
self-employed artist, had remarried and had two sons. His
former wife made four applications for an increase in
maintenance. He argued he could not even afford to pay
the current order of £60 per month and that, in any event,
the ex-wife would not be affected by an increase in the order
as the maintenance was deducted pound for pound from
her welfare benefits. Held: The courts had to bear in mind
the policies both of not casting the burden of maintaining
a spouse on the state and of achieving a clean break between
spouses where it would not cause undue hardship. The
husband was not devious but a genuine struggler. It was
not right to continue to force him to pay so a clean break
would be imposed.*
Ashley v Blackman (1988)

The courts will also look at whether imposing a clean break order will cause undue hardship to the wife. Wherever there has been a short marriage with no children and the parties are still young and able to look after themselves financially, a clean break is probable. In other cases, if the husband wants a clean break from the wife he will have to compensate her properly for giving up her right to maintenance.

The husband was a partner in a successful decorating business and the wife was a director. When the marriage broke up, the wife was ordered to be given the house and contents and maintenance of £1,800 p.a. He then sold the business for £1.8 million. The wife applied for an increase in maintenance: the husband asked for maintenance to be stopped either immediately or at some future date on payment of £40,000. Held: The proper sum for maintenance for the wife was £16,000 p.a. She could not adjust without undue hardship to termination of the payments and if the husband wanted a clean break he had to provide her with a sum sufficient to give her a comparable income to the right amount of maintenance. £40,000 was inadequate.

Boylan (1988)

Clean breaks are more often ordered where the husband and wife are richer (or poorer) than average. In the case of the average family with one main asset, the home, often there is not enough cash to buy out the wife's right to maintenance and there is no other option but for the husband to pay the wife maintenance until the children have left school or until she is able to earn a decent income in her own right.

The courts have also stressed more recently that 'mature' wives (in their fifties or so) who have not worked outside the home for a very long time are unlikely to have a clean break made against them, unless there is a lot of capital to go around and a sum of capital can be given to the wife which will support her for the rest of her life (perhaps combined with pension payments). Where the husband has a substantial pension fund, the wife may receive a pension credit in her own right which will enable her to have a clean break at least from the time she reaches pensionable age.

Note: clean breaks are limited to maintenance for a wife; courts will never order a clean break in respect of maintenance payments to children.

The children's maintenance

In any divorce, the court's overriding concern will be with the welfare of the children. So, proper maintenance for the children will take precedence over the financial claims of the parents. The court will want to do what is best for the children. For example, it may allow the wife to continue living in the home because she will be looking after the children – and their need for a home will take precedence over the father's desire to realize his share of the property's value. There are no longer any tax advantages in making maintenance payments directly to the children.

The amount of child support which will be payable is worked out according to the child support formula. The new percentage-based formula is much easier to calculate than previously. It can be affected by the amount of time the children spend with the non-resident parent – if for more than two days a week for example, the support is likely to be reduced (*see further* page 82).

The effect of remarriage on maintenance payments

A wife will lose her right to maintenance payments as soon as she remarries. However, her former husband will still be liable to pay maintenance to his children; that liability will be unaffected by the mother's remarriage.

If the ex-wife decides to cohabit permanently with another man, but not marry him, she may still forfeit her maintenance. The court always has the power to vary the amount of maintenance she should receive. However, it would be up to the husband to apply to the court to reduce the maintenance (*see* page 56). Mere sexual liaisons will not affect the wife's right to maintenance.

Property orders are not affected by a remarriage. So if a wife was given the matrimonial home in a clean break settlement and then remarried, the husband could not ask the court to reverse its previous decision. So a wife who is negotiating financial arrangements with her husband should ask for a high property settlement, or lump sum, and a low maintenance payment, if she plans to remarry afterwards. Although she must also disclose the fact that she will be remarrying, as concealing it could mean that the husband could ask for the order to be set aside.

The man's remarriage does not bring his maintenance obligations to an end. However, his new commitments may be a ground for his asking that the amount of the maintenance payments be reduced.

HOW TO APPLY FOR MAINTENANCE

A wife or husband can apply for a maintenance order whether or not divorce proceedings have been started. If divorce proceedings have begun, the application is made to the divorce court (i.e. the divorce county court or the High Court). If divorce proceedings have not begun, the application is made to the local magistrates' court, or to the divorce county court.

Both the divorce courts and the magistrates' courts

have wide powers that allow them to order one spouse to pay maintenance to the other, although in practice it will nearly always be the husband who is ordered to pay maintenance to the wife. In addition, the court can order maintenance to cover the needs of the children.

The principles used in the different courts are the same, although there are differences in the way in which the application to the court is made.

Although the different courts have similar powers to order maintenance payments, they have different powers when it comes to dividing up the family assets and property, such as the home and possessions. Basically, the magistrates' courts cannot make these orders, for it is only the divorce court that has these powers. So, if a wife (or husband) wants the court to divide up the family property in addition to ordering maintenance, then divorce or judicial separation proceedings must be begun.

Most maintenance applications are made by wives against husbands. However, it is possible for a man to apply for maintenance from his wife – for instance, if he is unable to work, or if the wife is wealthy, or if he gave up his job or home when marrying her, or if he is looking after the children.

Applying for maintenance in the magistrates' court

It is quite easy to apply for a maintenance order in the magistrates' court without the help of a solicitor. Only if the sums involved are large, or if there are any particular difficulties, is a solicitor advisable.

To start the proceedings the wife goes to the local magistrates' court; this can be any magistrates' court in the county where either her husband or she lives. Her application will be dealt with by the Family Proceedings Panel of the magistrates' court which deals with family and care matters only (and not criminal cases). If she is embarrassed about applying in a court near her home she can go to another court in the same county, although the proceedings could be transferred to her home town if that would be more convenient to everyone else. The wife should try to be at the court by 9.45 a.m.

At the court she should ask for the warrant officer and tell him that she wishes to apply for a maintenance order – and any other order she may be seeking, such as an exclusion order (*see* Chapter 7). The wife will then have to fill in a form, which is her formal complaint. She then appears before a magistrate, who will probably ask her a few questions before he issues a summons against the husband. The summons is the court's order telling him to appear at the court on a particular day to defend the maintenance claim. The issuing of the summons does not mean that the wife has been, or will be, awarded

maintenance; it just signifies the start of the legal proceedings. The court staff will arrange for the summons to be served on the husband.

It will probably be a week or so before the case is heard. In the meantime, the wife can apply to the DWP for income support – once she does so this will trigger an application to the Child Support Agency.

Both the wife and her husband will have to attend the court hearing. Maintenance applications are 'domestic proceedings' and must, therefore, be heard in private. There must be either two or three magistrates, picked from the Family Proceedings Panel, hearing the application, and, if possible, they should include members of both sexes.

Both the wife and her husband will be asked about their family finances, where they are both living, the age of any children, their income, and so on. It is helpful if they have documentary evidence to put before the magistrates so there can be no dispute as to their financial commitments – for instance, wage slips, bank statements, mortgage agreement, rent books, savings books and hire-purchase agreements.

Having heard the evidence in a fairly informal manner, the magistrates will decide whether the wife should receive maintenance and, if so, how much.

The court will order maintenance only if it is satisfied that the husband (or, exceptionally, the wife) has either:
- failed to provide the wife, or the children, with a reasonable amount of maintenance, or
- behaved in such a way that the wife cannot reasonably be expected to live with him, or
- deserted the wife.

The amount of maintenance will depend on the facts of the individual case. Magistrates' courts are generally more cautious than divorce courts. A survey by the DSS in 1990 showed that whereas the average weekly maintenance orders for children were £20 in the county courts, they were £15 in the magistrates' court (child support amounts have gone up considerably since then under the Child Support Agency regime). Magistrates' courts can also be more influenced by the good or bad conduct of the parties than are the divorce courts.

It should not be forgotten that the magistrates are unlikely to order the husband to pay a sum of maintenance that will leave him (and his new family, if he has one) on less than income support subsistence levels. In practice, the magistrates will probably make sure that the husband is left with:
- one-quarter of his net (i.e. take-home) pay; plus
- his rent; plus
- income support rate sums for himself (and for his new family, if any).

So the maintenance for the ex-wife will be limited to whatever figure would ensure that he is not left with less than this amount. If this means that she is left with insufficient maintenance, then she will have to claim income support.

Changing the amount of the order

The ex-wife can go back to the court at any time if she wants the amount increased, either for herself or for the children. Similarly, the husband can go back to the court if he wants it reduced. But the court will only increase or decrease the amount if good grounds for doing so can be shown – for instance, if the husband has had a wage rise or become unemployed. This can cover the situation where the ex-wife has been prevented from working because she has had another child by another man.

Following a consent order whereby the wife and child received periodical payments, the wife had another child by another man. She applied to increase the amount. Held: *The birth of the second child affected the wife's earning capacity. An increase in maintenance was ordered.*
Fisher (1989)

And also the situation where the ex-husband has additional financial commitments in the form of a new family.

The husband was ordered to pay £12 maintenance to the wife and their three children. He went to live with another woman and her son. The husband applied to vary the amount of the order but lost before the magistrates. He appealed. Held: *These were circumstances where a man had responsibility for his cohabitee and her child. The court must take into account all the circumstances.*
Blower (1986)

The amount of the maintenance can be increased any time after the original order – even if it is decades later.

A couple married in 1942 and lived together for two years. In 1945 the wife obtained maintenance of £2 per week, which was reduced to £1.50 per week in 1948. In 1953 she obtained a divorce because of her husband's desertion. She had a job until 1970, when she was forced to retire because of ill-health. In 1977 she was living on state benefits and the £1.50 per week maintenance. The husband was earning £110 per week. She applied for increased maintenance. Held: *She should receive £12 p.w. (which was approximately the value of £2 in 1945). She would have received more if the marriage had not been so short, and if it had not ended so long ago.*
McGrady (1977)

To prevent tedious repeated applications to court for an increase in maintenance payments to cover inflation, the amount of maintenance payments can be linked to, for example, the RPI. The wife can then ensure that the maintenance keeps pace with increasing living costs without having to shell out more legal costs for later court applications for a variation.

When does the maintenance end?

The wife's right to maintenance will automatically end if she remarries, or if she resumes cohabitation with her husband for a continuous period of six months. If the woman starts living permanently with another man, the ex-husband may be able to get the court to reduce (or even stop) the wife's maintenance – but not the children's – though only if the cohabitant is actually supporting the ex-wife. But the court will not force a woman indirectly to marry.

After divorce a consent order was made whereby the wife received periodical payments of £6,500. She began living with another man. She applied to increase the payments and the husband applied to stop them. Held: *Cohabitation was not the same as marriage. A court order should not place pressure on a former wife to regularize her position with a cohabitee so that he would assume a husband's obligations.*
Hepburn (1989)

Child maintenance

Even after the Child Support Act 1991 was implemented, couples who wanted to agree how much child maintenance would be paid rather than accept the child support formula could do so – their agreement was thereafter usually recorded in a consent order to court. (This did not apply where an application for welfare benefits (such as income support or family credit) was made by the mother, as then a child support assessment was triggered by the claim.) Under the new child support regime, which came into effect on 3 March 2003, a couple can no longer exclude the child support scheme by a consent order. When the court order is made after 3 March 2003, either party can apply after 12 months to the CSA for an assessment to replace the order. So for couples wishing to obtain consent orders, it makes sense now to ensure that the figures are as near as possible to what the CSA would direct. That will minimize the incentive for either parent to go to the CSA. If the parent with care goes on to benefits after the consent order has been made, the CSA will have jurisdiction (*see further* page 82). So it is still possible to apply to court by consent for children's maintenance, but how long is this likely to last (assuming neither party opts out after 12 months)?

A child's maintenance order will usually continue until the first birthday after he reaches the minimum school-leaving age of 16 (i.e. until he is 17). However, the court can order it to continue until he is 18 (e.g. if he is still at school) or completes secondary education, or even beyond that if the child is undergoing further education, or if there is some other reason justifying such an order (if the child is disabled and dependent, for example). The wife's and the children's maintenance will also end if the man dies, although both wife and children can apply to the court for a share of his estate (*see* Chapter 14). The child's maintenance will also end if he is adopted, as the parents' duty to maintain him will then cease.

Making sure the husband pays

If the man has a steady job, an attachment of earnings order can be a good way of enforcing the maintenance order. It is a court order telling the man's employer to deduct the maintenance from the man's wage packet and pass it on to the court. Thus, the maintenance is deducted before the man receives his wages. This type of enforcement can be asked for right at the start, when the order for maintenance is made. Since 1991, the wife does not have to wait until arrears have built up. Obviously, such an order is of no use when the man is unemployed, self-employed, or flitting from job to job.

If the husband stops paying

The husband is supposed to pay the maintenance to the wife every week (or month). If he stops paying, she will have to go back to the court to enforce the order. If she has a court order through the magistrates' court, she should go to the warrant officer and tell him she wishes to apply for 'an arrears of maintenance summons'. Some magistrates' clerks are reluctant to issue these summonses unless the arrears are considerable; however, they have no right to refuse to do so, even if there is only one week of arrears. So the wife should be prepared to insist on her rights. The summons will be issued and served on the husband by the court. When the date of the hearing arrives both husband and wife will have to attend court. The husband will have to explain why he has not paid the maintenance. If he can show good cause (e.g. he has become unemployed; he has moved in with another woman and so has additional financial responsibilities) then the magistrate may reduce the amount of the maintenance order. Generally, though, the husband is simply told to pay up.

The husband will probably be told to pay off the arrears of maintenance by instalments, but any arrears of more than 12 months will be written off. The magistrates may back up their order by threatening imprisonment.

If the magistrates are satisfied that the husband has not paid the maintenance because of 'wilful default or culpable neglect' (i.e. if he could have paid it, but didn't) then he can be sent to prison. But prison is the last resort and will be ordered only against a persistent offender and where an attachment of earnings order would not be appropriate. No more than six weeks' imprisonment will be imposed.

Often the magistrates will sentence the husband to prison but say that the sentence will be suspended if he pays the maintenance, plus the arrears, in instalments. Thus the man is given one more chance; if he does not keep up the payments, he will go to prison. Usually, these 'suspended orders' are successful, but in about 10 per cent of cases the husband still refuses to pay the money and so he ends up in prison.

Going to prison does not wipe out the arrears of maintenance. The husband will still be liable to pay them off when he comes out. But, in practice, the man will often avoid having to pay the arrears, because the court may decide to give him a fresh start by cancelling the debt ('remitting the arrears' is the term used), and, more important, he cannot be sent back to prison for a second time because of the same arrears. Thus the wife's chances of recovering these hardcore arrears are usually non-existent.

BENEFITS AND CHILD SUPPORT

If the mother has applied for child support via the CSA, and also claims welfare benefits, then if she claims income support, for example, up until 2001 the maintenance would simply reduce the income support – rather, in practical terms the maintenance would be used to pay the Treasury and not add extra to the mother's income. There was a small incentive so that a notional amount of 'savings' with the DSS could be built up by the mother, which could be drawn on if she ever went back to work. This pound-for-pound deduction did not apply to family credit (later replaced by Working Families' Tax Credit) where a 'credit' of £15 could be received. In other words if the father paid maintenance, £15 would be received by the mother and anything over and above that would be paid to the Treasury. Changes to the Child Support Act 1991 were introduced by the Child Support, Pensions and Social Security Act 2000 (*see further* page 82). Under the new child support regime, which became operational on 3 March 2003, a parent with care (the term for the parent looking after the child or children most of the time) on Income Support or income-based Jobseeker's Allowance will keep up to £10 a week of the maintenance paid for the children. This is called the 'child maintenance premium'. The £10 payment will not reduce the amount of benefit received by the parent with care. *See also* page 292.

Applying for maintenance in the county court (or High Court)

If a wife does not want to commence divorce proceedings she has two methods of obtaining a maintenance order against her husband:

1 she can apply to the magistrates' court (*see* above);

2 she can apply to the county court or High Court, under s27 of the Matrimonial Causes Act 1973, for an order for secured or unsecured periodical payments or for a lump sum.

In either case she must prove that her husband has failed to provide her with reasonable maintenance. In practice, it is rare to apply to the High Court – so the county court is most likely to be used if at all. Again, in practice, it is more likely that the wife will apply for divorce (or judicial separation) and make her application for maintenance in the divorce court, so what follows here is just a brief summary of the law.

The county court can make a maintenance order if there has been a failure to provide 'reasonable maintenance' for the other spouse. Basically, the court will decide an application on the merits of the case, using similar principles to those used in the magistrates' court and in the High Court on a divorce. In practical terms, it is often easier and simpler to apply in the magistrates' court. Also, public funding is more readily obtainable for magistrates' court applications and so most women do, in fact, apply to the magistrates' and not to the county court.

While it is usually possible to get a maintenance order in the magistrates' court within two or three weeks, it can take two or three months in the county courts. Another disadvantage of applying in the county court is that the county court cannot enforce its maintenance order if the husband defaults – to enforce a county court maintenance order, you generally go back to the magistrates' court (*see* page 57).

Applying for maintenance in the divorce court

When a wife (or a husband) files a petition for divorce, she can include in the petition a request for maintenance for herself and/or the children. She must indeed do so, even if she is not intending to ask the court for maintenance but instead hopes to reach an agreement with her husband. But the financial relief claims will lie dormant on the court file until activated by an application for maintenance (or for other financial relief).

Since 5 June 2000, the procedure for asking for maintenance has been changed nationwide, following the extension of what was previously an ancillary relief pilot scheme. An application in Form A needs to be filled in. The filing of a Form A triggers the court to set a timetable for dealing with the application. The first stage is a first appointment approximately 14 weeks after the Form A is filed. Five weeks before the first appointment date, a sworn statement of means (in Form E) must be filed by both husband and wife setting out their respective financial circumstances in detail and providing the court and each other with relevant documentation, such as bank statements, valuations of the family home and pension information. The Form A, filled in when filing the divorce petition, contains a section for requesting maintenance. There is no need to wait for the divorce to be granted before asking for maintenance.

Maintenance can be awarded before the divorce petition is heard. This is called *maintenance pending suit* and will only be a temporary award until a proper, final award is made. There is no obligation on a wife (or indeed a husband) to apply for maintenance pending suit. If a temporary agreement can be worked out between the couple then no application is needed.

An application for maintenance proper should be made as soon as the divorce proceedings are started. Public funding can cover maintenance disputes, even if the divorce itself is undefended.

Divorce court: If the husband stops paying the maintenance

If the husband stops paying, he will have broken the court order. The wife's remedy is to go back to the court and ask it to enforce the order against him – either by giving him a warning, applying for a warrant of execution or even sending him to prison.

However, it is easier to apply to the magistrates' court than to the divorce court. With a magistrates' court order the wife can simply go along to the court and a summons will be issued against her husband straight away; the case will probably be heard in a week or two. In the divorce court it is likely to be several weeks (or even months!) before the application is heard.

This difficulty can be overcome if the divorce court's maintenance order is registered with the magistrates' court – in other words, the divorce court makes the maintenance order but it then gives the magistrates' court the power to enforce it. If the husband stops paying, the wife can go along to the magistrates' court and issue an 'arrears of maintenance summons' in the usual way (*see* page 57). The procedure then is exactly as though the original maintenance order had been made by the magistrates' court and not the divorce court.

Is it worth applying for maintenance?

Many women have found that it is not worth applying for maintenance when they part from their husbands. Rather than go to the magistrates' court and ask for maintenance (*see* page 55) they wait until the divorce. In the meantime, if the woman herself has no source of income she can claim Income Support, or if she is working she can claim Working Tax Credit to top up her income.

If she does claim income support, this will automatically trigger a Child Support Agency assessment (although the same rule does not apply for Working Tax Credit). Where welfare benefits are involved, very often the best outcome (from the wife's viewpoint mostly) will be for the wife to get the matrimonial home (which will not prevent her claiming benefit), with no order for her maintenance. If the couple do not own their own home, but pay rent, then a lump sum will probably be better than regular maintenance (although problems can arise when it is more than £8,000 since she will then be ineligible for income support).

When the divorce is granted, the court can make maintenance orders and also property orders (for instance, giving the wife a lump sum or transferring the house to her). But, if resources are limited, the wife might be better advised to forgo maintenance for herself and negotiate instead for a lump sum and/or transfer of the home (or its tenancy) to her. This may be a more sensible course of action because:

1 The husband may not pay the maintenance.
2 Maintenance will affect her income support (or Working Tax Credit) eligibility. A capital sum of up to £8,000 will not (although capital of between £3,000 and £8,000 will reduce benefit). An even larger amount will be ignored by the DWP if it is to be used by the wife to buy a home.
3 A lump sum can be used as a deposit for a house purchase.
4 If she remarries, her maintenance payments would end, but she would not have to refund any lump sum she received.
5 If the home is transferred to her, the mortgage interest (but not the capital repayments) can be met by income support. Note that she can only claim for the mortgage interest payments to be met after some time has elapsed since her claim and not all the interest will be paid.

An out-of-court agreement

Often – in fact, in the majority of cases – the husband and wife will be able to work out a satisfactory financial arrangement between themselves, or through mediation, or by negotiation between solicitors. It is always advisable to have the terms of the agreement drawn up into a formal document which can then be placed before the divorce judge. He will then make a 'consent order' which confirms that both husband and wife agree to the terms and that it is now an order of the court.

There are dangers in not having a consent order drawn up by the court. Verbal agreements have a habit of unravelling over time as one or other spouse 'forgets' what was agreed. Even carelessly drafted orders can leave loopholes for a former spouse to exploit if the situation of the other improves in future.

Mr and Mrs Twiname were married in 1940 and divorced in 1971. Mr T remarried, Mrs T did not. Mrs T's divorce petition included a claim for 'such sums by way of secured provision and/or such sums by way of maintenance and alimony pending suit as might be just'. At the time of the divorce one of Mr T's companies was wound up and divided, 51 per cent to Mr T and 49 per cent to Mrs T, with maintenance for her too. The consent order made no mention of the lump-sum claim (usually this would be dismissed). In 1989 Mrs T applied not only for increased maintenance but also for a lump sum as Mr T had just sold his business for £6 million. Mr T argued that the late application would cause him hardship and was 'vexatious'. The court disagreed and allowed Mrs T's claim to go ahead. Twiname (1992)

If the court order does not entitle the wife to be paid any maintenance (for instance, she might be given the matrimonial home and in return agree to forgo maintenance), she cannot later change her mind and reapply to the court for maintenance. The courts say that when there is a clean break between the spouses in this way, the consent order should normally be binding. For instance:

Mr and Mrs Minton were divorced in 1972. In 1973 they reached an agreement about the family assets and it was agreed that Mrs Minton would be given the matrimonial home in return for £10,000 cash and for agreeing to forgo any maintenance. The agreement was made a consent order by the court. However, the bargain proved disastrous from Mrs Minton's point of view, for she soon found herself deep in debt, in poor health, and with the children to bring up. In 1976 she applied to the court for maintenance for herself. Held: She was not entitled to maintenance. By agreeing to the consent order she had forfeited her right to claim maintenance, and it was only fair on her husband that there should be a clean break between them. However, this did not, of course, prevent the court increasing the amount of maintenance for the children, their maintenance settlement being completely separate from that of their mother. Minton (1979)

This case of course predated the Child Support Acts, since which time it has been very rare to have court orders made for children (this is only by consent or where the CSA has no jurisdiction – for example if one parent lives abroad).

Note: if a clean break is to be achieved, the only way to do so is via a court order. Only the court can terminate spouses' obligations to maintain each other, which continue to exist even after the marriage ends. However firm the agreement for a clean break is, make sure that this is backed up by a court order so that each partner can truly start afresh financially without the fear of future maintenance applications being made.

TAX AND SEPARATION

How income tax personal allowances are treated

Following separate taxation and then the abolition of the married couples allowance in the tax year 2000/01, each spouse will continue as before in terms of tax allowances. They should each clarify who will be entitled to the Children's Tax Credit, introduced in the tax year 2001/02, which is usually paid to the parent who looks after the children.

Children's Tax Credit (not to be confused with the new Child Tax Credit) was a tax allowance which existed for two tax years (2001/2 and 2002/3). It was available to people on income below a certain amount and who were responsible for children. If you have not yet claimed for 2001/02 or 2002/03, you can do so now, or at any time up to a deadline of 6 years from the end of either of these tax years. Ring your local tax office for an application form. *See also* page 294.

Tax on maintenance payments

There are no longer any tax advantages in making maintenance payments directly to the children. The remaining tax reliefs which were available to 'old' orders for children pre-dating 1988 have also now been abolished, so there are sadly no income tax sweeteners on divorce.

Maintenance payments are not taxable in the hands of the recipients so ex-wives do not have to pay tax on maintenance payments received for themselves or for the children.

DEALING WITH THE FAMILY HOME

In addition to maintenance, a wife may be entitled to a share of the family home (together with other assets such as savings, endowment policies, the car(s) and house contents). New laws apply to pensions (*see* below).

When granting the divorce, the court has complete discretion as to how it divides up the property. As always, the main concern will be with the welfare of the children – and who is to have the home will often depend on who is to have the children.

The court's order will depend upon whether the home is owned or rented.

Owner-occupiers

Often the main substantial asset will be the family home in which the children are living (although the pension may also provide a substantial asset too). The problem with the home is that if the assets are to be divided up the house will sometimes have to be sold, and often the parent with primary care of the children will be unable to afford to buy another property. When this is the case, the courts insist that the financial entitlements of the two spouses should take second place to the needs of the children; the availability of the home for the children must be ensured.

In practical terms, there are usually three possibilities:

1 Transfer the house to one of the spouses

For instance, if there are children – and they will be living with the woman – the court might give the house totally to the wife. In practice:

● the court will rarely make such an order of its own accord (although it is sometimes ordered);

● it is quite common, however, for it to be agreed to by the parties as the best arrangement. Usually, in return for her husband's agreement, the wife will agree to abandon any right to maintenance for herself. Thus, there is a clean break – the husband gives her the house, and knows that he will not have the burden of maintenance payments hanging over him for years to come;

● similarly, such an arrangement might be agreed if the wife has left the home to go and live with another man. An ex-husband may then buy out her share for a lump sum payment.

2 Sell the property and divide the money

This may well be the best solution if neither can afford to keep the house or flat. Often it is agreed to sell the house so that the proceeds can be used to enable the wife to buy a cheaper home, with the husband giving her a larger-than-normal share of the proceeds in return for a reduced (or nil) maintenance entitlement.

A practical problem could theoretically arise if one (or both) of the parties is on public funding. This is because the Legal Services Commission, which is the body dealing with public funding costs, has the right to have legal costs paid straight away (rather than deferring payment until later) out of monies 'recovered or preserved' for a publicly funded party. This is called the 'statutory charge'. But there are some limits on how the statutory charge operates in family cases, which can help families struggling to provide a home for the children. (*See also* page 788.)

If the family home is not sold but is transferred to or kept by one spouse (and/or the children), then the Legal Services Commission will not ask for the legal costs to be paid straight away but will wait until the home is eventually sold before claiming repayment. In the meantime the Legal Services Commission will register a charge against the home (like a mortgage).

If the home is sold, then the Legal Services Commission can ask for the money to be paid straight away, unless the proceeds of sale are specifically to be used to buy a new home for the publicly funded spouse (and/or the children) within a year of sale of the old home. The Legal Services Commission will then register a charge against the new home when it is bought and again the costs will have to be repaid once this new home is sold. But if the new home is bought later than a year after the sale of the old one, then the legal costs will have to be paid straight away (so it is usually not worthwhile hanging around to see if a better deal can be obtained).

In both cases, a special form of wording must be used in the court order which deals with the family home. It is not enough to have a simple agreement or even a court order which does not say specifically what the sale proceeds will be used for. The wording (adapted as necessary for particular cases) is:

And it is certified for the purpose of the Civil Legal Aid (General) Regulations that the lump sum of £x has been ordered to be paid to enable the petitioner/respondent to purchase a home for herself/himself (or her/his dependants) [that the property (state address) has been recovered/preserved for the petitioner/respondent for use as a home for herself/himself (or her/his dependants].

If this special wording is used, then payment of the costs will be put off until the home (present or new) is sold in future. The drawback is that interest (at 8 per cent) will continue running on the unpaid legal costs until they are eventually repaid in full, but the advantage is that the home can be kept on and the publicly funded party (and children) will not be forced on to the streets.

If the property is sold, it is usually best to agree a percentage division rather than a fixed sum, especially in times of volatile house markets.

The wife was awarded a lump sum of £32,000 with an order that if the husband defaulted on paying this sum, the home should be sold. The husband's appeal was dismissed and the house was ordered to be sold – it was then worth £116,000. The husband kept on delaying and the house meanwhile increased in value to £200,000. The wife thus asked the court for an increased lump sum. Held: Supervening events had falsified the old order: the wife should receive 40 per cent of the sale proceeds. Hope-Smith (1989)

That case was decided when house prices were rocketing up, but its principle is just as important when house prices are falling or if houses take a long time to sell. Then the costs which must be deducted from the sale proceeds may increase and thus decrease the overall value of the home.

3 Keep the house for the wife to live in

This is the order that is often made if there are young children – indeed it is often the only feasible solution. The typical order will then be for the wife to live in the house with the children, and for the house to be sold when the youngest child reaches 18. For instance:

A couple married in 1956. In 1970 the husband left the matrimonial home and the wife obtained a divorce and custody of their only child, a girl. The wife asked for the house to be transferred to her. Both husband and wife were planning new marriages; the husband had already bought a house with his cohabitee, and the wife's new partner had transferred his house to his ex-wife. Held: The husband should not lose all of his share in the home. The property would be held jointly until the daughter was 17, when it could be sold. In the meantime, the wife should pay all the outgoings, including the mortgage. Mesher (1973)

That was a 1973 case, and since then the courts have refined the orders a bit. Now, generally, sale will also be ordered if the wife dies, remarries, or if she wishes to move home.

The problems with this sort of order are:
- that the wife can find herself homeless in middle age (when the youngest child reaches 18, or so), with only a share in the proceeds of sale – and a share that may not be enough to buy anywhere else (and a further difficulty may well be that her age and limited earnings prevent her from taking on a mortgage). To try to avoid this problem, some judges prefer to say that the property should be sold only on the wife's death, marriage, or her wishing to move (i.e. no mention of a sale on the children reaching 18). Thus the wife has long-term security but at the price of depriving the husband of his share of the capital for what may turn out to be a very long time – and many judges take the view that this is too unfair on the husband;
- that the husband may be liable for capital gains tax on the increase in value of the home after he has left once the principal private residence exemption no longer applies.

The root of the difficulties is, of course, that there is sometimes no satisfactory solution – very often there is not enough money available to finance the purchase and maintenance of two homes. Because of these difficulties, sometimes the court will order the husband to buy out the wife and so order a 'clean break' (*see* page 53).

The husband moved out after seventeen years' marriage, leaving the wife and the three children in the house (worth £18,500). The trial judge ordered that the property be kept until the youngest child left home and that it then be sold, with the proceeds being divided 50/50. In the meantime, the wife should pay 'rent' to the husband for the use of the house. On appeal, the court decided that this was an impracticable order, the wife would not have the money to pay any rent to the husband. Instead, the husband was ordered to accept the wife's offer to buy out his share in the house for £2,500. This would give him a deposit for a new house, and he would be able to afford mortgage repayments. The wife would be left with the house, which would give her long-term housing security, but no maintenance (she could claim supplementary benefit if necessary).   Scipio (1983)

Does it matter whose name the house is in?

It used to matter a lot. Before 1970 the courts adopted a very legalistic approach and were primarily concerned with whose name was on the title deeds. Often a wife was refused a share in the matrimonial home simply because her name was not on the deeds.

After years of agitation by Lord Denning and others, Parliament changed the law. Now the courts are not so concerned with whose name is on the deeds, although it is still a relevant factor.

If the house, or flat, is held in joint names (i.e. both spouses' names appear on the deeds) then it is virtually certain that they own the property jointly. If there were no children, and both husband and wife had contributed to the house bills, then both would probably receive half – especially if the wife was working. If there are children, the courts will be primarily concerned that they should receive a roof over their heads, so the wife might receive more than half of the property.

If the house is not in joint names (i.e. it is in the name of only one of the couple) then the position may occasionally be different. The courts will then be more ready to deny the other spouse a share of the home, but this will happen only in exceptional circumstances, such as with a very short marriage, or where the other spouse has behaved very badly, or is wealthy and yet did not provide any money for the house.

In the vast majority of marriages that last more than a few years the wife will be given often at least a half share, whether or not her name is on the deeds. Even though her husband may have put up all the money for the house, it is likely that the court will recognize her contribution in terms of being a home-maker, cook and mother, and so she will have earned her share in that way.

As Lord Denning said in *Wachtel*:

. . . Parliament recognized that the wife who looks after the home and family contributes as much to the family assets as the wife who goes out to work. The one contributes in kind. The other in money or money's worth. If the court comes to the conclusion that the home has been acquired and maintained by the joint efforts of both, then, when the marriage breaks down, it should be regarded as the joint property of both of them, no matter in whose name it stands.

Although the courts will usually give the wife a half share whether or not her name is on the title deeds, it is preferable for her to insist that the house be in their joint names. But it must be remembered that no two cases are the same; it is impossible to generalize, and there is no rule that says the wife must have a half share. It could be more; it could be less. See the warning on page 66.

The importance of staying at home with the children

The court will nearly always award the house to the spouse who has remained living there with the children. In practice this means that if the wife can remain in the house with the children, and get her husband out, she is almost certain to be awarded the property by the divorce court. As we have seen (above) this is likely to mean either:

- she occupies the house until the children grow up, whereupon it is sold and the proceeds divided between the spouses; or
- she becomes sole owner of the house immediately, forfeiting about one-third of her maintenance as payment for her husband's share.

Thus there is every reason for the wife to refuse to move out. Since her husband's legal advisers may well have informed him that if he moves out he is likely to lose the house, there is every likelihood of a domestic confrontation. Quite simply, neither dares move out. When this situation develops the law favours the wife, since she can get an occupation order ordering the man out of the house if the strain becomes too great and the balance of harm test shifts in favour of her and the children (*see* page 74). Otherwise both parties may be advised to sit it out until they reach an agreement or get a court order.

Stopping a sale or remortgage

If the house is not in joint names, but (for instance) in the sole name of the husband, there is an added danger; he may sell the house before the court makes an order and then disappear with the proceeds.

However, this can be prevented. A non-owning spouse has matrimonial home rights in the property under the Family Law Act 1996 and she can protect these by registration at the Land Registry and thereby stop the house being sold or mortgaged against her wishes. She can do this at any time – not just when she has fallen out with her husband. Her husband will probably not learn of the registration until he attempts to sell the property or to raise a new mortgage on it.

Once a charge has been registered on the property, this legally confirms the non-owning spouse's legal right to occupy the home and ensures that no one could buy the property (or lend money on its security) until she removes her registration or gives her consent. In effect, she can make sure that the property will not be sold behind her back. The only transaction that the registration is ineffective against is if the building society (or other lender) forecloses on the mortgage and repossesses the house because the instalments were not paid. But, otherwise, it gives her complete protection. Also, if her husband should try to evict her forcibly from the house she can apply to the court for an injunction (*see* page 76).

This matrimonial home right can be registered simply, easily and cheaply. It is best done by a solicitor, who should be asked to 'register a charge'. The solicitor's fee would probably be around £100 (the Legal Help legal-advice scheme might cover the cost, *see* page 789).

A non-owning spouse who has any doubts as to the loyalty of the other spouse is always well advised to register their matrimonial home rights, which last as long as the marriage lasts, i.e. until decree absolute. If necessary, even after the divorce, if the financial arrangements have not been worked out, this type of charge can be converted to another charge (technically called a 'pending action' charge) to continue the protection of the non-owning spouse's interest until the money disputes are concluded.

Ordering the other spouse out of the house

Once the divorce is heard the court can make whatever order it wishes and it may well order one of the spouses to leave the matrimonial home, under an occupation order. Although this type of order (often previously called an 'ouster' order) was extended by the Family Law Act 1996 to non-violent matters, more often than not the court will order a spouse out of the home *before* the divorce is granted only if he (or she) has been violent to the other spouse or to the children (*see* page 74).

Summary

With owner-occupied property, the woman has the following rights even if her name is not on the title deeds:

- she can live in the home until a court order is made evicting her;
- she can ask the divorce court to transfer the home to her sole name;
- in the meantime, she can prevent the home being sold, by registering her matrimonial home rights. She can also obtain an injunction if her husband tries to throw her out of the house.

Rented property

The divorce court can order that the tenancy be transferred to one of the spouses.

1 Privately rented property

The position depends upon the terms of the tenancy, and whether there is any restriction on the tenancy being assigned (i.e. transferred).

If there is no written tenancy agreement. It will be assumed that the tenant can assign the tenancy, even if the landlord does not want this. Thus the court will feel able to transfer the tenancy to the other spouse even if the landlord and the original tenant object.

If there is a written tenancy agreement. The position here is more complicated. There are three possibilities:

- If the agreement does not contain a clause forbidding the assignment of the tenancy, then the tenant is able to assign and so the court will feel able to transfer the tenancy to the other spouse. In other words, the position is identical to that when there is no written tenancy agreement.
- If the agreement contains a clause stating that the tenancy can be assigned only with the consent of the landlord, then the law will imply a qualification to this by saying that the landlord cannot 'unreasonably' withhold his consent. Thus, if the spouse to whom the tenancy would be granted is a 'reasonable' prospect as a tenant, then the landlord cannot object to the transfer of the tenancy. On the other hand, if it would not be 'unreasonable' for the landlord to object (e.g. the spouse cannot supply references, has no money, has previously been a bad tenant) then he cannot be forced to agree to the assignment. If the spouse is a 'reasonable' prospect then the court will feel able to transfer the tenancy, even if both landlord and tenant object. If the spouse is not a reasonable prospect then the court will not agree to the transfer. Usually, of course, there is no suggestion that the spouse (probably the wife) would not make a suitable tenant and so the problem rarely arises.
- If the tenancy agreement contains a clause stating that the tenancy cannot be assigned (and there is no clause saying that the landlord's consent is needed), then the landlord cannot be forced to accept an assignment. Thus, the court will probably feel unable to transfer the tenancy to the other spouse.

2 Council property

The council will transfer the tenancy from one tenant to another only if a court order has been made. The court can make an order on divorce or judicial separation and can also make an occupation order under the Family Law Act 1996. The position will therefore depend upon whether one or both of the spouses are tenants.

If the council flat or house is in joint names (i.e. both spouses' names are on the rent book) and the court does not order a transfer of the tenancy, then they can both stay there. This, frankly, is very rare – the court accepts that both need somewhere to live and it is unlikely that on divorce they can live amicably under the same roof. Under the Family Law Act 1996, the court has to weigh up the balance of harm test on the making of an occupation order – in other words, the spouse which will suffer the most if he or she has to leave is more likely to be allowed to stay. The court will look at whether either spouse can establish a priority need (if they have children or are vulnerable in some way) and thus be more likely to be rehoused by the council if they were ordered out.

If the council house or flat is in the name of only one of the spouses and the divorce court does not transfer the tenancy to the other spouse, then the other spouse will have to leave if ordered to do so by the spouse who is the tenant, once the divorce has been made absolute. Until that time, he or she has a right to remain in occupation. After the decree absolute, the spouse who is the tenant can apply to the county court for an eviction order (and if necessary an injunction) against the other spouse.

If the council house or flat is in the name of only one of the spouses and the divorce court transfers the tenancy to the other spouse, then the original tenant will have to leave. Generally, the court will transfer the tenancy to the spouse who has primary care of the children and will require the other spouse to leave.

Similar rules apply when renting from a housing association.

Does it matter whose name is on the rent book?

Generally, the answer to this is 'no' for, as explained above, the court can order that the tenancy be transferred from one spouse to another. However, if the rent book or lease is in the names of both spouses, then they can both continue living there unless the court says otherwise. So it is always an advantage for a spouse to have his or her name on the rent book or lease – in the same way that it is always better to have both names on the title deeds if the couple are owner-occupiers.

Sometimes a rented home will be in the name of the husband only and, following a matrimonial dispute, he simply walks out and does not return. When this happens, the wife can continue living in the home and she can insist that the landlord accepts rent from her as though she was the tenant; in effect, she takes over in place of her husband, although she will have to pay off any rent arrears that may have built up.

Ordering the husband out before there is a divorce

This is often ordered when the husband has been violent to his wife or the children. The husband can only rarely be ordered out if he has not been guilty of physical violence (*see* page 74).

PENSIONS

After the family home, private or occupational pensions can be the most valuable matrimonial asset. In fact, in some cases the pension can far exceed the value of the home. Airline pilots, for example, not infrequently have very valuable pension rights, valued at over half a million pounds if they have worked for a company for a long time. But how do pensions fit into divorce?

Before the Pensions Act 1995, the courts' powers were, by and large, restricted to compensating the non-pension scheme member spouse with extra capital (if any was available) for the loss of the pension benefits following divorce. Once decree absolute has been made in the divorce, then the marriage is over and a spouse is no longer a spouse but instead an ex-spouse and no longer entitled to pension benefits (in service or on and after retirement) if her spouse were to die.

However, nowadays the courts have more options. The first is to earmark a share of the pension so that the pension scheme member keeps his pension, but a share of it (say the lump sum payable on retirement and perhaps the pension following retirement) is earmarked for his ex-wife. There have been a number of problems with this arrangement, not least in that it depends on the ex-husband and ex-wife both surviving until retirement to gain any benefits and there has still been uncertainty over what proportion of the pension should be covered – should it just be the value of the pension over the marriage or that which accrues after the marriage is ended? Most importantly the provisions fly in the face of the clean break principle – both spouses are still financially tied together even though their marriage is ended.

Since December 2000, the courts can also order a pension to be shared or split so that the pension scheme member spouse gets to keep a reduced part of his pension while the non-pension scheme member spouse gets a pension in her own right – which she can either keep with the existing pension provider or move to another one.

Even a wife who has never worked outside the home can now get a pension in her own right.

A key issue is how best to value a pension. Personal pension plans, in which regular amounts are paid into the pension, are in some ways similar to a savings account and thus can be more easily valued. Occupational pensions are not so easy to determine. Take the example of employees of the Civil Service, whose pensions are 'unfunded': the government does not pay regular amounts into the pension scheme but makes a commitment that when the employee retires it will pay a pension broadly based on his or her final salary and the length of employment. It can be difficult in these circumstances to work out how much the pension will be worth, because neither the final salary – which would depend on promotion – nor the length of time the employee will work for the Civil Service is known.

In 1996 regulations were laid down that the value of a pension would be the 'cash equivalent transfer value' (CETV). This is the equivalent of how much a pension scheme holder would be paid if he or she were to take out the money from the current pension fund and transfer it to another. Pensions experts advise that this valuation method can undershoot the real value especially of occupational pensions, but it is more realistic for personal pensions. That said, this is the value which should be used.

Pension schemes can produce a CETV fairly simply, and most do so without a fee – you can simply write to them requesting that and an estimate of the value of the ex-spouse's lost pension rights. Under the Occupational Pension Schemes (Disclosure of Information) Regulations 1996, and the Divorce etc. (Pensions) Regulations 1996, pension schemes have to provide this information. In any event because the issue of pensions is very complex, it is important to obtain specialist legal advice from a solicitor about what rights might be claimed in respect of the pension.

See further on this topic Chapter 6.

When there is a lot of money

In a landmark decision in October 2000, the House of Lords changed the way that the courts look at working out the finances in divorce cases where the couple are very wealthy; where their available assets exceed their financial needs for housing and income. Following the House of Lords' decision in *White* v *White*, wealthy wives can expect a far larger share (up to half) of the family assets on divorce.

The facts in White

Martin and Pamela White had been married for 33 years. During that time they had built up a successful dairy farming business together, and accumulated property and other assets worth a total of £4.6 million. In their divorce proceedings, the High Court judge decided that Mrs White was entitled to only one-fifth of the total assets. That award was based on the traditional approach that the wife should get enough in a clean break divorce to satisfy her 'reasonable needs' (i.e. enough to buy a new house and maintain her). Under the traditional approach, anything over and above that amount should remain in the pocket of her earning spouse – so Mr White was left with more than the lion's share of the assets.

The House of Lords decided that from now on judges should be approaching matrimonial cases on the basis of splitting the assets equally. Mrs White was entitled to a sum that reflected her equal participation in the business and contribution to family life. On that basis, Mrs White's award was increased to two-fifths of the total assets. Lord Nicholls also emphasized that, although in this case there had been a true business partnership between the spouses, in cases where the wife stayed at home and brought up the children, there should not be a bias in the favour of the breadwinner when the courts came to divide up the assets on divorce.

White v White (2000)

Following the House of Lords' decision in the case of *White* v *White*, a number of husbands sought to establish that they should be entitled to more than 50 per cent of the matrimonial assets because of special or 'stellar' contributions to the acquisition of family wealth.

Mr and Mrs Cowan had been married for 35 years and had two children. Although there was some dispute about the wife's contributions to the building of the family companies at the beginning of the marriage, it was accepted that the husband's efforts had been of an exceptional or 'stellar' quality resulting in assets of about £11,500,000 at the end of the marriage. The Court of Appeal increased the lump sum awarded to Mrs Cowan to £3 million – but that only amounted to 38 per cent of the assets, leaving Mr Cowan with 62 per cent.

Cowan (2001)

However, the Court of Appeal in 2002 decided in the case of Harry Lambert that it was only in wholly exceptional cases that a husband's contribution would be found to justify a greater than 50 per cent share of the assets. Like Mr Cowan, Harry Lambert had been the business genius in the family and had built up a valuable empire from nothing. Shan Lambert, like Mrs Cowan, had played a conventional wife and mother role but the Court of Appeal held that she should, nevertheless, have half the fruits of the marriage.

SUMMARY: THE FINANCES OF A SPLIT-UP

This chapter has gone through the principles applied by the courts when working out maintenance and the division of the home and pension on a matrimonial breakdown. It will be clear that there are numerous factors to be taken into account and, accordingly, it is impossible to give simplified advice that will apply in every case.

The courts have become more flexible in recent years – they are now less likely to adopt rigid ideas of one-third or one-half. They also put greater emphasis on the position of the children and the desirability of the couple becoming financially independent.

The legal costs of divorce

Going to court for a full-blown battle over money is guaranteed to be very expensive – both emotionally and financially. Many couples have found this out to their cost too late, seeing all the family money swallowed up by lawyers' bills instead of being more fruitfully used for the benefit of the new halves of the family.

Warnings about costs are constantly being made in the courts. One judge, Mrs Justice Booth, issued these guidelines to lawyers in 1990:
- affidavit evidence should be confined to relevant facts;

- professional witnesses should avoid taking a partisan approach;
- extra care should be taken to decide what evidence should be produced – non-material emotive evidence should be avoided;
- avoid duplicating documents;
- both parties' solicitors should agree a chronology of material facts;
- if a case looks to be substantial, have a pre-trial review to see if settlement can be reached.

But what happens if one party wants to be reasonable and settle at a fair figure and the other refuses? The answer: damage limitation! The reasonable spouse can make an offer to the other spouse, called a Calderbank offer. Then, if the other spouse rejects the offer and pushes on to a full court hearing and the court ultimately makes an order of around the figure offered, the rejecting spouse can be penalized by having a costs order made against him or her, thus ending up having to pay most of both lawyers' bills, and may even end up having to pay interest on the lump sum he may eventually have to pay for a period since the offer to settle was received.

Usually costs orders follow the event – so in financial cases in divorce the winner will get an order that the loser should pay his or her legal costs. The amount of the costs ordered to be paid may not meet the full legal bill of the successful spouse, but it will certainly go a long way towards it. By making a Calderbank offer, the other spouse becomes more at risk on costs grounds.

Making a Calderbank offer is a gamble, but an experienced solicitor can help reduce the odds. In some cases the gamble pays off even if the offer is on the low side.

The husband made a Calderbank offer of £400,000 which the wife rejected. After a contested hearing the wife beat the offer and was awarded £435,000. But the judge refused to award the wife her costs because of her refusal to negotiate over the original offer. So she had to pay her own legal bill instead of this being awarded against the husband.

S *v* S (1990)

Calderbank offers are not just limited to rich families; they can be very useful in any case which involves the dividing up of assets, even just the family home.

MONEY MATTERS: CONCLUSION AND WARNING

Please remember what has been repeated again and again. In a book of this sort the author can give only general guidance. Please do not think (for instance) that a wife is automatically entitled to one-third income plus half the house. It is not as simple as that. Every case depends on its own circumstances – and the courts will throw away the rule book to do what is best in the particular circumstances.

6

Pensions – a Basic Guide to Retirement Provision

Pensions have attracted a great deal of interest and concern in recent years. There is increasing awareness that current levels of saving for retirement are likely to be inadequate as the result of dramatic falls in the value of equities and changing demographic patterns. People are living longer and retirement provision will be stretched to meet needs over longer life spans.

Various solutions are being debated ranging from encouragement for people to save more while they are in employment to extending working lives to enable people to make greater provision.

The aim of this chapter is to provide a brief overview of the different types of pension available. It will also look at what happens to pensions on divorce, early retirement and death.

WHAT ARE PENSIONS?

The term 'pension' is frequently used to refer to a whole range of retirement benefits. These include annuities, which are usually monthly payments made to a pensioner who has purchased an annuity from the fund accumulated by him during his working life to provide regular income on retirement. Pension benefits also encompass the payment of lump sums on retirement, payments to widows and other dependants and the payment of death-in-service benefits if the pension scheme member dies while in employment. Sickness or disability pensions may be available for those who have to retire early on health grounds.

There are two main types of pension arrangement:
- state benefits; and
- private arrangements.

State benefits

There are two state pension arrangements:

Basic state pension

The basic state pension is available to individuals who have reached state pension age, made sufficient National Insurance (NI) contributions and who make a claim for a state retirement pension.

The rate increases in April of each year. For the tax year 2003/2004, the full basic pension for a single pensioner is £77.45 a week (£4,027.40 a year). For married couples, it is £123.80 per week (£6,437.60 a year) in addition to which state pensioners receive a £10 Christmas bonus and a cold-weather payment in winter.

State pension age for men is currently 65. For women born on or before 6 April 1955, state pension age is 60. For those born between April 1950 and 1955, there will be a gradual increase in state pension age. At www.thepensionservice.gov.uk, there is a calculator to enable women to work out the date on which they will reach state pension age. From 6 April 2020, state pension for men and women will be 65.

Entitlement to a full state pension is built up by NI contributions. In some cases, people may be treated as having paid despite not being in work. To qualify for the full category-A basic state pension, the individual has to have paid or be credited with NI contributions for approximately 90 per cent of the tax years in his or her 'working life'. This begins on 16 April before your sixteenth birthday and ends on 5 April before you reach pension age. The maximum working life for a man (and for women born after April 1955) is 49 years and men therefore need to have contributed for 44 'qualifying years' to build up a full basic state pension. For women born before 1955, 39 qualifying years are needed and this will increase to 44 by 2020.

To build up basic state pension entitlement through NI contributions, it is necessary to pay for a whole year and for contributions to be of the right type. For the tax year 2003/2004, class 1 contributions are payable at the rate of 11 per cent by all employees earning in excess of the earnings threshold (£4,165 per annum or £89 a week). The upper earnings limit is £30,940 per annum or £595 a week.

From 5 April 2003, employees earning over £30,940 a year pay an additional 1 per cent and employers make secondary class 1 contributions of 12.8 per cent for those employees.

A reduced state pension may be payable to someone who has not worked for sufficient years or has had earnings below a certain level provided their NI contributions (or credits) qualify them for at least 25 per cent of the full basic state pension.

State second pension (S2P)

Until April 2002, the additional state pension was known as the state earnings-related pension scheme or SERPS. This depended on NI contributions paid by employees. From April 2002, S2Ps came into operation with the aim of benefiting people on low or moderate earnings. They also enable certain non-workers such as carers and people with long-term illnesses or disabilities to secure an additional state pension. For S2P purposes, earnings up to £11,200 a year in 2003/2004 are low earnings and earnings between £11,200 and £25,600 are moderate earnings. Those earning between £4,004 and £11,200 per annum in 2003/04 will be treated for S2P as if they had earned £11,200 in the relevant year. This allows the S2P to build up at twice the rate that SERPS would have provided.

Special rules apply to carers who are now able to build up an S2P for each full tax year in which they do not work or in which they earn less than the annual NI earnings limit provided:

- they are responsible for a child under 6 and in receipt of child benefit for that child; or
- they are looking after an ill or disabled person and qualify for Home Responsibility Protection (HRP); or
- they are entitled to a carer's allowance even if they do not get it because they receive a benefit which pays more.

Home responsibility protection

HRP helps carers to protect their basic state pension by reducing the number of qualifying years needed to build up a full basic state pension. Since 6 April 2002, it can also help to build up an additional state pension through the S2P.

To qualify for HRP, it is necessary for the carer to have looked after a child or a sick or disabled or elderly person for a full tax year for a minimum of 35 hours a week. The carer should not be in receipt of a carer's allowance or income support in his or her capacity as a carer.

Long-term sickness or disability

People who have worked and paid or are treated as having paid Class 1 NI contributions for at least one-tenth of their working lives by the time they reach state pension age will be entitled to an enhanced S2P if in receipt of incapacity benefit or severe disablement allowance on a long-term basis. For the years in respect of which they are in receipt of the relevant benefits or allowances, they will be treated as having earnings at the low-earnings threshold.

Contribution credits

Certain people are eligible to be credited with NI contributions when they are not working. This applies to people who are in receipt of certain state benefits, unemployed and available for and actively seeking work or incapable of work through illness or disability.

Voluntary NI contributions

Anyone with gaps in their NI record can pay Class 3 contributions on a voluntary basis. The flat rate in 2003/04 is £6.95 a week. It is now possible to go back 6 years to fill in contributions gaps.

Minimum income guarantee (MIG)

The MIG provided a means-tested income threshold or topping up of the basic state pension until October 2003. In effect, the MIG was a means of providing income support for single pensioners in receipt of £102.10 a week and couples in receipt of £155.80 a week.

From October 2003, MIGs have been replaced by pension credits which guarantee pensioners a minimum income but also reward them for savings.

Private pensions

Private pensions are a way of supplementing the state pension for those who are able to afford to make additional provision. A range of private pension schemes is on offer: occupational, personal and stakeholder pensions.

Occupational pension schemes

Many employers offer occupational pension schemes which provide a package of benefits including a retirement pension. Some employers contribute towards the occupational pension but most are contributory schemes to which the employee has to contribute.

There are two types of scheme: final salary and money purchase.

Final salary schemes

These are also known as defined benefit schemes. They are always employer-related and involve a promise of a benefit, frequently related to salary.

Final salary schemes reward employees for long service. The pension depends ultimately on the number of years of service, earnings at or near retirement and a fraction (usually one sixtieth) which indicates the amount of pension acquired for each year of service. Thus, someone who has worked for an employer for 40 years will be entitled to 40/60 of his salary at retirement. The benefits may be index linked. Since April 1997, the law has required final salary schemes to be supported by funding within the pension scheme. These schemes have become increasingly expensive for employers and few are now available outside the public sector. Example:

James has worked for the same employer and been a member of its non-contributory final salary scheme for 30 years. He is about to retire on a final salary of £50,000. His pension will be 30/60 x £50,000 or £25,000 per annum provided he does not elect to take a lump sum. If he takes a lump sum, his pension will be reduced by £1 for every £12 of the lump sum so that a tax-free lump sum of 1½ x salary will reduce his annual pension by £6,250 per annum to £18,750 per annum.

Money purchase schemes

These are also known as defined contribution schemes. Benefits are related to the sum of money accumulated over time. The accumulated sum is used at retirement by a pension the value of which depends on annuity rates at the relevant time. There is considerable uncertainty as to the final value of the pension which will depend on rises or falls in the stock market at the time the fund is cashed in to buy an annuity.

Stakeholder pensions

Stakeholder pensions are low-charge personal pensions of a money purchase nature. They were introduced in April 2001 to encourage lower earners and people who do not have access to occupational pension schemes or to good personal pensions to save for retirement.

Since October 2001, employers with five or more employees have been obliged to offer stakeholder pensions if they do not have an occupational pension scheme.

Since October 2003, stakeholder pensions have been available to part-time employees. People having a career break for childcare or other reasons can also contribute to stakeholder pensions.

Stakeholder schemes are flexible and management costs are low. It is possible for contributions to be varied, stopped and started again depending on circumstances. There should be no penalty on transfer between stakeholder and other pension schemes.

Despite these apparent advantages, stakeholder pensions have had very low take-up rates since their introduction in 2001. There has been resistance on the part of

insurers to setting up stakeholder schemes as a result of the 1 per cent cap on charges.

When are private pensions paid?

This depends on the scheme rules which normally set a minimum pension age. For post-1989 schemes, 50 is the lowest age before a pension can be paid with certain limited exceptions in the case of occupations where it is appropriate to retire earlier than 50.

Additional voluntary contributions (AVC)

Employees who entered occupational schemes late may be allowed to top up their pension rights by making AVCs into their employer's scheme.

Contracting out

It is normally possible to contract out of the additional state pension and to make private provision instead. Anyone considering contracting out has to balance the amount of state additional pension which will be given up against what he or she is predicted to receive from the replacement investment.

Where an employee contracts out of his employer's occupational pension scheme, both he and the employer pay lower NI contributions known as the contracted-out rebate. On retirement, the second pension comes from this scheme and not from the state.

The rebate of NI contributions will be paid into the personal pension scheme as will tax relief on the pension contributions.

Rate of income tax	Cost to you of every £100 that goes into your pension
22%	£78
40%	£60

Tax relief is applied regardless of whether it is an occupational, personal or stakeholder pension.

Tax considerations

Tax reliefs are available on pension contributions provided these fall within the permissible percentages. The percentage of earnings on which tax relief at the highest rate of income tax is available increases with age. Thus, it is 17.5 per cent for employees up to 35 years of age, 20 per cent for those aged between 36 and 45, 25 per cent between 46 and 50, 30 per cent between 51 and 55, 35 per cent between 56 and 60 and 40 per cent where employees are between 61 and 74 years of age. There is an earnings cap on income-tax relief which was £97,200 in the tax year 2002/03.

In addition to the tax relief on pension contributions,

part of the proceeds of occupational pension schemes and most personal pensions can be taken as a tax-free lump sum at retirement. Taking a tax-free lump sum reduces the amount of annual pension. The pensioner who is concerned about managing on the reduced pension can use the tax-free sum to buy a purchased life annuity. The figure which can normally be taken is one quarter of the pension fund.

Considerations for women

Women have a longer life expectancy than men with the result that pension provision has to be made for longer. However, average female earnings are lower than those for men which means that resources from which pension provision has to be made are scarcer.

Women frequently take career breaks to care for children or elderly or disabled relatives and this, too, affects their ability to build up adequate NI contributions to qualify for the full rate of basic state pension as well as to contribute to private pension schemes. It is thought that as many as 70 per cent of women of pension age do not have private pension rights.

It is hoped that the availability of home responsibilities protection and lower-cost stakeholder pensions may help women who have been affected by career breaks.

Pensions and divorce

Pension rights are frequently the largest assets available to a married couple besides the family home. In the great majority of cases, the rights belong to the husband. On divorce, many women lose valuable widow's pension benefits unless specific provision is made to transfer those benefits to them as part of a divorce order.

Pension sharing was introduced by the Welfare Reform and Pensions Act 1999. For all couples whose divorces commenced with petitions filed after 1 December 2000, the court can now divide a pension at the time of divorce so that the spouse, usually the wife, either becomes a member of the pension scheme in her own right or takes a transfer of a designated percentage into her own pension scheme. A pension-sharing arrangement is achieved by calculating the value of the member's accrued benefits at the time of divorce and allocating a percentage of the value to the spouse. If the spouse becomes a member of the scheme, this is known as an internal pension credit while a transfer of benefits into her own pension is known as an external pension credit.

The valuation used is the Cash Equivalent Transfer Value or CETV. An equal pension share will not necessarily give husband and wife equal pension rights. A pension credit for a wife may give her benefits of less value because of greater life expectancy.

In long marriage cases with older people, the availability of pension sharing has allowed for greater fairness on divorce. It has allowed women who have failed to make provision in their own right in reliance on their husbands' pensions to have secure benefits which do not depend on the former spouse following the divorce.

The spouse who receives a pension credit takes the pension at his or her own normal retirement age. Pension sharing does not apply to the basic state pension, as divorced people can replace their own contribution record with their husband's record for the duration of the marriage.

Early retirement

While current trends are to encourage people to work longer, early retirement remains an option particularly for those who are in poor health. There is no minimum age for retirement on health grounds. For those who qualify for early retirement on ill-health grounds, benefits levels are more generous than for those who take voluntary early retirement. It is often possible to obtain benefits calculated as though the individual had worked to his or her normal retirement date.

Occupational pension schemes may set their own limits on ill-health pension and related benefits which may be lower than the maximum the Inland Revenue allows.

Pensions for the self-employed

The self-employed are not normally eligible for occupational pension schemes and have to make private provision either through joining a personal pension scheme or a stakeholder scheme, or both if both can be afforded. For those whose earnings are erratic, stakeholder schemes may offer considerable benefit as they are flexible. Contributions can be as low as £20 a time at intervals which are regular or irregular and payments can be varied both in amount and in frequency.

Where the self-employed person wants to make the maximum allowable contributions but does not know until the end of the accounting year how much income he or she has had, one-off lump sum payments can be made into personal pension schemes. Advice can be obtained from independent financial advisers (IFAs) who are regulated by the Financial Services Authority (FSA). The FSA took over the regulatory duties of various other bodies on 1 December 2001. A good IFA should have sound knowledge of the private pension market and the track record of individual funds. They should also be able to advise on the best method of investing, whether it is by regular contributions of a fixed amount or by an annual lump sum payment once earnings for the relevant year have been assessed.

Death of the pensioner

On the death of the pensioner, there is a distinction between the operation of state and private pensions. State pensions may be available to a widow or widower based on their deceased spouse's NI record. Up to 100 per cent of the basic state pension may be available to the survivor. In addition, up to 50 per cent of any additional state pension may be available depending on the age of the deceased spouse at death.

Most occupational pension schemes and some personal pension schemes pay survivor's pensions to widowers, widows and other dependants of the deceased member on death in service or after retirement.

Death-in-service benefits frequently include:

- lump sum life insurance;
- a refund of contributions to the pension scheme;
- pension for the surviving spouse;
- pension for other dependants.

On death after retirement, the occupational pension may provide for a widow's pension, pension for other dependants including children and in certain cases a cohabitant.

For occupational pension schemes, tax rules allow two death-in-service benefits. The first is a lump sum of up to 4 x earnings and the second a pension payable to the widow, widower and/or other dependants. Generally, this is around two-thirds of the pension the deceased member would have received if he or she had retired on incapacity grounds. If more than one person is eligible to receive a pension, the total payable cannot exceed two-thirds of the incapacity pension.

On death after retirement, the spouse and/or dependants will generally get a proportion of the pension with a maximum of two-thirds. Again, if the pension is payable to more than one person, the total cannot exceed two-thirds of the deceased member's pension.

It is important for separated spouses to check their eligibility for widow's pensions. Unmarried and gay couples should also check the availability of dependants' benefits for unmarried partners. It is always sensible for the scheme member to lodge a notice of wishes in respect of the death-in-service or retirement benefits where unmarried dependants are involved. While trustees are not bound by a nomination of this kind, it will at least serve to inform them of the deceased member's wishes and obligations. Most occupational schemes provide standard nomination forms for the member to complete

and lodge with the trustees or administrators of the pension scheme. Personal pension providers usually make similar allowances for the expression of wishes.

A spouse who is under the age of 60 when he or she becomes entitled to an annuity on the death of a personal pension scheme member may elect to defer purchasing the annuity until the age of 60. This may serve to increase the annuity income on its eventual purchase. Where an annuity has already been bought by a member who subsequently dies, an annuity can be paid to a survivor being a widow, widower or dependant of the deceased member.

Planning for your future

A great deal of help and information is available from various organizations and websites. Your local Citizens' Advice Bureau may be able to offer basic help. Their website is at www.nacab.org.uk.

The Pensions Advisory Service (OPAS) can be contacted for information about any aspect of occupational, stakeholder and personal pensions on 0845 601 2923. The OPAS website is at www.opas.org.uk. You can write to OPAS at 11 Belgrave Road, London, SW1V 1RB.

There are numerous leaflets available from the Inland Revenue whose website is at www.inlandrevenue.gov.uk/leaflets.

The Financial Services Authority has a range of free consumer booklets and fact sheets explaining various pension options. The FSA can be contacted on 0845 606 1234. Copies can be downloaded from the website at www.fsa.gov.uk/consumer.

If your employer offers access to an occupational scheme, it is usually worth joining that scheme. For specific advice on pension options, contact an IFA but check the charges you will have to pay before seeking such advice.

Apart from your home, your pension is likely to be the most important investment of your life. It will determine the quality of your retirement. It is never too early to start investing in your future and you should monitor your investment regularly to provide a financially secure retirement.

7

Domestic Violence

The emotional trauma often associated with relationship breakdown can all too frequently erupt into physical abuse and/or violence – sometimes termed domestic violence. Domestic violence is no respecter of class or age: it cuts across all strata of society, economic and ethnic backgrounds. Such abuse may have been a long-term part of the marriage or relationship or it may more recently have reared its head when break-up is threatened. Although domestic violence most often occurs when men are the aggressors and women the victims, the fact that men can also be the victims of such abuse – from female partners or male homosexual partners – is increasingly better recognized. However for the purposes of this chapter the victim is usually referred to as she and the aggressor as he, to reflect the common pattern.

Domestic violence should never be tolerated. The police and courts have become increasingly aware of the damaging effects – short term and long term – not only on the individual adults concerned but also on their children. There are legal remedies available, but before looking at their individual merits, it should be stressed that:

- a cohabiting wife (i.e. a woman living with a man but not married to him) *can* get protection;
- people suffering violence from other relationships can get protection too – gay couples or a parent being attacked by a violent adult child, for example, can also seek redress under the law;
- the court procedures in domestic-violence cases can be pretty complex. This remains the case despite the introduction of new law and procedure under the Family Law Act 1996 Part IV. The law and the procedure for getting court protection can be somewhat (understandably) mystifying to a member of the public. It is always advisable to take legal advice and a victim should instruct a solicitor to act for her (or him).

The person charged with being abusive may also wish to seek legal advice. Public funding is available; since the partner's income will be ignored, many victims of violence will be eligible for free legal advice (*see* page 787).

HOW THE LAW CAN PROTECT A WOMAN AND CHILDREN

There are nowadays two different courses of action a woman can take to protect herself against further abuse. The first is now under the criminal law (and also the civil law), under the Protection from Harassment Act 1997 and the second is under the civil law, under the Family Law Act 1996 Part IV.

Remedies under the Protection from Harassment Act 1997

The Protection from Harassment Act 1997 was actually introduced to allay widespread public concern over the law's apparent inability to deal with what is commonly termed 'stalking'. Very often the laws are used to give added protection to victims of violence whose ex-partners, for example, are menacing and harassing them.

The essential characteristics of stalking are an obsessive harassment of the victim (usually, but not always, female) by someone who pursues her by physically following her, telephoning her and so on. A study in 2000 in *The Lancet* showed that stalkers who assault their victims are far more likely to be estranged lovers or acquaintances than crazy strangers – the most common victims are people who have fallen out with a former partner.

The study looked at case histories of 50 stalkers caught or investigated by police in North London – 20 of the 50 stalkers were former sexual partners of their victims, 18 were acquaintances while only 12 were total strangers. All cases had involved repetitive, unwanted communications with their victims or fear-inducing approaches over a time period of at least four weeks. Fourteen of the 20 former lovers violently attacked their ex-partners, while only eight of the other 30 stalkers had been violent to the victims.

The Protection from Harassment Act 1997 created an

offence of harassment, which thus became a crime, and also provides extra civil remedies to restrain offenders and to provide compensation (damages) for such behaviour.

Two new criminal offences are in fact created. The first offence, that of 'harassment', is fairly easy to prove. A second more serious offence, that of 'causing a fear of violence', is much harder to prove – not least because the Act requires that the individual incidents must cause a fear of violence, while with most stalking-type cases experts have commented that it is the totality of the behaviour that causes the fear and not individual incidents.

The summary offence of 'harassment' does not require that the accused should be warned that his behaviour could lead to a criminal conviction. But an accused will need to show a pattern of harassment – one or two incidents themselves will not be enough. The current CPS guidelines state that after one incident of harassment, the suspect should be warned that his behaviour is harassing and if a second offence is committed, he can be arrested.

The defendant had once assaulted his girlfriend and four months later had threatened her new boyfriend in her presence. Held: While the court accepted that the number of incidents which amounted to a 'course of conduct' need not exceed two, the fewer the incidents and the wider apart they were spread, the less likely it was that a finding of harassment could reasonably be made.

Lau *v* Director of Public Prosecutions (2000)

The numbers of stalking offences have far exceeded early governmental estimates of 200–300 prosecutions per year – in 1999 over 4,000 cases were prosecuted, making it the UK's fastest-growing crime.

For the criminal sanctions to be activated, a victim will need to contact the police and give full details of the harassment and be prepared to give evidence in court. However, if the police will not take any action she can still apply under the new law for an injunction under the Act – which created a new 'tort' (or civil wrong) of harassment. See below for an analysis of whether to use the civil court remedies under the Protection from Harassment Act 1997 or under the Family Law Act 1996, in circumstances where both options are available.

Comparing the Protection from Harassment Act 1997 (PHA) with the Family Law Act 1996 Part IV (FLA): Pros and Cons

- The powers of enforcement are probably better and simpler under the FLA than under the PHA – no power of arrest is available under the PHA. This in itself is a powerful argument in favour of FLA.
- PHA permits a damages claim in the same set of proceedings – if an applicant wants to claim damages she will not be able to do so under FLA proceedings but will have to make a separate claim. If getting monetary

recompense is an important factor, making a claim under the PHA is likely to be more attractive.
- PHA avoids consideration of the complex FLA concept of 'associated persons'.
- Solicitors are usually more familiar with FLA than PHA claims – this is not in itself a deciding factor, but it may influence the advice given to a client by a solicitor.
- Legal costs (the hourly costs a solicitor can charge) are likely to be slightly higher under the PHA than the FLA (although it is possible that standard fees might be introduced) if a client is paying privately: public funding in the form of Legal Representation should be available for both sets of proceedings if merits and means tests are met.
- If the perpetrator is under 18, a remedy is available under the PHA. Breaching a PHA injunction is a criminal offence and the youth court is able to make an injunction against a youth between 10 and 18 years old.

Civil remedies – Family Law Act 1996

The civil court using its powers under the Family Law Act 1996 Part IV can do two things: first, it can order the husband/man to stop assaulting or threatening the woman and/or children. This is called a non-molestation order. Second, it can order the husband/man out of the matrimonial home, so leaving the woman and children in peace. This is called an occupation order (previously often referred to as an ouster or exclusion order).

To an extent, the effectiveness of the court orders depends on how law-abiding the violent partner is (whether or not he will pay attention to a court document) and how determined the woman is to end the cycle of violence once and for all, and not accept dishonest promises to change by a habitually violent partner.

Who can apply?

In the past, the court could very often make these orders only if the parties were currently or had been living together. Since October 1997, many more categories of people are entitled to the law's protection against abuse. Broadly, however, the applicant for such an order needs to be:
- 'associated' (*see* below for the definition) with the respondent; or
- the applicant and respondent must be parties in the same family proceedings.

Someone is 'associated' with another person if:
(a) they are or have been married to each other;
(b) they are cohabitants or former cohabitants;
(c) they live or have lived in the same household, otherwise than merely by reason of one of them being the other's employee, lodger, or boarder;
(d) they are relatives;

(e) they have agreed to marry each other (whether or not that agreement has been terminated);

(f) in relation to any child, they are both parents or both have parental responsibility for any child (*see further* page 85)

(g) they are parties to the same family proceedings.

Spouses or ex-spouses and heterosexual partners or ex-partners come clearly within the definition. But a boyfriend and girlfriend who never lived together would not (unless they had taken the now rarer step of getting engaged). If they have lived together part of the time and separately part of the time, the law is likely to lean in favour of the victim:

A couple lived part of the week together and part of the week apart. He had been violent towards her. The magistrates refused to make a non-molestation order, but this was overruled on appeal. Held: Because the courts' powers were designed to give swift and accessible protective remedies to domestic violence victims, it would be 'most unfortunate' if sections were to be narrowly construed to exclude borderline cases. G v F (Non-molestation Order: Jurisdiction) (2000)

The orders will also be widely available to family members who have fallen out where one is abusive. So a daughter could, for example, apply for a non-molestation order against a violent stepfather. Or a parent could apply against an aggressive (perhaps schizophrenic) adult child.

Neighbours and ex-lodgers who are being harassed would not normally be able to get any protection under the civil law, but they could use the criminal law – the Protection from Harassment Act 1997 (*see above*).

Can children apply?

A child could, in principle, apply for a non-molestation order or an occupation order, although children under 16 have first to gain the court's leave (permission) to go ahead. This permission will only be given if the court is satisfied that the child has sufficient understanding to make the application. Applications for leave by children must be made to the High Court.

Special requirements for occupation orders

To apply for an occupation order, there are differences in the remedies available depending on whether the woman is classed as an 'entitled applicant'. Broadly, she will fall under this head if:

- she is entitled to occupy the home in question (if, for example, she is a joint tenant or can establish ownership in another way); or
- if she has 'matrimonial home rights' in respect of the home (if the wife is not the legal owner of the home but the home was her matrimonial home).

Ordering the man out of the home – special considerations

It is more difficult to persuade the court to grant an occupation order, ordering the man out of the home, than it is to obtain a non-molestation order, which merely orders him to stop assaulting and threatening the wife and children.

Whether or not an occupation order will be made will depend to some extent on all the background circumstances – in particular, how quickly the wife has gone to court, and the extent of the violence. It is important to realize that a domestic violence injunction is usually only viewed as a temporary remedy; under the old law, the courts took the view that it was reasonable to evict a man from his home for up to a few months but then permanent arrangements must be worked out.

Ms O'Neill and Mr Williams cohabited in a flat, which they owned in their joint names. In August he assaulted her and so she moved out. She hoped there would be a reconciliation and so it was not until October that she went to see solicitors. They applied for legal aid (to cover the costs of going to court for an exclusion order – the old term for occupation order – against Williams) but legal aid was not granted until February. The court then held that it was too late: exclusion orders are designed to give temporary, emergency, relief while long-term solutions are sorted out. Now that six months had passed, it would not be right to order Williams to leave the flat in which he had a half-share. So, the injunction was refused and Ms O'Neill would have to apply to the court for an order that the flat should be sold and the proceeds split 50/50. O'Neill (1984)

While such views still count under the new law, the courts' powers to make occupation orders are wider, and sometimes can provide a long-term solution even where there has not been any violence (*see further* page 63). This is because the courts have to weigh up the balance of harm test. In other words, the courts recognize that in making an occupation order, or in refusing to make an occupation order, each side might suffer some harm whichever route is taken. What the courts have to do is decide which party would suffer the most harm – and wherever there is a doubt, protecting the children from harm will sway the decision.

Apart from questions of delay or emergency, the court will also look at:

1 *Whose name is the property in (whether it is owned or rented)?* If the property is in the sole name of the woman, she is likely to find it easier to obtain an order than if it is in the sole name of the man. This is particularly so if the couple are not married.

2 *How large is the property?* Could it be divided up so that the couple can lead separate lives?

3 *Is there anywhere else for the husband (or boyfriend) to go?* Has he friends or relatives he can stay with?

4 *What assaults or threats have been made to the woman or children?* When was the most recent? Are further attacks likely? Has the man since made a sincere apology and promised to behave himself in the future? If so, what are the chances of him keeping his word?

5 *Is it likely to cause mental or physical suffering to the woman and/or the children if the man is allowed to continue living in the same house?* In short, is it impossible for her to continue living with him?

Which court to apply to?

There are three different courts that can help in domestic violence cases:

● The Family Proceedings Panel of the magistrates' court
● The county court (which can include the divorce court)
● The High Court

The procedure in each court is different, and each has its own particular advantages and disadvantages. Since the Family Law Act 1996 Part IV was introduced in 1997, the three different types of court have been given broadly similar powers, so there is less to choose between them. Your solicitor will be able to advise you which one would best suit your purposes.

Broadly still, the county court (or divorce court – this will be the court where you started your divorce proceedings and will most likely be a county court itself) has slightly greater powers than the magistrates' court, but the procedure in the latter court is more informal. The High Court has the greatest court powers of the three but the procedure is the most formal and the costs are likely to be higher.

If there is going to be a major dispute over the facts, it is better to go to the county court or divorce court, as the judges there usually have a lot of experience in deciphering the law. In particular, if there is a dispute over whether or not the applicant is legally entitled to property rights in the home, the application must be dealt with by the county court.

For unmarried couples, the choice is between the High Court, county court or the magistrates' court as, obviously, no divorce proceedings can be started.

Why do I need to go to court?

The nub of the problem is that the police are still reluctant to intervene in what they call 'domestic disputes', although their policy is improving across the country. Each police force is now required to appoint an officer with special responsibility for domestic violence issues, whose task is to monitor what action is already undertaken and make recommendations to improve practice if need be and to co-ordinate police responsibilities and actions in tackling domestic violence. Most police forces will now have a policy whereby every domestic violence incident must be properly recorded and the action taken also noted, which has overcome to some extent an outdated view that such incidents could be dismissed as just 'domestics'.

If the police do take action, this will usually be limited to talking to the couple involved in the incident and sometimes they will remove the violent partner from the home for a cooling-off period. If an assault has occurred, they should charge the assailant and then should ask the victim whether or not she would be willing to give evidence. The police may also now use the remedies under the Protection from Harassment Act 1997. However the police will also usually advise the victim to seek legal help and get an injunction to protect her.

Getting a power of arrest

The police's ability to deal with a violent partner is much strengthened if the injunction (non-molestation or occupation order) ordered by the court has a power of arrest attached to it. If there is a 'power of arrest' then the police will have no choice but to intervene if asked to do so and arrest the violent partner if he breaches the injunction in any way. Thus it is usual for the wife's lawyer to ask the court to attach a power of arrest to the injunction, so that the husband can be arrested if he breaks it.

A power of arrest will always be granted where there is evidence that the respondent has used or threatened violence against the applicant or a child. This is a change from the old law, when it was much harder to get a power of arrest. Nowadays the courts have a positive obligation to attach a power of arrest, which considerably strengthens the power of the injunction.

If there is a power of arrest and the man breaks the injunction, the police can keep him in custody for up to 24 hours before bringing him before a judge for punishment. If there is no power of arrest, then the police cannot intervene and the woman will have to give the man at least two days' notice if she intends to apply for him to be committed to prison because he has broken the injunction. During that two-day period the woman is often at risk.

How long does the power of arrest last?

While there was some doubt about how long a power of arrest could last, a 2000 case has clarified the position:

Powers of arrest attached to an order must be for the same period as that order. Injunctions also should not be for an open-ended period. In this case the judge restricted the duration of the order to 18 months.

M v W (Non-molestation Order: Duration) (2000)

What happens if the violent partner still breaches the order?

If the violent partner is still being violent and the ability to involve the police by using the power of arrest is not enough, the woman can go back to the court giving details of the breaches of the injunction and ask for the violent man to be committed to prison for contempt of court. She will need to detail the breaches very carefully – the contempt application must be very precisely set out as the courts have historically been unwilling to send a man to prison for this type of offence (although their views are changing and an increasingly tougher stance against domestic violence is now detectable). Legal advice should be sought.

If the court does not send him to prison straight away, it will usually issue a 'suspended sentence' – in other words if he breaches the order again then he will definitely be sent down. In contrast to the above case, it has now been held by the courts that a suspended committal order does not have to be restricted in time.

The husband (H) had already been in breach of a non-molestation and occupation order, and had been violent to his wife and two daughters. On an earlier application for committal, H was committed to prison for two months, but the prison sentence was suspended 'if and so long as' he complied with the terms of another non-molestation and occupation order made on the same date, expressed to last 'until further order of the court'. When H again breached the orders, he was committed by the judge to prison for six months. H then appealed, arguing that the original order was not valid in that its effect was to suspend indefinitely the prison sentence. However he got short shrift in the Court of Appeal. The court decided that the order was valid and the sentence would stand. Griffin (2000)

Applying 'on notice' or *ex parte*

Applications to a court are usually made after notifying the respondent (i.e. the man) of the date of the application and the type of order that the court is being asked to make. Such an application is said to be made 'on notice'.

However, it is not always necessary to warn the respondent beforehand. In emergency cases the application to the court can be made without notice; such an application is said to be made *ex parte*.

Usually, of course, the battered woman would prefer that the application be made *ex parte*, so that the man does not know about it until after the injunction or order has been granted. Naturally, she will be worried that he will assault her if he is given notice of the proposed application. However, *ex parte* applications are only for real emergencies – i.e. more-serious-than-average cases where there is real immediate danger of serious injury or irreparable damage.

While non-molestation orders can be obtained without difficulty *ex parte*, it is much more difficult to obtain an occupation order *ex parte*. This is because the courts are reluctant to exclude a man from his home without giving him a full chance of explaining himself to the court and of being able to call witnesses to support his version of events. This is particularly so when the home is either rented or owned in the sole name of the man. The woman's solicitor will be able to advise her whether the case is sufficiently grave to justify an *ex parte* application.

Obtaining the injunction

If she wishes, the woman can act for herself and apply to the court without the help of a solicitor. However, in practice it is advisable to use a solicitor since he or she will be more familiar with the procedure and can act more speedily. Public funding will usually be available (*see* page 787). Relatively few solicitors specialize in this sort of work so it is advisable to ask at a Citizens' Advice Bureau or Women's Aid Centre for the name of an experienced, competent solicitor. The Community Legal Service website at http://www.justask.org.uk/ might also be a good source of finding out the name of a specialist family law solicitor who undertakes injunctions. In some areas solicitors operate a local duty scheme whereby an emergency number can be contacted even outside office hours – the domestic violence liaison officer of the police may be able to provide more information.

The steps involved are:

1 The solicitor will complete an originating application Form FL 401 asking the county court to grant an injunction and specifying the type of injunction sought. Two extra copies will be made – one for the court and one for the man.

2 The solicitor will take a detailed statement from the woman, which will then be made into a sworn statement by the applicant, which should set out all the facts and matters on which her application relies – this will be her chief evidence. The procedure in the magistrates' court is slightly different – the application form must be accompanied either by a statement which is signed and is declared to be true or the applicant can give oral evidence.

3 The solicitor will then take the papers to the court and pay a £30 fee; public funding may pay the fee. In an exceptional emergency, the application can be made *ex parte*, and the hearing will take place immediately. In less exceptional circumstances the application must be on notice, and the man must be given at least four days' advance warning.

4 The application will be heard before the judge. The hearing will be in chambers, a private room, and not in a public courtroom.
5 If the case is heard on notice, the violent partner may attend and give an undertaking to the court not to attack the victim and/or the children. The drawback of an undertaking is that no power of arrest can be attached to it (*see* above), so it might be safer for the victim to try and get a full court order as in 6 below.
6 The judge makes his order. If he grants an injunction the solicitor will ask him to attach a power of arrest (*see* page 75). The importance of this is that the police must arrest the man if he breaks the injunction.
7 The injunction must be served on the man. Only then does it become effective, unless a power of arrest is attached. The solicitor will usually arrange for service.
8 If the man disobeys the injunction the position depends upon whether the injunction had a power of arrest attached:
- *if there was a power of arrest* the woman should contact the police, who will already have a copy of the injunction. They should arrest the man and keep him in custody until he appears before the judge, usually within the next 24 hours. The woman should attend that hearing, having sworn an affidavit setting out the details of how the injunction was broken.
- *if there was no power of arrest* the woman will have to go back to the county court. Her solicitor will try to arrange a speedy hearing in front of the judge who granted the injunction or accepted the undertaking. The man must be given at least two days' notice of the hearing and the woman will have to swear an affidavit setting out how the injunction was broken. In practice, there is likely to be a delay of at least a week between the woman contacting her solicitor again and the case being heard by the judge. This is the disadvantage of not having a power of arrest.

Either way, the judge will read the affidavits and listen to what the man has to say. The man may be given another chance or he may be sent to prison for contempt of court. However, if he tells the judge he is sorry and that he will not break the injunction again, he may escape prison. Similarly, if he is sent to prison he could be released as soon as he apologizes to the court and promises not to break the injunction again.

Domestic violence and contact with children

The courts are becoming increasingly aware of the links between domestic violence and applications for contact – in that the contact application may be itself a way of seeking revenge or control over the mother (*see further* page 113).

Where domestic violence has been established, there is no longer an automatic assumption that contact (access) with the children will automatically be granted.

For further help

The Women's Aid National Helpline number is 08457 023468, for any woman who faces violence and needs help and advice. They have a list of refuges nationwide where women and their children can flee if necessary. Their website is at www.womensaid.org.uk. Refuge also provides advice and can refer women and their children to refuges. Their helpline number is 0870 599 5443.

Survivors UK Ltd (www.survivorsuk.co.uk) has a helpline for men who have been victims of violence, sexual assault and rape: 020 7613 0808.

Everyman phoneline (020 7737 6747) is a national helpline for men who are violent or concerned about their violence and the consequences of it.

If the woman is homeless

The local authority has a duty to house homeless people who have a 'priority need' (*see* Chapter 94). Statutory guidelines on public housing say that victims of violence with dependent children living with them are always a priority need. If there are no children, the woman may well still be regarded as a priority need if she risks further violence from returning home (although a childless victim will have fewer 'points' to weight her claim for rehousing and may have to wait longer in the housing queue).

The local authority will not always expect a victim of violence to have to return to the home where the abuse was carried out, especially if the victim reasonably feels that, even with the benefit of a court order in her favour, she is still genuinely at risk of further attack.

Note: a local authority cannot argue that a victim of violence is 'intentionally' homeless in an attempt to avoid their duty to house: their guidelines state that a victim of violence who has fled the former family home should never be regarded as having become homeless intentionally, because it would clearly not be reasonable for her to remain.

8

Parents and Children

REGISTERING A CHILD'S BIRTH

Within six weeks of a child being born, the birth must be registered with the District Registrar for Births, Marriages and Deaths. Births are usually registered in the district where the child was born. But you can register the birth at a local register office if you have moved away from the area.

The registrar will take details of the date and place of birth (it is a good idea to telephone your registrar in advance of going down to register the birth to make an appointment, to avoid busy times when you register the birth).

The child's sex, place of birth, the child's names and the mother's details (name, surname and her address and place of birth) will always be entered. If the parents are married, then the father's details (name, surname, place of birth and occupation) will be included too. If parents are unmarried, then the father's details will be entered only in the circumstances set out below.

Who can register the birth

If the parents are married, either the mother or father alone can register the birth. If the parents are unmarried, only the mother can register the birth on her own but both parents can register it jointly.

The name of the father of a non-marital child can be added to a birth certificate only if:

- the father wishes it and the mother consents; or
- if the mother asks for his name to be registered and has a statutory declaration sworn by the father in which he declares he is the father; or
- on production of a court order showing the man to be the father.

The Adoption and Children Act 2002 provides that an unmarried father automatically acquires parental responsibility where he and the mother register the birth of their child (see also page 10).

Naming a child

Parents choose what name their child will be known by and are generally given a wide discretion over which names they choose, although their offspring will usually be more appreciative as they grow older if the parents stick to reasonably conventional choices! Children ordinarily take and are registered under their father's surname, but this need not be the case. Children can be registered under their mother's surname or a hyphenated version of their parents' surnames joined together. For example, Jane, the newly born daughter of John White and Jessica Black (who kept using her maiden name after her marriage) could be registered as Jane Black-White or Jane White-Black if the parents so choose.

Altering the register

If the child has already been registered but no person has been registered as the father, the register can be altered to show a man to be the father if the mother consents or if a court order is produced proving the man to be the father.

The register can also be changed within 12 months of registration, for example, if the parents want to change the name of the child or if there has been an error in the details recorded. In very rare cases of mistakes, the register can later be altered.

In 2000, Kerys Haines, a 27-year-old woman in Cardiff, discovered she had been registered as a male at her birth when she applied for a replacement birth certificate to get a passport. The registrar admitted there had been a mistake and as soon as it was discovered the register was changed as quickly as possible.

Barring such an unusual circumstance, the register cannot be altered unless the child is adopted. A later change of name, even by statutory declaration or deed poll, cannot alter the details on the certificate. Indeed, once a child's name has been registered for a period of a year, it is very hard to change that name.

The mother had registered the child with the surname of her former husband (under which she and her other children were known). The genetic father of her last child wanted the child to carry his own name. **Held:** *No. The fact that the father had taken a long time to act to change the surname counted heavily against him.*

Dawson *v* Wearmouth (1999)

The government announced proposals in December 2002 to change the law to allow transsexuals to marry in their adopted sex and to apply for substitute birth certificates showing their new genders (*see also* page 19).

BIRTH CERTIFICATES

There are two types of birth certificate.
1 The short version does not give full details of the parents and thus conceals the fact that a child is born outside marriage. One copy of this is provided free at the time of registration.
2 The long form of birth certificate includes the parents' details. The long and short forms are equally valid.

If you need an up-to-date birth (or marriage or death) certificate, the cheapest way of getting one is by going to the Public Search Room at the Family Records Centre, 1 Myddleton Street, London EC1R 1UW (Tel: 0870 243 7788). This will cost you £7. The time it will take will depend on how busy the Centre is.

Otherwise, you can apply by post to the General Register Office, PO Box 2, Southport, Merseyside, PR8 2JD (Tel: 0870 243 7788). The usual fee is £11.50 for a certificate sent by post, although if you already have the General Register Office reference for it, the price drops to £8.50. There is a premium for speed. The fee will be £27.50 if the certificate is needed urgently (sent within two working days) and the timescale for non-urgent applications will vary.

ADOPTED CHILDREN

When a child is adopted, the Registrar General enters the adoption in the Adopted Children's Register, which sets out the date, county, district and sub-district of the birth, the new names of the child, its sex, the name, address and occupation of the adopters, the date when the adoption order was made and the court that made the order. This is the child's new full birth certificate and effectively replaces the original one.

A short form of birth certificate can be obtained which makes no mention of the child's biological parents or of the fact that the child has been adopted.

Adopted people over 18 years old can trace the names

and particulars of their parents on the original birth register. If the adoption was made before 12 November 1975 this information will be made available only after the adopted person has seen a counsellor. Counselling services are provided by the Registrar General, local authorities and adoption agencies. Applications can be made to the General Register Office, PO Box 2, Southport, Merseyside PR8 2JD (Tel: 0870 243 7788).

An Adoption Contact Register was created by the Children Act 1989, kept by the Registrar General. Both people who have been adopted and their relatives (which includes anyone related by blood or marriage, not only the natural parents) can apply to have their names and addresses put on the Contact Register. This helps speed up the process for adopted children in tracing their birth family: details of relatives registered will be passed on to adopted children who themselves apply to be registered. But it is not a two-way process: birth parents cannot use the register to contact their adopted child without his/her knowledge and consent.

The information kept on the Contact Register is confidential and will not be disclosed to outsiders. In one rare case, the information was not even disclosed to the adopted person.

A man who had been adopted applied for an original birth certificate. He was being detained in Broadmoor, having been convicted for manslaughter. **Held:** *His application should be refused as there was a real risk that if the information were supplied, the applicant's natural mother would be at risk.* R *v* Registrar General *ex p* Smith (1990)

In December 1998, the President of the Family Division directed that the High Court can, during a child's minority, direct that details of the adoption register will not be disclosed to anyone without leave of the court. This provision was made because of fears that natural parents unhappy with the original decision for a child to be freed for adoption could inspect the Adopted Register and the security of the placement could be put at risk.

The Adoption and Children Act 2002 addresses the need for birth relatives and adopted people to have opportunities to be put in touch with one another. The Act gives birth relatives the right to ask for an intermediary service to contact an adopted adult and seek their views on renewed contact/communication. In the first instance, the service will only be available to adults involved in adoptions where the adoption order was made before 13 November 1975, so the adopted people affected will be at least 28 years old when the section is implemented in April 2004.

APPLYING FOR A PASSPORT

With effect from 5 October 1998, children can no longer be added to a parent's passport – they need to have their own separate passport. Children who are already on their parent's passport can continue to travel with that parent until they are 16 years old, the passport expires or the passport is submitted for amendment.

Otherwise, children now have to have their own separate passports when travelling abroad, however tiny they may be. The parent/applicant will need to obtain two photographs of the child and get one countersigned by a professionally qualified person (for example a solicitor, teacher or engineer) who usually has known you for at least two years and will also complete a section on the passport application. If the child is entitled to British citizenship, an application for a passport can be made by completing a special form available from post offices and sending it to the United Kingdom Passport Service (Tel: 0870 521 0410) with the birth certificate, two photographs and fee (currently £19.00).

You can also apply for a new passport, renew, amend or replace an existing one using the Passport Service's online application form (www.ukpa.gov.uk).

CHILDREN BORN OUTSIDE MARRIAGE

Over 40 per cent of children born in the UK are born outside marriage. It seems likely that most of these children were born into stable relationships, as around seven out of ten were registered by both parents living at the same address. However the fact of being born outside marriage does create some differences in the way the law treats a non-marital child.

Since the Family Law Reform Act 1987 came into force on 1 April 1989, much of the legal stigma of illegitimacy has been removed and the law gives marital and non-marital children broadly equal rights – for example, to claim maintenance and inheritance from the father.

But one major difference still remains: if the parents were not married at the time of the birth, then only the mother automatically has the legal rights and duties for the child, which are classed by the law as parental responsibility (*see also* page 85). If the father wants an equal say in the child's upbringing, then he has to acquire parental responsibility, which he can do either:

- with the mother's agreement; or
- by applying to court for a court order (*see* below); or
- by being appointed the guardian of the child on the mother's death; or
- by registering himself as the child's father on the birth certificate.

Change in the law

An unmarried father may acquire parental responsibility if he registers himself after 1 December 2003 as the child's father on the birth certificate. This change in the law only came into force (under the Adoption and Children Act) on 1 December 2003 and does not apply to unmarried fathers registered before that date.

Agreeing to share parental responsibility

If the mother agrees to share parental responsibility, both she and the father must sign a special court form called a parental responsibility agreement (reproduced on pages 86–7) to make that decision effective in law. Their signatures must be made in front of a court official as a witness at a local court and they must produce proof that they are who they say they are (unfortunately when these agreements were first introduced, some signatures were forged, so the new requirements seek to prevent that happening).

The mother or the father should lodge it (with two copies) at the Principal Registry of the Family Division, First Avenue House, 42–49 High Holborn, London WC1V 6NP. No fee is payable. A postal application will take around two weeks to process.

The mother should think carefully about taking such a step. In so doing she will be giving up her sole right to decide issues about the child and she will not be able to reverse her decision by herself later – only a court can terminate parental responsibility. The father will have an equal and independent say about the child's upbringing which will last until the child reaches 18 years old. However, if she refuses to sign an agreement, the father may well be able to gain parental responsibility anyway by applying to court for a parental responsibility order, and there are advantages in resolving something by agreement rather than having to go to court.

Parental responsibility by court order

If the mother refuses to sign the court form, the father can apply to court for a parental responsibility order under the Children Act 1989 s4. The court will grant this only where it is in the best interests of the child. The father will have to show that there is a good attachment between him and the child, that he is committed to the child and that his motives are in the child's best interests (i.e. that he is not making the application, say, on impulse to hurt the mother). As long as the father can successfully pass this threefold test – attachment, commitment and motive – he should be able to get a parental responsibility order. But in rare cases this will not be granted.

The father was found by the court to have caused worrying injuries to the child, suggesting cruelty and sadism, although the father denied it. The father argued that as he could prove attachment, commitment and motive, parental responsibility should be ordered. Held: No parental responsibility order. The three key factors were the starting point but not the only relevant ones. There was a risk to the son, especially as the father had not faced up to his actions. However, the father was able to get supervised contact with his son. Re H (1998)

The mother was suffering from a post-traumatic stress disorder, which she associated with the father, and feared him. The two children lived with the mother and had no contact with the father. The father wanted parental responsibility to be kept informed about the children. Held: No parental responsibility order. The mother's extremely negative reaction to such an order would have an adverse impact on the children. Re K (1998)

Parental responsibility can also be obtained by the father by a successful application for a residence order (*see* page 108).

Proving paternity

For the mother of a non-marital child to be able to get child support from the father or for the father to apply to court for an order (for parental responsibility, residence or contact, for example), paternity must be proved unless both parents accept that the father is the father. If there is any doubt, this can be resolved by way of DNA testing, which is newer and more accurate than the old blood tests and can provide proof positive of paternity.

DNA testing

DNA tests, a comparatively recent scientific development, examine bodily samples (this can be blood, semen or hair) from the parents and child and compare the genetic information. Because each person has a distinctive individual genetic fingerprint, the tests are claimed to be 100 per cent accurate.

Taking a test

For blood and DNA tests, samples will be needed from the mother, the father and the child. Consent on the child's behalf will usually be given by a parent or another person with parental responsibility (*see* page 85). Older children of sufficient maturity and understanding have the right to refuse to submit to testing.

If an application to court is made for a test, the court will usually agree to it. In very rare cases, the court can intervene to stop the blood test if it would be against the child's best interests. Thus, if a child is thought to be legitimate and the only effect of the test would be to make

him illegitimate, with no father, the court might refuse to allow the test to take place.

Refusing a test

The court cannot order a man to undergo a test, but it can draw its own conclusions if he refuses to agree to the test. If he does refuse, the court will usually take this as corroboration of the mother's claim that he is the real father.

If a mother of a non-marital child refuses to agree to blood samples being taken from a child, there is nothing the courts can do to order it.

The father gained an order under s20(1) of the Family Law Reform Act 1969 for blood tests to establish the paternity of a child who was the subject of legal proceedings. The mother refused to consent to the blood tests. Held: There was a need for consent under the Act and the court had no power to compel a mother to give blood samples to establish paternity or to order samples to be taken without her consent. In Re O (2000)

Fathers' applications

Under the old law, a man could not apply for a court order declaring him to be the father of an illegitimate child. Since 14 October 1991, when the Children Act came into force, a father can apply to court for a parental responsibility order even in the face of the mother's opposition. A parental responsibility order is not quite the same as declaring him to be the true father, but it does firmly establish his legal connection with the child. He could ask the court to order that a DNA test be carried out so that paternity would not be in doubt.

A father could also apply for a declaration of parentage, which resolves the question of paternity once and for all. In practice very few of these applications are made since they do not give the father any actual rights.

PARENTS, WELFARE BENEFITS AND TAX

Financial changes for married couples

In the not too distant past, there were a number of tax incentives for people to get and stay married. Since the last budget of the twentieth century these have pretty much all been scrapped. Since the tax year 2000/01, first, the abolition of mortgage tax relief and, second, the married couple's allowance, for those under 65 years, will both have hit most married partners, although some of that loss was offset by the 1 per cent cut in the basic rate of tax to 22 per cent. The Working Tax Credit and Child Tax Credit are intended to help parents with children under 16 (*see* page 293). However, the net effect of tax changes have left most 'average' middle-class married couples worse off. The only apparent bias towards the married state still surviving is the inheritance tax concessions. The inheritance tax thresholds will be £255,000 in tax year 2003/04. If a wealthy person wishes to give away his wealth, he will of course escape tax provided he survives for seven years.

Advice and help for parents

Raising a child can often be the most challenging task ever devised for adults for which no formal training is required! ParentLine (www.parentlineplus.org.uk) is a helpline run by trained volunteers who listen to parents and can direct parents to other useful contacts (it has now taken over the Stepfamilies helpline too.) The Helpline can be contacted on Tel: 0808 800 2222, and its hours of opening are 9–9 weekdays, 12–5 Saturdays, 10–3 Sundays.

Maintenance for non-marital children

A father of a child born outside marriage is legally bound to contribute towards his child's maintenance in just the same way as if the child had been born within marriage. It does not matter that the child may have been conceived on a 'one night stand' – if a man fathers a child he will be financially responsible for his offspring. The mother can ask the Child Support Agency to assess the amount of maintenance he should pay and the Child Support Agency will have the power to trace him and collect and enforce maintenance payments, assessed according to a formula (*see* below).

CHILD SUPPORT: THE NEW LAW

The new rules under the Child Support, Pensions and Social Security Act 2000 came into effect on 3 March 2003.

Broadly, they mean that a father will pay a percentage of his net income by way of child support, namely:

- 15 per cent if he has one child;
- 20 per cent if he has two children; or
- 25 per cent if he has three or more (25 per cent is the maximum he will pay).

A father has a net weekly income of £500 per week and has two children living with the mother (the 'parent with care'). The father's liability under the new rules would be £100 per week.

Those with income of less than £200 per week will pay reduced rates of maintenance. For high earners, there is a cap on relevant net income of £104,000 net per annum. In the case of a father whose net income is £104,000 or more per year, the maximum amount of child support he would have to pay is:

- £15,600 per annum for one child;
- £20,800 per annum for two children;
- £26,000 per annum for three or more.

When introducing the proposals in 1998, the then Social Security Secretary indicated that the average child support assessment would fall from £38 a week to £29 a week: the underlying philosophy being 'to ensure that more fathers pay, rather than that fathers pay more'.

The contentious phrase 'absent parent' in the old child-support legislation is replaced with the more neutral 'non-resident parent'. Another key aspect of the new law is that the mother's income (assuming she is the one looking after the children most of the time) will not be taken into account.

The amount of child support will be reduced if the child stays with the non-resident parent (NRP) for one night a week or more, on average, through the year. An NRP on benefit who shares the care of the child for at least 52 nights of the year will usually be exempt from paying the £5 flat rate. (NRPs with net income of £100 a week or less, and those on specified benefits including Jobseeker's Allowance and income support, pay a flat rate of £5 per week). There is concern that NRPs may seek to increase contact with children in view of the effect it will have on the child support maintenance rather than due to a genuine wish to spend more time with their children. The amount of child support will also be reduced to take account of all children in the NRP's current family, including stepchildren. The net income used to calculate maintenance will be reduced by 15 per cent for one child in the current family, 20 per cent for two children and 25 per cent for three or more children.

There is to be a benefit disregard of £10 a week, so lone parents who receive income support will actually get £10 more than their benefit a week if the father pays maintenance. The rest will go to the Treasury.

A father pays £15 a week child support and his ex-partner receives income support. She gets to keep her income support plus an extra £10 from the maintenance. The balance of £5 a week will be kept by the Treasury.

What constitutes net income?

For an employed NRP, net income is gross earnings less tax and national insurance. Pension contributions can be deducted before the maintenance calculation is carried out, provided contributions are paid to an Inland Revenue-approved scheme. Net income includes bonuses, overtime and pension income but excludes benefits in kind and investment income.

Net income for those who are self-employed is calculated as taxable profits or gross receipts, less tax and national insurance contributions. Pension deductions apply as above. Rental income and dividend income are not taken into account.

Parents will only be able to 'escape' the new formula for a period of 12 months. The government's intention was that if couples chose to make a court order by consent or make a written agreement dealing with child support, that would hold firm for a year afterwards. But after that either parent would be able to apply to the Child Support Agency – in other words it will be difficult for parents to make their own arrangements for child maintenance to sidestep the new formula, which will thus be more or less compulsory for all newly separated/divorced couples.

OLD LAW: BEFORE THE CHILD SUPPORT ACT 1991 CAME INTO FORCE

In 1989 the law was much simplified. Mothers could at that time apply for a maintenance order in the magistrates' court, county court or High Court for children born outside marriage. However, nowadays a mother will not be able to apply to the court for a court order for child maintenance unless the Child Support Agency has no jurisdiction – for example, if she, the child or the father lives outside England and Wales and is not 'habitually resident' here.

AFTER THE CHILD SUPPORT ACT 1991 CAME INTO FORCE

The Child Support Agency

It has been as it continues to be the duty of the Child Support Agency (CSA) to trace the father and collect maintenance payments from him, and enforce arrears if any become due. The Agency was a new and separate body, evolving from the DSS rather than the tax inspectorate (as in other countries where Child Support Agencies have had success in increasing payments made, like Australia). In the twenty-first century, the CSA was given wider power to liaise with the tax authorities, so that the previous limitations in its power to trace fathers who try to slip the net might be overcome. The CSA does of course have much greater powers than individual single parents to ensure prompt payments and it can get an order that maintenance collected by the Agency is deducted straight from the father's salary.

The Agency is most useful for cases where fathers are employed. Where they are self-employed and/or work as part of the black economy (cash up front, no questions asked), the Agency is just as likely to experience difficulties as any lone parent trying to extract maintenance on her own.

If the NRP fails to pay, the new child support regime has introduced new sanctions, some of which are quite draconian. It is now a criminal offence to fail to provide information requested by the CSA and, technically, if such an offence is committed, the NRP will be liable to a fine or imprisonment. The CSA can enforce the child support assessment by obtaining a liability order (leading to a garnishee or charging order which allows property to be taken in place of missed payments). An ultimate sanction is disqualification from driving for up to two years.

As before, if the parent with care fails to provide information and is in receipt of income support or income-related Jobseeker's Allowance, then the benefits can be reduced. The national CSA inquiry line (08457 133133) should be able to handle general queries.

The Child Support Act 1991

Once the Child Support, Pensions and Social Security Act 2000 came into force, this very much simplified the formula for working out child maintenance levels. The old formula – laid down by the Child Support Acts 1991 and 1995 – was horribly complex. The Child Support Agency was introduced because of the courts' poor record in ensuring that child support was paid – seven in ten lone parents on welfare benefit received no child maintenance from the fathers. However, the CSA, bogged down by the labyrinthine formula and difficulties in assessment, did not manage to improve this record much. The ridiculous complexity of the formula, needing over 100 pieces of information to produce an answer, meant that the CSA staff spent 95 per cent of their time assessing the formula and only 5 per cent of their time in ensuring that assessments were actually paid. Eighty-five per cent of assessments were still wrong and delay (the target of six months for an assessment is often missed) made the process even more miserable.

At the time of going to press, the hope was that by much simplifying the formula the CSA could get on with the job of working out efficiently and effectively what maintenance should be paid and then enforcing such payments if they were not paid. Time will tell whether the CSA has been able to put its poor track record behind it.

The old child-support formula

The old child support formula was complicated to work out. The following just provides a summary, as most people will find that their case will fall under the new rules.

The old formula was based on five different calculations:

1 the maintenance requirement;
2 exempt income;
3 assessable income;

4 deduction rate;

5 protected income.

The maintenance requirement

This represented the day-to-day expenses of raising a child and is based on income support rates. The weekly levels set for the children varied according to the child's age(s) plus a family premium and an adult personal allowance. Child benefit is deducted from the maintenance requirement.

Exempt income

This applied to both parents' income and represents their own essential living expenses. It covered a personal allowance, for day-to-day living costs, plus the costs of caring for their natural children living with them, plus their actual housing costs and travel-to-work costs if they had a long distance to travel. Debts were not automatically included, although an application could be made to deviate from the formula in very limited cases.

Assessable income

This was the part of a liable parent's income used for calculating the amount of maintenance due. It was the difference between the potential payer's net income (after deduction of tax, national insurance and half of pension contributions) and his exempt income. Assessable income was divided 50/50 between the children and the absent parent up to the amount of the maintenance requirement. Broadly, maintenance was capped once it reached a particular amount.

Deduction rate

Once the maintenance requirement was paid, if there is any extra assessable income belonging to the payer, a further sum of maintenance would be payable at a lower rate of deduction – i.e. 25 per cent of the maximum amount of maintenance.

Protected income

This was designed to prevent the payer's income falling to income support levels or below as a result of child maintenance commitments. The payer's income was not supposed to drop below the protected income level.

Now that the percentage formula applies, it will be much easier for anyone to work out how much child support should be assessed to be paid.

John and Jacqui have just separated. They have two children aged 3 and 4. John's net weekly income is £210. He will be assessed to pay child support of £42 a week. Jacqui's financial position will not affect this.

Transferring to the new system

People whose child support was assessed under the old child support formula will be transferred over to the new system at a date yet to be fixed by the government. If transferring over to the new system will entail a large change in the amount to be paid, it will be phased in over up to five years – so the amount of child support will increase gradually over that period to give people time to adjust.

Other financial provision for children

Mothers can also apply for a lump-sum order, secured periodical payments or property transfers (*see* page 49). Applications for financial relief for non-marital children are made in exactly the same way as applications for children born within marriage, save that paternity will have to be established too if the father denies he is the father.

The test was whether it is probable (not possible) that the man is the father. Corroborative evidence can include:

- an admission by the father of his paternity;
- evidence of sexual intercourse between the parents around the time of conception;
- proof of cohabitation;
- the man's name appearing on the birth certificate.

DNA tests can now conclusively prove whether or not a man is the father. If the father refuses to take a test, his refusal can itself amount to corroboration.

ABORTION

A man cannot get a court order preventing his wife or girlfriend from having an abortion. Nor can parents usually obtain an injunction to stop their teenage daughter from having an abortion.

A pregnant 16-year-old girl obtained medical approval for an abortion which her parents then tried to prevent. Held: The expectant mother had sufficient intelligence and understanding (both about the abortion and her obligations to her parents) to make up her own mind. Wren (1987)

The Abortion Act 1967 makes it lawful for a doctor to carry out an abortion during the first 28 weeks of pregnancy if:

- the continuance of the pregnancy would involve risk to the mother's life; or
- the continuance of the pregnancy would involve risk to the physical or mental health of the mother or her other children (social circumstances can thus be taken into account); or
- there is substantial risk that the child would be born

with a physical or mental abnormality that would make it seriously handicapped.

A Parliamentary bill in 1990 to reduce the period for lawful abortion to 24 weeks was unsuccessful.

The consent of two doctors is necessary. A doctor or nurse can refuse to take part in an abortion on the ground of conscience. The NHS will not always provide a free abortion and sometimes the mother may have to go to a fee-paying clinic. A mother who is having difficulty arranging an abortion should contact one of the pro-choice charities, which can usually be found under the Pregnancy Test Services section of *Yellow Pages*. Or contact a national advisory body like Marie Stopes (www.mariestopes.org.uk; Tel: 0845 300 80 90) or the British Pregnancy Advisory Service, Linkline number (www.bpas.org; Tel: 08457 30 40 30).

UNPLANNED CHILDREN

On a related topic, what happens if a man or woman has a vasectomy or sterilization operation but then has a child? Some judges have held that it is wrong for the parents then to be able to sue over the child's birth, but latterly the opposing view has gained ground.

A vasectomy was carried out properly but the doctor forgot to tell the man that it could not be 100 per cent guaranteed that he would not father a child. When a child was born, the man sued for breach of contract. **Held:** *Damages should be awarded. The man and his wife were awarded a total of £8,600 damages (£2,000 for her loss of earnings between the birth and the time the child started school; the rest being the cost of upbringing, based on supplementary benefit [the old equivalent of income support] rates).*　　Thake (1985)

Thus damages can be claimed if a sterilization or vasectomy operation goes wrong.

CHILDREN: WHOSE RESPONSIBILITY?

A brief history

In the 30 years or so culminating in the Children Act 1989, there was a dramatic shift in the way the law regulates relationships between parents and children. Children were once viewed as little more than objects over which parents had rights. The law then began to recognize that children had rights too. Thus the right of access (now called contact) to a child for a separated parent was seen as the child's right (not a parent's). Whether access would be awarded by the courts depended on what was in the *child's* (not the parent's) *best interests.*

Since 14 October 1991, when the Children Act 1989 came into effect, the focus has shifted yet again, with the emphasis now on parents' *responsibilities* towards their

children. The Children Act introduced the new concept of parental responsibility – a durable link between parents and children which will not be ended by divorce and which lasts until the child is 18 years old.

The change in the law was intended to produce a change in the way children and their families are treated by the legal system. So nowadays the courts will not interfere in the arrangements parents make for their children unless a specific problem arises. On divorce, for example, the courts will not make an order about where the children will live if the parents can agree this between themselves (*see* page 106).

The new, stronger legal requirement that children's welfare is the court's paramount consideration when considering any question about their upbringing or maintenance aims to put children first. The child's best interests will override the feelings of the parents.

Parental responsibility

Someone has to be legally responsible for a child until it grows up and reaches the age of 18. In law, the people responsible are those with parental responsibility.

Having parental responsibility is not the same as being a parent. Not all parents have parental responsibility automatically (*see* below). Also, people who are not parents can be given parental responsibility.

Parental responsibility is defined as 'all the rights, duties, powers and responsibilities and authority which by law a parent has in relation to the child and his property' (Children Act 1989 s3).

In practice parental responsibility covers the responsibility and right to, for example:

- maintain and protect the child;
- ensure he or she receives medical treatment;
- appoint a guardian to care for the child after a parent's death;
- make sure the child is educated between 5 and 16 years old and choose the child's school;
- name the child and register its birth;
- apply for the child's passport;
- choose the child's religion;
- decide where the child is to live.

Who has parental responsibility?

These people have parental responsibility automatically:
- married parents;
- unmarried mothers.

Married parents both continue to have parental responsibility even if the marriage breaks down. The only ways that they, or unmarried mothers, can lose parental responsibility are if the court makes an order terminating it (this is hardly ever likely to happen) or if the child is adopted.

Parental responsibility agreement

Parental Responsibility Agreement
Section 4(1)(b) Children Act 1989

**Read the notes on the other side
before you make this agreement.**

Keep this form in a safe place

*Date recorded at The Principal
Registry of the Family Division*

This is a Parental Responsibility Agreement regarding

the child   *Name*

Boy or Girl   *Date of birth*   *Date of 18th birthday*

Between
the Mother   *Name*
             Address

and the Father   *Name*
                     Address

We declare that   we are the mother and father of the above child and we agree that the child's father shall have parental responsibility for the child (in addition to the mother having parental responsibility).

Signed (**Mother**)   Signed (**Father**)

Date   Date

**Certificate of
Witness**

The following evidence of identity was produced by the person signing above:

The following evidence of identity was produced by the person signing above:

Signed in the presence of:
Name of Witness

Signed in the presence of:
Name of Witness

Address   *Address*

Signature of Witness   *Signature of Witness*

[A Justice of the Peace]
[Justices' Clerk]
[An Officer of the Court authorised by the judge to administer oaths]

[A Justice of the Peace]
[Justices' Clerk]
[An Officer of the Court authorised by the judge to administer oaths]

Notes about the Parental Responsibility Agreement

Read these notes before you make the agreement.

About the Parental Responsibility Agreement

The making of this agreement will affect the legal position of the mother and the father. You should both seek legal advice before you make the Agreement. You can obtain the name and address of a solicitor from the Children Panel (020 7242 1222) or from

- – your local family proceedings court, or county court
- – a Citizens' Advice Bureau
- – a Law Centre
- – a local library.

You may be eligible for legal aid.

When you fill in the Agreement

Pleaes use black ink (the Agreement will be copied). Put the name of one child only. If the father is to have parental responsibility for more than one child, fill in a separate form for each child. **Do not sign the Agreement.**

When you have filled in the Agreement

Take it to a local family proceedings court, or county court, or the Principal Registry of the Family Division (the address is below).

A justice of the peace, a justices' clerk, or a court official who is authorised by the judge to administer oaths, will witness your signature and he or she will sign the certificate of the witness.

To the mother: When you make the declaration you will have to prove that you are the child's mother so take to the court the child's full birth certificate.

You will also need evidence of your identity showing a photograph and signature (for example, a photocard, official pass or passport).

To the father: You will need evidence of your identity showing a photograph and signature (for example, a photocard, official pass or passport).

When the certificate has been signed and witnessed

Make 2 copies of the other side of this form. You do not need to copy these notes.

Take, or send, this form and the copies to **The Principal Registry of the Family Division, First Avenue House, 42–49 High Holborn, London** WC1V 6NP.

The Registry will record the Agreement and keep this form. The copies will be stamped and sent back to each parent at the address on the Agreement. If the Agreement is lodged by a solicitor, who needs a copy for his/her own records an additional (3rd copy) should be provided. The Agreement will not take effect until it has been received and recorded at the Principal Registry of the Family Division.

Ending the Agreement

Once a parental responsibility agreement has been made it can only end

- – by an order of the court made on the application of any person who has parental responsibility for the child
- – by an order of the court made on the application of the child with leave of the court
- – when the child reaches the age of 18.

Note: married parents who divorced before the Children Act came into force on 14 October 1991 will also both have parental responsibility.

Unmarried fathers can obtain parental responsibility by:

- making an agreement with the mother drawn up on a special court form (*see* page 80); or
- successfully applying to court for parental responsibility, or
- successfully applying to court for a residence order, or
- being appointed a guardian by the mother after her death.

Also, if an unmarried father (i.e. a father who was not married to the mother at the time of the child's birth) had an order predating the Children Act for custody, care and control or parental rights and duties in his favour, then as from 14 October 1991 that order will automatically include parental responsibility. The Adoption and Children Act 2002 amends the Children Act 1989 to provide that an unmarried father acquires parental responsibility where he and the child's mother register the birth of their child together. This part of the Act came into force on 1 December 2003. Unmarried fathers who registered their name on the birth certificate before 1 December 2003 will not automatically acquire parental responsibility.

In the past, stepfathers and stepmothers could not acquire parental responsibility on their own, but they could jointly apply for a residence order, which then gave them parental responsibility too. The Adoption and Children Act 2002 gives a step-parent the option of seeking parental responsibility for the child of his/her spouse, either with the agreement of all parents with parental responsibility or by order of the court.

Anyone with a residence order in their favour (this can include a grandparent looking after a child following a family split) will also have parental responsibility. In this case, parental responsibility lasts only as long as the residence order lasts.

If a care order has been made for a child, then the local authority looking after the child in care also has parental responsibility (but the local authority does not get parental responsibility if it is just providing accommodation for a child – the new Children Act term for voluntary care). However, parents do not lose their rights while children are in care; they still continue to have parental responsibility and they and the local authority have to work in partnership (*see* page 117).

What does having parental responsibility mean in practice?

One of the most important differences about the concept of parental responsibility is the increased amount of flexibility it gives to anyone who has it. Anyone with parental responsibility can act independently of others with parental responsibility and can make up their own minds about what is best for a child. They do not have a formal legal duty to consult anyone else with parental responsibility before making a decision (e.g. where the child should go to school), although on a practical level good parenting works best if the parents discuss issues about the children and make a joint decision. It is easy to see how this could work well while the parents are together or, for example, in an emergency. If, say, a mother has to take her child to casualty, she does not have to consult the father and obtain his agreement before giving the medical staff the go-ahead for an operation.

In practice, the parent having the day-to-day care of the child will very often have to make the majority of decisions affecting that child's upbringing. Some parents have expressed concern about how the concept of parental responsibility will work if the parents divorce, especially if the split-up is very bitter. Other parents have been glad that the courts do not now interfere unnecessarily. The philosophy behind the Children Act 1989 was: why should the courts *have* to intervene to regulate arrangements between parents on divorce, while they may have made a whole variety of different arrangements while the marriage lasted which would never have been looked at by the courts.

The important thing to remember is that while, on the one hand, the courts give parents a lot of flexibility to make up their own minds and will not interfere unnecessarily in family life, if disputes do arise which the parents just cannot sort out between themselves, either can apply for a court order. The new court orders that can be applied for are much simpler and the process for applying for them quicker and more streamlined (*see* page 108).

There are also a few legal restrictions and guidelines about the exercise of parental responsibility:

- The exercise of parental responsibility must not contravene any court order. If, for example, a father has a contact order to see the children at weekends, the mother cannot disappear with the children at the weekend to frustrate the contact order.
- A person with parental responsibility cannot give it away or transfer it, but they may arrange for some of it to be met by someone else acting on their behalf. Anyone looking after a child may do what is reasonable to safeguard the child.

GUARDIANS

Guardians can be appointed by the parents (under a will or in writing) or by the court to care for the children after the parents die. A guardian once appointed (which only happens after the parent has died) will have full parental responsibility just as if he or she were the parent. Not everyone is willing to take on the responsibility of becoming a guardian for children who are not their

Draft Deed of Appointment of Guardian

By this **DEED OF APPOINTMENT** I . . . . (*mother's name*)
of . . . . (*mother's address*) **APPOINT** . . . . (*guardian's name*)
of . . . . (*guardian's address*) to be the
GUARDIAN of my (*minor/infant*) son/daughter . . . . (*child's name*)
In pursuance of Section 5 of the Children Act, 1989.

Signed, sealed and delivered by the above named (*mother's name*) . . . .
(*signature*) . . . . In the presence of . . . . and . . . .
. . . . (*witnesses' names*)

. . . . (*first witness's signature*)

Address of witness
. . . .
. . . .

Occupation of witness
. . . .
. . . .

. . . . (*second witness's signature*)

Address of witness
. . . .
. . . .

Occupation of witness
. . . .
. . . .

Dated this . . . . day of . . . . 20 . .

---

own, so a potential guardian should be asked in advance whether he or she would be willing to undertake this role. An appointment of a guardian must be in writing. Most often this is achieved by a deed of appointment or via a will, either of which can be drawn up by a solicitor, who would probably charge around £50 upwards for preparing it. A blank draft deed is set out above.

If the parents were married at the time of the child's birth (even if they have divorced), in most cases the appointment of a guardian does not take effect until after both parents have died. This is to avoid battles between the surviving parent and the newly appointed guardian. But if there was a residence order in favour of the deceased parent, then the appointment of a guardian will take effect straight away. If both parents die and both have appointed different guardians who disagree, an application should he made to court for a section 8 order to decide who should act.

If the parents are not married, then only the mother can appoint a guardian, unless the father has parental responsibility too (*see* page 85). If he does not have parental responsibility, he will have no rights to look after the children after the mother's death. If the mother wants to appoint him as a guardian she must do so by deed or by will (although she can also appoint anyone else she chooses too). If the father does have parental responsibility, then he will automatically take over legal responsibility for the children after the mother's death as a married father would.

In summary, it is crucial that parents (especially unmarried mothers) do appoint guardians during their lifetime and do not just leave it to fate as to who will care for their offspring in future after their death.

MAINTENANCE

Parents have a legal duty to maintain children (whether or not they were married at the time of the birth). Since 1993 this will most likely be enforced through the Child Support Agency (*see* above). But fathers looking after children alone can also make an application for child support against the mother.

Children over 18 years old now also have their own right to ask for a maintenance order against a parent if they are in full-time education or training (whether or not they are earning money too – e.g. by working in a bar) if there was no maintenance order existing before the child was 16 years old and the parents have separated or divorced.

So the use that can be made of this legal 'right' is fairly limited. It is really designed to give the child the right to apply for maintenance if he or she has gone on to further education and in the meantime the parents have split up and the father has refused to pay the fees or living expenses.

TREATMENT WHEN ILL

The pre-Children Act test was that the parent must behave as a 'reasonable parent' would. If a reasonable parent would send for a doctor or allow an operation, then so should the child's parent. Now the test is that the child's welfare is the paramount consideration: parents' own views may well have to take second place.

If neither parent will consent to a necessary operation on the child, the hospital may inform the Social Services Department of the local authority. If the local authority has reasonable cause to suspect that the child is suffering, or is likely to suffer, significant harm, then it has a duty to investigate and decide whether it should take action to safeguard or promote the child's welfare. It could apply to the court for a child protection order (like a child assessment order or an emergency protection order). It could also apply for a specific issue order or for the child to be made a ward of court, although the court's permission would first have to be obtained. The court could then consent to the medical treatment on the child's behalf. *See* also page 117.

ASSISTED CONCEPTION AND PATERNITY

An estimated one in six couples is classified as 'infertile' – the technical definition of which means that they have not conceived within 12 months of trying to have a baby. With the advent of scientific advances and increased medical knowledge, many such couples are assisted in conceiving by IVF (in vitro fertilization), for example. If the sperm used is that of the woman's husband or male partner, in almost all cases the husband/father will be viewed by the law as the true father (but *see* the case of Diane Blood's baby, below). If the sperm is from a donor, the provisions of the Human Fertilization and Embryology Act 1990 usually apply.

Assisted conception and married couples

If the woman is married when she conceives, and provided her husband consents, her husband will be treated as the child's father. The consent must be given in writing and the husband must be given a suitable opportunity to receive counselling and information.

In 1997, a well-publicized case highlighted how the fast pace of medical advances was speeding ahead of legal change.

Diane Blood and her husband had decided they would like to have a child after they were married for three years. Sadly, the husband contracted meningitis and died. While he was unconscious in hospital, doctors removed a sample of sperm from Mr Blood at his wife's request. After her husband's death, Diane Blood asked for the required permission from the Human Fertilization and Embryology Authority (given the power and authority to decide such cases) for the semen to be released so that she could be artificially inseminated. The Authority refused, but on appeal it was held that the Authority's prohibition had not taken account of European law – specifically here Articles 59 and 60 of the EC Treaty. Eventually, Diane Blood was given permission to take the sperm to Belgium where she successfully obtained fertility treatment. Just before Christmas 1998, she gave birth to a son, Liam Stephen. However, in accordance with the provisions of the Human Fertilization and Embryology Act 1990, Liam is legally viewed as fatherless.

Another case that was covered in the national press in 2003 concerned the legal position of a husband when another man's sperm had mistakenly been used in the infertility treatment.

Two couples (A and B) were separately undergoing IVF treatment for their infertility. Mr B's sperm was mistakenly used to fertilize eggs from Mrs A. Mrs A went on to give birth to twins. The issue for the court was whether Mr A should be treated as the twins' father. Under section 28 of the Human Fertility and Embryology Act 1990 a husband should not be treated as the father of a child in circumstances where he had not given his consent to the placing in his wife of the actual embryo, which had been inserted in error, and ultimately resulted in the birth of a child. The Court of Appeal decided that, in these circumstances, it could not be said that the husband and wife had undergone 'treatment together'. Therefore, Mr B was the genetic and legal father.

Leeds Teaching Hospital *v* A and Others (2003)

Assisted conception and unmarried couples

Where a child is born to an unmarried couple as a result of artificial conception, the Human Fertilization and Embryology Act 1990 s28(3) provides that a man who is not the child's genetic father is nonetheless treated by law as father of the child, provided that the methods used to assist conception were carried out 'in the course of treatment services provided for [a woman] and a man together by a person to whom a licence applies'. So if an unmarried couple have together gained treatment through a licensed clinic, then the man is the child's father in law and he takes on all the consequences of paternity, including, of course, the obligation to maintain the child.

However, all the requirements of the Act must be met, as this case shows.

Miss U and Mr W (who was actually still married to someone else) travelled to Rome and received fertility treatment together there, which resulted in the birth of twins. Tests confirmed that Mr W was not the genetic father. Miss U and Mr W subsequently split up and Miss U sought a declaration of paternity that Mr W was the father of the twins so that she could get a child support assessment made against him. Held: No. Although the treatment services had been given to the couple together, it had not been at a licensed clinic. The twins were as a result legally fatherless and Mr W was not liable to maintain them.

U *v* W (A-G Intervening) (1997)

In October 2003, two women took their former partners to court, arguing that they should be able to use frozen embryos for IVF treatment. The frozen embryos had been created when the couples were still together. The male partners did not want a child to be born because the relationship had ended. Held: Embryos cannot be implanted in a woman unless both partners involved in their creation consent to the procedure. The women's claim failed.

Hadley and Evans (2003)

Assisted conception and sperm donors

Where a child is conceived in accordance with the provisions of the Human Fertilization and Embryology Act 1990, then the donor of the sperm is not treated as the child's father for any purpose. In contrast, where a woman conceives a child through a self-help method, then it is the donor, and not her husband or partner, who is the child's father in law.

SEX AND CONTRACEPTION

Girls over the age of 16 can consent to sexual intercourse. It is a criminal offence for a man to have sexual intercourse with a girl under 16, although the girl herself commits no offence. (There is no specific age limit for boys, although the law does not recognize that a boy is capable of having sexual intercourse until he is 14.)

But what if a girl under 16 intends to have sex and wants contraceptive advice?

Mrs Gillick, the mother of four daughters, wrote to her local Health Authority formally forbidding them to give any contraceptive or abortion advice to her children while under 16 and asking for their written agreement to her request. Receiving no satisfactory assurance, she commenced proceedings, which were appealed up to the House of Lords. Held: Young people have the right to make decisions about their lives and their bodies if they are old enough to have a mature appreciation of the issues and to make up their own minds.

Gillick (1985)

Department of Health guidelines advise doctors that they should normally seek parental consent for contraceptive advice but doctors can give advice and help if the patient 'is capable of understanding what is proposed and of expressing his or her wishes' (Lord Fraser in *Gillick*). The court avoided laying down a specific age limit. Doctors can thus give contraceptives to young people under 16 years old but doctors must not in any way encourage a breach of the criminal law. In practice, it will be up to doctors themselves.

SURROGACY

A surrogate mother is a woman who agrees to bear a child for a couple (usually because the woman of the couple is infertile). She agrees to hand over the child after the birth. Surrogate arrangements, although rare, are most often made between family members – say, a sister bearing a child for her sister who cannot carry a child to full term. While the law does not prohibit surrogacy, it prohibits payment to surrogate mothers of anything more than their costs involved in the pregnancy and birth (and for the period caring for the baby, if any). The law also protects the woman, allowing her in some cases to revoke her agreement to hand the baby over. The Human Fertilization and Embryology Act 1990 provides that a court can make an order in favour of a couple commissioning a surrogacy arrangement providing for a child to be treated in law as the child of the parties to a marriage. But various technical conditions must be met and a court would need to be satisfied that the woman giving birth gave her full and unconditional assent – the same applies to the parents-to-be too. This order needs to be applied for within six months of the birth and no money or other benefit must have been received.

Where such an order cannot be applied for, perhaps in non-mainstream cases, the usual recourse for the parents-to-be who wish to become recognized as parents by the law is to consider adoption or a residence order.

In 1999, a gay couple, two successful businessmen based in Essex, arranged for a surrogate based in the US to bear their child. Their overall costs for making this arrangement were reported to be £200,000. The surrogate became pregnant with twins (a boy and girl, who were later named Saffron and Aspen) fathered with a mix of both men's sperm. In 2000, after the twins were born and brought to this country, the two 'fathers' wished to apply to adopt. An alternative arrangement would be for them to apply jointly for a residence order for the twins.

In January 2000, the twins were granted unrestricted leave to stay in the UK, a decision made outside normal immigration rules because of the exceptional circumstances of the case.

ADOPTION

A child can be placed for adoption by a local authority, if the child has been taken into care. The natural parents must either consent to the child being adopted or the court must make a 'freeing order' if they do not consent. The local authority will have to show that the parents are not withholding consent unreasonably. This can sometimes be a considerable hurdle to cross.

A child aged 12 had been placed by the local authority with a comfortably off couple for some time. They expected to adopt her, but the girl said she did not want to be adopted. The natural mother had a history of failed relationships and alcohol and drug abuse. The adoptive parents-to-be sought an adoption order, on the basis that the girl would still have contact with her mother. **Held:** *No. The mother was not unreasonably refusing her consent, so an adoption order could not be made. A residence order was made instead.* Re M (Adoption or Residence Order) (1998)

See the chart on page 93 for the procedure on adopting a child. An adoption application can be made by: a married couple (both must be at least 21), parent and step-parent (but often a residence order will be preferred – *see* page 108), or a single person (who must be at least 21 and unmarried – or if married, spouse must permanently be living apart).

The Adoption and Children Act 2002 allows unmarried couples (including same-sex couples) to apply jointly to adopt a child. The couple would need to prove that they have a stable and lasting relationship and that they can provide a loving family environment for a child.

The Act represents the most radical overhaul of adoption law for 26 years. The other key changes are:

- an Adoption and Children Act Register has been operational since April 2002. The Register holds details of all children waiting to be adopted and all approved adoptive families. The aim of the Register is to reduce delays in the adoption process by enabling children and families to be matched more quickly;

- introduction of a new Special Guardianship order to provide security and permanence for children who cannot return to their birth families, but for whom adoption is not the most suitable option. The person appointed as special guardian will have responsibility for all the day-to-day decisions about caring for the child and for taking decisions about his or her upbringing. Unlike adoption, the order can be discharged or varied and the child's legal relationship with his or her birth parents is not severed. They remain legally the child's parents, though their ability to exercise their parental responsibility is limited;

- introduction of a new procedure for placing a child for adoption through an adoption agency. Two routes are provided: birth parents may give consent to placement or a local authority may secure a placement order from the court, authorizing it to place a child with adopters whom they select. The intention is to ensure that decisions about whether adoption is the right option for the child, whether the birth parents consent and, if not, whether parental consent should be dispensed with are taken earlier in the adoption process. The system aims to provide greater certainty and stability for children by dealing as far as possible with consent to placement for adoption before they have been placed, to minimize the uncertainty for prospective adopters, and to reduce the extent to which birth families are faced with a *fait accompli* at the final adoption hearing.

In practice, of course, the fundamental problem is finding a child to adopt. Begin by asking the adoption officer in the local Social Services Department to provide a list of adoption agencies. The number of babies to adopt has shrunk dramatically, although many older children have been freed for adoption and are waiting longingly for a permanent adoptive placement.

A study in the late 1990s was carried out by the Social

Adoption

The procedure when you have been offered a child

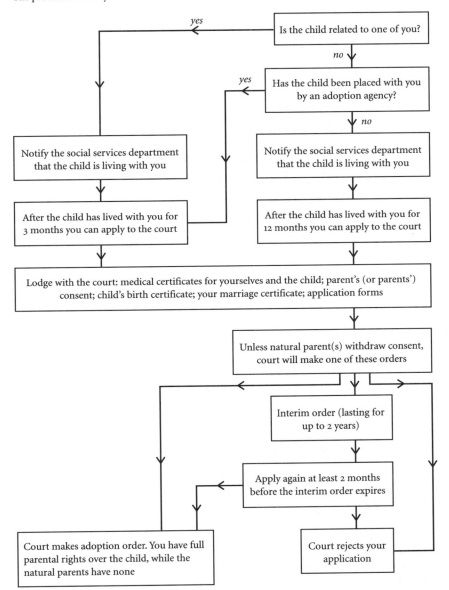

Services Inspectorate which showed that 2,400 children in England and Wales were ready for adoption and awaiting a match with a family while 1,300 approved families were unmatched. In 2000 the British Agencies for Adoption and Fostering (BAAF) subsequently published research involving a study of 1,437 children in care for whom no adoptive parents could be found.

The research compared the number of inquiries from potential adoptive families for different categories of children. It found that an average of 16 inquiries were made for each white girl aged 3–5 and most girls aged 6–10 could expect an average of five inquiries but no inquiries were made for half of all boys aged 6–10. On average, only one or two inquiries were made for other boys. The research gave ample evidence that if, and when, children are freed for adoption, what may actually happen to them will be much influenced by their age, sex and, indeed, ethnic origin as well as how many siblings they have (individual children find homes faster than siblings). Families interested in adopting a child can contact BAAF for their monthly newsletter, *Be My Parent* on Tel: 020 7593 2060 (www.baaf.org.uk)

INTERNATIONAL ADOPTION?

Another option sometimes sought by prospective adopters is to adopt a child from abroad. New laws passed in 1999 – The Adoption (Intercountry Aspects) Act 1999 – tightened up the loopholes in the law and ensured that people wanting to adopt a child from abroad will need to successfully pass the same tests and safeguards as those adopting a child in this country. The key aspects of the Act are that it:

- provides for automatic recognition of adoption orders where a child is adopted from a country which has ratified or acceded to the 1993 Hague Convention;
- establishes a Central Authority for each of England, Wales and Scotland to be responsible for the operation of the Convention;
- clarifies that local authority social services departments must provide an intercountry adoption service;
- changes the residence requirement before an adoption order can be made in the case of intercountry adoptions;
- confers British citizenship automatically on any child adopted in accordance with the Act in a country which has ratified the 1993 Convention; and
- makes it a criminal offence for someone who lives in the UK to bring into the country a child for adoption where the child habitually lives outside the UK unless the requirements set out in the regulations have been complied with.

INJURING THE CHILD

Obviously the parent has a duty to look after the child and to avoid injuring it. Deliberate injury or irresponsible neglect may well give rise to criminal proceedings or the local authority taking action. (Local authorities keep records of non-accidental injuries to children and a child abuse register for children at risk in their area.)

There is also the more general question of the parent's liability should he or she injure the child. The law allows the child to sue the parent for negligent injury. The most common form of this is when the child is a passenger in a car driven by its father and is injured; if the father was driving negligently, then he has broken his duty of care to the child and so he can be sued. In practice, of course, the father will have motor insurance to cover his liability for negligent driving and the child will be able to claim compensation from the insurance company. However, a child cannot sue in its own name (except in certain family proceedings), so the action is brought in the name of an adult who is said to act as the child's 'next friend' for the purposes of the action.

A child cannot sue its parents for injuries caused before its birth. For instance, if a child is born with disabilities because its mother drank alcohol during pregnancy, the child cannot sue its mother for negligence. But a local authority can take action to protect a child after the birth if the mother endangered its health during the pregnancy.

A mother who was a heroin addict bore a child prematurely: the child was suffering from withdrawal symptoms at birth. The local authority applied for a care order. **Held:** *The child should be taken into care. The court could have regard to events occurring during the pregnancy if they affected a child's health and development after birth.*

Re D (A Minor) (1986)

CORPORAL PUNISHMENT

Some countries, like Sweden, have introduced special laws to prohibit corporal punishment. Here, the law still allows parents to impose 'reasonable chastisement' on their children, although the attitude of the UK courts to corporal punishment is viewed with derision elsewhere in Europe. The test is whether a reasonable parent would impose that punishment. So a smack is allowed and will not be an illegal assault on the child. On the other hand, a punch in the face will be unreasonable and will be a criminal offence. In addition, of course, conduct of that sort is likely to lead to the local authority taking action to safeguard the child and any injuries to the head in particular will be taken very seriously as they can cause long-term damage to a child. Unnatural punishments, such as keeping the child locked up, are illegal.

A mother asked her boyfriend to 'smack' her 6-year-old boy for disobedience. The boyfriend hit the boy twice with his belt, bruising him. The social worker saw the bruises and the boy was taken to hospital. The boyfriend was prosecuted for causing actual bodily harm to the boy. **Held:** *He was guilty.*
Smith (1985)

The increasingly powerful influence of EC law on UK law may well operate to force a change in the law to provide greater protection to children against physical assaults by adults. In 1998, the European Court of Human Rights unanimously found that UK law allowing 'reasonable chastisement' breached children's human rights. The government accepted the judgment and announced it would consult on how to change the law. The Department of Health issued a consultation document 'Protecting Children, Supporting Parents' in January 2000. Pressure on the government to ban all forms of physical chastisement of children is growing, with an alliance involving major national children's charities seeking legal reform to give children the same protection as adults under the law on assault and to promote positive non-violent forms of discipline. In May 2003 the government announced plans to ban childminders in England from smacking children in their care. Despite pressure from child protection groups, it was decided that the smacking ban will not be extended to parents.

See page 102 about corporal punishment in schools.

VIOLENT PARENTS

Neighbours and relatives who think that a child is receiving excessive punishment should report their fears to the Social Services Department of the local authority or the National Society for the Prevention of Cruelty to Children (NSPCC). The NSPCC Child Protection Helpline is Tel: 0808 800 5000. The NSPCC will handle the matter confidentially and cannot be made to disclose a complainant's identity.

The NSPCC received a complaint about the mistreatment of a 14-month-old girl. An NSPCC inspector visited the parents and the mother called the family doctor, who examined the child and found it to be unmarked. The mother, who was very upset, sued the NSPCC and demanded to know the name of the informant. The NSPCC refused to disclose the informant's identity. **Held:** *The need for confidentiality overrode other claims and so the NSPCC was not obliged to disclose the identity of the informant.*
NSPCC (1977)

Since 14 October 1991, NSPCC records can be made available to a guardian *ad litem* in some family proceedings, but this should not affect the confidentiality of an informant's identity.

The NSPCC can itself apply directly to court for a care order for a child (*see* page 120).

If the father is violent towards the child, the mother can petition for divorce on the fact of her husband's unreasonable behaviour (*see* page 32). In addition, she will probably be able to obtain an injunction which forbids the father from hurting the child and which, in some instances, excludes him from entering the family home (*see* page 72).

CRUELTY TO CHILDREN

There are numerous criminal charges which can be brought against parents who assault or harm their children. The main offence is the 'cruelty to children' provision in the Children and Young Persons Act 1933, which protects children under 16. The accused person must have responsibility for the child (any person who has parental responsibility, or is legally liable to maintain, or otherwise has care of the child) and must have assaulted, ill-treated, neglected, or abandoned the child – which is sufficiently wide to cover general abuse and threats – so as to cause the child unnecessary suffering or injury to physical or mental health. But, in addition, the prosecution must show that the neglect was 'wilful', in that the act of cruelty was deliberate even though its effect was not anticipated. The offence is triable in the magistrates' court (maximum £2,000 fine and/or six months' prison) or the crown court (up to two years' prison and unlimited fine).

In practice, relatively few prosecutions are brought. The more sensible remedy is to remove the child from the position of danger. This is done either by the local authority taking action to protect the child or by the non-violent parent asking for an injunction stopping the violent parent from hurting the child or excluding them altogether.

The tragic death of 8-year-old Victoria Climbié in February 2000 resulted in pressure for radical reforms of child protection services in England. Victoria was repeatedly tortured and beaten by her aunt Marie-Thérèse Konao and her aunt's boyfriend Carl Manning. Both were jailed for life for her murder in January 2001. Victoria had been left in Konao's care by her parents, who wanted to give her a better life away from their native Ivory Coast. The little girl was seen by dozens of social workers, nurses, doctors and police officers before she died but all failed to spot and stop the abuse. A public inquiry into Victoria's death, headed by Lord Laming, identified social services departments in four London boroughs, two police forces, two hospitals, and a specialist children's unit who all failed to act when presented with evidence of abuse. Among the report's major proposals was the setting up of a children's commissioner to head a national agency. The national agency would report to a ministerial committee and attempt to improve co-ordination between groups responsible for child protection. In June 2003, the government appointed the first Minister of State for Children. Further reforms are to be announced in a Green Paper to be published later in 2003.

THE CHILD'S NATIONALITY

A child takes the nationality (i.e. citizenship) of its father (usually) or of the place where it was born. If these are different, the child can choose either, or alternatively sometimes it can have dual nationality by keeping both. This depends on whether both countries allow dual nationality: Britain, for example, allows dual nationality but the US does not; so if a child is entitled to both British and American nationality, eventually it will have to choose one of them only.

If a legitimate child, born abroad, has a mother with British nationality but a foreign father, the parents can apply for the child to be registered as a British citizen. The decision is in the hands of the Secretary of State.

A child born out of wedlock in the UK can inherit British citizenship only if the mother is a British citizen or settled in Britain. He or she does not get British citizenship simply by being born in Britain, unless he or she was born before 1 January 1983. An illegitimate child born abroad will be a British citizen if the mother is a British citizen, though this does not necessarily apply if the mother was herself born abroad.

If the child is born on a ship, aircraft or hovercraft which is registered in the UK, that child will be deemed to have been born in the UK. For example, if a child is born in the course of a British Airways flight to Iran, the child will be a UK national. However, if the flight was on an Iranian plane the child would not be of UK nationality unless its father has UK nationality.

GROWING UP

Although the law will rarely allow a contract to be enforced against a child, it does allow children to own money, possessions, and property, but not land (which includes houses). Generally, though, children's possessions are held in trust for them by their parents until the child is old enough to manage its own affairs. If the parent betrays the trust by using the money for his/her own uses, the child can sue the parent for the money lost. The parent is, however, allowed to withdraw money to pay for the child's upkeep, board and education.

Large amounts of money are usually held by independent trustees such as solicitors or bank managers. Generally, they will release money only for the child's maintenance and will not part with other sums unless the permission of the court has been obtained.

Taking a job

For the rules on the employment of children *see* page 406.

Babysitting

There are no rules specifying when a child/young person can babysit – in theory this can be done at any age, although a parent will want to assess a babysitter's suitability. The Children's Legal Centre recommends 16 years as the minimum age for babysitting.

Leaving home

Although the age of majority is 18 years old, the courts will intervene only rarely to stop a child in his mid- or late teens from leaving home.

Generally, if the child has reached 'the age of discretion' (approximately 16) the court will not intervene. Whilst the parents could apply for a section 8 order (*see* page 108), the court would be unlikely to intervene unless it could be shown that the child was in danger (e.g. keeping bad company).

Another possibility is for the local authority to take action to safeguard the child (which may involve taking him or her into care) if the child 'is suffering, or is likely to suffer, significant harm' (*see* page 118).

Generally, the child who has reached the age of discretion, has found a job and is leading a steady life is unlikely to be troubled by the law. The child will not be able to claim income support for himself or herself until aged 16, and then only in limited circumstances: where the child is caring for dependent children (although the amount of the income support will be less than for an adult) or is unable to work. Otherwise the child may be able to obtain a discretionary payment of income support to avoid severe hardship (this will depend on whether parents or relatives are willing to support the child).

Here is a brief list of what age you will need to be to do what.

Growing Up: The Law's Minimum Ages

Age

At birth	A bank or building society account can be opened in the child's name and he or she can own premium bonds. If the child travels abroad the child's own passport will be needed. The child can be handed to prospective adopters.
19 weeks	The child can be adopted. An adoption order can be made when the child is 19 weeks old, provided that the child has lived with the prospective adopters or one of them for the preceding 13 weeks. In the case of overseas adoptions, the child must have lived with the applicants for 12 months before an adoption order can be made.
5	The child must receive full-time education (*see* page 99) and can drink alcohol in private. The child will have to pay a child's fare on trains and on the public transport system in London.
7	The child can draw money from a TSB or National Savings account.

10   The child can:
- be convicted of a crime if it can be shown that he or she knew it was 'wrong' (*see* page 126);
- if a boy, be regarded by the law as capable of committing any sexual offence, including rape;
- open a current bank account, at the discretion of the bank manager.

12   The child can:
- buy a pet;
- see a 12 category film at the cinema or rent/buy such a film on video;
- If a child is getting a new passport, it must be signed by the child and not the parent(s).

14   The child:
- can take a 'light work' job part-time but cannot work for more than two hours on a school day or on a Sunday;
- can be convicted of a criminal offence as if an adult and can be fined by the Youth Court up to £1,000;
- can own an airgun;
- can go into a bar with an adult but cannot buy or consume an alcoholic drink.

15   The child can:
- own a shotgun and ammunition;
- be sent to youth custody in a youth offenders institution (part of the Prison Service);
- see a 15 category film at the cinema or rent/buy such a film on video.

16   The child:
- can get a National Insurance number;
- can marry if there is parental consent (*see* Chapter 3);
- can be assessed to pay child support if an absent parent, although it is unlikely that this will be enforced where the absent parent is still under 18;
- can receive income support in certain circumstances;
- can buy fireworks;
- can buy premium bonds;
- can leave school (*see* page 102) and then work full-time;
- can join a trade union;
- can drink beer, cider, porter or perry in a pub, but only with a meal in a part of the pub that serves meals, not at the bar;
- can drive a moped or tractor;
- can fly solo in a glider;
- can buy cigarettes (he or she can smoke at any age!);
- has to pay prescription charges;
- has to pay the full fare on public transport;
- can join the armed forces, with parental consent;
- A girl can consent to heterosexual intercourse. (Boys can consent to heterosexual intercourse at any age. There is no law against homosexual intercourse between women.)

17   The child can:
- donate blood without parental consent;
- drive a car or motor-cycle;
- go into a betting shop (but not bet);
- have an airgun in a public place;
- fly a plane solo;
- be tried on any charge in an adult court; can also be sent to prison;
- be fined up to £2,000.

18   The child becomes an adult and can:
- vote;
- sue in his/her own name;
- marry without parental consent;
- change his/her name;
- own land (including a house);
- enter into binding contracts;
- obtain credit (including HP) and have a cheque or credit card;
- be eligible for jury service;
- buy drinks in the bar of a pub;
- donate your body to science or donate body organs without parental permission;
- be tattooed;
- bet;
- if adopted, will no longer be adopted but can apply for a copy of the original birth certificate and apply to have his/her name and address put on the Adoption Contact Register;
- make a will;
- join the armed forces without parental consent;
- be admitted to a film rated 18;
- if male, consent to homosexual acts in private with another man also over 18;
- pawn an article at a pawnshop.

21   The adult can now:
- stand in a general or local election;
- apply for a liquor licence;
- drive a lorry or bus.

For more information on children's legal rights, contact the Children's Legal Centre, University of Essex, Wivenhoe Park, Colchester, Essex CO4 3SQ, Tel: 01206 873820.

PARENTS' LIABILITY FOR CHILDREN

Liability for contracts

In legal theory, a parent is liable for his or her children's contracts only if the parent told the child to make the contract or if they allowed the child to appear to be their agent (e.g. if the child orders groceries from the local shop the grocer is entitled to believe that the child is acting on its parents' behalf).

But, in practice, parents are often made liable for their children's contracts because the parent signs an indemnity or a guarantee agreement. This makes the parent personally liable if the child defaults on payment. Usually, no trader will accept a sizeable order from a child unless the child's parent signs a guarantee or indemnity (in which case the parent is liable).

The child itself is unlikely to be liable to carry out the contract. Only if the contract is for 'necessary' items, or if it is to his/her definite advantage, will it be enforced against him/her, and note that motorbikes and stereos would not be considered to be 'necessaries'. But if a child enters into an unenforceable contract and refuses to pay, the court may order the return of goods. The child can probably enforce the contract against the other, adult, party to the contract, although some lawyers dispute this.

Liability for the child's negligence

Negligence is a failure to take 'reasonable care'. But obviously a different standard of 'reasonableness' has to be applied to a child than to an adult. A child may therefore be able to do an act that injures another person or which damages property and yet not be legally liable, whereas if that same act had been done by an adult, the adult would be legally liable.

So the 'reasonable behaviour' test has to be modified when dealing with children. A 7-year-old boy who injures someone with a catapult will probably not be liable, for the court would be likely to decide that a typical 7-year-old would not appreciate the harm a catapult might do. But if the child was 10, the court might well think that a 10-year-old should have realized the dangers of a catapult and so he would be liable in negligence. The additional problem that arises when suing a child is that the child is unlikely to have any money with which to pay any damages. Usually, the child's parents will not be liable on behalf of their child and so they cannot be made to pay the damages. The practical result of this is that it is only rarely worth suing a negligent child.

But can the parent be sued for the child's negligence? Generally the answer will be 'no'. The parent is not automatically liable for the child's negligence and the parent will be liable only if he or she was negligent. For instance, the court might find that the parent was negligent to give a 7-year-old child a catapult, for if the child is too young to appreciate the dangers of a catapult, perhaps he or she should not be given one. Thus the person injured by the catapult might be able to sue the parent, not for the child's negligence, but for the parent's own negligence in letting the child have the catapult.

Anti-social behaviour

In the late 1990s, the then government was especially keen to show itself tough on crime and related activities and new laws were brought in to try and restrict anti-social behaviour, with particular regard to younger children who were outside the law in the sense that they had not been considered to be capable of criminal activity until they were 10 years old.

If a child aged 10 years or older is found to harass, or cause alarm or distress to one or more people outside his home, the magistrates may make an anti-social behaviour order against him, prohibiting him from doing anything detailed in the order.

Although children cannot be convicted of a criminal offence under age 10, if it is thought that the child is suffering or is likely to suffer significant harm and that the child is beyond parental control, then a care order can be made under the Children Act 1989.

Where a child under 10 has committed a criminal offence or has harassed, alarmed or distressed two people other than those living in your home, a child safety order can be made for up to three months. This places the child under the supervision of a social worker or a member of the youth offending team: Crime and Disorder Act 1998.

Children under 10 can also be the subject of a local child curfew scheme banning them from public places (except when accompanied by an adult) between 9pm and 6am: Crime and Disorder Act 1998.

The child's education

The Education Acts impose a duty on parents to ensure that their children are educated and a duty on local education authorities (LEAs) to provide suitable schools. In London, since the Inner London Education Authority (ILEA) was disbanded, its powers have devolved to 13 London boroughs, which have gained the status of LEAs.

If a child is of compulsory school age (between 5 and 16) he or she must receive full-time education at school or elsewhere – for example, at home: Education Act 1996 s7. This duty falls on the person with parental responsibility for the child (usually both parents) and if the local authority thinks that this duty is not being fulfilled, it can give the parent 14 days to prove that the child is receiving suitable education. If the local authority is not satisfied with the explanation offered, it can apply for an education supervision order on the parents. If this is ignored, the parents will be summonsed to appear in the magistrates' court.

Thus parents cannot refuse their child an education. However, it does not necessarily follow that the child has to go to school; the parents can discharge their duty to provide suitable full-time education by, for example, employing a tutor or teaching the child themselves. Parents who wish to offer home schooling for their children should contact the LEA who will visit the parents and take a view as to whether the education offered is 'suitable'. If there are concerns as to suitability, sometimes an educational social worker will be appointed.

Much is left to the discretion of the LEA, but it cannot insist that the child be taught the same range of subjects as is available at the local school or even that its education be as efficient. There is no need for the parents who are teaching their own children to be qualified teachers, although if they are suitably qualified that will be an important factor in deciding the authority's attitude.

If the parents cannot satisfy the LEA that the child's education meets the statutory standard they may first be given formal warning that the LEA intends to apply for an education supervision order. The parents may be able to delay matters by appealing against the LEA's choice of school, but the end result may well be the service of an education supervision order, to secure that the child is 'properly educated'. In addition, the LEA could apply for the child to be taken into care if it is not receiving official full-time education.

Types of schools

The Education Acts refer to a confusing variety of schools. Officially, the categories are:

1 *County schools*. Entirely financed by LEAs. Most primary and secondary schools come within this category.

2 *Voluntary schools.* These get some financial help from the LEA and are of three types:

- *controlled schools:* run by voluntary organizations, but the LEA will nominate two-thirds of the governors and pay all the running costs (and appoint the teachers);
- *aided schools:* receive 85 per cent of their running costs from the Secretary of State or the LEA. Two-thirds of the governors are appointed by the voluntary body (the others by the LEA);
- *special-agreement schools:* these are relatively rare (about 100 or so, mostly Catholic, although some are Church of England).

3 *Special schools.* For those with a 'learning difficulty' (*see* below).

4 *Direct-grant schools.* These receive some grant aid. Most are former grammar schools which opted to go 'independent' rather than be drawn more closely into the county schools system.

Some other, more specialist types of schools have more recently been established, for example City Technology Colleges (CTCs). Up to the age of 16, a child is still entitled to receive free full-time education. Schools, sixth-form colleges and CTCs are all free. There is no duty on LEAs to provide comprehensive education. A 1976 Act did introduce such a duty, but it was repealed in 1979, so now there is just a power for LEAs to impose the comprehensive system.

Choosing the school

The Education Acts give parents some say in the choice of their children's school. Parents' rights to choose a school for their child are being strengthened but schools still have a discretion about accepting pupils. Many schools operate admissions procedures, with priority being given to children within the locality and whose siblings attend the school, for example. These procedures must be fair. If the parents' chosen school refuses to accept their child, this is taken to be a decision of the local authority and can usually be appealed.

The choice of school is made by the person with parental responsibility for the child, which will usually, of course, be the parents.

Finding out about the local schools

Most parents will find about their local schools through informal contacts – friends, neighbours, etc. But, in addition, the LEA is obliged to provide certain basic information. The Education (School Information) Regulations of 1981 require that the local authority should let inquirers know:

- the number of children that will be admitted to a school in the coming year;
- the admission arrangements for children who do not live in the authority's area;

- transport arrangements (and whether help is given towards travel costs);
- the functions of the authority and the school governors as regards admissions.

The local authority's decision

The education authority need not accept the parent's choice of school. Under the Education Act 1981 s6, the authority can use one of three excuses:

1 *It would prejudice the provision of efficient education, or the efficient use of resources.* This is a very wide let-out clause but it will generally be used when there are no spaces available in the school, or if preference is to be given to children who live more locally to the school.

2 *It would be incompatible with the normal admission policy of the school* (e.g. a church school that only takes children from a particular parish).

3 *The child is refused admission because of 'ability or aptitude'* (e.g. if there is an 11-plus exam, which the child has not passed).

Appealing against the authority's decision

The authority should provide details of the appeals procedure, but all appeals must be in writing; a time limit for making the appeal will usually be laid down, but this cannot be less than 14 days. Usually, a simple letter of appeal will be enough but it is important to give a reason for the appeal. The sort of reasons that are more likely to be taken seriously are that: the child does live in the school's catchment area; brothers and sisters go to the school or to another school in that area; older brothers and sisters had been to the school that was being rejected (i.e. the parents have had one child there and do not want another to go); the child's home is very close to the school; there are genuine medical or social reasons (but try to get a doctor's certificate in support). On the other hand, the sort of reasons that are less likely to make the authority change its mind would include: convenience for mother's shopping or child-minding arrangements; parents wish to have the child educated at a single-sex (or co-ed) school; better sports facilities at a particular school; the child's friends will be going to the school.

In practice, it is difficult to win an appeal for a child who lives outside the school's catchment area. If a written appeal is made, there will eventually be a private hearing at which the parent can argue his/her case. After the appeal, a dissatisfied parent can complain to the Secretary of State for Education that the authority's admission arrangements are 'unreasonable', but in practice such complaints very rarely succeed.

Special schools

The Education Act 1981 saw a change in the way of dealing with children who have 'special educational needs'. The previous policy had been to send them to special schools but the 1981 Act introduced a policy, wherever possible, of keeping such children in ordinary schools (i.e. they are not to be segregated into special schools). In practice, this has been no more than a statement of intent because lack of money has prevented it being implemented.

The LEA can decide that a child has 'special educational needs', in which case the parent must be told, and be consulted. The LEA can then go on to make a formal assessment. The procedures are extremely complex but involve the LEA in preparing a written statement of the child's special needs (often colloquially referred to as being 'statemented'), which can be appealed by the parent. The parent can also ask for reassessment. Advice on the procedures (and the tactics of appealing) can be obtained from a Citizens' Advice Bureau or from one of the specialist educational advice bodies.

Truancy and school attendance

A parent technically commits an offence if the child does not regularly attend the school where it is registered, unless, of course, the child is receiving suitable full-time education elsewhere.

The offence is committed even if the parents were unaware that the child was not attending school. The only defences to the charge are:

- the child did not attend school because of sickness; or
- the child could not attend school because of some unavoidable cause affecting the child (i.e. not affecting the parent); or
- the child was absent on days set aside for religious observance (either the parents or the child must follow that religion); or
- the school is not within walking distance of the child's home, and the local education authority has not provided transport or arranged for transfer to a nearer school. ('Walking distance' for children under eight years old is two miles, and for those over eight years, it is three miles; distances are measured by the shortest practicable route, i.e. disregarding heavy traffic – but the child is not expected to use an isolated track.)

In practice, prosecution is a last resort. The first step will be for an education welfare officer to call on the parents to discuss why the child is not attending school. If it is simply because the parents are too poor to pay for a school uniform, the local authority may help with the cost. A prosecution for truancy (i.e. failing to secure regular attendance of a child at school) is a different offence from failing to register a child at school. If the parents do not register the child at school, then they will probably be served with an education supervision order (*see* page 99).

If it seems to be the parents who are at fault, the LEA will usually serve a warning notice on them. If there is no improvement, the parents may be prosecuted (maximum penalty: £400 fine and one month's prison).

If it is the child who is at fault, the case may go before the youth court. The court will consider reports from the education welfare service and will usually adjourn the case for four weeks to give the child a last chance. Most children heed this warning, but if the child continues to play truant, the next step will probably be a referral to a child guidance clinic. Alternatives would be an education supervision order or even (in extreme circumstances) for the local authority to apply to take a child into care (*see* page 118).

School rules

Local education authorities can lay down rules covering such matters as dress, length of hair and discipline, and these rules can apply not just while the child is at the school, but on his or her way to and from the school. If the child breaks these rules (e.g. because they are improperly dressed) then the school can refuse to admit them. The child's parents will then be failing in their duty to ensure that the child is being educated.

Exclusions

According to the Education Act 2002, exclusion means to exclude a child from a maintained school (that is, a school maintained by the state) on disciplinary grounds. Only the headteacher has the power to exclude a pupil from school. If a child is excluded, the headteacher must explain to the parents why the child is being excluded and how the parents might appeal against that decision.

There are two types of exclusion:

- *Fixed-period exclusion.* These exclusions are usually for a short period and include lunchtime exclusions. The pupil returns after the exclusion period has expired. In cases of more than a day's exclusion, work should be set and marked. A pupil may be excluded for up to a maximum of 45 school days in any school year.
- *Permanent exclusion.* This is also known as expulsion. This means the pupil cannot return to the school unless reinstated.

Ground for exclusion

A decision to exclude a pupil should be taken only:

(a) in response to serious breaches of the school's behaviour policy; and

(b) if allowing the pupil to remain in school would seriously harm the education or welfare of the pupil or others in the school.

A decision to exclude a child permanently is a serious one and is normally used as a last resort. There may however be exceptional circumstances (such as violence against another pupil or member of staff, sexual abuse or assault, supplying a drug, carrying a weapon) when it will be appropriate for the headteacher to exclude permanently for a one-off offence. It would not be appropriate for a pupil to be excluded for minor incidents such as failure to do homework, lateness, truancy, pregnancy or breaches of school uniform rules or rules on appearance except where these are persistent and in open defiance of such rules.

Duty to provide other suitable education
If a pupil is permanently excluded, the LEA has a duty to provide other suitable education. This may be a place in another school, a place in the local special educational unit, or the LEA may provide home or individual tuition.

Appeal process
When their child is excluded, the parents have the right to make representations to the school's governing body. If the governing body uphold a permanent exclusion, the parents can appeal against that decision to an independent appeal panel. The decision of the appeal panel is binding. The parents can challenge it only by judicial review.

Corporal punishment

Teachers no longer have a right to inflict corporal punishment on pupils whose education is paid for from public funds.

Children educated in the state sector or whose education is wholly or partly paid for out of the public purse (e.g. where boarding school fees are paid by the Ministry of Defence or where a local authority pays for a child to board) cannot be physically punished. If their teachers hit them, the teachers can be charged with assault.

Independent schools were brought into line with the ban on corporal punishment in state schools under the 1996 Education Act, as amended by section 131 of the 1998 School Standards and Framework Act. In 2002 the ban was challenged by Phil Williamson, a headteacher, and eleven other teachers. They argued that the legislation did not prevent a parent delegating to a teacher in an independent school the right to administer corporal punishment, in accordance with their religious beliefs. The Court of Appeal dismissed their case, holding that the statutory ban did not violate their right to manifest their religion or beliefs.

Starting school

Schooling is compulsory from the beginning of the first term after the child's fifth birthday. Many education authorities are prepared to take children before that age and, indeed, all 4-year-olds are entitled to a nursery or school place and many children are starting their formal schooling at age four.

Leaving school

The minimum leaving age is 16, but a child cannot necessarily leave on his or her sixteenth birthday. A young person can leave school on the last Friday of June if he is either 16 by that date or will reach the age of 16 during the summer holidays and before the beginning of the next school year: Education Act 1996; Education (School Leaving Date) Order 1997.

16-to-19-year-olds

The duty of the LEA to educate extends to 16-, 17- and 18-year-olds. The Further and Higher Education Act 1992 states that all young people are entitled to full-time education up to the age of 19. As regards those aged 19 and over, there is a duty to provide further education for those who want it (but since it need not be in the local area, this duty is – in practical terms – meaningless). As for fees, LEAs can charge for non-advanced further education (which means below GCE A-level standard); until recently, few LEAs did charge, but some authorities have now introduced charges. Universities have introduced annual fees of £1,000. Such fees are predicted to rise to £6,000 within the first decade of the twenty-first century.

The National Curriculum

One of the most important changes brought about by the Education Reform Act 1988 (certainly one which has generated much public debate) was the introduction of a National Curriculum. It forms part of an increasing seizure of power by central government of the education sector. The National Curriculum applies only to children between 5 and 16 years of age being educated in the state system; the private sector is exempted, although many of the private-sector schools also use the National Curriculum, if only as a benchmark to ensure that all the aspects designated are covered – in practice private schools often achieve much better results with their pupils.

The National Curriculum introduced ten foundation subjects which all children must study at school: English, mathematics, science, technology (and design), history, geography, a modern foreign language, music, art and physical education. From autumn 1989, all schools had to teach pupils aged 5–14 these foundation subjects. Attainment targets and study programmes for maths, science and English were introduced for 5-year-olds and for maths for 11-year-olds. The Act states that children must be assessed at ages 7, 11, 14 and 16 years, partly on the basis of teachers' own assessment and partly on the basis of national tests known as 'standard assessment tests'.

The first national *trial* assessment of 7-year-olds was in summer 1991. Teachers' criticism has led to the likelihood of some of the more time-consuming tasks of assessment being relaxed. The first national assessment of 7-year-olds, where the results were reported to parents, took place in summer 1992 and by summer 1993 the same applied to 14-year-olds. Doubts are still being voiced as to whether the over-concentration on such tests (SATs) is indirectly leading to a deterioration in children's education, while others point to the benefits of national standards and monitoring, whether or not those standards are being met across the country. The controversy about mandatory requirements over what schools teach has continued with the introduction of national literacy and numeracy targets since the late 1990s. For further information on this or any other issue relating to schooling, contact the Department for Education and Skills website (www.dfes.gov.uk).

The Parents' Charter

First published in September 1991, the Parents' Charter aimed to set out parents' existing rights and responsibilities, and talked of a partnership between parents and schools for children to receive the best education. It proposed changes like regular inspection of schools, written progress reports and annual published tables of performance for all local schools, and indeed these changes have now come into effect.

Sex education

Parents cannot insist that their children should not have sex-education lessons. There is no duty on the LEA to provide such lessons, and there is no right for the parent to object to such lessons. In practice, all the parent can do is to attempt to reach an informal agreement with the head that the child be excluded from those classes.

School uniforms

Head teachers can lay down rules that require the wearing of certain items and which forbid the wearing of others (e.g. Doc Marten boots). But the rules must be 'reasonable' and it would not be reasonable for the head to insist that particular types of garment (e.g. a special type of blazer) be worn when cheaper, otherwise similar, items can be bought elsewhere. But schools cannot discriminate on grounds of race, sex, culture or religion. If your religion dictates you must wear an item of clothing, the school cannot forbid it.

An orthodox Sikh boy, suing via his father, applied to court because his school had insisted that he remove his turban and cut his hair. The House of Lords held that this was unlawful discrimination under the Race Relations Act 1976.
Mandla (1983)

Similarly a girl refused the right to wear trousers (which boys could wear) was able to argue that this amounted to unlawful sex discrimination.

With regard to problems of appearance (e.g. long hair, jewellery, make-up), again it is back to reasonableness.

In practice, the head teacher is in a powerful position and failure to comply with the school rules as to uniform and appearance may eventually lead to suspension – it being treated as a discipline problem. The concerned parent should begin by discussing the problem with the head. The next step is to ask the LEA for a copy of its *Information for Parents* booklet to see whether the head teacher is complying with it (since 1981 regulations have required the LEA to publish details of its schools' uniform and dress rules). Otherwise, the only hope is to complain to the LEA.

The child and religion

Parents have no duty to bring children up with religious beliefs. The courts will not interfere unless the child is being exposed to a religious belief that will harm it – but, of course, such cases are few and far between.

Schools are required by law to start the day with collective worship and they must also provide religious instruction (RI) classes. Many schools ignore this legal requirement. A parent has a legal right to withdraw the child from the collective worship or from the RI classes. In county schools, the collective worship must be non-denominational.

School records

All schools keep records on pupils. In the past those records were viewed as confidential. However, subject to certain exceptions, since September 1990 a young person aged 16 years upwards is entitled to apply for access to his school records since 1 September 1989 which includes information from teachers, education social welfare officers, and other education support staff. Parents are also entitled to this information for their 16-plus children and parents have the right of access for under 16s: Regulations 4(1)(b) and 6(1) Education (School Records) Regulations 1989.

School charges

State education should be free. In practice, many schools ask parents to contribute towards the cost of books and craft materials, and also to pay for swimming and music lessons. Such charges could be argued to be illegal (certainly, the courts have held that fees for music lessons carried out on school premises are illegal) but given the ever increasing pressures on schools to raise funds for even basic school items, most parents would pay if they can afford to do so.

The school can certainly charge for activities and trips which are outside the normal curriculum, and since 1980 schools have been free to charge what they like for school meals (although these must be provided free to children whose parents receive income support). If school milk is provided (fewer and fewer schools do so), it will be charged for. As regards fares for school buses, the LEA cannot charge anything *if* the child lives further than 'walking distance' (*see* page 101 for what this means), but otherwise the authority can charge what it wishes.

Size of classes

In the past there was no fixed maximum number of pupils per class; the Direct Grant Schools Regulations 1959 simply stated that classes should not be 'over-crowded'. As from September 2001, a statutory requirement has been laid down to introduce a maximum class size of 30 for all 5-, 6- and 7-year-olds. Although maximum class sizes have generated much debate, there are at present no requirements for maximum class sizes for older pupils.

9

Disputes over Children

The Children Act 1989, which came into force on 14 October 1991, made dramatic changes in the law relating to children. Some of the most important changes were the new restrictions which affected when the law can be used to intervene in disputes involving children – both in private law (divorce and separation) and in public law (children in care). There is also a greater emphasis on *co-operation*; on parents being encouraged to try and sort problems out themselves without unnecessary court interference.

Although the Act has been in force for around a decade, some of its terms and concepts are still unfamiliar – even the media still use outdated terms like 'custody' and 'access', which have been consigned to the legal scrap heap. These old terms, as well as the new ones, are explained in this chapter, not least because some people may still have 'old-style' orders pre-dating the introduction of the Children Act 1989. Others may want to compare and contrast concepts which sound more familiar (even if they are outdated) with the new legal framework.

Main Aims of the Children Act 1989

- To change the way children are treated by the law, stressing adults' responsibilities towards children.
- To put children first: children's welfare is the court's paramount consideration in resolving disputes about them.
- To speed up the legal process and cut down delays in children cases.
- To reduce unnecessary court interference: courts can make an order only if it is better for the children to do so.
- To simplify the law so children are treated the same in the private (e.g. divorce) and public (e.g. children in care) law.
- To put local authorities under duties to provide services for children and to set local authorities standards that must be achieved.
- To respect family life: local authorities must promote the upbringing of children by their own families.

The Children Act 1989 had high ideals (*see* its aims above), many of which have been met, although some (like reducing delay) remain more of a wish list than a reality. Local authorities take the requirements of the Children Act seriously and have found their financial resources stretched to the maximum. The courts from time to time have found it hard to cope with the extra pressures on their timetables. But the Act has positive underlying messages for consumers (parents and children). Consumer power is considerably strengthened in the legal process: in theory parents now have more legal muscle to seek their proper rights, while they must also recognize their obligations towards their children. At the same time, children's views are being afforded increasing respect and courts have greater flexibility and creativity in deciding legal cases involving children. (*See* page 116 for the position on local authorities.)

The law on children faced a further shake-up, with the introduction of the Human Rights Act 1998 in October 2000 (*see* below for a summary of the key factors).

HUMAN RIGHTS ACT 1998 – ITS IMPACT ON FAMILY LAW IN ENGLAND AND WALES

The Human Rights Act 1998 ('the Act') was introduced into English law on 2 October 2000 and, thus, for the first time the UK courts are required to take these specific rights into consideration when deciding what to do in family cases (as well as other matters). Legal commentators anticipate that the most significant impact will be on children-related issues – although interestingly the Convention on Human Rights which is incorporated into the law here by the Act contains no specific rights for children. The key relevant section of the European Convention, Article 8, which is reproduced in the Act, is set out below.

Article 8

8.1 Everyone has the right to respect for his private and family life, his home and his correspondence.

8.2 There shall be no interference by a public authority with the exercise of this right except such as is in accordance with the law and is necessary in a democratic society in the interests of national security, public safety or the economic well-being of the country, for the prevention of disorder or crime, for the protection of health or morals, or for the protection of the rights and freedoms of others.

Three areas have been identified where the Act is likely to have an immediate effect: care proceedings, contact with an absent parent, and unmarried fathers.

Care proceedings

Any interference by a public authority must be 'in accordance with the law', Art 8.2. This means more than that there must be a legal basis for steps. Children cannot be taken into care by a local authority on the basis that it would be better for them to be cared for by foster parents: sufficient and weighty reasons must be given: *L v Sweden* (1984). Other important areas identified include the manner in which a child is taken into care and the way in which contact with the natural family is dealt with afterwards.

Contact with absent parent

A contact order (the new term for access order) even if it is made by the courts may be of little use if it is ineffective, and enforcement of contact may be an area which will be explored by the courts in future. In *Hokkanen* (1996), the state's failure to enforce a father's right to contact with his daughter was held to be in breach of Art 8.

Unmarried fathers

A recent case in the European Court of Human Rights held that it was not a breach of the European Convention on Human Rights for the current law in England and Wales to deny unmarried fathers automatic parental responsibility.

An unmarried father argued before the European Court of Human Rights that the law here was in breach of the Convention. The European Court of Human Rights thought otherwise. It held that this was discrimination that was objective and reasonably justified by the variety of relationships between unmarried couples. This ranged from ignorance and indifference to a close stable relationship indistinguishable from the conventional family-based unit:
see McMichael v UK, (1995), B v UK (2000)

This decision shows that the European dimension will not always provide the solution sought by those seeking redress.

Unmarried fathers who sign the birth certificate of their child may now acquire parental responsibility (*see further* page 80).

CHILDREN AND THE PRIVATE LAW: FAMILY BREAK-UPS

When parents decide to end their relationship, children can be caught in the middle as mother and father argue over who is to have them.

The law's paramount concern is for the welfare of the children and not the hurt feelings and pride of the parents. Generally, the courts take the approach that a child's welfare is best protected by ensuring that he or she retains links with both parents. Studies have shown that children cope much better with the trauma of separation and divorce if they continue to have regular contact with the parent who leaves as well as the parent who looks after them on a day-to-day basis. Children also are shown to benefit from being given lots of reassurance by both parents that while their own relationship as husband and wife has broken down, they will both still be there for the children and that they both love the children. Children appreciate clear explanations, appropriate to their age, about the separation and what practical arrangements will be made for the present and future. If parents can keep their own conflicts away from the children and let the children know that they will sort those issues out, again this has been shown to improve outcomes for children.

The law now gives parents who can co-operate with one another much greater flexibility to make their own arrangements for the children: courts will now make no court order unless it would be better for the children to do so. On the other hand, if parents (or even interested outsiders, like other family members) disagree over arrangements for the children, then the courts nowadays have wider powers to make simple but effective orders to sort out the problems.

The old law

The Children Act abolished the old familiar terms of 'custody', 'care and control' and 'access'. The new legal terms do *not* correspond exactly with the old law (*see* page 107. The boxes summarize the old and new concepts).

Old orders for children

Custody

This was the right to take the long-term decisions that affect the child. A parent with custody (properly called *legal custody*) had the ultimate legal responsibility for the child, but it did not necessarily follow that the child lived with that parent, since *legal custody* did not always equal *physical custody* of the child. Usually, the parent with custody also had actual physical custody of the child but not always. The most common order was for one parent to have sole custody, but sometimes a joint-custody order was made (custody to both parents jointly, but with only one of them having care and control).

The sort of decision that the parent with custody could make was choosing the method of education; the choice of religion; administering the child's property; vetoing the issue of a passport to the child; withholding consent to the child's marriage.

Care and control

This covered the day-to-day care of the child, and the responsibility for looking after it. It was called *actual custody* of the child, but did not include the right to make the sort of decisions that went with *legal custody*. Usually, of course, one parent was given both legal and actual custody of the child. But sometimes the court separated the two by making a joint order which gave legal custody to both parents jointly and actual custody to just one of them. By doing this, both parents were able to retain some influence over the child and neither felt totally excluded.

Access

This allowed the parent who did not have care and control to visit the child. The courts would only rarely refuse to allow access for they were always reluctant to sever a child's links with its natural parents. Only if the visits were likely to harm the child would access be refused, for the general rule was that the parent who failed to obtain custody would be granted access.

Usually, the court ordered 'reasonable access' (i.e. no fixed times) and would often allow more access as the child grew older. By the time the child was a teenager, he might be allowed to spend weekends with the parent or go away on holiday with him/her, although this would largely depend on the character and wishes of the child and the parents. These arrangements were usually agreed by parents – not ordered by the court.

The new law

Parental responsibility

Parental responsibility is defined as 'all the rights, duties, powers, responsibilities and authority which by law a parent of a child has in relation to the child and his property' (*see* pages 85–8 for what this means in practice):

Summary of Old and New Legal Concepts

The old law	The new law
Custody 'Custody' as interpreted by lawyers meant all the bundle of rights and responsibilities that parents have towards their children. It could be sole (in favour of one parent) or joint (shared between them). Sole custody gave a parent the right to decide issues about the child alone (although he or she should consult with the other parent). Joint custody meant that parents had to discuss and agree issues about children.	**Parental responsibility (PR)** PR means all the rights, duties, powers, responsibilities and authority parents have towards their children. PR is not lost on divorce. PR can be given to a non-parent. A person with PR can act independently of others with PR, but must not break any court order. Various 'section 8' orders can be made. The two principal ones are:
Care and control Care and control meant the day-to-day care of the child. It was sometimes called actual custody. Care and control could not be shared – it was given to one parent alone.	**1. Residence order** Residence orders state where the child will live and with whom. They can allow shared parenting (where children spend part of their time with mum and part with dad).
Access This allowed the parent who did not have care and control to visit the child and/or have the child to stay.	**2. Contact order** Contact orders require the person the child is living with to allow the child to visit or stay, or otherwise have contact, with the person named in the order.

Under the new law, all married parents have parental responsibility for their children. This lasts until the child reaches 18, whether or not the marriage lasts. (*See* page 10 for the position of unmarried parents.) The courts cannot take away parental responsibility from married parents unless an adoption order is made. The law thus recognizes the continuing blood tie that exists between children and their parents. The fact that each spouse will always have parental responsibility is intended to encourage absent parents (usually fathers) to take an active interest in their children's welfare. It means that fathers will not lose out on divorce since they keep parental responsibility (unlike under the old law, when they often lost custody).

Orders the courts can now make

All of the following orders are under section 8 of the Children Act 1989 and are thus referred to as 'section 8 orders'. They are intended to be much simpler than the old court orders and easier to grasp. So, instead of the old confusion about, for example, 'custody' – whether this meant legal custody or care and control (actual custody) – there is now a simple order for residence.

Residence order

This spells out where a child is to live. In most cases it will be with one parent (usually the mother). But it can allow for shared parenting, where children divide their time between their parents' homes.

Contact order

This requires the person with whom the child lives to allow contact (thus shifting the burden more to the parent looking after the child). It can be visits or stopovers, or can be by way of telephone calls or letters.

Specific issue order

This gives directions for the purpose of determining a specific question connected with parental responsibility – for example, which school the child should go to.

Prohibited steps order

This has the effect of restraining in some way the actions of a person in relation to the child. No step stated in the order can be taken without the consent of the court.

Both specific issue and prohibited steps orders have their origin in wardship proceedings, which have thus largely fallen into disuse. ('Wardship' means that the court becomes the legal 'parent' of the child and hence has the chief right to make decisions over the child's upbringing).

Although the courts have wide powers to make these section 8 orders, they are supposed *not* to use them without proper consideration. Court orders are now made only if it is better for the children to do so. There is, within the law, a presumption that it will usually be better for the children if their parents can agree between themselves how the children will be looked after (*see* also page 109).

Old cases

What happens where a court order under the old law has already been made?

Old orders

Where parents were married to each other when a child was born and where there is an existing order (usually an order for custody, care and control or access), then each will have parental responsibility for the child.

Where the parents were not married, the mother will have parental responsibility automatically; the father will have it automatically only if he had obtained an order for parental rights and duties or a custody or care and control order in his favour (but he can now apply for a parental responsibility order or a residence order which would give him parental responsibility).

If a parent, or anyone else, wants to change the old order, then the new application will be for a Children Act 1989 order.

Who looks after the children on divorce or separation?

On separation

Separating married parents can make their own voluntary agreement as to who will have primary care of the children and how much contact the other parent has. They both continue to have parental responsibility. Sometimes a provision about arrangements for the children is inserted in a *separation agreement* to record formally what the parents agree to do.

Such an agreement is not binding; parents can, in any event, apply to court for a residence order or contact order to regulate arrangements for the children. They do not have to wait until the divorce has been started to apply. An application can be made to the magistrates' court, a divorce county court designated as a Family Hearing Centre (*see* below) or the High Court.

The principle that the court will not make an order unless it is better for the children to do so will apply; but if arrangements are disputed, then it is likely that the court will make an order to resolve the problem. However, in by far the majority of divorce cases (90–95 per cent) parents do manage to make their own arrangements between themselves and no court order will be made.

Separating unmarried parents again can make their own agreement. The mother has parental responsibility automatically, so it is up to her usually to decide where the children will live. If the father too has parental responsibility (*see* page 85), he also has the right and responsibility to make decisions about the children's upbringing, so the parents should try to work out arrangements between themselves. If they cannot, consider mediation to resolve these issues (*see* page 40). As a last resort, again an application can be made for a residence or contact order.

On divorce

Divorcing parents both continue to have parental responsibility for the children even after the divorce. So they both technically have an equal say in what arrangements should be made for the children – where they will live, who will look after them, how often the other parent will visit and so on. In practice, the parent looking after the children on a day-to-day basis has more control over what happens to them.

In theory, this equal say can be exercised independently. That is, both parents can make up their own minds individually. But good parenting necessarily involves co-operation and negotiation, so parents should try to discuss with each other what will be best for the children. If they are still at stalemate, they could consider using their solicitors to try and negotiate for them or better still try mediation (*see* page 40). If there are still insoluble differences, then either can apply to court for a section 8 order.

No divorce decree can be made absolute without the court considering the arrangements for the children of the family. The court has to look at the arrangements and decide whether it is satisfied that a court order need not be made (*see also* page 45). In the vast majority of cases the divorce courts will not make court orders about the children but will leave it up to the parents to sort out arrangements between themselves.

'Children of the family' means the couple's own children (including adopted and legitimated children) and any child treated by them as one of the family. So arrangements made for a stepchild will also have to be put before the court.

Normally, only arrangements for children under 16 have to be put before the court. While parental responsibility lasts during the children's minority (until they are 18), court orders (i.e. section 8 orders) will not be made for children over 16 unless there are exceptional circumstances. But financial applications (e.g. for maintenance) can be made for a dependent child undergoing further education at any age.

When the parents agree about the children

Usually the parents are able to work out some satisfactory arrangement that they can both agree to. For instance, they may agree that the children are to live with the mother, while the father will look after them every other weekend and for a couple of weeks in the summer, alternating Christmas and other special days.

Parents now have more flexibility under the Children Act and can tailor-make arrangements to suit their own family. Agreements are encouraged under the law. If parents agree about where the children will live and who will care for them, they will be given the freedom to do so. The court should not reject arrangements just because they do not conform to traditional family patterns. So if parents want to share care of their children more equally, they can, for example, set up an arrangement so that the children spend term times with mum and holidays with dad. The test is whether the arrangements are in the best interests of the children. If they are, then the court will not interfere. But if the court thinks the proposals will put the children under stress, then it may intervene and will usually ask a court welfare officer to prepare a report to check that the children are coping satisfactorily.

Procedure at court

1 Before starting a divorce, the petitioner prepares a document called a Statement of Arrangements for the children and tries to agree its contents with the respondent. This form requires fairly detailed information about proposals for the children's upbringing, including details about:
   - the home (the number of living rooms and bedrooms, whether the house is rented or owned, who else lives at the home);
   - education (schools attended, any special educational needs, any fees payable);
   - child care details (which parent looks after the children, whether he or she works and, if so, who else looks after the children);
   - maintenance (payments made, whether or not under a court order, what agreements have been reached);
   - contact (whether the children see the absent parent and how *often*);
   - health; and
   - any other court proceedings.
   Present arrangements and any proposed changes must be set out.

2 If the petitioner and respondent agree with the contents of the form, they should both sign it. If the respondent does not agree with the contents of the form, he or she can file his/her own Statement of Arrangements once the divorce has started.

3 The petitioner starts off the divorce (*see* page 43), the papers are served by the court on the respondent and the respondent returns the acknowledgement of service.

4 Once the respondent has confirmed his/her consent to the divorce going ahead and the Statement of Arrangements, the district judge will look at the papers and consider the evidence.

   If satisfied that the court does not need to make an order about the children, the district judge will issue a certificate to this effect and neither husband nor wife has to go to court. No formal court order will be made. It will then be up to the parents to make the arrangements they have proposed work (although they can later apply to court for a court order if there are problems) or use mediation to resolve them.

If not satisfied that a court order need not be made (i.e. if the arrangements do not look as if they benefit the children or if for some other reason the district judge has doubts), the district judge may ask for more information. He or she will either set a date for a court hearing for the petitioner and respondent to attend personally, or ask for other evidence (usually statements) to be sent to court or ask for a welfare report so that a thorough investigation can be made.

5 If a court welfare report is ordered, the court welfare officer (often a trained probation officer) will visit both parents at home and discuss the children and their relationships with them. If the mother or father has acquired a new partner, then the officer may well want to know how she or he feels about looking after the children. The officer will also want to talk to other people who have relevant information, such as a social worker who has been involved with the parents and, sometimes, the children's schoolteachers. The children concerned may also be asked their own views, especially if they are old enough to have decided views and be able to express them. The welfare report will then go back to the court. The parents are entitled to copies of the report. If the district judge is then satisfied, a certificate will be issued.

6 Once a certificate is issued, the final decree of divorce (decree absolute) can be applied for.

For a summary of the steps in a divorce where the parents agree over arrangements for the children, *see* the chart on page 44.

When parents cannot agree

Mediation

If parents cannot agree but are healthily reluctant to become embroiled in a full-blown court battle, with its high emotional (and usually financial) costs, voluntary mediation is an option well worth considering (*see* page 40 for more details). Many courts around the country will require parents to try or at least consider mediation before they issue proceedings under the Children Act 1989, save in an emergency situation.

Going to court about the children

If the parents cannot reach agreement about arrangements for the children this will *not* make the divorce a 'defended divorce'. But it will mean that the divorce itself will take longer and may well be costlier.

In a disputed case, the petitioner or respondent will make an application for a section 8 order – usually a residence or contact order. The respondent will be able to send to the court his or her own proposals in another Statement of Arrangements. Applications for section 8 orders are best made by a solicitor; General Legal Help and/or Legal Representation should be available depending on the merits and financial criteria. An applicant may well be asked to attend a meeting with a mediator to explore the possibilities of mediation before the public funding application can be accepted, and mediation may well provide the forum for resolving the problems.

Once the court receives an application, it fixes a date for a preliminary hearing. That hearing is usually called a conciliation appointment (or 'in-court conciliation'), when a district judge and/or a court welfare officer will explore whether any agreement between the parents is possible. Other conciliation appointments can be set up if need be.

If the dispute is not then resolved, the court will make an order for directions. This will include a timetable for the preparation of evidence and a date when the case will be brought back to court for another hearing. Strict time limits apply. A parent who fails to comply with the time limits runs the risk of being accused of deliberate delay (recognized as being harmful to children by the Children Act) and will be in breach of a rule of court.

Separate representation for children

Children can make their own applications for section 8 orders under the Children Act, either by someone else (known as a 'next friend') or by themselves. The test for the court to hear an application made by a child him- or herself is whether the child has sufficient understanding to make such an application. This depends on the maturity of individual children: adolescents will certainly be covered but an articulate, mature 8-year-old may even be allowed to have a say.

A 'next friend' usually means the child's mother or father, but it could also be the official solicitor, who has power to act in children's cases in the High Court and the county court (but not in the magistrates' court). Public funding should be available.

In 2001, all the children's services – the Official Solicitor's Department, guardians *ad litem* and divorce court welfare officers – were brought together under one umbrella service. It is likely that the existing professionals will continue with their existing roles for the time being, but changes may occur over time as the bodies work together.

Evidence for the court

A welfare report will be prepared (by a different welfare officer than the one involved in any in-court conciliation) and copies will be supplied to both parents. This is a confidential document and must not be shown to anyone else (save the solicitors) without the court's permission. The solicitors will draw up formal statements setting out their clients' respective claims to the children and the reasons why the children should go to a particular parent (or whether contact should, or should not, be granted if there is a dispute about access). Sometimes other witnesses may be asked to give evidence – say, a grandparent or schoolteacher.

All evidence will be put before the judge or district judge when he or she hears the case, in private, in chambers. The courts try to take a clear, unemotional approach in children cases, even though the subject matter is highly charged for the parties. The judge will want both parents to be present so they can be questioned. The children may also be asked to attend court (usually from about nine years old); the judge may interview them in private but they will not be called in to witness the whole case. Often they will be asked to wait outside the court until the judge is ready to speak to them, so it is a good idea to arrange for an extra pair of hands to help with looking after them at court during the day.

The court's decision

The judge will then usually make an order. He or she will first have to consider whether making an order will be better for the children, but in a disputed case it is unlikely that no order will result unless the parents have reached a proper agreement and are both willing to make the agreement work in practice.

Judges are supposed to take objective decisions and not allow their own views to impinge on the outcome.

The father argued it was not in the best interests of the children to stay with their mother and her new partner, because the children had seen them naked and his six-year-old daughter had bathed with the mother's new partner (although they had since stopped behaving in this way). The father had involved the police and social services, who had seen no cause for concern. The court welfare officer was similarly unconcerned. Not so the judge, who found it 'startling' that this behaviour was acceptable. He awarded residence to the father. On appeal, the judge's views were found to be extreme. The judge had no basis to assume that the mother could not be trusted with the children. The case was sent back to another court for hearing.

Re W (Minors) (Residence Order) (1998)

In the great majority of cases, the judge will follow the welfare officer's recommendation, if any. If he or she does not, reasons must be given.

The decision as to who will have primary care for the children will usually be vital in deciding which spouse might be able to stay in the family home (i.e. via a possible transfer of a tenancy or transfer of an owner-occupied home), since the home will normally go to the spouse who looks after the children.

Which court?

Divorce

Most divorces are applied for in divorce county courts (or the Principal Divorce Registry at Somerset House, London). Under the Children Act, most divorce county courts have been designated 'Family Hearing Centres' and will be able to deal with contested applications as well as divorces alone. Some, however, will just be administrative centres, dealing with the paperwork for divorces; disputed cases will be transferred to the nearest Family Hearing Centre. Check with the local county court for details.

Children Act applications

Applications under the Children Act can be made in private law in the magistrates' court (Family Proceedings Court), Family Hearing Centre or High Court. The High Court is usually reserved for very complex or difficult cases (or those involving a lot of money in financial matters). If a divorce has already started, an application should be made in the divorce court. If this is a divorce county court, the court will transfer the case up to the local Family Hearing Centre. Public funding may be granted only for applications in lower courts (check with your solicitor).

The factors that decide a court case

The overriding principle is 'the child's welfare shall be the court's paramount consideration' (Children Act 1989 s1 (1)). In applying this principle, the court now has a checklist of matters it must look at. In particular:
- the ascertainable wishes and feelings of the child (in the light of the child's age and understanding);
- the child's physical, emotional and educational needs;
- the likely effect on the child of any change in circumstances;

- the child's age, sex and background and any characteristics the court considers relevant;
- any harm the child has suffered or is at risk of suffering;
- how capable each of the child's parents, and any other person in relation to whom the court considers the question to be relevant, is of meeting the child's needs;
- the range of powers available to the court.

The wishes and feelings of the child

The fact that the child's wishes and feelings have been placed at the top of the checklist emphasizes that children should be put first. The judge may ask to see the children in private in chambers without parents or legal advisers present, to talk to them and ask them what they want. More often their wishes and feelings will be explored by the court welfare officer when preparing the report.

Two children aged 10 and 11 wanted to stay in England and maintain contact with their father rather than go to Israel to live with their mother. The Court of Appeal quoted with approval the judge's words in an earlier (1992) case: 'Nobody should dictate to children of this age, because one is dealing with their emotions, their lives, and they are not packages to be moved around.'
M v M (1993)

The older the child, the more persuasive his or her views. Teenage children in any event 'vote with their feet' (i.e. live at the home of their choice). Little children may be asked to draw their wishes and feelings if they cannot put them into words. Often children will say that they just want their parents to get back together.

If the court suspects that children have been coached by one or other parent, 'their' opinions will carry little weight.

Although children's views will be respected, they should not be forced to choose unwillingly between two people both of whom they love. Ultimately it is up to the adults to make decisions.

The child's needs

The child's physical, emotional and educational needs are second on the list. If the child is very young or sickly or otherwise needs a mother's care, the mother is more likely to get the residence order. A good school near a parent's home where the child would be accepted as a pupil could also strengthen one parent's claim.

Splitting the family is always regarded as undesirable.

When husband and wife separated, one of their two children went to live with the mother, the other with the father. The mother appealed against the court order splitting custody and care and control between the parents. Held: Following divorce, siblings should, wherever possible, be brought up together so that they could give each other emotional support. The mother should have care and control of both children.
C v C (1988)

The effect of change

The courts have long acknowledged that changing the status quo will disrupt the child and thus compound the difficulties of adjusting to the parents' separation. So a parent who is already looking after the children will have a much stronger claim. This, however, does not apply if the children have been snatched from their usual home environment: the courts can act quickly to hand children back if they have been taken away from the parent best able to care for them.

Although the courts will normally want to make an order that will resolve a dispute for the foreseeable future (to ensure that the children are not going to and fro between the parents), in a borderline case the court may be forced to make the best short-term decision.

The wife went to live with another man. The husband stayed behind and looked after the daughter with the help of his mother and a woman friend. The mother applied for custody but failed; the court felt it was wrong to move a child from a home where she was happy to a home where she might or might not be happy. On appeal, held: This was a borderline case, decided in the child's best interests in the short term. The child should stay with the father but either parent could later apply to vary the order.
Thompson (1987)

The child's age, sex and background

In the past, generally the courts decided that a child's welfare was best protected by being with the mother rather than the father. This was only a general rule but it applied particularly to young children, especially babies. More recent cases have held that there is no presumption that the mother must always be considered as the primary carer over and above the father. It is not, for example, unusual for a court order to provide for older boys to live with their fathers. If one parent decides to leave and adopt a different lifestyle from the one the children are familiar with, the courts would take a critical view. However, if the mother has, in reality, been the chief carer of the children, then this situation is likely to continue after separation and divorce, although the children are entitled to be able to see their father regularly.

Harm or risk of harm

Alcoholism or violence (whether towards the other parent or the children) will prejudice a parent's case. A parent's homosexuality will be a factor taken into account but not necessarily a decisive one (unless the court thinks the children will be adversely affected).

If there is a risk of sexual abuse by a parent, that parent would definitely not get a residence order. A contact order might be given, but only if it would be in the child's best interests (e.g. if there is a strong bond between parent and child, if the parent is seeking treatment and if the contact is supervised properly).

At the end of the twentieth century, the Women's Aid Foundation mounted an awareness-raising campaign pointing out the links between applications for contact (access) to children and domestic violence. Where there were serious incidents of domestic violence, they pointed out that continuing contact with an absent parent could not be assumed automatically to be in a child's best interests. The campaign was given greater prominence and also made more poignant by a number of cases where contact with violent fathers was ordered and the children and/or their mothers were killed or brutally injured by the fathers.

The House of Lords, the highest court in the land, then decided appeals on four important cases which brought to an end the automatic presumption of contact where domestic violence had occurred. One of the cases, and the decision that applied in all four of the cases, is set out below:

There had been a series of violent incidents since the birth of the child in 1998 and the judge found that the mother's opposition to contact was based on a genuine fear of the father. Held: In a contact application where domestic violence has been proven, the court must consider the conduct of the parties to each other and the children, the effect on the children and the residential parent and the motivation of the parent seeking contact. The court should ensure, as far as it could, that any risk to the child was minimized and the safety of the child and the residential parent was secured.

In Re L (A Child) (Contact: Domestic Violence) (2000)

Capability of the parents and other carers

This can range from practical factors, like whether either parent works outside the home, to the ability to respond to the child's needs. Overall it is a matter of trying to assess which will be the better parent, and sometimes the claims of both will be equal.

Note: this does not refer to the parents' conduct as individuals and a distinction must be drawn between a person's behaviour as a parent and as a partner.

The husband was a clergyman. His wife had an affair and told her husband she wanted to leave, taking the children with her. The husband applied for custody. Held: Although the husband was of unimpeachable conduct, it was in the best interests of the children that they should be with their mother – despite the fact that she was the 'guilty' party.

Re K (1977)

A parent who can offer a stable home life (perhaps particularly if remarrying) will obviously have a stronger claim than a parent who is unreliable. A parent who walks out on the children or puts the interests of a lover above those of the children may well be at a disadvantage when making an application for a residence order.

Where relatives or other people (like nannies or child-minders) are involved in looking after the children, their capabilities too will have to be examined.

The courts' powers

The courts' powers under the Children Act are much wider; so they might be expected to come up with more creative solutions than in the past. For example, residence orders can be split between both parents. Thus if both parents are equally capable and the children want to share their time with each parent, the court could make a residence order specifying, for example, that the children would spend two weeks with the father and then two weeks with the mother so that the parents have the opportunity of sharing care of the children. But the court would have to be convinced that unusual arrangements are in the children's best interests.

Financial considerations should not weigh too heavily with the courts, as they have powers to make appropriate divisions of capital and maintenance orders so that children are properly provided for where possible.

Appeals

Successful appeals against first-instance decisions are extremely rare. The trial judge has wide discretion and appeals will be allowed only if the first decision can be shown to be 'plainly wrong'. This is so even if the Court of Appeal feels it would have come to another decision itself. However, if further important evidence comes to light, then an appeal might work.

Both husband and wife sought custody of the children. The father alleged that the mother had a violent temper and had committed adultery with D. The judge found that the mother was a liar with a bad temper and used bad language, but she would control herself and did not intend a permanent relationship with D. It was best for young children to be with their mother. The husband appealed, showing that D and the mother now lived together and that the mother had been violent. Held: The children should go to live with their father. The fresh evidence undermined the basis of the judge's findings.

A v A (1988)

Usually it will not be worthwhile appealing against an order. A parent unhappy with a court's decision would usually do better to wait for some time to pass (at least a year) and then reconsider whether circumstances have changed so that a fresh application to court might be warranted. For example, a father of a 10-year-old boy, when a residence order was given to his ex-wife, could wait until the boy becomes a teenager and then see if his son wants to come to live with him for longer periods of time.

Stepfamilies

Stepfathers and stepmothers occupy a special place, having taken on the burden (and joys!) of an actual parent but without being recognized by the law as such. However, under the new law the greater flexibility of the courts' new powers can be helpful for stepfamilies.

Step-parents do not automatically have parental responsibility during a marriage (or even after divorce) for their stepchildren. Parental responsibility belongs to both the father and the mother (if the parents were married at the time of the birth) or to the mother alone if the parents were unmarried. So step-parents cannot in law make decisions about a stepchild's upbringing themselves, although they will usually be involved in decision making via the parent (their partner).

To change this, and to become recognized by the law as having the role of a parent, a step-parent could apply for a residence order jointly with his or her new partner if the children are living with them. This indirectly gives him or her parental responsibility – residence orders can be made in favour of two people jointly.

The court will have to consider whether making an order is better for the children than making no order at all, but might grant such an application, particularly if the absent parent takes little or no interest in the children and the step-parent is particularly involved. The court would want to be satisfied that the new arrangement is stable.

Another option would be for the step-parent to apply jointly with his new spouse (the parent) for an adoption order. The courts are, however, unlikely to grant this as they are unwilling to terminate the links with natural parents.

On the death of the partner (the parent), the step-parent has no automatic rights vis-à-vis the stepchildren. If the parents were married at the time of the birth, then the other parent (not the step-parent) would automatically take over responsibility for looking after the children and the step-parent would be shut out. If the step-parent wanted to continue looking after the children, then again he or she would have to apply for a residence order.

To protect against this, particularly in situations where the absent parent has lost interest in the children, the parent (partner), while living, could make a will or deed appointing the step-parent as a guardian of the child on his or her death. But to make the position watertight, the step-parent and parent should apply jointly to the court for a residence order too, as otherwise the appointment as a guardian will not take effect until the death of the surviving parent (which defeats the object of an appointment).

Applications by grandparents and other relatives

When a marriage ends, sometimes the contact between children and their grandparents ends too, as families place themselves in opposing camps. This is rarely in the children's best interests: often children can be helped to cope with their distress by grandparents (or other mentors) who can offer a sympathetic (and non-partisan) shoulder to cry on.

Grandparents (or, for that matter, any other interested adult) can apply to the court for a contact order, a residence order or any other section 8 order. They do not have to wait until divorce proceedings have been started (as under the old law). If the parents divorced under the old law, grandparents can now make an application under the new law.

A grandparent (or any other interested adult) has the right to apply automatically to court for a section 8 order if:

- the child has lived with him or her for three years or more;
- they have the consent of the person with a residence order in their favour; or
- they have the consent of everyone with parental responsibility.

Otherwise, they have to get the court's permission to apply. The court will take into consideration:

- the nature of the proposed application;
- the applicant's connection with the child;
- the risk of harmful disruption to the child's life.

If grandparents have lost contact with the children over many years or had a bad influence on the children, then it is possible that their application for permission to apply to court will fail. But, usually, the court will grant permission to apply and leave an investigation of the facts to a full court case.

Applications for contact for grandparents will usually be granted unless there is deep bitterness between the families which would be exacerbated by making a contact order. Contact orders can be in the form of letters, cards and telephone calls, so the court may make an order for contact in stages, building up contact from letters and telephone calls before a face-to-face meeting if there has been no contact for a long time.

Applications for residence orders are unlikely to stand a chance of success unless the natural parents are in support.

The case involved a family of eight children (by five different fathers). One of the children caused serious problems and the mother sent her youngest son D to stay with a sister of his deceased father (i.e. his aunt) for the boy's own protection. After the problem sibling had left home, the aunt who was looking after D applied for residence although the boy, now 13, was anxious to return home. At the first hearing the justices gave a residence order in favour of the aunt. The mother successfully appealed. Held: While the welfare of the child was the test, there was a strong supposition that other things being equal, it is in the interests of the child to remain with his natural parents.

Re D (Residence: Natural Parent) (1999)

Taking a child abroad

The usual rule is that a parent who wants to take a child abroad (this includes going to Scotland) should obtain the other parent's written consent first. This is because it is a criminal offence to remove a child from the country without the written consent of both parents or the consent of the court.

Where a parent simply wants to take the child on holiday, if he or she has a residence order in his or her favour, he or she can take the child abroad for a period of up to a month. If the other parent objects, an application can be made to court for its permission by way of a section 8 order. (*See* page 116 concerning child abduction.)

If there is no residence order, the civil law says nothing either to permit or to prevent a parent from taking a child abroad. Again, if parents are in dispute, one or other should apply for a section 8 order.

But whether a residence order exists or not, the criminal law still applies.

Emigration

Emigration will of course affect children long-term and different considerations apply.

If a parent looking after the children wishes to emigrate with the children, in the past the court usually allowed him or her to do so, even if this meant that the other parent would have great difficulty in seeing the children in future.

Under the new law, however, the welfare checklist must be applied. It is arguable that if older children were adamantly opposed to the move and the other parent had sound plans for caring for them, an application to take the children abroad might be refused. By and large, however, a soundly based application to remove the children out of the country will be granted. In essence, the court's view is that there had to be some compelling reason to justify the court preventing the custodial parent from taking a reasonable decision to live outside the jurisdiction. This case is one of the few exceptions to that overall rule.

After the break-up of the marriage, the father (F) had contact with the daughter every third weekend with shared half-term and school holidays. The mother (M) told F she planned to marry Dr C and to move with him and her daughter to his home in Singapore – Dr C had a two-year contract to work as a doctor there. F applied for a prohibited steps order and a residence order – M cross-applied for leave to take the child out of the jurisdiction permanently. Held: The presumption that a child should be allowed to leave where a custodial parent had made a reasonable decision to move was outweighed by the fact that the child would be unable to bond with F and that it would ultimately result in her growing up in Singapore with, at best, only a few weeks a year with F and his family.

Re C (Leave to Remove from Jurisdiction) (2000)

The definitive case on removal from the jurisdiction is the Court of Appeal's decision in *Payne*.

The mother proposed moving permanently to New Zealand where her new husband had employment. The Court held that the reasonable proposals of the parent with a residence order wishing to live abroad carried great weight. Provided the Court was satisfied that the mother's motives were genuine and not intended to end contact between the child and the father, leave would normally be granted. It was important to look at the effect of refusal of leave on the applicant parent and the child's new family. Payne (2001)

The decision in *Payne* was further considered by the Court of Appeal in 2003 in the case of *Re B.*

The mother wanted to relocate to South Africa with her children. The fact that she was not in a position to marry her new partner was held to be unimportant. Her commitment to him was a decisive factor. The children's welfare could not be achieved unless the new family had an opportunity to pursue its goals and make choices without unreasonable restriction.

Changing the child's name

Under the Children Act, when a residence order is made parents cannot change the child's surname without consent (of the other parent or the court). But if no order is made, there is, theoretically, no legal requirement specifically preventing a parent with parental responsibility from changing the name. So, in theory, either parent, so long as they have parental responsibility, could change the child's surname; the other will have to apply to court for a prohibited steps order or a specific issue order to stop the change. As long as this is done quickly, the court will probably agree that the old family name should be kept. But if the child has had a new name for a long time and has adjusted to being known by the new surname, the court would probably take the view that to change the name back again would be confusing and so the new name could be retained.

The mother of a child born within a marriage had registered the child under her own (maiden) name. The father discovered this within a few months, but did not take any action for two years. He then applied for a surname change for the child under a specific issue order so that the child's name would either be changed to his own name or that his name should be added to the mother's for the child's surname, so as to make up a double-barrelled surname. Held: No. The father had not taken any action for two years and his application would be dismissed as it was not in the child's best interests for the surname to be changed.

A v Y (1999)

What if the child himself wants to change his surname? Since the case of *Gillick* was decided, a child of 'sufficient maturity and understanding' to appreciate the nature and importance of the proposed change of name would probably be allowed to change the surname himself or herself. This would definitely cover older teenagers; for younger children it will depend on their own individual maturity and articulateness. If there is any doubt, in any event a young person of 18 can change their name without any parental consent being needed.

Emergency disputes

Sometimes the court has to act quickly to protect a child. For example, the parents might break up and one of them might try to snatch the child and perhaps take it abroad. Similarly, the child may need to be prevented from doing something that would be to its own disadvantage – for instance, a 16-year-old might be planning to elope with someone wholly unsuitable. Under the old law, the solution was usually to make the child a ward of court, so that the court took over the role of legal parent. Children who were made wards of court were immediately prevented from leaving the country and no significant step could be taken concerning them without the court's permission.

Since the Children Act 1989 came into force, there are other court orders that can be applied for – prohibited steps orders and specific issue orders – that are effective and can be granted in an emergency. It is thus likely that applications for wardship will become less frequent. The new orders can stop children from being taken out of the country but otherwise will not freeze any other action; the remedies are specific, not blanket cover-alls.

The child's welfare will be the court's paramount consideration and the usual governing principles of the Children Act will apply: a court order will be granted only if it is in the child's best interests. Mature children will be given their own say too.

Child abduction

If a parent is suspected of intending to take a child abroad, action must be taken fast. Prevention is far easier than cure. Although there are legal remedies for the return to the UK of abducted children, these are time-consuming at best and useless at worst (if a child is taken to a country outside an international convention where signing countries agree to enforce each other's court orders).

The first step is to get legal advice (public funding should be available but will be subject to means and merits tests). The solicitor will usually apply for a prohibited steps order, which can be applied for *ex parte* (without telling the other parent in advance) on the same day, even by telephone if necessary. A prohibited steps order can prevent the other parent from abducting the child abroad, but the other parent must be physically served with the document.

If there is a real and imminent danger of the child being abducted (real and imminent means within 24 hours) a solicitor (or even a parent) can ask the police to issue a 'port alert'. The police will need personal details of the child and abductor, a description of their appearances and photographs if possible. They will want sight of any court order too. The police can then immediately notify all air and sea ports, whose officials will then be on the lookout for the abductor and child. Their task will be hard if the abductor flees from a busy terminal (and has been even harder post-1993 after the relaxation of border controls). If at all possible, try to supply specific details of which flight or boat crossing the abductor plans to take.

CHILDREN AND THE PUBLIC LAW: LOCAL AUTHORITIES AND CHILDREN

The burden of the responsibilities towards vulnerable children envisaged by the Children Act falls very heavily on local authorities. They have new duties not just towards children in care but towards all children who live in their area, with special extra duties towards 'children in need' (as defined in the Act).

Under the Children Act 1989, all children have a right to basic standards of care, nurture and upbringing. Where the parents fall short, local authorities are supposed to fill the gap. The services they provide are supposed to meet each child's identified needs and be appropriate in terms of the child's race, culture, religion and linguistic background.

In practice, the success of these aims has been curtailed by local authorities' limited resources. Many social services departments are already stretched to breaking-point, so while the rights set out here are laid down by law, in reality trying to exercise many of the more idealistic 'rights' might more likely lead to a complaint to the new complaints panels (which the local authorities also have had to set up) rather than direct effective action.

However, a recent case has opened up the possibilities of local authorities being held liable in negligence for their actions. This decision could force them to take action in areas where people feel strongly that they have been neglectful. At the time of going to press the final outcome was unknown, but you could check with a specialist solicitor to find out more.

Foster parents had spelled out their concerns to the local authority not to place their own children at risk by having any known sex abuser in their home when they fostered children for the council. A foster child, a boy who had already, unknown to them, committed acts of abuse, was placed with them and thereafter abused their own natural children. The foster parents tried to sue the council for damages in negligence for their psychiatric injury arising out of the placement. Held: 'It could not be said that the claim that there was a duty of care owed to the parents and a breach of duty by the defendants was unarguable, or that it was clear and obvious that it could not succeed.' In other words, the parents should at least be given the opportunity of pursuing the claim to trial. The hurdles they still face are significant – they may well have to ask the courts to extend the definition of psychiatric injury for one and also show that they fell within a category of primary or secondary victims. W v Essex County Council (2000)

Local authorities' duties to all children in their area

Local authorities have much greater powers to regulate and control services for all children in their area. Minimum standards of care and safety must be met by childminders and nurseries, all of whom have to register with the local authority. Nurseries and childminders who look after children under 8 years old for more than two hours per day for payment must apply for registration with the local authority and be vetted in advance. If they fail to do so the services they offer are illegal and they could face a fine.

Parents can check with the local authority for lists of registered childminders and nurseries (contact the local social services department), which should be provided free. If parents feel that the services fail to meet the standards laid down, they can complain to the local authority, which is under a duty to investigate.

Local authorities' duties to children in need

Children in need are defined by the Children Act 1989 thus:
- being unlikely to achieve or maintain or to have the opportunity of achieving or maintaining a reasonable standard of health or development without the provision for the child of services by a local authority;
- if the child's health and development is likely to be significantly impaired or further impaired without the provision for him of such services; or
- if the child is disabled.

The local authority is under two special duties towards children in need:
- to safeguard and promote the welfare of children within its area who are in need; and
- so far as is consistent with that duty, to promote the upbringing of such children by their families.

Disabled children

Local authorities must maintain a register of disabled children within their area. They must also provide services designed to minimize the effect of their disabilities and to give such children the opportunity to lead lives which are as normal as possible.

Services for children in need

Local authorities must provide three types of services for children in need (these services must be reviewed once every three years):

1 *Services for children in need who live with their families.* Under the umbrella aim of promoting children's upbringing within their own families, the local authority must provide a range of services designed to support the families who look after them. This includes advice and counselling, occupational and recreational activities, home help (which may include laundry facilities) and assistance enabling the families to have a holiday.

2 *Family Centres.* The local authority must provide 'such Family Centres as it considers appropriate' in relation to children in its area. The idea of Family Centres is to provide within a comparatively informal and homely setting a place where absent parents and children can meet (as an alternative to trailing around the park on a rainy day or McDonald's) and again where services for children can be centred. The law envisages that such services could include activities (occupational, social, cultural and recreational), advice and counselling, and even accommodation.

3 *Day care.* The local authority must provide day care for children in need under five not yet going to school, and for those of school age outside school hours and during school holidays.

Local authorities' duties towards children in care

Under the old pre-Children Act law (before 14 October 1991), when a child was taken into care the local authority usually took over parents' rights and responsibilities. This was the case whether the child was in voluntary care or under a proper care order.

Nowadays, parents retain their own rights and responsibilities, which they may share with the local authority. The concept of voluntary care has been abolished, and the right of local authorities to ask for a care order for children has been much restricted. Local authorities must provide accommodation for children who need it (*see* below under Provision of accommodation by local authorities), but providing accommodation for a child does not give them the right to assume the role of a parent.

Local authorities have to work in partnership with parents. They are under a duty to promote contact between children being looked after by them and their parents. What that means in practice is that they must first exhaust the possibilities of children being looked after by their own families before making other accommodation arrangements for them. Also, if they do make arrangements for children to be accommodated, they must work with the parents rather than making their own independent choices. Parents have to be given opportunities to have regular contact with their children and have a right to be consulted on arrangements made for them.

Provision of accommodation by local authorities
The Children Act stresses the fact that children should be brought up within their own homes and the need for partnership in working with children and their families, and for avoiding court appearances, except where necessary, to safeguard and promote the welfare of the child.

Local authorities are under a duty to provide accommodation for any child in need (*see* above for definition) within their area who appears to require accommodation as a result of:
- there being no person who has parental responsibility for him;
- his having been lost or having been abandoned; or
- the person who has been caring for him being prevented (whether or not permanently and for whatever reason) from providing him with suitable accommodation or care.

If the local authority provides accommodation for a child in need, both the child's wishes and the parents' role are important. Local authorities must find out what the child wishes to do and properly consider those wishes. The local authority also cannot continue to provide accommodation in the face of an objection from a parent with parental responsibility who is willing and able to provide a home (or arrange for accommodation to be provided).

Even more importantly, any person with parental responsibility for the child can take the child away from local authority accommodation at any time. (Under the old law, 28 days' notice had to be given; now the removal is allowed to take place immediately.) In practice, because local authorities want to have a degree of certainty in making arrangements for the children, they will try to make an agreement with the parent(s) about giving notice to take the child away.

Grounds for taking a child into care
Where local authorities:
1. are informed that a child who lives, or is found, in their area
   - is the subject of an emergency protection order; or
   - is in police protection; or
2. have reasonable cause to suspect that a child who lives or is found in their area is suffering, or is likely to suffer, significant harm, the authority shall make, or cause to be made, such inquiries as they think necessary to enable them to decide whether they should take any action to safeguard or promote the child's welfare.

Note: the local authority do not have to take action, just investigate.

Before a court will make a care or supervision order, it must be satisfied:
1. that the child has suffered or is likely to suffer significant harm; and
2. that the harm, or likelihood of harm, is attributable to
   - the care given to the child, or likely to be given to him if the order were not made, not being what it would be reasonable to expect a parent to give to him; or
   - the child's being beyond parental control.

These grounds have become known as the 'threshold criteria'. They are designed to prevent the knee-jerk response of taking a child into care. So, first the local authority must investigate before they can take action. Usually this will involve a full case conference (which the parents would normally be asked to attend). See chart opposite about taking a child into care.

Significant harm
The crucial phrase 'significant harm' turns on comparing the child's health and development with what could 'reasonably be expected of a similar child'. So it will not be enough simply to show that the child concerned would be better off living somewhere else than with the parent(s). The phrase 'similar child' can be argued to be read so as to take into account the parents' racial, social and cultural background. Most cases involve neglect or abuse – physical, sexual or emotional – in some shape or form, but all aspects of a child's development will be considered, as the following case shows.

This case concerned a 15-year-old girl who had been playing truant for three years. Many efforts had been made by the local authority to make her attend school, but none of these had worked. The council argued that if the girl's truancy was not stopped, it would have a profound effect on her ability to cope with adult life, and her emotional and social development would be threatened. Their view was

Taking a Child into Care

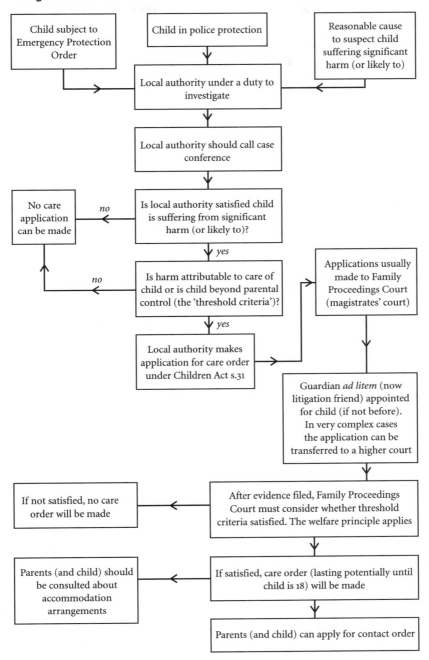

supported by the guardian ad litem. *It was said that her refusal to go to school 'will have a major impact on her self-esteem, her self-confidence and her perception of herself ... it will also seriously impair her ability to relate to peers and adults in a more formal way. This will inhibit [the girl's] development because school is, of course, not only about intellectual learning, it also provides young people with necessary social and relationship skills'.* Held on appeal: *It was open for the magistrates' court to come to the view that the girl's intellectual and social development was suffering and, hence, that she was suffering and was likely to suffer significant harm. The care order was confirmed.*

Re O (A Minor) (Care Order: Education: Procedure) (1992)

In cases of neglect or abuse, the local authority will usually have to prove that the parents were at fault. Where there are factual disputes – for example, over whether injuries were accidental or non-accidental, and who caused the injuries – then it will not be possible for any firm recommendations to be made as to what should happen to the child until these issues have been resolved. In such circumstances, the court will often order a split hearing – and direct an early hearing to deal with the factual issues in dispute.

An interim care order may be made instead of an indefinite order. These usually last for no more than four weeks, but at the first hearing an interim care order may be made for up to eight weeks as a one-off.

Beyond parental control

This would cover a child who persistently commits crimes (even if it is too young to be charged), persistently plays truant and gets involved with a gang of troublemakers or when the parents cannot control it any more. But the local authority should explore first whether steps can be taken to keep the child within the family by providing the family with help so that they can exert proper control over the child. This ground is used more rarely than the above ground, but could cover situations where a child has become addicted to drugs, or is sexually promiscuous, or has developed anorexia nervosa and the parents are powerless to influence the child's behaviour.

A child aged 13 was very seriously disturbed and behaving in an uncontrollable fashion, such that she was posing a serious risk to herself and to those around her, which the parents could do nothing to prevent. Held: *She should be taken into care.*　　M *v* Birmingham City Council (1994)

Interim care orders and exclusion orders

The Family Law Act 1996 introduced interim care orders as an adjunct to making an exclusion order to get someone out of the house where a child is living. The purpose of this two-fold approach is to give the courts extra power to take action if it is shown that a particular individual is harming or is likely to harm a child, and the parent himself or herself will take no action. If, for example, a mother started a new relationship with an abusive man and refused to end the relationship and get the man out of the house, even though she was aware he was abusive, an application could be made for an interim care order and exclusion order. This power has been available since October 1997. The exclusion order can be backed up by a power of arrest if necessary.

Special child protection orders

The old place-of-safety orders were abolished under the Children Act and the Act has also severely limited the use local authorities can make of the more flexible wardship proceedings. There are three types of child protection order which can be applied for by local authorities and the NSPCC:

1　Child Assessment Orders.
2　Emergency Protection Orders.
3　Recovery Orders.

Child Assessment Orders

The purpose of a Child Assessment Order (CAO) is to supplement the powers of social workers to organize an assessment of the child's emotional, physical and psychological well-being. They will probably be used where the grounds for an Emergency Protection Order (EPO) are not met but there is real concern about the child: for example, if a child suddenly fails to attend a local authority nursery without explanation or if a parent unreasonably fails to take the child for health visitor tests. However, the court should not make a CAO if the grounds are satisfied for an EPO and that would be a better order.

The CAO grounds are that the child is suffering or likely to suffer significant harm and an assessment is necessary to further determine the harm. A litigation friend should be appointed. Only the local authority or the NSPCC can apply and an order will last for a maximum of seven days.

Emergency Protection Orders

Emergency Protection Orders allow immediate compulsory intervention on a child's behalf, while the parents are given a reasonable opportunity to challenge the grounds for the intervention: they can be challenged after 72 hours.

They cover two main situations. First (most likely to be used where the child is in hospital and a parent unreasonably threatens to remove the child), if the child is likely to suffer significant harm if he or she does not remain in current accommodation (or if the child is not taken to this accommodation). Second, if the local authority's or the NSPCC's inquiries are being frustrated by being denied access to a child. In both cases the significant-harm grounds must also be proved and again a litigation friend will be appointed. EPOs will last for a maximum of eight days. Since October 1997, the court can also make an exclusion order against an actually or potentially abusive person getting him out of the house to protect a child. The exclusion order can be backed up by a power of arrest if necessary.

Recovery Orders

Recovery Orders allow a child to be recovered if someone has snatched the child: they order someone to produce a child who has been wrongly taken away. These are most likely to be used where parents are on the run, trying to avoid the local authority.

Secure accommodation orders

Another somewhat draconian step which can be taken by social services is to provide 'secure accommodation': where a child in care or being accommodated by social services can be locked up in a secure accommodation unit (a residential placement). Children must usually be between 13 and 18 to be placed in secure accommodation (a child under 13 can only be locked up with special permission), and the maximum stay is limited to 72 hours (three days) unless social services asks the court for a longer period. This provision can be used where a child has run away from a placement previously and social services are concerned it will happen again, or if the child has attempted suicide or might hurt other people.

Representatives for children

It is not often easy for children to voice their wishes and feelings; even when they do voice them, they can be ignored. To give children a proper say in adult proceedings, the Children Act provided for litigation friends to be appointed in any proceedings taken by the local authority.

They will act as the children's representatives in court, preparing for going to court by interviewing the parents, the child and anyone else who is concerned. They will have access to files which would otherwise be confidential – the local authorities' and NSPCC files, for example. Unlike private law proceedings (e.g. divorce or applications for a residence order), there is no test that a child has to satisfy before a representative is appointed for him or her. A litigation friend will always be appointed to act for the child and the child will also always have his or her solicitor (drawn from a panel of childcare specialists). Public funding for legal representation is available without a means test.

Litigation friends are usually trained family experts drawn from a panel of counsellors. Their role in court proceedings will be powerful and should act as a counterbalance to the adversarial stances often taken by the parents and local authorities. As mentioned above, there are structural changes planned to the way in which the service of the guardians *ad litem* operates but this should not affect the appointment of a guardian in a case.

Where children in care will live

Before the local authority decides where to place a child in care, it has to consult the child himself, the parents, anyone with parental responsibility, and even anyone else whose wishes and feelings the authority thinks to be relevant.

If a child already in a residential home is unhappy with the placement, he or she should complain to his or her social worker. Children can also complain about their treatment while in care: the new complaints procedures are designed to prevent another 'pin-down' occurring.

Contacting a child in care

It is not just the responsibility of parents of children who are in care to have contact with them. Local authorities are under a special duty to promote contact between children in care and their families, unless this is not 'reasonably practicable or consistent with the child's welfare'. If the local authority refuses to allow contact, then parents (including unmarried fathers), anyone who had a residence order made in their favour and even the child itself can apply to court for a contact order automatically (others have to seek the court's permission first). If the application is refused, then the applicant will have to wait for six months before applying again.

Access to confidential information held by social services

Children have a right to apply for access to social services files compiled since April 1989 provided they understand the nature of the request.

When children leave care

Local authorities are under a duty to provide aftercare services between the ages of 16 and 21 to a young person who was in care. They must 'advise, assist and befriend him with a view to promoting his welfare, when he ceases to be looked after by them'. This provision applies to young people who were looked after by a voluntary organization too.

The aim of aftercare is to smooth the transition between institutionalized care (which can often create dependency) and the harsh realities of an independent life in the outside world. The assistance can be in the form of cash. How much will depend very much on the local authorities' resources and, in practice, will sadly often be zero.

Contact the local social services department for further details.

10

Children, Safety and the Law

Every day three children die from accidents, 300 are seriously injured and 3,000 are taken to hospital. Levels of injury from accidents have reached what one television presenter (Anneka Rice) described in 1991 as 'epidemic proportions'. Of course, not all accidents can be prevented, but the law does provide some compensation for injuries and does set safety standards in a number of areas.

ACCIDENTS AT SCHOOL

A school is responsible for the safety and well-being of its pupils. If the school or a member of its staff is negligent, then the school will be liable in damages. Similarly, the school will be liable if the premises are unsafe.

Two boys were playing with a swing door. As a result of horseplay, a child put his hand through a glass panel in the door. The glass was an eighth of an inch thick. **Held:** *The school was liable. Whilst the glass was thick enough for normal domestic use, it was not suitable for the rough and tumble of school life.*   Lyes (1962)

Was it negligent to allow a child – aged seven years and two months – to select sharp-pointed scissors for use in an art class? **Held:** *The teacher had been negligent and the education authority was liable for £10,000 damages for the serious eye injury caused.*   Black (1983)

ACCIDENTS INVOLVING CHILDREN: GENERAL DUTY OF CARE

Anyone employed to work with children and young people, whether voluntarily or otherwise, is under a legal duty of care which has been interpreted by the courts as a duty to act as a careful parent would. This means that if a worker carries out his or her responsibilities negligently he or she, or the organization for which they

work, could be held liable under civil law and would have to compensate the child with damages.

Adequate records should be kept of any accidents or injury, or even altered behaviour, of children. The records may need to be produced in evidence in court.

Employees working with children ought also to be aware of health and safety legislation, as well as the duty under the Children and Young Persons Act to provide sufficient safety precautions if large-scale entertainments are planned involving more than 100 children (*see also* page 602).

ACCIDENTS IN PLAYGROUNDS

Parents can reasonably assume that playgrounds are safe. Owners or managers of playgrounds are under a statutory duty to equip and run playgrounds to ensure that children are not exposed to risks to their health and safety. They are liable for any injury which they could reasonably have foreseen; a higher duty of care must be shown towards children (even trespassers) under the Occupiers' Liability Act 1984.

If children are hurt because of unsafe equipment or the play area itself (from, for example, jagged broken netting surrounding it) or if there was no supervision and there should have been, claims could be made for resulting injuries.

DOGS AND CHILDREN

If a dog physically attacks a child (or adult) it must usually be destroyed: there is no rule that the dog is allowed 'one bite'. But you do not have to wait until a child has actually been hurt before action can be taken against a dog's owner. It is also an offence under the Dangerous Dogs Act 1991 to allow a dog to be dangerously out of control (maximum fine £2,000 or six months' imprisonment). If the dog also causes injury to anyone, this is an aggravated offence with a maximum penalty of two years' imprisonment. So, if there are good grounds for suspecting that a dog will injure someone – if the dog's owner refuses to secure the dog and it is trying to attack passers-by, for example – the police can take action. Owners can be ordered to muzzle or leash any breed of dog they consider dangerous (not just the four breeds mentioned below) and owners can be disqualified from having a dog.

Special breeds

Following the vicious attack on 6-year-old Rucksana Khan by a pit bull terrier in 1991, the government tightened up laws on some breeds of dog viewed as being dangerous: the pit bull terrier, the Japanese tosa, and the unlikely named dogo argentino and fila braziliero. Owners who wanted to keep their dogs had to obtain a certificate of exemption by 1 March 1992. Strict rules now mean owners of these dog breeds must:

- have third-party insurance to cover against the dog causing injury or damage; and
- keep the dog muzzled in public places and keep it on a lead in charge of someone aged at least 16.

Breaking any of these rules is a criminal offence and can result in a fine of up to £2,000 and the dog's destruction.

Parents may also have a remedy under the civil law if the dog is bred for fighting (like the American pit bull terrier, the Japanese tosa and 'bandogs'). Under the Animals Act 1971, the keeper of a dangerous animal (defined as a species or breed not commonly domesticated in the UK and which, when full grown, is likely to cause severe damage unless restrained) is liable in civil law for any injury or damage it may cause.

But what happens if the dog's owner does not have proper insurance cover for the dog? In practice, the first thing to do is to see if the dog's owner has a house insurance policy, since this will often cover liability for animals. If the dog owner does not have a policy, it may still be worthwhile making a claim against the owner if the victim has a domestic insurance policy: many of these policies have clauses which will pay damages and costs if the insured obtains a judgment in an action for personal injury and if that judgment remains unsatisfied. It is worthwhile seeking legal advice if a claim is intended to be made (*see further* Chapter 25).

ALCOHOL AND TOBACCO

There are specific laws which protect young people from the hazards of alcohol and tobacco.

Alcohol

The law allows children to go into pubs only in limited circumstances. It puts much of the responsibility for protecting children from alcohol on publicans (or other licence holders), who can be fined if they break any of the following regulations:

- children under five cannot be given alcohol except on medical grounds;
- children under 18 can be allowed into licensed premises at any time if they are accompanied by someone over 18, provided that the licensee holds a 'children's certificate';
- young people over 16 can go into a bar, but cannot drink alcohol until they are 18.

Children can be fined for breaking these regulations too. A young person under 18 who tries to buy, actually buys or drinks alcohol (thus covering every scenario) in licensed premises is liable to a fine of up to £400.

Under the Confiscation of Alcohol (Young Persons) Act 1997, the police may also confiscate alcohol from a young person if he is drinking in a public place or any place which has been entered unlawfully. They may also confiscate alcohol from anyone who intends that any of the alcohol should be consumed by the young person.

If a young person is over the age limit but looks young for his age, he may find it useful to carry a card proving his age – schemes operate in many areas. Sometimes publicans will refuse to serve someone unless they show their proof of age.

An older law can be used to punish parents too (although in practice this is hardly ever used). Under the Penalties for Drunkenness Act 1962, a person looking after a child under seven who is found in licensed premises can be liable to a fine of £10 or a prison term of up to a month.

Tobacco

Tobacco cannot be sold to anyone apparently under the age of 16, whether or not it is for his or her own use. Shopkeepers can be fined and even owners of cigarette-vending machines face fines if they do not take specific measures to prevent them being used by young people under 16 years old.

Park-keepers and police constables have a duty to confiscate smoking materials of anyone apparently under 16 years old smoking in a public place.

Body piercing

A young person can have his or her body pierced, although a parent may need to accompany them and provide consent.

CHILDREN AND THE INTERNET

A survey in 2000 conducted among 11,000 children using the internet revealed that a shocking 60 per cent of the them were being lured into 'cybersex' and 12 per cent had agreed to meet a stranger they had 'met' online. Parents are advised by internet experts to create and keep to a family internet policy that will keep their children safe online – for example, by using one of the software filters which restricts access to certain sites when the internet is being accessed by children.

CAR SAFETY

Some 230 children are killed and 20,000 injured every year on the roads. The laws are being increasingly tightened up in an endeavour to halt the escalating figures.

Driving

Children under 16 years cannot drive a moped and certain tractors. Children under 17 years could not drive a motorcycle, car or small goods vehicle but this age limit has recently been raised to 18 years (age limits for other passenger vehicles or goods vehicles are between 18 and 21 years).

When driven by a learner, the car must be fitted with 'L' plates and the learner-driver must have a learner's certificate issued (available from DVLA, Swansea) and be accompanied by a qualified driver over the age of 21 years sitting in the front passenger seat. For the first year following passing the driving test, the driver must now sport a green 'P' to show that he or she is still an inexperienced driver.

Seat belts

Legally, no person can travel in the front seat (or, since 1 July 1991, in the back seat if seat belts have been fitted) without using a seat belt. There are special extra regulations about children. It is up to the driver of the vehicle (whether or not they are the parents) to make sure that the laws are complied with.

Children in the car cannot be carried on adults' laps but must be restrained in a purpose-built restraint appropriate to the child's weight. An appropriate restraint includes:

- *for children under one year old*: a carrycot which is itself restrained by straps or a baby carrier;
- *for children between one and three years*: a child seat or safety harness or a booster cushion used with an adult belt;
- *for children over four*: an adult belt.

For further information on all aspects of child safety, including wearing seat belts, contact the Royal Society for the Prevention of Accidents, Edgbaston Park, 353 Bristol Road, Edgbaston, Birmingham B5 7ST, tel: 0121 248 2000 or visit their website at www.rospa.co.uk.

Safety campaigners have lobbied for restrictions on sale of secondhand car seats, because wear and tear (or even accidents) can, and will, damage their effectiveness, which parents will want to consider in any event. Wherever there is any doubt, the driver will bear the burden of responsibility.

In 1991, a mother was fined £50 because her 3-year-old child had undone the safety belt of the child's car seat in the back. A police car waiting next to the mother's car at traffic lights spotted that the child was unrestrained, and the mother was liable even though she had not noticed that the child had got out of her car seat.

There are some exceptions, so if all the available seat belts are used up (by adults or other children), extra children don't have to wear one. The theory behind adults taking priority in the use of seat belts is that the heaviest unrestrained passengers cause the most injury to others if thrown around in a crash. Children can also be medically exempted from using seat belts (but the child must be disabled and wearing a special belt or must be given a certificate by a doctor). In practice, as with adult seat belt regulations, few such certificates are granted.

CONSUMER SAFETY

It is a criminal offence under the Consumer Protection Act 1987 to supply unsafe consumer goods in the UK, although suppliers can offer as a defence that the product meets safety standards. There are extra regulations for children's goods. Pushchairs must be stable and have adequate brakes, an attachment for a safety harness and two separate locking devices.

Regulations for toys prohibit sharp edges and points, toxic paint and non-securely attached facial features. Plastic bags should also carry warnings about their dangers to young children. (*See also* page 420.)

FIRE

It is an offence for anyone over 16 years, looking after a child under 12 years, to leave the child alone in a room with an unprotected heater or open fire if the child is seriously injured or killed.

Children's nightwear (except terry towelling) is protected by special regulations. If a garment is marked 'low flammability to BS 5722', it has passed special safety tests. 'Keep away from fire' shows a less safe garment which has not passed tests.

The Furniture and Furnishing (Fire) (Safety) Regulations 1988 set new standards for furniture with foam filling: tests must prove it not to ignite quickly or emit high rates of toxic fumes.

FIREWORKS

While most restrictions on the sale of fireworks are voluntary controls by the industry, there are a few legal prohibitions. Fireworks must not be sold to any young person apparently under the age of 16 (leaving the decision up to the shopkeeper) and they must not be discharged in a public place. Fireworks must be packed in approved packaging and only 5 lb of fireworks should be exposed at any one time. (*See also* page 420.)

If a big neighbourhood party is planned, there are special rules too. If more than 100 young people under 14 years attend 'an entertainment', the provider of entertainment must ensure there are enough adults in attendance to ensure the children's safety and stop the admission of more children than can be accommodated.

SAFETY AT WORK

Children must be over school-leaving age (i.e. 16 years) before they can:
- work in industry (e.g. mines and manufacturing);
- carry a heavy load, operate a circular saw, handle poisons or use equipment without proper safety regulations.

Department of Health model guidelines (which may be enacted by local authorities as by-laws) propose that children must not work in collecting rubbish, delivering fuels or cleaning windows more than 10 feet from the ground. (*See* page 406 for the employment of children in general.)

11

Children and Crime

If a child is accused of a crime he or she will be treated differently from an adult; the principles and procedures are modified to take into account the age and circumstances of the child.

The laws which deal with children and crime (chiefly the Children and Young Persons Act 1969, the Children Act 1989 in the past, and now the Crime and Disorder Act 1998 and the Youth Justice and Criminal Evidence Act 1999 creating more fundamental change) were based on the premise that the child who commits an offence probably has social problems. The aim should be to help the child to mend his ways. Prosecution is normally seen as the last resort. It is used only when the child does not admit guilt or when, having admitted guilt, the 'social work' approach will not by itself reform him or her. Children in any event should still always expect to be prosecuted when they are accused of a *serious* crime.

More recently, there has been growing public concern that children and young people seem to be getting away with criminal actions for which their older brothers would face criminal proceedings, and specific laws have been brought in to try and restrict anti-social behaviour and other specific problems. A further refreshing, and very new, focus of the criminal law relating to young offenders is the idea of reparation – that instead of serving a sentence/punishment anonymously and divorced from the original crime, young offenders should be made to face up to the consequences of their actions. In future, they will very often meet the victims of their crimes face to face and have to listen to their (often painful) stories and recognize the implications of their crimes.

THE LAW

The Children Act 1989 requires every local authority to take all reasonable steps to discourage children from committing offences – for instance, by establishing youth and community services or by supporting parents in their role of encouraging children to steer away from crime. Similarly, local authorities must, wherever possible, reduce the need to bring criminal proceedings against child offenders. Whether either of these idealistic aims is realized remains in doubt because of local authorities' hard-pressed financial situations.

Children, or 'young offenders' as the law often called them, have different criminal responsibilities depending on their age.

Under 10 – children cannot be found guilty of any criminal offence and are immune from prosecution. That does not mean that the child can commit offences with impunity, because the local authority may apply for a child to be taken into care if he repeatedly breaks the law.
From 10 upwards – children are deemed to have full criminal responsibility for their actions and can be convicted of a criminal offence: Crime and Disorder Act 1998. If a child is male, from the age of 10 the law regards him as capable of committing any sexual offence, including rape: Sexual Offences Act 1993.

Although a child is technically deemed to have full criminal responsibility from age 10, the age of the child will probably still affect how he is treated by the judicial system. Younger children may be found guilty of a crime but it must be shown that they knew that they were doing wrong. If a child knows that its actions are *seriously* wrong and not just naughty or childish, then it will be assumed to know that they are *legally* wrong.

The courts adopt a commonsense rather than a legalistic approach. The child need not know that it has broken the law. Its actions at the time of the offence (such as planning, concealment or violent behaviour) are often a good indication of its state of mind.

A boy of 10 was convicted of murder when the evidence showed that, after killing a 5-year-old child, he had concealed the body and told lies about what had happened.

The closer a child is to the age of 14 years, the easier it is to show that he knew he was doing something legally wrong, although it is always necessary to look at his mental age. If, for instance, the mental age is under 10, it will be difficult to show that the child has criminal responsibility.

Anti-social behaviour

Part and parcel of the objective of preventing anti-social behaviour are new laws which target children's bad public/neighbourly behaviour. These laws apply not only to adults but to children aged 10 years and upwards too. Under the Crime and Disorder Act 1998, if an offender harasses or causes harm or distress to one or more people – this must be outside, not inside, his home – the magistrates can make an anti-social behaviour order, stopping the child doing anything set out in the order. The powers include creating an exclusion zone over certain streets or areas where the offender may not enter, and the maximum penalty for breach of an anti-social behaviour order is a hefty fine or five years' imprisonment for adults.

This Act is designed to provide powers to the courts to 'encourage defendants and their parents to address offending behaviour' (the encouragement is more in the format of a stick than a carrot) and provide a new national and youth focus on youth crime. Further reforms are set out in the Youth Justice and Criminal Evidence Act 1999 (*see* page 134).

These laws force local authorities to have a role in policing neighbourhoods alongside the police, although the new powers have not been popular with councils. In June 2000, the Home Secretary announced that only 80 anti-social behaviour orders had been applied for by councils within the first 14 months of their operation. The reasons cited for lack of take-up by the local authorities were that taking this action had proved costly and time consuming – since it often involved asking witnesses to come forward to give evidence. The government indicated that they would be requiring the local authorities to do more.

POLICE INVESTIGATIONS

Often the first the parent will know of the offence is when the police call at the house. If that happens, the parent should first discuss the case with them, out of earshot of the child. The police may then ask to speak to the child. If they do, then the parent should insist on being present.

It must be established that an offence was committed. For instance, in a shoplifting case, the child may have absent-mindedly left without paying. Here no further steps should be taken because there was no criminal intention. The nature of the offence should be explained to the parents to reduce the possibility of a child wrongly confessing to an offence.

If the offence is serious, it may be best for the child not to answer any questions until a solicitor has been instructed. Free access to a solicitor under the duty solicitor scheme is one of the important rights afforded to any accused person, whether child or adult (*see* page 797). It is available whether or not the child has been charged.

The police should not interview or arrest suspected young offenders at their schools other than in exceptional circumstances. The consent of the head teacher must be given and the interview or arrest must be in his or her presence.

Detention at the police station

If a young offender is arrested, his parents must be notified as soon as possible, and arrangements made for them to attend the police station. If a person *looks* under 17, the police must treat them as a young offender until they establish otherwise.

During police detention, the child must be kept away from adults charged with an offence, unless child and adult are charged with the very same incidents. This also applies when the child is travelling to court or waiting at court. If the young offender is a girl, she must be kept in the care of a policewoman at these times.

If a young person is detained by the police, he has the right to:
- have someone informed of his detention. If he is under 16, the police must take reasonable steps to inform his parents or guardian;
- consult a solicitor;
- consult the *Codes of Practice* which spell out his rights;
- have an 'appropriate' adult present when he is interviewed, except in certain limited circumstances.

These rights are especially important as the whole process of police detention and questioning is a frightening enough experience for adults and will be much more so for children. Police stations are a world of their own. Any detained person will, in some respects, be at the mercy of the police, who are to a great degree in control of what the suspect may or may not do while in the station. Any young offender can see the custody record at the end of his or her detention and may also ask to see it for up to one year after the record was made.

Rules for interviewing young offenders

The 'appropriate adult'

When a child is interviewed or asked to sign a statement, this must be done, if possible, in the presence of an 'appropriate adult'. This applies whether the child is a suspect *or* a witness to a crime. Copies of interview records and statements must be read and signed by the adult.

The adult's duty is to advise and help the young offender, and to ensure that the interview is fairly conducted. The young offender can consult privately with the adult at any time. The appropriate adult must not be involved in the crime for which the young offender was arrested.

If the parent or guardian is not available *or suitable*, the 'appropriate adult' could be a social worker or a representative of the local authority. As a last resort the adult may be any independent person over 18 who is not employed by the police.

A child aged 16 was interviewed by the police in the presence of his father. They chose not to ask for a solicitor. The father could not read and had a very low IQ. He was probably incapable of understanding the seriousness of his son's position. The High Court decided that he was not an 'appropriate adult' and the interview was excluded from the evidence. R *v* Morse (1991)

The police may waive the rules if the interview is 'urgent' – if a superintendent or higher-ranking police officer considers that a delay in interviewing the young offender would involve an immediate risk of harm to people or a serious loss of or damage to property.

Other police powers

Under the Police and Criminal Evidence Act 1984 and the Codes of Practice 1991, if a young person is detained by the police, they have the power, in certain circumstances, to:

- search him, including strip search him, without his parent's consent;
- carry out an intimate search without his parent's consent (although generally this should be done in the presence of an appropriate adult);
- take an intimate body sample from him, for example nail scrapings, saliva, hair, blood, semen, urine and dental impressions if the superintendent has reasonable grounds to believe it will prove or disprove his alleged involvement in a recordable offence *and* his parent's written consent has been obtained;
- take his fingerprints with parental consent.

Cautioning

The police must always 'caution' a suspect before questions are put to him or her. The purpose of cautioning is to make them aware of the importance of what they say. If the police fail to caution, any statements the suspect makes may be rejected by the court. The exact words used for cautioning are:

'You do not have to say anything. But it may harm your defence if you do not mention when questioned something which you later rely on in court. Anything you do say may be given in evidence.'

If a young offender is cautioned without an adult being present, the caution must be repeated in the adult's presence.

The right to legal advice

All suspects must be told of their right of access to a solicitor. A young offender must be told this in the presence of an 'appropriate adult'. If the adult feels that the child does need legal advice, then it should be provided. The child or the adult should then be allowed to communicate with a solicitor by telephone, letter or in person *at any time* and in private.

There is a duty solicitor scheme for those questioned in police stations. This service is funded by the government and organized by local solicitors, who arrange to be available both day *and* night to attend police interviews at police stations or elsewhere. This service is free to all those detained, regardless of income. The same solicitor who is present at the police station may represent the child in any subsequent hearing – for example, in an application for bail or at the trial. The child may later choose a different solicitor to represent him or her.

If the child admits the offence

If the child admits guilt, the police may simply caution him or her rather than prosecute. This 'caution' is different from the official 'caution', which is explained above. 'Cautioning' in this sense is in effect a 'dressing-down' from a senior police officer. The child is given a severe warning and told that he or she will not be dealt with so leniently next time. The caution does not go down as a criminal record, although reference can be made to it if the child appears before a youth or adult court in the future.

If the police are in doubt as to whether to give a caution, they may invite a 'Youth Offender Panel' (consisting of representatives of the probation, social and education services) to review the case. Nonetheless, the police have a complete discretion in deciding whether to prosecute for minor offences. If the young offender has been arrested and cautioned on several previous occasions (exactly how many varies with the different police forces – three is a common number) then prosecution will follow. Prosecution *must* follow if the offence is serious (e.g. rape, arson, aggravated burglary, etc.).

Sometimes, after cautioning, the child may be referred to agencies which provide guidance, support and involvement in the community. This may be to help with accommodation or benefits or work experience.

While cautioning a child as an alternative to prosecuting is clearly sensible, there is one major disadvantage. A caution will be given only to a child who admits guilt and, since many children regard a caution as 'getting off', there is a danger that the innocent child will say that he is guilty just to avoid the anxiety and worry of a youth court appearance. Thus the caution can sometimes be an inducement to the innocent to admit guilt. But care should be taken as the caution can be used as evidence of previous bad character if the child is prosecuted at a later date.

Some police authorities are now introducing schemes whereby an offender can make reparation to his victim – this could involve, for example, mediation between the young offender and a house owner he has burgled. The philosophy behind such schemes is to show the young offender the consequences of his actions – the distress and suffering caused to the victim, for example. While these schemes are in their early days at the beginning of the twenty-first century, the results look promising in the sense of actively discouraging re-offending (*see* further page 133).

If the child denies the offence

If the child refuses to admit to the offence, then the police will have to decide whether to prosecute or to drop the matter. The child cannot be given a caution as this would imply that they did commit the offence. In these cases it may be the courts' role to determine guilt or innocence.

Charging the detained young offenders

When the police have concluded their investigations, the child must be either charged or released. Any action should be taken in the presence of the 'appropriate adult'. Once charged, the young offender should be free to leave the police station unless the custody officer authorizes further detention on the grounds that:

- the child's address is unknown or uncertain;
- the officer believes that detention is necessary to prevent harm to the officer or others, or loss of, or damage to, property;
- the officer believes the child will fail to attend court or answer to bail; or
- detention is necessary to prevent interference with the administration of justice or the investigation of an offence.
- A young offender may also be detained after being

charged if the custody officer believes that this would be in the young offender's *own interest*.

As a general rule, young offenders should not be kept at the police station after being charged. They should be granted bail and released. If the young offender is remanded in custody (i.e. charged with an imprisonable offence), he or she should be sent to local authority accommodation, unless the circumstances justify keeping them at the police station.

A juvenile had been living at a local authority hostel. He had been convicted of a number of offences of theft and burglary, and was under arrest for further serious offences. He was denied bail to prevent him from interfering with witnesses. The local authority wanted him to go back to the hostel but the police custody officer refused. The local authority applied to the High Court to overrule the custody officer's decision. The High Court refused the application and decided that the custody officer had acted properly.

R *v* Chief Constable of Cambridgeshire *ex p* Michel (1990)

Young offenders should not be sent to *secure* accommodation (which they are not free to leave) if they are under 13 years. Secure accommodation orders may be used for young offenders between 13 and 18, usually where they have a history of absconding from local authority accommodation and it is necessary to protect the public from serious harm (*see* page 131).

When there is not enough evidence to charge the young offenders, the police must release him or her, unless the custody officer believes that detention is necessary to preserve evidence or to carry out further questioning.

GOING TO COURT

If the police decide to prosecute, their next step will be to issue a summons and serve it on the parents. This will tell the parents and the child to attend the youth court at the stated date and time. Only in serious cases will the police issue a warrant for the arrest of the child and take him or her to the police station. If this happens, the parents should contact a solicitor at once.

Even if the child is arrested, the police will usually release him or her on bail until the hearing of the case.

If bail is not granted, the child should be kept in the care of the local authority or in a remand centre if he is charged with a serious offence.

WHICH COURT?

Most children are tried in a youth court (formerly known as a juvenile court) and the trial will be by magistrates sitting without a jury – i.e. summarily. The magistrates are drawn from a specially trained panel and have knowledge and experience of children. They must be under 50 years (preferably under 40) when appointed and must retire at 65 years. The bench should consist of two or three magistrates, one of whom at least must be a woman.

In exceptional circumstances (for example, if a child is charged with homicide, including causing death by dangerous driving), a child may be tried in a crown court by a judge and a jury as if he or she were an adult. They may also be tried in a magistrates' court with a normal panel of magistrates (as opposed to a youth court).

For instance, a young offender charged with murder, manslaughter or any offence for which an adult may be punished with a prison sentence of 14 years or more will usually be committed by the magistrates for trial in a crown court. Following the killing of Jamie Bulger, his two killers, Thompson and Venables, were tried in the crown court – although this practice was later criticized in the European Court of Human Rights.

Where a child is charged jointly with an adult, he or she may be tried beside the adult co-defendant in a crown court or in a magistrates' court, though he or she may be referred to the youth court for sentencing.

A 16-year-old (juvenile) and an 18-year-old (adult) are accused of stealing a car. The 18-year-old can opt for trial in either the magistrates' court or the crown court. If he chooses a magistrates' court trial the 16-year-old will be tried with him. But if the 16-year-old is found guilty, he will be referred to the youth court for sentencing. However, if the magistrates wish to fine him, bind over his parents or give him an absolute or conditional discharge, they can impose that sentence themselves. If the 18-year-old elects to go for a crown court trial, the 16-year-old will still be tried with him, but if he is found guilty, he will almost always be passed back to the youth court for sentencing.

In theory, young offenders charged with linked offences to adults should be tried in the crown court only if it is necessary in the interests of justice. In practice, they are nearly always tried in the crown court. This is because the prosecution does not want to risk one offender being acquitted and the other being convicted on the same evidence in a different court.

PROCEDURE IN THE YOUTH COURT

The hearing may be either in a court which is used only for young offender hearings or in a normal magistrates' court. Although the youth court will be in the same building as the magistrates' court, it often has a separate entrance. When the youth court is in a normal courtroom, no adult criminal proceedings may be held in that room for at least an hour beforehand.

The procedure in the youth court is similar to that in the magistrates' court. The magistrates act as both judge and jury (*see* page 645), and are advised by a legally qualified clerk. Youth court cases are tried *summarily* (*see* above, Which Court?).

The proceedings are less formal than those of the normal magistrates' court. The object is to make the process less intimidating to young offenders. For instance, less legal terminology is used and young offenders will be asked whether they 'admit' or 'deny' an offence rather than pleading guilty or not guilty. Witnesses will promise to tell the truth as opposed to swearing on oath and young offenders will be referred to by their first name. Young offenders are not 'convicted' or 'sentenced' but are, instead, euphemistically 'dealt with'.

Giving evidence

The Youth Justice and Criminal Evidence Act 1999 (*see further* page 134) introduced a number of significant changes. Most importantly, the Act changed the law of competence as to when a child's evidence is admissible in criminal proceedings. The only test now is whether the witness can understand the questions being asked and give answers that are understood. In particular, all witnesses under 17 at the time of the hearing can be assisted with giving their evidence via special measures, including video-recording their evidence. A person who is under 14, or incapable of understanding the significance of the proceedings or the difference between truth and fabrication, will give evidence unsworn. The Act creates an offence of giving untrue evidence in this way. A witness older than 14, and capable of understanding the nature of the proceedings and the difference between truth and fabrication, will continue to be sworn and will commit perjury by lying on oath.

Hearings in youth courts are conducted in private; the general public may not attend. There may still be a surprisingly large number of people in the courtroom: lawyers, legal staff, the accused, his or her parents, the police, a representative of the local education authority and a probation officer. The press are also allowed in court but will rarely attend, as any information which may identify the young offender (e.g. the name, address or school of the child) cannot be published.

Parents are expected to appear and may even be ordered to do so. If there is a reason why the parents cannot be present (e.g. they are ill), then the magistrates will probably accept another family member, such as an older brother or sister, as a substitute. Should no substitute be available, the case may be adjourned, especially if the child does not have a solicitor representing him or her. In some courts, the child will be referred to the court's duty solicitor, who will then act for them. If the child remains unrepresented and if he or she denies the offence, a parent can help the young offender with their defence. The helper and the young offender may cross-examine the witnesses for the prosecution on such occasions. The court will generally assist by making sure that the young offender's case is properly put to the witnesses. In practice it would be unusual for a child to remain unrepresented, as public funding is generally freely available to young offenders.

The case may result in an absolute discharge, or a conditional discharge. Under the Criminal Justice Act 1982, the youth court also has the power to make an order requiring the offender's parents to take proper care of him and exercise proper control over him.

Home-surroundings reports

If a young offender is found guilty, the court will (in all but the most trivial cases) consider a report on his or her background and surroundings. If it has not been prepared by the end of the case, the court will adjourn so that social workers can prepare the report. Generally, bail will be granted (often with the parents as sureties). The procedure varies according to the age of the child.

Under 13 years – the police must notify the local authority of their intention to start the proceedings. The local authority must investigate the home surroundings, school record, health and character of the child. A report will be sent to the court. The court may ask the local authority to make further investigations. The child's attitude to the offence and any mitigating circumstances will be included in the report, which will in turn be supplemented by other reports produced by the local education authority or other body.

Thirteen years and over – prior notice must in this case be given to the probation office, which will then make the necessary inquiries and produce a report.

If the report is available at the hearing, the magistrates will immediately be able to sentence the young offender. The report need not be read out in court. The parents and the child can even be ordered to stay out of the courtroom while the report is being discussed. The court should, however, tell the parents and the child about any information in the report which will affect the sentence.

Statements by the parents

If the child is found guilty, the parents and child will be given the opportunity to make a statement 'in mitigation' on anything which the report may not have mentioned, to try to persuade the magistrates to deal with the young offender leniently. This is in addition to submissions made to the court by the child's solicitor. The magistrates will then consider the appropriate treatment for the child.

SENTENCING

A youth court can impose some adult sentences. There are also sentences only for young offenders.

Sentences specially for young offenders

Detention in a young offenders' institution

This is available only for children who have committed an imprisonable offence and who receive a custodial sentence. It is not available for children under 15 years old unless the child is found guilty of a very serious offence and has been in trouble many times beforehand. Under the Criminal Justice Act 1982 s1B, the length of sentence varies and the maximum can never be more than an adult sentence for the offence, or two years (whichever is less).

Secure training order (for young offenders of 12 to 14 years)

If a child is aged between 12 and 14 years, the court can make a secure training order. This again might happen if the offender has been in trouble a lot, has three convictions and has been on a supervision order (*see* below) which has been breached, or if the offender committed another offence while on a supervision order. If a secure training order is made, the offender will be sent to the Secure Training Unit in Medway, Kent (a closed unit where offenders are locked in or prevented from leaving). The minimum sentence is for three months and the maximum is 12 months.

Supervision order (for young offenders of 10 to 16 years)

This is the youth court's equivalent to a probation order (*see* page 655). The aim is to give young offenders long-term help without removing them from their home. The child will be under general supervision. Often conditions will be imposed, such as:

- to live with a certain person for a specified period;
- to have regular appointments with a 'supervisor' (*see* below);
- to have psychiatric treatment;
- to go to school regularly, if of compulsory school age;
- to have a curfew imposed;
- to refrain from participating in certain activities.

These conditions can be imposed only for a period of up to 90 days.

If the child does not comply with the order he can be brought back to the youth court and a different sentence may be imposed (e.g. a fine or an attendance centre order). A supervision order may last for a maximum of three years. If the offender is under 13 years the 'supervisor' will be the local authority; otherwise the supervisor will be a probation officer.

Supervision order with residence requirement

This is an order requiring the young offender to live in *local authority accommodation* for a maximum of six months. The residence requirement is intended to help a young offender whose surroundings are a contributory factor towards his behaviour. For example, the residence requirement would help a young offender who is living rough and stealing to survive, or where there is a lack of parental control.

It can be imposed only on a child who has committed a serious offence (one that would occasion imprisonment for an adult) while under supervision. The court must be satisfied that the child's home circumstances contributed to a significant extent towards his behaviour. A supervision order of this kind may also impose any of the conditions mentioned above. This sentence can normally be given only to a young offender who is publicly funded.

Probation order

Convicted young offenders who are 16 years upwards can be given a probation order for up to three years, an attendance centre order for a maximum of 36 hours or a community service order requiring them to undertake unpaid work in the community for between 40 and 240 hours. A combination order can also be made if the young offender is convicted of an imprisonable offence, placing him on probation for between one and three years and requiring him to perform between 40 and 100 hours' community service.

Detention (for under-18-year-olds)

Detention is the youth equivalent of adult imprisonment for under-18-year-olds who have committed serious offences (manslaughter and offences which would involve adult prison sentences of 14 years or more). It will be used when, because of the seriousness of the offence, there is no alternative to prison. The Home Secretary announced in March 2000 that there would be tariffs for under-18-year-olds to be set by the trial judge – and that the practice of detention during Her Majesty's pleasure would be ended. This followed the ruling of the European Court of Human Rights on the sentences imposed on Jon Venables and Robert Thompson, the two children who killed the toddler, Jamie Bulger. The court decided that government ministers should not set tariffs for young offenders sentenced to detention during Her Majesty's pleasure. In August 2000, the Lord Chief Justice issued further guidance, and said that the starting point for young offenders, in cases where an adult would be given a mandatory life sentence, would be 14 years. That term might be increased or reduced for aggravating or mitigating factors. Aggravating features would include evidence of a planned or revenge killing, or the killing of a very young or very old person – many other examples were cited too.

Detention under the Children and Young Persons Act 1933 (for young offenders of 16 to 18 years)

This is the young offender equivalent of adult imprisonment for children who have committed serious offences (for example, manslaughter and offences which would involve adult prison sentences of 14 years or more). It will be used when, because of the seriousness of the offence, there is no alternative to prison. The place and conditions of imprisonment are determined by the Secretary of State. It will usually be in a young persons' prison. The term of detention is limited to the maximum for the particular offence.

Detention 'during Her Majesty's pleasure'

This sentence must be imposed on young offenders under 18 years who are convicted of murder in the crown court. The young offender is held in custody for an indefinite period. The Home Secretary decides when he will be released.

Custody for life (for youths of 18 to 21 years)

This is imposed on young offenders and young people between these ages who have committed murder or any other offence which has a mandatory life sentence. It may also be given to those who are convicted of an offence where an adult *could* receive a life sentence (e.g. robbery).

Attendance centre order (for youths of 10 to 21 years)

This is ordered where the young offenders is guilty of an offence punishable with prison or has broken the terms of a supervision order. A mixture of firm discipline, physical training and the teaching of handicrafts and similar activities is used not only to take away the offenders' leisure time but to try to teach youths less anti-social uses of this time. The usual sentence is for a total of 12 hours (the maximum is 24 hours), to be served by between one and three hours on alternate Saturday afternoons. It is thus particularly suitable for football hooligans (i.e. when the team is playing at home), but generally it achieves little. An added problem is that few areas have enough attendance centres available (and so some other sentence has to be imposed). This sentence is only available for young offenders who have *not* previously been sentenced to periods of detention. If the child does not attend he or she can be brought back to the youth court and a different sentence will be substituted.

Exclusion order

A young offender may also be given an exclusion order – for example, to prevent him or her from attending a football match – *see* above.

Destruction order

In some circumstances, the court can also make a destruction order – for example, ordering that drugs be destroyed.

Sexual offences

If a young offender is convicted of, or even cautioned for, one of the sexual offences specified in the Sex Offenders Act 1997, his name will be entered on the sex offenders' register. However, if he was under 18 years at the time, registration is for half the time that an adult has his name registered under that Act.

'Adult' sentences used to punish young offenders

Community service order (for young offenders of 16 plus)

This is an order to do unpaid work. The sentence may be used only for offenders who have committed an imprisonable offence and who consent to the order. The offenders will work with volunteers.

The number of hours of community service which may be ordered for an adult is between 40 and 240 hours. The maximum for a child under 17 years is 120 hours. Adult rules apply to those over 17 years (*see* page 655).

Fines

Children may be fined and, until a child is 16 years old, the court can order the parents to pay unless it is unreasonable to do so. Once a young person reaches 18 years, he can be fined the maximum amount for the sentence.

Compensation

In addition to (or instead of) fines, the court can order payment of compensation up to £5,000 where injury is caused or property damaged. This can be instead of, or in addition to, any other sentence. Again, until a child is 16 years, the court can order the parents to pay, unless it is unreasonable to do so. If an offender cannot pay both compensation and fine, priority will be given to compensation.

Costs

A young offender may be ordered to pay legal costs. If the young offender is under 17 years, the amount must not be more than the maximum fine for the offence.

Responsibility of the parent

The parents of a young offender will be required to pay all fines, compensation and costs imposed on the young offender unless the parents cannot be found or it would be unreasonable to order them to pay. The parents must be given an opportunity to be heard before a payment order is made.

Discharge

Absolute and conditional discharges (*see* page 657) are both commonly used in youth courts. They follow a finding of guilt. A young offender granted an absolute discharge leaves the court with no criminal record. If he or she receives a conditional discharge, they will have no criminal record provided that they do not commit another offence within 12 months. Both kinds of discharge amount to a warning to the child, while at the same time avoiding the stigma that may be attached to a more serious sentence. Neither form of discharge is equal to an acquittal.

Binding over

The offender gives a written undertaking (or 'recognizance' as it is called) to promise to pay a sum of money (up to £1,000) if he or she re-offends within a given period.

The parents or guardians may be bound over to take proper care and control of their child. If the child thereafter re-offends and breaks the order, the parents can be fined up to £1,000.

Deferred sentence

This allows the court to put off passing a sentence for up to six months. When the court reconvenes it will be to consider how the child has behaved. If the child has not misbehaved during this time, he or she will usually be given an absolute or conditional discharge, or a fine (*see* above). In practice, the courts seldom use this sentence and will instead give the offender a conditional discharge.

Hospital orders

If during the course of the trial it becomes clear that the young offender has psychiatric problems he or she may be ordered to be detained in a hospital. If the mental condition is severe, and the court is satisfied that the young offender committed the offence, the court will make the order without making a finding of guilt.

APPEALS

Appeals against youth court decisions are normally made to the crown court. They should be made within 21 days and only the young offender may appeal. If the appeal is against sentence, the crown court may decrease or increase the sentence. Even if a custodial sentence is given, bail may be granted pending an appeal. In addition, either the young offender or the prosecution may appeal to the divisional court of the High Court on a point of law.

PUBLIC FUNDING

Young offenders may apply for public funding in the youth court. The parents may also apply on their behalf. Where the child is under 17 years the court may take into account either the child's or the parents' means. In all other respects public funding is assessed and granted following the same procedures as those used for adults who are charged with a crime (*see* page 797). As is the case with adults, a young offender who is charged with an offence for which he or she may receive a custodial sentence will almost certainly be granted public funding.

CHANGES TO THE YOUTH JUSTICE SYSTEM

The Youth Justice and Criminal Evidence Act 1999 aims for a more fundamental and deep-rooted further reform of the youth justice system, tackling the causes of crime as well as the crimes themselves. As a starter, the Act reforms the youth court and its powers. Young offenders now face a 'Youth Offender Panel' (YOP), made up of members of the public alongside members of the Youth Offending Team (drawn from the police, social services, the probation service, education and health services). The Act lays down selection criteria for members of youth offending panels.

The YOP has a particular focus on reparation to the community – seeing how a young offender can put right what he has done, as well as face up to the consequences of his actions. This will very often mean that he will have to face, in person, the victim of his crime. The Act has high ideals and adopts deliberately a fresh approach to get away from the destructive cycle of crime and punishment.

The views of the victim will always be sought, although their attendance before a YOP is not mandatory. Sometimes a separate meeting can be arranged between the victim and offender, away from the YOP. But if the victim declines to take part, or if this is a crime without individual victims, the offender will, in any event, be asked to make amends to the community as a whole. A community representative may be invited to attend meetings of the youth offender panel.

Referrals to a Youth Offender Panel

Not all young offenders will be referred to a YOP. However, where a young offender pleads guilty and it is his first time in court for an offence, he must be referred to a YOP unless:

- the offence is one for which the sentence is fixed by law;
- the court considers that the offence is serious enough to require a custodial sentence;

- the court intends to make a hospital order; or
- the court proposes to give an absolute discharge.

If a young offender is being tried for more than one offence and pleads guilty to at least one, but not all of the offences, the court has discretion over whether or not to refer him to a YOP.

When a referral order is made, the court will need to consider ancillary matters. Although it cannot be combined with other sentencing options apart from an absolute discharge, the court can, for example, order costs, compensation, licence endorsement or driving disqualification. It can also provide for exclusion under the football or licensing legislation, or registration on the sex offenders' register. An order lasts for between three and 12 months according to the seriousness of the offence. It is for the YOP which administers the order to determine its level of intensity. Provided the offender complies with its terms, his offence will be spent under the Rehabilitation of Offenders Act 1974 at its conclusion. That will leave the youth better served to seek employment without having to reveal any convictions. A failure to comply with the order will result in a return to court for a consideration of re-sentencing.

The contract with the offender

The outcome of the YOP will be a contract entered into by the offender including activities 'tailored to the individual circumstances of an offender to help them change the attitudes and behaviour that led to the offending in the first place'. The contract will always include some element of reparation to the victim or community and could also require young offenders to:

- participate in particular activities, such as family counselling or drug rehabilitation courses;
- undertake unpaid work in the community;
- comply with educational arrangements, such as attending school or a training scheme; or
- refrain from doing certain things or going to particular places.

Powers under the Act

The Act provides a wide range of powers 'to enable early, targeted interventions to deal with anti-social behaviour and to divert the very young from crime'. These powers include:

- local child curfew schemes to protect children under the age of 10 years from getting into trouble (*see* above);
- child safety orders, again aimed at children under 10 years;
- anti-social behaviour orders to deal with serious, although not necessarily criminal anti-social behaviour by children over 10 years;

- powers for the police to remove truants to designated premises.

Further powers for the police and courts to intervene spread nationwide in 2000/01. So a young offender in the twenty-first century might face:

- a final warning scheme, to replace police cautioning of young offenders;
- a reparation order requiring young offenders to make amends to their victims or the wider community;
- an action plan to tackle anti-social behaviour and its causes;
- a parenting order to help reinforce and support parental responsibility (this can be used in combination with an anti-social behaviour order or a child safety order);
- court-ordered secure remands – to remand certain alleged offenders to local authority secure accommodation;
- a detention and training order to provide a constructive and flexible custodial sentence with a clear focus on preventing reoffending.

The above powers show ample evidence of the high ideals of the youth justice reforms, tackling crime as well as the root causes of crime. It is, as yet, too soon to analyse how the ideals are translating into reality and what practical gains might ensue.

12

Wills

WHAT IS A WILL?

A will is the legal document by which people direct what should happen to their property after their death. A person who dies without making a will is said to have died intestate.

A properly made will appoints one or more people to carry out the terms of the will. They are called executors. If there is no will, the rules of intestacy determine who will administer the property of the intestate. They are called the administrators. Both executors and administrators are sometimes called personal representatives.

The property of the deceased is called their estate. Freehold land and leasehold property are described as real estate or realty, and all other property is described as personal estate or personalty. The main duty of the personal representatives is to gather in the assets of the estate, to pay the debts and liabilities and then to distribute what is left to those entitled.

There are various laws which ensure that the personal representatives carry out the duties which have been entrusted to them. These laws often describe the personal representatives as trustees, as the duties of a trustee can continue after the estate has been administered – for instance, when they have to continue looking after property which has been left to a child.

WHAT IS PROBATE?

Probate has two usual meanings. First, it can mean the document which confirms that the will is valid and states who the executors are. It authorizes the executors to gain access to bank accounts, shares, real property and other investments. It is known as 'Probate of the Will' and corresponds to 'Letters of Administration', which are granted to the administrators of the estate when a person dies intestate.

The second meaning of probate is wider and refers to the various laws and courts which deal with wills, intestacy, succession, inheritance, administration and disputes over estates.

While death may be the end of a person's earthly troubles, it can be just the beginning for those left behind. Until 1857 the Ecclesiastical Courts dealt with many probate matters but after that date the civil courts took over. Since that time Parliament has passed numerous laws relating to probate matters.

The probate laws have various objectives:
- to safeguard the dead person's creditors;
- to ensure that the provisions of the will are carried out (if there is a will);
- to ensure that the dead person's estate is shared out according to law (if there is no will);
- to determine what must happen if there is a disputed estate;
- to ensure that inheritance tax is paid (unless the estate is exempt).

The common law laid down its own rules for securing these objectives, but these laws have been replaced by Acts of Parliament, some still of nineteenth-century origin, which lay down rules as to how a valid will is to be made, how personal representatives are appointed, the extent of their powers and duties and, finally, how the assets are to be distributed and to whom.

WHY MAKE A WILL?

According to a Gallup poll, most of us think we should make a will but only one in three actually does so.

'I haven't decided who to leave it to yet.'
'I'm not going to tempt fate.'
'They can fight it out between themselves when I'm gone.'
'It will all go to the wife anyway.' (Not necessarily!)

Many people who die without making a will have had these phrases on their lips. They can leave a desperate muddle for their families.

If a person dies intestate, the property will pass to his or her relatives in accordance with the rules of intestacy (*see* page 162). Generally, this means that the surviving husband or wife receives the first £125,000 (or £200,000 if there are no children), plus a life interest in half the balance (or half the balance if no children). Problems, therefore, arise if the deceased does not want his or her spouse to take such a large share (for instance, they might have separated, or the spouse may have a large estate of their own) or wants them to receive a larger amount. Many lawyers these days advise that a surviving spouse should be left all the estate unless it amounts to well over £200,000 or they have significant funds in their own name. This is because inflation can soon reduce the value of that lump sum; even with inflation at only 3 per cent a year, £200,000 today would be worth only £147,485 in 10 years. So a man worth £200,000 with a wife and child would be well advised to make a will leaving everything to his wife, rather than rely on the intestacy laws (in which case his wife would get only £125,000, plus a life interest in half the balance of £75,000). There may also be significant income tax savings to be made by dividing such a sum between husband and wife during their lifetime, so a spouse thinking about making a will should also be thinking about equalization of assets and lifetime gifts. Do not forget the quotation, 'But in this world nothing can be said to be certain except death and taxes.' Think ahead.

So a will is advisable when the intestacy laws will not produce a satisfactory distribution of the estate. Since circumstances can change (for instance, a person might not think his estate is worth more than £125,000 or £200,000, but a few years of inflation can drastically alter the position), it is always sensible to make a will and avoid possible problems in the future. One way of reducing the impact of inflation on a will is to express gifts in terms of fractions or percentages of the estate so that the relative value of each gift is maintained at the same level.

In more complicated situations the advantages of a will are obvious. Apart from ensuring that the estate is given to the right people in the right proportions, a will can avoid family squabbles and jealousies, reduce the amount of inheritance tax payable, and also simplify the task of the personal representatives. In particular, a cohabiting couple, with or without children, should make wills as a cohabitant has no automatic entitlement to the estate of a deceased partner, no matter how long the couple have been together. An additional benefit is that the person who leaves a will can choose who will be his or her executors; if he or she dies intestate they will be selected by following a statutory set of rules (*see* page 162).

Making a will is not expensive. Solicitors generally charge from £40 or £50 upwards for drawing up a straightforward will but, despite this, many people put off making a will until it is too late: 'I feel better now, doctor' are famous last words. The eventual inheritance tax savings which can be made by having a will professionally prepared can be considerable. A solicitor should also draw attention to other ways in which a person can organize his or her affairs to advantage.

Do not forget lifetime gifts as an alternative to, or in conjunction with, a will. Annual exemptions are available and great inheritance tax savings can be made by the careful use of gifts. For others there is the simple pleasure of making the gift during their lifetime, when it may be most needed.

MAKING A WILL

The intention

Anybody who is over 18 years and of sound mind can make a will. But not every written document that sets out how one's property is to be disposed of on death is a will, for it must be intended to act as a will and to be its maker's 'last will and testament'.

Unless the document is intended to be a will it will not be enforced by the courts, or, to put this in more legal language, a will is only valid if it is made with the necessary testamentary intention. It must express a person's genuine wishes and they must understand and approve of its contents. Great care must be taken when encouraging an elderly member of a family to make a will to ensure that the will does not set out the wishes of the relative doing the encouraging. Thus, if someone is of unsound mind, or doubtful mental *capacity*, their will may be invalid. Even a person who is not of sound mind but is a patient under the Court of Protection may have a will made for them under the supervision of the Court of Protection. Because of this, when an aged and, perhaps, eccentric person makes a will, it is advisable to have a doctor as one of the witnesses, and the doctor should check that the old or infirm person is not only capable of making a will but that he or she understands what is written in the will. If the doctor makes a record of the examination it may be valuable evidence should the will ever be challenged on the grounds of mental incapacity. If an elderly person wishes to change a well-balanced will in favour of some other person, care must be taken to ensure that there has been no undue influence.

Foolishness, eccentricity or social pressure is not enough to invalidate a will. However, fear, fraud or coercion is; for instance, a person who signs a will at gunpoint is not making a valid will. Thus, if a solicitor or doctor takes advantage of his position of trust so that he benefits under the will, the gift to him may be challenged. Similarly, if a person is nagged and pestered by a begging relative or pressurized by someone who is looking after them, that too may amount to undue influence.

The formalities

There are detailed rules on how to sign and witness a will. These are set out in the Wills Act 1837 s9. The rules are that:

- the will must be in writing (so a video will would not be valid!); and
- it must have been signed by the testator or some other person in their presence and at their direction; and
- there must be signatures from at least two witnesses, who both saw the testator sign and who both then signed in his/her presence and in the presence of each other.

If the will does not comply with these requirements, it will be invalid. Its author will, therefore, die intestate, and his or her personal representatives may be forced by the intestacy rules to distribute the estate in a way that was not intended.

Although the Wills Act requirements seem straightforward, numerous wills have been turned down over the years because of a failure to meet the strict wording of the provisions. Although these rules may seem strict, the rules were even stricter before 1982 and it is likely that in the future many fewer wills will fail than was previously the case. For example, before 1982 testators had to sign at the foot of the will – if they wrote anything after their signature, then that part of the will was ignored. Now, they can sign wherever they like as long as it is clear that they want the whole document to be treated as their will. In practice, of course, the will should still be signed at the end so as to avoid any arguments, but the 1982 changes have meant that if a mistake is made it is now less likely to cause major problems. If the will consists of several pages, it is wise for the testator and the witnesses to sign at the bottom of each page.

Witnesses

As mentioned above, there must be at least two witnesses to the will. Any adult, except someone who is blind, can be a witness, but the witnesses must see the testator sign, and then sign the will themselves. The will is not valid if the witness does not see the testator sign or if the testator signs after the witness.

The witnesses need not see the contents of the will; all they are doing is witnessing the testator's signature, not the contents of the will. They are there as independent witnesses that the person signed the will freely and voluntarily. Because they are independent persons, they cannot benefit from the will, nor can their husband or wife benefit. Any gift to the witnesses (or their spouses) will be invalid and the property that would have gone to them will form part of the residue of the estate. However, if the witness and the beneficiary marry after the will is made this rule will not apply and the beneficiary can take the gift.

It is vital, therefore, that a beneficiary or the spouse of a beneficiary under a will should not witness it. If they do witness it, and so cause the gift to be forfeited, that will not affect the validity of the rest of the will; it will remain valid subject to their (or their spouse's) gift being struck out.

People sometimes ask close relatives to witness their wills. In such a case the witness should check whether they (or their spouse) will benefit from the will; if so, someone else will have to witness the will. This is most important!

Drafting a will

A will that complies with the rules and which was made with testamentary intention will be upheld by the courts as a valid and binding will. Therefore, the personal representatives will have to follow its instructions exactly – even if it is clear that the testator made a mistake when drafting it. This is because the law requires the written directions of the testator to be followed, and if he or she leaves clear and unambiguous instructions they must be obeyed. Only if there is some ambiguity or uncertainty in the will itself can the court consider other evidence, such as letters written by the deceased, or memories of conversations. Thus the language of a will must be clear and unambiguous, and the wording carefully chosen.

If ambiguous words are used, there are two possible consequences. First, the gift might not go to the correct people. For instance, suppose a man leaves his property to 'my children' and at the time of his death he has three children, including one stepchild. In such a case the law will construe 'my children' as meaning 'my own children of the whole blood', and so the stepchild will not receive anything. The property will all go to the other two children. There is a story, perhaps apocryphal, of the original 'lucky bastard'. A man is supposed to have made a will stating, 'I leave everything to my nephew Arthur.' There were in fact two nephews called Arthur, one of whom was illegitimate. On the construction of the will the court decided that the illegitimate nephew was the one intended to benefit under the will.

The second possible consequence of unclear wording is that the gift will fail altogether, because the court cannot decide what the testator meant. For an example of real trouble arising from a real will, look at the homemade will on page 151, and the resulting consequences.

The moral is to avoid difficulties by using clear, unambiguous language when drawing up a will. Sometimes testators fail to see inconsistencies in their wishes. They desire to leave everything to their spouse absolutely but they then contradict that desire by attempting to leave to their children what is left when their spouse eventually dies. They can say what will happen if their spouse dies first but otherwise a trust must be established and the spouse does not get an absolute interest.

Because of pitfalls such as these, words used in a will must be chosen with great care. While the layperson can draft their own will if it is simple (for instance, leaving all their property to one person), it is unwise to draft one's own will if there are several beneficiaries involved, or if the value of the estate is considerable. In these cases it is worth paying a small amount for a solicitor to draft the will. In fact, many solicitors make wills for a low fee in the hope that they will be asked to take over the rewarding work of administering the estate when the testator dies. There are firms which offer a will-writing service, but these may not be any cheaper than a solicitor and may not always have the broad view of the law necessary to advise on the best way to arrange one's affairs generally. Bear in mind also that inheritance tax can begin to bite on an estate worth over £255,000 (or even less if gifts have been made within the last seven years). Will-drafting by a solicitor may pay for itself many times over if the solicitor can draw up the will so as to reduce the IHT payable. Generally, therefore, it is wise to use a solicitor for drafting a will; this does not, of course, mean that there will be any obligation to let the solicitor administer the estate when the time comes. A person should think very carefully indeed before allowing their bank to arrange a will to be drawn up. The bank will inevitably put itself forward as executor and this will mean that the estate will have to pay the bank's administration charges, which are usually much higher than those charged by solicitors. A typical bank charge for administering an estate of £200,000, comprising a house worth £150,000 and a building society account of £50,000, could be as much as £6,000.

A person who is not prepared to go to a solicitor and who insists on writing his or her own will should use one of the will forms obtainable from stationers. These forms have the Wills Act requirements incorporated into them and give basic instructions for completion. Despite these precautions, people still make mistakes when using these forms. Also, the forms give little help on how to word the gifts correctly. Before completing one of these forms, however, read the home-made will on page 151, which contains several serious mistakes and ambiguities. Do not take any risks when making your will. Your family may be able to sue your solicitor if he or she is negligent when making your will. They cannot sue you when you are gone. If you are keen to make your own will you should read one of the numerous books offering advice.

Words in wills

Wills drawn up by solicitors sometimes seem verbose and full of antiquated legal jargon. Usually there is a reason for this; the solicitor is carefully using words and phrases that are known to have a well-defined legal meaning, usually as a result of court decisions which have laid down what these phrases mean. Generally, though, most people's wills can be written in modern English, uncluttered by the 'hereinafters', 'abovementioneds', 'herein beforementioneds', 'provided howevers' etc., that one frequently associates with legal documents. But whatever words they use – ancient or modern – the person drafting the document will need to choose their vocabulary with care, and also to ensure that the will envisages and deals with all possible eventualities. If you have a will prepared by a solicitor, do not be afraid to ask what a phrase means in ordinary English. It is your will, so you should understand it! If the solicitor can't explain it, do they understand it?

Words that are frequently used

bequeath The word 'bequeath' is used to refer to a gift of anything other than land. 'Land' includes houses, flats and open spaces. If the gift is of land, the word 'devise' is used. For instance, a testator 'bequeaths' a car, or a gift of £x, but he 'devises' his house. The words 'I give' are a good alternative.

children This includes both legitimate and illegitimate children, whether boys or girls. Adopted children are included if the will was made before or after the date of the formal adoption order, although there can be complications if the will leaves property 'to the children of . . . living at my death'. If the adoption takes place after the death, the child is treated as having been born after the death, even though their actual date of birth was before the death. Stepchildren do not always come within the definition of 'children' unless all the children are stepchildren and there are no other children alive at the date the will was made, or unless it is clear that the stepchildren were intended to be included.

descendants This means children, grandchildren, great-grandchildren, great-great-grandchildren, etc., whether male or female. If property is left to 'all my descendants', each individual descendant will have an equal share of the estate (referred to as '*per capita*'), whereas it may have been the intention of the testator that only their children should have an equal share, so that if a child has died leaving grandchildren, those grandchildren will share their parent's share (referred to as '*per stirpes*').

family This word has been held to have several different meanings. Generally, it means the same as 'children', but the careful will-drafter will avoid using the word 'family' because of the confusion over its meaning. In divorce proceedings, for instance, 'a child of the family' is one treated as one of the family whoever their parents. This can be quite different from 'a child of the marriage', who may be living with another family even though his parents are divorcing.

free of tax Although the law provides for the payment of inheritance tax from the residue of the UK estate, the testator can overrule that provision. If a particular gift is to bear its own proportion of inheritance tax, the will should make that clear.

infant This means the same as 'minor', i.e. a person under 18 years. People under 18 cannot own land and they cannot give a valid receipt to the personal representatives for money or chattels. It is risky for a gift to be passed direct to a minor as that minor could spend the money and then sue the personal representatives upon reaching 18 for failing to stop them from wasting the money. In the case of land, it will be held by trustees until the child is 18, and with other property the usual device is to word the will so that the gift goes to the parents or other trustees, who are asked to hold it for the child's benefit.

issue This has basically the same meaning as 'descendants', but occasionally it has been held to have a different meaning. Therefore, the word 'issue' should be treated with caution.

legacy This usually means a specific sum left to a beneficiary but it can also be a gift of a specific item.

nephews and nieces The general rule is that this phrase includes only the testator's own nephews and nieces, and not those of his/her spouse. For the avoidance of doubt, it is wise to name the children rather than simply describe them as 'my nephews and nieces'.

next of kin This will be the person who is the closest blood relative of the testator.

residue The residue is what is left after paying the testamentary expenses, the inheritance tax and all the specific legacies and devises (i.e. after all specific gifts have been made).

testamentary expenses These are the expenses of administering the estate: e.g. expenses of the executors, probate fees, lawyers' fees, costs of adverts, tracing beneficiaries, etc.

Making a will: thinking ahead

The person drafting a will has to think ahead and envisage all possible circumstances, such as the death of the main beneficiary, a change in the size of the estate or even a change in the tax laws. These are some of the points that a solicitor would want his or her client to consider:

- Are some people to be allowed to select mementoes or souvenirs from the testator's personal possessions? If so, it is wise to give very clear guidance to the personal representatives to enable them to avoid disputes which might otherwise arise over the identity and value of these items. It might also be sensible to give them authority to deal with disputes if any should arise.

- Is there a gift of the *residue*? The residue is the property that is not specifically given away as named items or as money legacies. If there is no gift of the 'remainder of my property', the residue will not pass under the will but be distributed as though the testator had died intestate (*see* pages 162–3). This is a very common omission in home-made wills, where the testator leaves exactly what they have got when they make the will. Remember that a person may win the lottery between making their will and dying.

- Is a gift to bear its own inheritance tax? Under the Inheritance Tax Act 1984 s211, all inheritance tax on the UK estate falls on the residue, unless the will provides otherwise. Would that be fair on the residuary beneficiary? Do not forget that a gift to a spouse is exempt and that there are other exemptions.

- If a house is to be given to a beneficiary, are any mortgages to be paid off? If so, it is the residue that will suffer. Would that be fair? At this point it is worth noting that confusion can arise over the effect of a mortgage protection policy. This is an insurance policy that pays out enough money on death to pay off the mortgage. However, it does not always follow that the insurance money must be used to pay off the mortgage; to avoid doubt it is wise to have a clause in the will which makes it clear that the policy monies are to be used to pay off the mortgage. In some cases the policy money may not be paid to the estate at all but direct to a spouse or a child, thus avoiding aggregation with the other assets of the estate for inheritance tax.

- Should a particular beneficiary be given a first option to buy a specific item from the estate and, if so, on what terms? This can cause problems if not carefully thought out. It may be better for the testator to make the arrangements direct with the beneficiary before making the will.

- What if a beneficiary should die before the testator? Normally, a dead person cannot inherit under a will. So, if the beneficiary is already dead when the testator dies, then the gift will fail. In this case, the property that should have gone to the dead person will remain in the testator's estate – and go to those people who are entitled to the residue. However, there is one exception. If the gift was to a child (or grandchild) of the testator, then it passes to that child's (or grandchild's) children. But, if the dead child did not have any children, then the gift will fail – it will pass into residue (and not, for instance, go to the dead child's spouse). It is, therefore, important when making a will to consider making substitutional gifts, to deal with the eventuality of someone else dying first. Bear in mind that if a specific gift does lapse, it will be added into the residue. Would that be an unfair benefit to the person entitled to the residue?

- What will happen if the person who is to receive the residue should die before the testator? Unless other arrangements are set out in the will the residue would then pass under the intestacy rules (*see* pages 162–3).
- Are there any adopted, legitimated or illegitimate children? Although such children are assumed to be included in the phrase 'children' (*see* above), it is best to avoid any doubt by specifically naming them.
- Does the will revoke all previous wills made by the testator?
- Is it possible that the testator will not own the property specifically named when they die? Obviously, if they do not own the property at the time of their death, they will not be able to give it to the beneficiary, and so the testator should consider this possibility by including an alternative gift when drafting the will. Lawyers say that a will 'speaks from death', which means that one must look at the position at the time of death, not at the time the will was written. For example, if a person makes a gift of 'my sports car' but by the time of his death has traded in the sports car for a saloon model, then the proposed beneficiary will take nothing; the correct way to word the will is to give 'my car' or 'my sports car or any other car I may own at the time of my death'. A gift that fails in this way is said to have been 'adeemed'.
- Does the testator have any infant children? If so, should the will appoint guardians in case the other parent also dies and the children are left without parents?
- If the estate is a large one, does it take advantage of the inheritance tax exemptions? In particular, do the respective wills of husband and wife both make gifts to the children in order to make the most of the £255,000 exemption available on each death?
- Is there a gift subject to a condition? Such a clause requires very careful drafting. The solicitor will word it so that the condition is for an event to happen before the gift is made, rather than for the gift to be forfeited on the event happening. Also, the condition should be drafted in such a way that it will be easy for the personal representatives to decide whether or not the condition has been satisfied.
- The will should name the executors. Should substitutes be named in case the named executors have died or are unable to take on the job? Two is generally regarded as the ideal number of executors. Are the executors to be paid for their services? If so, the will must specifically authorize their payment. It is usual to include a 'charging clause' in the will when there are professional executors such as solicitors or accountants. This, enables them to make normal charges for their services. Think twice before appointing the bank as executor, as their administration tends to be quite expensive,

especially for simple estates. Before naming someone as an executor, the testator should check that the person is willing to be an executor; a person named as an executor can decline to act. It is not essential to name executors: it will still be a valid will even if executors are not named.

- Does the will specifically state that it is 'signed by the testator in our presence and then by us as witnesses in his/her presence and in the presence of each other'? This confirms that the main requirements of the Wills Act have been observed and is called an 'attestation clause'. Its omission will result in the personal representatives being unable to prove the will until they obtain evidence from the witnesses that the Wills Act rules were observed. Accordingly, an attestation clause will save time, expense and inconvenience after the death.
- Should a trust be set up? It is often done inadvertently in home-made wills by clauses such as, 'I leave my estate to my wife, but if she remarries I leave it to my daughter.' Like it or not, the testator has created a trust which prevents the wife from having access to the capital even if she never remarries. A trust is an arrangement whereby property is given to someone to hold for another person's use until the occurrence of some event, such as their death. The concept is very simple but, unfortunately, the more one goes into it the more complicated it becomes. Suffice it to say that if I had £200,000 and an ex-wife, I might leave the money to a solicitor to hold on trust for my ex-wife until her death. Although the solicitor (the 'trustee') would be the legal owner of the money, it would be my ex-wife (the 'beneficiary') who would receive the benefit of the gift. However, she would not receive the capital sum itself; my solicitor would have to invest the money and my ex-wife would be entitled to receive only the interest or income from it – she could not touch the capital unless the will gave my trustee power to pay some of the capital to my ex-wife. On my ex-wife's death, the £200,000 would revert back into my estate and be distributed by my personal representatives in accordance with the terms of my will.

A trust is an effective method of giving a person the benefit of property without actually giving them the property itself. The beneficiary of a trust can be anyone – an infant, a Mental Health Act patient, a spouse, etc. – but the main use of the trust has been to enable wealthy families to pass their money down through the generations without the risk of it being squandered by one spendthrift member of the family. The trust is also used in schemes to minimize the amount of income tax and IHT paid by members of a family, and was greatly used in the past for estate duty avoidance schemes. If complex trusts are being contemplated, specialist legal advice will be essential. A trust giving a person a life interest should be approached with caution.

Making a will: a summary of the steps to be taken

1 Draw up a list of the estate. This will be all the assets, such as land, property, business, money, cars, valuables, etc., less debts (i.e. mortgage, bank overdraft, bills, etc.). The net figure is the likely estate.

2 Draw up a list of beneficiaries: the people who are to benefit.

3 Work out who is to receive what. How is inheritance tax to be paid? Check that all eventualities are covered. Is the bulk of the estate to pass under the gift of the residue or is that just a tidying-up clause?

4 Is there any property outside England and Wales (are two wills needed), are there any insurance policies written in trust, is there any jointly owned property (does it pass under the will or automatically to the survivor)? Have any gifts been made in the last seven years which might affect inheritance tax or which might result in one person getting more than their fair share?

5 The will should be set out on a clean sheet of paper. While it can be handwritten, it is advisable to type it and so avoid any problems of illegible handwriting.

6 The first clause of the will should set out the correct and full baptismal names of the testator. If he or she does not always use that name, the words 'sometimes known as . . .' should be stated. To avoid doubt it is best to state specifically that all previous wills are revoked. There is no need to start with the words 'This is the last will and testament of' although many lawyers use these words in order to avoid any doubts if an earlier will remains.

A typical opening might be:
'This will is made by me .... of ....'
The first clause should say:
'I revoke all earlier wills and codicils.'

7 The next clause should appoint the executors. Note that the executor(s) can be beneficiaries under the will (but witnesses cannot, *see* page 138). In a typical will the testator leaves all their property to their spouse and in such a case it is usual to appoint the spouse as the sole executor or executrix, with a named alternative in case the spouse cannot act for some reason. If a professional executor, such as a solicitor, is to be appointed, then the clause should specifically allow him or her to charge the estate for their work. (If everything is being left to the spouse there is seldom any need to appoint a professional executor.) In such a case, the testator should inquire what the executor's likely fee will be. A person should not be shy to ask what the fees will be if a bank is to be executor. A solicitor's charges will almost certainly be less.

8 The will should next deal with all the gifts of money and property other than land (which includes houses and flats). These are the legacies and bequests – the words 'personal chattels' are used to describe all such personal property, except for money. A typical clause will state: 'I give to (*name*) absolutely such of my chattels and effects of personal domestic or household use or ornament as are not hereby otherwise specifically disposed of'. The Administration of Estates Act 1925 provides a definition of 'personal chattels' which includes motor cars, horses, wines and domestic animals, as well as the more obvious items. The will can then go on to deal with specific gifts:
'I give the following specific items absolutely:
(a) to my daughter (*name*) my gold watch (be very careful to define which watch where the testator may have several gold watches);
(b) to my grandson (*name*) the tools which belonged to my late husband', and finally deal with pecuniary legacies: 'I give the following pecuniary legacies absolutely and free of all taxes:
(a) to (*name*) the sum of £*x*;
(b) to each of my grandchildren living at my death (absolutely and free of all taxes) the sum of £*x*.' If the sum is small it may be desirable to allow the parents to receive the legacy on behalf of the infant grandchildren in order to release the executors from long-term trust responsibilities.

9 Next come the devises of real property (i.e. land, houses and flats). Sometimes these devises are made via trusts, in which case complicated provisions may apply. Legal advice is then essential. Often, though, the property (generally the family house) will go to the testator's spouse along with all the other property. Then a simple will might read: 'I give the whole of my estate to my wife/husband subject only to the payment of my debts and testamentary expenses but if s/he should fail to survive me the succeeding provisions of this will shall take effect.' (*Then set out the alternative provisions.*)

10 Who is the residue (i.e. the net estate after making all the other gifts) to go to? Usually it is left to the surviving spouse in which case a clause similar to that above can be used. Otherwise, a different clause will be needed, such as: 'I give the residue of my estate to my two sons (*names*) equally, but if either of them dies before me leaving children then those children shall on reaching eighteen take equally the share which their father would otherwise have taken.' If the residue is not left to anybody it will be distributed under the intestacy rules (*see* pages 162–3). When working out entitlement under the intestacy rules, any benefits received under the will are taken into account. If a surviving spouse has already received £20,000 under the will then she will be absolutely

entitled only to £105,000 (£180,000 if there are no children) plus a life interest in half the residue.

11 What powers are to be given to the executors? There are various Acts of Parliament which set down certain powers but these can be quite restricting, so a testator will often want to give his or her executors wider powers, especially if they have money to invest or a business to wind up.

12 Does a testator have any declaration to make which would influence the executors? Here he or she would indicate, for example, whether they wished to be buried or cremated, and whether they wished to donate their body for medical research.

13 Finally, the testator should sign in the presence of the two witnesses. Remember that neither the witnesses, nor their spouses, can be beneficiaries. Typical wording is:

In witness whereof I have hereunto set my hand on the date set out at the beginning of my will

Signed by the above-named (*name*) in our presence and then by us in the presence of him/her and each other:

(*signature*)

(*signature of first witness*)
(*name, address, occupation*)

(*signature of second witness*)
(*name, address, occupation*)

14 The will should be kept in a safe place; it is advisable to make photocopies. Solicitors and banks will usually hold wills. Alternatively, the will can be lodged for safekeeping with the Principal Registry (at First Avenue House, High Holborn, London) – contact any district probate registry for details of this service (which costs £15). This ensures that the will is available when anyone attempts to become a personal representative and so there can be no risk of the testator dying intestate. The executors and the family should be told where the original will is kept and a note of the place written on a copy of the will kept with the other papers.

15 The really conscientious will-maker will try to make things easy for his/her relatives by making a comprehensive note of all the personal details that might be needed after death – for example, names and addresses of doctor, trade union, bank, accountant, solicitor, landlord, employer, building society, anyone who is a beneficiary or who should be told of the death. Also, where the following documents can be found: birth and marriage certificates, driving licence, insurance policies, title deeds, HP agreements, building society and bank books, rent book, passport, share certificates, NI card, etc.

16 It should be remembered that marriage revokes a will

so always make a new will on remarriage (as for divorce – *see* below).

REVOKING A WILL

The usual way of cancelling a will is by making a new one and commencing it with the phrase. 'I revoke all former wills and codicils made by me'. If the revocation clause was not included, the new will would revoke the earlier will only in so far as it was inconsistent with it.

As might be expected, the deliberate burning, tearing up or destroying of a will is assumed to destroy it. But merely writing 'revoked' across the face of the will may not be enough.

The revocation of a will may not always be effective if it was done on a false assumption. For example, suppose a testator makes a new will and then tears up their old will. If the new will should be held to be invalid for some reason, the testator would seem to be left without a valid will. However, in these circumstances, the court might say that the revocation of the old will was conditional on the new will being valid and, since that is not so, the revocation of the first will would be ineffective and it would still be a valid will. The jargon for this conditional revocation is 'dependent relative revocation' – a phrase that endows a straightforward idea with an unnecessary aura of complexity. For instance:

In August 1966, Mr Carey, a widower, made a will leaving his estate to his sister-in-law. He left the will with his solicitors but in 1972 he reclaimed it saying that he had nothing to leave and so he was going to destroy the will. In 1973 his sister died leaving him £40,000. In 1976 Mr Carey died without leaving a will. The sister-in-law asked the court to enforce the 1966 will on the basis that it had been revoked by Mr Carey in the mistaken belief that he had nothing to leave. Held: The 1966 will remained valid.

Re Carey (1977)

Marriage and divorce

Marriage

Revocation is automatic on the marriage of the testator. The logic behind this rule is that Parliament in 1837 assumed that most testators would want to leave their property to their spouse but a newly married testator might forget to alter their will, which might not mention the spouse as a beneficiary. Thus the Wills Act provides that unless the testator makes a new will after their marriage, they will die intestate and so the spouse will inherit some, if not all, of the estate under the intestacy rules (*see* page 162–3). The only exception to this rule is when the gift was clearly made in contemplation of the marriage, for then the testator can be assumed to have had their spouse-to-be in mind when they drafted the will; this applies even if the will leaves nothing to the spouse, for Parliament did not think it proper in 1837 to interfere with the right of a man to dispose of his property as he wished. Now, of course, the family provision legislation allows the courts to award shares of the estate to a spouse and other dependants (*see* Chapter 14).

If a will is made before a marriage it should always state that 'This will is made in contemplation of my marriage with . . .' If the marriage does not take place such a will would remain valid, and so it is usual to add 'and is conditional on the marriage taking place within . . . months'. Unless clear wording is used, the courts will not be able to uphold the will as having been made in contemplation of marriage. If a testator asks a solicitor to make a will in circumstances where the testator's cohabitant has taken the same surname, it is important to advise the solicitor, who may otherwise make wrong assumptions about inheritance tax liability and the like. If such a couple subsequently married, the will would become invalid and the intestacy rules would apply – not at all what might have been intended.

Divorce

Divorce does not invalidate a will but may make it largely ineffective. This is because any gift to the former spouse will no longer take effect, and nor will the appointment of the ex-husband/wife as executor. In effect, the ex-spouse is cut out of the will, as if they had died on the date of the decree absolute, but the rest of the will takes effect in the usual way. This rule is subject to there being no 'contrary intention' in the will – so if it is made clear that the spouse is to have the gift even if there is a divorce, then the gift will remain valid. Remember, though, that if the divorce is followed by a remarriage then the new marriage will invalidate the will (*see* above) and so the ex-spouse will get nothing – unless a new will is executed in which a gift is made to them (or unless they can apply to the court under the family provision legislation – *see* Chapter 14).

If a divorced spouse is cut out of the will in this way, then his/her share will go to the person who is entitled to the residue (i.e. all parts of the estate that are not specifically given to other people). So, if you are getting divorced, your ex-spouse will be cut out of the will – but you should think carefully about what will happen to his/her share. If you do not want it to go to the person who is entitled to the residue, then you should alter your will to deal specifically with the point. If you are paying maintenance under a court order you should seek legal advice on how best to deal with that matter under your will.

Can you agree not to alter your will?

The general rule is that a will is not a contract so disappointed beneficiaries cannot sue for breach of contract if they are not left what they were promised by the testator. This is because a person is free to alter his or her will as he or she pleases.

There are exceptions to this rule. For instance, two people may wish to enter into mutual wills in which each one undertakes not to change their will upon the death of the other. This is really a form of contract, which can cause serious problems if some unforeseen circumstances occur after the first death. In these cases it is generally unwise to rely on a verbal promise. Legal advice should be taken and a deed should be prepared setting out the arrangement.

Sometimes a person promises to leave money or an item in their will, but when they die, no mention of the gift can be found in the will. Usually the disappointed beneficiary would have no remedy (unless they were a dependant, cohabitant or close member of the family, in which case they might be able to apply to the court for reasonable provision under the Inheritance (Provision for Family and Dependants) Act 1975). However, in a recent case, a person who had worked for a wealthy bachelor farmer for many years was promised that the family business would be left to him. Unfortunately, the wealthy bachelor then met a young trainee solicitor, dismissed the employee, and left the property to the trainee solicitor. The court allowed the employee's claim on the employer's promise because the employee had relied on the promise and as a result had devoted his life to the farm. These were special circumstances but they do show that the court can take a flexible approach in some cases.

Alterations

Any alteration to a will should be treated as a new will, with all the Wills Act formalities being observed, even if the alteration or amendment is only minor. An amendment to a will is called a 'codicil'. A codicil is an amending document prepared and signed with all the formalities of a will. Apart from ensuring that the codicil is properly signed and attested, it is wise to state that 'in all other respects I confirm my will' so there can be no suggestion that the codicil was meant to revoke the whole will. However, if the layperson wishes to alter their will, it is better to rewrite the whole will in its amended form than add on codicils.

Three sample wills, one invalid, one defective but valid and one effective and valid, are shown on pages 145, 150 and 151.

After-death variations

It has always been possible to disclaim a benefit under a will, but the right to vary a will after the death is a comparatively recent development. Under the Finance Act 1984 variations can be made to wills or in the event of intestacy, so that adult beneficiaries can effectively agree who should get what. This redistribution must take place within two years of the death but it does enable the beneficiaries to reorganize the provisions of the will. A variation can be made to an infant's benefit provided the benefit is increased; otherwise the consent of the court will be required. These variations are subject to a number of conditions upon which legal advice should be obtained as soon as possible after the death, but it does mean that a will can be written for the deceased even if he or she never made a will before they died.

LIVING WILLS

These are not wills in the normal sense of the word. They set out how you would want to be treated if you were found to be suffering from a disease or incapacity which resulted in you being kept alive by intensive or painful treatment. You cannot use the living will to deal with your property or make funeral requests – you will need to make an ordinary will to do this.

A living will would be prepared after consultation with your doctor. It would set out the circumstances under which you would not want certain treatments or medication to be administered, even if that meant your life would not be prolonged.

A person who has all his faculties can make a decision about the medical treatment he wishes to have. If a person loses those faculties, having previously made a living will, the medical treatment he then receives should follow the wishes set out in the living will, provided that they are reasonable and have been discussed with that person's doctor.

Where the living will contains requirements about the future treatment (an 'advance directive'), the situation will be examined carefully. If the person making the request has done so without undue influence from third parties and following discussion with a doctor, the request would be binding provided that it did not ask for a treatment which would cause death without any beneficial effect (which would not be the case if the treatment was intended to ease suffering although it might hasten an otherwise inevitable death).

Information packs on living wills can be obtained from the Law Society or the Terrence Higgins Trust (52–54 Grays Inn Road, London WC1X 8JU, Tel: 08451 221200). *See* pages 146–9 for an example of a Living Will.

Three sample wills

An invalid will

John James wants to leave everything to his cohabitant, and nothing to the wife from whom he is separated.

> I John James of 2 Abingdon Cottages, London NE1 make this my Will, as set out in the Schedule below. Signed by me, John James, on the 2nd of November 2001
>
> ....
> (*signature*)
>
> Witnesses: Mabel Smith
>
> ....
> (*signature*)
>
> *The Schedule*
> I give the whole of my estate to my common-law wife Mabel Smith and nothing to my lawful wife Anne James.

Defects in this invalid will

1 The testator, John James, has not signed at the end of the will. This in itself would not make the will invalid, but the Probate Registry will probably query the signature (causing delay and probably expense).

2 The beneficiary is Mabel Smith, yet she is the witness. Even if there were two witnesses, the gift to her would therefore fail and the estate would pass under the laws of intestacy to Anne James, the testator's surviving spouse (and, if the estate was of sufficient size, to children or other relatives; *see* pages 162–3).

3 Even if there were two witnesses who were not beneficiaries, it is not stated that the witnesses saw the testator sign and that they then signed in his presence. While such a clause is not essential, the Probate Registry will not grant probate until it has been confirmed that the proper formalities were observed. If the witnesses cannot be traced, this can cause delay and difficulty.

4 The will does not state that it revokes all previous wills. If there is no revocation clause the will only revokes an earlier will in so far as it is inconsistent with it. In this example, it would probably make no difference but it is always wise to avoid doubt by inserting a revocation clause.

5 A properly drafted will would appoint executors.

Summary. The will fails completely. Thus John James will die intestate and all or part of his property will pass to his wife, Anne James, which is precisely what he wanted to avoid. The only hope that Mabel Smith, his cohabitant,

This is an important document. Before you fill it in, please read the notes which are attached to this form. We recommend that you discuss your Living Will with a doctor, but you do not have to.

Living Will declaration

Your details

I make this Living Will to record my wishes in case I become unable to communicate, and cannot take part in decisions about my medical care.

Name:

Address:

Daytime phone number: Evening phone number:

If you discuss this Living Will with a doctor before or after you fill it in, please fill in this section.

I have discussed this Living Will with the following doctor.

Doctor's name:

Doctor's address:

Doctor's phone number:

Living Will Advance directives

1 Medical treatment in general

Three possible health conditions are described below.
For each condition, choose 'A' or 'B' by ticking the appropriate box, or leave both boxes blank
if you have no preference. The choice between 'A' or 'B' is exactly the same in each case.
Treat each case separately. You do not have to make the same choice for each one.

I declare that my wishes concerning medical treatment are as follows.

Case 1 Life-threatening condition

Here are my wishes if:
- I have a physical illness from which there is no likelihood of recovery; *and*
- the illness is so serious that my life is nearing its end.

A *I want to be kept alive for as long as is reasonably possible
using whatever forms of medical treatment are available.*

B *I do not want to be kept alive by medical treatment. I want medical treatment to be limited
to keeping me comfortable and free from pain. I refuse all other medical treatment.*

Case 2 Permanent mental impairment

Here are my wishes if:
- my mental functions have become permanently impaired;
- the impairment is so severe that I do not understand what is happening to me;
- there is no likelihood of improvement; *and*
- my physical condition then becomes so bad that I would need medical treatment to keep me alive.

A *I want to be kept alive for as long as is reasonably possible
using whatever forms of medical treatment are available.*

B *I do not want to be kept alive by medical treatment. I want medical treatment to be limited
to keeping me comfortable and free from pain. I refuse all other medical treatment.*

Case 3 Permanent unconsciousness

Here are my wishes if:
- I become permanently unconscious and there is no likelihood I will regain consciousness.

A *I want to be kept alive for as long as is reasonably possible
using whatever forms of medical treatment are available.*

B *I do not want to be kept alive by medical treatment. I want medical treatment to be limited
to keeping me comfortable and free from pain. I refuse all other medical treatment.*

Living Will Advance directives

2 Particular treatments or tests

If you have any wishes about particular medical treatments or tests, you can record them here.
If you want to refuse a particular treatment or test, you should say so clearly. This is where to
write your views about treatment or tests while you are pregnant. You should speak to a doctor
before you write anything in this space.

3 Having a friend or relative with you if your life is in danger

You can fill in this section if you would like a particular person to be with you if your life is in
danger. It may not be possible to contact the person you name, or for him or her to arrive in time.

*If my life is in danger, I want the following person to be contacted to
give him or her a chance to be with me before I die.*

Name:

Address:

Daytime phone number: Evening phone number:

Tick this box if you fill in a name in this section, and you want to be kept alive for as long
as is reasonable to give the person you name a chance to reach you.

If you tick this box, any wishes you have stated above in Section 1 – *Medical treatment in general* and
Section 2 – *Particular treatments or tests* may be temporarily disregarded. This is explained in the notes with this form.

Living Will Health care proxy

I appoint the following person to take part in decisions about my medical care on my behalf and to represent my views about the decisions if I am unable to do so. I want him or her to be consulted about and involved in those decisions and I want anyone who is caring for me to respect the views he or she expresses on my behalf.

Name:

Address:

Daytime phone number: Evening phone number:

Signatures

This Living Will remains effective until I make clear that my wishes have changed.

Sign and date the form here in the presence of a witness.

Your signature: Date: /   /

The witness must sign here after you have signed the form.
The witness should then print his or her name and address in the spaces provided.
Please read the notes to this form to see who should not be a witness.

Signature of witness:

Name of witness:

Address of witness:

will have of inheriting any of the estate is to apply to the court under the family provision legislation (*see* Chapter 14).

A valid will

Sydney James wants to make a simple will leaving everything to his wife if she survives him and to his son if she does not.

This will dated 2 November 2001 is made by me Sydney James, of 2 Abingdon Cottages, London NE1.

1) I revoke all earlier wills.
2) I appoint my wife Emma James of 2 Abingdon Cottages, London NE1 to be the executor of this my Will but if she should be unwilling or unable to act as my executor I appoint my son, Harry James of 93 Clifton Road, London NE5, to be my executor.
3) I give the whole of my estate to my wife Emma James of 2 Abingdon Cottages, London NE1, but if she should pre-decease me I leave all my said estate to my son Harry James of 93 Clifton Road, London NE5.

In witness whereof I have set my hand on the date set out above

Signed by the above-named
Sydney James in our presence   Sydney James ....
and then by us in his and in the   (*signature*)
presence of each other:

Fred Evans
(1a Abingdon Cottages, London NE1, postman)

Mavis Evans
　　(1a Abingdon Cottages, London NE1, housewife)

Note. This will is for illustration purposes only. Do not risk adapting it to other circumstances. Many stationers sell pre-printed wills that can be used to cover most contingencies and one of those forms should be used if a solicitor is not used to draft the will, but consider the errors in the defective but valid will before taking the risk.

Even this would be an inefficient will in the following circumstances: if the estate of Sydney James was worth £200,000 and if his wife had investments of her own worth £150,000, the death of Sydney before Emma would incur no inheritance tax (all transfers to a spouse are free of tax). However, on Emma's death the combined value of £200,000 and £150,000 would incur inheritance tax of £38,000.

If, on the other hand, Sydney James had left £150,000 to his son and the balance of £50,000 to his wife, there would still be no inheritance tax to pay on his death

(£255,000 exemption covers the gift to the son and the balance passing to the wife is also free). On the wife's death she will have a total estate of £200,000 (£150,000 + £50,000), which is below the inheritance tax threshold of £255,000. This represents an overall saving of £38,000! Not all professionally drawn wills can save such a large amount, but a badly drawn home-made will can cost you dear.

A home-made will

How *not* to write your own will (see p. 151).

Here is a real example of a home-made will typed on to a will form. Only slight changes have been made for anonymity. The testator was an intelligent man but frugal. In saving the solicitor's fees by making his own will he has dropped several clangers.

The real property consisted of several acres of land, comprised in one set of title deeds, on which there were two houses. Ashfield House, occupied by the deceased, was left to his daughter, the other, Ashfield Cottage, was occupied by the daughter and her husband as tenants but was left to the son. The garage for Ashfield House stood at the end (not on the south side and not on the north side) of the communal carriageway. The deceased left money in a building society, but he also left stocks and shares. The value of Ashfield House was approximately equal to the value of Ashfield Cottage plus the money.

The testator has made several serious mistakes:

1　The will gives the daughter an empty house. What if she stays on as a tenant in Ashfield Cottage, left to her brother, and sells the testator's house, Ashfield House? The brother gets a sitting tenant.
2　The testator's garage, which serves Ashfield House, is at the end of the communal drive. It is not to the south or to the north of it. Who gets the garage which serves Ashfield House left to the daughter?
3　Inheritance tax was payable. Is it to be paid equally by son and daughter? The daughter had no money so she would have to sell Ashfield House, which she has inherited and hopes to live in, in order to pay the tax. What did the testator intend? Was the son to pay all inheritance tax from his 'money'? If so, the value of his inheritance was much less than the daughter's. The testator appears to have thought that he was sharing his assets out equally and the thought that tax would be payable had not occurred to him.
4　The will leaves the son 'all my money'. In law the meaning of 'money' must be ascertained from the context. What did the testator intend? He makes a mistake common in home-made wills: he tries to dispose of everything he owns at the time of making the will as specific items. He forgets to write in a clause which disposes of the residue of the estate.
5　The testator refers to his daughter's death. Does he mean that the property he leaves to her is to go to his

This is the last Will and Testament

of me   Edward Johnson

of   Ashfield House, Clodby

in the County of   Nottingham

made this   1st   day of   January

in the year of our Lord one thousand nine hundred and   ninety one

I HEREBY revoke all Wills made by me at any time heretofore. I appoint my son Darren Johnson

to be my Executor(s) and direct that all my debts and Funeral Expenses shall be paid as soon as conveniently may be after my decease.

I GIVE AND BEQUEATH   unto my son Darren Johnson all that property known as Ashfield Cottage, comprising house, workshop, buildings and land on the north side of the communal carriage way with all machinery, tools and all my money, half of my furniture and domestic goods.

I GIVE AND BEQUEATH unto my daughter Jane Fitzhenry of Ashfield Cottage all that property known as Ashfield House and paddock all that is at the south side of communal carriage way, the oak desk and cupboard and half of my furniture and domestic goods.

The communal carriage way is to be included in the property I leave to my son Darren Johnson.

In the event of my daughter Jane Fitzhenry's death, the property that I leave her shall not become the property of Silas Fitzhenry, but shall become the property of my grand daughter Tracey Fitzhenry.

If my wife Winnie survives me she shall have the use of all this property and money during her life and upon her death this Will shall be executed.

Signed by the said TESTATOR
in the presence of us, present at the same time, who at
his request, in his presence, and in the presence of
each other, have subscibed our names as witnesses.
If necessary to use next page, strike this out

C. Johnson

M. Cantor

Evelyn Cantor

granddaughter if his daughter dies before him or does he mean that his daughter is to get only a life interest in the property he has left to her, in which case she cannot sell Ashfield House? Furthermore, does he mean only the real property or all the property which she receives?

6 The testator's wife, Winnie, died before the testator, but if she had survived him a trust would have arisen which would have left the widow short of money but unable to sell the houses.

When wills like this are written they can cause trouble between families for a generation, and they can and do prove very expensive to administer, because a dispute of this type would have to go before a Chancery Court at a cost of many thousands of pounds. Do not forget the case of *Jarndyce* v *Jarndyce* in *Bleak House* (when the costs of the case extinguished the value of the estate before the case was concluded).

The moral of this story is, do not attempt to save the cost of having a will prepared by a solicitor if your estate is likely to incur inheritance tax or if you have any complicated provisions to make. Instead of a will costing, for example, £50, the estate had to pay several thousand pounds in additional costs before settling the case. Had it gone to court as a contested case, the costs would have been even greater and would probably have meant the selling of the testator's house left to the daughter. Neither party was happy about the settlement but neither did they want to risk losing any more of the estate in legal costs.

13

When Someone Dies

CHECKLIST OF STEPS TO BE TAKEN ON DEATH

Before personal representatives are appointed (*see* below) there are several administrative tasks that have to be carried out. Unfortunately, it is not always clear who is responsible for these tasks. Where families are close there should be no difficulty, but in other cases great care should be taken.

When a person dies leaving a will, the executors appointed by the will take on the mantle of authority immediately. If they are not close members of the family they will frequently delegate the funeral arrangements and the like to a member of the family.

When a person dies without making a will there can be difficulties because it may be several weeks or even months before letters of administration are granted, giving legal authority to the personal representatives. During that waiting period the funeral must be arranged. Some equally entitled members of the family may disagree about who should make these arrangements, about the place of burial or even the form of the funeral. More frequently there can be trouble because some members of the family enter the deceased's house and distribute cash and possessions wrongly, believing that they have authority or without understanding the strict rules that apply, perhaps forgetting the rights of the children of a deceased brother. A person meddling in this way can be in trouble because others may recollect that grandmother always kept her savings in the blue jug and where has that gone?

Immediately on death

If death occurred at home

The informant (usually but not necessarily a relative) should inform:

- the family doctor;

- relatives, and perhaps the priest, vicar, etc.;
- the department of anatomy of the local medical school if the deceased had donated his or her body for medical research. If the deceased was an organ-donor the nearest hospital should be informed;
- the police, if the death was violent, accidental or in suspicious circumstances.

If the doctor attended the deceased during their terminal illness, the doctor will give the relatives:

- a free medical certificate, showing the cause of death. This will be in a sealed envelope addressed to the registrar of deaths; and
- a formal notice stating that they have signed a medical certificate, and which also explains the procedure for registering the death.

Alternatively, the doctor will report the death to the coroner if:

- the deceased was not seen by a doctor during his last illness, or within 14 days of death; or
- if the cause of death is uncertain; or
- if the death was sudden, violent or caused by an accident; or
- if the death resulted from an industrial disease.

If death occurred in hospital

The ward nursing officer will inform the nearest relative of the death (the police will do this if the death followed an accident). The relative will have to attend the hospital to collect the deceased's possessions and also identify the body, unless the deceased had been an in-patient.

If the cause of death is clear, the hospital doctor will give the relatives a free medical certificate and a formal notice (as with a death at home, above). In addition, they will usually carry out a post-mortem, if the relatives agree.

Alternatively, they will report the death to the coroner if:

- the cause of death is uncertain; or

- the death was sudden, violent or caused by an accident;, or
- if the death resulted from an industrial disease; or
- if the death occurred during the course of an operation or while the deceased was under anaesthetic.

If the coroner is notified of the death

Whether the death was in hospital or not, the coroner will usually arrange for a post-mortem to be held; the relatives' consent is not needed, although they can retain a doctor to be present during the post-mortem.

The coroner may also decide to hold an inquest. He or she will generally do so if the cause of death:

- was violent; or
- was accidental; or
- resulted from an industrial disease; or
- remains uncertain.

If an inquest is held, the coroner will normally hold a preliminary hearing within a week or so of death. This hearing will be for purposes of identification only and formal evidence of the identity of the body will have to be given. The coroner will then release the body and so allow the funeral or cremation to take place. The inquest proper will usually take place some weeks later and will be an inquiry into the cause of death. The coroner may decide to sit with a jury. Relatives can attend the inquest and may wish to instruct a solicitor to attend if, for instance, the death was the result of a road accident (no public funding is available, however).

Before the burial can take place, the coroner must first issue a disposal certificate (either an order for burial or a certificate for cremation). This will normally be provided, free of charge, after the post-mortem or after the preliminary inquest hearing.

In addition, the coroner must also issue a cause of death certificate, so that the death can be registered. There are two possibilities:

- If the post-mortem shows that death was by natural causes, the coroner will normally provide a pink form addressed to the registrar of deaths in a sealed envelope. Sometimes he or she will simply send the form direct to the registrar, in which case the relatives will be notified of its issue.
- If a full inquest was held, the coroner will send a cause of death certificate direct to the registrar of deaths.

Registration of the death

Register the death with the local Registrar of Births, Deaths and Marriages (address in the telephone directory).

If the death has been reported to the coroner it cannot be registered until the coroner has provided the necessary pink form or certificate (*see* above). Thus there is nothing to be done until the coroner notifies the relatives that the pink form or certificate has been issued.

If the death has not been reported to the coroner, it must be registered within five days. Documents needed are:

- evidence of the cause of death (i.e. medical certificate provided by the doctor and/or pink form provided by a coroner);
- the deceased's NHS card, if available;
- the deceased's birth certificate and marriage certificate;
- any war pension order book of the deceased (if applicable and if available).

The registrar will want to know:

- date and place of death;
- deceased's usual address;
- full forenames(s) and surnames of the deceased (and maiden name, if a married woman);
- deceased's occupation (and that of her husband if a married woman or a widow);
- date of birth of deceased's surviving spouse (if applicable);
- whether the deceased was receiving any state benefits.

The registrar will then register the death and provide the applicant with:

- a certificate for disposal, unless the coroner has already issued one. This will have to be produced to the funeral director before the burial or cremation can take place;
- a certificate of registration of death. This is for social security purposes and upon production at the local DWP office will prove entitlement to bereavement allowance. Extra copies can be obtained at this stage for a small fee and may be needed for claims on insurance policies etc. They will cost more once the details have been passed to the Superintendent Registrar;
- pamphlets on welfare benefits that might be available and form PR 48, which gives guidance on obtaining a Grant of Probate.

The funeral arrangements

These cannot be finalized until it is known whether the death will be reported to the coroner, for this will affect the date when the body can be released for burial or cremation.

Check the deceased's will to see if it contains instructions as to whether he or she is to be buried or cremated. Note that there is no legal obligation on the executors or next of kin to follow these instructions: it is for them to decide whether to bury or cremate.

It is advisable to use a funeral director who belongs to the National Association of Funeral Directors (NAFD), since they are bound by a code of practice agreed with the Office of Fair Trading. In particular, an NAFD member must provide a full estimate in advance, and this must include the estimate for the cost of a basic, simple, funeral (i.e. exclusive of church fees, flowers, notices in local paper, but inclusive of a coffin, collection or delivery of the body up to 10 miles, care of the deceased, and provision of a hearse and one following car to the nearest local cemetery or crematorium, together with conductors and bearers as necessary).

If the estate has insufficient assets to cover the funeral an application should be made first to the DWP. If a person instructs an undertaker to deal with the funeral, that person is legally responsible for making the payment (although they will be entitled to a refund from the estate if they are the personal representative). Most of the assets will be available only when probate has been obtained, and that will take some time, so discuss the matter with the undertaker first. Most undertakers accept that there will have to be some delay before the bill can be paid. However, some institutions (e.g. building societies, banks) may be prepared to release up to £5,000 worth of assets on production of the death certificate alone (*see* steps 3 and 4, page 159).

The funeral cannot take place until a disposal certificate has been handed to the funeral director.

Burial

Check the deceased's personal papers and will to see if he or she has already paid for a plot in a graveyard or churchyard (the documents are called a grave deed or a deed of grant and a faculty, respectively). If not, a plot will have to be bought. The funeral director will provide details.

The burial will take place only when the following documents have been produced:

- either a certificate for burial (the disposal certificate) from the registrar of deaths, or, if there has been an inquest, the coroner's order for burial;
- application for burial – addressed to the cemetery and signed by the executor or next of kin. The funeral director will provide this form;
- grave deed or faculty, from the cemetery or diocese, which entitles the deceased to be buried in a particular plot.

Remember, some members of the family may have strong views about funerals. Should it be a lavish display or a simple one? Which church? Should it be a cremation? If the deceased was widowed twice, which wife should he join?

In the case of my grandfather, the churchyard was full but after negotiations the vicar agreed to allow him, as the deceased widower and father of eight children, to be squeezed into the only space left, on top of my grandmother, who had died some years before (and was known in the family as 'the hardy annual').

In some cases the relatives expect a good meal after the funeral. 'He was buried with ham' may be heard in Yorkshire after the funeral. This refers to the meal enjoyed by the mourners and not to some strange ritual at the burial.

Remember that a gravestone is not a testamentary expense. The executors must obtain the consent of the beneficiaries before ordering one.

Cremation

A cremation involves more formalities than a burial. It is necessary to have one of the following:

- a certificate for cremation (the disposal certificate) from the registrar of deaths, plus two cremation certificates. One is signed by the family doctor and the other by another doctor – both doctors will probably charge a fee;
- if the death was reported to the coroner, then after a post-mortem or inquest he or she will provide a free certificate for cremation. The following documents are also needed:
  – a cremation certificate signed by the medical referee at the crematorium. His/her fee will usually be included in the crematorium's charge;
  – two forms signed by the executor or next of kin. One applies for the cremation, while the other confirms the arrangements and gives instructions for disposal of the ashes.

Alternative funeral and burial arrangements

Most people who are responsible for organizing the funeral service of someone who has died will approach an undertaker with a request for a cremation or burial. They will then arrange for a service to take place either at the crematorium or at the church or chapel before the cremation or burial. There are however alternative funeral arrangements which are becoming more common.

Where it is felt inappropriate to have a religious funeral service there are a number of options available. Many people in that situation will opt for a cremation so that, instead of a religious service, the family can choose their own music and one or more of the mourners can give readings or speak about their memories of the deceased. The ashes can then be spread at a later date. It is also now possible to cremate organs at a later date when they have been held back for a post-mortem.

If the family wish to bury the deceased without a religious ceremony they can do so in a non-denominational cemetery, which may have some ground which is consecrated and some which is not. The British Humanist Association will provide an Officiant to conduct funerals or advice for those wishing to conduct the funeral themselves.

If the family wish to bury the deceased in the back garden or in land which is not designated as a burial ground, they should seek advice from the local planning authority and environmental health department who may object, although they should not if the intention is to bury only one or two people. Even if that consent is forthcoming the burial must also be registered at the Registry of Births, Deaths and Marriages within 14 days after the burial. The local planning authority will usually enter a record of the burial against the land where it took place and may impose conditions – so it is worth thinking about the effect it might have on the sale price of the home. If the family is contemplating such a burial they would be wise to obtain the necessary consents before any death has taken place.

The following organizations will be able to provide helpful advice for those going down the less conventional routes:

British Humanist Association, 1 Gower Street, London WC1E 6HD, Tel: 020 7079 3580.

The Natural Death Centre, 6 Blackstock Mews, Blackstock Road, London N4 2BT, Tel: 020 7359 8391. They can provide a list of Nature Reserve Burial Grounds in the UK together with helpful information about DIY funerals and ecologically friendly coffins, including those made of cardboard and woven willow.

Burial at sea

The coroner's approval must be obtained as such a burial is treated as though the body is being removed from the country. The consent of the Fisheries Inspectorate must also be obtained. Such burial is only allowed in a few areas.

Other steps to be taken

1 Return any pension book or welfare benefit book to the DWP; the book is the property of the DWP.
2 Go through the will to see who has been appointed executor. If no will can be found, make inquiries with likely solicitors and banks used by the deceased to see if they hold a will.
3 Work out who will be the personal representative(s) – *see* below. If the will appears complicated or if the estate includes a business or farm, you should immediately seek legal advice. If you intend to administer the estate yourself, turn to page 158. If there is no will, you must work out who is to be the administrator and contact them without taking any further steps yourself.

THE PERSONAL REPRESENTATIVES

The personal representatives, whether executors or administrators, are the guardians of the deceased's legal personality. They can sue on his/her behalf (strictly speaking, on behalf of his/her estate) if, for instance, he or she was owed money under a contract and, conversely, they can be sued (i.e. the estate can be sued) by the deceased's creditors.

The personal representatives are not personally liable to pay the deceased's debts, nor can they personally claim any damages recovered; it is the estate that is suing, or being sued, and the personal representatives are the mere nominees through whom the estate acts.

There are two types of personal representative – those appointed by a will and those not appointed by a will:

- personal representatives appointed by a will are called 'executors' (female singular: executrix, female plural: executrices);
- personal representatives not appointed by a will are called 'administrators' (female singular: administratrix).

Both types (collectively called personal representatives) have similar powers and duties. Only one personal representative is needed to administer an estate, although two will be required if there is an infant beneficiary or if a trust is created by the will or upon the intestacy.

A personal representative's task is similar to that of a trustee. Various statutes lay down detailed rules as to what a trustee or personal representative should, and should not, do. The basic rules are that they should be familiar with the terms of the will and not deviate from them; they must take care to preserve the property and assets as though they were their own; they must keep full accounts and keep the beneficiaries fully informed; they must consult with any other trustees, and not make unilateral decisions and, if in doubt, they should take legal advice. They must not make a profit from their position, unless they are professional trustees and the terms of the will give them the right to charge fees for work done, although they can recover their out-of-pocket expenses; neither must they put themselves in a position where there is a conflict of interest between themselves and the estate – thus a personal representative cannot buy anything from the estate unless all the beneficiaries are adults and they all consent.

If they fail to live up to the high standards required, the beneficiaries can sue them for negligence or fraud. If the claim is upheld they will be personally liable to compensate the estate, unless they can persuade the court that they acted 'honestly and reasonably, and ought fairly to be excused', in which case the court has a discretion to let them off.

Clearly, then, being a personal representative, or the trustee of a trust, is no sinecure. However, the prospective applicant should not be alarmed for, in practice, most estates are straightforward and are simple to administer, involving the personal representative(s) in little or no personal risk. In addition, of course, many personal representatives choose to seek the help of a solicitor and charge his fees to the estate.

Who will be the personal representative(s)?

Different rules apply depending upon whether there is a will or not.

If there is a will

If the will is valid and appoints you as executor you must decide whether you are going to administer the will yourself without legal assistance. You should not do this if the estate includes a firm or a business or foreign assets. You should think twice before administering any estate on which inheritance tax is payable without at least consulting experts to see how best to mitigate the effects of IHT, perhaps by a post-death variation. However, an executor is not obliged to act and if he or she does not wish to, he or she should make his/her position clear. This is best done by sending a written letter of 'renunciation' to the other people concerned, in case it is suggested that he or she has accepted some of the duties involved and so become obliged to take on all the responsibilities. It is quite common for an elderly widow to renounce probate of her husband's estate in favour of her children if she is bedridden or unable to act for some other reason – although it may be more convenient to appoint the children as attorneys in order to deal with the administration.

If the will does not name any executors, or if the named executors all renounce the job, someone else will have to apply for the grant. The persons entitled, in order of priority, are:

- the trustees and beneficiaries of any trust set up under the will; in practice, it is rare for there to be such a trust and so those next entitled are;
- the persons entitled under the will to the residue of the estate (*see* page 140);
- those entitled to inherit the estate under the intestacy rules (*see* pages 162–3). Whoever takes on the task will be an administrator, not an executor, since he or she was not appointed by will. In such a case an application will be made to the Probate Registry for 'Letters of Administration with the Will Annexed'.

Why appoint an executor?

It is sensible to appoint an executor – although it is not compulsory to do so. The best advice is to appoint a capable friend or relative. Alternatively, a bank or solicitor can be appointed. But if a solicitor or bank is appointed then your family will be committed to using that solicitor or bank to administer the estate. In the case of banks, this can be extremely expensive (*see* below). It might be much better simply to appoint a friend or relative, because at least that person will have the option of administering the estate themselves, rather than incurring professional fees. It is sensible to appoint two executors as there is less chance of both dying before the testator. Very elderly executors should not be appointed, and neither should an executor who lives abroad unless there are strong reasons for doing so. Another disadvantage of naming a particular bank or solicitor is if the person chosen should turn out to be inefficient and slow. If that happens, then there is not much that the beneficiaries (i.e. your family and relatives) can do to hurry matters up – except to complain to the relevant professional body if letters and phone calls to the person in question have failed. It is very difficult for beneficiaries to bring pressure to bear on a slow solicitor or bank. It would be much better if they themselves were the executors, in which case they could sack the slow bank or solicitor, and transfer the papers to someone who was likely to be more helpful.

If there is no will

If there is no will the estate will be vested in one or more administrators. Parliament has laid down an order of priority between competing applicants based largely on the closeness of the applicant's family links with the deceased. The order of priority is:

- surviving spouse; next
- issue (i.e. children, grandchildren etc., whether adopted, illegitimate etc.); next
- parents; next
- brothers and sisters of the whole blood (or their issue); next
- brothers and sisters of the half blood (or their issue); next
- grandparents; next
- uncles and aunts of the whole blood (or their issue); next
- uncles and aunts of the half blood (or their issue).

If there is no person with a beneficial interest in the estate the Treasury Solicitor will apply for the 'Grant of Letters of Administration'. The estate will then pass to the Crown, or the Duchy of Cornwall or the Duchy of Lancaster, if the death is in one of those areas.

A creditor of the estate may also apply if those entitled are unwilling to apply.

Between those of equal priority there is no order of priority (e.g. eldest son and youngest daughter have equal priority). Sometimes it may even depend upon who 'gets in first', but it is obviously better if the family can agree as to who will act.

Remember: this is just the order for deciding who is to be the administrator; there is a different order of priority for deciding how the estate is to be divided up (*see* page 162).

The appointment of the personal representative(s)

Once it has been decided who is entitled to become the personal representative(s), the prospective executor or administrator must apply to the Probate Registry for the court's written confirmation of his appointment. If the prospective administrator (no will) is a child under 18 years, testamentary guardians will have to be appointed to apply for the grant on the child's behalf.

The court's confirmation is in the form of a certificate called a 'grant', and this is the personal representative's formal proof that the deceased's estate is vested in him or her. The grant made to an executor (i.e. if appointed by the will) is called a 'Grant of Probate of the Will', while the grant to an administrator (i.e. when there is an intestacy) is a 'Grant of Letters of Administration'; in addition, there is also a 'Grant of Letters of Administration with the Will Annexed', which covers the hybrid situation of a will but no executors or a will which fails to dispose of the residue of the estate. Although these three grants have different names, their effect is the same – namely, to vest the deceased's assets and liabilities in the personal representative(s) as from the date of death, not just from the date of the grant. Thus there is no period of time when the deceased's legal personality is neither in the deceased nor in the personal representative(s), and so the presumption that death does not destroy the legal personality is preserved. Complications can arise where one person has partly administered the estate, believing that they have a right to do so when in fact they do not. If in doubt, take legal advice.

When there is no need for a grant

It may not be necessary to have a grant, because:
- small sums in National Savings etc. can be paid out without a grant (*see* page 162);
- cash, jewellery, etc. can be divided up between the relatives and beneficiaries (if they all agree) without a grant (*see* page 162);
- jointly held assets will normally pass automatically to the survivor (e.g. jointly owned house or bank account) and so a grant may not be necessary.

Do-it-yourself probate

Many personal representatives simply instruct a firm of solicitors to supervise the administration of the estate, and the duties of the personal representative are then restricted to signing forms prepared by the solicitors. The solicitor's fees will be paid out of the estate. Alternatively, a bank will usually be prepared to administer the estate, provided all the executors renounce probate and agreement can be reached over payment of the bank's (usually high) fees.

However, the personal representative need not retain a bank or solicitor to help him/her with his duties. He or she can instead do the administering of the estate alone and so save the legal fees that the estate would otherwise have paid. The savings can be considerable (*see* Legal fees in probate work, below).

In view of the potential liabilities of being a personal representative (above) DIY probate is not something that should be taken on lightly. However, when the estate is small or if there are few beneficiaries, it is usually a straightforward, if time-consuming, business of writing letters to banks, creditors and insurance companies. On the other hand, there are some more complicated situations when it is inadvisable to do the work oneself, and instead the executor or administrator should instruct a solicitor or a bank to administer the estate. This would generally be so if:
- the estate is worth a large amount (or, conversely, it is not large enough to pay the debts);
- the dead person has set up a trust;
- some of the beneficiaries cannot be traced;
- the dead person did not leave a will and it is known that there are untraced relatives who might have a claim on the estate;
- the testator was under 18 years old when he or she made the will;
- the will does not contain an attestation clause (*see* page 138);
- the will contains unsigned alterations;
- the will shows signs of burning, tearing, erasures or of another document having been attached (e.g. staple holes);
- the will gives a beneficiary a right to reside in a house;
- there is a business;
- inheritance tax may have to be paid;
- the will refers to another document or deals with property outside the UK;
- one of the beneficiaries under the will witnessed the will (or is married to one of the witnesses);
- the will is ambiguous or unclear (*see* the home-made will on page 151);
- the will does not dispose of the residue of the estate;
- there is a possibility of a relative or dependant making a family provision claim (*see* Chapter 14).

Legal fees in probate work

The saving of legal fees is likely to be the main reason why a personal representative decides to administer the estate himself.

Solicitors' fees are assessed on the same basis as fees in any other non-contentious (i.e. non-court) legal work, such as conveyancing. The nine factors to be considered when deciding what is a 'fair and reasonable' fee are set out on page 775. But with probate work, the size of the estate is usually taken as the most important single factor. If the solicitor charges on a time basis, the Law Society would generally approve a bill which comprised a charge for the time spent, plus 25–30 per cent typing and services, plus 1 per cent of the value of the gross estate. The total of these figures, in very rough terms, often works out in the region of 2 per cent of the gross estate. Do not expect a City firm (if it even deals with modest administrations) to have similar charges to a small provincial firm. You will be paying for expertise, but you will also be paying for the overheads of the firm acting for you.

If the solicitor is an executor under the will (especially if he or she is a sole executor with added responsibilities) it is usual to increase the 1 per cent charge to 1.5 per cent.

Grant only

If the solicitor takes out only the Grant of Probate or Letters of Administration, and takes no part in administering the estate, the 1 per cent is generally reduced to $^1/_6$ per cent.

As always, to avoid difficulties, it is advisable to obtain a firm estimate from the solicitor before instructing him or her to act. The difficulty for solicitors is to anticipate the complications which might arise and increase the work to be done.

Disputes over fees

Solicitors' fees for probate work come under the general non-contentious costs rules (*see* page 775). In particular, if the personal representative thinks the solicitor's fee is too high, he or she could ask the solicitor to obtain a remuneration certificate from the Law Society and can ask for the fees to be taxed (*see* page 775). This is one major advantage of using a solicitor rather than a bank: with banks, there are no controls over the fees charged (and, in any event, they nearly always charge more than solicitors).

Banks

Banks lay down their own scale of fees. Because banks usually charge a lot it is essential to discuss the fee before committing oneself to using the bank. Relatively few people realize just how much banks charge. Remember that fees are calculated on the *gross* estate before inheritance tax is paid. The bank also charges a 3 per cent withdrawal fee when any capital is withdrawn from a trust. There are other discretionary fees. Although the bank may reduce its charges if the estate is *unusually* simple, you should be ready for a very large bill if a bank

is the executor. Most other banks have a similar fee structure.

Generally, solicitors' charges are considerably less. As a rough guide, on an estate of £200,000 a solicitor might charge £3,000 (plus VAT) whereas a bank might charge approximately £6,000 (plus VAT). In addition, there would be disbursements (i.e. out-of-pocket expenses) incurred by the solicitor or the bank, the main one being probate fees paid to the court when taking out the grant. These are charged on the size of the *net* estate. The net estate is the amount left for distributing to the beneficiaries after paying funeral, probate and testamentary expenses.

Finally, if the property contains a house or flat, there will be solicitor's conveyancing fees for transferring the property to the beneficiary, or for acting on the sale of the property (*see* page 206 for conveyancing fees). If the property is sold, the solicitor's conveyancing fee will be calculated on the usual basis. However, if the property is merely transferred to a beneficiary (by what is called an 'assent') the fee will be much less, since little work will be involved.

ADMINISTERING AN ESTATE: A STEP-BY-STEP GUIDE

Obviously, no two estates are the same, but the procedure to be followed will always be similar. This checklist summarizes the main steps to be taken by personal representatives who decide to administer the estate themselves, whether they be an executor (i.e. there is a will) or an administrator (i.e. there is no will). If the estate is complicated or if it includes a business, a farm or a private company, it is essential to obtain professional advice at an early stage. If inheritance tax is payable, a post-death variation may be advantageous. Do not be afraid to take professional advice at an early stage. Failure to spot a problem early on can lead to serious consequences for the executor.

Before obtaining the grant

1 Follow steps to be taken on death, page 153.
2 Examine all the deceased's papers and find out where all the property is. A full list of assets and liabilities will eventually have to be prepared. Check that any property is properly insured, remove any valuables to safekeeping, redirect the post and consider whether the water system should be drained if the property is to remain empty.
3 Write to the bank for a statement showing balance, interest and any bank charges. What cheques have not yet been paid in? Ask whether the bank holds any

securities for the dead person. Ask a bank to open an executor's account; the account need not be with the deceased's own bank.

4 Find out the details of any life assurance policies held by the deceased. Write to the company notifying them of the death and enclosing a copy of the death certificate. Ask for details of the amount that will be paid; ask for a claim form. The amount due under the policy will not form part of the estate if either (a) it was taken out by the deceased's spouse, on the deceased's life, or (b) it was taken out under the Married Woman's Property Act (in which case the policy will be held for the wife and children).

5 Draw up a list of any shares held by the deceased. These will have to be valued as at the date of death; the bank manager will probably be able to find out the valuation. Otherwise, contact the brokers, or look up the shares – in the Stock Exchange official list for the date of death.

6 If there is a mortgage, notify the building society and enclose a copy of the death certificate. Ask for details of the amount owed at the date of death. It is wise in all cases to ask at this stage for any forms which may have to be completed before the bank or insurance company will pay out. Otherwise you will be sent the forms after you send the Grant of Probate, thus causing delays and increasing your work.

7 Obtain a probate valuation of any real property, such as a house or flat. The district valuer of the Inland Revenue will agree to fix a valuation after the papers have been lodged with the Probate Registry (*see* below). Seek expert advice if the deceased owned any property abroad.

8 Contact any pension fund (or employer) enclosing a copy of the death certificate and asking for full details of any sums due on death (e.g. under an occupational pension scheme). Ask whether the sum is to be treated as part of the estate or not, as this can affect the question of tax.

9 If the deceased held any savings certificates, write to the Savings Certificate Office, Milburn Gate House, Durham DH99 1NS, enclosing a copy of the death certificate. Ask for a full list of all certificates held, their date of purchase and value at the date of death.

10 If the deceased held any premium bonds, write to National Savings, Marton, Blackpool FY3 9YP, giving the full name and bond numbers. For the moment, the bonds can be left in the draw and only cashed shortly before the estate is distributed to the beneficiaries (bonds can remain in the draw for up to 12 months after death).

11 With savings, as in the National Savings Bank or a building society, send the savings book or deposit book to the institution, enclose a copy of the death certificate and ask for the book to be made up and

interest calculated to the date of death. Ask for a withdrawal form.

12 Value all the personal assets of the deceased. A valuer or secondhand furniture dealer can value the furniture if a personal estimate is felt to be insufficient. Use a garage to value a car, or look up its value in trade publications.

13 Had the deceased made any gifts in the seven years before his or her death? If the deceased left no will, it is essential to know whether he or she made any gifts to any beneficiary during his/her lifetime.

14 Was the deceased entitled to income from any trust or settlement? If so the trust will have certain formalities to complete and the value of the deceased's free estate (the estate he or she can leave as he or she pleases) will be added to the value of the trust assets to determine the total amount of inheritance tax payable.

15 Obtain details of any jointly held property. Does it pass automatically to the other joint holder or does it pass according to the deceased's will? Special rules apply for the valuation of half-shares in real property. Seek specialist advice if you become involved in such a case.

16 Notify the Inland Revenue of the death. Is the deceased entitled to a tax refund or does he owe tax?

17 Draw up a list of people who owed money to the deceased.

18 Draw up a list of people who are owed money.

19 Once all this information has been collected, the personal representative will be in a position to complete the forms needed to apply for probate or for letters of administration.

Applying for probate

1 Find out the address of the nearest probate registry and write or telephone for the forms you will require. You will be sent a guide for applicants acting without a solicitor (form PA2), which explains the procedure in simple terms. You will also receive the following documents:

- PA1   Probate Application Form
- IHT 205   Short Inland Revenue form for personal applicants
- IHT 206   Notes to help you fill in IHT 205

After reading form PA2 you will be able to fill in the application form (PA1). You will then have to fill in form IHT 205, setting out what assets were held by the deceased as well as particulars of any jointly owned assets, trust assets, foreign assets and details of any gift made in the seven years before the death. If the total assets set out in form IHT 205 exceed £240,000 it will be necessary to fill in an IHT 200 form upon which the inheritance tax will be calculated.

2 Send to the Probate Registry (not the probate office):
- PA1 and IHT 205 (and IHT 200 if the total on IHT 205 exceeds £240,000);
- the death certificate;
- the will (keep a copy in case the original is lost in the post);
- a covering letter.

As a personal applicant the personal representative will have to attend an interview, at either the Probate Registry or the probate office. He or she should state which they wish to attend and they should state any dates or times of the day when they cannot attend.

3 The applicant will be given an interview appointment. The object of the interview is to sort out any difficulties or ambiguities and to ensure that the forms have been completed correctly. Any inheritance tax will have to be paid before probate can be granted. The interview will be informal.

4 Some three or four weeks after the interview the applicant will be sent a set of forms. These forms are the application forms for the Grant of Probate. These should be completed and returned. The full list of items to be returned is:
- the Inheritance Tax Account form;
- the forms originally filled in;
- the Inheritance Tax Warrant, with a copy of the will annexed to it;
- a cheque for the inheritance tax in favour of the Inland Revenue. The amount of tax payable is set out on the Inheritance Tax Account form. In fact, few people have to fill in IHT forms – let alone pay any tax. The forms need only be filled in if the estate, including lifetime gifts, is worth more than £240,000, and tax will be payable only if it is worth over £255,000 (2003/2004 figures). However, it is not necessary at this stage to pay tax arising because of land (i.e. house, flat etc.) or certain shares in a private company. The personal representative may have to arrange to borrow money from a bank to pay the tax, for even if the amount in the deceased's own account is enough to meet the bill it cannot be touched until after probate is granted. However, if the account was a joint account the survivor can operate it and may be prepared to advance enough money, to pay the tax. There is also a special scheme to allow National Savings and other accounts to be used to meet the tax bill and funeral account; for details, contact the tax office or the bank.
- a cheque for the probate fee, payable to the District Probate Registrar;
- a covering letter requesting sufficient office copies of the Grant of Probate to avoid having to wait for the return of the original document every time it is requested by a company, bank or other authority. Each copy costs £1.

5 Some three weeks later the executor will be sent the Grant of Probate plus the office copies.

Administering the estate

1 Open a bank account in the name of the estate.
2 Collect any debts owed to the deceased, sums payable on insurance policies, sums in banks, building societies, unclaimed pension benefits, premium bonds, etc. If you have already obtained the relevant claim forms, you will be expected to send the completed claim form, the office copy Grant of Probate or Letters of Administration, the pass book or insurance policy and, in some cases, an official copy death certificate. Pay the monies into the estate's bank account, especially if it was overdrawn, to pay out the tax and other sums mentioned above (Applying for probate: 4). If the estate is under £5,000, it will not be necessary to produce a Grant of Probate, but the institutions in which the money is held will have their own forms which require completion. Insurance companies will wish to see an official death certificate.
3 Ask the Inland Revenue to pay over any tax refund.
4 Pay the debts owed by the deceased, funeral bills, testamentary expenses and IHT. If there is not sufficient cash available, sell off assets. Unless the will states which assets are to be used, the money should be raised, in order, from:
- property not dealt with under the will (i.e. property in respect of which the testator died intestate); next
- the residue; next
- property specifically left for the payment of debts (note that this property is *not* the first property used to pay the debts); next
- any fund left to pay pecuniary legacies; next
- property specifically devised or bequeathed (a proportion of the money from each).

5 Advertise for any creditors. Place adverts in the *London Gazette* and, if the deceased held land, in a local paper in the area. Forms can be obtained from Oyez Publishing Limited. The estate should not be distributed until two months after the placing of the advertisements, for otherwise the executor may be personally liable to the creditor. Once the two months have expired the executor is not personally liable, although the debt remains legally valid and the creditor can sue the estate and, if necessary, recover the money from the beneficiaries. If the advertisements result in claims these must be investigated before the estate is distributed.

6 Consider whether there is any possibility of a family provision claim (*see* Chapter 14) – that is, are there any children, including illegitimate children, mistresses, ex-wives, or others who might have a claim on the

estate? If there is any possibility of there being such a person, do not distribute the estate until six months after obtaining the grant.

7 Sell off assets that are not specifically devised or bequeathed, and which are not wanted by any of the beneficiaries. If they realize more (or less) than their original valuation, additional (or less) IHT may be payable.

8 Consider whether a post-death Deed of Variation could save IHT or achieve a fairer distribution of assets. Remember that all the beneficiaries must agree and be over 18 years, otherwise the consent of the court will be needed (not a simple or cheap exercise).

9 The next step is to distribute the assets. Note:
- the cost of maintaining any property specifically devised or bequeathed (e.g. insurance, packing, repairs) is borne by the beneficiary; similarly, legal fees on conveying land to a beneficiary are borne by the beneficiary;
- if property specifically devised or bequeathed produces income (e.g. dividends on shares), the beneficiary is entitled to all the income since the date of death;
- a pecuniary legacy accrues interest at 6 per cent per annum but generally this arises only from one year after the death.

Small estates – no need for probate

Small amounts of money due to the estate from building societies, the National Savings Bank, savings certificates, premium savings bonds, government stocks, banks, etc. may be payable without the need to obtain, or produce, a Grant of Probate. If the amount due from each institution is no more than £5,000, that institution may agree to pay out the money without the need for a Grant of Probate. However, the institution can insist on production of a Grant of Probate if it so wishes. Note that there can be up to £5,000 in each institution, so the total amount coming within this 'small estates' exception can be quite large. Also, any cash and personal effects (e.g. jewellery, furniture) can be dealt with without the need for a grant – provided that all the relatives and beneficiaries can agree on how it is to be split up.

INTESTACY: WHEN THERE IS NO WILL

If there is no will, the personal representatives will distribute the estate in accordance with the intestacy rules laid down in the Administration of Estates Act 1925 and the Intestates' Estates Act 1952. The order of entitlement laid down in these Acts was drawn up after a detailed examination of the way people tended to leave their property in wills, and so these Acts can be said to give effect to the 'presumed intentions' of the deceased – i.e. what he or she would have done had they left a will.

The rules are complicated and are best understood by considering, in turn, the position of the spouse, then the issue, and finally the other relatives.

The surviving spouse

If there are no surviving relatives, the spouse takes the whole of the estate.

If there is issue (i.e. children or grandchildren), the spouse takes the personal chattels (which include household goods, car, jewellery, wines, clothes and the like), a fixed sum of £125,000 and a life interest in half the balance. This means that the spouse will receive the interest from half the balance but will not have access to the capital.

If there is no issue but other relatives such as parents or brothers and sisters, the spouse takes the personal chattels, a fixed sum of £200,000 and half the balance.

The issue (i.e. children, grandchildren, etc.)

What the issue receive will depend upon whether the deceased parent left a surviving spouse:
- *If there is a surviving spouse*, the issue take one-half of the residue (i.e. the amount left after the spouse has deducted the chattels and £125,000). The other half of the residue will go to the surviving spouse for life and the capital will then pass to the issue on his/her death.
- *If there is no surviving spouse*, the issue inherit the whole estate. The estate is held for them so that they all have equal shares when they reach 18 years or when they marry (if earlier). If any children have already died leaving children (including adopted children), those children will share what their deceased parent would have received. If any of the children are illegitimate there may be difficulties if there is no affiliation order or other acceptable evidence of paternity.

In one administration a problem was solved by modern technology. A bachelor died leaving one accepted illegitimate child aged 3. The child's mother had obtained an affiliation order against him. Another woman then alleged that her 2-year-old child was also a child of the deceased and that she had been about to marry the deceased. Unfortunately she had no affiliation order or other evidence. Because both children were under 18 years old there could be no compromise. The matter was therefore expected to go to court in order for the 2-year-old, through his lawyers, to prove to the court's satisfaction that he was the son of the deceased.

The parties then considered genetic fingerprinting. Because the parents of the deceased were still alive, they were able to provide blood samples which, when combined with samples from the 2-year-old and his mother, proved he was indeed the child of the deceased. The matter was therefore solved relatively cheaply, without using up the modest estate in legal fees.

The other relatives (i.e. parents, brothers, sisters, or their children)

Entitlement here will depend upon whether there is a surviving spouse and/or any issue (children, grand-children etc.):

- *If there are any issue*, the other relatives will not receive anything.
- *If there is a surviving spouse but no issue*, the other relatives receive one-half of the residue left after the surviving spouse has deducted the chattels and £200,000. The half will go to the parents of the deceased in equal shares, but if there are no parents living, it will go to the deceased's brothers and sisters in equal shares. If any of those brothers and sisters have already died their share will be divided between their children.
- *If there is no surviving spouse and no issue*, the other relatives inherit all the estate. The order of entitlement is:
  - to the parents, but *if none*;
  - to brothers and sisters, *but if none*;
  - to half-brothers and half-sisters, *but if none*;
  - to grandparents, *but if none*;
  - to uncles and aunts of the whole blood (i.e. brothers and sisters of one of the deceased's parents), *but if none*;
  - to uncles and aunts of the half-blood (i.e. half-brothers and half-sisters of one of the deceased's parents), *but if none*;
  - the estate passes to the Crown or, in the appropriate areas, to the Duchy of Cornwall or the Duchy of Lancaster. In practice, the Crown (or the Duchies) will often pay all or part to someone who seems morally entitled to a share.

Note: if, under the intestacy rules, a share passes to a child, brother, sister, uncle or aunt who died before the deceased, then the share passes to that person's descendants (usually their children).

Fred Jones died intestate leaving an estate of £300,000. He was survived by his wife, Mabel, but they had no children. Other relatives include two nephews – the sons of Fred's brother Michael – and a niece – the daughter of his brother Frank. The estate will be divided as follows:

- his wife Mabel will take the personal chattels plus £200,000, plus one-half of the remaining £100,000 (i.e. £50,000). A total of £250,000 plus chattels.
- the *nephews* and the *niece* will take the share their parents would have taken. As brothers of Fred each would have been entitled to an equal share of the £50,000 left after Mabel had taken her share. Thus, the niece inherits £25,000 and the two nephews inherit £12,500 each.

Mistresses, cohabiting spouses

The intestacy rules only recognize the claims of relatives. Mistresses, lovers, close friends, and others do not have any claim under the intestacy rules. Contrary to popular belief, the term 'common-law spouse' is not recognized by the intestacy rules. If your partner is not your spouse, you both need wills – badly. They may be able to qualify as 'dependants' and so bring a claim under the family provision legislation for a share of the estate (*see* below) but there are no certainties and the claim may be expensive to pursue. Spouses of deceased relatives have no claim at all. Consider the following situation. A couple invite the husband's brother to come and live with them. The husband dies but his widow continues to look after her bachelor brother-in-law, who is rich but infirm. There is another brother but no one has spoken to him for many years. If the rich brother-in-law dies without having made a will his estate will pass to his estranged brother and his caring sister-in-law will get nothing.

Partial intestacy

If a person dies leaving a will, but the will does not dispose of all his estate, he is said to have died partially intestate. For instance, if the residue is left equally between two people, but one dies before the testator, then his share will pass as on an intestacy, unless the will makes the appropriate provision. Note that if the gift was to the two people jointly, then the survivor would take the whole gift.

The usual rules on intestacy apply to that part of his estate but the spouse and issue must take their benefits under the will into account when working out their shares under the intestacy rules. For instance, a widow who received £10,000 under the will would not take the first £125,000 of the undisposed-of estate, but only the first £115,000.

14

The Family Provision Legislation: Fair Shares for Family and Dependants

Only in 1938 did Parliament decide that a testator's moral duty to provide for his/her family should become a legal obligation.

It had long been a principle of English law that a man could dispose of his property as he wished. Thus a man was free to leave his family and dependants destitute – a principle that was alien to most Continental legal systems, and to the laws of Scotland too. The only relaxation of this strict rule was by virtue of several old common-law doctrines (such as dower, escheat and curtesy) that sometimes allowed the spouse and children to claim part of the estate, but these laws were repealed by a series of statutes from 1833 onwards. The law of the nineteenth century was a *laissez-faire* law, in which the right to dispose freely of one's property was inviolable. The family provision legislation of 1938 scotched this notion, and it provides yet another example of the free enterprise spirit of Victorian law being overturned by a twentieth-century Parliament which is more concerned with social justice than jurisprudential consistencies.

The Inheritance (Family Provision) Act 1938 was replaced in 1975 by the Inheritance (Provision for Family and Dependants) Act. This statute extended the protection to dependants such as mistresses, and did away with some of the more restrictive rules affecting the entitlement to provision and the form the provision was to take.

The 1975 Act (usually called the 'family provision legislation', despite the fact that it includes dependants who are not members of the family) envisages four categories of claimants:

- the surviving spouse (or unmarried ex-spouse);
- any person living with the deceased as husband or wife for a period of two years up to the date of death;
- the children (including any stepchild who was treated as a child of the family); and, finally
- other dependants whether members of the family or not.

The Act is strengthened by provisions which make it difficult for the testator to concoct schemes that may get around the legislation. Application under the Act is made by way of an originating summons to the High Court, either within the Chancery Division or within the Family Division, unless the net estate does not exceed £30,000, in which case the county court can hear the claim.

The application must be made within six months of the grant being issued by the Probate Registry, although the court does have power to allow late applications in exceptional circumstances (for instance, on the late discovery of a will). This six-month time limit poses a problem to many claimants, such as spouses who have been deserted by the deceased and who may not have heard of his/her death. To prevent the estate being distributed without his/her knowledge, the potential claimant can register a 'caveat' in the Probate Registry, which prevents a grant being made for the following six months without his/her knowledge and approval. An alternative and simpler safeguard is for the potential claimant to make a 'standing search' at the Probate Registry (fee £1) which entitles him/her to a copy of any grant during the next six months, and also to any grant taken out in the last 12 months. The search can, of course, be renewed every six months. If you register a caveat you will be warned if a probate action is commenced. You will then find yourself involved in the action. You would therefore be well advised to seek legal advice before registering a caveat.

Many such actions will be started with the words: 'It's not the money I mind about, it's the principle.' Unfortunately, such principles can be expensive, especially if the case has to be conducted through the Chancery Division of the High Court.

THE SURVIVING SPOUSE

The court will act as though it was considering the financial arrangements to be made on a divorce; thus the factors and principles considered by the divorce court (*see* Chapter 4) will be applied to the family provision claim. Most important, the issue before the court is not whether the deceased made reasonable provision for the *maintenance* of the spouse, but whether the deceased left his/her spouse (whether by will or under the intestacy rules) a 'fair share of the family assets' – which may, of course, be considerably more than is needed for maintenance alone. This test is more generous than that applied to the children and other dependants, who are only entitled to reasonable provision for their maintenance.

If the surviving spouse was divorced or judicially separated from the deceased, it is probable that there will have been an earlier court hearing when the family assets were divided between them. In such a case, although the surviving spouse can apply under the family provision legislation, the earlier division may well reduce the chances of a successful claim. If the former spouse remarries, he or she automatically loses all rights to maintenance or a share of the assets under the family provision legislation, and any order (e.g. for maintenance) is cancelled.

When deciding the sort of order to be made, the court has similar powers to those of the divorce court in matrimonial cases. For instance, the order can be for periodic payments, a lump sum (or a lump sum payable by instalments), or the transfer and purchase of property. A 'fair share' of the assets is determined on an objective basis, depending on the commitments and wealth of the deceased at the time of his/her death.

THE CHILDREN

The children do not fare as well as the surviving spouse. The test is whether the deceased parent made 'reasonable provision' for their maintenance. This is all they are entitled to – maintenance only, not a share of the family assets. 'Children' in this context includes any child of the family who was maintained by the deceased prior to his/her death; the child's age, marital status or illegitimacy is irrelevant. A child of the deceased who had not been born at the date of the testator's death would be entitled to claim if the will had divided the estate between named children.

OTHER DEPENDANTS

The final category of claimants under the 1975 Act is that of other dependants who were, partly or wholly, maintained by the deceased at the time of his/her death. This includes cohabiting wives and mistresses. Many cases of hardship arose from the exclusion of such people from the 1938 Act, for when the deceased died intestate the estate would pass to relatives (e.g. an undivorced, but 'separated', wife) and not to the cohabiting spouse. Although the cohabiting spouse is now included in the legislation, he or she is still discriminated against, for the Act only permits a claim for 'reasonable provision for maintenance', and not for a share of the family assets.

COHABITANTS

The effect of the Act was extended in 1995 to include a person living in the household of the deceased as husband or wife for a period of at least two years up to the date of death (who might not be dependants in the strict sense of the word).

FAMILY PROVISION LEGISLATION IN PRACTICE

A woman was brought up by her grandparents, having been rejected by her mother. When the mother died her estate was £172,000 but the daughter (then aged 58) received only a legacy of £200. The woman claimed that her mother had not made a reasonable provision for her. The woman lived on state benefits. The remainder of the estate was left to charities. The court decided that although the mother had no legal obligation to her daughter, there was a moral obligation to fulfil. She was therefore awarded £3,000 as a lump sum and £4,500 per annum maintenance.

Re Debenham dec'd (1986)

On the other hand:

A woman left everything to her natural son to the exclusion of her adopted daughter. The adopted daughter was independent and impecunious. She had also been wild, having served a three-month prison sentence. The testator stated in her will why she had left nothing to her adopted daughter. The judge considered the needs and financial resources, the size of the estate, the moral obligations and other matters. The adopted daughter failed to establish a right to be maintained. Williams v Johns (1988)

In another case, the adult child's entitlement changed after the value of the estate increased dramatically:

A man died leaving seven children and a widow. In his will, the father left a plot of land (worth £100,000 at the time) to his four sons, who used the land to carry on the family business. He bequeathed the family home and all the other money in the modest estate to his wife. The eldest daughter, Joan, who was 58 when her father died, did not receive anything under the terms of the will and she made an application under the 1975 Act. The family business was booming but her financial circumstances had always been precarious. Four years after the death of the father, the family business did a deal with Tesco involving the plot of land. The plot of land sold for £663,000. The court decided that although it had not been unreasonable for the father not to make provision for the eldest daughter in his will, due to lack of sufficient funds at the time, the subsequent windfall to the estate, following the deal with Tesco, changed the position. The sister was awarded maintenance of £3,000 a year. Snapes v Arram (1988)

What constitutes reasonable provision for the surviving spouse will depend on a number of factors, including the duration of the marriage, the contribution made by the applicant to the welfare of the family, and the provision which the applicant might reasonably have expected to receive if the marriage had ended in divorce:

The deceased, A, had been married to the claimant, B, for 54 years and they had 12 children. There had been one period of separation which lasted 18 months. A left B the household goods, his personal effects and a legacy of £10,000. However, B argued that the provision was not reasonable and wanted the family home. A's lawyers accepted that the provision was not reasonable, but said that the house was too big for B. The court held that, bearing in mind the duration of the marriage and the great contribution made by B in caring for 12 children and looking after the home and the needs of the deceased, the will did not make reasonable financial provision for B. The judge ordered that the family home should pass to B, but reduced her legacy to £5,000.

Elizabeth Adams v Julian James Lewis (Administration of the Estate of Frank Adams, dec'd) (2001)

A cohabitant can use the legislation to claim a share of the estate. For instance:

A former cohabitant claimed from the estate of the deceased. Their five-year relationship had ended two years before his death. She argued that he had promised to provide for her if she would live with him. Her claim failed but the court indicated that she would have succeeded had she been living with the deceased at the date of his death.

Layton v Martin (1986)

A couple had been living together since 1985, but did not share a bedroom and did not have sexual relations. The man continued working, providing most of the income for the running of the household and the woman was responsible for the housekeeping, washing, shopping, cooking and gardening. She also contributed towards some of the household bills. When the man died, the woman applied for reasonable financial provision from his estate. The court found that the couple were living together as husband and wife, despite the fact that they did not have a sexual relationship, and therefore the woman's claim under the 1975 Act should succeed. Re Estate of John Watson (1988)

Since the cost of taking a disputed case to court can often be a substantial part of the value of the estate, the courts discourage claims over relatively small estates.

Housing

Owner-Occupiers

Renting a House or Flat

The Home Owner and the Law

15

Owning Land

INTRODUCTION

'An Englishman's home is his castle' – or so the saying goes; and for Englishman you can also read Welshman, as the law is the same in both countries – and in the twenty-first century we should also be including English and Welsh women. But what does this mean? What rights do home owners have over their land? These are the subject matter of this part of the book.

CROWN OWNERSHIP

The property lawyer will tell you that in the eyes of the law, the Queen owns all the land in England and Wales; all you and I, her subjects, own is the right to *occupy* a piece of land for a certain length of time. Crown ownership comes about because of the Norman Conquest in 1066 when William of Normandy regarded all of the country as his by conquest. But don't worry, there is no risk of the Queen turning up on your doorstep demanding her land back!

FREEHOLD AND LEASEHOLD LAND

There are two different lengths of time for which you may be given the right to occupy a piece of land: freehold or leasehold. You will have seen reference to freehold or leasehold land when looking in estate agents' windows. Freehold means that you have the right to occupy the land for ever; leasehold means that you have that right for a fixed number of years, say 99, or even 999 years.

If you buy a freehold house, it will be yours to occupy, to sell or give away, for ever. And if you have the sole right to occupy the land for ever, the idea of the Crown owning the land is thus a bit of a nonsense. It is just a legal theory. The only significance of Crown ownership is that if a freeholder dies without making a will and without any close relatives, the Crown can then claim the land back.

In the case of leasehold land, this arises when the owner of the freehold lets someone else occupy his land for a fixed period, usually in return for a rent. The tenant (as an owner of a lease is called) then has the right of occupation to the exclusion of the owner of the freehold (called the landlord) until the end of the fixed period. The right to occupy will then go back to the landlord.

If you have a lease it is also possible to grant a sub-lease, to give someone else the right to occupy the land for a period shorter than your own. So, if you have a lease with 10 years left to run, you can grant a sub-lease to someone to occupy the land for any period less than 10 years – say seven years. This sub-tenant will then have the sole right to occupy for the seven years of his sub-lease. You will then get the occupation back for the remaining three years of your lease and then your landlord, the owner of the freehold, will get occupation back at the end of the 10 years granted to you.

Leasehold houses were once very common in some parts of the country, but virtually unknown in others. Many owners of leasehold houses have now exercised their right to buy the freehold from the landlord (*see* page 181).

Although leasehold houses are no longer very common, leasehold flats are the norm; it is most unusual to come across freehold flats. The reason for this is that, in the case of a block of flats, it is necessary for one person (or body) to be responsible for the repair and maintenance of the structure of the block and of the common parts. It would obviously be impracticable for each flat owner to repair the flat he owned – and who would be responsible for the common parts?

What is needed is some one person or body to be responsible for repair, etc. and then collect the cost from the individual flat-owners through the medium of a service charge. Unfortunately, the law does not allow covenants to repair or pay a service charge to be binding on future owners of freehold land. So if the flats were sold freehold, the first buyers would be bound to repair or pay the service charge, but this liability would not then be binding on future owners. This would obviously not be acceptable, so flats are sold off leasehold; in leases there is no problem of enforcing repairing obligations or payment of service charges. The problems flat-owners may have with services and service charges are dealt with on page 191. Note also that flat-owners can now club together and compel their landlord to sell them the freehold (*see* page 189).

A new way of owning property in a development which has communal facilities was introduced by the Commonhold and Leasehold Reform Act 2002. The new scheme, called commonhold, combines the security of freehold ownership with the management benefits of leasehold ownership. Individual flats are owned individually while the common areas are controlled collectively. *See further* below.

Freehold and Leasehold: The Main Differences

	Freehold	*Leasehold*
Duration of right to occupy	For ever, subject to (a) failure to comply with terms of any mortgage; (b) compulsory purchase.	For number of years laid down by lease, subject to (a) performance of covenants in lease; (b) failure to comply with terms of any mortgage; (c) compulsory purchase.
Mortgage availability	No problem for houses.	Mortgages on freehold flats available only from certain lenders. No problem for houses, subject to there being about 50 years of lease left unexpired at time of taking out the loan. In the case of flats, the lender will be concerned to see that there are adequate arrangements for repair and maintenance of the block.
Rent	No rent payable (exceptionally, in Manchester and Bristol areas a rent charge may be payable).	As laid down by terms of lease. May be subject to increase as laid down by terms of lease. In the case of a flat there will normally also be a service charge payable to cover repair and maintenance.
Obligation to repair	None, but: (a) it will be a term of any mortgage that the property is kept in good repair; (b) in the case of a building listed as being of historic or architectural interest, the local authority can require repairs to be effected.	In the case of a house, the lease will usually impose a repairing obligation. In the case of a flat, there will normally be a service charge payable to pay a part of the cost of the repair of the block.
Alteration, extensions, changes of use, etc.	No restrictions, but: (a) planning permission may be required; (b) consent of any mortgage lender will be required; (c) any covenants or easements affecting the property must be complied with.	The lease will usually require the landlord's consent to be obtained. In addition: (a) planning permission may be required; (b) consent of any mortgage lender will be required; (c) any covenants or easements affecting the property must be complied with.

Shared ownership

This is a hybrid form of home ownership – in effect it is a half-way house between owning the house (whether by having a leasehold or freehold) and renting it. It is only available to local authority and housing association tenants and it is a way of getting the less well-off on to the bottom rung of the home-ownership ladder. They might not be able to afford to buy a house outright, but they can with this method often afford to buy part of a house. For instance, a tenant may buy a 60 per cent interest in his or her house or flat from the landlord – usually with the aid of a mortgage loan in the usual way. The landlord will retain a 40 per cent interest in the house or flat and the tenant will continue to pay rent for that 40 per cent. At a later date, if the tenant can afford it, the tenant can buy an increased share in the house. If the house is sold before the tenant owns 100 per cent of it, the landlord will be entitled to a share in the profits equivalent to the size of the share he still owns.

Shared ownership is relatively uncommon now. It became fashionable in the mid-1980s and was encouraged by the property boom (when tenants were worried about being left out of the home-ownership market). The collapse of the property boom dissuaded many such people from wanting to own property. Although there has been a resurgence in the property market since the late 1990s, shared ownership has remained unpopular.

Timeshares

Timeshares for holiday purposes are now well known. Who hasn't been accosted by a timeshare seller on a continental holiday? Obviously, the legal systems in Spain and Portugal are completely different from our own, and before entering into a timeshare in another country specialist advice must be taken. Many are the horror stories of unsuspecting Britons losing their money in failed timeshare deals when the sellers go into liquidation, or it transpires that they actually never owned the land they were selling.

Timeshares are also available for those wishing to holiday in this country. How does a timesharing agreement fit into our legal structures? The answer is that it doesn't: lawyers have had great difficulty in finding a satisfactory legal framework for timeshares. The idea of a timeshare is that each 'owner' owns the right, for example, to a week's occupation for a fixed period of time, e.g. 90 years. Various legal devices have been used to set up timeshares. It is not possible for each timesharer to own the freehold in their unit, but one way is to grant each of the timesharers a lease for the week in question for each of the 90 years. This method has the advantage that the management scheme for the timeshare complex can then be based on the tried and trusted methods used in flat developments. So a management company will run the complex and each of the timesharers will pay a yearly service charge to cover their share of the costs of providing the various services. The problems, in practice, arise when a management company that is in financial difficulties owns the freehold of the property. If the management company has financial problems it often will not be able to afford to carry out essential maintenance work. As well as affecting the enjoyment of the property, poorly maintained property will be worth less and be difficult to dispose of. The best schemes will involve the participation of one of the major banks (or some other reputable institution), which will hold the land and property on trust for the timesharers. This means that although the bank will be the owner of the property, it will hold it solely for the benefit of the timeshare owners and not for its own benefit. *See also* page 428.

Commonhold

Leasehold land is often looked on as being 'second best' to freehold land. And this is not just because of the fact that a lease only gives you ownership for a limited length of time; in leases landlords commonly impose many more restrictions on the use to which the land can be put than is usual in freehold land. So the landlord's consent will usually be required before you can make any alterations or improvements to the land, before you can change the use and sometimes even before you can sell it. In May 2002 the Commonhold and Leasehold Reform Act 2002 introduced a new system of owning flats and similar types of property called commonhold. This allows the flat-owners to own the freehold in their own individual flats and also deals with the problem of the maintenance and repair of the block. Commonhold is looked at in more detail on page 196.

Rights of ownership

So what rights does a landowner have over his land? We have already mentioned one of the most important – the right to sole and exclusive occupation of the land. Whether you own the freehold or are a tenant under a lease, you have the right to exclude all others from the land – even your landlord. This is the origin of the phrase 'an Englishman's home is his castle'. However, in the case of leasehold land, the terms of the lease may allow your landlord access and, as we shall see, there are numerous other circumstances when the law allows others on to your land without your permission. Perhaps it would thus be more accurate to say that the owner of the land can exclude all others from the land *unless they have a legal right to be there.* But if you discover someone on your land who has no right to be there – a *trespasser* in legal jargon – then you are entitled to ask them to leave and then to use reasonable force to remove them if they will not go. However, force should be a very last resort as the court's idea of reasonable force might not be the same as yours and you could end up in court charged with assault (or worse).

Tony Martin, a farmer who lived alone in a remote farm house in Norfolk, opened fire on two trespassers who had broken into his home with the intention of stealing from him. One trespasser was killed and the other was wounded. Mr Martin unsuccessfully pleaded self-defence and was jailed for murder in August 1999. The Court of Appeal subsequently reduced the murder sentence to manslaughter.

As far as the use to which you can put your land, originally, the law allowed you to make whatever use of the land you wished. You could use and abuse it as you chose; you could build a house or a shop or a factory that polluted the environment. But as with the right of occupation, your right to do what you want with the land is now subject to legal controls in many ways. Neighbouring landowners may have rights over your land (*see* below) which restrict the use to which you can put it. If your land is leasehold, then the terms of the lease may well restrict the way in which the land can be used. Also, the law has long prevented a landowner from using his land in such a way as to cause a nuisance to his neighbours and the local council now has wide powers to control the use of private property in the general public interest. If you want to change the use of your land (for example, from a home to a dentists' surgery) or carry out any building work on your land, you will probably need planning permission (*see* page 247). Also, if your property is causing a nuisance to your neighbours, for example because it is in a dangerous state of disrepair, again the local authority may become involved. It has powers to order you to discontinue the nuisance. So today it is more accurate to state that a landowner can use his property in any way he wishes *provided there is no rule of law which prevents a particular use*. All these matters are looked at in Chapters 23 to 26 – The Home Owner and the Law.

Rights others may have over your land

We have seen that your rights of ownership are subject to any rights that others may have over your land. The more common of these are set out below.

Easement

An easement is a right exercised by one landowner over another's land. The classic example is a right of way, e.g. a right for one of your neighbours to walk (or drive their car) over your land to get to their own. Rights of drainage are also very common – a right for next door's drains to pass under your land. Of course, you may well have such rights over your neighbour's land yourself. Another common easement is a right of light – a right to have the light to one of your windows pass over the neighbour's land without any obstruction. For example, if a neighbour planted a tree on his land which blocked out the light to your window, they might be interfering with your right to light.

If your land is subject to an easement – or you have the benefit of such a right over your neighbour's land – then that easement cannot be obstructed in any way. So you cannot use your land in a way that interferes with the right of way, or the drains, or the light, as the case may be. An easement granted by a previous owner of your land will be binding on you – and this will still be the case if you did not know of the existence of this right when you bought the land.

The problem with easements is that they can be acquired over your land without your consent. If, for example, someone has been openly using a footpath over your land, without your permission, for 20 years or more, then the law will grant them a legal right to continue that use. This right will be binding on you and all future owners of the land and you will have no right to stop that use. The moral is obvious: if you see anyone using your land in any way, put a fence up, *stop them*, otherwise it may soon be too late and they will have a legal right to continue that use forever. This may well not only impede your enjoyment of the land, but also make it more difficult to sell. (*See also* page 256.)

If you sell off part of your land (e.g. part of your garden as a building plot), then the law may give the buyer easements such as rights of way, light, etc. over the land you are retaining. Such sales of part of land should never be done without taking legal advice.

Restrictive covenants

A covenant is simply an agreement to use (or not to use) your land in a particular way. It is common to find covenants restricting the use of a piece of land to residential purposes only, or preventing land from being used for industrial purposes. A covenant can only be entered into by an express agreement with your neighbours; it can never be imposed on you by the law. However, if a previous owner of your land entered into such a covenant, then it will be binding on you and all future owners. If, for example, the previous owner promised not to use the land for commercial use, this will be binding on you and so your use of the land will be restricted. There are various legal rules which must be complied with before you will be bound; in particular the covenant must be entered on the Land Register (*see* page 178), so you would have been aware of it before you bought the property.

The Householder Owns a 'Bundle of Rights'

The owner's 'rights'	The 'rights' that other individuals may have over the property	'Rights' vested in the community
• to live in the property; • to let the property; • to keep, sell or destroy anything on the property; • to build on the land; • to sell the land to anyone; • to give the land (or part of it) away; to bequeath it by will; • to fish in any river that flows through the land; • to do what he or she likes on the property; • to sue for trespass by other people or their possessions (including tree roots and branches); • to sue for nuisance, if the 'quiet enjoyment' is disturbed (e.g. by noise and vibration) etc.	• as tenant under a lease for more than 21 years (the 'rights' will be set out in the lease and in the Leasehold Reform Act 1967); • as tenant under any other lease (the 'rights' will be set out in the Rent Acts, Housing Acts, and in the lease, if any); • the building society or mortgage company that lent money on a mortgage (the 'rights' of possession and sale will be set out in the mortgage deed); • a neighbour's 'right' to prevent the home-owner from reducing the amount of light that enters the neighbour's buildings; • a neighbour's 'right' to prevent the home-owner from removing soil that would affect the support and structure of next-door property (including, perhaps, any buildings); • a 'right of way' to pass over the land; • a right of possession gained by 12 years' squatting on the land; • 'rights' under restrictive covenants to control and prevent development on the land or a change in its use; • 'rights' granted by custom, to graze cattle on the land, dig turf for fuel, etc.	• to enforce standards of hygiene and cleanliness; • to control development, erection of buildings, signs, conversions etc.; • to control a change of use of the property; • to control the quality and nature of building works; • to restrict the type of fuel burnt on the property; • to allow planes to trespass over the land and through its airspace; • to claim gold, silver and oil found on the land; • to claim any treasure trove found on the land, on behalf of the Crown; • to regulate the number of people living there; • to restrict the amount of water that can be taken from any rivers that flow across the land; • to prevent the property being used for certain dangerous purposes (e.g. involving radioactive fuels); • to sue for nuisance if the landowner disturbs others, or allows dangerous materials to escape from the land; • powers of entry given to police, gas board officials, etc.; • the right to compulsory purchase of the land; • the right for certain works to be carried out on the land (e.g. digging of pipes and laying of cables).

Positive covenants

The law distinguishes between covenants *not* to do something, i.e. restrictive covenants (*see* above), and those actually to positively *do* something. Positive covenants are not binding on future owners of the land (unlike restrictive covenants). So, if the person you bought the land from entered into an obligation to repair a fence, you will not be bound by that positive covenant when you buy the land. If he entered into an obligation to use the land for residential purposes only, then you will be bound by that restrictive covenant. This may seem illogical, but is based on the legal rule that someone should not be bound to do something unless they themselves have actually agreed to do it.

Note that the distinction between positive and restrictive covenants is one of substance not just in the wording used. So a covenant 'to use land only for residential purposes' is restrictive (albeit worded positively); what it really means is 'not to use the land for any other purpose'. Similarly, a covenant 'not to allow the fence to fall into disrepair' is positive; it really means 'to repair'. So always look at the underlying meaning – not just the actual form of words used.

Indemnity covenants

As we have just seen, if the previous owner of your land entered into an obligation to maintain a fence, this will not be binding on you. However, when the land is sold to you, the previous owner will still remain liable on that covenant. His promise 'to repair the fence' is deemed to be a promise to repair it forever (unless expressly stated otherwise). So it will be no defence to an action for disrepair that he has sold the land to you; otherwise everyone could simply escape any obligations they enter into by giving their land to a friend.

So you buy the land and do not repair the fence – you are not obliged to, remember. The person who sold you the land can then be sued for your breach. Hardly an ideal position for the seller to be in. In order to protect the seller's interests, it is likely that when the land was sold to you, the seller's solicitor would have insisted that you entered into an *indemnity covenant* with the seller. This is a promise that, if the seller is sued because of a future breach of the covenant, then you will indemnify him, i.e. pay to him the amount of any loss he has suffered because of the breach.

So although you cannot be *directly* sued if you breach a positive covenant, if you gave an indemnity in respect of it when you bought, you will be accountable to the seller (i.e. he can sue you) if you do break it.

Rights of occupiers

Persons other than the owner of the land may be in occupation of it or may have rights of occupation over it. This can cause problems to both the owner of the land and any potential buyer.

In cases where the matrimonial home is owned by one spouse alone, the other spouse is given a right to occupy it by the Family Law Act 1996. This is to prevent the owning spouse selling the house behind the other spouse's back. Although this right is only binding on a buyer if entered on the Land Register, a spouse can enter it on the register at any time prior to actual completion. It is essential, therefore, whenever you are buying a house from a single spouse to ensure that you obtain written confirmation from the other spouse that he will not make such a registration and will vacate the house prior to completion. Equally, if you are planning to sell in such a situation, you should ensure that your spouse is agreeable to the sale.

This right to occupy under the Family Law Act 1996 is only available to spouses, not cohabitants of the owner, no matter how long they may have lived in the house. However, under the Land Registration Act 2002, the rights of any person in occupation of the land will also be binding on a buyer. When a buyer discovers someone in occupation of the house as well as (or instead of) the seller, he should beware of this provision. If a person contributes to the purchase or improvement of a house, e.g. by helping with the mortgage repayments, then the law may imply that they should be given a share in the ownership of the house. Under the Land Registration Act 2002 this right would be binding on a buyer of the land if the person in question was in occupation. The buyer might then have to buy them out in order to be able to occupy the house himself. Again this is of concern to sellers as well as buyers. If it is discovered that anyone else is in occupation other than the seller, it is necessary to insist on that person declaring in writing that he will vacate the house prior to completion. The rights would then cease to be binding if there is no one in occupation on the day of completion.

The problem of occupiers' rights applies to any occupier, whether or not they are married to the owner. So the spouse, cohabitant, sister, brother or child of the owner may have acquired rights in this way and will need to confirm that they will vacate.

MORTGAGES

Non-lawyers often misuse the term 'mortgage'. A mortgage is *not* a loan from a bank or building society; you do *not* go to the bank to 'get a mortgage'. Rather, it is a right over land given by the owner to guarantee the repayment of a loan. You get a *loan* from the bank and give them a mortgage (i.e. a right over the land) in return.

Types of mortgage

There are innumerable types of loan available in the marketplace. Every lender seems to offer half a dozen (or more) various types of loan and it can be very difficult to find out which offers the best deal. Initially, mortgages can be divided into two basic types; repayment and interest only.

Repayment mortgage

With a repayment mortgage you repay the loan by making equal monthly payments over, for example, 25 years. Part of each payment comprises the repayment of the loan, most of it the repayment of the interest on the loan. At the end of the agreed loan period, both interest and loan have been paid in full.

Interest only mortgage

With an interest only loan, the repayments made to the lender consist only of the interest due on the loan; at the end of the loan period you will still owe the capital, i.e. the sum you originally borrowed. Some other arrangement needs to be made to deal with the repayment of the capital. Often an endowment assurance policy is taken out at the same time as the loan with the hope that this will produce sufficient by the end of the loan period to repay the loan. However, in recent years fears have been expressed that very many of these endowment mortgages have been mis-sold and that the policies will not produce enough to repay the loan in full. There is a suspicion that many borrowers were persuaded to take out endowment mortgages because of the high rates of commission paid to financial advisers for selling endowment policies.

Lender's rights over the property

So what rights do you give the bank or building society in return for your loan?

Possession

The lender has the right to the possession of your house as soon as you sign the mortgage deed, i.e. even though you are not in any arrears. However, most lenders will not actually exercise this right provided that you keep your payments up to date. However, if you do fall behind in your payments it is likely that the lender will then seek to take possession. Where you are still living in the house yourself, then the lender will need to obtain a court order to remove you from the property (unless you agree to leave voluntarily). When the lender applies to court, the court can refuse to order possession if you are able to make a sensible offer to make good the arrears within a reasonable time. What kind of offer would be acceptable will depend upon the precise circumstances of each particular case.

Sale

The lender's most important right is to sell the property in order to recover the money owed to it. The lender is entitled to sell in the circumstances laid down in the mortgage document. Normally, this will be if you fall behind with your mortgage payments or breach any other term of the loan. A lender will normally obtain possession first (*see* above), but once it has obtained possession, no further court order is required before the sale can take place. This makes the application for possession of even greater significance; if possession cannot be obtained, then there will generally be no sale; if possession is obtained, then a sale is likely to follow very quickly. When the lender sells, it must take reasonable steps to obtain the market price of the property. The lender is not entitled to keep all the sale proceeds, only sufficient to repay the loan (plus interest) and the costs of the sale. Any balance remaining will then be handed over to the lender, or to the next lender if there is a second mortgage on the property. The lender may sell by auction, or by placing the house in the hands of an estate agent in the usual way. Auction sales of repossessed property do not fetch very high prices, but as the sale was by auction, it is very difficult for a borrower to claim that the true market value was not achieved at the sale. It is always preferable, if there is no alternative to a sale, for the borrower to

conduct the sale himself. He may well achieve a higher price than a lender would and the costs of the sale are also likely to be lower.

Other rights

The terms of most mortgage loans are quite strict. The lender is always concerned that the borrower will not take any action that will in any way reduce the value of the land or cause any delay or difficulty in selling the land, should the lender need to do so to recover its loan. So you will not be able to let the house, or alter it, or extend it, or change its use without obtaining the lender's permission. Most lenders will charge you for the privilege of asking their permission (even if they turn you down) and may well insist on charging a higher rate of interest, particularly in the case of lettings.

Their mortgage conditions will allow them:

1 to charge a fee for considering the request; and
2 to charge a higher rate of interest if they agree to the request.

This is due to the higher risk that a tenanted property may be difficult to sell should they need to do so to get their money back. If you do not ask for permission when it is needed, you will be in breach of the terms of your mortgage and this would entitle the lender to obtain possession and sell the property.

SQUATTERS' RIGHTS

Yes, squatters do indeed have rights!

Historically, the way you proved the ownership of land was by showing that you had been in possession of it for a long time. This is no longer necessary, in the case of registered land, as we have a state-operated register which provides a written record of ownership. However, remnants of the historical principle still survive in the rule that if you occupy someone else's land for long enough, then you will become the owner of that land. Lawyers call this 'adverse possession under the Limitation Act 1980', referring to the legislation which sets out the rule.

Basically, if you occupy a piece of land for at least 12 consecutive years, without the permission of the owner, then *you* will become the owner of that land under the adverse possession rule. This is so even if the land is registered; on proof of your possession, the register will be altered and you will be entered as owner.

To amount to adverse possession, you must be in sole possession of the land to the exclusion of the true owner for a period of at least 12 years. Usually, this occurs when an owner abandons a piece of land and it is then 'taken over' by someone else, usually a neighbour. What amounts to adverse possession is a complicated legal problem and the answer will differ according to the nature of the property. For example, the way to acquire adverse possession of a house or flat is by living in it; if it is a piece of land then fencing it in with your own land and cultivating it in some way would be sufficient to amount to adverse possession. The moral for a landowner is clear: do not let someone occupy your land for any length of time – even if you have no present need for it – otherwise you run the risk of losing the ownership of the land forever. It is unusual for ownership of a house to be acquired by 12 years' adverse possession, but quite common in cases of vacant land. For example, an owner has no use for a piece of land and ceases to use it; a neighbour has some use for it and takes possession. A boundary fence or hedge falls down or is replaced, but not exactly in the same position as before; one neighbour loses a piece of land, the other gains a little.

There have been several recent high-profile cases of squatters acquiring the ownership of valuable pieces of property. For example, in 1999 Lambeth council lost the ownership of several houses worth many hundreds of thousands of pounds to squatters. These cases highlighted how the law was in desperate need of reform and the government responded with the Land Registration Act 2002, which radically changed the law. The Act introduced a new system in relation to adverse possession, which makes registered land virtually squatter-proof. (Registered land means that the owner's name and other details, such as the mortgage, are registered at the Land Registry. *See* page 178 'The Land Registry'.) Under the Act, after 10 years' adverse possession, the squatter will be entitled to apply to be registered as owner of the property in place of the existing registered owner. The owner can then object to the squatter's application. If the owner does object, the squatter will only be registered in very limited circumstances. The owner should then take action against the squatter to evict him from the land. He will have two years to get rid of the squatter – otherwise, the squatter can make a second application to the Land Registry two years after the first application and will be registered as proprietor. The Land Registration Act came into force on 13 October 2003. It will not affect squatters who have already acquired a right to ownership under the existing law and nor will it affect the law on adverse possession of unregistered land. People owning unregistered properties may wish to consider applying to the Land Registry for voluntary registration of their land in order to take advantage of the protection against squatters afforded by the Act. *See also* page 255.

OWNING PROPERTY JOINTLY WITH ANOTHER

It is very common for two and (occasionally) even more people to buy a house together. Often, they will be husband and wife. Whatever the relationship between the owners, they have to decide the legal way in which they will own the house. Note that the maximum number of owners permitted by the law is four. If more than four people wish to buy a property together, this will only be possible if a legal device called a 'trust' is used. The first four owners will become the owners of the land and will then hold it 'on trust for', that is on behalf of, themselves and the other owners.

When dealing with more than one owner of land (co-ownership, as the lawyers call it), the law lays down two different ways in which they can own land together. The owners must choose which method is suitable for their circumstances. To put it into legal jargon, they must decide whether they wish to own the land as *joint tenants* or *tenants in common*. What is the significance of this distinction?

Joint tenants

The first thing to realize is that the reference to *tenants* has nothing to do with renting the property; we are talking of people who do own the freehold in the house. 'Joint tenancy' is just a legal term describing how you 'hold' or own the land. It is derived from the Latin word 'to hold'; many English legal terms are of Latin or French origin.

So what is a joint tenancy? If you decide to be joint tenants, then on the death of one of the owners, that person's interest in the house will pass automatically to the survivor(s). So, if A and B buy a house together – and it does not matter whether they are husband and wife, the same sex or the opposite sex – when A dies his/her interest in the house will pass to B. This will happen despite any will that A may have left leaving the house to someone else.

So this is the first thing to think about when buying a house with someone else: do I want my share to pass to the other(s) on my death? If you do, then a joint tenancy may be the correct choice. If, on the other hand, you want to be able to leave your share to whomsoever you want, then you will need to choose a tenancy in common. Often, of course, in the case of husband and wife or other long-term relationship, you will want your share to go to the other owner. In practice, most husbands and wives do choose to be joint tenants.

Tenancy in common

If you choose a tenancy in common then on your death your share of the house will pass in the same way as all your other assets. It will pass either according to your will or, if you have left no valid will, to your nearest relative according to the rules of intestacy.

There may be another reason for choosing a tenancy

Adverse Possession – The New Procedure

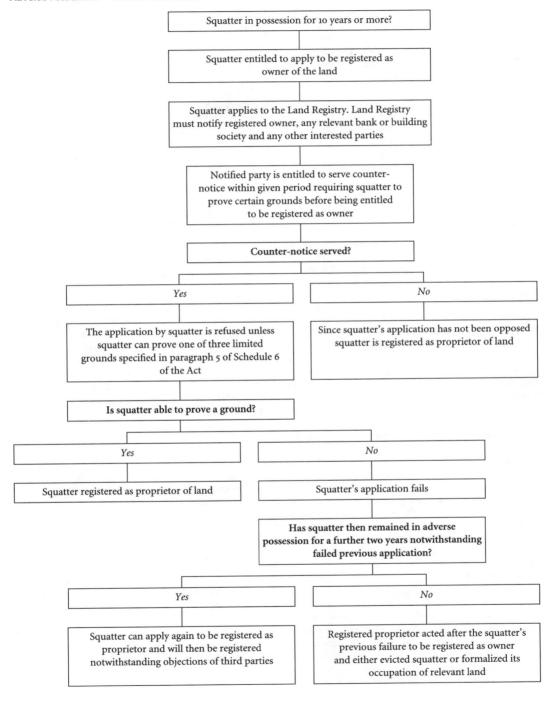

in common apart from freedom to leave it to whom you wish: with a joint tenancy, the shares of the owners have to be exactly the same. So if there are two owners, they must own half each, if there are three owners, they must own a third each, and so on. It is not possible to have a situation whereby A owns two-thirds and B one-third, to recognize the fact, for example, that A put up more money towards the house than B. But this is possible with a tenancy in common.

So if you decide to be tenants in common, you will also have to decide what share each owner is going to have, whether to reflect their respective contributions to the purchase price or for whatever reason. This will then be set out in the transfer, the deed that passes ownership from the previous owners to you.

Converting a joint tenancy into a tenancy in common

Most husbands and wives buying property together do start off by being joint tenants. On the death of one of them, they will want their share to go to the other – although this may not always be the case in a second marriage. It does not matter how much each of them contributed towards the purchase; in the first flush of love it is all 'ours' anyway. But, unfortunately, marriages, and other long-term relationships, do not always last. Couples split up or get divorced; what is to happen to the house in such a situation? Of course, financial matters are one of the main problems that need sorting out on the breakdown of any relationship, and whether the house is held as joint tenants or tenants in common the parties can agree any kind of solution that suits them. So the house may go entirely to one, or may be sold and the proceeds divided in whatever shares the court or the parties may decide.

But what if no agreement can be reached and there are no court proceedings? What if one of the parties dies before agreement can be reached or a court order obtained? With a joint tenancy, remember, that person's share will pass automatically to the other owner. Now the relationship has broken down, that may well be the last thing that the deceased wanted to happen – his spouse or partner may be the last person in the world that he or she wanted the house to go to.

Fortunately, if you decide to be joint tenants, it is possible at a later date to change your mind, to convert the joint tenancy into a tenancy in common so that you can leave your share in the house to whomsoever you choose. This is known as 'severance' of the joint tenancy. Severing a joint tenancy is simplicity itself. All you need to do is write a letter to the other owner(s) and either leave it at the house or send it to them by registered or recorded delivery post. A specimen letter follows:

> To: [*name and address of other joint owner*]
>
> *Dear ......*
>
> Re: [*insert full postal address of jointly owned property*]
> In accordance with Section 36 of the Law of Property Act 1925, I hereby sever our joint tenancy of the above property.
> Yours, etc.
> [*sign and print your name here*]

The downside of being joint tenants and then severing is that the joint tenancy rule will still apply, i.e. you will each own equal shares in the property. So that if there are two owners, on severance you will end up owning half each, notwithstanding that you may have contributed to the purchase price in completely different shares. If you wish those contributions to be reflected in your ownership, you should start off as tenants in common.

THE LAND REGISTRY

This is the government body which records the ownership of land in England and Wales. It is this register which is used to prove ownership of land when it is being bought and sold (*see* Chapter 18). Each piece of land registered is given its own 'title' (or reference) number, which must be quoted in all applications to the Land Registry relating to the land. There will be a separate title and title number for the freehold and for any lease affecting the land.

Although the ownership of the majority of land is entered on the register, some land which has not changed hands for many years has still not yet been placed on the register. Ownership is proved by producing the 'title deeds' to the land; there is no public register where the ownership of such 'unregistered land' can be checked. It is intended that the ownership of all land should be entered on the register within the next few years.

The register is open to public inspection (on payment of a small fee, currently £4 per title) and on completion of the appropriate form. If you do not know the title number of the property for which you require details, the Land Registry will provide this for you. The appropriate form can be downloaded from the Land Registry's internet site at www.landreg.gov.uk. You can also view property details on the internet using Land Registry Online at www.landreg.gov.uk/online/ on payment of a £2 fee by credit card.

The following information can be obtained by getting copies of the entries on the register relating to a property; these are known as Official Copies:

- the owner (or Proprietor, in Land Registry jargon) of the property;

- any mortgages over the land;
- any covenants affecting the land;
- details of *some* of the easements affecting the land;
- information about leases (over 7 years) affecting the land;
- the price paid for the property by the present owners – provided the purchase took place after April 2000.

The Land Registry is organized on a regional basis, with the ownership details of land in a particular area being dealt with by the appropriate District Land Registry. Details as to which District Land Registry deals with any particular area of the country can be obtained from any Land Registry (look in your local phone book) or from the Land Registry's internet site.

The Land Registry guarantees the accuracy of the information on the register; if anyone suffers loss due to a mistake in the register, then compensation may be available from the Land Registry.

TAX AND THE HOME OWNER

Income tax

For many years income tax relief was given on the interest paid on loans taken out to help finance the purchase of the borrower's only or main home. This was intended to encourage home-ownership. However, this relief was abolished in April 2000.

Capital gains tax

Capital gains tax is, as its name suggests, a tax on the gain made when property, including land, is sold or otherwise disposed of.

The gain is calculated by deducting the purchase price of the property from the sale price. (There are special rules for properties purchased prior to 1982.) This gain then has to be adjusted to take account of inflation. So, part of the increase in value will be due to inflation and allowance is made for this so that you do not pay tax on the increase caused by inflation. In addition, each taxpayer has an 'annual exemption', fixed in the budget each year. This allows gains made in a particular tax year up to the specified amount to be made without incurring liability to tax; tax is then payable on gains made over and above this annual exemption.

Capital gains tax will not be chargeable on the disposal by an individual of his only or main residence, provided various conditions have been complied with. The main condition is that the owner has lived in the house throughout the period of ownership. Certain periods of absence will be disregarded. These periods can be added together and include:

- any time spent working abroad;
- the last 36 months of ownership;
- any other periods of absence up to a total of 36 months; and
- up to 48 months spent working away in another part of the UK.

Special rules apply when the house has been let.

Married couples cannot claim the exemption in relation to more than one property, i.e. the husband cannot claim that one house is his main home and the wife that another is hers and so claim the exemption in relation to two properties.

Where part of the house is used exclusively for business purposes (e.g. a doctor who uses part of the house as his surgery) then only a proportion of the gain will be exempt from tax.

There are special rules relating to the sale of part of the garden of the house. Basically, as long as the area of the garden does not exceed 0.5 hectares, the sale will be capital gains tax free, but specialist advice should always be taken.

Council tax

Council tax is payable by occupiers of residential property. All residential properties in England and Wales have been 'banded' according to their value, Wales having a different range of bands to England. The amount of tax payable then varies according to the band in which the house has been placed, the higher-value properties paying more than lower-value properties. The charge accrues on a daily basis, so a new occupier becomes liable from the date of his occupation.

Generally, when property is let, the liability to pay the tax falls on the tenant and not the landlord. However, when the property is in multiple occupation, it is the landlord who is responsible. The definition of multiple occupation for council tax purposes includes any dwelling inhabited by persons who do not constitute a single household, all of whom either only have the right to occupy part of the house, or are licensees not paying rent. It is sometimes difficult to decide whether a group of people sharing a house do so as a single household. In cases of doubt, the landlord should include a provision in the tenancy agreement allowing him to increase the rent by the amount of any council tax he may be required to bear.

Four students at Sheffield University joined together to occupy a house for an academic year. Held: They were a single household and the house was not in multiple occupation. Barnes (1995)

In the case of a building containing ten bedrooms on four different floors, a kitchen and a bathroom in the basement, a living room on the ground floor and a second bathroom on a half-landing, where the property was let out under individual oral agreements for unspecified periods to up to nine single adults at a time, none of whom had any connection with the others, the house was held to be in multiple occupation. Rogers (1999)

Certain types of property and certain types of occupier are exempt from council tax. Exemptions include full-time students and properties empty for less than 6 months, for example, where the owner has moved to a new property to relocate for a new job but his old house has not yet been sold.

Discounts of 25 per cent are also available, irrespective of income, if the property is only occupied by one person aged 18 or over. There are also reductions available for households which contain a person with specified disabilities.

The government has announced a council tax revaluation of all properties in England to take effect from 1 April 2007. The National Assembly for Wales plans a revaluation to come into force in 2005, based on values as at April 2003.

16

Long Leases of Houses: the Right to Buy and Have an Extended Lease

INTRODUCTION

In certain areas of the country, such as South Yorkshire, it used to be common to find that houses were not sold freehold, which gives the right to occupy forever, but were sold on long leases. A lease gives the right to occupy for a fixed period; often in the case of house sales it would be 99 or even 999 years. Throughout the term of the lease a comparatively low rent would be paid. This is generally referred to as a 'ground rent' and is so named because the tenant pays a lump sum to buy the house at the start of the lease and then pays rent just for the land on which the house stands. Ground rents for older properties might only be a few pounds each year; for more recently granted leases, they might be a few hundred pounds each year.

Leasehold houses are often thought of as being inferior to freehold houses; not only because of the shorter length of time for which ownership will endure, but also because owners of leasehold houses are more likely to have restrictions placed on them as to what they can or cannot do in their property; for example building an extension or conservatory would usually require the landlord's permission. Furthermore, although a 999-year lease might appear to grant an ample period of occupation, a 99-year lease will approach its expiry date much more rapidly. And the nearer it gets to its expiry date, the harder it will become to sell it and so the lower in value it will get; the classic case of a depreciating asset.

WHAT HAPPENS AT THE END OF A LONG LEASE?

At the expiry of a long lease, a tenant does not immediately have to leave; he is allowed to remain in occupation as an assured tenant under the Housing Act 1988. His status as an assured tenant means the landlord cannot obtain possession unless he can prove one of the usual assured tenancy grounds (*see* page 217). But there is an extra ground for possession available: that the landlord needs possession because he intends to redevelop the site; this ground could obviously cause worries for a home owner.

But the most immediate impact that the home owner would face would be with regard to the rent. The ground rent the tenant had been paying throughout the lease – a rent that was perhaps fixed 99 years ago at a few pounds a year – would become a normal assured tenancy rent; the full market rent for both the land and the house. This could well be (depending upon the house, of course) several hundred pounds a month.

The right to buy the freehold or an extended lease

To mitigate the harshness of this situation, the Leasehold Reform Act of 1967 (the 'Act') confers on certain tenants of long leases of houses the right to acquire the freehold of their properties. This is often at a comparatively low cost. Lawyers sometimes refer to this as the right to 'enfranchise'. The Commonhold and Leasehold Reform Act 2002 introduced important changes affecting the enfranchisement of houses let on long leases. These changes came into effect on 26 July 2002 and are noted below.

Alternatively, the 1967 Act also gives tenants the right to acquire an extended lease at a ground rent.

For these rights to apply various conditions must be fulfilled.

The qualifying conditions in outline

There are four major requirements:

1 there must be a 'house';
2 let on a 'long lease';
3 for a 'particularly long term' (but only if the lease is a business lease);
4 the tenant satisfies the two-year ownership test.

Each of these will have to be looked at in turn in more detail.

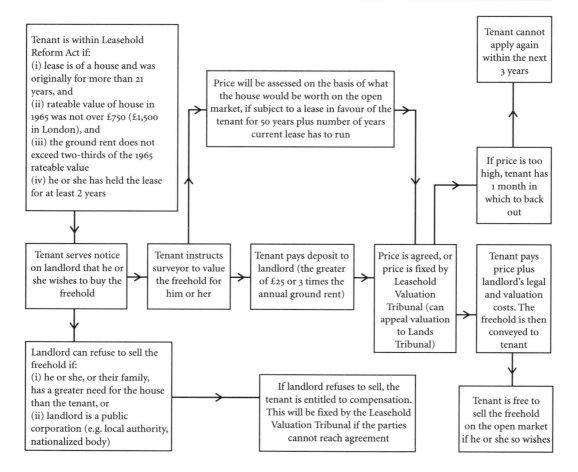

Tenant is within Leasehold Reform Act if:
(i) lease is of a house and was originally for more than 21 years, and
(ii) rateable value of house in 1965 was not over £750 (£1,500 in London), and
(iii) the ground rent does not exceed two-thirds of the 1965 rateable value
(iv) he or she has held the lease for at least 2 years

Price will be assessed on the basis of what the house would be worth on the open market, if subject to a lease in favour of the tenant for 50 years plus number of years current lease has to run

Tenant cannot apply again within the next 3 years

If price is too high, tenant has 1 month in which to back out

Tenant serves notice on landlord that he or she wishes to buy the freehold

Tenant instructs surveyor to value the freehold for him or her

Tenant pays deposit to landlord (the greater of £25 or 3 times the annual ground rent)

Price is agreed, or price is fixed by Leasehold Valuation Tribunal (can appeal valuation to Lands Tribunal)

Tenant pays price plus landlord's legal and valuation costs. The freehold is then conveyed to tenant

Landlord can refuse to sell the freehold if:
(i) he or she, or their family, has a greater need for the house than the tenant, or
(ii) landlord is a public corporation (e.g. local authority, nationalized body)

If landlord refuses to sell, the tenant is entitled to compensation. This will be fixed by the Leasehold Valuation Tribunal if the parties cannot reach agreement

Tenant is free to sell the freehold on the open market if he or she so wishes

A house

The Act applies only to houses and not to flats. If you own a flat, *see* page 185 which gives details of similar rights available to flat owners.

You might think that you know what a house is, but the Act provides a strict legal definition of the word for the purposes of deciding who qualifies.

'House' is defined to include any building designed or adapted for living in, notwithstanding that the building is not structurally detached, or was not or is not *solely* designed or adapted for living in, provided that it is 'reasonable' to call it a house.

Clearly this definition includes ordinary purpose-built houses, whether detached, semi-detached or terraced. These are buildings 'designed' for living in. It will also include buildings that were not originally 'designed for living in' (e.g. barns, warehouses, windmills, stables, etc.), which were later adapted for living in.

Some buildings do not fall so easily within the

definition. One problem that has arisen is with regard to shops with living accommodation – the classic 'corner shop', perhaps. The question of whether a corner shop, incorporating a flat, was a 'house' had to be decided by the House of Lords.

The case concerned a purpose-built shop with a flat above. Both were included in the lease to the tenant. Approximately 75 per cent of the property by area was attributed to the shop and 25 per cent to the living accommodation. The House of Lords held that it was reasonable to call it a house within the 1967 Act, even though it was also reasonable to call it something else as well, i.e. a shop.

It is a question of law whether it is reasonable to call a building a house, but this case does show that if the building is designed or adapted for living in, it is only in exceptional circumstances that it will not be reasonable to call it a house.

What about a property which was originally a house

which has been converted into flats? Large Victorian villas in inner city areas, too large for modern families, are often converted into several flats. The legislation makes it clear that an individual flat *cannot* be a house, but nevertheless the whole building may retain its characteristics as a house. For example, if the owner of a long lease of the whole house, who continues to occupy one of the flats, converts a house into four self-contained flats, sub-letting the others, the long leaseholder may be in a position to enfranchise. The building looked at as a whole can still reasonably be called a house, notwithstanding the internal sub-division.

However, this should be contrasted with the case of a purpose-built block of flats, let to a tenant who occupies one flat and sublets the rest; here, the block of flats could not reasonably be called a house; it's a block of flats.

Long lease

To be a long lease, the lease must have been originally granted for a term exceeding 21 years. Note that you need not be the original tenant to have rights under the Act, nor does it matter how long the lease has left to run; it is the original term which must exceed 21 years. So if you have bought a lease which has only five years out of an original 99 years left to run, this will still be a long lease for the purposes of the Act.

A particularly long term

This is a term which exceeds 35 years in length. This requirement that the lease must have been originally granted for a term of more than 35 years only applies to business leases.

Two-year ownership test

The Commonhold and Leasehold Reform Act 2002 provides that in order to qualify for enfranchisement or an extended lease the tenant must have held the lease for at least two years.

Death of the occupier

If the tenant dies before exercising rights under the Act and the tenancy passes to a member of his family, the successor can, in certain circumstances, add his own qualifying period of residence (post death) to the deceased's qualifying period of residence to make up the three-year minimum. This only applies, however, where the tenant dies while occupying the house as his only or main residence and the successor also resided in the house as his only or main residence and is still so resident at the date of the death of the tenant. 'Member of the family' is defined to include a spouse, children, parents or parents-in-law. Although not specifically included in the statutory definition, it is likely that the survivor of a couple in a long-term relationship would be held to be a member of

the deceased's family. This would be the case where the couple were of the opposite or the same sex.

The Commonhold and Leasehold Reform Act 2002 improves the rights of those who have inherited a leasehold house from a deceased leaseholder who qualified for the right to extend their lease and/or enfranchise at the time of their death. Personal representatives will have the right to enfranchise and/or extend the lease within two years following grant of probate or letters of administration.

Enfranchisement or extended lease?

The tenant who satisfies the above conditions will normally wish to enfranchise. This means that the landlord must convey the freehold to the tenant at a price, and on the terms, referred to in the Act. Alternatively, the tenant may elect to take an extended lease. Here, the landlord must grant the tenant a new lease for the unexpired remainder of the term of the existing lease plus a further 50 years. The new lease will be, broadly, on the same terms of the existing lease and the rent will be the same until the expiry date of the existing lease, but will then be replaced by a ground rent fixed to reflect modern values; this will be reviewed after 25 years of the extra 50 years.

As will be seen below, the price a tenant pays for the freehold will, for most properties, be very low. It is, therefore, preferable for a tenant to acquire the freehold if this is at all financially possible; it will be cheaper in the long run than taking an extended lease and having to pay an increased ground rent for the period of the extension. As this is a rent fixed to reflect modern values, it could be several hundred pounds per year, depending upon the size, location, etc. of the house.

Leaseholders can now buy their freehold even if their lease has already been extended. This is one of the important new rights introduced by the Commonhold and Leasehold Reform Act 2002. The 2002 Act also provides that where leaseholders extend their lease but do not buy the freehold, they will have the right to an assured tenancy when their extended lease expires. The procedures for enfranchisement of houses where the landlord cannot be traced are also simplified. Leaseholders will be able to apply to a county court for a vesting order and a Leasehold Valuation Tribunal (LVT) will determine the price payable.

The desire notice

The tenant must serve written notice, in the prescribed form, of his 'desire' to acquire either the freehold or an extended lease. This 'desire notice', as it is called, is normally the first step in the procedure to obtain the rights granted by the Act. The desire notice is deemed to be a contract to buy the land. The landlord must, within two months, serve a Notice in Reply admitting or objecting to the tenant's claim. The detailed procedure laid down by the Act is rather complex, but most landlords will accept the inevitable that they are going to have to sell, and will agree to a sale without the need to follow the statutory procedure. The main argument is going to be over the price to be paid (*see* below).

Transfer of right

Although the desire notice is deemed to create a contract, it is generally personal to the tenant and is not assignable to third parties. However, if the tenant assigns the lease, e.g. by selling it to a purchaser, he can assign the benefit of the desire notice to the purchaser at the same time. The purchaser could then proceed with the acquisition of the freehold or an extended lease even though he does not himself qualify under the Act. This can be very important to a tenant who, perhaps, cannot afford to buy the freehold, but is finding it difficult to sell his lease due to the short term remaining. The seller can serve the desire notice, assuming he has held the lease for at least two years, and then transfer the benefit of it to the buyer at the same time as he sells the lease to him. The buyer can thus buy the short residue of the lease and then buy the freehold without having to wait for a further two years.

The price of the freehold

The Act lays down the principles and formulae for calculating the price and the appeals machinery if it cannot be agreed between the parties.

There are two methods of ascertaining the price depending on the value of the house.

The valuation for most properties is very favourable to the tenant. It is assumed for valuation purposes that:
1 the landlord is selling the freehold subject to the lease; and
2 the lease has been extended for a further 50 years under the Act; and
3 the tenant is not the purchaser.

The valuation treats the property as if the freehold is being bought largely for its investment income. Anyone, other than the tenant, buying the freehold on this basis would simply be buying the right to receive the rent until the lease (assumed to be extended by 50 years) has come to an end. As that rent is likely to be fairly small, so will be the purchase price. The fact that the tenant can, on acquisition, merge the freehold and leasehold interests, and thus acquire the right to occupy the property for ever, is ignored. This 'marriage value', as it is sometimes called, is not taken into account for lower-value properties.

Often, therefore, the tenant will pay a very low price for the freehold, in some cases only about 10 times the amount of the ground rent.

For high-value properties, the basis of valuation is less favourable to the tenant. The increase in value created by the tenant owning both freehold and leasehold interests will be taken into account. Also, an assumption has to be made that the tenant has no right to extend the lease. This would again tend to increase the price that the tenant has to pay.

The method of deciding whether a house falls into the higher- or lower-value bands depends initially upon whether the house had a rateable value on 31 March 1990. If it did (and most houses in existence at that date would have had a rateable value), then the rule is that houses with a rateable value on that date of £500 or less (£1,000 or less in Greater London) will be classifed as lower value. Houses with a higher rateable value will be classified as higher value. Owing to the abolition of domestic rates, it is not possible to use rateable value as a determining factor in relation to houses which did not have a rateable value on 31 March 1990, i.e. basically houses built after that date. With regard to such houses a complex formula is applied based on the amount paid for the house on the grant of the lease and the length of the lease, and professional advice will be required.

Importantly, the Commonhold and Leasehold Reform Act 2002 provides that:
- marriage value is automatically disregarded where the lease has more than 80 years left to run; and
- where the lease has fewer than 80 years left to run, the marriage value should be split 50/50 between the leaseholder and the landlord.

In all cases where you intend to enfranchise, it is sensible to obtain the advice of a valuer at an early stage; this is particularly important in the case of larger properties because the price payable for a high-value property could be quite substantial.

In addition to the purchase price the tenant must pay the landlord's reasonable legal and surveyors/valuation fees. In lower-value properties, these will often exceed the amount of the purchase price. The LVT deals with disputes as to price.

For advice on making applications to the LVT, the Leasehold Advisory Service, an independent advice agency, funded by both government grant and private sector contributions, provides free advice to leaseholders, landlords, professional advisers, and others on the law affecting residential leasehold property.

Tel: 020 7490 9580 Fax: 020 7253 2043 Postal address: 70–74 City Road, London EC1Y 2BJ. Website: www.lease-advice.org. They can also provide contact details for your local LVT.

RIGHTS OF OWNERS OF LONG LEASES OF FLATS ACQUIRING THE FREEHOLD OR AN EXTENSION TO THE LEASE

Introduction

When you buy a flat, you normally do not buy the freehold, which gives you the right to occupy the property for ever, but instead acquire a long lease that gives the right to occupy for a fixed number of years. There are more than 1 million leasehold flats in England and Wales and there are a number of problems that are peculiar to them. Many 'long' leases are only for 99 years, or even less, and when there are less than 50 years left to run, it can prove difficult to find a buyer. This is because banks and building societies are often reluctant to lend money on such a comparatively short length of lease. These long leases are thus a wasting asset; they will decline in value as they get nearer to the end of the term.

Another problem with blocks of flats is that difficulties often arise with regard to the maintenance and repair of the block. This is normally in the hands of the landlord or a management company, the tenants paying a 'service charge' to the landlord as payment for the repairs and day-to-day maintenance. Tenants often complain that landlords do not undertake work that needs doing, or that they overcharge for the services, or both. For flat owners' rights in relation to service charge disputes, *see* page 191.

The Leasehold Reform, Housing and Urban Development Act of 1993 provides a solution to both of these problems. It gives flat owners the right to join together and collectively buy the freehold in their block – whether the landlord likes it or not. This enables them to take over the management of the block themselves. As they collectively own the freehold, they are also able to grant themselves new long leases when their existing leases become unsaleable.

It must be emphasized from the outset that if you exercise this right to buy the freehold, you must acquire the freehold in the whole block jointly with the owners of the other flats in the block. Even if you could afford it, you cannot acquire the freehold on your own; nor can you just acquire the freehold in your own individual flat; you will still only own a lease in that, but you, and the other flat owners, will together own the freehold in the whole block.

If you cannot afford to join the other flat owners in buying the freehold (and this might be quite expensive), flat owners are given the right to buy a new lease of their individual flats; this will extend their existing lease by 90 years. For many people, and particularly where the existing system of management of the block is working satisfactorily, this will be a better option than buying the freehold. It will solve the problem of the lease becoming less attractive to prospective purchasers. And importantly, you can exercise this right on your own whether or not the other flat owners wish to do so.

Both the right to buy the freehold ('collective enfranchisement', as it is sometimes referred to), and the right to buy a new long lease can be exercised without the landlord's consent. The building in which your flat is situated need not be let exclusively to tenants on long leases; some of the flats might be let out on short-term tenancies, for example.

Further, all of the building need not be let exclusively for residential purposes; there could be some parts of the building occupied for business purposes, e.g. as a shop. However, as we shall see, if a substantial part of the building is let for non-residential purposes, then there will be no right to buy the freehold (although there will still be a right to obtain an extended lease).

The Act did not receive a universal welcome from landlords; some landlords will, therefore, prove hostile to any claims under the Act and insist that the provisions of the Act are complied with to the letter. Faced with such a landlord, it takes a determined (and patient) group of tenants to succeed in an enfranchisement claim. But always remember, the law is on your side; the landlord can make you go through all the hoops laid down by the Act, but if you persevere, you will eventually prevail.

Other landlords will adopt a more fatalistic approach and be prepared to agree a sale without strict compliance with all of the Act's conditions.

As we shall see, the conditions that have to be met under the Act are somewhat complicated, but the Commonhold and Leasehold Reform Act 2002, which came into force in July 2002, made significant changes which will make it easier for leaseholders of flats to buy collectively the freehold of their building or extend their existing leases.

Qualifying conditions – buying the freehold

When does the Act apply?

Various conditions have to be fulfilled before you are entitled to the rights under the Act. These are somewhat complex, but basically both the tenants and the block of flats itself must 'qualify' under the Act, and a minimum number of the qualifying tenants must join in the purchase:

- the building and premises must contain two or more flats and at least two-thirds of those flats must be held on long leases;
- the right must be exercised by an RTE (Right to Enfranchise) company.

We will have to look at each of these requirements separately.

Am I a qualifying tenant?

A person will be a 'qualifying tenant' if he is a 'tenant' of a 'flat' under a 'long lease' and as defined by the Act.

Tenant

This is defined to include a sub-lease, so you still have rights under the Act even if your immediate landlord does not himself own the freehold. This might be the case, for example, where you have a lease from a management company which itself took a lease of the whole block from the owner of the freehold.

You will not be a qualifying tenant if you occupy the property for the purposes of a business or your immediate landlord is a charitable housing trust and the flat forms part of the accommodation provided by it for its charitable purposes.

Although these qualifying conditions seem very complex, in most cases a flat owner will have no difficulty in complying with them. Most blocks of residential flats are clearly just that – flats. And most (outside London, at least) are let on 99-year leases. In such a case a flat owner will clearly have a long lease of a flat, and as the lease was granted for more than 99 years, the amount of the rent is irrelevant. So if you buy a flat in such a block, even if there are only 25 of the original 99 years left to run, you will still be a qualifying tenant.

Flat

Most people will recognize a flat when they see one, but the Act provides a definition of 'flat' so that there is no uncertainty. 'Flat' is defined as meaning a separate set of premises, whether or not on the same floor, constructed or adapted for living in, where either the whole or some material part of the premises lies above or below some other part of the building of which it forms part. This sounds terribly complicated, but if you apply the definition to a flat in a block of flats, you will see that it works. The emphasis in the definition is on at least part of the flat being above or below another part of the building. Thus flats above shops will be included, as will what are sometimes referred to as 'maisonettes', i.e. two-storey dwellings above shops. What will not be included are some 'granny flats', i.e. those that are an extension to an existing building but not above or below part of it.

Long lease

This is defined to mean a lease that was originally granted for a term exceeding 21 years. It does not matter that you were not the original tenant, or that there are now less than 21 years left to run; you will still qualify.

Does the building in which my flat is situated qualify?

In order to be able to acquire the freehold, your flat must be situated in 'premises', as defined by the Act:

- the 'premises' must either consist of a self-contained building or a self-contained part of a building; and
- contain two or more flats; and
- at least two-thirds of those flats must be held on long leases.

So even very small blocks of flats come within the legislation. The requirement that two-thirds of the flats must be held on long leases emphasizes that tenants wishing to enfranchise need not hold all the flats in the block. In many blocks of flats, particularly in the London area, there will be a mixture of long leases and tenants renting under short-term leases. Some of the flats might be unoccupied. These blocks can still be enfranchised, subject to this two-thirds rule.

The premises must also be either a self-contained building or a self-contained part of a building. A building is a self-contained building if it is structurally detached. But what is a 'self-contained part of a building'? A self-contained part of a building consists of a vertical division of the building and its structure is such that that part could be redeveloped independently of the remainder. This all sounds very complicated, but is intended to deal with the common situation of long low blocks of flats, as opposed to tower blocks. These often have several separate entrances; one entrance leading to, for instance, flats 1 to 10, and the next to flats 11 to 20, etc. Assuming that each part could be developed independently, then the tenants in flats 1 to 10 will be in a self-contained part of a building and will able to enfranchise independently of those in the rest of the block, and vice versa.

What 'premises' are outside the Act?

Certain buildings are excluded from the rights given by the Act, even though at first sight they look as though they satisfy the conditions.

Buildings within the precincts of a cathedral, National Trust property, and property owned by the Crown will be outside the Act altogether.

Also excluded from the right to enfranchise only are buildings where any parts occupied or intended to be occupied for non-residential purposes (e.g. as a shop or office), exceed 25 per cent of the internal floor area of the premises as a whole. (In making this calculation, any common parts of the building are to be ignored.) This will exclude from the right to enfranchise most buildings with shops on the ground floor and flats above. However, qualifying tenants of such flats will still have the right to an extended lease.

In addition you will not be able to buy the freehold (but you can still buy a new lease), if the building is a converted property containing four or less flats and the owner of the freehold (or an adult member of his family) has lived in one of the flats as his only or principal home for the last 12 months and the resident landlord owned the freehold at the time of the conversion.

The right must be exercised by an RTE company

An RTE company is a private company limited by guarantee with membership restricted to qualifying tenants of flats in the building. Under the Commonhold and Leasehold Reform Act 2002 an initial notice (*see* page 188) can only be given by an RTE company. Before notice is given, all qualifying tenants must be invited to become participating members in that company. When notice is given, the number of leaseholders participating through membership of the RTE company must equal at least half the total number of flats in the building – except where there are only two flats in which case both long leaseholders must participate. The RTE company is the vehicle for the leaseholders' purchase and eventual ownership and management of the building.

What will we buy?

The qualifying tenants will buy not only the freehold of the premises in which the flats are situated, but also any separate garages or car-parking spaces and the grounds in which the block of flats is situated.

However, certain parts of the building may have to be 'leased-back' to the freeholder.

What is a lease-back?

This means that, although the tenants will be buying the freehold, they will have to grant a lease of some parts of the building back to the freeholder from whom they have just bought. This will be a lease for 999 years at a 'peppercorn' rent. In effect this means that no rent is payable for the property leased back. The parts to be leased back may include any parts of the building let on secure tenancies (*see* page 209), let for non-residential purposes or occupied by the landlord. So your erstwhile landlord will now become your tenant in relation to these leased-back parts.

Can the landlord oppose the sale?

A landlord can dispute the right to enfranchise if he can establish the applicants have not complied with one or more of the qualifying conditions.

A landlord can also oppose an enfranchisement claim if two-thirds of the long leases are due to end within five years and he can show that he intends to redevelop the whole or a substantial part of the premises. The best advice is to exercise your rights while there is still more than five years left unexpired.

How much will it cost?

This, of course, will in most cases be the crucial deciding factor as to whether the tenants wish to enfranchise or buy an extension. Most tenants' initial reaction to a request to join in an enfranchisement bid will be to ask how much it is going to cost.

It is essential to seek the advice of a qualified valuer or surveyor at an early stage so that some idea of the price to be paid can be ascertained. There is no point in starting down the road to enfranchisement until you are sure you can afford the cost.

Like the rest of the Act, the provisions for calculating the price are very complicated. Basically, you will pay the open market price, plus compensation to the landlord if your purchase of the freehold reduces the value of other property in the locality belonging to him. For example, if a landlord owns two blocks of flats in the same grounds, the acquisition of one block and the grounds by tenants may reduce the value of the other block. If that is the case, the tenants will have to compensate the landlord for that reduced value.

You will also have to pay the landlord's reasonable legal costs (as well as your own), and surveyors and valuations fees as well as the landlord's share of what is known as the 'marriage value'.

What is marriage value?

Marriage value is a very complex valuation principle. It is based on the concept that when the freehold and leasehold interests in the block are owned by the same people (as they will be after enfranchisement), the interests will then be worth more than when they were owned by different people.

A rather fanciful analogy can be drawn. Imagine a bowl of strawberries. Now imagine a carton of cream. Separately these two are quite appealing, but if you just have one without the other, there is something missing. Together they become much more attractive and thus they are more valuable together than separately. (If you prefer an alcoholic analogy, the same exercise can be preformed with a bottle of gin and a bottle of tonic; separately, these are not very attractive at all but together many would find them most attractive, and thus more valuable than the total of the two separate items.)

In the same way, the value of the block of flats increases when both the leasehold and freehold interests belong to the same person. If you own the freehold subject to the leases, all you are really entitled to is to receive the rent. If you own the lease, you have the right to occupy, but only for a limited amount of time, and the value of your lease will decrease as it gets shorter. So separately, the value of the lease and the value of the freehold might not be worth very much. When one person owns them both, that person has the right to occupy for ever, rent free; the value may then be much more than the combined total values of the freehold and leasehold interests valued separately.

For example, the value of the flat may be, for instance, £80,000. The value of the freehold subject to the lease may be £5,000 – a combined total value of £85,000. The value of the freehold and the lease when the same person owns them both may be £100,000. The increase in value of £15,000 is the marriage value. The landlord is entitled to 50 per cent of this marriage value. Marriage value is a real-life example of when 2 plus 2 really can make 5! However, there will be no marriage value payable on leases with fewer than 80 years left to run.

Who will be the new owner of the freehold?
The RTE company becomes the new owner of the freehold.

I'm interested. What do I do now?
The purchase is initiated by serving the appropriate notice on the freeholder. Under the Commonhold and Leasehold Reform Act 2002 this notice can only be given by an RTE company (*see* page 187). This is not something you can do without professional assistance. The Act requires that the initial notice requesting the purchase of the freehold is accompanied by a valuation prepared by a qualified valuer. You will also need legal advice when it comes to negotiating the terms of the acquisition. Probably the most sensible course of action, in the case of an acquisition of the freehold, is to discuss matters fully with the other flat owners and ensure that a sufficient number of them are interested. If sufficient are interested then the advice of a valuer should be sought as to the likely price. A final decision as to whether to proceed can then be made.

INDIVIDUAL ACQUISITION OF A NEW LEASE

Introduction

The right to buy the freehold must be exercised collectively, i.e. a majority of the tenants join together to buy it. Getting a sufficient number of tenants interested in buying might not always be possible; some might be unable to afford to join in, for example. The right to a new lease, however, can be exercised individually; you are not dependent on your neighbours joining in. The new lease will expire 90 years after the expiry date of the tenant's existing lease. It will be at a 'peppercorn' rent (i.e. a rent of no monetary value) but the tenant must pay a premium (i.e. buy the lease) calculated in accordance with a formula laid down by the Act. Although the lease is to expire 90 years after the end of the existing lease, it will take effect immediately in substitution for the existing lease. So, for example, in the case of a lease

with 23 years left to run, this will be replaced by a new lease for 113 years, i.e. 23 + 90.

When am I entitled to a new lease?

The tenant:
- must own a long lease (as previously defined); and
- must have owned the lease for two years before being able to exercise the right.

The difference from the enfranchisement conditions is that the flat need not be in 'premises' as defined by the Act, nor need there be a minimum number of flats in the building. So, as long as you are tenant of a flat under a long lease, and you have owned the lease for at least two years, you will have the right to have a new lease, even if there are no other flats in the building (e.g. a single flat over a shop) and even if the major part of the building is used for non-residential purposes.

Can the landlord oppose the grant?

Assuming that the qualifying conditions are satisfied, the landlord can only oppose the grant if the tenant's existing lease will end within five years from the date of the tenant's request and at the end of that lease the landlord intends to demolish or reconstruct the building and cannot do so without obtaining possession of the flat. If possible, it is best not to leave the application until the last five years of the lease so as to avoid this ground of opposition.

The amount of the premium

The Act contains complicated rules for the calculation of the price to be paid for the new lease. Professional valuation advice will be necessary at an early stage. You will be paying the full market price for the new lease, so it may not be cheap. Marriage value will only be payable on leases with fewer than 80 years left to run.

Effect of the grant of a new lease

Once the new lease has been granted, this will not prevent the tenant from joining in any future enfranchisement application. Indeed, the price to be paid for the freehold may well be reduced because of the existence of the new, longer lease.

WHAT HAPPENS WHEN MY LEASE RUNS OUT?

Ideally, you should never get to the position where your lease runs out; you should have exercised your right to a new lease or joined in with the other flat owners and bought the freehold and granted yourself a new lease. The reality of the situation may be that neither of these options was possible due to financial or other reasons, and the lease does expire. Fortunately, not quite all is lost.

You will not have to give up possession at the end of your lease; you will be allowed to remain in possession as an ordinary assured tenant. As to assured tenancies *see* page 217. Basically this means that you will have full security of tenure. However, you will have lost your capital asset, i.e. the value of the house that you bought. You are now just a tenant renting property, and as an assured tenant you will be paying the full market rent for the house, not just the ground rent you were paying before. The rent could well rise from a few pounds each year to hundreds of pounds per month. Furthermore, although you have security of tenure, the landlord will be able to obtain possession on one of the usual assured tenancy grounds. One of these grounds (Ground 6) allows a landlord to seek possession if he intends to demolish or reconstruct the property or the building of which it forms part. The best advice is to exercise your rights under the Act if at all possible.

TENANTS' RIGHT OF FIRST REFUSAL

Introduction

As well as the right given by the Leasehold Reform, Housing and Urban Development Act 1993 to buy the freehold, flat tenants are also given a right of first refusal in certain circumstances. This right is given by Part I of the Landlord and Tenant Act 1987 and requires a landlord who is intending to make various dispositions of the block in which the flats are situated, to offer first of all to dispose of the block on the same terms to the tenants. The tenants can then collectively accept or reject this offer. The Act only applies where a landlord is himself planning to dispose of his interest, unlike the 1993 Act where the tenants can insist on a sale at any time as long as the qualifying conditions are met.

The 1987 Act was rushed through Parliament shortly before the 1987 election and was not well thought out. Landlords often ignored it; but in 1996 it was revamped and made more effective. The advantage of taking the opportunity to buy under these provisions is that the price may well be lower than under the 1993 Act. Note also that the qualifying conditions are different from those under the 1993 Act, so that some tenants will find that they have rights under the 1987 Act but not under the 1993 Act – and vice versa. In particular there is no residence requirement under the 1987 Act, so tenants can join in a purchase of the freehold whether or not they are living in the flat.

Qualifying conditions

These are extremely complex and so only a summary can be given here. Basically, the following conditions must be satisfied before tenants can claim rights under the Act:
- the premises in which the flats are situated must come within the Act;
- the tenants must be qualifying tenants; and
- the landlord must be proposing to make a relevant disposal.

Each of these must be looked at in turn.

The premises

These must consist of a building divided into at least two flats occupied by qualifying tenants; and
- where not more than 50 per cent of the floor area is used for non-residential purposes; and
- where the number of flats held by qualifying tenants exceeds 50 per cent of the total number of flats in the building.

The building will be excluded if it has been converted into flats and the landlord lives in one of the other flats.

Note how these provisions differ from the 1993 Act; in particular the '50 per cent non-residential' rule, as opposed to the 10 per cent figure under the 1993 Act, will mean that many flats situated over shops or other commercial premises will have the right to acquire the freehold under this Act but not under the 1993 Act.

Qualifying tenants

Again, the definition is complex and includes tenants with long leases at low rents but not those with assured or assured shorthold tenancies.

Relevant disposal

For the right of first refusal to apply, the landlord must be intending to make a relevant disposal. Most dispositions are included, but the exceptions include:
- the grant of a tenancy of a single flat;
- the grant of a mortgage;
- a gift to a member of the landlord's family;
- a disposal within an associated group of companies, but only if the companies have been associated for at least two years.

Procedure

If a landlord proposes to make a relevant disposal, he must, prior to making it, serve a notice (a 'Section 5 notice') on at least 90 per cent of the qualifying tenants. The notice must detail the terms of the proposed disposition, including the price, and state that the notice constitutes an offer to dispose of the property on the same terms to the tenants. So the price will be the same as the landlord would have otherwise obtained had his intended disposition gone ahead. This offer must be accepted by at least 50 per cent of the qualifying tenants (cf. the two-thirds required under the 1993 Act). They must accept the offer within the period stated in the notice, which must not be less than two months after receiving it.

If the landlord decides to sell at an auction sale, a slightly different procedure applies. The Section 5 notice must be served not less than four months nor more than six months before the auction.

Criminal sanctions

The Act makes it a criminal offence for a landlord to make a relevant disposal without first serving a Section 5 notice on the tenants, or having served the notice without giving the tenants the chance to acquire under the Act. Where the landlord is a limited company, company directors, managers and company secretaries may be liable as well if they have consented to or connived in the disposal.

Effect of a disposal in breach of the Act

The disposal will remain valid, despite the imposition of criminal sanctions. However, the tenants are not prejudiced. They will have the right to acquire the property from the buyer on the same terms as it was acquired by him. Again, there are criminal sanctions for failing to comply with this obligation.

17

Owning a Flat – Repair and Maintenance

This chapter concerns lessees under long leases (i.e., in practice, people who have bought their flat). Repair and maintenance for people who rent is dealt with in Chapter 22.

Please note that the legal rights dealt with in this chapter apply regardless of whether the services are provided by the landlord or a management company. For ease of reference the term 'landlord' is used throughout this chapter to identify the person responsible for the provision of the services, whether it is the landlord or a management company.

INTRODUCTION

Rogue landlords

Unfortunately, rogue landlords exist in the long-leasehold sector as well as the short-term letting sector. In recent times, increased media coverage has exposed the problems which some flat owners have had to cope with. 'Landlords from Hell' are all too common, causing untold misery to flat owners.

Poor services and/or overcharging

There are two major and often interrelated problems with regard to services/repairs and service charges:
- the tenants complain that the necessary services are not provided, or are provided to an indifferent standard;
- the tenants complain that the amount they have to pay for the services is excessively high.

In the worst cases, both complaints apply: the services are abysmal, yet the charges are extortionate.

Threats of forfeiture

There then follows the third problem; if anyone dares to object to the level of the service charge demanded or to the poor standard of services/repair by withholding the service charge payment, the landlord threatens to bring forfeiture proceedings against the tenant.

Forfeiture means that the landlord brings the lease to an end prematurely – without the need to compensate the tenant for the capital asset that he is losing. It is available to a landlord when a tenant is in breach of any of the obligations under the lease, such as the obligation to pay service charge. The landlord has to go to court to enforce forfeiture. The tenant might have a defence to the action on the basis of the poor services, etc., but what tenant wants to put his home – and the money invested in it – at risk? What tenant wants to engage in lengthy, expensive and stressful litigation? The reality is that tenants pay up, grumbling to themselves (and anyone else who will listen) about the injustices of the system.

Lack of control by tenants

Flat tenants also complain about the lack of control they have over their homes. In theory, 'an Englishman's home is his castle', but a flat owner is in a much worse position than the owner of a freehold property. If the management of the block of flats is in the hands of the landlord or the landlord's agents, it will be the landlord who decides when the block is to be painted and in what colour, when repairs are to be done and by whom and in what way, what improvements are to be carried out and when and by whom. Flat owners can sometimes be forgiven for thinking that they are only there to foot the bill for all this.

Tenants' management company

In some cases the management of the flat is in the hands of the tenants themselves. This is usually through the medium of a tenants' management company, a company owned and controlled by the tenants. In that case, the tenants will have some control over the cost and quality of the services, subject to what the majority of the tenants can agree between themselves.

Often, the running of the management company is left in the hands of a few tenants only, due to the apathy of the majority. These few volunteers are not always the people best able to run the company efficiently. Disputes can arise between various factions of tenants. One group might want to replace the lifts or put in double-glazing, while the other group disagrees. Sometimes a compromise is reached on the basis of the lowest common denominator, which pleases no one. Sometimes no compromise can be reached; one group wants to replace the window frames with single glazing, the other with double-glazing, no agreement can be reached so the window frames are not replaced at all.

One solution to the problem of poor provision of services or overcharging, is to give more control to the tenants. Having said that, some of the worst-maintained blocks of flats are those where there is already a tenants' management company in charge. In many cases where a tenants' management company works well it is often due to the efforts of one or two people. If they move (or die), they may leave behind a vacuum in which things can go badly wrong.

The point is that there is no one ideal solution: what works well for one set of flat owners may not work for another. Some of the best-run blocks of flats are those with professional managing agents in charge. Good independent professional agents will have had training and experience in running blocks of flats, and this valuable expertise can be worth the cost of employing the agent. Some agents charge a percentage of the expenditure, but it is perhaps better if a set sum per flat is charged, as this will exclude any perception that the agents have no incentive to minimize the expenditure.

Problems usually arise when the landlord, or a company owned by the landlord, directly manages the block.

If you are thinking of buying a flat, it is sensible to take some time to find out how the block is managed. First impressions are very important; clean hallways and stairways and well-maintained flowerbeds are good signs. Your solicitor should obtain information about the level of the service charge, but it is as well to make your own inquiries as to the standard of service provided. If possible, ask someone else who lives in the block as well as the seller of the flat; the seller might just be selling because of management problems and may not be inclined to give full details of his reasons for moving. (If a seller actually tells lies about the level of service, or anything else, you may have legal remedies against him when you discover the truth. However, it is better to make other inquiries and find out the truth before you buy, so that you have the opportunity to back out of the purchase.)

POSSIBLE SOLUTIONS

There is a mountain of legislation giving flat owners rights with regard to services and service charges. The main problem is that most are dependent on some kind of court action being brought – and court proceedings are expensive and can drag on for a long time.

Obviously, it is best to avoid litigation whenever possible and make every effort to settle a dispute by negotiation. Gaining the support of the tenants' association (if there is one), will help to bring pressure to bear on a management company at company meetings. It will also strengthen your position in the negotiations if you can demonstrate a knowledge of the legal rights and obligations relevant to the problem in question.

The following potential solutions will be looked at in turn:

- the terms of the lease;
- obtaining information: Landlord and Tenant Act 1985;
- restrictions on the landlord's right to recover costs incurred: Landlord and Tenant Act 1985;
- appointing a manager: Part II Landlord and Tenant Act 1987;
- acquisition of the reversion: Parts I and III Landlord and Tenant Act 1987, and the Leasehold Reform, Housing and Urban Development Act 1993;
- taking over the management duties: Commonhold and Leasehold Reform Act 2002.

In addition to the introduction of a new statutory right to manage, the Commonhold and Leasehold Reform Act 2002 also improves the situation for leaseholders by giving them a number of new rights and protections regarding service charges and management. These will also be explored below.

THE TERMS OF THE LEASE

Introduction

In the case of a dispute, the service charge provisions in the lease should be studied carefully to see if there has been any breach of any obligation under them. If there has been a breach, normal remedies for breach of contract will be available.

Court remedies for disrepair

Specific performance

Specific performance is an order of the court, requiring the landlord (which includes a management company, remember) to actually carry out a stated task, e.g. to repair the roof. This is the obvious remedy where the landlord is refusing to carry out works which need doing.

Damages

Damages are compensation for loss suffered. The court will look at the facts of each case carefully to see what loss the tenant has actually suffered. The following are some of the possible losses, for which damages may be available:

- *Alternative accommodation.* Was the state of the property so bad that you had to move out? If so, the reasonable cost of alternative accommodation can be claimed.
- *Reduction in value of the premises.* If the flat, or block in which it is situated, is in a very poor condition, this may well reduce the value of the flat. If evidence of this can be shown, then this can also be recovered.
- *Inconvenience and discomfort.* This is something that will have to be assessed by the judge, but the inconvenience of living in a poorly maintained flat will entitle a flat owner to compensation.

Tenant's right of set-off

A flat owner's initial reaction to a failure to provide the services may well be to refuse to pay the service charge and/ or rent. This course of action is risky, as the landlord can bring court proceedings against you for non-payment. If the landlord does bring a claim against you, the law does provide the tenant with a remedy, known as 'set-off'.

'Set-off' is a right to deduct the amount of any claim you have against someone from the money that you owe them. So here, a tenant can deduct any loss he has suffered because of a breach of the repairing obligations from the service charge or rent due to the landlord. However, this right can be, and frequently is, taken away by the terms of the lease.

In the case of leases granted on or after 1 July 1995, an exclusion of the right to set-off may be void under the Unfair Terms in Consumer Contracts Regulations. These regulations state that a term *may* be void if it has the effect of 'obliging the consumer to fulfil all his obligations where the seller or supplier does not fulfil his'.

Deduction from rent of expenditure on repairs by the tenant

Another possible remedy not requiring court action is to do the repairs yourself, and then deduct the cost of those repairs from future payments. This right is only available if you have expressly told the landlord that unless he carries out the repairs within a (stated) reasonable time, you will do them yourself and deduct the cost from future payments. Doing the repairs yourself will really only be feasible when you are complaining about lack of repair to your own flat; it will not be possible in the case of the poor condition of the common parts.

OBTAINING INFORMATION

One particular problem that the law seeks to deal with is the question of information. Tenants often suspect that they are being overcharged for a service, but have no real proof. 'Does it really cost £x to cut the grass every year?' Information is not a remedy or solution to a problem in itself, but it may provide ammunition to use against a rogue landlord.

The Landlord and Tenant Act 1985

Tenants paying service charges have various statutory protections, over and above any rights given under the lease. These protections apply to leasehold houses as well as flats, but not to freehold premises.

Summary of costs

Whatever the lease might say, the Act gives a right for a tenant to make a written request to the landlord to supply him with a written summary of the costs incurred for the previous 12 months.

If there are more than four flats in the block, the summary must be certified by a qualified accountant as a fair summary and sufficiently supported by accounts, receipts and other documents, which have been produced to him.

These provisions are all well and good, provided that the tenants have the expertise to analyse the information when it is provided. Another problem is that the information may well come many months after the event, e.g. up to six months after the end of the relevant financial year. There is no 'quick fix' available.

Management audit

Under the Leasehold Reform, Housing and Urban Development Act 1993, tenants can require a management audit of the service charge functions. This right can be exercised without the need for court action (unless the landlord refuses to comply with the request). The audit will enable the tenant to check whether:

1 the landlord is discharging his management obligations effectively and efficiently; and
2 whether the service charge is being applied in an efficient and effective manner.

The audit will be carried out either by a qualified surveyor or a qualified accountant.

Similar information can also be obtained by the appointment of a surveyor to advise on the service charge. This right was introduced by the Housing Act 1996, following criticisms of the expense of a management audit. A recognized tenants' association may appoint a surveyor to advise it with regard to any matters relating to the payment of a service charge. The surveyor has extensive rights to inspect the property and access to documents in the landlord's control to enable him to advise on service charge matters.

Separate client accounts

Under the Commonhold and Leasehold Reform Act 2002 landlords are required to hold service charge funds in designated separate client accounts. Leaseholders have the right to ask for proof that this requirement has been met. Where leaseholders have reasonable grounds for believing that the landlord is not holding their service charges in a separate account, they can withhold their service charges.

RESTRICTIONS ON THE LANDLORD'S RIGHT TO RECOVER COSTS

Once you have discovered the full facts about the costs incurred, you can decide whether the landlord is actually entitled to charge those costs to the service charge account. The Landlord and Tenant Act 1985 lays downs restrictions on the landlord's rights to recover the costs he has incurred. The key word to remember is 'reasonable'.

Recovery of costs incurred

Costs can only be recovered to the extent that they are reasonably incurred, and where they are incurred in the provision of services or the carrying out of works, only if those services or works are of a reasonable standard.

Advance payments must be no greater than is reasonable.

Any agreement is void which purports to provide for the question of reasonableness to be determined in a particular way, e.g. by the landlord's surveyor. However, referring disputes to arbitration is allowed.

Costs incurred more than 18 months before the service charge demand is served cannot be recovered unless the tenant has been given written notice of those costs during the 18-month period. This is to stop landlords suddenly producing unexpected demands for cash in relation to old works, which might cause problems for the tenants who have not budgeted for that amount.

This protection for leaseholders has been further tightened up by the Commonhold and Leasehold Reform Act 2002. The 2002 Act obliges a landlord to provide a yearly summary of service charge costs relating to the last accounting year to each leaseholder, failing which payment of service charges can be withheld.

Determination of reasonableness of service charges

The landlord says that it cost £2,000 last year to cut the grass and you think that is unreasonable. You challenge the landlord, who says that it is reasonable. Where do you go from there? Obviously, if landlord and tenant cannot agree or reach a compromise, then some third party will have to make the decision. In the past, that would be the court, but since 1996 the Leasehold Valuation Tribunal (LVT) has also been given jurisdiction to make such decisions.

The LVT is a quasi-judicial public body that sits on a regional basis. Its members are appointed by the Lord Chancellor and consist of surveyors, lawyers and some lay persons. There were various reasons for giving the jurisdiction to the LVT. For a start, most county court judges will have no real knowledge of flat leases; the LVT should be able to approach matters with a degree of expertise in leasehold matters. Also, the procedure before the LVT is more informal than in court, and this should encourage more people to apply and appear before the tribunal on their own without the need for the expense of legal representation. And as the LVT cannot award costs, there is no risk if you lose of having to pay the landlord's costs. (It is likely, however, that in such a case, these will be added to the service charge! – but at least that shares them out between all the tenants.)

It remains to be seen what degree of success the LVT has had. The LVT was not fully prepared for the extra work involved, although the Lord Chancellor is now appointing extra members. There is still a long delay in getting a hearing in many parts of the country, upwards of six months in some cases. Even then, the decision is often reserved, i.e. you are not told the result at the end of the hearing, but have to wait for a written decision to be sent to you. This again is often months after the hearing. Also, there appears to be a lack of consistency between the decisions of the various regional tribunals, in that cases on what seem to be the same facts are being decided differently. (Although it has to be said that the same criticism probably applies equally to the decisions of different county courts.)

The LVT can be asked to make a declaration that costs were or were not reasonably incurred; that services or works are or are not of a reasonable standard; or that any advance payment is or is not reasonable.

A tenant may also ask for an order that any court costs incurred by the landlord in connection with court proceedings are not to be regarded as relevant costs when the tenant's service charge is calculated. This is to deal with the situation where a landlord has sued a tenant (e.g. for non-payment of service charges) and has lost. The court would have ordered the landlord to pay the tenant's legal costs. There is a danger that the landlord might then add all the costs, i.e. his own costs and those of the tenant that he has been ordered to pay, into the service charge account. The tenant can ask for an order to prevent this from happening.

Estimates and consultation

In addition to the reasonableness rule, there are other restrictions on the landlord's right to recover costs incurred on carrying out works. Where costs are incurred on carrying out works above the limit specified by legislation, the excess is only payable if the 'relevant requirements' have been complied with. This basically involves requiring the landlord to consult the tenants before the work is carried out and the expenditure incurred.

The specified limit is currently £50 multiplied by the number of flats in the building, or £1,000, whichever is the greater. So, in the case of a block of 25 flats, any works costing more than 25 x £50, i.e. £1,250, will be subject to the consultation procedure.

The 'relevant requirements' differ according to whether the tenants are represented by a recognized tenants association or not. The association can be 'recognized' by a notice in writing by the landlord. This recognition of the association shows that the landlord accepts the association's right to be involved in matters on behalf of the tenants. Whether the tenants are represented or not, the basic requirement is that the landlord must obtain at least *two estimates* for the works, one from a person wholly unconnected with the landlord, show them to the tenants and invite 'observations' from them. The landlord must then 'have regard' to any observations received.

This does *not* mean, however, that the landlord must comply with the observations of the tenants. All that the legislation requires is that he 'has regard' to them. He can quite properly 'have regard' to them, and then decide that he is right and that the work should still go ahead. There is still no real control for the tenants. Many critical observations might persuade the landlord to reconsider his plans. The criticisms might indicate that, if he does go ahead, the tenants will claim that the costs were not reasonably incurred. This procedure should, at least, make landlords think carefully before spending their tenants' money, and that cannot be a bad thing.

The court may dispense with these requirements, if satisfied that the landlord has acted reasonably.

Service charge demands

The Landlord and Tenant Act 1987 section 47 provides that where a written demand is made for rent or other sums due to the landlord under the tenancy (e.g. service charges), the following information must be included:

- the name and address of the landlord; and
- if that address is not in England and Wales, an address in England and Wales at which notices, including notices in proceedings, may be served on the landlord.

If the demand does not contain this information, any sum demanded which consists of service charges shall be treated as not due from the tenant until that information is supplied. So, you need not pay the service charge if this information is not included. But you do not get off the hook completely. Once the information is provided, then the money will become due from you and you will have to pay up. One problem tenants sometimes have is actually finding out who their landlord is – and if you do not know who he is, there can be problems in bringing any kind of proceedings against him. This provision should help solve this.

Restriction on forfeiture for non-payment of service charge

One weapon that landlords have long exploited is the right to forfeit a lease if the tenant is in breach of its terms in some way. This means that the lease is terminated prematurely, without any compensation to the tenant, who thus loses all his investment in the property. So if you paid £100,000 for your flat last year, you would lose all of this and have no claim for compensation against the landlord. Tenants threatening non-payment of the service charge because of its lack of reasonableness, are frequently 'reminded' by their landlord of his right to forfeit the lease, unless they pay up. And many tenants do of course, not wanting to run the risk that they may not win if the matter goes to court. No one wants to gamble with his or her home.

Some landlords take a subtler approach. They will simply inform your lender that you are not paying and that forfeiture is threatened. In the event of forfeiture, the lender would lose its rights over the property and risk not being able to get its loan repaid. So the lender will pay up – and then add the amount to the mortgage account, so you will pay anyway.

The Housing Act 1996 has attempted to put a stop to this intimidation. A landlord cannot forfeit for failure to pay a service charge unless the tenant has agreed to the amount of the charge or it has been determined by the LVT, a court or by arbitration.

This is an important provision. If the tenant disputes the service charge, then the landlord cannot forfeit unless the tenant agrees the amount due, or it is settled by the LVT, the court or arbitration. As mentioned above, the LVT has jurisdiction to determine whether the charge is reasonable or not. Any notice of forfeiture cannot be served until 14 days after the LVT has made its final determination. Alternatively, the landlord might sue for the payment of the money and the tenant could then raise the lack of reasonableness as a defence to the claim. At least this allows the issue of reasonableness to be ventilated without the threat of losing his home hanging over the tenant.

Appointment of manager under Landlord and Tenant Act 1987, Part II

The law recognizes that some landlords' attempts at managing a block of flats are so poor, either due to negligence or deliberate policy, that they have got to be replaced. One way is to apply to the LVT for a manager to be appointed to run the block in place of the landlord. The landlord thus still remains the owner, but someone else is put in charge of looking after the block. As we shall see, the tenants might also contemplate buying the freehold from the landlord as a way of getting rid of him permanently, but appointing a manager avoids the expense of having to buy him out. The drawbacks are that an application must be made to the LVT, which will involve some delay and expense.

When is it available?

A manager can be appointed if the LVT is satisfied that:
- the landlord is in breach of an obligation of the tenancy which relates to the management of the premises;
- and those circumstances are likely to continue;
- and it is just and convenient to make an order; or
- other circumstances exist which make it just and convenient for an order to be made; or
- the tribunal is satisfied that unreasonable service charges have been made or are proposed or likely to be made; and
- it is just and convenient to make the order;
- an additional ground introduced by the Commonhold and Leasehold Reform Act 2002 is where the landlord has failed to hold service charge funds in trust or in separate client accounts (*see* page 194).

There is thus a wide variety of circumstances in which a manager can be appointed. The longer the landlord's deficiencies (e.g. overcharging, bad management, etc.) have existed and the more serious his faults are, the more likely it is that the circumstances will continue and the more likely it is that it will be just and convenient to make the order.

Manager's powers, etc.

The manager may be appointed to carry out such functions of management, as the LVT thinks fit. The order may provide for remuneration to be paid to the manager by the landlord, or by the tenants of the premises or by all or any of those persons.

Acquisition of the reversion

In an extreme case, this should be seriously considered.

There is a right of first refusal under the Landlord and Tenant Act 1987; i.e. if the landlord wishes to dispose of his interest to someone else, he must first offer it to the tenants (*see* page 189).

There is also a general right to buy the freehold under the Leasehold Reform Housing and Urban Development Act 1993, albeit at a higher price than under the 1987 Act (*see* page 185).

Please note that all this legislation developed piecemeal as particular problems were identified. This means that the qualifying conditions for the 1987 Act and the 1993 Act are *not* identical, so one Act may sometimes apply but not the other. The 1987 Act will probably apply to flats situated over a row of shops; the 1993 Act will probably not. The various qualifying conditions must be considered carefully to see if they apply to the particular circumstances of each case.

Taking over the management of the building

The Commonhold and Leasehold Reform Act 2002 introduces a new right for the leaseholders to take over the management of the building from the landlord. There will be no need to prove any fault or inefficiency by the landlord and there is no requirement for purchase or payment of any compensation to the landlord. It will not need a court order, just the service of a notice on the landlord. The leaseholders will have to get together and set up a Right to Manage Company, and it is this company which will take over and run the building. This is obviously an important new right, allowing leaseholders to have a greater degree of control over the level of service charges set, and enabling them to appoint their own choice of managing agents and select their own insurers. The right to manage will not apply in certain circumstances, such as where the landlord is resident in the block or where the block has more than 25 per cent non-residential use.

COMMONHOLD – THE WAY AHEAD

A new scheme for owning flats, called commonhold, was introduced by the Commonhold and Leasehold Reform Act 2002.

What is commonhold?

Commonhold is a way of owning the freehold designed for properties like blocks of flats and offices.

Why is it needed?

The reason flats and offices in blocks are sold leasehold rather than freehold is because of the awkwardness in making arrangements for the repair of the block fit within a freehold structure. Obviously each tenant cannot be responsible for repairing their own part of it; and if they were, who would be responsible for the common parts, the hallways, etc.? The easiest way at the moment is for the landlord to be responsible for these things. But, as already discussed, this does not always work well.

Another problem with leasehold ownership is that as the term of the lease dwindles away, it reduces in value and becomes difficult to mortgage.

History

Other jurisdictions (such as Canada, the United States and Scotland) have had similar schemes for many years. No doubt you will have seen reference in American and Australian television shows to the 'condos' (condominiums) popular in those countries. These are arrangements where a development of flats (or apartments, as we are talking about America) is owned collectively by all of the occupiers of those flats. In England it is more usual for a landlord to own the development.

The Commonhold and Leasehold Reform Act, which introduced commonhold as a new form of ownership, came into force in July 2002. Commonhold will apply initially only to newly built flats or empty blocks, but will eventually replace leasehold.

How does it work?

It is *not* a completely new right over land but merely a type of freehold ownership with 'special statutory attributes'.

Each flat owner would own the freehold, i.e. the right to occupy for ever, in their respective flats, in the same way that people own the freehold in their houses. The freehold in the common parts would then be vested in a 'commonhold association' of which all the unit owners would be members. There would be thus no involvement by a 'landlord' or the developer of the block once the development had been completed.

All the unit-holders in a development will therefore have two interests in the property of the commonhold: a direct interest in the unit or units that they own and membership of the Commonhold Association which owns the common parts.

The Commonhold Association

The Commonhold Association will be a private company limited by guarantee, registered at Companies House. Membership of the Commonhold Association will be restricted to all the unit-holders within the development. It will have a standard set of memoranda and articles of association, which will be prescribed by the Lord Chancellor from time to time. These memoranda and articles of association will govern the management of commonholds. They set out voting rights of individual unit-holders and procedures for dealing with disputes. The Commonhold Association would be obliged to repair and maintain the common parts and the unit-holders would be obliged to pay a service charge. There would be mutual enforcement of the regulations between the unit-holders.

The Commonhold Association would be able to enforce payment of service charge obligations. As a last resort, the Association would be able to sell the freehold in the unit.

How will a commonhold be created?

This is the one potential problem area. Creation will be *voluntary*, both for new and existing developments.

In the case of a new development, the freeholder will apply to the Land Registry for the registration of a 'commonhold declaration' in relation to the land in question.

In the case of existing leasehold development, the freeholder can convert it into a commonhold, but only if 100 per cent of existing tenants consent. The consent of 100 per cent of lenders is also required. There is no method of compelling a landlord to create a commonhold. However, as tenants already have rights to acquire the freehold under the 1993 Act, the tenants could compulsorily acquire the freehold first and then set up a commonhold.

Remember, under the Leasehold Reform, Housing and Urban Development Act 1993 if you acquire the freehold, you will still only own a long lease over your flat, albeit a lease from the company which you yourself own along with the other tenants. If you set up a commonhold, you will own the freehold in your flat. A choice will have to be made between acquiring the freehold under the 1993 Act and setting up a commonhold. It is likely that the psychological effect of being able to own the freehold under the commonhold system will be very persuasive.

18

Buying and Selling Land – Conveyancing

INTRODUCTION

Conveyancing is the name given to the legal process whereby the ownership of land is transferred from one person to another. As it is a legal process, it is usual to employ someone legally qualified to undertake this work on your behalf, usually a solicitor or a licensed conveyancer. Although there is no legal reason why you should not do your own conveyancing, this is not something to be undertaken lightly. There are several books on the market offering guidance through the conveyancing process which will require careful study before embarking on a DIY transaction.

AN OVERVIEW OF BUYING AND SELLING A HOUSE

'Conveyancing' is the name given to the process of transferring the ownership of a house or land. The buyer is concerned to ensure that he gets good 'title' to the land, i.e. that the person selling the house actually has the right to sell it. You would not buy a piece of land from a man who is standing on that land and *says* he is the owner. As we have already discussed, the ownership of land often carries with it other benefits and burdens. So the house might have the benefit of a right of way over adjoining land, for example, the right to walk (or drive) across that other land. The house might also be subject to a right of way in favour of a neighbour. The house may also be subject to a covenant, for example, the obligation not to use the land other than for a specified purpose.

The system of conveyancing is designed to ensure that the buyer gets the land together with all the rights (or benefits) that go with it – and without any obligations other than those he knows about in advance. Problems ranging from disputes over boundaries and fences to granny refusing to move out on the day fixed for completion should be exposed, and resolved, by the conveyancing process.

A typical conveyancing transaction, whether a sale or purchase, contains two major 'landmarks': exchange of contracts and completion (which conveniently divide it into five stages).

1 Before contract stage.
2 Exchange of contracts.
3 Before completion stage.
4 Completion.
5 After completion stage.

The steps to be taken at each stage will differ according to whether you are involved in a sale or purchase. We will look at the sale and purchase separately.

What is involved in selling a house

Before contract stage

First of all, of course, you have to find a buyer. It may be that you are selling the house with the help of an estate agent, or perhaps just by advertising it yourself. Whichever way a buyer is found, the first thing to appreciate is that an agreement to sell to someone at a particular price is *not* legally binding. Either party can change their minds without the risk of any come-back or having to pay any penalty. Unfortunately, this rule enables the practices of gazumping and gazundering to flourish (*see* page 205). A contract for the sale of land is only legally binding when it is in writing and it will be some weeks yet before either party can safely enter into a binding contract.

A FEW WORDS OF WARNING!

Do not try and hurry things along and get the buyer to enter into a written contract at this early stage. The rule that there is no binding agreement until later is there to protect both buyer and seller and it could well be to your own disadvantage to do this. For all you know there could well be some reason why you might want to back out of the transaction and you would not be able to.

Assuming that you have a buyer and have agreed a

price, the first thing you must do as seller is to prepare a 'pre-contract package' containing a variety of information about the property, including proof of the seller's ownership and details of rights that others may have over the land, easements or covenants, for example. The pre-contract package will also contain the contract setting out the terms on which the seller is prepared to sell the house. (Time can be saved if you prepare this package as soon as you put the house on the market.) This package of information will include a Property Information Form. This is a questionnaire which the seller completes and which contains practical information about the property, such as who owns the boundary walls or hedges or whether there are any informal arrangements between neighbours affecting the property. It is important that the seller's Property Information Form is answered accurately and truthfully.

In the Property Information Form the sellers stated that there were no disputes with neighbours. However, there had in fact been a long-running dispute over the use of an access road, although at the time of the sale there was no problem because other neighbours had taken legal advice which had temporarily resolved the situation. After moving into the property, the buyers found themselves in the same sort of quarrels about the access road. They sued for fraudulent misrepresentation. The sellers argued that at the time of the sale there were no disputes – and that they could not be responsible for subsequent disputes. Held: The replies were inaccurate and there had indeed been fraudulent misrepresentation. There was a long-standing quarrel with the neighbour and this was precisely the kind of information that should have been disclosed to a potential purchaser. Thus, the sellers were liable in damages.

McMeekin *v* Long (2003)

The pre-contract package is sent to the buyer, who will consider all the information and the terms of the contract and consider whether he is prepared to enter into a legally binding contract. The buyer may wish to ask you a few more questions about the property, or your ownership of it, and may wish to renegotiate some of the terms of the contract. He will also be making various 'searches', i.e. finding out as much information as possible from various public records, such as those held by the local authority. Before he can enter into a binding contract the buyer will also need to ensure that he has the money available to buy. This will normally mean that he has to wait until he has received a formal offer of a mortgage loan from his bank or building society. He will also have to ensure that he has sufficient funds to pay the deposit of 10 per cent of the purchase price which is normally required on exchange.

This pre-contract stage is the longest part of the transaction – it will commonly take six, or even more, weeks. This can be reduced if you have your pre-contract package already prepared and ready to be dispatched as soon as a buyer is found.

Exchange of contracts

Eventually, after the buyer has made all necessary inquiries and is satisfied as to their results – and has also sorted his finances out – the parties will be in a position to enter into a legally binding contract. At this stage, they will have to agree on a completion date, i.e. the date when the buyer will hand over the balance of the money and will be entitled to move in. Completion will normally be fixed for a couple of weeks after exchange.

The way a legally binding contract is created in conveyancing is centuries old and is by 'exchange of contracts'. Two identical copies of the contract are prepared; the seller signs one and the buyer the other. The contract only becomes binding when the two copies are 'exchanged', i.e. the buyer gives the copy he has signed to the seller, and the seller likewise gives the copy he has signed to the buyer. The buyer will also pay over his deposit, usually 10 per cent of the purchase price. The logic behind the system of exchange is that now both seller and buyer have a contract signed by the other. Should either party subsequently allege a breach of contract and have need to commence court proceedings, the first thing the court would want is proof that there actually was a contract. As both buyer and seller now have the original contract signed by the other, either will have no difficulty in proving to the court that the other did enter into the contract. The same certainty could not be achieved by use of photocopies, which can all too easily be forged; courts generally insist on originals.

If there was only one copy of the contract, signed by buyer and seller, only one of them could keep the original. The person without the original would be placed at a disadvantage if he wished to sue the other.

On exchange, the buyer and seller are legally bound to go through with the transaction. Should either of them wish to withdraw (without a good legal reason), they will be in breach of contract and liable to the other for substantial damages for any loss suffered. In any event, the seller will be able to retain the deposit paid by the buyer on exchange, unless the seller is at fault in some way.

The deposit is handed over by the buyer to the seller on exchange. It is traditionally 10 per cent of the purchase price (although nowadays a smaller sum is often paid) and acts not only as part payment (i.e. the buyer only has to pay the balance of 90 per cent on completion) but, more importantly, as a guarantee that the buyer will go through with the transaction. Once contracts have been exchanged, if the buyer refuses to go on with the purchase, the seller is entitled to keep the deposit even if he suffers no financial loss. Thus the threat of losing the deposit acts as a financial incentive to the buyer to complete even if he does not really want to. Only in exceptional circumstances will a buyer be able to back out of the transaction without losing his deposit.

There is no similar guarantee to the buyer that the seller will not withdraw. Obviously, if the seller did refuse to go through with the sale for no good legal reason, he would be in breach of contract and the buyer would be entitled to sue for damages; the advantage of the deposit to the seller is that this money is available to him without the need for court action.

Before completion

Most of the seller's work has now been done. The buyer will draft the Transfer, i.e. the document which will transfer ownership to him from the seller, and this will be sent to the seller for approval. All the seller needs to do is to ensure that the terms of the Transfer accord with the terms of the contract, for example, that the price is correctly stated.

The buyer will also ask for details of the arrangements to be made for completion. This will include the venue where completion will take place, the arrangements for handing over the keys, and the arrangements for paying off any existing mortgage on the house.

The Transfer will then need to be signed by both buyer and seller and kept by the seller ready for completion. The seller must arrange to give vacant possession to the buyer on the day fixed for completion. This means that the house must be empty and suitable for the buyer to move in, i.e. no furniture or piles of rubbish left everywhere.

Completion

On the day fixed for completion, the buyer will hand over the balance of the money (usually this will be achieved by a direct electronic transfer between bank accounts) and he will, in return, receive the Transfer, the Land or Charge Certificate relating to the house, and of course, the keys.

After completion

There is little for the seller to do after completion – except congratulate himself on a job well done. If the property was subject to a mortgage, this would have to be paid off by the seller; no buyer will wish to buy a property burdened by someone else's mortgage. However, most sellers have a problem here: they will not have sufficient money to pay off the loan until the buyer pays over the purchase price. But the buyer will not be prepared to buy until the loan has been paid off. This 'Catch 22' situation is usually resolved by the seller's solicitor promising the buyer that, if the buyer hands over the money, the seller's solicitor will use it to pay off the mortgage. Promises (or *undertakings*, as they are called) like this made between solicitors are not only legally binding, but are also enforceable by the Law Society, the body which supervises solicitors. Where such an undertaking has been given, the seller's solicitor will have to deal with the discharge of the mortgage after completion and send evidence to the buyer that the loan has been paid off.

What is involved in buying a house

Before contract

Before you enter into a binding contract there are three areas that will need resolving: legal matters, financial matters and insurance.

Legal matters

You will need to investigate whether the seller is in fact entitled to sell the house and what obligations will be binding on you if you do buy it. You must also ensure that you will receive all the necessary rights over neighbouring land that you will need to enjoy the house properly, for example, if the drains pass through someone else's land, that you get a legal right to allow them to so pass.

The seller will supply you with a 'pre-contract package' of documents and information about the house. This will include the contract for the sale, which you must check to ensure that the terms are satisfactory, and details of the 'title' to the land. This is proof of the seller's right to sell, together with details of the rights and obligations affecting the land.

The seller does not have to supply to the buyer all the information a buyer needs in order to make his mind up whether to proceed with the transaction. For this reason the buyer must make various 'searches', i.e. inquiries of various public bodies, including the local council, to find out as much about the house as possible. For example, is there a possibility of road development? Was planning permission granted when the property was built? Are there compulsory-purchase proposals? Are there any tree preservation orders? Is the property connected to the mains sewer? Is the road a public highway? All these questions are printed on a standard form that is sent to the local authority. The cost of the local search will vary from council to council (generally it is £100). Also, some councils deal with search forms more speedily than others; generally a wait of two to three weeks is typical.

The buyer's solicitor should also request a copy of all Building Regulations consents. The absence of Building Regulations consents may indicate that work carried out on the property (such as an extension or a garage) is structurally unsound, or alternatively that the local authority did not grant its consent to the work. There is a risk that the local authority, if it did not consent to the building work, will take enforcement proceedings and require the building to be brought up to the required standard.

If anything untoward is discovered at this stage of the

transaction, remember that you are not legally committed to buy; you can walk away and look for another house without any liability to the seller. Equally, of course, the seller can change his mind and decide not to sell.

Financial matters

You must not enter into a legally binding contract to buy unless and until you are absolutely certain that you will be able to afford the purchase. There are two elements here: if you are buying with the aid of a loan, can you really afford the repayments? What would be your position if you (or your partner) lost your job, or your working hours were cut by your employer? Remember, a mortgage is a long-term commitment; you are borrowing the money over 20 or 25 years. It is not something to be entered into lightly. And also remember the 'health warning' on those mortgage ads: *'Failure to keep up your repayments can result in you losing your home.'* If you do not abide by the terms of the loan, the lender can take possession of the house and sell it to recover the money it is owed.

As well as this long-term view, you must also consider your finances in the short term. Taking into account all the expenses involved in the transaction, will you have sufficient funds to be able to hand over the full amount of the purchase price on completion? You will need to do your calculations very carefully, particularly where you are relying on the proceeds of sale of your present house.

If you will be relying on a loan of any kind, you must not enter into a legally binding contract unless and until you have received (and accepted if required) a formal offer of that loan. Do not rely on verbal 'assurances' that the loan will be forthcoming – it might not be. You must also check the terms of the loan offer to ensure that the amount that will actually be payable on completion will be sufficient for your needs. Lenders sometimes make deductions or retentions from the loan, for example, to cover repairs which need doing, so the amount you actually receive from them may be less than you expected.

As well as ensuring that you have sufficient funds with which to complete the transaction, you should also ensure that you will be able to pay the deposit that will be required on exchange. It is customary for 10 per cent of the price to be paid over on exchange; have you got sufficient savings to pay this? If not, it may be possible to borrow the deposit or, in the case of a sale and purchase, to use the deposit paid over to you by your buyer.

Insurance

In certain circumstances, the buyer will be liable to insure the house as soon as contracts are exchanged. If this is so, you must ensure that you are able to effect that insurance as from the day of exchange.

Exchange of contracts

When you are satisfied that you are able to afford the house, and that you have discovered all that there is to discover about the house – and, in the light of that information, that you still wish to buy it – then contracts can be exchanged. A completion date convenient to both buyer and seller will be agreed and both parties will then be bound to proceed with the transaction.

Before completion

The buyer must now draft the document which will actually transfer the ownership to him from the seller. This is called the Transfer and is a fairly simple standard form. When this has been drafted it will be sent to the seller for his approval. You will also need to inquire of the seller what arrangements are to be made with regard to completion, handing over the keys, etc. Immediately prior to completion a search will have to be made at the Land Registry. This is to do a last-minute check to ensure that no further entries have been made on the register of title which will adversely affect the ownership of the house. You must also ensure that the funds to be handed over on completion will be available to you on the completion date fixed.

Completion

On completion, you will hand over the balance of the purchase price, credit being given for the deposit, and you will receive in return the title deeds proving ownership of the house, together with the keys.

After completion

Although the transaction has been completed, your work is still not finished. You will have to pay any stamp duty required to the Inland Revenue and give them a form containing details of the transaction. Once you have received confirmation that any existing mortgage has been paid off, you will then need to register the purchase at the Land Registry so that your ownership of the house can be confirmed. There are strict time limits in which these steps must be taken and penalties for delay.

Warning!

This chapter only gives a brief overview of the steps in a typical conveyancing transaction. It is only intended to provide you with a 'flavour' of what is involved. It should not be relied on for guidance in actually carrying out the work.

Gazumping and gazundering – can they be avoided?

It seems that the evil of gazumping is once more stalking the land – or at least London and the South East; in some

Contract for sale

Each registered property has its own individual title number

The contract should set out the burdens attached to the land which will bind the buyer. Here the land is subject to covenants restricting the use to which it can be put.

The seller guarantees that there are no undisclosed problems with his ownership of the land.

In case of a delay in completion, the party at fault must pay interest on the purchase price at this rate. The Law Society's rate is 4 per cent above Barclay's Bank's base rate.

It is usual to pay a 10 per cent deposit on exchange of contracts.

Where chattels (e.g. carpets and curtains) are included in the sale, it is usual to state a separate price for them. This may result in a reduction in the amount of stamp duty payable, as this will only be payable on the price attributable to the land.

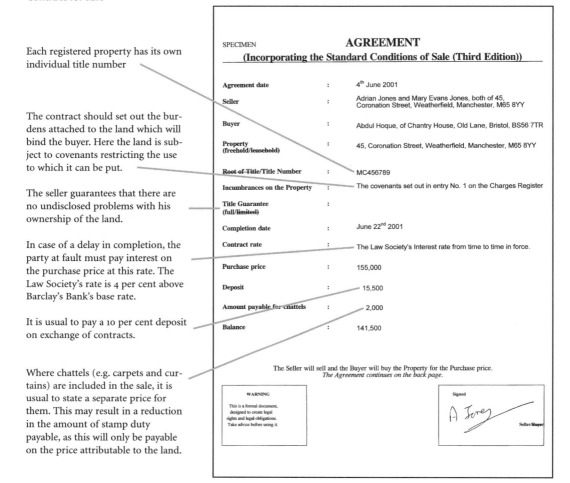

SPECIMEN

AGREEMENT
(Incorporating the Standard Conditions of Sale (Third Edition))

Agreement date	:	4th June 2001
Seller	:	Adrian Jones and Mary Evans Jones, both of 45, Coronation Street, Weatherfield, Manchester, M65 8YY
Buyer	:	Abdul Hoque, of Chantry House, Old Lane, Bristol, BS56 7TR
Property (freehold/~~leasehold~~)	:	45, Coronation Street, Weatherfield, Manchester, M65 8YY
~~Root of Title~~/Title Number	:	MC456789
Incumbrances on the Property	:	The covenants set out in entry No. 1 on the Charges Register
Title Guarantee (full/~~limited~~)	:	
Completion date	:	June 22nd 2001
Contract rate	:	The Law Society's Interest rate from time to time in force.
Purchase price	:	155,000
Deposit	:	15,500
Amount payable for chattels	:	2,000
Balance	:	141,500

The Seller will sell and the Buyer will buy the Property for the Purchase price.
The Agreement continues on the back page.

WARNING

This is a formal document, designed to create legal rights and legal obligations. Take advice before using it.

Signed

A Jones

Seller/~~Buyer~~

Reproduced by kind permission of the Solicitors' Law Stationery Society Limited and The Law Society of England and Wales.

SPECIAL CONDITIONS

1. (a)   This Agreement incorporates the Standard Conditions of Sale (Third Edition). Where there is a conflict between those Conditions and this Agreement, this Agreement prevails.

   (b) Terms used or defined in this Agreement have the same meaning when used in the Conditions.

2. The Property is sold subject to the Incumbrances on the Property and the Buyer will raise no requisitions on them.

3. Subject to the terms of this Agreement and to the Standard Conditions of Sale, the seller is to transfer the property with the title guarantee specified on the front page.

4. The chattels on the Property and set out on any attached list are included in the sale.

5. The Property is sold with vacant possession on completion.

(or) 5. The Property is sold subject to the following leases or tenancies:

6. The garden shed and greenhouse on the property are excluded from the sale.

If chattels are included, these must be clearly stated.

Normally, 'fixtures', i.e. things permanently fixed to the land, will be included in the sale. If this is not to be the case, this must be expressly stated.

Seller's Solicitors	:	**Dibb & Dobb**
Buyer's Solicitors	:	**Prim & Proper**

1995 *OYEZ*   The Solicitors' Law Stationery Society Ltd,
Oyez House, 7 Spa Road, London SE16 3QQ
©1995 **THE LAW SOCIETY**

Standard Conditions of Sale

Reproduced by kind permission of the Solicitors' Law Stationery Society Limited and The Law Society of England and Wales.

The Conveyancing Transaction

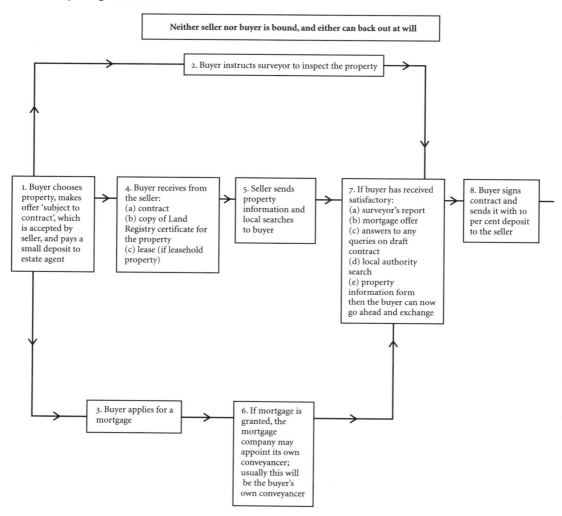

Neither seller nor buyer is bound, and either can back out at will

2. Buyer instructs surveyor to inspect the property

1. Buyer chooses property, makes offer 'subject to contract', which is accepted by seller, and pays a small deposit to estate agent

4. Buyer receives from the seller:
(a) contract
(b) copy of Land Registry certificate for the property
(c) lease (if leasehold property)

5. Seller sends property information and local searches to buyer

7. If buyer has received satisfactory:
(a) surveyor's report
(b) mortgage offer
(c) answers to any queries on draft contract
(d) local authority search
(e) property information form
then the buyer can now go ahead and exchange

8. Buyer signs contract and sends it with 10 per cent deposit to the seller

3. Buyer applies for a mortgage

6. If mortgage is granted, the mortgage company may appoint its own conveyancer; usually this will be the buyer's own conveyancer

parts of England and Wales the property market is still very depressed.

Gazumping

Gazumping is as old as the hills, or at least, as old as human nature. It became particularly prevalent during the property boom of the late 1980s. Everyone was so keen to get into the booming property market that people were prepared to pay ridiculous prices for property and cynical sellers were prepared to abuse the system to let them overturn previously agreed deals.

As we have seen, even when a buyer and seller 'agree' a price for a house, this agreement is not legally binding until written contracts are exchanged, perhaps six to eight weeks later. During this period of limbo, before exchange, the house remains on the market and estate agents will still show prospective purchasers around. They have to continue to market the property to cover themselves against the risk that the buyer might back out at the last minute. If that happens the seller will have wasted several weeks and then has to start marketing the house all over again.

In a market where prices are rising rapidly, there is a

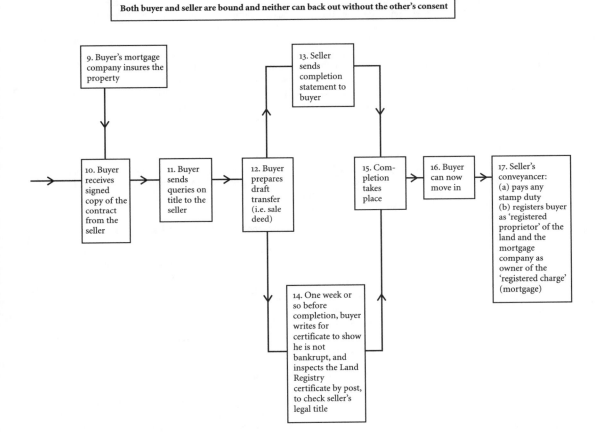

Both buyer and seller are bound and neither can back out without the other's consent

9. Buyer's mortgage company insures the property

10. Buyer receives signed copy of the contract from the seller

11. Buyer sends queries on title to the seller

12. Buyer prepares draft transfer (i.e. sale deed)

13. Seller sends completion statement to buyer

14. One week or so before completion, buyer writes for certificate to show he is not bankrupt, and inspects the Land Registry certificate by post, to check seller's legal title

15. Completion takes place

16. Buyer can now move in

17. Seller's conveyancer: (a) pays any stamp duty (b) registers buyer as 'registered proprietor' of the land and the mortgage company as owner of the 'registered charge' (mortgage)

risk that the seller will decide to accept a higher offer during this limbo period. Sometimes this occurs just before the original buyer was about to exchange.

The original buyer will have incurred the expense of surveys and searches and legal fees and has made plans to move in a few weeks' time. At the last minute he is told that the seller is going to sell to someone else at a higher price. He has been gazumped. Sometimes buyers are given the opportunity to make an increased offer for the house themselves – if they can afford to. Sometimes they are just told that the seller has accepted a higher offer and that the sale is off.

It is the long delay between the parties informally agreeing the sale and the sale becoming legally binding which allows gazumping to happen. Anything you can

do to reduce this delay, will reduce the opportunity for it to happen. You can, for example:

- arrange your loan in principle before finding a house;
- be sure that you (or your solicitor) are ready to commence the conveyancing work the day you agree to buy.

However, the delay cannot be avoided altogether and while there is this delay, there is always the risk of the seller accepting a better offer.

Lock-out agreements
The only way of preventing gazumping is to get the seller to enter into a legally binding agreement not to sell the property to anyone else during a specified period of time. This period of time will be long enough to allow you to undertake all the investigative work required before you

can safely enter into a binding contract to purchase. This agreement is known as a 'lock-out agreement'.

The snag with lock-out agreements is that although the seller is prevented from selling elsewhere, there is nothing to stop you, as buyer, changing your mind and deciding not to buy after all. The seller might take the view that it is unfair for you to expect him to agree to wait for you for (say) a month and then find that you do not want the house after all.

In times when the market is rising, i.e. prices are increasing rapidly, the seller might be reluctant to agree to locking himself into your deal and losing the opportunity of selling to someone else at a higher price, should the chance arise. The seller will probably take the view, 'Why should I deal with you if you insist on this lock-out agreement when I've got other people interested in the house who will deal with me in the normal way?' And there's the snag: most sellers would probably only agree to a lock-out agreement if they had become common practice in conveyancing transactions.

Insurance

It is not widely known, but it is possible to obtain insurance to cover you for the wasted expenditure should gazumping (or gazundering) happen to you. Such policies will often also cover you for wasted costs should the transaction fall through for other reasons, for example, problems with the seller's ownership. The premiums for such insurance are quite low. One building society, for example, offers its members such a policy for a premium of £30 for a buyer; £20.80 for a seller; and £45 when both buying and selling. Other lenders offer similar policies and such policies are also available independently of a lender.

Gazundering

Gazundering is the equivalent of gazumping in a market where house prices are falling. The buyer and seller agree a price and then, just when the seller was expecting to exchange, the buyer comes along and says he will only exchange if the seller agrees to a reduced price. Again, the long delay between agreeing a sale and exchange allows this practice to occur.

Government proposals for reform

In December 1998, the government undertook a survey of conveyancing practice and procedure. It found that although conveyancing in England took a lot longer than in most other countries, it was also much cheaper than in most countries. It was also found that gazumping occurred in only 3 per cent of transactions. Despite this, the government put forward proposals in December 1999 to reform the system of conveyancing with a view to reducing the delay between buyer and seller entering into an oral agreement and the contract becoming legally binding. It is this delay that creates the opportunity for gazumping to occur. Under the proposals, the seller would be required to gather all the information presently sought out by the buyer before exchange of contracts and give this to the buyer at the start of the transaction. There would then be no reason for a lengthy delay before contracts could be exchanged.

The package of information put together by the seller will be called a Home Information Pack. These proposals are included in the Housing Bill currently before Parliament, but are unlikely to be in force until 2005. One controversial aspect of the proposals is that the information provided by the seller should include a structural survey; few buyers currently undertake such a survey and providing one would add up to £500 to the cost of selling a house.

The costs of buying and selling a house

One reason people sometimes think of doing their own conveyancing work is in order to save money. There are not just legal costs involved and some costs cannot be avoided. The following costs may be incurred on a sale and purchase.

Sale

- Estate agent's fees for finding a buyer – perhaps 1 to 1½ per cent of the sale price, plus VAT at 17.5 per cent. You should shop around for the best deal, as fees differ.
- Land Registry fees – perhaps £4;
- Solicitors' fees for sale – you should shop around to get the best deal as fees differ enormously, but say £300 plus VAT for a sale. You should ensure that any quote obtained covers acting for the lender as well.
- Lender's and lender's solicitor's fees – if there is a loan on the property, lenders often charge various administration fees in connection with the repayment of the loan. These will include fees for sending the deeds to your solicitor and confirming that the loan has been repaid. These may amount to upwards of £100. Also, the lender will expect you to pay its legal fees in connection with the repayment of the loan. If you are instructing a solicitor to handle the legal work on the sale, his fee will normally include acting in connection with the repayment of the loan as well; if you decide to do your own conveyancing, the lender will still want a solicitor to act for it and will still expect you to pay the cost. This may well be about £50 – £100.

Purchase

- Solicitors' fees – again these vary, but you should be able to obtain a quote for around £300, plus VAT. You should ensure that any quote obtained covers acting for the lender as well.

- Lender's solicitor's fees – if you are buying the house with the aid of a mortgage loan, you will be expected to pay the lender's solicitor's fees. The lender, like you, will need to make sure that there are no legal problems with the land before lending the money. If you are instructing a solicitor to do your legal work, he will normally also act for the lender. Most of the work done for the lender is identical to that which would be done on your behalf anyway, so the fee quoted will normally cover acting for the lender as well. If you are doing your own conveyancing, the lender will still require a solicitor to check that you have done the work correctly, and you will have to pay the fee. This could amount to upwards of £150.

- Valuation for lender – if you are buying with the aid of a mortgage loan, your lender will require you to pay for a valuation of the property. The cost of this will vary according to the value of the property, but may be up to £200.

- Survey – this will also vary in cost according to the value of the property, perhaps as much as £500. However, if a valuation is also needed for a lender, the cost of this will be able to be saved by asking the person doing the survey to provide a valuation as well.

- Search fees – these will vary according to the location of the property, but may be as much as £150;

- Land Registry fees – after you have bought the house, you will have to pay for your ownership details to be registered at the Land Registry. The fees will vary according to the value of the property, but may be as much as £200.

- Stamp Duty Land Tax – this is a government tax paid by property buyers. This again differs according to the value of the property and is assessed according to the following scale:

    £0–£60,000 – no duty payable;

    £60,001–£250,000 – duty is assessed at 1 per cent of the purchase price;

    £250,001–£500,000 – duty is assessed at 3 per cent of the price;

    £500,001 and above – duty is assessed at 4 per cent of the price.

    Note that duty is assessed at the rates shown on the whole of the purchase price; thus, in the case of a house costing £300,000, duty will be assessed at 3 per cent on the whole of that amount, i.e. £9,000 duty will be payable.

    Houses in certain areas, that have been deemed 'Disadvantaged' by the government, are exempt from payment of Stamp Duty Land Tax up to and including a purchase price of £150,000. One can check which areas are disadvantaged by looking on the Inland Revenue website (www.inlandrevenue.gov.uk/so/disadvantaged.htm#l).

19

Renting in the Public Sector

INTRODUCTION

The law relating to renting houses or flats is extremely complex; it has been developed piecemeal over many years without any coherent underlying plan. It must be emphasized that the rules applying usually differ depending upon the identity of the landlord; thus the rules for private landlords are different from those for public ones and the rules for local authorities are different from those for housing associations.

COUNCIL HOUSING

Local authorities have traditionally been the principal providers of 'social housing' in the UK, with a duty to provide decent rented housing for those unable to afford high, commercially set rents. Increasingly, in recent years, the responsibility of providing new housing has passed to housing associations (or 'Registered Social Landlords', in bureaucratic jargon). Many existing housing estates have also been transferred to housing associations and this trend is likely to become even more common in the future.

The crucial point to note is that the rights of council tenants are not affected by such transfers.

The relations between landlords and tenants of privately rented properties are controlled by a complex set of rules under the Rent Act 1977 and the Housing Act 1988. The law for council tenants, on the other hand, is relatively straightforward. In short, council tenants have considerable protection from eviction, but little or no protection from rent increases.

Rent

A council tenant will have to pay whatever the local authority thinks is 'reasonable'. The tenant must be given four weeks' notice of the proposed rent increase. The increase does not have to be phased in any way, but a notice of increase must be served. Financial assistance with rent is available to council tenants through housing benefit, which is means tested.

Eviction

A council tenant can be evicted only by a court order. This will be made only if the landlord council can establish a 'ground' for possession, i.e. he must prove that one of the well-defined circumstances laid down by the law applies to his case. In addition to proving the ground, it must be proved that it would be reasonable to evict, or that alternative accommodation is available.

The provision of accommodation

Local authorities have considerable discretion in deciding to whom they should let council flats or houses. In a nutshell, the 'general management, regulation and control' of local authority housing is within the hands of the local council, but this is subject to influence and pressure from central government.

Sometimes a simple waiting list is the sole criterion in the selection of tenants, although it is more usual for it to be combined with a *points system* that takes into account such things as:
- room deficiencies, including mixed sleeping;
- whether the family has been broken up as a result of their poor housing conditions;
- the absence of facilities such as a bath, toilet, cooker, etc.;
- the fact that the accommodation is shared with other people;
- the inadequacy of the facilities provided (e.g. if the cooker is on the landing or the toilet is in the back yard);
- personal health, age and disability;

- length of time the family has been living in the borough;
- length of time the family has been on the housing waiting list.

Different councils award different numbers of points for these varying factors, for the government has not laid down any fixed guidelines. Councils must provide written summaries of their selection and priority rules if requested.

Councils are under a statutory duty to give a reasonable preference to persons in insanitary or overcrowded housing, persons with large families, or persons living under other unsatisfactory housing conditions.

When it is decided that an applicant should be offered a house or flat, the usual procedure is for him or her to be visited by a member of the council's housing department. The council official will try to form an impression of the applicant's general desirability as a tenant. Thus tenants are often informally graded, so that a high-quality home will not be given to an unsatisfactory tenant and a tenant with financial problems will probably be offered a cheaper property than would otherwise be the case.

Introductory tenancies

Local authorities can elect to introduce an 'introductory tenancy scheme'. If such an election is in force, any new council tenant is initially given a one-year trial period as a tenant, during which there is no security of tenure. So if the person does not prove a suitable tenant, the council can obtain possession without the need to prove any grounds or that it is reasonable to obtain possession. If the tenant does prove suitable, then neither landlord nor tenant need take any action; the tenancy will automatically become fully protected on the ending of the trial period.

THE COUNCIL TENANCY: A SECURE TENANCY

In law, a council tenancy is usually called a 'secure tenancy'. The rules on rent and eviction set out in this chapter apply only to secure tenants. This, in practice, includes the vast majority of council tenants.

But the following council lettings are excluded and will not be secure tenancies:
- houses contained in lettings of commercial or agricultural property, for example, the letting of a shop with a flat over it or a farm with a farm house on it;
- fixed-term lettings for a period of over 21 years;
- lettings to students;
- lettings to council employees when 'the house comes with the job'.

In addition, short-term temporary accommodation will not be protected. This includes property let:
- *As short-life lettings pending development of the land.* For instance, many councils allow squatting groups to occupy short-term property that is due for redevelopment or demolition; these squatters would not be secure tenants.
- *To homeless people under the Housing Act 1985.* There is a 12-month period before they become secure tenants, so during that time the council can evict them more easily. At the end of the 12-month period (or earlier if notified or rehoused elsewhere by the council) the tenant becomes a secure tenant and so has the benefit of the stricter controls on eviction.
- *When the council is itself a tenant under a short let.* If the council then lets the property, that tenant will not be a secure tenant.

The terms of the tenancy

When an applicant is offered a council house or flat they will have to accept the terms of the tenancy offered by the council. The terms will vary from council to council since there is no standardized set of terms laid down by central government.

Some councils require the tenants to sign a formal tenancy agreement, while others simply set out the main terms in the rent book. A rent book must be provided if the tenant pays his rent on a weekly basis.

Allowing the tenant to make improvements

One of the more absurd clauses that used to be found in council letting agreements was a restriction preventing tenants from carrying out improvements to their homes. The Housing Act 1985 now provides that the tenant must ask the council for permission but the council cannot unreasonably withhold its consent.

This applies to any alteration or improvement (e.g. changing bathroom fittings, erecting an exterior TV aerial, painting the outside). But in every case, the council's written permission must be asked for before the work can be done.

The council is not permitted to increase the rent on account of improvements lawfully carried out by the tenant at his own expense.

Sub-letting part

A lodger is a person who lives with the family – for instance, someone who shares meals and is taken into the home to live more or less as a member of the family. A council tenant need not obtain the council's prior permission before taking in a lodger. But if part of the property is let off to a sub-tenant, not a lodger, the council's written approval must first be obtained.

So the tenant must ask the council for permission and the council will want to know who is to be the sub-tenant. The council cannot unreasonably withhold its consent, but if there are reasonable grounds for refusing permission (for example, where there would be overcrowding) then the sub-letting will be prohibited. If the council gives a reason that seems unreasonable, the county court will decide the issue, but the burden would be on the council to show that it is not being unreasonable.

If part of the house or flat is sub-let unlawfully (because the council's permission was not obtained or because it was sub-let in defiance of the council's reasonable objections), the council will be able to evict him or her. However, the sub-tenant's own landlord (i.e. the council tenant) will not be able to use the illegality of the sub-letting as a ground for eviction; only the council can do that.

In practice, the sub-tenant will have little protection as against his own landlord, i.e. the council tenant. This is because the landlord will be a resident landlord and so the sub-tenant will have no protection under the Housing Act 1988.

Sub-letting/assigning the whole tenancy

If the tenant parts with possession of the whole of the property, he or she will no longer be a secure tenant, and nor will the person who takes over from them. The council would be able to obtain possession very quickly without the need to prove any grounds.

The general rule is that a secure tenancy cannot be given away or sold to someone else, unless, of course, the council will give its consent. But transfer is allowed:

- when one secure tenant exchanges (swaps) houses with another;
- when the court orders a transfer of the tenancy to the husband or wife in divorce proceedings;
- when the tenant dies and a member of his/her family 'succeeds to the tenancy' (*see* page 212);
- where the transfer is to a person who would be qualified to 'succeed to the tenancy' if the tenant were dead.

Evicting a council tenant

Under the Housing Act 1980, the council can only recover possession by establishing one of the 'grounds' or circumstances set out in the Act.

Need for a court order

Like any landlord, the council must obtain a court order before it evicts a tenant. If a tenant is evicted without a court order, it will be an illegal eviction and, generally, a criminal offence.

The procedure to be followed is in two stages:

1 the council must serve a preliminary notice on the tenant;
2 at least four weeks later, court proceedings can be begun.

The preliminary notice to the tenant

The first requirement is for the council to serve a notice of intention to seek possession on the tenant, stating and giving particulars of the ground on which the council will apply to the court for possession. It is insufficient merely to state the ground. Particulars must be given to indicate to the tenant what, if anything, he or she can do to avoid the commencement of proceedings. It must give at least four weeks' warning of the commencement of proceedings. Exceptionally, the warning period will have to be even longer – for instance, if the tenant pays his or her rent on a quarterly basis, then three months' notice must be given. Proceedings cannot be commenced until the warning period has expired.

The preliminary notice then has a life of 12 months. If proceedings are not commenced within that time, the council will have to serve a fresh notice and wait for the minimum period of four weeks to expire before starting the court proceedings.

COUNCIL TENANTS: GROUNDS FOR POSSESSION

Grounds where it must be 'reasonable' to evict

In the following cases the court will make a possession order only if it would be 'reasonable' to do so. For instance, not every act of damage will result in a court making an eviction order; the court will want to be sure that it is reasonable for that damage to lead to the tenant's eviction. The grounds include:

Ground 1 – Rent arrears or other breaches of the terms of the tenancy

In the case of rent arrears, the order will usually be made only if the tenant has a very bad rent record. If the arrears can be paid off by instalments, the court might make an order but suspend it. The order will then come into effect if the tenant does not pay the instalments. If the arrears are paid off before the court hearing, it is almost certain that no eviction order will be made.

In the case of breaches of other terms of the agreement, again no order will be made if the breach is only minor and the tenant agrees not to do it again.

Ground 2 – Nuisance, annoyance, illegality, immorality

This ground is an important weapon in the fight by councils to rid themselves – and their other tenants – of 'neighbours from hell'. The ground covers a variety of anti-social behaviour by the tenant, or any person living in, or visiting, the house. It includes conduct causing or likely to cause a nuisance or annoyance to anyone residing, visiting or engaging in a lawful activity in the locality, as well as convictions for using the house for illegal or immoral purposes or any arrestable offence committed in the house or in its locality. This ground has been widely used by many authorities, who employ specially trained staff to obtain evidence against the worst culprits. One problem with badly behaved tenants is that the neighbours are unwilling to give evidence against them due to fear of reprisals. The wording of the ground allows council staff to obtain the evidence that the conduct is *likely* to cause a nuisance or annoyance to the neighbours, without the neighbours actually being involved. If threats, etc. are made against the council officials themselves, this is also a part of the ground; they are engaged in a lawful activity and the conduct is causing them a nuisance or annoyance. Remember that possession will only be ordered if it is reasonable to do so; this will depend upon the extent and frequency of the conduct alleged and the attitude displayed by the tenant. Note also that councils are also able to obtain injunctions to prevent anti-social behaviour. Failure to comply with such an order will again be a relevant factor in deciding whether or not possession should be ordered.

Ground 2A – Domestic violence

This deals with the situation where the house was occupied by a married couple, or a couple living together as husband and wife, and one partner has been forced to leave the house due to the other's violence or threats of violence. In establishing the ground it does not matter which one of the partners is the actual tenant; the violent partner who remains in the house can now be evicted because of his behaviour. The reference to a couple living together as 'husband and wife' has always been interpreted by the courts as excluding a couple of the same sex who are living together; it remains to be seen, however, whether such interpretation remains valid following the passing of the Human Rights Act.

Ground 3 – Damage to the house

The tenant has damaged the property or allowed it to fall into disrepair. If a lodger or sub-tenant was to blame, the tenant must have failed to take steps to evict him or her.

Ground 4 – Damage to furniture provided by the landlord

Again, if the damage was caused by a lodger or sub-tenant, the tenant must have failed to take steps to evict him or her.

Ground 5 – False statement

The tenant, or someone at his instigation, made a false statement, knowingly or recklessly, to persuade the council to grant him the tenancy.

Ground 8 – Temporary accommodation

When the tenant has been allowed to live in the property while building works were being carried out to his own home, which was itself occupied under a secure tenancy.

Grounds where the council must provide alternative accommodation

In the case of the following grounds, the court will make a possession order only if it is satisfied that the council can offer the tenant suitable alternative accommodation. Basically, this means that the tenant must have security of tenure; it will be either another secure tenancy or a private sector assured tenancy; in addition the property must be suitable for the tenant and his family – distance from work, size, terms of the tenancy and any furniture provided will all be relevant in deciding this.

Ground 9 – Overcrowding

If the house is overcrowded, this ground enables the council to evict a tenant unwilling to transfer to more suitable accommodation.

Ground 10 – Demolition or reconstruction

The council reasonably needs possession to demolish or reconstruct the premises within a reasonable period.

Ground 11 – Charitable housing trust

The landlord is not a council but a charitable housing trust and the tenant's occupation conflicts with the charity's objects (for example, a person in housing for the blind is no longer blind).

Grounds where the council must prove it is reasonable to evict and must also provide suitable alternative accommodation

In these cases, a double test has to be satisfied: reasonableness *and* provision of suitable alternative accommodation.

Ground 13 – Disabled accommodation

The property is suitable for disabled persons but there is no longer a disabled person living in the house, and the council requires it for such a person.

Ground 14 – People difficult to house

If a housing association lets property to people who are difficult to house and the present tenant is either not within such a category or has been offered a secure council tenancy. People difficult to house would include, for example, people recently released from prison.

Ground 15 – Special needs

The property is one of a group let to people with special needs, where special services are provided, but the present tenant does not have special needs, and the council requires it for such a person.

Ground 16 – Overhoused

The accommodation is bigger than is reasonably needed. But the tenant must have been a 'successor' to the original tenant and the landlord must serve notice of court proceedings between six and 12 months after the death of the original tenant before this ground can apply.

Eviction of the tenant's family, etc.

What happens if the council tenant dies or leaves the rented property: do the people living with him or her have to leave as well or can they carry on living there?

When the tenant deserts his family

The abandoned husband or wife cannot automatically take over the tenancy, but the landlord is obliged to accept rent from him/her and the deserted spouse's occupation is to be treated as occupation by the tenant (Family Law Act 1996). Thus the landlord cannot argue that the tenant has left and that, accordingly, the remaining spouse must also leave.

Although the council must accept rent from the remaining spouse, they may refuse to transfer the tenancy to them unless the court has made an order to that effect. However, the court will make an order only in a divorce or judicial separation. If there are no divorce or judicial separation proceedings, then the court cannot order a transfer of the tenancy.

Other members of the family have no such right to remain in occupation. For instance, if the tenant is a single woman and she abandons her aged mother, her mother cannot demand to be allowed to stay in the rented property. Since the tenant has ceased to be in occupation, the tenancy has ceased to be secure and so the landlord will be able to obtain possession without the need to prove any grounds for possession.

On divorce

The divorce courts can order the secure tenancy to be transferred from one spouse to another, or from joint names into the name of one spouse only. If there are children, the tenancy is likely to be transferred to the spouse who resides with the children. The council is unlikely to transfer the tenancy unless there is a court order.

Cohabiting

The abandoned partner has no legal right to claim the tenancy or to insist that the council accept his/her payments of rent. However, if the unmarried couple originally took out the council tenancy together, then they will almost certainly both have their names on the rent book. Thus the departure of one of them would not affect the other, for he/she would still be tenant and would be able to carry on living there.

Notice to quit given by one of two joint tenants

If the tenancy is in joint names and only one moves out, the outgoing tenant can give the council/landlord notice to quit. This will terminate the tenancy even for the remaining tenant. The remaining tenant should seek a new tenancy agreement in his or her *sole* name.

The repair and maintenance of council properties

Councils are subject to the same laws on maintenance and repair of rented property as other landlords (*see* page 216).

THE COUNCIL TENANT'S RIGHT TO BUY HIS/HER HOME

The Housing Act 1985 allows council tenants to buy their homes. No such right is given to tenants of private landlords (except where the tenant has a long-term lease). The right to buy has proved extremely popular, having been exercised by over 1.1 million council tenants.

The tenant (or his/her spouse) must have been in occupation for at least two years. The price to be paid will be the open market price, less a discount which varies with the length of the tenant's occupation:

- up to two years, 32 per cent discount;
- over two years, 32 per cent discount plus 1 per cent for every year over two years (for example, 10 years equals 40 per cent) subject to a maximum discount of 60 per cent.

The discount is greater with respect to council flats, as an encouragement to those tenants to exercise their right to buy (for example, 44 per cent discount after two years plus 2 per cent for every year over two years subject to a maximum of 70 per cent).

However, the maximum discount in monetary terms cannot be greater than an amount fixed from time to time by the Secretary of State. This now varies according to the region of the country in which the house is situated. At the time of writing this varies between a maximum of £24,000 for houses in Wales, up to a maximum of £38,000 for houses in London.

The price will initially be fixed by the council but the tenant can appeal this valuation to the District Valuer within three months. The District Valuer's decision is final.

If the tenant resells within three years of his/her purchase he or she must repay all or part of the discount to the council:

Time since purchase	Percentage of discount to be repaid
under one year	100 per cent
after one year	66.6 per cent
after two years	33.3 per cent
after three years	nil

The tenant can claim a council mortgage to finance his/her purchase. This can be up to 100 per cent of the price, subject to the tenant's income entitling him/her to a loan of that amount. If the tenant cannot afford to buy, he or she can opt for shared ownership instead.

Some housing association tenants also have a right to buy (*see* page 215).

HOUSING ASSOCIATIONS

Housing associations are now seen as a major provider of state-financed housing. Basically, the idea is that a group of people can register themselves as a housing association with a view to constructing new homes or converting existing buildings into modern housing. If the government approves of the scheme, it will finance the building works and capital costs through full grants from the Housing Corporation, and when the work is completed the housing association will rent out the properties. Most local authorities, housing aid centres and Citizens' Advice Bureaux will provide a list of local housing associations and their properties.

The concept of housing associations is not new; it dates from the mid-nineteenth century. However, the early housing associations soon found that their economic-cost rents were too expensive for the 'labouring classes', for whom the accommodation was intended. Thus it was left to private foundations such as the Guinness, the Peabody and the Bournville trusts to subsidize various schemes, and it was not until the 1960s that the state began to take an active interest in financing housing associations. Since then, the housing association movement has expanded rapidly.

Housing associations are now one of the major providers of state-funded housing. Some are registered with the Housing Corporation (in England) or Housing for Wales (Ty Cymru) and are now referred to as 'Registered Social Landlords'. Some housing associations are also registered charities and must operate within their own charitable rules as well. Other housing associations are run on a co-operative basis where the tenants themselves own and manage the houses they live in.

Under policies developed by Conservative governments in the 1990s, registered social landlords have now become the main providers of new social housing, replacing local authorities in that role. Indeed, many local authorities have transferred some or all of their existing housing stocks over to housing associations. Such transfers require the consent of the Secretary of State (in England) or the Welsh Assembly and a local authority contemplating such a disposal must carry out a consultation exercise with the tenants affected. Several hundred thousand dwellings have already been transferred in this way and such transfers are still continuing.

The law relating to the security of tenure and rent control given to housing association tenants will depend not only on the type of housing association, but also on the date on which the tenancy was granted.

The position of the tenant in a housing association where tenancy was granted before 15 January 1989

For rent purposes the housing association tenant receives the protection of a private (Rent Act) tenant, but for eviction purposes the tenant is treated in the same way as a public (council) tenant.

Rent

Housing associations charge 'fair rents' as assessed by the Rent Officer (*see* pages 234–5 for more detail on the fair rent system).

Eviction

The tenant of a registered housing association has a 'secure' tenancy and can be evicted only by a court order obtained in certain well-defined circumstances. The position is exactly the same as for council tenants (*see* pages 210–12).

Eviction of the tenant's family, etc.

What happens if a housing association tenant dies, leaves the rented property or divorces his/her spouse? Briefly, the position of the spouse and family will be exactly the same as if they were in council housing. Similarly, the position of a cohabitant is as if the property were rented from the council (*see* page 212).

The position of the tenant in a housing association where tenancy was granted on or after 15 January 1989

Most new tenancies granted by housing associations on or after 15 January 1989 are governed by the Housing Act 1988 as part of the private sector. These are dealt with in Chapter 20. The new tenancy will be either an *assured tenancy* or an *assured shorthold tenancy*.

As housing associations exist to provide long-term housing for tenants, most tenancies will be ordinary assured tenancies with full security of tenure, although there is no legal rule preventing a housing association from granting a shorthold should it wish to do so.

Rent

There is no rent control. The tenant is obliged to pay the amount of rent specified in the tenancy agreement. There is no legal control over the amount of rent chargeable, even though one of the reasons for having housing associations is to provide accommodation at affordable rents. If the housing association wishes to increase the rent, it can do so only if either there is a clause in the tenancy agreement allowing them to do so or the tenancy is a periodic tenancy (weekly, monthly, etc.), by serving a notice of proposed increase under the Housing Act.

Registered social landlords should provide tenants with a written agreement specifying the rent to be charged, provisions as to increase and the other conditions of the tenancy. Tenants also have the benefit of a 'tenants' guarantee', which is an assurance from a landlord of good standards of management. Although not legally binding, the guarantee specifies the minimum contractual rights a tenant should be given with regard to taking in lodgers, making improvements, etc. It will also contain information on:

- the association's policies for selecting tenants and allocating houses;
- rent (which should be kept within the reach of people in low paid or no employment);
- management, maintenance and tenant participation.

HOUSING OMBUDSMAN SERVICE

All registered social landlords must be members of an independent housing ombudsman scheme approved by the Secretary of State. The housing ombudsman must investigate any complaint made to him which is not subsequently withdrawn. He *may* also investigate any complaint which is later withdrawn.

The ombudsman has wide powers: he may order the landlord to pay compensation to the tenant, or order that the landlord should not require payment of any outstanding rent. If the landlord fails to comply with the order within a reasonable time, the ombudsman may order the landlord to publish, in whatever way the ombudsman thinks fit, that the landlord has failed to comply with the determination. If the landlord fails to publish, the ombudsman has power to do so himself. The idea behind this is that the fear of adverse publicity will persuade the landlord to comply with the ombudsman's decision.

Transitional cases

If a new housing association tenancy is granted on or after 15 January 1989 it will not be governed by the Housing Act 1988 if:

- it is a renewal of a tenancy originally granted before that date; or
- it was entered into pursuant to a contract made before that date. Here, the old rules will continue to apply.

REPAIR AND MAINTENANCE OF HOUSING ASSOCIATION PROPERTIES

The normal rules as to the repair and maintenance of the rented property apply to housing associations (*see* Chapter 22).

TENANCIES TRANSFERRED FROM A LOCAL AUTHORITY

Former tenants of local authorities where the property has been transferred from the council to a registered social landlord will normally become assured tenants under the Housing Act 1988 (*see* page 217). However, such tenants retain their 'right to buy' even as against the new landlord. This is known as 'the preserved right to buy'.

THE 'RIGHT TO BUY'

Under the Housing Act 1996, most tenants of registered social landlords have the same right to buy as secure tenants (*see* page 212). However, this is subject to the property being built or purchased by the landlord with public money. This means that tenants of charitable and co-operative housing associations will probably not have the right to buy. As with council tenants, there is a residence qualification of a minimum of two years.

UNREGISTERED HOUSING ASSOCIATIONS

An unregistered housing association is one which is not registered with the Housing Corporation or Housing for Wales. This means that it does not qualify for state funding and is not supervised by a government body. Some housing associations have deliberately chosen not to be registered, preferring to act independently. This also means that they can set up shared ownership schemes, which is not possible with a registered association.

Tenancies granted on or after 15 January 1989

These tenancies will be assured or assured shorthold tenancies under the Housing Act 1988. They are thus governed by the same rules as private sector tenants (*see* page 217). They do not, however, have the benefit of the tenant's guarantee (*see* above).

Tenancies granted before 15 January 1989

Tenancies originally granted prior to this date will be subject to the Rent Act 1977 (*see* page 216).

CO-OPERATIVE HOUSING ASSOCIATIONS

Tenancies granted before 15 January 1989

Such lettings enjoy no security of tenure. However, as the tenants are in effect their own landlords due to the co-operative nature of the ownership of the freehold, they should be reasonably well protected, subject to compliance with the association's constitution.

As far as rent is concerned, the fair rent system will apply in the usual way (*see* pages 234–5).

Tenancies granted on or after 15 January 1989

A fully mutual housing association is exempt from the provisions of the Housing Act 1988, and so its lettings will have no statutory security of tenure. However, the tenant's guarantee will apply and the tenants remain their own landlords.

20

Renting from a Private Landlord

INTRODUCTION

Many rented houses, flats and bed-sitting rooms belong to private landlords. These landlords will include the owner-occupier who has surplus accommodation to let; the owner who is working abroad and letting his or her home while away; the large commercial landlord or company that owns numerous properties for rent; or the private individual who has decided to invest in a buy-to-let scheme. Unfortunately, there can be many pitfalls for both landlords and tenants in what has become an extremely complex area of the law.

Here are just a few of the questions that often arise:

1 Can the tenant be evicted when the tenancy ends (or even before it ends)?
2 What is the correct procedure for repossessing tenanted property?
3 What is the position if the landlord attempts to 'harass' the tenant into leaving?
4 Can the rent be increased or decreased?
5 Who is responsible for repairs to the property?

The responsibility for repair and maintenance will be dealt with in Chapter 22.

The law in relation to renting and letting houses can best be described as a mess. It is not contained in any single code or legislation, having developed higgledy-piggledy over many years. Often the answer to even the simplest question is far from clear. This is particularly so in relation to repairs.

Tenants of private landlords often have rights over and above those granted by the tenancy itself. So, even though the letting has expired, a residential tenant will often have the right to remain in possession for as long as he likes – and even though the landlord does not want him to. If this is the case he is said to have 'security of tenure'; if the landlord wishes to evict him he will have to have 'grounds for possession', i.e. establish one of the circumstances that Parliament recognizes as justifying evicting the tenant. Also, if the landlord wishes to increase the rent, he may find that he is only able to do so if he follows a procedure laid down by Parliament. Sometimes, indeed, tenants have the right to claim a reduction in the rent they have agreed to pay.

Entering into a tenancy

Legally a tenancy not exceeding three years in duration can be granted either in writing or by word of mouth. For longer tenancies a deed is essential. A deed is simply a written document in which the signatures of the parties are prefixed by the words 'Signed as a Deed' and then those signatures are witnessed. But many residential tenancies are for 12 months or less and although these can be validly granted orally, writing is best as there can then be no argument as to what precisely has been agreed.

The status of the tenancy

In answering almost any question in relation to rented property, the starting point is to decide the precise legal status of the letting in question. This will depend upon the date upon which the *original* letting between the parties was entered into. So, in the case of a tenant who was first granted a tenancy in 1988 and which has been renewed several times since, the relevant date for determining the status will be 1988.

There are two key dates: 15 January 1989 and 28 February 1997.

Lettings originally entered into prior to 15 January 1989 will fall within the protection of the Rent Act 1977. This gives tenants security of tenure and imposes substantial restrictions as to what rent the landlord can charge.

Lettings entered into on or after 15 January 1989 are subject to the provisions of the Housing Act 1988. This Act gave landlords a choice: they could either let on an assured shorthold tenancy, which gave the tenant no

Rights of Tenant/Occupier depend on 'Status of Occupier'

security of tenure but a limited degree of rent control or, alternatively, on an ordinary assured tenancy, which had no rent control but did give the tenant security of tenure. The rules relating to assured and assured shorthold tenancies changed radically in the case of lettings entered into on or after 28 February 1997. Although the basic choice given to the landlord remained the same, the rules relating to 'new' shortholds (i.e. those entered into on or after that date) must be distinguished from those relating to the 'old' shortholds entered into before that date.

Lettings entered into before 15 January 1989	The Rent Act 1977 applies	Tenant has security of tenure plus restrictions on rent
Lettings entered into after 15 January 1989	The Housing Act 1988 applies	Landlord can choose to let on assured shorthold tenancy or assured tenancy
Lettings entered into on or after 28 February 1997	Rules relating to 'new' shortholds apply	

All these provisions must now be looked at in detail, but bear in mind that some tenancies will not fall within either the Rent Act or Housing Act regimes. If, for example, the landlord lives in another part of the same house as the tenant, then the legislation will not give the tenant any protection over and above that which has been agreed in the tenancy agreement.

ASSURED SHORTHOLD TENANCIES

Assured and assured shorthold tenancies

The Housing Act 1988 'invented' two different types of tenancies of residential property; *assured tenancies* and *assured shorthold tenancies*. A landlord was able to choose which one he would use when he was letting property.

Assured tenancies give a tenant extensive security of tenure, i.e. at the end of the agreed term of the letting the tenant does not have to leave but has a legal right to stay on for as long as he wants, unless and until the landlord can establish one of the grounds for possession laid down by the Act.

An assured shorthold tenancy (or 'shorthold' as it is

usually called), gives a tenant no security of tenure after the ending of the agreed period of the letting. So a landlord is certain to obtain possession on or after the end of the term agreed. However, to do so he will need to go to court and follow the correct procedure. This basically involves giving the tenant at least two months' notice in writing. But there is no need for the landlord to prove anything else, or give reasons as to why he wants possession. It is for this reason that shortholds have proved very popular with landlords.

As far as rent is concerned, however, shortholds do have one slight advantage for tenants in that if the tenant considers the rent excessive, he can refer it to the Rent Assessment Committee for them to fix what would be a proper rent for the property. As we shall see, there are various time limits within which this right must be exercised and there is no question of the rent being reduced below the open market rent for the property. The provision only prevents the landlord from over-charging. It has to be said that, although this right exists, it is comparatively rare for tenants to avail themselves of it.

Most lettings on or after 28 February 1997 will be shortholds

Virtually all lettings of residential property made on and after 28 February 1997 will be shortholds. The Housing Act 1988 does lay down various conditions which have to be fulfilled, and we will look at these conditions later, but for the moment we can say that, unless special circumstances exist, a tenancy of a house entered into on or after 28 February 1997 is likely to be a shorthold – and remember, a tenancy can be validly created by word of mouth; writing is not essential.

Old shortholds and new shortholds

Before we go on and look at shortholds in detail, there is one more introductory matter that has to be understood. As stated, all residential lettings on or after 28 February 1997 will almost certainly be shortholds. We will call these 'new' shortholds.

However, shortholds could be granted before that date. Until 28 February 1997, to be a shorthold, a letting had to comply with various conditions, including serving a notice on the tenant prior to the letting stating that it was going to be a shorthold. We will call these 'old' shortholds.

If the conditions were not complied with, then the letting would be an ordinary assured tenancy giving the tenant full security of tenure.

So the position with regard to lettings made on or after 15 January 1989 can be summarized as follows:

Lettings made on or after 15 January 1989 until 27 February 1997 (inclusive)

All lettings would be *ordinary* assured tenancies *unless* notice was served to say there was to be a shorthold; there were also other conditions to be complied with before there could be a shorthold. These 'old shortholds' will be looked at on page 226.

Lettings on or after 28 February 1997

All lettings will be *shortholds* unless notice is served to say there is to be an ordinary assured tenancy.

The 'default' position has been completely reversed. As there are still likely to be many lettings around originally made prior to 28 February 1997, we will need to look at both sets of rules.

New shortholds: lettings made on or after 28 February 1997

Although it is highly likely that any letting of residential property made on or after this date will be a shorthold, there are various conditions that have to be fulfilled before one can say for certain that is the case. To be a shorthold, a tenancy must satisfy the conditions contained in the 1988 Act. Note that these conditions laid down in the 1988 Act apply to all lettings made on or after 15 January 1989, whether assured or shorthold tenancies (and whether new or old shortholds). Unless these conditions are complied with, the 1988 Act will not apply at all and the letting will have no security or rent control at all.

Qualifying conditions for assured tenancies and assured shorthold tenancies

A tenancy under which a house is let as a 'separate dwelling' will be an assured tenancy if and so long as *all* of the following requirements are met:
1 the tenant or each of the joint tenants is an individual; and
2 the tenant or at least one of the joint tenants occupies the dwellinghouse as his only or principal home; and
3 the tenancy is not specifically excluded by other provisions of the Act.
Each of these requirements must be looked at in detail.

Tenancy

There must be a *tenancy*. Licences to occupy houses are excluded from the definition. A licence is simply a permission to enter on to someone else's property for an agreed purpose. It will not be binding on future owners of the land and the occupier under it will not have Housing Act protection.

A tenancy is a contract under which the landlord gives the tenant the exclusive use and occupation of at least part of the property, either for a fixed specific term – for example, six months or one year (in which case it is referred to as a *fixed-term tenancy* or a *lease*) or on a periodic basis for an indefinite period, for example, from week to week, or from month to month (in which case it is referred to as a *periodic tenancy*).

The main factor that distinguishes a tenancy from a licence is the requirement that a tenant has *exclusive possession* of the property or some specific part of it – for example, a flat or a bed-sitter. A common situation that arises is the case of a house or flat 'shared' by several people. If each occupier has the right to exclusive possession of their own particular bedroom, this could amount to a tenancy, even though they might also share the rest of the house with the others. However, if the occupier does not enjoy exclusive possession of any part of the property, he is merely a licensee and will have no protection under the Housing Act.

The following case illustrates the courts' attitude to the question of whether or not an occupier does have a tenancy despite having signed what appears to be a 'licence'.

The case of **Street** *v* **Mountford** *decided by the House of Lords is a clear example of when the courts will hold the occupier to be a tenant, thus having protection, despite having signed a document called a licence. The owner, Mr Street, gave to Mrs Mountford the right to occupy furnished rooms forming part of a house in return for a 'licence fee' of £37 per week subject to termination by 14 days' written notice and to certain other conditions set out in the agreement. No person other than Mrs Mountford occupied those rooms. The House of Lords decided that Mrs Mountford was in fact the exclusive occupier of the rooms and that the agreement that she had with the owner was in reality a tenancy agreement.*

She therefore had legal protection as a tenant. The fact that the tenancy agreement was called a 'licence' could not alter the reality of the transaction. This was despite the fact that the agreement contained a clause stating that it was not intended to create a tenancy.

The case is authority for the proposition that (in the absence of exceptional circumstances) if an occupier is given exclusive occupation of a property (or a room) in return for a rent it will be a tenancy regardless of what the parties decide to call it.

House

There is no precise definition of 'house', but for these purposes it will be wider than the everyday use of the word. It will be a question of fact in each case whether what is let is a house or not but, basically, any building designed or adapted for living in is capable of being a house for these purposes. Thus, it will include lettings of whole houses, lettings of flats and also lettings of converted barns, windmills, etc.

Let as a separate dwelling

The property which is let, as well as being a 'house', must be let as a 'dwelling'. So the purpose of the letting is relevant. Thus, if a building that would otherwise qualify as a house is let for business purposes (for example, as an office), the tenant cannot claim that it is let on an assured or shorthold tenancy merely because he decides to move in and live there. (A tenant of business premises is likely to have other statutory protection, but this is outside the scope of this chapter.)

There must be a letting as a dwelling. It has been established that this means one single dwelling only. So if the property comprises two or more residential units, each intended for separate occupation (for example, the letting of the whole of a house which has been converted into several flats), that tenancy cannot be an assured tenancy. The sub-letting of each of the individual flats, however, could be within the definition.

There must be a *separate* dwelling. This is intended to exclude a letting of accommodation that lacks some essential feature of a dwelling, such as a kitchen. So the letting of a single room without kitchen and bathroom facilities would not be capable of being an assured or shorthold tenancy even though the tenant 'lived' in the room. However, if a tenant of such a room is given the right to share such essential facilities with others in another part of the building, the letting could then be an assured tenancy. In that case, the tenant must have the right to the exclusive possession of at least one room (otherwise it cannot be a tenancy at all). Note that if the facilities are shared with the landlord, the tenancy will be excluded from the definition of an assured or shorthold tenancy for different reasons (*see* resident landlords below).

These rules are important with regard to the common situation where a house has been converted into flatlets and each tenant is given exclusive occupation of his own bed-sitting room, but shares bathroom and kitchen with other tenants. The letting of each flatlet will be capable of being within the 1988 Act.

This situation can be contrasted with the position where each of a group of people is given a right to share the occupation of the whole of the house with the others. No one has the right to exclusive possession of any part of the house, and the arrangement can only give rise to a licence and not any type of tenancy.

If and so long as

The status of the tenancy is not to be determined once and for all at the commencement of the letting. Whether a tenancy is a shorthold can fluctuate during its subsistence according to changed circumstances. For example, one requirement of the definition is that the tenant must be occupying the house as his only or principal home. This may have been the case at the start of the tenancy, and so the tenancy would be within the 1988 Act, but if the tenant subsequently ceases to reside, the tenancy will no longer be within the Act. The landlord would then be able to obtain possession without having to follow the procedure laid down by the Act.

The tenant must be an individual

'Individual' in this context means a human being. So the letting must be to a human being, or to several human beings. Lettings to companies are thus excluded from the definition, even though a human employee or director of the company may well be in occupation of the house.

The tenant must occupy as his only or principal home

A person's 'home' is the place in which he intends to live permanently, rather than occupying it merely for a temporary period. The law recognizes that it is possible for a person to have more than one 'home'. If that is the case, then it is a question of fact as to which is the tenant's principal home. This could be a significant question, for example, for the person working in the City who has a flat nearby, in which he lives during the week, and a house in the country in which he lives at weekends. Which is his principal home? This will depend upon all the circumstances of the case. Only a tenancy of the principal home can be an assured or shorthold tenancy. A 'holiday home' would thus not be entitled to the protection of the Act.

Although the provision requires 'occupation', this does not mean continuous occupation. A mere temporary absence, due to holidays or hospitalization for example, will not deprive a tenancy of its status within the 1988 Act.

Tenancies specifically excluded from the definition

Various lettings which satisfy the basic definition of an assured tenancy will, in fact, not be protected if they fall within one of the following exceptions:

High-value properties

Following the abolition of domestic rates, a distinction has to be drawn between those tenancies granted before 1 April 1990 and those granted on or after that date. For tenancies granted before 1 April 1990, a tenancy of a house with a rateable value in excess of £750 (£1,500 in Greater London) cannot be an assured or shorthold tenancy.

If the tenancy was granted on or after 1 April 1990, it cannot be an assured or shorthold tenancy if the rent payable is £25,000, or more, per annum.

Tenancies at a low rent

This exclusion has also been affected by the abolition of domestic rates. Lettings made before 1 April 1990 cannot be assured or shorthold if the annual rent is less than two-thirds of the rateable value of the property. For tenancies granted on or after 1 April 1990, the exclusion applies to tenancies in which the rent does not exceed £250 per annum (£1,000 per annum in Greater London).

Business tenancies

A tenancy in which the premises are occupied for the purposes of a business, or for business and other purposes, is excluded from being an assured tenancy. This means that lettings of property used partly for business and partly for residential purposes cannot be assured tenancies, despite being occupied by the tenant as his only or principal home, etc. This would exclude, for example, a letting of the traditional 'corner-shop' with living accommodation over it. Such a letting may well, however, have some protection under the statutory protections given to business tenancies.

Tenancies of agricultural land

Tenancies of agricultural land will be excluded even though the tenant lives on the property. These tenants will probably have other statutory rights under the legislation relating to agricultural holdings, but this is outside the scope of this book.

Lettings to students

Lettings to students by specified educational bodies, i.e. most universities and colleges, are outside the definition of an assured tenancy. Note that this exception does not apply to lettings to students by landlords other than the specified universities and colleges; lettings to students by private landlords are capable of being assured tenancies, subject to the normal requirements being fulfilled.

Holiday lettings

A letting for the purpose of a holiday cannot be an assured tenancy.

Lettings by resident landlords

If the landlord lives in another part of the same building as that let to the tenant, it is likely that there will not be an assured tenancy. (For full details *see* below.)

Crown, local authority and housing association lettings

Although these are excluded from the definition of an assured tenancy, lettings by local authorities and housing associations may have other protections (*see* Chapter 19). Lettings by the Crown Estate, which administers property owned by the Queen in her private capacity, will be within the 1988 Act.

Rent under a new shorthold

The initial rent

There is no restriction on the amount of rent that can be charged on the grant of a shorthold tenancy. (This is so even if there is an existing registration of a fair rent for the purposes of the Rent Act 1977, as to which *see* page 234.) The amount of the rent under an assured tenancy is left to be fixed by agreement between landlord and tenant; 'market forces' will thus prevail.

However, a tenant may have a right to challenge the amount of the rent originally agreed by referring it to the Rent Assessment Committee (an independent, public body which operates on a regional basis).

Also, if the landlord subsequently wishes to *increase* the rent, he may not be able to do so unless he follows the correct procedure.

Referring the initial rent to the Rent Assessment Committee

A shorthold tenant can refer the rent originally agreed on the grant of the tenancy to the Rent Assessment Committee for a determination of the rent which, in the Committee's opinion, the landlord might reasonably be expected to obtain under the shorthold tenancy. However, the Committee cannot make such a determination unless there are a sufficient number of similar dwellinghouses in the locality let on assured tenancies *and* the rent payable under the shorthold is significantly higher than the rent which the landlord might reasonably be expected to obtain having regard to the level of rents payable under these other tenancies. The Committee thus proceeds by looking at the rents being charged for similar properties in the locality and then deciding what the rent for these premises ought to be.

There is, therefore, no question of the rent that is assessed being lower than the market rent for the premises. This is not a return to the 'fair rent' system as used under the Rent Act 1977, which frequently results in a rent of less than the market value being fixed.

A landlord is only at risk of a lower rent being fixed if he is charging 'significantly' more than the market rent for the house. Applications by tenants to the Rent Assessment Committee are comparatively few in number.

What is the effect of a determination by the Rent Assessment Committee?

The effect of a rent being fixed by the Rent Assessment Committee differs depending upon whether it is a fixed-term tenancy or a periodic tenancy.

In the case of a fixed-term tenancy, the rent will become the maximum rent chargeable for the property throughout the remainder of the fixed term. This is despite anything to the contrary in the tenancy agreement – and there is no provision for this figure to be increased during the fixed term, no matter how long that might be. It is for this reason that landlords are best advised to avoid granting long shortholds. In the case, for example, of a 21-year shorthold, a rent fixed in the first six months would continue to apply for the remainder of the term, despite any provisions in the tenancy agreement allowing the landlord to increase the amount of the rent.

In the case of a periodic tenancy, the rent will remain as fixed by the Committee unless and until the landlord is able to increase it using the statutory procedure for increasing rents in periodic tenancies (*see* below). Note that the landlord will be unable to use this procedure until 12 months have expired since the Committee assessed the rent.

The right to apply for the rent to be assessed is a once and for all right given to the tenant. Once the Committee has determined the rent no further application for the fixing of a different figure can be made by either landlord or tenant, even if market rents change in the meantime.

The rent determined by the Committee only applies during the particular tenancy in question, however. It will not limit the amount of rent chargeable under any subsequent letting of the same property, even if this is between the same landlord and tenant.

When is an application to the Rent Assessment Committee not possible?

A tenant can only apply to the Committee within the first six months of the tenancy. If a tenant has a succession of lettings (e.g. two successive lettings for three months), then he can apply within six months of the grant of the first tenancy to him. Apart from this situation, a tenant who does not apply for the rent to be assessed during the first shorthold granted to him, will not be able to apply during any subsequent letting; this is irrespective of whether an application was made during the original shorthold. Note also that only one application to the Committee can be made. Once the Committee has determined the rent, it cannot be resubmitted for a further determination, even if the original determination was many years before.

Contractual increases in rent

Under normal principles of contract law, a landlord cannot unilaterally vary the terms of a tenancy after it has been granted. He cannot, therefore, change the amount of the rent payable without the consent of the tenant, *unless* the terms of the tenancy allow the landlord to do so. Some landlords seem unable to grasp this point.

From a landlord's point of view, therefore, it is sensible for a term to be included in the tenancy agreement allowing the landlord to increase the rent, should he wish to do so. Many informally granted tenancies contain no such provisions and this could lead to unfairness to landlords. In the case of a long-term tenancy, a landlord could find the value of the rent he is receiving rapidly eroded by the effects of inflation with no chance of increasing that rent.

To relieve this potential unfairness, the Housing Act 1988 contains provisions enabling a landlord to increase the rent even though this is not permitted by the terms of the tenancy agreement. These provisions apply only to periodic (i.e. weekly or monthly) tenancies and the procedure is somewhat complex.

Statutory increases for periodic tenancies

If there is no provision in the tenancy agreement for an assured or shorthold tenancy allowing the landlord to increase the rent, he can do so by following the procedure laid down by the 1988 Act. This is a complex procedure requiring the landlord to serve a notice (in the prescribed form) on the tenant suggesting a figure for the new rent. The tenant can then refer this notice to the Rent Assessment Committee for arbitration if agreement as to the new rent cannot be reached. The Rent Assessment Committee will determine the rent at which the premises might reasonably be let in the open market. There is no suggestion that the assessed rent will be less than the open-market rent for the house. This is not a return to the old 'fair rent' system under the Rent Act 1977. (Under the Rent Act 1977 a rent lower than an open-market rent is frequently assessed – *see* page 234.)

If there is an express term in the tenancy agreement permitting rent increases, this will avoid the need to rely on the statutory procedure, as already stated. Without an express term in the agreement, if the landlord attempted to increase the rent without following the statutory procedure, the increase would be unlawful and could not be recovered from the tenant.

Rent increases for fixed-term tenancies

The statutory provisions only apply to periodic tenancies. There are no statutory provisions providing for a rent increase in fixed-term tenancies, for example, one for 18 months. In the absence of an express clause in the tenancy agreement the landlord will be unable to increase the rent during the fixed term without the agreement of the tenant.

Can the tenant transfer the tenancy or sub-let?

A tenancy 'belongs' to the tenant in just the same way as his car belongs to him. He can thus freely 'assign' it, i.e. sell it or give it away, to whomsoever he likes. Alternatively, he can sub-let, i.e. grant a lease shorter than his own, or take in lodgers, etc.

This is all well and good from the point of view of the tenant but will not necessarily be acceptable to a landlord.

There is little point in a landlord carefully checking the references, etc. of a tenant to find that the tenant can then assign the tenancy to a person who would have been unacceptable to him. It is usual, therefore to find that the landlord will include a clause in the tenancy agreement expressly prohibiting assignment, etc. If the landlord has included such a provision then this will be binding on the tenant. Sometimes the landlord will not completely prohibit assignment, etc. but will state that they are only permitted with his consent. This then gives him the opportunity to 'vet' any prospective new occupants in the same way as he would check up on any prospective tenant.

There is, of course, a risk that such a 'consent' clause could be abused by a landlord and any request for consent would be arbitrarily refused, or simply ignored altogether. To counteract this, the Landlord and Tenant Act 1927, and the Landlord and Tenant Act 1988 provide that a landlord cannot unreasonably withhold his consent and must respond to a tenant's request within a reasonable period.

If there is no such express provision prohibiting assignment, etc., the Housing Act 1988 may be of some assistance to the landlord as it implies this term into the tenancy agreement. The Act only applies to periodic shortholds (including statutory periodic tenancies). Like the provisions allowing increases of rent, it does not apply to fixed-term shortholds. Thus, in the absence of an express contractual prohibition, a fixed-term tenant will be able to assign or sub-let as he chooses.

Statutory prohibition

The term implied into a periodic tenancy by the 1988 Act is that the tenant shall not without the consent of the landlord:

1 assign the tenancy; or
2 sub-let or part with possession of all or part of the property.

Note that this statutorily implied prohibition does *not* prevent the taking in of lodgers or the sharing of accommodation with someone else, for example, a cohabitant.

The rules noted above (under the Landlord and Tenant Acts of 1927 and 1988) as to a landlord not being able to withhold his consent unreasonably, do *not* apply to consents needed under this statutory rule. So a landlord can be as unreasonable as he likes in refusing consent.

As these statutory restrictions do not apply to fixed-term tenancies, this is a potential problem for landlords granting assured shortholds. Although an assured shorthold tenant has no security of tenure, any sub-tenancy granted by an assured shorthold tenant is capable of being an assured tenancy with full security of tenure that can be binding upon the head landlord. Thus the head landlord will be entitled to possession as against the assured shorthold head tenant but not as against the sub-tenant, which is hardly satisfactory from the head landlord's point of view.

In *all* cases, a landlord granting a shorthold must avoid this potential problem, by ensuring that the tenancy agreement contains an *express* provision prohibiting sub-letting. With such a provision, any sub-letting would not be binding upon the head landlord.

What happens on the death of the tenant?

Fixed-term tenancies

As already stated, a tenancy 'belongs' to the tenant. It follows that when the tenant dies, his tenancy does not die with him – it will pass on in the same way as the deceased's other property. So, on the death of one of the joint tenants, the tenancy will become the property of the survivor(s). On the death of a sole tenant, the tenancy will pass to the person nominated in his will. If the will does not give the tenancy to a particular person, it will pass with the 'residue' of the estate, i.e. it will pass to the person who is given all the remainder of the deceased's property that has not been specifically disposed of.

If the deceased dies without leaving a valid will then he is said to die 'intestate' and legal rules then decide to whom his property, including the tenancy, will pass; often this will be his spouse.

Periodic tenancies

The Housing Act 1988 contains provisions dealing specifically with the succession to a *periodic* tenancy on the death of a sole tenant, which will override these normal rules.

On the death of a sole periodic tenant, the tenancy will pass to the tenant's spouse, notwithstanding the terms of the deceased's will. For this to happen, the spouse must have been occupying the dwellinghouse as his or her only or principal home immediately prior to the death.

'Spouse' is defined by the courts to include a person who was living with the tenant as his or her wife or husband even though they were not actually married. It will also include an established same-sex partner.

These succession rights will not apply if the deceased tenant was himself a 'successor', as defined, i.e. the tenancy became vested in him:

1 by virtue of this provision; or
2 under the will or intestacy of a former tenant; or
3 he is the sole survivor of joint tenants; or
4 he succeeded to the tenancy under the provisions of Rent Act 1977 (*see* page 231).

Thus only one statutory succession is possible. If X is tenant and dies, and then Y succeeds to the tenancy under this provision, there can be no further passing on of the tenancy under the Act, even if Y remarries and was living in the house with her spouse.

If there is no statutory succession because, for example, there is no qualifying 'spouse', or there has already been a succession, or the tenancy is for a fixed term, the tenancy will then pass under the will or intestacy of the deceased as set out above.

What is my position if I am a sub-tenant?

A sub-tenancy occurs when the person granting the lease is himself merely a tenant of the property. The law recognizes that a tenant can himself grant a lease giving the right to the exclusive possession of the property to someone else – known as a sub-tenant. The only restriction is that this sub-lease must be for a shorter duration than the unexpired length of the landlord's own lease. So a tenant with two years unexpired of his lease could grant a sub-lease for any period not exceeding one year and 364 days. The tenant would continue paying his rent to his landlord in the normal way, but would himself receive rent from the sub-tenant. This might be a sensible arrangement if the rent being paid by the sub-tenant was more than the rent due from the tenant to his landlord. A tenant can also sub-let part of the property to gain extra income while still living in the rest of the house himself.

As between any particular landlord and tenant, it is irrelevant whether the landlord owns the freehold interest in the property or is himself merely a tenant. If the conditions are complied with for the creation of a shorthold tenancy, then the sub-tenant, as against his own landlord, will have a shorthold. This will be the case even if the lease under which his landlord owns the property ('the head lease') prohibits sub-letting (*see* above).

The problem is that this sub-tenant may not always have any rights as against the head landlord. Thus, although the sub-tenant's own landlord will not be able to evict him until the end of any fixed term and then only by following the correct shorthold procedure, it may be that the head landlord will be able to obtain possession against him immediately.

The determining factor is whether the head lease prohibits the granting of sub-leases or not. If it does, either expressly or impliedly (*see* above), then the sub-tenant will have no protection as against the head landlord once the head lease has been brought to an end. Once the head lease has been brought to an end the head landlord will have an immediate right to possession without the need to prove any reasons or grounds for possession or serve the normal two months notice, or wait until the end of any fixed term. The head landlord, however, cannot evict the sub-tenant without obtaining a court order, although this will be available as a matter of right.

If the sub-tenancy was not prohibited by the terms of the head lease, the sub-tenant will have a shorthold binding both against his own landlord and any head landlord, irrespective of whether the head lease comes to an end or not.

What is my position if my landlord lives in another part of the same building?

This situation is often referred to as the 'resident landlord exception'. As stated above, most lettings by resident landlords that would otherwise fall within the definition of an assured or a shorthold tenancy will be excluded from the definition by virtue of this exception. Such lettings will thus have no security of tenure, and may also have only limited protection under the protection from eviction legislation (*see* Chapter 21).

For the resident landlord exception to apply various conditions must be fulfilled and these will be set out in detail shortly. As all lettings on and from 28 February 1997 will be shortholds, and as shortholds have no security of tenure anyway, the main significance of the resident landlord exception will be for tenants whose tenancies were entered into prior to 28 February 1997.

In the case of lettings on and after 28 February 1997, the effect of the resident landlord exception is that:

- the tenant has no right to refer the rent to the Rent Assessment Committee;
- the tenant is not entitled to the minimum two months' notice required to terminate a shorthold;
- the tenant does not have protection under all the protection from eviction legislation (*see* Chapter 21);
- the statutory succession provisions do not apply;
- the statutory rules on increasing the rent and not assigning will not apply.

What conditions must be complied with for the resident landlord exception to apply?

For the letting to be excluded from the definition of an assured or a shorthold tenancy *all* of the following conditions must be complied with:

1 the dwellinghouse which is let must form only part of a building; and
2 the building must not be a purpose-built block of flats; and
3 the tenancy was granted by an individual (i.e. *not* a limited company) who at the time of the grant occupied another part of the same building as his only or principal home; and
4 at all times since the tenancy was granted the interest of the landlord has continued to belong to an individual who continued so to reside.

The resident landlord exception thus covers the situation where the tenant lives in one part of a building and the landlord lives in another part of the same building, provided that the building is not a purpose-built block

of flats. So, if a landlord lives in a large house and lets part of it, or converts a house into several flats, lives in one and lets the others, the lettings will be outside the definition of an assured or a shorthold tenancy.

However, if the 'building' was constructed in flats (as opposed to being converted into flats) the lettings will be capable of being assured tenancies or shortholds even if the landlord lives in one of the flats himself.

Is it enough for the landlord to be resident just at the start of the letting?

It is not sufficient for the landlord merely to have been in residence at the commencement of the tenancy; he must be in occupation throughout the tenancy. If the position of landlord is held by two or more individuals, only one of those persons need be in residence at any one time.

Note that periods of absence by the landlord, while on holiday or in hospital for example, will not end his residence. Also, although on a change of landlord, the new landlord must take up residence for the exception to apply, certain periods of absence on a change of ownership or on the death of the landlord will not have the effect of ending the exemption from security of tenure.

What if my landlord moves in after the grant of the tenancy?

The landlord must be resident at the start of the tenancy. If he is not, then the exception will not apply, even if he moves in at a later date and is still in residence when possession is being sought. Further, if a tenant has an assured tenancy, i.e. there is no resident landlord, and the landlord then moves in and grants him a further tenancy, this second tenancy will *not* be subject to the resident landlord exception even though the landlord was in residence at the start of the tenancy and remains so throughout the letting. This is an anti-avoidance provision designed to ensure that a landlord does not deprive existing tenants of their protection as assured tenants by moving in and then granting a new tenancy to the existing tenants.

What happens when a shorthold expires?

When a fixed-term shorthold (e.g. one for six months) ends, the tenant is allowed to remain in possession as a statutory periodic tenant. Alternatively, the parties may agree on the grant of a new tenancy – probably at a higher rent. However, whether there is a new tenancy or not, the tenant still has no security of tenure. That means that the court must still make an order for possession if the landlord follows the correct procedure. This involves the service on the tenant of not less than two months' notice stating that the landlord requires possession (*see* below).

In the case of a shorthold which is a periodic tenancy, this can only be brought to an end if the landlord obtains a court order for possession and this will again require the service of not less than two months' notice.

How does the tenant terminate the tenancy?

It is not always appreciated by tenants that a tenancy is a contract and places obligations on them as well as on the landlord. So if a tenant enters into a 12-month fixed-term, he cannot terminate the letting before the end of those 12 months without the landlord's consent. If he does attempt to terminate it before the end of the period without consent – by just leaving, or sending the keys back to the landlord – the landlord is entitled to claim the full amount of rent from him until the end of the fixed period.

In the case of a periodic tenancy, the tenant can only terminate it, unless the landlord agrees otherwise, by serving notice on the landlord in writing. This must be one month's notice in the case of a monthly tenancy and four weeks' notice in the case of a weekly tenancy. As well as being the correct length, the notice must also expire at the end of a completed period of the tenancy. This is sometimes referred to as the 'corresponding day rule', as the notice always has to expire on the same day of the week or month. This means, for example, that for a weekly tenancy beginning on a Monday, the notice must expire on a Sunday (technically, the tenancy ends at midnight on the Sunday, so a notice terminating on a Monday would also be acceptable). For a monthly tenancy commencing on the 23rd day of a month, the notice must expire on the 22nd day of a subsequent month, although the 23rd day would also be acceptable. But, in either case, no other day or date will be acceptable.

How does the landlord obtain possession?

The court must order possession on or after the coming to an end of a shorthold, provided that the landlord follows the correct procedure. This involves the landlord serving a notice on the tenant (the 'Section 21 notice') giving the tenant at least two months' notice that he requires possession. However, in the case of both fixed-term and periodic shortholds, the court cannot order the tenant to give up possession before six months have passed since the grant of the tenancy. This is so even if the fixed-term letting was for a shorter period, for example, three months. Further, if the tenancy is a fixed term then the notice cannot expire before the end of the fixed term.

The Housing Act does not specify a 'prescribed' form of notice but it must be in writing and it must require possession to be given up after a specified date which must be at least two months after the notice has been served on the tenant.

Note that:

- the two-month period is the minimum – longer notice can be served if desired;
- the two-month period runs from the date the notice is given to ('served on') the tenant and not from the date that it is signed. Service is best effected by handing it personally to the tenant, as there can then be no dispute that it has been received;
- if the tenancy is a periodic tenancy, or the fixed term has expired before the notice is served, then the date after which possession is required must be the last day of a rental period. So, if the tenancy is a monthly tenancy and the rent day is the 15th of the month, the date specified must be the 14th of a subsequent month at least two months after the date of service.

Commencing court proceedings

If the tenant does not leave voluntarily, then the landlord must obtain a court order to evict him. Provided the landlord has followed the correct procedure (e.g. the Section 21 notice was correctly served), the court must order possession to be given within 14 days of the making of the court order – or within 42 days in cases of exceptional hardship. There is a special *accelerated possession procedure* available in the county court for the area where the property is situated. This is designed to ensure that the order can be obtained without any undue delay. The forms for the procedure and an explanatory leaflet on completing them can be obtained from the county court.

Landlord's duty to provide a statement of the terms of the tenancy

It is always best to have a written tenancy agreement setting out all of the terms relating to the letting. Many tenancies are still granted orally and this can often lead to a dispute between landlord and tenant as to what exactly was agreed between them.

The Housing Act 1996 places an obligation on a landlord of a new shorthold tenancy to provide the tenant with details of some of the more important terms of the tenancy. The tenant must make a request in writing and the landlord must provide details of the following terms:

- the commencement date of the tenancy;
- the rent payable and the dates on which it is payable;
- any terms providing for rent review;
- the length of a fixed-term tenancy.

It is a criminal offence to fail to provide the information within 28 days, unless the landlord has a reasonable excuse. For example, if the landlord was away on holiday when the request was served, this might amount to a reasonable excuse.

This right only exists where the terms are not already evidenced in writing. So the provision only relates to oral tenancies, or those in writing which do not contain any reference to one or more of the specified matters.

Old shortholds: lettings made before 28 February 1997

The requirements for an old shorthold start off as being identical to those for a new shorthold, i.e. there must be a tenancy of a house as a separate dwelling, etc. All the qualifying conditions that apply to new shortholds must be complied with. *In addition*, however, there were other conditions that had to be complied with:

- the letting had to be for a *fixed* term (i.e. not a periodic tenancy), of at least six months in length (note: for new shortholds, any kind of letting is permitted);
- there had to be no provision in the agreement allowing the landlord to terminate the tenancy during the first six months; and
- before the grant of the tenancy, the landlord had to serve a notice on the tenant, in the form laid down by Parliament. This notice warned the tenant that he would have no security of tenure if he entered into the letting.

If these extra conditions were not complied with, then the letting would not be a shorthold but an ordinary assured tenancy. This would give the tenant full security of tenure. He would, however, have no right to refer the rent to the Rent Assessment Committee.

The other significant difference between new and old shortholds is that, under an old shorthold, the tenant could refer the rent to the Rent Assessment Committee at any time during the letting but a tenant under a new shorthold can only make such a reference during the first six months.

ASSURED TENANCIES WHICH ARE NOT SHORTHOLDS

Introduction

As previously stated, the Housing Act 1988, which applies to lettings entered into on or after 15 January 1989, invented two new types of tenancy: the assured shorthold tenancy, which we have just looked at, and the 'ordinary' assured tenancy.

Lettings entered into on or after 15 January 1989 but *prior* to 28 February 1997, would be assured tenancies *unless* the requirements for an 'old' shorthold were complied with (*see* above). Lettings entered into on or after 28 February 1997 would be shortholds unless a notice was served by the landlord stating that it was to be an ordinary assured tenancy.

So ordinary assured tenancies can arise in these two different circumstances, but the rights given to tenants will be the same in both cases.

If an assured tenancy has been created, then the 1988 Act gives to the tenant several rights over and above any agreed to by the landlord. In particular the tenant is given 'security of tenure'. This means that at the end of the tenancy the tenant does not have to move out of the property; he has a legally enforceable right to stay in possession.

The landlord can only require him or her to leave if he can establish a valid reason as to why he wishes to obtain possession. The only valid reasons for requiring possession are those set out in the Act. They are known as 'grounds for possession' and include situations where the tenant has not been paying the rent regularly or the landlord wishes to occupy the house himself.

Some of the grounds for possession are known as 'mandatory grounds'. With these, on proof of the ground, the landlord has an absolute right to possession.

The others are 'discretionary grounds'. In the case of these grounds the landlord will only be entitled to possession if, in addition to the ground, he can also establish that it is reasonable for him to insist on possession.

Merely having a ground for possession is not sufficient: with both mandatory and discretionary grounds, the landlord still has to apply to court, following the correct procedure, for a court order before he can actually obtain possession.

Definition of an assured tenancy

The conditions which must be met before a tenancy will qualify as an assured tenancy were set out above when we were looking at shortholds (*see* page 218). There must be a letting of a house which is let as a 'separate dwelling' and all of the following requirements must be met:

1 the tenant or each of joint tenants is an individual; and
2 the tenant or at least one of the joint tenants occupies the dwellinghouse as his only or principal home; and
3 the tenancy is not specifically excluded by other provisions of the Act.

Just as these requirements are identical to those for shortholds, the exceptions set out there are also identical. All lettings complying with these conditions entered into on or after 15 January 1989 and before 28 February 1997 will be ordinary assured tenancies unless the relevant conditions for an old shorthold were complied with.

Assured tenancies today

In the case of lettings on or after 28 February 1997, even though the above conditions are complied with, the letting will be a shorthold, *unless* the landlord serves a notice on the tenant that the letting is to be an ordinary assured tenancy. This notice can be served before or after the tenancy has been entered into or can be included in the tenancy agreement itself. There is no prescribed form laid down for this notice; any form of words will be sufficient as long as it is clear that the letting is intended to be an ordinary assured tenancy. Nowadays, most landlords let on shortholds to prevent their tenants enjoying security of tenure.

What security of tenure does an assured tenant have?

An assured tenancy can only be brought to an end by the landlord obtaining a court order for possession. Thus, in the case of a periodic assured tenancy, a notice to quit is of no effect. If a fixed-term assured tenancy is brought to an end otherwise than by a court order or by surrender, the tenant is entitled to remain in possession as a statutory periodic tenant.

'Surrender' consists of an agreement between landlord and tenant that the tenancy should come to an end and the tenant will leave the property. Note: the tenant can in no way be required by his landlord to enter into this kind of agreement and that any agreement to terminate, etc. contained in the tenancy agreement itself will be ineffective.

The statutory periodic tenancy will be on the same terms as the previous fixed-term tenancy (although there is a little-used procedure for changing those terms under the Housing Act 1988 Section 6).

How can landlords obtain a court order?

The landlord can obtain a court order for possession only if he follows the correct procedure and can establish one or more of the grounds for possession set out in the Housing Act 1988. Although some of these grounds are mandatory grounds (i.e. the court must order possession if the ground is established), many of them are discretionary grounds. On proof of the discretionary ground, the court will order possession only if it considers it reasonable to do so.

The procedure for obtaining possession involves the landlord serving a notice on the tenant (a 'Section 8 notice'), in the prescribed form. The Section 8 notice must specify the ground(s) upon which the landlord intends to rely and must give at least two weeks' notice of the landlord's intention to commence possession proceedings. (Sometimes two months' notice has to be given, depending upon the ground being used; *see* below.)

The proceedings must then be commenced not earlier than the date specified and not later than 12 months from the date of service of the notice.

It is possible for the court to dispense with the requirement for a Section 8 notice (unless Ground 8 is being relied upon), but only if it considers it 'just and equitable' to do so.

Note: in most cases it is not possible for the landlord to obtain possession during the continuance of a fixed-term tenancy. So if the landlord grants a tenancy for a fixed term of two years, and after three months the landlord wishes to obtain possession, this will normally not be possible even if he can establish one of the grounds laid down by the Act. The landlord will be bound to wait until the end of the two-year term he granted to the tenant. However, some of the grounds can be used to obtain possession before the end of the fixed term unless the tenancy agreement contains a term allowing the landlord to repossess before the end of the fixed term.

What are the grounds for possession?

Mandatory grounds

Grounds 1 to 8 are the 'mandatory grounds'. On proof of one of these grounds the landlord will be automatically entitled to an order for possession. Most of the mandatory grounds require the landlord to have served a notice on the tenant at the start of the tenancy warning that the ground might be used against him.

Assured shorthold grounds

Schedule 2 Housing Act 1988 sets out the statutory grounds on which a landlord can recover possession of an assured shorthold. The table below sets out which are mandatory and those which are discretionary, and how much notice is needed for each.

Ground 1: landlord is owner-occupier or requires property for his/her own occupation
The following conditions must be satisfied.
(**a**) *Prior notice.* On or before granting the tenancy, the tenant must have been given written notice that possession might be required on this ground. If this notice was not given, the landlord cannot use Ground 1, unless the court is of the opinion that it is just and equitable (i.e. fair) to dispense with the notice. For example, if the tenant was told that the landlord previously occupied the property, but the landlord failed to give a *written* notice, the court might dispense with the requirements of a written notice.
(**b**) *Prior residence.* Prior to the tenancy, the landlord (or

		Mandatory	Discretionary	2 weeks' notice	2 months' notice	No notice period
1	L's main or only home now required by L or spouse	✓			✓	
2	Mortgagee wants to sell	✓			✓	
3	Holiday let	✓		✓		
4	Student letting	✓		✓		
5	Minister of religion's accommodation	✓			✓	
6	L intends to substantially redevelop	✓			✓	
7	T has died (and no one can succeed)	✓			✓	
8	T owed 2 months' rent (monthly) or 8 weeks' rent (weekly)	✓		✓		
9	Suitable alternative accommodation available		✓		✓	
10	Rent arrears		✓	✓		
11	T persistently late with rent		✓	✓		
12	T broken other non-rent obligation		✓	✓		
13	Condition deteriorated		✓	✓		
14	Resident caused nuisance etc		✓			✓
14A	Domestic violence caused partner to leave house		✓	✓		
15	Furniture condition worsened		✓	✓		
16	Ex-employee of L		✓		✓	
17	False statement by T		✓	✓		

L: landlord
T: tenant

one of them if there is more than one landlord) must have occupied the property as his or her only or principal home. In other words, the landlord must have previously been an owner-occupier. If this is not so, *see* 'No prior residence'.

(c) *No prior residence.* If the landlord did not personally occupy the property prior to the tenancy, the landlord must show that he or she now requires possession for himself or herself, or for his or her spouse, as his or her only or principal home. Ground 1 is not, however, available if the landlord bought the property during the currency of the existing tenancy. This is to stop landlords buying up rented property cheaply and then seeking to get possession on the basis that they want it for themselves.

(d) The Section 8 notice must give two months' notice before proceedings can be commenced.

Ground 2: landlord's mortgage lender requiring possession in order to sell with vacant possession
The following conditions must be satisfied:

(a) *Existing mortgage.* The house must have been mortgaged to the lender *before* the tenancy was granted. If the mortgage was taken out after the tenancy was granted, Ground 2 is not available.

(b) *Lender selling.* The lender/mortgage company must show that it is entitled to sell the property. This normally means that the landlord/borrower has defaulted in his/her mortgage payments or his/her obligations under the mortgage deed.

(c) *Prior notice.* On or before the date of the tenancy the tenant must have been given notice under Ground 1 or, if no such notice was given in writing, the court must be satisfied that it is just and equitable (i.e. fair) to dispense with that notice.

This ground can be used in the case of a fixed-term tenancy which has not yet expired, provided the tenancy agreement contains an appropriate clause stating that the ground can be so used.

Two months' notice of proceedings is required for this ground.

Ground 3: out-of-season holiday accommodation (winter lets)
The following conditions must be satisfied.

(a) *Prior notice.* On or before the date of tenancy the landlord gave a written notice that possession might be recovered on Ground 3.

(b) *Fixed term.* The tenancy must be for a fixed term of not more than eight months.

(c) *Previous occupation for holiday purposes.* During the 12 months prior to the tenancy, the property must have been occupied for holiday purposes.

Ground 4: out-of-term student accommodation

If the property belongs to a university, polytechnic or college, and in the last 12 months the property was occupied by their students, the landlord is entitled to possession if the landlord gave notice, on or before the date of the tenancy, that possession might be required on this ground.

Ground 5: minister of religion's house

If, on or before the date of the tenancy, the landlord gave written notice that possession might be recovered on Ground 5 and the court is satisfied that the house is now required for occupation by a minister as a residence, the court must make a possession order.

Two months' notice of proceedings is required for this ground.

Ground 6: demolition or reconstruction

The following conditions must be satisfied.

(a) The landlord intends to demolish or reconstruct the entire property or a substantial part of it or to carry out extensive works.

(b) The intended work cannot reasonably be carried out while the tenant is still living there or the tenant will not allow the landlord access to carry out the work or is not willing to accept a tenancy of a part of the property not affected by the work.

(c) The landlord did not *buy* the property subject to the tenancy. In other words, only the original landlord (or someone who inherited on the landlord's death or acquired the property as a gift) can use this ground.

If the landlord succeeds on this ground, he is required to pay the tenant's removal expenses.

Two months' notice of proceedings is required for this ground.

Ground 7: death of a periodic tenant

If the tenancy is periodic (as opposed to a fixed-term lease) and the tenant dies without leaving a resident 'spouse' (as defined by the Act) living in the home, the landlord can seek possession within 12 months of the tenant's death. (For details of what will happen if the tenant is survived by a resident spouse, *see* page 223.)

Ground 8: two months' or eight weeks' rent arrears

If the tenant is at least two months (if the rent is payable monthly) or eight weeks (if the rent is payable weekly or fortnightly) in arrears with rent when the landlord serves notice that he intends to bring proceedings (*see* page 227) and that amount of arrears still exists at the date of the hearing, the landlord is entitled to possession *as of right*.

The rent must be 'lawfully due'. If the tenant has a valid claim against the landlord for lack of repair (*see* Chapter 22), this may have the effect of reducing the arrears to less than the amount specified in the ground. It is only if two months'/eight weeks' rent is lawfully due at the date of the hearing that the court can grant possession under this ground. So if the tenant can reduce the amount due by making a partial payment prior to the hearing, then the ground will fail.

A further point which the tenant will need to check is whether or not the landlord has served a notice in writing giving the tenant an address at which documents, etc., can be served on the landlord. This is required by the Landlord and Tenant Act 1987 Section 48.

If no such notice has been served prior to the current proceedings, the rent is not lawfully due, unless and until the landlord complies. If the landlord's address is set out in the tenancy agreement, this will be sufficient to comply with the Act. Particular attention should be paid to cases where the identity of the landlord has changed during the tenancy; the address in the tenancy agreement will no longer be accurate and a written notice of the new landlord's address will need to be served.

This ground can be used during the continuance of a fixed term, provided notice to that effect is included in the tenancy agreement.

Discretionary grounds

Unlike the previous eight grounds, the remaining grounds are discretionary. Proof of one of these grounds will not inevitably result in a possession order being made. The court will only order possession if it considers it 'reasonable to do so'. This will be a question of fact in each case, but this proviso does allow the court to take into account all the relevant factors before deciding whether or not to order possession. So, for example, the hardship that will be suffered by both the landlord and the tenant, depending upon whether an order is, or is not made, can be taken into account.

Ground 9: suitable alternative accommodation

If the tenant has been offered suitable alternative accommodation but chooses not to accept it the court may order possession against the tenant. The alternative accommodation must be similar in size, quality and proximity to the tenant's place of work and afford to the tenant similar security of tenure. The offer of alternative accommodation may come from the landlord him- or herself, from a local authority or from some other landlord. If the landlord does succeed on this ground, he must pay the tenant's reasonable removal expenses.

Two months' notice of proceedings is required if this ground is to be used.

Ground 10: rent arrears

This applies to any rent lawfully due but unpaid.

Unlike Ground 8, where the court has no discretion but to order possession, if the landlord is relying on Ground 10 the court must be satisfied that it is reasonable to order possession in the circumstances. For Ground 10 to apply, however, there must again be some rent lawfully due at the time when the landlord served notice of his/ her intention to bring proceedings and also on the day when proceedings were begun.

This ground can be used prior to the ending of a fixed-term letting, provided the tenancy agreement contains a provision permitting it.

Ground 11: persistent delay in paying rent

Even if there are no rent arrears, the fact that the tenant is persistently late with the rent payments can be a ground for possession. What amounts to 'persistent delay' is a question of fact in each case.

Like the other grounds based on rent arrears, this ground can be used during a fixed-term letting provided the tenancy agreement permits.

Ground 12: breach of other tenancy obligations

If the tenant has broken the terms of the tenancy agreement (other than failure to pay rent) the court may, if it is reasonable, grant possession on this ground.

This ground can also be used during a fixed-term letting provided that the tenancy agreement contains a provision permitting it.

Ground 13: deterioration of property through neglect or default

This ground applies if the condition of the property has deteriorated because of the neglect or default of the tenant or of any person residing with the tenant.

This ground can be used during a fixed-term letting, provided that the tenancy agreement permits it.

Ground 14: nuisance or annoyance to adjoining occupiers

This applies where the tenant or a person residing in or visiting the house has been guilty of conduct causing or likely to cause a nuisance or annoyance to any person residing, visiting or engaging in a lawful activity in the locality. It will also apply if the tenant or a person residing in or visiting the house has been convicted of using the property for illegal or immoral purposes, or of an arrestable offence in or in the locality of the house.

This ground can be used during a fixed-term letting, provided that the tenancy agreement permits it.

Ground 15: damage to furniture

This applies where the landlord's furniture has been broken or damaged by ill-treatment by the tenant or a person residing with the tenant.

This ground can be used during a fixed-term letting, provided that the tenancy agreement permits it.

Ground 16: tenant a former employee of the landlord

This applies where the property was let to the tenant while he was an employee of the landlord (or a previous landlord) and the tenant is no longer so employed.

Ground 17: false statement by tenant

This ground applies where the landlord alleges that he was induced to grant the tenancy by a false statement made knowingly or recklessly by the tenant or someone acting at his instigation.

This ground can be used during a fixed-term letting, provided that the tenancy agreement permits it.

How much rent can the landlord charge for an assured tenancy?

There is no restriction on the amount of rent that can be initially charged on the grant of an assured tenancy. The amount of the rent under an assured tenancy is a matter of agreement between landlord and tenant. 'Market forces' will thus prevail. Assured tenants do *not* have the same right as shorthold tenants to refer the rent to the Rent Assessment Committee. Once the tenant has entered into the agreement, he is stuck with the amount of rent agreed, even though he may subsequently realize that it is excessive.

If the landlord subsequently wishes to increase the rent, he may not be able to do so unless he follows the correct procedure. This is the same as set out for shorthold tenancies above.

Can the tenant transfer the tenancy or sub-let?

The position for assured tenants is the same as set out for shorthold tenants.

What happens on the death of the tenant?

Again, the position is the same as that for shorthold tenants (*see* page 223). It should be noted that on the death of a periodic assured tenant, if there is no succession under the provisions of the Act, the landlord would be able to use mandatory Ground 7 in order to obtain possession, should he wish to do so (*see* above).

What is my position if my landlord lives in another part of the same building?

The 'resident landlord exception' is also the same as for shorthold tenants (*see* page 224). It is of particular significance to an ordinary assured tenant. If the exception applies, the loss of security of tenure, which goes with his status as an assured tenant, will place him in a much worse position than a shorthold tenant who has a resident landlord.

OLD TENANCIES – THE RENT ACTS

Introduction

This section deals with pre-1989 lettings. Such lettings will fall within the protection of the Rent Act 1977. The provisions of the Rent Act are in many ways very similar to those of the Housing Act 1988, but there are also important differences in the protection given to tenants. Rent Act tenants have security of tenure very similar to that given to ordinary assured tenants, but, in addition, there is statutory control over the amount of rent the landlord can charge. This is popularly known as the 'fair rent' system. Another difference is that on the death of a Rent Act tenant, there is a wider class of members of the tenant's family who can succeed to the tenancy than for assured tenancies.

Although the Rent Act basically applies to lettings entered into prior to 15 January 1989, remember that what is relevant is the date of the *original* tenancy between the parties. So, if the first tenancy was entered into in 1988 and this has been renewed on various occasions since then, each of the lettings will be a Rent Act tenancy, even if entered into this year. This will be so whether or not the tenancy is of the same premises. So, if you had a tenancy of 1 Coronation Street, and the landlord then grants you a new tenancy of 8 Coronation Street, that new letting will still be a Rent Act tenancy, even though it was entered into recently. For this rule to apply, however, there has to be no gap between the end of the original Rent Act tenancy and the grant of the new one; if there is, then the new tenancy will be governed by the Housing Act 1988 in the usual way.

There are, therefore, still many thousands of Rent Act tenancies in existence today, although their numbers are likely to decline as the years go by and tenants leave.

Protected tenancies

Protection under the Rent Act is given to 'protected tenancies' and 'statutory tenancies', which must be considered separately.

There will be a protected tenancy where a dwellinghouse was 'let as a separate dwelling'. (Please see the discussion of the similarly worded requirement for an assured tenancy under the Housing Act 1988 at page 218 above.)

Note: unlike the position under the Housing Act, there is no need for the letting to be to an individual, nor does the house need to be the tenant's only or principal home. Thus, a letting to a limited company, or a letting of a 'second home', can be a protected tenancy.

There are various exceptions which are generally very similar to those for assured tenancies, for example, lettings by resident landlords, holiday lettings, tenancies at a low rent.

Protected tenancies can be either periodic tenancies or for a fixed term, and there are no maximum or minimum periods. They have rent control and succession rights, but not necessarily security of tenure. To have security of tenure, a Rent Act tenant must qualify as a 'statutory tenant' on the ending of the protected tenancy.

Statutory tenancies

This is the device by which security of tenure is given. If the landlord terminates the protected tenancy the tenant will be allowed to remain in possession only if a statutory tenancy then arises. The tenant will become a statutory tenant only *'if and so long as he occupies the dwellinghouse as his residence'*.

So, although occupation as a residence is not necessary for the letting to qualify as a protected tenancy, it is necessary for the tenant to be given security of tenure. While he satisfies this definition of a statutory tenant, the tenant continues to have the benefit of rent control and succession rights, and will also have security of tenure, i.e. he can only be evicted if the landlord goes to court and establishes one of the grounds for possession laid down by the Rent Act.

Only an individual can occupy as a residence. A company tenant can be a protected tenant but not a statutory tenant; this is so even if one of the directors or employees of the company is living in the property.

As a statutory tenancy only arises on the ending of a protected tenancy, it does mean that in order to obtain possession against a protected tenant, a landlord must first of all terminate that protected tenancy, for example, by serving notice to quit in the case of a periodic tenancy. If the tenant does not qualify as a statutory tenant, for example, in the case of a company tenant, the landlord will be immediately entitled to a court order for possession. If a statutory tenancy does arise, the landlord will only be entitled to possession if he goes to court and can establish one (or more) of the grounds for possession laid down. As with assured tenancies, some of these are mandatory and so the court must order possession on proof of the ground, but many are discretionary and the court can only order possession if it considers it reasonable to do so. Many of the assured tenancy grounds for possession were based on Rent Act grounds and reference should be made to the equivalent assured tenancy ground where relevant. The Rent Act 1977 grounds are called 'Cases'.

Discretionary grounds for possession

Case 1

Where any rent lawfully due from the tenant has not been paid, or any obligation of the protected or statutory tenancy . . . has been broken or not performed.

This Case should be compared with Grounds 8, 10, 11 and 12 for assured tenancies. Note, in particular, that non-payment of rent is only a discretionary ground, no matter how great the amount of the arrears.

Case 2

Where the tenant or any person residing or lodging with him or any sub-tenant of his has been guilty of conduct which is a nuisance or annoyance to adjoining occupiers, or has been convicted of using the dwellinghouse or allowing the dwellinghouse to be used for immoral or illegal purposes.

This Case is similar to assured tenancy Ground 14, but is far less wide-ranging in its application.

Case 3

Where the condition of the dwellinghouse has, in the opinion of the court, deteriorated owing to acts of waste by, or the neglect or default of, the tenant or any person residing or lodging with him.

This Case is virtually the same as assured tenancy Ground 13.

Case 4

Where the condition of any furniture provided for use under the tenancy has, in the opinion of the court, deteriorated owing to ill-treatment by the tenant or any person residing or lodging with him or any sub-tenant of his.

This Case is identical to assured tenancy Ground 15.

Case 5

Where the tenant has given notice to quit and, in consequence of that notice, the landlord has contracted to sell or let the dwellinghouse or has taken any other steps as the result of which he would, in the opinion of the court, be seriously prejudiced if he could not obtain possession.

This Case has no equivalent under assured tenancies. The rationale for the availability of this ground to Rent Act tenancies is that a statutory tenancy, with security of tenure, arises on the ending of the protected tenancy no matter how it may have ended. So, on a tenant himself

giving notice to quit, a statutory tenancy will still arise and the landlord will not be entitled to possession unless he can prove one of the grounds laid down by the Act. This could place him in difficulty if, thinking that the tenant is about to vacate the property, he enters into a contract to sell with vacant possession or let the house to another tenant. If it was not for the existence of this Case, the landlord would have no right to possession if the tenant should subsequently change his mind and decide not to vacate after all.

Case 6

Where, without the consent of the landlord, the tenant has . . . assigned or sublet the whole of the dwellinghouse . . .

This Case will apply whether or not there is any express prohibition on assignment (i.e. transferring the tenancy) in the tenancy agreement.

Note that the ground will not apply to a sub-letting of only part of the house, or where the tenant takes in a lodger. However, if this were prohibited by the terms of the tenancy agreement, then the tenant would be liable to an order being obtained under Case 1.

Case 7

This has now been repealed and is thus no longer applicable.

Case 8

Where the dwellinghouse is reasonably required by the landlord for occupation as a residence for some person engaged in his whole-time employment, and the tenant was in the employment of the landlord or a former landlord, and the dwellinghouse was let to him in consequence of that employment and he has ceased to be in that employment.

This Case is similar to assured tenancy Ground 16.

Case 9

Where the dwellinghouse is reasonably required by the landlord for occupation as a residence for:
(**a**) himself, or
(**b**) any son or daughter of his over 18 years of age, or
(**c**) his father or mother, or
(**d**) the father or mother of his wife or husband,
and the landlord did not become landlord by purchasing the dwellinghouse or any interest therein . . .

It should also be noted that a court cannot order possession under this Case if, having regard to all the circumstances, it is satisfied that greater hardship would be caused by granting the order than by refusing to grant it. Obviously, the question of hardship will depend upon the facts of each particular case, but factors such as the availability of alternative accommodation to the respective parties and their respective financial circumstances will be relevant to this.

This Case will be available to a landlord whether or not he has resided in the property prior to the letting and there is no need for any warning notice to have been served on the tenant prior to the letting (cf. Case 11 and assured tenancy Ground 1).

This ground will not apply if the landlord became landlord by purchasing the property. This means that a landlord who buys a house with a sitting tenant will not be able to use this ground.

The landlord recovered possession of the Rent Act property by falsely claiming that she intended to live in the property. Held: The landlord had misrepresented her intentions. The court awarded the ex-tenant £30,000 damages. The case serves as a warning to those landlords who might be tempted to abuse the owner-occupier recovery provisions.

Clemens *v* Simmonds (2002)

Case 10

This allows possession to be claimed if the tenant has sublet part of the house at a rent greater than legally permitted. This ties in with the fair rent system, which fixes the maximum rent which can lawfully be charged on a Rent Act letting. It is little used.

Suitable alternative accommodation

Although not allocated a Case number, the Rent Act 1977 also allows the court to order possession on this ground but, again, only if it considers it reasonable to do so. As to what amounts to 'suitable alternative accommodation', *see* the discussion on assured tenancy Ground 9.

Mandatory grounds for possession

If the landlord can establish one of these *mandatory* grounds, then the court has no discretion and must order possession, regardless of whether it is reasonable to do so or whether any hardship will be caused to the tenant.

Case 11

Where a person who occupied the dwellinghouse as his residence [in this Case referred to as 'the owner-occupier'] let it . . . and

(a) not later than [the date of the commencement of the tenancy] the landlord gave notice in writing to the tenant that possession might be recovered under this Case, and

(b) the dwellinghouse has not . . . been let by the owner-occupier on a protected tenancy with respect to which the condition mentioned in paragraph (a) above was not satisfied, and

(c) the court is of the opinion that . . .

One of the following conditions is satisfied:

(i) the dwellinghouse is required as a residence for the owner or any member of his family who resided with the owner when he last occupied the dwellinghouse as a residence; or

(ii) the owner has died and the dwellinghouse is required as a residence for a member of his family who was residing with him at the time of his death; or

(iii) the owner has died and the dwellinghouse is required by a successor in title as his residence or for the purpose of disposing of it with vacant possession; or

(iv) the dwellinghouse is subject to a mortgage, granted before the tenancy, and the mortgage lender is entitled to exercise a power of sale and requires possession of the dwellinghouse for the purpose of disposing of it with vacant possession; or

(v) the dwellinghouse is not reasonably suited to the needs of the owner, having regard to his place of work, and he requires it for the purpose of disposing of it with vacant possession so that he use the proceeds to purchase another house as his residence which would be more suited to his needs.

This Case must be distinguished from the superficially similar Case 9. Unlike Case 9, it is dependent upon the service of a warning notice prior to the letting and the landlord must have resided in the house at some time prior to the letting. There is no requirement for this written notice to be in any particular form. If the court is of the opinion that it is just and equitable to make an order for possession, it has the power to dispense with the notice requirement. This might be the case, for example, where a landlord made it clear to a tenant before the letting that the house was his home and that he might want it back at some future date, but did not actually put this in writing.

The basic ground is that the landlord requires possession from the tenant so that the house can be used as a residence for himself or a member of his family. Note that in the case of a family member, he must have lived in the house with the landlord when he resided in the property, otherwise the ground will not be established.

This Case also deals with the possibility that possession might be required after the death of the owner, either for sale or as a residence. Possession is also recoverable to enable a sale with vacant possession to take place either by a mortgage lender or if the landlord has changed his place of work.

Case 12

This allows possession to be claimed by a landlord who has purchased a house as a prospective retirement home, but lets it in the meantime. There is no need for prior residence (cf. Case 11), but the availability of the Case is again dependent upon a warning notice having been given no later than the commencement of the tenancy.

This notice can, however, be dispensed with in the same circumstances as in Case 11. The landlord will then

be entitled to possession on retirement or in the circumstances set out in paragraphs (ii) to (iv) of Case 11.

Case 13

This Case is virtually identical to assured tenancy Ground
3 (i.e. lettings of holiday accommodation out of season)
and requires the giving of a warning notice prior to the
letting.

Case 14

This Case is relevant to lettings of student accommodation by specified educational institutions. It is almost
identical with assured tenancy Ground 4, and is again
dependent upon the giving of a warning notice prior to
the letting.

Case 15

This Case involves the letting of houses kept for occupation by ministers of religion and is identical with assured
tenancy Ground 5.

Cases 16, 17 and 18

These Cases relate to lettings of farm houses and lettings
of houses to persons employed in agriculture and the
house is required for occupation by a new employee.

Case 19

This is the Case that gave the landlord of a protected
shorthold tenancy a mandatory right to possession. Protected shorthold tenancies were the forerunners of the
present-day assured shorthold tenancies and are now
obsolete. Any new letting on or after 18 January 1989 to a
protected shorthold tenant would be an assured
shorthold.

Case 20

This Case allows members of the armed forces who
acquired houses during their service and let them in the
meantime, to obtain possession in similar circumstances
to owner-occupiers under Case 11.

The fair rent system

What is it?

Both protected and statutory tenancies are subject to
control as to the amount of rent that the landlord can
charge for the property. The Rent Act 1977 set up a register
of 'fair rents' for dwellinghouses. Once a rent has been
registered in relation to a property then that becomes
the maximum chargeable under any present or future
protected or statutory tenancy of that property. The existence of a registered fair rent does not limit the amount
of rent chargeable under an assured or assured shorthold
tenancy.

The rent is assessed by a rent officer, a local authority
official, in accordance with criteria laid down by the Act.
The criteria are designed to exclude any scarcity element
from the calculation of the rent. Under normal market
forces, the rules of supply and demand, a high demand
for rented property and a small supply would tend to
push up the price, i.e. the amount of the rent. For many
years there was a scarcity of accommodation to let which
tended to push up the amount of rent chargeable beyond
the means of many people. By requiring the rent officer
to assume that there is no shortage of accommodation to
let (even though there might be) the assessed rent is often
considerably lower than it otherwise would be.

The existence of the fair rent system is a valuable asset
for Rent Act tenants, but is viewed less favourably by
landlords who consider that it prevents them from receiving an adequate return on their investment. In recent
years there has not been a shortage of accommodation to
let in many parts of the country and fair rent levels are
being set at, or very nearly at, the ordinary open market
rental levels.

Applying for a fair rent

The tenant can apply for a fair rent at any time during
the continuance of the tenancy. The fair rent then
becomes the maximum payable, despite the existence of
a higher agreed figure in the tenancy agreement. Further,
the fair rent cannot then be exceeded in any new letting
of the house, whether to the same or a different tenant.
The only way in which the landlord can increase the rent
is by applying himself to the rent officer for the assessment
of a higher fair rent. He cannot make such an application
within two years of an earlier fair rent having been
assessed.

By an order made in 1999, the government has limited
the amount by which a fair rent can be increased to the
increase in the Retail Price Index plus either 5 per cent or
7.5 per cent, depending on the circumstances.

What if I have been paying too much rent?

Any rent over and above the amount permitted by the
Rent Act under the above provisions is 'irrecoverable' by
the landlord. This means that the tenant does not have
to pay it and the landlord cannot bring court proceedings
to claim it or bring possession proceedings based on
non-payment. Any sums already paid can be recovered
from the landlord by the tenant but only for a maximum
period of two years.

Succession to Rent Act tenancies

On the death of a statutory or protected tenant, that
person's spouse (or a person living with the tenant as
husband or wife) will become the statutory tenant of the

house and thus entitled to all the benefits of security of tenure and rent control.

In the past, the courts interpreted the requirement that a person not actually married to the tenant must have been living as 'husband or wife' as meaning that the successor must be of the opposite sex to the tenant. A cohabitant of the same sex was not entitled to succeed to the tenancy. Previously, a gay partner could only be a successor to an assured tenancy as a member of the deceased tenant's family (*see* below). That distinction has now been abolished, as being in breach of the Human Rights Act 1998.

If there is no surviving spouse (or person who lived with the tenant as husband or wife), then for deaths occurring prior to 15 January 1989, any member of the deceased's family who had lived with him at the time of death and for at least six months prior to death would have become statutory tenant. For deaths taking place on or after 15 January 1989, for a family member to succeed he needs to have been living with the deceased for at least two years prior to death.

In the case of such deaths the family member will only become entitled to an assured tenancy and *not* a statutory tenancy. The main effect of this is that, although the tenancy will still have wide-ranging security of tenure, it will lose the benefit of the fair rent system.

In the case of deaths prior to 15 January 1989, two successions were permitted, i.e. on the death of the 'first successor' a second 'transmission' would take place in favour of the first successor's spouse or family member, the same succession rules applying. In the case of the death of a first successor after 15 January 1989, a second transmission is only possible in very limited circumstances. A person is entitled to a second succession only if they were *both* a member of the original tenant's family *and* a member of the first successor's family, *and also* if they had resided with the first successor for at least two years prior to the first successor's death.

Note that there is no requirement for this second successor to have lived with the original tenant at all; it is sufficient if he is a member of the original tenant's family, although often, of course, he will have resided with the original tenant.

This complicated formula is designed to cover the situation where the original tenant was (say) a man living in the house with his wife and child. On the death of that original male tenant, a first transmission will occur in favour of the spouse. On the death of the spouse, a second transmission is then possible in favour of the child, provided that the child satisfies the residence requirement.

Note that this second successor will always take the tenancy as assured tenant.

21

Protection from Unlawful Eviction and Harassment

INTRODUCTION

Regardless of whether or not the tenant has the protection of the Housing Act 1988 or of the Rent Act 1977, virtually *all* residential occupiers have a right not to be unlawfully evicted or subjected to harassment. Under the Protection from Eviction Act 1977, virtually *all* residential occupiers, whether they are tenants or merely licensees, who lawfully occupy the property can only be lawfully evicted if the landlord obtains a court order. There are criminal penalties for landlords who resort to unlawful eviction or harassment.

The need for a court order

Where any premises have been let as a dwelling and the tenancy comes to an end, but the occupier continues to reside in the premises, the owner cannot enforce his/her right to recover possession other than by court proceedings. This prevents the landlord from simply walking back in and repossessing the property. It is a criminal offence to breach this requirement. The protection extends not only to tenants but also to other residential occupiers, for example, someone who only has a licence to occupy a house because they do not have exclusive possession (*see* page 219). It does not, however, extend to squatters or trespassers.

However, there are some specific cases that are excluded from this protection. These are referred to as excluded licences or tenancies.

Excluded licences or tenancies

These include:
- where the occupier shares accommodation (e.g. a kitchen, a lounge or a bathroom) with a resident landlord or member of the landlord's family;
- holiday lettings;
- where the occupier does not have to pay any rent (i.e. a gratuitous arrangement).

Even in these excluded cases, although a court order is not required, the landlord cannot use violence to gain re-entry. Using violence to gain re-entry is a criminal offence under the Criminal Law Act 1977. The landlord can be fined or imprisoned if convicted.

Notice to quit – periodic tenancies or licences

In certain cases, if the tenancy or licence is periodic (e.g. weekly or monthly), the landlord must serve a notice to quit before the tenancy or licence can be terminated. This notice must be served before any proceedings are commenced for possession and it must be a *valid* notice to quit. To be valid it must comply with:
- the rules of common law; and
- section 5 of the Protection from Eviction Act 1977.

Note: notices to quit are *never* required in the case of assured or assured shorthold tenancies under the Housing Act 1988, or in the case of fixed-term tenancies. Instead, the landlord is required to serve a 'notice of intention to commence possession proceedings'; this is considered at page 225 above.

The common law rule

At common law, the landlord can terminate a periodic tenancy by giving a notice to quit to the tenant which must be at least equal to the length of a rental period (e.g. at least one calendar month in the case of a monthly tenancy) *and* must expire at the end of a rental period. For example, if a tenancy is a monthly tenancy that commenced on 12 January, a notice to quit must be at least one calendar month in length and must expire on the 11th or 12th of a subsequent month. (The rental period technically ends at midnight on the 11th, but either date can be specified in the notice.) The tenancy agreement may specify different rules but the tenancy agreement cannot modify the minimum requirements of Section 5 of the Protection from Eviction Act 1977.

Section 5 of the Protection from Eviction Act 1977

This provides that no notice by a landlord or a tenant to quit a dwelling is valid unless

- it is in writing, and contains the prescribed information; and
- it is given not less then four weeks before the date on which it is to take effect.

The current prescribed information is as follows:

Failure to provide this information renders the notice invalid

It is emphasized that four weeks is an *absolute minimum* and that a longer notice may be required in many cases. For example, if the tenancy is a monthly tenancy, at least one full calendar month's notice is required at common law and, therefore, four weeks would be insufficient.

These rules apply not only to periodic tenancies but also to periodic licences, so that even if the occupier does not have a tenancy in the strict sense, he is still entitled to a minimum of four weeks' notice in the prescribed form.

The excluded tenancies and licences detailed above are also excluded from the notice to quit requirements. Even in these excluded cases the landlord must still give a *reasonable* period of notice before seeking possession. What counts as a 'reasonable period' will depend on the circumstances. In some cases one week has been held to be too short for a residential occupier, but each case must be looked at on its own merits.

Unlawful eviction

If the landlord evicts the tenant or occupier without a court order (e.g. by throwing out the tenant's furniture and/or changing the locks while the tenant is away), this constitutes unlawful eviction. The remedies are dealt with below.

Harassment

Harassment is any act done with the intention of causing the tenant to give up possession of all or part of the property or to refrain from exercising his or her legal rights. It also includes acts which are *likely* to have this effect – even if the landlord did not intend that result to happen.

Harassment can take many forms but here are a few examples:

- changing the locks;
- assaulting, or threatening to assault, the tenant or his/her family;
- turning off the gas, water or electricity without good cause;
- taking up floorboards every weekend on the pretext of repairing the electric wiring;
- removing slates from the roof;
- deliberately blocking access to a shared toilet;
- leaving a hi-fi on so as to disturb the tenant;
- the landlord kicking the door every time he passes it;
- frequently shouting abuse at the tenant or making threats of eviction;
- interfering with the tenant's hot water supply;
- removing light bulbs from the hall so that the passage becomes unsafe.

Such acts can amount to the offence of 'harassment' under the Protection from Eviction Act 1977, even if they are not successful and the tenant stays put.

In cases of unlawful eviction and harassment there are several remedies available.

Remedies for unlawful eviction and/or harassment

Court injunction

The tenant can apply to court for an injunction, i.e. a court order reinstating the tenant and/or prohibiting the landlord from continuing his/her unlawful conduct. If an injunction is obtained and the landlord breaches it, he or she is liable to imprisonment. In most cases the county court is the appropriate court. In an emergency situation an injunction can be obtained very swiftly.

Criminal prosecution

The local authority normally deals with criminal prosecutions for unlawful eviction and harassment. Under the Protection from Eviction Act 1977 it is a criminal offence for any person unlawfully to deprive a residential occupier of his/her occupation of premises or any part of it or to attempt to do so. It is also an offence to do acts likely to interfere with the peace or comfort of a residential occupier or members of his/her household or persistently to withdraw or withhold services reasonably required for occupation of the premises if the landlord knows or believes that such conduct is likely to cause the residential occupier to give up occupation of the property or to refrain from exercising any of his/her rights. The offence is punishable by a fine and/or imprisonment for up to six months (and in some cases up to two years). The court also has power to award compensation to the tenant, although this is likely to be less than that awarded by the county court (*see* below). It is a defence if the landlord had reasonable cause to believe that the residential occupier has ceased to reside in the premises.

Damages

The tenant who suffers loss as a result of being unlawfully evicted or harassed into leaving the premises has always had the right to sue the landlord for compensation. This will basically cover the loss actually incurred because of the landlord's behaviour, for example, the cost of alternative accommodation, the value of the tenant's goods that have been damaged, or compensation for pain and suffering if the tenant has been assaulted.

Under the Housing Act 1988, the measure of damages has been enormously increased. Basically, it is the gain that the landlord will make by his unlawful eviction and is calculated by taking the difference in the value of the house subject to the tenancy and the value with vacant possession, i.e. free of the tenancy. This is intended to deter landlords from unlawful eviction or harassment. For example:

Value of landlord's interest in property with vacant possession (i.e. free of tenancy) £75,000
Value subject to tenancy £44,000
Difference in value £31,000

Thus the unlawfully evicted tenant was entitled to £31,000 damages under the Housing Act 1988.

Tagro *v* Cafane (1991), Court of Appeal

Some other cases of high damages being awarded under these provisions include £34,000 (*Weston* v *Maloney* [1991], Blackpool County Court) and £20,278 (*Chappel* v *Panchall* [1991], Preston County Court).

In order to succeed, the tenant must show that he has been unlawfully deprived of possession of the property or has left because the landlord (or someone on his or her behalf) has done acts likely to interfere with the peace and comfort of the occupier or his/her family, or persistently withheld or withdrew services reasonably required for occupation.

However, more recent cases have shown that if the tenant has no security of tenure (e.g. under a shorthold tenancy) the difference in value will be slight. Remember that with a shorthold tenancy, the landlord can lawfully insist on possession simply by giving two months' notice, so the difference in value could well be quite small. In *Mason* v *Nwokorie* (1993) the Court of Appeal awarded £4,500 in damages and in *King* v *Jackson* (1997) only £1,500, in such a situation.

Defences/mitigation of damages under the Housing Act 1988

Belief that residence has ceased
If the landlord can show that he genuinely and reasonably thought the tenant/occupier had already moved out before the conduct complained of, this is a defence.

Misconduct by tenant/occupier
The damages can be reduced if the tenant or someone living with him or her has been guilty of unreasonable conduct that makes it fair for the damages to be reduced. This must be judged on the facts of each case.

Reinstatement
It is a defence if, before the legal proceedings are disposed of, the tenant is reinstated or the court, at the tenant's request, makes an order reinstating him/her. So under the 1988 Act a tenant cannot get damages *and* reinstatement; however, he/she can obtain the ordinary measure of damages mentioned above *and* reinstatement.

Offer of reinstatement
The damages can be reduced if the landlord offers to reinstate the tenant, who unreasonably rejects that offer. The offer must be made *before* the court proceedings are commenced. If the court takes the view that the tenant was right to reject the offer (e.g. because he feared that the landlord might do the same thing again), there will be no reduction in damages.

22

Rented Property: Repair and Maintenance

INTRODUCTION

One of the major issues arising in the case of rented property is that of maintenance and repair: who is responsible if the roof starts leaking, the central heating system breaks down or someone is injured after tripping over a broken paving stone in the path leading to the house. The law in this area is complex and often unclear, as it is not contained in one single piece of legislation; even when it is established that one party or the other is liable, it can also be difficult to ensure that the person liable actually carries out the repairs.

Although when dealing with security of tenure, it is necessary to distinguish between lettings from private landlords and those from local authorities or housing associations, the law relating to repairs generally makes no such distinctions. So unless stated otherwise, you can assume that the identity of the landlord is not relevant to the situation.

MEANING OF REPAIR

As we shall see below, in many cases there will be an express or implied obligation on either the landlord or the tenant to 'repair' the house. So we need to establish precisely what the law means by the term 'repair'. Legally speaking, the word 'repair' must be distinguished from:

- improvements to the house;
- the total or substantial renewal or rebuilding of the house;
- bad living conditions caused by design faults or construction defects.

'Repair' has been defined as:

restoration by renewal or replacement of subsidiary parts of the whole. Renewal ... is reconstruction of the entirety, meaning by the entirety not necessarily the whole but substantially the whole. *Lord Justice Buckley, 1911.*

So, if the only way to 'repair' a building is virtually to pull it all down and start again, that will not be a 'repair' and so not within the obligation to repair included in a tenancy agreement.

Equally, repair must be distinguished from improvements. If you are under an obligation to 'repair' a building, you must restore it by replacing or renewing defective parts, but you need not improve it. Obviously, in one sense, every repair is an improvement; if there is a broken window letting in the wind and rain, repairing it will be a great improvement to the quality of life enjoyed by the occupiers. The legal distinction between repair and improvement can be explained as follows:

If the work which is done is the provision of something new for the benefit of the tenant that is ... an improvement; but if it is only the replacement of something already there which has become dilapidated or worn out, then, albeit that it is the replacement by its modern equivalent, it comes within the category of repairs and not improvements.
Lord Denning, 1956.

So, repair includes:

- remedying a defective damp-proof course;
- repointing brickwork;
- eliminating dry rot and replacing the affected joists, etc.;
- renewing crumbling plaster;
- rewiring;
- replacing a broken window;
- renewing burst or defective water pipes.

Improvement includes:

- putting in a bathroom;
- installing extra electrical sockets when rewiring;
- installing a damp-proof course;
- installing double-glazing.

Alternatively, the house may be unpleasant or unhealthy to live in, perhaps because of condensation, but where the fault is not due to a lack of 'repair'.

Mr Quick was a tenant of a local authority. The house suffered severe dampness due to condensation caused by metal window frames and inadequate heating and ventilation. Although his decorations and clothes and furnishings were damaged as a result of the condensation, the actual fabric of the house was not damaged in any way. The problem was faulty design and, as this had not resulted in any damage to the building, remedying the condensation was not within the landlord's obligation 'to repair'.

Quick (1986)

Note, however, that if the faulty design and construction *had* caused damage to the actual building, then this would be within the meaning of repair. So, where the condensation had caused damage to the plaster in the house, replacing the plaster was within the landlord's repairing obligation (*Staves* (1992)). However, if the landlord had agreed to keep the house 'in good condition' (rather than just to repair it), then the landlord would be liable to cure damp and condensation whether or not the building was damaged (*Welsh* (2000)). A similar problem arose for Mr Mills and various other tenants of a London borough council. Their flats had wholly inadequate soundproofing, such that they could hear almost all aspects of everyday life being carried on in the neighbouring flats. However, this was caused by poor construction standards and not lack of repair and so the council was not liable to remedy the problem (*Mills* (1999)).

WHAT IF LANDLORD WANTS TO REPAIR BUT TENANT WON'T ALLOW IT?

Most of this chapter deals with the position when a landlord is reluctant to repair and so a tenant has to use a legal remedy to ensure that the necessary repairs are carried out. However, it sometimes happens that the position is reversed; it is the landlord who wants to carry out building works but the tenant refuses to give his or her consent. What can the landlord do?

First, a landlord has the right to enter the property (after giving reasonable notice) and carry out *necessary* repairs if:

• there is a specific clause in a lease or tenancy agreement that gives him/her that right; or
• the repairs are his/her legal responsibility.

Otherwise, the landlord cannot force repairs on the tenant, and if he or she tries to do so may be liable for harassment (*see* page 237).

Second, the landlord might want to improve, modernize, extend or convert the property, as opposed to merely carrying out repairs. If so, does he or she have the right to enter the property and carry out the work? Generally, the tenant can refuse entry unless there is a specific clause in the lease that allows it. However, as most tenants from private landlords will have assured shorthold tenancies with no security of tenure (*see* Chapter 20), a tenant may be faced with a classic 'Hobson's Choice' – either agree to the landlord's request or be evicted.

WHO IS LIABLE TO DO THE REPAIRS?

Landlord and Tenant Act 1985

The starting point is the Landlord and Tenant Act 1985: sections 11–14 apply to lettings of houses and flats if the term is for less than seven years and impose some repairing obligations on landlords. The Act will also apply to periodic tenancies (e.g. weekly and monthly) even if they have actually lasted longer than seven years. Its provisions will still apply even if the landlord has inserted contrary provisions in the tenancy agreement.

Thus this covers most rented accommodation. Most lettings are either for short fixed terms or are periodic. Further, it applies to all lettings entered into on or after 24 October 1961 – the 1985 Act replaced an earlier Act.

Note that the obligation on the landlord is only to repair and maintain; he or she need not, for instance, install water heaters or gas fires if they were not there when the tenant first rented the property.

Summarized, it makes the landlord liable for the repair and maintenance of the structure of the building and of the electrical, gas and plumbing systems (*see also* below). Although 'structure and exterior' are not defined by the Act, 'structure' clearly includes the main fabric of the dwelling, including walls, foundations, roof and window frames, as opposed to the decorations and fittings. 'Exterior' has been held to include steps or paths that form an essential means of access to the property.

The words 'structure and exterior' of the dwelling can cause problems in the case of flats. What if the repairs are required to the communal parts of the building, and not to the specific flat let to the tenant? The courts originally held that the repairing obligations did not apply to the whole of the building in which the flat was situated, but were limited to the flat itself.

However, if the tenancy was granted on or after 15 January 1989 the landlord will now be liable for communal parts if he owns the entire building, as the legislation has been amended, but only for lettings entered into on or after that date. However, if these repairs cannot be done without gaining access to the flat or other flats and such access is refused, the landlord will be able to defend proceedings on the basis that he or she used all reasonable endeavours to obtain access. Further, there is no liability unless the disrepair interferes with the enjoyment of the tenant's flat.

Despite these drawbacks, the remedy will often be the main remedy available to tenants.

Gas escapes

A claim against the landlord for a defective gas appliance (typically for carbon-monoxide poisoning) can be made under one of three heads:

- Section 4 Defective Premises Act 1972. Section 4 of the Act provides that a landlord has an obligation to see that all persons who might reasonably be affected by defective premises are kept safe from personal injury or damage to property. This duty will cover most claims arising from defective gas appliances.

A gas fire in residential premises leaked gas and fumes, causing the tenant to suffer brain damage from carbon-monoxide poisoning. The fire had never been serviced by the landlord. The tenant, who had an assured shorthold tenancy agreement, brought proceedings against the landlord under the Defective Premises Act 1972 for damages. Held: The tenant did not have to show that the landlord knew about the defect in the gas fire. The tenant merely had to show that the landlord had failed to take reasonable care to see that the tenant was safe from personal injury. Thus, the landlord was liable in damages, although the tenant's damages were reduced by 80 per cent as a result of his contributory negligence in failing to do anything about an obvious defect. Sykes v Harry (2001)

- Section II Landlord and Tenant Act 1985. As mentioned above, this obliges the landlord to keep in repair and proper working order the installations in the house for heating. Liability only arises after the landlord has been made aware of the defect. This can make claims under the 1985 Act difficult.
- Gas Safety (Installation and Use) Regulations 1998. These make it clear that a landlord must carry out an annual gas safety check and ensure that relevant gas fittings and flues are maintained in a safe condition. Each appliance and flue must be checked for safety within 12 months of installation and then at least every 12 months. A record of every check must be kept for a period of two years from the date of the check. In addition, the landlord may only use a Corgi-registered gas installer for the safety work and the landlord must give a copy of the inspection record to the tenant within 28 days. Moreover, a copy of the last inspection record for each appliance or flue has to be given to any new tenant before that tenant takes up occupation. In practice, a large number of landlords do not comply with the 1998 Regulations. The claim in the case referred to above (Sykes v Harry) pre-dated the 1998 Regulations, but failure by a landlord to carry out an annual inspection as required by the Regulations, might now result in the court deciding that the landlord ought to have known of any defect for the purposes of a damages claim under Section 4 of the Defective Premises Act 1972. Plus, breach of the Regulations is a criminal offence.

The tenant's use of the property

The landlord will be able to avoid liability if the disrepair arose because the tenant did not behave reasonably. This is called 'failing to behave in a tenant-like manner'.

Thus, if the tenant is going away for the winter, he must turn off the water and empty the boiler. He must clean the chimneys when necessary, and also the windows. He must mend the electric light when it fuses, he must unstop the sink when it is blocked by his waste. In short, he must do the little jobs about the place which a reasonable tenant would do. *Lord Denning, 1954.*

So if the water pipes burst due to the pipes freezing when the house was left unheated, then the landlord would not be liable to repair them, even though the pipes are within his obligation under the Act.

Consequential loss

Even if the landlord is clearly liable to repair the property, there may be a dispute as to the cost of loss and damage caused by the defect. For example, if the roof leaks and rain damage is caused to interior decorations and the tenant's possessions, who will pay for the cost of redecorating and can the tenant hold the landlord responsible for the cost of his damaged possessions? Even worse, suppose the roof leaks so badly that a bedroom ceiling falls on the tenant, injuring him. Can he sue the landlord for his personal injury and loss of wages while off work? As regards the cost of repairing the roof and the ceiling, there can be no argument, for the Act clearly makes this the landlord's responsibility. But as regards the consequential loss (i.e. the cost of redecoration, the injury compensation, loss of wages, etc.), the landlord will be liable only if he had notice of the defect. Thus, if the tenant had earlier warned the landlord that the ceiling looked unsafe, the landlord would be liable. Or if the landlord's builder had inspected the property and seen the defect (or if he *ought* to have seen it), the landlord would be liable. But not otherwise.

Mr O'Brien was the tenant of a flat. In 1965 he had complained to his landlord about stamping on the ceiling from the flat above, although he had not suggested that the ceiling was defective in any way. In 1968 the ceiling fell in and Mr O'Brien was injured. He sued the landlord, arguing that there had been a breach of the Act. Held: The landlord was only liable to remedy the defective ceiling when he knew that it was defective; he had not been given notice of any defect and so he was not liable. O'Brien (1973)

So the advice for any tenant is to carry out regular inspections of rented property and give the landlord written notice of any possible defect; always keep a copy of any notices or letters sent to the landlord.

The main drawbacks of this remedy are that:

- it cannot be used to require structural alterations or

improvements (and installing a damp-proof course would probably come within this category, although the landlord would have to repair an existing one);

- it cannot be used for consequential loss when the landlord does not have notice of disrepair;
- it cannot be used to require hot water or space heating if there was none in the property at the start of the letting;
- it does not apply to communal parts (e.g. shared hallway or a toilet on the landing), if the tenancy was entered into before 15 January 1989.

The tenancy agreement

If sections 11–14 of the 1985 Act do not cover the repair in question, then the next matter to consider is the terms of the tenancy agreement itself. A well-drafted agreement – and many short-term letting agreements aren't – will set out precisely who is responsible for what. Remember, though, that if the 1985 Act applies, i.e. there is a letting for a period not exceeding seven years etc. (*see* page 240), then the inclusion of a provision in the agreement saying that the tenant will be responsible for the repairs within the Act will have no effect; the provisions of the Act will still apply.

However, in relation to lettings outside the 1985 Act (e.g. for longer than seven years), or in relation to repairs not covered by the Act (e.g. internal decorations), then the tenancy agreement will be conclusive as to who is responsible. Often responsibility for repairs outside the 1985 Act will be placed on the tenant.

Some leases exempt the tenant from responsibility for damage, etc., caused through 'fair wear and tear'. This exempts the tenant from liability for repairs that are caused by things wearing out because of normal use and because of the passage of time. However, if further damage flows from that wear and tear, he must remedy that further damage. So, if a slate came off the roof due to fair wear and tear, the tenant would not be liable to replace it. However, if the hole in the roof let in the rain which caused damage to the interior of the house, that further damage would be the tenant's responsibility; that further damage was not caused by fair wear and tear.

What if the tenancy agreement does not deal with the repairs in question?

In many cases, though, the tenancy agreement may not mention repairs at all, or deal with repairs that need doing. Indeed, in some cases there may well not be a written tenancy agreement at all. What happens then?

Assuming that the 1985 Act does not apply (*see* page 240), there may be other situations in which the law will impose liability to repair on the landlord.

Implied 'correlative' duty by landlord

If the tenancy agreement makes the tenant responsible for internal repairs and decoration but does not state that the landlord must look after the exterior, the court may imply such an obligation on the landlord independently of the 1985 Act. If it can be argued that doing the internal repairs and decoration would be pointless (because, for example, penetrating dampness caused from outside means the wallpaper keeps peeling off), it will be an implied term that the landlord must repair the outside in order to enable the tenant properly to perform his obligations to repair the inside.

Common parts

In the case of blocks of flats, houses converted into flats etc., the Landlord and Tenant Act 1985 does not always require the landlord to repair the 'common parts', i.e. the parts of the building not let to the tenants, such as the hallways and stairs etc. (*See* page 216 as the Landlord and Tenant Act obligations only apply to the common parts if the tenancy was granted on or after 15 January 1989.) However, there will, in such cases, be a separate obligation implied by the law to keep in repair the essential means of access to each of the flats, for example, the steps, stairs, passages, etc.

Getting the landlord to do the repairs

Having decided that the landlord is liable to do the repair in question, the next problem is how do you actually make him do those repairs?

The first thing, of course, is to tell the landlord that the repair needs doing. Whether the landlord is liable because of the 1985 Act, or because of a term in the tenancy agreement, he must have notice of the repair. He will not be liable for failing to carry out the repair unless, and until, he fails to carry out the repair within a reasonable time of being advised as to what needs doing. What amounts to a reasonable time will depend upon the nature of the work required. If there are major works necessary, a reasonable time may well be several weeks, or even longer. A landlord needs time to obtain estimates and find a builder to do the work. If the problem is a burst pipe, or the central heating breaking down in the middle of winter, a reasonable time may well be only a day or so.

If the landlord fails to carry out the repairs within a reasonable time – or disputes that they are his responsibility – then, basically, the tenant is going to have to go to court and commence proceedings against the landlord in order to get the repairs done – this can be expensive and time consuming. (For circumstances where the local authority may be prepared to take action against the landlord *see* page 243.)

By going to court, the tenant will be able to obtain an order that the landlord should carry out the repairs in question and may also be entitled to an order that the landlord pay the tenant compensation ('damages' in legal jargon) because of his failure to carry them out, and to cover any loss the tenant has suffered. The appropriate court will be the county court for the area in which the house is situate. Your local county court (address in the telephone book) will be able to provide details as to which is the correct court and also the appropriate forms, details of court fees, etc. However, the court officials will not be able to assist you or advise you in connection with a particular problem.

Damages

The landlord is liable, as from the date he or she knew of the defect, for damages and can be sued by the tenant, generally in the county court. The compensation will depend on the circumstances of each case. The tenant may be able to claim general damages for discomfort, ill-health/injury, mental distress and disappointment resulting from disrepair. If the condition is such that he or she has no alternative but to move into temporary accommodation while the repairs are done, he or she can claim the expenses of that temporary accommodation. Any actual expense attributable to the landlord's breach (e.g. cleaning and redecoration, damage to tenant's possessions) can also be recovered.

Getting the repairs done – court order

This is the tenant's main concern. The court can, in addition to or instead of awarding damages, make an order requiring the landlord to carry out the repairs within a stated reasonable time. This is known as an order for 'specific performance'. If the landlord still fails to carry out those repairs without good reason, then he will be guilty of contempt of court and could ultimately be committed to prison for such contempt.

Doing the repairs yourself

Going to court can be slow, expensive, time consuming and frustrating. As an alternative, tenants can get the work done themselves and deduct the cost from future payments of rent. However, the danger of this is that the landlord will say that the tenant has failed to pay the proper rent and bring proceedings claiming arrears of rent or claiming possession because of arrears of rent. To try and avoid this danger, the tenant should give the landlord written notice of his or her intention. The landlord should be given a chance to do the work – say, 28 days, or seven days if it is really urgent. The tenant should obtain more than one estimate for the work and send them to the landlord, giving him a chance to challenge them. Only then should the work be done and deducted from future rent payments. Obviously, the tenant should

be sure that the landlord is legally liable to do the work before he or she risks doing the work themselves and deducting the cost from the rent.

As a less risky alternative, tenants could still do the work themselves but then sue the landlord in the county court for the cost, rather than deducting the cost from rent payments. That way the tenant cannot be said to have got into rent arrears.

Council tenants have a special 'self-help' scheme for getting repairs done. It applies only to repairs costing between £20 and £250 and details are given in the Secure Tenancies (Right to Repair Scheme) Regulations 1985. The scheme is limited to 'qualifying repairs', which means any repairs for which the landlord is responsible, other than repairs to the structure and exterior of a flat. Basically, it involves the tenant completing a form describing the work to be done and why it is needed. The landlord then has 21 days either to confirm or refuse the tenant's repair claim. The landlord may refuse the claim if it intends to carry out the work itself or the works will cost more than £250.

Note that it is not compulsory for council tenants to use this scheme. It is simply an alternative to the ordinary legal rules. It is probably simpler for the tenant to use the ordinary legal rules and to ignore this scheme.

All of these self-help remedies presuppose, of course, that the tenant has the money to actually pay for the repairs in the first place. If he has not, then it may be possible to get the local authority involved.

Local authority's powers and duties

The next two remedies can be enforced by either the tenant or the local authority. They are speedy and effective remedies, and are derived from environmental or public health legislation, which reflects society's concern that everyone should live in hygienic, healthy surroundings. However, in practice, local authorities are reluctant to get involved in anything that might require them to spend money and so often it is only in the worst cases that they are prepared to intervene, despite the wording of the legislation.

Sections 79–82 Environmental Protection Act 1990

If the premises are 'prejudicial to health' or a 'nuisance', then the local authority must serve an abatement notice on the landlord requiring him to 'abate', i.e. remedy the nuisance, etc. The unusual feature of this remedy is that it *requires* the local authority to take action against the landlord if the public health provisions have been broken. The local authority has no discretionary powers.

The remedy applies to two different sets of circumstances: first, when the premises are a legal 'nuisance' and, second, when they are 'prejudicial to health'. It is the 'prejudicial to health' claim that is likely to be of most use to the tenant. To the lay-person, the idea of a breach of the Environmental Protection Act conjures up images of a house infested with rats and cockroaches, or with foul drains. Although the Act covers such blatant examples of uncleanliness, it also encompasses much less obvious health hazards that might not, at first sight, seem to be environmental health matters. For example, dampness, defective sanitary fittings, ill-fitting windows or doors, leaking rainwater drains, defective roofs, damp plaster-work, etc.

But it must be appreciated that it is not the defect itself that gives rise to an environmental health remedy; it is the *consequence* of the defect that raises a matter of environmental health concern. As an illustration, consider a window that will not open because the wooden frame has rotted. In itself this will not be an environmental health matter, but if that window is the only one in the room, the result will be that there is no ventilation and that could be an environmental health matter (particularly if it is in a bedroom), since it is 'prejudicial to health' to occupy an unventilated room. Similarly, suppose the defect is a hole in a roof. Of itself, that will not be an environmental health matter, but as soon as it rains and water enters the house, it becomes a public health concern, for the defect has now caused a situation that is 'prejudicial to the health' of the occupants.

But, as with repairs (*see* page 239) there must be a defect in the property. Otherwise the remedy will be of no use. This can be a particular problem with condensation, as this case illustrates.

Council tenants lived on an estate in which the buildings had gas or electric background heating systems. These systems were expensive to run and, in practice, none of the tenants used them. The result was that the buildings suffered from condensation The tenants complained that the buildings were 'injurious to health' because of the extensive condensation. Held: The council was not liable. There was an adequate heating system which was not defective. If the tenants used the heating system provided, then there would be no condensation problem. Even though the court felt that the tenants were not acting unreasonably in not using the expensive heating systems, the fact remained that the council was not liable.   Dover District Council (1982)

However, if the damp and condensation is not the fault of the tenants and it is prejudicial to health, then the requirements of the Act will be complied with (*Issa* (1996)).

Thus a tenant can use the public health remedy only if he or she can tie up the defect to an environmental health aspect. If there is no health hazard resulting from the defect, the remedy cannot be used. An environmental health hazard of this sort is called a 'statutory nuisance' and this is the term that the tenant should use when making a complaint.

Enforcing the remedy: enforcement by the local authority

The local authority must enforce the remedy. The appropriate local authority is the district, unitary or London Borough Council in whose area the house is situated. If the environmental health officer thinks that the defects amount to a 'statutory nuisance' he or she must serve an 'abatement notice' on the landlord, specifying the defects and fixing a date by when they should be remedied. The landlord has a right of appeal, within 21 days, to the magistrates' court if he or she wishes to dispute the notice. If the landlord does not appeal and does not comply with the notice, he or she is guilty of an offence, unless he or she is able to show there was a reasonable excuse for non-compliance. However, it is up to the local authority whether or not to prosecute.

Alternatively, or in addition, the local authority can itself do the necessary work and recover the cost from the landlord. But this assumes that the local authority is helpful and prepared to act on the tenant's behalf. Most local authorities have enormous pressures on their limited resources and will only be prepared to intervene in the most extreme cases.

If the council fails to serve an abatement notice, the tenant is able to start proceedings against the landlord himself.

Enforcing the remedy: enforcement by the tenant

The tenant may find it quicker to take action himself rather than wait for the local authority to do so. The tenant should go to the local magistrates' court and ask them to issue a summons under the Environmental Protection Act 1990 Section 82. Once the summons has been issued, the court will serve it on the landlord and arrange a date for the hearing of the case. The tenant will need to employ an expert in environmental health matters to give evidence of the disrepair, and that it is prejudicial to health.

If the magistrates decide there is a statutory nuisance, they must issue an abatement notice. Some magistrates' courts take a fairly robust view of what constitutes a health hazard and is thus a statutory nuisance. However, it must be remembered that several seemingly trivial defects can, when taken together, amount to a statutory nuisance. Although this is undoubtedly the law, some magistrates' courts are reluctant to convict in such cases, and need to be reminded of the law.

Mr Patel issued a summons against his landlord. At the hearing the evidence was given by a self-employed public health adviser and by the local council's environmental health officer. Both described the property's defects in detail and stated that they were 'prejudicial to health'. Despite this expert evidence, the magistrates did not convict the landlord. They said that it appeared from the unchallenged evidence that the alleged defects to the premises existed and that the standard of those premises was undesirably low. The majority of the defects were trivial and appear to have been contributed to if not caused by the neglect of the occupiers (i.e. the Patels). They constituted an inconvenience rather than a health hazard. Mr Patel appealed to the Divisional Court. Held: The magistrates were ordered to convict the landlord. Magistrates should not substitute their own opinion for those of informed expert witnesses.

Patel (1980)

If the local authority is itself the landlord, a tenant's only choice will be to go to court himself. After all, the local authority can hardly commence proceedings against itself. It should be noted, however, that public funding is not available to the tenant who wants to take the case to court himself. However, if the court finds in favour of the tenant (whether the local authority or the tenant commences the proceedings) the court can be asked to make a compensation order against the landlord. This is to compensate the tenant for loss or damage arising out of the state of the property. However, it is likely that such an award would be less than the damages which would be ordered in the county court if proceedings had been commenced there.

Houses unfit for human habitation

If the property is in such a bad state that it is unfit for human habitation, the local authority has wide powers to deal with the situation under the Housing Act 1985. Again, getting the local authority to act is not always easy. A local housing advice centre may be able to help in lobbying the Housing Department, the Environmental Health Department, a local councillor or your MP. The tenant could issue a complaint to a magistrate under section 606 of the Act, but again public funding is not available for this.

The various powers that local authorities have are complicated. Briefly, the main powers are:

- to serve a repair notice;
- to make a closing order;
- to make a demolition order;
- to provide for area clearance.

Many of these powers depend on whether or not the house (or flat) is 'unfit for human habitation'. This is dealt with in section 604 of the Act. A house is deemed to be 'unfit' if, first, *in the opinion of the local authority* it fails to meet one of the requirements listed in section 604 (*see* below) and, second, in consequence, it is not reasonably suitable for occupation.

The list includes:

- structural instability;
- serious disrepair;
- dampness prejudicial to the health of the occupier;
- inadequate lighting, heating and ventilation;
- inadequate water supply;
- inadequate facilities for preparation and cooking of food, including sink and hot and cold water;
- unsuitably located toilet, bath or shower and wash-basin;
- inadequate drainage.

There are additional requirements in the case of flats in relation to the entire block.

Repair notice

If the local authority decides that the most satisfactory method of tackling the problem is repair, it may serve a 'repair notice' on the person 'having control' of the premises – which normally means the landlord. The notice must specify what work is needed. The landlord can appeal within 21 days to the county court. If the notice is not complied with, the local authority can (if it so chooses) carry out the work itself and recoup the cost from the owner.

The repair notice procedure can also be used in cases where the house is not 'unfit' in the legal sense. Under section 190, it can be used where the property is in such a state of disrepair that although not unfit for human habitation, the condition is such as to interfere materially with the personal comfort of occupying tenants.

Similarly, the procedure can be used where substantial repairs are required to bring the property up to a reasonable standard. Failure to comply with a valid repair notice is a criminal offence and the local authority can prosecute the landlord.

Closing order or demolition order

These measures are worth considering only if the house is unfit for human habitation and the tenant wants to be rehoused. If the local authority resolves to make either of these orders, the result will be that the property will be closed down or demolished (although if the local authority has itself purchased the property, the property can be used for temporary accommodation). There is a right of appeal against a closing/demolition order to the county court if the owner objects. If a tenant is displaced as a result of either type of order, and suitable alternative accommodation is not available, the local authority must provide accommodation. Compensation may be payable to the tenant.

23

Home Improvements and Planning Permission

Householders who wish to modernize, convert or improve their property have three hurdles to overcome before they can put their plans into effect.

First, they must raise the money. A local authority grant (*see* below) might possibly cover part of the cost, but they will almost certainly need to raise money by loan or mortgage. Second, once it is clear that finance is available, they must next consider whether planning permission is needed. Finally, they must obtain any other necessary consents – for example, from their mortgage lender or from neighbours under any covenants affecting the property.

Only then can work start.

RAISING THE MONEY: LOCAL AUTHORITY, ETC., GRANTS

The days of extensive grants from local authorities for home improvements have gone. Grants may be available if you intend to put in basic amenities (e.g. a bath or indoor toilet) or in the case of insulation for lofts, hot water tanks, etc. However, funds are limited. You should check with your district, unitary or London Borough Council to see what is available in your area.

Special grants for listed buildings

Buildings of 'special architectural or historic interest' may be eligible for special grants. In addition, the Historic Buildings Council can award grants for buildings of architectural or historic interest.

RAISING THE MONEY: BORROWING TO FINANCE THE WORK

If you need to borrow the money to pay for the work then a baffling choice of loans faces you – the press is full of advertisements for mortgages and personal loans. Where do you start?

Perhaps the first thing to decide is whether you want a personal loan or a secured loan (i.e. mortgage).

A personal loan is not secured on your property, so you can sell the house without having to repay it. But personal loans are often repayable over a comparatively short length of time – say five years – and are usually limited to a maximum of £15,000. Because there is no security, interest rates will be higher than a mortgage loan. If you are considering borrowing only a relatively small amount of money (e.g. £5,000) and can afford to repay it within a few years, a personal loan may be a sensible choice – but shop around for the best deal; interest rates vary enormously.

For larger loans (e.g. £15,000 plus), the lender will require security (i.e. a mortgage) over your house. The interest rate will normally be lower than for a personal loan and the repayment period longer. But if you move, you will have to repay the loan, just like any other mortgage, and there may be valuation fees and legal fees because of the need to register the mortgage over the property at the Land Registry. Often, with a little shopping around, a lender can be found who will pay these charges for you.

With a secured loan you have three basic choices:

1 Approach your existing lender. They will know you and your payment record and will normally be sympathetic to a proposal that increases the value of the property.

2 Obtain a second mortgage from another lender. Interest rates on second mortgages are usually higher than on first mortgages.

3 Remortgage the house. Whether you go to your existing lender or another lender, you must choose whether to take out an extra loan for the amount you require only or whether you want to remortgage. Remortgaging consists of taking out a new loan sufficient to pay off your existing mortgage and to cover the cost of the improvements. You may find that with a remortgage

you can get a much better rate of interest for the new loan than you are paying at the moment, thus saving considerable amounts of money. Again, it is a question of shopping around – and studying the small print of the various offers very carefully.

Tax relief is no longer available on loans for the purchase or improvement of private residential property.

OBTAINING CONSENT FROM THE LOCAL AUTHORITY

The householder will have to consider whether planning permission is needed.

Planning permission

The wish of the householder to improve, modernize or convert his or her home must be balanced against the effect the works will have on the local area and its amenities. The control of development, in the public interest, is provided by the planning system introduced in 1948 by the Town and Country Planning Act.

Planning permission is needed for any *development*. The word 'development' is given an unusually wide definition by the planning laws. Thus, it covers not only straightforward building work such as the erection of an extension, but also any change in the use to which the building or land is put. For example, converting a house into two flats, or into an office, will be a change of use and so require planning permission; this is so even if no building work is needed to carry out the change of use.

The result of this wide definition is to bring most projects for the improvement, modernization or conversion of houses within the scope of the planning laws. Fortunately, the fine detail of the legislation exempts many – but not all – minor household 'developments' from the need to apply for planning permission, even though, technically, they count as development.

The summaries (*see* below) set out the rules that apply to the more usual household developments.

Applying for planning permission

Forms can be obtained from the district, unitary or London Borough Council. It is wise to discuss the plans with the council officers before filling in the forms. They will usually give informal advice as to whether your planned work will need planning permission and, if so, of the likelihood of that permission being granted.

Detailed plans will have to be lodged with the application unless outline planning permission only is being sought. Plans can be expensive to prepare, so if you are unsure whether permission will be granted, outline

permission can be applied for. This will ascertain whether the council will, in principle, permit the kind of development you wish to carry out. For outline permission, detailed plans are not required, just an outline of the kind of development proposed, for example, building a three-bedroomed bungalow. Once outline permission has been granted, the expense of detailed plans can then be safely incurred. The outline permission would have to be followed up by a further application to approve all the details before the development can be started; this is called an 'application for approval of reserved matters'. The outline planning permission procedure is not available for a 'change of use' application.

Applications generally take about two months to process. A fee is payable. If permission is refused, or is granted subject to conditions, the council must give an explanation to the applicant, who then has six months in which to appeal to the Secretary of State.

Opposing a planning application

There are various rules requiring the local authority to publicize planning applications. Often this will consist of a site notice, i.e. a notice fixed to a lamp post or similar near the site stating that an application has been made and asking for any objections to be made by a certain date. Many local authorities will, as a matter of course, write to neighbouring owners advising them that an application has been made. For an objection to carry any weight, it must be based on planning grounds. The planning laws are there to protect the interests of the whole community, not necessarily individuals, so the fact that a particular development might overlook your house, or spoil a view or reduce it in value might not be a valid ground for objection. What would be relevant would be a development that affected the amenity of the whole area – such as setting up a noisy industrial process in a residential area. If you wish to object it is sensible to attend at the council offices and view the plans and then discuss any concerns you have with the planning officials to see whether you have any valid ground for opposing the application. Normally, applications for extensions and the like will be permitted provided they fit in with the area and the existing building, for example, similar colour bricks and tiles.

Flouting the planning laws

Do not be tempted to ignore the need for planning permission and assume that once the development has been completed the local authority will be unable, or unwilling, to do anything about it. In such a case you are likely to be served with an 'enforcement notice' requiring that the property be put back to its original (undeveloped) condition, regardless of the cost and inconvenience of doing so. If the 'enforcement notice' is not obeyed, the local authority may start criminal proceedings against you. The local authority may begin by serving a Planning Contravention Notice, which requires that information be given to the council about the use to which the property is being put. Again, there are criminal sanctions for failing to reply. If that use is in breach of a condition attached to a previous planning permission, then the council can issue a Breach of Condition Notice, which is a far more straightforward and simple procedure than an enforcement notice.

If the unauthorized development involved building works, then an enforcement notice must be served within four years of the works being carried out. Once the four years have expired it is too late for the council to serve an enforcement notice and so the unauthorized development is allowed to stand. If the unauthorized development did not involve building works but was a change of use (e.g. converting an office into a flat) then there is a 10-year time limit for serving an enforcement notice.

Is planning permission needed?

The summaries set out the usual position for household developments, but bear in mind that:

- they deal with houses (for flats and maisonettes the answers may be different);
- an existing planning permission may cover the property and lay down special conditions that override the normal rules;
- where conditions are stated, if these are not to be complied with, then planning permission will be required;
- special conditions can apply in conservation areas and to listed buildings. Also, the position in London may be different by virtue of the London Building Acts;
- the full details are set out in the Town and Country Planning General Permitted Development Orders;
- these normal rules can be disapplied by the local authority in particular parts of their area by what is known as an 'Article 4 Direction'.

Is Planning Permission Necessary?

Aerials and satellite dishes	No.	Subject to compliance with size rules.
Tank for central heating: oil or gas	No.	Provided the tank is for domestic heating purposes and is in the garden; there are rules as to the size of the tank and its location in the garden.
Demolitions	No.	Generally permission is not needed unless the building is listed or is in a conservation area.
Detached structures	No.	This covers such separate buildings as a shed, greenhouse, aviary, kennel, summer-house, swimming pool, sauna cabin, etc. However, there will be a need for planning permission if the structure is not for the sole use of the residents of the main house, and if the size and location rules are not complied with.
Extensions	Yes.	But if the extension is for the use of the residents of the house (i.e. it will not be a separate dwelling), there will be no need for planning permission if conditions as to size and location are complied with.
Fences and walls	No.	Provided that it does not exceed one metre in height if adjoining a highway or two metres in height elsewhere.
Flats	Yes.	There is a material change of use. In particular, permission is needed to convert a house into two or more flats. Permission is needed even if no building works are needed for the conversion.
Greenhouse		See 'Detached structures'.
Hardstanding for a car	No.	Provided that it is for the use of the occupiers of the house.
Hedges	No.	See 'Fences and walls'.
Improvements	No.	Unless the front line of the house is extended in any way. Thus changing flat sash windows into bay windows might require planning permission, whereas a change from sash window to casement window or installing UVPC double-glazing would not. (But if the house is listed or in a conservation area, permission will be needed.) *See also* 'Internal alterations' and 'Maintenance'.

Internal alterations	No.	Unless there is a change of use (e.g. erecting a new staircase for the purpose of converting a house into a flat and an office) or unless it is a listed building. Otherwise, there is no control over internal alterations. *See also* 'Extensions', 'Improvements', 'Maintenance'.
Keeping a boat or caravan in the garden	No.	Unless the caravan is used as a separate dwelling. However, many local authorities have local by-laws that restrict the keeping of boats and caravans in gardens, so check with the local council.
Loft conversion	No.	Subject to size and height restrictions; see 'Extensions'.
Maintenance	No.	For example, redecorating the inside and outside, stone-cladding, repointing brickwork, pebble-dashing, sandblasting, fitting shutters to windows. All of these can normally be done without planning permission, even if the external appearance of the house is altered. Different rules apply in conservation areas and to listed buildings.
Office or other business use	Yes.	Using part, or all, of a house as an office will be a change of use and so will need planning permission. Similarly, a householder who decides to work from home, give lessons at home, or store business goods in a spare room, will technically require planning permission, although councils will often turn a blind eye to minor infringements.
Porch	No.	Conditions as to size and location must be met.
Shed	No.	See 'Detached structures'.
Sun-lounge	Yes.	See 'Extensions'.
Tree lopping or felling	No.	But check that the council has not made a tree preservation order. Permission will also be needed in a conservation area.
Walls	No.	But see conditions in 'Fences and walls'.

Changing the use of a property

Planning permission is needed for 'a material change of use'. Thus it will be needed if, for instance, a house is to be changed into a shop. This is so even if no building works are needed to bring about the change.

In particular, the Town and Country Planning Act 1990 states that the conversion of one house into two or more dwellings is a material change of use and so planning permission is needed. All conversions of houses into flats must therefore be approved by the planners.

Not all changes of use are so clearly within the planning laws. The difficulty lies in deciding what is a 'material' change of use.

Basically, a proposed change of use constitutes development only if the new use is *substantially* different from the old. A change in kind will always be material (e.g. from house to shop, or from shop to factory). A change in the degree of an existing use may be 'material' but only if it is very marked. For instance, the fact that lodgers are taken privately in a family dwellinghouse would probably not constitute a material change of use in itself so long as the use of the house remains substantially that of a private residence. On the other hand, the change from a private residence with lodgers to a declared guesthouse, boarding house, or private hotel would be 'material'. A nice 'grey area' would be the family in a holiday area who take in a few bed and breakfast guests in the holiday season. Is this still primarily a private residence or is it now a guesthouse, for which planning permission is needed? Often permission is not obtained in these cases.

More likely to need permission is the doctor or dentist who uses a few rooms in his house as consulting rooms. If this is only done on an occasional, emergency basis, no permission would be needed, but if it is done on a regular basis, there is likely to have been a material change of use.

The General Permitted Development Order

The basic rule is that any 'development' needs planning permission. But, because the word 'development' is defined so widely, it would cover virtually any works that anyone wanted to do to their property (as well as any change of use). To overcome this, the Town and Country Planning Acts allow certain types of development to be carried out without the need for planning permission. These exceptions – when permission is not needed – are mainly set out in the General Permitted Development Order (GPDO). As its name indicates, certain types of development are 'permitted', i.e. can be carried out without the need for planning permission.

Extensions: Is Planning Permission Necessary? *(and see page 248)*

Yes
extension is larger than
15 per cent of the size
of the original house,
and is larger than 70 m³

Yes
extension is in front of
the original house

road

No
extension is within the
15 per cent (70 m³) size
limit

No
extension does not face
a road and is at the rear
of the original house

road

1930 house
1971 garage

Yes
extension is within the
15 per cent size limit,
but the limit has already
been taken up by the
garage

original house
extension
unclassified road
drive
classified road B123

Yes
extension has a new
access on to a classified
road

Yes
extension is above the
limit of the original house.
Front fence (facing road)
can only be up to 1 m high

road

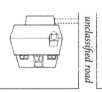

unclassified road
classified road B123

No
extension has a new
access but it is not on
to a classified road

No
extension does not exceed
the height of the original
house

road

For instance, the GPDO allows certain developments within the grounds of a dwellinghouse (e.g. enlargement, improvement or other alteration, erection of a porch, enclosure of a swimming pool), provided that certain conditions as to size and location are complied with.

Similarly, the GPDO permits certain minor building operations to be carried out: for instance, the erection of gates and fences (subject to height limitations).

The rules are extremely complex and you should always check with the local planners before starting any work. In particular, the permissions granted by the GPDO might have been taken away by conditions attached to an earlier planning consent, or by the local authority making an Article 3 Direction.

There are also important rules on when one can change the use of premises without the need for planning permission. The basic rule is that any change of use amounts to 'development', and therefore requires planning permission. However, certain types of change of use are exempt from the need to obtain planning permission. Many types of use are very similar and the Town and Country Planning (Use Classes) Order groups many of the similar uses together into 'classes'. For instance, Class A1 covers shops; Class A2 covers financial and professional services; Class A3 covers premises selling food and drink; Class B1 is general business and offices; Class B2 is general industrial. There are many further subclasses, but these are the main ones encountered.

The rule is that you can change the use of premises from one use to another within the same-use class. For instance, if premises are currently being used as a newsagent's shop (Class A1), then the use can be changed to any other category A1 shop (e.g. a greengrocers) without the need for permission. On the other hand, it would not be possible to change to a different category (e.g. a shop selling drink or food, which is Class A3) without the need for permission. Similarly, a surveyor's office would be covered by Class B1 (offices), and those premises could be changed to the offices of a market researcher since that would still be an 'office' use, and thus within the same class (B1).

There are occasions when it is possible to change from one class to another, provided the change is to one less detrimental to the amenity of the area, for example, it is possible to change from Class A3 (food and drink) to Class A1 (ordinary shops). Similarly, it is possible to change from Class A2 (financial and professional services) to Class A1 (shops) if the premises have a display window at ground-floor level. It is also possible to change from Class B2 (general industrial use) to Class B1 (business offices).

As can be seen, these are complicated rules. The key point to appreciate is that any development needs planning permission; this includes any change of use of premises. The GPDO exempts much 'development' from this rule; in particular, changes of use within the Use Classes Order do not need permission.

Because of the complexity of the rules, it is always advisable to check with the local planners before carrying out any 'development' (i.e. building works or change of use).

Finally, it should not be forgotten that any building works carried out should comply with the relevant building standards. Building Regulations are laid down to ensure that building work is carried out to proper standards and using good-quality materials. The work has to be inspected (often by the local authority) to ensure compliance with the regulations and there are criminal sanctions for failure to comply.

Listed buildings

Listed buildings are subject to special planning controls. There are three grades of listed buildings:
- Grade I: buildings of exceptional interest (only about 2 per cent of listed buildings are in this category);
- Grade II: these are particularly important buildings of more than special interest;
- Grade III: these are buildings of special interest that warrant every effort being made to preserve them.

As well as planning permission, work to listed buildings will also need special 'listed building consent' to ensure that the buildings are not irreparably changed.

Conservation areas

A district or county council can designate an area as being of special architectural or historic interest: this is a conservation area. There are about 6,300 conservation areas in England.

If a property is within a conservation area, it follows that the planners will give special attention to the desirability of preserving or enhancing the character of the area whenever they are considering a planning application. The basic rule is to say that the planners start with a presumption in favour of preservation.

The GPDO (*see* above) normally allows certain development works to be carried out without planning permission. But within a conservation area those exceptions are severely restricted so that planning permission will nearly always need to be applied for.

In addition, any tree within a conservation area is automatically protected (as though there were a Tree Preservation Order in respect of that tree).

Obtaining other consents

Even if the householder has raised enough money to finance the improvements or modernization, and has obtained any necessary planning permission from the local authority, it still may not be possible to do the work. There may be other people whose consent has to be obtained before starting work. In particular, it may be necessary to ask permission of someone with the benefit of a restrictive covenant over the land; a ground landlord; the lender that gave the mortgage to buy the property; or a tenant who lives in it. Your house insurers will also need notifying.

Restrictive covenants

Restrictive covenants may limit the freedom of the freeholder to do what he or she likes with a property. Frequently, such restrictions are imposed by the developer of a building project when selling off the plots, so as to preserve the character and amenities of the area or of a neighbouring piece of land. Typical restrictive covenants prohibit building work without the consent of a neighbouring landowner or prohibit business use. The law on restrictive covenants is complicated and in some respects out of date. Detailed rules decide when a restrictive covenant is enforceable. The solicitor who acted on the purchase of the property should be able to advise the owner whether the land is subject to any restrictive covenants, and if so, may also be able to say who now has the benefit of them, i.e. who can enforce them.

In practice, many of the restrictive covenants in title deeds are unenforceable because they have become obsolete over the years, or do not comply with the strict rules as to enforceability. Such covenants can be safely ignored by the householder, but obviously this is something that should be done only after taking full legal advice.

If there is a valid restrictive covenant that affects planned building work, then there are four possible lines of action:
1 Approach the person who has the benefit of the restrictive covenant and negotiate (i.e. buy) permission.
2 Apply to the Lands Tribunal for the restrictive covenant to be cancelled or altered. Basically, the landowner will have to prove that:
   ● there has been a change in the character of the area; or
   ● no one would be injured by the cancellation or amendment; or
   ● the restrictive covenant impedes the reasonable use of the land.
In practice such an application is impractical except in cases of major developments, e.g. housing estates and the like; the landowner has to make out a very good case, and may well have to pay compensation. The

legal costs may well run into thousands of pounds and there will be a long delay while the case waits to be heard.
3 If the plans involve the conversion of a house into two or more flats or dwellings, the landowner can apply to the county court (not the Lands Tribunal) for the restrictive covenant to be cancelled or altered. Once again, cost and delay are factors to be borne in mind.
4 The householder can take out insurance, so that if the restrictive covenant should be enforced against him or her, the insurance company will pay compensation. Obviously, cover is available only when it is most unlikely that the covenant is enforceable. A single, one-off, premium is payable. Premiums vary considerably but start from about £250.

Is a restrictive covenant enforceable?

Suppose my land has the benefit of restrictive covenants affecting my neighbour's land. Can I enforce the covenants? Only if:
● the covenant makes it clear that the restrictive covenant is to benefit my land; and
● it was intended that it should be enforced by someone other than the original party to the covenant; and
● the covenant is properly entered at the Land Registry against your neighbour's property.
These are complicated rules, so always take specialist legal advice.

Covenants in a long lease

In the same way that a freeholder's rights may be limited by restrictive covenants, a leaseholder's rights may be limited by clauses in the lease. Moreover, the advantage of a lease is that it allows positive covenants (e.g. to spend money on repairing a fence) to be enforced. This is why most flats are sold on a leasehold, not freehold, basis.

Most long leases (i.e. leases for over 21 years) require the leaseholder to obtain the landlord's consent before erecting an extension or carrying out any other building work. Such consent should always be obtained, for otherwise the landlord will be able to terminate the lease for breach of covenant by the tenant; the absence of consent will also make it difficult to sell the house, should you wish to do so.

Mortgage lender's consent

Most mortgage deeds require the borrower to obtain the lender's consent before carrying out any alterations or building works or change of use. Usually, obtaining consent is no more than a formality since the lender will be only too pleased to approve works that increase the value of the property. However, the consent should always be obtained, for otherwise – in theory, anyway – the mortgage company would be entitled to take possession and sell the house in order to recover its loan. Often, the lender will charge an administration fee for deciding whether or not to give consent.

Party walls

A neighbour may have a 'right of support' from the land or buildings on the householder's land. If so, the householder must not carry out any works that would interfere with that right. In effect, both property owners are prevented from pulling down the party wall.

In London there are special laws that allow a householder to develop a party wall after giving notice to the neighbour. If the neighbour will not consent to the works, permission to carry them out can be obtained from the court, which can also order the neighbour to contribute towards the costs of the works if he or she will benefit from them. Architects and surveyors can advise on how these rules work.

Access to neighbouring land

Sometimes the only way to carry out repairs or improvements to property is to go on to your neighbour's land, for example, if the wall of the house is right up against the boundary line. However, going on to someone else's land is trespass and it is no excuse that you need to do so in order to repair your own property. Usually, of course, access will be freely granted out of neighbourliness; occasionally, the deeds may grant an express right of access to carry out repairs. But what if the neighbour steadfastly refuses to allow access? What can you do about it?

Until the Access to Neighbouring Land Act was passed in 1992, the answer was that little could be done. The Act has changed that. It lays down a procedure whereby a landowner can apply to the court for a court order permitting access to a neighbour's land if this is reason-ably necessary in order to carry out repairs or improvements. Any costs and expenses incurred by the neighbour will have to be met and the court can also order payment of an amount to compensate the neighbour for loss of privacy and inconvenience during the access. Bearing in mind these provisions and the costs and delay of going to court, it will always be beneficial to arrange access rights out of court, if this is at all possible. However, the existence of the Act may be useful as a bargaining tool.

Rights of light

Check that any building works will not interfere with a neighbour's right of light (*see* page 260).

A tenant's consent

If there is a tenant living in the property, it may well be necessary to obtain their consent before any building work can be carried out. A landlord will normally have a right of access to carry out repairs (on giving reasonable notice) but will only be able to carry out improvements if the terms of the lease allow him.

House insurers

You will also at the very least have to notify your buildings and contents insurers. You are under an obligation to let them know of anything which may increase the 'risk' to them, i.e. the chance of a claim being made on the policy. Carrying out building work, changing the use, etc. may well involve an increased risk and the insurers will want full details. They may decide to charge an increased premium or impose conditions as to how the work is to be carried out. If you do not inform your insurers and a claim then needs to be made on the policy, the insurance company would be within its rights to refuse to honour the claim.

24

Neighbours

Every house owner has certain rights, and similarly his or her neighbours will have rights over their property. At times, these rights and interests will clash, and then the law must resolve the ensuing dispute.

But the law is a clumsy instrument for dealing with the delicate relationship which exists between neighbours and the wise house owner will do almost anything – short of moving house – to avoid getting the law involved in a neighbour dispute. Sometimes even moving will be cheaper and less stressful in the long run. Try tact, diplomacy, persuasion, concession, anything, rather than move in with a blunt statement of legal rights. All solicitors know from experience how neighbour disputes can easily erupt into lengthy, expensive and bitter litigation, with the real cause of the argument being lost in a web of hurt feelings and self-justification. Often, too, neither party is satisfied with the outcome; the only winners are the lawyers who will collect their fee no matter who wins and no matter how many people get hurt in the process.

NEIGHBOURS FROM HELL

Neighbours from Hell was the title of a successful television series, highlighting the problems that can arise between neighbours – often people who were once friends – and providing the voyeuristic public with a chance to thank their lucky stars that it is someone else, and not them, caught up in the horror. More often than not, there is fault on both sides and feelings are exacerbated when one side or the other starts quoting their legal 'rights'. However, if the parties cannot reach a satisfactory compromise, what is the legal position? What are the rights and responsibilities of the house owner *vis-à-vis* his neighbours?

MY RIGHTS – MY NEIGHBOUR'S RIGHTS

We have already seen that your rights to do what you want with your land – or your neighbour's rights to do what he or she wants, for that matter – are restricted by the rights that others may have over a piece of land. These may be rights granted to individuals or to the community at large, and this section of the book looks at the ways the law tries to regulate these clashes between the rights of various people. As a reminder there are:

- rights vested in the community (e.g. to enforce public health standards of hygiene on the property or to control the erection and design of buildings);
- rights that other individuals have over the property (e.g. a right of way to walk over the land or the power to stop nuisance-making activities).

These are the sorts of rights that neighbours can have over one's land, and are therefore the concern of this chapter. Thus my right to use and enjoy my land freely is limited by my neighbour's rights. Conversely, the extent of my rights over my neighbour's land affects the neighbour's ability to use and enjoy that neighbouring property in the way that he may wish.

The point to be repeated (again and again!) is that the law should be the last resort, not the first, in a neighbour dispute. Conciliation, not confrontation or litigation, is likely to yield the best results. And even moving may be easier in the long run; no, it is not giving in and 'leaving your home because of them'; it is often plain common sense.

Trespass

'Keep Out – Private Property' is a concise statement of the law. If someone owns a plot of land, a house or a garden, it is up to them to decide who can come on to the property. This is, of course, subject to the community's right to send in the police if a criminal offence has been committed or to allow gas pipes to be laid, etc.

and even these rights of entry are strictly limited and controlled by the law. But, as regards other private individuals, such as neighbours, the owner can generally say 'Keep Out – Private Property: You Are Trespassing'.

What if the trespasser defies the owner's wishes and comes on to the property; what can be done? First, the landowner can eject the trespasser, after first asking him or her to leave, using no more force than is reasonably necessary. But this is unwise, for the trespasser might allege (and prove) that unnecessary force was used and so prosecute or bring civil proceedings for assault. The much-publicized case of farmer Tony Martin in April 2000 demonstrates that it is not lawful to shoot a trespasser unless self-defence can be established under normal legal rules.

Second, the landowner could sue the trespasser for damages, to obtain compensation for any loss caused. Unless the intruder had damaged the house, trampled on the garden or broken a fence, it would be unlikely that the landowner would have suffered any loss and so claiming damages would be a pointless exercise. The owner would probably recover only nominal damages of a few pounds, and the court might show its disapproval of suing over such a petty matter by not awarding any legal costs.

Does this mean that there is no remedy against the trespasser? Against the casual trespasser – such as the country walker who takes a short cut across a field – the answer is 'yes', for in practice the landowner can do nothing unless real damage is caused. However, in the case of a persistent trespasser, the landowner could ask the court for an injunction, ordering that person not to trespass in the future; if that order was ignored then the trespasser would be in contempt of court and so liable to a fine or even imprisonment. Thus, if a person regularly uses someone else's back garden as a short cut, or if they frequently park their car on someone else's lawn, the law can be used to stop the trespass.

As for signs that proclaim 'Trespassers Will Be Prosecuted', these are pure bluff on the part of the landowner. Trespass is a wrong to the landowner, who can sue in the civil courts for damages and/or an injunction. But the landowner cannot prosecute, since trespass is not, of itself, a criminal offence. So the police may not be overinterested in cases of trespass as no criminal offence has been committed. They may attend in order to prevent a breach of the peace, but it may be the violent landowner they arrest for this and not the peaceful trespasser. Exceptionally, the person who trespasses in a building by squatting may be committing a criminal offence, and many public or quasi-public bodies, such as railways and airports, have special Acts of Parliament which makes trespass on their land a crime, but the general rule remains that trespass is a civil, not a criminal, wrong.

Squatters' rights

As we have seen (page 175), if someone trespasses on land by taking possession of it for 12 years they may acquire the legal ownership of that land. Until then, however, squatters are merely trespassers and can be evicted as such. A court order is generally advisable and a speedy procedure is available in the county court which allows the eviction of any squatters, even if their names are not known.

Removing squatters

The main remedies available against squatters are:

- possession order: as already mentioned, a speedy procedure is available in the county court to obtain a possession order against a squatter. This is a relatively expensive process, though;
- interim possession order (IPO): IPOs were introduced as an emergency procedure to short-circuit standard squatter possession procedures. The aim was that IPOs would be available in about a week. In practice, if a local county court is busy, then it will not be much quicker than a standard squatter application. One advantage is that if the squatter fails to leave within 24 hours of being served with the court papers, then he can be arrested. The claim for an IPO must be issued within 28 days of the landowner knowing that the premises are being squatted in, the court forms must be served within 24 hours of being issued by the court and the landowner has to attend the court proceedings;
- legal forced entry: if you go away for a few days and then return to find squatters in occupation of your home, you may be entitled to use force to gain entry to your home (under section 6 of the Criminal Law Act 1977). However, this remedy is more theoretical than practical as the police will rarely assist;
- changing the locks when the squatters are out: this may seem a cheap and immediate remedy, but it rarely works. Section 6 of the Criminal Law Act 1977 makes it an arrestable offence for any person to use or threaten violence to enter premises if they know that there is someone present on the premises opposed to their entry. Therefore, you have to be absolutely certain that the building is empty before breaking in and changing the locks. If you do not, then it will be an illegal forced entry. In practice, most squatters are usually smart enough to leave someone on the premises;
- police power to impound vehicles and arrest the trespassers (sections 61 and 62 of the Criminal Justice and Public Order Act 1994): this allows the police to intervene by arresting or impounding where there are two or more people on open land acting abusively, threateningly, or damaging property (and/or if they have six or more vehicles on the land). In theory, it provides an admirable remedy when squatters are on

'open land', in that it is cheap to the landowner, gets an immediate result and there is also a power of arrest. In practice, it is useless because the police simply will not use their powers.

Travellers

A traveller may own the land on which he has parked his caravan but, in most instances, such use of the land will be unlawful. In that case, the local planning authority can take action to remove travellers from the land. In particular, the local authority may attempt to obtain an injunction to remedy a breach of the planning laws. However, if the travellers apply for planning permission, then it will be extremely difficult for the local authority to obtain an injunction pending the outcome of the planning decision.

The Criminal Justice and Public Order Act 1994 introduced powers for the police to remove those involved in an unlawful occupation of land involving six or more vehicles and this power can be used to evict travellers. However, the Association of Chief Police Officers announced that no police force in the country had either the time or the manpower to become involved in removing travellers from sites.

The only real alternative lies in a civil court action for possession. Typically, this will take about two weeks, although it can be quicker if the landowner chooses to enforce the order for possession through private bailiffs rather than waiting for court officials to effect the eviction.

Rights of way

The general rule is that a person who goes on to another's land without permission will be a trespasser. But footpaths and other rights of way allow the use of private land without trespassing.

Private footpaths

A person may have an easement (*see* page 172) to use a footpath across private land. As we have seen, that right can be acquired by an express grant by a previous landowner, or by implication of law when part of a piece of land is sold, or by using the footpath for a sufficiently long period, i.e. 20 years without permission.

If a person has a right of way across another's land then they will not be a trespasser as long as they keep to the footpath. If they deviate from the path, they will become a trespasser.

Public rights of way

In the same way that an individual can acquire a private footpath right, so the public at large can gain a public right of way. Public rights of way can be created after 20 years' use, but only if the route is used:

- by the public at large (i.e. not just by the owners of a neighbouring piece of land); and
- as of right (i.e. without permission having been asked for or given); and
- over a defined route.

After 20 years' use by the public, the law presumes that the landowner has dedicated the land as a public highway (Highways Act 1980). To avoid this happening, a landowner should publicly show that a public right of way is not being created. This can be done by displaying a sign stating that the land is not being dedicated as a public highway, or by depositing a formal notice with the local authority. Alternatively, the landowner can protect his or her position by blocking off the road or path for one day every year, so as to assert ownership and indicate that the use of the path is by courtesy only.

Types of use permitted

A right of way, whether public or private, can be restricted to a particular method of use. In the case of a private right which has been expressly granted, then the deed creating it should be looked at. Does it allow access merely on foot, or is vehicular access also allowed? Was the right granted for use all day and every day, or only during daylight hours or not at weekends? Use in an unauthorized way will amount to trespass.

In the case of easements acquired by long use, the type of use over the 20-year period will dictate the use permitted in the future. So, 20 years' use on foot will not permit use by vehicles.

In the case of public rights of way, you should inspect the local authority's definitive map showing all highways in their area. All public rights of way have to be categorized as either:

- *footpaths* – pedestrians only;
- *bridleways* – pedestrians and horses only;
- *by-ways open to all traffic* – i.e. cart-ways open to pedestrians, horses, carts and cars.

The district, county, London Borough or unitary council will keep copies of the definitive map, which shows the location and classification of every public right of way. If a path is marked on a definitive map that will be conclusive evidence that it is open to the public, but just because a path is not on the map it does not follow that it is not open to the public. So public paths can still be created and can therefore exist even when not marked on the definitive map. Obviously, in such a case it is sensible to ask the council to include the path on the definitive map when it is next revised.

A public footpath cannot be lost by disuse; once a footpath exists it remains a footpath, until closed by an order made under a statute. Such an order might be made, for example, to divert a path in order that a building estate can be constructed.

Common land

It has been a criminal offence since 1925 to drive a vehicle over common land. That means that it is not possible to acquire an easement by 20 years' use to drive a vehicle across common land to get to one's house. Thus, the fact that a landowner may have driven a vehicle over a common for more than 20 years will not have given him an easement. The end result is that the common's owner (often a local authority) can demand a ransom price to allow the vehicle access to continue.

This problem has been addressed by the Countryside and Rights of Way Act 2000. The Act deals primarily with the right to roam across the countryside, but section 68 makes it possible for an easement to be granted giving vehicular rights over common land. A property owner who can show 20 years' usage over the privately owned access way (which is part of the common land or village green) can now claim a statutory easement. The access owner is entitled to compensation, but instead of holding the property owner to ransom he will instead get compensation assessed under a statutory formula. Most properties will pay 2 per cent of their current open market; properties in existence by 1930 will pay 0.5 per cent, and those in existence before 1905 0.25 per cent.

Use of a footpath

A public footpath can be used by anyone, but only for passing along it in the course of a bona fide journey. While the walker can stop for a rest he or she cannot use the footpath for camping on or for some other use unconnected with travelling along the path. If the path is not used for its proper purpose, the walker becomes a trespasser.

A footpath ran beside a field where horses were trained. A journalist walked backwards and forwards over a 15-yard stretch of the path for an hour and a half, making notes on the performance of the various horses. Held: He was a trespasser since he was not just using the path for a bona fide journey. While it would not be unreasonable for a walker to sit down to rest, or even to stop to make a sketch, it was unreasonable to use the footpath as a means of spying on the training of horses. Hickman (1900)

However,

When 21 people gathered on a public right of way to protest about their exclusion from Stonehenge, it was held that they were not trespassing. The public's right was not restricted to the right of passage and matters incidental or ancillary to that right. Rather, the public had the right of use for such reasonable and usual activities, including peaceful assembly, as were consistent with and did not obstruct the general public's primary right of passage. Jones (1999)

The general rule is that it is a criminal offence to ride a motor bike or drive a car on a footpath or bridleway. Although horse riders are not allowed to use footpaths they do not, in fact, commit any criminal offence in doing so; the only remedies are for the council to put up barriers (but leaving sufficient space for walkers), or for the landowner to sue for trespass. Finally, a walker can take a dog on a footpath, but obviously it must not be allowed to stray on to the neighbouring land.

Maintenance of footpaths and bridleways

The general rule is that it is the duty of the county or unitary council, or London Borough Council, to maintain public footpaths and bridleways in its area; the only exceptions are footpaths created since 1949 which the council has not agreed to maintain. By the Highways Act 1980 section 130, county councils have a duty 'to assert and protect the rights of the public to the use and enjoyment' of paths in their area and 'to prevent as far as possible the stopping up or obstruction' of paths.

The council's duty is to maintain only the surface of the path. There is no duty to maintain the subsoil on which it rests. For example, if a towpath collapses into a canal the council need not repair the path since it has now disappeared!

A council is not expected to maintain a path in perfect condition. As long as it is safe and fit to carry its usual amount of traffic that will be sufficient. The rambler cannot expect a little-used path to be fully cleared. Ministry guidelines to councils state:

Where paths are used mainly for pleasure by ramblers, it will no doubt generally be sufficient that they should be free from obstructions or impassable water or mud, and that they should be inconspicuously but sufficiently signposted or marked where necessary. The main consideration is clearly that they should serve their purpose, whether business or pleasure, and not that they should conform to some arbitrary standard of construction.

If the county council, as the highway authority, fails to maintain paths to this standard, it can be taken to court by any private individual and ordered to repair the path or bridleway. However, note the limitations placed on this.

Where a council had allowed a bridleway to be encroached on to by adjoining owners, which seriously obstructed the use of the bridleway, they could not be compelled to remove the obstructions on the basis that the bridleway was out of repair. Removing obstructions did not amount to repair. Westley (1998)

In addition, if the authority fails to inspect the paths reasonably often and then carry out any necessary works, it may well be liable in damages to anyone injured because of the lack of repair. However, it is rare for such a liability to arise since the courts do not expect councils to carry out frequent inspections of their footpaths.

Mrs Whiting was injured while walking on a footpath. She stepped into undergrowth beside the path to let another walker pass and hurt herself on a concealed tree stump. She sued the council, but the council argued that it had not been negligent. The path had been inspected in July, cleared the following February, and the accident happened a month later. Held: The council had acted reasonably and was not liable. Whiting (1970)

While the duty to maintain the surface of a footpath falls on the council, the duty to maintain stiles and gates rests on the owner of the land. The obligation is to keep stiles and gates 'in safe condition, and to the standard of repair required to prevent unreasonable interference with the rights of persons using the footpath or bridleway' (Countryside Act 1968). The council must contribute at least a quarter of the maintenance costs. If the landowner does not maintain the stiles and fences, the council can give 14 days' notice and then do the work itself, but at the expense of the landowner and without any contribution from the council. Alternatively, the council or any private individual can apply to the magistrates' court for an order requiring the landowner to do the necessary works.

In theory, county councils are under a duty to put up signposts whenever a public right of way meets a metalled (i.e. tarmac) road. But the Act does not lay down a time period within which this must be done and so, in practical terms, councils cannot legally be forced to put up signposts, although most have done so.

Obstructions on footpaths and bridleways

Anyone who 'wilfully obstructs the free passage along a highway' can be fined (the Highways Act 1980 section 137). The prosecution need not be brought by the highway authority but can be brought by a private individual or even an amenity group, for example, the Ramblers' Association. A prosecution was brought in January 2000 against Mr Nicholas Van Hoogstraten for the alleged obstruction of a disputed footpath across his estate in East Sussex.

The Countryside and Rights of Way Act 2000 considerably toughened sanctions against landowners and occupiers who persistently obstruct footpaths or bridleways. People convicted of deliberately obstructing a highway can be fined £1,000 and ordered to remove the obstruction. If they do not, they can be fined up to £5,000 or face a prison sentence. Further fines of up to £250 can be imposed for every day the obstruction remains.

It is not necessary that the obstruction should completely block the path; it is sufficient that it blocks part of it or that it makes walking along the path more difficult. For instance, a farmer who dumps refuse on part of the path or who padlocks a gate can be prosecuted. Similarly, if a farmer allows crops to grow on the footpath or bridleway that, too, may be an obstruction.

The ploughing up of a path or bridleway is not of itself an obstruction, unless, of course, it makes it impossible to use the route. However, ploughing is dealt with by the Rights of Way Act 1990. In essence, a farmer can plough a right of way, provided he does this for the purposes of 'good husbandry' (i.e. efficient farming) and provided the path is reinstated within 14 days. If the farmer does not reinstate the path within 14 days, then the highway authority can prosecute (but the highway authority can extend the 14-day period).

The Rights of Way Act 1990 also makes it an offence for a farmer to allow any crop (except grass) to encroach on a footpath or bridleway so as to make it inconvenient for the public to exercise their right of way. Another offence puts an obligation on the farmer to take necessary steps to ensure that the line of the highway on the ground is indicated. In other words, a farmer cannot simply plant crops and leave it to the public to guess which is the correct line of the footpath. Moreover, the Act lays down minimum widths for footpaths in these circumstances.

Note that any individual or organization can prosecute for breach; this is obviously important for pressure groups wishing to preserve rights of access to the countryside.

If a walker or rider comes across an obstruction it can be removed, but only in so far as it is necessary to be able to continue the journey. So if the path is only partly obstructed the walker cannot remove the obstruction if it is possible to continue the walk without removing it. The walker can only do what is essential.

Mr Slama had a café by the sea front in Hastings. Access to the café was by three public footpaths which crossed Mr Seaton's land. Mr Seaton erected a fence which blocked all three paths. Slama took down 180 yards of fence and burnt part of it, claiming that he was exercising his right to remove obstructions from a public footpath. Held: No. The judge said: 'If the gate is locked he may be entitled to break the lock. If there is a fence across the entrance to the way he may be justified in removing a sufficient part of the fence to enable him to have free access to the way. But he could do no more than that.' Seaton (1932)

In addition, this form of self-help is available only to someone who is genuinely using the path for a journey. So a rambler who sets out with the sole object of removing obstructions cannot claim to be acting lawfully; apart from being sued for trespass, the rambler might be prosecuted for criminal damage. In practice, of course, it would be difficult for the landowner to prove that the rambler did not genuinely intend using the path for a journey.

The experienced walker will probably come across two other problems – usually resulting from farmers who resent public use of footpaths. First, there is the 'misleading sign' ploy (e.g. a 'Private' sign). This is illegal if the sign is designed to deter the use of a public right of way marked on the definitive map. Report the offence to the county council. Under the Countryside and Rights of Way Act 2000, landowners who put up misleading signs, stating that there is no public right of way where one legally exists, will be liable to fines of £200. The second tactic is the 'bull in the field' ploy. Since 1981 all dairy bulls have been banned from fields that are crossed by public paths, and other types of bull can be permitted only if accompanied by cows or heifers. Prosecution is difficult, however, because no specific criminal offence arises (although the police might decide that the farming business being carried on is endangering the public, and so prosecute under the Health and Safety at Work laws).

The right to roam

Walkers and other environmental pressure groups have for many years been pressing for an unrestricted 'right to roam' over private land. This campaigning finally bore fruit in November 2000 when the Countryside and Rights of Way Act 2000 was enacted. This allows people to walk on open country which is shown on maps produced by the Countryside Agency. The legislation does not provide a new 'right to roam' as it is commonly referred to, but rather a right of access to land that has been designated as 'access land'. Any walking on private land in accordance with the right to roam will no longer be a trespass – indeed it will be a criminal offence to prevent or obstruct this right to roam.

However, this right should not be overstated. It will only grant a right to roam over uncultivated land, so walkers will not be able to roam at will through a field of growing crops – or someone's back garden! There is some concern that the publicity given to the right to roam has emphasized the right without sufficiently stressing its limitations and this may encourage some to claim a right to roam where none exists. Many landowners fear the damage which may be caused. There are also genuine uncertainties. What is uncultivated land? Obviously open moorland is included, but what about a field left fallow on a rotational basis; will it be subject to a right to roam one year and not the next? Anyone seeking to exercise this right to roam will need to study its provisions very carefully, as will landowners likely to be affected.

The promised access over four million acres of open, uncultivated country will not be available anywhere at all until at least the summer of 2004, when areas of southern England will see the new rights introduced, and will not be available over the whole country until the end of 2005, when approved maps of the whole country will be completed.

- Certain land is specifically excluded from the new statutory right of access, including cultivated land, golf courses, race courses, railways and buildings.
- The Act gives no new rights to cycle, ride horses or use boats or vehicles, though where these rights already exist, they will not be affected.
- Activities such as running, walking, bird-watching and climbing will be allowed.
- People on access land must not light fires, damage plants, animals or property, feed livestock or bathe in water. Those who break these rules will lose their right of access for 72 hours and will be treated as trespassers.
- Landowners can exclude or restrict access to their land for up to 28 days a year, for example during the lambing season, but not at weekends or public holidays.
- Landowners who disagree that their land qualifies as open country will have a right of appeal.
- The Act redesignates more than 4,000 miles of rights of way as 'restricted byways', a new category of public highway giving access to all traffic except motorized vehicles. This will give greater access to horse riders, walkers, cyclists and drivers of horse-drawn carriages.
- The Act updates the Wildlife and Countryside Act 1981, creating a new offence of 'reckless disturbance' of wildlife, which could be used against those who use scrambler bikes or play war games on wildlife areas or in the vicinity of rare birds. In September 2001, a wild birds' egg collector became the first person in the UK to be jailed under the legislation. He was sent to prison for four months by magistrates who were told that his hobby was damaging the country's bird population. The 2000 Act allows courts to impose a jail sentence of up to six months. (*See also* page 275.)

Airspace

The rules of trespass are not confined to the land itself. In legal theory, a landowner owns not only the surface of the land, but the air above it and the soil beneath it. Thus an unreasonable intrusion into another person's airspace will be a trespass, although whether that person will be awarded any damages will depend upon their being able to show a resulting loss.

Mr Kelsen had a tobacconist's shop in Islington. His landlords allowed a tobacco company to erect a large 'Players Please' sign which projected eight inches into the airspace above his shop. Mr Kelsen sued for trespass. Held: Yes, it was a trespass and the sign should be removed.

Kelsen (1957)

But it is not always necessary to claim damages. Simply getting an injunction may be enough to cause great inconvenience to the trespasser. This has proved to be the case with large cranes. Often, the property developer will install a crane on a plot of land in order to carry out building works. But modern cranes are so large that the booms often overhang neighbouring land. If this happens, there will have been a trespass. It follows from this that anyone who wishes to use a crane must ensure that neighbours give consent before a crane boom passes over their land. If this consent is not given, then an injunction can be obtained against the trespassing crane. In practice, this means that the developer will have to buy permission to use the airspace from the neighbour.

The developers of a major dockland site erected large cranes. But the owner of a neighbouring site objected because the booms of the tower cranes over-sailed his land from time to time. The developer argued that it would be wrong for an injunction to be granted; after all, the crane booms were at such a height that they were in no way interfering with the normal use of the neighbour's land. **Held:** *The crane booms amounted to an invasion of airspace and this was trespass. That being so, an injunction would be granted.*

Anchor Brewhouse (1987)

When planes first started flying, their pilots faced trespass claims from the owners of the land flown over. To get around this problem, the Civil Aviation Act 1949 exempts over-flying aircraft from trespass claims, for otherwise homeowners near airports would be able to obtain injunctions against the airline operators and so ground all flights. However, the Act does not protect planes that are flying 'unreasonably low' and in that case there may be a trespass; generally, the minimum height for a light aircraft is about 1,000 feet and 2,000 feet for other aircraft except, of course, when landing and taking off.

The protection given by the 1949 Act covers any flight which is at a reasonable height, even when the object of the flight is not just to pass over the land en route to the plane's destination.

Skyviews took aerial photographs of people's houses and then offered to sell photographs to the house owner. One person whose home was photographed in this way was Lord Bernstein. He took exception to this invasion of his privacy – he had warned the firm before they took the photographs not to over-fly his land – and sued Skyviews for trespass. In their defence, Skyviews relied upon the protection given by the Civil Aviation Act 1949. **Held:** *A landowner has rights only in his airspace to such a height as is necessary for the use and enjoyment of his land. The flight by Skyviews had been at a reasonable height and was thus protected. There had been no trespass.* Bernstein (1977)

Light

Although landowners own the airspace above their property, there is no automatic right to have light enter their airspace or land. Thus, if a neighbour wants to build a high boundary wall (or grow a high Leylandii hedge) that will put your house into shade, there may be nothing that can be done about it, beyond opposing the neighbour's application for planning permission to erect the wall (*see* page 247) and below 'High Hedges').

However, it is possible for a landowner to have acquired a 'right to light', either by written agreement with the neighbour or by long use, i.e. by having actually enjoyed the light for over 20 years. So, if the house is over 20 years old, the house owner will probably have acquired a right to light and will be able to prevent the erection of any structure that would seriously reduce the amount of light to its windows.

Note that the right to light is a civil right; there can be no prosecution for infringing such a right. A county court injunction would be required to prevent building works which obstructed the right. Although, as we have stated, court action should normally be a last resort, if you delay too long before seeking an injunction to prevent building work (e.g. by allowing the building work to be substantially completed before you object to it), then the court may refuse to grant an injunction and award damages by way of compensation instead.

The right to light only exists in relation to light for buildings, and not for gardens and other open spaces, such as allotments; so if the proposed wall would put a rose garden into shadow the landowner could never claim a right to light to prevent its erection (but a greenhouse is a building and so may have a right to light – *see* below).

The extent of the right

If a right to light exists, it is not a right to prevent any obstruction, but just a right to ensure that a minimum level of light is maintained. If the light is reduced, but the selling and letting values of the house are unchanged and the comfort of its occupants not reduced, then there will not have been any infringement of the right to light. Thus the question is not 'How much light has been taken away?' but 'How much light remains?'

In deciding what is the minimum level required the court will consider such factors as the nature of the locality and the type of room affected: for instance, a bedroom needs less light than a sitting room. Conversely, if the normal use of a building requires it to have an unusually high level of light, e.g. an artist's studio, then the right to light will have been infringed if the level is reduced to a level which is insufficient for its normal use.

Mr and Mrs Allen had a greenhouse in their back garden. It had been there for over 20 years, so when their neighbours erected a fence beside it, they asked for the fence to be removed on the grounds that it infringed their right to light. In particular, their tomatoes no longer grew properly because the greenhouse was now in shadow. The neighbours refused to move the fence and argued that a right to light only covers a 'normal' amount of light – not the exceptional amount needed by a greenhouse. Held: A right to light extends to the amount of light needed by a building for its normal use. The greenhouse needed a lot of light, and so the right to light had been infringed. The fence had to be taken down. Allen (1979)

If a house owner does not have a right to light (e.g. if he or she owns a new house on a new estate) there is nothing that can be done to prevent neighbours from blocking off the light, apart, of course, from using this as a ground for opposing the granting of planning permission. If, despite these efforts, planning permission is granted, the house owner will just have to accept the resulting inconvenience and reduction in the value of the property. His neighbour has the right to build on his own land and in so doing is not infringing any right of the house owner.

Preventing a right to light being acquired

Finally, a word of warning: it is possible to own a 20-year-old house and yet not have a right to light. This can happen when the title deeds specifically say that a right to light cannot be acquired. For instance, if a house owner sells off half the garden for development, a clause might be inserted preventing a right to light being acquired by the buyer and his successors; otherwise, if the seller wanted to build on the other half of the garden in over 20 years' time, this might be challenged on the ground that the proposed building would infringe the other property's right to light. By suitably wording the original deed transferring ownership, a seller can prevent the right to light being acquired.

It is not unusual for the deed to state that the buyer cannot acquire a right to light over the seller's land, while specifically giving the seller a right to light over the buyer's land. This will then prevent the buyer building on his land so as to obstruct the light to the windows of the seller's house. However, due to the uncertainties of the right to light (e.g. the amount of light to which you are entitled) it is probably preferable for the light to windows to be protected in a different way. The buyer, as part of the purchase deal, can be required to enter into a covenant (i.e. a formal promise) not to build on the land unless the seller approves the location and plans of the building. The seller can then refuse consent to any building which might infringe his light. Alternatively, if the buyer refuses to agree to this as he thinks that this will give the seller too much control, a 'building line' can be used. The buyer covenants not to build within a stated distance of the boundary fence – and this distance can be sufficient to ensure that any building will not cause the seller any inconvenience.

Mr Howells decided to put up an extension. His neighbours, the Pughs, objected, pointing out it would interfere with their right to light. Despite clear warnings on this, Mr Howells went ahead. The Pughs then went to court, asking for an order that the extension be removed. Held: The extension did interfere with the light to the Pughs' house. Howells had been given ample warning but decided to go ahead nonetheless. An order was made that the extension should be knocked down. Pugh (1984)

High Hedges

The government is giving strong support to a private members' bill, the High Hedges Bill, which is consequently very likely to become law. Under the Bill a residential occupier can complain to the local authority about a high hedge. The hedge must be an evergreen, over 2 metres high and unreasonably restricting light to the property. If the local authority is satisfied that action should be taken, then it will issue a 'remedial notice' on the hedge owner (e.g. to reduce the height). Failure to comply could lead to a £1,000 fine, and further daily fines for non-compliance. For further information, or to keep an eye on the progress of the Bill, visit Hedgeline's website at www.hedgeline.org. Hedgeline is a group campaigning for legislation to deal with problem hedges in residential areas.

Protecting a view

English law does not recognize the right to a view from one's house and, unlike a right to light, it is not possible to acquire the right to an uninterrupted view by 20 years' usage.

Thus, a house owner cannot go to court if a neighbour erects a building or plants a tree that will ruin the view, even if it takes thousands of pounds off the value of the householder's property. However, on a sale of part of your land, your right to a view can be protected by requiring the buyer to enter into a covenant as mentioned above, i.e. not to build without your permission and approval of the plans. You can then ensure that any building work will not spoil the view – or obstruct the light.

Nuisance

Trespass covers *physical* intrusions by a neighbour but if the interference with a householder's rights is of a less tangible nature, trespass will be of no use; for instance, noise and smells cannot be stopped by bringing an action for trespass since there has been no physical encroachment on to the property. However, for these intangible intrusions, the law provides another remedy – bringing an action for 'nuisance'.

When a lawyer talks of a 'nuisance', the word is being used in a well-defined legal sense. Not every anti-social act by my neighbour will be a legal 'nuisance', although I might well regard it as a 'damned nuisance'!

The 'nuisance' claim covers behaviour that causes injury to land or, alternatively, substantially interferes with the enjoyment of land. Vibrations from a nearby factory that cause damage to the foundations of a house; heavy smoke from a coal fire; strong smells from a neighbour's septic tank or pigs; noise from machinery in a factory or noise from late-night parties – these are the sort of anti-social acts that can amount to a legal 'nuisance'.

The law expects neighbours to give and take. When people live in close proximity to one another they must be prepared to compromise and to take account of the reasonable wishes of their neighbours. In fact, the word 'reasonable' occurs again and again in the courts' decisions on nuisance cases, for the courts apply an objective test of how the 'reasonable man' (or woman) would behave and how he (or she) would react to the behaviour in question.

Does a 'nuisance' exist?

The first step is to consider whether the plaintiff (i.e. the complainant) is justified in going to court. Clearly, if he or she or their land has suffered material physical damage, they are entitled to bring a claim (e.g. if crops have died from factory fumes). If the complaint is an interference with the use and enjoyment of land (e.g. unpleasant smells) then the courts will want to be sure that there is a serious or substantial interference, and that the plaintiff is not being over-fussy or fastidious. Thus the extent and duration of the interference becomes relevant (e.g. a party every night is unreasonable, but one a month is probably not). What is the nature and character of the harm? Is the plaintiff's use of the land suitable for the neighbourhood and locality (e.g. he or she may want peace for their animals to graze – in the country this might be reasonable, but in central London it would be unreasonable)? Could he or she have easily avoided the consequences of the neighbour's behaviour or are they just being bloodyminded?

If the plaintiff passes these hurdles on the 'reasonable man' test, the court goes on to consider the behaviour of his troublesome neighbour, the defendant. An important factor will be whether their use of the land is reasonable for the area and locality (e.g. keeping a dozen pigs may be reasonable in the country, but it would be considered unreasonable in central London). Is the defendant's aim innocent or is he or she, in fact, acting with malice by trying to annoy the plaintiff (e.g. is the sole motive for practising drum solos to annoy the neighbour or is the defendant really a music student with nowhere else to practise?)? Has he or she taken all reasonable steps to minimize the effects of their actions (e.g. do they try to muffle the sound of their drums? Do they practise in daylight hours only?)? Once again, a 'reasonable man' test is applied, and if the defendant has not behaved reasonably the court will award damages to the plaintiff and probably grant an injunction ordering the defendant to stop the nuisance-making activities.

Clearly, then, what will be a nuisance in one part of the country may not be a nuisance in another area; what may be a nuisance to one plaintiff will not be a nuisance to another plaintiff. As a judge said in one case over a hundred years ago: 'What would be a nuisance in Belgrave Square would not necessarily be so in Bermondsey'. It all depends on the facts of the case and whether our 'reasonable man' (or woman) would tolerate the neighbour's behaviour. A factor to bear in mind is the question of planning permission. Before a landowner can change the use of his land or build on it, he will need permission from the local authority. What if the person causing the alleged nuisance has got planning permission, does this justify the nuisance and act as a defence to any claim brought by an aggrieved neighbour? It may do.

The operators of a commercial dock had been granted planning permission and within that permission operated on a 'round the clock' basis so that heavy lorries continuously passing to and fro caused serious disturbance in the adjoining residential district. Held: *The grant of planning permission had altered the character of the neighbourhood from residential to commercial and the question of nuisance would be judged in relation to the character as changed and not as it was previously. On the facts there was no nuisance.* Medway (Chatham) Dock Co. Ltd (1993)

On the other hand:

In a classic neighbours from hell scenario, the defendants obtained planning permission to erect a large pig unit within a few metres of the plaintiff's house. The smell was unbearable. In an action for nuisance it was no defence that planning permission had been obtained.

Wheeler (1996)

Nuisance claims are not confined to such obvious complaints as noise and smells. Anything that substantially interferes with a householder's or landowner's enjoyment of his property can be a nuisance.

Two prostitutes lived in a house in Mayfair. Their neighbours applied to the court for an injunction ordering the girls not to use their house for prostitution, on the ground that the frequent callers and the general misbehaviour was a legal nuisance. Held: *Yes, there was a nuisance, and an injunction was granted.* Thompson-Schwab (1956)

A company bought a shop in an area that was residential, but which included restaurants, snackbars, etc. Previously the shop had been a dress shop; the company converted it to a sex shop, with illuminated signs describing its wares. Local residents brought a nuisance claim against the company, claiming damages and an injunction. **Held:** *A sex shop could be a legal 'nuisance'. Anything that was an affront to the reasonable susceptibilities of ordinary people and which interfered with reasonable domestic enjoyment of property could be a nuisance. An injunction would be granted.*
Laws (1981)

A motor company had a lease on premises next to some open land owned by the local council. Gypsies moved on to the land and, despite complaints, the number of gypsies increased over the years. The council got a court order against the gypsies but never evicted them. The garage company sued for damages – complaining that they had suffered a major loss in trade due to the presence of the gypsies. **Held:** *The council were liable in nuisance. They owned the land and should have taken more prompt steps to get rid of the gypsies.*
Page Motors (1981)

Noise

When considering a nuisance claim for noise, the court will consider all the factors mentioned above. For example, in a 1914 case a hotel was able to stop building operations on an adjacent plot because they prevented the residents from sleeping and after-dinner speakers from making themselves heard. But the court ordered the builders to stop their pile-driving only between 10 p.m. and 6.30 a.m. – so what may be a nuisance at night need not be a nuisance in the daytime.

The nature of the locality will also be important.

Mr Leeman bought a house in an area that was partly residential and partly rural. His neighbour had an orchard 100 yards away, in which he kept 750 cockerels. The crowing of the cockerels prevented Mr Leeman from sleeping, so he brought a nuisance claim against his neighbour. **Held:** *The cockerels were a nuisance, although they would probably not have been a nuisance in a non-residential area.*
Leeman (1936)

Why does the plaintiff need peace and quiet? Is a neighbour's noise really a nuisance or is the plaintiff being fussy? For instance, when the vicar of a Brighton church went to court over the hum from nearby electrical machinery, his claim failed because the court did not regard the noise as a sufficiently serious annoyance, since he was still able to preach and conduct services.

Sometimes it is a new neighbour who has just moved into the area who complains about the defendant's noisy behaviour. The defendant might argue, 'I was making the noise before he came; he didn't have to come and live here.' That argument will not succeed, and the defendant will have to stop his anti-social behaviour if it is a nuisance to his new neighbour – as with Mr Leeman's neighbour who kept the cockerels in his orchard (*see* above). The fact that Mr Leeman was new to the area did not prevent him from having an existing nuisance stopped.

Mrs Kennaway owned land beside an artificial lake, which was used by a water-skiing club. The club had been using the lake since the early 1960s. In 1969 Mrs Kennaway got planning permission to build a house which she started occupying in 1972. From 1969 onwards the motor-boat activities steadily increased and by 1977 the lake was used each weekend for races and practice. In 1977 Mrs Kennaway started court proceedings. She wanted an injunction but the trial judge would only award her damages (£1,000 for past nuisance, and £15,000 for future nuisance). She appealed. **Held:** *An injunction would be granted allowing only limited use of the lake by the club. Damages should only be awarded in place of an injunction in the most exceptional circumstances.*
Kennaway (1980)

On the other hand, the defendant may be able to use the 'long-usage' defence against a neighbour who has tolerated it for 20 years or more: for example, if Mr Leeman (or the previous owner) had waited 20 years before complaining, he might well have lost his case.

Even noisy children can be a legal nuisance.

Mr and Mrs Dunton owned a small hotel with a pleasant garden and grazing land beyond it. The council built a housing estate on the grazing land, with a playground next to the hotel garden. The playground was open from dawn to dusk and was used by children of all ages. The noise was so intolerable that Mrs Dunton moved out of the hotel. Mr Dunton brought a nuisance claim against the council. **Held:** *The playground was a nuisance. The council was ordered to limit its use to children under 12 years of age, and to restrict the opening hours to between 10 a.m. and 6.30 p.m. In addition, Mr Dunton was awarded £200 damages.*
Dunton (1977)

If an injunction is granted, it may be suspended in order to give the defendant time in which to reorganize his or her business:

Mr and Mrs Allison lived in a council house next door to a hospital boiler room. The noise, a continuous low-pitched hum, interfered with Mr Allison's sleep and caused him a significant degree of nervous agitation, as well as bouts of depression. **Held:** *The noise was a nuisance. The hospital would be given 12 months in which to cure the noise. In the meantime, the Allisons would be paid £850 damages.*
Allison (1975)

The problem is, of course, that going to court – and asking for an injunction – is usually an expensive process.

Other remedies for noise

Bringing an action for nuisance is only one of the remedies available against noisy neighbours. Because of the cost of bringing such a civil action, the house owner will probably be reluctant to sue for nuisance and might prefer to try a cheaper remedy. The Control of Pollution Act 1974, the Environmental Protection Act 1990, the Noise and Statutory Nuisance Act 1993 and the Noise Act 1996 all contain powers enabling local authorities to control excessive noise.

The first step is to complain to the Environmental Health Department of the local authority that the noise is a 'nuisance' or 'prejudicial to health' under these Acts. Evidence that it interferes with sleep, or causes disturbance, will probably be needed. If the council agrees that the noise is a nuisance, it can serve a noise-abatement notice on the owner or occupier of the building. The notice will forbid the making of the noise, or restrict it to certain noise levels, at certain times of the day. If the noise-abatement notice is not complied with, the council can prosecute in the magistrates' court, and the offender will be convicted unless it can be shown that the 'best practicable means' were used to avoid making the noise (e.g. the latest, quietest machinery was installed with all the usual noise-reduction devices).

Prosecution under these Acts is entirely separate from bringing a civil injunction.

Major construction work was being carried out next door to a branch of Lloyds Bank. So much inconvenience was being caused that the bank sought an injunction limiting the hours of building work. The injunction was granted. However, at the same time the local council issued a notice under the Control of Pollution Act 1974 which also limited the hours of work, but which was less strict than the court injunction. The builders argued that the injunction should now be cancelled. Held: The two legal remedies were entirely distinct and separate. The injunction could remain in force.

Lloyds Bank (1987)

If the council refuses to issue a noise-abatement notice, or if it refuses to prosecute for its breach, the house owner can complain to the magistrates' court. A summons is issued in the usual way (*see* How to bring a private prosecution, page 640) and if the magistrates agree that the noise is a nuisance, they will issue a noise-abatement notice. As with a notice issued by the council, the offender can be fined if he or she does not observe the terms of the notice. A house owner who applies to the magistrates' court for a noise-abatement order should produce evidence to support the contention that the noise is a nuisance (e.g. statements of other neighbours, a note from a doctor as to the effect the noise is having on the house owner and family, etc.).

Another way of taking action against noise is to prosecute under local by-laws. Most local authorities have by-laws that can be used to control noise. (By-laws are local laws which only apply in a particular area, rather than being universally applicable, as ordinary laws are.) Usually, a private individual can prosecute for breach of the by-laws, although it is always advisable to try to persuade the council to prosecute. The house owner should check whether there are relevant by-laws by inquiring in the Environmental Health Department of the district, London Borough or unitary council. The following are typical anti-noise by-laws.

Radio, stereo, etc. Such noise is prohibited if it is so loud and so continuous that it is an annoyance to occupiers of premises in the neighbourhood. Generally, the complainant must first give 14 days' written notice to the offender that he or she regards the noise as a nuisance, and the notice must also be signed by two other householders within hearing distance. Only if the noise continues beyond the 14-day period can the offender be prosecuted in the magistrates' court.

Alarm bells. It is often an offence to leave an alarm bell ringing for so long that it becomes an annoyance to local residents. However, the offender will usually have a defence if he or she can show that the noisy alarm was not his/her fault (e.g. there was an unknown electrical fault).

Noisy animals. It is usually an offence to keep a noisy animal if it causes a serious nuisance to residents in the neighbourhood. As with the radio and stereo by-law, the offender must first be given 14 days' notice, signed by a total of three householders.

Music near houses. It is usually an offence to play any 'musical or noisy instrument' or sing in a street or public place that is within 100 yards of a house or office. However, the noise must have been sufficient to have interfered with the ordinary activities carried on in the building (e.g. sleeping, if outside a house at night) or to have been otherwise unreasonable.

Two other common sources of noise are also subject to legal restriction.

Car horns. The Road Traffic Act 1974 makes it illegal to sound a horn while the car is stationary or to sound the horn on a moving car in a restricted road (unless there is danger to another moving vehicle) between 11.30 p.m. and 7 a.m. Both offences carry a maximum penalty of a £1,000 fine. Prosecutions are extremely rare.

Chimes and loudspeakers. The Control of Pollution Act 1974 makes it illegal to operate a loudspeaker or chime in a street. The main exception is for food and drink vehicles, which can use loudspeakers and chimes between noon and 7 p.m., but only if the noise does not cause unreasonable annoyance to local residents. Thus short bursts on an ice-cream chime are allowed but long tunes are not.

The maximum penalty, on conviction, is a £2,000 fine and £50 for each day the noise continues after conviction.

Non-disclosure of noisy neighbours

The sellers replied to pre-contract inquiries (see page 199) by saying they knew of no dispute about the property or any properties neighbouring theirs. But, they omitted to mention the complaints they had made about their neighbours (and that they had given evidence at possession proceedings brought by the neighbours' landlord). The unhappy buyer, saddled with the same noisy neighbours, was entitled to damages.

Noisy vehicles

Maximum noise levels for vehicles are laid down in the Motor Vehicles (Construction and Use) Regulations. The maximum fine for breach is £1,000.

In practice, these noise restrictions are of limited value because the police lack the facilities for monitoring noise levels. In addition, it can often be difficult to prove that a particular vehicle was causing excessive noise if it was one of several vehicles on the road at that time.

Complaints about routing and regulation of traffic should be made to the local traffic authority. However, if the traffic complained of is mainly going to (or coming from) a particular site, then there may be liability by that site owner in nuisance.

Noise from planes

There is little that can be done about noise from planes. The normal remedies of applying for a noise-abatement order or of bringing a nuisance action do not apply, since various statutes exempt aircraft from these controls.

Complaints about noise from aircraft using an airport should be made to the airport operator. Complaints about military aircraft should be made to the Ministry of Defence or to the station commanding officer.

The owners of a stately home brought nuisance proceedings against the Ministry of Defence because of screeching Harrier jets landing at an adjacent airfield. The noise was extreme and double-glazing was not practicable because it was a Grade 1 listed building. Held: There was a breach of the owners' human rights ('everyone has the right to respect for his private and family life, his home and is entitled to the peaceful enjoyment of his possessions'). Damages were awarded. It should be noted, however, that this was a relatively extreme set of circumstances and is not necessarily an encouragement to others who live near airfields.

Dennis *v* MoD (2003)

Smells

What if a neighbour has a compost heap in his garden and, because of the exceptionally dry weather, it smells? Probably there is no nuisance, because it is only a temporary annoyance and it is quite reasonable to have a compost heap in one's garden. However, if the neighbour uses the heap as a general dump for all household refuse, that would probably be unreasonable and so a nuisance.

What is an objectionable smell in one neighbourhood may be perfectly normal elsewhere. A person who lives in a steel town is expected to tolerate smells that would be regarded as a nuisance in other areas. Thus the smell from a fish and chip shop was held to be a nuisance, even though it would not have been a nuisance in a less fashionable district one mile away.

As with noise, the house owner who suffers from offensive smells in the neighbourhood may have additional remedies apart from an action for nuisance. Complaint should be made to the environmental health officer of the local authority, for there are several statutory provisions that can be used to control the source of the smells.

Building works

The nuisance action can sometimes be of help to the landowner disturbed by nearby building operations. If noise, dust and fumes result, it may be possible to obtain an injunction to stop the work continuing, although the court will probably confine the ban to the night hours and insist that the builders take all reasonable steps to minimize the inconvenience (as in the hotel case on page 263). However, some disruption and inconvenience may have to be accepted by the landowner, for it is not unreasonable to build on one's land (or carry out DIY works) as long as the inconvenience to others is minimized.

Local authorities have special powers to control noise from building sites (under the Control of Pollution Act 1974), so complaint should be made in the first place to the local authority.

Subsidence

But what of the damaging effect that the building works may have on one's own property? If a neighbour digs a hole on their side of a boundary fence, it may well cause subsidence to the soil on the other side. Can the neighbour be ordered to stop digging, in order to prevent the subsidence? The answer is 'yes', for a neighbour cannot excavate land if it will cause another's soil to fall in.

But this right of support applies only to earth and soil – it is not assumed to apply to buildings. This may seem ridiculous, but if the excavations cause a neighbour's house to collapse the neighbour may not have any remedy – unless the soil would have fallen in anyway, whether or not there was a building there. In short, the right of support covers only soil and earth, not buildings.

However, it is possible to acquire a right of support for buildings, so that they are protected in the same way as soil and earth. This could be done by a written deed or restrictive covenant, but the usual method is to acquire it by 20 years' usage (i.e. *prescription*) in the same way that a right to light is acquired after 20 years (*see* page 260). If the house has had the benefit of a support for 20 years or more, then the law presumes that it has the right to be supported by next door's soil. Also, if a house stands on the site of an old house that had itself acquired the right of support, then the new house will probably inherit that right. Once acquired, the right continues for ever. Otherwise there is no right of support for a house, just for the earth and soil. But there is an exception to this: if subsidence is caused to a house by a neighbour's tree roots, the landowner can sue even if there is no right of support (*see* below).

TV reception

We have seen that although you may have a right to light, there is no right to a view. But what about a right to view television? What if your neighbour's building work interferes with your television reception, is that an actionable nuisance?

The defendants constructed a 250-metre-high stainless steel clad tower building at Canary Wharf. This interfered with the plaintiff's television reception. **Held:** *This was not a nuisance. If a person can build on his land so as to block sunlight from reaching the plaintiff's land, the same must also apply to a structure which blocks television signals.*

Hunter (1997)

Trees

Trees can also amount to a nuisance at law.

Overhanging branches

If the branches of a neighbour's trees interfere with the enjoyment of an adjoining property, it may amount to a legal nuisance.

The usual way of tackling a legal nuisance is to take the matter to court and ask for damages and/or an order that the offending item be removed. This is an unnecessarily complicated and expensive procedure for so small a matter as an overhanging branch. If the neighbour refuses to prune the tree, the landowner is allowed to resort to self-help and cut off the branches. However, the branches will still belong to the neighbour (and so will the fruit on them), so the law-abiding landowner should return them to the neighbour.

This is one of the few occasions when the law does not frown upon self-help, for generally the courts do not approve of people taking the law into their own hands. It is, though, important that the landowner be able to show that it was reasonable to chop off the branches; probably the best safeguard is to write a letter to the neighbour setting out the complaint, and stating a date by when the tree should be pruned, failing which the landowner will prune it himself.

If the tree branches do not overhang the landowner's property, but merely block the light, there is probably no remedy for the landowner unless there is a right to light (*see* page 260).

Tree roots

As with tree branches, so with tree roots; if the roots of a neighbour's tree intrude into another's property, the landowner can either cut off the roots or take the neighbour to court for damages and/or an order that the roots be removed. In view of the cost of digging up tree roots, it is usually advisable for the landowner to obtain a court order beforehand, rather than do the work and then try to recover the cost from the neighbour. Apart from paying for the cost of digging up the roots, the neighbour would also be liable for incidental expenses, such as returfing a lawn.

The tree owner will also be liable for any damage caused to neighbouring buildings. This does not just apply to trees owned by neighbours; it also applies if the trees are on the council's pavement.

In the early 1900s, the Church Commissioners erected 19 blocks of flats, collectively known as Delaware Mansions, Maida Vale, London W9. In 1989, structural engineers reported that blocks 9 to 12 had sustained structural damage caused by the encroachment of roots of an 80-year-old plane tree, for which the defendant council was responsible as the highway authority. The engineers advised that either the tree should be felled, which would have ended the nuisance at very little cost, or that the blocks should be underpinned. The council declined to fell the tree on the basis of their wish to preserve mature plane trees in central London. As a result, underpinning of the blocks was necessary at a cost of £570,735 to the claimants. **Held:** *The council was liable for the cost of the underpinning.*

Delaware Mansions *v* Westminster City Council (2001)

But this does not mean that every council is liable for all damage caused by trees on pavements.

Eight metres from a house was a 60-foot-high horse chestnut tree. In the 1976 drought, the roots dehydrated the soil and caused subsidence. The house owner sued for the cost of the £5,000 underpinning. **Held:** *The council was not liable. The risk of this sort of damage arising had been too vague and remote. It would not be right to make the council liable.*

Solloway (1981)

The moral of this case is to make sure that the council is given good advance notice if there is any possibility that the roots might cause damage. Legal liability does not arise until the landowner has – or ought to have had – knowledge of the nuisance and then had time to abate it.

It is no defence for the tree owner to argue that the damaged building should have been constructed more soundly.

A block of flats was built near the boundary of a plot of land. On the other side of the boundary were tall trees. Within ten years the foundations of the flats were affected by subsidence, caused by the trees which were reducing the moisture level of the soil. The tree owner was sued, but he argued that the flats were of faulty construction. **Held:** *The tree owner was liable. He could not blame the faulty construction of the building; that would be relevant only if the defects had been so overwhelming as to make the effect of the roots insignificant. Moreover, the fact that the trees had been there before the block of flats was no defence in a nuisance claim. The tree owner was liable for the full cost of repairs.* Bunclark (1977)

Nor is it a defence to argue that one's trees planted themselves (as opposed to having been planted by man). The landowner is responsible for all trees on the land, irrespective of how the trees came to be on the land in the first place.

Falling trees and branches

The owner of any item or piece of property is liable for damage or injury caused if he or she was negligent. So it is with trees, and the house owner will be liable for damage caused by a falling tree or branch – but only if he or she was negligent. So if the accident occurred without warning (e.g. because of an exceptional gale, lightning or other unforeseen weather conditions) there would not have been any negligence. But if the tree fell down because of old age or disease the landowner would probably have been negligent for not inspecting the tree regularly, and so would be liable in damages. The prudent tree owner would probably be expected to inspect all trees at least once a year and, perhaps, twice a year.

Tree-preservation orders

A tree-preservation order (TPO) is an order made by the local planning authority which makes it illegal to prune, fell, uproot or lop that particular tree. When a TPO is made the owner is given notice by the local authority, and then has 28 days in which to make representations.

The TPO is binding on all subsequent owners of the land, not just the person who was the owner at the time the order was made. This is so even if the offender does not know of the existence of the TPO.

Mr Mortamer cut down an oak tree that was subject to a tree preservation order. He was prosecuted but argued that he could not be guilty since he had not known about the TPO. **Held:** *This was not a defence. He was guilty.* Maidstone (1980)

The planning department of the local authority can tell you whether a particular tree is covered by a TPO. This information should also have been discovered by your solicitor when you bought the property and he would have been negligent if he did not discover it or did not tell you about it. The maximum penalty for felling a protected tree is a fine of £2,000, or up to twice the timber value of the tree, whichever is the greater. For otherwise damaging a protected tree, the maximum penalty is a £1,000 fine.

Even if a tree is not subject to a TPO, the owner may be subject to restrictions on lopping, pruning, felling or uprooting the tree. If it is within a conservation area at least six weeks' notice must be given to the local authority so they can decide whether to make a TPO. Failure to give notice is an offence (same penalties as for breach of a TPO). A person who thinks that a particular tree should be subject to a TPO should apply to the local planning authority for an order to be made.

Liability for escaping water, oil, etc.

If householders choose to store water on their land, will they be liable if it escapes? For example, suppose the house owner builds a rock garden with fountains and fish ponds; what happens if the supporting walls give way and the escaping water floods a neighbour's cellar? The courts would say that the house owner was liable even if there was no reason to suspect that the walls might give way; thus his having acted 'reasonably', without negligence, would be irrelevant. The court would simply say that if someone chose to store water on their land, they did so in the knowledge that it might cause damage if it escaped. Anyone should appreciate the risks and it would be for the house owner to compensate the neighbours if an accident occurred. This strict rule was laid down in a case that is famous among lawyers – *Rylands* v *Fletcher* (1868):

Mill owners built a reservoir to hold water for their mill. Unfortunately, the water percolated down disused mine workings and flooded a nearby mine. The mill owners had not been negligent, but it was held that they must compensate the mine owner for the damage done. A person who, for his own purposes, brings on his land and collects and keeps there anything likely to do mischief if it escapes, must keep it at his peril. Rylands (1868)

Since then, this approach has been extended to cover the storage and escape of other potentially dangerous substances, such as electricity, smuts, gas and even sewage in a septic tank. Similarly, if the house owner builds a tank to hold central-heating oil, but the tank fractures and the escaping oil ruins his or her neighbour's garden, then the house owner will be liable to the neighbour – whether or not it was the householder's fault.

It is this element of *strict liability* (irrespective of negligence, nuisance, reasonableness and the other usual tests of liability) that makes the rule in *Rylands* v *Fletcher* so unusual. However, if the escape was caused by the actions of a trespasser (e.g. who deliberately let the substance escape) then there will be no liability on the landowner – unless the acts of the stranger could have been foreseen by the landowner who was negligent in not preventing them.

Generally, English law disapproves of strict liability. Normally, negligence by the neighbour must be shown; if it *is* shown then he or she will be liable on that basis.

A basement was used for storing goods. The next-door building was derelict and the basement owners made lots of complaints about tramps wandering around the next-door building. Eventually, burglars broke through the dividing wall and stole valuable goods. Held: The owners of the derelict building had been negligent in not taking reasonable security precautions. Perl (1983)

Rivers, fishing rights

Although a landowner owns the air above and soil below his or her property, this ownership does not include the water that runs across his or her land in rivers.

Navigation

The public can navigate on a tidal river up to the point where the tide ebbs and flows. Beyond that point the public have a right to navigate only if such a right has been acquired by long usage over the years (in the same way that the public can acquire a right of way over land – *see* page 256).

Fishing

The public can fish in a tidal river up to the point where the tide ebbs and flows. Beyond that point, fishing rights belong to the landowner. Even if the public have acquired a right to navigate over this non-tidal part of the river, that navigation right will not include the right to fish.

Abstracting water

A landowner used to be able to take water from rivers and streams that flowed through his or her land. However, the Water Resources Act 1963 now generally requires the landowner to obtain a licence to abstract from the local water authority.

Boundary fences and walls

'Good fences make good neighbours', wrote Robert Frost. But the law does not usually require a landowner to fence property or even to maintain an existing fence or wall.

Despite this, neighbours often have disputes over the responsibility for maintaining their boundary fences. The first point to note is that there is only rarely a legal obligation on a landowner to fence a property. Generally, this will be as a result of a covenant in the title-deeds or lease which obliges the landowner to fence. Conversely, the property may be in an open-plan estate, in which case it is likely that the title deeds will contain a covenant prohibiting the erection of a fence.

But in the absence of such a legal obligation, the house owner is free to decide whether or not he or she wants to fence a property, and similarly whether to continue maintaining an existing fence or wall.

If your neighbour owns the fence or wall, but there is no obligation on him to maintain it, then there is nothing much you can do about it. If you were to repair the fence yourself, technically that would be trespass, although it is difficult to see what kind of damages the neighbour could obtain if you have actually improved the value of the fence. However, it might not lead to good relations with the neighbour. More sensible would be to ask the neighbour first if you could repair the fence. Often, he will say yes, if you are footing the bill. The only other alternative is to erect a new fence, on your land, immediately next to (but not touching) the old fence. As long as you do not trespass on his land, or obstruct a right to light he may have (*see* page 260) and obtain any necessary planning permission (*see* page 248), there is no way your neighbour can legally object to this. However, once again, this may not lead to good neighbourly relations.

Fences

If the deeds make no provision, a general guide for deciding the ownership of a fence is to say that it belongs to the land on the side that the fence posts or vertical supports are placed. This is based on the logic that the person erecting the fence would have erected it so that the outer edge of the fence was right up to the actual boundary with the fence posts on his own land; remember it would be trespass to put the posts on the neighbouring land.

Boundaries

When it comes to considering the ownership (and even the location) of a disputed boundary, the court will look, first, at the title documents to see if they give any guidance, for example 'T' marks. 'T' marks are the way lawyers indicate on plans who owns a boundary wall or fence. The rule is that the stem of the 'T' rests on the fence in question and the side of the fence that the 'T' is placed indicates that the owner of that land is the owner of the fence. But often the deeds are of little help, being imprecisely worded or incorporating a map of such a small scale as to be useless. However, if there is a hedge and a ditch, the court will assume that the person who dug the ditch did so at the boundary of his or her own land, and then planted the hedge on top of the earth from that ditch; so the boundary is then assumed to run along the edge of the ditch furthest away from the hedge. The rather strained logic behind this rule – once explained as being based on the presumption that the landowner would put the hedge on his side of the ditch so that *his* animals would not fall into it – can be overruled by other evidence; for example, if the other landowner has traditionally maintained the hedge, it might be held that it – and not the ditch – formed the boundary. Similarly, if the title-deeds define the property by reference to Ordnance Survey maps, the 'hedge-and-ditch' rule might not apply, for the OS always draws boundaries along the middle of hedges rather than along the edges of ditches.

25

Responsibility for Damage Caused by Animals

What if a pet escapes and causes damage to a neighbour's garden or injures the neighbour; can the neighbour sue? Generally, the answer will depend upon whether the pet's owner was negligent, and this will be judged according to the standard set by the mythical 'reasonable man' (or woman).

Thus, if an animal wanders out on to the public highway and causes an accident, the owner will be liable only if their behaviour fell below that expected from the 'reasonable man'. For example, it may be reasonable to leave an untethered dog in an ungated garden if the property is beside a quiet country road; however, if the same behaviour took place in the centre of a town the owner would almost certainly be liable if the dog ran out into the road and caused a motor-cyclist to swerve and fall off.

Ms Sudron bought a pedigree puppy. To stop it escaping she had repairs done to her fence and gate. One afternoon, when she was out, her boyfriend failed to notice that a visitor had forgotten to close the gate. The puppy darted out and caused a moped-rider to crash. He sued. Held: Ms Sudron was not liable. She had not been negligent since she had taken all the precautions that one could reasonably expect. The injured moped-rider went without compensation. Smith (1982)

Although the animal owner will normally be liable only if he or she was negligent, there are three exceptions to this rule.

1. Dangerous animals

If a person chooses to keep an animal belonging to a dangerous species they do so at their own risk. So they will be liable if the animal escapes and causes damage, even if they were not negligent and could not be blamed for the accident.

Certain animals are obviously dangerous, such as lions,

tigers, elephants, etc., and so if one of these animals escapes from a zoo, the zoo would be liable whether or not the accident was their fault. The Animals Act 1971 says that an animal is of a 'dangerous species' if it is not usually domesticated in this country and is, when fully grown, likely to cause severe damage unless restrained. Thus, a camel is not normally domesticated in this country and so is a dangerous species under the Act, even though it is normally domesticated in some overseas countries. The size of a fully grown camel does mean that it is likely to cause severe damage.

2. Animals that are normally harmless but for some reason are dangerous

The same rule of strict liability without the need to show negligence will apply to damage caused by animals that are not from a 'dangerous species', yet have unusual characteristics known to the owner. This is because an animal may normally be harmless but, in a particular set of circumstances, can be dangerous. For example, a dog is not normally dangerous, yet if a bitch has a litter of puppies it is quite likely that she will bite an approaching stranger; thus the owner of the bitch should keep her under strict control during this dangerous period. Similarly, a dog with rabies is, in the circumstances, dangerous and so if it bites someone the owner will be liable – assuming, of course, that the owner knew it had rabies.

It is this requirement that the owner should know of the special circumstances that makes the animal dangerous which gives rise to the phrase 'every dog is allowed one bite'. Until that first bite, the owner has no reason to suppose that a seemingly normal dog is unusually aggressive and dangerous; however, after that bite the owner is assumed to know of its dangerous temperament and so should take precautions to ensure that it does not hurt anybody. But there is no need to show that the animal was known to be vicious – merely that it was bad-tempered may be enough.

A groom was injured while leading a horse into a trailer. The horse, which was known to be temperamental and nervous, suddenly became violent and her arm was crushed. Held: The stable owner was liable. There was no need to show that the horse had a vicious tendency to injure people: it was known to be unpredictable and unreliable, and that made it dangerous. Wallace (1982)

On the other hand:

A postman rode up to a house on his moped; he got off to deliver his letters and was met by the house owner's 100 lb Rottweiler dog called Boots. The postman turned tail and fled and was chased for 100 yards by Boots before the postman fell over and injured himself. Held: The owner was not liable for the injuries to the postman. There was no evidence that the defendant knew that Boots had a propensity to chase people. Boots was not dangerous, said the judge; he was 'friendly, albeit boisterous', 'a gentle giant'. Paul (1998)

It is now clear that an owner will be strictly liable when a horse (or other animal) is frightened and causes an accident on a highway or elsewhere.

A car driver was seriously injured when her car crashed into a horse on the road. The horse had panicked (for some unknown reason) and broken through the fencing around its field, before galloping down the road. The fencing had been adequate and there was no negligence on the part of the horse owner. Despite that, the horse owner was liable. Mirvahedy v Henley (2003)

Although this case involved a horse, it is important to appreciate that the Animals Act 1971 covers any non-dangerous, commonly domesticated, animal in the UK. Thus, it would apply not only to horses but, for instance, to dogs, cats and cattle. Accordingly, if you own a cat or a dog, then you are strictly liable for its actions – however absurd that may seem. Presumably, the wise pet-owner will now take out insurance. *See also* page 601.

3. Straying livestock

We have seen that an animal owner is not usually liable if a pet strays, unless there was negligence. However, for livestock the position is different, and an owner may be liable even if there was no negligence; this applies when the animals stray on to private property, such as a neighbour's front lawn.

This strict liability rule applies only to livestock, as defined in the Animals Act 1971. The definition includes cattle, horses, asses, mules, sheep, pigs, goats, fowls, turkeys, geese, ducks, pigeons, peacocks and other poultry; it does not include cats and dogs.

Thus, if a householder chooses to keep a goat in the garden, and the goat enters his or her neighbour's garden through a hole in the hedge, the house owner will be liable for any damage caused by the goat – even if it was thought that the goat was properly tethered and even if the owner did not know about the hole in the hedge. The only defence would be if it was the neighbour's own fault (e.g. in leaving a gate open), or if the livestock strayed on to the neighbour's land from the public highway (if they were lawfully on it in the first place).

Remember that if livestock stray on to the road, then the owner will be liable only if he or she was negligent (*see* page 270).

Guard dogs

The Guard Dogs Act 1975 lays down special rules for the use of guard dogs on commercial premises; the Act does not apply to private houses or to agricultural land.

The main requirement of the Act is that the dog should be under the immediate control of its handler or, alternatively, that it be tethered so it cannot roam freely. In addition, a warning notice must be displayed. Breach of these laws is a criminal offence. However, breach of the Act does not automatically mean that the dog's owner would be liable in damages if a civil claim was brought (e.g. if someone was mauled by an untethered guard dog). This is because the Act is concerned only with the criminal law, and not with the civil law of damages for injury and loss caused to someone else.

The Animals Act 1971, however, includes special provisions to deal with the case where a trespasser has been injured by a dangerous animal – and this applies to all types of property, including houses. Although an owner is normally liable for injury caused by a dangerous animal – for example, a dog known to be vicious – there will be no liability to a person trespassing if the animal was not kept for protection or, if it was, if keeping it for protection was not unreasonable. So keeping a lion or cobra for protection would be unreasonable but, perhaps, not a fierce dog. Thus held Lord Denning in 1977, saying: 'True, it was a fierce dog. But why not? A gentle dog would be no good. The thieves would soon make friends with him.'

Note that these provisions only apply to injury to trespassers caused by a dangerous animal. If injury is caused by an animal not known to be dangerous, then there would be no liability, unless it could be shown that the owner had been negligent in some way. In the case of a trespasser, this would be very difficult to establish.

Note, finally, that certain visitors to your property will not be trespassers, even if you have not expressly invited them on to your land. So post office employees, waste disposal operatives, persons delivering goods, and the like, will not be trespassers and so these provisions of the Animals Act will not apply to any injury caused to them. The ordinary rules as set out above would apply, i.e. has the owner been negligent?

Keeping animals

Most domestic animals need not be licensed. It is a common belief that cats are beyond the law, and that a cat owner cannot be responsible for the actions of the cat; this is not true, and a negligent cat owner will be liable in the same way as any other pet owner, although, in practice, proof of such negligence would probably be extremely difficult.

A local authority licence is, however, needed to keep a dangerous wild animal (e.g. alligator, cobra, cheetah, lion, gibbon, ostrich, etc. – a full list is set out in the Dangerous Wild Animals Act 1976).

Dogs and the criminal law

Various statutes contain provisions aimed at controlling dogs, and also at protecting animals from their owners. In practice, prosecutions are rare: apart from the difficulties of identifying the owner of a particular dog the police tend to refuse to prosecute in all but the most serious cases.

Dogs roaming in the road

Local authorities can designate particular roads as being roads in which any dog must be on a lead.

Dangerous dogs

The Dogs Act 1871 allows the magistrates to take action against dogs that are both dangerous and not under proper control. The mere fact that a dog is dangerous is not sufficient; the magistrates will also want to be sure that it is not under sufficient control. In practice, the easiest way to prove that a dog is dangerous is to show that it has attacked someone; once again, therefore, there is some truth in the adage that 'every dog is allowed one bite'. But it is not essential that injury be caused before a prosecution can be brought.

If the case is proved, the magistrates can order the owner to keep the dog under proper control, or they can order its destruction. Other remedies include ordering that a male dog be neutered, and the magistrates can disqualify the owner from dog ownership for a period of time. A fine of up to £400 can also be imposed.

The Dangerous Dogs Act 1991 was introduced to deal, primarily, with the threat from particularly vicious dogs – such as pit bull terriers. A registration system has been introduced for such dogs. But a more important change brought about by the 1991 Act was to introduce an offence of having a dog that is dangerously out of control in a public place; this is a more serious charge than anything covered by the Dogs Act 1871. Prosecution can be brought only if the dog was out of control in a 'public place', and if it was also 'dangerously out of control' – a far stricter test than under the 1871 Act. On conviction in the magistrates' court, there is a maximum penalty of £2,000 (or six months' prison); if the dog actually injured someone, then it is possible for the case to be heard in the crown court (which could impose an unlimited fine and imprisonment).

Collarless dogs

Under the Control of Dogs Order 1930 it is compulsory for a dog on a highway or in any 'place of public resort' to wear a collar stating the name and address of the dog's owner. Maximum penalty for breach of the order is a £2,000 fine.

Fouling the footpath

Most local authorities have by-laws which provide that 'no person being in charge of a dog shall allow the dog to foul the footpath . . . provided that a person shall not be liable if he satisfies the court that the fouling of the footway was not due to culpable neglect or default on his part'. Maximum penalty is usually a £100 fine. Private prosecutions are permitted.

Beaches

Many seaside local authorities have now adopted by-laws prohibiting or restricting the access of dogs to beaches during the holiday season. This is to prevent health hazards to children due to fouling.

Noisy dogs

By-laws usually contain provisions that can be used to control noisy dogs.

Worrying livestock or poultry

Under the Dogs (Protection of Livestock) Act 1953 it is an offence for a dog to 'worry' livestock on agricultural land if it could reasonably be expected to cause injury or suffering to the livestock. Maximum penalty is a fine of £200. If the dog actually injures cattle or poultry, or chases sheep, it can be treated as a 'dangerous dog' (*see* page 270). Private prosecutions are permitted.

The Animals Act 1971 makes the owner liable if the dog kills or injures livestock. The owner can be sued for damages and it is not necessary for the farmer to show that the dog's owner was negligent or that there was reason to think the dog might attack the animals.

A trespassing dog can only be shot if it is worrying or about to worry livestock and there is no other reasonable means of ending or preventing the worrying. A dog can also be killed if the worrying has ceased but it has not left the area, is not under the control of anyone and there is no practicable means of ascertaining to whom it belongs. In both cases, however, the person killing the dog must notify the police within 48 hours.

Cruelty to dogs

Under the Protection of Animals Act 1911, it is an offence to be cruel to any animal, including a dog. The maximum penalty is a £50 fine and three months' imprisonment, plus disqualification from keeping a dog for a stated period. Private prosecutions are permitted and are often brought by the RSPCA.

Abandoning a dog

The Abandonment of Animals Act 1960 makes it illegal temporarily or permanently to abandon any animal without reasonable cause, if it is likely to cause unnecessary suffering to the animal. The penalties are the same as for cruelty. Private prosecutions are permitted.

26

Accidents at Home

What happens if someone is injured because of a defect in the home, such as an uneven path or a falling slate; is the house owner liable for the state of the property?

The simple answer is 'yes'. The general rule is that the owner of the premises will be liable if he or she was negligent. This is the rule applied if the person injured is on the road or if he is the next-door neighbour. Thus, if a slate falls off the roof and hits the neighbour's car, the question to be asked is: was the house owner negligent? If he or she knew the slate was loose, or had not inspected the roof for a long time, then he or she would be liable. On the other hand, if the falling slate was the result of an unusually fierce storm, he or she might not be liable, since then he or she might not have been negligent.

The same rule applies if a tenant has a flat and is injured by something falling from the landlord's part of the building:

Mrs Cunard was injured when part of the roof and some guttering fell on her. Mr and Mrs Cunard were tenants of part of the building, but the roof and guttering were maintained by the landlord. Held: The landlord had been negligent and so he was liable to pay damages to Mrs Cunard.   Cunard (1932)

VISITORS, ETC.

Complications arise if the accident involves someone who is visiting the house. While the general rule is that the occupier is liable if he or she was negligent, the rule has to be modified to deal with uninvited guests: burglars, squatters and other trespassers. It would be unfair to make the occupier liable to these trespassers and so the law provides that the occupier is not liable even if there was negligence. For instance, if burglars trip over an uneven step, they cannot sue the house owner. But even this rule is subject to exceptions:

1 The occupier cannot take advantage of this freedom from liability deliberately to lay traps that might injure a trespasser. For instance, it is wrong to leave a mantrap to catch a burglar, and the house owner who did so would be liable in damages. In short, the house owner need not take steps to ensure that trespassers are not injured but must not deliberately take steps that will cause them to be injured.

2 Children cannot be expected to stay off private property. Children are naturally adventurous and curious. The house owner must therefore take precautions to prevent children from entering dangerous property – otherwise, if children are injured, it cannot be argued that they were trespassers. The precautions to be taken will largely depend upon the extent of the risk.

But this is not an absolute duty. The occupier (or the owner of the land) just has to take the precautions that a sensible and humane adult would. It is a matter of protecting children from themselves, but there is a limit to the precautions that can reasonably be taken:

Northampton Council owned a rubbish tip. At one end the tip adjoined houses, but the railings between the two had been broken down. The council knew that children played on the tip, and staff chased them off whenever dumping was being carried out. It would have been prohibitively expensive to fence the whole site. Several children lit a fire on the site and one of them threw an empty aerosol can into it. It exploded, burning one of the children. Held: The council was not liable. The risks did not warrant the expensive precautions required to make the site child-proof.
Penny (1974)

The Southern Electricity Board were held to owe a duty to ensure that an intelligent 14-year-old boy was prevented from climbing up a pole to reach an electricity installation mounted on it; an anti-climbing device should have been installed.   Adams (1993)

On the other hand:

The old British Rail was held not liable when another 14-year-old boy climbed on to the roof of a railway carriage and suffered severe burns from the overhead electric power-lines. No reasonable person could have done more to prevent this kind of thing happening.   Wiltshire (1992)

So, if a person is injured on someone else's property (or if their property is damaged), they will be able to sue the negligent house owner, unless they themselves were trespassers.

Occupier's liability for open spaces

It is important to appreciate that what the occupier is required to make safe is the visitor, rather than the premises. The law does not necessarily require an occupier to spend large sums on repairing dangerous structures; depending on the circumstances, it may be that an adequate warning sign will be just as effective. If the property is inherently dangerous, and obviously so, it may be that the occupier is not even required to give a warning, since this would not make the visitor any safer than he or she already is.

A visitor to Hardwick Hall, a country estate owned by the National Trust, drowned while swimming in the pond, which was about three metres deep. The National Trust was not keen on visitors swimming and there were occasional patrols to discourage people. However, there was no set system for preventing use of the pond and there were no notices to discourage swimming and no life-saving equipment. The court held that there were no 'swimming' risks in the pond which would not be perfectly obvious to any competent swimmer. Thus, warning notices would not have told the visitor anything that he did not already know.   Derby v National Trust (2001)

But, in addition, there may be other people who can also be sued:

The landlord

If the property is rented, the landlord will probably be liable for accidents caused by defects in the property. (*See* Chapter 22 for when a landlord is obliged to repair a tenant's home.) However, the landlord will only be liable if he or she:

- knew of the defect; or
- should have known of the defect. Most landlords will be under a duty to repair because of the Landlord and Tenant Act 1985 (*see* page 240); under this Act, the landlord is also given a right to enter the property to

see what repairs need doing. This right to check on the state of the property will mean that he ought to know of any defects that would have been revealed by such an inspection.

A landlord let out a property as a bedsit hostel, but without imposing adequate fire prevention arrangements on the tenants. A resulting fire damaged neighbouring property. Held: **The landlord was liable to the neighbour for the nuisance caused by the tenant.**   Ribee v Norrie (2000)

See page 241 for landlords' liability for gas escapes.

Building contractors

If the house owner employs a contractor to carry out work and a visitor is injured through the contractor's negligence, the contractor will be liable.

Building contractors were employed to remove a sloping ramp leading to the front door of a house. They told the house owner to use a side route until the work was completed. The side route passed close to a small sunken area. One night a 71-year-old friend of the house owner left by the side route and was injured. Held: **The negligent contractors were liable to her.**   Billings (1957)

Professional advisers

They owe a duty to all people who might reasonably be on the property.

During demolition works, an architect advised that a wall was safe and that it could be left standing. In fact, it was not safe – as any expert should have known. A labourer was hurt when the wall collapsed. Held: **He could sue the negligent architect.**   Clay (1963)

The right to roam

The right to roam under the Countryside and Rights of Way Act 2000 enables any person to enter and remain on access land for the purposes of open-air recreation (so long as no damage is caused and the general restrictions in Schedule 2 to the Act are observed – such as not lighting fires or swimming in non-tidal waters). The landowner's duty of care to a rambler exercising the right to roam is the same as that owed to a trespasser, except that there is no duty in respect of risks resulting from natural features of the landscape, such as rocks, trees, rivers, streams, ditches or ponds. Nor will the landowner be liable if someone is injured when climbing over or through a wall, fence or gate. But occupiers must not recklessly put visitors directly at risk (e.g. by carelessly operating dangerous machinery). (*See also* page 259.)

PART THREE

Welfare Benefits and Tax Credits

27

Introduction to Social Security Law

INTRODUCTION

We are all likely to need to claim social security benefits at some time in our lives. The welfare state exists to support people during vulnerable periods – such as during pregnancy, retirement or ill health. Unfortunately, social security law is notoriously complicated and many people are uncertain of their entitlements or how to make a claim.

This chapter aims to provide a basic introduction to the welfare state in the United Kingdom. All the rules discussed apply equally in Scotland. Northern Ireland is not directly covered by the same welfare law, although separate, but almost identical, legislation does apply.

We will look at the individual benefits and also the circumstances in which people can claim. It is only possible to outline the main rules that apply to social security benefits in this book but potential claimants can use this to point them in the right direction, and also to help them recognize when more specialist advice or guidance is required.

AN OVERVIEW

The welfare state as we know it has its roots in the sixteenth and seventeenth centuries with the Elizabethan poor laws. Significant development came with the first National Insurance Act in 1911, which formalized the idea that all people should pay into a central fund which could then be accessed by individuals in times of unemployment, incapacity, widowhood and retirement. These early works were built upon by the reforms of Beveridge in the 1940s and, following the Labour landslide victory in the election of 1945, his reforms were largely incorporated into English law. A key reform that Beveridge advocated was the extension of state assistance to those who were not able to provide sufficient contributions. Means tests were used to assess entitlement to state assistance. This form of financial assistance has expanded rapidly since then to the extent that many people who are entitled to contribution-based benefits will also be entitled to a means-tested top-up to bring their income to a sufficient level.

It is a startling fact for many that every single person in the country is likely to come into contact with welfare benefits at one time or another. If they do not, it is likely that they have either missed out on their rightful entitlements, or have managed to avoid all contact with the social security and tax systems. Benefits are often associated with poverty and many who have to rely on them do, in fact, live in poverty. As new governments have come into office over the decades it can be seen that each has tried their hand at reforming the social security system and eradicating poverty. The recent round of reform is another attempt to do this – although an unfortunate by-product of successive alterations of the benefits system is an increasingly complex area of law.

Part of the welfare reform programme has placed an increasing responsibility on benefit claimants to provide accurate information and to meet on-going rules of entitlement. In return, the development of computer technology and integration of social security into the tax system may help ensure that benefits are claimed by all that are entitled. However, even with such development, there is still an estimated £6 billion of unclaimed benefits each year. It is vital for everyone to be aware of potential entitlement to welfare benefits and tax credits. We all contribute to them via tax and National Insurance contributions and we all may need to claim at some point in our lives.

SOCIAL SECURITY LAW

There are four main Acts of Parliament that provide the basis of most social security law:

- the Social Security Administration Act 1992;
- the Social Security Contribution and Benefits Act 1992;
- the Social Security Act 1998; and

- the Tax Credits Act 2002.

These provide the framework for all benefits rules and enable the Secretary of State for Work and Pensions to make regulations in the form of Statutory Instruments, to pad out the detail. Where there is dispute about the interpretation of the law there are routes to challenge decisions, and higher appeals are directed to the Social Security Commissioners. Their decisions also form a body of case law that can be relied on when interpreting the primary and secondary legislation. In turn, higher courts (Court of Appeal, House of Lords and the European Court of Justice) can decide appeals from the Commissioners where important points of law are at issue.

Social security is an area of civil law that is particularly complex and prone to lengthy legal challenges. One reason for this is that social security law has a substantial impact on the lives of some of the most vulnerable members of our communities. It also affects most of our lives, since benefits can be claimed both by the rich and poor, the able-bodied and those with a disability, and the old and young. Most of the significant life changes that we may face in a lifetime can lead to benefit entitlement: maternity, birth, school, work, sickness, disability and retirement and bereavement.

STRUCTURE OF SOCIAL SECURITY BENEFITS

Welfare benefits can be split into three main groups:
- contributory benefits;
- non-contributory benefits;
- means-tested benefits and tax credits.

It is useful to have a basic understanding of the differences between the types of benefit because entitlement to a benefit in one category may exclude or reduce entitlement to benefits in another.

Summary of Differences

Contributory benefits	Non-contributory benefits	Means-tested benefits and tax credits
Entitlement depends on paying NI (National Insurance) contributions.	Entitlement does not depend on paying NI or means testing.	Entitlement does not depend on paying NI. Entitlement depends on the individual's financial circumstances (including whether they are receiving the other benefits).

Contributory benefits

The first grouping is contributory benefits, for which entitlement is based upon a person having paid sufficient contributions into the National Insurance fund. The National Insurance scheme can be compared to any other insurance scheme. Any person who pays into the fund insures against any one of a number of defined risks. They are able to make a claim irrespective of any other income or capital they may have, just as is the case if a claim is made on a car insurance policy. This rule is by no means rigid since successive governments have helped to substantially erode this basic principle. So, for example, where someone claims contribution-based Jobseeker's Allowance, occupational pensions over a set level will prevent full payment of benefit. Reforms to Incapacity Benefit in 2001 brought in similar measures for Incapacity Benefit.

These benefits replace earnings lost because you have suffered an 'insured risk' such as unemployment. Therefore, you cannot get paid more than once. So if you become unemployed and claim Jobseeker's Allowance and then fall sick, your Jobseeker's Allowance will stop being paid and you will have to claim Incapacity Benefit instead.

Non-contributory benefits

These benefits are paid out of general taxation and have no means-testing or contribution conditions attached to them. Most of them are non-taxable and are generally paid for indefinite periods, as long as the qualifying conditions for entitlement are met. Apart from Child Benefit, their role is mainly to compensate for the extra costs and needs associated with caring and disability. They are a source of extra income that is always worth checking for.

Some of the non-contributory benefits can be claimed in addition to all other benefits. Disability Living Allowance is an example of benefit that is claimed by people with personal care and/or mobility needs. Its payment has no effect on contributory or means-tested benefits (in fact its payment generally increases entitlement to some means-tested benefits). Other benefits in this group, such as Child Benefit and Industrial Disablement Benefit, can also be paid in addition to contributory benefits.

Means-tested benefits and tax credits

The final group of benefits is often described as a financial safety net. People who are not entitled to contributory or non-contributory benefits and have limited resources may qualify. There are complex rules for each benefit in this category but the overriding feature common to them all is that they compare a claimant's income and resources

This chart gives examples of the range of benefits that could be claimed depending on different family circumstances. Several different types of benefit may apply and there may be other benefits that could apply that do not appear in every box.

	Contributory	Non-contributory	Means-tested
Pregnant	Maternity Allowance Incapacity Benefit (Statutory Maternity Pay paid by employer)	Child Benefit (for other children)	Sure Start Maternity Grant, Income Support, Housing Benefit, Council Tax Benefit, Free milk and vitamins, health benefits
Sick and incapable of work	Incapacity Benefit (Statutory Sick Pay paid by employer)	Industrial Injuries Benefits, Disability Living Allowance	Income Support, Housing Benefit, Council Tax Benefit, health benefits
Long-term disabled	Incapacity benefits	Disability Living Allowance, Attendance Allowance, Child Benefit	Income Support, Housing Benefit, Council Tax Benefit, health benefits
Children	Increases for most contributory benefits. Statutory Maternity Pay, Statutory Paternity Pay, Adoption Pay	Child Benefit, Disability Living Allowance	Increases in means-tested benefits, Working Tax Credit, Child Tax Credits
Caring		Carer's Allowance	Income Support, Housing Benefit, Council Tax Benefit, health benefits
Working		Child Benefit, Industrial Injuries Benefits, Disability Living Allowance	Working Tax Credit, Child Tax Credit, Income Support, Housing Benefit, Council Tax Benefit, health benefits, Jobseeker's Allowance
Widowed	Bereavement benefits	War widow's pensions	Social Fund funeral payments, all means-tested benefits
Retired	Category A and B Retirement pensions	Disability Living Allowance, Attendance Allowance, Child Benefit, Category D (over eighties) Retirement Pension	Housing Benefit, Council Tax Benefit, health benefits, Pension Credit, Child Tax Credit
Separated	Pensions based on spouse's contributions		Working Tax Credit, Child Tax Credit, Income Support, Housing Benefit, Council Tax Benefit, Health Benefits, Jobseeker's Allowance
Unemployed	Jobseeker's Allowance (contribution-based)		Jobseeker's Allowance (income based), Income Support, Housing Benefit, Council Tax Benefit, health benefits, Child Tax Credit

Below are listed some of the standard rates for benefits and tax credits that applied between April 2003 and April 2004 (unless otherwise stated). They should only be used as a guide to levels of entitlement.

Attendance Allowance	£
higher rate	57.20
lower rate	38.30

Bereavement Benefits

Bereavement payment (lump sum)	2,000
Widowed parent's allowance (basic allowance)	77.45
(for first child)	9.55
(for each additional child)	11.35
Bereavement allowance (55 and over)	77.45

Child Benefit

only or oldest child	16.05
each subsequent child	10.75

Disability Living Allowance

Care Component

Highest	57.20
Middle	38.30
Lowest	15.50

Mobility Component

Higher	39.95
Lower	15.15

Guardian's Allowance	11.55

Incapacity Benefit

Short-term lower rate (first six months of sickness)	54.40
Short-term higher rate (second six months of sickness)	64.35
Long term (one year and onwards)	72.15

Income Support

Personal Allowances

18 to 24	43.25
25 or over	54.65
lone parent 18 or over	54.65
couple and one or both 18 or over	85.75

Dependent children

birth to September following 16th birthday	38.50
from Sept. following 16th birthday to day before 19th birthday	38.50

Premiums for specific circumstances

family	15.75
disability – single	23.30
disability – couple	33.25
disabled child	41.30
carer	25.10

Pension Credit

Basic Minimum Income Guarantee

Single	102.10
Couple	155.80

Additional amounts	£

Severe disability

Single	42.95
Couple one qualifies	42.95
Couple both qualify	85.90
Carer	25.10

Savings credit threshold

Single	77.45
Couple	123.80

Industrial Injuries Disablement Pension

Payment depends on level of disablement assessment	23.36–116.80
Maximum reduced earnings allowance	46.72
Maximum retirement allowance	11.68

Carer's Allowance

Basic Benefit	43.15

Maternity Allowance

£100 a week or 90% of average weekly earnings

Retirement Pension

State pension	77.45
Pension based on spouse's contributions	46.35
Over-eighties pension	46.35

Statutory Maternity Pay

Lower rate £100 a week or 90% of average weekly earnings

Statutory Sick Pay	64.35

Working Tax Credit

Elements	Annual amount
Basic element	1,525.00
Couple or lone parent element	1,500.00
30-hour element	620.00
Disability element	2,040.00
Severe-disability element	865.00
50+ element working 16–29 hours per week	1,045.00
50+ element working 30 or more hours per week	1,565.00
Childcare element – 70% of eligible childcare costs.	
Maximum *weekly* amount payable for one child	94.50
For two or more children	140.00

Income threshold

With or without child tax credit	5,065.00

Child Tax Credit

Elements	Annual amount
Basic family element	545.00
Family element baby addition	545.00
Child element, per child	1,445.00
Disability element	2,155.00
Severe-disability element	865.00

Income threshold

Claiming child tax credit only	13,230.00
Second income threshold	50,000.00

with a set amount. The set amount takes account of the particular circumstances of the claimant and any dependants they also claim for. If the claimant's available resources are below the set amount, then benefit may be payable. Therefore, each claimant will receive a different amount of benefit, depending on the level of resources they have and also the circumstances of any family members included in his/her claim.

This table sets out the different forms of financial support that are available under the three benefits.

Non-contributory benefits	Contributory benefits	Means-tested benefits and tax credits
Attendance Allowance	Incapacity Benefit	Income Support
Disability Living Allowance	Widowed Parent's Allowance	Jobseeker's Allowance (income-based)
Carer's Allowance	Bereavement Payment	Council Tax Benefit
Child Benefit	Bereavement Allowance	Housing Benefit
Guardian's Allowance	Maternity Allowance	Health benefits
Retirement Pension for over 80s	Retirement Pensions	Working Tax Credit
	Jobseeker's Allowance (contribution-based)	Disabled Person's Tax Credit Pension Credit
Industrial injuries benefits		The Social Fund Child Tax Credit

A case study helps to illustrate how a claimant may get benefits from each of the three groups of benefits described above. It also shows that there are many options open to claimants depending on their circumstances.

Jackie and Paul live in a mortgaged house that they both own. Jackie is not employed but cares for her mother who receives the highest rate of Disability Living Allowance (DLA) because she needs a lot of help with her personal care. Paul has recently been made redundant and has been trying to find work. His redundancy and notice pay has just run out and their savings are only likely to cover one more month's living expenses for them both.

Jackie is able to claim Carer's Allowance (CA) even before Paul lost his job. His former income would have no effect on her level of benefit. Her contribution record would not *be relevant as CA can be paid to anyone who cares 35 hours or more for a person getting higher rates of DLA. Once Paul's notice period has run out he may be able to get contribution-based Jobseeker's Allowance (JSA) if he has paid the correct amount of National Insurance contributions. Even if he does not qualify for the contribution-based JSA, he could also claim income-based JSA, which can also include extra amounts to cover mortgage interest liabilities after a waiting period. Jackie's CA will be counted as income for the income-based JSA but, because she is classed as a carer, they will get an additional amount of JSA. They will also be able to claim Council Tax Benefit. If Paul does not want to claim as unemployed, Jackie could claim Income Support instead as a carer.*

> **Paul**, who is unemployed, can claim *JOBSEEKER'S ALLOWANCE*
>
> He and Jackie can also claim *COUNCIL TAX BENEFIT*

> As a carer, **Jackie** can claim *CARER'S ALLOWANCE*
>
> She can also claim *INCOME SUPPORT*

> **Jackie's mother** receives *DISABILITY LIVING ALLOWANCE*

Administrative structure

There have been major changes to the structure of administration of social security benefits in recent years. Jobcentre Plus, an executive agency of the DWP, administers most benefit claims. The Pensions Service, another executive agency of the DWP, administers State Retirement Pension and will progressively take responsibility for Pension Credit (formerly known as Income Support Minimum Income Guarantee).

The Disability and Carer's service is responsible for claims for attendance allowance and disability living allowance. The Carer's Allowance Unit administers claims for carer's allowance.

The administration (but not the judicial function) of welfare benefits and tax credit appeal tribunals is the responsibility of the Appeals Service, which is another executive agency of the DWP. The Inland Revenue administers Working Tax Credit, Child Tax Credit, Child Benefit and Guardian's Allowance. Employers have responsibility for Statutory Sick Pay, Statutory Maternity Pay, Statutory Paternity Pay and Statutory Adoption Pay. Housing Benefit and Council Tax Benefit are both administered by the local authority.

28

The Benefits and How to Qualify

NON-CONTRIBUTORY BENEFITS

Disability Living Allowance

For people with an illness or disability, this is an important benefit to think about claiming. Disability Living Allowance (DLA) can be paid to people who need help in getting around outside and also to those who need help looking after themselves. Any income or capital does not affect the outcome or level of payment of a claim and it can be paid on top of almost all other benefits. Where a person receives Income Support he can claim extra amounts based upon his entitlement to DLA.

Disability Living Allowance has two parts (or components) that can be claimed separately or together:
- the *mobility* component; and
- the *care* component.

Each part is paid at different levels depending on the type and extent of disability. The claim form asks for self-assessment of how disabilities affect a claimant, so it is important to think carefully about the types of activities where help is needed and to fill in the form as completely as possible in all areas. It is also important to note that DLA can be paid whether or not another person provides attention or supervision for the claimant.

Main qualifying rules

Mobility Component
- *Low rate* – paid to people who need guidance or supervision from another person when walking outside on an unfamiliar route. People who suffer from panic attacks, who are deaf or who have epilepsy may be entitled to claim if they can show that they are at risk without someone else on hand to help them get to their destination or find their way.
- *Higher rate* – a higher rate is paid where someone is either unable to walk at all or they are treated as virtually unable to walk. This has a technical meaning that looks at the distance, time, speed and manner of walking. A rough benchmark for distance is 50 metres

or less but, when claiming, it is important to explain any discomfort or problems that walking causes. There are several other routes to qualify including where the claimant's health would be put at risk if he were to walk, for example, when he suffers from a serious heart condition.

Care Component
- *Low rate* – if there are problems preparing and cooking a main meal. For example, where there is a restriction in the use of the hands, the lower rate of the care component may be payable. The other route is to show that there is a limited need for help with personal activities for around an hour in any one day.
- *Middle rate* – someone can qualify for this rate if they need help with personal activities frequently in the day or night time or they need regular supervision. For example, they may qualify if they are at risk of hurting themselves or causing an accident in the home when left alone. The rules are harder to meet for the night time because many people will generally be able to sleep through the night.
- *Higher rate* – where someone meets the entitlement rules in both the day and night time they can get the highest rate of benefit.

Since 1992, when the benefit was introduced, these tests have been the subject of many legal challenges and, on occasion, these have reached the House of Lords. If in any doubt about whether you qualify, a claim should always be made – preferably with the help of someone who has experience in completing the claim form, such as a Citizens' Advice Bureau or Welfare Rights worker. It can also be worthwhile challenging a negative decision as many people are awarded benefit after making several challenges (*see* Challenging Social Security Decisions, Chapter 30).

Other benefits

Where the higher rate of the mobility component is paid, this can be used to buy or lease a car or wheelchair under the Motability scheme (Goodman House, Station Approach, Harlow, CM20 2ET, Tel: 01279 635666; website: www.mobility.co.uk). This scheme offers very favourable terms on the hire or purchase of cars or wheelchairs for disabled motorists. There is also road tax exemption and motorists can also apply for a blue badge from their local authority to avoid many parking restrictions.

The higher rates of DLA care component can help in claims for sickness benefits like Incapacity Benefit. Where means-tested benefits like Housing Benefit and Income Support are claimed, a successful claim for DLA can lead to extra amounts being paid. If there is a carer who looks after the disabled person, they may be able to claim Carer's Allowance. If someone needs extra space or adaptations to their home, they may also qualify for a reduction in their council tax liability.

Those who care for someone who receives middle- or highest-rate care component of DLA, may, from 6 April 2002, start to build up additional pension through state second pension. Carers who receive Carer's Allowance will get NI credits towards their basic state pension. The Disability Living Allowance Customer Care Helpline is 08457 123456.

Attendance Allowance

This is a close relative of DLA. It is paid at two rates and the rules mirror those described above for the middle and highest rates of the care component of DLA. The main difference is that it is only paid to people who first claim when they are over 65 years old. There are also no equivalent payments for mobility problems.

Mrs Jacobs is 58 years old and has just been awarded the highest rate care component of DLA because she needs attention in the day and night. She has diabetes, incontinence and arthritis throughout her legs and back and now needs to sleep downstairs. She has also been awarded the higher rate of the mobility component because she can only walk about 20 yards before she has to stop because of pain. She lives with her daughter who helps to look after her and who gets Carer's Allowance.

Now that she has got the higher rate of mobility component she could use this to buy a new car under a Motability agreement.

Alternatively, if she or her daughter already has a car, they can apply for road tax exemption and a blue badge to make parking easier when they go out.

They should also check if their council tax bill could be reduced because a room has been adapted for her use.

Mrs Jacobs may also be entitled to Income Support because of the DLA award.

For further information, ring the Benefit Inquiry Line for People with Disabilities: 0800 882 200.

Industrial Injuries Benefits

Work-related injuries and accidents may give rise to a civil or even criminal claim against an employer. The Industrial Injuries Benefits (IIB) can be paid without having to show fault on the part of the employer but the claimant must be classed as an employee. There must also be a clear link between an accident or disease and that person's employment. IIB are non-contributory so can be paid on top of other contributory benefits, although they are counted as income when means-tested benefits are worked out. The most common benefit is Disablement Benefit and the main qualifying rules are described below.

Main qualifying rules

- Only employed earners can qualify. If an accident or disease occurs during unemployment or self-employment benefit will not be payable.
- The claimant's injury must be caused by a disease that is recognized in the benefit regulations or by an accident.
- Disability is assessed by the decision makers, who consider the evidence before them, including a doctor's opinion. There must be a disability assessment of at least 14 per cent to receive a payment. Some disabilities have set percentages: for example, where the claimant is blind in both eyes, he will automatically be assessed as 100 per cent disabled. The amount of the benefit depends on the extent of the disablement, as assessed.
- Disablement Benefit is paid weekly, normally over a fixed period. Assessments can be varied if a condition changes – a new medical assessment will help the Benefits Agency decide if the benefit can be increased or if it should continue at the end of a fixed-term award.

Other benefits

Other Injuries Benefits can be paid on top of the basic Disablement Benefit. For example, where an accident or disease occurred before October 1990, Reduced Earnings Allowance may be payable if earnings capacity was reduced as a result of the accident or disease. Where injuries are severe, Constant Attendance Allowance can be claimed. There are several other benefits in this group so it is always vital to check with a union representative or benefits adviser to see if there are any potential claims.

Paul was a coal miner for five years until 1988 when the pit shut down. He suffered from a bad back after a pit prop fell on him but has never claimed anything for this injury. He has since changed jobs but finds that he cannot sit for too long before his back plays up and forces him to get up and move about. He has also had a lot of time off because of back pain.

He should apply for Disablement Benefit since his injury was caused by an accident at work. If his disability is assessed as more than 14 per cent he will receive a weekly pension.

He should also think about claiming Disability Living Allowance if he finds any aspect of personal care difficult.

He may also get Reduced Earnings Allowance if he can show that he can no longer earn as much as he did in his previous job.

It is unlikely that he could make a civil claim against his employer as too much time has passed since the accident but if his injury has only gradually come to light it would be safest to check if a claim is appropriate with a solicitor.

Carer's Allowance

There are thousands of full-time carers in the UK. They can be children, relatives or friends and neighbours. They provide support and indispensable help for many disabled people who, without their help, would have to rely solely on social services. Carer's Allowance (CA) aims to compensate carers for the time that they spend caring. It is non-contributory and is not means-tested, although there are rules about the amount of earnings that can be received. Before 6 April 2003, you could receive an extra amount of CA if you were also looking after a child or children. After that date, increases for children were abolished and replaced by Child Tax Credit. A person in receipt of the child dependency increase before 6 April 2003 will continue to receive it.

Main qualifying rules

- The carer must spend at least 35 hours a week looking after the disabled person.
- The person cared for must receive either Attendance Allowance or the middle or higher rate of Disability Living Allowance.
- The carer cannot earn over a set amount in a week and cannot be in full-time education.
- The carer can still receive the benefit during limited breaks from caring.

Other benefits

If there is entitlement to CA, the claimant can also receive additional amounts of Income Support, Housing Benefit and Council Tax Benefits if they meet the normal rules for these benefits. The fact that someone is a carer means that they are not required to sign on in order to receive means-tested benefits or to receive credits of National Insurance.

Child Benefit and Guardian's Allowance

Perhaps the commonest of non-contributory benefits, Child Benefit is paid in respect of almost every child in the country. To be eligible, the person who claims must be classed as responsible for the child. In general terms this means they have the child living with them and they pay an amount equal to the amount of Child Benefit towards keeping the child. It is not necessary to be the parent of the child.

Disputes can arise as to who should claim the benefit where two parents share the care of the child.

In a 2002 case, it was held that the Secretary of State for Work and Pensions has no power to split child benefit between two parents (where, for example, they share the care equally), as may have been previously thought (*R. Barber* v *Secretary of State for Work and Pensions* (2002)).

To obtain further information about Child Benefit, ring the Child Benefit Office: 0845 302 1444.

Main qualifying rules

- The child must be under 16 years old (or under 19 and still in full-time education).
- Benefit can be paid beyond the age of 16 even when a child has left school. The child must be registered with a careers service as unemployed and looking for work and/or training under the current Work Based Training for Young People scheme.
- The claimant must either be living with the child or contribute towards the maintenance of the child.

Other benefits

People on a low income who claim Child Benefit may be able to claim any one of the means-tested benefits. If the claimant or their partner works for 16 or more hours a week they may be able to get Working Tax Credit (*see* page 294). Child Tax Credit can be claimed on its own or in addition to other means-tested or non-means-tested benefits. Income from Child Benefit is ignored for the purpose of calculating tax credits.

Guardian's Allowance

The rules for this benefit closely follow those for Child Benefit and it can be claimed in addition to Child Benefit. Guardian's Allowance may be payable where both parents of the child have died or where one has died and the other is serving a long-term prison sentence.

To obtain further information ring the Guardian's Allowance Unit: 0191 225 2151.

Retirement Pension for people over 80 years old

This is a non-contributory pension that is paid at a similar rate to other state retirement pensions but entitlement does not depend upon having paid any National Insurance contributions. Where someone becomes entitled to this pension on reaching 80 years old it is worth checking if they are receiving all the means-tested benefits to which they may also be entitled. In 2001 research revealed that three million pensioners were missing out on £1.3 billion in unclaimed benefits each year.

CONTRIBUTORY BENEFITS

Incapacity Benefit

Every person who becomes too ill to work can be entitled to Incapacity Benefit (ICB). If they are in work they may be able to get Statutory Sick Pay from their employer for up to 28 weeks (*see* page 300). If their Statutory Sick Pay runs out or if they are not working they may be able to claim ICB straight away. It depends upon recent National Insurance contributions; people with insufficient contribution records will not qualify. They may still be able to claim Income Support and also Child Tax Credit if they have children (*see also* page 294). Benefit is paid at three rates depending on the length of time that a claimant has been sick.

In general, the claimant must pass a personal capacity assessment, which will test whether they are incapable of work. The assessment will be based on a medical examination.

The medical examination is split into two parts:

1 The first part of the examination looks at both mental and physical restrictions based on the ability to perform defined activities. Physical activities include such things as walking, sitting and reaching. A points score is given depending on the level of restriction on a particular activity. Mental activities include assessing abilities to cope with daily life or pressure. They also attract a points score. To pass this first test a claimant must score a set number of points from physical, mental or a combination of both sets of activities.

2 The second part of the examination takes a more subjective approach and concentrates on a claimant's abilities to overcome any illness or disability. The assessment identifies any aids or appliances that might help someone work. It looks at ways to overcome problems in getting to a job, risks that work may impose on a claimant and how levels of energy or stamina may affect the claimant's ability to work.

A decision maker will make a decision based on the first report while the second assessment will be used by an employment adviser to help them assess whether the claimant is capable of some form of work.

Main qualifying rules

- Must have paid sufficient National Insurance contributions in the last three years.
- The claimant must be assessed as incapable of work. The test is normally as described above but where someone has recently worked an inability to carry out the normal occupation is all that is required.
- Normally, if the claimant works while claiming benefit, the benefit will be withdrawn. Work done on the advice of a doctor and within certain limits may still be allowed.
- Benefit stops once a claimant reaches pensionable age.
- Young people aged 16 to 19 who are incapacitated may be able to qualify for Incapacity Benefit without having to satisfy the normal NI contribution conditions. Young people aged 20 to 24 may also qualify if they were in education or training for three months immediately before they attained the age of 20 years.
- An extra amount may be claimed for an adult dependant or someone who looks after your children. Increased amounts for dependent children were replaced with Child Tax Credit for claims made from April 2003.
- For claims made from April 2001, most pension payments affect the amount of Incapacity Benefit payable. Incapacity Benefit is reduced by half of the amount of gross weekly pension payments over £85. This reduction does not affect people receiving the highest rate of disability living allowance care component.

Other benefits

People on a low income may also qualify for a top-up of Income Support and other means-tested benefits. If you stop claiming in order to try out work, you may be able to go back on to your old rate of benefit if you fall sick again within a year.

The tests that assess incapacity for work are initially based on a self-assessment so it is important to read the claim form very carefully and complete it as fully as possible. It is advisable to assess restrictions of physical or mental abilities as they are on a bad day and then say how often these bad days occur. A claimant will be best placed to explain the effects of an illness and if this is done at the outset the claim is more likely to succeed without having to mount further challenges down the line.

Jobseeker's Allowance

Many years ago, if you lost a job you were classed as unemployed and if you had paid enough National Insurance contributions it was relatively simple to receive unemployment benefit for up to a year.

Contribution-based Jobseeker's Allowance

The unemployed are now all described as 'jobseekers' and contribution-based benefit is only paid for a maximum of six months.

Means-tested Jobseeker's Allowance

If you have made insufficient contributions or your income is low, a claim can be made for means-tested Jobseeker's Allowance. There are common rules for both types of Jobseeker's Allowance which are described below.

All newly unemployed people have to go to a new jobseeker's interview. This is where the Jobcentre Plus worker checks their claim and begins to draw up a job-seeker's agreement. This agreement sets down the type of work that is suitable for the person applying and the steps needed to find work. At this stage it is important for the claimant to be realistic about what can be done to find work. Once signed, the agreement will be binding and any breaches could lead to sanctions – i.e. suspension of the benefit. An example of such a breach is where the Jobcentre Plus notifies the jobseeker of an interview and the jobseeker fails to attend the interview.

Main qualifying rules for both types of Jobseeker's Allowance

- You must be available for work. All claimants have to be ready to start work immediately and show that there is a real chance they can get work if they have placed restrictions on the type, hours or pay rate of the work. For example, a farm labourer restricts the type of work he is looking for to manual labour. If there are very few vacancies for this type of work, the Jobcentre Plus may say he must look for other types of work. If he does not, it may be decided that he does not have a reasonable chance of securing employment and benefit may be stopped.
- You may be sanctioned if you have left your job voluntarily or have lost your job due to misconduct.
- You must be actively seeking work. This involves showing that reasonable steps have been taken to find work, for example, drawing up a CV or looking at job adverts.
- A jobseeker's agreement must be signed. You do not have to stick rigidly to the agreement but changes should always be agreed with an employment adviser in advance to avoid possible sanctions.
- You must not be working for 16 hours or more a week. Any earnings from this work will reduce the level of benefit received.

Additional rules for contribution-based Jobseeker's Allowance

- You must satisfy the National Insurance contribution conditions. There are strict rules about how many contributions a claimant has paid as an employed earner or has been credited with in recent years. In general your contributions must have been paid or credited in the last two tax years before the year in which the claim is made.
- Receipt of pension payments above £50 a week will reduce the amount of benefit, pound for pound.

Other benefits

Where income is low, means-tested benefits and Child Tax Credit can be claimed. It is important to make all claims as soon as possible as there are only limited circumstances where benefit can be backdated.

Maternity Allowance

If you are pregnant and not entitled to Statutory Maternity Pay from your employer, you may be able to claim Maternity Allowance from the Department for Work and Pensions (DWP). It is a weekly benefit and payments can start from 11 weeks before the expected date of birth of the baby. Payments can last for a maximum of 26 weeks, the earliest payment being 11 weeks before the expected date of birth and the latest being the day after the baby is born. The pregnant woman can claim extra Maternity Allowance if she is also maintaining an adult. *See also* page 390.

The claim form is available at antenatal clinics or the Jobcentre Plus. Medical evidence about the expected date of birth must be provided. This is available from the midwife or GP (maternity certificate form MATB1). Self-employed women may also be eligible for Maternity Allowance.

Main qualifying rules

- You must not be working at the time of claim; and
- you need to have been working for at least 26 weeks out of the last 66 weeks before the expected week of birth; and
- you must have paid National Insurance on those earnings or you earn at least £30 a week. In the latter case, benefit will be paid at a rate equal to 90 per cent of earnings.

Other benefits

Statutory Maternity Pay cannot be paid at the same time as Maternity Allowance but other means-tested benefits could be claimed to top up a low income. If there is no entitlement to Maternity Allowance, the DWP should then check to see if Incapacity Benefit is payable. They often do not do this so it is best to remind them of their obligation. People on low income and in receipt of certain other benefits may also qualify for a Sure Start Maternity Grant from the Social Fund.

Some people may be able to get statutory paternity pay

for up to two weeks. Some adopters may be able to get statutory adoption pay for a period of 26 weeks (*see* page 392).

State Retirement Pension

There are two basic types of contributory pension:

Category A pensions (the state pension) are based on National Insurance contributions paid over the contributor's lifetime.

Category B pensions are based on your spouse's contribution record.

The start date for payment is when pensionable age is reached, which is currently 65 years for men and 60 years for women. Pensionable age for women is to be gradually increased to 65 years between 2010 and 2020.

You can continue to work after you have claimed the pension and you can also defer a claim to a later date. This can lead to an increased entitlement when a claim is eventually made. Although everyone who has worked will be entitled to this pension, it is not automatically paid. Claims for pension can only be actioned if a valid claim is received (except pension for people over 80 years and certain widows). Claim forms are normally sent out four months before the potential claimants reach pensionable age and it is important to send them back promptly because only three months' backdating will be paid.

Main qualifying rules

- You must satisfy the two contribution conditions:
  – you or your spouse has paid National Insurance on a set amount of earnings in any one tax year. This set amount is called the lower earnings limit (£4,004 in 2003/2004);
  – you or your spouse has paid or been credited National Insurance for earnings up to the lower earnings limit for each year in your (or your spouse's) working life. If this condition is not met in every year pension is normally reduced (*see* the illustration below).
- For the Category A pension, you have to be over pensionable age to claim.
- For the Category B pension for married women, you and your spouse have to be over pensionable age and your husband has to be entitled to his Category A pension.

At the moment, a married man cannot get a basic state pension on his wife's National Insurance contributions record. This will change from 2010 when the state pension age for women begins to change.

Men need to have 44 qualifying years to be entitled to the full basic state pension (£77.45 a week in 2003/04). For women who reach the age of 60 before 2010, they need to have worked for 39 qualifying years to get the full basic state pension.

Other benefits

Additional amounts are payable for spouses and adult dependants who are caring for a child. If income is low, pension credit, tax credits, housing benefit and council tax benefit can be claimed.

Mr Jacks is 64 years old and wants to check the level of pension he is due to receive. To get a full pension in this case he will need to have paid National Insurance for at least 44 years. This is his 'working life' minus five years. 'Working life' is calculated by adding the years between the age of 16 years and pensionable age (currently 65 for men and 60 for women). Because of the length of Mr Jacks's working life he is allowed to have five years where he need not have paid National Insurance. The number subtracted may be less if the length of working life is reduced. Years spent caring for a child or disabled person may reduce the length of 'working life' used in the calculation of pension entitlement. Mr Jacks knows that he has only paid National Insurance for 22 years. This means that he will only be entitled to half the standard entitlement to a pension, as 22 is half of his working life (calculated as 44 years). His earnings will not affect the level of pension but it may be worthwhile for him to check if he could claim any other means-tested benefits.

BEREAVEMENT BENEFITS

This section describes the benefits that can be claimed by a spouse when the other spouse dies. Since April 2001, both men and women are able to claim bereavement benefits and the main changes are also outlined in this section. For all these benefits the level of earnings or savings does not affect the amount of benefit received. The new system will not affect women who were already getting bereavement benefits under the previous scheme.

Bereavement Payment

This is a one-off lump sum payment of £2,000. Entitlement depends on whether the claimant's late spouse has paid enough National Insurance contributions. A claim must be made within twelve months of death. If the late spouse has not paid sufficient contributions, the widow/widower may still qualify if he/she died as a result of an industrial injury or industrial disease.

Widowed Parent's Allowance

This is a weekly benefit paid to widows who are pregnant and to widows and widowers who look after a child of the marriage or a child who was a part of the family before the spouse died. The definition of 'child' is the same as for Child Benefit. If the late spouse has not paid sufficient contributions, the widow/widower may still qualify if the late spouse died as a result of an industrial injury or industrial disease and in receipt of Child Benefit or is pregnant.

Bereavement Allowance

This is a weekly pension paid to widows and widowers who are 45 years old or over when their spouse dies. Again, the spouse must have paid sufficient National Insurance contributions over their life. It can be claimed up to the age of 65 years. Payments will only be made for a maximum of 52 weeks after a bereavement (beginning on the date of death). Bereavement allowance may be reduced where the late spouse has not paid sufficient contributions. If the late spouse has not paid sufficient contributions, the widow/widower may still qualify if he/she died as a result of an industrial injury or industrial disease. This allowance is paid at a reduced rate when the widow/widower is aged under 55 when the spouse died.

Other benefits

If income is low, means-tested benefits can top up bereavement benefits. Other contributory benefits may be claimed but these overlap so that only the highest would be paid to the claimant. Where a widow or widower starts cohabiting, bereavement benefits will be suspended and they can be reclaimed only if they become single again. Where a widow or widower remarries, entitlement will cease.

Mary's husband dies in September 2000. She has three children and after the death receives a life insurance payment of £20,000. She has no income except Child Benefit for the children.

- *She can claim a lump sum bereavement payment as long as she claims within twelve months of her husband's death.*
- *She may also be entitled to a Widowed Parent's Allowance because she cares for children from the marriage. This will include a basic amount for herself and extra amounts for each of her children.*
- *Once her children have grown up she will be able to transfer to Bereavement Allowance as long as she does not remarry.*
- *While her capital exceeds £16,000 she will not be able to receive any means-tested benefits but she will be entitled to Child Tax Credit. If she starts full-time work, she can claim Working Tax Credit.*

MEANS-TESTED BENEFITS

Income Support

This is a key means-tested benefit, which is aimed at providing a safety net for anyone who has a low income but who is not required to look for work. The entitlement rules are complex but broadly claimants must satisfy two tests.

1 *First, claimants must show that they fit into a class of persons who may qualify.*
   The main groups are:
   - people under 60 on a low income;
   - those who are incapable of work because of illness or disability;
   - lone parents;
   - carers;
   - some groups of pupils over 16 years or students.
   Claimants must also not be working for 16 or more hours in any week that a claim is made. If a partner works, they must not be doing so for 24 hours or more a week.
2 *Second, the claimant must pass a means test.* This involves comparing your income and savings with your individual needs and the needs of your family.

How are your needs assessed?

The Department for Work and Pensions uses standard amounts to work out the total minimum amount of money that the law says is needed to support a claimant and his family. The final amount is often called the applicable amount and this is arrived at by adding together three different sets of figures:

1. *Personal allowances.* These are amounts that apply to a single person or couple. Amounts for children are now claimed through Child Tax Credit.
2. *Premiums.* These are extra amounts for specific circumstances of the claimant and/or their partner.
3. *Housing costs.* If there is a mortgage, Income Support can include an amount towards the mortgage interest payments. The DWP uses a standard interest figure to calculate this and housing costs are not generally paid at the start of a claim.

How is income assessed?

This is worked out by looking at all types of income that are received in each week. It will include things like: other benefits, part-time earnings, and maintenance payments. If there are savings or capital over £3,000, this will be treated as producing a weekly income. For every £250 above £3,000 you will be treated as having £1 per week income.

When these calculations have been done, total income is deducted from the needs assessment and the claimant is paid the difference.

Julie Mason has just separated from her husband. She has stayed in her house which has a mortgage. She gets Child Benefit for her 6-year-old child. Her husband is giving her £30 a week maintenance but she is struggling to pay all the bills and make ends meet. She is not working so she claims Income Support. Her benefit is worked out as follows:

		£
Applicable amount:	*personal allowance for Julie as a single parent*	*54.65*
Income:	*maintenance*	*30.00*
	Child Benefit	*17.55*
	Total income	*47.55*

The amount of income support that she would receive would be £7.10, which is her applicable amount minus her income. Her mortgage interest can also be included but there are waiting periods before the full amount may be paid. She will also need to claim Child Tax Credit, which replaced additional amounts for single parents and families with children previously paid through income support from April 2004.

Claiming Income Support

A claim for Income Support is made by completing the correct form and supplying all the information and evidence of identity that is asked for on that form. These rules are much stricter than is the case for other benefits – for which the only requirement is that a claim is made in writing. The reason behind this stringency in the case of Income Support is an attempt to reduce fraudulent claims and also to impress upon claimants the seriousness of asking for money from the state.

If the form is not correctly completed it is usually returned to the claimant. Provided that the corrected form is returned to the local benefits office within a month, the claim will run from the original date of receipt. If it takes longer than this, benefit will normally only be paid from the date the fully completed form is received. If in doubt seek help from an advice agency.

Since 7 April 2003, lone parents with children who make a new claim for income support have to attend an interview with a personal adviser. The benefits office will also visit him or her to issue and complete a maintenance application form for child support. The Child Support Agency treats parents with care who claim income support or income-based Jobseeker's Allowance as if they have applied for child maintenance unless they opt out. Those who do opt out may have their benefit reduced if they ask the CSA not to arrange child maintenance. *See also page 56.*

Other benefits

Most other benefits are counted as income and will reduce the final amount of Income Support that is paid. It is still important to claim other benefits because if they are paid they may enable extra premiums to be paid with your Income Support. For example, if a claimant receives Invalid Care Allowance, he will get a Carer premium with his Income Support. The total amount of money from all of his benefits will be more than if he had not claimed the Care Allowance. Free health benefits come with Income Support entitlement, as do free school meals for your children.

Jobseeker's Allowance (income-based)

Most of the means-testing rules described above apply to the part of Jobseeker's Allowance that is means-tested. The major difference is that all the rules connected to job searching which are explained in the section on contribution-based Jobseeker's Allowance must be passed. It is not possible to claim both Income Support and Jobseeker's Allowance at the same time but there are circumstances where someone can choose which to claim. For example, a lone parent who wants to look for work would be able to choose which benefit they claim even though the amount of benefit would be exactly the same. There are new rules for people bringing up a child or children whose parent lives somewhere else in the United Kingdom. When you or your partner claim income-based Jobseeker's Allowance it will be treated as an application for child maintenance unless you or your partner opt out.

Pension Credit

This used to be called the Minimum Income Guarantee. In October 2003, the Minimum Income Guarantee was replaced by a new means-tested benefit called Pension Credit for those of pension age who normally live in the UK. Some types of income are ignored when assessing entitlement to Pension Credit. Pension Credit is made up of two parts: a guarantee credit if you are aged 60 or over which tops up your income to a guaranteed level, and a savings credit if you are aged 65 or over and have certain types of income or capital. Either or both parts may be claimed depending on individual circumstances.

Additional amounts of Pension Credit can be claimed if you or your partner have a severe disability, are a carer or are liable for mortgage payments. Those who continue to work after reaching pension age may be entitled to Working Tax Credit and those with children may claim Child Tax Credit.

Housing Benefit

This is paid to people on a low income who pay rent. People can get this whether they are working full-time or not and entitlement does not depend upon National Insurance contributions. The claimant has to be treated as liable to pay rent. This means that there must be some legally enforceable agreement.

Not everyone can get Housing Benefit. For couples, only one partner can claim. If a tenant pays rent to a close relative who also lives with them, the scheme excludes them from benefit. Most asylum seekers cannot get Housing Benefit and full-time students are not usually eligible (unless they are disabled or have children). Local councils administer the scheme and it involves a very similar means test to that used to calculate Income Support except that additional amounts are allowed for the circumstances of the claimant and their family. For private sector tenants, the local council will also assess whether the rent is a reasonable one in relation to the local average and the quality and suitability of the property for the tenant. They can restrict the maximum level of rent they will pay where they feel it is too expensive. This will lead to a tenant having to spend more money on their rent even where they are claiming subsistence benefits such as Income Support which do not include amounts to cover rent. It is, therefore, always worthwhile seeking a local council determination on the level of rent before you accept a tenancy. Potential tenants can do this by completing a form called a Pre-tenancy Determination which is available from local council offices. If the council does restrict the level of benefit it pays, this decision can be appealed. Challenges should be directed to your local authority in the first instance.

The government has proposed to give local authorities the power to impose Housing Benefit sanctions where the recipient has been behaving in an anti-social way.

Main qualifying rules

- You must have income below your level of assessed needs – needs are assessed using standard amounts as for Income Support, but additional amounts are added for children;
- your capital or savings must be less than £16,000, although anything above £3,000 will be treated as generating weekly income;
- you must be liable to pay rent on your home;
- you must be living in your home, although short absences do not necessarily prevent benefit from being payable;
- if the claimant has other people living in their home, their Housing Benefit may be subject to non-dependant deductions, as it is assumed that the others will make a contribution to the rent. This also applies to Council Tax Benefit (*see below*).

Other benefits

If a claimant also qualifies for Income Support, income-based Jobseeker's Allowance or the guarantee credit of

pension credit while in a rented house he will get the maximum amount of Housing Benefit allowed by the local council. If he stops claiming these benefits because of work he can get an extended payment of Housing Benefit as long as he claims quickly. He may also qualify for health benefits or tax credits.

Ms Quigley is 26 years old and has recently moved into a two-bedroom flat costing £55 per week. She earns £60 a week and applies for Housing Benefit. The local council decides that the flat is too big for her and restricts her maximum rent to £40 per week. After applying the means test they assess their contribution of Housing Benefit as £33.50. Such an outcome is not uncommon, where a rent restriction leaves tenants with very little money left after paying their rent. There is a way to appeal the rent restriction and she should do this or try to find someone else to share her liability.

Council Tax Benefit

If you are liable to pay Council Tax for your home then you can try to apply for Council Tax Benefit. The local authority also administers this and most authorities allow claims to be made on the same form as for Housing Benefit. The calculation is also very similar to Housing Benefit. Needs are compared to income and a proportion of the difference is paid towards Council Tax liability.

Second adult rebate

There is a second type of benefit called second adult rebate that does not depend on income and savings but rather looks at the circumstances of the other adults in the house.

For example, a person who lives alone would normally qualify for a reduction of 25 per cent in their Council Tax bill because they live alone. They would lose this reduction if another adult moves in. However, if that second adult has a low income and therefore cannot afford to make up the loss, a second adult rebate of up to 25 per cent of the Council Tax bill could be claimed.

Tax credits

Tax credits are a benefit that is administered by the Inland Revenue. They are very similar to other means-tested benefits in that they rely on a means test to determine the amount payable. They are also governed by similar rules about how decisions are made or challenged. Tax credits are aimed at topping up low incomes for employed or self-employed single people and couples – whether or not they also have children. Tax credits are paid through the pay packet where the claimant is working. Otherwise, they are paid directly to the claimant. Employers do not foot the bill. They recoup the money from all the tax and National Insurance they have deducted from all their workforce.

In April 2003, Working Tax Credit replaced Working Families' Tax Credit, Disabled Person's Tax Credit and Employment Credit within New Deal 50 plus. At the same time, Child Tax Credit replaced Children's Tax Credit and increases for child dependants for those receiving Incapacity Benefit, Severe Disablement Allowance, retirement pension, Carer's Allowance, Widowed Parent's Allowance.

In April 2004, Child Tax Credit replaced amounts for children within Income Support and income-based Jobseeker's Allowance. Those claiming Income Support or income-based Jobseeker's Allowance for children on 6 April 2004 receive Child Tax Credit without having to make a separate claim.

There is no limit to the amount of capital or savings you may have.

Working Tax Credit – main qualifying rules

- you are aged 16 or over;
- you usually live and work in the UK;
- you are working for at least 16 hours per week *and* responsible for a child or young person *or* have a relevant disability *or* are a member of a couple and qualify for a '50 plus element';
- you are aged 25 or over and work at least 30 hours per week;
- your income is low enough;
- If you are a member of a married or unmarried couple, you must make a joint claim.

Child Tax Credit – main qualifying rules

- you, or your partner if you have one, are responsible for at least one child or young person who usually lives with you;
- at least one child is aged 16 or under;
- your income is low enough;
- in certain circumstances, Child Tax Credit can be paid until the child is aged 19.

Tax credits are normally paid from the date of claim to the end of the current tax year. The tax year runs from 6 April to 5 April. Where a claim is made after the beginning of a tax year, the annual amount of tax credit is reduced proportionally.

Any change in the income or household circumstances of the claimant or their family must be reported within three months. Failure to report a change of circumstances may cause tax credits to be overpaid. In these circumstances, the Inland Revenue will ask for these to be repaid and may also impose a penalty of up to £300.

Parents and carers can get help with the cost of childcare through Working Tax Credit – this is known as the childcare element. It is worth up to 70 per cent of childcare costs up to £135 per week for one child and £200 for two or more children.

To calculate the maximum award, the different elements relevant to the individual, couple or family are added up (*see table* on page 282).

Those with an income below the threshold of £5,060 per year will qualify for the maximum amount of Working Tax Credit. The threshold income for those entitled to Child Tax Credit only is £13,320 per year. Those with an income above the threshold will receive less than the maximum – the award being gradually reduced at the rate of 37 pence for every pound of gross income above the threshold. Child maintenance payments, most non-taxable income and certain benefits are disregarded as income.

The reduction on account of income is first applied to the elements of Working Tax Credit except the childcare element, then the childcare element and finally the child elements and any disability or severe disability elements for the child or children within Child Tax Credit.

The family element of Child Tax Credit, including the baby addition, will not be reduced until income rises above £50,000 per year and entitlement to other tax credits has been withdrawn. This element will then be reduced at the rate of £1 for every £15 of income above £50,000.

Patrick is aged 26 and is single with no children and works for 35 hours per week. His gross annual income is £7,500. Patrick is entitled to Working Tax Credit of £23.80 per week.

Simon and Michelle are a couple in their thirties with one child aged 3. Simon works full-time and Michelle has a part-time job. They have a joint gross annual income of £10,000. They are entitled to Working Tax Credit of £22.90 per week and assistance with childcare costs. They are also entitled to Child Tax Credit of £38.00 per week.

Health Benefits

The main help that can be obtained for health-related costs are:

- free prescriptions;
- free sight tests and glasses;
- free dental treatment;
- fares to hospital.

Generally those who receive Income Support, income-based Jobseeker's Allowance and tax credits can get all of the above. If you have a low income it is still possible to get partial help towards the above, apart from prescriptions which is an all-or-nothing means test.

The Social Fund

This is a cash-limited fund that is split into two parts. The first can make payments to help with the costs of funerals, maternity and cold weather. In general, where someone receives a means-tested benefit they may qualify.

The second part of the fund has a more restricted set of rules. It is cash limited and people can apply for lump sums to meet essential needs. They can be awarded either a grant or a loan, which is repayable out of future benefits and income. It can be a useful source of extra money to help with unexpected or intermittent costs – such as money needed to replace a faulty cooker, provide emergency living expenses or to set up home after a period of unsettled living. Because the fund is cash limited it can be difficult for many to qualify unless their need is great.

29

What to Claim if Circumstances Change

In this chapter, we will examine how welfare benefits may provide support and assistance during major life events.

PREGNANCY

Which benefits may be relevant?	Main points
Maternity Allowance	Depends on NI contributions
Statutory Paternity Pay	Payable to the spouse or partner
Statutory Maternity Pay	Alternative to Maternity Allowance
Incapacity Benefit	Where the woman is not entitled to MA or SMP
Income Support	If the woman is pregnant and cannot work
Working Tax Credit	If in full-time work
Child Tax Credit	If there are other children
Sure Start Maternity Grant	Where IS, JSA (income-based), certain elements of WTC or CTC or Pension Credit is payable
Free NHS prescriptions and dental treatment	All pregnant women

There are various benefits and social security payments that can be accessed by a pregnant woman (*see also* page 391). For those in work or who have recently worked, the main payment is Maternity Allowance (MA) (*see* page 289), which is a contributory benefit. It is closely linked to a woman's employment and National Insurance record. It can be claimed if a claimant is not entitled to Statutory Maternity Pay (SMP). Where a woman is not entitled to either SMP or MA it is possible to claim Incapacity Benefit from six weeks before the expected birth until two weeks afterwards.

A pregnant woman may also be able to top up payments of SMP or MA with other means-tested benefits. Income Support (IS) (*see* page 291) can be payable if the claimant is pregnant and too ill to work, or there are less than 11 weeks to go before the expected week of birth. If the pregnant woman has a partner, she should be the main claimant of IS otherwise her partner would have to claim Jobseeker's Allowance (unless he meets other qualifying rules for IS). If the partner is working it may be possible to claim Working Tax Credit (WTC) (*see* page 294). If there are other children Child Tax Credit may be payable.

Where IS, JSA (income-based) or certain elements of WTC, CTC or Pension Credit are payable, it is possible to claim a Sure Start Maternity Grant. It is also worth trying to get a grant or loan from the Social Fund for additional maternity expenses, as long as it can be shown that the application is for expenses that are not specifically covered by the payment. Any pregnant woman is entitled to free NHS prescriptions and dental treatment. If she or her partner receives IS or JSA (income-based), they can get all health benefits free, including vitamins and milk tokens.

Josy lives alone and had been unemployed for about nine months after being laid off as a care assistant in a private nursing home. Some three months ago her old employer offered her old job back and she has been working since then, earning between £100 and £150 per week. She is pregnant and her baby is due in ten weeks' time. She has now stopped work and wants to claim any welfare benefits to which she is entitled. Her home is mortgaged and in her name only, since this was transferred to her following the break-up of her marriage five years ago. She has a new partner who lives in a rented council flat. She has no other children and no savings.

Josy cannot get SMP from her current employer because she has not worked continuously for 26 weeks or more with them.

She may get MA as long as she has worked 26 weeks out of the last 66.

She will be able to claim IS straight away and she should claim for mortgage interest payments and Council Tax Benefit as part of her IS claim. If she gets IS she will also be able to get a Sure Start Maternity Grant, and the full range of health benefits.

CHILDREN

Which benefits may be relevant?	Main points
Child Benefit	Everyone is entitled
Child Tax Credit	There must be a child in the family
Free sight tests, dental treatment and prescriptions	All children under 19 years old, who are still in education, are entitled

A new addition to the family is a special event but the joy of a new baby also brings worries about the extra costs involved with raising a child. The first step in accessing social security is to claim Child Benefit (*see* page 287). This is a standard amount payable, irrespective of income and circumstances. Once Child Benefit is being paid, the claimant may become entitled to other benefits, or the benefits that he is already receiving may be increased.

For people who receive contributory benefits such as Incapacity Benefit and retirement pension, if there is a dependent child, Child Tax Credit may be claimed. Additions for children within contributory benefits were removed for claims made from 6 April 2003. Most parents in receipt of these additions prior to this date will qualify for transitional protection and these will be retained.

Since April 2004, amounts for children are no longer included in the assessment of means-tested benefit, except Housing Benefit and Council Tax Benefit. Child Tax Credit must now be claimed instead. Help with childcare costs may be available from Working Tax Credit. Parents who were receiving additional benefit for children with their Income Support and income-based Jobseeker's Allowance prior to 6 April 2004, had these additional amounts replaced with Child Tax Credit.

For Housing Benefit and Council Tax Benefit, higher amounts are payable for lone parents and other families with children.

It will depend very much on the family's circumstances as to what benefits may be payable. It is always important to check on a regular basis whether entitlement has been gained. If a benefit claim was refused because of too much income, as children grow up this may mean that entitlement is gained with the passage of time. All children under 19 years old who are still in education can get

free sight tests, dental treatment and prescriptions, no matter what the income of their parents.

Children with a disability

Which benefits may be relevant?	Main points
Disability Living Allowance	For children with extra personal care needs or mobility needs
Child Tax Credit	There are extra amounts for disabled children

There are additional benefits and payments that can be claimed where a child has a disability. A parent can claim Disability Living Allowance (*see* page 285) if the child has personal care needs that are in excess of those for a healthy child of their age, or if they have mobility needs. Where this is paid it will also enable extra means-tested benefits, such as Income Support and Housing Benefit, to be paid (*see* pages 291–2).

Young people aged 16 to 19 who are incapacitated may be able to get Incapacity Benefit without having to pay any National Insurance contributions in the past. Where a child is severely disabled it may also be possible to seek extra help outside social security; The Family Fund, PO Box 50, York YO1 9ZX (Tel: 0845 130 45 42; website: www.familyfundtrust.org.uk) can give grants to families to help with the special needs of a disabled child.

When children grow up

Many parents will say that a child never really leaves home. However, social security law sees things differently. Most benefits tie in entitlement to child-related benefits to school leaving. Child Benefit (*see* page 287) can continue for a limited period after a child leaves school – however, in the case of a lone parent claiming Income Support, they can no longer claim Child Benefit when their last child reaches 16 years.

Children who have left school but who are not yet 18 years old will *not* be able to claim benefits if they are unemployed – but their parents also cannot claim. Where children are estranged from their parents they can sometimes get benefit from the age of 16 years but, in general, this age group tends to be left to rely on their parents until they reach 18 years.

Mr and Mrs Polesworthy have just had their first child. Mr Polesworthy is working and his wife has taken maternity leave and receives Statutory Maternity Pay from her employer. They rent their house.

Their current income is made up of wages and Statutory Maternity Pay. While Mrs Polesworthy is off work they should check to see if they could get Working Tax Credit or Child Tax Credit since their income is low. They can claim Child Benefit, and they may also qualify for Housing Benefit to help towards rent payments and also Council Tax Benefit. If they still qualify for these benefits as the child reaches school age they may get education benefits to pay for school uniform. The eligibility rules for this may vary depending on where they live because each education authority decides their own rules. When their child reaches 16 years they may also get more means-tested benefits, as the amounts included in the calculation increase once a child reaches 16 years.

WORK AND LOW PAY

Means-testing was planned to provide a safety net for those who were unable to work because of unforeseen circumstances. The social security net has, in recent decades, caught more and more people. There is now a minimum wage, currently set at £4.50 an hour; however, if you are supporting a family and paying a mortgage in a low-paid job, you are likely to need to rely on social security to top up your income. Tax credits aim to alleviate some of these problems, and changes to the system in 1999 enable higher payments and the disregard of childcare costs and maintenance payments. If one member of a family works they can still access Housing and Council Tax benefits. Where the worker is disabled there is also the Working Tax Credit that tops up low earnings. Such a worker may also be able to get Disability Living Allowance since this benefit does not stop if work is attempted, although it is advisable to inform the paying office if you have started work.

The fact remains that for a family to come off means-tested benefits completely they need a substantial income. An increasing threshold under which National Insurance contributions are paid does help to increase the wages in the pay packet. Increases to Child Benefit and child allowances in other means-tested benefits also help to increase a family's income.

Some benefits can continue to be paid while you are working. If someone is a carer in receipt of Carer's Allowance they can work and earn up to £50 per week without losing the benefit. Even those who are sick and receiving Incapacity Benefit can work up to 16 hours on medical advice. There are also many incentives for those claiming sickness benefits to attempt work. For example, work can be attempted for up to 52 weeks and if things do not work out, maybe because the person found work too difficult to manage with their disability, they can return to their old rates of benefit.

Accidents at work

If you experience an accident at work you should always report this to your employer and make sure it has been entered in an accident book. It is also useful to report an accident to the DWP in case you want to claim benefit in the future. Many injuries may only cause problems many years after an accident. Reporting an accident early can help speed up the claims process at a later date.

Pensions and benefits in respect of accidents or diseases caused by work can continue even where the worker is able to return to work. They are an important source of compensation for injury. Statutory Sick Pay (*see* page 327) will be paid for the first 28 weeks of sickness and then you will need to check entitlement to other social security benefits such as Incapacity Benefit and Disability Living Allowance.

RETIREMENT

Which benefits may be relevant?	*Main points*
State Pension	Must have paid NI
Income Support	Must pass means test
Winter Fuel Payment	One-off payment for over 60s
Attendance Allowance	Over 65s who need extra help

Everyone who pays National Insurance over at least a quarter of his or her working life will be able to claim a pension. This will be payable on reaching pension age, which is currently 65 years for men and 60 years for women. For those who are not entitled, perhaps because they have never worked, Income Support can be claimed on reaching the age of 60 years if the means test is passed. Occupational pensions may top up other income and these have no effect on state pension payments. All workers earning between £9,000 and £20,000 are now encouraged to have access to some form of occupational pension.

Remember that you may be entitled to a state pension based upon your spouse's contribution record, such as the married women's category B pension. A general point to bear in mind is that retirement pensions are taxable – you may be better off to forgo entitlement if you can, instead, continue to receive a non-taxable benefit, such as Severe Disablement Benefit.

If you are 60 years or over you will qualify for a winter fuel payment which is a one-off lump sum to help towards the extra costs of winter. Where there are disabilities or a need for assistance with day-to-day personal care, Attendance Allowance might be payable if you are over 65 years.

Benefits are also accessible if you go into residential care and have limited income or capital. Means-testing rules apply, although these are modified to take account of the special situation of people either in temporary or permanent care. If one member of a couple needs to go into care or into hospital, resources and circumstances will eventually be assessed as if there are two single people – which may mean benefits can be claimed that were not accessible before. The rules are complex and it is best to seek expert advice from agencies such as Citizens' Advice Bureaux or Age Concern (details in local phone directories).

As with any other stage in life, there could also be entitlement to other means-tested benefits depending on income, capital and individual circumstances.

SEPARATION

If a couple separate, one person (usually the woman) may be left in a jointly owned property with no income to cover basic housing and life needs. They may also have children to care for. Apart from issues around splitting property proceeds, the benefits system recognizes the harsh results of separation. A parent can claim Income Support immediately on separation if they meet the normal rules of entitlement. Where a mortgage or rent is payable, and the non-resident partner refuses to pay, benefits can pick up these payments to ensure the home can be maintained.

The parent caring for the children may need financial support from the absent parent. The Child Support Agency (CSA) now administers child maintenance. The CSA will require the parent looking after the children to provide authorization for them to pursue the absent parent (*see* page 82). Any payments due are counted in full for the purposes of Income Support but they are ignored for Working Tax Credit and Child Tax Credit.

The whole range of means-tested benefits can be claimed. However, where there are no children a person who is newly separated will have to sign on as unemployed and seek work in order to qualify for benefit. Sometimes a claimant may be treated as a member of a couple when they feel that they should not be. This is often the case where people of opposite sexes live in the same property, for example, in a landlord/lodger relationship. The Benefits Agency must show, on balance, that there is a couple relationship. As with any decision there is a right to dispute this.

Advice on maintenance, benefits and other money matters is available from the National Council for One Parent Families. Their Lone Parent Helpline is 0800 018 5026.

Mr Jones leaves his partner, Ms Gee. They jointly rent their home and have two children who remain with Ms Gee in the house. She works and, before he moved out, Mr Jones had stayed at home to look after the children. Now he has left the family home, Mr Jones is classed as single. He can claim Jobseeker's Allowance and Housing Benefit for any new property he rents.

Since Ms Gee is working, she may qualify for Working Families' Tax Credit, and if she now has to pay for childcare this will be taken into account in the calculation of benefit. Mr Jones may have to pay a minimum amount of Child Support maintenance. If he starts work, Ms Gee could apply for the Child Support maintenance to be increased. Ms Gee may also qualify for Housing Benefit and Council Tax benefit. She should inform the Council Tax billing authority, as she would get a discount if she is the only adult in her home.

BEREAVEMENT

Which benefits may be relevant?	Main points
Bereavement Payment	A lump sum that must be claimed within twelve months
Funeral Payment	Must be claimed within three months
Widowed Parent's Allowance	Where surviving spouse is supporting children
Bereavement Allowance	Where there are no children
Guardian's Allowance	Where child is orphaned, carer can make claim

Since April 2001 both men and women can access benefits following the death of their spouse. This section looks at how these rules operate. When there is a bereavement in the family it is important for family members to be aware of benefits that the deceased was claiming and also the potential entitlements of the surviving relatives.

To claim benefits following a death the claim must be made promptly. For example, a lump sum Bereavement Payment (*see* page 290) must be claimed within twelve months, as must a Funeral Payment from the social fund. Where there are children, a Widowed Parent's Allowance (*see* page 291) may be payable and, generally, £10 of this will be ignored when assessing entitlement to means-tested benefits. If there are no surviving children, a Bereavement Allowance can be claimed for a year after the death – after that you would be subject to normal benefit rules. In addition to these benefits for bereavement, means-tested benefits can be claimed. If a child has no surviving parents, his carer can claim Guardian's Allowance in addition to Child Benefit (*see* page 287) and additional amounts of means-tested benefits for the child.

Where the deceased has claimed benefits in their own right, any uncashed payments need to be returned. If there is any form of overpayment after a person has died then this can be recovered from the estate of the deceased.

UNEMPLOYMENT

The benefit system is aimed at providing a bare minimum of income to ensure that the basics of modern life can be maintained following redundancy or dismissal (for whatever reason). The main benefit is Jobseeker's Allowance. It is important that you approach your local employment service office as soon as possible to arrange an interview and get relevant claim forms. Depending on your circumstances, contributory Jobseeker's Allowance can be claimed. This may be topped up by the means-tested JSA if there is a mortgage. Some interest payments are included but, for most people, there is a waiting period before full costs can be paid following a new claim for benefit.

Where both partners in a couple are unemployed, only one of them has to meet all the labour market conditions, such as being available for work. It is a requirement from 2001 that both members of certain couples have to be available for and actively seeking work. However, where there are children or one member of the couple is sick, this requirement will not apply. If an unemployed claimant is sick and has lost a job then sickness and disability benefits, including Income Support, should be considered.

Income-based Jobseeker's Allowance is commonly described as a 'passport' benefit. This means that if it is paid it leads to automatic entitlement to other benefits. These include health benefits, maximum amounts of Housing and Council Tax benefits, and access to the full range of Social Fund payments. Although there are many benefits available to someone who is unemployed, the level of income is still likely to be substantially lower than that obtained from full-time work. It is useful, not only to be aware of benefit entitlements, but also to seek money advice to prevent any lenders (e.g. the bank holding a mortgage over your house) taking recovery action unnecessarily.

SICKNESS, DISABILITY AND CARING

Which benefits may be relevant?	Main points
Statutory Sick Pay	Where you have to give up work
Incapacity Benefit	Payable after six months of receipt of SSP
Industrial Disablement Benefit	If work caused the disability
Severe Disablement Benefit	Where the disability/illness is not related to work

Suffering from illness, accident or disability can be a traumatic change in your life, both on an emotional and financial level. There are many social security benefits that may be payable and these have different qualifying rules and span the three types of benefit described in Chapter 27: contributory, non-contributory and means-tested. It is an area of social security where specialist advice is essential to ensure that entitlement is gained.

For those who have to give up work, Statutory Sick Pay and, possibly, contractual sick pay from the employer will be payable for the first six months (*see also* page 327). Even where you are paid sick pay by your employer, after six months Incapacity Benefit can be claimed. Depending on the duration and degree of the illness, Disability Living Allowance or Attendance Allowance may be appropriate. If work could be a cause of the disability, Industrial Disablement Benefit should be claimed and you should think about consulting a solicitor in case there is a civil claim against the employer.

Means-tested benefits take account of long-term illness by allowing extra premiums, and they generally pay extra once you have been sick for a year or more. If a claimant needs to stay in hospital there are complex rules about what benefits can still be payable. Some benefits will be suspended while others are reduced after different periods. If the home is adapted or an extra room is used because of disability, the council tax bill can be reduced. For those who have been ill or disabled and who start work again the Working Tax Credit can help top up low wages. For people who care for a disabled person, Carer's Allowance (*see* page 287) can be claimed along with Income Support if the carer's income is low. Bear in mind that this can affect the benefits of the person being cared for, so it is important to check any possible implications with a specialist adviser before claiming as a carer.

Mr Jackson breaks his leg at work and, following complications in an operation, is unable to walk without great pain. He receives Statutory Sick Pay for 28 weeks and then he is dismissed from his job, as he is not likely to recover enough to return to any jobs that his employer can offer. He has two children and a mortgage. He has to sleep downstairs as he now finds it difficult to climb stairs.

He will get Incapacity Benefit if he has paid sufficient National Insurance contributions and he may get Disability Living Allowance mobility component based upon his walking problems. He already gets Child Benefit for his children and may also qualify for Income Support to top up the other benefits he gets. Income Support will pay an amount towards the cost of his mortgage, and he will get an additional premium because he is incapable of work and gets Disability Living Allowance. He may also get Industrial Disablement Allowance because the accident occurred at work. He should also claim a reduction in his council tax bill since he has adapted the use of his home because of his disability and also Council Tax Benefit to reduce his payments further.

30

Challenging Social Security Decisions

The basic idea behind challenging social security decisions is very simple. Anyone dissatisfied with a decision about benefits can dispute that decision through a revision, supersession or appeal to an Appeal Tribunal. The original decision may then be reversed, changed or confirmed. Officials acting on behalf of the DWP, Inland Revenue or local authority, commonly known as decision makers, decide most welfare benefit or tax credit matters. There is a framework of very short time limits, normally of one month, in which to lodge a dispute. There are only limited grounds to extend the relevant time limit.

Some of the decisions do not have a right of appeal. An example is whether to accept a claim not made on a valid claim form. Although there is no right of appeal, the Secretary of State can be asked to revise the decision or it can be challenged by applying for judicial review.

MAKING A VALID CLAIM FOR BENEFIT

An appeal can only be brought against a decision about a valid claim for benefit. A tribunal cannot have jurisdiction to hear the appeal unless a valid claim is made in the first place.

In general, if a claim is not made on the correct claim form the Secretary of State can decide that an alternative form or written document is acceptable. This is a decision that does not have a right of appeal. However, once the Secretary of State has decided that a valid claim has been made in an acceptable way it is still up to the decision maker to decide what the claim is for and the date from which it will run. This decision can be appealed.

A claim can be amended or withdrawn before a decision about benefit is made. This could be important, for example, if circumstances change before a decision is made.

Information in support of a claim

If a person fills in the wrong form, or fills in the right form incorrectly, the Secretary of State should still treat it as a valid claim if the mistake is corrected within one month. If the requested information is not supplied, benefit can be suspended. Claims for Jobseeker's Allowance and Income Support must be made on the correct claim form with the main parts completed fully and correctly, with all relevant information and evidence provided. Proof of identity and a National Insurance number is required for all benefit claims.

Time limits for claiming

Each benefit has a time limit for bringing a claim. If a claim is made outside the appropriate time limit, benefit is not normally paid for any period before the claim unless 'good cause' for the late claim can be shown. There must be an application for a claim to be backdated and it can be backdated for up to three months. Some benefits, such as Incapacity Benefit and Child Benefit, have automatic backdating rights, while others, such as Attendance Allowance and Disability Living Allowance, cannot be backdated at all. Housing Benefit and Council Tax Benefit can be backdated for up to one year from the date that backdating is requested.

Decisions on benefit claims

Once a valid claim has been made, a decision maker will decide whether the benefit should be granted. The decision maker must normally give his decision in writing, including a statement of reasons and details of any right to request a revision, supersession or appeal. If this is not forthcoming there is a right to request a statement of reasons within one month of the date of the decision and this should then be provided by the decision maker within 14 days.

The following paragraphs explain the different ways in which a claimant can dispute a decision. Note that it is more important to challenge a decision within the relevant time limit than to use the right terminology.

Disputing decisions

There are three main ways of challenging a benefit decision: revision, supersession and appeal.

Revision

The right to dispute a decision through a revision is at least as important as the right of appeal to an Appeal Tribunal. It can be a quick way to change a decision, and it also gives the applicant two chances to challenge the decision. If the revision is not completely favourable, there is a further right of appeal within one month of receiving the revision notification. The new decision following the revision should take effect from the date of the original decision. For tax credit decisions, unless you are just reporting a change of circumstances, it is usually better to appeal than request a revision.

Time limits

A decision can be revised either by an application by the claimant or on the decision maker's own initiative:

- *Within one month* – a decision can be revised on any ground if the application is made within one month of the decision being notified to the claimant.
- *Within 13 months* – it will be possible to request a revision outside the one-month time limit, and up to 13 months after the issuing of the original decision, if it is 'reasonable' to grant the application and there are 'special circumstances'.
- *At any time* – if the decision arose through 'official error', or, if the original decision created an overpayment of benefit through a failure to disclose or a misrepresentation on the part of the claimant. For tax credits, there is a five-year time limit for a revision of a decision. This time limit runs from the end of the tax year in which the decision was made.

If a request to revise a decision is made late, there is a general test of reasonableness when deciding if it can be accepted. Reference will be made to the length of a delay, the merits of the appeal and any special circumstances that made it difficult for the claimant to apply within the time limit. These are the same tests that are applied to late supersessions. Since the terms are not restrictively defined it is always worth trying to secure a late revision if there are any circumstances that go some way towards explaining a delay.

The Basic Appeals Procedure and Time Limits

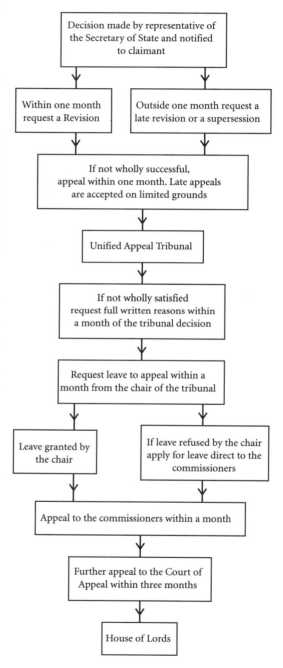

Supersession

Supersession is another way to change a decision unless it is a tax credit decision, to which the supersession procedure does not apply. This method is generally available if certain changes have occurred since a claim was made. Decisions can be superseded where there has been, or there is likely to be, a change in the applicant's circumstance or if there is some sort of mistake about the facts or the law. The date that the superseded decision takes effect is generally the date when the application is made.

If the applicant's circumstances change in a way that is advantageous to his claim, the superseded decision will take effect from the date of the change of circumstances and backdated payments could be made. On the other hand, if the applicant's circumstances change in a way that is disadvantageous to his claim, he may have to repay benefits from the date of the change of circumstances if it is decided that he failed to disclose or misrepresented the facts in any way.

Appeal

The other way of challenging most benefit decisions is to appeal. An appeal to the Appeal Tribunal can be further pursued to the Social Security Commissioner and, ultimately, to the Court of Appeal, the House of Lords or the European Courts. An appeal can be made against an original or later decision. If the decision maker agrees to change the decision in the claimant's favour, even in part, the appeal will lapse. The time limit for making an appeal is restricted to one month. A late appeal may be allowed provided that the appeal has a reasonable chance of success and that it is in the interests of natural justice. There is an absolute time limit of 13 months to bring a late appeal. A legally qualified tribunal member makes these decisions. Any changes of circumstances after the original decision are ignored when looking at the appeal so it is important to put in a new claim while any appeal hearing is being arranged if circumstances change.

Writing an appeal letter

An appeal must be made in writing and sent to the office that made the decision. Appeal forms can be obtained from the office which made the decision, but a letter signed by the claimant may be accepted as long as it contains sufficient details of the decision and reasons for appealing. The style of the letter is not as important as the content, which should contain enough fact and argument for the decision maker to be likely to change their decision so that there is no need for an appeal. The appeal request can also give the name of a representative, if one has been agreed, and also state whether the appeal papers should be sent to them as well as to the claimant.

After the appeal is lodged

After the appeal is lodged, the decision maker will look at the decision again and may revise it in whole or part, particularly where further evidence has been supplied. If the decision is revised in part only, the appeal will lapse and it is necessary for a further appeal to be lodged. If the decision is not revised, the relevant office will prepare a bundle of documents containing all the relevant papers concerning the claim and also any supporting evidence, medical reports or correspondence. These are then forwarded to the claimant who will, for the first time, know in detail what the relevant office will be saying and how they have come to their decision.

The Benefits Agency will also issue an inquiry form to the claimant asking if they want an oral or paper hearing. It is always best to ask for an oral hearing as these are more likely to succeed than one that is decided on the papers alone. The inquiry form should be returned to the local Appeals Service within 14 days. The next contact will be in the form of a notice of the hearing which provides a minimum of 14 days' notice. If there is not enough time for collecting evidence, or if the date is impossible, then a letter should be sent to the Appeals Service to ask for the tribunal to be postponed, giving reasons for the request. Occasionally, it will just be impossible to attend on a particular day and in this situation it will help to provide a written argument for the tribunal to consider.

There are circumstances where an appeal may be struck out, which means it is cancelled. This can be done by a clerk to the tribunal or by a legally qualified panel member. An appeal could be struck out if it has been made outside the time limits or if the claimant has failed to provide information as directed by the Secretary of State. All is not lost at this point because there is still a right to request that the appeal be reinstated.

Tribunal procedure

The Appeals Service has overall responsibility for administering all social security appeals. They have an administrative system with a president and regional chairs. The Lord Chancellor is responsible for appointing these people and also controls the appointment of tribunal panel members. There is also a clerk who is appointed by the Secretary of State who is responsible for the general organization of the appeal. All tribunal hearings are held in public unless you request a private hearing, or the legally qualified panel member is of the opinion that intimate personal or financial circumstances may have to be disclosed or issues of public security are involved.

Tribunal panel members

Appeal Tribunals comprise one, two or three members, one of whom must be legally qualified. The exact composition and number will depend upon the type of issue that is being looked at. Other members are drawn from a panel of experts.

The members of the panel will have experience in four areas:

- Legally qualified panel members are often known as chairs. Their main functions are to introduce the proceedings, chair the tribunal, determine the structure and order of the tribunal and chair the decision-making process after the hearing.
- Medically qualified panel members are doctors who have at least 10 years' practice experience, or who are named on a specialist register.
- Financially qualified members will be qualified accountants.
- People with disability experience – either a disabled person or someone who has experience of disability issues in a voluntary or professional capacity.

Who sits on the tribunal?

The Clerk to the Tribunal has responsibility for summoning the correct members to the different types of tribunal.

Type of claim to be considered by the appeal	Who must sit on the appeal tribunal panel?
Severe Disablement Allowance and Industrial Injuries Benefits	Legally qualified panel member + one or two medically qualified panel members
Incapacity Benefit	Legally qualified panel member + medically qualified panel member
Disability decisions regarding Disability Living Allowance and Attendance Allowance	Legally qualified panel member + medically qualified panel member + someone with experience of disability
Child Support appeals	Legally qualified chair alone, unless there are issues related to business accounts or if there is also a medical/disability question

A single, legally qualified, chair will generally consider all other types of appeal. There is also provision for the inclusion of additional members to the above tribunals (up to a maximum of three in total) to help monitor the standards of the tribunal and to provide experience for the additional members.

Others present at the tribunal

In addition to the members of the Tribunal there may be a number of other people present in the Tribunal room.

The presenting officer

The presenting officer is the representative for the Secretary of State for social security and child support appeals, the representative for the local authority for Housing Benefit/Council Tax Benefit appeals or the representative for the Inland Revenue for Tax Credit and Child Benefit appeals.

The presenting officer will probably not be the same as the one that made the initial decision. The role of the presenting officer is not supposed to be that of an advocate but rather to ensure that all the relevant facts are before the tribunal. They should also refer the tribunal to all the relevant decisions of the Social Security Commissioners. In practice, the approach of presenting officers can be like that of an advocate who is arguing for a decision against the claimant.

The Clerk to the Tribunal

A clerk is appointed by the Secretary of State to service each appeal tribunal. This is a marked change to the previous system of appointment by the Regional Chairs. The clerks' independence has been reduced, along with an increase in their powers to determine questions relating to appeals. A clerk's main functions are: to receive the appeal documents; ask the claimant if an oral or paper hearing is required; consider requests for postponements; notify claimants, their representatives and the Secretary of State of the tribunal's decision; and to pay travel expenses (meals and loss of earnings can also be claimed). During the course of the tribunal, the clerk should take no active part in the proceedings, and may wander in and out of the room dealing with people in the waiting room.

The hearing

Appeals are either heard at 'oral' or 'paper' hearings. An oral hearing of a case will be allowed if any party to the appeal, or the chair, requests one. Otherwise they will be dealt with on the basis of the paperwork available for the hearing. There is also limited scope to request a domiciliary hearing in a claimant's home, but the appeals service makes every effort to avoid arranging these due to the additional costs. Statistics show that oral hearings are more likely to succeed. This is understandable because

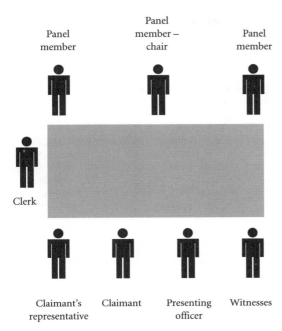

Panel member

Panel member – chair

Panel member

Clerk

Claimant's representative

Claimant

Presenting officer

Witnesses

of the additional evidence that can be presented. An oral hearing should be requested whenever possible for this reason.

Those present at the tribunal usually sit around a single table with the panel members on one side and the claimant, his representative, the presenting officer and any witnesses on the other.

The order of the tribunal is at the discretion of the individual chairperson of the tribunal. There are three basic ways the tribunal may run:

1 the claimant argues their case first, followed by the presenting officer;
2 the presenting officer puts the reasons for the decision first, followed by the claimant answering;
3 the tribunal members lead, with the chair of the tribunal taking the major leading role and identifying the issues and questions that need answering.

It is best to be prepared for any of the alternatives but, if necessary, the chair can be asked if a particular procedure could be adopted.

The key to getting a successful result at a tribunal is to be well prepared. However, it is also necessary to be able to cope with new arguments or facts that arise during the hearing. A tribunal can ignore anything that was not raised in an initial appeal so it is important if new issues are raised after the appeal has been lodged to make a case for their inclusion. There is no advantage to gain by 'springing' new arguments on the tribunal or withholding

evidence from it and this could seriously affect the outcome of the appeal.

Presenting your case to the tribunal

If there is no representative the chair will generally lead the process and ask questions, although a claimant is free to present his case if he wishes. There are several elements to presenting a case at a social security tribunal. A basic plan for an argument would look something like this:

● explain the decision the tribunal is being asked to make;
● clarify the facts and the relevant background to the claim;
● explain how, from the evidence presented to the tribunal, the Acts, Regulations and Commissioners' Decisions support a different interpretation and a different decision;
● answer the points raised in the Secretary of State's submission;
● sum up.

It is always best to write down arguments and if they are lengthy hand them in before the tribunal hearing. The advantage of a written argument is that it is easier to keep a record of what has been said and what is intended to be argued.

Like a claimant, the presenting officer has a right to be present, although in practice they often do not attend. They will tend to rely heavily on the written submission in the appeal papers but may bring forward new facts or quote different Regulations or Commissioners' Decisions. If any new information makes a material difference to the case an adjournment can be requested to give time to think about the new information. A full adjournment for another day may be arranged if the tribunal feels that further information is needed.

The tribunal decision

The tribunal will normally make its decision immediately after the hearing. A short decision notice will be given out, giving the terms of the decision and the main reasons. The tribunal may decide to issue a full decision or either side can request one within one month of the summary decision having been issued. A copy of the full decision is essential if a further challenge on the case is being considered. It is also useful to request a copy of the chair's handwritten notes of evidence. Even if the decision is negative, this does not mean that all is lost because there are a number of ways in which the decision can still be challenged.

Further appeals

Either the claimant or the Secretary of State has a further right of appeal to the Social Security Commissioner from a tribunal decision. The procedure below is described from the claimant's point of view, but it applies equally to the Secretary of State. If the Secretary of State appeals, then payment of benefit will normally be suspended until the appeal is heard.

Grounds for appeal

There is a right of appeal to the Social Security Commissioner on a point of law only. This is a technical term and it is generally best to seek specialist advice before taking a case further. There are no costs involved and it is possible to run a case without further advice.

A tribunal may have committed an error of law for the following reasons:

● an interpretation of existing law can be disputed or is wrong;
● the decision is supported by no evidence;
● the facts found lead to one decision but the tribunal has come to a different decision;
● the record of the decision does not contain adequate reasons or findings on the important questions of fact;
● there was a breach of the rules of natural justice – this means that there was some unfairness in the way the proceedings were conducted.

How to appeal

Before an appeal can be made, leave to appeal has to be obtained. This is done by applying to the tribunal chair within one month of the tribunal's decision. If the chair rejects an application or refuses leave to appeal, then a further application can be made to the Commissioner within one month of the refusal. Once leave to appeal has been obtained, a copy of the appeal will be sent to the office that administers the benefit for their comments. A copy of these will then be sent to the claimant and his representative for their further comments. The process continues until each side has said all it wishes to. The Commissioner usually decides the case on the basis of these written submissions, but may decide to hold an oral hearing. The Commissioner has the power to either give the decision he considers the tribunal should have made or to refer the case back to another tribunal with directions for its determination. Once a Commissioner has made a decision this can be appealed further to the Court of Appeal. In the majority of cases, the Commissioner will refer the case back to a tribunal for it to redetermine and make a new decision.

Setting aside

A tribunal chair or the clerk to the tribunal has the power to correct an accidental error in its decision at any time. A tribunal also has the power to set aside a decision and allow the case to be heard afresh. There are limited grounds for this to happen which include where:

● documents have gone missing or were not shown to the claimant;
● the claimant was not notified of a hearing date and did not attend;
● the tribunal chair feels that an error of law has occurred.

An application to have a decision set aside should be made in writing to the appeal tribunal clerk. It has to be made within one month and be accompanied by the written reasons for the tribunal decision.

Employment

Introduction

Modern employment law, in its many guises, touches the working lives of all individuals who work for another person or business. Until relatively recently, the over-riding principles were founded in law on the subservient basis of a 'master' employing 'servants'. Since the 1970s such age-old principles have been almost entirely over-ridden. There now exists in their place a considerable volume of protective legislation, designed to provide employees with a 'floor' of employment rights. Employment law is constantly evolving, often as a result of new European directives and decisions. This part of the book will guide you through the existing maze of employment legislation.

31

Employment Status

WHEN IS AN EMPLOYEE NOT AN EMPLOYEE?

Historically, the answer was quite simple – an employee is not an employee when that individual is self-employed. However, in the past decade the more significant distinction is between an employee and a 'casual worker'. The distinction between an employee and a person who is self-employed or a casual worker has great significance legally. The legal rights of each are different. An employee is entitled to a considerable level of statutory and common law protection, much more than if that person was self-employed or a casual worker.

THE IMPORTANCE OF BEING AN EMPLOYEE

An employee is entitled to the following rights:
- protection against unfair dismissal;
- redundancy pay;
- notice of termination of employment;
- guaranteed payments in respect of lay-off and short-time working;
- written particulars of employment;
- itemized payslips;
- equal pay;*
- maternity rights;
- protection from race discrimination;*
- protection from sex discrimination;*
- protection from trade union victimization;
- protection of employment upon the transfer of a business;
- time off to fulfil trade union duties;
- to be protected by reasonable health and safety measures;
- not to have unlawful deductions made from wages;
- to be paid Statutory Sick Pay;
- protection from discrimination on the grounds of disability;*

- national minimum wage;*
- paid annual leave;*
- limitation on working time;*
- parental leave;
- the right not to be discriminated against on the grounds of religion or belief or sexual orientation.*

These rights will be examined in detail later. With so much at stake, the importance of ascertaining employment status is self-evident.

Casual workers are only entitled to the rights marked with an asterisk (*) above.

A self-employed person is only entitled to the right not to be discriminated against on any of the above grounds and only then if he or she executes the work done personally.

What is a casual worker?

Lawrence works at National Power Limited as a tour guide. His contract states that he must be available for work 'as and when required'. He works for National Power Limited for two years until he is dismissed for misconduct. His claim for unfair dismissal fails because he is a casual worker and not an employee. This is because the employer was not under an obligation to provide him with work, even though he was under an obligation to do the work provided.

THE DEFINITION OF AN EMPLOYEE

An employee is employed under a 'contract of service' or a 'contract of employment' and is different from a self-employed or independent contractor who would typically work under a 'contract for services'. What the parties call themselves and how they label the agreement is not the decisive factor. If there is a dispute, or where there is no written agreement at all, the court will try to ascertain the true nature of the relationship between the parties.

The law does supply a definition of an 'employee' and

regards it as an 'individual who has entered into or works under a contract of employment'.

Note that this will include an apprenticeship. This definition may be quite clear when the individual in question has been issued with a document by his employer entitled 'contract of employment'. Where there is no written contract of employment the position is much less straightforward.

The practical definition

The court will take into account a range of factors in deciding whether an individual is an employee or is self-employed. The starting point for the court is to ask:

1 whether the 'employer' is *obliged to provide* work for the 'employee'; and
2 is the 'employee' obliged to *personally perform* work for the 'employer'?

These mutual obligations are a strong indicator that the worker is an employee. Without mutuality of obligation, there can be no contract of employment. Once this prerequisite is satisfied, the court will look at other important factors in determining the status of a worker, which are detailed in the table below. In practice, the court will look at all the factors and make a balanced decision. The test is known as the 'multiple-factor test' and all of the issues are given equal scrutiny.

Sally is a bookkeeper for ABC Ltd. She works three days a week and has done so for five years. When at the office she uses ABC's equipment and resources. She works for no other employer and is subject to the day-to-day direction and control of the Finance Director. Due to the installation of a new computer system ABC wishes to dispense with Sally's services. They regard her as a self-employed contractor and give her one week's notice.

In fact, applying the above test, Sally is a part-time employee. As such, she is entitled to:
- *statutory notice; and*
- *redundancy pay.*

She may also challenge the dismissal if she feels it is unfair in the circumstances.

Factor	Employee	Self-employed
Is there a mutual obligation to provide and do work?	Yes	No. Worker may be a casual worker or self-employed
Does the person work under the orders or regular control of another?	Works under the daily control of another	Not generally under ongoing direction and control. Often taken on to perform or complete a specific task
Does the person work exclusively for the other party?	Yes	No. Can do work under two or more contracts, with different parties, at the same time
Does the person work as part of the other's business?	Yes, an integral part of the other party's business or organization	No – is used as and when required
Does the person provide their own plant and equipment?	Other party provides all tools and equipment required	Most often provides their own tools and equipment
Does the person provide their own support staff?	Other party provides all required support staff	Provides own team of support staff, as required and pays them directly at own expense
Is the person responsible for own profit and loss?	No overriding ability to increase profits over and above wage received	Ability to enhance profit by maximizing efficiency
Tax, NI and VAT arrangements?	All dealt with by the other party automatically – subject to PAYE rules	Undertakes own accounts
Is the arrangement designed purely to achieve tax advantages and/or to avoid employment legislation?	If yes, it is likely to fail and the individual will be regarded as an employee	No
Does the worker receive paid holiday?	Yes. The worker is an employee or a casual worker	No

The contractual provisions

This will often be the starting point for the court if a document entitled 'The Contract' or 'The Contract of Employment' (or similar) is in existence. Many people believe that if there is no written contract or document, there can be no contract. This is not the case in law. Where there is nothing in writing, the court will consider the 'contract' to include everything orally agreed, the working relationship of the parties in practice and the custom and practice of the parties.

Avoidance of legislation

Where a contract is called a 'contract for services' and purports to be self-employed in nature but, in applying the above tests, is clearly nothing of the kind, the court will not be fooled. Unscrupulous employers will fail if seeking to use this method to avoid the rigours of employment legislation. Similarly, where an individual has openly requested of another party to be self-employed, for example to reap tax advantages, the court will be wary if that person, when times get hard, claims employment status.

SPECIFIC RELATIONSHIPS

There are some types of individual who, over the years, have been considered by the courts with regard to their being employees or self-employed. It is useful at this stage to list these types and indicate the court's view on their status.

Directors

Strictly speaking, a director is not an employee. There need be no contract of employment between a director and the company for which he works. Normally, there is a contract called a 'service contract' or 'service agreement'. Particularly where the director is required to perform specific tasks in return for a regular salary, the court will usually decide that this contract is a contract of employment.

Most of the cases where a director is not an employee involve small private family companies. A director of such a company may work full-time for that company and not be an employee. The key to the distinction is that a director of a small private company is under different obligations than his counterpart within a large organization.

Partners

Partners are not employees. They are self-employed, receiving for payment a share in the profits generated by the business. There is a distinction, however, between an 'equity partner' and a 'salaried partner'. If the former owns part of the business and, therefore, takes a share of the profit, that person will be self-employed. A 'salaried partner' does not own a distinct part of the business and receives payment by way of salary only. Such an individual is highly likely to be an employee, being a 'partner' in name only.

Homeworkers

This group of workers are so called due to their working in their own home away from the premises (if any) of the other party. In such situations the court will, once more, look at the true relationship between the parties. That said, the court decided in a 1994 case that homeworkers who worked flexible terms and dictated when and in what quantity they wanted work were, in fact, employees and entitled to use any protective legislation available to them.

Pam works from home packing greetings cards into boxes for Happy Birthday Ltd. Materials are delivered to her home twice a week and the work she has completed is collected. Pam is paid 20 pence for each box she packs. She is free to work whatever hours she chooses and can do as much or as little work as she likes, subject to a minimum requirement of 100 boxes per week.

In Pam's circumstances, it is highly likely she will be regarded, in law, as an employee and will therefore be entitled to all the statutory protection and benefits listed above.

Temporary workers supplied by an agency

For such workers there would normally exist two contracts. One between the worker and the agent and another between the agent and the direct recipient of their services (usually the company). In many such arrangements the agent places the worker and pays the worker direct. In most cases of short periods of temporary relief work, such workers will not have a relationship of employment with either the agent or the company with whom they are placed.

The agreement with the agent is regarded as a separate type of contract and quite distinct from one of employment. However, the problem area is the relationship between the worker and the recipient company or other party. Over a period of time it is possible for this relationship to develop into something akin to an employment contract. The usual tests stated earlier in this chapter will be applied.

In addition, to add to the confusion, under new legislation (*see* page 401) agency workers are defined as 'employees' for the purpose of statutory paid annual leave, statutory minimum wage, rest breaks, a limit on average weekly working time to 48 hours (optional) and a limit on night workers' average normal nightly working time to eight hours. The aim of the legislation is to protect the health and safety of workers and not just employees, hence the inclusion of agency workers within its remit.

Rights for 'workers'

In fact, although the concept of an 'employee' does remain important for unfair dismissal and redundancy payments, an increasing number of employment rights are vested in casual 'workers' as opposed to employees. For instance, the working time rules, the minimum wage, the Part-time Workers Regulations, the Fixed Term Work Directive and the Public Interest Disclosure Act 1998 all apply to 'workers' as well as 'employees'. The discrimination laws and also the Equal Pay Act 1970 all use a broader definition of 'worker', and not employee. Regulations introduced in October 2002 to prevent fixed-term employees being treated less favourably than comparable permanent employees cover employees doing seasonal or casual work, but not agency workers (*see* page 335). Similar regulations introduced in July 2000 to protect part-timers cover the wider category of 'workers'.

EXCLUDED EMPLOYEES

Even where employment status unquestionably exists, there are circumstances in which certain employees are denied the benefits of some or all of those rights as listed above. This section will briefly catalogue the main excluded employees.

Illegal contracts

Any person employed under an illegal contract is not entitled to the protection of the law with one important exception. This is a matter of public policy. A wrongdoer must not be seen to benefit from their misconduct. A prime example of an illegal contract is one that commits a fraud upon the Inland Revenue. For example, where an employee is listed in the 'books' as being paid £100 per week (with tax and National Insurance being paid on that sum) but in fact is given an extra amount of £25 'cash-in-hand', this is illegal. Any person receiving payment in a similar fashion will not be entitled to the protection of the employment legislation so long as they are actively participating in the fraud.

Another illegal contract would be where the performance of duties under the contract of employment involves an illegal act. For example, where an employee was required under contract to obtain prostitutes for the customers of his employer.

It should be noted that any employee or worker engaged under an illegal contract may still claim discrimination.

Diplomatic and state immunity

In short, in very restricted circumstances, employees of consuls and foreign diplomats residing in this country are excluded from the protection of employment legislation.

Crown employees

These are employees who work for a government department. Most statutory rights are available to crown employees. The most notable exceptions are the rights to statutory redundancy pay and to a minimum period of notice. Members of the armed forces are crown employees, but are generally not eligible for any statutory rights save protection from race, disability and sex discrimination.

Employees over the age of retirement

For the purposes of this exclusion 'over the age of retirement' means:
- over the age of 65 years;
- over the normal retirement age of their employer's business (provided the normal retirement age for that business is the same for both women and men) or, where there is no normal retiring age, over the age of 65 years.

Such employees are excluded from claiming statutory redundancy pay and from applying for unfair dismissal before an employment tribunal.

Short-term and temporary employees

This category of workers is usually excluded from claiming unfair dismissal or statutory redundancy pay because, in practice, they do not work for the employer long enough to obtain the continuous service necessary to bring such actions. An employee must have worked for the employer for one year to be eligible to make a claim for unfair dismissal, and two years for statutory redundancy pay.

Casual workers are not employees and therefore cannot claim.

Part-time workers

Part-time workers used to be denied the right to claim redundancy payments or unfair dismissal until they had worked for the employer for five complete years. This is no longer the case. A House of Lords' decision in 1994 maintained that this unfairly discriminated against women and the five-year qualifying period was abandoned. Part-time workers now require two years' continuous service to claim redundancy pay and one year's service to claim unfair dismissal (i.e. the same as full-time workers).

However, a part-time employee will be considered to have been unfairly dismissed (or selected for redundancy) regardless of length of service if the dismissal is related to asserting rights under the Part-time Workers (Prevention of Less Favourable Treatment) Regulations 2000. (*See* page 334.)

Employment outside Great Britain

In order to seek the protection of British employment rights it follows that the contract of employment must have been made or be applicable in Great Britain. Where an employer is international it is usual for the contract of employment to state quite clearly which country's law will apply in the event of a dispute between the parties. Where the contract is silent and the employee works in and from more than one country the issue of applicable law can be complex. Suffice it to say, the first issue the court will look at is where the contract was made, how long the worker has worked in the UK relative to other countries and where the worker is presently working. That said, employees who do not wholly work outside the UK will qualify for the rights referred to.

Miscellaneous

Police officers, share fishermen and merchant seamen are all excluded from claiming unfair dismissal and from receiving a statutory redundancy payment.

AVOIDING STATUTORY RIGHTS

It is unlawful for an employer to privately agree with an employee that the statutory rights will not apply. Any such agreement will be null and void. An example of this is a 'final settlement', where a sum of money is paid to the employee who, in return, agrees not to take his employer to the employment tribunal. To the great surprise of many employers, such final settlements are unlawful and will not prevent the employee from pursuing his rights before an employment tribunal. Such settlements will only be lawful if they have been approved by the Advisory, Conciliation and Arbitration Service (ACAS), or where the employee has taken independent legal advice before signing a 'Compromise Agreement'.

32

The Contract of Employment

FORMATION OF THE CONTRACT

A contract of employment, like any other legal contract, is regulated by basic common law principles. There are also a number of other legal requirements imposed by statute in respect of the form and content of the contract of employment. For a contract to exist in law between two parties (in this case the employer and the employee) there must be the following elements:

- an offer;
- acceptance; and
- payment or benefit.

Put simply, that means there must be a clear offer of a job from the employer to the employee. The employee upon receiving that offer must equally clearly have communicated his acceptance to the employer. And lastly, the deal must be to work for money or some other benefit and not to undertake employment as a free volunteer.

The offer and acceptance (either or both) may be oral or in writing. There will still be a legal contract between the employer and employee even where no written documentation has changed hands. The importance of written terms and conditions of employment is that, in the event of a dispute, it is easier to prove before a court what the parties agreed.

In practice, it is common for a job to be offered orally at the end of an interview and to be accepted verbally by the employee. Usually, the employer will formalize the agreement at a later date by issuing the employee with a letter of appointment, expressing the main terms and conditions, or a full contract of employment.

John attends an interview with Big Shot Ltd. The interview goes very well. The next day the boss of Big Shot Ltd telephones John and says the job is his if he wants it. John accepts the job there and then over the telephone and they agree he will start work on Monday. John turns up for work Monday morning to be told the boss has changed his mind and is entitled to do so since nothing has been signed.

In law, Big Shot Ltd are in breach of contract and John is entitled to receive notice of termination of the contract of employment or payment in lieu of notice.

TERMS OF THE CONTRACT

Just as the contract itself does not have to be in writing, nor do the terms and conditions of that contract. To determine what the parties have actually agreed, courts or tribunals will consider the following types of contract term:

- express terms;
- implied terms;
- incorporated terms.

A contract of employment may, in reality, have some of each type of term, so it is important to be able to recognize the nature of the terms.

Express terms

Such terms may be either written or oral. They represent what has been specifically expressed and agreed between the parties. These terms are usually quite clear and, most often, confirmed in writing. The importance of express terms is that in law, in the event of a dispute, they will override all other terms of the contract. They have priority.

Implied terms

A term may be implied into the contract of employment when its existence is so obvious that it must have been contemplated by the parties, even though they did not confirm it specifically in writing. An obvious example is the implication that the employee is to be paid for the work they perform. If the express terms of the contract do not state how much the employee will receive, the court may imply that a reasonable sum of money was to be paid for their work.

Another example of an implied term accepted by the courts in the past includes the right to reasonable notice of termination of the contract to be given to both the employee and the employer.

The following common law duties are implied into every contract of employment.

Duty to provide work

This applies where the employee is paid according to what they produce (e.g. piece work). The employer is under a duty to provide work to allow the employee to earn money. In all other situations (non-piece work) the employer is only under the obligation to pay the agreed wage.

Duty to indemnify employees

Where an employee necessarily incurs expense in the performance of their duties, the employer, impliedly, must meet those expenses.

Health and safety

The employer is under a general duty to provide employees with a safe working environment. Employees are doubly protected in this regard since there is also a statutory duty to provide the same. Moreover, employers must, by law, have insurance to cover their liability to employees should they be injured at work. The employer's duty extends to providing safe equipment for the employees' use.

Trust and confidence

The law has determined that every employment relationship requires there to be mutual trust and confidence between the parties. When this trust and confidence is completely undermined by the actions of one party, the contract of employment may be regarded by the other as being at an end. The elements of trust and confidence are another way of expressing the need for respect for each other and co-operation.

Competence

Implied into every contract of employment is the term that the employee will undertake his work with the required degree of skill and care in order to safely and effectively complete the tasks for which he was employed.

Obeying orders

Employees are under an implied duty to obey reasonable and lawful management instructions. Failure to do so may legitimately lead to dismissal. The instruction will be 'lawful' if it comes from such a person with relevant authority. Whether or not it is 'reasonable' is often open to argument and can be a common area for dispute. As a rule of thumb it will be reasonable if it is either:

- within the job description in the contract;
- without being demeaning, is reasonably within the capability of the employee concerned;
- has been performed by the employee before, without protest.

It follows that where an employee is requested to perform a task which is quite clearly outside of the (implied or express) contract terms, the employee will be under no obligation to comply with that request.

Faithfulness

Sometimes referred to as the 'duty of fidelity', in essence, this is the implied duty to work in good faith for the employer and not to engage in work for another or for oneself that may compete with, or damage, the employer's business. An employee should not be able to make a personal profit by breaching the duty of good faith to the detriment of his employer. It follows that if an employee was to 'moonlight' in competition with the employer's business, the duty of faithfulness would undoubtedly be breached, bringing the contract of employment to an end. That said, 'moonlighting' in some capacity unrelated to the business of the main employer is unlikely to affect the relationship of good faith between the parties.

Confidentiality

In most employment relationships the employee will, from time to time, come into possession of commercial information which is by its nature confidential. To disclose it could damage the employer's business. For example, if lists of clients and their terms of business with the employer were to fall into the hands of a competitor, great financial damage could be caused to the employer. Therefore, implied into every contract of employment is a duty on the employee not to disclose obviously confidential information to a third party. Breach of this duty could, once more, bring about the termination of the contract of employment if the employer so desired.

Not all information is protected by this implied term. During employment, protected confidential information is not necessarily restricted to 'trade secrets' – a wider category of information may be protected. Following termination of the contract of employment, only that information which by its nature is a 'trade secret' and patently confidential is protected. In fact, much of the information an employee is given during their employment falls outside of this category of confidential material.

In trying to distinguish between confidential information caught by the implied term and that which is not, the following guidelines are often used by the courts:

- Has the employer made it clear to the employee that particular information was to be regarded as confidential?

- Is the confidential information in question readily distinguished from other general information in respect of an employer?
- Would a third party have an alternative means of legitimately accessing the information other than being told by the employee?
- The nature of the employment will be examined including the status and responsibility of the employee concerned and the frequency with which they dealt with such information.

Custom and practice

Finally, on this section dealing with implied terms, it is possible for a term to be implied into the contract through custom and practice. That is, although there is no verbal or written agreement between the parties, the employer or employee, through habit, so act that their conduct becomes an implied term of the contract. There are many examples. One, typically, would be where a van driver, as a matter of fact, always drives the company vehicle home at night and back to work in the morning even though no express permission has been given by the employer. After a period of time – usually months rather than weeks – this custom and practice will become a term and condition (an employee's right) under the contract. In practice, much depends on the custom itself and the period of time over which the conduct has taken place. Each 'acquired' implied term will ultimately depend on the particular facts of each case.

Incorporated terms

The prime example of an incorporated term is one that becomes part of an employee's contract by reason of it being negotiated by a trade union with the employer on behalf of the employee (or usually group of employees). The agreement is not made directly between the two parties to the contract, the employee and employer, but by a third party – the union.

In law, the unions can only negotiate terms which may be incorporated into the employee's individual contract if it:

1 has the right to negotiate with the employer, i.e. it is recognized by the employer for the purposes of collective bargaining; and
2 the matter to which the negotiations relate is within one of the following categories and relates to:
   - terms and conditions of employment;
   - the physical conditions of employment;
   - engagement, non-engagement, termination or suspension of employment;
   - allocation of work;
   - discipline;
   - membership or non-membership of a trade union;
   - facilities for trade union officials;
   - facilities for negotiations or consultation in relation to any of the above matters.

STATUTORY REQUIREMENTS

The law requires every employer to provide the employee with written details of the job within eight weeks of the employee starting work. The written statement must include the following:

1 the name of the employer and employee;
2 the date upon which employment commenced;
3 the date upon which the employee's period of *continuous* service began, whether or not different from the date upon which employment commenced;
4 the rate of pay and interval between payments (weekly/monthly, etc.);
5 hours of work;
6 holiday entitlement, holiday pay and the rate of accrual;
7 sickness/injury pay or entitlement;
8 pension entitlement and whether a contracting-out certificate is in force in respect of any occupational pension scheme in place – statements must be provided even if the employer makes no provision over and above the state pension scheme;
9 the length of notice which the employee is entitled to give, and to receive, in order that the contract of employment may be terminated;
10 job title;
11 the employee's place of work (or, if variable, the employer's address);
12 if the employment is temporary, the time period of that intended employment;
13 if the contract is for a fixed period of time, the date upon which that fixed-term contract will end;
14 any collective agreement that may affect the terms and conditions of employment;
15 where the employee is required to work outside the UK for more than one month, the written statement must provide the following information:
   - the period of working outside the UK;
   - the currency of remuneration;
   - any additional remuneration and benefits;
   - any terms and conditions relating to the employee's return to the UK;
16 any disciplinary rules applicable to the employee;
17 a person to whom the employee may complain if dissatisfied with any disciplinary decision;
18 a person to whom the employee may complain if they wish to raise a grievance in respect of any aspect of their employment.

Where an employer has less than 20 employees on the date that the employee started employment, there is no obligation to provide disciplinary rules. The only obligation is to identify the person to whom the employee may raise a grievance. Note though that the Employment Act 2002 removes this 20-employee threshold, so small businesses will have to provide information on both disciplinary and grievance procedures. The government has still not set a date in 2004 when this part of the Act will come into effect.

The names of the parties

Both employer and employee must be named. This is particularly important where there has been a change of employer, for example, following a recent takeover of a business.

The date employment commenced

This date will be crucial if the employee is seeking the protection of some of the employment legislation provisions (*see* page 332). For example, if the employee is claiming unfair dismissal, he will need to be able to calculate when he started work and how long he has worked for his employer. Where an employee has rejoined an employer after a short break elsewhere, he is entitled to know the starting point for that subsequent period of employment *and* whether it may be added to a previous period of service for the purpose of calculating continuous service.

Pay

All details of remuneration should be clearly stated, including bonus and commission payments, shift premiums and benefits in kind, such as luncheon vouchers where applicable. The pay interval must be stated.

Pay cannot be less than the current national minimum wage. That is:
- £3.80 per hour for 18- to 21-year-olds, increasing to £4.10 per hour in October 2004;
- £4.50 per hour for workers aged 22 and above, increasing to £4.85 in October 2004;
- £3.80 per hour for workers doing accredited training.

No benefits in kind (such as the provision of meals) count towards the national minimum wage (except accommodation, in respect of which, the amount that can count towards the national minimum wage must not be greater than £19.95 per week). Tips only count if they go through the payroll.

Hours of work

This should include details of the core working hours of the week and within what times of the day they should be worked. Lunch times and other breaks should be stated along with details of overtime where applicable, such as the rate of pay and whether it is voluntary or compulsory. The right to lay-off staff in periods of work shortage should also be detailed in this section of the written particulars, along with any contractual right to vary the hours of work upon issuing reasonable notice of the change to the employee concerned.

An employee need not work more than an average of 48 hours per week, but has a free choice to do so if he wishes. In that case, the employee should sign a statement that he is prepared to waive his right to limit his hours of work to 48 per week. The average number of hours is usually worked out over a period of 17 weeks or the period worked to date if the employee has been employed less then 17 weeks. The employer is under no obligation to keep appropriate records of weekly hours worked but it is good practice to do so.

An employee is entitled to an uninterrupted break of 20 minutes when the daily working time is more than six hours. The break may be paid or unpaid and this is subject to agreement between the employer and employee. An adolescent employee (over school leaving age but under 18 years old) is entitled to a rest break of 30 minutes when the daily working time is more than 4½ hours. The rest break should not be at the beginning or the end of the working periods stated above.

The entitlement to a rest break does not apply to employees in a range of circumstances:

1 where an employee's activities are such that his place of work and place of residence are distant from one another or his different places of work are distant from one another;
2 where an employee is 'engaged in security and surveillance activities', i.e. where there is a need for round-the-clock presence;
3 where an employee's activities include the need for continuity of service or production, i.e. workers in hospitals, residential institutions, prisons, docks, airports, press, radio, television, postal services, gas, water and electricity production, agriculture, etc.;
4 where there is a foreseeable surge of activity, i.e. this may apply to workers in agriculture, tourism and postal services;
5 where an employee's activities are affected by an occurrence due to unusual and unforeseeable circumstances, or exceptional events, the consequences of which could not have been avoided, or an accident, or the imminent risk of an accident. In these circumstances, the employee is entitled to 'an equivalent period of compensatory rest'.

Night work limits

An employer is required to take all reasonable steps to ensure that the normal hours of his night workers do not exceed an average of eight hours for each 24 hours over a 17-week period. The averaging period may be extended in certain circumstances. Night time is a period of at least seven hours, which includes the period from midnight to 5 a.m. The parties can decide which hours the employee will work within those parameters (for example, 10 p.m. to 5 a.m. or 12 p.m. to 7 a.m.). In the absence of such an agreement it will be 11 p.m. to 6 a.m.

A 'night worker' is any worker whose daily working time includes at least three hours of night time:

- on the majority of days they work;
- on such a proportion of the days they work as is agreed between the employer and the workers in a collective or workforce agreement; or
- sufficiently often that they may be said to work such hours as a normal course.

Holidays

This section should include the number of days of holiday entitlement, the rate of pay, the rate of accrual and the employee's entitlement (if any) to public or bank holidays. Please note that, contrary to popular belief, there is no statutory right to take public or bank holidays, let alone to be paid for them! There is, however, a statutory right to a minimum of four weeks' paid leave each year for all employees and casual workers. This leave includes the eight statutory bank holidays. Employees become entitled to four weeks' paid leave from the first day of work. The entitlement will accrue on a month-to-month basis, at the rate of one-twelfth of annual entitlement for each month. Part-timers are entitled to a proportionate amount of leave in accordance with hours worked. Where a part-timer works variable hours, an average is taken over the previous 12 weeks worked.

Allan resigns from his job after 16 weeks' service. Under his contract of employment he was entitled to 20 days' holiday per year. He took no holiday since joining his ex-employer but was paid for a summer bank holiday Monday. Allan's ex-employer refuses to pay him any holiday entitlement after Allan leaves.

Allan built up holiday entitlement during his employment. Under his contract, he was entitled to take 1.66 days of holiday per month (20 days divided by 12 months). He worked for his employer for three months. His entitlement upon leaving is, therefore, 3 × 1.66 = 5. Having received 1 day's holiday for the bank holiday this is reduced by 1 day and his ex-employer owes him 4 days' holiday pay.

Sick pay

The agreement should state what the employee's entitlements are if he becomes sick or injured. The agreement may refer only to the provisions of the Statutory Sick Pay (SSP) (*see also* page 300) scheme or provide that the employer pays a contractual amount above the basic entitlement. There should also be available full details of the rules for qualifying for SSP or other sick pay scheme, and for how long such payments will be made and whether any amount paid over and above SSP is a contractual entitlement, or at the discretion of the employer.

Pensions

Details of any company pension scheme must be provided and whether the employer is contracted in or out of the state pension scheme.

Notice period

The employer must provide details of notice required to terminate the contract. However, the notice period must never be less than the statutory minimum requirement. The statutory minimum requirement provides that the employer must give the employee the following periods of notice, depending on how long the employee has worked for that employer:

Period of employment	Statutory minimum notice period
Less than one month's service	**None**
Between one month's and two years' continuous service	**1 week's** notice
Between 2 years and 12 years	**1 week for each complete year** of service
Over 12 years' service	**12 weeks'** notice

The employee, on the other hand, must give the employer at least one week's notice where he has one month's service or more, but this does not increase with the length of service. Both parties to the contract of employment may agree to a different period of notice than the statutory amount. However, it must never be less than that amount as stated above.

For employees who have worked less than one month, they are not entitled to statutory minimum notice. However, they may make a claim for reasonable notice (which will be less than one week) or a claim for contractual notice if there is an express contractual clause.

Sarah works for Superstores Limited as an employee. After five years' employment her contract is terminated by way of redundancy. She is entitled to statutory notice of five weeks. However, if her contract provides for a greater notice period she is entitled to this longer period. If the employer fails to provide due notice (or pay monies in lieu of notice), she may claim wrongful dismissal and recover the unpaid monies by way of damages.

Employees dismissed for gross misconduct are not entitled to contractual or statutory minimum notice, provided the gross misconduct is objectively justified.

Before Sarah is made redundant, she commits an act of theft at work and is dismissed that day. Her claim for wrongful dismissal would fail provided that the employer had reasonable grounds to dismiss for gross misconduct.

Job title

This should adequately and appropriately describe the job and duties the employee is required to undertake. It is quite lawful for the employer to keep this broad and add such phrases as, '. . . and to perform any other duties reasonably within your capability and skills as the interests of the business dictate'. A job description or title is most often a combination of what is expressed within the contract or written statement of particulars and what the employee does in practice. It is of particular importance to female employees since it may assist in defining the role to which they return after maternity leave.

Temporary employment

Temporary employees are also entitled to a written statement of all these details – provided that the temporary contract of employment is to last more than one month.

Disciplinary rules

At the present time, small employers (i.e. those who employ less than 20 members of staff) are given some latitude by the legislation. They do not have to provide details of disciplinary rules and procedures. However, where they exist as a matter of practice, a note specifying what the procedure is, or referring to a document which contains it, must be included within the statement.

Under the Employment Act 2002, all employers, regardless of size, will have to operate a minimum standard compulsory disciplinary and grievance procedure. These statutory procedures will be an implied term of all contracts of employment. The government has yet to

specify a date in 2004 when these provisions of the Act will come into force. *See further* Chapter 37.

Grievances

The statement of particulars should provide details of who to complain to and the procedure for complaining, stating:
- in what form, oral or written, the grievance should be made;
- the time period in which the grievance will be considered by the employer;
- whose decision is final;
- how and when that final decision will be communicated.

Finally, it should be noted that the content of the written statement of particulars is the bare minimum statutory requirement. A good employer will go far beyond this statement, adding and clarifying many other terms and conditions of employment. A good contract of employment is a source of reference for both employee and employer, in the event of a disputed term or condition.

STATUTORY TERMS AFFECTING THE CONTRACT OF EMPLOYMENT

The Equal Pay Act 1970

Implied into every woman's contract of employment is the right to pay equal to that of a man where the woman undertakes work which is:
- like work to a man;
- work rated as equivalent to work done by a man;
- work of equal value to that done by a man.

The provisions of the Equal Pay Act were deliberately designed to combat the problem of discrimination in pay between the sexes. Note that the Act applies to men as well as to women. The way that the right to equal pay works in practice is that any term in the employment contract relating to pay which is unequal will be changed so as to provide equality.

The only defence to a claim for equal pay is for the employer to argue that the variation between a woman's and a man's contract is genuinely due to a material factor which is not the difference of sex. The law in this area can be complex and it is sufficient for the purposes of this section to state that the law requires such material factors, where they are alleged to exist, to be objectively justified by the employer.

A claim for equal pay may be brought before an employment tribunal and, if successful, the amount awarded will be the difference in pay between that of the claimant and the 'equivalent' employee. The claim can be backdated for up to six years. This topic is covered in more detail in Chapter 33.

Discrimination

It is implied, by statute, into every contract of employment that discrimination against an employee on any of the following grounds is unlawful:

- sex;
- marital status;
- colour;
- race;
- nationality;
- ethnic origin;
- national origin;
- disability (where the employer has 15 or more employees, but note that this exemption will be removed in October 2004);
- religion;
- sexual orientation;
- belief.

Discrimination is discussed in detail in Chapter 38. Workers and self-employed persons executing work as a personal service also have the right to claim discrimination.

Health and safety at work

Broadly, legislation in respect of health and safety provides that certain standards must be maintained by the employer. The employee has the right:

- to enjoy generally a healthy and safe place of work;
- to be protected by the employer from risks to his health and safety arising out of or in connection with his work;
- to be protected from substances hazardous to health that are used or kept at the workplace.

Employers are placed under various duties by the Health and Safety at Work Act 1974 and regulations made under that Act. *See* Chapter 40.

The Patents Act 1977

This Act covers the inventions of employees created in the course of work and clarifies whether the employer or the employee owns that item or substance in law.

Inventions generally belong to the employer where:

- the invention was made during the employee's normal duties;
- the employee had a particular responsibility or special obligation to further the interests of the employer's business.

The Copyright, Designs and Patents Act 1988

This covers similar issues to the Patents Act (*see* above), but deals with ownership of the copyright of literary, musical or dramatic works, rather than a particular item or substance in tangible form.

The Employer's Liability (Compulsory Insurance) Act 1969

Implied into every contract of employment is the obligation on the employer to have adequate insurance to cover personal injury (including industrial disease) inflicted on the employee during the course of their employment duties arising out of the employer's negligence or breach of statutory duty.

The Factories Act 1961

This Act implies duties on the factory employer in respect of:

- cleanliness;
- working temperature;
- ventilation;
- lighting;
- safe machinery.

The Offices, Shops and Railway Premises Act 1963

This is similar to the Factories Act (*see* above) but applies to smaller working environments.

The Employer's Liability (Defective Equipment) Act 1969

An employer is under an implied duty to pay damages to any employee injured as a result of using defective equipment provided by the employer, while in the normal course of their employment.

The Employment Rights Act 1996

Under this Act the employee has the right in certain circumstances not to have deductions made from their wages. (The subject of deductions is dealt with in detail on pages 324–5.)

TERMS NOT CONSIDERED TO BE CONTRACTUAL

In this chapter we have discussed terms and conditions that are considered to form part of the contract of employment whether express, implied, or incorporated via collective agreement or statutory requirement or obligation. To complete the picture, it should be noted that some terms will not always be considered to be part of the contract.

Many employers provide policy statements that may cover various matters such as carrying out routine work, not smoking on the employer's premises, or the procedures to be adopted in the event of redundancy. Policy statements dealing with these matters will not always be part of the actual contract. Much will depend on the facts of any particular case. The crucial point to grasp is that if a term is non-contractual and it is breached by employer or employee, the aggrieved party may have no legal redress.

It is often difficult to tell whether such policy statements are intended to form part of the body of the contract of employment. A key factor that may indicate that the term is intended to be part of the contract is if it provides for the employee to be disciplined by the employer in the event of breach. Other than that, there is often no simple solution and the court will arrive at its decision by setting the policy statement in the context of other documentation and the custom and practice of that particular place of work.

It should be noted however that a failure to follow a non-contractual procedure may still give rise to a discrimination claim (*see further* Chapter 38).

33

Pay

FORM OF PAYMENT

By virtue of legislation which took effect from 1987, manual workers no longer have the right to be paid in cash, or 'coin of the realm' as it was known. The method and form of payment is now a matter of private agreement between the employer and the employee. However, there remain a great number of manual workers who are still paid cash. For those workers there now seems little doubt that, provided their employer gives reasonable notice and has some business reason for the change, they may impose a cashless pay system. That is, one in which a credit transfer is made into the bank account of the employee concerned at a regular interval.

Technically, if an employer were to forcibly impose a cashless pay system on a previously cash-paid employee, this could constitute a breach of contract. It seems that courts would not be inclined to award anything other than nominal damages in such cases, in particular where the employer provides some business reason for the change, for example an efficiency or security reason.

ITEMIZED PAY STATEMENTS

Employees have a legal right to an itemized pay statement unless they are:
- engaged in police service;
- employed as a share fisherman or merchant seaman.
  The pay statements must contain the following details:
- the gross amount of wage or salary (i.e. before tax has been deducted);
- the net amount of wage or salary (i.e. after tax has been deducted);
- amounts of (and reasons for) any variable or fixed deductions;
- where different parts of the net amount are paid in different ways, the amount and method of payment of each part payment.
  It is a further requirement that the statement be given to the employee on or before the date pay is normally due under the contract. In respect of fixed deductions the following information is required:
- a cumulative statement of aggregate fixed deductions;
- the amount of the deduction;
- the interval at which it was made;
- the purpose for which it was made.

A statement of fixed deductions may be amended by the employer by notice in writing to the employee containing details of the amendment. A standing statement of fixed deductions will only remain effective for 12 months, after which time the employer must re-issue the statement, with any amendments.

Should an employee believe that his pay statement is incorrect, incomplete in any way, or non-existent, his ultimate remedy is to take the matter before an employment tribunal for compensation or a declaration as to his rights. If the employment tribunal finds that deductions were made which were not properly notified, it can order the employer to reimburse the employee the amount of any such unnotified deductions made in the 13 weeks immediately before the employee lodged the complaint.

DEDUCTIONS FROM WAGES

In the mid 1980s legislation was introduced to protect employees from rogue employers who claimed back large sums of money by way of deductions from their wages for various reasons. Often, deductions were made without notice to the employee and for reasons far from clear, let alone agreed by the employee concerned. A statutory framework for regulating deductions is now contained in the Employment Rights Act 1996. The Act covers most, but not all, forms of deduction.

Excluded from the provisions are those deductions made:

1 to reimburse the employer for a previous overpayment of wages;

2 further to a right to deduct wages contained in a written contract of employment;

3 further to a statutory provision (e.g. tax, National Insurance contributions);

4 as a result of any disciplinary proceedings made under any statutory provision;

5 where the employer is bound by statute to deduct and pay over an amount to a public authority (e.g. an attachment of earnings order of the county court);

6 to pay a third person, where the employee consents in writing to such payment and the third person has notified the employer of that amount (e.g. a payment to a private pension company);

7 further to the employee's participation in a strike or other industrial action, and the deduction relates to this action;

8 further to the satisfaction of an order of a court or tribunal for the payment of an amount by the employee to the employer.

Other than these exclusions, the general rule is that any deduction from the wage of an employee will be unlawful *unless* the employee has given the employer *prior written consent* to make that deduction. Any deduction made unlawfully will allow the employee to take the matter before an employment tribunal to reclaim the sum involved and to have the deduction declared unlawful. The practical effect of having the deduction declared unlawful is important, since it will prevent the employer from recovering that sum through any other legal channels, even if there was a good case for arguing a right to recovery.

Albert employs Bill. At Bill's request, Albert loans him £1,000. Bill is slow to repay the debt and, in frustration, Albert deducts the outstanding sum owed of £300 from Bill's wages. This deduction is not permissible under the written contract of employment. Also, Albert does not have Bill's prior written consent to do this. The deduction is unlawful. Should Bill take the matter to an employment tribunal for a declaration that the deduction was unlawful, Albert would be penalized and barred from recovering the loan by any other court action.

'Prior written consent' means exactly what it says. Any written consent of the employee obtained after the deduction has been made will be unlawful. In addition, the consent must precede not only the deduction itself but also the event or conduct giving rise to the deduction. Equally, any contractual provision must be in writing and clearly indicate that in particular circumstances a sum may be deducted from the employee's wage.

The definition of 'wage'

Wage, for the purposes of this statutory provision, will include the following sums payable to the worker:

- fees;
- bonus payments;
- commission;
- holiday pay;
- Statutory Sick Pay;
- statutory maternity pay;
- guarantee payments (in respect of lay-off – *see* later in this chapter);
- any sums ordered to be paid by an employment tribunal for reinstatement/re-engagement;
- earned overtime;
- basic wage or salary.

'Wage' does *not* include:

- an advance under a loan agreement or an advance of wages;
- expenses;
- pension payments;
- a compensatory payment for loss of office;
- redundancy payments;
- other payments that may have been made to the employee but were so done in some capacity other than that of an employer and employee relationship;
- a non-contractual payment in lieu of notice.

Retail workers

Special provisions apply to workers within the retail industry in respect of cash shortages and stock deficiencies. The maximum deduction on any pay day must not exceed 10 per cent of the gross wages on that day. This ceiling figure of 10 per cent will not apply to a retail worker's final wage or salary. In order to deduct money from a retail worker's pay the employer must:

- inform the employee, in writing, of their total liability to the employer in respect of stock shortages or deficiency;
- make a written demand for payment which is on a pay day.

The demand can be made on the first pay day after written notification to the employee. However, generally shortages and deficiencies which occurred at some time before the last 12 months up to the point of demand are not recoverable by the employer.

Remedy

An employee must take his complaint of an unlawful deduction from wages before an employment tribunal. The claim must be made within three months less one day of the date of deduction. Where a series of allegedly unlawful deductions have been made the three-month less one day period will run from the date of the last deduction. However, where an employee was only informed that the deduction was made a month after the termination of his employment, he was allowed to bring a claim within three months of that date and not the expiry of his contract.

Jane's contract of employment is terminated on 15 August. The employer fails to pay her for the work in August. Jane must issue her claim for unlawful deduction of wages by 14 November. A claim received by the employment tribunal on 15 November would be one day late and out of time.

The employment tribunal has the authority to declare the deduction unlawful and to order the employer to make a repayment to the employee.

ATTACHMENT OF EARNINGS

Where an employee owes money to a creditor, the court can make an attachment of earnings order. Under the order the debtor's employer must pay part of the debtor's wages at a regular interval directly to the court office. Such payments are typically ordered by the court in respect of the following matters:

- child support;
- maintenance for the employee's ex-wife or cohabiting wife;
- judgment debts (provided they are for more than £50);
- payments under an administration order (in the case of a series of debts being owed to various creditors);
- criminal fines further to a conviction;
- payment under a public funding contribution order.

Under an attachment of earnings order the employer is under a legal obligation to make the requested deduction and forward it to the court. Certain provisions exist to limit the amount that may be deducted from the employee's wage. The definition of 'earnings' which may be subject to attachment is wide and includes:

- wages;
- salary;
- bonuses;
- commission;
- overtime payments;
- certain pension payments.

The court will calculate the level of earnings that the employee requires for his basic needs. The court will not order a deduction which would leave the employee with less than this amount. More than one attachment of earnings order may be made against an employee at any one time. Priority will be given to the orders chronologically. The employer must comply with the order, or risk a conviction and fine. In addition, the employer may charge the employee, by way of a deduction from the wage, a small sum of money to cover the administration cost of each deduction made. Notice of this deduction must be given in writing to the employee. (*See also* page 753.)

STATUTORY GUARANTEE PAYMENTS

An employee has the right to receive a statutory guarantee payment from their employer if the employer fails to provide work due to:

- a reduction in the employer's business that affects the work of the employee;
- some other occurrence that affects the employer's business and, in turn, the work of the employee.

An example of the first point would be a reduction in business orders due to the economic conditions in a particular market. The second is designed to cover situations such as a power cut.

In order to be eligible for the payment, the employee must have been employed for one month before the first day without work and must not be working under a fixed-term contract of three months or less. In addition, the employee must not unreasonably refuse to undertake other similar duties within their capability if requested by the employer, in an attempt to find suitable alternative work for the employee. What is 'reasonable' is a matter of degree but there will be an obligation on the employee not to be deliberately obstructive.

The maximum amount payable is £17.30 per day for the first five workless days in any three-month period. Less than £17.30 may only be paid if the employee would normally earn under that figure per day.

If the employee is normally required to work less than five days a week, the entitlement cannot exceed the number of days the employee is required to work per week under their contract.

It is important to note that an employer does not have any right to lay off employees unless such a right exists in the contract of employment. This means that where the right exists the employer can simply enforce the statutory guarantee payment system as the needs of the business dictate. Where the right does not exist, in order to reduce pay by any amount at all, the employer must actively seek the agreement of those employees to be affected. Otherwise, a reduction in pay or guarantee pay where no right to lay off exists and without the agreement of the employee, will be a breach of contract. If the employer fails to make a guarantee payment the employee can make an application for payment to an employment tribunal. The application must be made within three months of the day for which a guarantee payment is claimed.

THE INSOLVENT EMPLOYER

It is an unfortunate fact of life that, occasionally, an employer may be forced out of business due to economic circumstances. When this happens, employees are often left out of pocket, with unpaid wages still owed to them. Some pay may be owed under the contract of employment, for example, arrears in wages and accrued holiday entitlement. Other pay may be due as a statutory right, for example, notice and redundancy payments.

When the employer is bankrupt or, if a limited company, made insolvent, the assets of the employer are sold off. The creditors of the business will then be paid in strict prioritized order. Secured creditors (e.g. the Inland Revenue or banks who have lent money to the employer on the security of particular assets) are paid first. Employees are next in line to be paid. Creditors lower down in the pecking order (e.g. suppliers of materials to the employer's business) may only receive a fraction of what is actually owed to them.

Employees are entitled to receive the following, provided that there is any money left after the secured creditors have been paid:

- all wages and salary for up to four months immediately prior to insolvency (including Statutory Sick Pay and statutory guarantee payments);
- all accrued holiday entitlement up to the date of termination of the contract of employment by reason of the employer's insolvency.

In any event, any sum payable relating to the points above is subject to a maximum of £800 per employee. It is evident, therefore, that these provisions can prove harsh. For this reason, certain debts are guaranteed to be paid by the state where the employer has no money to make the payments owed. The following guaranteed debts are recoverable:

1 pay arrears for up to eight weeks subject to a maximum amount of £260 per week. (This will include commission due, overtime payments, etc.);
2 accrued holiday entitlement up to six weeks subject to a maximum of £260 per week;
3 employment tribunal basic award if dismissal by the employer was proven to be unfair;
4 the statutory minimum period of notice (one week for each complete year of service up to a maximum of 12 weeks), subject to a maximum of £260 per week;
5 apprentices and articled clerks are entitled to reimbursement of their fees;
6 statutory maternity pay;
7 redundancy payments.

In the case of unpaid pension contributions by the insolvent employer, special provisions apply for the state to make such payments and to determine the amount payable. If an employee feels they have not been paid their full preferred and guaranteed entitlements, they may apply to an employment tribunal for determination as to precisely how much is due.

THE RIGHT TO PAYMENT DURING NOTICE

Where an employee tells his employer that he is leaving but is not ready, or willing, to work his notice period, he will not be entitled to any payment in lieu of notice. He will only be entitled to pay up to and including his last day of work. However, where he does offer to work his notice but is not wanted or falls sick during the period of notice, the employee will be entitled to the statutory period of notice to be paid by the employer at his normal rate of pay. This will be simple to calculate where the employee receives a normal rate of pay. Where a week's pay varies according to the amount of work done, there exists a formula for calculating a 'week's pay'.

Where pay is variable, a week's pay is calculated as being the average hourly rate multiplied by the number of normal working hours in a week. The average hourly rate is calculated by referring to the period of 12 weeks immediately preceding the first day of the notice period where there are normal working hours. The average hourly rate is based on the hours actually worked by the employee (including overtime) and on the money they were paid for those hours. If there are no normal working hours, a week's pay is the average weekly pay over the last 12 weeks before the first day of notice.

Martin, in a wild mood swing, dismisses Kevin, telling him to collect his things and go. Kevin is not sure what his entitlements to pay are. His contract refers to one month's notice.

He has no right to demand to work his notice. Because Kevin was ready, willing and able to work his notice but was not required to do so, Martin must pay him one month's money in lieu of working his notice. Martin can pay the notice in one of two ways. He can pay Kevin weekly in the normal manner, until the expiry of one month and, if he does, the contract will continue for that month and Kevin will be on 'garden leave'. Alternatively, Martin can bring the contract to an immediate end and pay Kevin one month's money up front, in lieu of notice.

In addition, Kevin is entitled to all benefits for the one-month notice period or compensation for their loss.

See further page 348.

STATUTORY SICK PAY

Statutory Sick Pay (SSP) must be distinguished from other forms of sick pay that may be payable under an individual's contract of employment (*see also* page 300). Statutory Sick Pay is the minimum amount of sick pay that all employees are entitled to (subject to qualification). If eligible, the employer must pay the employee this amount of sick pay. In a great number of cases the employer will, as a benefit to the employee, pay over the

Statutory Sick Pay

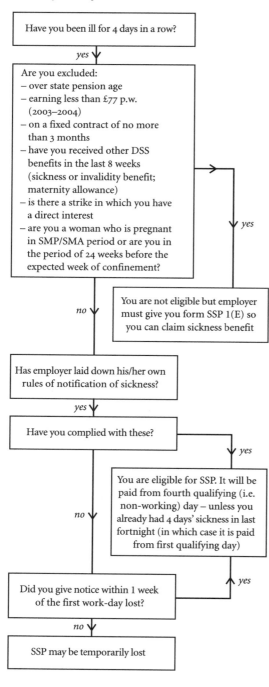

Have you been ill for 4 days in a row?

yes ↓

Are you excluded:
– over state pension age
– earning less than £77 p.w.
  (2003–2004)
– on a fixed contract of no more
  than 3 months
– have you received other DSS
  benefits in the last 8 weeks
  (sickness or invalidity benefit;
  maternity allowance)
– is there a strike in which you have
  a direct interest
– are you a woman who is pregnant
  in SMP/SMA period or are you in
  the period of 24 weeks before the
  expected week of confinement?

yes →

You are not eligible but employer
must give you form SSP 1(E) so
you can claim sickness benefit

no ↓

Has employer laid down his/her own
rules of notification of sickness?

yes ↓

Have you complied with these?

yes →

You are eligible for SSP. It will be
paid from fourth qualifying (i.e.
non-working) day – unless you
already had 4 days' sickness in last
fortnight (in which case it is paid
from first qualifying day)

no ↓

yes ↑

Did you give notice within 1 week
of the first work-day lost?

no ↓

SSP may be temporarily lost

SSP amount and anything up to the full rate of pay for periods of sickness. Such a payment will be payable under the contract. This section deals with SSP only.

The following employees are *not* entitled to SSP:

- employees aged 65 years or over on the first day of sickness;
- employees under a fixed-term contract of three months or less;
- employees who earn (currently) less than £77.00 per week. Known as the 'lower earnings limit';
- employees who go sick within eight weeks, or 52 weeks of having received certain social security benefits;
- those who have performed no work for the employer under the contract of employment;
- employees who are off sick during a stoppage at work due to a trade dispute (unless that employee can prove no direct interest in that dispute);
- employees who are pregnant and go off sick during the maternity pay period;
- those who are already due 28 weeks' SSP from their employer(s) in any one period of incapacity for work (or any two or more 'linked' periods, i.e. separated by eight weeks or less period of entitlement of three years – *see* below);
- employees who have already been due 28 weeks' SSP from a previous employer and on joining a new employer and again going sick, the gap between the period of incapacity is eight weeks or less;
- employees in legal custody on the first day of incapacity;

Provided none of the above exclusions apply the requirements for qualification are that the employee:

1 must have four or more consecutive days of sickness (including non-work days and holidays) during which they are too ill to work;
2 must notify the employer of their absence;
3 must supply evidence of the incapacity, usually:
(a) a self-certificate for the period of four to seven calendar days;
(b) a doctor's certificate of illness from the eighth day of sickness onwards.

The payment period

A period of sickness of four days or more is called the 'period of incapacity for work' (PIW). Two or more PIWs which are separated by eight weeks or less are said to be 'linked' and are counted as one PIW. During a PIW, SSP is payable only:

- where there is a period of entitlement; and
- for the days within the PIW which are 'qualifying days'.

Qualifying days

Statutory Sick Pay is only paid in respect of 'qualifying days', which will usually be the days when the employee is normally at work. If the normal working days are Monday to Friday, they will be the qualifying days.

Working days

Statutory Sick Pay is not payable for the first three qualifying days in the period of entitlement. It is the fourth day of sickness which triggers the SSP entitlement. Payment will only be made from the fourth day (including that day) onwards.

Periods of incapacity for work can be linked where they are not separated by more than 56 calendar days. Where they are linked there are no waiting days for the second period of incapacity. For example, an employee who is off for two weeks comes back to work for a month and then goes off for a further five days. They will receive SSP for the second PIW of five days because it is linked in time with the first. Absences of less than four days do not constitute a PIW and no SSP is payable.

Periods of entitlement

Statutory Sick Pay is currently payable for a maximum of 28 weeks. This need not be a single period but could be a series of linked PIWs within a maximum period of entitlement of three years. Once the 28 weeks has been exhausted the employee must look to the state for any sickness benefit.

Statutory Sick Pay rates

The rate of SSP depends on the employee's average gross weekly earnings during the eight weeks preceding the PIW. Rates are reviewed annually and currently stand at £64.35 per week for a maximum of 28 weeks. Maximum SSP payable is, therefore, £1,801.80.

Leaver's statement

When an employee's contract of employment comes to an end the employer must issue a leaver's statement (Form SSP1(L)). A new employee should give his leaver's statement to the new employer. If the employee falls sick within the first eight weeks of new employment the information on the statement may affect the employee's entitlement to SSP.

Withholding Statutory Sick Pay

Statutory Sick Pay may be withheld by the employer if they have reason to believe that the employee was not ill or failed to comply with the employer's notification of absence procedure. The employer may set rules in respect of notification, providing they are reasonable. Where SSP is withheld, the employee has the right to request a written statement from the employer specifying the days on which SSP was and was not paid and, in respect of the latter, the reason for non-payment.

If the employee feels SSP has been unreasonably withheld, he may make a complaint to an Inland Revenue adjudication officer. The officer will ask both parties to provide written observations before he makes his formal decision, and the officer hearing the appeal will try to decide it by agreement between the employer, the employee and the original officer. If all parties are unable to agree, the appeal will be considered by the Tax Commissioners.

OVERPAYMENT OF WAGES OR SALARY

There are two types of mistaken overpayment:

1 a mistake of fact; and
2 a mistake of law.

Mistakes of law are not easy to determine (even for the courts) and involve the interpretation of contract or statute. Most mistaken overpayments are mistakes of fact. Clerical errors, miscalculations, wrong data input and computer errors are all mistakes of fact. Mistakes of fact are normally recoverable.

It follows that should an employee receive an overpayment in their wage packet, it is likely to be recoverable by the employer if they find out. Spending the overpayment will not provide the employee with a legal defence. There may be occasions when the employee is genuinely unaware that he has received an overpayment by way of clerical error. This, as said, will be recoverable by the employer. If the error has taken place over many months, the employee could have received a considerable amount and have spent some or all of the money involved. In such cases, it would be unreasonable for the employer to demand repayment in a lump sum and the employee should seek to negotiate an agreeable staged repayment.

The only legal defence open to an employee in receipt of a mistaken overpayment is if he can persuade the court that in good faith he changed his position and incurred expenditure which would not otherwise have been incurred. The 'good faith' element of this defence is important, as it implies that the employee did not know, nor should he reasonably have known, that he was being overpaid.

EQUAL PAY

The provisions of the Equal Pay Act 1970 require equal pay for 'equal work' regardless of the employee's sex. The right to equal pay applies to:

- women employed in Great Britain whether or not they are British citizens; and
- men as well as women.

In practice, most cases under the provisions are brought by women, which is reflected in the remainder of this chapter. The Equal Opportunities Commission (www.eoc.org.uk/) may assist individuals in bringing an equal pay claim. Their contact telephone number is:

England	0845 601 5901
Scotland	0845 601 5901
Wales	029 2034 3552

The Equality Clause

The Act provides that an 'equality clause' is impliedly included into a woman's contract of employment where one does not already exist. The clause operates so that:

- a term which is less favourable is modified to become as favourable as that within a corresponding man's contract;
- any beneficial term in a man's contract but not in a corresponding woman's will be deemed to be included in the woman's contract.

The comparison

The woman can compare herself with a man employed by the same or an associated employer if:

- they do 'like work'; or
- a job-evaluation scheme has rated their work as equivalent; or
- her job is of equal value.

A woman may be regarded as employed on 'like work' with men if her work and theirs is of the same or of a broadly similar nature. This means that any difference that may exist between the two roles are not of practical importance. The work must be 'like work'. The woman cannot claim, for example, if her work involved greater responsibility or skill but was less well paid.

With regard to a job-evaluation study, it must be remembered that the employer is under no legal duty to conduct such a study. However, where they do and a woman's work is rated equivalent to that of a man's by considering effort, skill, qualifications and responsibilities, etc. this will facilitate an equal pay claim.

If the work is not 'like work' and no job-evaluation study has been conducted, the woman may bring an equal pay claim if she can show that her work is of 'equal value' to that of a corresponding male. The question of equal value is very complicated and normally requires expert evidence. It requires an assessment of skill, effort, responsibilities, etc., just as with a job-evaluation study. Recent case law also suggests that a woman may bring an equal value claim where the work she is doing is, in fact, of greater value than her male counterpart's. It should also be noted that a claim may be brought for unequal pay for like work based on grounds of race or disability.

The employer's defence

Apart from where the employer can demonstrate that the woman's work is not 'like work' or work of 'equal value' which relies on differences of *practical* importance, the law provides a defence where there exists a 'material difference' between the man's job and that of the woman which is not the difference of sex.

Material differences are regarded as those which are concerned with *who* does the work rather than relating to *what* work is done. The work might be like work, work rated as equivalent or work of equal or greater value but, nonetheless, the employer is afforded a defence if there exists a material difference in respect of who actually undertakes the work. The difference must be significant and relevant and may well go beyond what an individual brings to any job in question in terms of skill, experience, training or productivity.

An example of a material difference would be where a man doing similar work to a woman is paid more because of a sales-related bonus that was available to both or because he happens to have been employed longer by the employer and it is their business policy to reward long service.

Remedy

Any employee wishing to bring an equal pay claim may do so upon application to an employment tribunal at any time during employment or within six months of the effective date of termination of employment. An employee can serve an Equal Pay Questionnaire on her employer within 21 days of filing her complaint at the tribunal or, if tribunal proceedings have not been started, within six months of her last day at work. The employee can use the questionnaire to request key information from her employer. The employer has eight weeks in which to respond and the tribunal can draw inferences from a deliberate refusal to answer or from an evasive or equivocal reply. The tribunal may make a declaration as to the inequality and is, as a result of recent case law, empowered to award up to six years' arrears of pay up to the point where proceedings were commenced. However,

Equal Pay
If you are getting less pay than a man

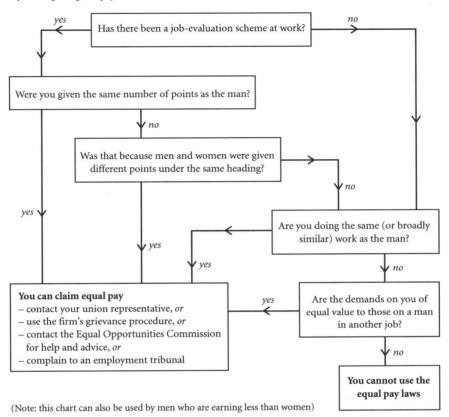

yes   Has there been a job-evaluation scheme at work?   *no*

Were you given the same number of points as the man?

no

Was that because men and women were given different points under the same heading?

no

yes

yes

yes

Are you doing the same (or broadly similar) work as the man?

no

You can claim equal pay
– contact your union representative, *or*
– use the firm's grievance procedure, *or*
– contact the Equal Opportunities Commission for help and advice, *or*
– complain to an employment tribunal

yes   Are the demands on you of equal value to those on a man in another job?

no

You cannot use the equal pay laws

(Note: this chart can also be used by men who are earning less than women)

in certain cases a longer period may be argued where there has been deception on the part of the employer.

The Equal Opportunities Commission can provide invaluable advice to anyone contemplating an equal pay action, in particular as to the prospects of a successful claim given the particular facts and circumstances. As this section has indicated, such claims are notoriously complex for the unassisted litigant.

Regulations implemented in December 2003 allow the six-month time limit for presenting an equal pay claim to a tribunal to be extended in certain circumstances where the employer has concealed any relevant fact. The Regulations also give employment tribunals the power to determine the question of whether work is of equal value itself or to appoint an independent expert to prepare a report into any aspect of that issue.

34

Unfair Dismissal

THE PRINCIPLE

The law provides protection for an employee from being unfairly dismissed from his job or from being forced out of his work by the actions of his employer. To claim unfair dismissal the employer must have clearly terminated the contract of employment orally, in writing or by his conduct.

Where there has been no dismissal but the employer has acted so unreasonably as to force the employee to resign his position, this is known as 'constructive dismissal' and the employee may act as if dismissed by the employer. It should be noted that the law will only recognize an employee's right to claim constructive dismissal where it can be shown that the employer has acted in *serious* breach of contract. A minor breach will not be enough to warrant resignation and a constructive unfair dismissal claim. Similarly, unreasonable behaviour by the employer of itself is irrelevant unless it constitutes a breach of mutual trust and confidence. This is because unreasonable behaviour is not a breach of contract and for this reason constructive unfair dismissal is difficult to prove and most claims fail.

Examples of serious breaches would include imposing, against the employee's wishes, changes to hours, pay, work location and the nature of the task to be performed or being in serious breach of the implied term of mutual trust and confidence (*see* Chapter 32). In most cases, an employment tribunal hearing a constructive dismissal claim would have expected the employee to have first exhausted all internal avenues of grievance with the employer and not to have resigned as a first option. Constructive dismissal is largely an action of last resort. 'Resign or be sacked' situations resulting in a resignation would also be covered by an application to an employment tribunal for constructive dismissal.

Finally, it should be noted that the non-renewal of a fixed-term contract by the employer is a dismissal and can, therefore, amount to an unfair dismissal. It is no longer possible for employees employed under fixed-term contracts to agree to waive their unfair dismissal rights.

Time limits

An employee must bring a claim for unfair dismissal within three months less one day of the date of termination. A claim received by the employment tribunal after this deadline will be out of time. Tribunals will reject such claims unless it can be shown that it was not reasonably feasible to bring the claim within the time limit. If the employer dismisses the employee with notice, the date of termination will be the end of the notice period so long as the employee actually works until that date.

Dan is dismissed for not being capable of performing his work on 15 May. He has worked for the company for four years. The employer pays Dan the two months' notice that he is entitled to under his contract of employment. Dan's unfair dismissal claim must be received by the tribunal by 14 August to be in time.

The safest way of calculating the date of termination is to determine the last day on which the employee physically attended work. Evidence of the date of termination can also be found in the P45 tax document.

THE EXCLUSIONS

Not all employees are protected from being unfairly dismissed. The following conditions apply:
1 the employee must have been employed for at least one year's continuous service (but see exceptions below);
2 the employee, male or female, must not at the time of dismissal (or resignation) be over their normal retirement age for that employer or, where none exists, over 65 years old;
3 the provisions do not apply to share fishermen;
4 in certain situations employees dismissed in connection with a lock-out or strike, are prevented from

claiming protection against unfair dismissal. (An employee is protected for the first eight weeks of participation in official industrial action, or if the employer has failed to take reasonable procedural steps to resolve the dispute);

5 those employed in the police service are excluded.

If the employee is excluded by reason of one of the above, he will not be able to challenge the unfairness or unreasonableness of his employer's actions, whatever the circumstances. His only hope of redress will be a claim for breach of contract (sometimes confusingly called 'wrongful dismissal') against the employer. This is dealt with in detail later.

THE EMPLOYER'S DEFENCE

The employee must first prove that he has, in fact, been dismissed or constructively dismissed. Once this is done, and in most cases this is straightforward, the employer is then under a legal obligation, if challenged by the employee, to show that the dismissal was for one of five permitted potentially fair reasons for dismissal. It follows that these reasons may afford the employer a defence to his act of dismissal. They are:

1 capability or qualifications;
2 the employee's conduct;
3 redundancy;
4 statutory requirements;
5 some other substantial reason.

Capability and qualifications

Generally, 'capability' will include the following elements:
- the employee's skill in the performance of his duties;
- the aptitude of the employee concerned in relation to the job for which he is employed;
- the employee's physical and mental ability to perform the tasks required.

'Qualifications', on the other hand, is described as any degree, diploma or other academic, technical or professional qualification relevant to that person's position as an employee. The absence of capability or qualification need only exist in relation to a significant part of their job. The employer need not show that *all* the tasks an employee is requested to undertake are affected by the lack of these two factors.

Conduct

Conduct or, more to the point, misconduct, is for obvious reasons a potentially fair reason for dismissal. The law supplies no definition of 'conduct'. However, it does include acts of gross misconduct, for example:

- theft;
- fraud;
- violence;
- damage to the employer's property;
- an act of dishonesty;
- sexual harassment;
- inciting racial tension or hatred;
- a significant act of negligence;
- alcohol abuse at work;
- insubordination, etc.;

(*This list is not exhaustive.*)

Conduct will also include acts of ordinary misconduct such as:

- persistent poor time-keeping;
- persistent absenteeism;
- attitude problems;
- carelessness, etc.

(*This list is not exhaustive.*)

An act of gross misconduct and one of ordinary misconduct are, as the lists show, quite different in nature. Gross misconduct is so serious that the employer can bring the contract of employment to an immediate end without warning or notice to the employee – *provided always* that the employee has had an opportunity to defend his position against the initial allegation before the employer decides to dismiss. An act of gross misconduct will, therefore, provide an employer with a potentially fair reason for dismissal.

Ordinary misconduct does not bring the contract to an immediate end. In order for the employer to have a defence against dismissal for ordinary misconduct he must usually have followed a fair disciplinary procedure and given the employee a number of warnings. In practice, tribunals will look to see whether the employer has followed the ACAS Code of Practice on Disciplinary Practice and Procedures. The ACAS Code requires the employer to go through four stages before dismissing the employee:

1 a verbal warning;
2 a first written warning;
3 a final written warning;
4 dismissal.

The employee should be given an opportunity to state his case prior to *each* stage of the procedure. Failure to follow a similar procedure may take away the employer's defence of a potentially fair reason for dismissal.

Redundancy

It is a potentially fair reason for dismissal where an employee's contract of employment has been terminated because his job has diminished considerably or ceased to exist at his normal place of work. In short, because he is no longer required by the business and is redundant. (*See* Chapter 36.)

Statutory requirements

This potentially fair reason for dismissal is aimed at those situations where an employer has to dismiss an employee because he is not able to continue in that job without falling foul of some law. For example, a van driver who loses his driving licence for 12 months because of a drink-driving conviction, will no longer be able to undertake driving duties for his employer without being in contravention of road traffic law.

Some other substantial reason

This fifth, potentially fair reason, was designed to be a 'catch-all' for those reasons that did not fall neatly into the other four categories but, nonetheless, should rightfully, on their facts, provide the employer with a defendable position in law. Over the years one common type of dismissal persistently presents itself within this group. That is, where an employer reorganizes his business and as a necessary part of that restructuring is forced to impose contract changes on the employee. The business reorganization will fall short of a full-blown redundancy but will similarly be driven by economic factors. In such situations, to dismiss an employee who refuses to accept such contract changes will be a potentially fair dismissal 'for some other substantial reason'.

Peter works for George in his pizza restaurant. For the last two years he has worked five days per week from 6 p.m. to 11 p.m. George's restaurant is doing very well and he needs Peter to work 4 p.m. to 11 p.m. and to be able to help out at weekends. Peter refuses to extend his hours so George is forced to terminate Peter's contract of employment with due notice. Peter claims unfair dismissal at an employment tribunal. He loses his case. The tribunal accepts Peter was dismissed fairly for 'some other substantial reason' driven by George's pressing need to reorganize his business.

AUTOMATIC UNFAIR DISMISSALS

Up to now we have dealt with those situations which are potentially fair and which allow the employer a defence. There are also a number of types of dismissal which, if proven on their facts, will be 'automatically unfair' and will not allow the employer any defence at all.

You will recall that in most cases, an employee must have been employed for at least one year before he can bring a claim of unfair dismissal in the employment tribunal. For those sub-sections below marked by an asterisk (*) this one-year rule does not apply and employees over the normal retiring age or over the age of 65 years are not barred from pursuing a complaint.

Trade union membership*

It is automatically unfair to dismiss an employee because they were, or proposed to become, a member of an independent trade union.

Trade union activity*

Where an employee is dismissed for having taken part, or having proposed to take part, in the activities of an independent trade union, outside working hours or within working hours if permitted by the employer, he will be deemed to have been automatically unfairly dismissed.

Closed-shop dismissals*

It is automatically unfair to dismiss an employee for refusing to become, or refusing to remain, a member of an independent trade union.

Assertion of a statutory right*

Where an employee seeks to assert a statutory right (for example, to demand a written statement of particulars of employment) and is dismissed, that employee will be deemed to have been automatically unfairly dismissed. The reason behind this law is to prevent employers from victimizing employees using fear of dismissal if all they seek is the enforcement or application of their statutory rights.

Rachel has worked for Dodgy's Taxi Cabs for 12 weeks. When she started she was promised a contract of employment that would outline the terms and conditions of employment agreed at her interview for the job. None has been issued. Rachel is told if she keeps 'nagging' Dodgy's for a contract she could end up being dismissed.

Rachel is entitled to a written statement of terms and conditions of employment within the first eight weeks of service. If she is dismissed for asserting this statutory right she will be able to claim that she has been automatically unfairly dismissed. However, if Rachel is dismissed for asking for a contract of employment her claim will fail. This is because the law does not entitle an employee to a written contract of employment but merely to a written statement of terms and conditions.

Part-time workers*

It is automatically unfair to dismiss a part-time employee if the reason, or the main reason, for the dismissal is that:
- they exercised or sought to enforce rights under the Part-time Workers (Prevention of Less Favourable

Treatment) Regulations 2000, refused to forgo them or alleged that the employer had infringed them; that

- they requested a written statement; or that
- they gave evidence or information in connection with proceedings brought by an employee under the Regulations; or that
- the employer believed the employee intended to do any of these things.

The Regulations aim to protect part-time workers by ensuring that they are treated no less favourably in their working conditions (salary, benefits, training and holiday) than comparable full-timers, unless the less-favourable treatment is justified on objective grounds. Part-time workers who believe that they have been treated in a manner which infringes the Regulations have the right to make a request in writing to receive, within 21 days, a written statement from their employer giving the reasons for the treatment.

While only employees can complain of unfair dismissal (*see* page 311), workers who are not employees can complain to an employment tribunal that they have suffered a detriment if their contracts are terminated for any of the above reasons. Compensation will be awarded on the same basis as for unfair dismissal. It is also unlawful to subject any part-timer to a detriment for any of the above reasons.

Fixed-term workers*

The Fixed-term Employees (Prevention of Less Favourable Treatment) Regulations 2002 provide fixed-term employees with similar protection to part-timers under the Part-time Workers Regulations (described above), although in the case of fixed-term employees the right is not to be treated less favourably than comparable permanent employees. It is automatically unfair to dismiss a fixed-term employee for the same reasons as under the Part-time Workers Regulations. Employees are also protected from detrimental treatment which falls short of dismissal for these reasons.

Tax credits*

Working Tax Credit was introduced in April 2003. It is automatically unfair to dismiss an employee if the reason, or the main reason, for the dismissal is:

- that they are entitled, or will or may be entitled, to Working Tax Credit; or
- that they took (or proposed to take) any action with a view to enforcing or otherwise securing a right conferred by regulations under the Tax Credits Act 2002; or
- from the same date, that their employer was prosecuted or fined as a result of such action.

It is also unlawful for an employer to subject employees to any other detrimental treatment.

Spent convictions

It is automatically unfair to dismiss an employee for having a conviction that has become spent under the Rehabilitation of Offenders Act.

Pregnant employees*

To dismiss an employee solely because she is pregnant, or for any reason predominantly connected with her pregnancy, or on grounds related to childbirth or maternity leave will be regarded in law as an automatically unfair dismissal. Employees also have the right not to be subjected to any detriment or victimization for reasons related to pregnancy, childbirth or maternity.

Health and safety related dismissals*

Employees are protected from dismissal where they:

1 carry out health and safety activities on behalf of their employer;
2 bring to the attention of the employer a concern over a risk to health and safety;
3 propose to leave, or leave the workplace and refuse to return while danger persists, in the event that they reasonably believe their well-being is in serious and imminent danger which cannot reasonably be averted;
4 in the circumstances immediately above, take appropriate steps to protect themselves or others from danger.

There is no maximum on the amount of compensation that can be awarded by the tribunal in these circumstances.

Shopworkers and Sunday trading*

From August 1994 the law has recognized types of shop worker in respect of Sunday trading:

- the protected shopworker;
- the opted-in shopworker;
- the opted-out shopworker.

It is automatically unfair to dismiss a shopworker for refusing to work on a Sunday where he is either a protected or an opted-out worker.

In brief, the protected shop worker is one who, before August 1994, was not employed to work Sundays. Where the employee is asked to work Sundays and has no objection, by written notice to the employer the employee thereby becomes 'opted-in' and no longer a 'protected shop worker'. The employee is under no legal obligation to comply with the employer's request in such circumstances. The employee has freedom of choice. The notice to the employer must be:

- written;
- signed;
- dated; and
- clearly stating that there is no objection to working Sundays.

An 'opted-out' worker is one who is not protected but, in complying with similar formalities above, has given his employer clear notice of his objection to Sunday working. To prevent the disturbance to the employer that may ensue if employees were allowed to opt in and out with regularity, the employer may insist that, for a period of three months after having received an opting-out notice, the employee undertakes Sunday work.

Every new employee has the right to receive from the employer an explanatory statement that they may choose to work or not to work on Sundays. If the employee wishes to object to Sunday work and does so within the first eight weeks of service the employer is discharged from the obligation to provide an explanatory statement. In these circumstances, workers who object will become 'opted-out' shopworkers. The right to work or not to work on Sundays as a shopworker applies irrespective of length of service.

Official industrial action and dismissal*

The dismissal of an employee for participating in official industrial action will be automatically unfair if it occurs during the first eight weeks of such participation. A dismissal will also be unfair after that period if the employer has failed to take reasonable procedural steps to resolve the dispute. Unfairly dismissed strikers will be entitled to reinstatement (i.e. to go back to their old jobs) only after the strike is over.

There is no equivalent protection for employees participating in unofficial industrial action.

Unofficial industrial action and dismissal

The major difference between dismissals for unofficial and official industrial action is that, where unofficial, the employer is given greater latitude by the law and is allowed to select which employees to dismiss and re-engage without penalty. This, in practice, will allow an employer to dismiss the perceived 'ring-leaders' of the industrial action.

Industrial action will not be considered unofficial where:

- the employee is a trade union member and the action is authorized or endorsed by the union;
- the employee is not a trade union member but trade union members are taking part in the action, and it has been authorized or endorsed by that union.

Industrial action may become unofficial if repudiated by the trade union. It will be classed unofficial with effect from the working day that immediately follows the date of repudiation.

Pressure dismissals*

An employer who dismisses an employee because of pressure from a trade union, by way of the threat of industrial action, will be dismissing that employee unfairly.

Dismissals on a transfer of an undertaking

To dismiss an employee 'further to' a business transfer will be regarded as, on the face of it, unfair. The dismissal may be before or after the transfer and the employer is only afforded a defence if he can show that the reason for dismissal was either an economic, technical or organizational reason which would necessarily lead to changes being required in the workforce.

A transfer of a business takes place where a business or part of a business is sold or otherwise disposed of to another business or individual. In these circumstances, the law protects the employees who are disposed of with the business. The employees cannot, generally, be dismissed by either the seller or the purchaser of the business and cannot have their contract terms interfered with by either without their agreement.

Dismissal and the National Minimum Wage*

It is automatically unfair to dismiss a worker simply because the employer does not wish to pay the National Minimum Wage (NMW), or because the employee has taken action to enforce his rights to the NMW. In addition, if a worker is 'subjected to any detriment', such as hours being reduced, he may bring a claim in the employment tribunal from the first day of employment.

Dismissal for Public Interest Disclosure*

The Public Interest Disclosure Act 1998 protects employees who 'blow the whistle' about wrongdoing. In certain circumstances, disclosures are protected and the employees who make them are similarly protected. Employees are protected from unfair dismissal and from suffering any other detriment from their employer. Detriment may take a number of forms, such as denial of promotion, facilities or training opportunities which the employer would have otherwise offered.

Certain kinds of disclosure qualify for protection, for example, where the employee reasonably believes one or more of the following matters is either happening, took place in the past, or is likely to happen in the future:

- a criminal offence;
- the breach of a legal obligation;
- a miscarriage of justice;
- a danger to the health and safety of any individual;
- damage to the environment; or
- deliberate covering up of information tending to show any of the above five matters.

It may subsequently be discovered that the employee was wrong in his reasonable belief. This will not matter provided it was a reasonably held belief in the circumstances at the time of disclosure. The employee may make the disclosure to the employer or a third party if he reasonably believed he would be subject to a detriment by the employer if disclosure were made to him.

Employees protected by the provisions who have been dismissed or have suffered other detriment can complain to an employment tribunal. The complaint should be made within three months of the dismissal or detriment. For unfair dismissal claims, interim relief is also available, provided the claim is made within seven days of the effective date of termination of employment. There is no limit to the amount of compensation that may be claimed.

Working time cases*

It is automatically unfair to dismiss an employee for refusing to forgo a right conferred on him by the Working Time Regulations 1998 (e.g. the right to four weeks' paid annual leave) or refusing to comply with a requirement imposed on him by the employer in contravention of those Regulations (e.g. refusing to work on average over 48 hours per week). In addition, it is also unlawful to subject an employee to a detriment for reasons related to the Regulations.

Pension scheme trustees*

An employee's dismissal is automatically unfair if the reason relates to the employee performing his functions as a trustee of a pension scheme related to his employment.

Trade union recognition*

It is automatically unfair to dismiss an employee on grounds related to compulsory trade union recognition or de-recognition, and it is unlawful to take adverse action short of dismissal on these grounds.

Dismissal for exercising right of accompaniment at disciplinary hearings*

An employer who dismisses an employee for exercising his statutory right to be accompanied at a disciplinary hearing, or for accompanying another employee, will be dismissing that employee unfairly. An employee also has the right not to be subjected to any detriment on these grounds.

Parental leave dismissals*

The dismissal of an employee for taking parental leave is automatically unfair and it is unlawful to victimize him for reasons relating to parental leave, for example, by freezing an employee's salary upon his return to work when similar employees have enjoyed an increase in pay.

Time off for family emergencies dismissals*

If the reason for dismissal relates to the employee exercising his right to time off to deal with family emergencies, that will be automatically unfair. In addition, it is also unlawful to subject an employee to a detriment for reasons relating to time off for family emergencies, for example, by denying an employee a training opportunity or promotion merely because the time he took off to cope with the family emergency was inconvenient to the business.

Adoption leave dismissals*
The dismissal of an employee for taking adoption leave is automatically unfair (*see further* Chapter 39).

Paternity leave dismissals*
The dismissal of an employee for taking paternity leave is automatically unfair (*see further* Chapter 39).

Requesting flexible working*
It is automatically unfair to dismiss an employee if the reason or principal reason for that dismissal is that the employee:
- made or proposed to make an application for flexible working time;
- exercised or proposed to exercise a right under the procedure;
- brought proceedings against the employer; or
- alleged the existence of circumstances which would be unlawful.

It is also unlawful to subject an employee to a detriment on any of these grounds (*see further* Chapter 39).

Claiming for Unfair Dismissal or Redundancy

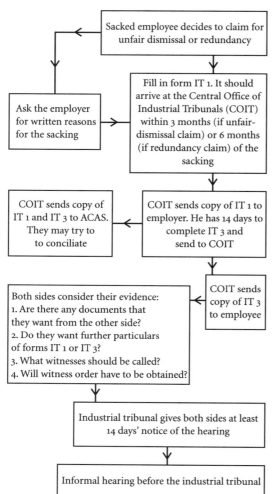

Sacked employee decides to claim for unfair dismissal or redundancy

Ask the employer for written reasons for the sacking

Fill in form IT 1. It should arrive at the Central Office of Industrial Tribunals (COIT) within 3 months (if unfair-dismissal claim) or 6 months (if redundancy claim) of the sacking

COIT sends copy of IT 1 and IT 3 to ACAS. They may try to to conciliate

COIT sends copy of IT 1 to employer. He has 14 days to complete IT 3 and send to COIT

Both sides consider their evidence:
1. Are there any documents that they want from the other side?
2. Do they want further particulars of forms IT 1 or IT 3?
3. What witnesses should be called?
4. Will witness order have to be obtained?

COIT sends copy of IT 3 to employee

Industrial tribunal gives both sides at least 14 days' notice of the hearing

Informal hearing before the industrial tribunal

Employee representatives*

A dismissal will automatically be regarded as unfair if the reason relates to the employee carrying out his functions as an employee representative (or a candidate for election as such a representative) on a transfer of an undertaking or where the employer proposes to make collective redundancies.

Redundancy*

To be selected for dismissal on the ground of redundancy for any of the reasons stated above (other than that on a transfer of an undertaking).

THE FAIRNESS OF DISMISSAL

No analysis of unfair dismissal would be complete without there being some attempt to understand how the courts view a fair dismissal within the five categories of potentially fair dismissals (*see* above). It is the role of an employment tribunal to consider all the facts of a particular case and to determine whether in all the circumstances the dismissal was fair and reasonable. Having dismissed an employee, the employer will be under an initial burden to defend his action and show that it was based on one of the five potentially fair reasons for dismissal. Having done that, the tribunal will then look into the following factors:

- Was the reason for dismissal sufficient given the facts of the case?
- What are the size and administrative resources available to the employer?
- Was there sufficient investigation by the employer prior to the decision to dismiss?
- Was there a fair hearing for the employee prior to the decision to dismiss?

Having looked at these elements, the tribunal must then ask itself whether, in accordance with equity and the substantial merits of the case, it believes the employer acted reasonably in dismissing the employee.

FAIRNESS AND THE FIVE POTENTIALLY FAIR REASONS FOR DISMISSAL

Capability and qualifications

For an employer to dismiss an employee on the grounds that they were incapable of performing the tasks required of him the employer must satisfy the tribunal that he honestly felt this to be the case. In exceptional cases the employer may come to this decision without following any formal procedure with the employee concerned. For example, when it can be demonstrated that the employee clearly knew what was expected of him and was equally clearly incapable of reaching that standard of work or of improving to reach that standard in the foreseeable future. In most cases, before such a conclusion may be drawn, the employer must adopt a fair procedure.

Fair procedure

Such a procedure would be expected to include the following:

- monitoring of the employee;
- face-to-face meetings with the employee to discuss the problem openly;
- clear details of the employee's shortcomings;
- implementation of a fair warnings procedure (*see* Chapter 37) if the employee fails to improve their performance;

- reasonable opportunity to improve;
- careful consideration of training requirements by the employer;
- consideration of alternative work for which the employee may be more suited.

The Employment Act 2002 will introduce new statutory dismissal and disciplinary procedures. These statutory procedures will be implied in every contract of employment and must be followed by employers. It will be unfair for an employer to dismiss an employee without meeting their obligations under the statutory procedure. An employee will be entitled to a minimum of four weeks' pay as compensation where they are found to have been unfairly dismissed and the statutory procedure has not been complied with. Importantly, the Act will also alter the way that unfair dismissals are judged so that, provided the minimum standards set out in the Act are followed and the dismissal is otherwise fair, procedural shortcomings can be disregarded. Employers will have to follow the basic procedures, but will no longer be penalized for irrelevant mistakes beyond that – provided the dismissal would otherwise be fair. These provisions of the Act were due to be implemented in April 2004. *See further* Chapter 37.

Lying about qualifications

Dismissal of an employee for not having the required qualifications is rare, since most of the relevant information should have been checked by the employer at interview stage or shortly thereafter. If an employee misleads an employer at interview or within the job application in respect of qualifications and the employer subsequently discovers the truth, the employee may reasonably be dismissed if the required qualifications are essential for the performance of the job. Also, the dismissal may be without notice for gross misconduct because of the dishonesty involved on the part of the employee. If, however, during the course of employment a qualification is taken away (e.g. loss of driving licence) the employee should only be dismissed if it is not reasonable or possible to provide suitable employment in some other capacity. Employees who are offered another job by the employer in those circumstances must be prepared to change their contract of employment accordingly, possibly to the extent of accepting less pay if the job is of a lower grade.

Ill-health

An employee may become incapable of working due to ill-health. Before dismissing an employee who is ill, the employer is obliged to consider any medical evidence reasonably available. Often this will necessitate requesting the permission of the employee to approach his doctor or consultant for a report. The employee may refuse permission, but if they do, the employer will be able to

make a decision on his future employment without the benefit of an expert medical opinion. This decision may not favour the employee. Having obtained a report from the employee's doctor, the employer is in a position to make a reasoned decision as to the employee's future employment with the business. The employer must consider:

1 the needs of the business;
2 the prospects of a quick return to work by the employee;
3 the availability of lighter duties to help the employee in getting back to work;
4 the employee's past record of health;
5 the nature of the illness and the likelihood of illness recurring;
6 the likelihood of a full recovery and return to full duties;
7 finally, the employer should consult the employee before taking any decision to dismiss him.

Failure to follow the above procedure may well be viewed by the tribunal as an unfair dismissal.

The employee's conduct

Many of the procedural requirements which make dismissal for misconduct potentially fair are dealt with in Chapter 37. It is sufficient at this stage to outline the requirements. Other than in cases of gross misconduct, a dismissal for misconduct must have been subject to the following:

1 proper investigation of the facts by the employer. (This applies equally to gross misconduct);
2 implementation of a fair warnings procedure;
3 a fair hearing of the employee's case at *each* stage of the warnings procedure;
4 the implementation of a reasonable disciplinary sanction at each stage of the warnings procedure;
5 credit must be given to the employee in respect of 'old' warnings that may reasonably be deemed to have lapsed by passage of time (usually 12 months or more);
6 consistent treatment with similar misconduct.

In the case of an allegation of gross misconduct, the employer is still required to convene a disciplinary hearing. If at that hearing the employer has an honest belief, based on reasonable grounds after all reasonable investigation, that the employee did act as alleged, there may be a finding of dismissal without notice on the ground of gross misconduct.

Redundancy

Redundancy is dealt with in detail in Chapter 36 since, in its own right, it has proven to be a hotbed of dispute and litigation over the years. What may be emphasized at this stage is that for a dismissal on the ground of redundancy to be potentially fair there must be:

- prior meaningful consultation with any relevant employee;
- a fair selection of the employee(s) for redundancy;
- full consideration of any alternative work available;
- full consideration of any methods whereby redundancy may be avoided;
- a situation where the job at that place of work has diminished considerably or ceased to exist.

Statutory requirements

The mere fact an employer may be able to genuinely show, due to contravention of law, that he is no longer able to employ a certain individual, will not absolve him from the responsibility of following a fair procedure in implementing that dismissal. The procedure should include:

- a full consultation with the employee concerned;
- full exploration (if appropriate) of suitable alternative employment with that business.

Some other substantial reason

As previously stated, two main types of dismissal which habitually fall into this category are those involving a business reorganization and changes to the employee's contract of employment. In each of these cases, and in all the others within this category of dismissals, formal procedures on consultation and hearings are prerequisites before the dismissal will be regarded as potentially fair. Whatever the pressing business needs of the employer, the tribunal will invariably not accept that any commercial situation is so urgent that employees may be unfairly treated in substance or by the failure to observe procedural fairness and ordinary principles of natural justice.

WRITTEN REASONS FOR DISMISSAL

Every employee who has at least one year's continuous service with their employer and who is dismissed, is entitled to request a written statement of reasons for that dismissal from the employer.

The employee may make his request orally or in writing and the employer must comply with the request within 14 days. In addition, an employee who is dismissed during pregnancy or maternity leave, irrespective of length of service, is entitled to a written statement of reasons for dismissal without having to request it. In practice it is well worth making the request and many employers make the mistake of supplying reasons which in fact only lend support to a claim for unfair dismissal. The written statement is admissible in evidence in any tribunal proceedings.

Should the employer refuse the request, on that point alone the employee may bring a complaint before an employment tribunal. Application may also be made where the reasons supplied are inadequate or untrue. The claim must be presented within three months from the effective date of termination of employment (that is, the last day of the notice period – or, immediately, in circumstances where notice is not applicable).

If well-founded, the complaint may lead to an award against the employer to pay the employee a sum equal to two weeks' pay and a declaration as to what the real reasons were for the termination. Equally, if the employment tribunal finds that the real reason for the dismissal is not the reason originally given by the employer, the employee may recover two weeks' pay.

UNFAIR DISMISSAL – THE REMEDIES

When an employee has succeeded in his claim for unfair dismissal, he is entitled to choose whether he wishes to return to the job or compensation. Returning to work is known as reinstatement or re-engagement.

The difference between the two is that reinstatement provides return to the same job while re-engagement is the return to a comparable job if that is practicable.

Reinstatement

This is an order made by the tribunal that the employer shall treat the complainant (ex-employee) in all respects as if he had not been dismissed. The tribunal will consider:

1 the wishes of the complainant;
2 whether it is practicable for an employer to comply with such an order if it were made;
3 the conduct of the complainant when he was working for the employer, in so far as whether it would be just to make an order for reinstatement.

In practice, the employer is entitled to object to an order being made and the tribunal will consider evidence from the employer in respect of the following:

(a) whether further conflict or industrial unrest would follow;
(b) the resources of the employer;
(c) whether it would lead to a redundancy situation if the complainant had already been replaced;
(d) whether it would result in overmanning.

If the employer's argument against reinstatement fails, and the order for reinstatement is made, the tribunal will specify:

- arrears of pay;
- other financial benefits payable;
- the rights which must be restored to the complainant upon returning to work;

- the date by which the employer must comply with the order.

Re-engagement

If the tribunal makes an order for re-engagement, the employer will have to take the complainant back on in a job that is comparable with the one from which he was dismissed. If, in the time between dismissal and the tribunal decision, the original business has been taken over by another, the tribunal has the power to order the successor to re-engage the complainant. The tribunal will hear objections to the order and take into account the points raised in the reinstatement section above.

Where the tribunal makes the order it will specify:
- the employer (in the event of a takeover situation);
- the type of employment;
- the wage or salary to be paid;
- arrears of pay;
- other financial benefits;
- rights to be restored to the complainant upon return to work;
- the date by which the employer must comply with the order.

Generally

It should be noted that while a tribunal will consider the changed circumstances of the employer post-dismissal, it will not allow the employer to get out of reinstating or re-engaging the claimant simply because someone has been hired to replace the employee. That would make the avoidance of reinstatement and re-engagement orders too easy. The employer must show that it was necessary to hire a replacement or that a temporary replacement pending the deliberation of the case by the employment tribunal was not practicable in the circumstances.

The employer refuses to reinstate or re-engage

This is the situation where a tribunal orders reinstatement or re-engagement but, for whatever reason, the employer flatly refuses to comply with the order. In such circumstances the tribunal is empowered to make what is known as an additional award. This is an amount of compensation of not less than 26 and not more than 52 weeks' pay, up to a maximum of £260 per week.

The maximum amount is therefore: 52 × £260 = £13,520.

The additional award is made (as it implies) on top of other awards, typically the basic and compensatory awards.

The basic award

Where it is impractical to order reinstatement or re-engagement, the employee must look to financial compensation. An award of compensation can be made up of two elements: the basic award and the compensatory award.

The first element of compensation will be the basic award which is payable when there is a finding of unfair dismissal. The amount to which the employee is entitled under the basic award depends on:
- the age of the employee;
- their length of service (up to a maximum of 20 years);
- their average gross weekly wage (up to a maximum of £260 per week).

The employee is entitled to:
- one and a half week's pay for each year during which the employee was aged 41–64 inclusive;
- one week's pay for each year during which the employee was aged 22–40 inclusive;
- half a week's pay for each year during which the employee was less than 22 years of age.

The maximum basic award is: 20 × 1.5 × £260 = £7,800

In the event that the effective date of dismissal falls after the employee's 64th birthday, the basic award will be reduced by one-twelfth for each complete month by which their age exceeds 64 years.

The amount of the basic award may be further reduced in the following circumstances:
- where the conduct of the complainant prior to dismissal would make it just and equitable to do so;
- where the complainant has unreasonably refused an offer made by the employer which would have had the effect of reinstatement prior to the tribunal hearing;
- where the complainant has already received from his employer an *ex gratia* payment of an amount that is sufficient to cover the amount of any basic award;
- where a redundancy payment has been awarded by the tribunal or paid by the employer, by the amount of that payment (provided the employee was redundant).

Exception

The amount of the basic award will be 2 x £260 (two weeks' pay) where the reason for the dismissal was redundancy and the employee:
- unreasonably refused or left suitable alternative employment;
- was re-engaged or reinstated by the employer and there was, in effect, no dismissal.

Compensatory award

The amount the tribunal may grant as a compensatory award may be anything up to a maximum statutory ceiling figure of £53,500. (This amount is altered annually.) Until October 1999, the amount that the tribunal could award was limited to £12,000. Although the average employment tribunal awards are still normally only a couple of thousand pounds, this change opened the door on new types of claim (e.g. share scheme claims) and new types of claimant (such as senior managers). The sums at stake are now much larger, and this will give increased negotiating strength to senior employees in many cases.

In deciding how much it should award, a tribunal will take into account several factors:

1 the loss to the complainant, including:
   (a) expenses reasonably incurred as a result of the dismissal;
   (b) loss of employment rights.

Other damages are assessed in accordance with their net value and include:

2 loss of wages, from the effective date of termination to the hearing;
3 future loss of earnings;
4 loss of personal use of a company car;
5 loss of benefits in kind. For example, medical insurance, free accommodation, free roadside assistance membership, contribution or payment of telephone bills, loss of use of mobile phone or lap-top computer;
6 pension rights. Particularly in respect of final salary schemes;
7 loss of statutory rights. This covers the loss of employment protection for the first year of service, statutory redundancy pay and the entitlement to statutory minimum notice. Awards are commonly in the region of £260 for loss of statutory rights. However, there is no science behind this amount and the law requires clarification.

Reducing the compensatory award

As with the basic award, the compensatory award may be reduced by the tribunal. Factors taken into account include:

- contributory fault on the part of the complainant while in employment. The tribunal is at liberty to reduce the amount by 100 per cent;
- did the unfairness of the dismissal make any difference?
- mitigation;
- payments already made by the employer.

Edward has three years' service with International Carpet Warehouse Ltd. At first he was a reliable employee. Of late, his timekeeping has been lamentably poor and he has received a single written warning requesting improvement. He turns up late yet again and his boss sacks him on the spot saying, 'It is the last straw!'

At tribunal there is a finding of unfair dismissal because the warnings and disciplinary procedure were inadequate. However, the tribunal takes into account evidence of Edward's conduct in the months prior to his dismissal and reduces the award of compensation for unfair dismissal by 70 per cent.

The unfairness of the dismissal

The tribunal may reduce the size of the award if the unfairness of the dismissal would not have made any difference to the ultimate decision to dismiss. This factor is now of less importance to the tribunal than it had been for some years. The tribunal will consider what would have happened if a fair procedure *had* been adopted. For example, it may be provable by the employer that even if a fair procedure had been implemented, due to economic necessity, several weeks later a genuine redundancy would have been imposed on the employee in question.

Finding another job

The complainant is obliged to attempt to mitigate his loss. In essence, this means that after he has been dismissed, the complainant must take all reasonable steps to find suitable alternative work. Otherwise, the tribunal will penalize him by reducing the amount of compensation it awards. It is for the employer to prove that the complainant has not made every effort to reasonably mitigate his loss. Any necessary expenditure (such as travel costs) incurred by the complainant in attempting to mitigate his loss will be recoverable as part of the compensatory award.

Other sums paid to the complainant

As with the basic award, any amounts paid to the complainant by his former employer will be taken into account in the assessment of the compensatory award.

Deduction of state benefits

The complainant may have received state benefits after he was dismissed. In that case the tribunal will deduct the amount of state benefits received from the part of the award that covers lost earnings. Significantly, the deduction will not be applied if the parties agree the amount of compensation. It is only applied if the employment tribunal itself determines the amount of compensation to be paid.

Tom wins his claim for unfair dismissal. The tribunal invites the parties to try to agree on the amount of his losses. Tom's total loss is £12,000 but he has received £3,000 worth of state benefits (Jobseeker's Allowance and Income Support). If the tribunal awards £12,000, £9,000 will be paid to Tom and £3,000 will be repaid to the Department of Work and Pensions on Tom's behalf. Tom agrees to accept £10,000 from the employer and the parties inform the employment tribunal of their agreement. In these circumstances, there will be no deduction of state benefits.

Order of deductions

The order of deductions is as follows:

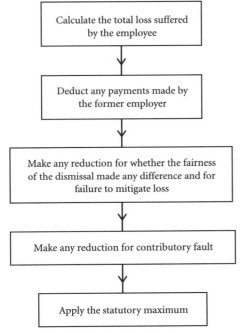

It is important to note that the statutory maximum is only applied after the reductions have been made.

Interest on tribunal awards

Interest will accrue on awards made by an employment tribunal at the rate of 8 per cent per annum, starting 42 days after the tribunal's decision is dispatched to the parties in the case. Interest is simple rather than compound and accrues on a daily basis. Awards of costs or expenses do not carry interest.

SETTLEMENT

There are two forms of settlement acceptable in law.

ACAS settlements

Once proceedings have been issued before an employment tribunal, an ACAS officer in that region will automatically become involved with the case in an attempt to resolve the dispute by settlement through negotiation. Where agreement is achieved, the details of the settlement are formalized in a document drafted by the ACAS officer, known as a COT3 Settlement (so called after the form upon which it is written). COT3 Settlements are binding on both parties and are in effect full and final – i.e. once agreed, the parties may take no further legal action against each other in respect of that particular dispute.

Compromise agreements

Where there is a dispute between employer and employee that could lead to proceedings being issued, their differences can sometimes be settled using the compromise agreement facility. The agreement is usually (but not always) drafted by the employer's lawyer on the ground that they have more available resources than the employee.

The compromise agreement is a simple means of resolving disputes but a number of conditions must be satisfied. For the agreement to be valid in law it must:

1 relate to a particular dispute between the parties;
2 be in writing;
3 have been agreed to by the employee, who must have received independent legal advice from either a qualified lawyer (i.e. a solicitor or barrister not being the employer's lawyer) or a competent trade union officer or official or a competent advice centre worker before having signed the agreement;
4 identify the independent adviser;
5 provide for insurance of the independent adviser against claims for professional negligence;
6 contain a declaration that the formalities stated above are satisfied.

If the conditions are satisfied the agreement will be legally binding on both parties and will act as full and final settlement of the particular dispute, i.e. once agreed, the parties (in practice, the complainant), may take no further legal action against each other in respect of that particular dispute or any other matter relating to the employment of the complainant which is within the knowledge of that person at the time they signed the agreement.

Paul sues his employer for race discrimination and unfair dismissal. The employer offers Paul £20,000 to settle his claims. Paul seeks legal advice and decides to accept the sum of £20,000 and signs the compromise agreement. Some months after he signs the agreement, Paul discovers that the employer has sent an unfavourable reference to a prospective employer. He is also told by a friend that his original claim was worth £100,000. Paul sues his former employer for unfair dismissal, race discrimination and for the production of the discriminatory reference. His claim for unfair dismissal and race discrimination fails because of the compromise agreement, which prevents such claims. Costs are awarded against Paul for bringing these misconceived claims. His remedy is to sue the legal adviser for negligence if it is true that his claim was worth £100,000.

However, Paul's claim for the discriminatory reference is allowed to proceed because the reference was produced after the compromise agreement was made.

It is theoretically possible to prevent future claims in a compromise agreement, although this is not what Parliament intended. The courts have said that if the parties wish to compromise future claims they must do so in clear and unequivocal language and they have added that they will only permit such clauses in exceptional circumstances.

The only other method of determining an employment tribunal claim once it is issued is by order of the employment tribunal. This order would state that the matter has been withdrawn upon the parties agreeing settlement terms. If the tribunal claim is settled but not in the form of a compromise agreement, ACAS settlement or tribunal order, such settlement is ineffective.

Paul is offered £20,000 in full and final settlement of his claims against the company. He accepts the sum and signs the agreement but does not take independent legal advice before signing it. The agreement was drawn up by the employer and is not in the form of a compromise agreement. Paul sues for unfair dismissal and race discrimination. The employment tribunal allows his claim to proceed because it has not been settled in a manner recognized in law. If Paul is successful at the tribunal, the monies received previously would be set against any damages awarded.

35

Wrongful Dismissal

THE DEFINITION

Wrongful dismissal should not be confused with unfair dismissal. The latter is the statutory right not to be dismissed unfairly. Wrongful dismissal derives from common law and is where the employer decides to terminate the contract of employment by dismissing the employee without notice. The employer is then in breach of contract, and the employee may claim damages.

Until relatively recently, a wrongful dismissal claim could only be brought before a county court or High Court but it may now be brought before an employment tribunal. The amount claimed by the employee will determine which court forum may be used. In some cases the employee will have a choice (*see* the table below).

Amount in dispute	Type of court
Less than £25,000	Employment tribunal *or* county court
Greater than £25,000	County court *or* High Court (it may be given fast-track status subject to level of complexity)

In order to bring such a claim the employee must be able to show that:
1 he was dismissed in breach of contract and received no notice or less than the statutory minimum period of notice or less than the contractual notice, whichever is the greater; and
2 he has suffered financially as a result of the employer's breach of contract.

WHICH FORUM?

Where the employee has a choice of court or tribunal in which to bring his action he should consider the advantages and disadvantages of each.

The employment tribunal

For lower-paid employees, whose wrongful dismissal claims are worth less than £25,000, the employment tribunal is normally the appropriate forum. This is because:
- there are no fees to be paid at the employment tribunal;
- the employment tribunal is a specialized forum and better understands wrongful dismissal situations;
- costs are not awarded against the complainant if he loses his claim (unless his claim is misconceived);
- wrongful dismissal claims are normally heard more quickly in the employment tribunal than in the county court or High Court;
- it is normally appropriate to bring a wrongful dismissal claim in the same forum and at the same time as bringing an unfair dismissal claim. Often employers who fail to pay proper notice act unfairly as well as wrongfully in respect of the dismissal.

The disadvantage of bringing the claim in the employment tribunal is that the time limit is much stricter than the civil court time limit (*see* page 349).

County court or High Court

Higher-paid employees and senior executives will normally sue for wrongful dismissal in the county court or High Court. This is because their contractual claim is worth more than £25,000. However, the significant risk with such claims is that the loser must pay the winner's legal costs. The advantages of the civil court forum include the ability to obtain summary judgment and interim payments (*see* below).

If an employee brings a wrongful dismissal claim in the county court or High Court, he may invoke a number of useful procedural devices that are not available in employment tribunals.

Summary judgment in the High Court and county court

In the High Court and county court, the employee may apply for summary judgment where he can show that the employer has no real defence to the claim. Summary judgment means that the case does not have a full trial – the outcome is determined by the court at a very early stage in the proceedings. The result can be very quick payment for the employee by order of the court, or the employer being ordered to pay money into court as a condition of being granted leave to defend. This can be a very useful tactic for the employee to apply pressure to pay on an employer who is procrastinating or ignoring his claim. The court has the power to strike out a so-called defence of its own choosing. Before filing the Allocation Questionnaire, the claimant can simply write to the court asking the District Judge to determine whether the defendant's reply should be treated as a defence. This is appropriate where the reply is an obvious play for time.

Interim payment

There is also a procedure in the county court and High Court whereby an employee may be able to seek an interim payment from the employer. This is possible where the employee has a strong case for payment and he will suffer financial hardship if payment is unduly delayed. The three basic grounds on which an interim payment may be claimed are where:

1 the employer has admitted liability but contests the amount of damages; or
2 the employee has obtained judgment against the employer for damages to be assessed; or
3 if the action proceeded to trial, the employee would obtain judgment for substantial damages against the employer.

Conversely, wrongful dismissal claims in the county court for less than £5,000 will normally be heard in the small claims track, in which costs are not awarded against the losing party. In addition, such claims are heard in private. Also, it should be noted that wrongful dismissal claims for more than £5,000 may attract legal aid (now called public funding). If the complainant obtains public funding, they will be protected against any costs award.

Counter-claim

The county court, High Court and employment tribunal all have a procedure whereby the employer can put in a counter-claim. That is, the employer counter-claims that the employee owes him money for some reason. The circumstances in which an employer can bring a counter-claim are much more restricted in the employment tribunal. This restriction may be to the advantage of the employee.

WAS THE EMPLOYEE DISMISSED?

There are several ways in which dismissal may be established.

Dismissal with notice

This is the most straightforward way of establishing dismissal. This is where the employer terminates the contract of employment by giving the employee contractual notice or by complying with the statutory minimum period of notice, whichever is the greater. It follows that any dismissal by the employer that fails to comply with either the contractual or statutory notice is a breach of contract and wrongful dismissal.

Where a contract of employment contains no provision for notice the court is entitled to impose what it considers to be a reasonable period of notice. This may not be the statutory period of notice.

Arnold, a salaried employee, has been working for six months under a contract of employment. The contract says nothing about the provision of notice. Arnold is paid regularly at monthly intervals. His employer terminates the contract and seeks to apply the statutory minimum period of notice by paying one week only. It is for Arnold to bring an action for wrongful dismissal on the basis that, by implication, he is entitled to one month's notice by reference to his pay interval and his level of pay. Arnold will be relying on the court to agree that on the facts, a reasonable period of notice would have been one month and no less.

This example is common in practice and, in most cases, the court would find in favour of the employee's claim, if for no other reason than the employer should be penalized for failing to clarify the period of notice in the contract. Where the employee in question is particularly skilled, highly paid or in a position of seniority, it is not inconceivable that the court would be prepared to imply a reasonable period of notice of three months to one year, should the contract be silent.

Dismissal without notice

Dismissal without notice may occur where the employee is allegedly guilty of gross misconduct, which may include gross negligence or gross incompetence.

In this case the employer is entitled to terminate the employment without notice. Put simply, the employer's right to sack on the spot arises when the employee has acted in such a way as to completely undermine the relationship of trust and confidence between himself and the employer. The employee, by their act or omission, is often said to have destroyed the contract of employment, rendering it inoperable from that point onwards. Another way in which such acts are commonly described is to say that the employee has acted in repudiatory (i.e. fundamental) breach of contract upon which the employer is entitled to respond by imposing summary dismissal.

However, not just any breach of contract by the employee will entitle the employer to sack on the spot. The employer must always be able to justify the dismissal without notice. If the employer fails to prove that the employee has committed a repudiatory breach, the employee may regard himself as having been wrongfully dismissed. In that case he will be entitled to claim damages for breach of contract, based upon the period of notice to which he is entitled under contract or statute.

In bringing an action for wrongful dismissal in such circumstances, the employee is, in effect, challenging the reason for summary dismissal. The court or tribunal will look at the alleged fault by the employee to determine whether the employer's response was justified. Depending on the facts, this may or may not be in the best interests of the employee.

To assist an employee in deciding whether to bring an action for wrongful dismissal following summary dismissal, it may be useful to consider the following:

1 Had the employee previously acted in a similar way during his employment?
2 If yes, had the employer regarded the matter with such gravity?
3 Had other employees similarly acted without being summarily dismissed?
4 In all the circumstances, did the act or omission *completely* undermine the relationship of trust and confidence between the parties?

The first three points above are important, since the court or tribunal will look at the consistency of approach by the employer. If there is no consistency, a finding of unjustified summary dismissal is likely.

Amanda works as a telesales operative for Keith Haddock Promotions Limited. She has six months' service. Keith can be a difficult boss and is particularly concerned about timekeeping. Amanda arrives late for work for the third day in a row due to a delayed train service beyond her control. In a fit of temper Keith says 'It's the last straw. I'm sacking you with immediate effect for gross misconduct – collect your things and go!' Keith refuses to pay Amanda her one month's contractual notice.

Amanda is advised that although the poor timekeeping is deeply frustrating for Keith, it is, at worst, ordinary misconduct for which Amanda should receive a verbal warning. The conduct is not serious enough to be gross misconduct warranting immediate termination of the contract. Amanda applies to an employment tribunal claiming wrongful dismissal. That is, a claim for money she should have received for the contractual period of notice (one month) and accrued holiday entitlement up to the end of the notice period. Amanda's claim is successful.

THE EMPLOYEE RESIGNS

If the employer acts in such a way as to breach a fundamental term of the contract (for example, by failing to pay due wages or salary) they will be acting in repudiatory breach of the contract of employment. The employee then has a choice. He can continue with the contract and waive the right to take action for the repudiatory breach. Conversely, the employee may resign and sue the employer for breach of contract as if he had been dismissed.

The employee resigns in breach of contract

Typically, the situation is this: under the employment contract the employee is obliged to provide notice of his intended resignation from his position with the employer. The required notice may be one week, one month, six months, or more, depending on the nature and wording of the contract. For one reason or another, usually because the employee has a better job offer to go to, the employee fails or refuses to give the employer the required period of notice under the contract. This failure is a breach of contract on the part of the employee. The employer may, in theory, bring an action for damages against the employee. The employer would have to bring his action before the High Court, since he is not entitled to issue proceedings against an employee in an employment tribunal.

In most cases it is not in the employer's best interests to sue the errant employee. Working out what loss the employer has suffered as a result of the employee's breach can be difficult. Certainly, the employer cannot restrain the employee from leaving inside the notice period, since to allow such a legal remedy would be tantamount to slavery and unsupportable on the grounds of public policy. What then, if anything, can an employer do against the employee?

The answer is that only in a limited number of cases, with exceptional facts, will the courts be willing to prevent an employee from leaving an employer in breach of contract. Such cases would be where the employee is of significant importance to the employer, such as the editor of a national newspaper. Even then, no court order will demand that the employee works out the period of notice. Instead the employee is put on what is called 'garden leave'. That is, he is relieved of all duties and paid his salary at the normal interval for the duration of the notice period he should have given under the contract. In return, for that period he is restrained from taking up employment elsewhere.

THE EMPLOYEE IS DISMISSED WITH PAY IN LIEU OF NOTICE

There are many occasions where the employee is dismissed by the employer and instead of being asked to work out the statutory or contractual period of notice he is paid 'in lieu' of notice; i.e. receiving an equivalent sum of money to that which he would have earned had he worked out the period of notice.

Where this occurs the general principle is that the employee will have no claim for wrongful dismissal. This is because the courts will view the payment in lieu as damages for wrongful dismissal, thus effectively taking away from the employee a right of action. It is important that the employee is put in the same financial position as he would have been in if notice had been given. For example, if he had a company car for personal use, he should be compensated for loss of that car during what would have been the notice period (*see* Quantifying damages, pages 349–51).

Two important aspects of this situation should be noted. First, the employer has an absolute right to pay in lieu of notice, whether or not this right is expressed in any way within the contract of employment. The second point is the logical reverse; no employee has the right to demand to work his period of notice. The reason the courts adopt this approach is an unwillingness, for obvious reasons, to force an employer or employee to work for or with one another.

Since pay in lieu of notice is regarded as damages for breach of contract, impliedly, the employee should receive payment for the notice period net. That is, receive the same amount as they would have received had they worked that period. However, it is commonplace for employees to be paid gross in lieu of notice. Such amounts may, depending on the wording of the contract itself and the custom and practice of the employer, be liable to tax and National Insurance as earnings. Generally, there is great uncertainty as to the taxability of such payments and the employee should take as much care as the employer to ensure that liability is met or lawfully avoided. In any event, any damages are taxable to the extent that they exceed £30,000.

Discretionary clauses

There is an important distinction between non-discretionary and discretionary payment in lieu of notice (PILON) clauses. An example of a non-discretionary PILON clause is where the clause says that 'in the event of termination, the employee *would* be entitled, other than in the case of gross misconduct, to a period of notice or an equivalent payment in lieu'. If the employee is dismissed without notice, and without any compensation, he will be able to sue for the full amount of the payment in lieu of notice. This is because the clause will be interpreted by the courts as being non-discretionary (i.e. the employer has no choice but to pay it). Also, the employer will not be able to argue that the employee could have mitigated his loss, so as to reduce the amount that he can claim – i.e. by getting earnings from another job during the notice period.

Where the PILON clause is discretionary, the situation is different.

The employment contract said that 'the employer may make a payment in lieu of notice to the employee'. The court decided that the clause was discretionary and therefore the employee was under a duty to mitigate his loss.

Cerberus *v* Rowley (2001).

If the PILON clause is discretionary ('may') then an employer who wants to dismiss an employee assuming there is no gross misconduct has three choices:

- give notice and allow the employee to work out that notice; or
- pay money in lieu of notice (i.e. under the PILON clause); or
- do nothing. This will put the employer in breach of contract and will result in the employee suing. The employer can then reduce his liability by arguing that the employee should mitigate his loss during the notice period. In practice, most employees will have to mitigate their loss.

It should be noted that an employer who adopts the third option will be in breach of contract and accordingly will not be able to enforce any restrictive covenants or other post-termination provisions. (*See further* page 351.)

WRONGFUL DISMISSAL AND RESTRICTIVE COVENANTS

The employee's contract of employment may contain restrictive covenants. He must comply with these in the event of termination of the contract of employment.

Examples of restrictive covenants are:

- not to work for a competitor of the employer within a specified period of time (usually six months to one year);
- not to work for a competitor of the employer within a

defined geographical area (usually linked to the time period above);

- not to solicit clients, or potential clients, of the employer for a specified period of time after termination of the contract;
- not to entice away from the employer existing members of staff for a specified period of time after termination of the contract.

Other similar restraints may be agreed under contract. Chapter 41 deals with this issue in more detail. Should the employer wrongfully terminate the contract of employment, there will be a question mark over his ability to enforce such conditions against the employee. The principle applied by the courts is that they will not support a wrongdoer, in this case the employer, in respect of other contract terms and conditions.

TIME LIMITS

Wrongful dismissal is a claim for breach of contract and the normal time limits for bringing a claim based on a contract will apply. All claims in the county court and High Court must be brought within six years of the breach of contract.

Recently, as already mentioned, the jurisdiction to hear breach of contract claims, including those for wrongful dismissal, has been extended to employment tribunals. They may now hear claims where the amount in dispute between the parties is less than £25,000. The employee must present his claim to the tribunal within three months from the effective date of termination. Where there is no such date, time will run from the last day upon which the employee worked in employment for that employer. Only in exceptional circumstances will the time limit of three months be extended.

The courts will only extend the time to submit a defence if evidence is presented which shows that in all the circumstances of the case it was not reasonably practicable for the employee to present his claim in time. Breach of contract claims may only be made to an employment tribunal where the employee's employment has terminated. Existing employees must therefore make such a claim to the county or High Court.

If the employee brings a claim in the employment tribunal for unfair dismissal or some other right resulting from the termination, the employer may argue that he should not have the right subsequently to sue for wrongful dismissal in the civil courts when he should have brought the claim together with his other employment claims in the employment tribunal.

SETTLING A CLAIM FOR WRONGFUL DISMISSAL

The employer may admit wrongful dismissal and wish to settle the dispute with the employee rather than go to court. In respect of an action that may be taken in the county court or High Court, the law provides that the parties can reach an agreement not to proceed to court provided that the employee receives 'valuable consideration'. 'Valuable consideration' is some benefit (usually financial but not always) that is granted to the employee by the employer in return for the case being dropped. The complicating factor is the emergence of employment tribunals in respect of wrongful dismissal claims.

WRONGFUL DISMISSAL AND UNFAIR DISMISSAL – A SIMULTANEOUS ACTION

In theory, provided the employee is in no way excluded from bringing either action, he may bring claims for unfair dismissal and wrongful dismissal at the same time. This can now happen in two ways:

1 both actions are brought before an employment tribunal;
2 an action for unfair dismissal is brought before a tribunal and/or additional action for wrongful dismissal before either the county court or High Court.

If both actions are before a tribunal, the facts relating to each claim will be heard at the same time and a decision will be made by the tribunal on each in a single judgment.

Where the wrongful dismissal claim is brought before the county court or High Court it is usual for the employer to request that the tribunal proceedings are stayed (put on hold) until the outcome of the wrongful dismissal action. Such a request will normally be granted. The reason for staying the tribunal action is because it is most commonly the least important financially of the two claims. However, this may be less true today when employment tribunal claims can exceed £50,000.

It is a principle of law that the employee will not be entitled to recover twice for the same loss. Any award made in a tribunal may be taken into account by the county court or High Court and vice versa.

QUANTIFYING DAMAGES

Generally, the employee is entitled to damages that equal the amount of wages or salary that he would have earned if the employer had not prematurely terminated the contract of employment. Additionally, the employee may claim for any benefits in kind that would have been received during the notice period had it been worked.

The period of time over which these entitlements are

assessed is from the point of wrongful termination to when the contract may have been lawfully terminated by the employer. In most cases this will be no more (and no less) than the period of notice that should have been given to the employee. In assessing the loss which is recoverable, the courts will consider two factors:

1 the employee must have been contractually entitled to the wage, salary or benefit in kind;
2 the period over which these amounts were due must be ascertainable. (In most cases the notice period is self-evident or the court will have little difficulty in implying a reasonable notice period over which to make the calculation.)

Wages and salary

The amount of basic salary, whether expressly stated in the contract or included by implication, will be recoverable. The most common and reliable method of calculating the amount of basic salary over the period of notice is to assess the net salary over the relevant period. This sum should then be 'grossed-up'. The employee should then receive the amount remaining after tax and National Insurance liabilities have been deducted from the grossed-up sum. In many cases this will amount to the net sum payable over the period. Employees should be aware that taxation is likely to affect the amount of money received by order of the court. In addition, social security contributions received by the employee over the relevant period will be deducted from the amount recoverable.

Additional amounts

An employee may customarily, or under contract, be in receipt of payments over and above that of basic salary. Such amounts include:

- commission;
- profit-related pay;
- bonus entitlement;
- gratuities (i.e. tips).

The court will look at the following to work out how much the employee should receive:

- the wording of the contract;
- oral agreement;
- past performance;
- custom and practice.

In looking at commission, profit-related pay and bonus payments, the court will not necessarily assume that these would be payable in the amounts paid up to the date of dismissal. It may be possible for the employer to show that business was poor post-dismissal and that would have affected the amounts payable under such provisions – the court will listen to this evidence. However, in most cases, the courts will look at past payments and apply an average amount payable over the relevant notice period.

Discretionary bonus payments

Depending on the wording of the contract of employment, many bonus payments are discretionary by nature. If they are discretionary they will not be regarded as a contractual entitlement and are, therefore, not recoverable by the employee. They may however be recoverable if they have become contractual by custom and practice. They may also be recoverable under a discrimination claim.

Holiday pay

Holiday pay is another typical additional amount recoverable in wrongful dismissal actions. The amount payable will depend on the terms of the contract and any statutory entitlement. The minimum statutory entitlement is 20 days and any contractual term which provides for a lesser period is unlawful. Generally, then, the annual entitlement will be 20 days unless the contract provides for a longer period. To calculate the entitlement the employee should divide the annual entitlement by 52 (representing the weeks in one year). This figure is then the rate of weekly accrual. This weekly figure should be multiplied by the number of weeks in the holiday year up to and including the date upon which the contract would have ended had due notice been issued. Finally, any holiday taken in that holiday year should be deducted, leaving the amount recoverable under the wrongful dismissal action. This amount is recoverable net since it is a right derived under contract.

Benefits in kind

These will include:

- company car;
- accommodation;
- pension contributions;
- medical insurance;
- interest-free, or low-rate, loans while in employment.

The basis of calculating all these amounts is the net value to the employee for the duration of the notice period.

Other losses

A claim for damages may include an amount to compensate the employee as a result of the employer failing to follow a contractual disciplinary procedure. The employee will be able to claim damages for the time it would have taken the employer to go through the procedure (*see* Chapter 37).

Losses not recoverable

Generally, damages for injury to feelings, mental stress and anxiety may not be claimed in breach of contract actions. Recent case law would suggest that such losses are also not recoverable in unfair dismissal actions. The House of Lords has also stated that they would not normally allow a complainant to recover loss of earnings over and above the notice period in a wrongful dismissal claim. The reason for this is that Parliament has only given employees with more than one year's service the right to claim unfair dismissal and long-term loss of earnings caused by dismissal. The court will not effectively allow unfair dismissal losses to be claimed in the form of a wrongful dismissal claim.

Imran's contract of employment was terminated after nine months' service. His employer pays him two weeks' notice. He does not have one year's qualifying service to bring an unfair dismissal claim. However, he believes that the employer sacked him at that time to avoid his acquiring the necessary service. He also believes the manner of dismissal was unduly harsh. He claims loss of earnings from the dismissal until he finds new employment and injury to feelings for the manner of dismissal. His claim will largely fail and is misconceived. He is not entitled to the loss of earnings nor to compensation for injury to feelings. However, he is entitled to the balance of his notice monies.

Compensation for the manner of dismissal has no place in damages awarded in wrongful dismissal actions. However, in very limited circumstances, damages for loss of reputation (stigma damages) may be recoverable.

Perhaps the only other exception to this strict rule is that of an apprentice under a contract of apprenticeship (usually two years) who is wrongfully dismissed, and who may recover a sum of damages to reflect the loss of future prospects, having been denied the opportunity of completing his apprenticeship contract. The amount will be based on the cost of retraining elsewhere.

MITIGATION

As discussed in Chapter 34 in relation to the compensatory award for unfair dismissal, the employee will be under a general duty to mitigate his loss. This includes actively looking for alternative employment and not unreasonably refusing such employment should the opportunity arise. The onus of proving the employee has failed to mitigate his loss is on the employer. The duty to mitigate *only* begins once the contract has been breached by the employer – even where the employer has indicated in advance that he will dismiss the employee.

Moreover, the obligation to take reasonable alternative employment is more flexible towards the employee than

at first it may appear. For example, just because an alternative job offers a similar wage or salary, this may not make it a suitable alternative position. The status and responsibility offered by the new position are matters the employee is entitled to take into account when making his decision to accept or reject the offer. On the other hand, to hold out for exactly the same salary, status and responsibility in difficult economic conditions may be regarded as a failure to make a reasonable effort to mitigate loss.

If a new position is secured, the employee will have mitigated his loss. This could be in full or in part. The new job may be lower paid. As a general rule the amount earned by the employee in his new job will be taken into account by the court and deducted from the total of the wrongful dismissal claim. The period between dismissal and new employment will remain recoverable, as will any shortfall in wage or salary between the old and new job for the duration of the notice period.

However, if the employer terminates the contract by making a payment in lieu of notice under an express clause of the contract which permits this, then the employer must pay the relevant amount in full, without any deduction for mitigation. This is because the employer has contractually promised the payment regardless of mitigation. However, see page 348 for where the payment in lieu of notice clause is discretionary.

UNFAIR DISMISSAL COMPENSATION

Rarely is the basic award for unfair dismissal deducted from the damages awarded for wrongful dismissal. The compensatory award is a different matter. Amounts paid under a compensatory award may be deducted in so far as they correspond to heads of damages in the wrongful dismissal claim. This would mean that a certain proportion of the amount awarded for loss of earnings or additional payment at tribunal may reduce the value of the wrongful dismissal claim. In practice, this calculation is not simple. Suffice it to say in this context, that employees should be aware of a possible reduction in their damages as a result of this reasoning.

ACCELERATED RECEIPT

This is not applicable in the great majority of wrongful dismissal actions, for the simple reason that most people's entitlement to notice, whether contractual or statutory, is short. It may apply to those employees who are entitled to a period of notice of say one or two years, where the court makes its decision and awards damages before the expiry of the period of notice. In most cases the leaving date is some time after the expiry of the last day of notice had it been given.

Accelerated receipt is a mechanism used by the court to reduce an amount of damages awarded. It takes into account the possibility of occurrences that might affect employment until the end of the stated period of notice such as death, medical incapacity or the employee deciding to resign before the unexpired portion of the notice period. It also takes into account that the employee will be receiving a proportion of wages as damages, up front. Investment of these funds will in itself create some wealth that would not have been possible had the contract been worked by the employee. A normal rate of reduction is between 2 and 6 per cent.

INJUNCTIVE ACTION

There may be occasions when the employee is not satisfied with claiming damages for wrongful dismissal but wishes to prevent the employer from dismissing him. A possible remedy would be an application to the court for an injunction to restrain the employer from acting as he intended.

The general rule is that injunctions for such matters are granted only in exceptional cases. The reason for this is the courts' reluctance to compel an employer to retain an employee, since to do so may result in conflict between the two parties and may adversely affect the employer's business. As stated earlier in this section, an injunction sought by the employer to restrain the employee from leaving inside the notice period is a similarly rare occurrence but for different reasons.

The exception to the general rule against granting an employee an injunction is where it can be manifestly proven that the relationship of trust and confidence between the parties is intact and that damages in themselves would be an inadequate remedy. In addition, the courts will give consideration to the size and resources of the employer. Large organizations and local authorities, for example, are more likely targets for a successful application for an injunction by an employee who has been wrongfully dismissed.

The test applied by the court to an injunction application is known as the 'balance of convenience'. The court will look at:

- the likelihood of success by the employee at full trial;
- the adequacy of damages as a remedy;
- whether there is an issue of 'real significance' at stake?;
- the impact of the injunction, if granted, on the employer's business.

To reiterate, in the vast majority of cases, the employee will stand little or no chance of persuading a court to grant an injunction restraining the employer from dismissing him wrongfully. Most claims are for damages for breach of contract. Therefore, there can be little doubt that damages will be considered an adequate remedy.

36

Redundancy

THE GENERAL SCHEME

In broad terms, the statutory redundancy payment scheme entitles any employee with two years' service, who is dismissed for redundancy, to a lump sum tax free. The amount of the lump sum is calculated according to the employee's age, length of service and gross weekly wage. This is the redundancy payment scheme.

There is also the issue of whether a redundancy constituted an unfair dismissal. There are four situations in which a redundancy may give rise to an unfair dismissal claim:

1 When the redundancy is a sham.
2 When the employee is unfairly selected for redundancy. Normally, the last-in-first-out principle applies and an employer requires a good reason to depart from it.
3 When any available suitable alternative employment is not offered (or it is offered but not for the statutory four-week fixed trial period).
4 Where there has been no or no adequate consultation.

THE DEFINITION

The redundancy situation must exist on its facts. It must not be used as a convenient vehicle for removing an employee with whom the employer is, for some reason, dissatisfied. The statutory definition provides that the dismissal must be attributable wholly, or mainly, to the fact that:

1 the employer has ceased, or intends to cease, to carry on the business for the purposes for which the employee was employed, or has ceased, or intends to cease, to carry on that business in the place where the employee was employed; and/or
2 the requirements of the business for the employee to carry out work of a particular kind in the place they were employed have ceased or diminished, or are expected to cease or diminish.

Typically there are three scenarios which give rise to a redundancy situation:

1 the employer closes his business or the part of his business in which the employee works;
2 due to an economic downturn in demand, the employee is no longer or will be no longer gainfully employed in his present position;
3 due to a business reorganization for economic and/or reasons of efficiency the employee's job has gone or been significantly reduced.

Most redundancy situations will fit into one of the three categories above. When it does, the dismissal for redundancy which follows will in all likelihood be potentially fair. It will only be made unfair if the employer fails to follow the correct procedure for implementing the decision or fails to pay the employee what is rightfully due to him under contract or law. Employees should remember that where they suspect the redundancy situation is bogus, the burden of proving that a redundancy situation actually exists on its facts rests with the employer, if challenged.

At that place of work

To be within the definition, the redundancy situation must apply to the employee at his place of work. One problem which can occur is where the employee selected for redundancy is subject to a mobility clause within his contract of employment. That is, the contract has a term incorporated into it either expressly or impliedly (through custom and practice) that in the event of there being no work at one of the employer's sites, he may demand that the employee moves to another where there is a plentiful supply of similar work.

The test for determining the place of work is primarily a factual one, although the employee's contractual terms may provide evidence of the place of work. Thus, if an employee has, as a matter of fact, worked in only one location, then the existence of a contractual mobility clause enabling the employer to move him to another site does not change the place of work. Therefore, the employer cannot avoid paying the statutory redundancy payment by relying on a mobility clause. In one case, the employee claimed that the employer should have utilized the mobility clause and moved the redundant staff to another location. However, the tribunal decided that the mobility clause should not be taken into account when considering whether a person has been made redundant at a particular place of work.

TIME OFF

Assuming the redundancy is fair and has been fairly implemented, any employee given notice of termination on the ground of redundancy, is entitled to reasonable time off during the notice period to look for other work or make arrangements for necessary training.

What is 'reasonable' is largely a matter of common sense and is deliberately not more precisely defined in law. The time off should be paid by the employer. The right is dependent upon the employee having two years' continuous service at the date upon which the dismissal notice is due to expire.

Most time off taken by employees is to attend interviews at the offices of prospective employers or with recruitment or employment agents. Even if the employee is attending two or three interviews per week, this number of appointments is likely to be regarded as reasonable if challenged by the employer. The employer has no right to demand proof of the appointments but it follows that to refuse to comply with a request may be seen as obstructive and could be unhelpful to the employee's claim that time off to attend such interviews is reasonable.

THE REDUNDANCY PAYMENT

Where a redundancy situation exists on its facts, the employee will be entitled to a redundancy payment. This entitlement remains whether or not the employee is fortunate enough to have secured alternative work with another employer. There are conditions to the payment:

- the individual must be an employee (not self-employed or a casual worker – *see* Chapter 31);
- the individual must have been employed for a continuous period with that employer of not less than two years;
- the employee must have been dismissed;
- the dismissal must be by reason of genuine redundancy.

Continuous employment (entitlement to statutory payment)

One of the conditions of entitlement to a redundancy payment is that the individual must have worked for the employer for a continuous period of not less than two years. Holiday leave and time off sick will not break the time that counts towards the continuous period of two years. The employee must have done some work for the employer during any week in which they were under contract of employment.

Put another way, any break in employment of more than seven days to undertake work elsewhere, or to do no work at all by choice, may break continuity of service. Much depends on the facts of any particular case and what has been agreed between the parties. The transfer of ownership of a business from one employer to another will not break continuity.

The relevant date for the purpose of calculating the continuous period of two years will be:

1 where the employee is given notice, the date upon which that notice expires;
2 where no notice is given, the date upon which termination takes effect;
3 where the employee is paid in lieu of notice either:
   (a) the last day of work, where the notice is paid in a lump sum; or
   (b) the date on which notice expires where the employee receives normal payments but is relieved of all duties for the duration of the notice period;
4 where the employee works under a fixed-term contract, the date upon which that contract expires.

It should be noted for those employees dismissed and having just under two years' service that they are permitted in law to add to the end of the relevant termination date a period of one week. This represents the statutory minimum period of notice. If, in adding the one week, the employee then has two years' continuous service, he may claim his statutory redundancy payment.

The requirement of dismissal

The employee must have been dismissed. This may be deemed to have occurred in the following circumstances:

- the employer terminates the contract by issuing notice to the employee;
- the employer terminates the contract but does so summarily, without notice;
- the employee works under a fixed-term contract and that contract expires without being renewed;
- the employee terminates the contract with or without notice by reason of the employer's conduct (constructive dismissal situations).

Are you within the redundancy-payments legislation?

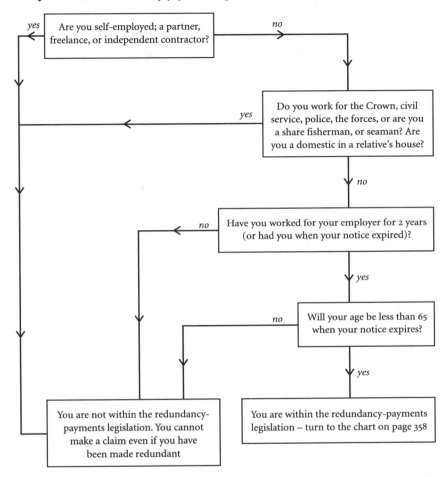

There will be *no* dismissal and therefore no entitlement to statutory redundancy payment where:

- the employee's fixed-term contract is renewed;
- the employee is issued with a new contract of employment without there either being a break in service, or if there is a break, for a period of less than four weeks;
- the employee is offered a different job with the same, or an associated employer, and accepts the new position;
- the employee has resigned *before* notice of termination for redundancy has been issued to him by the employer.

With regard to the last point, it should be distinguished from the situation (as often happens) where the employer has issued notice of termination for redundancy and during that period of notice the employee leaves prematurely to take up alternative work. In these circumstances, the employee in question will normally remain entitled to statutory redundancy pay. However, if the employer objects to the employee's premature departure and serves on the employee a written request not to leave early, warning him that if he does so the employer will contest any liability to make a redundancy payment, he may lose his right to such payment. If the employer withholds the redundancy payment in these circumstances, the employee may apply to an employment tribunal. The tribunal will consider whether the employee's action in leaving prematurely was reasonable or unreasonable in the circumstances. An employee will not be entitled to any payment in lieu of notice for a period in which they were not ready, willing and able to work.

John owns an ornamental plant centre and is experiencing trading difficulties. He specializes in palm trees and it has been a particularly wet summer. The public, it would seem, do not want to buy his stock of exotic trees. Claire is 26 years old, earns £250 a week and has been working for John for six years. She is one of only three staff at the centre who all do similar work and have similar skills, qualifications and experience. Out of the three staff, Claire has been working for John for the shortest period of time.

John is aware that if business does not get better soon he will have to make one of his staff redundant. He is aware of the requirement for consultation and at a meeting with all his staff informs them that a redundancy in the future may be a possibility.

Claire is alarmed at this news. She panics, looks for another job the next day and accepts an offer of employment with a local florist on lower pay. She tenders her resignation to John in writing stating she is willing to work one week's notice and that she looks forward to receiving her statutory redundancy pay. John seeks legal advice.

Claire is not entitled to statutory redundancy pay. The reason being she was not dismissed for redundancy and resigned before John issued formal notice of redundancy. John had only just begun the consultation process. If Claire had secured alternative employment after formal notice of redundancy had been issued, she would have been entitled to resign within the notice period and statutory redundancy pay would have been payable had John not objected to her premature departure. Given her age, gross weekly wage and length of service her redundancy entitlement would have been as follows.

5 × £240 (maximum weekly wage) = £1,200 tax free
Claire's impatience cost her dearly.

LAY-OFF AND SHORT-TIME WORKING

A redundancy situation in law can arise in situations of lay-off or short-time working imposed by the employer. The definitions of each are, therefore, important. An employee is deemed laid-off when the employer fails to provide work for the employee during a week under which a contract of employment is in existence. The employee must be available for work during such time. Short-time is where an employee receives less than half a week's work and pay during any week in which a contract of employment exists. Where these situations exist, subject to conditions, the employee may serve written notice on the employer for redundancy payment. The employee must have been:

- laid-off or kept on short-time for four or more consecutive weeks; or
- laid-off or kept on short-time for six weeks or more within a total of 13 weeks, and not more than three of those six weeks were consecutive.

The employee must serve notice within four weeks of the last day of lay-off or short-time working to make his claim. The employer may counter-claim where there is a reasonable expectation that within four weeks of the notice being served by the employee, full-time working will resume and continue for at least 13 weeks. The employer must serve this counter-notice in writing on the employee within seven days of the employee's original notice.

If the employee disagrees with the reasonable expectation of work resuming made by the employer, he may apply to the employment tribunal to decide the matter. He should make the application without delay. The employee must first terminate his contract of employment by giving contractual or statutory notice (one week) to the employer – whichever is the greater.

No claim can be made for any week in which the lay-off or short-time working was as a result of employee's industrial action against the employer or due to the employer's imposed lock-out for similar reasons.

EXCLUDED EMPLOYEES

The following employees cannot claim a redundancy payment:

1 employees who have reached, or are over, the *normal age of retirement* for their employers. Or, where there is no express or implied normal retirement age, employees who have exceeded the age of 65 years (this applies to both men and women);

2 *share fishermen*;

3 civil servants and other *public employees*;

4 employees who have accepted an offer from the employer of a *suitable alternative job* to the one from which they were made redundant;

5 employees who have *unreasonably refused to accept an offer*, by their employer, of a suitable alternative job;

6 employees who initially accept alternative work as suitable, commence such work under a statutory four-week trial period and *unreasonably resign* their position during that trial period;

7 employees who, during the period of notice of termination for redundancy, are *dismissed for misconduct* (given the short periods of notice that typically apply, most of these situations in practice involve the employee having committed an act of gross misconduct);

8 employees who, working under a fixed-term contract of employment, have agreed in writing with the employer, prior to commencement of work of two years or more under that contract, to *exclude their right to claim* a statutory payment in the event of a redundancy situation. However, the waiver clause will only be valid where it was signed before 1 October 2002. Under the Fixed-term Employees (Prevention of Less Favourable Treatment) Regulations 2002, any

waivers inserted into contracts agreed, renewed or extended after 1 October 2002 will not be valid and fixed-term employees will have a right to statutory redundancy payments if they have been continuously employed for two years or more;

9 certain groups of employees affected by the operation of an *exemption order* as imposed by the government. This order may be made in respect of an employer and excludes them from liability for making statutory redundancy payments, where contractual terms are more advantageous to their employees.

TIME LIMIT FOR MAKING A CLAIM

If the employee believes that he is redundant and has made a claim to that effect in writing to his employer, but the employer refuses or fails to make due payment, the employee may apply to an employment tribunal to decide the matter and order payment.

The application to the tribunal must be made within six months less one day from the original claim to the employer or from when the employer has clearly refused to comply with the request. Where the employee is dismissed without payment, the employee must bring his claim within six months less one day from the date of termination.

THE PAYMENT

The amount the employee receives as his statutory redundancy entitlement is dependent upon his age, length of service and gross weekly wage (*see* Table 36.1, page 358). The amount payable is based on the following method of calculation:

1 one and a half week's pay for each complete year of employment during which the employee was aged 41 years or over but was less than 65 years of age (or under the employer's normal retirement age where less than 65 years);

2 one week's pay for each complete year of employment during which the employee was aged 22–40 inclusive;

3 half a week's pay for each complete year of employment in which the employee was aged 18–21 inclusive;

4 service before the employee's eighteenth birthday will not count.

Calculation is made by working backwards from the effective date of termination to take into account those years of service which provide the greater entitlement. The calculation of 'a week's wage' is described in Chapter 32. The amount is subject to a statutory ceiling of £260 per week (as at 1 April 2003). The maximum period of service taken into account is 20 years. *The maximum payment is therefore currently £7,800.* The ceiling figure of £260 per week is subject to annual review.

In the case of an employee being made redundant in their sixty-fourth year of age, the amount payable will fall to be reduced by one-twelfth for every complete month by which their age exceeds 64 years. This incremental reduction does not apply where the employer's normal retirement age is less than 65 years. Statutory redundancy pay is not subject to tax or National Insurance deductions.

WRITTEN STATEMENT

The employee is entitled to receive from the employer a written statement as to how the redundancy payment has been calculated. There are two penalties for the employer's failure depending on the circumstances:

1 where the employer fails to supply the statement he may be fined up to £200;

2 where the employee has, in writing, requested a statement and the employer has failed to comply, he is liable to be fined up to £1,000.

These awards may be made by an employment tribunal upon application by the employee.

SUITABLE ALTERNATIVE EMPLOYMENT

The employer may be in a position to offer the redundant employee an alternative job within the business. If the alternative on offer is 'suitable', the employer can avoid having to make a redundancy payment. If the alternative job is suitable, it may not be unreasonably refused by the employee.

Two problem areas emerge:

1 when is an alternative job offer *suitable*?

2 what will be considered an *unreasonable* refusal?

When presenting the alternative job to the employee, the employer is under an obligation to clearly identify the new position and to set out the differences between it and the original job which is redundant. Only when this has been done will the employee be in a position to make a reasoned decision. The offer of the new role must be made before the existing contract of employment comes to an end and must take effect within four weeks of the expiry of the original contract. The employee is entitled to turn down the new job and state the reasons why he believes the position is unsuitable.

There may be many reasons for unsuitability such as:

- it involves an inconvenient geographical relocation;
- it involves greater travelling time to and from work;
- terms and conditions interfere with unavoidable or important family commitments;
- it requires the employee to accept terms and conditions (e.g. hours, pay, holiday entitlement) which are less advantageous than the redundant position;

Service (years) Age (years)	2	3	4	5	6	7	8	9	10	11	12	13	14	15	16	17	18	19	20
20	1	1	1	1															
21	1	1.5	1.5	1.5	1.5														
22	1	1.5	2	2	2	2													
23	1.5	2	2.5	3	3	3													
24	2	2.5	3	3.5	4	4	4	4											
25	2	3	3.5	4	4.5	5	5	5	5										
26	2	3	4	4.5	5	5.5	6	6	6	6									
27	2	3	4	5	5.5	6	6.5	7	7	7	7								
28	2	3	4	5	6	6.5	7	7.5	8	8	8	8							
29	2	3	4	5	6	7	7.5	8	8.5	9	9	9	9						
30	2	3	4	5	6	7	8	8.5	9	9.5	10	10	10	10					
31	2	3	4	5	6	7	8	9	9.5	10	10.5	11	11	11	11				
32	2	3	4	5	6	7	8	9	10	10.5	11	11.5	12	12	12	12			
33	2	3	4	5	6	7	8	9	10	11	11.5	12	12.5	13	13	13	13		
34	2	3	4	5	6	7	8	9	10	11	12	12.5	13	13.5	14	14	14	14	
35	2	3	4	5	6	7	8	9	10	11	12	13	13.5	14	14.5	15	15	15	16
36	2	3	4	5	6	7	8	9	10	11	12	13	14	14.5	15	15.5	16	16	16
37	2	3	4	5	6	7	8	9	10	11	12	13	14	15	15.5	16	16.5	17	17
38	2	3	4	5	6	7	8	9	10	11	12	13	14	15	16	16.5	17	17.5	18
39	2	3	4	5	6	7	8	9	10	11	12	13	14	15	16	17	17.5	18	18.5
40	2	3	4	5	6	7	8	9	10	11	12	13	14	15	16	17	18	18.5	19
41	2	3	4	5	6	7	8	9	10	11	12	13	14	15	16	17	18	19	19.5
42	2.5	3.5	4.5	5.5	6.5	7.5	8.5	9.5	10.5	11.5	12.5	13.5	14.5	15.5	16.5	17.5	18.5	19.5	20.5
43	3	4	5	6	7	8	9	10	11	12	13	14	15	16	17	18	19	20	21
44	3	4.5	5.5	6.5	7.5	8.5	9.5	10.5	11.5	12.5	13.5	14.5	15.5	16.5	17.5	18.5	19.5	20.5	21.5
45	3	4.5	6	7	8	9	10	11	12	13	14	15	16	17	18	19	20	21	22
46	3	4.5	6	7.5	8.5	9.5	10.5	11.5	12.5	13.5	14.5	15.5	16.5	17.5	18.5	19.5	20.5	21.5	22.5
47	3	4.5	6	7.5	9	10	11	12	13	14	15	16	17	18	19	20	21	22	23
48	3	4.5	6	7.5	9	10.5	11.5	12.5	13.5	14.5	15.5	16.5	17.5	18.5	19.5	20.5	21.5	22.5	23.5
49	3	4.5	6	7.5	9	10.5	12	13	14	15	16	17	18	19	20	21	22	23	24
50	3	4.5	6	7.5	9	10.5	12	13.5	14.5	15.5	16.5	17.5	18.5	19.5	20.5	21.5	22.5	23.5	24.5
51	3	4.5	6	7.5	9	10.5	12	13.5	15	16	17	18	19	20	21	22	23	24	25
52	3	4.5	6	7.5	9	10.5	12	13.5	15	16.5	17.5	18.5	19.5	20.5	21.5	22.5	23.5	24.5	25.5
53	3	4.5	6	7.5	9	10.5	12	13.5	15	16.5	18	19	20	21	22	23	24	25	26
54	3	4.5	6	7.5	9	10.5	12	13.5	15	16.5	18	19.5	20.5	21.5	22.5	23.5	24.5	25.5	26.5
55	3	4.5	6	7.5	9	10.5	12	13.5	15	16.5	18	19.5	21	22	23	24	25	26	27
56	3	4.5	6	7.5	9	10.5	12	13.5	15	16.5	18	19.5	21	22.5	23.5	24.5	25.5	26.5	27.5
57	3	4¼	6	7.5	9	10.5	12	13.5	15	16.5	18	19.5	21	22.5	24	25	26	27	28
58	3	4.5	6	7.5	9	10.5	12	13.5	15	16.5	18	19.5	21	22.5	24	25.5	26.5	27.5	28.5
59	3	4.5	6	7.5	9	10.5	12	13.5	15	16.5	18	19.5	21	22.5	24	25.5	27	28	29
60	3	4.5	6	7.5	9	10.5	12	13.5	15	16.5	18	19.5	21	22.5	24	25.5	27	28.5	29.5
61	3	4.5	6	7.5	9	10.5	12	13.5	15	16.5	18	19.5	21	22.5	24	25.5	27	28.5	30
62	3	4.5	6	7.5	9	10.5	12	13.5	15	16.5	18	19.5	21	22.5	24	25.5	27	28.5	30
63	3	4.5	6	7.5	9	10.5	12	13.5	15	16.5	18	19.5	21	22.5	24	25.5	27	28.5	30
64	3	4.5	6	7.5	9	10.5	12	13.5	15	16.5	18.5	19.5	21	22.5	24	25.5	27	28.5	30

Table 36.1. Calculator for statutory redundancy entitlement. (The figures represent the numbers of weeks' pay to which the employee is entitled.)

- it does not carry the level of status and responsibility which the employee enjoyed in his previous position;
- it requires considerable re-training.
  (*This list is not intended to be exhaustive.*)

Where reasons for unsuitability are put forward by the employee and they appear reasonable in the circumstances, a tribunal will be reluctant to force the employee to accept the alternative job offer. However, merely stating the offer is unsuitable, without further supporting reasons, is unlikely to be acceptable. It follows that sound reasons for declining the job offered will allow the employee to be viewed as reasonably refusing the position. Although often borne out of the same facts, the issues of suitability and the reasonableness of refusal are looked at separately by the tribunal should the matter be put before them.

Susan works for Web-site Wonders Limited. Her employer is moving premises to the next town two miles away. Susan is told her job will transfer to the new site in its entirety. Web-site Wonders are not willing to pay Susan redundancy pay since they believe that although her job has ceased to exist at the old site, they are able to offer a suitable alternative at the new site on the same terms and conditions of employment.

Susan has an elderly mother who depends on her to prepare and cook a meal at lunchtime. The location of the new site would not allow Susan to visit her mother at lunchtimes in the future since she cannot drive and public transport is irregular. Susan claims her redundancy pay and the tribunal accepts that, in light of her caring responsibilities, the employment offered on the new site is not a suitable alternative position to that which was made redundant.

Trial period

Where an employer offers an alternative position and the new role involves a change to the existing terms and conditions of employment or is work of a different nature, the employee is entitled to request a four-week trial period. The four weeks is a statutory period and may be extended by the parties with agreement. Whether four weeks or more the agreement must:

- be in writing;
- be made before the commencement of the trial period;
- specify the date upon which the trial period is to end;
- state clearly the terms and conditions of employment which will apply at the end of the trial period.

There may be three distinct outcomes of the trial period:

1 *Employee accepts the new position.* If the employee is satisfied with the new role and continues after the expiry of the period, he will have accepted the new position. There will be no dismissal in law, no entitlement to redundancy pay or notice and continuity of employment will be preserved.

2 *Job is unsuitable.* At the end of the trial period the employee or employer may decide the role is unsuitable. Reasons for unsuitability must then be put forward. If the employer terminates the contract, the fairness of the dismissal will be assessed at the end of the trial period and not at the end of the original contract.

3 *Employee leaves.* The employee may leave before the expiry of the trial period. In this situation the employee will be treated as having been dismissed on the date upon which their original contract came to an end.

The employee must be able to provide reasons for unsuitability, since failure to do so may be regarded as an unreasonable refusal of alternative work and disentitle them to a redundancy payment. The reason for termination will be regarded as the same reason for which the original contract was terminated; usually redundancy.

CHANGE OF EMPLOYER

If, following the transfer of the business into new ownership, the employer changes, the transferred employees will not be entitled to a statutory redundancy payment just because of the change. This is because a transfer preserves continuity of employment and there will be no dismissal in law. Should the new employer make the employee redundant shortly after transfer of the business, the new employer will be liable to pay the redundancy entitlement for the *whole* of the period of employment with both (or more) employers.

REDUNDANCY AND UNFAIR DISMISSAL

An employee may claim unfair dismissal by reason of redundancy before an employment tribunal provided he has one year's continuous service. Current legislation imposes on an employer a number of obligations when considering dismissal by reason of redundancy:

- employees have the *right to be consulted* prior to the decision to dismiss; and
- the *right not to be unfairly selected* for redundancy.

This section deals with these two issues in turn.

Consultation – union and/or elected employee representatives

Not all employers recognize a trade union for the purposes of collective bargaining. In fact, they are under no general legal obligation to do so, unless a majority of the employees join a union or vote in favour of recognition of the union in a specially organized ballot. Where they do, the employer is under a statutory duty to consult with that union where it is proposed to dismiss 20 or more employees. The consultation must be with the category of workers represented by the union, and must take place within a period of 90 days or less.

Appropriate representatives

If the employer does not recognize a trade union, it must consult with the 'appropriate representatives' of the employees whom the employer is proposing to dismiss. The 'appropriate representatives' may be either:

- employee representatives already elected by the employees (provided that they are deemed to have the authority of the affected employees); or
- employee representatives specifically elected for the purpose of consulting with the employer about the collective redundancies.

Election of employee representatives

The law sets out a number of criteria that must be satisfied in relation to an election of employee representatives. These include ensuring that all affected employees are entitled to vote and that none of the affected employees is unreasonably excluded from standing for election. The voting process should be secret. The employer can determine the number of representatives to be elected (subject to ensuring that there are sufficient representatives to represent the interests of the affected employees) and their term of office (subject to enabling the consultation process to be properly completed). The employer can also decide whether the employees should be represented by a representative for a particular class of employees, or by representatives for the entire group.

Employees who participate in an election of employee representatives are entitled not to be dismissed, or subjected to a detriment, on that ground. In addition, employee representatives and trade union officials are entitled to time off during working hours for training to perform their functions in relation to consultation. Where 'union consultation' is referred to in the rest of this section this should be read as including consultation with employee representatives where appropriate.

The consultation process

The employer must commence its consultation with the union as soon as redundancies are forecast. Consultation must in any event begin:

- where 100 or more redundancies are proposed at one establishment within a 90-day period, at least 90 days before the first of the dismissals takes effect;
- where 20 or more redundancies are proposed, at least 30 days before the first dismissal takes effect.

Furthermore, the employer must disclose in writing to the union representatives the following information:

- the reasons for the proposed redundancies;
- the number and descriptions of employees whom it is proposed to make redundant;
- the total number of employees of any such description employed by the employer at the establishment;
- the proposed method of selection;
- the proposed method of carrying out the dismissals with due regard to any agreed procedure;
- the proposed method of calculating the amount of any non-statutory redundancy payments.

The consultation must involve discussing ways to avoid the dismissals, reducing the number of employees to be dismissed and mitigating the consequences of the dismissals. Such consultation undertaken by the employer must be done so with a view to reaching agreement with the trade union representatives. The employer must consider and reply to any representations made by trade union representatives, giving reasons for any representations rejected.

Complaint to tribunal

Should the union feel the employer has failed to meet these requirements it is entitled to make a complaint on behalf of its members to an employment tribunal. The tribunal is empowered to make a 'protective award' in favour of all employees within the relevant group. The amount of the award is one week's pay for each week of the 'protected period'. The length of the protected period is itself dependent upon how many employees it is proposed to make redundant at any one place of work. If the proposal is to dismiss:

1 100 or more employees = 90 days
2 20 or more employees = 30 days

The maximum protective award for failure to comply with the consultation obligations on collective redundancies is 90 days' pay for each employee. If one employee is awarded a protective award by an employment tribunal, theoretically all employees made redundant at that time also become entitled to such an award (subject to time limits). Finally, where collective redundancies are proposed, an employer must also send written notification in a prescribed form to the Department of Trade and Industry.

Consultation – individual employees

Regardless of whether they are a union member or one of many redundancies, each employee is entitled to be consulted individually *prior* to the decision to dismiss being made by the employer. The purpose of the consultation is for the employer and employee to look at ways of avoiding the dismissal.

The consultation should discuss and explain to the employee the following key issues:

- the economic or business need for the proposed redundancy;
- the selection criteria used;
- the reasons why that individual has been provisionally selected for redundancy;
- suitable alternative employment – if available.

Employees should be advised that the redundancy proposals are not finalized and invited to consider them and make any suggestions or comments they feel appropriate. It follows that such consultation will take time, at least several days and probably a week or more. Consultation does not mean the employer informing the employee that they are redundant and then asking for a response. The consultation must take place *prior* to the decision to implement dismissal by reason of redundancy.

Failure to consult properly or at all will allow the employee to claim unfair dismissal before an employment tribunal.

Selection

Unfair selection for redundancy can lead to an unfair dismissal.

The tribunal will look very carefully at how employees have been selected for redundancy where the selection process appears to depart from the custom and practice of the business or contractual procedures and where there was no special reason for justifying a departure from such arrangements.

Selection for redundancy should be in accordance with agreed procedures where they exist. Where there are no agreed procedures, custom and practice should be followed, which invariably is, '*last in, first out*' (LIFO). The order of priority is therefore:

1 select employees for redundancy by following agreed contractual procedure – written or oral;
2 follow custom and practice (usually last in, first out).

Who is last in?

The correct selection procedure should be identified and followed, together with the necessary consultation process (*see* above). Where LIFO is the criterion for selection, care should be taken in working out which employees have been working for the business for the longest time. The employee is entitled to count the length of continuous employment only (i.e. a single unbroken period of employment). He cannot add together periods of work (e.g. a month here and a couple of months there) where there are breaks between each period. A series of fixed-term contracts could constitute a single unbroken period of employment for the purposes of LIFO.

The employer can choose to select employees for redundancy only from the area or areas of the business where manning cuts are necessary. The employer must not only consider the job descriptions of the employees concerned but also what functions those employees perform in practice.

Special reasons for not following agreed procedure

The employer may wish to deviate from an agreed or customary procedure. To do this he will require special reasons. Cases on 'special reasons' indicate that the following factors may be acceptable:

- skills;
- experience;
- qualifications.

The employer may consider the above factors, both in contemplating what he requires at the time of the decision to dismiss for redundancy and what he reasonably believes will be his requirements in the future. Any criteria used must be objective and verifiable by reference to data such as attendance records, length of service, measurable efficiency and skills audits.

Unfair selection

Finally, employees should be aware that attempts to select them for redundancy based on vague subjective criteria such as quality of work, inter-personal skills or attitude are, on their own, very likely to be regarded as unfair. An employer cannot use redundancy as a 'convenient' method of getting rid of an employee when he is otherwise disenchanted with the employee's performance. Performance problems must be dealt with by using an appropriate disciplinary procedure. Redundancy will stand or fall on its own economic facts and circumstances. The conduct of the employee should never be used as a single reason for selection by the employer. Where an employee feels that this is the real reason behind the bogus redundancy, he should not hesitate to go to the employment tribunal claiming unfair dismissal, having first exhausted all internal avenues of grievance.

37

Disciplinary Practice and Procedure

THE REQUIREMENT

There is a common theme running through UK law that nobody should be punished unjustly for an act or omission which was not their responsibility. Employment law is no exception. To be disciplined for an act of misconduct can have a grave effect on the employee concerned. At best, it acts as a 'blot on the copybook' and, at worst, it could lead to dismissal. It follows that the law requires certain procedures to be closely followed by employers before any disciplinary sanction may reasonably be imposed on the employee concerned. Failure on the part of the employer to follow the correct procedure will allow the employee to claim unfair dismissal before an employment tribunal where he has more than one year's continuous service.

According to ACAS, disciplinary rules and procedures are necessary for promoting fairness and consistency in the treatment of individuals and in the conduct of industrial relations. They also assist an organization to operate effectively. Rules set standards of conduct at work; procedures help to ensure that the standards are adhered to and also provide a fair method of dealing with alleged failures to observe the rules. It is, therefore, vital that employees know what standards of conduct are expected of them. The law requires employers, in the written particulars of employment, to provide information about certain aspects of their disciplinary rules and procedures.

The importance of disciplinary rules and procedures has also been recognized in law in respect of dismissals, since the grounds for dismissal and the way in which the dismissal has been handled can be challenged before an employment tribunal. Where either of these is found by a tribunal to be unfair the employer may be guilty of unfair dismissal and ordered to reinstate or re-engage the employee concerned or may have to pay compensation to him.

ACAS have produced *The Code of Practice on Disciplinary and Grievance Procedures in Employment*. The aim of the ACAS Code is to help employers, trade unions and individual employees, wherever they are employed, and regardless of the size of the organization in which they work. In smaller establishments it may not be practicable to adopt all the detailed provisions, but most of the features listed later in this section could and should be adopted by employers and incorporated into a simple procedure.

FORMULATING POLICY

The ACAS Code of Practice clearly states that it is management who are responsible for maintaining discipline within an organization and for ensuring that there are adequate disciplinary rules and procedures. However, if they are to be fully effective, the rules and procedures need to be accepted as reasonable by those employees who are to be covered by them and those who operate them. Management should therefore aim to secure the involvement of employees and all levels of management when formulating new or revising existing rules and procedures.

Rules

It is unlikely that any set of disciplinary rules can cover all circumstances that may arise. The rules required will necessarily vary according to particular circumstances such as:

- type of work;
- working conditions;
- the size of the employer.

When the employer draws up the rules he must try to specify clearly and concisely what is necessary for the efficient and safe performance of work and for the maintenance of satisfactory relations within the workforce and between the employees and management. Rules should not be so general as to be meaningless.

Rules should be readily available and the employer should make every effort to ensure that employees know and understand them. ACAS suggest that this may be achieved by giving every employee a copy of the rules, and by explaining them orally. In the case of new employees this should form part of an induction programme. Finally, employees should be made aware of the likely consequences of breaking rules and in particular they should be given a clear indication of the type of conduct that may warrant summary dismissal (i.e. sacking on the spot).

ESSENTIAL FEATURES OF DISCIPLINARY PROCEDURES

In their Code of Practice, ACAS indicate what should comprise a good and effective disciplinary procedure. They also state that procedures should not be viewed primarily as a means of punishing an employee. They should also be designed to emphasize and encourage improvement in individual conduct.

According to the Code, the disciplinary procedures should:

1 be in writing;
2 specify to whom they apply;
3 provide for matters to be dealt with quickly;
4 indicate the disciplinary actions which may be taken;
5 specify the levels of management which may have the authority to take the various forms of disciplinary action, ensuring that immediate superiors do not normally have the power to dismiss without reference to senior management;
6 provide for individuals to be informed of the complaints against them and to be given the opportunity to state their case before decisions are reached;
7 give individuals the right to be accompanied by a trade union representative or a fellow employee of their choice (this is now a statutory right);
8 ensure that no employees are dismissed for a first breach of discipline, except for gross misconduct;
9 ensure that disciplinary action is not taken until the case has been carefully investigated;
10 ensure that individuals are given an explanation for any penalty imposed;
11 provide a right of appeal and specify the procedure to be followed.

It is important to note that although the Code of Practice is *not* law, it is admissible as evidence before an employment tribunal and, in practice, tribunals are keen to see that employers are following the procedures as closely as possible. Where they are not followed and there is no good reason, a finding of unfair dismissal is likely. That is to say, a failure to follow a procedure laid down in the Code can turn an otherwise fair dismissal into an unfair dismissal.

THE PROCEDURE IN OPERATION

According to ACAS the employee should expect the implementation of the following procedure:

When a disciplinary matter arises, the supervisor or manager should first establish the facts promptly, before recollections fade, taking into account the statements of any available witnesses. In a serious case, such as where there is a reasonable belief that an act of gross misconduct has taken place, it may be necessary for the employer to suspend the employee while the case is investigated. Unless there is a provision in the contract of employment to the contrary, this period of suspension should be on full pay. The period of suspension should be for no longer than is reasonably necessary in the circumstances. It cannot be used by the employer as an excuse to do nothing more, that would be unfair on the employee who in all probability will be keen for an outcome, good or bad.

Before any decision is made by the employer or any penalty imposed against the employee, the individual should be interviewed and given the opportunity to state their case. The employee should be advised of their statutory right to have a trade union representative or colleague from the workplace present at the hearing. Where the facts of the case appear to call for disciplinary action, other than summary dismissal, the following procedure should normally be observed:

1 In the case of minor offences the individual should be given a *formal oral warning*. It is recommended that the warning be confirmed in writing.
2 If the misconduct continues or the first offence is more serious, the employee should receive a *first written warning*. This warning should set out the nature of the offence and the likely consequences of further offences. In either case, the individual should be advised that the warning constitutes a formal stage of the disciplinary procedure.
3 Should further similar misconduct occur, the employer should issue a *final written warning*. This should contain a statement that any recurrence will lead to either dismissal or some other penalty.
4 Should similar misconduct continue, the final stage of the procedure is the implementation of *dismissal, disciplinary transfer or disciplinary suspension* according to the nature of the misconduct (but in the case of the latter two, only if these are allowed for by an express term of the employment contract). Periods of disciplinary suspension without pay should not normally be for prolonged periods of time.

In summary, the procedure that an employee guilty of misconduct (other than gross misconduct) can expect is one of four stages:

1 oral warning;
2 first written warning;

3 final written warning;

4 dismissal.

At each stage the employee should be told of any right of appeal, how to make it and to whom.

There must be a fair hearing prior to the implementation of *each* stage. The employer must not prejudge the situation. Classic examples of prejudgement which may render the warning invalid are where the employer:

- without consultation sends the warning by post to the employee;
- holds a disciplinary hearing only to hand a *pre-written* warning to the employee at the end of the meeting.

A reasonable period of time should elapse between each warning to allow the employee an opportunity to improve and for the employer to properly monitor the employee's performance. What is a reasonable lapse of time is not defined in law but will depend on the facts of the case and the type of misconduct or poor performance. For example, instances of insubordination may be met with a different stage of the disciplinary procedure on each occasion. A general complaint of poor performance would have to be monitored over a period of time to allow any meaningful analysis of improvement or continued unsatisfactory work.

Employers are not generally entitled to progress on to the next stage of the procedure where a substantially different type of misconduct has occurred from the original warning. For example, it would be unfair for the employer to issue a final written warning for poor workmanship, if the employee is in receipt of a verbal warning and first written warning for poor timekeeping. The correct procedure would be to issue a verbal warning for the unsatisfactory level of performance. The employee in that example would then be on a first written warning for timekeeping and a verbal warning for performance. The law expects employers to recognize this differential.

EXCEPTIONAL CASES

There are certain situations where special consideration should be given to the way in which disciplinary procedures are to operate.

Trade union officials

Disciplinary action against a trade union official can lead to a serious dispute at the workplace if it is seen as an attack on the union's functions. Of course, trade union officials are not exempt from normal disciplinary standards, but no disciplinary action beyond an oral warning should be taken until the circumstances of the case have been discussed with a senior trade union representative or full-time official.

Criminal offences outside employment

There may be occasions when an employee commits a criminal offence away from the workplace out of work time. These should not be treated as automatic reasons for dismissal. The employer must consider whether the offence has any relevance to the employee's job. The main considerations should be whether the offence is one that has undermined the relationship of trust and confidence between the parties or made the individual unsuitable for their type of work or unacceptable to other employees. Employees should not be dismissed solely because a charge against them is pending or because they are absent through having been remanded in custody.

Paul works for Luvvies Limited, a media consultancy. At a football match outside of work hours one Saturday, he is arrested for chanting racist abuse at a particular football player. He is charged and given police bail.

His employers suspend him immediately, undertake an investigation and call him to a disciplinary hearing. Paul argues that the incident is unrelated to his employment and has no effect on his ability to perform his job as a client liaison officer. Luvvies dismisses Paul with immediate effect for gross misconduct. Paul claims unfair dismissal.

The tribunal finds in favour of Paul's employers and accepts their argument that the nature of the misconduct had a direct bearing on the relationship of trust and confidence between the parties because of Paul's close contact with a range of multi-ethnic clients. The tribunal accepts all trust and confidence has been completely undermined by Paul's actions.

Employees in particular working environments

Special provisions may have to be made for the handling of disciplinary matters among nightshift workers, or those in isolated locations or work sites, since there may be no one present with the necessary authority to take disciplinary action or no trade union representative available. Employees in these working environments are still entitled to be treated fairly and reasonably.

INVESTIGATION

Before an employer may reasonably make a decision as to whether or not an employee deserves to be disciplined, a full investigation of the facts is important. The employer cannot act against an employee on the basis of mere suspicion and should treat with great caution matters of hearsay. The employer must have an honest and genuine belief, based on some proof, following reasonable investigation, that the employee is guilty of the alleged misconduct. Reasonable investigation is a necessary ingredient of any fair disciplinary process.

The employer is under a duty to gather together all available evidence. Possession of all the facts should come before a reasonable decision as to what action (if any) is necessary. A good example of where an employer has failed to undertake proper investigation is when he presents the employee with a general allegation of misconduct unsupported by references to incidents or events. When faced with a 'blanket' allegation an employee is entitled to reply with a 'blanket' denial and this will not be held against him by a tribunal.

Details of the allegation

The employer must, well in advance of any disciplinary hearing, provide the employee with *specific* details relating to the allegation, including the following information where reasonably practicable:

- date;
- time;
- place;
- the people involved;
- the witnesses;
- all facts relevant to the act of misconduct;
- why the incident is regarded as misconduct by the employer;
- if the employer regards the misconduct as a potential sacking offence, this must be made clear to the employee.

Ideally, this information should be given to the employee in writing, both to avoid doubt and for future reference.

Delay

The employer should not unnecessarily delay the disciplinary proceedings in undertaking investigation. There is a balance to be struck between having possession of most of the facts and acting promptly before recollections fade. Where the period of investigation is seen to be unnecessarily lengthy and the employee is subsequently dismissed, a claim of unfair dismissal may be possible if he can show that the employer's delay in implementing the disciplinary procedure was prejudicial, i.e. the evidence was stale, witnesses were not available or specific detail was insufficient. The employer must undertake investigation at the earliest opportunity, which will usually be as soon as he becomes aware of the facts. Failure to act promptly will allow the employee to claim unfair dismissal, since to be aware of the conduct and to do nothing may be viewed as the employer's acceptance that such conduct is permitted in the employee's performance of his duties.

Witnesses

In conducting the investigation, witnesses should be interviewed and statements taken. The employer need not interview every available witness once the facts surrounding the misconduct have been clearly established. Should the employer overlook a key witness, the investigation may be flawed. Where the evidence of a witness is used against an employee, as a general rule the employee is entitled to question the witness. The employee is allowed to do this in order to test the accuracy of the witness's account of events and to establish whether there exists any ulterior motive for the allegation.

Anonymous witness

The problem is complicated where the witness or informant wishes to remain anonymous and the employee at the centre of the allegation is thereby potentially disadvantaged. In such situations the courts have provided the following guidelines to ensure a fair hearing, while protecting the request for anonymity:

1 The informant's statement should be reduced to writing in full.
2 In taking this statement the employer must note the date, time and place of each observation or incident and the informant's opportunity to observe clearly and accurately.
3 The employer should consider whether the informant had any reason to fabricate evidence.
4 Having taken the statement, the employer should then undertake further investigation with a view to finding other independent supporting evidence.
5 Inquiries should be made into the character and background of the informant.
6 A decision must then be made as to whether to hold a disciplinary hearing.
7 If possible, the informant should be personally interviewed by the employer with a view to deciding what weight should be given to his evidence.
8 The informant's statement should be made available to the employee and his representative in advance of the disciplinary hearing.
9 Should the employee or his representative have any reasonable questions to ask the informant, wherever practicable the employer should put the questions to the informant and refer back with answers.
10 Careful notes should be taken at the disciplinary hearing where informants are involved.

Employees faced with allegations based on the evidence of an informant have no legal right to demand to question them. However, an employee is entitled to request that the employer follows a procedure, as outlined above.

CRIMINAL PROCEEDINGS PENDING

Where it is alleged that the employee has committed a criminal act, inside or outside the workplace, and the police are proceeding with a prosecution, this can cause problems for the internal disciplinary hearing. In such circumstances, it is rarely acceptable for the employer to do nothing until the outcome of the criminal hearing. They should do their best to come to a decision as to the employee's guilt and whether, if at all, this affects the employment relationship. This requires a hearing to be held and a decision to be made. If the decision is to dismiss the employee and this is implemented and then the employee is acquitted of the criminal charge, the dismissal will not necessarily be unfair. Fairness will depend on the procedure adopted and the facts available to the employer at the time of the decision.

STANDARD OF PROOF

The purpose of a fair disciplinary process is to ensure that the employer comes to a reasonable decision on the facts of the case. The employer is not required to prove the case against the employee beyond all reasonable doubt. That requirement is for the criminal courts and has no place in a civil employment environment.

The employer is required to be satisfied on the 'balance of probabilities' that the employee acted as alleged. That is, on the evidence available, having investigated the facts and heard the employee's story, it was *more likely than not* that the employee committed the alleged misconduct. Provided the employer satisfies this standard of proof any subsequent dismissal will be potentially fair.

THE DISCIPLINARY HEARING

Having decided to proceed with a disciplinary hearing, the employer must conduct such proceedings fairly in the interests of 'natural justice'. This is necessary because a person's job is at stake. A serious breach of the rules of natural justice will make a dismissal unfair.

The employee states his case

The purpose of a hearing is twofold:
1 to investigate whether or not misconduct has been committed; and
2 to allow the employee to put forward a reason or explanation for his conduct.

The employee must be given an opportunity to state his version of events and explain any mitigating circumstances. What may seem obvious misconduct to the employer may have a perfectly innocent explanation.

Archie is accused of being in 'a drunken state' by his employer. He is dismissed on the spot. Archie claims unfair dismissal. His action is successful on the ground that had his employer adopted a fair procedure prior to dismissing him, they would have been given medical evidence demonstrating that he was not intoxicated through alcohol, as alleged, but through medication he was given for toothache. Archie was given no possible indication of this side effect and was, in fact, quite blameless.

Only in extraordinary cases may an employer not hear the employee's side of events and the dismissal still be regarded as fair, such as where the employee is not willing to attend the hearing. Furthermore, the employee should be given an opportunity to speak to the person who will actually make the disciplinary decision. The decision maker should not hear of the case third-hand. Should the employee be given the opportunity to explain his conduct but fail to do so, a subsequent dismissal will be potentially fair.

Details of the allegation

As stated earlier, the employee should know of the case against him well in advance of the hearing. This is to allow him to prepare and present a defence. The employer who 'springs' a disciplinary hearing on an employee may well invalidate the proceedings. Moreover, once the employee has been given details prior to a hearing, there should be no 'surprise' new allegations added at the hearing itself. If this happens, the employee would be acting reasonably in declining to comment and requesting an adjournment of the hearing in order to prepare a proper defence.

Any evidence upon which the employer is seeking to rely in making the allegations must be given in advance to the employee. The allegations and their specific facts will be the focus of the disciplinary hearing. Where witness evidence is being used, the witness must be made available for questioning at the hearing if the employee so requests. The hearing itself should not be over-formal. It is not a court of law but rather a forum for questioning by both employer and employee and for general investigation.

The decision maker

Where the resources of the business allow, the person investigating the misconduct on behalf of the employer should not be the decision maker. The investigator should assemble evidence to be put before another person – the decision maker. This is to allow the decision maker to make an objective assessment of the facts at the hearing, without having already prejudged the situation during the investigation. In addition, the decision maker should not have a direct interest in the outcome of the disciplinary hearing. That would be an unfair bias against the employee. The chances of bias should be minimized by the employer whenever reasonably practicable.

Representation

The employer does not have to allow an employee to be legally represented. After all, this is an internal disciplinary hearing, not a court of law. However, if the contract of employment states that the employee 'has the right to be represented' (or words to that effect), the employee may ask for his solicitor or other advocate to state his defence to the allegations.

In any event, a worker attending a disciplinary or grievance hearing has a statutory right to be accompanied by a union representative or fellow employee of his choice. The individual must be:

- selected by the employee;
- permitted to address the hearing (but not to answer questions on the employee's behalf);
- permitted to confer with the employee during the hearing.

The employer is free to select an initial date for the hearing, but he must reschedule the hearing date if the employee's chosen companion is not available on that date. The employee must propose an alternative time which is reasonable and which falls within a period of five working days (excluding weekends and bank holidays), beginning with the first working day after the day proposed by the employer.

The employee's companion must be given time off during working hours to accompany the employee for these purposes. An employee may complain to an employment tribunal where an employer has not allowed a companion to attend a hearing or where the employer has failed to reschedule a hearing. The tribunal can order an employer to pay compensation of up to a maximum of two weeks' pay to the employee.

The decision

Only in very clear-cut cases should the employee expect a decision at the end of the hearing. Usually the decision will follow some time after the hearing has been concluded. The employer is under an obligation before making a decision to bear in mind all relevant factors. The ACAS Code of Practice states the relevant factors are:

- the employee's general record, age, position and length of service;
- whether the disciplinary procedure indicates what the

likely penalty will be as a result of the particular misconduct;
- the penalty imposed in similar cases in the past;
- any special circumstances, for example, provocation;
- any mitigating factors, for example, the employee's health or domestic situation;
- the gravity of the offence;
- the range of sanctions available within the disciplinary procedure.

APPEALS

Where the contract of employment provides for an appeal procedure it should be followed. Where there is no right to appeal in the employment contract, failure to allow one may be grounds to claim unfair dismissal. An appeal procedure should clarify:

- the time period within which the appeal must be lodged;
- to whom the appeal should be made;
- whether the appeal should be oral or submitted in writing only;
- whose decision is final;
- how that decision will be communicated;
- the time period within which the decision will be made.

Once more, depending on the resources available to the employer, the appeal should be heard by someone other than the first decision maker, to allow an objective review of the facts and circumstances of the case. The conduct of the appeal hearing and the composition of the appeal 'panel' is therefore important. Unless otherwise stated, the contract of employment will be effectively terminated at the point in time when the original decision to dismiss is communicated to the employee. The contract will not remain live until the outcome of the appeal. If the appeal is successful and overturns the decision to dismiss, then the employee will be treated as having been suspended pending the outcome of the appeal. Impliedly such suspension will be with pay unless there exists a contractual provision to the contrary.

Finally, it should be noted that where an employee has failed to make use of an available appeal procedure offered by the employer following dismissal, an employment tribunal has the power to reduce any unfair dismissal compensatory award by up to two weeks' pay. Similarly, if the employer denies access to an appeal, compensation may be increased by up to two weeks' pay.

THE IMPORTANCE OF LENGTH OF SERVICE

Remember that the ACAS Code of Practice on disciplinary procedures is not law. However, it is well established that breach of the Code may well render a dismissal unfair. It will also be an error of law for the employment tribunal to fail to consider the code in a misconduct dismissal case. However, in Chapter 34 we explained that in order to claim unfair dismissal before an employment tribunal, the employee must have one year's continuous service. Without that length of service, no matter how blatant the breach of the Code or how unfair the dismissal, the employee cannot challenge the decision on its merits. The employee will only be able to claim for money owed under the contract of employment in a wrongful dismissal claim.

If, however, the contract of employment is so worded that the disciplinary procedure (if any) outlined within it is contractually binding from day one of the commencement of employment, it follows that an employer's subsequent failure to follow the procedure will be a breach of contract. Where the employer is in breach of contract the employee is entitled to claim damages before an employment tribunal or county court.

Damages should be assessed on the basis of the amount of wages or salary that would have been earned by the employee had the employer gone through the disciplinary procedure in the contract, subject to the employee's duty to mitigate his loss and actively seek employment elsewhere. To date, claims such as these are few in practice. But there is nothing, in theory, to prevent such a claim. It may be worth a try, particularly before an employment tribunal where the procedure for application is simple and there is so little to lose.

Future developments

The Employment Act 2002 introduces new statutory procedures for dismissal, disciplinary and grievance procedures. The procedures will be implied in every contract of employment. In summary, the key changes are:

- all dismissals will have to be preceded by a meeting with the employee. This will apply to all dismissals (not just disciplinary dismissals), including dismissals resulting from redundancy, poor performance or long-term sickness;
- there will always be a right of appeal against a dismissal. At the present time, appeals are usually limited to disciplinary cases – in future, it will even extend to dismissals for (e.g.) redundancy;
- all appeals will have to involve meetings at which the employee can explain his or her case;
- tribunals will be able to vary compensatory awards by up to 50 per cent where the employer or the applicant has failed to use the minimum statutory procedures;
- an employee who fails to follow the first step of the statutory grievance procedure (by raising a written grievance) will not be able to rely on that grievance in future claims. So, if an employee complains to a tribunal about a grievance he could have raised with the employer, but failed to do so, then the tribunal will not hear that complaint;

- it will be unfair for employers to dismiss an employee without meeting their obligations under the statutory dismissal and disciplinary procedure. However, tribunals will be obliged to disregard failures by employers to take procedural actions outside the framework of the statutory procedure (i.e. the minimum requirements laid down by the Act), in unfair dismissal cases, if following full procedures would have made no difference to the decision to dismiss;
- an employee will be entitled to a minimum of four weeks' pay as compensation where they are found to have been unfairly dismissed and the statutory procedure has not been complied with.

These provisions of the Act were due to be brought into force by April 2004.

RECORDS AND DATA PROTECTION

The employer is obliged to keep records detailing the nature of any breach of disciplinary rules, the action taken and the reasons for it. Details of appeals, where lodged by the employee, should also be kept. The employer should keep these records safely and confidentially.

After a period of time, a warning will become lapsed and may be disregarded. Where the contract of employment says nothing about the duration of a warning, the normal common law rule is that it will lapse after a period of one year. The contract, or the warning itself, may state a shorter period of time. If longer than one year the contract term may be challenged as unreasonable and, if an employee is dismissed as a result of its application, it may be claimed to be unfair before an employment tribunal. The importance of a warning having lapsed is that in the event of further similar misconduct by the employee, the employer will have to 'go back' to the preceding live warning, if any.

The Data Protection Act 1998

Under the Data Protection Act 1998, which came into force in March 2000, employees have the right to receive a copy of their personnel files on request and to demand that any inaccuracies be corrected or removed. They also have the right to be told whether, and for what purposes, personal information relating to them is being processed, the nature of the data and the people to whom the information may be disclosed.

It is important to note at the outset that transitional provisions set out in the Act give employers a period of several years to comply with the new provisions in relation to existing paper-based records.

The principles

The Act contains eight basic principles:

1 Personal data shall be processed fairly and lawfully and shall not be processed at all unless certain conditions are met in relation to personal data and additional conditions in relation to sensitive personal data. The conditions are:
   - the data subject has given his consent to the processing; or
   - the processing is necessary for the various purposes set out in the Act.
2 Personal data shall be obtained only for one or more specified and lawful purposes.

   Personal data shall not be processed in any manner incompatible with that purpose or those purposes.
3 Personal data shall be adequate, relevant and not excessive in relation to the purpose or purposes for which they are processed.
4 Personal data shall be accurate and, where necessary, kept up to date.
5 Personal data processed for any purpose shall not be kept for longer than is necessary for that purpose.
6 Personal data shall be processed in accordance with the rights of data subjects under the Act.
7 Appropriate technical and organizational measures shall be taken against unauthorized or unlawful processing of personal data and against accidental loss or destruction of, or damage to, data.
8 Personal data shall not be transferred to a country or territory outside the European Economic Area unless that country or territory ensures an adequate level of protection for the rights and freedoms of data subjects in relation to the processing of personal data.

Access and information

Under the Act, employees have the right, on request:
- to be told by the employer whether personal data about them is being processed;
- to be given a description of the data concerned, the purposes for which it is being processed, and the recipients or classes of recipients to whom it is or may be disclosed;
- to have communicated 'in an intelligible form' the personal data concerned, and any information available to the employer as to the source of the data;
- to be informed in certain circumstances of the logic involved in computerized decision making.

The employer is not obliged to supply the information mentioned above unless the employee has made a written request and has paid a fee, currently £10. The employer must comply with the request within 40 days.

The Data Protection Act, together with the questionnaire procedure for discimination claims, is the most useful device for gathering evidence from an employer.

Correction of inaccurate data

An employee has the right under the Act to apply to the High Court or to a county court on the grounds that the personal data relating to them is inaccurate. If the complaint is upheld, the court may order the employer to rectify, block, erase or destroy that data and any other personal data which contains an expression of opinion based on the inaccurate information. If the inaccurate data has been disclosed to third parties, the court may also order the employer to notify those third parties that the inaccurate information has been corrected.

Notification

The Act introduces a simplified system of 'notification' of information in place of the registration scheme that existed under the earlier legislation. The details that an employer will be obliged to notify under the Act include a description of the personal data being processed and of the category or categories of data subject to which it relates, the purposes for which the data is being processed, and any person to whom the employer intends to disclose the data.

Enforcement

The Act confers extensive powers of enforcement, including powers of entry and inspection, on the Data Protection Commissioner. If a data controller has contravened the data protection principles, the Commissioner may issue an enforcement notice. This notice will formally request notification of any particular failing, error or wrongdoing by the data controller within a specified period of time and set out the consequences of failing to comply with the notice. The Commissioner may also issue a notice requiring the data controller to provide information for the purpose of determining whether a data protection principle has been breached. Failure to comply with a notice amounts to a criminal offence. Individuals may also apply to the Commissioner in certain circumstances for an assessment as to whether the provisions of the Act have been complied with, and in many instances they will be able to recover compensation from the data controller if a breach has taken place.

Implementation

For paper-based personnel files the following will apply:
- 'new' processing, i.e. processing commencing on or

after 24 October 1998, is subject to all relevant provisions and to each of the eight principles;

- 'old' processing, i.e. processing already under way immediately before 24 October 1998, was exempt until 23 October 2001 from each of the eight principles, from the provisions governing employees' rights of access and right to correct inaccurate data, and exempt from principles 1–5 (only) until 23 October 2007.

38

Discrimination

RECOGNIZED DISCRIMINATION

Presently, UK employment law recognizes three types of discrimination: sex, race and disability. From December 2003, discrimination on the grounds of sexual orientation, religion or belief in employment or vocational training is also unlawful (*see* page 377). It is anticipated that legislation outlawing age discrimination will come into force in December 2005.

Difficulties of proof

Discrimination is always denied. Often the discriminator is unaware that he or she is discriminating or is in self-denial. Discrimination can be unwitting or unconscious. Due to the unusual difficulties of proving discrimination claims the burden of proof was partially reversed by EU legislation. This means that once a complainant of sex discrimination brings evidence to show that she may have been treated less favourably on the grounds of her gender (or marital status), it will be up to the employer to prove they have not discriminated against the victim. It is no longer possible for the employer merely to provide a possible explanation for the unfavourable conduct. Instead, they will have to actually disprove the existence of discrimination.

A similar change was introduced for race discrimination claims (*see also* page 378) and for religion, belief and sexual orientation discrimination claims. These new rules of proof will be applied to disability discrimination claims in 2004 and to age discrimination claims in 2005.

There is also a special questionnaire that a complainant of discrimination can request the employer to complete. This can help greatly with gathering evidence in support of the claim. Model questionnaires can be obtained from the Commission for Racial Equality, the Equal Opportunities Commission and the Disability Rights Commission (*see* page 384 for contact details).

Time limits

A claim for any type of discrimination must be received by the employment tribunal within three months less one day of the act of discrimination. Claims may be brought by workers applying for work or who are at work or who have been dismissed because of discrimination. Often the discriminatory treatment causes the victim to suffer ill health and to take sick leave. Some advisers mistakenly believe that the time limit does not apply when the victim is on sick leave. In fact, it does. This is because the sickness absence is not a form of discrimination, although it may be a consequence of it.

The time limit for presenting a claim may be extended if it constitutes a 'continuing act of discrimination'. If the act is continuing against the employee, the time limit is continually refreshed and ongoing. The claimant will have to show that each of the incidents of discrimination are linked. The key points to grasp about continuing acts are:

- where the contract of employment includes a term making the conduct an unlawful act, the act shall be treated as extending throughout the duration of the contract;
- any act extending over a period shall be treated as having been done at the end of that period;
- a deliberate omission by the employer shall be treated as done when the person in question decided upon it (i.e. the point in time when the employer, or any appropriate member of their staff, made the decision to act in a manner which constituted a deliberate omission).

An example of the last point would be where a personnel manager fails to consider female part-timers within a pool of employees for a particular training programme.

The time limit can also be extended where the tribunal considers that it would be just and equitable to do so. The tribunal will look at all the circumstances including the relative prejudice to the parties in granting the extension, the harm done to the chances of a fair hearing and whether the worker was trying to conciliate the potential claim.

If the claim is late because of negligent advice from a legal adviser, the tribunal may take this into account in deciding whether to extend the time limit. The tribunal's discretion to extend time is very wide and much broader than the test to extend time for unfair dismissal claims. Provided that the applicant had a good reason for the delay the tribunal will invariably extend time beyond the three-month less one day limit. Having said that, it is always advisable to submit a claim within time.

A claim will be received by the tribunal on a particular day if it arrives by fax or e-mail before midnight. Ignorance of the time limit is no defence. The tribunal will not look at what the complainant knows, but what he or she ought to have known. Most people who have employment-related problems ought to have taken legal advice and therefore ought to have known the time limit. If they do not know, they will need to explain their ignorance.

When the last day for submitting a claim falls on a Sunday or a bank holiday, time is not normally extended to the next working day for any tribunal claim. Finally, a complainant who has missed the deadline for presenting their claim must ask the tribunal for an extension of time. The tribunal is not under a duty to consider such an extension without being asked to do so.

REMEDIES

The following remedies are available in respect of any discrimination claim, whether based on race, gender, disability or any other form of discrimination.

Declaratory order

The tribunal may issue an order declaring the rights of the complainant and the respondent in relation to the act about which a complaint has been made.

Recommending remedial action

The tribunal may recommend that an employer, within a specified period of time, take some form of practical action to avoid or reduce the adverse effect presently experienced by the complainant. A recommendation can be made to improve the workplace even after the complainant's employment has ended if that recommendation would alleviate the suffering of the complainant.

An employment tribunal cannot order that the employer provides an apology. This is because it is believed that an apology which is compelled is insincere.

Compensation

A monetary award can be made if the complainant has suffered loss – this can include a sum for injury to feelings and compensation for loss of opportunity in the labour market. There is no ceiling on the amount of compensation that can be awarded. However, in 2002 the Court of Appeal laid down guidelines for tribunal awards of compensation for injury to feelings, which will apply in race and sex discrimination cases. The court decided that there were three broad bands of compensation. In the top band, an award of between £15,000 and £25,000 would be appropriate in the most serious cases (e.g. where the victim had been subjected to a lengthy campaign of harassment). In the middle band, which would apply to serious cases, an award of between £5,000 and £15,000 would be appropriate. The bottom band was for less serious cases (for example, where the discrimination was a one-off or isolated occurrence) and compensation between £500 and £5,000 would be suitable. The court added that awards of less than £500 should be avoided.

Aggravated damages

A complainant of discrimination may also claim aggravated damages where the discriminatory acts are carried out in a high-handed, insulting, malicious or oppressive manner.

Punitive damages

Theoretically, a complainant may also seek exemplary or punitive damages for acts of discrimination which are intentional and which are either an abuse of power (e.g. by a government department or a powerful organization or individual) or were calculated to make a profit for the employer.

Punitive damages are measured against the turnover or the profitability of the employer and seek to punish the wrongdoer, rather than to measure the damage done to the victim. Hence, a minor discriminatory act carried out by a multinational company could theoretically lead to a seven-figure compensation payment. However, there has yet to be an award for punitive damages for discrimination in the UK.

Personal injury

A victim of discrimination must also claim compensation for any personal injury caused by the discrimination in the employment tribunal. Personal injury includes clinical depression, psychiatric damage and physical injury. Personal injury losses are broader than injury to feelings losses and can include compensation for pain, loss of amenity and suffering, disadvantage in the labour market, loss of the potentially more lucrative future employment and the cost of care. Expert evidence from a medical consultant is normally required to prove this aspect of the claim.

It is possible to recover greater damages than can be claimed for personal injury caused by negligence. For negligence claims, a victim can only recover reasonably foreseeable losses, whereas for discrimination claims the victim can claim any personal injury loss caused by the discrimination, whether it was reasonably foreseeable or not.

Loss of earnings

Loss of earnings can be claimed where a dismissal is found to be discriminatory. It can also be claimed where a job applicant is denied a post because of discrimination or a worker is refused a promotion because of discrimination. In addition, it can be claimed where a worker loses income as a result of being on sick leave due to discrimination.

Where the victim has been dismissed because of the discrimination he or she may claim loss of earnings from the date of the dismissal up to the date of the tribunal hearing. Also, if they have yet to find a new job or have found a new job on a lower salary, they may be able to claim future loss of earnings beyond the tribunal hearing date. However, this is unlikely to extend to more than one year's future loss because most workers will find work within such a period of time.

Mitigation

Complainants of discrimination (or unfair dismissal) are under an obligation to reduce their losses – principally by seeking new employment if they have been dismissed. They should keep a record of jobs applied for and should actively seek new employment. If they are too ill to seek work, a doctor's report will normally be required to prove this at any tribunal hearing.

Interest

Interest may be claimed on the above losses at 8 per cent per year over the whole period of the discrimination and loss.

Reinstatement

The employment tribunal does not have the power to order reinstatement in discrimination cases. Nor can the tribunal recommend that the victim of discrimination should be offered the next available post at the company, as this would constitute positive discrimination (*see* page 376). The tribunal can order reinstatement where victims win their unfair dismissal claim.

References

The tribunal does not have the power to order that a company provides a reference to the complainant. However, a failure to provide a reference may give rise to a claim of victimization or discrimination.

SEX DISCRIMINATION

The Sex Discrimination Act 1975 provides that women and men may bring claims of discrimination on the grounds of their sex or marital status or if victimized on those same grounds. It follows that a person may be discriminated against in one of three ways:

1 directly;
2 indirectly;
3 via victimization.

Most sex discrimination claims of whatever type are brought by women. For that reason, this section will concentrate on unlawful discrimination against women, although men may also apply of course if similar discrimination is evident.

Direct discrimination

This occurs where a woman, because of her sex, is treated less favourably than a man or if married is treated less favourably than a single person. Any woman making such a claim must be able to show not only that her treatment is *different* but that it is also *unfavourable*. The latter is a key ingredient. A typical example of direct discrimination is where a female employee is told by her employer that she would have been promoted but for her being a woman. The test applied by the courts is, therefore, would the employee have been treated more favourably 'but for' her sex?

The main examples of direct discrimination are:

- a female employee who applies for a job is not offered the position because the employer decides that they would have offered her the position but for her sex;
- a female employee is appointed but offered less favourable terms of employment because of her sex;
- deliberately failing or refusing to offer employment to a woman because of her sex.

There is no defence to a claim of direct discrimination. If an employer is found to have treated a woman unfavourably on the grounds of her gender, it cannot avoid liability by stating that the treatment was objectively justified or that it did not intend to treat her differently or unfavourably.

Indirect discrimination

This form of discrimination is less obvious to detect. It might not, quite genuinely, have ever been intended by the employer. It occurs when an employer applies a criterion, practice or provision to the workforce which has the effect of disadvantaging women. Indirect discrimination occurs where:

- the proportion of women or married persons who are able to comply with it is considerably smaller than the proportion of men or unmarried persons; and
- the employer cannot show it to be justifiable, irrespective of the sex or marital status of the applicant; and
- the condition is to the applicant's detriment because she is unable to comply with it.

In each case of indirect discrimination the key issue is whether the requirement is justifiable in the light of the duties to be performed. The intention or motive of the employer is largely irrelevant. The test is what impact the treatment had on the victim.

The Box Company Limited advertises for a packer and applies a minimum height requirement of six feet. Maureen is five feet eight inches tall and applies for the job. She is turned down. Maureen claims sex discrimination. Her claim is successful because the height requirement indirectly discriminates against women in that statistically more women than men are under six feet and the condition could not be justified by the company.

Where such a criterion, practice or provision is applied by the employer and a claim of discrimination is made against them, they must show that it is objectively justified for an economic, administrative or other reason. A balance has to be struck between the discriminatory effect of the criterion, practice or provision and the reasonable needs of the employer. The courts must ask themselves how many women will suffer as a consequence of it and how seriously they will suffer.

Victimization

The idea here is to prevent employers from penalizing employees for taking action against the employers under the provisions of the sex discrimination legislation. Discrimination will occur when the victimized employee is treated less favourably by the employer by reason that she has:

- brought, or threatened to bring, proceedings against the employer or some other relevant person;
- given evidence or information in connection with proceedings brought by any person against the employer or other relevant person;
- otherwise done anything under, or by reference to, the sex discrimination legislation, in relation to the employer or other relevant person;
- alleged that the employer or other relevant person has committed an act which would contravene the sex discrimination legislation.

These instances are called the 'protected acts'. This will also include situations where a person is victimized by the discriminator because they intend to do any of the above or the discriminator suspects they will do any of them.

The test applied by the tribunal in respect of victimization claims is different to that applied to direct discrimination claims. In direct discrimination cases the complainant must show that the disadvantage was caused by the discrimination, i.e. that but for the discrimination the complainant would not have suffered any disadvantage. The test for victimization is what the reason was that the complainant suffered disadvantage. This means that the tribunal must look at the employer's state of mind when perpetrating the less-favourable treatment to see if they were consciously or subconsciously affected by the fact that the complainant carried out a protected act.

Sharon raises a grievance of sex discrimination because of sexist language at work. She secretly tape-records her male line manager calling her a sexist name. When the tape-recording is discovered, Sharon is dismissed for gross misconduct. It is likely that she will lose her subsequent claim for victimization because the reason for her dismissal (the less-favourable treatment in this case) was her breach of trust, in secretly recording her line manager – and not the fact that she had previously complained of discrimination. This is so despite the fact that the need to record the line manager and gather evidence of the discrimination was caused by the fact that she had raised a grievance.

The need for comparison

A successful discrimination claim depends on a woman being able to show that she has been treated less favourably than a man because of her sex. The person with whom she compares herself should be a man in an identical or very similar situation. In the absence of such a person, the comparator can be hypothetical. Like must be compared with like, even where a hypothetical comparator is used. In defending a claim, the employer can compare a female claimant with a hypothetical man but only by reference to the same employment with the same members of staff involved. The issue of comparability can be complex.

Clothing and personal appearance

Discrimination can occur when the employer insists on enforcing different rules for clothing or appearance for men and women at their place of work. Most people will have conventional ideas about the way the sexes should dress, keep their hair or have earrings.

The approach of the employment tribunal when faced with cases like these is to consider the clothing or appearance rules as a whole, rather than garment by garment. The tribunal is looking to see if the rules are more restrictive for one sex than the other. They take a pragmatic approach, men and women are different and therefore it is expected that the rules will also differ. Provided the employer enforces the rules even-handedly they are unlikely to be regarded as having discriminated against one or other sex. For example, if the rules state women must wear make-up and men must not wear beards, they are even-handed and unlikely to be seen as discriminatory provided they are enforced in equal measure.

Pregnancy

In the case of a pregnant woman, the question has arisen whether comparison with a man is possible or necessary. Pregnancy is a condition unique to women and when a pregnant woman believes she has been treated less favourably by her employer because of her condition, to search for an analogous male comparator is somewhat artificial.

The comparison test in pregnancy cases is now outdated and any woman dismissed where the primary reason can be shown to be her condition or because of absences from work due to maternity-related illness, is entitled to claim that the dismissal is automatically unfair and that she has been discriminated against on the ground of her sex. There is a 'protected period', which runs from conception until the end of the maternity leave period.

Advertising

When an employer advertises a position there are rules that must be complied with to avoid discrimination. The responsibility not to discriminate will extend to the publisher of the advertisement. Job applicants should look out for the following signs of discrimination:

- stereotyped words or phrases, for example, 'postman' or 'hostess'.
- does the job description in the advert deter women from applying?
- if there are pictures or illustrations along with the advert, do they discourage women from applying, for example, by showing only men in that working environment?
- are there any conditions or requirements within the job specification as advertised which could be indirectly discriminatory?
- is the advert placed in a newspaper or magazine read predominantly by one sex?

A woman can only bring a claim for sex discrimination based on a discriminatory advert if she actually applies for the post in question and is unsuccessful. If she does not apply, she cannot bring a claim. However, the Equal Opportunities Commission can take action to make the employer comply with the law.

Interviews

Discrimination often takes place at the interview stage where:

- male and female candidates are asked different questions;
- questions are asked which are based on stereotypical assumptions;
- sexist questions or remarks are made by the interviewer;
- unnecessary questions, not relevant to the job, are asked of the interviewee in respect of domestic circumstances.

Belinda applies for a job as a trainee solicitor with Crusty and Co. At the interview she is quizzed by Mr Crusty as to her future plans to have a family, get married and whether she could foresee difficulties in balancing a home life with children and a career as a busy solicitor. Belinda did not get the job and she claimed sex discrimination. Her claim was successful. At her interview she was treated less favourably than a man based on stereotypical assumptions and an inappropriate and irrelevant line of questioning. She was awarded £2,000 for injury to feelings.

Opportunities

Once in employment, a woman can expect not to be discriminated against in the way in which the employer provides her with access to opportunities for promotion, transfer or to any other benefits or services.

Dismissal

If an employee is dismissed on the grounds of her sex or marital status this will be unlawful sex discrimination and an unfair dismissal. This applies to constuctive dismissals, as well as actual dismissals (*see* page 332).

Other detriment

A woman will be entitled to claim sex discrimination if she is subjected to any other detriment – other than dismissal – such as demotion, wage cut or withdrawal of employment privileges on the grounds of her sex.

This protection includes and extends to any situation where the woman feels that she has been put to a disadvantage and a reasonable worker would also consider that she has been disadvantaged.

Pensions

Many employers contract out of the state pension scheme and provide benefits to their employees under a private scheme. The employer will be acting unlawfully if they do not allow equal access to the scheme for men and women. Note here that to deny part-timers access to a pension scheme will be to indirectly discriminate against women since, in the UK, more part-time workers are women.

Positive discrimination

The 1975 Act does not allow positive discrimination since that would involve deliberately appointing a woman because of her sex where candidates are equal. This approach would lead to discrimination against men and the Act is in place to protect both sexes. However, encouraging women to apply for a position is permissible by:
- providing training for women; and
- advertising.

Such action is only permitted if the employer can show that in the preceding 12 months there have been no women, or only a small proportion of women, carrying out particular work.

Positive discrimination is permissible through the operation of genuine occupational qualifications and genuine occupational requirements.

Genuine occupational qualification

If the employer can establish that being a man is a genuine occupational qualification (GOQ) for a job, they may discriminate lawfully in certain respects. This permitted discrimination will cover advertising, interviewing, offers, refusing opportunities for promotion, training or transfers. Being a man is a genuine occupational qualification for a job in the following circumstances:
- physiology, dramatic performance, entertainment or authenticity;
- for reasons of decency or privacy – where the job involves close physical contact or state of undress with other employees, customers or persons;

- the work is in a private home and involves close physical or social contact with, or intimate details of, a person;
- the employee lives in and only single-sex sleeping accommodation is available;
- the job is being carried out at an establishment which is single sex – for example, a male health clinic;
- personal services for the welfare or education of individuals are being provided, and the recipients could identify better with a member of their own sex;
- the work is being carried out outside the UK and the laws and customs of that country prohibit a particular sex from carrying out that work;
- the work requires a married couple.

Genuine occupational requirement

Since 2002, employers may also discriminate in favour of a woman provided that they can show a genuine occupational requirement (GOR) applies to the post. GORs are a wider concept than GOQs. A GOR can apply to any post, provided that the employer can show that gender is a genuine and determining occupational requirement for the job and that it is proportionate to apply that requirement (*see also* page 380).

Part-timers

Twenty-eight per cent of the workforce in the UK work part-time. Of those, 88 per cent are women. More women than men are unable to meet the requirement for full-time working. This may mean that they do not receive the same employment benefits as full-timers, for example, bonuses, holiday and contractual sick pay. If this differential cannot be objectively justified by the employer it may be viewed as indirect discrimination against women if, as is usual, the part-time workforce in question is predominantly female.

Sexual harassment

Sexual harassment is normally unlawful because it constitutes direct discrimination. Harassment will of itself amount to unlawful sex discrimination when the new EU laws are introduced in the UK (*see below* 'Changes to the law'). It occurs when the conduct towards a woman complainant is viewed by the victim as:
- unwanted; or
- unreasonable; or
- offensive.

It will also include situations where the employer or a member of their workforce uses such conduct as a basis for deciding on promotion, an appraisal or other employment matters. The conduct must be such that the victim felt:

- intimidated; or
- the subject of hostility; or
- humiliated.

What is the position where a particular woman regards certain conduct as sexual harassment but most other women would not take exception to the conduct? The law states that, provided the employee has made it clear that the conduct is unwelcome, any repetition may amount to harassment. Of course, many forms of conduct are objectively hostile or offensive and these do not require the employee to indicate that they are unwelcome before they may constitute harassment.

The employer has a duty to properly and thoroughly investigate an allegation of sexual harassment, and to take whatever disciplinary action is appropriate against the perpetrator of the conduct. Unless the employer can show that reasonable steps were taken to prevent sexual harassment they may be held responsible for the acts of the perpetrator. Employees who feel they are being sexually harassed at work should first raise a formal grievance with their employer. If this fails to address the problem adequately, they may consider reporting the matter to the regional office of the Equal Opportunities Commission for further investigation, or to a local solicitor.

Changes to the law

The UK and other Member States have until 5 October 2005 to implement the Revised Equal Treatment Directive. This will require some amendments to the Sex Discrimination Act 1975. The key changes that must be made are:

- a new definition of direct sex discrimination which will mean that a person will be able to complain about sex discrimination even if the discrimination is not on the grounds of that person's own sex;
- a new definition of indirect sex discrimination which will not require proof of statistical disadvantage in the same way that existing law requires;
- a definition of harassment for the first time in legislation in the field of sex discrimination. In fact the definition is narrower than that required under existing case law in the field of sex discrimination;
- rights to judicial protection after the employment relationship has ended.

Transsexuals

Discrimination on the grounds that a person intends to undergo, is undergoing, or has undergone gender reassignment is unlawful. The employer may apply any genuine occupational qualification (as listed above) provided that, in so doing, they are acting reasonably, given the particular facts and circumstances of the case.

Religion, belief and sexual orientation

From December 2003, new Regulations have prohibited discrimination on the grounds of religion, belief and sexual orientation. Religious discrimination covers recognized religions, such as Catholicism, Judaism and Islam. Belief discrimination will cover any system of belief with a profound philosophical basis. Belief discrimination will not extend to political beliefs. It is not yet clear whether these new types of discrimination will extend to cult religions or less recognized belief systems. It is likely that protection may be linked to the number of people who are members of a particular religion or belief system.

Sexual orientation discrimination extends to less-favourable treatment on the basis of a person's heterosexual, homosexual or bisexual orientation. The Regulations are not intended to cover sexual practices and preferences (e.g sado-masochism and paedophilia).

Steven pokes fun at John at work because of John's belief in the Order of the Jedi Knight. Steven says that the Star Wars-inspired belief is fictional nonsense. John retorts that the Jedi Knight is as real as God. Steven, who is an Anglican, brings a grievance against John complaining of religious discrimination. John responds by bringing a grievance against Steven for belief discrimination. Separately, Susan brings a grievance against Steven because she believes that he is anti-gay because of his religious beliefs. It is likely that Steven's grievance would be upheld by an employment tribunal and that John's grievance would fail because the Order of the Jedi Knight is not considered to be a recognized belief. It is unlikely that Susan's claim will succeed, in the absence of any actual anti-gay conduct by Steven, in that Steven states that his religion is not homophobic.

It is likely that expert evidence will be required to prove what constitutes a religion or belief system and to specify the rules of conduct of that religion or belief system.

THE EQUAL OPPORTUNITIES COMMISSION

The Equal Opportunities Commission (EOC) was set up specifically to work actively towards the elimination of discrimination, to promote equality of opportunity between men and women generally, and to keep under review the working of the Sex Discrimination Act 1975.

The EOC issues codes of practice and, if it thinks fit, is empowered to conduct a formal investigation for any purpose connected with the carrying out of its duties. In undertaking this investigation, the EOC may issue a notice requiring the production of written information or documents from the employer. It also has the power to examine witnesses. As a result, the EOC may make recommendations to the employer for changes in their procedures (*see also* page 384 for contact details).

Non-discrimination notice

The EOC may issue a non-discrimination notice during its investigations if it is satisfied that an employer has committed or is committing:

- an unlawful discriminatory act;
- a discriminatory practice;
- a breach of the provisions in respect of advertising, instructions to discriminate or pressure to discriminate;
- a breach of a term modified or included by virtue of an equality clause.

The non-discrimination notice may require the employer not to commit any such acts and to change their practices and other arrangements. If the errant employer does not comply with the notice, the EOC may apply to the county court for the issue of an injunction.

The EOC may give assistance to claimants if their case is of some complexity or raises a question of principle. Assistance will include trying to obtain a settlement, advice and legal representation if necessary. The cost of assistance may be recovered by the EOC on an award of costs by the tribunal or from any agreed settlement.

The future of the EOC

In May 2002, the government announced plans to abolish the EOC, the Commission for Racial Equality, and the Disability Rights Commission and to set up a single equalities watchdog dealing with discrimination on the grounds of race, gender, disability, sexual orientation, age and religion. The new body is unlikely to be operative before 2006.

RACE DISCRIMINATION

Discrimination on racial grounds is unlawful under the Race Relations Act 1976. The provisions of that Act are very similar to those of the Sex Discrimination Act. Broadly, the Act outlaws discrimination in three ways: where it is direct, indirect or by way of victimization. In order to determine whether a person has been discriminated against, a comparison is necessary with someone of similar ability and qualifications in similar circumstances. Like must be compared with like.

Direct discrimination

This will occur where an employer or potential employer treats a person less favourably than he treats or would treat others on the grounds of their race.

Indirect discrimination

For claims of race discrimination based on colour or nationality an employer will discriminate indirectly if, on racial grounds, they apply to one person a requirement or condition which they apply or would apply equally to persons not of the same racial group but:

- it is such that the proportion of persons in that racial group who can comply with it is considerably smaller than the proportion of persons not of that racial group who can comply with it;
- which the employer cannot show to be justifiable irrespective of the colour or nationality of the person to whom it is applied; and
- which is to the detriment of that other person because he cannot comply with it.

This is a stricter test than the test for indirect sex discrimination. The other point is that there is now, very confusingly, a two-tier system for indirect race discrimination claims, with one set of rules where the claim is based on the applicant's colour or nationality and another where the claim is based on the applicant's race or national or ethnic origins (*see also* page 380, 'Changes to the law').

Imran, who is Asian, applies for the post of local authority lawyer. It is a condition or requirement of the job that the applicant is a qualified solicitor and has an upper-second-class law degree. The advertisement for the post also states various 'desirable qualities' that the ideal applicant will possess. These include that the applicant has worked for that local authority previously. Imran believes that he does not get the job because he did not work previously for the local authority. His claim for indirect race discrimination fails because working for the local authority was not a condition or requirement. By contrast, it is a criterion, practice or provision and hence the same claim would succeed if Imran's claim was based on his race or national or ethnic origins (as opposed to his colour or nationality).

Victimization

This takes place where the person victimized is treated less favourably than the discriminator would treat others because the victim has:

- brought proceedings against the discriminator or any other relevant person under the terms of the Race Relations Act;
- given evidence or information in connection with proceedings brought by any person against the discriminator or any other person under the Act; or
- otherwise done anything under or by reference to the Act in relation to the discriminator or any other person;
- alleged that the discriminator or any other relevant

person has committed an act which amounts to contravention of the Act.

This will also include situations where a person is victimized by the discriminator because they intend to do any of the above or the discriminator suspects they will do any of them.

What is race discrimination?

Race discrimination, direct or indirect, takes place following less favourable treatment on *racial grounds*. Racial grounds covers a number of possibilities including a person's:

- colour;
- race;
- nationality or national origins;
- ethnic origin.

Clearly, nationality is quite different from race or colour and much wider in its application and would include, for example, Northern Europeans who are discriminated against on the grounds of their country of origin. Ethnic origin is added because it too can be different from a person's nationality or race. Ethnic groups can span a variety of racial or national origins and could include Sikhs or Jews. To establish an ethnic origin, the group of people must have:

- a long shared history, of which the group is conscious and which distinguishes it from other groups;
- a cultural tradition of its own including family, social customs and manners, often associated (but not necessarily) with religious observance.

The following characteristics are also relevant:

- common geographical origin, or descent from a small number of ancestors;
- common language (not necessarily peculiar to the group);
- common literature;
- common religion, different from neighbouring groups or the general community;
- being a minority, or being in an oppressed or dominant group within a large community.

Case law has established that Sikhs, Jews and Romany gypsies comprise ethnic groups, but Rastafarians and Muslims do not. Interestingly, the Scots and the English have been held to be separate groups. There are many others yet to be tested.

From December 2003, Muslims can seek protection from race discrimination and Rastafarians may be able to seek similar protection against religion or belief discrimination. It is a question of fact whether a belief system or religion constitutes a protected belief or religion (*see also* page 377).

The Race Relations Act 1976 (as amended) prohibits discrimination on racial grounds and not merely discrimination on the grounds of a person's race. Hence a white person can claim discrimination when he is discriminated against because he objects to the racist actions of his employer towards black or ethnic minority staff (or customers). Similarly, as all that is required is a difference on racial grounds it is perfectly permissible for a race claim to be brought by, for example, a Black African applicant against a Black Caribbean employer or vice versa.

Discrimination in employment

Employers are prohibited from discriminating on grounds of race at every stage of employment at any establishment within the UK. This includes applications for jobs, treatment at work and certain treatment after work has ended. Employment is given a wider definition than usual and includes employees, apprentices and contract workers. It also covers other categories of workers such as the police – who are not covered under other areas of employment legislation.

Advertisements

It is unlawful for an employer to advertise a position which indicates an intention to discriminate unlawfully. It will only be lawful if there exists a genuine occupational qualification for the job (*see* page 380).

Engagement

It is unlawful for an employer to discriminate on grounds of race in relation to:

- the arrangements they make for the purpose of determining who should be offered employment;
- the terms on which they offer employment;
- refusing or deliberately omitting to offer employment.

This will cover short-listing, processing of application forms, interviewing and the offer of terms of employment itself.

Training

No discrimination is permissible by an employer on racial grounds in the way in which the employee is afforded access to opportunities for promotion, transfer or training or other employment benefits, facilities or services.

Other detriment and dismissal

Dismissal on racial grounds is almost always unfair. A claim, therefore, before an employment tribunal will deal with both the unfairness of the dismissal and the element of race discrimination as separate issues derived from the same facts. Subjecting an employee to any detriment other than dismissal on the ground of their race is also unlawful. Other detriments normally will include demotion or a wage cut or harassment (*see* below). Constructive dismissal is also covered.

EXCEPTIONS TO RACE DISCRIMINATION

The exceptions listed under this section are generally narrowly construed when tested before the courts or tribunal – i.e. the employer will not be given the benefit of the doubt.

Employment outside the UK

The provisions of the Act do not apply where the employee works wholly or mainly outside the UK or on a British-registered ship, aircraft or hovercraft, wholly outside the UK.

Private household

Except for the provisions relating to victimization, the Act does not apply to the employment of domestic staff in a private household.

Public facilities

The Act will not apply if the employer is concerned with the provision of facilities, benefits or services to the public. For example, an employer offers a service to the public but not to an employee by virtue of a provision under the contract of employment. Provided this restriction is implemented even-handedly by the employer there will be no discrimination.

Genuine occupational qualification

Discrimination will be lawful by an employer where the selection of job candidates is based on a genuine occupational qualification for the job. The requirement by an employer that an employee must belong to a particular racial group is justified only where:
- the job involves participation in a dramatic performance or other entertainment in a capacity for which a person of that racial group is required for reasons of authenticity;
- physiology requires a particular colour or race (e.g. an artist's model);
- in a public restaurant or bar, where authenticity

requires members from a particular racial group (e.g. Chinese staff in a Chinese restaurant);
- in the provision of personal welfare services to a particular racial group, where it would be better provided by someone of the same racial group (e.g. in a group promoting the welfare of Afro-Caribbean mothers, the work may be carried out more effectively by someone of the same Afro-Caribbean origin).

Genuine occupational requirements are also permissible (*see* page 376).

Acts done under statutory authority

No race discrimination will occur if the employer acts in accordance with any condition required by law.

Positive discrimination

Positive discrimination (i.e. favouring people of a particular racial group) in order to provide access to training and work is permissible provided that, if at any time within the preceding 12 months:
1. there were no people from that group doing work at that establishment; or
2. the proportion of people from that group doing work at that establishment is small in comparison with:
   (a) All other staff employed;
   (b) The population of the area from which the employer normally recruits their workforce.

RACIAL HARASSMENT

Racial harassment of an individual can amount to race discrimination but it attracts fewer cases than its counterpart, sexual harassment. The harassment may be verbal, non-verbal or physical. Such activity must amount to a detriment. For example, for security guards to search every black entrant into a premises and not every white could be regarded as harassment. Insults may also amount to harassment but only where it can be shown that the employee has been in some way disadvantaged by the language used. The fact that distress has been caused will not in itself be enough for it to be an unlawful act.

In a recently decided case it was held that it was racial harassment based on a person's national origins where the employer failed to prevent colleagues subjecting the employee to Irish jokes and comments.

Changes to the law

Changes to existing race discrimination law to comply with a European Union Race Directive came into force in July 2003. The new Race Relations Regulations, which implement the EU Directive, apply to discrimination on grounds of race or ethnic or national origins, but not colour or nationality (because the definition of 'race' in the Directive is narrower than under the Race Relations Act 1976). The 1976 Act (as unamended) will therefore still apply to discrimination on grounds of nationality and colour. This confuses an already complex area of law, introducing a two-tier system, with one set of provisions governing the legal position where the discrimination is on the grounds of race, ethnic or national origin and a different set of provisions applicable where the discrimination is on the grounds of nationality or colour. The new Regulations apply not only to employment, but also to social protection and advantages and access to goods and services, including housing. The key changes under the Regulations are:

- a wider definition of indirect discrimination, which will mean that less reliance will be placed by tribunals on statistics and complainants will also be able to complain about informal practices at work that indirectly discriminate against them;
- an explicit right not to be subjected to harassment. The Regulations define harassment as unwanted conduct on the grounds of race or national/ethnic origin which has the purpose or effect of violating dignity or creating an intimidating, hostile, degrading, humiliating or offensive environment. Regard will be had to all the circumstances including, in particular, the perception of the 'victim', to see whether the conduct amounts to harassment as defined;
- a new definition of GOQs. Being of a particular race, ethnic origin or national origin must be a genuine occupational requirement for a particular post and it must also be a determining requirement for that post – i.e. it must be decisive. Even then, it must be proportionate to apply the requirement;
- a shift in the burden of proof requirements. Once the complainant establishes a *prima facie* case of discrimination, the onus will be on the employer to prove that he did not commit an act of unlawful discrimination or harassment.

In addition, new statutory disciplinary and grievance procedures will apply in all discrimination cases (*see* page 368). Where an employer has failed to follow the statutory procedures, the tribunal has the discretion to uplift the compensation awarded by between 10 and 50 per cent.

COMMISSION FOR RACIAL EQUALITY

The 1976 Act established a Commission for Racial Equality (CRE) whose function is to work towards the elimination of discrimination, the promotion of equality of opportunity, good race relations and monitoring the working of the Act. Where an employee or job applicant

believes they have been subjected to race discrimination, they may make contact with their regional CRE office which is empowered to assist with the investigation of their complaint. The CRE also issues codes of practice, which employment tribunals must not ignore.

The Commission for Racial Equality and non-discrimination notices

In addition to undertaking, on request, investigations against employers who are allegedly acting in a discriminatory fashion, the CRE in the course of their inquiries may serve a non-discrimination notice on the employer, requiring them:

- not to commit such acts; or
- to change certain practices or arrangements.

To do this the CRE must first be satisfied that the employer is committing, or has committed, an unlawful discriminatory act or practice or is guilty of placing or publishing an unlawful discriminatory advertisement or has applied pressure to discriminate unlawfully.

The CRE may require verification from the employer that they have complied with the notice. This must be supplied to the CRE within a specified period of time and not later than five years from the date the notice became final.

As can be seen, the CRE have a wide range of powers to prevent or curtail race discrimination at the workplace. Employees who believe they have a valid complaint should not hesitate to contact the CRE whose subsequent process of investigation is taken seriously by most employers. Local employment offices and Job Centres are also a useful source of primary information (*see also* page 384).

DISABLED EMPLOYEES

The Disability Discrimination Act 1995 has as its central objective the elimination of discrimination against disabled people, particularly at their place of work.

The meaning of disability

Under the legislation a person is regarded as having a disability if they have a physical or mental impairment which has a substantial and long-term adverse effect on their ability to carry out normal day-to-day activities. We will look at each part of this definition in more detail.

Impairment

Mental impairment includes an impairment resulting from, or consisting of, a mental illness only if it is a clinically well-recognized illness (for example, mentioned in the World Health Organization's International Classification of Disease).

Long-term effect

A long-term effect is defined as one which has lasted at least 12 months, or where the period for which it lasts can reasonably be expected to be at least 12 months. Of course, this prediction would be required to be supported by an appropriate medical report.

Day-to-day activities

The impairment must affect normal day-to-day activities. This will be deemed to have occurred when the impairment affects one or more of the following:

- mobility;
- manual dexterity;
- physical co-ordination;
- continence;
- ability to lift;
- ability to carry or otherwise move everyday objects;
- speech;
- hearing;
- eyesight;
- memory;
- ability to concentrate or learn;
- ability to perceive physical danger;
- substantial and adverse effect.

In determining whether an impairment has an adverse effect on a person's ability to carry out activities, the fact that a person can, with difficulty and great effort, carry out the activities does not mean that their ability to carry them out has not been impaired. In addition, where the person is on medication, consideration must be given to how the activities would have been affected without medication. Substantial means more than 'minor' or 'trivial'. In general, asthma, epilepsy, ME, post-traumatic stress disorder, ureteric colic, and depression being treated by Prozac have all been held by tribunals to be disability within the meaning of the Act.

Unfortunately, normal day-to-day activities do not appear to include the actual work done by the complainant. The complainant's status as a disabled person is determined by his capability outside of work – not by reference to his duties at work.

Jack works at a DIY superstore. He injures his back playing football. Afterwards he cannot lift heavy objects at the store. He is dismissed for lack of capability. His claim for disability discrimination fails because he is not found to be disabled. This is because his back injury does not sufficiently adversely affect his normal day-to-day activities (such as lifting a kettle or climbing a flight of stairs), even though it does prevent him from being able to carry out his tasks at work. In other words, lifting heavy objects is not viewed as a normal day-to-day activity.

Discrimination in employment

It is unlawful for an employer to discriminate against a disabled person in the arrangements made for determining to whom he should offer employment, the terms upon which employment is offered, refusal to offer, or deliberately not offering, employment. In much the same way that the race and sex discrimination laws operate, it is also unlawful to discriminate against a disabled person in the terms and conditions, opportunities for promotion, transfers and training provided by the employer. Disabled employees must not be dismissed on the ground of their disability or subjected to any other detriment.

Constructive dismissal is also covered, together with certain post-employment acts of discrimination.

Treated less favourably

Less favourable treatment of a disabled employee will be discriminatory unless the employer can justify the treatment. There are four specified conditions in which justification can be established as reasonable in the circumstances:

1 the disabled person is unsuitable for the employment;
2 the disabled person is less suitable for the employment than another applicant who was appointed;
3 the nature of the disabled person's disability significantly impedes, or would significantly impede, the performance of their duties;
4 the nature of the disabled person's disability would significantly reduce the value of any training provided by the employer.

Closely linked to less favourable treatment is the employer's duty to take such steps as are reasonable to prevent any work arrangements or any physical features of the employer's premises from placing a disabled applicant or employee at a substantial disadvantage compared to non-disabled applicants and employees (*see* below). If an employer has not complied with his duty to make adjustments, the defence of justification is only available if the less favourable treatment would have been justified even if the duty had been complied with.

Duty to make reasonable adjustments

In certain circumstances a specific duty is placed on the employer, in law, to make changes to work arrangements or to any physical feature (e.g. stairs) of the work premises which places the disabled person at a substantial disadvantage in comparison with able-bodied persons. The duty on the employer is to take all reasonable steps in the circumstances to alter the arrangements or physical feature, or to prevent them from having that effect.

The disabled person may be either an applicant or present employee. If a conclusion may be drawn that an arrangement or a physical feature does treat the disabled person less favourably, the employer, to defend their position, must then show that to alter the arrangements or physical feature would be unreasonable in all the circumstances.

An employee may, therefore, expect an employer, or prospective employer, to make reasonable adjustments to the workplace in order to overcome the practical effects of the disability. That does not mean the employer is under a duty to make the best adjustment possible in the circumstances but to do what may be reasonably expected.

Reasonable adjustments may include:

- widening doorways or making other adjustments to premises;
- re-allocating some of the disabled person's duties;
- transferring them to fill an existing vacancy;
- altering their hours of work;
- assigning them to a different place of work, or allowing them to work from home;
- allowing them to be absent during working hours for assessment or treatment;
- providing training;
- acquiring or modifying equipment;
- modifying instructions or manuals;
- providing a reader;
- providing supervision;
- modifying testing and assessment procedures.

In determining what steps it is reasonable for an employee to take, the following will be relevant:

1 Is it practicable for the employer to take the steps?
2 What are the costs?
3 What are the employer's resources?
4 Is any financial or other assistance available to the employer?

In addition, there is no general duty on an employer to require them to adapt their workplace or change their working practices to make them accessible in anticipation of possibly having a disabled applicant or employee at some time in the future.

Anthony applies for a job with Gossip Radio FM. Gossip Radio have 36 employees. He is interviewed by Kevin McDifficult. Anthony is blind, and has been so since birth. He is applying for a job as a receptionist. At the interview Kevin says that although he does not have anything against taking on a blind person, the receptionist's console, as it stands, can only be operated by a sighted operator. In addition, Kevin says he is allergic to Golden Labradors such as Anna, Anthony's faithful guide dog. One week later Anthony receives a letter from Kevin saying his application for the position was unsuccessful. Anthony seeks legal advice.

Gossip Radio have more than 15 employees and, therefore, the provisions of the Disability Discrimination Act apply. Upon investigation, which Kevin was not prepared to undertake because he was too busy, it was discovered that the receptionist's console could be adapted for use by a blind person for the small cost of £250. Anthony files a claim of disability discrimination against Gossip Radio and is successful. The tribunal find that Gossip Radio should have undertaken the 'reasonable adjustment' to their reception console since Anthony (on all other criteria) was the best candidate for the job. Anthony is awarded £16,000 compensation to cover his losses and injury to feelings. Kevin's alleged allergy to Golden Labradors is ruled as irrelevant.

SMALL EMPLOYERS

Where the employer employs fewer than 15 staff they are exempt from claims of disability discrimination. However, they are encouraged to follow good practice guidelines. This exception is to be removed in 2004 (*see* below).

Changes to the law

The Disability Discrimination Act 1995 (Amendment) Regulations 2003 will amend the Disability Discrimination Act 1995 to ensure the Act is consistent with the requirements of the EU Employment Framework Directive. It is planned that the new regulations will come into effect on 1 October 2004. The main changes to the law on disability discrimination will be:

- where the reason for the less favourable treatment is merely that the person has a disability, that can never be justified. An example of the sort of situation where the employer will not be permitted to justify their actions is where a disabled job applicant is rejected without any consideration of whether he would be able to do the job;
- the introduction of a new offence prohibiting harassment against disabled employees on the grounds of their disability;
- the removal of the small-employer exception, so that employers with fewer than 15 employees will be covered by the Act;
- the possibility of justifying a failure to make a reasonable adjustment is to be removed;
- instructions and pressure to discriminate will be made unlawful (e.g. a parent company putting pressure on one of its subsidiaries to dismiss a disabled employee);
- making unlawful certain acts of discrimination and harassment after employment has ended;
- employment on ships, planes and hovercraft, firefighters, prison officers and specialized police forces will be covered.

In addition to the European agenda, the UK government has also indicated that it will extend the definition of disability to cover progressive conditions such as cancer and MS automatically from the point of diagnosis.

Bringing a claim

The disabled employee who believes they have been discriminated against by their employer or prospective employer may bring an action for compensation before an employment tribunal. The tribunal's powers are similar to those which apply to complaints of race and sex discrimination. There is no upper limit to compensation. In addition, an amount may be awarded for injury to feelings.

The National Disability Council and the Northern Ireland Disability Council established under the Act are responsible for drawing up codes of practice which affect disabled people in the workplace.

The Disability Rights Commission

The Disability Rights Commission (DRC) has statutory powers of enforcement, as are afforded to the EOC and the CRE. The DRC's mission is to work towards the elimination of discrimination against disabled people. It also promotes the equalization of opportunities for disabled people with those of non-disabled people, promotes good practice among employers and service providers, advises the government on legal issues concerning discrimination against disabled people and is a central source of advice for employers and business.

Useful sources of information

Commission for Racial Equality (CRE)
St Dunstan's House
201–211 Borough High Street
London SE1 1GZ
Tel: 020 7939 0000; Website: www.cre.gov.uk

Equal Opportunities Commission (EOC)
Arndale House
Arndale Centre
Manchester M4 3EQ
Tel: 0845 601 5901; Website: www.eoc.org.uk

Disability Rights Commission (DRC)
Freepost MID 02164
Stratford-upon-Avon CV37 9BR
Tel: 08457 622 633; Website: www.drc-gb.org

London Discrimination Unit
Tel: 020 7737 9770; Website: www.no-dis.org
Provides advice and representation to people living or working in a London borough.

National Association of Citizens' Advice Bureaux (NACAB)
Myddleton House
115–123 Pentonville Road
London N1 9LZ
Tel: 020 7833 2181; Website: www.nacab.org.uk

Disability Alliance
Universal House
88–94 Wentworth Street
London E1 7SA
Tel: 020 7247 8776; Website: www.disabilityalliance.org.uk

Disability Law Service Free Legal Advice
39–45 Cavell Street
London E1 2BP
Tel: 020 7791 9880; e-mail: advice@dis.org.uk

Discrimination Law Association
PO Box 36054
London SW16 1WF
Tel: 020 8769 2020; e-mail: info@discriminationlaw.org.uk

Law Centres Federation
Duchess House
18–19 Warren Street
London W1T 5LR
Tel: 020 7387 8570; Website: www.lawcentres.org.uk

Lesbian and Gay Employment Rights (LAGER)
Unit 1G Leroy House
436 Essex Road
London N1 3QP
Tel: 020 7704 6066 (gay men's helpline); 020 7704 8066 (lesbian helpline); 020 7704 2205 (administration and general inquiries); Website: www.lager.dircon.co.uk

Maternity Alliance
45 Beech Street
London EC2P 2LX
Tel: 020 7588 8582; Website: www.maternityalliance.org.uk

Rights of Women
52–54 Featherstone Street
London EC1Y 8RT
Tel: 020 7490 5377; Website: www.rightsofwomen.org.uk

Stonewall
46–48 Grosvenor Gardens
London SW1W 0EB
Tel: 020 7881 9440; Website: www.stonewall.org.uk

Employment Tribunal Service Central Office
Central Office of the Employment Service
19–29 Woburn Place
London WC1H 0LU
Tel: 020 7273 8575; Website: www.employment tribunals.gov.uk
For access to published information about how to apply to a tribunal, addresses of tribunals.

39

Maternity and Parental Leave

INTRODUCTION

There are many rights which currently exist in the UK specifically to protect pregnant women, to provide a period of leave for the mother immediately before and after the birth of her child and to allow her to return to her place of work. The statutory rights in relation to maternity are, broadly:

- time off for ante-natal care with pay;
- the right not to be unfairly dismissed or suffer any other detriment for a reason connected to maternity;
- maternity pay;
- the right, in certain circumstances, to return to work after childbirth.

MATERNITY RIGHTS DURING PREGNANCY

Any pregnant woman who has, on the advice of her doctor, health visitor or midwife, made an appointment for ante-natal care has the right to reasonable time off during working hours to enable her to attend the appointment. She is entitled to be paid during her absence at the normal hourly rate.

No employer must unreasonably refuse time off for ante-natal care. Ante-natal care includes medical examinations, parent craft and relaxation classes. There is no minimum service or working hours per week requirement before the woman may enjoy these rights.

In return, the employee is expected to act reasonably and, except for the first appointment for ante-natal care she must, if requested by the employer, produce for inspection:

1 a certificate from her doctor, midwife or health visitor stating that she is pregnant; and
2 an appointment card.

The employee should be paid her normal hourly rate of pay during her time off for ante-natal care. This rate is calculated by dividing the amount of a week's pay by the number of normal working hours in a week. The normal working hours will usually be clearly stated in a contract of employment, letter of appointment or written statement of particulars of employment. If the hours are variable, an average should be taken over the preceding 12 working weeks. If 12 weeks have not been worked the hours should be reasonably estimated by reference to custom and practice. Overtime is only counted if the employee is contractually obliged to work additional hours as the needs of the business dictate.

Remedies

A woman who believes she has been unreasonably refused time off for ante-natal care may complain to an employment tribunal within three months from the date of the appointment concerned. This may be extended if there are practical reasons why a complaint within this time period was not possible. If the complaint is upheld, the tribunal will make a declaration to that effect and order payment of the money due.

DISMISSAL FOR REQUESTING OR ASSERTING THE RIGHT TO TIME OFF

Any employee who is dismissed for seeking to assert, or asserting, the right to time off for ante-natal care will have been dismissed unlawfully. A claim for unfair dismissal may be brought before an employment tribunal. There is no service requirement, i.e. the woman need not have worked for the employer for a minimum amount of time.

Dismissal for Pregnancy

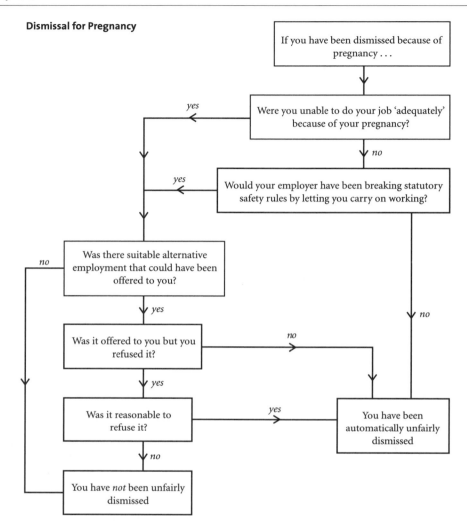

PREGNANCY – PROTECTION FROM DISMISSAL

Regardless of length of service or weekly hours, it is automatically unfair to dismiss a woman if the reason or principal reason is the following:

- that she is pregnant;
- any reason connected with her pregnancy;
- any reason connected with her having given birth to a child;
- because she took advantage of the benefits of maternity leave;
- that, because of her pregnancy, she was selected for redundancy in preference to other comparable employees.

A dismissal in connection with pregnancy may also amount to sex discrimination (*see* Chapter 38). A woman also has the right not to be subjected to any detriment for reasons relating to pregnancy, childbirth or maternity.

Exceptions

Where the employee is dismissed with due notice because her pregnancy-related incapacity or because her continued employment would lead to a breach of the law (usually on grounds of health and safety) she will not be entitled to claim unfair dismissal.

Any dismissal which is on grounds largely or wholly unrelated to pregnancy or childbirth. For example, a genuinely coincidental redundancy situation.

Written statement of reasons for dismissal

Normally an employee requires one year's continuous service before being entitled to a written statement of the reasons for dismissal. However, if the employee is dismissed during pregnancy or statutory maternity leave, irrespective of her length of service, the following will apply:

1 she will be entitled to an accurate written statement of the reasons;
2 she need not formally request this statement.

If the employer fails to provide a statement or it is unsatisfactory or allegedly untrue, the employee may complain to an employment tribunal within three months less one day of the refusal or receipt of the inadequate reasons.

Remedies

Any claim for automatic unfair dismissal for a reason connected with pregnancy or childbirth must be brought before an employment tribunal within three months less one day of the dismissal.

MATERNITY LEAVE AND THE RIGHT TO RETURN TO WORK

Rather confusingly there are potentially three situations where the employee has the right to return to work within a specified period of time. Two are statutory; one is contractual. The legislation no longer refers to a right to return. Instead, it refers to a right to take either ordinary maternity leave or additional maternity leave. The three situations are as follows:

1 the right to 26 weeks' ordinary maternity leave;
2 the right to 26 weeks' additional maternity leave beginning at the end of ordinary maternity leave;
3 the right to any greater period of maternity leave/absence within the contract of employment or as otherwise agreed between the employer and employee.

Ordinary maternity leave period

All pregnant employees are entitled to at least 26 weeks' statutory maternity leave. This applies regardless of their length of service or hours of work.

Commencement

The 26 weeks' leave may commence at any time after the beginning of the eleventh week before the expected week of childbirth (EWC). If the employee is absent due to a pregnancy-related illness before the date she intended to take her leave, the maternity leave period starts automatically on the day after the first day of absence following the beginning of the fourth week before the expected week of childbirth. If childbirth occurs before the date the employee has notified (or before she has notified any date), the maternity leave period starts automatically on the day after the date of birth. It follows that the basic 26 weeks' leave can commence in one of three ways:

1 by childbirth itself;
2 pregnancy-related illness;
3 by the employee giving notice to the employer of the date on which she wishes to commence her maternity leave.

In return for the benefit of the 26 weeks' leave the employee must comply with certain procedural requirements to be fair to the employer. She must:

1 tell the employer that she is pregnant – in practice at the earliest opportunity;
2 notify the employer of her expected week of childbirth by way of appropriate medical certificate;
3 provide notification of the date when she wishes leave to commence;
4 give notification to the employer:
   (a) not later than the 18th week before the EWC;
   (b) as soon as reasonably practicable if the notice provision cannot be complied with for good reason.

Written notice of pregnancy is not essential. Notification of the date of commencement of maternity leave need not be given in writing unless the employer requests written notification. The employee can change the date on which she intends to start leave by giving at least 28 days' notice. The employer must respond to this notice within 28 days, in writing, stating the date it understands the employee will return from maternity leave. If an employer fails to give this notification, then it cannot prevent the employee from returning early should she wish to do so.

Joanna is employed by Richard, the owner of the Lovely Motor used car emporium, and has eight months' service. She is six months pregnant. She is unsure of her entitlement to leave and maternity pay, and whenever she asks Richard, his smooth-talking fails to provide her with either answers or reassurance. Joanna would also like to return to work on reduced hours once the baby is born. She seeks legal advice.

Joanna will have 26 weeks' service by the 14th week before the EWC and will, therefore, be entitled to ordinary maternity leave of 26 weeks and additional maternity leave of 26 weeks. This leave may commence any time after the eleventh week before the EWC. When Joanna chooses to commence leave she will be entitled to statutory maternity pay (SMP) for the duration of the ordinary maternity leave; the first six weeks at 90 per cent of her pay and the remaining 20 weeks at the lower rate of SMP – £100 or 90 per cent of pay, whichever is less.

She should notify Richard of the date she wishes to

commence leave no later than the 15th week before the EWC or as soon as possible. Joanna's contract of employment will continue throughout her maternity leave and she will be entitled to all contractual benefits during leave, for example, her company car, private health care payment and employer's pension contribution. She will also continue to accrue holiday entitlement while on leave.

With regard to her wish to return to work part-time, she is advised to raise this with Richard at the earliest opportunity. Richard must carefully consider her request and must not reject it out of hand. Richard must accommodate a part-time return where there is no good business reason to refuse her request. If the job requires full-time hours, Richard should also consider the possibility of a job share (see page 389).

Early return

This is possible if the employee provides the employer with at least 28 days' notice of her intended early return date.

Return on the due date

An employee need not give notice of return if she intends to return at the end of her ordinary maternity leave period. She can simply present herself for work.

Extension

This may occur in the following situations:

1 the baby is overdue, in which case the 26-week period is extended to the date of the birth, plus a minimum of two weeks, since it is unlawful for a woman to return to work less than two weeks after childbirth;

2 where health and safety reasons, which are related to the recent birth of the child or breast feeding, prohibit the mother from returning. Where this occurs the period of 26 weeks will be extended until it is safe for her to return.

Sickness at the end of maternity leave will not postpone return. Instead, normal sick leave procedures at the woman's place of work will apply. A woman who fails to give proper notice of taking or returning from maternity leave will be treated as being on unauthorized absence and liable to disciplinary action, but she will not forfeit her maternity rights.

Payment during ordinary maternity leave

The employee is entitled to all benefits *except* pay. She may, therefore, receive all contractual benefits such as:

- private health care;
- use of the company car (if applicable);
- accrued holiday;
- pension contributions;
- other service-related benefits.

Additional maternity leave period

A woman will only acquire the right to additional maternity leave in certain circumstances. To qualify she must have 26 weeks' continuous service with her employer by the beginning of the 14th week before the EWC.

The additional maternity leave entitlement

Provided she qualifies, the employee will be entitled to additional maternity leave of 26 weeks, which begins at the end of ordinary maternity leave. Thus, a woman who qualifies for AML will be able to take a total of 52 weeks' maternity leave.

Childbirth

It is possible that the woman may have a still-birth or miscarriage. To take this factor into account the statutory provisions state that the definition of childbirth is the birth of a living child or the birth of a child whether living or dead after 24 weeks of pregnancy. Should a miscarriage occur before the end of the twenty-fourth week of pregnancy and the employee is off sick as a result, she will not be regarded as absent through childbirth (although a dismissal for this absence may amount to sex discrimination – see Chapter 38). Ordinary contractual or statutory sick pay provisions will apply.

Early return

The employee can provide the employer with at least 28 days' notice of her intended return date if she intends to return earlier than the end of her additional maternity leave period.

Return on the due date

An employee can simply present herself for work at the end of her additional maternity leave period.

Contractual rights during additional maternity leave

The contract of employment continues during the additional leave period. The employee is entitled to the benefit of her employer's implied obligation to her of trust and confidence, and any terms and conditions of her employment relating to:

- notice of termination;
- redundancy compensation;
- disciplinary and grievance procedures.

Likewise, the employee is bound by her obligation to her employer of good faith and any terms and conditions of her employment relating to:

- notice of termination;
- disclosure of confidential information;
- acceptance of gifts;
- participation in any other business.

Resumption of work

The employee is entitled to return to the same job with the same terms and conditions of employment as if she had never been away from work. Furthermore, if in her absence there have been made any general improvements to the terms and conditions of employment by her employer, she is entitled to benefit as if she had been at work. However, an employee on AML is entitled to return not to the same job but to a substantially similar post.

If a genuine redundancy situation has arisen while the employee was on maternity leave and her original job no longer exists, the employer or any associated employer must offer her a suitable alternative vacancy where one is available. The new job must be:

- suitable and appropriate in the circumstances;
- on no less favourable terms than the original contract.

It will be regarded as an unfair dismissal if a suitable vacancy exists but the employer fails to offer it to the returning mother. If, for a reason other than redundancy, it is impracticable for the employee to return to her original position, she must be offered a suitable alternative vacancy and the same two conditions will apply. In practice, there is a very strong obligation on the employer to allow return to the *same* job – any comparable position will not do without an extremely good business reason.

As detailed above, a woman who fails to return from additional maternity leave will be treated as being on unauthorized absence and liable to disciplinary action, but she will not forfeit her maternity rights.

Small employers

Businesses which employ less than five people (including employees of any associated employer) immediately before the end of the additional leave period are not subject to the automatic unfair dismissal provisions provided that it is not reasonably practicable to permit the employee to return to a suitable job. To deny return legitimately they must be able to show why their action is reasonable and practicable in the circumstances.

Returning to part-time work

If the employer allows a request to return part-time, there is no problem in law and no break in service. The terms and conditions, in particular the hours, are deemed to have been varied by mutual agreement. However, the right is to return to the same job and that means in theory to the same hours as under the original contract. That said, the employer is under a duty to carefully consider the employee's request for fewer hours. If the request is rejected for no good reason, the woman may bring a claim of indirect sex discrimination before an employment tribunal. She may bring this claim even where she returns to full-time work under sufferance.

Increasingly, employers are considered to be acting in a discriminatory fashion if they do not consider or accommodate an employee's request in this regard. Sound business reasons must exist for the refusal to allow part-time work to be justifiable.

New right to request flexible working

From April 2003, employees who are parents of young children have the right to request flexible work patterns. Employers must give the request serious consideration. Note that this is not a right to work flexibly – only a right to request a new work pattern relating to e.g. hours worked, shifts or place of work (including working at home).

In order to qualify for this right a parent must:

- be an employee (not an agency worker);
- have been continuously employed for at least 26 weeks at the date of the application;
- have a child under 6, or 18 where the child is disabled;
- be responsible for the child as its parent or as the partner of the parent (including adoptive and foster parents);
- be making the application to enable them to care for the child; and
- have not made another application to work flexibly during the past 12 months.

If the request is agreed, this will form a permanent change to the employee's terms and conditions. There is a prescribed procedure for making the application and the employer must follow the timetable stipulated in the legislation. The timetable specifies time limits for meeting to discuss the application, notifying the employee of the decision, setting up and holding an appeal meeting. The employer must justify a refusal in writing, giving a sufficient explanation of the business reasons for doing so and setting out the appeals procedure.

Where the employer rejects the request for flexible working, there are only limited grounds for complaining to an employment tribunal. Complaint may be made that the employer:

- failed to hold a meeting to discuss the application, or
- failed to hold an appeal meeting, or
- failed to give notice to the employee of the decision on the application or on the appeal, or
- refused the application on a non-specified ground, or
- rejected the application on incorrect facts.

Where the complaint is upheld the tribunal can order that the application should be reconsidered and award compensation up to a maximum of 8 weeks' pay.

It is automatically unfair to dismiss an employee for making or proposing to make an application for flexible working time and an employee cannot be subjected to a detriment for the same reason.

Break in employment

The period of maternity leave will not break continuity of service and will count as service for the purpose of calculating statutory notice or redundancy entitlement.

Maternity suspension

An employee may be suspended from work on maternity grounds if a specified health and safety regulation prevents her from doing her normal tasks and duties because either:

- she is pregnant; or
- she has recently given birth; or
- she is breast feeding.

Should this occur the woman will have certain rights, which, broadly, are:

- to be offered any other suitable work available before being suspended;
- to be paid at her normal rate of pay for the duration of suspension – however long;
- protection from dismissal because of a health and safety provision which does, or could, give rise to necessary maternity suspension.

These rights apply irrespective of the length of the employee's service or weekly hours. Any complaints in respect of the above may be made to an employment tribunal. The pregnant woman is entitled to full pay during the period of suspension.

MATERNITY PAY

There are two entitlements to money for maternity (*see also* page 296). The first, Maternity Allowance (MA) is paid directly by the Department of Work and Pensions. The second, Statutory Maternity Pay (SMP), is administered and paid by the employer (although at least some of it can be recouped by the employer from National Insurance contributions that would otherwise be paid). Broadly, the difference between the two is the status of the woman, i.e. whether she is unemployed or employed respectively.

Maternity Allowance

This is normally payable where:

- the woman is unemployed from the eleventh week before the EWC;
- the woman is employed or self-employed from a week of her choosing, but no earlier than the eleventh week before the expected week of childbirth.

The entitlement to MA has conditions. These are:

1 the woman must be pregnant and have reached, or have given birth before reaching, the eleventh week before the expected week of childbirth;
2 she must have been an employed or self-employed earner for at least 26 weeks in the 66 weeks ending with the week before the expected week of birth;
3 she must *not* be entitled to SMP.

The payment period is 26 weeks, payable any time after the eleventh week before the expected week of confinement. The right to claim MA may be lost if the mother does not make the claim within 12 months of the birth. The rate of pay over that period is as follows:

Standard rate – £100 per week or 90 per cent of the woman's average weekly earnings, whichever is less.

The figures quoted in this section are subject to government review in April each year (*see also* page 289).

Statutory Maternity Pay

Eligibility for SMP is dependent upon the employee fulfilling the following conditions:

1 she must have been continuously employed by her employer for at least 26 weeks continuing into the fifteenth week before the expected week of birth (the fifteenth week is known as the Qualifying Week (QW));
2 she must have stopped working for the employer wholly or partly as a result of pregnancy or confinement;
3 she must have average weekly earnings of not less than the lower earnings limit in force at the time for payment of National Insurance contributions for the period of eight weeks ending with the QW (the current (1 April 2003) lower earnings limit is £77.00 per week);
4 she must have become pregnant, and still be pregnant, at the beginning of the eleventh week before the expected week of birth, or have given birth;
5 she must give notice to the employer that she intends to stop working because of her pregnancy (*see* page 387);
6 she must provide her employer with medical evidence for her expected week of giving birth.

SMP is not conditional on an intention to return to work after the maternity leave.

The qualifying week

This is simply calculated as the fifteenth week before the EWC.

Continuous service

Employment for any part of each of the 26 weeks will be sufficient to preserve continuity. The following will also count as continuous weeks of service:

- where the employee is incapable of work due to sickness or injury;
- she is absent from work due to a temporary cessation of work;
- she is absent from work in circumstances that, through the custom and practice of the employer, are regarded as continuing employment;
- she is absent from work, wholly or partly, because of pregnancy or childbirth.

A transfer of a business resulting in a change in the woman's employer will not affect continuity of service for the purposes of SMP.

Medical evidence

Statutory Maternity Pay can only be paid where the employer is in receipt of evidence of the expected date of childbirth. This is usually complied with by providing for the employer form MAT B1 (Certificate of Maternity).

Payment

Statutory Maternity Pay is regarded as earnings and will therefore attract tax and National Insurance contribution deductions. It may be paid on the employee's normal pay days for the duration of the payment period or paid in a lump sum.

The maternity pay period

Statutory Maternity Pay is payable for a 26-week period. It only becomes a shorter period if:
- the woman is taken into legal custody;
- she goes outside countries which are members of the European Union or the European Free Trade Agreement;
- she works during the period;
- she dies.

In general, when it starts depends upon when the employee gives notice and stops work (*see* below).

Working during the period

The woman does not have to leave employment at the fifteenth week before the expected week of confinement. She could carry on working right up to childbirth, provided no health and safety regulations restrain her. The first week of the period may not be earlier than the eleventh week before the expected week of childbirth, nor later than the first week which immediately follows childbirth. It may be in the woman's interest financially to continue working for as long as possible given the rate

of SMP she is to receive as compared to her wage or salary.

The rates of SMP

There are two rates: the lower and higher rate.

The lower rate – £100 per week or 90 per cent of pay, whichever is lower.

The higher rate – 90 per cent of the average weekly wage.

The higher rate is payable for a maximum of six weeks, the lower rate then becomes payable for up to the remaining 20 weeks of the period. The lower rate is subject to government review in April each year.

MISCELLANEOUS POINTS ON STATUTORY MATERNITY PAY

Non-payment

If the employer decides not to pay or to stop paying SMP, the woman is entitled to reasons for the decision provided for her on form SMP1. Disputes over non-payment go before an Inland Revenue Officer for a formal decision. One can appeal against their decision to a Tax Commissioner. The employment tribunal does not have the jurisdiction to order SMP during the course of employment.

Multiple births

One amount of SMP only is payable irrespective of how many babies are expected by the mother.

Multiple employers

Provided the employee qualifies according to the payment rules, there is nothing in theory to prevent SMP being payable by two or more employers.

Insolvency

Where SMP is payable but the employer becomes insolvent, the Secretary of State is obliged to pay the employee. In other words, even if the employer goes bust, the employee's statutory entitlement is guaranteed.

CONTRACTUAL MATERNITY ENTITLEMENTS

This section has concentrated on the statutory rights in respect of maternity. That is, what represents the 'floor of rights' beneath which the employer may not go. However, there are a number of employers who are willing to provide entitlements to both leave and pay over and above the statutory minimums. As with all contractual matters this may occur through express provision of the contract of employment, oral agreement or be implied through custom and practice as a term and condition of employment. In such cases, the statutory provision becomes a 'fall-back' position for the employee which may or may not need to be relied upon. Should enhanced contractual entitlements exist, but be breached by the employer, the employee's remedy is one for damages for breach of contract before an employment tribunal, county court or High Court, depending on the amount in dispute.

Paid Paternity Leave

Since April 2003, employees have had a statutory right to take paternity leave on the birth of a child, or placement of a child for adoption. Paternity leave may be taken by employees who:

- have or expect to have responsibility for the child's upbringing; and
- are the biological father of the child or the mother's husband or partner (includes same-sex partners); or
- are the spouse or partner (including same sex) of a child's adopter – who is themself taking adoption leave (*see* below); and
- have 26 weeks' continuous service with their employer leading up to the 15th week before the EWC or in the case of adoption, 26 weeks ending with the week in which the child's adopter is notified as being matched with the child.

Employees who qualify are able to take up to two weeks' leave. The leave may be taken in a two-week block or a one-week block but the two weeks cannot be taken at separate times. So if a one-week block is taken, there will be no opportunity to take the other week at a later date. The leave cannot start until the birth of the baby or the day of the child's placement for adoption and must be taken within 56 days of the birth or placement. If the child is born prematurely, the leave must be taken within 56 days of the first day of the original EWC. The employee is only entitled to one period of leave, even if there is more than one child as a result of the same pregnancy.

The employee must give the employer notice that they want to take paternity leave by the 15th week before the EWC (unless that is not reasonably practicable). In cases of adoption, notice must be given no more than seven days after the adopter was notified of having been matched with a child for adoption. Employers can ask for a self-certificate confirming the employee's eligibility to claim paternity leave and pay. This self-certificate must be produced in order to qualify for Statutory Paternity Pay, which is £100 per week or 90 per cent of average weekly earnings (whichever is lower). Employees with average weekly earnings below the lower earnings limit (currently £77 per week) will not qualify for statutory paternity pay. Dismissal on the grounds that an employee took or sought to take paternity leave will be automatically unfair. Furthermore, the employee cannot be subjected to any detriment at work for the same reason.

Adoption Leave

Employees who are eligible to take adoption leave are entitled to 26 weeks' ordinary adoption leave and a further 26 weeks' additional adoption leave – but only one parent of an adopted child can take adoption leave (though the other could take parental leave or paternity leave for adopters). Adoption leave is not available where the child is already known to the adopters, as in step-family adoptions or adoption by existing foster carers.

Employees who are eligible to take adoption leave are those who:

- are newly matched with a child for adoption (a child is defined as a person under the age of 18); and
- have 26 weeks' continuous service leading into the week of the notification of being matched; and
- provide such evidence of the match as is required by the employer.

For those who qualify, Statutory Adoption Pay is £100 per week or 90 per cent of pay, whichever is the lower, for 26 weeks during the whole of the ordinary adoption leave period. The employee's rights during leave and right to return are the same as under the maternity leave provisions. Adopters must inform their employers of their intention to take adoption leave within seven days of being notified by the adoption agency that they have been matched with a child for adoption (unless not reasonably practicable). As with maternity leave, once an employer has received notification that an employee intends to take the leave, it must notify the employee (within 28 days) of the date on which the leave will end. The notification requirements for returning early from adoption leave are the same as for maternity leave.

If an employee is dismissed for taking or seeking to take adoption leave, that will be automatically unfair. Again, the employee is protected against detriment which is attributable to the fact that they took or sought to take leave.

PARENTAL LEAVE

Since 15 December 1999, there has been a new right of parental leave, introduced in order to comply with the EU Parental Leave Directive. The law entitles an employee to be absent from work on parental leave in order to care for a natural or an adopted child.

The main provisions of the parental leave scheme are:

1 A right for natural mothers and fathers (as named on the child's birth certificate) and adoptive mothers and fathers to each take up to 13 weeks' *unpaid* time off work to care for a child during the first five years of its life (or the first five years after adoption, up to age 18 years). The right applies to children born after 15 December 1999 or children under 18 years adopted after that date. Parents who have acquired formal parental responsibility for a child born after 15 December 1999 who is under five years old also qualify. In the case of twins, 13 weeks' leave must be provided for each child.

2 Parents of disabled children born after 15 December 1999 are able to use their entitlement to 13 weeks' unpaid leave over a longer period, up until the child's eighteenth birthday. A disabled child is a child for whom disability living allowance is awarded.

3 Employees qualify if they have one year's continuous service with their employer.

4 The employee remains employed while on parental leave, his job must be kept open and he must not lose any of his seniority and pension rights that he had built up before taking parental leave.

5 The employer is not required to keep records, but he can reasonably ask for evidence to support a request for parental leave. When an employee changes jobs, employers are free to make inquiries of a previous employer or seek a declaration from the employee about how much parental leave he has taken. If an employee behaves dishonestly in claiming entitlement to parental leave, the employer is entitled to take disciplinary action.

The government has proposed a 'fallback scheme' for parental leave, which will automatically apply where employers and employees have not agreed their own scheme. The key elements outlined above must be part of any agreed scheme, although it can be more generous. For example, employees must be able to take the equivalent of 13 weeks' leave, whether the agreed scheme allows this to be in days, weeks, one long block or as reduced working hours or a mixture of all of these. Subject to this requirement, collective or workforce agreements can set aside the government's fallback scheme and replace it with a different set of arrangements entirely. Arrangements can cover matters such as how much notice of parental leave must be given, arrangements for postponing leave when the business cannot cope, and how it should be taken.

If no scheme is agreed, the fallback scheme also provides the following:

- leave must be taken in blocks of one week, up to a maximum of four weeks' leave in a year (for each child). If leave is to care for a disabled child, leave may be taken a day at a time or longer if they wish;
- 21 days' notice must be given by the employee;
- the employer can postpone leave where the operation of the employer's business would be unduly disrupted by the employee taking leave, but not for more than six months;
- leave cannot be postponed when an employee gives notice to take it immediately after the time the child is born or placed with the family for adoption.

An employee may complain to an employment tribunal where his employer has unreasonably postponed a period of parental leave or has prevented him from taking parental leave. Employees also have the right not to be subjected to any detriment for reasons relating to parental leave and any dismissal on these grounds is automatically unfair.

Ben works for Albion Ltd, a small family-run construction company. His wife Eileen is expecting their first child in two months' time. Ben asks his employer for one week's parental leave immediately after the birth of the child. Albion refuse Ben's request, saying that it would be inconvenient since the proposed leave coincides with a busy contract period for the company. Albion have no parental leave agreement in place for their workers.

The 'fallback scheme' applies. Since Ben has given his employer 21 days' notice and is requesting leave immediately after the birth of the child, Albion's business commitments cannot be used to postpone Ben's request on this occasion. Ben is advised to repeat his request once more and, if his employer continues to refuse it, he should apply to an employment tribunal for a declaration and enforcement. Should Albion dismiss Ben, he has the right to claim unfair dismissal (irrespective of his length of service) since he will have been dismissed for asserting the statutory right to take parental leave.

TIME OFF FOR FAMILY EMERGENCIES

In addition to parental leave, there is a right to take a reasonable amount of time off work to deal with family emergencies. This is *unpaid* leave and there is no minimum service requirement.

The government has given the following examples of cases that will be covered:

- to provide assistance or make arrangements for the provision of care if a dependant falls ill, is injured or assaulted, or gives birth;
- dealing with the consequences of the death of a dependant, for example, dealing with funeral arrangements and attending the funeral;
- dealing with the consequences of a child being involved in an incident at school or during school hours;
- where child care, or other arrangements for the care of a dependant, break down.

For these purposes, a 'dependant' generally means a spouse, child, parent or a person living in the employee's household as part of the family. In the first and last example of cases covered, 'dependant' also includes any person who reasonably relies on the employee for assistance, or to make arrangements for the provision of care, in the event of illness or injury.

The employee is obliged to tell his employer the reason for his absence as soon as reasonably practicable and how long he expects to be absent. An employee may complain to an employment tribunal where his employer has failed to permit him to take time off. Employees also have the right not to be subjected to any detriment for reasons relating to time off for family emergencies and any dismissal on these grounds is automatically unfair and not subject to a service requirement.

Molly is a single mother and has been working as a receptionist at a large telecommunications company for three months. Molly is telephoned at work by the head teacher of her son's school. She is told her son Jack has been caught smoking cannabis behind the school bike sheds. The head teacher is considering suspending Jack and demands Molly meets her at the school immediately to discuss the matter. Molly asks her boss for permission to go to the school. She is told she cannot leave her post. In a high state of distress she says she simply has to attend the school and walks out of her employer's premises. Having resolved the family crisis, Molly seeks advice on her employment situation.

Molly was entitled to unpaid leave to attend the school given that the situation was a genuine family emergency. She is entitled to take the time off without pay. Her employer unreasonably refused her request and was at fault. Molly is advised to attend for work the following day with a written explanation and if she is dismissed or disciplined she will have the right to take the matter before an employment tribunal and claim compensation.

40

Health and Safety

THE COMMON LAW DUTY

The health and safety of employees is protected by numerous statutes and by the common law (i.e. the principles of law which have developed through cases decided in the courts). In this chapter we will outline the various protections enjoyed by employees, and the duties placed on employers under Acts of Parliament and case law.

The common law places a duty on all employers to take such steps as are reasonable and necessary to ensure the safety of their employees. If the employers fail in their duty they will have committed a wrong against the employee who is injured or killed as a result of their negligence. The employee's claim will be for damages.

In order to further protect employees who may suffer at the hands of their employer, the law requires all employers (irrespective of the size of the business) to have Employer's Liability Insurance. As a result, should the employee have a claim against the employer it is in practice brought against their insurer who must meet or defend the claim for damages.

The duty of care employers owe to their employees is measured by the application of the following test, which requires the employer to provide:

- a safe place of work;
- a safe means of access to their place of work;
- a safe system of work;
- adequate equipment and materials;
- competent fellow employees;
- protection to employees against unnecessary risk of injury.

Should the employer fail in any of the above, the employee who has suffered as a result is likely to have a reasonable claim for damages.

Safe place of work

The employer's premises must be in good repair and regularly inspected. A place of work that is normally safe can become temporarily unsafe, for example, if oil is spilt on the workshop floor and is not cleaned up promptly or properly. If the employer sends an employee to another place of work (for example, to a contractor's premises) he has a general duty to check that place of work is safe for his employee, in so far as is reasonably practicable. This duty cannot be delegated to the contractor.

Safe means of access

This means that approach paths, private roads and thoroughfares at the place of work or on the employer's premises must be safe for the employees coming to and from work. For example, failure to remove ice on a footpath within the work site, which causes injury, would be a breach of this duty.

Safe system of work

This, in essence, means that the method used to carry out the work must be safe. Short-cut procedures, which increase productivity at the expense of health and safety considerations, will not be a safe system of work. The employer is afforded a defence provided he can show that he has taken all reasonable steps to ensure that a safe system of work is in operation.

Safe equipment and materials

This includes the provision of safety equipment for employees where appropriate, for example, steel toe-capped boots, a hard hat, gloves, ear defenders or goggles. Materials delivered to a workplace should be checked for safety and any defects which may cause harm to employees who would handle them in their normal course of work.

Competent fellow workers

Should an employer hire an incompetent, inexperienced or unqualified co-worker whose actions cause injury to another employee, the employer is likely to have breached his duty of care.

Protection from injury

The employer is under a duty to do all that is reasonably possible in the circumstances to eliminate risks at the workplace (*see also* page 599).

VICARIOUS LIABILITY

The principle of vicarious liability makes an employer responsible for the negligent acts of any of his employees committed in the course of their duties. This would mean that a hammer carelessly dropped by one employee on to another's foot and causing injury, could lead to a claim by the injured party directly against the employer under this principle. Each case will depend on its own facts and circumstances. There is no vicarious liability if the negligent act committed by the employee is so far removed from what he is authorized to do, that he can be said to be on 'a frolic of his own'. (*See further* page 596.)

CONTRIBUTORY NEGLIGENCE

As with all common law actions for negligence, the amount of damages an injured employee may be awarded by a court must take into account whether he committed any contributory negligence. That is, in some way, he failed to take reasonable steps to ensure his own safety. Where there is deemed to be some element of contributory negligence the court may reduce the award by a percentage – the reduction can, in theory, be by anything up to 100 per cent.

THE OCCUPIERS' LIABILITY ACT 1957

Under this Act, among others, the employer is under a legal duty to his employees to:

take such care as in all the circumstances of the case is reasonable to see that the [employee] is reasonably safe in using the premises for the purposes . . . of their work.

THE WORKPLACE HEALTH AND SAFETY AND WELFARE REGULATIONS 1992

Employers are under a duty to their employees (among others) in the interests of general health and welfare to ensure that their factories and other work premises are:

- clean;
- not overcrowded;
- at a minimum temperature;
- well ventilated;
- well drained;
- well lit;
- able to provide fresh drinking water;
- able to provide washing facilities;
- able to provide accommodation for clothing and seating;
- able to provide adequately fenced machinery;
- safe for access;
- generally well maintained;
- safe in respect of dangerous substances.

Enforcement

An employee may claim for any breach under the Regulations provided always that he can establish that the breach caused the accident and injury. The Health and Safety Executive is empowered to enforce the provisions of the Regulations.

THE HEALTH AND SAFETY AT WORK ACT 1974

This Act has been effectively described as an attempt to balance the degree of risk to employees' welfare against the cost and reasonable ability of the employer to minimize that risk. It follows that under the provisions of the Act a number of duties are placed on employers.

Employer's duties

Broadly, the Act is designed to give statutory force to the common law duty of care an employer owes his employees. Such duty of care of an employer can be expressed as:

- a general duty to ensure, in so far as is reasonably practicable, the health, safety and welfare of all his employees;
- he must provide and maintain plant and systems of work that are safe;
- arrangements must be made to ensure safety and minimize risk with regard to the use, handling, storage and transport of articles and substances;
- the employer must provide all employees with such

information, instruction, training and supervision necessary to ensure health and safety at the workplace;

- the place of work must be well maintained and kept in a safe condition, including access to and from that place, in order that it presents no risk to the health and safety of the employees;
- the provision and maintenance of a working environment which is safe and without risk to health and has adequate facilities and arrangements for the staff.

Anna works for Bob as a shelf stacker in his ice cream warehouse. On many occasions ice cream is spilt on the warehouse floor. Bob has the floor cleaned twice a day and does not like it cleaned at any other times since it distracts an employee from their core duty to stack shelves. Anna slips on some spilt ice cream and breaks her arm. She seeks legal advice.

Bob has failed to provide a safe place of work, a well-maintained place of work and a safe system of work. Clearly, cleaning spilt ice cream only twice a day is inadequate, as it should be cleaned on every occasion it is spilt at the earliest possible opportunity. Anna is advised to bring an action against Bob for her injury. As Bob is insured, Anna's action will, in effect, be against the employer's liability insurer.

Health and safety policy statement

Employers are obliged under the 1974 Act to provide a general written policy with regard to the health and safety at work of their employees and the arrangements for carrying out that policy. The content of the policy must include:

- a general statement of policy concerning health and safety;
- organizational arrangements for implementing the policy;
- identification of specific hazards and a statement of the rules designed to deal with them.

Such information must actively be brought to the notice of the employees. However, employers with fewer than five employees are exempted from the obligation to provide a policy statement.

Safety representatives

Safety representatives and safety committees must be appointed and constituted where a trade union is recognized and a collective agreement exists between the employer and the employees' union. Employers must allow safety representatives time off with pay to perform the functions of investigating potential hazards and complaints about the health and safety or welfare of any employee or group of employees. Safety representatives should be regarded as points of health and safety information. They may make representations to the employer, represent the employees in consultation with inspectors of the Health and Safety Executive and conduct inspections of the workplace.

EMPLOYEE'S DUTIES

All employees, while at work, have a duty to:

- take reasonable care for their own health and safety and of other persons who may be affected by their acts or omissions at work;
- co-operate with their employer in ensuring that requirements or duties are complied with that are imposed on the employer in law.

Stuart is employed as a gardener with the local council. The council provide steel toe-capped boots for Stuart to use when he uses a lawn mower. Because Stuart thinks the boots are 'uncool' he refuses to wear them. The council is now threatening to discipline Stuart if he continues to fail to wear the boots provided. Stuart seeks clarification of his position.

Stuart could rightfully be disciplined by his employer, since they are under a legal duty not just to provide the boots but to ensure that they are worn. Furthermore, if Stuart is injured while not wearing the boots, any claim he may have against the council could be heavily reduced as a result of his contributory negligence.

EMPLOYEE INTERFERENCE WITH SAFETY MEASURES

If an employee deliberately or recklessly interferes with health and safety measures provided by the employer, he may be guilty of a criminal offence. The offence is punishable by a fine, for which there is no maximum amount.

PROVISION OF SAFETY EQUIPMENT

Given the nature of the duty imposed on employers to take all reasonable precautions and to provide all reasonable apparatus to minimize the risk to the health and safety of their workforce, it follows that compliance can be expensive. The law does not permit the cost of health and safety items to be passed on to the employee by the employer. An employee cannot be forced to pay for his own safety equipment. Should any such attempt be made by the employer, the employee should complain to the local Health and Safety Executive Office.

ACCIDENTS AT WORK

Any employee who suffers an injury in the course of his work, which results in him being incapable of work for four consecutive days or more, must report the accident to the employer. The report may be made orally or in writing. Normally, reporting will lead to information being recorded in an 'accident book' which all employers with more than ten employees are required to keep at the workplace.

To allow for proper independent investigation, the employer is under a duty to report to the Health and Safety Executive:

- any accident which results in the employee being off work for more than three days;
- any accident which results in the death or major injury of an employee;
- any notifiable dangerous occurrence;
- the death of an employee within one year of being injured as the result of a notifiable accident or dangerous occurrence;
- any suffering by an employee of a specified work-related disease;
- incidents relating to gas release.

Any employee who is injured severely or suffers serious illness while at work or as a result of work should check with the local Health and Safety Executive Office to see whether they received any notification from the employer. The inspection carried out by the Executive could assist the employee's legal claim against the employer for damages.

FIRST AID

Employers must ensure that there are adequate first aid provisions for their employees. What is 'adequate' will depend on:

- the size of the business;
- the nature of the work;
- the employer's resources;
- location of the workplace;
- number of employees.

First aid boxes, and, where appropriate, travelling first aid kits must be made available. 'Suitable persons' must be provided by the employer to administer first aid in an emergency. A 'suitable person' is deemed to be:

- a person who holds a current first aid certificate issued by a Health and Safety Executive (HSE) approved organization; or
- any other properly trained and/or qualified person approved by the HSE.

As a guideline, during normal working hours, the employer should provide at least one first aider for every 50 employees. In hazardous work environments this ratio should be increased. Information in respect of first aid arrangements should be conspicuously displayed in the workplace, providing names of first aiders and the location of equipment.

DANGEROUS SUBSTANCES

Regulations exist controlling substances classified as hazardous to health. The employer must assess the risks associated with hazardous substances in the workplace and take steps to eliminate or control those risks. The regulations apply to:

- substances which are listed as toxic, very toxic, harmful, irritant or corrosive;
- substances with maximum occupational exposure limits;
- harmful micro-organisms;
- substantial quantities of dust;
- other substances which create a comparable hazard to the health of an employee.

Employers must take all reasonable steps to limit exposure to such substances, to provide protective equipment and/or clothing and to monitor the hazardous substances. They must also provide their employees with adequate information, instruction and training in order for them to take appropriate precautions and limit their exposure to the substance.

NOISE

In a working environment where the daily noise exposure is no less than 85 db (A), the employer must assess the noise level and inform all employees if ear protection is required and, if so, provide adequate ear protection. Furthermore, the employer must do all reasonably within his capability to limit or reduce noise at the place of work. However, employers are under no legal duty to require employees to take regular hearing tests.

VISUAL DISPLAY UNITS

It is now quite common in an office environment for many employees to have on their desks a VDU or other display screen equipment (DSE). Health hazards are created by long use and exposure to such apparatus. Regulations now exist requiring employers to take steps to protect the health and safety of VDU/DSE users. Workstations must be assessed to establish whether any risk to health exists, particularly in respect of stress and fatigue. Equipment must be:

- adjustable;
- glare free;
- appropriately lit;

- maintained at an appropriate temperature.

Where an employer works for many hours in front of DSE, regular work breaks or changes in activity must be provided. DSE users are entitled to appropriate eyesight tests, which must be paid for by the employer. Should spectacles be prescribed to correct vision defects as a result of DSE work, the cost of such spectacles must be borne by the employer. Overuse of DSE can lead to:

- eye strain;
- headaches;
- stress;
- limb strain;
- dermatitis (facial);
- epileptic fits.

Compliance with the regulations is designed to combat these complaints.

LIFTING AND CARRYING

Manual Handling Operations Regulations exist to ensure that injury sustained through lifting and carrying at the workplace is controlled and the prospect of injury minimized. The regulations require assessment of the risks by the employer with a view to making sensible procedural changes if required. Consideration must be given to the capabilities of the employees involved in such activity and they must be trained to handle and move heavy loads safely. Where appropriate, moving or lifting equipment should be provided for the employees.

MACHINERY

Machines, whether manual or automated, present an obvious hazard in the workplace. Statutory requirements in respect of new equipment are in place which ensure:

- the adequate maintenance of machinery;
- its suitability for the job;
- the provision of information about its use by the employee;
- instructions for use;
- training for use;
- European standard conformity.

For existing equipment as at 1 January 1997 further requirements are in force covering:

- dangerous parts of machinery;
- protection against specific hazards;
- temperature extremes;
- control systems;
- power isolation;
- stability;
- lighting;
- markings and warnings.

The purpose of these regulated matters is to provide the employee with a safer working environment where it involves the use of machinery in the performance of his duties.

FIRE

Employers are under a duty to minimize the risk of fire, and to inform the employees as to:

- escape routes;
- fire drill;
- the use of extinguishers/fire blankets where appropriate;
- precautionary measures;
- warning systems.

All employees should be clearly aware of the procedures to be adopted at their place of work in the event of a fire and of the need generally to prevent it, how to prevent its spread and the importance of keeping fire exit points free from obstacles.

MAINTAINING THE WORKPLACE

Maintaining the workplace has often been described as 'good housekeeping' measures. In fact, the regulations which exist in this regard place specific duties and obligations on the employer, and any breach which adversely affects the well-being of an employee may lead to a legitimate claim for damages. Regulations exist in respect of the following matters:

- workplace, equipment and work systems maintenance;
- ventilation;
- workplace temperature;
- lighting;
- cleanliness;
- room dimensions of the workplace;
- floor condition;
- traffic routes;
- falling objects;
- windows, doors, gates, walls, skylights, ventilators;
- lifts and moving walkways;
- sanitation;
- toilets;
- washing facilities;
- drinking water;
- accommodation for clothing, changing and eating meals;
- rest room accommodation for non-smokers.

THE HEALTH AND SAFETY EXECUTIVE

The Health and Safety Executive (HSE) has overall responsibility for enforcing the existing health and safety laws and regulations and is the main enforcing authority.

The laws and regulations are very strictly enforced, with a presumption in favour of the claimant.

The employee was injured when carrying a door down an awkward set of steps. He argued that this was a breach of the Manual Handling Operations Regulations 1992. The court held that despite the fact that the risk of falling down the stairs was slight and the defendants were not at fault for not providing assistance (i.e. there was no negligence), the defendants had failed to comply with the Regulations. On the facts, it was found that the best practice would have been to provide a second man to help carry the door down the steps. Hawkes (2000).

In respect of certain workplaces and premises the local authority also has powers of enforcement. For example:

- offices;
- shops;
- public houses;
- sports centres;
- restaurants.

An HSE inspector is empowered to enter premises with or without a police officer for the purpose of inspection, examination or investigation. They may take with them equipment to assist them in their purpose and take samples of anything found on the premises. Further to their investigations, they may interview representatives of the employer and employees without interference. Upon the recommendations of the inspector's report the HSE may order an improvement or prohibition notice.

Improvement notice

This may be issued where the employer:

1 is contravening one or more statutory provisions; or
2 has contravened such provisions in circumstances where it is likely that contravention will continue.

The improvement notice requires the contravention to be remedied within a specified period of time of not less than 21 days.

Prohibition notice

The notice must:

1 state the inspector's belief regarding the risk of serious personal injury;
2 specify what is responsible for the risk;
3 state the inspector's belief that an actual or potential breach of a statutory provision is involved;
4 direct that the unsafe practice or activity must not continue.

Prosecution

In certain circumstances, the employer's actions are such that criminal proceedings may be issued against them. Generally, such action would be considered by the HSE where the employer has:

- failed to discharge a general duty under the statutory health and safety provisions;
- breached health and safety regulations;
- made a false statement or entry in a register, document, etc. required to be kept by law;
- failed to comply with an improvement or prohibition notice;
- obstructed an inspector in the course of their duty.

Where the employer is a limited company, it is possible in law for criminal proceedings to be brought against a specific director or officer of that company where the breach is committed with the consent, connivance or neglect of that person. Such proceedings are rare. Summary proceedings before a magistrates' court must be brought within six months from the date upon which it was known by the enforcing authority that a breach of the statutory regulations had been committed. Penalties include fines and/or imprisonment.

Employer's defence

A common thread runs through most of the statutory provisions relating to the health and safety of employees in the workplace. That is, employers are obliged to act under the regulations in so far as is reasonably practicable given the circumstances of the case. It follows that a defence is provided in law for the employer where he can show that such an obligation has been discharged, i.e. he has done all that was reasonably practicable.

UNFAIR DISMISSAL AND HEALTH AND SAFETY

This is dealt with in Chapter 34.

WORKING HOURS AND REST BREAKS

Long hours and lapses in concentration can cause serious injury and, in some cases, can be fatal. To protect employees in these circumstances the Working Time Regulations were introduced into the UK in 1998. The provisions currently apply to all categories of workers except workers employed in the following sectors:

- air transport;
- rail transport;
- road transport;

- sea transport;
- inland waterways and lake transport;
- sea fishing;
- other work at sea;
- doctors in training;
- armed forces;
- police;
- civil protection services;
- domestic servants in private households.

The reason for the transport industry exclusion is that alternative provisions protect employees against long continuous hours of work, for example, tachograph regulations.

Forty-eight-hour week

All workers under a contract of employment (including agency workers), other than those specified above, are, from 1 October 1998, subject to a maximum working week not exceeding 48 hours. The worker's average hourly week is calculated over 17 weeks. This is called the reference period. Employees may agree (either by collective agreement through trade unions or a workforce agreement) to extend the reference period from 17 weeks to 52 weeks.

Workers and employers can also agree that the 48-hour maximum week will not apply. Such agreements must be in writing and should have a notice of termination clause not exceeding three months. Being on call at home will not generally count towards working time.

Kevin works for Keith's photocopier leasing company, Copymagic. Kevin sells photocopy paper to Copymagic clients and his sales area is extensive, covering the whole of the south coast of England from Cornwall to Rochester. As a result, Kevin works very long hours, travelling considerable distances each day between clients in his area in the execution of his duties.

Since commencing employment with Keith, Kevin's circumstances have changed. His wife has given birth to their first child, Esmerelda. Due to family commitments, Kevin no longer wishes to work the 60 hours a week he has worked in practice over the last three years. Kevin would like to reduce his hours. He has approached Keith about the matter but Keith is unsympathetic and points to a clause in Kevin's contract of employment which states:

You will work such hours as are necessary for the better performance of your duties as a Copymagic sales person.

Kevin is desperate to spend more time with Esmerelda and his wife. He seeks legal advice.

Taking a reference period of 17 weeks, Kevin works, on average, more than 48 hours per week. Kevin may, with immediate effect, legitimately refuse to work more than 48 hours per week – on average. This is a statutory right and,

as such, overrides any provision to the contrary within his contract of employment with Copymagic. However, if Keith dismisses Kevin for asserting his statutory right or imposes any other detriment, Kevin may claim unfair dismissal and/ or compensation (whichever is appropriate), provided he brings his claim before an employment tribunal within three months of the act complained of. Travel required by the job counts as working time.

Holidays

See page 320 for statutory entitlement to paid leave.

Rest breaks

Adult employees (18 years of age or over) are entitled to 11 hours of rest in every 24-hour working period. They are also entitled to not less than 24 hours' rest in each seven-day period, or 48-hours' rest in each 14-day period. The employer may decide which of these to apply. Employees are also entitled to 20 minutes' rest break during the working day where daily working time is more than six hours. These rest breaks must be uninterrupted.

Young workers (over minimum school leaving age but under 18 years of age) are entitled to 12 hours' rest in any 24-hour working period, 48 hours' rest (starting from midnight) in each seven-day working period, and 30 minutes' rest break during the working day where daily working time is more than 4.5 hours. Again, these rest breaks must be uninterrupted. Young workers' weekly rest period of 48 hours in each seven-day period may be reduced to 36 hours if justified by technical or organizational reasons.

Breaks are unpaid. The entitlements can be modified or excluded altogether by collective or workforce agreement, subject to the employee being permitted to take an equivalent period of compensatory rest (*see* below). Where work is of a monotonous nature or hazardous to health, the employer must ensure adequate breaks are taken.

Night workers

The regulations state maximum hours that can be worked during the night. Employers are required to take all reasonable steps to ensure that night workers (unless they fall within an exempt category or derogation) do not work more than an average of eight hours in any 24-hour period. Any employee who works at least three hours of their daily working time during the hours of 11 p.m. and 6 a.m. is a night worker. Workforce, collective or individual agreements may be drafted to include a night period different to that specified, but the period must be of at least seven hours, which must include midnight to 5 a.m. There is a reference period of 17 weeks to calculate the number of hours worked. Unless modified, health and safety bodies can use a snapshot of any 17-week period during the working year to calculate hours worked.

All night workers are entitled to a free health assessment before starting night work and at regular intervals thereafter. This can be done by the completion of an initial health questionnaire, then referral to a doctor if necessary. A night worker is entitled to be transferred to day work on request if they have medical evidence indicating that night working is affecting their health. They are not entitled to transfer with any enhancements such as extra pay. The employer is not required to dismiss a day worker to make room for such a transfer but is required to reassign workers, if possible, subject to their agreement. Employers must not contract out of the right to health assessment or transfer.

Derogations/exceptions

Unmeasured working time

This covers workers whose time cannot be measured or predetermined and covers managing executives, family workers, workers officiating at religious ceremonies in churches and religious communities. Such workers are not subject to regulations governing a 48-hour week, length of night work or rest breaks.

Work-specific activities

Includes security and surveillance workers and 24-hour service providers, for example, dockers, medical workers, hotel staff, postal workers, farmers, tourism workers, refuse collectors, gas, water and electricity providers. Regulations relating to night work and breaks do not apply.

Note that, although exempt, these workers are entitled to compensatory rest, which constitutes a rest period equivalent to that specified in the regulations to be taken at times other than those specified in the regulations.

Shift workers

These are workers whose work schedule is part of shift work, whereby each worker replaces another at the same continuous workstation, for example, factory machine workers. Such workers are exempt from the rest break provisions.

Note that although exempt, these workers are entitled to compensatory rest, which constitutes a rest period equivalent to that specified in the regulations to be taken

at times other than those specified in the regulations. The employer must observe the entitlement to compensatory rest.

The above derogations are subject to any relevant Health and Safety Regulations, health and safety being the prime consideration at all times.

Enforcement

Employment tribunals will enforce rest breaks, annual leave and compensatory rest. Claims must be brought within three months of the act complained of and, if successful, awards of compensation may be made. The employer must not subject employees to any detriment as a result of the rights and obligations arising under the regulations; such treatment would give rise to a claim. It is also automatically unfair dismissal to dismiss an employee for a reason related to the regulations, irrespective of their length of service.

Health and safety bodies will enforce the maximum working week, maximum night work, and duty to provide health assessment. Sanctions include criminal penalties such as conviction, fine and imprisonment. Health and safety bodies have a right of access to information and records. If an employer fails to comply, criminal sanctions are available. Employers must keep proper written records of night workers, all hours worked, compensatory rest periods, work patterns and leave.

Workforce agreements

These agreements must be in writing and specify the start date. They will only apply to relevant members of the workforce. To be valid, they must be signed prior to the start date by the majority of those who are relevant members of the workforce (only if there are 20 or fewer workers employed by the employer) or by elected representatives. These representatives must be elected by secret ballot. The employer is free to determine the number of representatives to be elected and the term for which they are elected. All members of the workforce are eligible to stand as candidates and all of them are entitled to vote. To be valid, the workforce must have seen copies of the agreement prior to signature together with guidance to assist their understanding. The agreement must have effect for no more than five years.

Individual agreements

These are agreements entered into voluntarily by the employee and employer, for example, to work in excess of the weekly working time limit. They must be in writing.

Collective agreements

These are agreements reached between an employer and a trade union recognized by that employer for collective bargaining purposes. They do not have to be in writing but to be enforceable they must be incorporated into the contract of employment either by reference or expressly.

41

Miscellaneous Matters

INTRODUCTION

There are a number of aspects of employment law about which an employee should know. Often they do not fit neatly into a wider area of employment law even though individually they may be of considerable importance and touch the working lives of many people. The purpose of this final section is to address the main miscellaneous areas of employment law not detailed previously but which are, nonetheless, worthy of note.

REFERENCES

Contrary to popular belief, an employee in the UK has no legal entitlement to a reference from his previous employer, even where failure to provide a reference will almost surely lose the applicant the opportunity of employment with a prospective employer.

Should an ex-employer provide a reference, whether orally (over the telephone) or in writing, for a prospective employer, it must be accurate and the person giving the reference must believe its content to be true. If it is inaccurate and untrue, particularly if driven by spite or malice, it could well be defamatory, allowing the employee a right to claim damages for libel (if in writing) or slander (if oral). However, before considering such an action against an ex-employer, the individual would need good evidence and should be aware that such actions are notoriously costly and are not eligible for public funding.

Providing a reference on an ex-employee without the consent or request of that person may be a breach of the Data Protection Rules, produced by the Information Commissioner under the Data Protection Act 1998. Employers should find out when an employee stops working whether or not the employee wants references to be provided to future employers.

Recent House of Lords' decisions have allowed claims for sex, race and disability discrimination relating to matters which occur after the termination of employment.

These decisions extend to the giving of or failure to give a reference.

The new Race Relations Regulations that came into force in July 2003 (*see* page 380) also allow former employees to bring claims of race discrimination against their former employers where the event complained of occurs after the employment relationship has ended. This would cover a failure to give a reference or giving an adverse reference. Since December 2003, it is unlawful discrimination for an employer to refuse to provide a reference, or to provide an adverse reference, because of the employee's religion, belief or sexual orientation or because they brought discrimination proceedings against the employer on these grounds.

There is one further consideration on the matter of references and that is their position in relation to a settlement. Often following the termination of employment, there is a dispute between the employer and ex-employee. In most cases, an amicable settlement is achieved. An agreed reference can become an important aspect of the settlement and ex-employees in that situation would be well advised to be fully aware of the commercial value of a good reference. An extra £500 on a sum in settlement may appear attractive, but what price a reference which may secure further employment?

ACCESS TO MEDICAL REPORTS

Often, when an employee has been off work, injured or ill for some time, an employer will seek to assess the situation by requesting a medical report either from the employee's own doctor or an independent consultant. Under the Access to Medical Reports Act 1988, the employee has the right to access to any such medical report before the employer has had a chance to look at it.

A medical report for the purposes of the Act includes any report relating to the physical or mental condition of its subject. It covers reports compiled by the employee's own doctor, any consultant or company-appointed doctor. The employer must not approach the employee's doctor without the employee's permission *in writing*. The employer's request for permission to approach the doctor for a medical report must also state the employee's right to:

- withhold consent;
- demand access to the report before it is sent to the employer;
- gain access to the report after it has been delivered to the employer;
- ask that the report be amended;
- refuse to allow the report to be sent to the employer.

Under the rules of access, the employee is entitled to a copy of the report, or to sight of the original. The employee's right to make amendments to the report exists where he believes any part of it is incorrect or misleading. The employee may request that the doctor makes changes to the report. If the doctor agrees to the changes, it is amended before being sent to the employer. If the doctor refuses to make changes, the employee cannot insist that they are made. Instead, a copy of the employee's objections is attached to the report before it is sent to the employer.

There are situations where the doctor need not give the employee access to the whole or part of the medical report. This occurs where disclosure would:

- in the doctor's opinion, be likely to cause serious harm to the physical or mental health of the employee, or anyone else;
- indicate the doctor's intentions in respect of the individual;
- be likely to reveal information about another person;
- be likely to reveal the identity of another person who has supplied the doctor with information in respect of the employee.

If the doctor wishes to rely on any of these exemptions he must notify the employee accordingly. Should any of the provisions of the Act not be complied with by the employer or the doctor, the employee may complain upon application to the county court, which is empowered to order compliance.

More generally, the Access to Health Records Act 1990 allows an employee, or any individual, to request in writing access to their health record or any part of it from a doctor, including a company doctor. Where this request is made within 40 days from the date on which the record was made, the record must be produced within 21 days of the request without charge. Where the record is more than 40 days old, a charge (currently £10) may be levied. The cost of copying and posting may also be charged.

The right to access to health records does not apply to any records made before 1 November 1991. Moreover, for those records made after that date there exist exclusions where:

- to provide access could cause harm to the physical or mental health of the patient;
- another individual could be identified by the information (excluding health care professionals).

REHABILITATION OF OFFENDERS AND EMPLOYMENT

The Rehabilitation of Offenders Act 1974 provides that after a set period of time those individuals who have committed certain criminal offences are entitled to regard the conviction as spent. The meaning of 'spent' means that in certain circumstances when a person is asked about their criminal record, he can regard the offence as never having been committed.

Within an employment environment, job applicants are often asked at interview or within an application form whether they have any criminal convictions. Provided the conviction is spent, subject to certain excluded professions, the employee is under no duty to disclose the conviction if asked. Failure to disclose a spent conviction is not dishonest if it is acting in compliance with the law.

An employer may not dismiss an employee merely because he discovers that the employee has a spent conviction. People in certain occupations and professions *are* obliged to disclose spent convictions and may be dismissed or excluded from employment because of the conviction. These occupations are:

- doctors;
- nurses;
- midwives;
- dentists;
- barristers;
- solicitors;
- accountants;
- judges;
- teachers;
- police officers;
- directors and officers of building societies;
- those who have access to children in the normal course of duties;
- veterinary surgeons;
- opticians;
- chemists;
- traffic wardens;
- firearms dealers;
- probation officers;
- prison officers;
- securities dealers.

The Rehabilitation Periods

Sentence	Period before conviction is spent
Life imprisonment	Never
Imprisonment for 30 months or more	Never
Imprisonment for a period between 6 months and 30 months	10 years
Imprisonment for 6 months or less	7 years
A criminal fine	5 years
Detention of a child or young person for a period between 6 months and 30 months	5 years
Detention of a child or young person for 6 months or less	3 years
Conditional discharge, probation, care or supervision order, a bind-over to keep the peace	1 year or the duration of the order, whichever is the longer
Disqualification from driving	The length of disqualification but where there is a fine, 5 years
Absolute discharge	6 months
A criminal fine for a child or young person	2½ years

See further pages 665–7.

People banned from working with children

Unless a court believes that it is unlikely that an offender aged 18 or over will commit a further offence against a child the person will be banned from working with children if they have been convicted of certain specified offences against those aged under 18 (or 16 in some instances) and given a hospital or guardianship order or a custodial sentence of 12 months or more. Suspended sentences of 12 months or more are also treated as qualifying sentences. Young offenders (i.e. those aged under 18) will only be banned if it is judged that they are likely to commit further offences against a child.

The specified offences include:
- homicide and threats to kill;
- abduction and false imprisonment;
- wounding and causing grievous bodily harm;
- assault occasioning actual bodily harm;
- rape and indecent assault;
- intercourse with a girl under 16;
- incest and cruelty to children;
- offences relating to prostitution;
- offences relating to child pornography;
- abuse of trust; and
- supplying a class-A drug to a child.

Those people who commit a specified offence will be given a disqualification order as part of their sentence. Offenders will be able to seek a review of the order only after ten years have elapsed (five years for young offenders). At such reviews, it will not be sufficient for individuals to prove that they are no longer a risk to children. Rather, they must prove that they are now positively suitable for such work before a tribunal will be satisfied that there are grounds for lifting the disqualification order. Working with children is defined in the Criminal Justice and Court Services Act 2000 as working in a 'regulated position'. This includes employment in those establishments that cater mainly for children, such as schools, children's homes and children's hospitals. It covers most employment in day-care premises but not, for instance, cleaners who enter the premises each day after children have left. As well as caring for, training, supervising or being in sole charge of children, the definition also covers a position where normal duties involve unsupervised contact with children. This would cover, for example, a mini-cab firm whose drivers are routinely employed to transport unaccompanied children on a regular basis, but not those who do it on an irregular or one-off basis. The definition also covers child employment. (*See further* page 668.)

THE EMPLOYMENT OF CHILDREN

The employment of children is governed by legislation. There are a number of restrictions which must be complied with when considering employing a child. In this context, a 'child' is a person who has not yet attained minimum school leaving age. In England and Wales, a child can leave school on the last Friday in June if they are 16 years or will be 16 years before the start of the next school year.

The restrictions

The main provisions which restrict the employment of children are set out below. As a general rule, a child may not be employed (whether the work is paid or unpaid):
- if he is under the age of 14 years; or
- to do any work other than light work; or
- during school hours on any school day; or
- before 7 a.m. or after 7 p.m. on any day; or
- for more than two hours on any school day; or
- for more than two hours on any Sunday; or
- for more than eight hours (or if he is aged under 15 years, for more than five hours) on any Saturday, or

any other day on which he is not required to attend school (other than Sundays); or

- for more than 35 hours (or if he is aged under 15 years, for more than 25 hours) in any week in which he is not required to attend school; or
- for more than four hours in any day without a rest break of at least one hour; or
- at any time in a year unless he has had or could still have at least two consecutive weeks off during a school holiday.

Failure to comply with any of the restrictions set out above may lead to criminal prosecution and the imposition of a fine of up to £1,000.

What is light work?

Light work means work which is not likely to be harmful to the child's health, safety, development, attendance at school or participation in work experience. A health and safety risk assessment must be carried out and information on the outcome provided to the parents.

The employment of children is prohibited for work:

- which is beyond their physical or psychological capacity;
- which involves harmful exposure to toxic or carcinogenic agents or agents which cause heritable genetic damage or harm to the unborn child or which in any other way chronically affect human health;
- which involves harmful exposure to radiation;
- which involves the risk of accidents which it may reasonably be assumed cannot be appreciated or avoided by a child owing to his insufficient attention to safety or lack of experience; or
- in which there is a risk to health from extreme cold, heat, noise or vibration.

In addition, no child can be employed in any industrial undertaking, i.e. mines, quarries, factories, building and works of engineering construction and transportation. (*See also* page 125.)

Powers of the local authority

In addition to the restrictions set out above, local authorities have the power to pass by-laws concerning the employment of children. For example, certain by-laws may authorize the employment of children under the age of 14 years by their parents or guardians in light agricultural or horticultural work, or may authorize the employment of children aged 13 years in certain categories of light work as specified in the by-law.

Since each local authority has its own powers, it is important that employers check with their local education authority to see whether there are any by-laws of which they need to be aware.

Note that breach of a by-law is a criminal offence and again a fine of up to £1,000 will apply.

Requirement for work permit

Each local authority generally has the power to supervise the employment of children in its geographical area. Many local authorities require the employer to obtain a work permit enabling the child to carry out the particular work. In summary, the local authority may require details of how the child is employed and at what times and for what periods before a permit is granted.

Work experience

The rules above are relaxed where the child is in their last academic year of schooling and the job is for work experience and the arrangements for such employment are made or approved by the local education authority.

Young persons

A 'young person' is defined as an individual who is no longer a child (above school leaving age) but who is under the age of 18 years. Generally, there are few restrictions on the employment of young persons, whether in offices, shops or factories but the law was tightened up in 2003 (*see* below).

There is one important aspect of the employment of young persons that should not be overlooked – an exception to a general legal rule. In nearly all other areas of law, a person under the age of 18 years is deemed a minor and, therefore, not able to enter into a legally binding contract. Employment contracts for young persons between school leaving age and 18 years are an exception. Such contracts, provided they are freely entered into, are binding and enforceable in law should the young employee be in breach of its terms and conditions. Apprenticeship agreements are similarly regarded.

Employers who routinely engage the services of school leavers should be aware that from 6 April 2003, youngsters aged 16 and 17 cannot work:

- more than 40 hours a week;
- more than 8 hours in one day;
- between 10 p.m. and 6 a.m. or 11 p.m. and 7 a.m.

These limits are absolute. Young people under the age of 18 will not have the right to opt-out of these upper limits (whether they wish to or not). Nor will it be possible to average their working hours over a 17-week or agreed longer period (as continues to be the case for workers aged 18 and over).

SERVICE LETTINGS

It is common practice in a number of industries (e.g. catering) to offer a person a residence along with the job. Difficulties can arise when the employment comes to an end. Generally, an ex-employee will only retain the right to continue residing in the employer's premises if the occupancy amounts to a separate tenancy. A service occupier in law never becomes a tenant and the employer never becomes a landlord. The relationship remains one of master and servant, that is, one of employment.

In most cases, the right to reside in any particular premises as part of the job offer is clearly stated within the contract of employment. Where it is so stated there can be no confusion and no creation of a separate tenancy. The circumstances of employment and residence may also imply a relationship that creates a service letting and not a tenancy. The facts of each particular case must be assessed on their own merits. Where there is no express statement of a service letting but it is clear the accommodation was offered for the better or more effective performance of an employee's duties it is very likely to be regarded by the courts as a service letting.

Termination of employment – implications for the service letting

If the contract of employment is brought to an end for whatever reason under a service letting, the employee's contractual right to occupy the property ceases. Usually the employer will provide a reasonable period of time within which the property must be vacated by the ex-employee, for example, 28 days. If the ex-employee remains in the property after such time he will be acting unlawfully and the employer may seek a court order for possession of the property. Should the employer seek to evict the ex-employee forcibly or in any other way harass the ex-employee, this may constitute a criminal offence and the police should be informed.

Ex-employees in this situation should be aware that if the employer has good grounds for possession of a true service letting, and seeks a court order to that effect, the employer may also claim damages based on the unlawful possession of the property by the ex-employee from the point in time when he no longer had the right of residence. These damages will be based on the reasonable rent which could have been taken for the property in question and could be considerable by the time the court orders possession in favour of the employer.

For an employer to seek an order for possession he must show that:

- the property was occupied by the employee for the term of employment and for the better and more effective performance of his duties;

- the contract of employment has been effectively terminated;
- reasonable or proper notice of possession has been given to the ex-employee;
- no new tenancy arrangement has been created between the parties.

RESTRAINT OF TRADE

It is now quite common for a contract of employment to contain clauses that seek to restrain the employee in some way after the contract has been terminated. These restraint of trade clauses are sometimes referred to as restrictive covenants – the two terms are interchangeable.

Such clauses are included to restrict certain activities, most typically:

- working for a competitor;
- working in the same industry;
- the soliciting of the ex-employer's clients or customers;
- the soliciting of the ex-employer's staff;
- breach of confidentiality;
- the passing of trade secrets.

For the court to uphold such clauses against the employee it is essential that two conditions are fulfilled. The nature of the restraint must be reasonable between the parties, and be in the public interest.

In essence, employers must only use these clauses to protect legitimate business interests. They will not be upheld if they are intended to punish the employee for leaving the employer, and act to prevent the ex-employee from earning a living in the only business they know. A balance has to be achieved between these two competing interests. The main points to remember in respect of restraint of trade clauses are:

1 they are unlikely to be enforceable if they are drafted in vague or uncertain terms;
2 some attempt must be made to define the geographical area of restraint and the time limit within which activity is restricted;
3 the clause must be reasonable and not punitive;
4 the question of reasonableness is ultimately one for the courts;
5 any definitions within the clauses must be certain and clear;
6 the courts will not rewrite badly drafted clauses in order to make them effective and enforceable;
7 they must be no greater than is necessary to protect legitimate business interests;
8 restraint of trade clauses will be examined within their context; each profession, trade or industry will have different levels of acceptability;
9 if an employer dismisses an employee wrongfully (in breach of contract), normally they will be prevented from seeking to impose any restraint of trade clause that exists within the contract of employment;

10 employers can legitimately protect only the following:
(**a**) trade secrets;
(**b**) confidential information;
(**c**) trade connections;
(**d**) goodwill;
(**e**) existing staff.
The following will always be considered by the court:
1 the nature of the employer's business;
2 the scope of their business;
3 the geographical area of intended restraint;
4 the duration in time of the intended restraint;
5 the status and responsibilities of the employee.

Should the clause not offend any of these 'rules' the employer may enforce its terms against an employee in breach, by seeking an injunction in the county court to restrain the employee from continuing his activities. The employer may also claim damages where the financial loss to his business is quantifiable.

Alex works in central Birmingham as a hairdresser. Victoria, her boss, insisted Alex sign a contract of employment when she started work that included a restraint of trade clause. In the contract Alex is prohibited for two years from working as a hairdresser on her own account, or for any other business, within a five-mile radius of Victoria's salon. In addition, she is not to solicit clients of the salon for 12 months after the termination of her employment with Victoria. Alex wants to leave Victoria's employment and work for Keith two miles across town, and seeks advice.

The geographical prohibition is punitive. It goes beyond the protection of Victoria's legitimate business interests and would, if upheld by the court, force Alex out of the centre of Birmingham. That part of the clause is, in effect, unenforceable. The restriction on soliciting Victoria's clients is probably reasonable but the court is unlikely to view it in isolation. As such, Victoria will not be able to rely on either restriction and Alex is free to join Keith.

SEASONAL EMPLOYEES

Those individuals who work for a limited period of time, for example, a summer or winter season, are nonetheless regarded as employees by the law. Most, by the nature of their short period of work, will not have the right to claim unfair dismissal or a statutory redundancy payment upon termination of the contract of employment. However, many will work for four weeks or more and, therefore, be entitled to a statement of written particulars of employment. All will be entitled to the statutory minimum period of notice on termination.

In certain situations, particularly where the employee concerned is habitually re-engaged time and time again by the same employer, the employee may retain continuity of service between each period of work. This is possible where the period without work is regarded in law as a temporary cessation of work. Where this is so, full employment rights may accrue after one year's service with the same employer. As with all employment law, each case must be assessed on its own particular facts and circumstances.

Joan is a 66-year-old cleaner at the local school. She has been employed for three years. During the school holidays Joan does no cleaning and receives no pay, but resumes her duties when the children return to school. The school wishes to retire Joan in line with Educational Authority policy. Because of the breaks in her employment during the holidays, the school assumes Joan has less than one year's continuous service and terminates her contract with one week's notice. Joan seeks advice.

The periods of school holiday are likely to be regarded in law as a temporary cessation of work thereby not breaking continuity of employment. Joan is entitled to at least three weeks' notice.

FIXED-TERM CONTRACTS

Increasingly, employers are placing employees on fixed-term contracts. There are two main reasons for this occurrence:
1 a properly formalized fixed-term contract can be a convenient method for the employer to avoid liability for statutory redundancy payments after two years of continuous service (but *see* below); and
2 such contracts can 'bind' a key employee into the business.

The definition of a fixed-term contract is one which has a specific beginning and end, usually characterized by the phrase,

. . . you will be employed with effect from (date) and continue in employment until (date).

Regulations introduced in October 2002 gave fixed-term employees protection against being treated less favourably than permanent employees. Less favourable treatment could occur when, for example, a fixed-term employee does not get a benefit that a comparable permanent employee gets, such as free membership of a workplace gym or paid bank holidays or a bonus. It could also mean that fixed-term employees are dismissed or selected for redundancy purely because they are fixed-term. The Regulations cover fixed-term employees including employees doing seasonal or casual work, employees on fixed-term contracts providing cover for maternity leave, and employees hired to cover for peaks in demand. They do not apply to agency workers. Employers have to show that the different treatment can be objectively justified, for example, because there is a genuine business objective to be achieved.

If fixed-term employees believe they have been treated

less favourably or their employer has infringed any of their other rights under the Regulations, they may present their case to an employment tribunal within three months of the date that the right was infringed. The tribunal can order the employer to pay compensation if the employees' complaint is upheld.

Fixed-term employees have the right to ask their employer for a written statement giving the reasons for any less favourable treatment and the employer must produce the statement within 21 days. This statement can be produced at the tribunal hearing.

Importantly, the Regulations abolish the provisions enabling fixed-term employees to waive the right to a redundancy payment.

Any waivers inserted into contracts agreed, renewed or extended after 1 October 2002 will not be valid and fixed-term employees will have a right to statutory redun-dancy payments if they have been continuously employed for two years or more. Where the waiver clause was signed before 1 October 2002, the waiver would still apply and the employee would not be entitled to statutory redundancy payments if their contract expired and was not renewed. However, if the contract was renewed or extended after 1 October, any waiver clause would not be effective. The Regulations also give fixed-term employees the right not to be unfairly dismissed after one year's service.

Should the employee be dismissed within the defined period of the contract for no valid reason, they may bring a claim for damages in respect of breach of contract against the employer. Damages are based on what the employee would have earned over the remaining period of the fixed term. The employee will always be under a duty to mitigate their loss and actively seek comparable work. This may act to reduce the amount claimed.

Introduction

It is estimated that consumer complaints about faulty goods and services are now running at just under 1 million a year. The Director General of Fair Trading (DGFT), for example, believes that this is just the tip of the iceberg and that tens of millions of transactions for goods or services cause problems for consumers.

Defective goods, substandard service and poor information cost UK consumers an estimated £8.3 billion a year. At the top of the list of consumer complaints are problems with defective goods or substandard services, followed by problems with high-pressure selling techniques. And it's not only consumers that lose out. Taking advantage of consumers is also bad for business; it gives reputable traders and better businesses a bad name.

Despite the high levels of reported abuse, UK consumers are – or should be – protected by some of the most developed and sophisticated consumer law in the world.

Consumer law in the UK is a curious mix. In many areas, consumer law is left to the individual consumer to enforce. For example, the law states that consumers are entitled to a certain quality or standard in respect of goods and services which they purchase, and individual shoppers must take steps themselves to exercise and enforce these legal rights (in court if necessary) when things go wrong.

But that is not the end of the story. There are also many laws and regulations operated on a wider level by bodies such as 'consumer policemen' and watchdogs. These laws, dealing with fundamental issues such as consumer safety, dishonest and incompetent traders are often backed by the criminal law – and could result in the payment of a (hefty) fine or even imprisonment. In the criminal area of consumer law fall familiar Acts of Parliament, such as the Trade Descriptions Act 1968 and the Food Safety Act 1990 (covering food standards and hygiene).

Much of this consumer protection legislation is enforced by local authority trading standards departments.

It is their job to enforce and advise on a wide range of consumer protection law.

Some consumer law is operated at a national level by the DGFT who heads the Office of Fair Trading (OFT). Set up in 1973, the OFT is a non-ministerial government department. Its main roles are to identify and put right 'dodgy' practices and consumer scams; regulate consumer credit (*see* pages 433–4); and deal with anti-competitive practices.

Falling somewhere in the middle is a new breed of legislation that allows consumer watchdogs to apply to the courts to stop, through a court order, poor practices that have a detrimental effect on consumers generally.

Supplementing this 'hard' law is the fertile area of self-regulation. Many local and nation-wide self-regulatory initiatives, often in the form of codes of practice promoted by trade associations, also play an important role in protecting consumers' rights. These codes offer a higher level of consumer protection and service than the safety net provided by consumer law. They also tend to offer greater flexibility and are targeted at specific areas and specific issues.

All change?

Many of the laws mentioned in this chapter are tried and tested. Some are relatively new and their full use is still to be established, while others are in the process of change. And yet more change is on the horizon.

In July 1999, the Secretary of State for Trade and Industry launched the government's Consumer White Paper, *Modern markets: confident consumers*. The White Paper, produced following an intensive period of work over the early part of the summer, contains 90 specific initiatives 'committed to putting consumers centre-stage'. They range from building on open and competitive markets, to helping consumers get redress and keeping consumer law up to date. Most importantly, the DGFT has been asked to review the OFT's consumer protection functions.

The government has produced a detailed implementation plan with commitments on timing. Some of the White Paper's commitments have already been met. Others will require new legislation.

Details are highlighted within the following chapters (Chapters 42–51).

42

Buying Goods

If you buy something that turns out to be faulty – it is scratched, falling to bits or just does not work – you have two ways to sort out your problem.

Is there a guarantee?

First, you may have a guarantee from the manufacturer. This is usually in small print and sometimes attached to a registration card or some other similar marketing blurb. It sets out what the manufacturer promises to do if there are problems with the goods. It may last for six months, a year, or whatever period is specified. It may cover replacement and it may cover parts or labour. Usually, it tells you how and when to notify claims to the manufacturer or its servicing firm. Sometimes guarantees are free; sometimes you have to pay for cover, particularly for longer periods. In addition to these guarantees you also have legal rights against the seller.

Your legal rights

Every time you buy goods from a shop, street market, mail-order company or the internet, or from any other kind of supplier, you enter into a contract with the seller. This contract, supplemented by legislation, gives consumers basic legal rights.

Although it started life as a law for business, consumer lawyers often consider that the Sale of Goods Act 1979 is the basic charter of rights for consumers. This legislation is largely a consolidating measure building upon the Sale of Goods Act 1893. It lays down that all goods supplied by business to consumers must:

1 fit the *description* used in any advertisement, label, packaging and so on relating to them – the year or make, type, colour, size or materials used, for example, must all be accurately described;

2 be of *satisfactory quality* – the goods should work

properly, have no major or minor defects, be safe and, if new, look new and be in good condition;

3 be *fit for their purpose* – if you made it clear to the retailer when choosing goods that you needed them for a specific purpose, the goods must fulfil those requirements.

If you place an order on the basis of samples of the goods which you intend to buy (material for a sofa cover, for example), the finished goods must correspond with that sample. If they do not, you have a claim against the retailer for breach of contract.

These requirements cover all goods (apart from land and homes) – from the most sophisticated computer systems to a simple bunch of flowers.

SATISFACTORY QUALITY

At the heart of the Sale of Goods Act is the buyer's right to receive goods which are of satisfactory quality.

What does it mean?

The concept of satisfactory quality is fairly recent in legal terms and has not had much real testing in the courts. Before satisfactory quality was introduced into consumer law, legislation had for many years referred to the buyer's right to receive goods of 'merchantable quality'. This was found in the original Sale of Goods Act dating back to 1893 – and lasted well over 100 years into the tail end of the last century.

Merchantable quality was defined for the first time in the Supply of Goods (Implied Terms) Act 1973. Nobody at that time suggested that a change in the law was intended or took place. Many lawyers assumed that the previous case law on the meaning of the phrase still held good. Then, in 1977, it was suggested that the 'new' definition had changed the law in a significant way. The issue was put fully into the spotlight when it came to the attention of the Consumers' Association (CA). One of its members, Mr Summerfield, wrote to the association about his Reliant Scimitar car. Although the car suffered from 29 separate faults, Mr Summerfield had been advised by counsel that he had no right to redress since none of the defects rendered the car unmerchantable. The CA obtained two barristers' opinions on the meaning of merchantable quality in its general application to consumer sales. From the CA's point of view the lawyers' opinions presented a gloomy picture. Leading academics and practising legal experts in consumer law were then consulted. They prepared their own opinions, each differing from the next. A seminar was convened by the CA in June 1978. After the seminar the CA published, under the general editorship of Professor McAllen of Liverpool University, a publication called *Merchantable Quality – What Does It Mean?* It set out an agenda for reform.

In November 1978, at the CA's suggestion, the Supply of Goods (Amendment) Bill was introduced by Donald Stewart, with the aim of altering the definition of merchantable quality. In January 1979, the Minister of State for Prices and Consumer Protection, John Fraser, told the House of Commons that, as a result of the introduction of the bill, the government was referring the issue to the Law Commission. The reference was wide; it included an assessment of the question of merchantable quality. Eventually, a Joint Report was published in May 1987. It recommended updating the 1979 Act in a number of respects. In particular, the report recommended changing the term 'merchantable quality' to 'acceptable quality' – amending it to a new legal definition, specifying that goods should have an appropriate appearance and finish, be durable, safe and free from minor defects.

The new definition

These recommendations, modified and updated, became law in 1995 as a result of a private member's bill introduced by David Clelland. Most importantly the bill, which became law as the Sale and Supply of Goods (Amendment) Act 1994, implemented the most significant Law Commission recommendation to replace the outdated phrase 'merchantable quality' with a more up-to-date phrase 'satisfactory quality' (which was the Law Commission's 'acceptable quality'.) There was also a new definition making the law clearer that satisfactory quality includes fitness for purpose, appearance and finish, freedom from minor defects, safety and durability.

When Mr Brown's £6,000 jet ski started to misfire just over a year after he bought it, he complained to the seller that it was not of satisfactory quality. Backed by an engineer's report confirming that an engine part had failed, Mr Brown sued for compensation. The court awarded him the full cost

of repairs, £2,371.97, plus the cost of towing the jet ski to the repairers.

REDRESS

If goods you have bought do not fit their description, are not of satisfactory quality or are not fit for their purpose, you can claim compensation for breach of contract from the retailer who supplied the item. Some retailers claim that it is not their responsibility to sort out problems with faulty goods and that the responsibility lies with the manufacturer. Do not be fobbed off in this way.

Depending on how quickly you act, you are entitled to:

- a full refund; or
- money compensation, which usually works out to the cost of repairs.

You do not have to accept a credit note, free repair or replacement item if you do not want to – though often this is the easiest way to resolve a problem. Agreeing to a repair does not necessarily stop you from claiming your money back if the repair does not solve the problem.

Getting a refund

If you pay for goods with cash, a credit/debit card or by signing a cheque, the law gives you a right to reject them if faulty or there is another problem. However, your right to reject goods (to terminate the contract) and get your money back is lost once you 'accept' the goods.

Accepting the goods

Under the Sale of Goods Act you are taken to have accepted goods when you retain them for a 'reasonable time' after delivery, without intimating to or telling the seller that you have rejected them. What is a reasonable time is a question of fact, decided by the courts in the light of each individual case

The consequences of the law are highlighted in a notorious consumer law case called *Bernstein* v *Pamson Motors (Golders Green) Ltd* (1987).

The engine in Mr Bernstein's new car seized up, owing to a manufacturing defect, just 27 days after he had bought and taken delivery of it. The car had been driven for only 120 miles. A High Court judge decided that Mr Bernstein had accepted the new car and was, therefore, prevented in law from rejecting it and getting his money back.

So, for some time it became accepted that consumers who buy goods containing a hidden or latent defect had no effective, meaningful legal right to end the contract and require the return of the purchase price. This seemed very unfair. Whether the buyer had accepted the goods was judged by how long it took him to discover the defect and time started to run from when he bought the goods – not from the time when the defect actually came to light.

Other contracts for the supply of goods – contracts of hire, hire-purchase, barter and conditional sale agreements – are, as a matter of law, treated differently from contracts of sale for the purpose of 'acceptance'. They are subject to the common law principle of 'affirmation' – which is much kinder to the buyer.

Other contracts – affirmation

Broadly speaking, the principle of affirmation means the owner of defective goods loses his right to reject goods only after he knows about the defects and does some act intimating that he wants to keep goods. The test is not subject to the lapse of time. Another car case, *Rogers v Parish (Scarborough) Ltd* (1987), illustrates the point. A claim to reject a car was upheld after it had done 5,000 miles and after it had been kept for six months, during which time several attempts at repair had been made, but without success. This case was one of a conditional sale – not a sale for cash. So the matter of rejection was subject to the common law principle of 'affirmation' rather than 'acceptance' (which applied to Mr Bernstein). Since the buyer had not affirmed the contract he was still able to exercise his right to end the contract and get a refund.

Reform – the new position

The *Bernstein* problem can be summed up like this. As already discussed, the buyer is taken to have accepted goods (and will, therefore, lose his right to a refund) when he keeps the goods for a 'reasonable time' after delivery, without intimating to or telling the seller that he has rejected them. In deciding whether there has been a lapse of a 'reasonable time', the crucial issue is whether the buyer has had a reasonable opportunity to examine the goods.

An opportunity to reform the law arose during the passage through Parliament of the Supply of Goods (Amendment) Bill in 1994. The government spokesman, the Consumer Affairs Minister, Earl Ferrers, said 'examine' should be interpreted in a wide context. Examination means more than just an examination in general terms – a cursory examination. It means an examination or inspection to see whether, among other things, the goods are in conformity with the contract. It is an examination to see whether the implied terms of the contract are satisfied. So a buyer should have a chance to see whether the goods are likely to be durable, safe, free from minor defects and so on, before a buyer is deemed to have accepted them and so lost the right to reject and get a refund.

What this all means is that now, under the Sale and Supply of Goods (Amendment) Act 1994, consumers have better, stronger rights to insist that the goods they get – the goods they pay for – are okay and up to a reasonable standard.

No longer will retailers be able to say 'You've had this car for three weeks, you can't get your money back'. Excuses like this are no longer acceptable, and short time limits during which refunds are 'offered' will be meaningless. It is true that the courts will still be left to decide whether a consumer has had a chance to examine defective goods. But if they interpret the law in accordance with the statements provided by ministers during the parliamentary debates, consumers will be able to examine and test goods to see that they are in good order, before losing their right to a refund.

While this falls short of a full-blown right to reject, which the CA had initially campaigned for, it does mean that consumer rights are improved and that courts should not adopt a similar approach to that used in *Bernstein*. This is because of a (relatively) new rule concerning the way courts interpret Acts of Parliament. In its landmark decision in *Pepper (Inspector of Taxes) v Hart* (1992), the House of Lords ruled that courts can refer to reports of debates and proceedings in Parliament as an aid to construing ambiguous or obscure legislation. The technique was, for example, used by the House of Lords in another case involving a prosecution for giving false price indications under the Consumer Protection Act 1987 section 20, *R v Warwickshire County Council, ex p Johnson* (1992).

Proving your claim

It is often difficult to show that goods were inherently faulty when purchased if you have had them for some time, but to have a successful claim you will need to prove that this was the case, and you may need technical evidence from an expert to add weight to your claim. You may contact the retailer and ask whether he will agree to abide by the decision of an independent expert. This will save on the costs of both parties getting technical evidence.

Second-hand

When you buy used goods from a trader – a secondhand car from a dealer or a used computer – you have the same rights under the amended Sale of Goods Act 1979 as if the goods were new. They should fit their description, be of satisfactory quality and reasonably fit for their purpose.

However, you cannot expect a secondhand car, for example, to be in the same condition as a new car, but you are entitled to expect it to be roadworthy. The quality and condition you are legally entitled to depends on the price paid, appearance, and any description used to sell the item 'in perfect running condition', for instance. (For more information *see* www.oft.gov.uk)

When shopping for used goods it really pays to examine and test them before buying.

Time limits

Any claim under the Sale of Goods Act can be brought against a seller at any time within six years from the date of purchase. However, the seller is only responsible if the fault or failure of the goods to meet the requirements laid down in the Act is due to some defect which was present at the time when they were sold.

In Scotland you have five years in which to complain from when you discover the fault.

Once you spot a defect in goods, act quickly: contact the retailer (telephone or go back to the shop), make it clear what you want – a refund or free repair, for example, and what you will do if you do not get a satisfactory response.

New rights for purchasers of faulty goods

In March 2003, a European Directive on the sale of consumer goods was implemented in the UK through the Sale and Supply of Goods to Consumers Regulations 2002. The aim of the Directive is to encourage people to shop across borders, knowing they have protection if anything is wrong with the products they buy. The Regulations update the existing Sales of Goods Act and apply to anyone who is a 'consumer' (i.e. a natural person, acting outside the purposes of his trade, business or profession).

The Regulations state that if a fault appears in the goods within the first six months, it will be assumed that the fault was there when the consumer bought the goods, unless the seller can prove otherwise. This reverses the current situation where the buyer has to prove that the goods were defective at the time of purchase. If goods are defective within the first two years (within one year if the goods are secondhand), the consumer can, in the first instance, require the seller to repair the goods or replace them free of charge. If repair or replacement is not possible, consumers have the right to a refund or compensation. Also, manufacturers' guarantees will become legally enforceable. Another new obligation for retailers under the Regulations is the requirement that anyone offering goods for sale which come with a guarantee must be able to provide a consumer with a copy on request. This must be within a reasonable time.

Mail order

You may have extra protection under the codes of practice governing mail order purchases. If you pay when you order in response to an advertisement which carries the Mail Order Protection Scheme (MOPS) logo, you are offered special protection. If the newspaper or publication carrying the advertisement belongs to MOPS, you can reclaim any money you may have sent if the firm goes out of business. Remember to keep a copy of the advertisement.

If paying on your credit card, you have extra protection if the goods cost more than £100 (*see* below). The Consumer Protection (Distance Selling) Regulations 2000 (*see* below) also protect mail order transactions.

In practice, mail order companies which belong to trade associations such as MOPS also generally agree to replace goods free of charge if they have been damaged in transit. Check with the association to see what is covered by the relevant scheme. You may also have some comeback against a supplier who is not a member of any trade association. If the supplier cannot prove that the goods left its premises in perfect condition, you have a claim to be reimbursed for the cost of the goods.

If it can be proved that the goods were damaged in transit, you have a claim against the carrier. In the case of the Post Office, you should complete form P58 (available at any post office) and send it to the Head Postmaster. Remember to keep a copy of your correspondence. If you can show that a parcel was damaged in the post, you will be entitled to compensation on a sliding scale, but this may not always reflect your actual loss.

Private sales

When you buy goods from a private individual, the only responsibilities on the seller are that he must own the goods and that the goods must correspond with any description you have been given. So if you buy a car from a private advertisement in a newspaper, you cannot complain if it breaks down after a week unless it was described, for example, as being in perfect working order.

In the sales

If you buy goods at a reduced price in a sale, you still retain all your rights under the Sale of Goods Act. However, if you are buying goods described as 'seconds', be certain to find out before you buy them exactly what defect makes them not of first quality. You cannot complain later about *that* defect, but if the goods develop a *different* fault you can complain about that fault to the retailer. Notices in shops to the effect that no refunds are made on sale goods have no basis in law – if the goods are faulty, you are entitled to a refund. Such notices are unlawful unless they say 'This does not affect your statutory rights', and should be reported to your local trading standards department.

Late delivery

The law does not normally regard time as a crucial element in contracts for consumer goods. If it is important that the goods you have ordered are delivered to you by a particular date, you should make this clear to the supplier by stating that 'time is of the essence' in writing when placing your order. If the goods ordered subsequently do not arrive on time, the supplier is in breach of contract and you are legally entitled to receive a full refund of the price that you paid. And if it costs you more than the price you paid with your order to get the same goods elsewhere, you are also entitled to receive the difference in price from the initial supplier.

If the supplier agrees to deliver the goods but no date for delivery is fixed, the Sale of Goods Act 1979 says that the supplier must send the goods to you within a reasonable time. However, as in other instances, there is no hard-and-fast rule about what is 'reasonable'. It depends on the circumstances – the type of goods, their availability, and so on.

Sometimes it is clear, either from a catalogue or from the nature of the goods themselves, that the goods are required by a particular date. If you order goods from a Christmas catalogue, or the goods themselves are particularly seasonal (Christmas cards, say), then it is clear that they must be delivered in time for Christmas. If such goods are not delivered in time, you are entitled to cancel your order and to ask for a full refund of the purchase price.

E-commerce

When you buy goods over the internet from businesses based in the UK, you have the same rights as when you buy from a shop. However, the nature of internet trading can cause additional problems, for example, it may be difficult to trace the whereabouts of an internet trader, making it difficult to get a refund if the goods turn out to be faulty or not as described.

You should check whether a trader belongs to an online code of practice. There are several, including the CA's *Which?* Web Trader scheme for UK-based internet traders (*see* www.which.net/webtrader). Each has different provisions but they all aim to set standards for internet traders to adhere to. These will usually include your rights to return the goods, delivery times and prices.

Because there are several codes, the Alliance for Electronic Business (AEB) and the CA launched a government-backed scheme called Trust UK, which sets out minimum standards for online codes. Trust UK has launched an 'e-hallmark' which traders can display on their websites, the presence of which will guarantee to consumers that the trader subscribes to a code of practice that meets these minimum standards. Only traders whose code has been accredited by Trust UK can display this e-hallmark. The minimum standards include having in place a complaints procedure, an efficient dispute resolution service, a procedure to guarantee consumers' privacy, and good practice in relation to security of information. Traders will also have to comply with the Consumer Protection (Distance Selling) Regulations, which protect consumers in distance contracts (*see* below) and the Electronic Commerce (EC Directive) Regulations 2002.

The Electronic Commerce Regulations 2002 stipulate that businesses which advertise or sell goods online must provide certain information to end users, including the full name of the business, contact details and a clear indication of prices, including delivery or tax charges. Online orders must be acknowledged without undue delay and customers must be given a chance to amend their orders. Depending on the exact nature of the non-compliance, end users may cancel their order, seek a court order against the business, or sue for damages for breach of statutory duty if they can demonstrate that they have suffered a loss as a result of the failure of the business to comply with the Regulations.

In addition, the Director General of Fair Trading and Trading Standards Departments can apply to the courts for a Stop Now Order if the failure to comply with the Regulations harms the collective interest of consumers. If a business fails to comply with a Stop Now Order, it may be held to be in contempt of court and could face a fine and/or imprisonment.

If a trader sends unsolicited commercial communications by e-mail (e.g. an e-mail advertising goods or services which is sent to a recipient who has not requested it), the Regulations stipulate that the trader must ensure that recipients are able to identify them as such as soon as they receive them. Possible ways of meeting this requirement include placing the words 'unsolicited advertisement' or 'unsolicited commercial communication' in the title of the e-mail. The purpose of this requirement is to ensure that recipients or their internet service providers can block or delete the e-mail without the need to open and read it.

Stop Now Orders

This is a new form of injunctive relief (in the civil courts) that can be applied for by a variety of bodies (OFT, industry regulators, local authorities, as well as Shelter, the Consumers' Association, and other organizations that exist to protect the collective interests of consumers).

Stop Now Orders apply to legislation associated with the EU Directives covering misleading advertising, contracts negotiated away from business premises, consumer credit, broadcasting, the package and travel industry, advertising of medicines, unfair contract terms, timeshares, distance selling and sale of goods and guarantees. *See also* page 437.

Buying from traders based abroad

If you are buying goods via the internet from overseas, the law applicable to the contract (unless otherwise stated) could be that of the country you are buying from. This may differ significantly from UK legislation and may offer different protection. Furthermore, the practicalities of enforcing your rights against a non-UK trader will be difficult and costly, and you may not be able to take your claim to a local court.

Distance Selling Regulations

The Consumer Protection (Distance Selling) Regulations 2000 are designed to give basic legal protection to consumers who buy goods and services via the internet, through mail order, telephone, or any other contract where the consumer and the supplier do not come face to face. However, it does not cover holiday and travel arrangements, or deliveries of goods for everyday consumption (e.g. milk). Financial services will have their own regulations in 2004 when the EU Directive on Distance Marketing of Financial Services is implemented.

Under the Regulations you will have the right to:

- basic pre-contract information, such as the name and address of the supplier, the price, and the right to withdraw;
- written confirmation of the order;
- a cooling-off period of seven working days (during which time you can change your mind about entering into the contract);
- the contract being carried out within 30 days unless otherwise agreed;
- a refund of all money taken through fraudulent use of a credit or charge card;
- a complete ban on the supply of unsolicited goods and services where supply involves a demand for payment;
- an opt-out from receiving spam (junk) e-mail.

SAFETY

There are special laws dealing with unsafe products. For example, the General Product Safety Regulations 1994 (implementing an EU Directive) impose a general duty on all suppliers of consumer goods to supply safe products. Amazingly, this basic protection was missing before this law came into force.

The Regulations cover new and secondhand goods (including clothes, medicines, food and drink, nursery items, cars and so on), except products that are covered by specific European safety legislation.

Products must provide the safety that consumers may reasonably expect. Safety takes into account factors such as the product's characteristics, instructions and warnings, and whether likely users, such as children, need extra care. Relevant UK or European standards may be considered.

The legislation also deals with product recalls from suppliers. Recalls of unsafe or faulty products already sold to consumers is a difficult area, currently dealt with by a voluntary system.

Trading standards departments enforce this law. With cars, for example, trading standards officers can inspect vehicles on garage forecourts to see if they are safe.

Traders supplying an unsafe product can be punished by a fine of up to £5,000 for each offence, and/or three months in prison.

Some specific types of goods are also covered by targeted rules.

Fireworks

Fireworks supplied in the UK must be authorized by the Health and Safety Executive, and there are stiff fines if fireworks do not meet specific fireworks regulations. (*See also* page 125.)

Furniture

Furniture bought since 1988 is covered by the Furniture and Furnishings (Fire) (Safety) Regulations 1988. These set down stringent fire resistance tests for upholstered furniture, and limit the effects of fires in the home.

Toys

Toys are covered by the Toys (Safety) Regulations 1995. The Regulations again implement an EU Directive. Basically, all toys supplied in the UK (and the rest of the EU) must satisfy essential 'safety requirements' and bear the 'CE' mark. Trading standards officers can take unsafe toys off the shelves and take legal action. Supplying unsafe toys can result in a fine of up to £5,000 or six months in prison, or both.

Compensation for unsafe products

You are entitled to claim under the Sale of Goods Act 1979 for any damage caused by faulty goods. If, for example, your washing machine breaks down and damages the clothes that are in it at the time, you are entitled to claim compensation from the retailer for those items, as well as for the machine. You may, however, need evidence that the clothes were damaged by the machine. Photographs can help. Also keep the damaged items until your claim is settled.

The Consumer Protection Act 1987 also establishes that manufacturers (or 'producers') are strictly liable for harm caused by defective products. If you can prove that a defect in a product caused you personal injury, or damage to your property over £250, you can claim compensation from the manufacturer, not from the retailer. Anyone injured can claim – the right to do so is not restricted to the purchaser of the goods. The law applies to consumer goods and products used in the workplace, but used not to apply to primary agricultural products and game. Since December 2000 these exceptions have disappeared and all products are covered.

Under the 1987 Act you are entitled to compensation for the time you have had to take off work, lost wages, and the pain and suffering caused by the injury. The amount of compensation you can claim may be considerable, depending on the seriousness of the injury and the nature of the 'loss of amenity'. If you are a builder, for instance, and cannot do manual work for six months, you will be entitled to claim more for this element than someone who does not have to perform physical tasks for a living. It is important to get legal advice from a specialist personal injury solicitor before making any claim.

43

Services

When you ask someone to carry out a service for you – such as building work, plumbing, dry-cleaning, furniture removal, hairdressing, and so on – you enter into a legally binding contract which gives you basic legal rights. As well as the right to receive the service that is defined within the terms of the contract (types of materials that will be used, dates by which the work will be done, and so on), you also have rights read ('implied') into the contract by law.

The Supply of Goods and Services Act 1982 (common law in Scotland) lays down that services must be carried out with reasonable skill and care. It also says that if your agreement with the supplier does not specify precise dates or prices, the work must be carried out within a reasonable time and for a reasonable price. It is not always clear what is 'reasonable'. It will often depend upon whether or not another supplier would have done the same as the firm you are claiming against.

If something goes wrong as the result of a service – your new plaster starts to crack, or the roof which you had mended still leaks – in the first instance ask the contractor to put the defects right. If the contractor will not do so, you are legally entitled to employ another contractor to rectify the problem – and then claim the cost from the first contractor.

ESTATE AGENTS

Estate agents are usually instructed by and act on behalf of sellers of properties. Their work is regulated by the Estate Agents Act 1979, and regulations and orders made under the Act. The purpose of these laws is to make sure that estate agents act in the best interests of their clients and that both buyers and sellers of property are treated honestly, fairly and promptly. The Director General of Fair Trading (DGFT) is responsible for the working and enforcement of the law. Trading standards departments and, in Northern Ireland, the Department of Enterprise,

Trade and Investment help to enforce the law in this area.

Also, the Property Misdescriptions Act 1991 states that property misdescriptions are illegal. If an agent lies about the size of a room, in property particulars, for example, he faces a large fine. This law is enforced by local trading standards officers.

If you instruct an estate agent to sell your home, your legal position is governed by the law of contract. This means it is largely up to you to lay down the services you require, and to make sure that the agent agrees to perform them. (Laws – see below – make this relatively easy for consumers.) You also have rights to a reasonable service under the Supply of Goods and Services Act 1982 (common law in Scotland).

In addition, under the common law of agency, the estate agent is obliged always to act in the best interests of the client. Unfortunately, there are no hard-and-fast rules about what precisely estate agents have to do to find a purchaser, so when choosing an estate agent you should contact several offices to find out exactly what services are offered.

One problem area often focused on is estate agents' commission. This is normally a percentage of the price at which the property is sold. It is, however, important to check what is included in the price. Ask if it covers photographs, a 'for sale' board and advertisements in the local press. You can usually opt for the following deals:

- *sole agency* – you instruct only one agent;
- *joint agency* – you instruct two agents. Both agents have to agree to this, and on who gets the commission on the sale;
- *multiple agency* – you instruct as many agents as you like. The one who comes up with the buyer earns the commission. The fee for this type of arrangement is normally higher than sole or joint agency.

Information the agent must give you

Before you agree to an estate agent acting for you, the agent must give you specific information about their services in writing. In particular, the agent must give you advance written information about fees and charges. You must also be told about any services offered by the agent to potential buyers – such as arranging mortgages. Any technical phrases used, such as 'sole agency', must be spelt out in definitions prescribed by the Office of Fair Trading. If you are not given this information in advance, the agent will not be able to enforce payment of fees without a court order.

It is normally advisable to choose a no sale, no fee deal: that way, you pay commission only if the agent introduces you to someone who actually buys your home. Beware of contracts that say that you will have to pay the fee 'in the event of our introducing a purchaser who is able and willing to complete the transaction'. Under this arrangement, you could end up paying a fee if your home was not sold because you took it off the market, or if you found the eventual buyer yourself.

Estate agents are required to reveal promptly and in writing any personal interest they have in a transaction. During negotiations, estate agents must make sure that everyone involved is treated equally and fairly. That means, for instance, that sellers must be given written details of all offers received from potential buyers promptly – except those which the seller has told the agent not to pass on. Estate agents must also tell sellers whenever a potential buyer asks them to provide a service, such as arranging a mortgage. It is illegal to mislead buyers or sellers in any way, for example by giving misleading information about offers.

Complaints

If you are not happy with an estate agent or the service provided by them, remember that you can take your house off their books. In the first instance, problems with agents should be directed to the manager or owner of the office. If this does not resolve your problem, see if the agent is a member of a professional association, such as the National Association of Estate Agents, Arbon House, 21 Jury Street, Warwick CV34 4EH or the Royal Institution of Chartered Surveyors, 12 Great George Street, London SW1P 3AD. Both bodies have a code of practice and disciplinary mechanisms to deal with bad service.

If the agent is a member, also complain to the Office of the Ombudsman for Estate Agents, Beckett House, 4 Bridge Street, Salisbury SP1 2LX (www.oea.co.uk). The ombudsman runs a code of practice which says, for example, that members must put up a 'for sale' board only with the seller's permission and agree not to directly, or indirectly, harass anyone to gain instructions. The ombudsman can also order estate agents to pay up to £25,000 compensation to a client. Unfortunately not all estate agents are part of this scheme. It is generally operated by large estate agencies. Many thousands of the smaller estate agents are not governed by the scheme (though they are eligible to join), so check whether the agent that you have chosen is covered by the scheme before using that complaints procedure. The scheme costs you nothing.

If your estate agent does not belong to the scheme, and your dispute remains unresolved, your only option is to pursue your claim in court. In Scotland, solicitors often sell property and so act like estate agents.

GARAGES

If you ask a garage to service or repair your car and it is damaged in the process, or fails to function for a reasonable time after the repair because the work has not been carried out properly, then the garage is in breach of contract. You are entitled to claim compensation for any loss or damage arising from this breach, which usually means the cost of getting the damage repaired. However, you should also be compensated for any expenses you incur which were reasonably foreseeable by both you and the garage at the time the contract was made, such as the cost of alternative means of transport while your car was off the road. But you must do what you can to ensure that your claim is kept to a minimum. If you cannot show that you have minimized your loss in this way, you run the risk of not being able to recover all your costs if the matter does eventually go to court.

The price

When you ask a garage to repair or service your car, you are obliged to pay only for work you have authorized. So make sure you know exactly what you have agreed to before allowing the garage to carry out any work, preferably by putting it in writing. If the price is not agreed beforehand, the law says that you are obliged to pay a reasonable price for the work. There are no hard-and-fast rules about what a reasonable price is: it depends on the type of repair or service that was undertaken. If you feel that the price you have been charged is too high, you will have to demonstrate that the price is unreasonable, so get evidence in the form of quotations for the same work from other garages, or from a motoring organization if you belong to one. A useful tip is to ask the initial garage to give you an estimate as soon as the problem has been diagnosed.

If you are forced to pay as a condition for recovering your car, you should make it clear, preferably in writing, that you are paying under protest. This keeps your rights open to seek redress later.

What if the garage damages the car?

When you take your car into a garage for repairs, the garage is legally obliged to take reasonable care of it. If your car is damaged while in the possession of the garage – for example, on the garage forecourt or in a car wash – the garage is responsible, under the law of bailment, for that damage unless it can prove that the damage was caused through no fault on its part. Garages may try to restrict your legal rights by displaying notices denying responsibility for any loss or damage to vehicles left in their possession. Any such attempts by garages to wriggle out of their legal obligations are covered by the Unfair Contract Terms Act 1977 and the Unfair Terms in Consumer Contracts Regulations 1999 (*see* page 435).

One option to help avoid problems is to look for a local garage registration scheme. Trading standards departments in about 30 local councils throughout the UK run such schemes. Each is slightly different, but runs on broadly the same lines. Participating garages sign up to a code of practice, covering standards, customer care, complaint handling, and so on. Failure to stick to the code means a garage could get kicked off the scheme. Contact your local council to see if a scheme operates in your area.

COWBOY BUILDERS

Cowboy builders are a consumer nightmare, especially with regards to home maintenance and installing double glazing. For generations, consumers have complained that they do not know which businesses offer good value and service. More still do not know where they stand when things go wrong.

Finding a reputable builder

If you are looking for a builder, and want to avoid the cowboys, help is finally on its way. In June 2000, the government launched a register of builders who meet minimum standards of skill, workmanship, qualification and financial stability. Consumers can use the register to find a reputable builder who has been awarded the Quality Mark. Approved builders should also offer an insurance-backed warranty, covering the consumer against poor workmanship and builder insolvency. Linked to this, the builder will be required to have an effective complaints and discipline procedure.

Following successful pilots in Birmingham and Somerset, the government announced in March 2002 that the Quality Mark scheme would be rolled out across England and Wales over a three- to four-year period.

To apply for the mark, builders will have to submit references from satisfied customers, and their work may be inspected as part of the application process. To keep them on their toes, they will also have to re-register each year. Consumers using a Quality Mark builder will be covered by a warranty against shoddy workmanship or the builder going bust. There is a complaints system to resolve any disputes.

Problem areas

Consumer complaints about building, plumbing and other home maintenance work focus on overcharging, delays and substandard work. Some of these problems can be avoided or, at least, reduced by taking some precautions in advance of employing the contractor. An obvious tip is to discuss the job with two or three contractors and ask them to provide detailed estimates of the work. It also pays to use a contractor recommended by a friend or relative. Also ask to see work done for other clients, and talk to them about the quality of the contractor's work.

The price for the job

Once they have sized up the job, you may be given a provisional price or a firm one. If the document gives precise details of the work with detailed costs, the price should be binding. A rough price is only a general guide: when he eventually sends you his bill, the contractor may charge you more. But the total still should be 'reasonable'. What is reasonable depends on how much work has been done and the type of job that was undertaken.

Put it in writing

With everything other than straightforward jobs, it also helps to have a proper written contract drawn up between you and the contractor. In this way everyone should be clear about what is involved and it will be easier for you to prove exactly what you and the contractor agreed should any problem arise.

A typical, simple contract which you draw up yourself should include:

- your name and the name of the contractor;
- the standard of workmanship and materials to be used, including a statement that the work will be in accordance with any given plans and specifications: these specifications may refer to appropriate British Standards or Codes of Practice;
- the date on which the work will be started;
- the date on which the work will be finished. You may also include a clause stating that the contractor will pay you reasonable compensation if the completion is

delayed. You should specify a degree of flexibility as regards the completion date, due to delays being caused by unusually bad weather or other circumstances beyond the contractor's control;

- a clause to the effect that the contractor should leave the site in a tidy state at the end of the work;
- clarification as to which party is responsible for obtaining planning permission;
- precise details of how changes to specifications will be agreed;
- a stipulation that the contractor must be properly insured;
- a precise definition of circumstances in which you or the contractor can terminate the contract;
- the total cost of the work and how the bill will be paid – in a lump sum at the end, or in stages as the work progresses;
- a requirement that the contractor should return to put right any defects that manifest themselves in the work after it is completed, and to rectify any damage caused to your property, at his expense;
- a requirement that in the event of a dispute over the cause of any defects you may appoint an expert to report on the faulty work and/or materials and the contractor will agree to accept the findings of that expert and, if the report proves the liability of the contractor for the faulty work and/or materials, the contractor agrees to pay the cost of that report.

If the contractor offers his own contract for the work, read it very carefully and check it against this list before signing. If the contractor has reservations about the contract you want to use, discuss it to see if you can reach a sensible compromise. If you are considering major building work, it can pay to instruct an engineer or architect. This gives you greater protection against things going wrong.

Every time a contractor agrees to carry out work for a client, the client enters into a contract with him. Along with the specific rights given in the contract (e.g. the types of materials that the contractor should use) the client also has rights under the Supply of Goods and Services Act 1982 (common law in Scotland), which entitle the client to have the work carried out with reasonable skill and care, and within a reasonable time. If the contractor does not carry out work as specifically agreed in the contract (e.g. if he uses the wrong type of roof tiles) or does not carry out the work with reasonable skill

and care, the client can claim for breach of contract. This means that he is legally entitled to have the work put right free of charge.

Time

If it is important to you that the work is completed by a particular date, get the contractor to agree in writing to a specific date for completion of the work, and also make clear in writing that 'time is of the essence'. By doing so you give yourself stronger legal rights in the event of the work not being finished on time – if the contractor does not complete the job on time, you could, for example, cancel the contract and call in another contractor to complete the work; if this costs you more than the first contractor's estimate, you can claim the extra cost from the original firm.

The law does not normally regard time as a crucial element of building contracts, so if the work is not done on time, and you have not agreed that time is of the essence, you may claim compensation for breach of contract if you have suffered financially as a result of the delay – you have been compelled to eat out because of the unfinished state of your kitchen, for example – but the contract will still stand and you will not be entitled to call in another contractor to finish the job.

If you have not agreed a completion date, you are entitled to have the work carried out within a reasonable time. This period is not defined by law but it depends on the size and type of work involved. If the work is delayed you should give the contractor written notice that you are making time of the essence and fix a reasonable date for completion. Then, if the work is not finished on time, you can safely consider the contract at an end.

Substandard work

If work is substandard, yet the contractor fails or refuses to put it right, get two or three quotes for the cost of finishing the job properly. This shows you are serious and that you will, if necessary, call in another contractor to carry out remedial work.

If this does not work and you eventually have to get another firm to put the work right, you are legally entitled to ask the first contractor to foot the bill. You may, however, need a detailed report from the repairer or an engineer backing your claim for compensation. Essentially, this report needs to be a diagnosis of what went wrong and what was needed to put it right.

44

Holidays

BASIC RIGHTS

Tour operators selling air travel as part of the holiday package must have Air Travel Organizers' Licences (ATOLs). These protect you from losing money or being stranded abroad if the operator goes out of business.

When your package holiday booking is accepted (usually by the issue of a confirmation invoice), a legally binding contract is made between you and the tour operator – the company that organizes your holiday. The contract is not with the travel agent and, if things go wrong, your claim is against the tour operator. On the other hand, travel agents do owe you a legal duty of care and if they do not do a competent job you will have a claim against them.

Descriptions in the travel company's brochure of the hotel and the resort form part of your contract with the tour operator, and are therefore part of your legal entitlements. These descriptions must be factually accurate – the hotel facilities specified in the brochure must exist as described; a 'quiet' hotel must be quiet, and the dates and times of flights must be correctly stated too.

Along with the specific right to features described in the brochure, you also have rights implied into the contract by previous case law. Broadly, these cases have established that the accommodation provided must be of a standard of cleanliness and quality to be reasonably expected from the type and price of holiday booked.

Special requirements that you have communicated to the tour operator before making your booking, and which have been accepted by the tour operator and written on the confirmation form, are also part of your contract: so if you have specified a room with a sea view, or a ground-floor room for an elderly relative, for example, you are legally entitled to find them available when you arrive.

PROBLEMS

If, when you arrive at your destination, you find that the tour operator has failed to provide the holiday you booked, make sure you complain immediately to the tour operator's representative. The representative may be able to rectify the problem by offering to move you to another room or hotel, for example. If you do not complain and put up with the situation the tour operator can argue that you failed to reduce your loss and this may mean that you are not entitled to as much compensation. Even if the representative is unable to rectify the situation you will be able to argue that you tried to mitigate (reduce) your loss. In all cases you should ensure that you have filled out a customer dissatisfaction report. If complaining at the time does not resolve your problem, write to the tour operator when you get home.

The Association of British Travel Agents (ABTA) is the main representative body for both travel agents and tour operators. It operates a bonding scheme to ensure holidaymakers do not lose their money when member companies go out of business. It also operates a code of conduct for both tour operators and travel agents which sets standards of service that are binding on members.

ALTERATIONS BEFORE DEPARTURE

Tour operators' booking conditions usually reserve the right to 'make minor alterations' to your holiday arrangements without paying you compensation. However, under an EU Directive, incorporated into UK law by the Package Travel, Package Holidays and Package Tour Regulations 1992, if a tour operator makes a significant change to your holiday, it must tell you as soon as possible. You are entitled to cancel and get a refund (and possibly compensation if you suffer additional losses), or opt for compensation. A significant change would be moving you to a different resort. If, as a result, you choose to cancel your holiday, and it costs you more money to book a similar holiday, you can claim the difference in value as well as a refund.

If despite the alteration you decide to go on the holiday, you should write to the tour operator stating that you accept the alteration under protest and reserve your right to claim compensation on your return.

Any attempt by the tour operator to limit your right to complain or to make changes to your holiday after booking must be fair and reasonable, otherwise you may have a claim under the Unfair Contract Terms Act 1977, or be able to take action under the Unfair Terms in Consumer Contracts Regulations 1999.

PROBLEMS AFTER DEPARTURE

A tour operator's failure to provide you with the precise accommodation you booked is, on the face of it, a breach of contract on the tour operator's part. Under the Package Travel, Package Holidays and Package Tour Regulations 1992, in addition to the ABTA code, operators must take due care to ensure that problems such as overbooking do not happen. However, many tour operators' brochures contain a term in the booking conditions denying liability for changes of plan caused by overbooking, which will probably prevent you claiming compensation so long as the alternative accommodation provided is of the same standard as that booked and is in a comparable part of the resort. But if the alternative offered is of a lower standard, or in a different resort, for example, you will be entitled under the Regulations to be repatriated and to compensation if you make a reasonable decision that the alternative is not suitable.

The Regulations also make the tour operator liable to you for any damage caused by the negligence of any suppliers of the services under the holiday contract. So if you become ill by eating contaminated food on an all-inclusive holiday abroad, you can sue the tour operator in this country rather than pursuing a claim against a hotel in a foreign jurisdiction. For this type of claim you should always seek legal advice.

Sometimes, if a number of people become ill, for example, solicitors will bring a joint claim called a 'group action' to get compensation.

COMPENSATION

The amount of compensation you could reasonably expect to receive depends to a large extent on the amount of enjoyment you were able to derive from your holiday. There are four basic components of holiday compensation.

1 *Loss of value* – the difference between the value of the holiday you got and the one you paid for.

2 *Loss of enjoyment* – something to compensate you for the disappointment and frustration of your holiday going wrong.

3 *Out-of-pocket expenses* – the refund of any reasonable expenses you incurred as a result of the tour operator's breach of contract.

4 *Pain and suffering* – if you have suffered an illness or injury on holiday, you may be entitled to compensation. Consult a solicitor about the amount you can claim. (*See further* pages 599 and 613.)

For their honeymoon, Steve and Jo Roake booked two weeks at Unijet's Club Antigua Hotel. The total cost was £2,586. On arrival they found their honeymoon room had twin beds, not the double bed promised in the brochure. They found the general attitude of the hotel staff to be sloppy and the Unijet representative seemed unconcerned and unhelpful.

When Unijet failed to offer the Roakes satisfactory compensation, they claimed in the small claims court. The court awarded them £1,000, plus the court issue fee, and £60 each for earnings they had lost in attending the hearing.

SAFETY

It is worth checking about safety issues with the Foreign and Commonwealth Office, particularly if you are straying well away from the beaten track. The Foreign and Commonwealth Office website www.fco.gov.uk/travel includes advice to help British travellers avoid trouble, especially threats to their personal safety arising from political unrest, lawlessness, violence, natural disasters, epidemics, anti-British demonstrations, and aircraft safety.

PLANES

If your tour operator changes your charter flight, look at the booking conditions in the brochure: unless the conditions allow such changes, the tour operator is not entitled to do this. Unfortunately, most booking conditions, and the ABTA code, do allow minor changes to flight times. However, you should be given a full refund, or some kind of compensation, if you decide to cancel when the operator makes such a major change. In this instance, major and minor are not precisely defined and depend on the circumstances of each case.

Under the Warsaw Convention (incorporated into English law by the Carriage by Air and Road Act 1979), airlines are obliged to compensate you if they fail to get you to your destination within a reasonable time of your scheduled arrival. On a long-haul flight, a 'reasonable' time is usually considered to be about six hours. The strength of your claim depends on what causes the delay.

If it is a factor outside the airline's control – bad weather, for example – you do not stand much chance of recompense. But if your delay is a result of overbooking, or any other cause within the airline's control, you do have a valid claim and it is worth persisting.

There is also an EU Regulation covering overbooking on scheduled flights from European destinations. If you turn up at an airport within the EU and are denied boarding because the flight you have booked is already full, you will be entitled to a full refund of the unused ticket, or a seat on the next available flight of your choice. The airline must also offer you on-the-spot cash compensation: you are currently entitled to about £120 for flights of up to 3,500 kilometres, and £240 for longer flights. These amounts are halved if the airline can get you to your final destination within two hours (or four hours for flights over 3,500 kilometres) of your original scheduled arrival. You must also be given a free telephone call to your destination, meals throughout the delay and overnight accommodation if it is necessary.

If your luggage is lost, damaged or even delayed on an international flight, you may have a claim against the airline for compensation. The Warsaw Convention allows you to claim a maximum sum, currently about £15, per kilogram of checked-in baggage. This limitation applies whether your case is full of expensive designer clothes or old T-shirts and jeans, so you should always make sure you have adequate travel insurance. If your luggage is returned to you damaged, you must make your complaint to the airline within seven days of getting it back.

Mr M booked a non-smoking club class seat with British Airways for a return flight to Hong Kong. It cost £4,200. On the plane he found that his seat was immediately in front of a row for smokers. Unable to move because the plane was full, five heavy smokers made Mr M's 12-hour flight unbearable. In court the judge decided that as he had been allocated a non-smoking seat it was reasonable for Mr M to expect it to be reasonably smoke free. It was not and he was, therefore, awarded £600 compensation for his discomfort.

TIMESHARE

In 1990, in response to a request from the Secretary of State for Trade and Industry, the Director General of Fair Trading conducted an inquiry into the timeshare industry and published a report on its problems. That report included a comprehensive list of recommendations for action, one of which was a right for the consumer – the 'offeree' – to withdraw from the contract without penalty during a 14-day cooling-off period. Because of the European dimensions of timeshare, the government asked the European Commission to bring forward a directive

addressing the problems outlined in the report. The Commission reacted positively and drafted a directive.

At the tail end of 1991 the European initiative was overtaken when a private member's bill was introduced into the House of Commons by Andrew Hunter. The purpose of the bill, the Timeshare Bill, was simple: it imposed a minimum 14-day cooling-off period.

The bill became the Timeshare Act 1992. It provides for a 14-day (minimum) cooling-off period in timeshare contracts provided that either:

- the contract is signed by either party within the UK; or
- the contract is subject to the laws of the UK.

The Act also makes it a criminal offence to enter into a timeshare agreement without first giving consumers notice of their rights to cancel the contract at any time during the cooling-off period. A cancellation form for the customer to complete and return should be attached to the notice setting out the cancellation rights. If consumers cancel during the cooling-off period, they are entitled to recover any money paid in connection with the contract.

The Act also provides for a minimum cooling-off period of 14 days in the case of most timeshare credit agreements – in other words, where there is a provision for credit with which to pay for the timeshare. As with timeshare agreements, the Act requires a statement of consumers' rights to cancel during the cooling-off period, to which a cancellation form should be attached. It also sets out arrangements for repayment of credit if the agreement is cancelled. In line with other laws covering credit, it is not, however, a criminal offence to fail to hand over a notice of consumers' rights to cancel a timeshare credit agreement.

Be particularly careful if you sign a contract outside the UK as you probably will not be protected by UK law. Check if the timeshare contract claims to be covered by UK law and get legal advice before signing.

If timeshare is bought anywhere in the European Economic Area (EEA), consumers have minimum rights to protect them. These are:

- a minimum 10-day cooling-off period in the EEA countries in which to cancel the contract;
- timeshare sellers cannot seek or take deposits during the cooling-off period;
- the right to a brochure and a written contract setting out basic information on the timeshare property in the buyer's own language.

Products with no legal protection

There are a number of timeshare-related products which are not subject to timeshare law and consequently do not offer the same protection and rights. These are:

- holiday or vacation club schemes – where membership

of the club is not linked to any rights in any particular property;

- timeshare resale;
- timeshare in floating vessels (such as narrow boats, pleasure boats and houseboats);
- timeshare lasting less than three years.

Complaints about timeshare

Problems relating to timeshare should be referred to your local trading standards department (www.trading standards.gov.uk), who are responsible for enforcing the timeshare law within the UK. The Timeshare Consumers' Association offers consumers advice and information on many problems relating to timeshare and holiday clubs (Tel: 01909 591 100; website: www.timeshare.org.uk). The Association of Timeshare Owners' Committees (TATOC) is a non-profit-making body representing the interests of timeshare owners, owners/resort committees and associations. It can provide information and advice on timeshare resale, maintenance fees, exchanges and VAT/tax issues. Tel: 0151 638 8239. The Organization for Timeshare in Europe (OTE) is a trade association which represents timeshare, holiday clubs and resale companies located throughout Europe. It represents about 40 per cent of the industry. All of its members follow a strict code of practice and it also provides a free advisory and conciliation service for anyone who deals with its members. For information, advice and help telephone: 00 322 533 3069.

45

It Isn't What It Says It Is

FALSE DESCRIPTIONS

The Trade Descriptions Act 1968 is probably the most quoted and yet perhaps the least understood consumer law. At the core of the 1968 Act are measures to stop businesses misdescribing goods and services to consumers.

Accurate and reliable information is essential if consumers are to make the right choices. The 1968 Act was introduced with this very much in mind, and updated laws on this theme dating from the nineteenth century. The Act's two main provisions concern:

- statements about goods; and
- statements about services, accommodation and facilities.

The Act makes it a criminal offence for traders to give false or misleading information about the goods and services they supply. Misdescription of goods, for example, covers statements made on the packaging, in the brochure, by a salesman in adverts, and so on. So a tour operator's brochure that shows a hotel next to a quiet beach when it is really in the middle of town falls foul of this law. The Act is enforced by local trading standards departments.

A mail order company was prosecuted under the Act for claims that one of its gadgets, a £10 TV antenna, was 'crammed with space-age circuitry'. It was not. The court fined the supplier £1,500 plus costs of £3,500.

At present the Act treats services differently to goods. If a trader misdescribes goods (e.g. a car) he commits an offence, irrespective of whether he intended to mislead. However, if a trader misdescribes services (e.g. a car repair), he commits a crime only if it can be proved that he did so knowingly or recklessly. With services the enforcement authorities must establish that the trader knew the statement was false at the time he made it, or that he had been reckless.

It has long been recognized that there is no real justification for the different treatment under the Act of false or misleading statements relating to goods and those relating to the supply of services. As long ago as 1976 the Director General of Fair Trading (DGFT), in a major review of the Act, recommended that the Act's treatment of goods and services should be brought into line. Since then an increasingly large share of consumers' income has been spent on services, such as holidays. And the growth of services being delivered over the internet is a further reason why it is important to ensure that consumers have confidence in information.

The White Paper *Modern Markets: Confident Consumers* proposes a change to the way that services are treated under the 1968 Act. It is proposed that the Act should treat the supply of services in the same way that it does the supply of goods.

Since it is a criminal law, the Act cannot help you directly if you want to make a claim for compensation (*see* below), but threatening to report the matter to the local trading standards department may indirectly lead to a quick settlement of any compensation claim you may make.

CLOCKING

Many cases brought by the enforcement authorities under the Trade Descriptions Act 1968 involve cars that do not match their description (including mileage). In addition, the government has announced a package of measures aimed at tackling the problem of 'clocking'. 'Clocking' is illicitly tampering with the mileage gauge of a vehicle so that the vehicle appears to have done fewer miles. The Driver and Vehicle Licensing Agency (DVLA) is considering a requirement that mileage be reported on vehicle registration and vehicle licence renewal forms, while plans to computerize the MOT testing system would allow mileage to be recorded at each MOT. The Office of Fair Trading (OFT) has also announced that it would remove or refuse to grant or renew credit licences to car dealers who are shown to undertake unfair practices, such as selling unroadworthy vehicles.

MISLEADING ADVERTISING

Advertising in the UK is mainly subject to self-regulation, and control through codes of practice. Non-broadcast advertising, in magazines and papers, for example, is overseen by the Advertising Standards Authority (ASA). It aims to ensure compliance with the British Codes of Advertising and Sales Promotion. These codes are, broadly, the rules drawn up by the advertising industry – and with which industry agrees to comply. At their core, the rules require advertisements to be legal, decent, honest and truthful.

In addition to the Codes, the Control of Misleading Advertisements Regulations 1988, which implement the EU Misleading Advertisements Directive, require the DGFT to investigate complaints and empower him to seek an injunction from the courts stopping misleading advertisements, where necessary. The DGFT usually leaves it to the ASA to resolve complaints before acting though. The DGFT also investigates complaints under the Control of Misleading Advertisements (Amendment) Regulations 2000, which deal with adverts which do not comply with the conditions under which comparisons are permitted with advertisements.

Television and radio advertising is covered by codes of practice operated by the Independent Television Commission and the Radio Authority.

The Sale and Supply of Goods to Consumers Regulations 2002 (*see* page 418) will make advertisers more wary of the claims they make about their products. This is because among the factors that must now be taken into account in deciding whether goods are of 'satisfactory quality' will be any public statements made in relation to the specific characteristics of those goods by the seller, the producer or his representative 'particularly in advertising or labelling'. So advertising claims can be enforced against the seller. A retailer has a defence if he can show that he was unaware of the statement, but this is unlikely to be of any assistance in the case of packaging claims. If a manufacturer's TV advert leads a reasonable consumer to expect a certain quality of goods then a retailer may face demands from dissatisfied purchasers. Bear in mind that this new provision does not apply to second-hand or auction sales.

PRICES

The law recognizes goods advertised for sale in a shop or on an internet trader's website as simply an 'invitation to treat', i.e. an invitation for you, the consumer, to make an offer to buy which the trader is entitled to refuse. Unfortunately, if the goods have been wrongly priced (for example £5 rather than £500) you cannot insist that the trader sells you the goods at that price.

On the other hand, if your offer to buy is accepted by the trader before it has been discovered that the item is wrongly priced, and you can show that the contract is concluded then you can insist that the trader supplies you with the goods. Evidence, such as an order confirmation or paying a deposit, is helpful in this respect. If the trader fails to supply the goods, you can buy the same goods elsewhere and, if they cost you more, you can claim the difference in value from the first trader. The trader could try to argue that a mistake had been made which could make the contract void. For this to succeed the trader must be able to show that you must have known that the offer was not genuine. This will be easier to prove where there is a large discrepancy in the price.

However, it is basically up to traders to charge what they like for consumer goods and services. But they must not give misleading prices to consumers, for example, by failing to include extras, like delivery, and VAT in their prices. This is laid down by Part III of the Consumer Protection Act 1987. A code of conduct under this Act helps traders stay on the right side of the law by giving guidance on good practice. The trading standards departments enforce this legislation.

Price rip-offs are dealt with by other controls. Overpricing because of price rigging is covered by competition law, for instance (*see* page 528). Overcharging by tradesmen who work on the basis of an initial estimate is dealt with by laws laying down that they can only charge a *reasonable* price for their services (*see* page 424).

To help consumers make value-for-money comparisons, the Price Marking Order 1999 lays down rules requiring prices for many pre-packaged consumer goods to be displayed with unit prices. So, a packet of cheese should include the price per kilogram, for example. The rules also cover goods sold from bulk. This law was updated in March 2000 so that goods offered for sale in a shop should have easily identifiable price tags. Consumers should also be able to compare prices more easily.

There is also other legislation on displaying prices covering:

- theatre and other tickets;
- bureaux de change;
- hotels and guest houses;
- restaurants and bars;
- information where costs differ according to the method of payment.

WEIGHTS AND MEASURES

Sometimes you buy goods by reference to weight, volume, length, area or capacity – 10 tomatoes, 10 litres of petrol, four metres of cloth, and so on. These deals are, generally, covered by the Weights and Measures Act 1985 and detailed legislation made under it. These laws, which are generally backed by fines and other penalties, are aimed at protecting consumers from being sold short measures, and at providing information about the weight or volume of goods to enable consumers to make informed decisions before they buy. They are largely enforced by local trading standards officers.

Among other things, the 1985 Act gives enforcement authorities wide powers of entry to business premises to check that the law is being followed. It also requires them to maintain local and working standards to ensure that all trade measuring equipment is accurate. These are traceable to national standards.

Since October 1995, legislation has required all pre-packed goods – such as shrink-wrapped cheese – to be marked with metric measurements. Goods sold loose from bulk – such as fruit and vegetables at the green-grocers – should also now be sold in metric units. Pounds and ounces were banned from January 2000. It is, how-ever, likely that old, imperial measurements will be found in common, if not legal use, for some time to come.

COMPENSATION FOR MISREPRESENTATIONS

If you enter an agreement on the basis of a statement (e.g. on the packaging or made by a salesman) claiming to be a fact but which turns out to be untrue, you have the right to cancel the deal and get your money back if you act quickly, or to compensation. This is laid down by the Misrepresentation Act 1967, and, in Northern Ireland, the Misrepresentation Act (N.I.) 1967. The Act does not apply to Scotland. However, Scottish law is broadly similar.

In addition:

- goods such as cars are also covered by the Sale of Goods Act 1979 (*see* page 415). So, if you buy a secondhand car that turns out to have been clocked, and there was no indication (e.g. a sticker) warning you that the odometer may have been wrong, you will have a claim under the Act for misdescription.
- with services, you also have a claim for compensation for breach of contract.

The amount you can claim generally works out to be equivalent to what you have lost as a result of the misdescription.

46

The Right to Cancel

CAN I CHANGE MY MIND?

Most contracts become legally binding – and, therefore, legally enforceable – as soon as they are made. Both the consumer and the supplier must go through with the deal. The supplier must supply the goods or services which are the subject of the contract, and the consumer has to pay the purchase price. As a general rule, consumers cannot get out of a binding contract simply because they change their mind. Failure to go through with a contract – for example, cancelling because you have changed your mind – is usually a 'breach of contract'. And that typically means having to pay the (innocent) supplier compensation.

However, in particular situations, consumers do have the right to cancel during what is commonly known as a 'cooling-off period'. Your rights vary when buying any product or service in the home, depending on how the visit from the sales rep came about, whether there is an element of consumer credit, and whether the goods or services fall into specific categories (e.g. timeshare). The policy reasons behind these distinctions are not always clear.

Only specific types of contract can be cancelled safely, without penalty, after signature. They are:

1 *credit agreements* – the Consumer Credit Act 1974 provides for a five-day cancellation period for credit contracts that are signed anywhere other than at the creditor's or trader's business premises;

2 *timeshare contracts* – *see* holidays (page 428);

3 *contracts made at home* – the Consumer Protection (Cancellation of Contracts Concluded Away from Business Premises) Regulations 1987 give you a seven-day cooling-off period, during which you have the right to cancel a contract which is made during an 'unsolicited' visit.

CREDIT

If you have just signed a credit agreement for some new furniture, for example, whether or not you can get out of the deal – because you cannot afford the payments, for example – broadly depends on where you made the agreement and whether it was signed by the trader at the same time you signed. The law in this area is set out in the Consumer Credit Act 1974.

Consumers who sign a credit agreement on trade premises – at the furniture store, for instance – have no cancellation rights if the trader signs at the same time.

However, some credit agreements do not come into force as soon as the consumer signs, since the company also has to sign before the agreement becomes binding. The trader or credit company may want to run credit checks to see whether the customer is a good loan risk before going ahead. In these circumstances, a consumer may be able to cancel and get out of the deal even if the contract was signed at the trader's premises. In this type of situation consumers should tell the trader as soon as possible that they are withdrawing from the contract, before the trader has completed the credit checks and signed the agreement.

Consumers who sign credit agreements at their home or off trade premises have the right to cancel without penalty. But they must act quickly. The 'cooling-off' period (time in which consumers can change their mind without risk of paying compensation) lasts for five clear days. Note that:

1 when consumers sign up for credit they must be given a notice of their cancellation rights along with a copy of the credit agreement;

2 the five-day cooling-off period does not start to run until the consumer receives the second copy of the agreement from the credit company with a notice of the cancellation rights;

3 both copies of the agreement must mention the right of cancellation;

4 the second copy must be delivered by post. The countdown to the fifth day of the cooling-off period does not begin until the consumer has received the second copy, and does not include that day;

5 if the credit company or trader fails to comply with the formal procedures set down by the 1974 Act, the credit agreement cannot be enforced by the company.

To cancel, consumers must give written notice to the credit company or to an agent who conducted the negotiations, such as the salesperson. If a consumer posts a cancellation notice, it takes effect as soon as it is posted. Consumers are best advised to make sure they get a certificate of posting from the Post Office. The effect of the cancellation is to bring the whole agreement to an end and to absolve the consumer from any future liability. If a deposit has been paid, it must be refunded.

CONTRACTS MADE AT HOME

The Consumer Protection (Cancellation of Contracts Concluded Away from Business Premises) Regulations 1987 gives consumers a seven-day cooling-off period during which they have the right to cancel a contract which is made during an 'unsolicited visit' by a salesman to their home.

An 'unsolicited visit' means that the consumer has not expressly requested the salesman to call – that includes appointments made as a result of unrequested telephone calls, or after delivery of a card proposing a visit. If consumers have asked the salesman to call, they are not protected by the Regulations.

The Regulations apply to most cash and credit contracts over £35, but do not cover agreements for the sale of food and drink and other goods supplied by regular roundsmen. The salesman must give consumers a notice of cancellation rights at the time the agreement or offer is made. If the company representative or salesman does not give a copy of the notice, the contract is null and void. It is also a criminal offence to fail to deliver the required written notice of cancellation rights. Trading Standards Departments are responsible for enforcing this aspect of the Regulations.

Consumers are not penalized for cancelling at any time within the cooling-off period and consumers who have paid a deposit can demand its return. To cancel an agreement consumers should either send the cancellation notice or write to the trader and keep the goods safe until they are collected by the trader.

INDUSTRY-LED PROTECTION

Some trade associations offer their own cooling-off protection. For example, solar power companies belonging to the Solar Trade Association (The National Energy Centre, Davy Avenue, Knowlhill, Milton Keynes, MK5 8NG; Tel 01908 442290; www.solartradeassociation.org. uk) must give customers a cooling-off period of seven days for all contracts signed away from business premises – whether or not a sales representative's visit is solicited. Check with individual trade associations to see if their members provide this cover.

47

Unfair Contract Terms

SMALL PRINT

It is all too easy for consumers to lose out as a result of small print in contracts which they are unable to scrutinize or negotiate for themselves. For many years consumer bodies have campaigned to stop bad small print. Back in 1974, for example, the Consumers' Association's *Which?* reported how James Bennett drowned in the swimming pool at a holiday camp. A judge found the owners of the camp 50 per cent to blame, but Mr Bennett's widow got no compensation because the holiday booking form excluded liability for personal injury, including death caused by negligence. The Consumers' Association's campaign for reform led to the involvement of the government's law reform body, the Law Commission. In November 1976 the Consumers' Association promoted the idea of a private member's bill which was taken up by Michael Ward. The law reached the statute book as the Unfair Contract Terms Act 1977.

Under the 1977 Act, small print cannot be used to exclude or restrict responsibility for causing death or personal injury as a result of negligence. Also, the small print in contracts for the sale of goods or hiring to consumers cannot take away basic Sale of Goods Act rights. Generally, other types of small print attempting to limit responsibility when things go wrong must be fair and reasonable. Whether a term is or is not unreasonable is for the court to decide.

Since July 1995 we have had (European) law dealing specifically with unfair terms in consumer contracts, such as terms which are baffling or illegible, which allow the trader to change the contract or increase the price after the consumer has signed. Until recently, the law:

1 gave individual consumers the right to challenge small print if its use becomes an issue in an individual case; and

2 enabled the Director General of Fair Trading (DGFT) to bring court proceedings for an injunction to stop the use of any small print in general use.

This law changed in 1999, and the new legislation, the Unfair Terms in Consumer Contracts Regulations 1999, now allows other qualifying bodies, including statutory regulators, trading standards departments and the Consumers' Association to mount legal challenges to unfair terms in consumer contracts. This is the first of many expected changes which will empower consumer organizations to launch court challenges on behalf of consumers generally.

Although much progress has been made ridding contracts of unfairness, there is plenty of work still to do. The Office of Fair Trading (OFT) Unfair Contract Terms Unit recognized that its first 12 months of operation, for example, was a 'very busy first year'. Contrary to its expectations, the Unit's experience of these first months led it to believe 'that the use of unfair terms in consumer contracts is widespread and amounts to a serious problem in the United Kingdom'. More recently, the OFT has noted that it continues to deal with 'a high volume of complaints'. That continues.

STANDARD CONTRACTS

The Regulations say that a consumer is not bound by a standard term in a contract with a seller or supplier if the term is unfair, i.e. that it unfairly tips the contract against you and in favour of the business. If a term is 'unfair' it is invalid and will not affect your claim for redress.

The Regulations generally cover all contracts entered into by consumers. They do not cover terms in contracts between small traders, larger businesses, or contracts between private individuals, such as private sales.

'Standard terms' are terms that are pre-prepared by the business. Standard terms are usually found in printed conditions of business, often in brochures or on the backs of invoices and quotations, and popularly known as 'the small print'.

The following terms are not covered by the Regulations:

- contract terms which you have individually negotiated with a business;
- contracts relating to employment, to succession rights (e.g. inheritance), to family law matters (e.g. maintenance payments) and to the setting up and running of businesses;
- core terms, i.e. terms that define what you get and how much you pay. So the Regulations cannot be used to argue that a contract does not, for example, represent fair value for money;
- 'mandatory terms' are terms which, by law, have to be included in contracts.

However, core terms and mandatory terms must still be written in plain and intelligible language. Core terms which are very difficult to read or understand can still be deemed to be unfair by a court.

WHAT IS 'UNFAIR'?

Only a court can say definitely whether a term is fair or unfair. In assessing fairness, a court will also consider:

- the type of goods and services involved;
- all the other terms of the contract (including core terms);
- all the circumstances surrounding the making of the contract;
- the relative bargaining strengths of the consumer and the business.

Examples of possible unfair terms

- *Penalty clauses* – requiring you to pay disproportionately high compensation if you break a contract in any way or you want to end the contract early, for example redemption penalties.
- *Hidden terms* – binding you to terms which you have had no real opportunity of seeing before signing the contract, for example terms which force you to buy other products, such as insurance.
- *Obstacle clauses* – preventing you from paying your debt more quickly.

The effect of an unfair term

Consumers are not bound by an unfair standard term. What this means in practice depends on the nature of the term. For instance, a business would not be able to rely on a term that unfairly tried to make you pay more than the originally agreed price if it went to court to try to enforce the extra payment. Similarly, a builder would not

be able to rely on small print saying a consumer had no right to compensation for poor workmanship.

The fact that a business cannot enforce an unfair term against a consumer does not mean, however, that the rest of the contract collapses, so long as it is capable of continuing to exist without that term.

Arbitration clauses

Another control on unfair small print operates through the Arbitration Act 1996 (in Scotland, the Consumer Arbitration Agreements Act (Scotland) 1984). This lays down that consumers are not legally bound by small print saying that disputes must be referred to arbitration. If you are claiming under £5,000 in England and Wales (or £750 in Scotland), you have the choice of taking your claim to court or arbitration.

RIP-OFFS

There are plenty of examples of greedy, unscrupulous traders ripping off consumers. Often this happens because markets – the new car market, for example – do not work effectively and are rigged to prevent real consumer choice. Monopolies and other anti-competitive practices keep prices high and exploit consumers.

A recent investigation by the competition watchdogs, the Competition Commission and the OFT, found that UK consumers are paying 'over the odds' for new cars. In recent years, for example, prices of cars in the UK have been between 10 per cent and 20 per cent higher than prices in France, Germany and Italy. Taking the Commission's work further, the government announced that it was committed to taking strong action to force car manufacturers to lower prices and to putting the interests of ordinary consumers first. This resulted in the introduction of the Supply of New Cars Order in September 2000. One of the main provisions of the Order requires suppliers to offer dealers who purchase volumes of cars outright equivalent discounts to those offered to fleet customers who purchase similar volumes. The intention of this provision is to close the price gap between cars offered to fleet customers and those offered through dealers to private buyers. The new EC Cars Block Exemption, which came into force in October 2003, should help reduce UK prices by increasing competition and providing greater freedom to import cars from other Member States.

Competition law in the UK had its biggest overhaul in years with the introduction of the Competition Act 1998, the teeth of which are now starting to bite.

The aim of the law, modelled on European competition law, is to make markets work properly. It has wide-ranging measures preventing all sorts of anti-competitive practices, such as secret deals to rig prices, and bullying behaviour by big business.

The OFT, and certain other watchdogs, were given tough and extensive new powers to investigate anti-competitive behaviour, including the possibility of dawn raids on suspected offenders. The law is backed by severe criminal penalties, such as large fines.

Victims of anti-competitive practices (such as price fixing) can also sue for compensation. This type of claim would be based broadly on difference between the price you have paid for an item and the price you would have paid had the market worked properly.

ROGUE TRADERS

There are plenty of unscrupulous and dishonest traders whose practices endanger the safety of consumers. Consumer watchdogs, including the OFT and trading standards departments, have long complained that there are too many of these operators who try to flout consumer law, getting away with daylight robbery and, in some cases, endanger lives – the car mechanic who deliberately fails to repair an unsafe car, for example.

Operating on the wrong side of the law and hoodwinking consumers – or rogue trading as it is known – is covered by Part III of the Fair Trading Act 1973, and enforced, at present, by the OFT.

Part III provides a means of dealing with traders who ignore consumer law and operate their businesses in a way that is unfair to consumers. It gives the OFT power to seek written assurances from traders who have 'persisted in a course of conduct' that is unfair and detrimental to the interests of consumers. The Act sets out the type of behaviour that is considered unfair.

If the trader refuses to give an assurance or breaches one he has already given, the OFT can apply to the court for an order that the trader refrains from continuing the course of conduct. If the trader then breaches the order he can be guilty of contempt, which is punishable by a fine and/or imprisonment.

In October 1999, a car mechanic was sent to prison for 15½ months for persistently carrying out shoddy work and selling shoddy cars, despite repeated warnings from the courts and the OFT.

In practice, the law has often missed its mark, failing to stop rogue traders in their tracks. There has long been some concern on the part of the OFT and others that Part III is ineffective, slow and cumbersome. The OFT has also said that its experience is that courts considering applications require a very large number of instances of unlawful conduct before they will find that a person

carrying on business has 'persisted' in a course of conduct.

Reform of Part III of the Fair Trading Act 1973

The Stop Now Orders (EC Directive) Regulations, which came into force in June 2001, give new, focused and effective powers to enable the OFT and trading standards officers to take quick and effective action against rogue traders. The Regulations enable consumer bodies to tackle unscrupulous traders for whom existing sanctions are not a sufficient deterrent. The Regulations contain two new main powers:

1 the power for a court to grant an *injunction* against a trader found to have engaged in a course of conduct involving breaches of a criminal or civil obligation which causes detriment to consumers;

2 the power to *ban from trading* a person whose pattern of conduct, taking into account various breaches of his legal obligations, leads the court to conclude that a ban is necessary to protect consumers.

The power to apply for an injunction is available to every local trading standards department and to the OFT. In addition, the Regulations specify ten public bodies which have the full power to take action against breaches of the consumer protection legislation. These bodies are collectively known as UK Public Qualified Entities. The OFT has a duty to coordinate action under the Regulations and any enforcement partner intending to seek a court order in the UK must consult the OFT first.

Under Part III, the courts have set a high threshold before they will find that the trader has 'persisted in a course of conduct'. The Regulations drop the requirement for persistence, and replace it with a requirement that an enforcement authority must demonstrate that a person has *engaged in* a course of unfair conduct. This should make it easier for enforcement authorities to catch up with rogue traders – particularly those who disappear or move on – and bring a prosecution.

The Regulations also cover Northern Ireland. *See also* page 419.

Fast track consumer law

It is not always easy to predict the sort of fast practices that rogue traders will adopt in response to new laws and new business opportunities. To deal with this problem Part II of the 1973 Act provides a fast track method for dealing with abuse.

Part II of the Act gives powers to the Secretary of State, any other minister or DGFT to refer doubtful trade practices to a body known as the Consumer Protection Advisory Committee ('the Committee'), for its consideration. In particular, the DGFT may include in his reference to the Committee proposals for the Secretary of State to legislate to stop a consumer trade practice that appears to him to have adverse effects on consumers. His proposals are intended to lead, subject to the Committee's views, to an Order under Part II which will prevent the continuance of that practice, or cause it to be modified.

The Secretary of State may make an Order in respect of the trade practice if the Committee concludes:

1 that the practice does adversely affect the economic interests of consumers in one of the following ways:
   - it misleads consumers as to their rights and obligations under the transaction; it otherwise misleads or confuses consumers;
   - it subjects consumers to undue pressure, or it causes the terms and conditions to be so adverse to consumers as to be inequitable; and
2 it agrees with the DGFT's proposals to remedy the problem. It can also modify his proposals in its report, if it considers that the modifications are proportionate and will tackle the problem more successfully.

These Orders are enforced by local trading standards departments within their area and are subject to criminal penalties.

Although well intended, there are problems with the existing law and the process has not been used as much as it might. These criticisms have led the government to propose wide-sweeping changes in its consumer White Paper *Modern Markets: Confident Consumers*. If these proposals are adopted, the Committee would be scrapped and a new streamlined law-making mechanism put in its place. Under the new proposals, the DGFT will be able to investigate all sorts of trade practices and then report and make recommendations to the Secretary of State. He will then be able to make law (an 'Order') stopping or changing the sharp practice in question.

FOOD SAFETY

There has been huge concern in the recent past about food safety and standards. Recent scares have highlighted an inability to ensure effective food safety controls. Regulation has been weak at ensuring prompt and effective action when there is a threat to public health. Around 94,000 people were reported as having food poisoning in 1998. There is also the BSE crisis, of course, which has led to people tragically contracting new variant CJD – and has cost the taxpayer billions of pounds.

The Food Standards Agency

The government's response was the Food Standards Agency Act 1999, which established the Food Standards Agency (FSA) (www.foodstandards.gov.uk) in April 2000.

The FSA has three key objectives:

1 to improve the enforcement of food law, such as the Food Safety Act 1990;
2 to support consumer choice; and
3 to promote healthy and safe eating.

European proposals

At the European level, a new European Food Safety Authority was created in 2002. This followed a series of high-profile food scares – such as dioxins in Belgian meat and sewage sludge used in French animal feed. The primary responsibility of the Authority is to provide independent scientific advice on all matters with a direct or indirect impact on food safety. The Authority can examine all stages of food production and supply, from primary production to the safety of animal feed, right through to the supply of food to consumers. It can respond to scientific questions from the European Commission, the European Parliament and the Member States and it can also initiate scientific investigations on its own behalf.

Food Safety Act 1990

In the UK, there are also masses of specific laws dealing with food safety and labelling, including the Food Safety Act 1990 and rules labelling modified products. These laws are enforced by local environmental health and trading standards officers.

The key provisions of the Food Safety Act 1990 make it a crime to:

1 render food 'injurious to health';
2 sell or keep for sale food that does not comply with food safety requirements – basically food that is unfit for human consumption or so contaminated that it would not be reasonable to expect it to be fit for human consumption;
3 sell food which is not of the 'nature or substance or quality' demanded by the buyer; and
4 falsely describe, advertise or present food.

Enforcement officers have wide powers to inspect food and to seize food suspected of being unsafe. They also have power to enter business premises to see if the law is being followed.

Magistrates' courts can condemn food if it is found to be unsafe and can generally impose fines up to £5,000 and/or send someone to prison for six months. More serious offences are dealt with by the crown court which can impose unlimited fines and/or send someone to prison for up to two years. Courts can also issue legal orders stopping the sale or preparation of food where there is a health risk. Government ministers are also given powers to make emergency orders aimed at protecting health and safety.

A free booklet The Food Safety Regulations gives further detailed information. It is available from Food Standards Agency, PO Box 369, Hayes, Middlesex UB3 1UT; Tel: 0845 606 0667; foodstandards@eclogistics.co.uk.

Other regulations include rules covering, for example:

• food names;
• listing ingredients;

- how additives should be described;
- wine labelling;
- which ingredients should go into certain foods, for example bread and flour, cocoa and chocolate;
- slimming foods; and
- flavourings.

Food poisoning

If you think you have eaten unsafe food and have suffered food poisoning, visit your GP. Your GP has to report all cases of suspected food poisoning to the local environmental health department who may investigate as appropriate. Signs of food poisoning include nausea, diarrhoea, vomiting, stomach pains, sweating, fever and, in severe cases, shock and physical collapse. Vomiting and diarrhoea can lead to dehydration and can be particularly dangerous for children and older people, so replace lost fluids immediately.

In cafés and restaurants your rights to compensation for poor food or poor service are covered by the law of contract. So descriptions of food and wine on the menu, which form part of your contract, must be correct – 'home made soup', for example, must be home made and not tinned. Also, under the Supply of Goods and Services Act 1982 (common law in Scotland), restaurants must prepare food with reasonable skill and care: so frozen food must be properly defrosted, for example, and cooked food must not be raw.

If you think that what you have ordered does not match the description or has not been prepared with reasonable skill and care, do *not* start eating. Complain immediately and ask for something else. If you do not manage to get things put right, you can deduct what you think is a fair and reasonable sum from the bill. Alternatively, you can pay under protest and claim compensation later.

Service charges

If a service charge is automatically added to the bill, this must be clearly indicated both outside and immediately inside the door. You have to pay it unless the service was not of a reasonable standard for that type of restaurant. If it was not, you can refuse to pay all or part of the service charge. The reasonableness of the service is judged by the type of restaurant you are in and the price you are asked to pay for the meal and service. If it is the restaurant's fault that you have had food or drink spilled on you, the service would not be reasonable and you would not have to pay a service charge. You could also claim the cost of cleaning clothes damaged by the spillage. If, on the other hand, a service charge is not indicated, you do not have to pay – it is up to you whether or not to tip and, if so, by how much.

HEALTH

Recent scandals, including the *Shipman* and the Bristol heart surgery cases, have resulted in proposals for major reform of the systems that govern doctors and other healthcare professionals.

NHS Patients' Charter

With the NHS, a charter for patients sets out patients' rights and responsibilities. Broadly, your rights are:
- to be registered with a GP;
- to change your GP quickly and easily if you wish;
- to receive information on local health services, including what to expect and maximum waiting times;
- in virtually all cases, to be guaranteed admission for treatment by a specific date, no more than two years after being put on a waiting list by a consultant;
- to receive information from your GP about the services provided and to see on request the practice leaflet;
- to receive a health check on joining a practice if you have not seen a GP in the last three years, or yearly if you are over 75 years old;
- to have any proposed treatment clearly explained – including any risks and alternatives – before you decide whether to have it;
- to be referred to a consultant or for a second opinion (but only when your GP agrees);
- to have access to your health records;
- to be able to opt out of medical research or student training;
- to have any complaints investigated and to get a quick, full, written response.

The Charter also includes aims covering respect for privacy, dignity and personal beliefs; the time taken by ambulances to arrive at accident scenes; hospital casualty waiting times, and so on.

Complaints

Complaints about the service or treatment you receive from the NHS – whether it is from a hospital, GP, nurse, optician, pharmacist or dentist – should first be referred to the individual concerned. This procedure is known as 'local resolution' and is particularly useful if you want an explanation or apology. If you prefer to talk to someone who was not directly involved in your care, it is possible to involve a 'complaints manager'. If you complain about a family practitioner then the staff in the surgery or the complaints manager in the health authority will probably investigate. The complaint must be made within six months of the problem coming to your notice.

If this does not resolve your complaint, you can ask

for the matter to be looked at by an independent review panel, but this must be done within 28 days of the written reply to your complaint. The written reply should inform you whom to contact. Although you have the right to request an independent review, you do not have an automatic right to have one carried out. If a review panel is set up, it will fully re-examine your complaint and send a final report within 12 weeks. The chief executive of the trust or health authority will write to inform you of any action to be taken.

If your request is turned down you can get help from a Community Health Council (CHC). These are independent patient watchdogs which help, support and advise patients. Look under 'community' in the phone book for your nearest CHC.

It is also possible to appeal to the Ombudsman (known as the Health Service Commissioner). He is independent of the NHS and the government, and his services are free. As well as complaints about NHS services, he can investigate complaints about how the complaints procedure is working if, for example, you want to appeal against a refusal to set up an independent review panel. You must appeal to the Ombudsman in writing within a year of the event. The Ombudsman cannot award compensation, but can ask the NHS authority or trust to remedy or compensate for any injustice or hardship suffered.

If you think a health professional has behaved unethically or unprofessionally, you can complain to the professional body with which he or she is registered (*see* table below).

Clinical negligence

Claims for financial compensation because of clinical negligence are handled by the courts. Crucially, you should get advice from a specialist solicitor. Action for Victims of Medical Accidents (a national charity) can put you in touch with a solicitor and support groups. The Helpline (0208 686 8333) is open Monday–Friday 10–12 a.m. and 2–4 p.m. You can also request an information pack by e-mail to admin@avma.org.uk

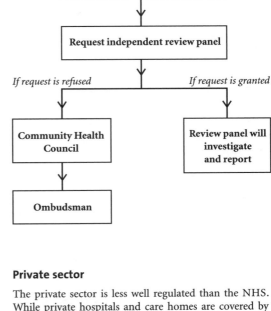

Local Resolution: talk to individual concerned or complaints manager

↓

Request independent review panel

If request is refused — *If request is granted*

Community Health Council

Review panel will investigate and report

↓

Ombudsman

Private sector

The private sector is less well regulated than the NHS. While private hospitals and care homes are covered by the Registered Homes Act 1984, for example, this requires health authority inspections only twice a year. Significant problems can, and have, fallen through the gaps.

For complaints about private medical treatment your only option is to take the matter up yourself with the practitioner concerned. You can also complain to a professional body such as the General Medical Council. If you cannot get a satisfactory response, and you wish to claim compensation, you may have to consider court action. New standards to protect older people in care homes were published in March 2001. They came into force in April 2002 and aim to drive up the quality of care, increase protection for older people and guarantee consistent quality of care.

Type of health professional	Professional body	Contact details
Doctor	General Medical Council	178 Great Portland Street, London W1N 5JE (020 7580 7642)
Dentist	General Dental Council	37 Wimpole Street, London W1G 8DQ (020 7887 3800)
Optician	General Optical Council	41 Harley Street, London W1G 8DJ (020 7580 3898)
Nurse, health visitor, midwife	United Kingdom Central Council for Nursing, Midwifery and Health Visiting	23 Portland Place, London W1B 1PZ (020 7637 7181)

49

Insurance and Money

INSURANCE

Insurance law can be highly technical and specialized. For consumers, the focus is often on how to make a claim on your policy. Most of the law here is basic contract law. Your side of the contract includes paying the premium, of course, and telling the truth about what you want covered and what you are claiming for. Insurers, for their part, have to pay out under the terms of the policy if you make a legitimate claim.

To make your claim, contact your insurance company (or broker, if you are insured with Lloyd's). Once it has your claim form your insurer may arrange for a loss adjuster to check if your claim is valid. While loss adjusters are independent of insurers, they are hired to investigate and advise on claims on the insurers' behalf. So they may not always help *your* claim. If you want, you can appoint a loss assessor. Unless the sums involved are large this may be costly, since you have to pay the assessor's fee for representing you.

Buildings insurance

Like other insurance, buildings insurance is intended to provide cover for specific damage or loss – fire, flooding, subsidence, or whatever – not to pay for running repairs. If your insurance company is not prepared to settle your claim, you will have to prove that the damage you are claiming for is covered by the policy. With a subsidence claim you will have to prove that your home was damaged as a result of subsidence – and not lack of maintenance, for example. Some claims are not straightforward and you may need expert evidence backing you up. So take photographs of the damage as soon as you can and ask for a contractor, a builder or an engineer, for example, to give you a written report detailing the work needed to remedy the problem and commenting on the cause.

Contents insurance

Home contents insurance covers your household possessions, but only against certain eventualities such as theft. If your property has been stolen, you often have to report the theft to the police. If you do not, your insurance company could refuse to meet your claim. Check the wording of your policy for the claims procedure.

Policies can offer different types of cover. If, for example, your policy offers 'new for old' cover, you are entitled to claim the cost of new items to replace those destroyed or stolen; with other cover you may only be entitled to claim the cost of replacing the item less an allowance for age and wear and tear.

Not all insurers settle your claim by paying cash. Many arrange for free repairs or replacements. If you are claiming for something that has been damaged but can be repaired – a scratched table, for example – you can usually only claim the cost of repairs.

Some claims need to be made on both your contents and building policies, particularly if you are with different insurers. Burglary, for instance, may lead to a claim for the damage to the structure of the property on your buildings insurance – if a door or window is smashed – and a claim for compensation for stolen items.

Holiday insurance

Lots of things can go wrong with holidays, so it pays to take out comprehensive insurance when you book.

Travel insurance should start from the time of booking your holiday just in case you have to cancel before you are due to depart. Pack a copy of the policy and take it with you on holiday since you may have to follow a claims procedure (which may involve contacting the local police or tour operator's rep, for example). If you have to claim, also get evidence before you return home; keep relevant receipts and bills.

Most holiday insurance policies cover theft, injury,

medical bills, cancellation, and so on. Check the wording of your policy to see what is included. But note that policies are not generally designed to compensate you for any loss of enjoyment through illness or travel delays, for example. Instead, they are aimed at compensating you for actual losses that hit your pocket.

Insurance companies may deny your claim if they consider that you have failed to take reasonable care. This rule can apply to all insurance but is particularly relevant on holiday. It means, for example, that you should not leave valuable goods on the beach unattended when you go for a swim. Nor should you generally leave a car with keys in the ignition. Whether or not you took reasonable care will depend on the circumstances of each case.

A consumer stopped, as usual, to pick up his newspaper shortly after 7 o'clock one winter morning. Although he was inside the newsagent's shop for about 20 seconds, he heard his car being driven off as he came out. The keys had been left in the car. The insurer rejected his claim, stating that leaving the keys in the car was in breach of the policy condition that he 'should take all reasonable steps to safeguard' his car. Because the consumer usually took his car keys with him, and had left them due to a momentary oversight, the Ombudsman (see below) upheld his complaint and the insurer agreed that the consumer had not deliberately courted a known risk or acted recklessly.

Car insurance

You must have car insurance by law. The legal minimum you need covers claims made against you for personal injury to other people (including passengers) and their emergency medical expenses, damage to other people's property caused by you, and limited legal expenses. Most drivers want more cover than this and opt for 'third party' cover. This gives the legal minimum cover extended to all public and private roads, plus cover for damage and injury to other people caused by your passengers. One step up from this is 'third party, fire and theft', which provides third party cover, plus cover in the event of your car and/or property fitted to it (such as the radio) being stolen or damaged by lightning, fire and explosion, or of the car being damaged during theft or attempted theft. This kind of cover does not include the contents of the car, for example, a briefcase or sports bag. Top of the range is fully comprehensive insurance. This gives you third party, fire and theft cover, plus cover for damage to, and theft of, your car, and its contents (up to a financial limit), your medical expenses (again often up to a limit) and the cost of taking your car to a garage and then home again after an accident.

If your car is written off following an accident, but not totally destroyed, you will usually be entitled to its market value at the time it was stolen or damaged. If you get a low offer from your insurer, you will have to prove that the car is worth more than the insurer's valuation and, to do this, you may need expert help. The Institute of Automotive Engineer Assessors will give you the name of an assessor in your area who can provide a valuation – or ask the RAC or AA if you are a member.

If your vehicle is involved in an accident and you do not have comprehensive insurance, you will have to claim your losses from the driver of the other vehicle involved. Even if you are covered, you will usually have uninsured losses such as any excess you have to pay on your own policy, loss of no-claims discount, compensation for personal injuries, loss of earnings, damaged clothes or other personal items and the reasonable cost of alternative transport. You will be able to claim only if the collision was caused by the other driver's negligence, e.g. because the other driver did not look where he was going. You would not be able to claim if no one was to blame for the collision.

Ombudsman

If you have worked your way through the insurance company's complaints procedure (set out in your insurance policy) and you are still not happy, contact the Financial Ombudsman Service (0845 080 1800) (*see* page 446).

Membership of the Financial Ombudsman Service is compulsory for insurance companies. It deals with the unfair treatment of customers, poor service and maladministration. You do not have to wait until the insurance company has gone through and completed its complaints procedure. Once the insurer has had eight weeks to deal with the complaint, you can contact the Financial Ombudsman Service. Awards recommended by the Financial Ombudsman Service are binding on companies up to £100,000, although claims for more than this can be considered. Awards are not binding on consumers, so you can still go to court later. Awards can be made in respect of distress and aggravation suffered by the consumer, as well as for actual financial loss. It will not be compulsory for insurance brokers to be members of the service until February 2005. In the meantime, insurance brokers can join early on a voluntary basis, but few have done so to date. If your complaint is about an insurance broker who is not a member, the Financial Ombudsman Service is still likely to be able to deal with the problem on the basis that the insurance company who is the underwriter of the policy is responsible for the broker's actions.

MONEY

A revolution has happened to the way financial services are regulated. The Financial Services and Markets Act 2000 has transformed the whole area of regulation of personal finance and money. In particular, there is a single focus for regulation, the Financial Services Authority (FSA).

Two of the FSA's statutory objectives are to protect consumers and to promote public understanding of financial services. Broadly speaking, the FSA has the same functions as all of the old regulators it replaced.

The FSA authorizes firms which offer financial services, and only firms which have this authorization can offer these services. It deals with consumer inquiries, complaints and compensation schemes, oversees the training of people providing financial services, and has the power to investigate and discipline firms breaking its rules. The FSA has also appointed a 'consumer panel', which advises the FSA on the implications for consumers of any new policies it develops.

The FSA provides a consumer helpline (0845 606 1234 – calls charged at local rates) which you can ring if you have a financial complaint or problem and are unsure where to go for help. However, at present it cannot deal with the problem itself, though it can direct you to the correct regulator or ombudsman. The FSA website is at www.fsa.gov.uk/consumer.

Consumer credit

The Consumer Credit Act 1974 regulates consumer credit and consumer hire agreements for amounts up to £25,000. It covers credit agreements between traders and individuals, sole traders, partnerships and unincorporated associations.

This complex and difficult Act lays down rules covering:

- the form and content of agreements;
- credit advertising;
- the method of calculating the annual percentage rate of interest (APR) of the total charge for credit;
- the right to a cooling-off period if you sign a credit agreement (*see* page 433);
- what happens if you cannot pay or want to pay off the debt early;
- extortionate credit bargains.

Under the Act, all traders who credit deals covered by the Act must be licensed by the Office of Fair Trading (OFT). Along with the OFT, the Act is enforced by local trading standards departments. For further information contact your local trading standards or the OFT.

Traders do not have to lend you money or give you credit, nor do you have the right to be told why you may have been turned down for credit. You do, however, have the right to see any information from a credit reference agency file on which lenders may have based their decision. The Consumer Credit Act 1974 sections 157–60 allow you to challenge the basis on which you may have been refused credit. If you write within 28 days of being turned down, asking whether a credit reference agency has been used in considering your application, the trader is obliged to tell you whether an agency has been used and to give its name and address. You can then write to the agency, requesting a copy of the file relating to your case. The agency is obliged to send you a copy of it for a fee, currently £2. If the information on the file is incorrect, you are entitled to have it amended or removed. You can reapply for credit.

Some lenders use a point scoring system to assess creditworthiness. The process is generally automated whereby a computer allocates points to each answer in a series of questions. The total number of points determines whether you get credit.

If your loan payments are exorbitant, or if the rate of interest you are being charged is very high, you are legally entitled to ask the creditor to reconsider the matter. Your right to do so is laid out in the Consumer Credit Act 1974 sections 137–40. You must convince the court that the loan is extortionate, and the court will assess how expensive the loan is in relation to the risk to the lender that the loan may not be repaid. Court action can be slow and expensive – if you would have difficulty in financing such action contact your local Citizens' Advice Bureau or the Money Advice Association (in Scotland contact Money Advice Scotland).

Credit cards

Paying by credit card (but not a charge card or a debit card) gives you the added protection of the Consumer Credit Act 1974, provided the goods or services cost over £100 and under £30,000. If you pay by this means, the credit card company, as well as the supplier, is liable for any breach of contract. So you can claim for faulty goods or defective or inadequate services against the supplier, the credit card company or both. Write to both when you are making your claim. You will not get two lots of compensation, but you will increase your chances of getting the problem sorted out.

Mr Cowe arranged for replacement front and back doors to be supplied and fitted to his house. He paid the bill, around £1,500, using his credit card. Shortly after installation, things started to go wrong – the locks would not work and the frames were poorly made. When the supplier failed to put things right, Mr Cowe wrote to the credit card company.

He got three quotes for the cost of repairs and sent these on. The credit card company agreed to pay for replacements, costing nearly £2,300.

You are also entitled to claim from the credit card company if the retailer or supplier goes into liquidation. This cover is particularly useful if you have made a payment in advance, such as a deposit, to a company that subsequently closes down, for you would otherwise have to take your chances as an unsecured creditor.

Buying on hire purchase

If you buy something on hire purchase (HP), your contract is with the finance company – the lender – not the retailer who supplied the goods. You have the same basic rights as if you had paid cash; goods must meet their description and be of satisfactory quality, but your rights are covered by a different law, i.e. the Supply of Goods (Implied Terms) Act 1973.

When it comes to rejecting faulty goods your rights last longer if you have bought on HP than if you have bought them for cash. If you are paying on HP, you have the common law right to reject faulty goods throughout the duration of the agreement. If you find a problem with the goods and want to reject them, stop paying the instalments, write to the HP company and state what the problem is – that the goods are unsatisfactory, for example – that you are rejecting them, and that they are available for collection by the company. If you reject the goods in this manner, the HP company must refund the payments you have made. There is a risk that if you stop your instalments the HP company will sue you. Although you will have a defence because the goods are faulty, you may not wish court proceedings to be started against you.

Alternatively, rather than stopping your payments, tell the HP company that you are paying your instalments under protest until the matter is resolved.

If you do not want to reject the goods, but would like, for example, a free repair, you should write to the company, explaining what is wrong with the goods and that you would like a free repair.

You are also entitled to claim compensation for any expenses you incur which were reasonably foreseeable by both you and the company at the time you entered the HP agreement; for example, if you bought a car on HP and it proved faulty, the cost of alternative means of transport while the car was being repaired would be an allowable expense.

Once you have paid all the instalments on your goods, your consumer rights become the same as if you had paid cash.

Bank or building society accounts

All the usual rules governing contracts to supply a service apply here as they do with other services (*see* page 422). There is also a banking code of practice covering good practice within the banking industry. It aims to build on your legal rights. It includes the following:

- *fair conduct* – banks and building societies should always act 'fairly and reasonably' in dealings with customers;
- *information on changes* to your account – you must be told of any changes to the terms and conditions, charges and interest rate of your account within specified time periods. If your savings and investment account is superseded by a new type of account, your account must either be kept at the same interest rate as a new account with similar features, or switched to another with similar features;
- *cards* – for any type of plastic card, credit card, bank card, and so on, your maximum liability for money taken without your agreement is £50, or nil if the card is lost or stolen before it reaches you. You will lose this protection only if you have been 'grossly negligent' by, for example, writing your personal identification number (PIN) on the card – it is up to the bank or building society to prove that this is the case. Where you have never let the card out of your possession, and an unauthorized debt appears on your statement, you do not have to pay the first £50;
- *confidentiality* – your personal financial details will not be passed to other companies in the banking group – such as their insurance or investment arm – without your consent. In practice, this probably means that new customers will be given a straight 'yes/no' choice of whether to give their consent, and existing customers (who are deemed to have agreed to this sharing of information) will be given the right to object;
- *complaints* – all institutions must set up proper internal complaints procedures and tell you what these are.

If your cheque book is stolen, you are not liable for any fraud provided you let your bank or building society know of the theft as soon as possible. But fraud using cheques that you have already written is another matter.

Unless you write out cheques using specific wording (*see* below), a thief can fake the signature of the person to whom you are paying the money (the 'payee') on the back of a cheque you have already written out, even if you have crossed it, pay it into his own account and, when it clears, withdraw the money and disappear. You would have no claim against either the bank where the cheque was paid in or your own bank which paid the cheque.

However, the Cheques Act 1992 states that if you write the words 'Account Payee' or 'a/payee' with or without the word 'only' on the face of a crossed cheque, you are protected against the cheque being transferred to a thief's account. If the bank where the cheque is paid in negligently credits an account other than that of the payee named on the face of the cheque, it will have to make good the payer's loss.

If you cannot resolve your problem at your branch or by writing to the bank or building society, contact the Financial Ombudsman Service. Both the banking and building society ombudsmen became part of the Financial Ombudsman Service (FOS) in December 2001.

Some insurance words explained

All-risks – insurance that covers loss or damage by an accident or misfortune not specifically excluded by the policy.

Averaging – the amount paid in settlement of a claim being reduced by the proportion of any under-insurance (e.g. a piece of property worth £10,000 is insured for £5,000, and £5,000-worth is stolen; under the average clause, payment will be only £2,500).

Betterment – the amount by which an insured person would be better off after a claim; it has to be repaid, or will be deducted from settlement (e.g. old car in accident, after repair paid for by insurance, car has new wing instead of rusty old one, so consumer has to pay appropriate proportion of cost).

Excess – a specified amount of a claim – say, £25 for storm damage – which the insured person will bear him- or herself; if the whole claim comes to less than the amount, nothing will be paid by the insurer.

Ex gratia – payment made as a gesture of goodwill when the insurer does not have to do so on a strict interpretation of the terms of the policy.

Index linking – the sum insured goes up automatically in line with increased prices or building costs.

Knock-for-knock – in motor insurance, where two cars are involved, an agreement that the two insurers will each pay their client's claim, irrespective of which one was to blame for the happening.

Ombudsman – *see* page 443.

Uninsured loss – in motor insurance, amounts not met by the policy (e.g. hire of substitute car while damage done is being repaired).

50

Utilities

ELECTRICITY AND GAS

Increasing numbers of consumers can now choose their electricity and gas suppliers, with different companies competing to supply electricity.

If you are unhappy with the amount of your electricity or gas bill, or have any other complaint about the service, contact your supplier first. If you are unhappy with the response you get, contact the Gas and Electricity Consumers' Council, also known as energywatch. Energywatch is an independent consumer organization providing advice and information to gas and electricity consumers, representing their views and referring complaints to the Office of the Gas and Electricity Markets (Ofgem) for possible enforcement action. Energywatch was set up in November 2000 following the merger of the Gas Consumers' Council and Ofgem's regional offices. You can contact energywatch on: Tel: 0845 906 0708 (gas complaints)/0845 601 3131 (electricity complaints). Calls are charged at local rate. In Northern Ireland, you can refer your complaint to the General Consumer Council.

Ofgem (*see* www.ofgem.gov.uk) is the watchdog set up to regulate and promote effective competition in the gas and electricity industries and to ensure that they comply with their statutory obligations. In Northern Ireland, the watchdog is called the Office for the Regulation of Electricity and Gas (OFREG).

Ofgem may, for example, intervene in cases of proposed or actual disconnection in exceptional circumstances, e.g. a pensioner's home being cut off during the winter. However, suppliers are entitled to disconnect a supply for non-payment, though cases of hardship should be dealt with reasonably and sensitively. Alternative payment options may be offered, e.g. a prepayment meter.

With electricity, Ofgem has set out guaranteed standards of performance. This includes compensation of a fixed sum, currently £50, for power cuts if caused by technical breakdowns or negligence, but not severe weather. If an engineer fails to keep an appointment, customers receive another sum, currently £20. Various delays (in giving customers notice of supply interruptions, dealing with company fuse failures, giving estimates of connection charges, and in dealing with meter problems, voltage complaints and charges and payment queries) also attract compensation. Payments are automatic for most of the standards and are normally made by reducing the customer's next electricity bill (though for delayed supply restoration and lack of notice of supply interruption, it is necessary to submit a claim).

Some electricity suppliers already offer rebate and voucher schemes. Full details can be obtained free from your supplier, or by asking Ofgem for a fact sheet comparing the different deals on offer.

British Gas and other gas suppliers promise to meet certain standards with regard to service. Failure to meet these standards may result in compensation:

- *missed appointments* – you receive compensation if British Gas or your supplier fails to turn up for an appointment, unless the supplier gave you 24 hours' notice that it could not keep the appointment;
- *special treatment for older, disabled or chronically sick customers* – British Gas maintains a Gas Care register and invites older, disabled or chronically sick customers to register for services including a free annual gas safety check. Similar services may be available from other suppliers.

Full details can be obtained free from your supplier.

WATER

Water companies in England and Wales are regulated by the Office of Water Services (OFWAT). The equivalent bodies in Scotland and Northern Ireland, respectively, are the Water Industry Commissioner for Scotland, and the Water Services Office of the Department of the Environment. Complaints about water quality should be directed to the watchdog or the Drinking Water Inspectorate.

The watchdogs are responsible for ensuring that water and sewerage companies provide their customers with a good-quality and efficient service at a fair price. Each supplier must have a code of practice that sets out what services are offered, gives details of charges, advises customers what to do in an emergency and lays down a procedure for making complaints. There are also codes of practice covering leakage. Leaflets explaining all these codes are available from your local water company: look under Water in the telephone directory or ask OFWAT.

Following the Water Industry Act 1999, water disconnections have been banned. If you encounter difficulties paying your bills, ask your company about special assistance under the 'Vulnerable Groups' regulations. Water companies must also operate a Guaranteed Standards Scheme. Customers are entitled to claim a set amount, currently £20, every time there are unplanned interruptions of water supply lasting longer than 12 hours (unless the burst is on a strategic main), or if it takes longer to restore the water supply than the customer was told. Customers are entitled to a further £10 for each 24-hour period the supply remains unrestored. You may also claim a refund of your sewerage bill each time your property suffers sewer flooding, subject to a limit of £1,000 per incident (limited to one per year).

TELEPHONES

All telecommunications – phones, faxes and the internet – are currently covered by the Office of Telecommunications (OFTEL) (*see* www.oftel.gov.uk). If you have a complaint you should contact OFTEL. There are also currently a number of bodies whose function is to advise OFTEL. They are:

Consumer Communications for England,
50 Ludgate Hill, London EC4M 7JJ.
Tel: 020 7634 8773

Scottish Advisory Committee on Telecommunications,
28 Thistle Street, Edinburgh EH2 1EN.
Tel: 0131 226 7275

Welsh Advisory Committee on Telecommunications,
4 The Science Park, Aberystwyth, Ceredigion SY23 3AH.
Tel: 01970 636 413

Northern Ireland Advisory Committee on Telecommunications,
22 Great Victoria Street, Belfast BT2 7QA.
Tel: 028 9024 4113.

Advisory Committee on Telecommunications for Disabled and Elderly, which represents the interests of disabled and elderly people, and Communications for Business, which represents the interests of small businesses, can be contacted at Consumer Communications for England (above).

The Communications Bill will, when its provisions are enacted, radically overhaul the communications industry. It is proposed that by the end of 2003 a single powerful regulator, the Office for Communications (OFCOM) will replace the five existing regulators, including Oftel. An OFCOM Consumer Panel will be created to take over the responsibilities of all six advisory committees described above.

With BT it is also possible to take your claim to arbitration, run by the Chartered Institute of Arbitrators. Arbitration under this scheme is totally independent of BT. The claim is handled in writing so you do not have to attend a hearing. Any decision is legally binding. You will have to pay a small fee with your application, which will probably be refunded if the arbitrator finds in your favour (this is left to his/her discretion). You do not have to pay any other costs.

Under its guarantee scheme, BT also promises an agreed date of appointment for installation of your telephone line. It also guarantees to repair line faults by the end of the day following the day when they were reported. If BT falls short of an agreed installation or repair target, including weekends, you can claim compensation of one month's line rental charge per day (up to £600). Alternatively, if you suffer financial loss as a result of BT's failure to meet its targets, you can claim up to £1,000 compensation. You have four months in which to register a claim.

RAILWAYS

The Health and Safety Executive is responsible for the regulation of rail safety. If your complaint relates to the service itself, for example if your journey was delayed or you were unhappy about the facilities on the train or at a station, you should address your complaint to the train company that provided the service. Your local Rail Passengers' Committee (RPC) should be able to tell you which train operating company provided the service. The RPCs are regional bodies responsible for representing passenger interests, and they also mediate complaints that passengers and train companies cannot settle (www.railpassengers.org.uk/). The Strategic Rail Authority (SRA) is responsible for consumer protection matters such as fares, quality of service, overcrowding and complaints handling. It is also responsible for letting and managing passenger rail franchises. The SRA can be contacted at Tel: 0207 654 6000; www.sra.gov.uk.

The Office of the Rail Regulator's principal function is

to regulate Railtrack's stewardship of the national rail network.

POSTAL SERVICES

Postwatch, the Consumer Council for Postal Services, champions the interests of customers of Royal Mail, Parcelforce Worldwide, Post Office Limited and any other licensed provider of postal services. If you have already complained to your postal provider and are still unhappy, Postwatch will take up your complaint on your behalf. Their customer helpline is 08456 013265. Postwatch can also refer a failure by a licensed mail provider to comply with the terms of their licence to the industry regulator, Postcomm, with a request for an enforcement action to be taken.

51

Codes of Practice and Other Laws

CODES OF PRACTICE

Business-led codes of practice have the potential to offer protection that goes beyond consumer law. However, experience of trade association voluntary codes of practice, as they currently stand, has been very mixed.

Logos of trade associations, institutes and guilds might look impressive in traders' adverts, but trade association codes of practice can present a chaotic jumble. They do not all cover the same things. Some are more like a book of rules for members, while others cover technical standards or procedures in great detail. Some trade associations check standards are being generally met, but will not get involved in disputes about issues like costs or delays in completing a job. Others are little more than advertising schemes to attract business for their members, and offer no real consumer benefits.

Research by *Which?*, for example, has shown a significant problem with consumer protection in this area. Most worryingly, it revealed that many of these organizations have little to offer consumers.

In response, the government has proposed to strengthen the regime that deals with codes of practice by enabling the Office of Fair Trading (OFT) to approve codes which are effective in protecting consumers, and to take a tough line with those that are not.

If implemented, these proposals will mean that consumers should see codes that cover: truthful adverts; clear, helpful and adequate pre-contractual information; clear, fair contracts; staff who know about and meet the terms of the code as well as their legal responsibilities; an effective complaints handling system run by the business; if problems cannot be resolved in-house, an effective and low cost redress mechanism; publicity about the code from the business and the sponsors, including a report (to the OFT) on the operation of the code. Behind the scenes sponsoring bodies will be required to have the set-up to deliver all these things.

Buying and selling online – e-commerce – is one area ideally suited to the self-regulatory, code, approach. At the start of 2000 a new body, Trust UK, was set up to approve e-commerce codes that accord with certain core principles. It comprises the Alliance for Electronic Business and Consumers' Association and has government backing. The Trust UK 'hallmark' of approved codes should appear on the websites of e-traders belonging to codes of practice, such as *Which?* Web Trader, approved by Trust UK.

The government will also work within Europe to encourage the development of an EU-wide code and with the OECD on its guidelines for consumer protection in e-commerce.

OTHER LAWS

Other laws affecting consumers include:

The Disability Discrimination Act 1995

Part III of this Act came into force in October 1999. Among other things, it deals with the adjustments that service providers, including shops, hotels and restaurants, have to make to ensure access for disabled people to their services – for example providing those who are hard of hearing with written information, or allowing guide dogs on to premises. (*See also* pages 381 and 502.)

The Contracts (Rights of Third Parties) Act 1999

Before this Act you could take legal action to enforce a contract only if you were a party to it. So, if you bought a birthday present for someone and it turned out to be faulty, say, the recipient of the gift would, strictly speaking, not have any claim for compensation against the shop because he was not a party to the contract. The 1999 Act changes this, and brings the law in England and Wales into line with Scotland. It now allows the recipient to take action provided that at the time of making the contract the purchaser specifically agrees with the retailer that the recipient (or 'third party') is to have the benefit and that the Act applies. This should be done in writing.

Personal information and junk marketing

It is against the law for a commercial organization to hold personal data on an individual without being on the Data Protection Register.

Under the Data Protection Act 1998, which came into force on 1 March 2000, you have the right to be informed by an organization whether it holds personal data on you and to have access to any such data. If it is appropriate, you have the right to have such data corrected or erased.

The law sets rules for processing personal information (including facts and opinions) and applies to paper records as well as those held on computers.

Anyone processing personal data must comply with eight rules. These rules stipulate that data must be:

1 fairly and lawfully processed;
2 processed for limited purposes;
3 adequate, relevant and not excessive;
4 accurate;
5 not kept longer than necessary;
6 processed in accordance with the data subject's rights;
7 secure;
8 not transferred to countries without adequate protection.

The Act is supervised by the Data Protection Commissioner.

If you do not want to receive advertising circulars and other junk mail by post, you can write to the Mailing Preference Services (MPS) and request that your name and address be removed from the companies' lists. This is a free service set up and funded by the direct mail industry to enable consumers to have their names and addresses taken off or added to lists used by its members. More than 100 companies subscribe to the MPS.

If you want to stop unsolicited mail from member companies write to the MPS at Mailing Preference Service, DMA House, 70 Margaret Street, London w1w 8ss or e-mail mps@dma.org.uk.

Marketing over the phone or by fax is subject to laws introduced in May 1999. Under these laws it is unlawful to make unsolicited direct marketing phone calls or to send unsolicited sales and marketing faxes to consumers who have indicated they do not want such calls or, with faxes, have not given prior permission.

Other industry-led schemes allow you to register if you do not want to receive unwanted sales and marketing messages on the telephone or by fax. To register with the Telephone Preference Service online visit www.tpsonline.org.uk. For faxes *see* the Fax Preference Service at www.fpsonline.org.uk

Insolvency

Introduction

An individual or organization is said to be 'insolvent' if they are unable to pay their debts at the time they are due for payment. The formal arrangements for dealing with money problems differ according to whether the debtor (i.e. the person or business that owes the money) is an individual or a company. One of the main differences is that an individual who cannot pay his debts can be made bankrupt. A company, on the other hand, can be put into liquidation. Individual insolvency is dealt with in Chapter 52 of this part and corporate insolvency is discussed in Chapter 53. In either case, informal negotiations with creditors should always be attempted.

Informal arrangements

People may well be able to resolve their financial problems by coming to an informal arrangement with their creditors. Creditors (i.e. people to whom money is owed) should always be approached on this basis whenever someone finds themselves in financial difficulties, in the hope of preventing the situation getting out of control. In many cases, it will be possible for the parties to agree satisfactory payment arrangements without the need to go to court or put formal arrangements in place.

The debtor may be able to negotiate direct with creditors or use the services of a money adviser or some other professional, such as an accountant or solicitor, to negotiate on his behalf.

It is important that people with debt problems do not bury their heads in the sand. If someone has problems meeting his financial commitments, he should contact his creditors immediately, and before the debts get out of control. It is generally not advisable to try and borrow your way out of debt. This usually leads to an increasing spiral of debt, as the individual finds that he now owes more than he did before and soon finds that he is still unable to keep up with his payments.

Being in debt can be a stressful experience. People may be so afraid of making contact with their creditors that they do not pick up the telephone, answer the front door or open their mail. There is still a degree of guilt attached to being in debt and some people are afraid of asking for advice in case they are criticized or humiliated. Once they have plucked up the courage to go into an advice agency, many of these people speak of the sheer relief at being able to talk over their debt problems with an adviser who adopts a non-judgemental attitude to their situation.

Helpful organizations

There are many agencies which provide free, impartial and confidential money advice services to individuals, while others may charge a fee. Money Advice Centres, law centres and Citizens' Advice Bureaux are able to deal with money advice and debt problems. Look in the telephone directory for addresses and telephone numbers. The Money Advice Association (Tel: 01476 594970; website: www.m-9-9.org.uk) can give details of the nearest adviser for people living in England and Wales. The National Debt Line (Tel: 0808 808 4000; website: www.nationaldebtline.co.uk) also provides free information for people living in England and Wales.

Advice agencies can assist someone by:

- finding out to whom they owe money, how much is owed and what steps, if any, have been taken by creditors to recover their debts. The agency also checks that the person is legally liable for the debt;
- identifying any emergencies, such as eviction from their home, disconnection of fuel supplies, bailiff action, or imprisonment, for example for non-payment of a fine. Emergency situations are dealt with first;
- maximizing income (e.g. possible social security benefit entitlement, availability of additional work, raising a lump sum) and minimizing expenditure; essentially this involves identifying non-essential

expenditure while maintaining a reasonable standard of living, the aim being to enable the person to budget so that the debt problems do not recur;

- prioritizing debts: some creditors can impose severe sanctions for non-payment of their debts, for example eviction for rent/mortgage arrears, recovery of possession of goods on hire purchase/credit sale, disconnection for non-payment of electricity, gas and telephone, use of private bailiffs and possible imprisonment for non-payment of fines and local taxes. Payment arrangements will be negotiated with these creditors first of all, which will usually involve clearing the arrears over a period of time while keeping up with the current payments;

- drawing up a realistic financial statement: this contains details of the person's regular income, essential expenditure, creditors and any surplus income that is available for a sustainable payment arrangement;

- deciding a strategy for non-priority creditors. All other creditors can only use the county court in order to recover their debts and should not harass the person for payment by, for instance, telephoning them at work, contacting neighbours, telephoning or visiting their home at anti-social hours, using threatening or intimidating language, or making repeated telephone calls. The strategy can range from asking creditors to write off their debts where there is no realistic prospect of payment through to offering token payments with the situation being reviewed when the person's financial situation improves. Other proposals include making payment offers based on each creditor receiving a regular payment proportionate to the size of their debt (known as 'pro rata payments').

Peter owes £1,500 to Bigwoods plc, on their store card. He used the card to buy a television, a stereo and most of the Christmas presents for his family last year, but he fell behind with the payments when he was out of work for six months. Bigwoods have sent him three letters asking for payment. The last letter threatened that they would start court proceedings against him. Peter visited his local Citizens' Advice Bureau, who helped him to work out his income and outgoings, and put together a realistic proposal for paying off

the debt by instalments over 30 months, with interest on the debt being frozen.

Formal arrangements

A drawback of dealing with debts on an informal basis is that the arrangement will not be legally binding, so a creditor who had informally agreed to let the debtor pay off only part of the debt could always decide to claim the whole debt at a later date.

Where negotiations fail, or where more certainty is required, the law provides a number of formal solutions to both creditors and debtors faced with an insolvency situation. The main attraction of these formal solutions is that:

- they allow the debtor to wipe his slate clean and make a fresh start after the arrangement has run its course;

- all the debts are lumped together and dealt with at the same time;

- in the meantime, most creditors will not be able to take unilateral court action against the debtor to recover their individual debt. It should be emphasized, however, that secured creditors do not have to go along with a formal arrangement unless they choose to be included.

On the downside, in the case of individual voluntary arrangements and bankruptcy, the debtor loses control over his own finances and in all cases there is some expense involved (e.g. court fees) and the arrangement is a matter of public record, so other people can find out about the individual's money problems.

Changes in the law

A major new piece of legislation, the Enterprise Act 2002, is set to overhaul radically the existing insolvency legislation. It will affect both personal (bankruptcy, individual voluntary arrangements, etc.) and corporate insolvency (liquidation, company voluntary arrangements, etc.). These changes are likely to be implemented during the course of 2003 and 2004. Any changes to the current position by the new Act will be referred to where appropriate.

52

Individual Insolvency

Apart from informal arrangements, there are three separate ways in which an individual can reach a formal agreement with his creditors through the courts:

- administration order;
- individual voluntary arrangement;
- debtor's bankruptcy petition.

The table below summarizes the main points about the different options.

ADMINISTRATION ORDER

Who would opt for this?

Shane has a number of credit card debts and is in arrears with his electricity, gas and council tax. Altogether he owes £3,600. The council has taken him to court and obtained a county court judgment against him for his overdue council tax. The council are threatening to send the bailiffs to his flat. Shane is on a low income and cannot afford to offer to pay his creditors by substantial instalments.

Shane could opt for an administration order because:
- *his debts are not more than £5,000 in total; and*
- *one of his debtors has obtained a court judgment against him for the payment of money.*

If Shane obtains an administration order, instead of making payments to individual creditors, his debts will be lumped together and he will make one payment every month into court. He can also ask the court to order that he need only pay part of his debts if it would take him more than three years to pay them off.

	Administration order	Individual voluntary arrangement	Bankruptcy
Who takes control of the debtor's assets?	The court distributes payments to the creditors	The supervisor	The trustee in bankruptcy
Who divides the assets among the creditors?	The court	The supervisor	The trustee in bankruptcy
Can the debtor continue to run his business?	Yes	Yes	It is unlikely, because of restrictions on trading, running a company and obtaining credit
Can individual creditors take court action against the debtor?	No, in general	No, in general	No, in general
What expense is involved?	Court fees	Court fees plus fees of the insolvency practitioner	Court fees plus deposit and fees of the trustee in bankruptcy
Is it a matter of public record?	Yes	Yes	Yes (bankruptcy still carries the most stigma)

Summary of procedural steps

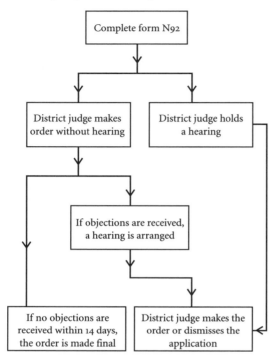

It is relatively easy to apply for an administration order. The debtor simply completes form N92, which is available free from any county court. The debtor must list all his debts and sources of income on the form. There are notes for guidance on completing the form and advice agencies (such as those already mentioned above) will be happy to help. There is no court fee payable on the application but, if the administration order is made, the court will charge a 10 per cent 'handling fee' (which is added to the debts).

On the form, the debtor can:

1 offer to pay by instalments over any period of time (there is no maximum amount of time within which the debts must be paid); or

2 ask to pay only a proportion of the total debts; for example, the debtor can ask to pay only 50 pence in the pound, so that half of his debts would be wiped off the slate. This is known as a composition order. The court will normally allow this where it would take an unreasonable length of time (usually considered to be more than three years) to repay the debts in full at the rate the person can afford.

If the debtor is employed, the court will collect the monthly payments due under the order direct from his employer (through an attachment of earnings order). If the person does not want this to happen, he must indicate this on the N92 and state his reasons. A good reason might be if the debtor would lose his job if his employer finds out about the administration order.

Making the order

If any objections to the application are received, a hearing is arranged before a district judge. No court fee is payable for the hearing. Creditors may object to their own or another creditor's debt(s) being included in the order, to a composition order, or to the rate of payment. The applicant may also raise objections, for example he may object to a creditor not being included in the order, to the rate of payment ordered, or to the refusal to make a composition order.

If, instead of making an order outright, the court decides to hold a hearing, notice of the hearing must be given to the applicant and all creditors named in the N92. The district judge has complete discretion to:

● allow or disallow any creditors' objections;
● grant or refuse to grant the administration order; and, if granted, to
● include or exclude any creditor from the order;
● make a composition order;
● fix the rate of payment;
● provide for a review of the order (*see* below).

Advantages and disadvantages

Advantages

The main advantage of an administration order to an individual is that, once he pays all the instalments due under the order (including a composition order), he can wipe the slate clean and creditors can no longer take any action against him to recover their debts.

Other advantages include:

● instead of making payments to individual creditors, the person is only required to make one monthly payment to the court;
● creditors included in the order cannot petition for the individual's bankruptcy (*see* below) without leave of the court, unless the debt exceeds £1,500 (the normal minimum figure is £750) and the petition is presented within 28 days of the creditor receiving notification of the application for the administration order;
● creditors included in the order, and also any other creditors who were included in the N92, cannot take any enforcement action against the person or his property without leave of the court;
● the court can decide that only a proportion of the debts

is to be paid and overrule any creditor's objections to the terms of the order or the rate of payment;

- the court costs to the individual are substantially less than those involved in either individual voluntary arrangements or bankruptcy (*see* below).

Disadvantages

However, there are a number of disadvantages, including:

- the £5,000 upper limit for total indebtedness is too low for most people to be able to make use of the procedure;
- a judgment is required for at least one of the debts;
- the order is registered at the Registry Trust in the same way as a judgment, which may affect future credit;
- if the order is revoked because the debtor fails to make payments, the debtor can be made subject to the same restrictions as an undischarged bankrupt in regard to obtaining credit, being a director of a company or running a business (*see* below) for a period of two years;
- creditors can successfully object to being included in the order;
- although further debts can be 'added' to the order even if this takes the total indebtedness over the £5,000 limit, in those circumstances the court could decide to revoke (i.e. cancel) the administration order instead, so depriving the person of the protection of the order;
- if only the arrears of a credit or other debt are included in the administration order and the individual is unable to keep up the ongoing payments, the creditor will be able to take enforcement action in respect of the balance and so defeat the purpose of the order.

Reviews

If the debtor defaults on paying the instalments due under the administration order, the district judge can order a review hearing. In addition, either the individual or one of his creditors can request a review of the administration order at any time, or the court can order a review on its own initiative, for example where it is made aware of anything that makes it desirable to review the order, such as an additional debt.

When the order is reviewed the district judge may:

- suspend the order if the person cannot maintain the payments; or
- vary the order if there has been a material change of circumstances since the order was made, for example to add further arrears accrued on an existing debt; or
- revoke the order if the person has failed to comply, or if it is otherwise just and expedient so do so, for example where the person deliberately failed to disclose the existence of debts that would have taken the total indebtedness over the £5,000 limit; or

- make an attachment of earnings order to secure the payments due under the administration order. (An attachment of earnings order is a court order requiring the debtor's employer to deduct a set amount from the debtor's take home pay at the end of each pay period.)

INDIVIDUAL VOLUNTARY ARRANGEMENT

What is it and who would choose this?

An Individual Voluntary Arrangement (IVA) is an alternative to bankruptcy but has the great advantage of not having the same automatic restrictions apply, e.g. the potential loss of all or most of your assets. For this reason alone, wherever a debtor has income or assets available to pay creditors, an IVA should always be considered in preference to bankruptcy (*see* page 464).

An individual voluntary arrangement (IVA) should always be considered where the debtor has at least £100 to £200 a month available for payment to his creditors, whether or not he also has assets. An IVA lasts for a set period (usually not more than five years) and so should also be considered where an informal payment arrangement is likely to last more than 10 years. There is no maximum or minimum level of debt but, in view of the costs involved (*see* below) it is unlikely to be appropriate unless the individual has debts of at least £10,000.

Summary of steps: reaching IVA

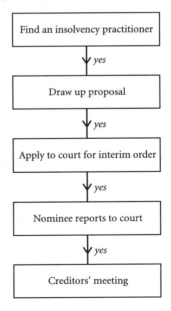

Find an insolvency practitioner

↓ *yes*

Draw up proposal

↓ *yes*

Apply to court for interim order

↓ *yes*

Nominee reports to court

↓ *yes*

Creditors' meeting

Overview

To summarize, to reach an IVA the individual will come up with a proposal for paying the creditors. If the proposal is acceptable to at least 75 per cent in value of the creditors, the IVA will be made. While the creditors are considering the proposal, the individual should ask the court to make an interim order, which will put a freeze on all bankruptcy and other court proceedings against him. An insolvency practitioner will supervise the IVA and pay the creditors in accordance with the accepted proposal.

The proposal

The first step is to find an insolvency practitioner who is prepared to act in the IVA. The insolvency practitioner will draw up a 'proposal' for the person's creditors and the court. In the proposal the individual will make a repayment offer to the creditors. The proposal has to be accepted by at least 75 per cent in value of the creditors, so it should be a more attractive financial offer than what the creditors could get if they made the individual bankrupt. That will mean paying a higher dividend more quickly to the creditors and the proposal will set out how the individual will achieve this.

The individual should take as much information as possible to the insolvency practitioner regarding his financial affairs. Advice agencies will assist in preparing a statement of the individual's income and expenditure and a list of his debts and assets to show to the insolvency practitioner. Any information revealed to the insolvency practitioner at this stage is confidential.

Finding an insolvency practitioner

Many advice agencies have referral arrangements with insolvency practitioners and may be able to arrange for an initial free consultation. The local county court may be able to provide the names of local practitioners and a list is available for people to look at in the local Official Receiver's office. Otherwise, details of insolvency practitioners in the locality can be obtained from The Insolvency Practitioner Unit, The Insolvency Service, PO Box 203, 21 Bloomsbury Street, London, WC1B 3QW. The insolvency practitioner's fees are agreed as part of the IVA. A typical fee is £3,000. Some insolvency practitioners do not charge up-front fees, but are paid as they go.

The insolvency practitioner appears in many different guises during the course of the IVA. Once he has signed the proposal he becomes the individual's nominee. Later on in the IVA, the insolvency practitioner becomes the supervisor of the arrangement. The insolvency practitioner's role as 'supervisor' of the IVA is to implement it and ensure that the debtor carries out his side of the arrangement as agreed. The insolvency practitioner has a duty to ensure a fair balance between the interests of the debtor and the creditors. He can seek guidance from the court, if necessary.

The terms of the proposal

Information that must be contained in the proposal includes:

- details of the proposed arrangements, including why an IVA is the appropriate solution and likely to be accepted by creditors. IVAs do not usually provide for payment of the individual's debts in full. They normally provide for his available income and the proceeds of the sale of any assets to be distributed to creditors on a pro rata basis, with the balances being written off, i.e. a composition;
- the anticipated level of the person's income during the period of the IVA (unlike bankruptcy, the individual will be able to keep trading);
- details of all assets (together with their estimated value) and of any assets being made available by third parties (such as a relative or friend who is prepared to make a payment to prevent the individual from going bankrupt);
- details of any charges on property in favour of creditors and of any assets that the individual proposes to exclude from the arrangement;
- details of the individual's debts and of any guarantees given for them by third parties;
- the proposed duration of the IVA and the arrangements for payments to creditors, including the estimated amounts and frequency. IVAs do not normally last longer than five years;
- details of the supervisor and of the fees to be paid to the nominee and the supervisor.

An experienced insolvency practitioner will be aware of what proposals are likely to be acceptable to creditors and the court and which are not, and will ensure that the proposal complies with the requirements of the Insolvency Act 1986. The insolvency practitioner is required to sign the notice of the proposal to indicate that he is prepared to act and will not do so unless he is satisfied that the proposal is reasonable and viable. Following the making of the proposal, the individual must prepare a statement of his affairs containing detailed particulars of the matters contained in the proposal.

Interim order

Once the insolvency practitioner has signed his acceptance of the proposal and become the individual's nominee, the next step is to apply to the court for an 'interim order'. The effect of the interim order is that:

- the creditors cannot try to make the individual bankrupt while the interim order is in force; and
- no court proceedings or enforcement action (e.g. sending the bailiffs to the individual's house) can be taken against the individual without the court's permission.

The application must be made to the county court for the insolvency district in which the individual resides. In London, the application is made to the High Court. It must be accompanied by an affidavit (a sworn statement) and a copy of the notice of the proposal signed by the insolvency practitioner endorsed with his consent to act. A court fee is payable.

The court sets a hearing date to consider the matter and gives two days' notice. Any court proceedings or enforcement action against the individual are frozen (or 'stayed') while the court decides whether to make the interim order.

The court can make an interim order provided that:

1 it is satisfied that the proposal is 'serious' and viable, i.e. it has not been made just to delay the making of a bankruptcy order and with no benefit to creditors;
2 the insolvency practitioner is prepared to act as nominee;
3 there has been no other application for an interim order in the previous 12 months; and
4 the individual is either an undischarged bankrupt or could petition for his own bankruptcy.

The IVA cannot be made unless the creditors support the arrangements. The next step is for the court to consider whether it will be worthwhile holding a meeting of the creditors to consider the terms of the individual's proposal. The nominee will submit a report to the court (either at this stage or when the application for the interim order is made), evaluating the proposal and indicating whether in his opinion a creditors' meeting should be called.

If the court rejects the nominee's recommendations, the interim order is discharged and any proceedings or enforcement action can continue.

Creditors' meeting

Assuming the court accepts the nominee's report, the insolvency practitioner will inform all creditors of the date and time of the meeting, which is normally held in the insolvency practitioner's offices and is chaired by the nominee. The individual is usually required to attend. The creditors will consider the proposal and eventually vote on it. Although the proposal can be amended, the individual must consent to any modifications. It is not unusual for IVAs to contain provisions for any 'windfall' payments received by the individual during the period of the IVA to be taken into account.

The proposal must be approved by 75 per cent in value

of the creditors voting on the proposal, i.e. if someone has £50,000 worth of debts and a creditor is owed £10,000, that creditor's vote counts as 20 per cent. Certain creditors, such as banks and the Inland Revenue, always vote at meetings and, as they also tend to be the largest creditors, any proposal is unlikely to be approved unless these creditors can be brought on board. The nominee may well discuss the proposal with creditors prior to the meeting in the hope of obtaining agreement. The meeting cannot approve a proposal that would affect the rights of a preferential creditor in bankruptcy (such as the Inland Revenue) or the rights of secured creditors (such as a mortgage lender) without their consent.

Usually, the nominee's appointment is approved at the meeting and he then becomes the 'supervisor' of the IVA. If the proposal is approved, it takes effect immediately and is binding on every creditor who received notice of the meeting and was entitled to vote. The outcome of the meeting must be reported to the court within four days. The court will record the effect of the report and discharge the interim order.

Challenging the IVA

The individual, or any of his creditors, can appeal to the court against the IVA within 28 days of the report of the creditors' meeting being made to the court, but only on the grounds that:

1 there were irregularities in the way the meeting was held, for example the proposal contained misleading or inaccurate information; or
2 the arrangement unfairly prejudiced the rights of a creditor.

An example of the latter might be where the debtor and his wife were jointly liable for a number of unsecured debts and the majority of the creditors accepted the debtor's proposal that no creditor should be able to pursue his wife in respect of those debts because their joint income was being used to fund the IVA. A creditor who might otherwise have been able to pursue the wife as co-debtor might object to the IVA on that basis.

If the court considers that the challenge has been made out, it may:

- revoke (or suspend) the agreement; or
- direct that a fresh creditors' meeting be held either to consider a new agreement or reconsider the existing agreement (and renew the interim order).

Conduct of the IVA

The supervisor will ensure that the individual complies with the terms of the IVA, including arranging the sale of any assets that need to be sold. The supervisor will collect the payments due from the individual and distribute them to creditors. If the individual's circumstances change, the original arrangement can be modified at a creditors' meeting called for that purpose and provided all the creditors agree.

Provided the individual complies with the IVA he will be discharged from his liability to all creditors covered by the IVA at the end of the period. The IVA will not, however, automatically discharge any co-debtor, including the person's spouse or partner, and provision for this will have to be specifically included and agreed. If the terms of the IVA are not complied with, then the arrangement will usually provide for the supervisor to petition for the individual's bankruptcy.

Advantages and disadvantages

Advantages

The advantages of an IVA include:
- the lack of stigma or publicity attached to bankruptcy;
- if the individual runs a business, it can continue to trade and provide income to fund the arrangement;
- drawing up an IVA to meet the individual's situation, so that assets, such as the family home, can be excluded so long as the creditors agree, for example because overall the creditors will be better off than in a bankruptcy;
- creditors should receive higher payments than they would in a bankruptcy because of the lower costs involved;
- unsecured creditors who voted against the IVA will still be bound by it;
- the individual is not subject to the restrictions imposed on bankruptcy and so can still be a company director and use a business name.

Disadvantages

Disadvantages include:
- the individual must have at least three unsecured creditors and unsecured debts of at least £10,000–£15,000 for an IVA to be a suitable option;
- the individual will generally be required to make higher payments over a longer period than in a bankruptcy;
- the costs of an IVA are relatively high and may have to be paid in advance (although it should be possible to find an insolvency practitioner who does not require up-front fees);
- assets are at risk if the creditors do not agree to exclude them;
- the individual may still be made bankrupt if the IVA fails and the costs of the unsuccessful IVA will be added to the debts;
- the individual will be closely monitored by the supervisor during the period of the IVA;
- IVAs are a matter of public record and so future applications for credit could be affected.

DEBTOR'S BANKRUPTCY PETITION

Who can apply?

A creditor, or the debtor himself, can apply to the court for bankruptcy.

Petitioning the court

In order to make himself bankrupt, an individual must 'petition' the court on the ground that he is unable to pay his debts. This involves completing the form for bankruptcy petition (form 6.27) together with a statement of affairs (form 6.28). The bankruptcy petition is a fairly straightforward document to complete and reflects the fact that most bankruptcies involve people who have been in business.

The forms are presented to the local county court with bankruptcy jurisdiction, or to the High Court in London. There is a court fee of £140 payable together with a deposit of £250. Although the fee may be waived where the individual is in receipt of specified social security benefits or remitted on the ground of financial hardship, the deposit must always be paid. This anomalous situation has been unsuccessfully challenged in the courts. In many cases, the fee and deposit have to be borrowed from friends or relatives, and local charities may also help.

Statement of affairs

The statement of affairs requires a considerable amount of information to be supplied, much of which may not be readily available, for example asset valuations. Although there are Guidance Notes (form B44.24), these are not comprehensive. Many agencies will assist the individual to complete the debtor's petition and statement of affairs.

Bear the following points in mind when completing the statement of affairs:
- pages C1/C2/C3 require details of assets. Any money in a bank or building society account which is needed to cover everyday living expenses should be withdrawn before the form is completed. 'Bottom book value' (i.e. the price the goods are likely to fetch at auction rather than by private sale) should be used as the value of any motor vehicle. If it is subject to hire purchase or conditional sale, the creditor is the owner of the vehicle. When calculating the value of household items and furniture, use the figure that they would fetch at auction rather than their new or replacement value. If any valuables are listed they are likely to be claimed by the Official Receiver. Under current legislation, any pension policies

The Steps to Bankruptcy

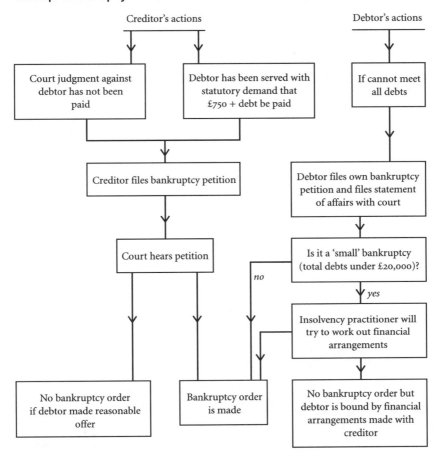

or interests in occupational pensions should be disclosed and the value given as 'to be advised';

- page D requests details of any levies against goods by creditors. The creditor will, however, only be allowed to keep the benefit of any distress or execution if it has been 'completed' before the making of the bankruptcy order;

- page E requires details of any current court action by creditors, including attachment of earnings orders. Such action will be stayed, i.e. halted, once the petition is presented;

- page F requires information to enable the court to decide whether an IVA might be more appropriate (*see* page 464). Only include attempts to make arrangements with creditors generally, not attempts to make arrangements with individual creditors;

- page G requires details of the individual's monthly income and expenditure. Only include details of regular income. Although page G suggests that any available income will be taken for creditors, in practice the trustee will only require payments if it is economical for him to administer them (*see* below).

Once the forms are completed they must be taken to the court to be sworn and filed, together with the fee (or application for exemption or remission on form EX160) and deposit (*see* above). The court will arrange for the forms to be put before a district judge. Some courts arrange a hearing either immediately or later in the day which the individual must attend, but other courts deal with the matter without a hearing.

Considering whether an IVA is more appropriate

In some cases, the court will refer the case to an insolvency practitioner to consider and report on whether an IVA (*see* above) is a more appropriate option. This will happen where the debtor's debts are less than £20,000 and he has money and property worth at least £2,000 – provided that he has not been the subject of bankruptcy proceedings in the previous five years.

The individual does not have to pay the fee for this report. In practice, there are usually insufficient assets for the insolvency petitioner to recommend an IVA, and the bankruptcy proceeds.

If the case is not referred to an insolvency practitioner, the court will still not automatically make a bankruptcy order. Where it appears, for example, that the debtor's assets exceed his liabilities or that the debtor is otherwise able to pay his debts, the district judge can dismiss the petition. Otherwise, the bankruptcy order will be made.

'Fast-track' official receiver IVAs

The Enterprise Act 2002 introduces a new fast-track IVA for undischarged bankrupts. The official receiver (OR) will act as nominee and put forward proposals to the creditors on a 'take it or leave it' basis. There will not be a creditors' meeting or any opportunity to make any proposed amendments. If the proposal is approved, the OR will act as supervisor and notify the court so that the bankruptcy order can be annulled. His fees will be a flat rate and therefore are likely to be cheaper than those of an insolvency practitioner. In practice, it is not anticipated this new regime will be heavily used, unless for example by individuals who did not properly consider the state of their pre-bankruptcy finances.

Certificate of summary jurisdiction

In some cases, the individual can ask the court to discharge him from bankruptcy after only two years instead of the normal three years. This shorter form of bankruptcy is called a 'certificate of summary jurisdiction'.

The individual should ask the court to issue a certificate of summary jurisdiction where:
- his total unsecured debts are less than £20,000; and
- he has neither been bankrupt nor subject to an IVA in the previous five years.

Another advantage of the certificate of summary jurisdiction is that the individual's affairs will not normally be investigated, nor will a creditors' meeting be held and the individual will not face examination as to his financial affairs in open court.

It is important that the individual asks the court to consider the issue of a certificate of summary administration

at the hearing as it cannot be issued retrospectively. Otherwise, after the bankruptcy order is made, the procedure is the same as that following a bankruptcy order made on a creditor's petition (*see* pages 466–71).

Under the Enterprise Act, the summary administration of bankruptcy cases will be abolished.

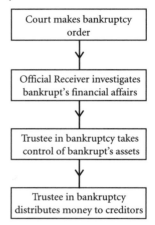

Advantages

There are a number of advantages to bankruptcy, including:
- it can remove the uncertainty and anxiety caused by negotiating with a large number of creditors simultaneously;
- there can be a sense of relief for the bankrupt;
- he usually pays less;
- it can be a fresh start;
- the process is certain;
- after discharge (*see* page 470) most debts are written off and cannot be pursued by creditors.

Disadvantages

However, there are also many disadvantages, including:
- the bankrupt will almost certainly lose any assets of value that can be sold off;
- if there is equity in the family home (i.e. it is worth more than the mortgage), it will probably be sold;
- if he owns a business and employs people, or the business has a value, his employees may have to be dismissed and the business sold;
- if he has mortgage or rent arrears, the family home will be at increased risk. This is because his mortgage lender or landlord may conclude that because of the bankruptcy their arrears are unlikely to be paid and they should, therefore, take possession proceedings on the grounds of those arrears;
- he cannot obtain credit of more than £250 without disclosing that he is an undischarged bankrupt and it will probably be difficult to obtain a bank account;

- the process is very expensive;
- he must allow his financial affairs to be scrutinized by officials who may take criminal action if any irregularities are discovered;
- he cannot hold certain public offices (e.g. MP, magistrate or councillor) or practice certain professions (e.g. accountant, solicitor);
- his future credit rating will continue to be adversely affected and this will probably make running a business or buying a home in future very difficult;
- he may feel judged and humiliated. There is still a stigma attached to bankruptcy;
- he cannot be a company director (without leave of the court) and cannot trade under any other name than the one used at the date of bankruptcy order;
- the names of people who are made bankrupt are published in the *London Gazette* and also in the local press. Friends and neighbours may find out about his financial difficulties;
- he must report any changes in circumstances during the bankruptcy to his trustee. Even after discharge, he may still have to co-operate with the trustee and Official Receiver in the administration of his assets;
- not all debts will be written off at the end of the bankruptcy, for example fines, maintenance/child support payments;
- secured creditors are not affected by bankruptcy and can still enforce their security;
- joint debts are not written off in the sense that creditors can still pursue the non-bankrupt debtor. If she is the bankrupt's partner, the family will still be in financial difficulties.

CREDITORS' PETITION

A warning to creditors

Creditors who are considering making an individual bankrupt need to bear in mind that the process is intended to benefit *all* creditors and not just themselves. They could bear all the costs of obtaining a bankruptcy order only to find that other creditors receive more and they could even end up with nothing at all if the individual has no assets or income to speak of.

Who can apply?

A creditor can apply for someone to be made bankrupt where he is owed at least £750, which the person 'appears unable to pay'.

The creditor can only satisfy the court of the individual's inability to pay in one of two ways:

1 by serving a 'statutory demand' on the individual with which he fails to comply; or

2 by unsuccessfully attempting to enforce a court judgment against the individual by 'execution against goods'. This means that the bailiff must have made serious attempts to enter the debtor's home and seize property. It is not enough if the bailiff has merely visited the individual's home and been unable to gain access. The attempt to enforce a court judgment is unsuccessful if the money due under the judgment is not paid in full.

What is a statutory demand?

A statutory demand is a document (form 6.2) demanding that the individual pay the debt in full or in part in a manner acceptable to the creditor, which could be by instalments.

The statutory demand does not have to be issued by the court or even seen by it at this stage. If the individual does not comply with the statutory demand within 21 days, the creditor can issue a creditor's petition and ask the court to make a bankruptcy order. A creditor does not need a judgment in order to be able to serve a statutory demand for the debt. However, without a judgment, the creditor might find that the individual is able to challenge the existence of the debt and so prevent the issue of the petition (*see* 'Setting aside a statutory demand', below). A creditor who does have a judgment is not required to attempt to enforce it by means of execution against goods first of all. He can serve a statutory demand instead.

Responding to the statutory demand

Although some creditors use statutory demands as a means of debt collection with no intention of making the individual bankrupt, statutory demands should never be ignored (unless the individual has decided that he wants to go bankrupt). On receipt of the statutory demand, the person should consider the following options:

- whether to apply for an administration order or propose an IVA (*see* above);
- make payment(s) to either clear the debt in full or reduce it below the £750 bankruptcy limit;
- make an offer to pay the debt by instalments. If the debt is subject to a judgment, as well as trying to negotiate with the creditor, the individual should apply to the court to vary the judgment to enable payment by instalments with a view to arranging this before the creditor can obtain a bankruptcy order;
- offer a charge over his property as security for the debt. This is a short-term solution and the individual should also arrange to pay the debt as soon as possible to prevent the creditor from enforcing the charge by selling the property;
- apply to set aside the statutory demand.

Setting aside a statutory demand

If individuals wish to challenge the statutory demand and avoid being made bankrupt, they must do so within 18 days after service of the demand. The day the demand is served is ignored for the purpose of calculating this time period. Likewise, if the demand is received after 4 p.m. on a business day, on a weekend or a bank holiday, these days can be ignored too in calculating whether 18 days have expired. An application will need to be made to the county court to 'set aside' the statutory demand. It is important that the time period to set aside the demand is complied with, although the court does have a discretion to extend this provided a good reason is given, e.g. the debtor has been away on holiday. The grounds for applying to set the statutory demand aside are:

- there is a substantial dispute about the money said to be owed, i.e. the individual has a reasonable prospect of being able to establish that the money is not owed. Where the creditor has obtained a judgment in respect of the debt, that will usually prevent the individual from claiming that there is a valid argument that the money is not owed;
- the individual has a cross-claim against the creditor which exceeds the amount of the debt;
- the creditor holds security which equals or exceeds in value the amount of the debt.

A court fee of £60 is payable on the application and this, together with a sworn statement setting out the ground(s) will need to be filed at the court. The application will be put before a district judge. If the district judge considers there are no grounds for the application, he can dismiss it without a hearing. Otherwise a hearing will be arranged at which the district judge will consider the application.

The court will not set aside a statutory demand on the ground that the creditor has unreasonably refused an offer of payment or security or even on the ground that the creditor has refused to consider such an offer. Nor will the court set aside a demand on the ground that it is for an excessive amount. In such a case, the individual is supposed to pay the amount admitted to be due and only apply to set aside as to the amount in dispute. The court will not 'do a deal' with the individual to set the statutory demand aside on condition that payment is made. Neither will the district judge set aside the demand where it is based on a judgment and no appeal or application to set aside the judgment has been made. If an appeal or application to set aside the existing judgment has been made, the application to set aside will be adjourned pending the outcome of that application. Nonetheless, where the court is satisfied that the individual has a genuine and serious counterclaim, then in these circumstances their application to set aside the demand is likely to succeed.

If the application to set aside the statutory demand is dismissed, the creditor will be given leave to present his bankruptcy petition. However, should the individual succeed with his application to set the demand aside, he is likely to be able to make a claim for costs against the other side.

The petition

The next step is for the creditor to present a bankruptcy petition (on the appropriate form) to the court. There are different forms depending on whether the creditor is an unsatisfied judgment creditor or has served a statutory demand.

Together with the petition, the creditor must send to the court:

- an affidavit (i.e. a sworn statement that the facts stated in the petition are true); and
- a court fee of £180; and
- a deposit of £300.

Responding to the petition

The petition must be served personally on the individual. It is still not too late for him to prevent a bankruptcy order being made, but he must give at least seven days' notice to the court and to the creditor of his intention to do so. He can still pay the debt, or make an offer to do so, or seek an IVA.

Bankruptcy hearing

The hearing will be before a district judge. At the hearing, the creditor must prove that he has served the petition on the individual (and the statutory demand, if relevant) and file a certificate to the effect that the debt is still owing.

The court has a discretion to refuse to make a bankruptcy order in certain circumstances, including where the creditor has, in the court's opinion, unreasonably refused to accept an offer to pay the debt by instalments or a reduced sum in full and final settlement of the debt.

It is not unusual for the parties to reach agreement about payment of the debt and the hearing of the petition can be adjourned.

IVA supervisor's petition

Where the individual is subject to an IVA, the supervisor can petition for a bankruptcy order on the grounds that:

- the arrangement was based on false or misleading information supplied by the individual; or
- the individual failed to comply with the terms of the IVA.

Where this happens, the supervisor will usually become the individual's trustee in bankruptcy.

Who will deal with the bankruptcy?

On the making of the bankruptcy order, the court will notify the OR, a Department of Trade and Industry official. Soon after the bankruptcy order is made, if not on the same day, the bankrupt will be summoned to the OR's office.

The OR's primary functions are to investigate the bankrupt's conduct and financial affairs, and report to the court (unless a certificate of summary administration has been issued) and to obtain control of his property and any relevant documents. The OR will advertise the bankruptcy and invite creditors to 'prove' their debts, i.e. submit claims.

The bankrupt is required to co-operate with the OR. Unless the bankruptcy order was made on his own debtor's petition, the bankrupt must draw up a statement of his affairs for the OR. He must give up possession of his assets (with limited exceptions *see* below) and hand over any papers reasonably required by the OR. His bank account will be frozen. The OR can arrange for him to be examined in public by the court as to his financial affairs and the causes of his bankruptcy, although this rarely happens. The OR can arrange for his mail to be redirected, if appropriate. The OR will usually visit any business premises and may also visit the bankrupt's home, but this is rare. If the OR does visit, he may remove any items of value.

The OR must decide within 12 weeks after the bankruptcy order is made whether or not to summon a creditors' meeting for the purpose of choosing a trustee in bankruptcy. If no trustee in bankruptcy is appointed, the OR will become the trustee in bankruptcy.

What does the trustee in bankruptcy do?

The trustee in bankruptcy is responsible for gathering in and selling the bankrupt's property and distributing the proceeds to the bankrupt's creditors. However, the trustee will not sell property unless it is economical to do so, i.e. there will be a return for creditors after taking into account the costs of sale. In the case of jointly owned property, the trustee must either obtain the consent of the co-owner or obtain a court order. Special provisions are made for the family home (*see* below).

There may be property which either cannot be disposed of or involves obligations which would be detrimental to the bankrupt's estate, for example a lease. The trustee can dispose of such 'onerous' property. If the bankrupt acquires any property before the bankruptcy is discharged, he must inform the trustee and the trustee can then decide whether or not to claim the property for the estate. The bankrupt must not dispose of the property in the meantime.

It is a criminal offence for the bankrupt to intentionally conceal information or property from the trustee (or OR) or to deliberately mislead the trustee (or OR) about such property, whether he had it before or after the date of the bankruptcy order.

Effects of bankruptcy

Once a trustee is appointed following a creditors' meeting (or if the OR becomes trustee), ownership of the bankrupt's property (known as the bankrupt's 'estate') automatically passes to the trustee. There are exceptions to this (*see* below).

Attempts to sell off property

Any attempt by the bankrupt to dispose of property during the period between the bankruptcy petition being presented to the court and the trustee's appointment is void. The trustee will be able to reclaim the property, unless either:

1 the court confirms the transaction; or
2 a purchaser of the property either:
(**a**) did not know of the petition; or
(**b**) paid full value for the property; or
(**c**) otherwise acted 'in good faith'.

Where the bankrupt's bank honours a cheque after the date of the bankruptcy order, the transaction will not be void if either:

- the bank did not have notice of the bankruptcy order before honouring the cheque; or
- it is not reasonably practicable to recover the payment from the person to whom it was made.

Property which does not pass to the trustee

The bankrupt can keep the following items:

- tools of the trade, including a vehicle, which are *necessary* and used by the bankrupt *personally* in his work; and
- household items (such as clothing, bedding and furniture) which are *necessary* for the *basic* domestic needs of the debtor *and his family*.

However, if the value of the property is more than the cost of a reasonable replacement, the trustee can claim the property and purchase a reasonable replacement, provided there are funds available. The trustee must make the claim within 42 days of becoming aware of the property.

Although assured, protected and secure tenancies (*see* Chapter 20) do not vest automatically in the trustee, if they have a value then the trustee can claim them, again within 42 days.

What happens to the bankrupt's earnings?

The bankrupt is entitled to retain sufficient income to enable him and his family to have a reasonable standard of living, i.e. the bankrupt is not restricted to basic or income support levels.

If the trustee cannot agree a figure with the bankrupt, he can apply to the court for an 'income payment order'. The order will require the bankrupt to pay part of his wages, salary or other income to the trustee. Trustees and courts are relatively generous in this regard, and a payment is unlikely to be required unless the bankrupt has at least £100–£200 a month available. An order can last for a maximum of three years (including post-discharge). The court can also order that an employer should pay the bankrupt's salary direct to the trustee.

Can the trustee take money from a pension?

Personal pensions are part of the bankrupt's estate and must be paid to the trustee regardless of whether they become payable during or after the bankruptcy. If the bankrupt has acquired rights under an occupational pension scheme prior to the date of the bankruptcy order, the position currently depends on whether or not the scheme contains a 'forfeiture clause'. A forfeiture clause provides for pension rights under the scheme to be forfeited in the event of bankruptcy. Any payments are then made at the discretion of the scheme trustees, usually to a member of the bankrupt's family. If there is no forfeiture clause, the bankrupt's pension rights vest in the trustee (i.e. ownership passes to the trustee).

Even in cases where a pension does not actually vest in the trustee, any income (including a lump sum) could be made the subject of an Income Payments Order (*see* 'What happens to the bankrupt's earnings?', above).

Since May 2000, rights under a tax-approved pension scheme have been excluded from the bankrupt's estate; i.e. they can no longer be claimed by the trustee, other than by way of an Income Payments Order in appropriate cases.

Following Regulations that came into force in May 2000, unapproved pension arrangements may be protected on bankruptcy if the pension is the bankrupt's sole or main pension (apart from any state pension). The exclusion of such a pension from the bankrupt's estate can either be by application to the court, or by an arrangement made between the bankrupt and the trustee. However, it should be appreciated that the Regulations are complex and, most importantly, the bankrupt must apply for exclusion within 13 weeks from the date of the estate or pension rights vesting in the trustee. That time limit is applied strictly.

What happens to the family home?

The bankrupt's share in the family home is one of the assets that automatically vests in his trustee in bankruptcy. If there is sufficient equity in the home, the trustee will want to sell it as soon as possible. Otherwise, he will register a 'restriction' at the Land Registry (to alert potential buyers of the property to the fact that he has an interest in the home) and may order a sale in the future. Alternatively, he may put a charge on the property. This means that even after the bankrupt has been discharged from bankruptcy, the trustee will retain his interest in the property and can apply to the court to sell it.

The Enterprise Act 2002 changes the position with regard to the bankrupt's home. When this part of the Act comes into force (expected in April 2004), the bankrupt's home will cease to be part of the estate after three years. At the end of three years from the date of the bankruptcy, the bankrupt's home will vest in the bankrupt (without the need for any transfer). What this means in practice is that the trustee will have only three years to sell the house. After that time, the bankrupt can deal with his property as he did prior to the bankruptcy. The trustee cannot hold on to the property even after the bankrupt has been discharged from the bankruptcy and wait for property values to increase (to the distress of the bankrupt and his family). Even where the bankrupt's home is vested in the trustee, then where this is of low value (yet to be defined by the legislation) any application to realize this interest will be rejected by the court.

If the home is jointly owned, the trustee will try to sell the bankrupt's share to the co-owner (e.g. the bankrupt's husband or wife). If there is little equity, the trustee will usually be prepared to sell for a nominal sum plus legal costs (typically £250). If the bankrupt lives in the home with a wife, she has a right to live there even if she is not a co-owner. In such cases, or if the bankrupt's wife will not purchase his share, the trustee will probably apply to the court for an order for the sale of the property. If children live in the home, he must obtain a court order.

In deciding whether to order a sale, the court must consider:

- the creditors' interests;
- whether the wife contributed to the bankruptcy;
- the needs and resources of the wife and any children (the legislation does not mention partners or other dependants); and
- any other relevant circumstances (but *not* the bankrupt's needs).

In practice, family homes are not sold for at least a year after the bankruptcy unless all parties agree. After a year, the interests of creditors outweigh all other considerations, unless there are exceptional circumstances. The loss of the home is not considered 'exceptional'.

Selling off goods at a low value

A debtor who anticipates that he may be made bankrupt may attempt to put his property out of the reach of the trustee by selling it (or giving it) to friends or family for less than the market value. This is called an 'undervalue transaction'. The trustee can ask the court to set aside the transaction where:

- the transaction was carried out within five years prior to the date of the bankruptcy order; and
- the bankrupt was insolvent at the time; or
- the transaction was carried out within two years of the date of the bankruptcy order, regardless of whether the debtor was insolvent or not.

If the transaction is set aside the court can restore the position of the parties to what it was before the transaction was entered into or the payment made, for example by requiring any property or money to be returned to the trustee or ordering that the trustee should be paid for goods or services. Protection is given to third parties who act in good faith without notice of the circumstances.

Giving priority to a creditor

The trustee can also ask the court to set aside a payment made by the bankrupt to an unsecured creditor in order to put that creditor in a better position than he would have been in if he had to prove the debt in the bankruptcy. For example, the debtor may attempt to divert money to a business partner or spouse before the bankruptcy order is made, in order to put that creditor in a better position than other creditors. This is called a 'preference'.

The following conditions must be satisfied:

- the effect of the payment was to put the creditor in a better position than if he had to prove the debt in the bankruptcy; and
- the bankrupt had this intention; and
- the bankrupt was insolvent at the time; and
- the payment was made six months before the date of the bankruptcy order (or two years where the preference was to an 'associate', i.e. wife or other relative, business partner or employer/employee).

Can creditors bring proceedings against the bankrupt?

Once a bankruptcy petition has been presented the court may halt any action, execution or other legal process against the individual. This is called a 'stay' of proceedings.

Once the bankruptcy order has been made:

- no creditor who has a bankruptcy debt (*see* below)

shall have any remedy against the person or property of the individual in respect of that debt; or

- may commence any action or other legal proceedings in respect of the debt without the leave of the court.

It should be noted that a stay of proceedings is not automatic, but must be applied for and that the court can allow proceedings to be commenced or continue. The purpose of these provisions is to protect the individual's assets for the benefit of all his creditors.

Bankruptcy offences

Bankruptcy is not a criminal offence as such, although in the past it was treated as a quasi-criminal process. In addition to non-disclosure (*see* 'What does the trustee in bankruptcy do?', above), the main points to note are:

- it is an offence for an undischarged bankrupt to fail to disclose his status to anybody from whom credit of more than £250 is sought (including HP or conditional sale agreements);
- it is an offence for an undischarged bankrupt to act as a director of a limited company or to be involved (directly or indirectly) in running a company. It is also an offence for an undischarged bankrupt to run a business in any other name than that in which he was made bankrupt.

Payments to creditors

As noted above, the OR will advertise for creditors to contact the trustee. They will be asked to 'prove' their claims, i.e. show that they are owed the amount claimed. This must be done on a prescribed form (form 6.38). The only debts which cannot be proved are:

- fines;
- maintenance orders (and Child Support Agency orders);
- debts arising from certain other orders of the criminal courts.

In other words, in these cases the creditors concerned cannot make a claim in the bankruptcy and the court has no power to prevent the creditors attempting to enforce payment. The Enterprise Act 2002 will abolish what is known as Crown preference. This relates to debts incurred by the bankrupt in respect of income tax, VAT and social security, etc. Prior to the new Act being implemented, the OR had to settle these debts first from any assets of the bankrupt before any other creditors could be paid. Now this has been abolished, the entire assets of the bankrupt can be spread among the unsecured creditors, with no one taking priority.

Secured loans do not need to be proved because the rights of secured creditors are not affected by bankruptcy.

In theory, secured creditors can agree to release their security and ask to be included in the list of creditors. If they have already forced a sale of the secured property, they can be included as creditors for any shortfall.

Any surplus will be returned to the bankrupt.

How long does bankruptcy last?

If the court has issued a certificate of summary jurisdiction, the individual will be discharged from bankruptcy after two years.

In all other cases, i.e. the majority of bankruptcies, discharge is automatic after three years from the date of the bankruptcy order. However, the trustee can ask the court to delay this if he believes that the debtor has failed to carry out his obligations. The court can then suspend automatic discharge and the bankrupt will have to apply for discharge and persuade the court that he has now complied.

When the Enterprise Act 2002 comes into effect in April 2004, nearly all bankrupts will be automatically discharged after a maximum of 12 months. Moreover, the OR may file a notice saying the bankrupt is to be discharged even earlier than one year (if he thinks an investigation of conduct is unnecessary, or has been concluded). Where the bankrupt has been guilty of fraud or reckless behaviour, the OR will be able to apply for a 'restriction order' preventing the bankrupt from obtaining credit, acting as a director of a company or taking part in its management or trading in a different name from that in which he was made bankrupt. These restriction orders can last for up to 15 years.

Restriction Orders will be made where:
- the bankrupt failed to keep records or produce information;
- the bankrupt entered into a transaction at an undervalue or gave a preference;
- the bankrupt incurred a debt that he had no reasonable expectation of being able to pay;
- the bankrupt failed to provide goods or services despite being wholly or partly paid for them.

There are some provisional measures under the Enterprise Act 2002 to deal with individuals who have been made bankrupt prior to the new Act being in force. If a bankrupt is due to be discharged less than one year after the new Act comes into force, there will be no change to the date of discharge. However, if a bankrupt is due to be discharged more than one year after the new Act comes into force, then that period will be reduced to one year from the date of the Act, unless a court order is made to suspend the discharge date.

The provisional measures described above will not apply though to anyone who has been bankrupt more than once in the previous 15 years and who is still undischarged when the Enterprise Act 2002 comes into force. Any bankrupt who falls into this category will not be discharged until five years have elapsed from the date of the new Act.

After discharge, the individual can require the court to issue a certificate of discharge. All the bankrupt's debts remain unenforceable, except the following:
- secured creditors (if the property was sold but the sale price was insufficient to pay off the secured debt, then the shortfall is no longer secured, but will remain unenforceable provided the mortgage or secured loan was taken out prior to the date of the bankruptcy order, even if the property was not sold until after discharge);
- fines;
- maintenance and other family court orders;
- debts from personal injury claims;
- debts incurred through fraud;
- debt arising from certain other orders of the criminal court;
- student loans made under the Education (Student Loans) Act 1990.

Occasionally the trustee has not completed the realization of assets, e.g. the sale of the family home, when the bankrupt is discharged. In such cases, that asset will still be realized and distributed despite the fact that the creditors could not otherwise obtain payment (but see page 468 for changes introduced by the Enterprise Act 2002). The duties of co-operation with, and to provide information to, the OR and trustee continue after discharge for so long as is reasonably required.

Annulment

A bankruptcy order can be annulled, i.e. cancelled, at any time by the court if the bankrupt has either:
- repaid the debts and bankruptcy expenses in full; or
- has provided full security for them; or
- if there were insufficient grounds for making the order in the first place.

This will not enable the individual to recover any property already disposed of by the trustee or distributed to creditors, but any property still vested in the trustee will revert. The individual also becomes liable again for all his debts.

A bankruptcy order can also be annulled where a creditors' meeting has approved an IVA proposal.

BANKRUPTCY OR IVA?

An individual often has no choice over whether or not to go bankrupt. However, in practice, individuals are often faced with deciding whether or not to oppose bankruptcy. The possibility of obtaining an IVA should always be considered before deciding on bankruptcy, particularly where the individual needs to remain in business if he is to be able to pay creditors or needs time to sell assets in an ordered way. Bankruptcy is likely to be the preferred option only if an individual has a number of debts, no assets (or no equity in his home), a low income and it is unlikely that this situation will change. He must also have no need for credit in the medium term. An IVA should be the preferred option if the individual has income and/or assets and is able to make a substantial offer but is unable to persuade his creditors to accept an informal arrangement. However, IVAs do not end in automatic discharge, as does bankruptcy (after two or three years).

The following factors should be taken into account.

Risk to current assets

Property owned by an individual is directly put at risk in bankruptcy. In practice, many things which a person uses may be owned by someone else (e.g. a partner) and these goods cannot be taken. However, jointly owned property, particularly the family home, will be indirectly at risk, because the trustee may be able to sell it in order to realize the bankrupt partner's share. In the case of an IVA, there is less risk to assets because creditors are being offered regular payments.

Future assets

In considering either bankruptcy or an IVA, the individual should bear in mind the potential risk to any future assets, particularly where he expects to inherit property or already owns assets which are likely to increase in value over the next few years. Although it is possible to arrange for potential donors to change their wills, asset transfers may well be caught by the undervalue transaction provisions discussed above.

Effect on future credit

Both bankruptcy and IVAs are a matter of public record. It is very unlikely that a lender would give credit to a bankrupt person and it is likely to be more expensive to obtain credit after discharge. In addition, it is an offence for an undischarged bankrupt to obtain credit of more than £250 without disclosing his bankrupt status (including ordering goods and then failing to pay for them). For people who want to run their own business, the need to make this declaration may make this impossible because they are unlikely to be given further credit. Although utilities cannot insist on payment of pre-bankruptcy arrears as a condition of continuing to supply services, they may well require a security deposit or insist on the installation of pre-payment meters. It may, therefore, be necessary to transfer the accounts to a non-bankrupt member of the family. The individual is unlikely to face these problems with an IVA.

The effect on employment or office

Being an undischarged bankrupt prohibits anyone from being an MP, a councillor, a magistrate or an estate agent. The professional rules of solicitors and accountants make it virtually impossible for people who have been bankrupt to work in these professions. Other employers may be unwilling to employ a bankrupt person, especially if he is responsible for money. Charity law limits the ability of people who have been bankrupt to serve on management committees. A bankrupt usually cannot be a school or college governor. The bankruptcy of a sole trader does not necessarily mean that the business will close, but it will be difficult for it to continue:

- if there are items of business equipment used by the bankrupt's employees rather than by him personally, he will not be able to claim exemption for them (*see* page 467) and the trustee may insist on a sale. Stock in trade is not exempt from sale by the trustee;
- if the business needs credit, the bankrupt must disclose his status to anyone from whom he obtains goods or services on credit and they are unlikely to give credit in these circumstances, and may even be creditors whose debts are included in the bankruptcy;
- the bankruptcy will be advertised locally and this may damage the reputation of the business as well as of its proprietor, as it is an offence for him to trade in another name other than that in which he was made bankrupt;
- an undischarged bankrupt cannot be a director of a limited company or be concerned (directly or indirectly) in the management of a company without the court's permission;
- he will find it extremely difficult to operate a bank account, not only because of the credit restrictions but also because of the possibility of the trustee making a claim against any credit balance in the account.

These restrictions do not apply to someone with an IVA.

The effect on housing

If the bankrupt owns his home and is forced to move, for example because the trustee forces a sale, it will be impossible for him to obtain another mortgage, at least during the period of his bankruptcy. Even if he does not own his home, the restrictions on obtaining credit may cause difficulties in renting a new property because a deposit and/or rent in advance often have to be paid.

Type of information	Where are records kept?	Is there a fee?	How long are records kept?
Details of IVAs: the name and address of the debtor, the name and address of the supervisor, the name of the court that made the interim order, the date of the IVA, the date the IVA was completed and whether it succeeded or failed	IPCU, 2nd Floor, East Wing, Ladywood House, 45–46 Stephenson Street, Birmingham B2 4DS. Telephone: 0121 698 4000	No fee	Indefinitely – but the information is only made available for 2 years after completion of the IVA
Details of bankruptcies: the name and address of the debtor, the date of the bankruptcy order, the name of the court that made the order, the name and address of the OR dealing with the case	Bankruptcy Search Room, 2nd Floor, West Wing, Ladywood House, 45–46 Stephenson Street, Birmingham B2 4DS	No fee – but the information can only be obtained by visiting in person or writing	Indefinitely
Details of company receiverships, liquidations and disqualified directors	Companies Registration Office, Cardiff. Telephone: 02920 380801	This information is available from the website at www.companieshouse.gov.uk	Indefinitely

The effect on reputation and stress

Bankruptcy can be a very humiliating experience for many people. It is a possibility that there may be a public examination of the debtor's conduct and financial affairs in open court. There will be an advertisement in a local paper. Bankruptcy could add considerably to a person's stress. Individual voluntary agreements do not carry the same stigma, but can be time-consuming to draw up and gain agreement for and could, therefore, add to stress.

Are there resources available?

If an individual wants to petition for his own bankruptcy he has to pay a deposit in addition to the court fee, unless this can be waived. Lack of resources sometimes prevents this. Most insolvency practitioners will require at least £750 in advance of setting up an IVA, although a free initial interview may be available. A person may well pay more for the 'privilege' of avoiding bankruptcy.

Searching public records

The table above provides details of how you can find out whether a person has been made bankrupt or is subject to an IVA. It also shows how you can find out if a company has gone into liquidation or a director has been disqualified (*see* Chapter 53).

53

Corporate Insolvency

A limited company is a legal entity in its own right; it is owned by its shareholders (called 'the members') and is run by a board of directors (*see* page 481). In the same way that an individual may run into money problems and have to go bankrupt, or come to some other formal arrangement with creditors, a company may need to take steps to reorganize its finances in order to keep the business afloat. This section considers the various ways in which the insolvency of a limited company can be dealt with.

SUMMARY OF OPTIONS

Currently, the insolvency of a company can be dealt with in four ways (*see* below). However, the Insolvency Act 2000 and the Enterprise Act 2002 have made significant changes. In particular, the scope to appoint administrative receivers is going to be curtailed and, in addition, a major new out-of-court procedure is to be introduced whereby the company, its directors and holders of certain floating charges can appoint an administrator. The reforms under the Insolvency Act were introduced in January 2003 and the changes under the Enterprise Act 2002 are expected to come into force in September 2003.

The insolvency of a company can be dealt with in the following ways:

- company voluntary arrangement;
- administration order;
- administrative receiver;
- compulsory liquidation.

In a nutshell, administration orders and company voluntary arrangements are ways of reorganizing a business and re-establishing its finances with a view to saving the business. Even when a company is in administrative receivership it may still be able to trade, and so can be sold as a going concern. Compulsory liquidation is the end of the line for most companies – the usual end result is the loss of the business.

COMPANY VOLUNTARY ARRANGEMENT

A company voluntary arrangement (CVA) is the company equivalent to the IVA for individuals.

Outline of the procedure

The directors of the company will need the assistance of an insolvency practitioner to develop proposals for getting the company out of its financial difficulties. The proposals must be filed at court and meetings of the company's shareholders and creditors must be held to vote on the proposals. The plan must be approved by both the shareholders and the creditors. Preferential creditors (e.g. the Inland Revenue) and secured creditors (e.g. a mortgage lender) cannot be bound by the arrangement without their consent. Subject to that, assuming the required majorities are achieved, any dissenting creditor who received notice of the meeting will be bound by the majority decision.

Can creditors take enforcement action in the meantime?

The Insolvency Act 2000 introduced on 1 January 2003 made important changes to CVAs by making them easier and quicker to obtain. The changes however only apply to small companies that have:

- assets of less than £1.4m;
- sales of less than £2.8m;
- fewer than 50 employees.

Once the application to the court is made, an automatic moratorium is in place for 28 days, or until the creditors' meeting is convened. This means that during this period no hostile action to enforce debts can be taken by any creditors. Provided the above conditions are met, a CVA will operate in the same way as an IVA, i.e. immediate protection from creditors once the court papers are filed.

ADMINISTRATION ORDER (AO)

The AO procedure is intended for insolvent companies that have a reasonable prospect of being able to survive their current financial problems – possibly through arrangements with their creditors or through disposal of part of the company's operation as a going concern. The procedure is designed to enable the company to avoid being wound up or the sale of the company's assets by secured creditors at knock-down prices.

	Who can apply?	*What happens?*	*Who takes control?*	*Effect on the company?*
Company voluntary arrangement	The directors	A plan to reorganize the company's financial affairs is put into place	The plan is supervised by an *insolvency practitioner*	The aim is to save the company
Administration order	The directors Under the Enterprise Act 2002, floating charge holders can apply	Company is put under the control of an administrator	An *administrator*	The aim is to save the company
Administrative receivership	Any creditor with a floating charge	Creditor appoints administrative receiver to recover its money	An *administrative receiver*	The aim is for the creditor to get its money back
Compulsory liquidation	A creditor owed at least £750	Liquidator sells off assets and pays creditors	The *liquidator*	The company ceases to exist

Outline of the procedure

The directors of the struggling company must apply to the court for an AO. The application should be supported by an 'independent report' on the company's affairs by the insolvency practitioner who is proposed as the 'administrator', to the effect that an AO is appropriate. In practice, it will not usually be possible for the company to obtain the AO without a favourable report. The court will not grant an AO unless it is satisfied that it will achieve the aim of either enabling the company to survive, or come to satisfactory arrangements with creditors for payment, or allow the company's assets to be sold off in a more advantageous way.

Can creditors take enforcement action in the meantime?

The application for the AO effectively prevents any (further) enforcement action against the company until the application has been dealt with by the court. This means that:

- no winding up order may be made;
- no steps may be taken to enforce any security over the company's property or to repossess goods in the company's possession (including goods on HP or subject to a retention-of-title clause) without the leave of the court;
- no other proceedings and no execution (distress against goods) or other legal process may be commenced or continued without the leave of the court.

If the AO is actually made, this protection against enforcement action by the creditors will continue.

What effect does an administrative order have?

The immediate effect of an AO being made is to remove certain threats to the company and its assets. For example, any application to wind up the company will be dismissed and no administrative receiver can be appointed.

The next step is for the administrator to call a meeting of creditors, who must approve the directors' survival plan for the company. If the proposals are not approved by the creditors, the court can discharge the AO. If the proposals are agreed, the administrator will do whatever is necessary to implement the plan.

Although the making of an AO ends any administrative receivership, the creditor who is entitled to appoint an administrative receiver can effectively pre-empt this by appointing an administrative receiver on receiving notice of the application for the AO. This is because the court is required to dismiss an application for an AO if an administrative receiver has been appointed.

Reform of the administration system

In addition to changes to individual insolvency (*see* Chapter 52), the Enterprise Act 2002 reforms the administration system, with the aim of making it more accessible, cheaper and less bureaucratic. The key change is the removal of the need for a court hearing before an administration order is granted. Under the new regime (which is anticipated to be in force by September 2003), an administrator may be appointed by either (a) a company or its directors or (b) the holder of a qualifying floating charge, without the need for a court to be involved. When an administrator is appointed, a moratorium takes effect.

The directors of a company wishing to appoint an administrator will need to show that the company is, or is likely to become, unable to pay its debts and that at least five working days' notice have been given to any floating charge holders. When seeking to appoint an administrator, a statutory declaration will be needed but the requirement for a detailed report is no longer necessary. The administrator takes office when the Notice of Appointment is filed with the court, identifying the administrator and including a statement from the administrator agreeing to the appointment. Attached to this will be a statutory declaration stating that the company's application meets the necessary criteria. As soon as the Notice of Appointment is lodged at the court, the freeze on creditors (the moratorium) takes effect and the company is protected.

Once the administrator has been appointed, he will send the Notice of Appointment to the company and creditors as soon as reasonably practicable. An administrator is an officer of the court with a duty to act fairly. Therefore, he is obliged to perform his functions quickly, efficiently and reasonably practicably. Failure to do this may result in an application to the court by a creditor who claims to have been harmed by the administrator's actions. The administrator under these new provisions must therefore act with the interests of all the creditors in mind.

A representative of the company must then within 11 days of the administrator's request provide a statement of the company's affairs. The administrator has a maximum period of eight weeks from his appointment to provide all the creditors with a formal statement setting out his proposals for the company. The administrator will then hold an initial creditors' meeting within 10 weeks of the administration. At this meeting, when the administrator tables his proposals, the creditors can vote on whether or not to accept them. This meeting will either approve the implementation of the CVA (75 per cent of the creditors need to vote in favour) or vote in favour of a creditors' voluntary liquidation.

Administration will eventually replace administrative receivership as the principal means of enforcing full, fixed and floating securities. Administrative receiverships will become increasingly rare. It should not be forgotten that the administrator will owe duties to all creditors, while an administrative receiver's duties are traditionally owed primarily to the secured creditor. Moreover, the new procedure makes it clear that the primary objective of the administrator will be to rescue the company as a going concern – irrespective of who is responsible for his appointment.

Another significant change to corporate insolvency by the Enterprise Act 2002 is the abolition of Crown preference. The intention behind this is to make funds available to unsecured creditors. This is to be achieved by means of a cut of the assets ('the prescribed part') that would otherwise go to floating charge holders being set aside for unsecured creditors if the net property exceeds a prescribed minimum. The prescribed minimum is set at £10,000 and the prescribed part is 50 per cent of net property up to £10,000 and 20 per cent of net property over £10,000. The maximum amount of the prescribed part is £600,000.

ADMINISTRATIVE RECEIVER

Any creditor who has a 'floating charge' can appoint an administrative receiver (but *see* 'Reform' on page 476).

What is a 'floating charge'?

Only a limited company can grant a floating charge; no other organization or individual can do so. The easiest way to explain what a floating charge is, is to contrast it with a 'fixed charge'. A 'fixed charge' is a security over a *particular* property or asset. A floating charge, on the other hand, can be over the *whole* of a company's assets and undertakings. On the happening of certain events, for example on the company going into liquidation or applying for an AO, the floating charge will crystallize. The charge then 'fixes' on the assets comprised in the charge.

Who is the administrative receiver?

Floating charges are a device favoured by banks to secure company overdrafts. An administrative receiver is an insolvency practitioner appointed by a bank under the terms of its floating charge to recover its loan from the company. He cannot be appointed until the bank has made formal demand for repayment of the loan. The bank may decide to act because it feels that its security is inadequate or is at risk if the company continues to trade as it has done.

The administrative receiver's primary duty is to act in the interests of the bank that appointed him in selling off the company's assets. Unlike administrators, administrative receivers are not required to carry out their functions in such a way as to ensure the survival of the company. The administrative receiver has the power to carry on the business of the company, but only for the purpose of getting a better price for it through being able to sell it as a going concern.

The administrative receiver can apply to the court for permission to dispose of any assets or property subject to a charge free from that charge on the ground that by doing so he will be able to obtain a better price for the company's assets than if the property was disposed of subject to the charge. He must then use the proceeds of sale to discharge those secured debts. He must pay preferential creditors out of the proceeds of sale of the assets comprised in a floating charge *before* accounting to the creditor who holds the floating charge itself. Any surplus is paid back to the company out of which it will have to pay its secured creditors.

Reform

Under the Enterprise Act 2002, the holder of a floating charge will no longer be entitled to appoint an administrative receiver (and so block the making of an administration order). The main exception to this is an existing floating charge (i.e. prior to a prescribed date which has not yet been laid down – because these provisions of the Enterprise Act 2002 are not yet in force). Under the new provisions contained in the Enterprise Act, when directors use the out-of-court route to appointing an administrator they will need to give floating charge holders five days' notice of the proposed appointment. Any charge holders can then elect to appoint their own administrator instead. To do this, all a floating charge holder has to show is that the charge is enforceable and the company is not in liquidation.

COMPULSORY LIQUIDATION

Who can apply?

A creditor who is owed an amount exceeding £750 can apply to the court for a winding up order against the company.

Obtaining the winding up order

The creditor will file a petition at court (usually the High Court) together with a sworn statement. The creditor must also pay the court fee of £150 and a deposit of £500 on account of the OR's fees. The petition must be advertised in the *London Gazette*. If the creditor does not

attend the hearing, the petition is usually dismissed. If the company demonstrates that it has a reasonable defence to the creditor's claim, the court will dismiss the petition and a creditor who anticipates that a company will oppose a petition on this ground should obtain a judgment first of all.

If the company admits that the debt is due and that it has not paid it in spite of demands for payment, the court will usually make a winding up order. The court cannot refuse to make a winding up order solely on the ground that the company has no assets, or that its assets are fully mortgaged, but a winding up order will generally not be made unless it will result in some benefit to the creditor.

Effects of the winding up order

If the court makes a winding up order, it immediately informs the OR. The order is advertised in both the *London Gazette* and a local newspaper for the area where the company's registered office is situated.

On the making of a winding up order, all directors and employees of the company are automatically dismissed. Floating charges crystallize (if they have not already done so).

Can the creditors take enforcement action?

Once a winding up petition has been presented, the court may put a stop to any proceedings or enforcement action against the company. Following the making of the order, no proceedings or action may be commenced or continued against either the company or its property without leave of the court. Any enforcement action taken against the company's assets after the winding up petition has been presented will have no effect if a winding up order is made and, unless the creditor has 'completed' the enforcement action by the date of the presentation of the winding up petition, he will not be allowed to retain the benefit of it. This is wider protection than that provided in bankruptcy, where the relevant date is the date of the actual bankruptcy order.

Disposals of property

Any disposals of company property after the date the petition was presented are void unless the court otherwise orders (again, this is wider protection than that provided in bankruptcy). For example, if the company pays a debt to one of its creditors following the presentation of a winding up petition, the creditor may have to repay it unless the court is satisfied that the payment was made in good faith in order to carry on the company's business. If the creditor behaved unreasonably and the company obtained no benefit from the transaction other than to have satisfied its indebtedness to that creditor, the court is likely to decide that the money should be repaid.

What does the OR do?

Following the making of a winding up order, the OR becomes 'liquidator' of the company unless and until someone else is appointed. The OR's duties include investigating the company's dealings and reporting to the court.

Role of the liquidator

The liquidator (or the OR if no liquidator is appointed) is an agent of the company. The company's assets do not vest in him (in the way that an individual's assets vest in his trustee in bankruptcy) and he deals with them under statutory powers rather than as owner.

The liquidator's functions are:

- to recover and realize the company's assets;
- to distribute the assets or proceeds of sale to the company's creditors (the categories of preferential and ordinary creditors are the same as in bankruptcy); and
- if there is a surplus after the company's debts have been discharged in full, to distribute that surplus to the company's shareholders.

The liquidator has similar powers to those enjoyed by a trustee in bankruptcy.

The final stages

When the liquidator (but not the OR) decides that the winding up of the company's affairs is complete, he must call a final meeting of creditors to present his report on the conduct of the winding up and to request his release from his appointment as liquidator. He then gives notice to the court and to the Registrar of Companies.

In the case of the OR, he must give creditors notice that the winding up is complete and he then gives notice to the Secretary of State for Trade and Industry, and the Registrar of Companies.

The Registrar dissolves the company three months after receiving notice from the liquidator or the OR. The company then ceases to be a legal entity.

POSITION OF DIRECTORS

The general rule is that a company, being a legal entity in its own right, is solely liable for its own debts. However, company directors can also find themselves liable.

Personal guarantees

Many creditors, particularly banks and other lenders, will not give credit to a limited company unless the individuals actually in charge of its affairs, i.e. the directors, personally guarantee the company's liability. In this way, if the

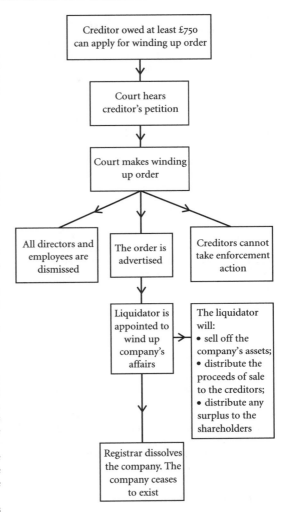

company is unable to pay the debt and there are no assets out of which the creditor can obtain payment, the creditor can enforce the liability against the individual director and his assets (e.g. his house).

Fraudulent trading

If, in the winding up of a company, it appears that the company's business has been carried on with intent to defraud the company's creditors or for any fraudulent purpose, the liquidator (and only the liquidator – not a creditor) can apply to the court for an order that any director or any persons in the company who were a party to the carrying on of the business in this way is liable to make a contribution to the company's assets of such amount as the court thinks fit. This involves proving that the person actually *knew* that the company would be unable to pay its debts. In practice, because of the high burden of proof (beyond reasonable doubt) this is very rare. It is also a criminal offence.

Wrongful trading

The liquidator can apply for an order against a director who knew, or should have concluded, that there was no reasonable prospect of the company avoiding an insolvent liquidation. It is a defence for the director to show that he took every step he ought to have taken to minimize the potential loss to creditors.

This is a subjective test. A director will be judged not only by reference to his actual general knowledge, skill and experience but also the general knowledge, skill and experience that may reasonably be expected of a person carrying out the same functions as those of that director.

Similar to fraudulent trading, the liquidator can apply to the court to make the directors personally liable to contribute towards any debts of the company. However, only a liquidator can pursue this course of action and not a creditor. The standard of proof that needs to be shown is the balance of probabilities.

Directors' disqualification

The court can also disqualify from acting as a director for between two and 15 years any person who is or has been a director of an insolvent company and whose conduct makes him unfit to be concerned in the management of a company. Breach of the order is not only a criminal offence, but the individual may also be made personally liable for any debts incurred by the company while he was acting as a director.

Practical steps to be taken by directors to avoid future problems

There are various measures that directors should consider if, and when, the company gets into financial difficulty.

Doing the following may militate against the possibility of being pursued for either wrongful or fraudulent trading:

- ensure minutes are taken of all board discussions;
- keep up to date with the company's financial position;
- consider carefully the company's ability to pay before entering into contracts for further goods or services;
- consider carefully any actions that could potentially weaken the position of creditors;
- make known their opinion, preferably at a board meeting, if there is the likelihood of insolvency.

If despite a director's best efforts, his views at board level are not accepted, he should therefore consider whether or not to remain a director. A powerless director who carries on in office despite not being able to exert any influence over the board is exposing himself to future problems.

PARTNERSHIP INSOLVENCY

Partnership insolvency involves elements of both individual and corporate insolvency:

- a partnership can be the subject of a CVA and an AO and can be wound up in the same way as a limited company;
- individual partners can arrange IVAs or be made bankrupt.

A winding up petition may be presented against the partnership alone, without presenting bankruptcy petitions against the partners themselves, or there may be petitions presented against both the partnership and one or more individual partners. A partner may arrange an IVA or be made bankrupt without involving the partnership itself.

In the event that the partnership assets are insufficient to pay the partnership creditors, the individual partners are likely to find themselves bankrupt. The shortfall in the partnership debts can then be proved in the individual's bankruptcy, thus ensuring a greater return to partnership creditors and a (possibly) lower return to individual creditors.

Business

54

Choice of Business Structure

A person who is thinking of setting up on his or her own in business, or considering joining a business as a partner, director or even shareholder will face a vast web of rules, regulations and laws. Their most immediate concern will be leaving their current employment and deciding upon the type of business structure to run. There is a wealth of information available to the fledgling businessperson and the main sources of assistance are set out at the end of this chapter.

DIFFERENCES BETWEEN SOLE TRADERS, PARTNERSHIPS, LIMITED LIABILITY PARTNERSHIPS AND LIMITED COMPANIES

The basic choice of business structure is as follows:
- sole trader;
- partnership;
- limited liability partnership; and
- limited company.

There are other less popular choices available and these include, an unlimited company (e.g. a co-operative) or a limited partnership. These are much less common, so we shall focus here on the four main choices listed above.

Ease of creation

The key considerations are speed and cost. Both sole traders and partnerships can simply come into existence although, in the case of a partnership, it is preferable for the partnership to have a Partnership Agreement or Deed (*see* Chapter 55). The business is established from the moment trading commences. A partnership must also fulfil the legal definition of a partnership under the Partnership Act 1890 section 1: 'partnership is the relationship which subsists between persons carrying on a business in common with a view of profit'. This means there must be at least two people carrying on a trade, occupation or profession together, intending to make a profit.

A limited liability partnership (LLP) despite its name is really much more like a limited company than a partnership, e.g. it is recognized in law as being a separate legal entity and so can enter contracts etc. in its own right. It has been possible since 6 April 2001 to set these up where two or more persons wish to carry on a lawful business with a view to profit. A limited liability partnership is registered at Companies House like a company. Furthermore, and again just like a limited company, certain formalities must be complied with, such as keeping accounting records, filing an annual return and accounts at Companies House and maintaining records of changes of membership details.

Limited companies must be formed through application to the Registrar of Companies. This apparent disadvantage can be reduced by the use of an 'off the shelf' or 'shelf' company (i.e. a pre-formed company that can be bought from a company formation agent – *see* Chapter 55). Extra formalities are also required for running the company, such as maintaining the company books (register of directors and directors' interests, secretaries, shareholders and charges), preparing minutes of meetings and filing audited accounts and the annual returns.

Ownership of assets

A sole trader is, as the name suggests, the sole owner of the assets in his business. In a partnership, all the partners own all the assets equally, unless the partnership agreement says otherwise. In a limited liability partnership, ownership of the assets will belong to the limited liability partnership as it is recognized in law as a separate legal entity from its members. Likewise, a limited company too is recognized in law as having its own legal personality and exists independently of its owners (shareholders) and its managers (directors). As a result, the company owns the business assets in its own right.

Management of business

Even where a sole trader engages staff to assist in the business, he has the sole right to make all decisions affecting the business.

Partners share the right to run the business although they may agree to limit the right to one or more of their number; for example, a sleeping partner may agree not to be involved in day-to-day matters.

In a limited liability partnership, the members will be responsible for running the business. They may designate particular functions to particular members and will do so in a document known as a members' agreement. Members, like directors of a limited company, act as agents for the business.

The director, or board of directors, runs the business as the company's agent. An agent is someone who has authority to act on behalf of another. The directors exercise the powers that are given to them in the Articles of Association (*see* page 486). Usually, the board of directors will appoint different people to be responsible for various aspects of the business, for example finance director or sales director. This does not absolve them from responsibility for management of the company as a whole.

Shareholders may take no part in managing the business, unless they are also directors. Shareholders have the right to make decisions on important issues reserved for them by the Companies Act 1985, or the Articles of Association, for example changing the company's name, dismissing and appointing directors, and issuing new shares.

Liability for business debts

The personal assets of a sole trader or partnership, as well as their business assets, are at risk should the business fail or be unable to pay its debts. In other words, creditors of the business can sue a sole trader or partner and go against their personal property and bank accounts: ultimately, the owners may face bankruptcy.

By contrast, because it has a legal personality separate from its shareholders and directors, the limited company alone is liable for its debts. Consequently the shareholders' personal assets will not be jeopardized. Their liability is limited to the value of their investment (i.e. the price they have paid or agreed to pay for their shares). The apparent advantage of this limited liability can be undermined where creditors insist upon the directors personally guaranteeing the company's liabilities. The company's bankers and the landlord of leased premises are likely to require personal guarantees from directors – particularly where the company has not been trading for very long.

Just like a limited company, limited liability partnerships are a separate legal entity from their members. This means that generally any liability for business debts will lie solely against the limited liability partnership and not the individual members. Their liability, should the business become insolvent, will be limited to the amount they have contributed to funding the business by way of capital or loan. This will not stop the members becoming personally liable for debts of the limited liability partnership if they have provided personal guarantees.

Raising money

Both limited companies and limited liability partnerships have a distinct advantage over sole traders and partnerships because they can offer security for finance in the form of 'floating charges'. A floating charge gives a lender continuing security over all assets such as stock and equipment. It is flexible in that the company can continue to buy and sell those assets which are the subject of the floating charge. This would not be possible with a normal mortgage or charge over assets as the lender's consent would be needed for the sale of each item – with ever-changing levels of stock, this would prove an awkward and cumbersome way of going about things.

A sole trader or partnership can offer a fixed charge over assets (such as a mortgage over business premises owned by the business) but cannot then deal freely with those assets.

Venture capitalists (*see* page 489) are less likely to be interested in a sole trader or partnership, due to the risks associated with unlimited liability.

Publicity

Generally, financial and internal affairs of a sole trader and partnership remain private (the exception being accounts and tax returns to the Inland Revenue). By contrast, the limited company is obliged to make information available to the public through the Registrar of Companies. Information accessible by the public includes:

- annual accounts and directors' statements;
- details of company directors and shareholders;
- the Memorandum and Articles of Association;
- annual returns with updated information regarding changes in directorship/shareholders;
- details of mortgages/charges.

Reporting requirements are enforced by Companies House, which has the power to impose criminal sanctions (mainly fines) on defaulting companies or directors.

The price to be paid for limited liability partnerships enjoying limited liability is the public availability of financial statements. The following must be filed at Companies House:

- annual accounts which must include the name and profit share of the highest paid member;
- the name and address of every member; and
- annual return.

Death and retirement

Both limited companies and limited liability partnerships will be relatively unaffected by the death or retirement of their personnel. This is because both are separate legal entities from the directors, shareholders and members. Of course, if a key member of the company or limited liability partnership dies or retires, this may affect the future prosperity of the business.

Although the law treats limited companies and limited liability partnerships like individuals in the sense that they have separate legal personalities, neither can die – they can only be brought to an end by being wound up.

By contrast, if a sole trader dies the business will end. Unless the partnership has a Partnership Agreement that deals with the situation, the death or retirement of one of its partners will mean the business will come to an end. Although the remaining partners could form a new business, they will need to purchase the departing partner's share. Unless the Partnership Agreement fixes the terms of purchase there may be complications agreeing the valuation of business assets such as premises and stock.

Taxation

Sole traders and partners are charged income tax on the profits they make and capital gains tax on gains from the disposal of assets. All profits are taxed whether or not they are retained in the business.

A limited company pays corporation tax on profits and capital gains. The director of a company will pay income tax on his income, as will any other employee. If excess profit is left in the company, rather than paid to the employees, it will be subject to corporation tax.

Although limited liability partnerships resemble limited companies in being recognized as separate legal entities, they are treated quite differently for tax purposes. Limited liability partnerships are not subject to corporation tax. Provided they carry on a trade or profession, they are not in fact taxed on their income or capital gains at all. Instead, the members are taxed on their shares of the limited liability partnership's profits and gains, just as partners in a partnership are currently taxed.

Taxation is dealt with in detail in Chapter 58.

Overview of differences between sole traders, partnerships, limited liability partnerships and limited companies

Limited liability partnership	*Partnership*	*Limited company*	*Sole trader*
Separate legal entity	Not a separate legal entity	Separate legal entity	Not a separate legal entity
Governed by Limited Liability Partnership Act 2000	Governed by Partnership Act 1890	Governed by Companies Act 1985	Not subject to any Act
Incorporated at Companies House	Few formalities. Can be created orally. Must comply with Business Names Act 1985	Incorporated by registration at Companies House	No formalities. Must comply with Business Names Act 1985
Can be formed by 2 or more persons	Can be formed by 2 or more persons	Can be formed by 2 or more persons	Formed by an individual
Tax transparent, i.e. not taxed on its income or gains	Tax transparent, i.e. not taxed on its income or gains	Not tax transparent. Is a taxable entity – liable to pay corporation tax	Not tax transparent. Is a taxable entity – liable to pay income tax and capital gains tax

SOURCES OF ASSISTANCE

Government departments

The Department of Trade and Industry (DTI)provides free publications to help new and existing businesses. Call the General Inquiries line on 0207 215 5000 or visit the website at: www.dti.gov.uk

Training and Enterprise Councils and Local Enterprise Councils

These are based in the local community and provide training and support to the small business.

Business Link

Backed by the DTI, Business Link is networked across the country and has small business advisers to assist with problems and opportunities and to provide support.
Tel: 0845 600 9006 or visit the Business Link website at: www.businesslink.org

Chambers of Commerce

Members of Chambers of Commerce are entitled to receive the range of business support services with particular emphasis in developing opportunities in the UK and abroad.

Trade associations and business federations

There are numerous organizations formed to cover a particular market sector (e.g. the trade association for newsagents is the National Federation of Retail Newsagents) or to represent small businesses in general. Their function is to provide information and support services and to promote the interests of their members.

Business professionals

Many accountants, solicitors and banks provide advice on business start up. Solicitors who are members of the 'Lawyers for Business' scheme provide at least half an hour's free legal advice to businesses on issues connected with setting up and running a business. The scheme offers various free publications and may be contacted by telephone on 020 7316 5521.

Rural development

For businesses in rural areas, the three main sources of advice, information and rural grants are the Countryside Agency (www.countryside.gov.uk; Tel: 01242 521381), the South-East England Development Agency (SEEDA) (www.seeda.co.uk; Tel: 01483 484 200) and the Rural Development Service of the Department for Environment, Food and Rural Affairs (www.defra.gov.uk; Tel: 08459 335577).

55

Forming the Business

Once the businessperson has decided which type of business structure to opt for, he or she will wish to get the business 'on its feet'. This chapter deals with the initial issues connected with establishing the business.

LEGAL FORMALITIES

Sole trader

As already mentioned, there are no forms to fill in, people to notify or legal formalities connected with starting business as a sole trader. The Inland Revenue and Customs and Excise must be informed.

Partnership Agreement

The number of partners in a partnership is now unlimited. The restriction that used to limit the number to no more than 20 has now been abolished.

It is advisable for a partnership to have a written Partnership Agreement to regulate relations between the partners and reduce the risk of dispute. Where the Partnership Agreement is silent on a particular point, the provisions of the Partnership Act 1890 will apply. The Act has its limitations: for example, it treats partners equally and does not enable a partner to be expelled or retire from the partnership without the business being brought to an end. It is preferable for the partnership agreement to include terms covering the following points:

- names of partners and their duties;
- name of firm and main trading activities;
- start date of partnership and how long it will last (i.e. will it be for a fixed period of time or will it last indefinitely);
- ownership of the assets used in the business;
- amount of money each partner invests in the firm;
- sharing of profits and losses;
- frequency and amount of drawings of profits and salaries;

- allocating the authority to make decisions between the partners;
- what happens when a partner wants to retire or leave;
- what happens when a partner dies or is unwell;
- expelling a partner from the business and buying the outgoing partner's share in the firm;
- restrictions on partners from competing or poaching clients or staff once they have left the business.

CREATING A LIMITED COMPANY FROM SCRATCH

A minimum of two people will be needed to start a limited company. The businessperson must decide who will be the directors (managers) and who will be the initial investors in the company (shareholders). A company secretary must be appointed and if there is only one director, he cannot also be the company secretary.

To form a limited company, four documents must be sent to the Registrar of Companies at Companies House in Cardiff, together with a fee (currently £20). The documents are:

1 *Form 10* – stating the proposed registered office address and details of first directors and company secretary. The registered office need not be where the company carries on business but it must be an address at which someone can 'find' the company should, for example, a creditor wish to serve court documents on it. The registered office is often the address of the company's accountant or solicitor. The company books (*see* 'Ease of creation', page 481) must be kept at the registered office.

2 *Form 12* – this is a sworn declaration by the director, company secretary or solicitor involved in forming the company that all legal formalities have been complied with.

3 *Memorandum of Association* – this governs the external workings of the company and states the name of the

company, the country where the registered office is situated, the fact that the shareholders' liability is limited, the amount of authorized share capital (maximum number of shares that can be issued and basic value of each share) and the names of the first shareholders. It will also set out the purposes of the company and what it is allowed to do – known as the 'objects clause'. Standard wording in many precedent Memoranda of Association refer to the company as a 'general commercial company'. This clause ensures the company can diversify its business without encountering restrictions on what it can do (*see 'Ultra vires acts of a limited company'*, page 507).

4 *Articles of Association* – these govern the internal workings of the company and form a contract between the company and its shareholders. The Articles will usually deal with procedure for transfer and allotment of shares, the powers of directors and conduct at meetings. A standard set of Articles is issued by the Department of Trade and Industry (DTI) and is called 'Table A'. Table A will be adopted as the company's Articles, unless the company changes or restricts Table A in any way.

Once Companies House has approved documents 1–4 above it will bring the limited company into existence and issue a Certificate of Incorporation. Most companies then hold a meeting of directors to deal with matters such as opening a company bank account, ordering stationery, appointing an accountant and allotting shares.

Shelf companies

To save time and expense, a businessperson can buy a pre-incorporated company from a company formation agent. The cost is between £80 and £200. The shelf company will not have been trading but would have been formed in anticipation of someone wanting to buy it.

Employees of the company formation agent will have been named as first directors and members of the company. The directors will resign and appoint the buyers as directors at a board meeting. The members will transfer the shares to the buyers by signing Stock Transfer Forms.

The company's name and registered office can be changed by its new owners as it may not be suitable. Although the Memorandum and Articles of Association will be fairly standard, any changes can be effected with the approval of shareholders.

Checklist of requirements common to most types of business

1 *Insurance* – (*see* pages 490, 503).
2 *Environmental* – businesses involved in producing, disposing or recycling waste may be regulated by the Environmental Protection Act 1990 or the Waste Management Licensing Regulations.
3 *Licences* – depending upon the type of business activity, a licence may be required from:
  (**a**) local authority licensing department – for pet shops and pet boarding kennels, public entertainment venues, taxi companies, residential and care homes;
  (**b**) local authority environmental health department – for hotels, restaurants, hairdressers and body piercers;
  (**c**) magistrates – liquor licence for public houses, shops, clubs, restaurants and hotels;
  (**d**) Office of Fair Trading – for moneylenders, debt collectors and hiring, leasing or rental of goods;
  (**e**) Information Commissioner – any business processing (i.e. using or recording) data about an individual may need to be registered with the Commissioner under the Data Protection Act 1998 at a cost of £35.
4 *Tax, National Insurance and VAT* – the business will need to register with the Inland Revenue for tax and National Insurance purposes. If VAT is payable, then Customs & Excise will need to be informed (see Chapter 58):
5 *Health and safety* – for health and safety purposes, the business may need to register with the Health & Safety Executive or the local authority (*see* page 502).

Choice of business name

A businessperson will want to choose a name for his or her business that portrays an accurate image of the business and its activities. Some names cannot be used, due to legal restrictions on the use of certain names or because another business has a prior claim to the name. It is important to establish this before the business is named. Changing the name at a later date may affect trade and will certainly result in wasted stationery and costs.

Availability of name

Limited companies:
1 a company name must end in 'Limited' or 'Ltd';
2 Companies House will refuse to register the name if:
  (**a**) it is the *same* as that of an existing company; or
  (**b**) its use would constitute a criminal offence (e.g. a name inciting racial hatred); or
  (**c**) it is offensive (e.g. a sexually explicit name);
3 Another limited company may object to a new name appearing in the Companies' Index within 12 months if that new name is too *similar* to its own.

Restricted names – all business types

The use of certain 'sensitive' words in a business name will require the approval of the Secretary of State. Words are usually sensitive if they imply a certain prestige or eminence. For example, names suggesting a connection with HM government, the royal family, local authorities or international dealings (e.g. European Pig Traders Ltd) are sensitive.

If a new business starts operating under the same or similar name to another established business, the use of the name by the new business may be subject to a 'passing off' action in the courts. The court will assess whether the public are being confused and misled by the use of the name and if so the new business will be prevented from trading under the name. Another consideration to bear in mind when choosing a name is whether the business name or logo has been registered as a trademark by another business (*see* Chapter 61).

Name check: summary of sources to check

- Companies Index at Companies House;
- Trade and Service Mark Registers at the Patents Office, Cardiff;
- Register of business names maintained by London Chamber of Commerce & Industry;
- trade journals;
- *Yellow Pages*/phone directories.

Business stationery

By law, a firm's stationery must contain certain information. With the growth of e-business, it is important to note that the same rules apply to e-mail. There are different requirements depending upon the type of business.

Sole trader

The name of the owner and the business address must be stated on business letters, written orders, invoices, receipts and demands for payment. The owner's name and address must also be displayed at any business premises.

Partnership

The name of each partner and the business address must appear on business letters, written orders, invoices, receipts and demands for payment. For a partnership of over 20 partners, the stationery need not state all the partners' names but it must refer to the fact that a list of partners is available for inspection at the business premises.

Limited liability partnership

The name of a limited liability partnership must end with LLP, e.g. Sunshine Products LLP. A limited liability partnership cannot use the same name or a similar name to one that is already in use and registered at Companies House. In addition, the name must be clearly affixed on the outside of all premises where it trades and also appear, together with its address, place of registration and regis-

tered number on all business letters, notices, orders, cheques, bills and invoices.

Limited company

The required information on business letters and order forms is set out in the example below. Directors' names do not need to be disclosed but if they are, all names must be included. A limited company may operate under a business or trading name, in which case the documents must include the company name and an address in the UK for service of documents on the company.

Other documents including notices and publications must state the full company name. The business name must also be displayed outside any business premises and at the registered office.

With all three types of business, the VAT registration number must be stated on invoices if the business is VAT registered.

(*at top of page*)

Sunshine Products

2 Station Yard
Smithton
Smithshire
SM2 1RY

(*at bottom of page*)

Sunshine Products (UK) Ltd
Registered Office: 66 Main Road, Smithton, Smithshire, SM2 1DU

Registered in England & Wales
Company Number 521233334

Raising finance

Money to finance a business can basically come from four different sources:

- family/friends;
- the owner's own savings;
- banks; or
- venture capitalists/business angels.

Before applying for money, the businessperson must decide:

- what the finance is needed for (i.e. long-term funding to buy business premises or short-term to provide working capital);
- how much is required;
- the practical and financial implications of the type of funding sought (i.e. the cost of making repayments or providing security).

Business plan

Most lending institutions will want to see a business plan before deciding whether, and to what extent, they will invest in the business. The plan should outline a strategy and objectives for the particular business. It should include:

1 *A summary of what the businessperson is proposing to do* – a short introduction to tempt the lender to read on, including a list of objectives, how much finance is needed and a description of the business.
2 *Background about the business* – the type of business being planned and personal details about the applicant, including any previous business experience he might have.
3 *Information about markets/products/services* – what sector of the public makes up the anticipated client base and where the products will be sold; whether there is a demand for the suggested products/services, who the competitors are and what their comparative strengths and weaknesses are.
4 *People* – details of other people involved in the business, for example employees and proposed suppliers.
5 *Business premises and equipment* – what is required/proposed.
6 *Finance and cash flow* – prices, budget, anticipated sales and pre-tax profits, and monthly cash flow forecasts.

Loans from financial institutions

If satisfied that a business can afford to repay both capital and interest, a financial institution will lend the business money for a fixed period of time. The period of the loan will depend upon the amount borrowed and the purpose of the loan.

Repayment of the loan will typically be in periodic (monthly or quarterly) instalments. The lender will have calculated the level of repayment required to ensure the full loan plus interest is paid within the term agreed. More unusually, some loans provide for repayment upon the happening of a particular event, for example the sale of particular property. These loans will still provide a long stop date for repayment.

The lender will charge interest on the loan at a fixed rate or by reference to percentage points above the bank's base rate (often shown as, e.g., 2.5 per cent/b.r. or 2.5 per cent above bank's base rate from time to time). It is essential that you read the small print, as often bank conditions will allow the bank to charge penalty interest (i.e. at a higher rate than that which was originally agreed) if the business fails to keep up with repayments.

The Banking Code of Practice sets out the standards of service that bank and building society customers are entitled to receive. If disputes between a lender and a business cannot be resolved internally, then the matter can be referred to the Financial Ombudsman Service for investigation.

Loans from other sources

The Small Business Service (SBS) Small Firms Loan Guarantee Scheme

Changes to the government Loan Guarantee scheme came into effect on 1 April 2003. For a business that is unable to get conventional finance, this scheme guarantees loans from banks and other lenders. Loans are available for periods of between 2 and 10 years on sums from £5,000 to £100,000 (£250,000 if the business has been trading for over 2 years). The SBS guarantees 75 per cent of the loan and in return the borrower pays the SBS 2 per cent per year on the outstanding amount of the loan. To qualify, the company must not have an annual turnover greater than £3 million (£5 million if the company is a manufacturing company). For further details, contact Business Link 0845 600 9006.

The Business Start-up Scheme

Through local Training and Enterprise Councils, loans are offered to unemployed people thinking about setting up in business.

The Prince's Youth Business Trust

The Trust provides grants and low interest loans to young people (aged 18–29) unable to raise money to start a business.

Overdrafts

Although easy to set up and flexible in terms of the amount of money that can be borrowed, the disadvantage is that an overdraft is repayable 'on demand' – this enables the bank to 'pull the plug' at any time.

The bank will negotiate overdraft limits with the business. If drawings exceed the overdraft limit without the bank manager's consent, the bank will charge the business or call in the overdraft.

Personal guarantees

Where a lender requires security for business borrowings, it may demand a personal guarantee. This frequently occurs where a bank is lending to a small limited company – the lender will require the directors to guarantee personally the borrowings of the limited company. The guarantee in turn may be secured against the directors' own homes by a mortgage (*see* below). The directors will have a strong personal interest in seeing the business borrowings repaid, as failure to do so will result in the bank calling in the guarantee.

In view of the personal risk involved, directors should try to persuade the bank to accept alternative security, i.e. insurance policies or charges on business premises.

Mortgages/debentures

In Chapter 54 we contrasted fixed and floating charges – the latter only being available to limited companies. A lender may wish to secure any borrowings by a fixed charge over assets such as premises or a floating charge over fluctuating assets, i.e. stock or book debts. Failure to repay the borrowings will result in the bank taking possession and selling the assets charged.

Venture capitalists and business angels

Where large outside investment is required (say, £200,000 or more) this may be sought from a venture capitalist organization. Traditional venture capitalists will only invest in companies with a proven track record and the potential for rapid growth. The organization will aim to sell its investment and make a large gain when the company's shares are listed on the London Stock Exchange.

The venture capitalists will require a substantial shareholding in the company and usually take a seat on the board of directors, for which they will require a fee. More details can be obtained from the British Venture Capital Association (BVCA), 3 Clements Inn, London WC2A 2AZ Tel: 020 7025 2950; website: www.bvca.co.uk

Of more interest to smaller businesses is sourcing finance from private individuals known as 'business angels'. This is how a number of well-known businesses, such as The Body Shop, got started. Business angels tend to be people with business backgrounds willing to invest time, money and expertise into a new or growing company in return for shares in the company. A business angel will often group with others to form an investment syndicate where large amounts of money are involved. They can be reached through organizations such as the National Business Angel Network (NBAN), Third Floor 40–42 Cannon Street, London EC4N 6JJ. Tel: 020 7329 2929. Website: www.nationalbusangels.co.uk.

The Enterprise Investment Scheme (EIS) is a scheme to encourage business angels by a series of tax incentives. Individuals may invest up to a total of £150,000 per tax year in qualifying companies and receive tax relief at the lower rate, currently 20 per cent, on the cost of qualifying investment. The investment is exempt from capital gains tax when sold provided the investment is held for five years (for shares issued after 5 April 2000, the period is three years). Should the business fail and the investor suffer a loss, loss relief is available against other taxable income or capital gains, at the investor's highest rate of tax – currently 40 per cent for a higher rate taxpayer.

For other sources of help try contacting your local government office or Business Link (*see* page 484).

56

Business Premises

WORKING FROM HOME

Technological advances, such as fax, e-mail and the internet, are revolutionizing the way that we work. Working from home has become a realistic alternative to commuting into an office.

What are the implications of choosing to work from home?

Planning

Under the planning laws, a domestic property should be used for residential purposes only. Planning permission is usually required to change the use of a property, for example from residential use to business use. If you are conducting your business from home, you may not be in breach of the planning legislation particularly where you are just using a single room, because this would not be regarded as a material change of use. It is however sensible to keep a low profile in any case. It is particularly important not to upset your neighbours because many local authority investigations start from a neighbour's complaint. Failure to be discreet may alert the local authority (who enforce the planning laws) and prompt an investigation into whether your property's use has been changed to a mixed residential and business use.

If the local authority decide that you have changed the use of your property, then they can take enforcement action. Their powers include serving an enforcement notice to require you to stop carrying on the business from your home.

The local authority will not be concerned with minor or occasional business use. An example of minor use, which will not fall foul of the planning laws, includes a hairdresser cutting hair in the front room of her home. Equally, using a bedroom as an office will not breach the planning regulations – bear in mind that the crucial issue is whether the business use has transformed the overall character of the property. Factors that will be relevant include whether the rooms can still be used for domestic purposes and whether the business is a nuisance to neighbours because of excessive traffic noise, smells, etc.

Restrictive covenants

Examine your title deeds and/or lease to check that your property is not subject to any restrictions either prohibiting you altogether from carrying on a business or excluding certain types of business from being carried out.

If you have a mortgage, your title deeds will usually be stored with your lender or your conveyancing solicitors may have a copy of the deeds. If the title to the property is registered, the local land registry will hold information about the property, including whether there are any restrictive covenants.

Mortgages

Ask your lender whether there is a clause in the mortgage deed forbidding you from running a business at home.

Insurance

Check with your insurers that by working from home you are not in breach of either your buildings or contents insurance policy conditions.

Business rates

Business rates, as opposed to council tax which is payable on domestic properties, will not normally be due unless the business use materially detracts from the domestic use. An example of this is where part of the property is used as a school or a dentists' practice. This is similar to the position under the planning legislation. Factors that will be relevant include the frequency of use and whether or not the particular room can still be used for domestic purposes, for example, if you use a room as a study and also allow your children to use the room to do their homework then business rates will probably not be due.

Capital gains tax

If you sell your own home at a profit then you are normally exempt from having to pay any capital gains tax (CGT). However, if you use part of your home exclusively for business purposes then you may be liable to pay CGT, which will be assessed on any gain on the business proportion of the house. In other words, if one or more rooms are used entirely for work, then there will be CGT to pay on a proportion of the gain on any sale. The proportion of the property used solely for the business will have to be agreed with the tax inspector. This is often calculated by reference to the number of rooms used or their floor area.

This can be avoided if you can show that the rooms in question were not used solely for business purposes and so form an integral part of the house. If you are in any doubt, check the position with your accountant.

SEARCHING FOR BUSINESS PREMISES

You are most likely to find business premises to buy or rent in the local newspaper, or through commercial estate agents. The following factors should be considered.

Space

What are my present requirements and is there additional room for expansion if the business takes off?

Location

Although still a factor, particularly if your business is retail, the growth of e-business on the internet means that location may not be as crucial as it once was. Bear in mind the general rule that the better the location the higher the purchase price or rent will be.

Facilities and services

Are there adequate fixtures and fittings, partitions, computers, telephones, electrical points, heating, lighting and alarms? If not, then the additional cost of upgrading the facilities must be taken into account.

Cost

As well as the purchase price or the rent, there are other significant costs that should be considered. These include surveyor's fees, lender's fees, solicitor's costs, stamp duty, removal expenses, land registry fees and contractors' costs if works need to be carried out. There will also be everyday expenditure on amenities such as heating, lighting, telephone and insurance. It is essential to take these extra costs into account before you commit yourself to taking on business premises.

Planning

It is vital that you know the permitted planning use of the premises to avoid falling foul of planning regulations. Your solicitor will investigate this issue on your behalf if you go through with the purchase or lease but you will avoid wasting time and money by making your own enquiries at an early stage. The agent or seller/landlord should be able to tell you the current planning use of the premises. This information is also held on the planning register at the planning department of your local authority. The planning register is a document of public record and the local planning authorities are usually happy to assist with any enquiries. Clearly, if a change of use is required to run the business from the premises, then this needs to be taken into account both in terms of cost and timing, as obtaining planning permission may cause some delay.

Do you buy or rent?

The answer to this question usually comes down to how much you can afford. Purchasing a freehold property will be more expensive than renting and is unlikely to be within the grasp of a new business.

Buying freehold premises

Generally, if you buy a freehold property you will own the land for ever until you sell or otherwise dispose of it. As the owner, you will also have wide powers to use the property and the land on which it stands as you see fit (see Housing, Chapters 15–18). This flexibility of use means that buying the freehold is more desirable than leasing but the cost is often considerably more. You should also consider the following factors.

1 If the land is registered, the freehold title (i.e. proof of who owns the land) will be registered at the Land Registry. If the land is unregistered, the title will be set out in a series of documents, some of which will be decades old and phrased in antiquated legal language. Conveyancing can be a complicated exercise,

particularly in the case of unregistered land, and it is advisable to instruct a solicitor to act on your behalf in the purchase. Solicitors' costs are often based on a percentage of the purchase price, plus VAT. Other expenses, or 'disbursements', which you will have to pay whether or not a solicitor acts for you, will include the local authority search fee, Land Registry fees and stamp duty (a government tax). The amount of stamp duty payable depends on the purchase price of the property. The rates of duty currently payable are: 1 per cent of the purchase price between £60,001 and £250,000, 3 per cent of the purchase price between £250,001 and £500,000 and 4 per cent of the purchase price over £500,000. There is no stamp duty payable where the purchase price is £60,000 or less.

2 Under English law, a seller is not obliged to disclose any structural defects in the property he is selling. You will need to instruct a surveyor to carry out a full structural survey of the premises before you commit yourself to the purchase. You should insist that any problems revealed by the survey should be put right or negotiate a reduction in the purchase price to balance the extra expense of carrying out the remedial work yourself. The cost of instructing a surveyor will not be cheap, but if there are any defects in the property you may save money in the long run.

3 A freehold owner does not necessarily have unlimited rights to use the property as he pleases. Apart from planning restrictions, there may be other limitations or 'covenants' affecting how your property can be used. These covenants will be recorded on the deeds of title to the property. If any covenants interfere with your ability to use the property for the intended purpose then your solicitor should bring these matters to your attention as quickly as possible. Your solicitor should also check that the intended use of the premises complies with planning regulations and that you have adequate rights of access.

4 Any structural alterations are likely to require building regulation approval from the local authority. If you are not sure whether you need local authority approval you could make enquiries with the building regulation department at your local authority or speak to your surveyor, preferably before they have carried out the survey.

5 Finally, do not forget to insure the building and its contents once you are the owner. Normally the surveyor in his survey report will recommend a suitable amount to insure the property against loss or damage, i.e. the cost of rebuilding the property if damaged or destroyed by fire.

Buying commonhold premises

Under the Commonhold and Leasehold Reform Act 2002 that is likely to be introduced in December 2003, it is going to be possible to buy commonhold premises.

Commonhold is a new system of owning freehold land where there are interdependent properties, e.g. shops, offices, etc. The idea is that commonhold will avoid the need to use a lease and so reduce the problems associated with leasehold properties, i.e. service charge disputes, leases that need renewing on their expiry, poorly drawn-up leases, etc. The principle is that each property in the development will be called a 'unit' and each unit owner will own the freehold of their respective unit. The freehold interest in the common parts of the development, e.g. car park, parts of the structure or service media (pipes, wires, cables) etc., will then be vested in a 'commonhold association' of which the unit owners will be members. Unit owners will therefore have two interests. First, they will own the freehold of their unit. Second, they will become members of the commonhold association that owns and maintains the common parts. The commonhold association will be a private company limited by guarantee and registered at Companies House. The association will be responsible for repairing and maintaining the common parts and will be entitled to levy a service charge on the unit owners called 'common assessment'. This will be a percentage of the association's expenses. Until the new system of commonhold ownership develops, it is impossible to know whether it will be preferable to owning leasehold premises and also how much more expensive it is likely to be.

Renting business premises

For many businesses, particularly new or small businesses, buying a freehold property will be too expensive. The alternative is to rent premises. Renting has other advantages quite apart from cost. The main plus point is flexibility, in so far as the business will be free to move to alternative premises at the end of the lease if it requires more space.

A lease is essentially a contract between two parties – the landlord and the tenant. The tenant will have the use of the property for a fixed period of time and will normally have to pay rent to the landlord.

There is no reason why renting premises should be problematic provided the following simple guidelines are adhered to.

1 You should resist the temptation to move in without entering into a written lease. Although it is possible to create a business tenancy by verbal agreement, they are generally less regulated. This means there is less scope for the courts being able to imply certain terms into the agreement, for example who is responsible for carrying out repairs.

2 Be wary of agreeing to accept a 'licence' or a 'tenancy at will' instead of a lease. A licence will exist where the tenant does not have exclusive possession, i.e. the landlord can gain access at any time. A tenancy at will is created where the landlord either by express

agreement or implication has the right to end the agreement at any time. In both cases the occupier will have little or no protection from eviction. This can be disastrous, particularly where a business is starting to take off or where money has already been spent on the premises. (*See also* page 219.)

3 Having said that, genuine licences can be particularly suitable for new businesses. Serviced offices are a typical example of a situation where a licence may be suitable. This is where office space and other facilities, such as the reception, are shared with other businesses. Often there will be support services, such as equipment, receptionists and interview rooms, which can be made available on a flexible basis according to need. The advantage of a licence arrangement in this context is the flexibility it affords: very often the minimum of formalities is required and occupation can be taken up immediately. The period of notice that must be given before quitting the premises is also normally short, often as little as a month, so if things go wrong payments can be quickly ended.

4 Before you sign the lease it should be checked by a solicitor specializing in landlord and tenant matters. Leases can be complex documents and therefore need careful scrutiny. All the clauses should be explained to you before the lease is signed. It is not unusual for the landlord or his/her agent to ask the tenant to pay their legal fees. Unless you agree to this, there is no legal obligation to pay. If you do agree, then it is sensible to specify a maximum amount that you will contribute towards the fees. VAT will also normally be added to this amount.

Other considerations

Duration

Think very carefully about how long you wish to occupy the premises. Although a longer term may seem more attractive, bear in mind that you will be potentially liable to pay the rent and comply with the other obligations in the lease for the whole of that period. This will be a financial burden if you are unable to find someone to take over the lease. It may also restrict the expansion of your business if you are tied to premises that are unsuitable. If in doubt, it is safer to opt for a shorter period or to try to negotiate what is known as a 'break clause'. A 'break clause' in a lease provides a means of ending a lease earlier than the fixed term.

'The tenant shall be entitled to terminate this lease in 3 years' time from the date of this agreement (the 'break date') by giving not less than 6 months' prior written notice and provided prior to the giving of notice and up to the break date the tenant has materially observed and performed the covenants contained in the lease.'

However, avoid agreeing to break clauses that are subject to conditions, such as the one above, i.e. that the clause cannot be exercised if the tenant is in breach of any of the conditions in the lease. Even if there has been a minor breach by the tenant he will not be able to exercise the option.

Rent

Agree the amount of rent that is to be paid, how it is to be paid and when. The rent will be payable in arrears unless the lease states otherwise. The landlord is likely to require rent in advance together with a deposit and/or guarantor. A new tenant starting in business should try to negotiate with the landlord to pay the rent in arrears. You should also clarify whether the lease is going to contain upward-only rent review clauses, which allow the landlord to increase the rent periodically. Rent review clauses can be complex and your solicitor should explain how they are to operate and what steps you should take when a rent review is imminent. Essentially, the review is likely to involve instructing a commercial valuer to act on your behalf in the negotiations on the new rent with the landlord and his/her representatives.

Also watch out for the landlord electing to charge VAT on the rent, which he/she is entitled to do. If you are not VAT registered then this may cause significant cash flow problems, as the VAT paid on the rent cannot be claimed back.

Stamp duty

Stamp duty is also payable on a lease. Where a landlord has an option to charge VAT on the rent but has chosen not to do so, stamp duty will still be based on the presumption that VAT has been added to the average rent. However, this will not apply where there is a specific agreement in the lease that the option to charge VAT will not be exercised by the landlord.

From 1 December 2003, stamp duty is charged at the rate of 1 per cent on all rents payable under the lease (although future rents will be discounted by 3.5 per cent). There is a threshold figure (below which no stamp duty is paid) of £150,000 for non-residential property (£60,000 for residential property).

Repairs

You must clarify who will be responsible for internal and external repairs of the premises. If the tenant will be responsible for repairs, a surveyor should carry out a full structural survey before the lease is signed. You will then be fully aware of what repair work needs to be done and the likely cost. In general, if the lease is for less than five years it is more likely that the landlord will be responsible for all repairs.

Even if the landlord agrees to be responsible for repairs, the tenant may still have to make a contribution towards the cost if the lease contains a service charge clause. A service charge is a payment that tenants are required to make towards the cost of repairing and maintaining the premises. If the lease does contain a service charge clause then again it will be sensible to have the premises surveyed before signing. There is no statutory control over how much a landlord can charge under a service charge contained in a business lease. The amount that can be charged will be governed solely by the wording used in the service charge clause in the lease. It is therefore sensible to try to fix the proportion of the expenses for which you will be responsible, e.g. by reference to the floor area of your building expressed as a percentage of the overall floor area of the premises, and to define very carefully what items will be covered by the service charge.

User

Finally, you will need to obtain the landlord's agreement to your intended use of the premises and any alterations to the property you intend to carry out. For maximum flexibility as a tenant you should try and negotiate as wide a user clause as possible. As well as allowing you to diversify your business it may make the lease easier to dispose of in the future. As far as alterations are concerned, these should be agreed with the landlord right from the outset. Most leases will impose fairly tight restrictions on the alterations that are allowed, particularly those of a structural nature, and these will normally require the consent of the landlord.

WHAT IS THE EFFECT OF THE LANDLORD AND TENANT ACT 1954?

Unless the business lease you are proposing to enter into is within one of the limited exceptions set out below, it is highly likely that your new lease will be affected by the Landlord and Tenant Act 1954. This Act applies to virtually all commercial leases, whatever the type of premises being used, provided there is a business use. Even where premises have a mixed residential and business use, for example a flat above a shop, the Act will apply. It is immaterial whether the agreement is written or verbal.

The main aim of the Act is to provide security for business tenants by allowing them to stay on in their premises even though on paper the lease has come to an end. The only way a landlord will be able to avoid renewing the tenant's lease is by proving one or more of the seven grounds set out in the Act. In that case the landlord may have to pay compensation to the tenant.

Exceptions

The 1954 Act will not apply to a licence, tenancy at will or short, fixed-term tenancies.

A licence

Under a licence, you occupy someone else's property but do not have the right to keep the owner out. An example of a licence arrangement is where you share a space within a building with other businesses, such as a shop within a shop. It is not always easy to tell whether an agreement is a lease or a licence and the courts have struggled over the years to produce a clear definition of the difference. Landlords sometimes attempt to dress up a lease as a licence in order to deny the tenant the protection of the 1954 Act.

A tenancy at will

A tenancy at will is basically a right to occupy property wholly at the landlord's will. There must be no suggestion of any right to stay for a particular period because if it is a tenancy at will, the landlord can ask the tenant to leave at any time. It will therefore be fatal if the landlord asks for the rent to be paid in advance, because this will create the impression of a periodic lease, i.e. from week to week, month to month, etc. As there is no right to occupy the premises for any defined period of time, a tenancy at will is unlikely to be attractive to a tenant, except perhaps for a short period of time, i.e. a short-term occupation just before the lease is signed.

Short, fixed-term tenancies

The Act will not apply to a tenancy with a fixed term of up to six months, provided there is no condition allowing the term to be extended or renewed. The period must be fixed, i.e. three months, four months, etc. A tenancy that is renewed every week or month (i.e. a periodic tenancy) will not be a short, fixed-term tenancy. When the fixed term runs out the landlord can grant one more fixed term of six months or less. Only two fixed terms of a maximum of six months each can be granted because, once a tenant has been in occupation for more than twelve months under a series of fixed-term tenancies, he/she will enjoy the protection of the 1954 Act.

If a prospective tenant wants to move in before the lease is signed because, for example, negotiations over the lease are still taking place, then it will be safe for the landlord to give the tenant a fixed term of less than six months – this is preferable to granting a licence and getting into an argument about whether it is in fact a lease. From the tenant's point of view, the short, fixed term arrangement will give him the opportunity to start trading and settle in the premises but he may be in a weaker position when it comes to negotiating the terms of the lease. If the landlord tries to impose onerous terms in the lease, the tenant will be faced with the choice of either having to accept these or move out when the fixed term expires.

Contracting out

A landlord and tenant can both agree that the Act should not apply to their business lease. This is called 'contracting out of the Act'. This is only allowed where both parties agree to accept this arrangement and it will only apply to a written, fixed-term lease. The court's approval of the arrangement is required – before the lease takes effect – although this is usually granted. Both parties must apply jointly to the county court on a Part 8 claim form (form N208). The court fee is currently (1 April 2003) £130. If a solicitor is not involved, the court will often want the parties to attend a hearing before granting the exemption to ensure that the tenant understands the position. It will usually be possible to obtain the appropriate order to contract out of the Act within four weeks. Contracting out of the Act is normally only suitable where the term of the lease is to be relatively short. As a tenant will be losing the protection of the Act he/she should generally insist on paying a lower rent and ensure that the repairing obligations are minimal.

If one of the above exceptions applies then you will be unprotected by the 1954 Act. This will mean if you are occupying business premises the owner can ask you to leave either by giving you notice, or on the expiry of the agreement. You will have no automatic right to stay on and demand a new agreement from the owner.

Reform of contracting out

The time, inconvenience and expense involved in obtaining a court order where the parties to a lease wish to exclude security of tenure have long been a source of criticism. In June 2002, the government published proposals to reform the contracting-out provisions of the Landlord and Tenant Act 1954. The intention is to scrap the procedure whereby a joint application has to be made to a court to approve the contracting out. Instead, the normal procedure will be that, at least 14 days before the grant of the lease, the landlord will have to serve a 'health warning' notice on the tenant explaining what rights are to be excluded and urging the tenant to take appropriate legal advice.

The government proposes that the 'health warning' will read as follows:

IMPORTANT NOTICE

You are being offered a lease without security of tenure. Do not agree to it unless you have read this message carefully and discussed it with a professional adviser

Business tenants normally have security of tenure – the right to stay in their business premises when the lease ends.

If you sign the lease you will be giving up important legal rights.

- You will have **no right** to stay in the premises when the lease ends.
- Unless the landlord chooses to offer you another lease, you will need to leave the premises.
- You will be unable to claim compensation for the loss of your business premises, unless the lease specifically gives you this right.
- If the landlord offers you another lease, you will have no right to ask the court to fix the rent.

It is therefore important to get professional advice – from a qualified surveyor, lawyer or accountant – before agreeing to give up these rights.

If you want to ensure that you can stay in the same business premises when the initial lease ends, you should consult your adviser about another form of lease that does not exclude the protection of the Landlord and Tenant Act 1954.

However, there will also be a speedy procedure to use if notice cannot be served 14 days in advance. In that situation, the landlord must serve notice on the tenant before the lease comes into effect, and the tenant will then have to make a statutory declaration that he has received the notice and accepts the consequences of the lease being excluded from the Landlord and Tenant Act 1954. Both the notice and the statutory declaration must then be referred to in the lease. It is anticipated that the changes (and other proposed reforms referred to below) will not come into effect before summer 2004. The present system will stay in place until that time.

Understanding how the 1954 Act works

If you are a tenant who is happy with your business premises then you will be in no hurry to move. The protection afforded by the 1954 Act means that this is perfectly possible to achieve. This is because the main purpose of the Act is to allow a tenant occupying business premises to stay on in those premises and obtain a new lease from the landlord. However, where the landlord wants the tenant to leave, the tenant will have to take certain procedural steps in order to assert his right to stay. The procedure can be complex and there are strict time limits to follow. It is advisable to seek legal advice from a solicitor specializing in landlord and tenant law to ensure that your protection under the Act is not lost.

We will examine some common situations and note whether the Act applies and what steps should be taken by a landlord or tenant to preserve their rights under the Act.

1 *There is either a written lease which has expired or a verbal agreement which has expired under which the*

tenant was, for example, paying rent monthly to the landlord: provided the tenant is occupying the premises to carry out his business the Act will apply. It makes no difference whether the lease is in writing or not. If the parties do nothing the lease continues automatically. It does not matter that the written lease has expired because under the Act it just continues on exactly the same terms. (In the absence of a rent review clause coming into effect on the last day of the lease or the tenant's consent.) The landlord cannot therefore suddenly increase the rent. Likewise the tenant must continue to pay the same amount of rent as he/she has been paying.

2 *The tenant has decided, during the fixed term of the lease, that he does not want to continue his business at the premises when his written lease eventually expires:* as long as the tenant has completely moved out of the premises by the end of the lease then he does not have to give the landlord any notice of his intention to leave. The lease will come to an end on its expiry date and will not be automatically continued under the Act. Until the lease expires the tenant will still have to pay rent even if he has moved out in the meantime.

Before leaving prior to the end of the term, the tenant should check his lease to ensure that it does not contain a clause providing that he must keep the premises open for business throughout the term. This will often be the case if the tenant is occupying a unit in a large shopping centre. The clause may tie the tenant in and prevent him from leaving early.

3 *The tenant has a verbal agreement and is paying rent weekly. He has decided to cease trading and leave the premises:* this arrangement is called a 'periodic tenancy' as it will carry on from week to week until the parties decide to end the arrangement by giving 'notice' to the other party. To end the lease the tenant needs to give the landlord just one week's notice. Similarly, if the rent is being paid monthly then one month's notice should be given.

4 *The landlord does not want the existing lease, which has ended, to continue under the Act:* this decision could be made for various reasons. The landlord may want to get rid of the tenant because, for example, he wants to reoccupy the premises for his own use. Another reason could be that the landlord wants to increase the rent. Whatever the reason, to bring the existing lease to an end the landlord must serve a special type of notice on the tenant called a 'Section 25 notice'. This notice, in order to be valid, has to conform to a particular format and include certain important information. The form can be obtained from a legal stationer. The notice must state the date when the lease is to end and this must be between six and 12 months ahead. A tenant will therefore always be given at least six months' notice. The date for ending the lease cannot be earlier than the date the lease would normally have come to an end. For example, if the lease is for five years ending on 30 June then the date in the Section 25 notice cannot be earlier than 30 June. The notice must also say whether or not the landlord will oppose the tenant's application to the court for a new tenancy. If the landlord wants to oppose the tenant's application then he has to set out in the notice full details of the grounds upon which he intends to rely (*see* paragraph 6 below).

5 *What action should a tenant take on receiving a Section 25 notice?* There are two steps that a tenant must take if he wants to protect his right to obtain a new lease. If a tenant overlooks either one of these steps the right will be lost and he must leave the premises on the date specified in the notice.

Step 1: within two months of receiving the Section 25 notice the tenant must give the landlord a written counter-notice stating that he would like a new lease. Unlike the landlord's Section 25 notice, the tenant does not have to use any special form for the counter-notice. A dated letter addressed to the landlord stating 'I would like to renew my lease' will be acceptable.

Step 2: not earlier than two months but no later than four months after receiving the landlord's Section 25 notice or after requesting a new tenancy, the tenant must apply to the county court for a new lease. This is, of course, assuming that in the meantime a new lease has not been agreed and signed by both the landlord and tenant. If a tenant is negotiating a new lease he must not overlook the need to make an application to the court within the above time limit. This is because, if the negotiations break down and an application to the court has not been made, then the tenant will lose the right to be granted a new lease under the Act.

6 *The landlord opposes the tenant's request for a new lease:* the court will give the tenant a new lease unless the landlord is able to show that one or more of the following reasons exist:
   (a) the tenant has failed to repair and maintain the property as required by the lease;
   (b) the tenant has persistently delayed in paying the rent;
   (c) the tenant has committed other substantial breaches of the lease, for example a breach of planning laws;
   (d) the landlord can provide the tenant with suitable alternative premises;
   (e) the tenant is a sub-tenant of part only of the building and the landlord wants to sell or lease the whole building;
   (f) the landlord intends to carry out building works or demolish a substantial part and requires possession in order to do so;

(g) the landlord wants to occupy the premises for his own business or residential use.

Grounds (a) to (c) can be used by the landlord where the tenant has broken terms in the lease. If you are a tenant and the landlord is trying to use these grounds then do not despair. Even if you have broken the terms of your lease the court may still give you a new tenancy if you can persuade the judge that you will rectify any problems, for example by bringing the rent up to date or by repairing the property.

To rely upon grounds (f) and (g) the landlord must show an intention to carry out his plans. In the words of the court, 'the proposals need not be cut and dried but must be more than mere contemplation'. In addition, ground (g) cannot be used unless the landlord has been the landlord of the premises for at least five years. However, this difficulty can be overcome if the landlord also intends to carry out work or demolish and needs possession to do the work under ground (f).

7 *The landlord and tenant cannot agree the terms of the new lease:* if the landlord and tenant cannot agree on the terms of the new lease then the court will decide what the terms will be. The court will take into account the existing terms. The maximum length of the new lease will be 14 years and the rent will be what is known as an 'open market rent'. This means that the court will ignore the tenant's occupation, any goodwill associated with the tenant's business and any tenant's improvements.

8 *The court refuses to grant a new tenancy:* if the tenant's application fails, then he has twelve weeks to leave the premises. If the tenant is refused a new lease because the landlord has successfully opposed on grounds (e), (f) or (g) (i.e. the tenant is not at fault) then the tenant will be entitled to compensation. The idea is to compensate the tenant for the disruption to the business of having to find alternative premises. The amount will depend upon how long the tenant has been occupying the premises. The rates are complex and advice should be obtained from a commercial property surveyor. As a general rule, however, if a tenant has been in occupation for less than 14 years then he will receive a sum equal to the rateable value of the premises. If he has been in occupation for over 14 years then the tenant will receive twice the rateable value of the premises.

9 *Can a tenant start the procedure for a new lease?* A tenant need not wait for a landlord to serve a Section 25 notice to start the procedure under the 1954 Act. It may be the case that a tenant's lease has ended and he wants the peace of mind of knowing that he has another fixed term of occupation. The tenant starts the procedure by serving what is known as a 'Section 26 notice' on the landlord. Like the landlord's Section 25 notice, a special form must be used. Within two months the landlord must serve a counter-notice stating whether or not he will grant the tenant a new lease. If the landlord fails to serve a counter-notice he cannot then oppose the tenant's application to the court for a new tenancy. To avoid losing the right to renew following receipt of the landlord's counter-notice, a tenant must apply to the court no earlier than two months but not later than four months after requesting a new tenancy. Even if the landlord has failed to serve a counter-notice the tenant must still apply to the court for a new tenancy. Failure to do this will mean the right to a new lease is lost.

10 *What if the fixed term has ended and the tenant wants to leave?* Under the Act the old lease continues automatically. If the tenant does not want the lease to continue then he must give at least three months' notice expiring on a quarter day (these are 25 March, 24 June, 29 September, and 25 December). In the meantime, a tenant will be liable to pay the rent until the notice runs out on the appropriate quarter day.

Reform of the 1954 Act

In addition to proposals to reform the contracting-out procedure under the 1954 Act (*see* page 495), the government plans (as part of the same package of reforms) to improve the procedures for renewing business tenancies as described above. The aim is to modernize and streamline the procedures, so that business tenants will face less risk of missing deadlines and losing the right to renew their business tenancy. The key changes are:

● the requirement for the tenant to serve a counter-notice to a landlord's Section 25 notice within two months will be abolished;

● the landlord (as well as the tenant) will be entitled to apply to the court for renewal of the tenancy, and will also have the right to apply for an order confirming termination of the tenancy where renewal is opposed on any of the permitted statutory grounds;

● while the existing time limits for the tenant's application to the court for a renewal will be preserved, the parties will be able to extend the time limits by agreement;

● tenants as well as landlords will be able to apply for an interim rent;

● where a tenant holding over after expiry of the contractual term wishes to terminate his tenancy, three months' notice will suffice in future (rather than at least three months ending on a quarter day, as at present);

● the maximum length of a new lease that can be awarded by the court will be extended from 14 to 15 years;

● abolition of the current trap whereby a tenant, who is

an individual who later sets up a limited company, loses his protection under the Act because he is no longer regarded as carrying on the business (despite the company often being owned and controlled by the individual).

These changes will not come into effect before summer 2004.

ASSIGNING YOUR LEASE

It is not uncommon for a tenant to want to dispose of his lease before it has ended, often because he wants to sell his business or move to alternative premises. In legal jargon this is known as 'assigning' the lease.

The first thing to do is to check your lease to see if the landlord's consent to assignment is required. A well-drafted lease will contain such a term, with an added proviso in most cases that the landlord's permission to assignment is not to be unreasonably withheld. If the lease has been poorly drafted (from the landlord's point of view) and there is no restriction on assigning, then the tenant is free to dispose of the lease to whomever he likes. Equally frustrating, from the tenant's perspective, will be a clause in the lease prohibiting any assignment whatsoever. The effect is that the tenant cannot assign the lease at all which could be disastrous, particularly if the tenant is trying to sell his business and the potential buyer wants to trade from the same premises.

Where the landlord's consent is required he will want assurances that the proposed new tenant will be capable of paying the rent and obeying the other conditions in the lease. Before agreeing to the assignment, the landlord will want to know all about the proposed new tenant's financial background. The landlord will expect to see at least three years of accounts together with references from former landlords and banks.

A landlord who is given a written request for permission to assign the lease from an existing tenant, is under a statutory obligation to deal with the application within a reasonable period of time. Previous cases have suggested that the courts will expect landlords to treat a tenant's request for assignment with a good deal of urgency. If a landlord refuses to consent to the assignment, then he must give reasons for this decision. A landlord's refusal will be perfectly justified, for example, where he is unhappy with the financial standing of the proposed new tenant. Understandably, a refusal will be regarded as unreasonable if it is based on a person's race or sex.

If the tenant takes the view that the landlord is unreasonably refusing consent, then he could go ahead and assign the lease. This course of action is not recommended and the suggested way forward is to apply to the court for what is known as a 'declaration'. In other words,

the court will be asked to decide whether or not the landlord's refusal to consent is unreasonable. If the court finds in the tenant's favour then as well as allowing the assignment to go ahead, the landlord may have to pay damages.

Liability after assignment

Until a change in the law on 1 January 1996, the original tenant was liable to the landlord for rent arrears and other breaches of covenant committed by his successors, even after the lease had been assigned. This harsh rule arose because the original lease was regarded as a contract. Under contract law the parties to a contract are bound by its obligations and it is difficult for anyone else to take over those obligations during the remaining term of the contract.

Old law for pre-1996 leases

Under the old law, which applies to all leases entered into before 1 January 1996, the original parties to the lease remain bound by the contract. This means that if a subsequent tenant fails to, say, pay the rent or carry out repairs, the original tenant can be forced to pay. The only respite for a tenant in this position is to pursue the tenant who took over the lease. This will not help, however, if the person who took over the lease has since become insolvent.

There is some protection under the Landlord and Tenant (Covenants) Act 1995 even for those leases entered into before 1 January 1996. A landlord must now notify former tenants and their guarantors, if any, within six months of the current tenant's default, otherwise the landlord cannot sue them. If the landlord remembers to serve the notice within six months then, if the original tenant pays up, he becomes entitled to an 'intervening lease', between the landlord and the current tenant who has defaulted. Although this sounds very complex, the idea is that by being given a new lease, expiring three days after the original lease, the former tenant has something of value which can be assigned later if he wishes.

Furthermore, if the original lease has been varied after the original tenant assigned, then the original tenant will escape all liability if a subsequent tenant defaults. Variations do not, however, include rent reviews.

Current law for post-1996 leases

The Act contains a number of complex provisions. The main change is that the original tenant escapes future liability, usually in return for guaranteeing the performance of the next tenant who takes over the lease. This is called an 'Authorized Guarantee Agreement'. It allows landlords and tenants to specify conditions that will have to be satisfied before the landlord can agree to an assignment. Each tenant will be automatically released from the Authorized Guarantee Agreement when the person to whom they assign the lease in turn assigns the lease to a third party.

TYPICAL COVENANTS FOUND IN A LEASE

A series of promises contained in a lease are known as 'covenants'. The covenants to which the parties have agreed will be set out in the lease. If the lease is not in writing, or it is silent about certain matters, then the following covenants will be implied into the agreement.

By the landlord:
1 a covenant for quiet enjoyment;
2 a covenant not to derogate from the grant.

By the tenant:
1 a covenant to pay the rent;
2 a covenant to use the premises in a tenant-like manner.

In a well-drafted lease it would be normal to find detailed covenants dealing with such matters as repairs, insurance, alterations, use, assigning, sub-letting, entry and inspection. The scope of these covenants and who is to have the benefit of them will be down to the negotiating skills and relative strengths of the parties and in practice, very often, market forces. Particularly in a long lease, it is often the case that the tenant is responsible for many of the most important covenants. Nonetheless, the effect and importance of the landlord's implied covenants of quiet enjoyment and non-derogation from grant should not be ignored.

Covenant for quiet enjoyment

If there is no reference to this covenant in the lease then it will be implied. This covenant will be breached by a landlord where there is a substantial interference with a tenant's enjoyment of his property. To make a claim, the interference must be substantial. Examples of the covenant being broken include the landlord erecting scaffolding in front of a tenant's shop and blocking the entrance, damage to property caused by a landlord failing to repair a drain, a landlord removing doors and windows to make a property uninhabitable and a landlord making violent threats to evict the tenant.

Covenant not to derogate from grant

Again, if this is not set out in the lease it will be implied. This covenant overlaps with the covenant for quiet enjoyment and it is sometimes difficult to tell the difference.

The covenant will be broken if the landlord does something which is inconsistent with the purpose for which the tenant took on the lease. For example, a breach of the covenant occurred when a landlord let premises for the storage of explosives and then decided to build on the adjoining land. The tenant's licence to store the explosives was conditional on there not being a building nearby. The landlord's proposed building works would have completely undermined the purpose of the tenancy, i.e. to store ammunition. The court accordingly took the view that this was a derogation from grant.

To date the courts have been reluctant to extend this principle to stop landlords letting adjoining premises to new tenants who are intending to carry out the same or a similar business to an existing tenant. A tenant should therefore ask his solicitor when drawing up the lease to check if the landlord will agree not to let adjoining premises to new tenants in the same line of business.

To pay the rent

This is an implied covenant by the tenant to pay to the landlord the agreed rent on the agreed day. The term is implied only where there is no written lease. It follows that in the absence of a written rent review clause the landlord cannot increase the rent.

To use the premises in a tenant-like manner

This imposes a limited obligation on the tenant to look after the premises in a way that a reasonable tenant would do. The tenant would not be obliged to carry out major repairs under this implied covenant.

BREACHES OF COVENANT

The rules are complicated and legal advice from a solicitor should be sought in every case. Nonetheless, there are certain basic guidelines to follow. Breaches of covenant will generally occur where either the landlord or the tenant fails to obey a condition in the lease, e.g. a failure to pay rent, carry out repairs, etc. For historical reasons non-payment of rent is dealt with differently from other breaches of other covenants.

Landlord's remedies for non-payment of rent

If the tenant has failed to pay the rent, the landlord has three options. Only one of the following can be used at any one time.

Forfeiture

This is legal jargon for the landlord having the right to re-enter the premises where the tenant is in breach of covenant, i.e. fails to pay the rent. The effect will be to bring the lease to an end and this can only occur if the lease contains what is known as a 'forfeiture clause'. This is a potentially draconian remedy that allows the landlord the right to enter a tenant's premises without any prior warning to seize their goods. Certain goods are exempt, including cash, perishable goods, clothes, bedding and tools of trade. Most well-drafted leases will contain such a clause. In addition, generally the rent has to be formally demanded by the landlord. Once again, most well-drawn leases contain a clause to get around this problem. The landlord can choose whether to go through the courts to have the lease forfeited or to take direct action himself by, for example, padlocking up the premises while the tenant is out. Whichever method is adopted the result will be the same; the lease comes to an end, the tenant must leave the premises and is not liable to pay any future rent.

Distress

This is an ancient remedy that gives a landlord the right to enter a tenant's premises to seize their goods. Certain goods are exempt, including cash, perishable goods, clothing, bedding and tools of the trade worth up to £150. Perishable goods are items that cannot be returned in the same state and condition they were in before they were taken, for example milk, fruit, grain, or flour out of a sack.

Sometimes, the goods are not taken away immediately. When this happens, the tenant is given a list of the items that are to be removed and this is called a 'walking possession agreement'. The tenant is then given five days to pay the outstanding rent. If the tenant is still unable to pay the arrears, the goods can be sold in order to pay the outstanding rent. Distress can be a very effective method of enforcement. The landlord normally instructs a certified bailiff to carry out this task.

Court action

There is nothing to stop the landlord from suing the tenant for non-payment of rent. As with all court action to recover money, there will be no point in committing time and money to court proceedings unless the tenant has the means to pay the rent arrears.

Landlords' remedies for other breaches of covenant

The remedies are either forfeiture, court action for damages or, in emergencies, an injunction.

Forfeiture

The same rule applies as for forfeiture for non-payment of rent, i.e. in order to end the lease there must be a forfeiture clause. Where a tenant has broken a covenant and the landlord wants to forfeit the lease, the landlord must take care not to lose the right by 'waiving the breach'. This means doing something, like accepting rent, which implies to the tenant that the landlord is happy for the lease to continue.

The next step is to serve a special type of notice on the tenant called a 'Section 146' notice. This notice must inform the tenant of the breach, how it can be put right (if it can) and the amount of any compensation that is to be paid. If the tenant fails to put the problem right after being given a reasonable period of time or if the breach is incapable of being rectified, then the landlord can forfeit the lease.

One of the most common situations where a landlord will use a Section 146 notice is where a tenant is in breach of his repairing obligations under the lease. The notice will refer to the clause in the lease that has been breached, give details of why the clause has been breached (e.g. water has entered the building) and set out the amount of compensation required. The amount of compensation will relate to the loss, if any, suffered by the landlord. This will be the amount by which the value of the freehold has diminished as a result of the tenant's breach. In practice, this means any compensation will be the amount by which the saleable value of the property has decreased because of the tenant's failure to repair.

Damages/injunction

The landlord may decide that he does not want to end the lease because, for example, he wants the rent to continue and it is difficult to re-let the premises. His other option is to sue the tenant for damages, for example, for the cost of repairs if the tenant has failed to carry out the appropriate repair work. For more serious breaches, such as carrying out major building works in breach of a covenant in the lease, the landlord may wish to apply for an injunction to stop the work immediately.

What a tenant should do if the landlord forfeits the lease

The tenant must examine the lease straight away to check whether or not it contains a forfeiture clause. If there is no forfeiture clause then the landlord is acting illegally and can be stopped. Where the landlord legitimately forfeits for non-payment of rent, the tenant can apply to the court within six months of the lease ending for what is known as 'relief against forfeiture'. If the tenant pays all the rent arrears and the landlord's costs to the court, the lease will be reinstated. A tenant can also apply to the court for relief where the landlord forfeits for breach of any other covenant. The court will have a discretion whether or not to agree to the tenant's request, but will usually require the breach(es) to be remedied and the costs paid.

What a tenant should do if the landlord levies distress

The tenant should check the lease to see whether or not the landlord must formally demand the unpaid rent. Technically, unless the rent has been demanded, it is not overdue. If the lease has been well drafted, however, it will contain a clause stating that the rent is due whether or not it has been formally demanded. If the lease is silent on this point, the landlord must make a formal demand for the rent before the bailiffs can be sent to the premises. The rent can only be formally demanded between sunrise and sunset on any day except a Sunday. If the rent has not been formally demanded then any distress is illegal.

The distress will be illegal if the landlord forfeits the lease first (by locking up the premises, for example) and then takes away the tenant's goods. Distress can only occur when the lease exists – not after it has ended. Equally, the landlord cannot levy distress against licensees. This is because the remedy can only be used where there is a lease. If the landlord or the bailiffs force entry (unless they had previously entered and taken what is called 'walking possession') or take away goods that are considerably more valuable than the amount of rent owed, then the distress will be illegal.

Tenant's remedies for breaches of covenant

A tenant also has means of redress where the landlord breaches a covenant in the lease. This can happen when, for example, the landlord fails to repair the premises as he is required to do under the lease. In this situation, the tenant's main remedy will be a claim for damages. It is also possible, in cases of emergency, to obtain from the court what is known as an order for 'specific performance'. This will have the effect of forcing the landlord to carry out the repairs within a given time period. A tenant may also have the right to 'set off' the cost of repair against future rent. This cannot be done where the lease specifically excludes the right to set off. Before exercising this right, the tenant should allow the landlord a reasonable time to repair. The tenant should also warn the landlord, preferably in writing, that he will carry out the repairs if the landlord does not do the work. Finally, the tenant should obtain more than one estimate from a reputable company for the cost of carrying out the repairs.

OTHER FACTORS TO CONSIDER

Business rates

Uniform business rates are payable on most business premises. They are calculated by the Valuation Office Agency, which is an executive agency of the Inland Revenue. The calculations for business rates are complex and advice should always be taken from a chartered surveyor.

The basis of the valuation is the amount of annual rent the premises can command, i.e. the rateable value of the premises. Your local council works out your business rates by multiplying your rateable value by the multiplier which the government sets each year on 1 April. This is changed each year in line with inflation. The valuation office carries out a revaluation every five years and the next one is due to take place in April 2005.

There are transitional arrangements to assist in meeting any increases. Where the rateable value of the property is less than £12,000 (£18,000 in Greater London) increases will be restricted to 5 per cent in the first year and 7.5 per cent thereafter. For large premises, the increases are capped at 12.5 per cent for the first year, 15 per cent for the second year and 17.5 per cent thereafter.

There should be added to these percentages any increase in the annual rate of inflation. If the property is sold, the buyer can use the seller's transitional relief.

Business rates are an allowable expense for tax purposes. This means that similar to other allowable expenses, such as staff wages, the amount of business rates can be deducted in order to calculate your annual profit. This will have the effect of reducing your tax bill.

If the premises are empty for more than three months then you will only have to pay half your normal bill. Where the premises consist of both business and residential use, business rates are paid on the non-domestic part and council tax is paid on the residential part.

If you feel your rates bill is too high, then you can appeal. Although you can represent yourself it is sensible to use a chartered surveyor. You should certainly avoid using unqualified advisers who will often charge for providing information that you can obtain free from your local valuation office.

For more advice about the valuation of your premises or how to appeal, you should contact your valuation office. Look under valuation office in your phonebook or log on to their website at www.voa.gov.uk

Business rates are collected by the local authority. You will receive a new bill each year. In most cases you will be allowed to pay your business rates by instalments, in the same way that council tax is paid on a residential property.

If you fail to pay an instalment, the local authority must inform you in writing that the payment is overdue.

The right to pay by instalments will be lost if you fail to pay the amount within seven days from the date of the council's letter. This can be disastrous because the remainder of the rates due for that year must then be paid within a further seven days.

If you default on your instalment payments for a second time in the same financial year, the local authority do not have to write to ask you to pay the missing instalment. The right to pay by instalments is immediately lost when you default for the second time and you have seven days to pay the full amount outstanding.

Local authorities have wide enforcement powers, including sending in the bailiffs and ultimately, in cases where the ratepayer deliberately refuses to pay, imprisonment.

Health and safety

The various requirements for protecting the health and safety of employees are contained in Acts of Parliament and regulations. The rules are enforced by the Health & Safety Executive (HSE). The rules stipulate matters such as the number of washrooms and lavatories and heating, lighting and ventilation that must be provided in business premises. Further guidance can be obtained from the HSE. They also publish free information booklets which can be obtained from their information line on Tel: 01787 881165.

Fire regulations

Even if you employ only one person, fire regulations must be complied with. Business premises must have a fire certificate, which can be obtained from the local fire officer. If you are considering buying or renting premises, you should ask to see the current certificate. Check whether the certificate covers your type of business. You will need to approach the local fire authority for a new certificate if you are planning to alter the premises. Failure to do so may be expensive – the fire authority may insist on further changes being made to the premises before they will issue a new certificate.

Access for disabled people

Under the Disability Discrimination Act 1995, it has been unlawful for service providers to treat disabled people less favourably for a reason related to their disability. Since 1 October 1999, service providers have had to make 'reasonable adjustments' for disabled people in the way services are provided.

From 1 October 2004, service providers will have a duty to make 'reasonable adjustments' not only to the way services are provided but also to any physical feature of their premises that makes it impossible or unreasonably difficult for disabled people to make use of a service. A service provider is anyone who provides services to members of the public. It makes no difference whether the public have to pay for the service. Nor is there an exemption for small businesses although their resources will be taken into account when considering what it is reasonable for them to do.

Anyone who provides access to and use of any place which members of the public are permitted to enter, is defined under the Act as a service provider. This means that the landlord of a shopping centre who provides a car park will be caught by the Act, as will the individual tenants who provide services to the public in their respective shops.

On 1 October 2004, if you provide services to the general public, you will be required to take such steps as are reasonable in all the circumstances to overcome any physical feature to enable disabled people to use your services.

Physical features are not just doorways and stairs. They may also include:

- steps, exterior surfaces and paving;
- parking areas;
- building entrances and exits, including emergency escape routes;
- internal and external doors;
- toilets and washing facilities;
- lighting and ventilation;
- lifts and escalators;
- telephones, counters or service desks.

In order to comply with the Act, you will be under a duty to take reasonable steps to do the following:

- remove the feature, or
- alter it, or
- provide a reasonable means of avoiding it.

When it comes to the question of what is reasonable, there is no clear-cut answer to this question. Nonetheless, the Code of Practice that supplements the Act says what is reasonable may vary according to:

- the type of service being provided;
- the nature of the service provider, its size and resources;
- how practical it is to take the steps;
- the financial and other costs of doing this;
- how disruptive it would be;
- how much money and other resources the service provider has available to spend on this;
- how much money they have spent already.

Some examples of reasonable adjustments include the installation of additional lighting, the widening of doors, the installation of handrails along passages and the rearrangement of furniture to allow wheelchair access.

In order to make any reasonable adjustments, it may be necessary to apply for planning permission, building regulation approval or any other permission you might need, including your landlord's consent. The Disability Discrimination Act now implies into all leases that the tenant is entitled to make an alteration to comply with the Act, whatever the lease says. There is also implied into the lease a term that if an alteration is required under the Act, then the landlord's consent cannot be unreasonably withheld. This will always be a question of fact in each case. However, an example where a landlord may be regarded as behaving unreasonably is if they refuse consent to alter the front of the premises on the ground that it is out of keeping with the other shops in the parade or shopping centre.

The Disability Discrimination Act allows individuals to bring a claim in either the county court or employment tribunal. Any damages awarded are unlimited and may be substantial and can also include compensation for injury to feelings. It will therefore be prudent to have your business premises audited to ensure you meet the requirements of the Act. The Centre For Accessible Environments (Tel: 020 7357 8182) can provide advice and assistance in this respect.

Help and advice is also available from the Disability Rights Commission helpline on Tel: 08457 622633.

Insurance

By law, if you employ staff you must have employers' liability insurance cover. This requirement is intended to protect employees if they are injured at work. The minimum amount of cover is £5 million and the insurance certificate must be displayed prominently at the business premises.

Although not compulsory, it is sensible to also take out public liability insurance. This will cover you if a member of the public is injured while on your premises, for example if they are hurt after slipping on some ice on your pathway.

Other types of insurance to consider are:

- road traffic insurance (this is compulsory for some risks, e.g. injury to third parties);
- 'key man' insurance (in case the owner or key director of the business is unable to work due, e.g., to illness);
- credit insurance against bad debts; or
- business insurance (protection against stock damage or theft, temporary interruption of business, product liability or legal costs).

57

Internal Workings of a Business

DAY-TO-DAY RUNNING OF THE LIMITED COMPANY

Appointment of directors

The first directors of the company will be those named on Form 10 when the company is being formed (*see* Chapter 54). Subsequent directors can be appointed by an ordinary resolution (*see* below) of the members or by a resolution of the board of directors. The appropriate procedure will be stipulated in the company's Articles of Association.

The incoming director must sign Form 288a indicating his consent to act as director – the form is lodged at Companies House.

If a director works full-time for the company he/she is often described as an 'executive director'. A non-executive director is someone who is only involved with the company on a part-time basis as an adviser or supervisor.

Duties of directors

The directors are responsible for the day-to-day management of the company. Their powers are authorized by resolutions passed at board meetings. A resolution is simply a decision that is made by the board and formally recorded in the minutes of the meeting.

In cases of conflict between the shareholders and directors, although the shareholders cannot overrule the directors' decisions, they can restore the balance of power by removing certain directors from the board or changing the Articles of Association to take powers from the board.

The duties of directors fall into three categories: fiduciary, common law and statutory.

Fiduciary

This means serving the interests of others rather than furthering personal interests. The key fiduciary duties are:

- the duty to act in good faith – the directors are required to act in the best interests of the company;
- the duty not to exceed or abuse their powers – the directors must only use their powers for the purposes for which they were given and not, for example, to force other members/directors out of the company;
- the duty to avoid conflicts of interest – the directors must not put themselves in a situation where their personal interests conflict with their duty to the company. For example, if in the course of his duties a director discovers a business opportunity, he must not exploit it for his personal benefit, to the detriment of the company.

Common law

Directors are expected to act with the degree of reasonable care and skill to be expected of persons with their knowledge and experience. Therefore a higher standard is expected of a professionally qualified director than a director with no previous business experience.

Breach of any of the fiduciary or common law duties will entitle the company to bring an action against the director to recover any loss suffered or any profit made by the director.

Statutory

The Companies Acts impose extra obligations on directors. These include:

- presenting annual accounts to shareholders;
- submitting an annual return to the Registrar of Companies;
- disclosing any personal interests in matters to be discussed at board meetings. For example, where board approval is being sought of a director's service contract (which will deal with salary, period of service and payment on loss of office) the director must disclose his personal interest in the issue. The company's Articles will determine whether an interested director can vote with the board.

Restrictions/liability of directors

1 *Substantial property transactions* – the sale or purchase of an item of *requisite value* by a director in his personal capacity to or from the company must be approved by an ordinary resolution of the members. An asset under £2,000 is not of requisite value. An asset valued above £2,000 will be of requisite value if it is worth more than 10 per cent of the company's net relevant assets or £100,000 (whichever is the lower). Failure to obtain approval of a transaction that takes place will make the director liable to the company for any loss and also accountable to it for any profit made.

   An example of a substantial property transaction would be where a director sells premises owned by him/her to the company for £150,000, the company's net relevant assets being £500,000. The members must approve the sale by passing an ordinary resolution.

2 *Loans to directors by the company are unlawful* – there are limited exceptions including where the loan is small, i.e. not exceeding £5,000.

3 *An undischarged bankrupt cannot act as a director.*

4 *The Company Directors Disqualification Act 1986* – this Act enables the court to disqualify a person from holding the office of director. The period of disqualification ranges from 2–15 years depending upon the seriousness of the offence. *See* page 478 for further details.

5 *Wrongful/fraudulent trading* – this involves misconduct by a director prior to a company going into insolvent liquidation. *See* pages 477–8 for further details.

6 *Breach of warranty of authority* – if a director exceeds his actual or apparent authority (*see* 'Liability for acts of agents of limited company', page 507) in contracting on the company's behalf, the third party can pursue the director for breach of warranty of authority.

7 *Disclosure* – a director should make it clear when he is acting as agent for the company in a transaction, rather than in his personal capacity. Failure to do so will result in him/her being personally liable to the other party to the contract.

An important point to note for those involved in running a limited company is that a person can be a director even if not validly appointed. There are two types of 'director' who, although not formally appointed, are treated in law as holding the position of director:

1 *'de facto' director* – this is someone who, although not validly appointed as a director, calls himself a director and undertakes tasks that usually only a director would do; and

2 *shadow director* – is not appointed but his/her co-directors are accustomed to act in accordance with their directions or instructions (this will usually exclude professionals advising the company in a personal capacity).

De facto and shadow directors have the same duties, restrictions and liabilities imposed on them in law as properly appointed directors.

Board meetings

Any director can call a board meeting on giving reasonable notice to all his/her co-directors in the country at the time. What is reasonable notice? Basic issues can be dealt with on five minutes' notice if all directors are present. Seven days' notice may be more appropriate for complex or sensitive matters.

Although all directors are entitled to attend and vote at the meeting, Table A (the standard Articles of Association which apply by default) requires the presence of a minimum of two directors who are entitled to vote on the matter in question.

Decisions are made by majority vote (i.e. over 50 per cent of the directors must vote in favour) and each director has one vote. If no majority is achieved, the chairman can prevent the resolution from failing by exercising his casting vote (if the Articles allow this).

To relieve the burden of complying with these formalities, most boards of directors delegate the authority to make day-to-day decisions to a managing director. Important decisions are usually reserved for approval by the board as a whole.

Another way to save time is by adopting a written resolution procedure. The directors can approve the resolution by signing and returning it to the company secretary. This avoids the need for a board meeting.

Removal of directors

The company's Articles will dictate the circumstances in which a director can be removed from office. They may require a director to vacate his office if, for example, he/she is of unsound mind or fails to attend meetings.

A power that cannot be taken away from the members (i.e. the shareholders) is the ability to remove a director by passing an ordinary resolution at a meeting. Twenty-eight days' notice of the meeting must be given to the company. A company seeking to remove an executive director should also consider the contract and employment law implications of removing him/her and the manner of removal. A botched dismissal may result in a monetary claim against the company for wrongful dismissal (i.e. breach of contract), unfair dismissal or redundancy.

Duties of a company secretary

The role of a company secretary is an administrative one. Although no professional qualifications are needed, a company secretary should familiarize himself with company law and regulations. The position will involve attending meetings and preparing minutes, filing forms and returns to Companies House and maintaining company books.

There are financial penalties that can be imposed on the company for non-compliance with Companies House requirements. The secretary is accountable to the company in this respect and failure to carry out his duties may result in his dismissal or removal by the board of directors. Remember that a sole director cannot also be the company secretary.

Rights of shareholders

A shareholder is a member of the company who holds shares in that company. Usually a shareholder will be entitled to vote at members' meetings and receive a dividend, although these rights may be varied by the class of share allotted to him. For example, shareholders with preference shares are entitled to dividends in priority to the holders of ordinary shares.

The company may allot new shares to a potential shareholder or existing shares may be transferred from a shareholder to a buyer. To effect the transfer of existing shares, the selling shareholder completes and signs a stock transfer form. The form and share certificate are given to the buyer who must pay a tax known as stamp duty (currently 50p per £100), unless the shares are a gift. Once the company has the form and certificate it must issue a new certificate to the new member and update the Register of Members.

As mentioned above (see 'Duties of directors') a dissatisfied majority of members can change the way that the company is run. A minority shareholder may also challenge the acts of the majority shareholders where a fraud is being committed on the minority.

Where a minority shareholder feels that the company is being conducted in a prejudicial way, which is affecting him in his capacity as member, he can present a petition of *unfair prejudice* to the court. Examples of unfair prejudice include non-payment of dividends to a particular member or 'freezing out' or excluding a member from involvement in the company to the extent that he is forced to leave. The court can make any order it thinks fit but often the appropriate solution is for the complaining party's shares to be bought out by the other members at a fair price.

As a last resort, a member can apply to the court to have the company brought to an end (or wound up) on the ground that it is just and equitable to do so. Winding up may be the only solution where management is in deadlock. The result of the order is that the company will cease to exist, any goodwill value in the company will be lost and the employees will lose their jobs.

Many companies have a Shareholders' Agreement, which forms a contract between its members. The agreement will deal with issues such as availability of information, formalities at meetings and purchase of outgoing members' shares. Such an agreement may help to reduce the potential for dispute.

Members' meetings

Although the directors carry out the day-to-day running of the business, some decisions must be approved by the shareholders at a general meeting. There are two types of general meeting:

1 *Annual general meeting (AGM)* – this is held once a year and in a large company it is an important opportunity for shareholders to question the directors on financial issues such as directors' salary awards. The shareholders will also be provided with the annual accounts. In small companies the AGM may be unimportant, as the shareholders are often directors as well. In this situation, all members can agree to dispense with the need to call an AGM by passing an 'elective resolution'.

2 *Extraordinary general meeting (EGM)* – despite its name, an EGM is every general meeting other than the AGM.

Usually, directors call general meetings, although the shareholders may also have the right to do so, for example to get rid of a director. Written notice convening the meeting must be given to all members. Depending upon the type of meeting and proposed resolution (see below), either 14 or 21 days' notice of the meeting must be given. In some circumstances the members can agree to receive shorter notice of the meeting.

Types of resolution

Special resolution

This resolution must be passed by a 75 per cent majority of voting members. Twenty-one days' notice of the meeting is required. A special resolution is required for decisions such as changing the company's name or Articles of Association.

Ordinary resolution

A simple majority of the members can pass an ordinary resolution. Twenty-one days' notice is required if the resolution is to be raised at an AGM, 14 days for an

EGM. Members can use an ordinary resolution for most decisions unless legislation or the company's Articles state otherwise. Ordinary resolutions are used for the appointment and removal of a director and the approval of a dividend payment.

Extraordinary resolution

For the resolution to be passed, a 75 per cent majority is required. Twenty-one days' notice is required for an AGM, 14 days if the resolution is proposed at an EGM. Extraordinary resolutions are rarely used. An example of when an extraordinary resolution will be required is where the members want to approve putting the company into voluntary liquidation.

Elective resolution

All of the company's shareholders must vote in favour of the elective resolution for it to be passed. Twenty-one days' notice is required. This resolution is used to dispense with the need to call an AGM (*see* above).

Voting

The members can vote by:
- a show of hands; or
- a poll vote.

A vote taken on a show of hands means each member has one vote, irrespective of the number of shares he has. A poll vote enables a member to have one vote for each share he owns. Usually voting will be on a show of hands, although a poll can be demanded.

If a member cannot attend a meeting, he can appoint a proxy to attend and vote on his behalf. Usually a proxy can only vote on a poll, not a show of hands.

After the meeting, the company secretary will write up the minutes of the meeting and is required to send copies of each special, extraordinary and elective resolution to the Registrar of Companies within 15 days. Most ordinary resolutions do not need to be filed.

As with directors' decisions, to avoid the need to call a meeting, most resolutions can be passed by way of written resolution.

LIABILITY OF THE LIMITED COMPANY

In the daily running of the business, the company is likely to be involved in buying or selling goods or supplying services. The business will incur certain obligations, for example to pay for products or to provide the service promised – the responsibility to fulfil these obligations is the company's 'liability' under the contract.

Liability is an important issue because if the company does not meet its contractual obligations the repercussions could be legal action or ultimately insolvency.

Ultra vires acts of a limited company

As mentioned on pages 485–6, the company's Memorandum of Association must have an objects clause. The objects clause sets out the purposes of the company and what it is allowed to do. If the company exceeds the activities authorized by the clause (e.g. by moneylending when the objects clause does not allow this), that activity is said to be *ultra vires*. In other words, the company has acted beyond its powers.

Once a legal obligation has been incurred (e.g. by advancing the loan monies) the *ultra vires* transaction will be valid and binding on the company and the other party involved. An aggrieved member cannot challenge the transaction but can claim against the directors for breach of duty.

If the unauthorized activity has not yet occurred, a member of the company can ask the court to grant an order restraining the company from acting in such a way.

Liability for acts of agents of limited companies

The directors and company secretary are known as the company's 'agents'. The agents may have actual authority or apparent authority to act. In either case, the company will be bound by their actions. Apparent authority can arise:
- where a third party contracting with the company is told by a company officer with actual authority that a particular agent is authorized to act in a certain way; or
- by virtue of the position the agent holds within the company.

A third party is entitled to presume that a director would have authority to enter into contracts on behalf of the company and is not expected to check whether this is in fact the case. A company can only escape liability on a contract entered into by a director without authority if the outsider was acting in 'bad faith' – i.e. fraud or deception was involved.

Shareholders can apply to the court to prevent a proposed unauthorized act of an agent. As previously mentioned in this chapter (*see* page 504), where a director breaches his duties to the company or exceeds his authority, the company will be able to recover any losses from the director.

DAY-TO-DAY RUNNING OF THE PARTNERSHIP

Types of partners

A partner may be a general partner, a sleeping partner or a salaried partner. A general partner participates fully in the running of the firm and shares the profits and losses of the firm. A sleeping partner may be entitled to a share in the firm's profits as a result of his capital investment in the partnership, but may be restricted from managing the firm. A salaried partner receives a salary instead of a share in the profits and his duties and rights are usually set out in an employment contract.

Partners' duty of utmost good faith

Partners are required by law to act in good faith towards one another and act in the best interests of the business. This means, for example, that partners must divulge all relevant information concerning the business and not make a secret personal gain to the detriment of the firm.

Breach of this duty will entitle the partners to recover any loss incurred by the firm from the errant partner. Equally, the partners will be entitled to recover any profit made by the partner at fault.

Partnership decision making

As mentioned in Chapter 54, a partnership should have a Partnership Agreement, which can establish matters such as the functions of each partner, and how decisions will be made.

The firm may agree that some of the partners should not be permitted to authorize large transactions without the approval of the other partners. Unless the Partnership Agreement contains such restrictions, all of the partners will be entitled to take part in the decision-making process.

A simple majority on a show of hands is all that is required to approve most decisions of the partnership. Unanimous consent is required to bring in a new partner or change the business.

LIABILITY OF THE PARTNERSHIP

In a partnership, all the partners or just one of the partners may enter into contracts. If the partners did not approve the obligation collectively, they may argue that the business is not liable on the basis that the partner did not have their authority to enter into the contract. If the firm is not liable then the individual partner may be.

The partnership will always be liable for contracts that were *actually authorized* by the partners. Actual authorization may arise where:

1 the contract was entered into by all the partners; or
2 the partners have agreed that one of the partners has authority to do certain acts on the partnership's behalf. This may be expressed verbally or in the Partnership Agreement. For example, a partner may be authorized to buy and sell goods up to a certain value; or
3 authority can be implied due to the fact that the partners have always acted in such a way and there are no restrictions on the partners' activities.

Even if an activity is not actually authorized, a firm may be liable if the contract between the partner and an outsider is *apparently authorized*. Apparent authorization may arise where:

1 the activity relates to the type of business usually carried on by the firm. For example, this is unlikely to be the case if a partner in a firm of solicitors orders a large quantity of luxury foods; and
2 the transaction is one for which a partner in that type of business would usually have authority to act. For example, the firm is unlikely to be bound where one partner enters into a contract to sell the business premises.

Where the above can be satisfied, the firm and the partner concerned are liable for the transaction. The firm will not be liable if:

1 the outsider knew or had reason to suspect the partner had no authority to act; or
2 the outsider did not know the person he/she was dealing with was a partner.

Personal liability

Even if the firm is not liable, the contracting partner will be personally liable to the outsider. So, in the first example above, the solicitor would be obliged to pay for the luxury goods from his own resources.

Where the firm has been made liable due to a partner entering into a contract by virtue of apparent authority but without actual authority, the partner must compensate the other partners for any loss they sustain.

Joint and several liability

Where a firm incurs a liability, the partners can be sued jointly or individually – this is known as 'joint and several liability'. Where one partner is sued although the whole firm is liable, that unfortunate partner can claim an indemnity from the other partners so as to share the debt. This rule of joint and several liability will also apply to salaried partners. A salaried partner is really an employee but anyone dealing with the partnership can treat him in the same way as an equity partner having a share in the business. If a partnership gets into financial difficulties, the salaried partner will be equally at risk of being personally sued as partners who are entitled to a share in the profits of the business.

Outgoing partner

A partner is personally liable for all of the firm's debts where the obligation arose during his time as partner. Even after the partner has left the firm, he remains liable on contracts made while he was a partner. He is not liable for new contracts entered into after his departure, provided that the outsider is aware that he is no longer a partner. The departing partner should therefore send letters to everyone who has had dealings with the firm, stating that he is leaving and the leaving date. An advertisement should also be placed in the *London Gazette*.

A creditor who can show he did not receive notice in this manner can hold the former partner liable.

It is also important for the firm to alter the business stationery to delete reference to the former partner. If a non-partner is held out to be a partner in the firm (e.g. either on the firm's stationery or verbally), that person may be liable to a creditor if:

- the creditors relied on the statement that the person was a partner; and
- the non-partner knew he was being held out as a partner.

DAY-TO-DAY RUNNING OF A LIMITED LIABILITY PARTNERSHIP

Structure

Under the Limited Liability Partnership Act 2000, a limited liability partnership does not have a Memorandum or Articles of Association like a limited company or any specified management structure. Nonetheless, like a partnership, although it is not compulsory, it is important that the members enter into an agreement, known as a members' agreement, which should cover as many of the issues that you would expect to find in a well-drawn-up partnership agreement. If this is not done, the default provisions under the Act apply and will result in equal profit/loss sharing, equal shares in capital, equal rights to take part in the management of the business, unanimous approval for the introduction of new members, no right to remuneration and no right to expel a member. This fall-back provision under the Act will rarely be appropriate and therefore a members' agreement must be drawn up and address the following:

- capital contributions made by members, together with any increases in capital;
- withdrawal of capital, including what happens when members retire;

- shares of profit and loss;
- are there to be special tiers of members with different rights, obligations and duties?;
- decision-making. Who makes them? Do all the members have a say or is day-to-day management delegated to a board or executive committee?;
- new members. How are they admitted?;
- designated members. Who are they?;
- retirement and expulsion. When and how and on what grounds?

It is very important that the members' agreement is comprehensive because the law relating to partnerships and limited companies does not apply.

Every limited liability partnership must appoint at least two designated members at all times. If there are fewer than two, then each member is deemed under the Act to be a designated member. A designated member is really the equivalent of the company secretary as they have various important administrative duties to perform as follows:

- appointing an auditor;
- signing the accounts on behalf of the members;
- delivering the accounts to the Registrar at Companies House;
- notifying Companies House of any membership changes, change of name or change of registered office;
- preparing, signing and delivering the annual return to Companies House;
- acting on behalf of the limited liability partnership if it is wound up or dissolved.

Designated members are accountable if they fail to carry out these functions and the Registrar at Companies House can impose penalties broadly similar to those imposed on directors.

LIABILITY OF THE LIMITED LIABILITY PARTNERSHIP

In the normal day-to-day operation of running a business, a number of contracts will be negotiated and entered into by the limited liability partnership. The contracts are made with the limited liability partnership and not the individual member who negotiated the terms. This is because limited liability partnerships, like limited companies, are recognized in law as having their own legal identity and can therefore enter into contracts in their own right. This means that the responsibility for complying with any contracts rests solely with the limited liability partnership. If things go wrong, then only the limited liability partnership can be sued, not the individual members.

Liability of the members

Any claims should only be made against the limited liability partnership. If this happens, it could be liable for the full extent of its assets, depending on the size of the claim made against it. In this case, similar to a limited company, the liability of the members will be limited to the value of their capital in the business. This contrasts with the position of a partner who is potentially personally liable for all claims made against the partnership, whether he was personally to blame or not.

There may however be certain rare circumstances where an individual member could become personally liable, e.g. a civil action for negligence where the individual member assumed personal responsibility for the advice given and where the client relied upon that assumption and it was reasonable to do so – *Williams & another* v *(1) Natural Health Foods Ltd (2) Richard Mistlin* [1998] 1 WLR 830.

Dealings with third parties

Members, like company directors, are authorized to act on behalf of the limited liability partnership, unless of course the members' agreement restricts this. Third parties can assume that the member is authorized to act on behalf of the limited liability partnership unless they know he is not authorized to do so or that he is not a member.

A former member is still a member unless the third party has notice that he is not a member or a notice to that effect has been delivered to Companies House.

For more information and guidance about limited liability partnerships, look at Companies House website www.companieshouse.gov.uk and the Inland Revenue website: www.Inlandrevenue.gov.uk

58

Tax and VAT

Once an appropriate business structure has been chosen (the three main options being a sole trader, partnership or limited company), you should consider your responsibilities in relation to tax, national insurance and value added tax (VAT).

WHO SHOULD BE INFORMED?

The Inland Revenue and Customs & Excise must be informed that you are starting up in business on your own account. There is a £100 fine for failing to notify the Inland Revenue within three months of starting self-employment.

The Inland Revenue are responsible for collecting income tax, corporation tax and national insurance contributions. Customs & Excise are responsible for collecting VAT. Both of these departments can be notified at the same time by completing form CWFI1, which is contained in a leaflet *Thinking of working for yourself?* (PSEI1). This leaflet, which also contains a lot of useful information and advice, can be obtained from your nearest Inland Revenue office. The completed form should be sent to the Inland Revenue National Insurance Contributions Office, Self Employment Directorate, Longbenton, Newcastle upon Tyne, NE98 1ZZ. Your details will subsequently be passed to the Inland Revenue who will also notify Customs & Excise should you either be required, or volunteer, to register for VAT.

INCOME TAX AND THE SOLE TRADER

Employed or self-employed?

The primary issue that must be established with the Inland Revenue is that you are a sole trader (i.e. self-employed) and not an employee. This is because the Inland Revenue makes a distinction between the two categories and applies different rules in calculating any tax that is due.

It will be quite obvious that you are self-employed and a sole trader if, for example, you own your own shop. It will be less clear what the position is if, for example, you are a heating engineer and have a regular contract one or two days a week to service a local hotel's heating and hot water system. To determine whether or not you are self-employed, the Inland Revenue will look at the overall circumstances and in particular focus on the following:

- do you work mainly for one business?
- do you have to carry out the work personally or can you use someone else?
- do you take orders as to how and when you do the job?
- do you work set hours weekly, monthly, yearly?
- do you receive overtime, sickness or holidays?
- do you provide your own equipment?
- if you make a mistake are you required to bear the cost of putting it right?

You can challenge a decision by the Inland Revenue as regards your status but this is likely to be costly and time consuming. With this in mind, before you start your business venture you must take advice from an accountant as to how your status is likely to be defined by the Inland Revenue.

What is income tax?

As the name suggests, income tax is payable on your income. The Inland Revenue has devised various schedules (which are sometimes sub-divided into cases) and if an item of income comes within one of these schedules, then income tax will be due. A sole trader will pay income tax on the actual profits of the business. These are assessed for income tax under Schedule D Case 1.

Can I choose my accounting year?

A sole trader will have to pay income tax to the Inland Revenue on business profits for the accounting year ending during the current tax year. Tax years run from 6 April to 5 April the following year. Although your accounts will be made up annually, you can choose which day is to be your year's end. You may decide that it is to coincide with a tax year, i.e. 6 April–5 April next, or you may choose another suitable date. The date chosen could save you tax and you should therefore take advice on this.

Business profits

Business profits can be calculated by preparing what is known as a profit and loss account. This involves adding up all the income earned by the business and then deducting any permitted expenses. The resulting figure will be either a net profit or loss. It will be on this figure that income tax is paid.

Business expenses

Any money that is paid out 'wholly and exclusively' for the business can be claimed as a business expense and deducted from your taxable profits. It is not always clear whether an expense can be claimed or not. For instance, in some cases the Inland Revenue will not allow you to claim a deduction for an expense for something that is used for both business and private purposes, such as clothing bought mainly for work. On the other hand, if your telephone and other utilities at home are used for the business, you may be able to claim a proportion of the expenses, i.e. part of the telephone bill, heating, lighting, etc. The table lists some examples of allowable and non-allowable expenditure.

Can be claimed	Cannot be claimed
All staff costs, wages, bonuses, gifts, NI contributions	Drawings on account of profits by sole trader/partner
Counselling services for redundant employees	Self-employed NI contributions Classes 2 & 4
Heating, lighting, telephone, etc.	Business entertainment
Rent on business premises	Donations to political parties
Business rates	Travel expenses between home and work
Repairs	Cost of improvements, extensions and additions to premises
Interest on business loans	Equipment
Business postage, stationery	Taxes, fines and penalties
Business travel	Legal fees on forming a company, drawing up a partnership deed, acquiring assets such as leases
Accountancy fees	Gifts to customers
Bad debts written off	Fines
VAT – only if you are not registered for VAT	Depreciation on capital equipment

How are business profits calculated?

The profits of a business are (in Inland Revenue jargon) the chargeable receipts of the trade less its deductible expenditure. In plain English, this means the profits of a business can be calculated by adding up all its income and then deducting various permitted expenses.

How to calculate business profits:

James runs a shop employing two part-time shop assistants. He rents his premises.

Turnover (Total Sales)		£50,000
LESS ALLOWABLE EXPENSES		
Staff wages	£15,000	
Rent	£10,000	
Business rates	£5,000	
Advertising	£500	
Heating, lighting, telephone	£1,000	
National Insurance	£600	£32,100
	Business profit	**£17,900**

Capital allowances

In order to operate the business you will probably need to spend money on plant and machinery (which covers most of your ordinary business equipment), vehicles, patents and know-how. The expense incurred is called 'capital expenditure'. In each year that you own any of the above assets, you can deduct a percentage (normally up to 25 per cent) of the purchase price as a business expense. This is called a 'capital allowance' and can be deducted from your business profits for the year in order to reduce your tax bill. In the first year that you own the asset, you will deduct a percentage of the initial purchase price (e.g. if the asset cost £10,000, in year 1 the capital allowance is 25 per cent of £10,000 = £2,500). In subsequent years, the percentage calculation will apply to the balance of the purchase price (e.g. in year 2, the balance of the purchase price is £7,500; 25 per cent of £7,500 = £1,875).

Generally, capital allowances are not allowed for what you spend on business premises, but exceptions are made for industrial and agricultural buildings.

For small- and medium-sized companies and sole traders there are two important cases where the capital allowance on certain types of assets is significantly higher.

First, from April 2000 for four years there is 100 per cent capital allowance on computer software and internet-enabled mobile phones in the first year of purchase. This has been introduced by the government to encourage more businesses to go online and invest in e-commerce and new information technology. Second, there is a first year capital allowance of 40 per cent on new and second-hand plant and machinery (not cars). To qualify for the above, the following conditions must be met by the business:

- turnover less than £11.2 million;
- assets less than £5.6 million;
- less than 250 employees.

A construction company buys a crane for £20,000 – the capital allowances are as follows:

Year 1 – 40 per cent of £20,000 = £8,000 (written down allowance). This is then deducted from the value each year.

Year 2 – 25 per cent of £12,000 = £3,000

Year 3 – 25 per cent of £9,000 = £2,250

etc . . .

If you later sell the asset having claimed a capital allowance, it will be necessary to compare the reduced balance of the cost at the time of sale with the actual sale price. If you make a profit, then this may be added to your tax bill.

How income tax is assessed

Income tax is assessed on the business profits for the accounting period ending in the current tax year. This is known as 'the current year basis'. For example, if your accounting year is from 1 January to 31 December each year, then for the trading year ending 31 December 2000, the income tax year will be tax year 2000/2001 (6/4/2000–5/4/2001). However, special rules apply to the first and sometimes the second tax year of trading.

The first tax year

In the first tax year of your business, income tax is paid on any profits made from the first day of trading to the end of the tax year (5 April). If your accounting year does not follow the tax year, i.e. 6 April–5 April next, then tax is paid on a proportion of the profits up to 5 April.

James started his business on 4 August 1999. He decided his accounting year is to end on 3 August each year. His first year's profits amounted to £14,000. His first year's tax payment would be based on his profits from 4/8/99 to 5/4/2000, which is eight months' trading.

8/12 of £14,000 = £9,333.

The second tax year

Income tax is based on your profits for the 12 months up to the end of the accounting period which ends in that tax year.

James' first accounting year ends on 3/8/2000, which falls in tax year 2000/2001 (6/4/2000–5/4/2001). Income tax will be paid on profits made in the first accounting year i.e. £14,000.

Third and subsequent tax years

Income tax will be paid on profits for the 12-month accounting period which ends in the tax year.

In his second accounting year ending 3/8/2001, James made a profit of £20,000. His second accounting year ends in tax year 2001/2002 (6/4/2001–5/4/2002).

If these rules result in some of your profits being taxed more than once, you will be entitled to an adjustment when your business ends, or when there is a change in accounting date. However, if you choose a 5 April year end, there will not be an overlap.

When does income tax have to be paid?

Any income tax that is due is collected by the Inland Revenue in two equal half-yearly payments on 31 January and 31 July. The first two payments on 31 January and 31 July are called 'payments on account' and are based on your tax bill for the previous year. The third payment, due on the following 31 January, is to cover the balance of any outstanding tax owed over and above the amount paid in the two previous instalments on 31 January and 31 July.

James' first accounting year runs from 4 August 1999 to 3 August 2000 and will form the assessable profits for two years, 1999/2000 and 2000/2001. The total profit achieved was £14,000. In the second year ending 3 August 2001, the assessable profits amount to £20,000 and these will be taxed in the 2001/2002 year.

The first year's profit needs to be apportioned to determine the taxable amount in the 1999/2000 year, i.e. 5/4/2000: 8/12 of £14,000 = £9,333.00 – total income tax payable £2,000. This tax will have to be paid by 31 January 2001.

In addition to the payment for the 1999/2000 liability, a payment on account for the 2000/2001 year must also be made on 31 January 2001 and this payment on account is half of the final liability for the previous year, in this case £1,000. A further payment on account for the 2000/2001 year is due on 31 July 2001 and again this is half of the previous year's liability.

The taxable profit for the 2000/2001 year is £14,000 on which a total liability of £3,000 arises. James will already have made two payments on account totalling £2,000 and so a final 'balancing' payment of £1,000 will need to be made on 31 January 2002. However, you must also make his first payment on account for the 2001/2002 year on this day and this will be £1,500 with a further £1,500 due on 31 July 2002. The final liability for the 2001/2002 year is £4,000 and so a balancing payment for this year of £1,000 will be due on 31 January 2003 together with a payment on account of £2,000 for the 2002/2003 year. This system then continues for the life of the business.

Interest on underpayments and overpayments

Under the self-assessment rules you are required to make two payments on account towards your tax bill on 31 January and 31 July. A final payment for any tax due is then paid on the following 31 January. Interest is charged on any underpayment and final balancing payments and is based on the average rate of borrowing. It may be the case, however, that you have been making overpayments and, if so, the Inland Revenue will refund any overpayments made together with interest based on the average investment return.

Surcharges

In addition to any interest charges, any balancing payment due at 31 January and not paid by 28 February will be subject to an automatic surcharge of 5 per cent of the amount outstanding. A further 5 per cent surcharge will be added to any outstanding amounts that still remain unpaid at 31 August.

How to calculate the amount of income tax to pay

Income tax is paid on the profits of the business less allowable expenses and capital allowances. From this amount, you can set off your personal allowances. Every taxpayer under 65 years old will receive a personal allowance of £4,615 (April 2003). On income above your personal allowance tax is payable at 10, 22 or 40 per cent depending on how much you earn. These rates are set by the government and are often changed each year when there is a Budget.

How to pay income tax

Payment can be made to the Inland Revenue by post, bank giro, cheque, or cash at the Post Office, or by electronic fund transfer through BACS or CHAPS.

Self-assessment – what is it?

Self-assessment was introduced for the 1996/97 tax year. It was a major change as it put the onus on taxpayers to assess their own tax liability. Self-assessment forms (Form SA100) are normally sent out each April. When you complete the form you are informing the Inland Revenue of your tax position.

If you would like the Inland Revenue to calculate your tax liability then you have to return the form by 30 September following the end of the previous tax year (which will have ended on 5 April). If you miss this date, you may have to calculate your own tax liability. This is because the Inland Revenue will not guarantee to calculate your tax liability by 31 January, which is the latest date for returning your self-assessment form without incurring a penalty. Failure to have returned the form by this date may result in a fine of £100, unless the outstanding tax liability that remains unpaid is less than £100. In this case the penalty will be reduced in line with the outstanding amount. In addition, the Inland Revenue have a discretion to charge another £60 per day until the form is returned. There is also a further fine of £100 to be paid if the form has still not been returned by 31 July.

Completing the self-assessment form

This can be a complex exercise. The Inland Revenue has a telephone help line, practical help sheets and tax inquiry centres and these can provide you with assistance. Nonetheless, there are clearly advantages in consulting a professional to both complete the form and work out your tax liability.

The basic form consists of eight pages and this is supplemented by extra pages depending on your individual circumstances. The extra pages cover such matters as employment and self-employment. The form requires you to complete full details of your income, claims for reliefs and allowances. It is a good idea to keep a photocopy of your completed return. There is normally no requirement to send in accounts with your return but you will need to include accounts information in the appropriate section of the form. If you want to calculate your own tax, the Inland Revenue provide a tax calculation that may be useful.

Duty to keep records

It is now compulsory for all taxpayers to keep records for a minimum period of time. If you are a sole trader, partner or limited company then you must keep records for five years and 10 months from the end of the tax year. If the Inland Revenue have started a formal inquiry into your tax affairs, your records must be kept until the inquiry is concluded. Records will include payments, receipts, invoices, bank records, statements, paying-in books and cheque stubs. If adequate records are not kept a penalty of up to £3,000 may be charged.

Trading losses

A new business

A sole trader can claim very generous reliefs if losses are made during the early years of a new business. If you make a loss during your first four years' trading, this can be carried back and claimed against any income received in the three years before the loss was incurred. This will be particularly beneficial if the amount of tax paid in one or all of the previous three years was at the higher tax rate of 40 per cent.

An established business

If you have been in business for a few years and make a loss, this can be set against any other income received in the same or previous tax year (provided you were still in the same business in that tax year). Another option is to carry the loss forward to set off against a future profit. It is generally sensible to set off any losses against income in previous tax years because otherwise, if you want to set off losses against future profits, it can take some time to receive the benefit.

INCOME TAX AND A PARTNERSHIP

The profits of a partnership are taxable in the same way as that of a sole trader (*see* above), i.e. income tax and capital gains tax will be payable where appropriate and the rules relating to self assessment will apply. The following additional requirements must also be considered.

Who pays?

The profits of the partnership will be divided between each of the partners in accordance with the profit-sharing agreement contained in any partnership deed. If there is no such agreement, the profits will be divided equally. Each partner is therefore treated as if they were running their own business. From his total income a further deduction for personal allowances can be made. Income tax is then paid at the rate of 10, 22 or 40 per cent depending on income. In the past, if one or more of the partners failed to pay income tax the Inland Revenue could look to the other partners to pay. It is no longer the case that each partner is jointly and severally liable for the partnership's overall tax bill. A partner is now only liable to pay income tax on his or her own share of the profits.

Change of partners

This will happen if one of the following occurs:
- retirement of a partner;
- expulsion of a partner;
- resignation of a partner;
- death of a partner;
- bankruptcy of a partner.

Provided at least one of the other partners remains in the partnership, a change in the composition of the partnership will not be treated as if the partnership had ended. This was not the case under the old rules and, consequently, an election had to be made to the Inland Revenue to treat the partnership as continuing. Now, when a partner joins or leaves the partnership he or she will be assessed for income tax based on the same rules that relate to a sole trader either starting or finishing a business.

Trading losses

The same principles apply to partners as sole traders. Each partner is now individually assessed for income tax and trading losses may be claimed by each partner independently of each other. However, the carry-back rules that apply for the first four years of any new business will only apply to a new partner joining the business and not to the existing partners.

Self-assessment

In addition to the partners completing their own tax returns, the partnership has to complete a separate tax return (Form SA800). A statement must also be sent stating the names, addresses, tax districts and tax references for each partner, together with their share of the profits/losses and tax deducted or credited. When the partnership's turnover exceeds £15,000, accounts details known as 'standard accounts' must be included in the partnership return.

Each partner's own tax return must also include details of his share of the partnership income and any gains on his share of the partnership assets, for example property. Class 4 national insurance contributions must also be included in the return.

Deadline date for the partnership tax return

The partnership return must be sent to the Inland Revenue by 31 January following the end of the previous tax year, i.e. by January 2001 for the tax year 1999/2000. A fixed penalty of £100 will be due from each partner and also from the partnership as well if the return has not been sent in by 31 January. A further penalty of £100 will again be due from each partner if the return is more than six months late, i.e. not returned by 31 July.

NI contributions for sole traders and partners

If you are a sole trader or partner over the age of 16 years old then, subject to one or two exceptions, you will have to pay National Insurance contributions (NICs). These contributions are now collected by the Inland Revenue.

There are two classes of contributions to pay: Class 2 and Class 4. Class 2 is a flat rate and always payable, whereas Class 4 is based on a percentage of your profits and is only payable if those profits exceed a certain figure which is set annually by the government.

Class 2 Contributions

Unless your net income is less than £4,025 (from April 2002) you will have to make a flat rate payment of £2.00 per week. This can be paid by various means, including monthly by direct debit. The direct debit form is in the back of the Inland Revenue's leaflet CWFI *Thinking of Working for Yourself?*. You can also pay quarterly in arrears.

Payment of Class 2 contributions will entitle you to receive incapacity benefit, basic retirement pension, bereavement benefits and maternity allowance. However, it will not qualify you to receive either Jobseeker's Allowance or the state earnings-related supplement (SERPS) to retirement pensions.

More than one job

If you have more than one self-employed job, you will only have to pay one Class 2 weekly contribution, i.e. £2.00. If you are either employed and self-employed, or you have two jobs and are employed in both, then NICs under Classes 1, 2 and 4 may be potentially payable for each employment. There is a ceiling on the amount that can be paid and when the maximum is exceeded you can apply for a refund from the Inland Revenue. If you know in advance that you are likely to exceed the maximum figures, you should apply to the Inland Revenue for a deferment. This will avoid having to wait until the end of the tax year for a refund. Applications for a deferment can be made on form CA72(b). This form, together with other information about deferment, is contained in booklet CA72 *National Insurance contributions – deferring payment.*

Class 4 Contributions

If your profits exceed £4,615 (from April 2003) Class 4 NICs are payable in addition to Class 2 contributions. Your profits are calculated in the same way as for income tax, although trading losses are treated differently. Class 4 contributions are payable at 8 per cent of your profits between £4,615 and £30,940 (2003/2004) per year and 1 per cent above £30,940 per year. These rates are usually changed annually by the Chancellor in the Budget. Unlike Class 2 contributions, Class 4 contributions do not entitle you to any state benefits. They are simply another tax on your profits.

Class 4 contributions are collected and assessed by the Inland Revenue and paid at the same time as income tax under the self assessment rules, i.e. half-yearly on account every 31 January and 31 July for the previous year's profits. The same penalties apply to late payment of Class 4 contributions as to the late payment of income tax.

Further information about national insurance contributions can be obtained from the government's Employers' Helpline, Tel: 0845 6070143.

CAPITAL GAINS TAX FOR SOLE TRADERS AND PARTNERS

General principles

If you make a gain from selling, exchanging or giving away land, goodwill or plant and machinery, you may be liable to pay capital gains tax (CGT). Working out the CGT liability can be complicated as there are a multitude of rules concerning how any gain is calculated and whether various reliefs can be applied to reduce the gain. Professional advice from an accountant should be sought in most cases. Nonetheless, the general principles are as follows.

Step 1

When the asset is disposed of you can deduct from the sale proceeds:

- the original cost of acquiring the asset;
- certain items of expenditure that have increased the value of the asset (this does not include normal repair and maintenance cost). An example would be having a painting restored;
- incidental costs of disposal (e.g. agents' fees, solicitors' fees, advertising costs).

Where there is a disposal of a partnership asset, each partner will be treated as owning a share of the asset in accordance with the Partnership Agreement. If there is no agreement, then the value of the asset will be shared equally between each partner. Each partner will therefore have a separate calculation to make to work out his capital gains tax liability.

Step 2

What is known as an 'indexation allowance' can then be applied to any gain. This relief has the effect of reducing any gains caused by inflation since March 1982. For sole traders and partners, indexation allowance cannot be claimed after April 1998. Indexation allowance is calculated by applying to the original cost of the asset (usually the purchase price) the increase in the retail price index between the month when the asset was acquired or March 1982 if later, and the month of disposal of the asset up to April 1998. The retail price index is published monthly by the government. The formula and calculation for indexation allowance is:

$$\frac{\text{Indexation figure for month asset disposed of}}{\text{Indexation figure for month asset acquired}} -1$$

Asset acquired in December 1987 and sold in March 1998

Retail price index figure for December 1987 is 103.3

Retail price index figure for March 1998 is 160.8

$$\frac{160.8}{103.3} -1 = 0.557 \text{ (55.7 per cent)}$$

Indexation allowance ceased to be available for sole traders and partners in April 1998. It has now been replaced by 'taper relief', which reduces the gains on a sliding scale in line with the period of time the asset has been owned to allow for the effects of inflation. There are different rates depending on whether the asset is a business or non-business asset. The maximum amount of taper relief available on a business asset is 75 per cent, leaving just 25 per cent of the gain chargeable. You become entitled to the benefit of this maximum relief if you own the business asset for more than four years.

By applying steps 1 and 2, you will be able to calculate what is known as 'the chargeable gain'.

Asset acquired in December 1987 at a cost of £15,000 and disposed of in March 1998 for £30,000. Indexation allowance is 55.7 per cent (see above example). The chargeable gain is:

Disposal price		£30,000
Acquisition cost	£15,000	
Indexation allowance	£8,355*	£23,355
Chargeable gain		£6,445

(*calculated by taking the gain value of £15,000 and multiplying the figure by 55.7 per cent).*

Step 3

Every person has an annual exemption. This is available to both husbands and wives and is currently £7,700 for tax year 2002/2003. This can be used to reduce the chargeable gain. In the above example, the annual exemption will wipe out the chargeable gain, so no capital gains tax will be payable.

Step 4

If the gain is not wiped out by the annual exemption, the following further reliefs may be available. They can have the effect of reducing or postponing the payment of tax for a period of time:

- *Roll over relief* – if you sell assets and then purchase certain replacement assets, payment of capital gains tax can be postponed. To qualify you must reinvest in a replacement asset within either three years, or one year before the previous asset was sold. This relief applies to land, buildings, goodwill, fixed plant and machinery.
- *Hold over relief* – if you make a gift of certain assets, then it is possible to defer the payment of capital gains tax. The effect of this relief is that capital gains tax is not paid until the person who receives the gift disposes of the asset. Once the asset has been disposed of by the donor (the person who made the gift) to the donee (the person receiving the gift), only the donee is liable to pay capital gains tax. The person who made the gift will therefore avoid paying capital gains tax.

When is capital gains tax paid?

Capital gains tax is paid to the Inland Revenue and is due by 31 January following the end of the tax year. It is possible in certain circumstances to pay the tax in instalments.

What is the rate of capital gains tax?

The first £7,700 of any gain will be exempt. Any gain made which exceeds this amount will be taxed at income tax rates.

TAXATION OF LIMITED COMPANIES

A limited company, unlike a partnership or sole trader, does not pay income tax or capital gains tax. Instead, a limited company pays corporation tax. Nonetheless, many of the taxation principles that apply to income tax and capital gains tax also apply to corporation tax. In particular, the way in which gains and profits are calculated is very similar, as is the treatment of capital allowances. Some of the main differences are set out below.

Basis of charge

Corporation tax is paid on both the profits of the company and on its capital gains.

What are the rates of tax?

The tax rates are fixed by reference to financial years, which run from 1 April to 31 March the following year. This can be contrasted with the income tax year, which runs from 6 April to 5 April the following year. Financial years are also described by reference to the period they begin, so the corporate year running from 1 April 2002 to 31 March 2003 is financial year 2002. The rates of tax are as follows:

- a lower small company rate of zero per cent on profits up to £10,000;
- a marginal rate calculated at 19/400 on profits between £10,001 and £50,000;
- a small company rate of 19 per cent on profits between £50,001 and £300,000;
- a marginal rate of 11/400 on profits between £300,001 and £1,500,000;
- a full company rate of 30 per cent on profits of £1,500,001 or more.

When is corporation tax paid?

For businesses that are classified as small companies, i.e. profits below £1.5 million, corporation tax is due nine months and one day after the end of the company's accounting period.

If a company's accounting period ends September 2003, then corporation tax is due on 1 July 2004.

Interest on overdue corporation tax is charged at 5 per cent per annum.

Self assessment

Like sole traders and partners, companies are required to assess their own corporation tax liability in a company return. The Inland Revenue will no longer issue estimates or formal assessments. Unlike sole traders and partners, companies cannot request the Inland Revenue to work out their tax liability.

Accounting periods

A company is free to choose its accounting period, but it cannot exceed 12 months. If the accounting period falls between two tax years, then the profits of each period will be apportioned on a time basis. Remember, the corporation tax year runs from 1 April to 31 March.

If a company's accounting period runs from September to August, the apportionment will be 7/12 of profits (seven months from 1 September to 31 March) for one tax year with the balance of the profits 5/12 (five months from 1 April to 31 August) due the next tax year.

Losses

If a company suffers a trading loss it can set off the loss against current profits. If this fails to absorb all the loss, the loss can be carried back against any profits made in the previous financial year.

If this still fails to absorb the loss then the loss can be set off against future profits of the same trade until the loss is absorbed. This will not apply where there is a change of ownership. 'Of the same trade' means the type of business in which the company was engaged, for example property. If, for instance, a property company changes its trade from property to financial services, it could not set off any unabsorbed losses of the company while it was involved in property against the future profits of the company when it became involved in financial services.

Directors' pay

A director's main sources of remuneration usually consist of a salary and/or a dividend payment and other fringe benefits (often called 'benefits in kind').

Salary

Where the director is paid a salary, income tax and Class 1 national insurance contributions will be deducted under what is known as the Pay As You Earn scheme (PAYE). The amount of the salary is a matter for negotiation, but if you do have a contract of service, it must be above the national minimum wage which is currently £4.20 per hour for employees aged 22 and over. The rate is due to be increased to £4.50 in October 2003 and £4.85 in October 2004. The salary paid to a director is a deductible expense, so it can be deducted in calculating the company's annual profit.

Dividends

Dividends can only be paid out of the profits of the company and are paid to shareholders in proportion to the numbers of shares they hold. Payment of a dividend can be attractive to a director/shareholder as there will be no national insurance contribution to pay. However, from the company's perspective, the disadvantage of paying a dividend is that it is not an allowable expense, so it cannot reduce the company's tax bill.

New rules have recently altered the tax treatment of dividends. Under these rules, the net dividend paid to the shareholder is deemed to be received net of a 10 per cent notional tax. This rate of 10 per cent is now the liability of basic rate taxpayers. For higher rate taxpayers dividend income is taxed at a rate of 32.5 per cent, which after taking off the deemed 10 per cent deducted at source, means that a further 22.5 per cent tax will be due. If you are a higher rate taxpayer, you will therefore have to pay a further 22.5 per cent out of the 90 per cent net dividend received.

Unfortunately, these new rules are very confusing. The main point to grasp is that if you are a basic rate taxpayer, no additional tax is payable on the dividend. If, however, you are a higher rate taxpayer, then you have to pay additional tax on the dividend at a rate of 22.5 per cent (having taken into account a tax credit given automatically of 10 per cent).

Finally, remember, dividends cannot count as pensionable income. This will be particularly important for a director close to retirement, as it may reduce the final salary figure which is used to determine the amount of pension paid under a final salary occupational pension scheme. A director who is regularly paid by dividends, instead of a salary, will not be paying national insurance contributions. This could jeopardize his/her entitlement to various state benefits.

Fringe benefits

These may include, for example, contributions by an employer to an approved pension scheme, a company car, health insurance or accommodation. Generally speaking, most fringe benefits will be taxable, unless you are either:

- an employee who is not a director and earning less than £8,500 per annum; or
- a full-time director earning less than £8,500 per annum (includes salary + the value of the benefits) and having no material interest in the company (i.e. owning less than five per cent of the ordinary share capital of the company).

If you do not meet the above conditions you are known in Inland Revenue jargon as a 'P11D employee'. This means that the Inland Revenue will endeavour to assess what the benefit is worth in cash and add this amount to the taxpayer's income for the year. This is called the 'tax charge' or 'taxable benefit'.

Pensions

Contributions by an employer to an approved Inland Revenue pension scheme are one of the few fringe benefits to P11D employees that do not attract tax or national insurance. In addition, the company's contributions to the employee's pension will be deductible in calculating its profits for corporation tax.

Cars

In 6 April 2002, a new system for calculating the cash-worth of this benefit was introduced. The main aim of the new system is to reward company employees who drive cleaner and more fuel-efficient cars. This is to be achieved by:

- removing any incentive to save tax by driving unnecessary extra miles;
- giving employees and employers a tax incentive to buy more fuel-efficient vehicles.

The amount of tax due is based on a percentage of the list price of the car, graduated according to the level of the car's carbon dioxide emission. There is a minimum tax charge of 15 per cent of the car's list price each year. In addition, your tax charge increases by one per cent of the list price for every five grams per kilometre of carbon dioxide your car produces above 155 grams per kilometre. In the tax year ending 5 April 2004, the maximum tax charge payable will be 35 per cent of the list price for cars producing 255 grams per kilometre.

Your company car is valued at £19,000 and has carbon dioxide emissions of 200g/km. Your car will be taxed on 24 per cent of the list price, i.e. £19,000 × 24 per cent = £4,180. Therefore, your taxable charge will be £4,560 and this is the figure to go in your tax return.

The cash-equivalent value of your car is based on the list price of the vehicle in accordance with existing rules. (The list price is the manufacturer's price for the vehicle when it was new – not the dealer's price. This information can be found in a publication called *Glasses Guide*.)

The following are a variety of sources available to find out how much carbon dioxide your car emits:

- ask your dealer;
- obtain a free guide from the Vehicle Certification Agency (www.roads.detr.gov.uk);
- for cars registered from November 2000, the carbon dioxide emissions figure for tax purposes will be recorded in the vehicle registration document (V5).

However, as there is no reliable data on carbon dioxide emissions for cars registered before 1 January 1998, they will be taxed on their engine size as follows:

- 0–1,400cc   15 per cent;
- 1,400–2,000cc   22 per cent;
- 2,001cc +   32 per cent.

There will be an extra three per cent charge for diesel cars, subject to the maximum charge of 35 per cent of the list price. This is because diesel engines generally produce higher levels of other pollutants.

When choosing a new company car, it will be sensible to take into account emission levels, because cars with lower emissions will attract less tax.

How is the Inland Revenue notified about fringe benefits?

Employers must keep a record of an employee's benefits on form P11D. Copies of the form must be given to the employee and the Inland Revenue by 6 July following the end of the tax year. If the employee is required to complete a tax return, the details contained in the P11D must be included. Finally, do not forget that all taxpayers are required to keep a record of their tax liabilities, so P11D must be kept safely for at least 22 months from the end of the tax year.

IR 35

What is IR 35?

These are the Inland Revenue's regulations on the taxation of contractors – i.e. individuals who provide services to a client through a company, or in certain cases, a partnership. This sort of arrangement is particularly common in the IT industry. In 1999, the Inland Revenue decided to introduce new regulations in order to limit this way of operating, as it was being used as a ploy to reduce the payment of tax and national insurance.

The position before IR 35

Before IR 35 came into force on 6 April 2000, it was usual for the client to enter into a contract with the individual's service company, rather than with the individual himself. Payment for the work was accordingly made to the service company. First, this arrangement benefited clients because they were able to avoid paying tax and national insurance and having to provide the usual employee benefits like holiday pay, sick pay and maternity leave. This was because, as the contract was made between the client and the individual's own company, the individual who did the work was not the client's employee. Second, the arrangement benefited the individual because he/she was able to reduce tax and national insurance payments when taking money out of the company. This was done by paying themselves a low salary and taking the rest as dividends. Remember, no national insurance is paid on a dividend.

How does IR 35 change things?

The individual providing the services is classified as an employee of their service company. To determine whether or not the rules apply, the Inland Revenue looks carefully at the relationship between the client and the individual providing the service.

How does this affect the tax and National Insurance position?

The Inland Revenue regards the income received by the company from the client as a deemed salary. As a consequence, by 19 April each year, the service company will have to pay tax and national insurance due on the amount paid by the client for the work. In calculating the deemed salary, service companies will be able to deduct certain allowable expenses such as VAT, professional indemnity insurance cover and employee Class 1 national insurance contributions, together with an additional flat rate deduction of five per cent of the gross fee received. The individual will also have to pay more income tax because income tax and national insurance must be paid on earnings from all the work carried out.

How does the Inland Revenue decide if you are an employee?

The following various tests will be applied although no single factor will be conclusive:

- Does the individual bear the financial risk if the job overruns, is more complex than anticipated or is not done correctly?
- Does the individual give instructions on what is to be done and supervise the project?
- Does the individual work for just one client and if so for how long? Specifically, the Inland Revenue has indicated that if an individual provides a service for more than a month, then there will be a presumption that the new rules apply.
- Does the individual work standard hours?
- Does the individual have the normal appearance of an independent business? i.e. provide his/her own equipment/materials, invest in their own company or put capital at risk?

A 'yes' answer to these questions (apart from the question about whether the individual works fixed hours) would tend to indicate self-employment. This is a new and complex area. You will need an accountant to advise you as to whether or not your business is subject to these far-reaching changes in taxation and NI. It is also possible to obtain a ruling from the Inland Revenue as to whether or not you are caught by these changes by sending them your contract to be examined.

VAT

What is VAT?

VAT stands for value added tax and is charged on the supply of most goods and services:

- a sale of goods;

- a supply of a service;
- an exchange of goods/services;
- a gift.

The VAT that you pay on any goods/services that you buy for your business is called 'input tax'. The VAT that you charge your customers on supplying goods/services is called 'output tax'.

There are three main rates of VAT:

1 *Zero rate* – no VAT is charged. This applies to goods such as food, children's clothing, books, drugs and medicines on prescription.
2 *Reduced rate* – this is charged at five per cent and applies to domestic fuel and power and the installation of energy-saving materials, for example loft insulation, etc.
3 *Standard rate* – this is charged at 17.5 per cent and applies to the majority of goods and services.

Registration

You must register for VAT if:

- your annual turnover exceeds £56,000 on a 12-month rolling basis; or,
- you have reasonable grounds for believing that your turnover in the next 30 days will exceed £56,000.

Notification to Customs & Excise is made on form VAT1. If you contact your local VAT office they will send you this form to complete. In due course you will be given a VAT registration number, which you must show on all invoices.

It is also possible to voluntarily register for VAT even if your turnover is below the current threshold. Although this will result in extra paperwork, it may be advantageous because you will be able to claim back the VAT you have incurred on paying for any goods and services (input tax). This is particularly useful when you are starting a new business as you may need to use solicitors and accountants and their fees will normally have VAT added.

How does it work?

You charge VAT on any goods/services you supply (output tax) and you are charged VAT on any goods/services for which you pay (input tax). You account to Customs & Excise if your output tax exceeds your input tax, or you recover the difference if your input tax exceeds your output tax.

Robert buys goods for £117.50, inclusive of VAT. His input tax is £17.50. He later sells the goods for £200 before VAT. The final sale price including VAT will therefore be £235.00. The VAT charged of £35 will be Robert's output tax. Robert will then deduct his input tax from his output tax, i.e. £35.00 minus £17.50, and will pay the difference of £17.50 to Customs & Excise.

Paying VAT

You are required to make quarterly returns on Form VAT100 to Customs & Excise showing your input and output tax. The normal tax period for VAT is three months. Any VAT due must then be paid within one month from the end of the quarterly period. If you regularly claim a VAT refund because you pay out more VAT than you collect, it is possible to have a one-month tax period rather than the usual three months.

Keeping a record

Records must be kept of all transactions. The following should be kept for at least six years:

- invoices for all sales or supplies;
- a VAT account for each tax period;
- the VAT returns sent to Customs & Excise.

Providing a VAT invoice

When you supply goods or services to another person/company who is VAT registered, you must provide and keep a copy of the invoice. The invoice must contain the following information, unless the tax-inclusive price is less than £100:

1 identifying number (usually an invoice number);
2 your VAT reference number, name and address;
3 the customer's name and address;
4 the tax point – normally the date when the goods are supplied or the customer is billed;
5 type of supply, for example sale, rental, etc;
6 a description which identifies the goods or services and includes:
   - the quality of goods or extent of service;
   - the cost excluding VAT;
   - the rate of VAT;
7 the total amount paid excluding VAT;
8 the total VAT paid.

Special schemes

The following are special schemes to make things easier for certain types of businesses.

Cash accounting scheme

Small businesses (turnover less than £600,000) can pay VAT on a cash accounting basis. This means VAT is only paid on money actually paid and received, instead of invoices. This can be of considerable assistance to a small business because you do not need to account for VAT until you have been paid. If you are not paid by a customer, you will enjoy automatic bad debt relief.

Annual accounting scheme

You can join this scheme as soon as your business is registered and has a turnover of less than £600,000. Instead of completing returns and paying quarterly, you can instead pay instalments by direct debit and send in just one annual return. Your VAT liability is estimated on the previous year's payments and is divided by ten. Nine equal monthly payments by direct debit then have to be made, with the annual return and final payment following within two months after the end of the year. The advantage of this scheme is that only one return has to be made and you know in advance how much VAT to pay.

Retail schemes

These are for businesses, such as shops, which would find it very difficult to account for VAT in the usual way. There are three separate schemes, and you should ask your accountant's advice before deciding on the most appropriate one for your business.

Flat-rate scheme

This scheme is open to small businesses whose turnover is less than £100,000. The aim of the scheme is to simplify the way small businesses account for VAT so that they need to spend less time and money keeping VAT records and calculating the VAT payable to Customs. Under the flat-rate scheme, businesses do not have to identify and record the VAT on sales and purchases. They simply record all business supplies and apply a flat-rate percentage to the total in each period. Further details of the scheme are contained in the Customs and Excise Notice 733.

Penalties

Blank VAT returns are sent out by Customs & Excise for completion for each VAT period (generally three months). Customs & Excise have extremely wide powers to penalize for late, incorrect or incomplete returns, ranging from fines, charges and seizure of goods to imprisonment. You must therefore ensure that you account for VAT correctly and on time. Further details can be obtained from Customs & Excise who have published a notice entitled *What if I don't pay?* (VAT notice 930).

WHAT SHOULD A BUSINESS DO IF IT IS THE SUBJECT OF AN INLAND REVENUE INVESTIGATION?

How will I be notified?

The first indication that you are subject to an inquiry will usually be when the Inland Revenue write to you. The Inland Revenue may just want to clarify some aspect of your annual return. A reply dealing with the issue may often resolve the matter. However, you may be invited to visit your tax office. The Inland Revenue has 12 months from the final filing date to let you know that you are subject to a tax inquiry.

What is an investigation?

There are two different types:
1 an *aspect* inquiry is fairly straightforward. This means the Inland Revenue have noticed something that is not quite right in your return. Provided you can deal with these points that should be an end to the matter;
2 a *full* investigation is more serious. The Inland Revenue will want to examine your finances in great detail and go through all relevant documents, such as bank statements.

It is also normal practice during a full inquiry for the Inland Revenue to ask you to attend a meeting to discuss the business records and often your own personal financial affairs too. Ideally, you should seek representation from a solicitor or tax expert before attending such a meeting.

What should I do?

- Seek advice straight away from an accountant or tax adviser familiar with Inland Revenue inquiries;
- do not agree to attend an interview without your accountant/tax adviser being present;
- do not admit to keeping inadequate records;
- be polite when you deal with the inspectors;
- try and co-operate wherever possible; however, remember the Inland Revenue cannot visit your home/business without your consent. If you refuse, then they will have to obtain a warrant;
- ask the inspector to clarify the nature of the investigation;
- be sure your accountant/tax adviser is present and gives you advice before you sign any statements or agreements.

What happens next?

Once the inquiry is concluded, you will have to pay any tax owed together with interest at the official rate. You can also be charged a penalty of up to 100 per cent of the tax that you owe. In very serious cases, the ultimate penalty is imprisonment. Note that the extent of any penalty depends not only on the seriousness of the offence, but also on the level of co-operation from the taxpayer. Being obstructive could therefore prove to be counter-productive.

APPEALS AND COMPLAINTS AGAINST THE INLAND REVENUE

If you disagree about the amount of your tax bill, then initially you should exhaust all avenues within the Inland Revenue to agree a settlement. As a starting point, you should raise the matter with your tax inspector. If the dispute cannot be resolved, you can firstly appeal to the Commissioners. Although there are two types of Commissioners, most appeals are dealt with by the General Commissioners. They are not tax experts, but often local business people who act in a voluntary, unpaid capacity with the assistance of a clerk who will have expert knowledge. The hearing is conducted in private. There is a right of appeal from the Commissioners' decision to the High Court.

If you are unhappy about the manner in which the Inland Revenue has handled your tax affairs, you should first complain to your tax inspector. If this fails to resolve the problem, then complain to the Director responsible for your tax office. As a last resort, you can complain to the Independent Revenue Adjudicator. They will deal with errors, excessive delay or discourtesy.

59

Trading Arrangements

COMMERCIAL AGENTS

A business wishing to expand its sales into a different market or a new range of products may instruct a self-employed *agent*. An agent is simply someone who represents a person or firm in business. The business instructing the agent is known as the *principal* and will hope to benefit from the agent's local trade connections. The arrangement will also save the principal money, as it will not have to recruit new employees or open new branches.

Traditionally, agency arrangements have been very popular with businesses but regulations brought into force in 1994 (*see* below) have introduced tighter controls over what can be agreed between the parties. As a result, in some situations an agent will be in a stronger position than an employee; if, for example, the principal terminates the arrangement, a court can award an agent unlimited financial compensation.

Types of agency arrangement

There are two types of agency:
1 *Sales agency* – the agent will be authorized to enter into contracts with customers on behalf of the principal. The principal will have a direct contract with the customer through the agent's actions.
2 *Marketing agency* – the agent may only effect an introduction between the principal and the customers. The agent does not have authority to enter into contracts on the principal's behalf.

Form of agreement

The Commercial Agents (Council Directive) Regulations 1993 ('the Regulations') govern the relations between commercial agents who *buy and sell goods* in the UK and their principals. The Regulations do not apply to agents who *provide services*.

The Regulations provide protection for agents by stipulating that the contract will include certain terms. These terms deal with payment, ending the agency and the respective duties of the parties, such as requiring the principal to provide certain documents, for example commission statements. Principal and agent cannot agree to exclude certain terms, such as the requirement for the principal to pay compensation to the agent if the contract is ended.

The Regulations require the parties to sign a written agency agreement if one of the parties requests this. Even if the Regulations do not apply or neither party requests it, a written agreement is advisable to avoid uncertainty.

The agreement should include:
1 the area in which the agent is due to operate (known as the *territory*);
2 description of products to be sold/marketed;
3 type of agency – sales or marketing (*see* above);
4 whether the agent has:
   - *sole agency* – the principal may not appoint any other agents in the territory although the principal can still seek business in the territory;
   - *exclusive agency* – no other agents or distributors may operate in the territory nor may the principal;
   - *non-exclusive agency* – the agent cannot prevent the principal or other agents from operating in the territory;
5 duties and obligations of both parties, for example sales targets to be achieved by agent;
6 how long the agreement will last, for example fixed term or indefinitely;
7 payment;
8 restraint of trade (i.e. restricting agent's activities after the agreement has ended);
9 termination – notice to end agency and compensation for termination.

Effect of agency

The principal will need to keep a close check on the sales agent, as any contracts with third parties agreed by the agent will be binding on the principal.

The agent will not be liable under a contract negotiated with a third party on behalf of the principal. The principal cannot sue the agent if the third party does not comply with the contract nor can he be sued by the third party if the principal defaults.

Payment to agents

Agents are usually paid a percentage of the net sales value of the goods marketed for the principal – this is known as *commission*. The commission rate will usually be agreed verbally or in writing. If nothing has been agreed, the agent will be entitled to 'reasonable remuneration' having regard to what is normal in their industry (e.g. the type of products being sold).

Under the Regulations, the agent is entitled to commission on sales effected *during the period he/she is an agent* where:

- the transaction is concluded as a result of his/her efforts; or
- the customer acquired by the agent has placed a repeat order.

Even after the agency has ended, the agent will be entitled to commission on a sale if it is mainly attributable to the agent's efforts while he/she was working for the principal. The agent will similarly be entitled if the order reaches the principal before the agency contract has ended. However, if the sale is effected more than a reasonable period after the agency has ended, commission will not be payable. 'Reasonable period' can be defined in the agency agreement but otherwise will be what is normal in the industry. For example, if an agent is selling expensive technical products to a small customer base and has been working on a sale for a considerable time, a 'reasonable period' is likely to be longer than, for example, an agent selling fruit drinks.

If the agreement is silent about when the agent must be paid, the Regulations require the principal to pay commission when the goods have, or should have been, delivered or when the customer pays for the goods.

Termination of agency

If the agency contract is for a *fixed period*, the agency will end when the period expires, if it is not renewed. To end the arrangement during the fixed term, the party wanting to end the contract would have to show either:

1 a fundamental breach of contract (*see* below); or

2 that the contract allows it.

If neither 1 nor 2 above apply then the party ending the agency will be in breach of contract and liable to the other for any loss. If the Regulations apply, the agent will probably be able to claim compensation too (*see* below).

An agency for an *indefinite period* can be ended on reasonable notice given by one party to the other. What is reasonable will often be based upon how long the agent has worked for the principal, for example one week for an agent of three weeks' service. Notice means a warning given to the other party that the relationship will end on a particular date.

Where the Regulations apply, there are minimum notice periods:

1 one month's notice for the first year of the agency;

2 two months' notice for the second year which *has begun*;

3 three months' notice for the third year which *has begun* and *all subsequent years*.

For example, an agent who has worked for one year and one month is entitled to two months' notice. An agent who has worked for five years is entitled to three months' notice.

Whether it is the principal or agent who has given notice to end the agency, the principal can require the agent to work during the notice period. In practice, if the relationship between the parties has broken down, the principal will often pay the agent in lieu of notice rather than requiring him to work. The principal may be concerned that if the agent works out his notice, he may have a damaging effect on the business.

An important exception to the rules requiring either reasonable notice or notice under the Regulations is the concept of *fundamental breach of contract*. This means that the agent or principal has been guilty of serious misconduct which undermines the whole foundation of the contract; for example, if an agent refuses to visit customers then sales will be lost and the whole purpose of the agency arrangement is undermined. In these circumstances the aggrieved party can immediately end the contract and sue for losses.

The Regulations provide that commercial agents are entitled to be either indemnified or compensated when the agreement is terminated. This concept is quite different from the compensation provisions that normally apply under English law, i.e. damages are only payable where a party is in breach of contract. Under the Regulations the principal will be required to make redress to the agent simply when the contract ends. The agent is not required to show any breach of contract or fault on the part of the principal. An agent will be entitled to a payment on termination of the agency agreement where:

- the agency agreement is terminated by the principal;
- the agent dies;
- the agent is too old or ill reasonably to continue.

Ascertaining how much an agent is entitled to receive

under either the indemnity or compensation measures, when the agreement has terminated, is not easy to determine and has caused the courts a great deal of difficulty. This is because the termination provisions are EU concepts and the Regulations give little or no guidance on how to work out termination payments.

Unless an agreement specifically provides for the indemnity measure, the agent will be entitled to receive compensation. Broadly speaking, the indemnity measure focuses on what the principal has gained from the efforts of the agent. On the other hand, the compensation measure focuses more on the loss to the agent and is to compensate the agent for the agreement being brought to an end.

The indemnity measure is capped at one year's commission. The Regulations state that an agent is entitled to an indemnity where the agent has brought in principal new customers or significantly increased the volume of business with existing customers and the principal continues to derive substantial benefits from the business with such customers. Factors that are taken into account when trying to work out how much to pay the agent on termination include:

- how much new business the agent has brought the principal;
- the amount of the gross commission for the last year of the agency on new and increased business;
- the maximum figure allowed under the regulations, one year's gross remuneration, compared with an average of the previous five years;
- adjust to take into account the equity of the situation, e.g. downturn in the business.

If an agent is entitled to a compensation payment on termination of the agreement, then the following factors are taken into account:

- how much commission the agent was earning;
- the amount the agent would have earned had the agreement continued, and for how long;
- whether the agent increased sales;
- the period of time the agent had worked for the principal;
- the age of the agent.

There have been various attempts in this country to follow French case law that allows for a straightforward payment of two years' gross commission without any deductions. However, in this country the position at present still remains that the two-year rule should not necessarily always be followed and is regarded as too simplistic. Factors such as the length of the agreement, whether the agent has built up a big customer base, the value of the agency as an asset before termination, will all be relevant.

Although it is difficult to give any guidance, payments between one and two years' net commission seem to be a rough rule of thumb. If and when any offers to settle are made, always ensure they are made without prejudice. Also ensure that any payments made are on a 'full and final settlement' basis. This will stop the agent accepting the money and then coming back for more.

Finally, the agent is only entitled to remuneration on termination if they inform the principal of this within one year of the agreement being ended.

DISTRIBUTORS

Another sales arrangement for a business is the distribution agreement. This may arise where a supplier or manufacturer wishes to have his goods sold in a new area but does not wish to open a branch office in that area. A distributor buys goods from the supplier/manufacturer and resells them to his customers in the new territory at a profit. There is no contract between the supplier/ manufacturer and the customer as the distributor deals with the customer direct.

Types of distribution agreement

Exclusive distribution agreement
Only the distributor is allowed to sell the goods in the territory allocated to him. The supplier/manufacturer is prevented from doing so.

Non-exclusive distribution agreement
The supplier/manufacturer may appoint more than one distributor to sell the products in the territory. No one distributor will have the sole right to do so.

Sole distribution agreement
No other distributor may be appointed by the supplier/ manufacturer to work in the territory.

Selective distribution agreement
The supplier/manufacturer will appoint more than one distributor but will restrict the number and type of business to whom he supplies. The supplier may also try to restrict the sales the distributor makes. This type of agreement is more frequently used with quality, high-value products. Care has to be taken to ensure the selection is not applied in a discriminatory way as otherwise the agreement may fall foul of competition law (*see* pages 528–9).

FRANCHISES

Business franchising involves a company (the franchisor) allowing another company (the franchisee) to operate an established business system. The business system involves

Differences between agency and distribution agreements

	Agency agreement	Distribution agreement
1	Agent seeks to conclude a sale between principal and customer	Distributor buys from supplier/manufacturer and sells to customer
2	Agent often has power to bind principal to a contract with the customer	Distributor has no power to create a contract between supplier/manufacturer and customer
3	Due to 2 above, agent requires closer supervision by principal	Less supervision necessary for distributor
4	If agent is operating in unfamiliar markets (e.g. abroad) there is more risk to the principal due to 2 above	A distributor may be more appropriate for an unfamiliar market as the supplier/manufacturer need not operate there itself
5	Agent is remunerated by payment of commission	Distributor receives commission or profits from sales to customers
6	Agency arrangement preferable where goods marketed are to be tailor-made or modified to suit client's needs	Distribution agreement can work well where goods are standard and relatively easy to market
7	If products sold are defective, the principal (rather than the agent) is liable to the customer	Liability for defective products rests with the distributor although his ability to recoup any loss in turn from the supplier/manufacturer is governed by the distribution contract
8	Even in the absence of a written agreement, an agent's position is considerably strengthened by the Commercial Agents (Council Directive) Regulations 1993, e.g. particularly regarding compensation for termination	The Regulations do not apply to distributors, so an aggrieved distributor will have to rely on provisions in the distribution agreement (if one exists) or general contract law

a common form of activity, branding, administration and managing.

It is an extremely common type of business arrangement, involving activities ranging from sale of pet products to fast food restaurants, for example McDonald's.

The key to a franchise is that it is a *proven business system with an established track record.*

The franchisor owns the trademarks/trade names, which he allows the franchisee to use for an initial fee. The franchisor will provide the franchisee with support in setting up and running the business in the form of advertising, training and administration. The franchisee will have a continuing obligation to pay for that support.

Although the franchisee is self-employed, he must run the business in accordance with the *Franchise Agreement and Franchise Operating Manual.* It is essential for a would-be franchisee to take legal and financial advice *before* signing the agreement, to reveal any hidden 'nasties' such as unexpected costs, restrictions on sale or ending the franchise or time limits on the franchise.

The British Franchise Association, through their members, promotes good franchising practice in the UK. The Association can provide advice and literature on buying a franchise and can be contacted on Tel: 01491 578050; website: www.british-franchise.org.uk.

Many high street banks have franchise departments that can provide information to businesses.

Checklist of advantages and disadvantages of a franchise

Advantages

1 *For franchisor* – means of expansion without capital outlay.
2 *For franchisee* – benefit of using a tried and tested business concept with support from the franchisor.
3 *The franchisee* receives the benefit of the franchisor's experience and a franchise business is statistically less likely to fail.

Disadvantages

1 *For franchisor* – poor performance by franchisees may damage his reputation.
2 *For franchisee* – he must run the business within the confines of the *Franchise Agreement and Franchising Operating Manual,* and that may be unduly restrictive.
3 *Franchisee* is vulnerable to ability of franchisor to promote the business concept and maintain standards with other franchisees.
4 Initial fee and continuing payments required from the franchisee are often significant.

COMPETITION LAW

The Competition Act 1998

The Act replaced a number of laws governing competition in the UK and applies to businesses of all sizes and types. If left unchecked, some companies will attempt to dominate the market to sell more products or services. This usually damages competing businesses and restricts choice for the consumer. Competition law aims to regulate the power of companies in the market place to ensure they do not abuse a dominant market position or enter into agreements restricting prices of goods or services.

The Act is divided into two main parts: Chapter 1 outlaws anti-competitive agreements such as excessive pricing and Chapter 2 outlaws an abuse of a dominant position in the market, for example refusal to supply certain businesses.

Anti-competitive agreements – Chapter 1 of the Act

Step 1

Where a business is operating in such a way as to prevent, restrict or distort competition it may be infringing the Act. Examples include:
1 fixing buying or selling prices of goods;
2 agreeing to produce only a fixed amount of products each year;
3 market sharing, i.e. businesses agreeing to carve up the territory between themselves.

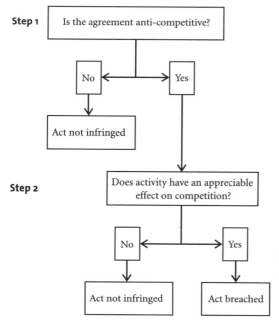

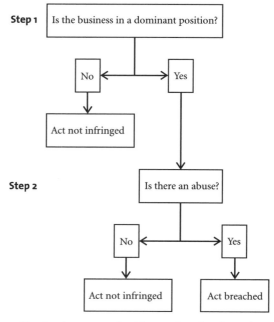

The Act is concerned with ensuring that by maintaining free competition consumers receive benefits in the form of lower prices and better quality services.

Step 2

The activities of the business must have an *appreciable effect* on competition in the market in which it operates. The activities would usually have an appreciable effect if the parties involved in the anti-competitive behaviour make up more than 25 per cent of the market share. However, price fixing, market sharing and maintaining minimum resale prices will usually have an appreciable effect regardless of the business's market share.

Abuse of dominant position – Chapter 2 of the Act

Step 1

As well as anti-competitive agreements, the Act prohibits abuse of a dominant position in the market. Whether a business is in a dominant position will usually depend upon its size and position in the market. It is unlikely to be considered dominant if its market share is less than 40 per cent.

Step 2

What is abuse? Examples include:
1 *predatory pricing* – where a business fixes low prices to force out smaller businesses with the intention of raising prices above a competitive level once they have gone;

2 *refusal to supply* – a dominant undertaking would have to justify refusing to supply *existing customers*, for example for non-payment of invoices. A business retains the right to refuse to deal with a *new customer* unless, for example, the supplier controls 'essential facilities' such as a port.

3 *tied sales* – where a customer is obliged to buy a second product because he had bought the first, for example selling computers only if the computer software is purchased as well.

Enforcement

The Office of Fair Trading (OFT) administers and enforces the Act. The regulators of the gas, electricity, water, telecommunications and railway industries have equivalent powers to enforce the Act in their sectors.

The Director General of Fair Trading (DGFT) has extensive powers to investigate if he has reasonable grounds for suspecting the Act has been broken. His two main powers are:

1 requiring production of documents or information relating to the matter being investigated;

2 'dawn raids' or on-the-spot investigation of documents at premises.

Penalties

Once the DGFT has established that a business has breached the Act, he can direct the parties to vary or end the infringing agreement or conduct.

The financial penalty on the company is 10 per cent of its UK annual turnover for each year of infringement, up to a maximum of three years.

Summary

All businesses, small, medium or large are affected by the Act and owners need to closely scrutinize any trading arrangements that are or may be anti-competitive. The penalties are harsh for those who do not comply. Some comfort is offered by the OFT, which has the power to offer total immunity or reduced penalties if the company 'blows the whistle' about its own activities.

Anyone adversely affected by anti-competitive behaviour can complain to the OFT and if sufficient evidence is provided, the DGFT will investigate. The Act also allows the aggrieved party to bring a court action; however, this is less attractive due to the cost involved.

Competition Act Enquiry Line at the OFT: Tel: 08457 224499; e-mail: enquiries.competition@oft.gov.uk

60

Safeguarding the Business

TERMS AND CONDITIONS OF TRADING

The Consumer section (Chapters 42–51) of this book deals with terms that are implied by law into a contract between a customer and a business, for example regarding the quality and standard of the goods or services. This chapter examines how a businessperson can safeguard his/her business by ensuring, as far as possible, that the contract is performed on terms favourable to his/her business.

Many businesses do not have terms and conditions of trading, and many contracts can be entered into without any written record of the agreement. Often contracts are made verbally or implied by the parties' conduct. For example, a customer purchasing a bag of carrots from a greengrocer will not be expected (nor expect!) to sign a contract agreeing to the terms of purchase. The contract will be concluded by the customer taking the carrots to the till, the shop assistant ringing up the price and the customer paying for the carrots.

Although often there will be no doubt that there is a contract between the parties, in more sophisticated transactions problems can arise as to what the parties agreed. In commercial transactions it is common for the parties to negotiate for some time before reaching agreement. If the parties then fall out and, for example, one party refuses to perform an aspect of the contract, it will be much easier for the courts to decide on the parties' intentions if the terms are in writing.

If you are in business, a written agreement signed by the parties is binding even if they have not read the terms. The court assumes that all the terms agreed are encompassed in the written contract. Rarely will the court allow outside evidence to contradict the written terms. The only exception is if one party has misled the other party about the content of the agreement, i.e. by fraud or misrepresentation. In these circumstances, the court may allow the aggrieved party to get out of the contract altogether and/or claim damages against the other party.

Battle of the forms

All businesses, other than those engaged in the most straightforward of transactions, are well advised to have a commercial solicitor draw up a document setting out the standard terms on which they will trade. The cost is likely to be in the region of £150 to £1,500 depending upon the complexity and length of the document. It is extremely important that the terms are clear and unambiguous. If the clause cannot be interpreted in a straightforward way this will work against the person trying to rely upon the clause.

The next hurdle is to *ensure the terms form part of the resulting contract*. To do this the business must show the other party had reasonable notice of the terms and he/she absolutely accepted them.

Reasonable notice

Many businesses make the mistake of only printing their terms and conditions on an invoice which is supplied at the end of the transaction, i.e. after the goods have been delivered. This is not usually sufficient to show that the terms form part of the contract, as the party should have notice of the terms when the contract is formed. The timing is the key here; the parties must know the terms upon which the contract *will be performed*. The law does not allow terms to be imposed after the event (unless of course the parties agree). Terms on an invoice may be sufficient if the seller can show a regular and consistent course of dealings with the buyer over a period of time.

Unusual or onerous terms (such as exclusion clauses) should be made more prominent or pointed out to the other party. A business should also ensure the terms are printed on something that the other party may consider likely to contain contract terms, i.e. a ticket rather than a receipt.

It is fairly standard practice for companies giving quotations to have terms and conditions on the reverse of the quotation. This is good practice as long as the face of the quotation refers to the fact that there are terms and conditions on the reverse and that if the customer accepts the quotation the contract will be governed by those terms and conditions.

The best way of ensuring that the other party does not deny ever receiving the terms and conditions is to require the customer to sign and return a duplicate form containing the terms. This may not be practicable for each contract, so at a convenient stage in the parties' relationship (say when the customer's credit account is opened), the business should send out the terms and conditions asking the other party to sign a form confirming that all future transactions will be governed by those terms and conditions.

In the context of transactions concluded on the internet, it is important that the terms and conditions of trading are posted on the website. A common practice has developed whereby the customer is required to complete an order form online. On the form there is a hyperlink (key words that link the web pages) to the terms and conditions, which are stated to apply to the contract.

Acceptance of terms

If a supplier delivers goods subject to his terms and conditions of trading and the customer simply takes delivery with no further comment, then it is clear the contract is governed by the supplier's terms and conditions. Similarly, if a customer places an order for goods specifying the terms and conditions to apply to the contract and the supplier delivers with no further exchange of correspondence, then the customer's terms and conditions apply.

By contrast, if a business supplies terms and conditions to a customer who then replies with different terms of his own, this will be a counter-offer rather than acceptance and the customer will not be bound.

Company A is approached by Company B to supply machine tools. A issues a quotation to B and refers to her terms and conditions of trading which will apply to the contract. B replies, accepting the quotation but saying that his terms and conditions will apply.

If A acknowledges B's order without further comment, she will be bound by B's terms and conditions. In this scenario B is putting forward a counter-offer which will form a contract once accepted by A without further comment.

If A replies to B's letter noting his acceptance but stating that A's terms and conditions will apply, there will be no contract. This is because, although B has accepted the quote, he has not accepted A's terms and is seeking to impose terms of his own. As long as the parties continue not to accept the other's terms there will be no contract.

For internet sales, it is safer for the supplier to specify that the contract will not be formed until he has communicated acceptance of the order (usually by e-mail) to the customer. In this way, if a customer places an order that the business cannot fulfil, he is not bound to deal with it and can simply reply declining the order.

Price and payment

The price in a contract may be fixed or determined, for example, by the number of hours worked or items produced. If a price or rate is not agreed then the buyer must pay a reasonable price.

What is a reasonable price is a question of fact and will depend upon factors such as the type of business involved, whether the work was urgent or whether the buyer specially commissioned it. To avoid arguments, the contract should be clear about the price.

Other matters to be addressed in the contract are:

1 Is the price stated inclusive or exclusive of VAT?
2 Are there any other costs (e.g. transportation and insurance)?
3 When is payment due (e.g. on completion of the product or 30 days from receipt of the invoice)?
4 If stage payments are agreed, can the seller end the contract if the buyer does not make a stage payment when due or can he refuse to deliver?
5 What form of payment is required (e.g. cash on delivery or cheque)?
6 Is interest payable on late payments? (*See* page 535.)
7 Where the buyer also supplies the other party, provision can be made for any debts under each contract to be offset against the other. For example, A supplies B with machine components which, as yet, are unpaid. Under a separate contract, B has carried out servicing work on the boiler at A's factory. A cannot refuse to pay for the service just because B has not paid him for the components. The contract would have to specifically allow offsetting or contra-payments. Even if the two debts are offset, if one debt is higher than the other, the excess must be paid to the party concerned.

Ownership and risk

The contract should be clear as to when ownership and risk (i.e. responsibility for loss or damage) in the goods passes to the buyer. For example, if the buyer is collecting the goods, does he acquire ownership and risk at that stage or when they reach the buyer's premises? This is important because if the goods are damaged in transit, the contract will determine who bears the loss.

Usually the buyer will only acquire the risk in the goods once he acquires ownership. The parties' intentions regarding the passing of ownership and risk are paramount and these can be ascertained from the contract, their conduct or surrounding circumstances. If no intention is apparent, the provisions of the Sale of Goods Act

1979 section 18 will apply. Section 18 sets out various rules that apply depending upon, for example, whether the goods need to be weighed or in some way put into a deliverable state or are supplied on a sale or return basis. The rule that applies to most sales states that ownership passes to the buyer when *the contract is made*. Therefore, if a customer goes into a shop and agrees to buy a sofa for delivery the next day, ownership and risk has passed to the customer. If the sofa is destroyed in a fire at the shop overnight, strictly speaking, the customer will bear the loss. In practice, however, the retailer will usually have insurance to cover the loss.

Where the contract contains a retention of title clause (*see* below) the supplier will want to specify that risk passes on delivery.

Retention of title

A business wishing to ensure that a buyer does not acquire ownership of goods until payment has been made can insert such a provision in its terms and conditions of trading. If there is no such provision, ownership of the goods will pass to the buyer when the contract is formed, regardless of whether the goods have been paid for or delivered.

Retention-of-title clauses are also known as *Romalpa* clauses – the name stems from the name of a company involved in a case concerning retention-of-title clauses.

The main benefit of an enforceable retention-of-title clause is that in the event of the buyer's insolvency, in theory the seller can reclaim the goods for himself rather than relying on the availability of funds in the debtor's estate to pay the invoice. If the Insolvency Practitioner disposes of the goods, the seller would be entitled to sue him for interfering with the goods. The amount of the claim would be for the market value of the goods.

There are a number of hurdles to overcome to persuade the insolvency practitioner that the retention of title clause is valid:

1 to rely on the clause, the seller must show the buyer had reasonable notice of the term and the clause formed part of the contract (*see* 'Battle of the forms', p. 530);

2 to reclaim goods, the seller must be able to identify the products supplied – i.e. by markings or codes on the goods themselves, cross-referenced with details on the invoice. This is fine for some goods but problematic for others, for example two tonnes of top soil;

3 it is advisable for the terms and conditions to require the buyer to store the goods separately (to assist with their identification) and for the seller to be given a right of entry to the buyer's premises. It is unlikely, however, that a seller could rely on such a clause to gain entry to a private individual's home without a court order allowing him to do so;

4 what happens if the buyer sells the goods or uses them in the manufacture of another product? Unless expressly provided for in the agreement, the seller's retention of title will usually fail at this stage. There are additional legal complications that make most clauses extending ownership to third parties or manufactured products unenforceable.

Some retention-of-title clauses retain ownership on the goods delivered until *all debts and obligations* owed by the buyer have been paid – this is known as an *all monies* clause.

Delivery

Delivery usually means the physical handing over of goods to a buyer or providing means of access to them (e.g. keys to a warehouse).

The buyer is obliged to collect the goods from the seller's business premises at a reasonable hour, unless otherwise agreed. If the contract provides that the seller will deliver, it should specify whether he will deliver the goods personally or by a carrier. If the latter, the seller will probably specify that delivery takes place when the goods are given to the carrier.

Late delivery is a fertile area for disputes between businesses. The parties should agree a date for delivery and this should be stipulated in the contract. Failure to meet the deadline will entitle the seller to reject the goods and walk away from the contract. If no fixed date for delivery has been agreed, then the goods must be delivered within a reasonable period of time. What is reasonable will vary from case to case.

Where delivery has not been made by what the buyer believes to be a reasonable time, he should 'make time of the essence' by giving the seller a final deadline for delivery. This should be a reasonable period of time, e.g. not the next day. If the seller then fails to deliver on time, the buyer can refuse to take delivery and end the contract.

If time is not of the essence, the buyer may still be able to sue the seller for damages for late delivery.

Exclusion clauses

The Consumer law section of this book (Chapters 42–51) has examined exclusion clauses in contracts and the implications of the Unfair Contract Terms Act 1977 and the position under the Unfair Terms in Consumer Contracts Regulations 1999.

Despite their unpopularity with the courts, most commercial agreements will contain exclusion or limitation of liability clauses. They are useful protection for a business opposing a futile yet aggressive attempt by a customer to hold the business responsible for some minor problem connected with the transaction. Clearly, if a business constantly relies on an exclusion clause to excuse the business from not providing a good service, then it will soon be out of business.

The law is less restrictive when dealings are between two businesses – a clause which would otherwise be disallowed if the business was dealing with a consumer, will be allowed (subject to it being reasonable) where the transaction is between two businesses. For example, it is not possible to exclude the implied terms contained in the Sale of Goods Act as to title, description, quality, fitness for purpose and sample in a consumer sale. However, such implied terms (save for title) can be excluded in a non-consumer sale if the clause is reasonable. The 'reasonableness' test is discussed in Chapter 47.

Exclusion clauses are scrutinized closely by the courts and will be construed strictly against the person trying to rely on them. The clause will therefore need to cover the liability, which is the subject matter of the dispute. They can be useful to put a cap on the amount of damages an aggrieved party can claim from the business if the contract is not fulfilled. For example, often the terms will restrict liability to the buyer to the amount of the contract price. This would ensure that even if the buyer sustained other losses, for example loss of profit, he could not claim this from the seller.

A common restriction imposed by sellers is to require the buyer to notify him of any defects, damage or non-delivery within a certain period of time. The term often states that if the buyer fails to do so, the goods will be presumed to be free from defect/damage.

A prudent buyer will incorporate in his terms and conditions a right to reject goods that do not conform with the contract. The buyer could also seek an indemnity from the seller to protect him in the situation where the buyer sells defective goods to a customer and is sued by that customer.

Boilerplate provisions

'Boilerplate provisions' simply means standard clauses that are common to most commercial agreements. These include:

- *cancellation* – the party will probably wish to terminate the agreement if the other is in breach of the agreement or becomes insolvent. It is common to have such a clause in terms and conditions and for the contract to specify what happens after termination, for example a wind-down of operations;
- *law and jurisdiction* – stating which country's laws are to apply and which courts are to deal with the case. This will rarely be necessary if all parties are based in England and the contract is to be performed in England;
- *notices* – specifying how and where any notices under the agreement must be sent, for example in writing, by recorded delivery to the company's registered office;
- *force majeure* – if a party cannot perform his/her contractual obligations due to circumstances beyond his/her control (e.g. acts of God, civil war) a force majeure clause allows him/her to be excused from liability.

CREDIT CONTROL AND COLLECTING DEBTS

Businesses operating on a cash-on-delivery basis (like shops) need never be concerned about credit control. Even shopkeepers, however, may experience a bad debt from time to time, for example where a customer's cheque has bounced. Bad credit control can have a damaging effect on a business, as it may be unable to pay its own suppliers and be forced to either borrow the money or perhaps go out of business.

Creditworthy customers

Once a new customer has agreed to the terms of trading, an account can be opened up. The customer should complete a form providing full name, address and contact details. The next step is to give the business a credit check. This is particularly important on high-value debts. There are various ways to obtain information about a business or person:

- *credit reference agencies* – for a fee, an agency will provide a recommended credit rating for the customer. The rating will be based upon information obtained from Companies House (i.e. accounts and mortgages), the register of county court judgments and information from other suppliers. Reports can usually be supplied on the same day, as most of the information is available 'on line';
- *Companies House* – information on limited companies is maintained by Companies House and is available on request and payment of a fee. The information includes accounts, current and disqualified directors and mortgages. Directors' reports of public limited companies and their large private subsidiaries give a useful indication of the average time they take to pay their suppliers. Contact telephone number: 029 2038 0801;
- *register of county court judgments* – this is maintained by Registry Trust Ltd in London on behalf of the Court Service. It contains details of all county court judgments and can be searched by providing the Registry with the customer's name and address and £4.50 fee. The search will reveal the date and amount of the judgment, defendant, court and case number. After six years, a judgment is removed from the register. Contact telephone number: 020 7380 0133;

- *bank/trade references* – if the customer agrees, a reference can be obtained from his bank. As the bank will only use standard wording in its reply, it is best to ask specific questions such as 'is A Ltd good for £3,000 per month on 30 day terms?'. Be wary if the bank provides a guarded reference.

   Alternatively, approach suppliers of the business for a reference. Questions to be asked include payment terms and payment history;
- *Insolvency Service* – based in Birmingham, the Insolvency Service is an executive division of the DTI and keeps information regarding individual voluntary arrangements and bankruptcy. The search can be conducted in person or by post upon production of the customer's name, address (and date of birth or approximate age for bankruptcy searches). Contact telephone number: 0121 698 4000.

How to reduce risk

If the customer has checked out to your satisfaction, the account can be put into action. This can be done by writing to the customer setting out levels of credit to be allowed (based on the results of the credit check) and re-emphasizing the payment terms.

For riskier customers special terms could be imposed, such as:
- cash on delivery or part payment in advance of the service being provided;
- reduced credit periods, for example 14 instead of 30 days.

A clear and accurate invoice should be sent to the customer without delay once the job is concluded.

To aid cashflow, many businesses factor or invoice discount their debts. Factoring involves the business selling its invoices to a factor that will pay up to 80 per cent of the value of the invoice immediately. The factor will chase debts and collect payments and may also advise the business on the creditworthiness of its customers. Factoring is unlikely to be available to retailers or business sectors involving a high level of disputes or to a business with a projected turnover of under £100,000. The factor will charge service fees of between 1 and 2.5 per cent of the overall debts and interest will also be charged on the uncollected debts until payment is made.

Invoice discounting is similar to factoring in that a business receives payment for its invoices. It is, however, without the extra facilities provided by a factor such as administration of the business's sales ledger and credit management. The business collects the debts itself and remits the monies to the discounter.

Collecting the debt

Once the invoice has been dispatched, it is important to monitor payment. A business should set its own timetable for chasing debts. With large debts, consider calling before the due date to ensure payment is being processed and there are no problems.

Once the invoice has fallen due, payment can be chased by telephone or, if the debt is large, by a personal visit to the debtor. It is important to remember that although reasonable efforts to collect debts are acceptable, harassment of debtors or their families can be a criminal offence, for example persistent telephone calls at night.

A reminder statement can be sent when the account becomes overdue and a polite reminder letter can follow this. Many firms find that a chasing fax to a named director at the debtor company will ensure prompt payment.

Date
Dear Sirs,

   Despite various requests for payment, my invoice (number) dated (date) in the sum of £ (amount owed) still remains outstanding.

   In the circumstances, I would be grateful if you would please arrange payment of this invoice as a matter of urgency and in any event by no later than (7) (or) (14) days from the date of this letter.

   In addition, I wish to draw your attention to the fact that I reserve the right to charge interest under the Late Payment of Commercial Debts (Interest) Act 1998 on the overdue amount at the rate of x per cent per annum until payment is received.

   I look forward to hearing from you.

   Yours Faithfully,

Once the account is over one month old and the above efforts have been ignored, it would be appropriate to send a strong final demand threatening further action to collect the debt.

Date
Dear Sirs,

   My invoice of (date) for £ (amount owed) still remains outstanding despite my letter of (date) requesting payment.

   In the circumstances, I am now writing again to formally demand payment of the amount owed within (7) or (14) days from the date of this letter. Should payment not be forthcoming, then please note I shall issue legal proceedings against you without further notice.

   If I am forced to take action against you, in addition to the money owed, I will also make a claim against you for costs and interest.

   I hope that, despite the clear intention of this letter, legal proceedings may still be avoided and I look forward to receiving payment within the time stated.

   Yours Faithfully,

Interest is now available on overdue debts even if the parties do not specify this in their terms and conditions of trading. The Late Payment of Commercial Debts (Interest) Act 1998 contains the following provisions:

- for contracts entered into after 1 November 1998 interest is payable on overdue debts at the rate of eight per cent above base rate per annum. The base rate is set by the Bank of England and is often mentioned in the press (in particular the *Financial Times* and can also be found by visiting www.payontime.co.uk). Calculating the appropriate base rate is now a much more straightforward exercise following a recent change to the legislation. Instead of having to make adjustments following any change to the base rate, the base rate for the purposes of the Act is now fixed for a six-month period. The Bank of England base rate on 31 December is used as the base rate for calculating any interest due between 1 January and 30 June and the Bank of England base rate on 30 June is used as the base rate for any interest due between 1 July and 31 December. To work out what interest rate you should use when calculating interest on a late payment, you need to add 8 per cent to the appropriate base rate that covers the six-month period in which the debt became late;
- interest runs from the date the invoice fell due for payment to the date of final payment. If nothing has been agreed then the payer has 30 days' grace from the date of the invoice or when the goods were delivered or services provided. After that time interest can be charged;
- when it was first introduced the Act only applied to small businesses (meaning having 50 employees or less) as against large businesses (meaning having more than 50 employees) and the public sector (i.e. government departments and local/public authorities);
- from 1 November 2000, the right to claim interest was extended so that small businesses can claim interest from other small businesses on contracts agreed after that date;
- all businesses and the public sector are able to claim interest from the other where the contract has been agreed after 1 November 2002;
- in addition to interest, the following charges can be recovered and added to the debt:

Size of unpaid debt	Debt recovery costs
Up to £999.99	£40
Between £1,000 and £9999.99	£70
Over £10,000	£100

Parties to a contract are free to agree different late payment penalties in a contract. When the Act first came into force there was concern that small businesses would be pressurized into accepting terms less attractive than those provided for by the Act. However, the courts have the power to strike out a term that does not provide a substantial remedy for late payment. No doubt many businesses will now include such clauses (providing for a 'substantial remedy') so as to avoid the statutory provisions. At the moment, we have no authority on what a 'substantial remedy' will be, although it is clear that the courts will have to consider such factors as the equality (or inequality) of the parties' bargaining positions. Plus, government guidance suggests that the courts will also look closely to see whether the parties agreed a credit period significantly different from custom and practice in that industry, or which is different from other supply contracts operated by the debtor, and also whether the parties agreed an interest rate that is significantly lower than the statutory rate, or if there are excessive information requirements on the creditor before any credit period starts to run under the contract. There is an excellent Users' Guide at www.payontime.co.uk

When reminders are being issued, the creditor should mention that he is claiming interest under the Act and the daily rate at which interest is payable.

If the final demand is ignored, the business has five options:

1 *Solicitors* – a powerful letter from a solicitor threatening court action or statutory demand may provoke payment. Most solicitors will be prepared to charge a fixed fee of around £30 for sending a letter before action (*see* page 738).

2 *Debt collectors* – most act on a 'no collection, no fee' basis and usually charge a minimum of five per cent of the amount collected. Be wary of 'cold calling' debt collectors who offer their services upon payment of a large upfront fee. There are many rogue traders in the debt collection business who will take payment and never be seen or heard of again! To carry on business, most debt collectors require a credit licence from the OFT. So, if in doubt, check with the OFT.

3 *Court action* – for debts up to £5,000, a creditor can pursue the debt himself through the small claims court. The procedure is fairly straightforward and the first step is to contact your local county court to obtain a claim form N1 together with the court service guidance booklets on how to proceed.

For debts over £5,000, although a creditor is not obliged to instruct a solicitor, the procedure is less straightforward if the debtor defends the action.

Before spending out on the court fee to issue court proceedings, ensure that the debtor is in fact worth suing, i.e. he actually has sufficient funds/assets to cover the debt. This is because even when a creditor has a judgment against a debtor, if the debtor still does not pay, enforcement action will have to be taken (*see* Chapter 97 – Enforcement of money judgments). If the debtor has nothing to enforce against, the creditor will either have to write off the debt or bide his time until the debtor's financial circumstances improve;

4 *Statutory demand* – a legal form sent by the creditor, solicitor or debt collector giving the debtor 21 days to pay, failing which application can be made to wind up a limited company or petition for the bankruptcy of an individual. Statutory demands must not be sent in the case of a genuinely disputed debt. The forms are available from a legal stationer;

5 *Negotiation* – contact the debtor to agree a repayment plan or deferred payment date. If the amount of the debt is disputed, non-court action can include mediation, conciliation or arbitration. A leaflet concerning alternative dispute resolution is available from your local county court.

E-COMMERCE

Virtually all types of business, particularly small businesses, can benefit by using the internet to sell goods and services. This is known as electronic commerce or e-commerce. In the UK, 22 per cent of the population regularly use the internet, with 33 per cent of organizations using or intending to use the internet for buying and/or selling purposes. The advantages include:

- a cheap way of setting up a worldwide business as it can avoid intermediary/distribution costs;
- provides even the smallest business with an international presence. The internet will enable a business to reach customers worldwide;
- speed – a contract made over the internet can be formed almost instantly;
- a significant cost saving in offices and manpower, as there will be less need to have branch networks;
- an inexpensive way of advertising your business. It is no longer essential to send out publicity material/ brochures;
- enables a business to operate 24 hours a day all year round;
- the ability to contact your customers instantly to provide them with updated information, for example about new products/services;
- the ability to find out quickly and easily what your competitors are doing in the market place.

Although e-commerce is of growing importance, the law is still evolving to fully address problems specific to the medium. This area is still largely governed by principles of our existing laws, in particular the laws of contract and intellectual property. You should, where appropriate, refer to other chapters in this book that will deal with these issues in greater depth. In this chapter, we will outline some of the key considerations.

Domain name

Any business wanting to use the internet will need a domain name. This is computer jargon for an internet address so that you can be located on the internet. A domain name begins with the prefix 'www'. This is followed by your chosen name. After the name there is a two- or three-letter suffix which will indicate the type of organization operating the site, for example a business name will be followed by either co or com. Finally, there will usually be a two-letter suffix indicating the country of registration. An example of a domain name having all these characteristics is that of Virgin, which is www. virgin.co.uk.

Domain names are allocated on a first come, first served basis. For this reason, each domain name is unique and this can lead to arguments where more than one party wants to use the same domain name. This has caused particular problems where someone registers a well-known company's name as a domain name, and then attempts to sell it back to the company concerned at a premium. This is often referred to as 'cyber squatting'. The UK courts have so far taken a robust view of such behaviour and decided that it amounts to trademark infringement and passing off. As a result, the courts have ordered the domain names to be transferred to the appropriate businesses.

To avoid getting into a dispute, before choosing a domain name, it is important to carry out the following searches:

- a registered trademark search at the Trade Mark Registry;
- a search at Companies House to see if there is a limited company with the same or similar name to the one which you propose to use;
- a domain name search at http://www.netnames.co.uk;
- check for the same or similar names in relevant trade journals, telephone directory, *Yellow Pages*, etc.

Although the law regarding the use of domain names is developing all the time, the following guidelines should be noted:

- do not register well-known domain names with a view to selling them to the trademark owner;
- do not register a domain name which is the name of a limited company;
- do not register a domain name which is the same as or similar to a registered trademark.

Doing any of the above may involve you in an action for breach of trademark and/or passing off. Nominet, the registration body who allocate many of the domain names in the UK, insist that the registration of a domain name must not, to the best of the applicant's knowledge, interfere with or infringe the right of any third party. Clearly, if you have failed to carry out the relevant searches, you may find that the registration company withdraws your domain name if another business has a better claim to it, for example because they have a registered trademark.

If a dispute arises over the use of a domain name, then as an alternative to taking court action, it may be sensible to refer the matter to Nominet under their dispute resolution service. Further details about this service can be obtained from Nominet.

Once you have chosen your domain name, it will need to be registered. There are at least 200 domain registration bodies throughout the world and they all have different requirements. In this country, Nominet offers the suffixes co.uk; org.uk; ltd.uk; and plc.uk. Nominet can be contacted on telephone number 01865 332211 or at www.nominet.org.uk. The registration fee for a domain name is £80 plus VAT and there is a renewal fee payable every two years.

Type of website

Once a business has registered a domain name, the next step will be to design and develop the website. This will often involve using outside technical help and there is an increasing number of businesses offering this type of service. The definition of a website is a digital work containing graphics and text, with video and sound often included.

Considerable thought will need to be given to the type of website your business requires. Will the website be passive and essentially just a means of advertising your business (i.e. where it is located, the type of goods/services offered, etc.)? Alternatively, will the website be more sophisticated, and enable customers to access various services or buy goods online?

Whichever type of website is chosen, it is essential to ensure that where a website designer is contracted to design it, they assign any copyright in the design and underlying software to you. You should therefore use a solicitor to draft a contract to deal with these issues.

The website designer may also arrange hosting of the website on a server that is physically connected to the network. Hosting is necessary so that the website is accessible to anyone over the internet. Again, a solicitor should vet the hosting agreement. Particular attention should be given to provisions relating to what happens if the server crashes, making the website unavailable.

Advertising and selling on the internet

Using your website to advertise either your business or goods and services does not mean you can ignore the various laws that control business advertising and trade. Particular attention should be paid to ensure you:

- comply with the regulations covering the sale and supply of goods and services, e.g. the Sale of Goods Act 1979, the Supply of Goods and Services Act 1982 and the Sale and Supply of Goods to Consumers Regulations 2002;
- comply with the E-commerce (EC Directive) Regulations 2002, which require businesses advertising or selling goods or services on a website to include certain information on the website about the supplier, its products and services. For example, the business must provide the full name of the business and contact details including the geographic address. The business should also acknowledge receipt of orders electronically and without undue delay and customers must be given an opportunity to amend their orders. If the requisite information is not provided to users 'easily, directly and permanently' trading standards or consumer bodies could apply to the courts for a 'Stop Now Order' to force the site owner to amend its site, or face criminal penalties. In addition, if the key information criteria are not met, the sale will not be valid and the customer will be entitled to a refund. The customer may also be able to sue for damages. The Regulations also apply to businesses advertising or selling by mobile phone, by e-mail or by interactive television. (For more about 'Stop Now Orders' *see* pages 437 and 419);
- comply with the Consumer Protection (Distance Selling) Regulations 2000, which apply to most e-commerce contracts where the other party is a consumer. Before the contract is made the consumer must be given, in a clear and comprehensive manner, certain information including the name and address of the supplier/seller, the price (including all taxes) and the delivery arrangements. Following the decision to buy, the consumer is entitled to details of after-sales services and guarantees, a proper address for complaints, and details of the consumer's right to cancel orders. The consumer will have the right to cancel the order within seven working days. The right to cancel can be extended for up to three months if the supplier fails to provide notice of the seven-day cooling-off period. In addition, if the contract is not performed within 30 days, then unless otherwise agreed, the consumer is entitled to a refund;
- comply with the voluntary code of the Advertising Standards Authority, which requires all advertisements to be legal, decent, honest and truthful;
- comply with the Trade Descriptions Act 1968 and the Consumer Protection Act 1987 on misleading prices and false descriptions applied to goods;
- comply with the Control of Misleading Advertisements Regulations 1988, which deal with advertising that deceives customers;
- comply with trademark law. You may fall foul of trademark law by using another business's trademark to sell

either the same or similar goods and services, or by including wording on your website advertising someone else's trademark without their permission, to show that you supply their goods/services;

- have suitable wording on your website to make it quite clear that only the law of England and Wales will apply to your advertisement. This is to avoid the complications that may arise because your website can be viewed in any part of the world, and consequently may inadvertently fall foul of the laws of other countries;
- comply with the laws relating to the particular products or services that are being sold, for example liquor licensing, financial services or consumer credit;
- do not ignore data protection or defamation issues.

Contracts on the internet

Under English law, provided there is offer, acceptance, consideration and an intention to create legal relations, there will be a legally binding contract. There is an additional requirement that certain types of contracts, for example those for the sale of land, must be made in writing and signed by the parties. Many of these factors give rise to problems when the internet is used to sell goods and services. To avoid these complications, the following steps should be taken:

1 make sure your website distinguishes between offers and 'invitations to treat'. The act of displaying goods in a shop is recognized in law as an invitation to treat – in other words, inviting customers to come in, look around and make an offer. The customer cannot insist on buying a particular item, nor can you be required to sell it. Difficulties can arise where you make a statement that indicates an intention to be bound by the customer's response, for example 'special promotion, £20 off for first 20 customers'. This might constitute an offer – if it does, and the customer accepts it, you could be forced to honour the bargain.

To minimize the risk of inadvertently being bound by an offer, you should clearly explain on your website the different stages the customer must follow in order for a contract to be made: for example, stipulate that the customer must initially complete an order form and e-mail this to you for your consideration;

2 set out which country's law and courts will apply to the contract in the event of a dispute. For convenience, this will usually be the country where the business is based.

There are various conventions governing this difficult area. Conventions are treaties that certain countries have voluntarily adopted, in order to help regulate and promote international trade. They will only apply if the countries where the parties are based

have signed them. The conventions provide that if the parties to the contract are both in business, then if the contract specifies which court and laws apply, this will prevail. If the contract is silent, then the laws and courts governing the dispute will be those of the country in which the contract is being carried out (the place of performance). Unless otherwise agreed, the place of performance will be the place where the goods are delivered. Therefore, if you sell goods on the internet and fail to say where the place of performance will be, it will be in the country where the buyer resides.

In many transactions, businesses will be dealing with consumers. The European Commission adopted Regulation 44/2001 which came into force on 1 March 2002 and contains special rules that apply to consumer contracts. Most sellers using the internet will want to specify their home country as having the appropriate jurisdiction to deal with disputes. However, this new Regulation provides that if the seller has a commercial activity in the consumer's member state, or 'directs its activities' to that state, then the consumer's home state will deal with the dispute. The seller is not given any choice in the matter. This could prove costly and very inconvenient to your business;

3 ensure that you have written terms of business and that these terms are clearly drawn to the customer's attention before the contract is made. Merely making the terms and conditions available somewhere on your website will not be sufficient. This is because under English law, the customer is only bound by the terms if he/she was aware that the contract was subject to those terms, or if the seller did what was reasonably necessary to give the customer notice of the terms and conditions. This is particularly important where your terms and conditions try and exclude or limit liability.

The most effective way of incorporating your terms and conditions into the contract is to ensure the customer can only purchase or order goods/services after they have clicked on a box to confirm they have read your terms and conditions beforehand.

Digital signatures

The UK's Electronic Communications Act 2000 aims to ensure that electronic signatures are legally recognized. This should enable websites to be more secure and reduce the risk of third parties denying the existence of a contract. An electronic signature is not a handwritten signature scanned into the computer. Instead, it is a security device available for purchase by proof of ID, which when supplied with a CD can be loaded into a computer. Subsequently, a PIN number or code is supplied which means that the operator can send emails or contracts that are digitally signed.

61

Intellectual Property

Many businesses, both large and small, need to protect the commercial value of ideas, information, names, designs and innovations. The legal terminology for these, often valuable, rights is intellectual property (IP). Legal action to protect the rights may range from stopping a competitor using the shape of a bottle, to the protection of the company's logo or domain name.

Intellectual property law broadly deals with copyrights, patents, designs and trade marks. This area of law is highly specialized and complex. Advice must be obtained from either a solicitor with the relevant expertise, or a patent/trade mark agent. You will find both patent and trade mark agents listed in *Yellow Pages*. Alternatively, you can contact the Chartered Institute of Patent Agents (Tel: 020 7405 9450) who should be able to put you in touch with someone suitable. In addition, the Patent Office (Tel: 0845 9500 505; website: www.patent.gov.uk) can provide further information as well as some helpful guides.

The following categories of intellectual property are available for businesses to use to protect themselves.

Trade marks

A trade mark can be anything, including a word, symbol, smell or sign, used to distinguish the goods and services of one business from those of another. Trade marks can be registered or unregistered and are protected either by:

- registration at the Patent Office – if the trade mark is capable of being registered;
- the common law action of passing off – if the trade mark is unregistered.

A trade mark describes the origin of the goods rather than the nature of the goods. Its main function is to protect the symbol of recognition of the business, so that the customer associates the trade mark with a particular quality of product or service, and can distinguish quickly and easily between similar products or services. A trade mark must therefore be distinctive.

Registered trade marks

Recent changes in the law have widened the scope of types of trade marks that can be registered. These can now include three-dimensional shapes, sounds, smells and tunes, in addition to the more usual names and logos. Well-known examples of registered trade marks include invented words such as Kodak, Pentium and Coca-Cola; ordinary words such as Mars, Penguin; shapes such as the Coca-Cola bottle and the Toblerone chocolate bar; smells such as dewberry; or words and numbers such as 7UP and Windows 2000.

If you are intending to register your trade mark, you should employ a trade mark agent. They will make the necessary searches once you have chosen your potential name, to see whether or not it is either the same as, or too similar to, an existing trade mark. If this is the case your application will be rejected. The fee for making a trade mark application is £200.

It is important to be aware that your proposed trade mark must be distinctive, otherwise it will not be registered. All invented or ordinary words chosen must not have a direct association with either the goods or services or the way in which the goods/services are used. If they do, they will be rejected as not being distinctive enough. You should also avoid using either generic names such as bread, or place names such as Godalming. You will stand a better chance of getting your name registered if it is an invented name, for example Coca-Cola. An ordinary company name like J Smith Ltd will not be distinctive enough.

Generally, your application will be handled within two months, and there is then a period of between three and six months during which time you will have the opportunity to deal with any objections or queries. Once an application is made, the letters TM must be used until the trade mark has been approved. Once your trade mark is registered, this protection will last for 10 years. On payment of a renewal fee, your trade mark can be renewed thereafter every 10 years.

Once the trade mark is registered, you will effectively have a monopoly in the mark where it is applied to the goods/services which it is registered under. This means you can take action where a third party uses the same or even a similar mark in relation to the goods/services for which the mark is registered. Finally, remember the registered trade mark will only protect your goods/services in this country. If you trade overseas, in particular the EU, it may be advantageous to apply for a Community Trade Mark (CTM). This is similar to a trade mark that is registered in this country. A CTM provides protection by means of a single registration covering the whole of the EU. It will last for an initial period of 10 years and can be renewed. Registration of the trade mark is granted by the Office for the Harmonization of the Internal Market (Trade Marks and Designs) located in Alicante, Spain. This can often be cheaper than paying for your trade mark to be registered separately in each country.

Passing off

If a trade mark is unregistered, it may still be protected by the law of passing off. This will apply where a business uses a similar name, goods or packaging that are associated with another business and so tries to take advantage of that business's name and reputation. To succeed, you have to be able to demonstrate to the court that deception has taken place. This will involve proving that customers are being misled into thinking they are buying your goods/services when, in fact, they are buying the other business's goods/services. A recent example occurred when a well-known biscuit manufacturer who made the Penguin biscuit managed to bring a successful passing off action against a rival biscuit manufacturer who introduced the Puffin biscuit.

In addition, the court is unlikely to find that passing off has taken place where the parties are in a different field of business from one other. This is because it will be difficult to show that customers have been confused. For example, the owner of the London nightclub 'Stringfellows' failed to stop the marketing of frozen chipped potatoes also being sold under the name 'Stringfellows'. Although the chip manufacturer's advertising campaign showed people dancing in the kitchen as if in a discotheque, the court felt that each party traded in a different line of business and so there was no common field of activity and no real possibility of the public being confused.

A passing off action is likely to be expensive to pursue, and also often fraught with difficulty. In addition to proving that you have a particular goodwill in relation to

your goods/services, you also have to prove that customers are being misled. Realistically, this means that only a well-established business is going to stand a chance of bringing a successful court case. Even if the business is successful, goodwill is very often local to the area where the business is based. This means if a business trading in Guildford finds out that another business in Manchester is using the same name, they will not be able to bring a passing off action. Obviously, if the business has a national reputation, then it will stand a better chance of being successful in establishing passing off. For all these reasons, passing off is much more difficult to prove than breach of a registered trade mark.

Mercedes took action against a small clothing store in Carnaby Street, called Merc, that had been selling clothes and shoes for over 30 years. Mercedes sued for passing off and trade mark infringement, with part of its case resting on the fact that the defendant's business was aimed at mods, skinheads and casuals, none of which groups Mercedes wanted to be associated with. Mercedes lost. The judge took the view that Mercedes had extensive goodwill in its trade mark registered 'Merc' in relation to vehicles, but not to clothing. Moreover, there was no evidence that the public would be confused between the defendant's and the claimant's products within the clothing sector.

Daimler *v* Alavi (2001)

Copyright

As the word indicates, copyright is the right to stop others from copying, adapting or reproducing your work. Copyright protects original literary, dramatic, musical and artistic works, films and television broadcasts. Copyright therefore covers a vast area and includes newspapers, books, tapes, CDs, photographs, drawings, videos, films, internet websites, computer programs and trade catalogues.

Despite copyright protection being extremely wide, there are some very important exceptions. First, you cannot copyright a name, as this is not regarded as a literary work. Second, you cannot copyright ideas, only the actual expression of the idea. (For example, the idea for a novel or a play would not be protected until it was written down.) Third, you cannot copyright three-dimensional designs, e.g. furniture or tools. To protect these, you have to rely on registered and unregistered designs.

Copyright protection is free and automatic, as there is no system of registration. Any work that is original, in the sense that you have used skill and effort in producing the work, becomes the subject of copyright. This paragraph you have just read is subject to copyright protection, as indeed is the whole of this book.

Normally, the author of the work owns the copyright.

This will not be the case, however, where the author is an employee and the work has been produced in the course of the employee's employment. In that case, the employer will own the copyright. As copyright cannot be registered, it can sometimes be difficult to establish that you own the copyright and also the date when the work was first published. To minimize these problems, it is suggested you do the following:

- ensure all works clearly identify the author's name and date when the work originated;
- write the word 'copyright' or the symbol © and then add the year of publication and the author's name;
- place a copy of the work in a sealed envelope and deposit it with a solicitor or bank;
- if you are able to, ask a third party to provide written information of the date and originality of your work;
- send a copy of your work in a sealed envelope addressed to yourself. On arrival keep the envelope sealed. The Post Office's date on the envelope will provide additional evidence of the date of the work.

In the UK, copyright protection in a literary, dramatic, musical or artistic work (including photographs) lasts 70 years after the death of the author. Sound recordings, broadcasts and cable programmes are protected for 50 years. It is also possible that the copyright can be protected in other countries. This is because nearly all the major countries, including the UK, are signatories to various international conventions.

Copyright will be infringed when a substantial part of your work is copied without your permission. Unfortunately, there is no general test, and whether or not there has been a breach of copyright will depend on the facts. Nonetheless, if the most vital part of the work is copied, even if it only amounts to a small section, this may be considered to be a substantial part. There are some limited exceptions which permit work to be copied without permission, i.e. where copying is done for research, private study, for the purpose of criticism or news reporting.

Another aspect of copyright protection is the right to be able to claim what are known as moral rights. These consist of:

- *Paternity right* – the right of the author of a literary, dramatic, musical or artistic work and the right of a director of a film to be identified as such, whenever the work is performed in public or exploited;
- *Right to object to derogatory treatment* – this gives the author the right not to have their work added to, deleted, altered or adapted in a way which is prejudicial to their reputation;
- *False attribution* – this is a right not to have work falsely attributed to them as the author;
- *Right to privacy* – this allows someone who has had a photograph or film made for private and domestic purposes (weddings, christenings) to stop the work

being made public, despite the copyright still belonging to the author, for example the photographer.

Bear in mind that it is permissible to waive your moral rights.

Patents

Patents exist to protect the technical effects of ideas, discoveries and inventions. In order to obtain a patent, the invention must be new or novel. This means that the invention must not have been disclosed to the public before the first filing date at the Patent Office. It is therefore important not to publish or demonstrate the invention before making an application. In addition, your invention must involve an inventive step, i.e. your invention must not merely be an obvious development on what has been done before. That is why it is helpful to keep contemporaneous memoranda which set out the difficulty of any problem that the invention solves and why existing technology is not satisfactory. These memoranda must remain confidential until the patent is published. There are certain things that cannot be patented. These include:

- animal or plant life;
- methods of diagnosis, therapy or surgery;
- methods of doing business;
- rules and methods of playing a game.

A patent is obtained from the Patent Office and involves filing an application, together with technical specifications. This can be a lengthy and complex exercise and you should use a patent agent to deal with your application. It can sometimes take as long as two years to obtain a patent. Once a patent is granted it will allow you to have exclusive use of your invention for 20 years.

Designs

The law governing the protection of designs is concerned with enabling the designer to protect the way their article looks, and to stop anyone else manufacturing either the same or a similar-looking article. Somewhat confusingly, design protection takes two forms:

- registered designs;
- unregistered designs.

Registered designs

To obtain a registered design it is necessary to make an application to the Patent Office. The application for registration will require drawings and/or photographs of the article, together with a model of the product. Registration will normally take about six months to complete. Once the design is registered, it will last for five years. It may then be extended on four further occasions (each renewal lasting five years), up to a maximum period of 25 years.

In order to register a design, the article must:

- be novel, i.e. it must differ from prior designs by more than immaterial details;
- possess individual character, i.e. if the overall impression it produces on the informed user is materially different from the impression made by another design.

These changes were implemented by the Registered Designs Regulations 2001, which came into force on 9 December 2001. There is no longer a requirement for 'eye appeal' or a requirement for the design to be industrially exploited, i.e. designs can now be hand-made one-off designs such as bespoke jewellery, clothes, furniture, etc.

The above criteria are judged with reference to designs that have been made available to the public before the date of the application. There is a period of grace allowed of 12 months during which designers are allowed to market their products prior to an application for registration. This so-called 'grace period' is useful where a designer wants to market or test a product before deciding whether or not to register the design.

The whole or any part of a product can be registered, even if the part will not be sold separately, e.g. the wing mirror of a car. The Regulations also widen the definition of design so that it includes two- and three-dimensional shapes, lines, contours, textures, materials and graphic symbols (such as a computer icon).

Unregistered design right

This right is similar to copyright because it arises automatically and cannot be registered. An unregistered design right will exist where:

- there is an original shape or configuration of an article. Two-dimensional shapes such as textiles or wallpaper are therefore excluded;
- the design is not commonplace. Designs that are well known, mundane or routine are excluded. However, unlike registered designs, there is no requirement for aesthetic quality and the design right can apply to both the exterior and interior of the article. An example of the difficulty in demonstrating that the article is not commonplace occurred in a recent case where a drink company failed to convince the court that their tall-necked bottle was significantly different from any other tall-necked bottles. As with registered designs, 'must fit, must match' designs are unprotected.

An unregistered design lasts for 10 years from the date of first marketing the article in the UK, subject to a maximum of 15 years from creation of the design. Similar to copyright, as the right cannot be registered, it is sensible to keep full details of when the design was first recorded in a material form.

Protecting a design in Europe

The Community Design Regulation created a new type of intellectual property asset – the registered community design (RCD), which protects designs throughout the EU:

- unregistered designs: the unregistered community design has been in existence since March 2002. Like copyright, no application is needed to secure an unregistered community design, which arises automatically. It provides the holder with the exclusive right to use the design and prevent unauthorized deliberate copying. But, protection only lasts for three years from the date on which the design was first made available to the public within the EU;
- registered design right: the RCD is much wider and has much greater benefits. It protects a 'design', which is some aspect of the appearance of a product or some of its parts. Examples include designs for clothing, jewellery, textiles, shoes, cars and tableware. A design can be registered as an RCD if it is 'new' and has 'individual character'. To be 'new' the design cannot have been made available anywhere in the world before the application is filed, so it is important to file an RCD as soon as possible after a design is finalized. 'Individual character' will apply if an informed user would have a different overall impression of the design as compared to other designs in the market.

RCDs can protect logos, packaging, graphic symbols, typefaces, computer icons and numerous other items (but not computer programs).

RCDs have a number of benefits over registered trade marks which makes it worthwhile to register both (e.g. there is no requirement to use the design; the design can be descriptive or non-descriptive – unlike a trade mark; one registration covers all goods). The drawbacks compared to registered trade marks are mainly that RCDs last for 25 years, whereas trade marks can be renewed indefinitely. Also, there is the novelty 'new' test which does not exist for registered trade marks; and RCDs only apply to goods and not services.

Remedies available if your intellectual property rights are infringed

As will be apparent from the above summary, intellectual property is a complex area of law. If you believe that your rights are being adversely affected by a third party, it is important you take advice from a solicitor who specializes in this area. The Law Society should be able to provide you with further details. The following remedies are available.

Injunction

This is probably the most effective remedy, as an injunction takes immediate effect to stop the infringing act. Sometimes in cases of real emergency, the third party will not even be notified in advance that an injunction has been applied for and granted by the court. Failure to comply with an injunction is contempt of court, which can be punished with imprisonment.

Damages

This is a claim for financial compensation. The amount of compensation will normally be based on what a reasonable licence fee to use the owner's right would have cost if permission had been given.

Account of profits

This offers the injured party the opportunity to claim the profits made by the infringing party. A choice must be made between claiming damages and claiming an account of profits – the claimant cannot claim both, but he can wait until the conclusion of the main court hearing before deciding which to claim. In practice, it is often difficult to establish what proportion of the defendant's profits derived from the infringing act.

Delivery up and destruction

This gives the successful claimant a right to seize goods and have the infringing material or goods handed over.

Criminal penalties

Both copyright and trade mark infringement are criminal offences. Enforcement action is carried out by trading standards departments.

62

Cessation of Business

THE LIMITED COMPANY AT AN END

There are many reasons why a limited company may cease to exist; it may be that the owners and managers are retiring and cannot sell the business as a going concern or that the company is being forced out of business due to financial difficulties.

Whatever the reason, the main class of people who will be concerned about the status of the company are creditors. If the limited company ceases to exist then the creditor will be unable to pursue the company for payment. As was mentioned in Chapter 54, a limited company has an identity separate from its shareholders (owners) and its directors (managers). Only in limited circumstances can the individual people involved in the company be liable to creditors, for example where a director personally guarantees the company's liabilities. (*See* Chapters 53 and 57 for further information.)

If a creditor or customer of a limited company is told that the company is going out of business, he/she may wish to know what this entails and/or whether there is anything he/she can do to stop it.

Striking off by Registrar

The Registrar of Companies at Companies House can bring a limited company to an end if he believes the company is no longer carrying on business. The Registrar may take this view if:

1 letters sent to the company's registered office have been returned undelivered; or

2 the company has not sent the Registrar the documents it is obliged to by law, i.e. annual return or audited accounts.

The Registrar will make enquiries about the business to ensure it is defunct and reminders are usually sent to the directors requesting overdue information. If the directors do not wish the company to be struck off they should provide the requested information. The directors may also be criminally liable for failure to comply with Companies House requirements.

If the Registrar is satisfied that the company is no longer in business, he will advertise his intention to strike off the company in a publication called the *London Gazette*. Three months later, unless the Registrar has upheld objections, i.e. from the company or its creditors, the company will be struck off. This will be advertised in the *London Gazette* and the company is then at an end – known as 'dissolved'.

When the company is dissolved, any assets that were held by the company will belong to the Crown – this is called *bona vacantia*. For this reason the Registrar will seriously consider objections to striking off. A creditor may object because, for example, they are owed money by the limited company, which has ceased trading but still has sufficient assets to pay its debts. The creditor will want to see the assets sold to pay creditors, probably in the course of voluntary liquidation (*see* below).

If a company is struck off, any interested party, for example a shareholder, can apply to the court to get it restored to the register. The application must be made within 20 years of the dissolution. Grounds for ordering restoration include the fact that a person did not receive notice of the company's application.

Striking off on company's application

A company may apply to the Registrar to be struck off. This commonly occurs where the business has ceased trading because the owners/managers have retired and are not replaced. Other situations may arise where the company is no longer needed, for example where a company is set up for a particular project which never came to fruition and the company is not needed for any other purpose.

Creditors can object to the company's application to be struck off, so it is not an easy way for a company to get out of paying its debts. Certainly, if a company cannot pay all of its debts or come to an arrangement with creditors, it should consider compulsory winding up or liquidation (*see* below) before applying for striking off.

The directors make the application by submitting form 652a together with a £10 fee to the Registrar of Companies. Within seven days the directors must send a copy of the form to the shareholders, all existing and potential creditors, employees, those directors who have not signed the form (if any) and trustees of any employee pension fund.

The Registrar will not allow the application if the company has carried on business or changed its name in the previous three months. Otherwise, the Registrar will advertise the application in the *London Gazette* and strike off the company after three months. The striking off will also be advertised and the company will be dissolved.

As mentioned above, the Registrar will consider objections to the company's application. Valid objections may include, for example, the fact that court proceedings are being pursued against the company, the company is being wound up or the directors are committing a fraud.

There are serious repercussions if the directors do not deal with the application properly, for example by failing to notify an interested party or applying when the company should not be struck off. The directors may be fined or disqualified from being directors or even in some circumstances imprisoned.

Compulsory winding up

When a business fails, the court can wind it up and the company will cease to exist. The application to the court to wind the company up may be made by:

- a creditor – because the company cannot pay its debts; or
- the shareholders of the company.

Another situation where the court may be asked to wind up the company is where the company is in deadlock (*see* Chapter 57, p. 506). Chapter 53 deals with the conditions and procedure for compulsory winding up.

Voluntary liquidation

A company will cease to carry on business if it resolves to voluntarily wind up. (*See* Chapter 53 for further details.)

Phoenix companies

This is a ploy used by directors of a failing business to avoid paying the company's debts. The directors allow the failing company to go into liquidation and then set up a 'new' company with a clean slate, using the same assets, the same staff, run from the same premises and selling the same product or service. The new company appears to have risen from the ashes of the failed company – hence the term 'phoenix company'.

Unless the statutory procedure is followed, the Insolvency Act 1986 prohibits directors of a company placed in insolvent liquidation from trading through another company (whether limited or not) with the same or similar name. This restriction lasts for five years and prevents the person from being a director or being involved in the promotion, formation, management or trading of another business of the same or similar name. The prohibition applies to anyone who was a director or shadow director (*see* page 505, 'Restrictions/liabilities of directors') within 12 months before winding up.

A person who breaches the restriction commits a criminal offence and may be personally liable for the debts of the old company.

Creditors who are concerned about the creation of a phoenix company should check with the liquidator as there are exceptions to the rules allowing him/her to sell the goodwill in the company name.

Dormant companies

When a company is not trading and no significant accounting transactions are taking place, it is described as 'dormant'. A businessperson may buy a company with no intention of carrying on business through the company until a later date. The benefit of having the company 'lined up' is that no one else can incorporate a company under the same name – thus the name is preserved. For example, a sole trader operating under the trading name of Beautiful Brides may wish to buy a limited company and register the name as Beautiful Brides Limited. In this way, if the sole trader decides to 'go limited' in future the existing trading name is reserved for him.

The dormant company must file an annual return to Companies House, but it can be exempted from other requirements. The shareholders can pass a special resolution exempting the company from appointing auditors or filing audited accounts. The directors must file a signed balance sheet stating that the company was dormant during the financial year.

Share/asset sale

At some stage a businessperson may decide to sell off his or her business in order, for example, to reap the rewards of many years of hard work or to get out while the company is thriving, in anticipation of being forced out of the market by up and coming competitors.

With a limited company, the sale can be either:

- a share sale; or

- an asset sale.

With a share sale, only the shares are transferred and the assets remain owned by the same company. The company continues to exist as before albeit with different owners.

An asset sale is different because all or most of the assets used in the business will be sold, including premises, stock, goodwill and contracts. Customers will be affected and technically they should be consulted. Parties to contracts (such as those for the provision of cleaning services or catering facilities to the company), must be consulted as their consent to the transfer of the contract to the new owners must be obtained.

With share sales, as no assets or contracts change hands, generally no one need be consulted before the sale. Any liabilities remain with the company. As a result, most sellers prefer share sales to asset sales.

Unless specifically agreed, the buyer of the assets in an asset sale will not take over the selling company's liabilities to creditors. This may cause some concern to creditors. Although the company remains liable for its debts, the fact that its assets have been sold means that it is practically valueless and will not be worth suing by creditors. In certain circumstances, there is protection for creditors if a company 'asset strips' before going into insolvent liquidation (*see* Chapter 53).

Company sales can be extremely time consuming and will take several months to achieve.

Depending upon the complexity and financial worth of the sale or purchase, most businesses will need a team of advisers to assist them – usually a commercial solicitor, an accountant and sometimes a surveyor. The solicitor will ensure early on in the transaction that a 'confidentiality agreement' is in place. This is necessary because during negotiations between seller and buyer, sensitive financial and commercial information may be exchanged that either party may not want disclosed should the sale not proceed.

The next step will be for the buyer's advisers to gather together information and documents about the target company – this is called 'due diligence'. The advisers will check contracts, property deeds and financial information to ensure the buyer knows exactly what he is buying and there are no hidden 'nasties'.

Disclosure of information early on in the transaction is important – obviously it may affect the price the buyer is willing to pay or other terms upon which he is prepared to buy.

It is usual for the buyer's solicitor to draft the sale and purchase agreement, dealing with the terms upon which the business is being sold. For example, the agreement will deal with the price to be paid for the company's shares or assets, how and when payment will be made and warranties (or promises) made by the seller about the business that the buyer will rely upon, for example that all equipment used in the business is in good and serviceable condition and is owned by the seller.

Any qualifications to the warranties will be stated in a 'disclosure letter'. Using the above example, where the seller has warranted in the sale and purchase agreement that all equipment used in the business is in good and serviceable condition, he may state in the disclosure letter that one particular piece of equipment is defective. In this way the buyer knows what the situation is regarding that one piece of defective equipment but can rely on the assurance he has been given regarding the other equipment.

Once signed, the buyer and seller are bound by the agreement. Failure to comply with its terms will entitle the wronged party to recover compensation from the other. In some circumstances the wronged party will be granted a court order to force the defaulting party to take steps to comply with the agreement.

DISSOLUTION OF A PARTNERSHIP

How does it occur?

Dissolution of a partnership means that the legal relationship between the partners comes to an end. It does not necessarily mean that the business ceases, as some of the partners may continue in a new partnership together.

There are three ways in which a partnership can be brought to an end:

1 under contract law; or
2 under the Partnership Act 1890 (note that unless the partners provide to the contrary in a Partnership Agreement, the Act will apply); or
3 by court order.

Contractual provision

1 The partnership can be brought to an end if all partners agree; or
2 there is a term in the Partnership Agreement expressly allowing the partnership to be ended in this way; or
3 where a partner has been induced to enter into the Partnership Agreement by the fraud or misrepresentation of his co-partners, he can end the agreement; or
4 by a partner where co-partners have breached the Partnership Agreement in a serious way, for example by stealing money from the business.

Partnership Act 1890

Unless the partners provide to the contrary in a Partnership Agreement, the Act will apply.

1 *Notice under the Act* – the partnership can be dissolved at any time by one partner giving 'notice' to the others. All this means is that the partner must tell the others that he does not wish the partnership to continue any longer. The notice can take effect immediately and although sometimes not required by law, practically

the notice should be in writing to pre-empt any dispute regarding the date of dissolution.

A partnership that can be brought to an end by notice is called a partnership 'at will'. Most verbal agreements to carry on a business as a partnership will be partnerships at will. This is because it is unlikely that the partners will have verbally agreed to exclude the provisions of the Partnership Act. Although providing flexibility to the partners, a partnership at will is an unstable arrangement as the partnership can be brought to an end at any time.

Provision is often made in the Partnership Agreement for the partnership to end only after a fixed period of notice, for example after six months. This is preferable as it gives the partners the opportunity to decide what to do with the business, for example to sell the business as a going concern.

2 *Death and bankruptcy* – under the Act, a partnership will dissolve if a partner dies or is made bankrupt. To avoid this happening, provision should be made in the Partnership Agreement for the remaining partners to continue the business and pay for the bankrupt or deceased partner's share in the business.

3 *Retirement* – if a partner wants to retire, he can give notice to his co-partners but this will cause the partnership to dissolve. The Partnership Agreement should specify when a partner can retire (without dissolving the partnership) and for purchase of his share by the remaining partners. Often retiring partners are required to give three to six months' notice of their intention to leave.

4 *Expulsion* – under the Act, expelling a partner without his consent can only be effected by dissolving the partnership. Expulsion is an important power for aggrieved partners where, for example, a partner is damaging the business. It is therefore important for the Partnership Agreement to provide a power to expel – covering the grounds for expulsion, how the power will be exercised and how the departing partner's share will be paid for.

The court's powers

A partner can apply to the court to order dissolution of the partnership. Such an application is only necessary when a partner is 'locked into' a partnership by an agreement that does not allow him to leave or dissolve the partnership. Obtaining a court order avoids the partner being in breach of contract.

The grounds upon which the court may order dissolution include conduct by the other partners calculated to harm the running of the business, wilful or persistent breach of the Partnership Agreement or that a partner is incapable of doing his job properly.

What happens after dissolution?

If dissolution occurs because one partner leaves (i.e. through expulsion, death, retirement or bankruptcy), the other partners may wish to continue in business together and will need to negotiate for the purchase of the outgoing partner's share. The Partnership Agreement should contain provisions dealing with this scenario, including how the business's assets will be valued and the terms of purchase.

Sometimes a partner will be entitled to payment of his share in one lump sum. Many firms will find it difficult to raise the necessary amount and therefore the Partnership Agreement should allow the firm to pay the partner's share by instalments. In these circumstances, the outgoing partner is often entitled to interest on his share.

An outgoing partner must take certain steps to ensure that he does not continue to be responsible for the firm's debts (*see* page 509).

The remaining partners may take the opportunity to restructure the business, reallocating the former partner's duties and responsibilities to others. The firm may also decide to replace the partner either by promoting an existing employee or recruiting someone externally.

Many Partnership Agreements provide that if agreement cannot be reached regarding the purchase of the outgoing partner's share in the business, the dispute will be referred to arbitration. If there is no means of settling the dispute, the business will be sold. Usually more money can be obtained for a business sold as a going concern. This is because the goodwill of a successful business will have significant value.

If a buyer cannot be found, the business will have to be broken up and the assets sold separately. If necessary, a partner can apply to the court for the business to be wound up and the assets sold. If there is a dispute between the partners, or assets are at risk, a partner can apply to the court for appointment of a receiver, or receiver and manager. The appointee is an officer of the court and can deal with the assets, sell the business and if also a manager, can run the business.

When partnership assets are sold, the money must be applied in a set order. First, debts and liabilities of the firm (excluding claims by partners) will be paid. If there are insufficient partnership funds, the partners will have to contribute personally from their private assets, sharing the loss in accordance with the Partnership Agreement. The partners will share the loss equally if the Agreement is silent on this point. Second, money lent by partners to the firm must be repaid plus interest. Next, each partner will be paid their capital entitlement and, finally, if there is a surplus, it will be divided amongst the partners in accordance with the Partnership Agreement (equally if no agreement).

This may happen for all the reasons referred to earlier concerning limited companies, i.e. all the members decide to retire, the business is in financial difficulties, etc.

There are various ways that a limited liability partnership can cease to exist and these are again similar to a limited company, i.e. striking off by the Registrar, voluntary liquidation and compulsory liquidation.

For further details, refer to Companies House website www.companies-house.gov.uk, which has a very helpful guide on winding up a limited liability partnership or removing it from the register.

PART EIGHT

Motoring

The Driver

The Vehicle

Accidents

Prosecution and Penalties

Motoring

Involvement with a motor vehicle brings the individual up against a set of laws that are complicated and constantly changing. Changes to vehicles and road design, the influence of Europe, the growing number of vehicles and the place of the motor car in popular culture combine to make motoring law interesting and widely discussed.

The next four chapters examine legal requirements, some common problems and offences and the particular procedures and penalties found in road traffic cases. However, what must not be forgotten is that a motor vehicle is an item of personal property and as such many other parts of this guide will apply apart from this specific motoring section.

The Basic Requirements

Anyone over the age of 17 years can apply for a driving licence unless suffering from epilepsy, severe mental handicap, disabling giddiness, fainting or bad eyesight (i.e. unable to read a number plate at 20.5 metres in daylight, while wearing glasses if necessary).

A learner driver receives only a provisional licence (valid to age 70 years), but is required to display 'L' plates and be accompanied by a driver in possession of a full licence, who is 21 years or older and has held a full licence for at least three years. To charge for driving instruction a person must fulfil certain standards and be registered with the Department of Transport.

On passing the driving test, a motorist is entitled to a full driving licence and this will not require renewal until he reaches his seventieth birthday. After 70 years it can be renewed every three years, but an applicant must disclose any disability and may be required to submit to a medical examination, and agree to his medical records being examined.

Separate from licence applications, there is a duty on licence holders to notify the DVLA of the onset of a relevant disability. (The DVLA is the Driver and Vehicle Licensing Agency based at Swansea. It is the body set up by the government to administer driver and vehicle licensing and take decisions on behalf of the Minister of Transport.) Doctors will often advise patients on this point but if in doubt it would be wise to ask. Failing to heed a known disability would increase the seriousness of a motorist's position were there to be an accident.

A licence must be signed as soon as the licence holder receives it. If the licence holder changes his address (or name) he must return the licence and supply the new particulars.

A disqualification from driving for more than 56 days revokes a licence and the motorist would need to reapply for a licence; it is not an automatic process.

Common Offences

WHAT IS 'DRIVING'?

This section describes some of the most serious, and the most common, offences that are a direct result of a motorist's behaviour. It may be useful at the start to establish what constitutes 'driving'. It is not necessary for a vehicle to be under the power of its engine for there to be 'driving' – the law is more concerned with control in the sense of movement and steering. A motorist seated at the controls of a car in motion will almost certainly be found to be driving, however that motion is achieved.

Use of the engine is not conclusive proof of driving:

A motorist who was sat at the steering wheel of a stationary car with the engine switched on was not at that time necessarily driving the vehicle.   Leach (1993)

In the situation of a two-wheeled vehicle:

A moped rider sat astride his moped, which was faulty and would not start. The rider propelled the machine with his feet. The rider was shown to have excess alcohol in his body and was prosecuted for driving in that condition. Held: the rider was properly convicted, he had control of the moped and it was moving regardless of how the movement was achieved.   Gunnell (1993)

DRIVING OTHERWISE THAN IN ACCORDANCE WITH A LICENCE

It is an offence to drive otherwise than in accordance with a driving licence. The offence may be committed in two main ways. First, a would-be motorist could drive without any licence having been issued. The offence is clear. The offence could also be committed if a licence was revoked (for medical reasons or following disqualification) or if the licence is suspended (when it is not produced following a court order). In all these situations there is no licence.

In the second type of situation a licence has been issued

but the motorist does not comply with the conditions of its use. The breach of conditions might be driving the wrong class of vehicle or more usually it will involve a learner driver not having 'L' plates or supervision.

Whatever the actual ingredients of the offence, the offence is endorsable. If there was no driving licence to start with, the endorsement is recorded on the DVLA computer.

FAILING TO PRODUCE DRIVING LICENCE

This offence has much in common with failing to produce a test certificate and failing to produce insurance; the matters often go together, as motorists tend to carry all documents or none. A police officer can require a motorist to produce his driving licence on the basis of any one of the following justifications:

- the motorist is driving on a road;
- the officer believes the motorist was the driver of a vehicle when an accident occurred owing to the presence of the vehicle on a road;
- the motorist is believed to have committed an offence;
- the motorist was supervising a learner to whom one of the previous points applied.

If the motorist cannot produce his driving licence then and there, he has seven days to attend in person at a police station with his licence. Note that he cannot post his licence and other documents to the police station – he must attend in person to produce his documents. With the increased use of fixed penalties, licences are sometimes 'in the system' rather than with the motorist. In these circumstances, if the motorist produces the receipt for his licence he need not produce his licence until it is returned from the fixed penalty process.

DRINK-DRIVING

All solicitors have a steady flow of clients who come into their office with drink-driving summonses, expecting that some sort of defence can be put up to the charge. For the vast majority of these people, the best advice is to plead guilty and not waste money on legal fees. It may be a difficult fact for the disgruntled motorist to accept, but in the overwhelming majority of drink-driving cases there is no defence to the charge and they would be well advised to start the inevitable period of disqualification as early as possible.

In practice, once the police have shown that the motorist was 'over the limit', then the chances of acquittal are remote. The only possible defences are based on legal and scientific technicalities, and these apply only in the most exceptional cases.

There are in fact five basic offences:

1 driving or attempting to drive with excess alcohol;
2 being in charge of a vehicle with excess alcohol;
3 driving or attempting to drive while unfit through drink or drugs;
4 being in charge of a vehicle while unfit through drink or drugs;
5 failing to give a specimen (of breath, blood or urine) at a police station (there is also a less serious offence of failing to give a roadside specimen).

The 'being in charge' offence covers motorists who are not driving – perhaps because they are so drunk that they are slumped across the steering wheel, for example.

All of the first four offences must have been committed in a public place – so if the motorist was on private property all the time, it may be that no charge can be brought. In practice, of course, this is highly unlikely. Note that whether a place counts as 'private' or 'public' does not depend upon whether it is privately owned. If the public have access then it is likely to be a 'public' place (e.g. a pub car park is likely to be a public place during opening hours). Many offences may be committed in a 'public place' as well as a road.

B was seen driving in a multi-storey car park operated by a private company at 12.45 a.m. when only two other cars were parked in the car park. The prosecution produced evidence of use of the car park by the public and the absence of a barrier. Held: *The car park was a public place.*

Bowman (1991)

In theory, the police cannot carry out random breath tests. In practice, however, they require very little justification to carry out a test. All the police need to show is that they had suspicions that the driver had consumed alcohol. The police need not have suspected that the driver was over the limit; it is enough that they suspect the driver has had some alcohol, and so merely leaving a pub car park may be sufficient grounds for suspicion.

Alternatively, the police can carry out a test if there has been an accident (the victim of an accident can be tested) or if the motorist has committed a moving traffic offence (e.g. one wheel crossing over a white line or a flickering rear light). Their powers to stop and test are extensive, and while the police cannot simply set up random breath tests as and when they wish, they do, in practical terms, have more than sufficient powers to stop drunk drivers. The result is that it is almost impossible for motorists to raise a defence based on the argument that the breath test was not legally justified, unless they can show that the police acted in bad faith.

The popular belief prevails that there are loopholes in the drink-driving law that can be exploited by a clever lawyer. In fact, the drunk driver will almost certainly be convicted. For instance, there used to be a dodge known as the 'hip flask defence', under which the motorist would have a quick drink after being stopped by the police and before having a breath test. Under the present law, the chances of that defence working have been drastically reduced, since motorists must now prove that they would otherwise have been under the limit – and in practical terms that is often very difficult to prove. Similarly, under the old law there were complicated procedural steps that the police had to take, and the smallest breach of those rules would make the breath test invalid; under the present rules, most minor procedural mistakes are ignored.

The level of alcohol

There are various ways of measuring the alcohol level. Motorists will be guilty if they have more than 80 milligrams of alcohol in 100 millilitres of blood; 107 milligrams of alcohol in 100 millilitres of urine or 35 micrograms of alcohol in 100 millilitres of breath. The last of these three tests is most commonly used, usually by means of an Intoximeter machine. To avoid the risk of mistakes, the police do not prosecute if the breath reading is less than 40 micrograms (even though the legal requirement is 35 micrograms). In practice, therefore, there is little chance of a motorist being wrongly convicted on the basis of an incorrect breath test.

Where a breath specimen provided at the police station shows a reading of less than 50 micrograms of alcohol in 100 millilitres of breath, the motorist will be offered an opportunity to provide an alternative specimen of blood or urine. If offered, the option should be taken: the way that alcohol is absorbed in the body means that the new specimen should show a lower reading. While this new reading will rarely be below the limit, it will be used in evidence in court and the penalty handed down by the court will relate to the lower reading.

The penalty

Motorists convicted of driving with excess alcohol in their body, driving while unfit or failing to give a police station specimen face a maximum penalty of up to six months in prison or a fine of £5,000 or both, and disqualification for at least one year. The penalties for being in charge of a vehicle (i.e. not driving) are less. In practice, disqualification is nearly always ordered; it will be for at least 12 months or for at least three years if there has been another such disqualification in the previous ten-year period. Refer to the penalty chart (pages 581–3) for typical sentences for first-time offenders.

Prison for drink-drivers

In most parts of the country repeat offenders and those with very high alcohol readings are likely to receive a prison sentence. A second offence within a few years or a measurement of twice the permitted level of alcohol in the body places the motorist in special difficulty and they cannot assume they will receive a fine. Even though they may have no defence to the case, it may be necessary to instruct a solicitor to represent them in court and argue against a prison sentence. Aside from prison, more constructive sentences, such as community service or probation with an alcohol education programme, are now widely used where the defendant's alcohol level is high but not extreme.

Avoiding disqualification

The crucial question for motorists is not: 'Will I be found guilty?' (because, in the vast majority of cases, they will almost certainly be found guilty), but, 'Will I be disqualified?' Once again, the answer is that it is extremely likely that they will be disqualified. However, where there were 'special reasons' surrounding the commission of the offence, they may be able to avoid disqualification.

The special-reasons argument can be raised only in exceptional cases. This is because the 'special reasons' must apply to the way in which the offence was committed – not the effect that the disqualification will have on the motorist. The essential point to grasp is that the special reasons must, in some way, explain how the offence was committed; they are not to be confused with circumstances special to individual motorists that would make disqualification particularly inconvenient for them.

In practice, few motorists are able to argue 'special reasons'. The following are all examples of cases in which motorists were *not* able to show special reasons (and so they were disqualified):

- the defendant is a careful person who would not have driven had he realized that he had drunk too much;
- he is a diabetic;
- although he failed the breathalyser tests, his driving ability was unimpaired;
- the excess alcohol level in his blood or urine was very small;
- drinking on an empty stomach caused the drinks to have an unusually powerful effect.

A sudden emergency can amount to a special reason. The defendant must prove that he was forced to drive by a sudden emergency and that he would not otherwise have driven.

A mother telephoned her baby-sitter and was told that someone had made numerous telephone calls threatening to attack her daughter with a knife. After trying unsuccessfully to get a taxi, the mother drove home, fearing an imminent assault on her daughter. She had been drinking and would not otherwise have driven. Held: *The mother had shown a 'special reason' and therefore would not be disqualified.*　　　　　　　　DPP *v* Knight (1994)

The defendant's sister telephoned him to tell him that their mother had been taken to hospital as an emergency patient. He had been drinking at home and was not expecting to drive. Without enquiring further about the mother's state of health, he drove several hundred miles to the hospital. Held: *No special reason existed for him having to drive with excess alcohol.*　　　Thompson *v* Diamond (1985)

The court will take into account the acuteness of the emergency, whether there was an alternative means of transport or help, and the standard of the defendant's driving.

Laced drinks can also be a special reason. The defendant will have to prove that his excess alcohol level was due to alcohol that was put into his glass unknown to him. Note that a person who laces another's drinks when he knows that they are driving can himself be prosecuted.

The defendant drank one and three-quarter pints out of two pints of lager beer which had, without his knowledge, each been laced with a double Bacardi rum. He had thought the lager tasted strange, but thought that was due to a faulty pump, about which he had been told a few weeks previously. Held: *The defendant had shown a 'special reason' and so he was not disqualified. The court was satisfied that, but for the addition of the Bacardi, the defendant would not have been over the limit.*

DPP *v* Youngs (1990)

(Note that wherever there is an allegation that somebody's drinks have been laced, expert evidence will be needed to prove that without 'lacing' the alcohol level would not have been above the legal limit.)

Since drink-driving is an absolute offence, it makes no

difference whether the prescribed limit is exceeded by a large or a small amount. In either case the accused is guilty and the court will take into account the amount of alcohol that has been consumed only when deciding on the length of disqualification or other punishment. Similarly, it is irrelevant that the drink consumed did not actually affect the driving of the accused. On conviction, disqualification for a minimum of 12 months is automatic. Where the conviction is the motorist's second drink-driving conviction in the last ten years, the disqualification will be for at least three years.

CAUSING DEATH BY DANGEROUS DRIVING

The Road Traffic Act 1988 created the offence of dangerous driving, and a separate offence of causing death by dangerous driving. There is no offence of causing death by careless driving – so when a death occurs due to a small degree of carelessness on the motorist's part, he can be charged only with careless driving. This apparent loophole in the law has been the subject of much controversy – particularly from the relatives of victims of road accidents. To meet public concerns a new offence was created of causing death by careless driving where the motorist was also drunk.

The four offences mentioned can be summarized:

1 dangerous driving – one offence;
2 careless driving – a second less serious offence;
3 causing death by dangerous driving – a third offence;
4 causing death by careless driving while having excess alcohol in the body or while unfit – the new fourth offence.

This leaves a somewhat odd situation in relation to offences. A motoring death caused by a drunk driver or a motoring death caused by a careless driver does not lead to an offence based on the death; the offences would simply be drunken or careless driving. The offence charged and the maximum penalty on conviction will not relate to the death. However, a motoring death caused either by a dangerous driver or by a drunken and careless driver gives rise to an offence based on the death, with much higher maximum penalties. Such offences must be dealt with at the crown court and substantial prison terms are common.

Dangerous driving

For a motorist to be guilty of dangerous driving, it must be shown that more than mere carelessness or bad driving was involved. The motorist must have been driving in a way far below the standard of a competent and careful driver, with an obvious risk of danger. Without exception, any motorist facing such a charge should seek legal representation.

The sort of situations that lead to a dangerous driving charge (as opposed to the less serious charge of careless driving) are: a major accident caused by going through red lights, overtaking on a bend, or going the wrong way on a dual carriageway. Often the charge is brought together with a charge of the lesser offence of 'careless driving'. It is then left to the court to decide whether the driving was so bad as to be dangerous.

Dangerous driving is an offence that can be tried in either the crown court or the magistrates' court. The charge of causing death by dangerous driving can be heard only in the crown court. The attitude of the courts (and the public) to offences involving death or serious injury has hardened significantly in recent years. The strong likelihood of a substantial prison sentence where death is involved has already been noted. A simple offence of dangerous driving where no death results is in itself serious; prison is often the outcome with occasional use of community service or probation orders. Disqualification will always be ordered and often the offender will also be ordered to retake the driving test.

Careless driving

The official definition of this offence is: driving 'without due care and attention, or without reasonable consideration for other persons using the road'.

This is a charge that is frequently brought after an accident. The test to be applied is: did the motorist exercise the care and attention that a reasonable and prudent driver would have done? If the answer is 'no', they are guilty. Bad driving can lead to a conviction even if there was no accident. Basically, even the most minor error of judgement will be careless driving and, although not every breach of the Highway Code will be sufficient for a conviction, the offence is one that is easy to commit. For the purposes of the test, it is assumed that the prudent motorist observes the Highway Code. Many motorists commit the offence every day of the week.

Whether an offence is careless driving or dangerous driving is all a matter of degree. For instance, in the case of the motorcyclist riding through a town at 75 m.p.h., an accident might be dangerous driving; if he had been doing 40 m.p.h. then that would have been careless driving. Similarly, running into the back of the car in front is careless driving; but driving into the back of it at a high speed, after a risky overtaking manoeuvre, would be dangerous driving.

Learner drivers doing their 'incompetent best' are subject to the same standards as other drivers – so, too, are the drivers of emergency vehicles. Police, fire brigade and ambulance drivers cannot, for instance, jump red lights; they are subject to the same standard of driving care as other road users.

A policeman answered an emergency call on a motorway. He drove along the hard shoulder and collided with a stationary lorry. The policeman was prosecuted for careless driving but argued that he was on an emergency call and so had a defence to the charge. The court would not accept that argument. The policeman's standard of driving should be the same as that of other road users. There are no special standards for policemen. [Note that with speeding there is an exception, for emergency vehicles can exceed the speed limit if their use would otherwise be 'hindered'.] The policeman was guilty. However, the fact that he was on an emergency would be very relevant in determining what was the proper sentence. Wood (1977)

In practice, careless driving is another difficult charge to defend. Endorsement will be ordered unless there are special reasons. A fine of between £120 and £180 (plus 3–9 points) will usually be imposed (*see* the penalty chart, pages 581–3).

The allied offence of inconsiderate driving covers drivers who, for example, cause other drivers to make sudden avoiding manoeuvres. The victim, i.e. the person denied the consideration, could be a cyclist, a pedestrian or even a passenger in the motorist's own vehicle.

SPEEDING

The opinion of two people (whether police officers or not) is enough to secure a conviction for speeding. More usually, the evidence will be that of one police officer who followed the accused for three-tenths of a mile and was watching the police vehicle's speedometer, or who noted the speed on radar equipment. The opinion of any one person about a speed is insufficient to support a conviction unless that person's opinion is supported by reference to instrumentation.

Chief constables have produced guidelines on police action to be taken against speeding motorists: when to use a caution, when to use a fixed penalty and when to send a case to court. The individual police officer retains a discretion to act according to the circumstances of individual cases but the general scheme is as follows:

- up to 10 m.p.h. over the limit – the motorist will receive a warning or caution, which may be a signal from an officer operating a radar gun, or a firm ticking-off from a traffic officer on the motorway or a written warning;
- over 10 but less than 25 m.p.h. over the limit – the motorist will be given a fixed penalty;
- over 25 m.p.h. over the limit – prosecution will normally follow.

Since speeding is an absolute offence, it is no defence to argue that the speeding did not cause danger to anyone. If the speeding was dangerous, then the more serious charge of careless or dangerous driving may also be brought.

In built-up areas, if the streetlights are less than 200 yards apart one can be sure that there is a 30 m.p.h. speed limit, unless there is a sign to the contrary. If the lights are over 200 yards apart then it will usually be an unrestricted zone, or, to use the language of the Highway Code, the national speed limit will apply. The national speed limit is 70 m.p.h. on a dual carriageway and 60 m.p.h. otherwise. Lower speed limits apply in certain circumstances to passenger vehicles, goods vehicles and vehicles towing (for example, those towing caravans).

If a motorist is detected speeding by a camera, it will be almost impossible to dispute the speed alleged; the point in issue is usually the identity of the driver. The camera will have captured the registration number of the speeding vehicle. The registered keeper of the vehicle (as recorded in the DVLA records) will be sent documents requiring identification of the driver. If the driver is not identified without good reason the keeper will face a penalty including endorsement of any driving licence held. There have been cases of companies, who of course do not hold driving licences, accepting the penalty for failing to disclose who was driving a company car, rather than disclosing the fact that the driver was a director or a senior employee. If it could be shown that individuals planned such a course of conduct it could amount to the very serious offence of conspiracy to pervert the course of justice.

Any interference with cameras or radar is an offence but it is not an offence to have the means to detect the existence of such apparatus.

It is notoriously difficult to defend a speeding charge successfully. Police officers have little difficulty in finding motorists who are speeding and so it is difficult to persuade a court that the police were mistaken and that the offence was not committed. Usually, it is alleged that the motorist was breaking the limit by at least 10 m.p.h. and so it is difficult to argue that there was a misreading, or that the police officer's speedometer was inaccurate. It is particularly difficult to defend the charge if the motorist was caught in a radar trap. Then the only hope is for the motorist to argue that the police identified the wrong car, but few magistrates are impressed by such an argument.

A conviction will result in endorsement, and from 3–6 penalty points, unless special reasons apply (*see* the penalty chart on page 586).

TAKING A MOTOR VEHICLE WITHOUT CONSENT

The Theft Act 1968 created a special offence of taking a vehicle without consent. This is because the charge of theft can apply only when the offender intended to 'permanently deprive' the owner of his vehicle. The joyrider has no intention to permanently deprive, and so cannot be guilty of theft – but he can be guilty of taking a vehicle without consent. It is also an offence, and generally considered as serious as taking a vehicle, for a person to allow himself to be carried in a vehicle knowing it to have been taken without consent.

Defendants will have a defence to the charge if they can show that they believed they had the owner's permission to take the vehicle or that the owner would have consented had they known the circumstances. The defendant has to prove only one of these points on a 'balance of probabilities' to be acquitted. If the owner's consent is obtained by trickery, offenders cannot be prosecuted for taking the vehicle, although they can be prosecuted for deception.

Disqualification is common, although the youth of many offenders leads many courts to avoid disqualification so as not to damage employment (and thus rehabilitation) prospects. Since joyriders often damage the cars they borrow, it is worth remembering that the court can order the offender to pay compensation to the victim. Where damage or injury occurs after a vehicle is taken the more serious offence of 'aggravated vehicle taking' is committed. (For the penalties, *see* the penalty chart in Chapter 72.)

PARKING – BASICS

The offence generally called 'illegal parking' encompasses many different offences. Roadside parking has different rules to off-street parking, local by-laws play a large part and London has a separate scheme from the rest of the country. A few basic generalizations are possible.

The mere absence of a 'no parking' sign does not mean parking is always permitted. Local by-laws will often lay down the details of parking zones and ignorance of these is no defence. Similarly, the rules as to parking meters vary from place to place, but generally motorists cannot feed the meter (i.e. add money for a second time) or move their car directly into a bay in the same group of meters (a different group will be marked by two white lines).

If the parked car causes an obstruction, the motorist can be prosecuted for the offence of obstructing the highway. In practice, though, they are more likely to be charged with a similar offence contrary to the Road Vehicle (Construction and Use) Regulations 1986. This covers 'causing unnecessary obstruction of a road'. It is for the magistrates to decide whether the car did cause an 'unnecessary obstruction', but the law can be applied strictly. For instance, in one case a taxi driver was found guilty when he had waited in the road to turn right, so holding up heavy traffic. In another case, a doctor answering an emergency call parked his car so as to cause an obstruction and was found guilty. Likewise, a motorist who boxed in another car by bad parking was convicted

of causing an obstruction and fined. The fact that ten other cars were doing the same thing, or that others parked after you and created the problem will not alter the basic situation.

Often the offence commonly called 'illegal parking' is the breach of a local 'no waiting' order. However, these orders almost always have an exception to allow for the loading and unloading of vehicles. Not within the exception is the purchase of shopping items, use of a bank or a bank machine or indeed anything other than loading and unloading.

When a ticket is written out, motorists can opt to pay the fixed penalty (usually £20) within 21 days. If they do so, there will be no offence and no conviction. However, if they do not pay the fixed penalty and are subsequently fined in the magistrates' court, this will count as a criminal conviction and, theoretically, will need to be reported to their insurers before their policy is renewed. The offence is not endorsable and the typical fine is about £40. If the obstruction involved a complete disregard for other people (e.g. blocking a fire station access) a heavy fine would be imposed. A heavy fine is also likely where the road involved is a London priority route – the so-called 'red routes'. Parking within a pedestrian crossing or where a double-white-line system is used is endorsable and a typical fine will be £150.

Parking – tracing drivers

Drivers are rarely with their vehicles when the traffic warden or police officer detects that a car is illegally parked. This often leads to a fixed penalty being sent to the individuals recorded by the DVLA as the registered keepers. Unless the keeper follows a strict procedure for identifying who was driving at the time of an offence, the keeper will be liable for the penalty. This is called owner's liability and it can be applied in ways that seem unfair.

A motorist left his car with a garage for three weeks for repair. While the car was being looked after by the garage it was illegally parked. Notices of a penalty were fixed to the car but removed before it was returned to the owner. The owner did not know of the parking offences. **Held:** *The owner could not challenge the penalty notice. The owner was presumed to be responsible for the vehicle until the DVLA were notified of disposal.* Wandsworth (1998)

Parking – clamping

Immobilizing vehicles has proved to be an effective way of enforcing parking restrictions. Particularly in London and large cities where tracing the drivers responsible for parking is difficult, immobilization and removal to a pound is a relatively efficient way of keeping main roads uncluttered. While the high charges for release are clearly unpopular there is a degree of acceptance that the traffic authorities must take action. The public appears to approve less of private 'clamping'.

The wheel clamping of cars on private property is not a matter of road traffic law; it is generally covered by the law of 'tort'. An illustration from a case may assist.

A motorist parked without authority on private property. On the property were notices advising motorists that wheel clamping was in operation and that charges would be made for the release of vehicles. The vehicle was clamped. The angry motorist returned with a tow truck and tried to remove his vehicle with the clamp still in place. Held: When a motorist parks in these circumstances, particularly having regard to the notices, he consents to the clamping. Clamping would in other circumstances be an unlawful act. The fact of the notices and the reasonableness of the release charges placed the motorist in the wrong both for the parking and for seeking to remove his vehicle. Arthur (1996)

This area of law has developed further recently. On the one hand courts will look at whether release charges are reasonable (arguably supporting the motorist's position) but on the other hand the courts will not be impressed by motorists who fail to see a notice that is there to be seen (perhaps supporting the landowner's position).

A motorist who was feeling unwell parked on private land without seeing notices warning that cars would be clamped. A clamp was applied and in due course a release charge of £105 was paid under protest. The motorist challenged the legality of the charge. Held: The motorist was liable to pay the charge. The notice was found to be properly displayed. The charge (£65 for the clamping company and £40 for the landowner) was found to be reasonable. Vine (2000)

Numerous stories of abuse of the law by private firms of wheel-clampers have led to the passing of the Private Security Industry Act 2001. A new body was set up under the Act, the Security Industry Authority, to regulate criminal elements within the private security industry, including wheel-clampers. From July 2004, all operatives in organizations that provide wheel-clamping or towing-away services will have to be licensed. Failure to have a licence will be a criminal offence.

Private landowners who are not connected with wheel-clamping or towing away carried out by others will not require a licence. Thus, if a landowner contracts out the service, the landowner will not need a licence. In fact, the landowner will not even be required to check that the contractor is licensed.

The Basic Requirements

ROAD FUND LICENCE

Road tax, properly called 'vehicle excise duty', must be paid for any vehicle kept, parked or used on the road. This includes an 'old banger' that needs mechanical attention before it will go. Payment of road tax is evidenced by the display of a road fund licence (or tax disc as it is commonly known) in the front windscreen of the vehicle. The only occasions when a licence is not needed are when the motorist is driving to and from a prearranged MOT test, or when the car is being used during the 14 days' grace informally allowed after expiry of the last licence. Note that the period of grace applies only if a new licence was applied for before the old one expired, not if the application is made in the 14 days following expiry of the licence. During the 14-day period the old licence should be displayed on the windscreen; it is not enough to display a 'licence applied for' sign.

Application for a new licence can be made by post or in person at local vehicle licensing offices (in the telephone directory under 'Transport, Department of'), and at some post offices. Documents required are the vehicle registration document, insurance certificate, MOT certificate (if applicable), the completed form and requisite fee, and the old licence (if applying at a post office). Failure to tax a car, and failure to display the tax disc, are separate offences (*see* the penalty chart, pages 581–3). If a tax disc is lost, a replacement can be obtained by completing form V20. If a licence is surrendered before its expiry date, a refund can be obtained for complete calendar months by completing form V14.

Displaying a tax disc on a vehicle, which is taken from a separate vehicle, is a serious offence, even in circumstances where the latter has been scrapped with an unexpired period remaining on the tax disc. The proper course is to claim a refund and obtain a licence for the second vehicle rather than use self-help methods. The display of another vehicle's licence will be treated as fraudulent; it may horrify a motorist to find that in these circumstances they have acquired a conviction for dishonesty.

MOT CERTIFICATE

A current MOT certificate is needed for any vehicle that has been registered for three or more years. The requirement arises at the third anniversary of the first registration; it is not sufficient to wait until the next vehicle excise licence application after that date. Similarly, cars imported from abroad need an MOT certificate as soon as they are three years old; the three years does not run from the date of importation.

The MOT test covers steering, brakes, tyres, lights, seat belts and anchorage points, exhaust, flashers, washers, wipers, warning lights, horn, body and suspension. It is not a certificate of roadworthiness, and the possession of a current MOT certificate will not be a defence in a prosecution for a vehicle defect, even if the defect in question was the subject of a recent test. Evidence of recent testing could, however, provide some mitigation if carefully used.

The police can ask a motorist to produce his MOT certificate in the same circumstances they can ask to see his driving licence (*see* page 554). (Penalties for MOT offences are set out in the penalty charts.)

REGISTRATION DOCUMENT

Some people still use the term 'log book', although the registration document is no longer a book. It shows who is the registered keeper of the vehicle but it does not show who is the owner. Although a registration document should always be handed over when a car is sold, it is not proof that the seller owns the car. The DVLA must be informed immediately when a car is sold – by both the seller (who fills in the tear-off part of the registration document) and the buyer. Buyers cannot simply wait until they next need to tax the car.

The address of the DVLA is The Driver and Vehicle Licensing Agency, Swansea SA99 1BU.

Great care should be taken by both seller and buyer to make sure that the DVLA is notified. It is unsafe to rely upon assurances that the other party will see to the notification, even if the other party is a car retailer. Every week hundreds of former owners are issued with fixed-penalty tickets that should belong to someone else. The DVLA records are used by all police forces to trace owners and, like all computers, the DVLA computer will continue to give false information until it is given the new data.

The number of former owners of a vehicle is noted on the registration document, but their names and addresses are not stated (except for the last owner). The registered keeper can obtain these details, free of charge, by writing to the DVLA. Lost registration documents can be replaced by applying on form V62. Penalties for registration document offences are set out in the penalty chart, pages 581–3.

INSURANCE

The law tries to ensure that anyone who suffers injury through a motorist's negligent driving should recover damages for any serious personal injury that is caused. Parliament has insisted that all motorists insure against that possible liability; this is known as third-party liability. It is all that the law requires – simply insurance against injury to other people (including passengers). The motorist need not be insured for damage to other people's property and possessions although in practice, most policies do cover damage to property and possessions. The position is developed when we deal with offences, in the next chapter.

VEHICLE MAINTENANCE

The duty to have a safe and roadworthy vehicle is not limited to the time of the annual MOT test. The Road Vehicle (Construction and Use) Regulations set out – in some 109 provisions and 14 schedules – the legal standards required at all times from any car on the road. Many of these detailed regulations will be met by the vehicle manufacturer and are unlikely to concern the motorist (e.g. the dimensions and turning circles of the vehicles). However, the regulations insist that these requirements are met at all times and both the owner and the driver of the vehicle can be prosecuted for any breach.

The Construction and Use Regulations cover virtually all aspects of vehicle design, safety and maintenance; the provisions on horns, brakes, overloading, steering, tyres,

mirrors and noise are of particular importance. A similarly detailed set of regulations deals with lighting requirements. Most of the offences do not carry penalty points (or endorsement), although the rules on dangerous loads, brakes, steering and tyres are exceptions to this. (For penalties *see* the penalty chart, pages 581–3.) There are separate and, thankfully, simpler regulations for pedal cycles (including mopeds) and for invalid carriages.

Motorists can be convicted of using a vehicle in breach of the Construction and Use Regulations even when they did not know of the fault. This is because they are absolute offences: the offence was committed or it was not – there can be no halfway house. The charge is one of 'being in breach of the Regulations', it is *not* 'knowingly being in breach of the Regulations'. For instance, headlights must be in perfect working order during the day, and not just at night; the motorists driving in the daytime may not know if their headlight bulb has broken since they last used the lights, but they will still be guilty of an offence. However, in such a case the court will usually find the motorist guilty but give an absolute discharge, recognizing technical guilt but not imposing punishment.

If the charge is one of 'causing or permitting' the vehicle to be used by someone else in breach of the Regulations, then the defendant must be shown to have 'known' of the fault. Whereas 'using' the vehicle is an absolute offence, 'causing or permitting' its use is not.

Spot-checks

Breaches of the Construction and Use Regulations usually come to light when the police inspect a vehicle after an accident or during a spot-check. A uniformed police officer can, at any time, stop a vehicle and ask to check its brakes, steering, silencer, tyres, exhaust, lights and reflectors. However, the driver can say that it would be inconvenient to have an immediate inspection and can insist that it be arranged at any convenient time in the next 30 days. If the police officer feels that the vehicle should be checked immediately, either because it has been in an accident or because it seems to have a serious defect, the inspection cannot be postponed. If serious defects are found, the police may order that the vehicle should not be driven any further.

Brakes

The handbrake and the brakes on the four wheels must be effective and capable of stopping the car in a reasonable distance. As a guide, the Highway Code gives the shortest stopping distance of a typical car with good brakes, including thinking time. Precise requirements will depend upon the type and age of the vehicle. In general, the more modern the vehicle the more stringent the requirement.

It is also an offence to leave a motor vehicle without switching off the engine and setting the handbrake. Separate brakes are needed on trailers weighing more than 750 kilograms and on smaller trailers manufactured after 1997.

Horn

All private motor vehicles must have a horn capable of giving proper warning of the vehicle's position. Bells, two-tone horns and sirens are not allowed. There are restrictions on sounding horns at night and sounding them unnecessarily. You may be surprised to hear that anti-theft alarms must have cut-off devices to limit the time for which they sound to five minutes.

Lights

Both lights and reflectors must be kept clean and in full working order, even in daytime. It is illegal to have a red light at the front of the car or a white light at the rear (except when reversing). It is also illegal to have rear fog lights that are wired to the brake lights. Lighting-up time is the period between sunset and sunrise. Dipped or full headlights are compulsory at night outside built-up areas (i.e. where the streetlights are more than 200 yards apart), and in all areas if there is poor visibility, due to factors such as fog or heavy rain.

When parked at night, a car must have sidelights on, unless it is on a road with a 30 m.p.h. speed limit, in the light of a street lamp and not on a main bus route. It must also be parked at least 10 metres from any junction and be facing in the correct direction for driving off.

Mirrors

All vehicles must have a rear-view mirror; modern vehicles and all goods vehicles and large passenger vehicles need wing mirrors in addition. Modern vehicles require an offside wing mirror and either an internal mirror or a nearside mirror. The internal mirror must be made of safety glass and all mirrors must be adjustable.

Number plates

These must display the vehicle's number in regulation-approved size and style of lettering. Use of the spacing or styling character to personalize a plate is unlawful. An offence is committed if the vehicle is driven with number plates that are so dirty as to be unreadable. Clearly using number plates from another vehicle is a serious offence.

Silencer

An effective silencer is compulsory. The precise performance required of a silencer will depend upon the vehicle's age. Standards have risen sharply in recent years to match environmental concerns. Powers now exist to test exhaust emissions and devices are available to do so.

A police officer in uniform may stop a vehicle at any time to enable an authorized examiner to make a check that regulations governing the construction and use of vehicles are being complied with. Exhaust gas must pass through a silencer and the silencer must not be modified to increase the noise. The relevant regulations then provide limits both for noise and exhaust emissions. The precise limits depend upon which of 14 possible classes a vehicle is allocated to; the broadest level of generalization would be to say that any emission of smoke or visible vapour should be avoided.

Speedometer

A speedometer must be fitted to nearly all post-1937 vehicles and vehicles first used after 1 April 1984 have been required to show speed in kilometres per hour as well as in miles per hour. (*See also* page 430 for 'clocking' offences.)

Windscreen wipers

Wipers are compulsory unless the driver can see clearly over or through the windscreen without them. Windscreen washers are also compulsory. The test is whether the two devices used together can effectively clear the windscreen so therefore the blades must be adequate in the wiper and the washer tank has to contain water.

Seat belts

The fitting of seat belts in new cars has been compulsory for many years (generally since 1964), but it is only since 1983 that the wearing of seat belts in the front of a car has been compulsory. There are only a few exceptions: when reversing; for delivery roundsmen, taxi drivers, police and other emergency services; and if a medical exemption certificate can be produced. In practice, few people are entitled to medical certificates, since most GPs apply the rules strictly. There is no exemption for pregnant women, although clearly a pregnant woman could be the subject of a medical certificate. Since 1991, the wearing of seat belts in the rear has also been compulsory for adults where a belt is fitted. If a person does have a certificate of exemption, then it must be shown to the police on request (or produced at a police station within seven days).

The defendant was a newsagent; he collected bundles of newspapers and was returning to his premises when the police stopped him for not wearing a seat belt. **Held:** *Local rounds meant a series of visits or calls and the defendant's trip did not qualify, whatever use the vehicle might be put to at other times.*　　　　　　　　　　　　　Webb (1988)

Children under three years are not allowed to travel in a front seat unless they are using an appropriate child restraint, i.e. not an ordinary seat belt and not being held by an adult. Children aged between three and 13 years inclusive are allowed in front seats, but must be strapped in (as, of course, must any adult). If a child is not strapped in, then the driver can be prosecuted. All rear-seated children must be belted-up if belts are fitted.

Except where the passenger is a child, the driver is not criminally liable where a passenger fails to use a seat belt provided. The normal rules of 'aiding and abetting' do not apply to this law. However, the driver would be in serious difficulty regarding his or her civil liability if no attempt to encourage the use of a belt had been made. Failure to wear a belt seriously weakens a person's position in any civil legal action relating to an accident, as it will be regarded as contributory negligence.

CYCLES

Cyclists are subject to the same laws as other road users and, although they cannot be imprisoned or disqualified, they can be fined. For instance, a cyclist who disobeys a police officer's signal is subject to the same maximum fine, £2,500, as a car driver. There are, of course, various provisions that apply only to cyclists.

Dismounted cyclists who are pushing their bikes are legally 'riders', not 'pedestrians'. Thus, they commit an offence if they wheel their bikes past red traffic lights. However, there is an exception for cyclists who wheel their bikes over pedestrian crossings; for those purposes they are not cycling.

Cycles are subject to special parking controls. It is illegal to leave a bike in a dangerous position, on a footpath or on a traffic clearway. But cyclists need not obey painted yellow lines. Thus, cyclists can leave their bikes on the kerb beside a double yellow line, unless it is in a dangerous position or on a clearway.

A cyclist can be convicted of being drunk in charge of a bike. The normal breathalyser laws do not apply and, of course, there can be no disqualification (merely a fine of up to £1,000). There is no scientific test for drunkenness in the case of a cyclist; the evidence is normally the opinion of a police officer and there can be no breath test.

66

Common Offences

USING A VEHICLE WITHOUT INSURANCE

While this offence clearly covers the person who drives a car without insurance, it goes further and includes a person who has a car on the road that is capable of being used.

A vehicle remained parked on a road for seven months during which time its insurance and MOT certificate expired. Dilapidation resulted in the car becoming incapable of being driven or towed without repair. Held: The vehicle was being used even though its wheels would not turn. Pumbien (1996)

On the other hand, if a car is completely beyond repair, and cannot be moved, then the owner cannot be said to be using it. The test seems to be whether the vehicle was available for use in the sense that it could have been made to move under its own power with a reasonable amount of repair.

The compulsory insurance laws are applied strictly. Even if motorists believe they are insured but in fact are uninsured, they will still be committing an offence even if they are making an honest and genuine mistake. For instance, if Smith borrows a car from Jones after being told (incorrectly) by Jones that the insurance covers Smith, then both will be guilty of breaking the compulsory insurance laws. However, it may be that Smith, but not Jones, can avoid endorsement and penalty points if he was misled. Anyone who is misled rather than mistaken over the existence of insurance should seek legal advice.

Failure to have insurance is a serious motoring offence and will lead to the endorsement of penalty points (between six and eight) and sometimes disqualification (*see* the penalty chart, pages 581–3). However, there is a special defence for employees who innocently drive their employer's vehicles without insurance. For this defence to succeed, employees must satisfy the court that it was more likely than not that:

- the vehicle did not belong to them, and they had not hired or borrowed it; and
- they were using the vehicle in the course of their employment; and
- they did not know, and had no reason to believe, that they were not insured.

CAUSING OR PERMITTING A VEHICLE TO BE USED WITHOUT INSURANCE

This offence is aimed at the person who lends out his or her car without checking that the driver is insured. If owners tell drivers that they cannot use the car until they obtain insurance, then the owners will not be liable. But this would need to be clearly and expressly stated; casual comments and assumption will not excuse an owner.

What happens if a car is loaned to a person for a third party to use?

Fisher loaned his car to another on the understanding that the other person would provide a driver with proper documentation. An uninsured driver used the vehicle and, when prosecuted, Fisher claimed he had made a proper arrangement with the person to whom he loaned the car. Held: This did not help Fisher. He had permitted his car to be used without any direct contact with the driver so he could not have satisfied himself about the insurance. Fisher (1991)

The obligation to insure (and indeed to have a driving licence and MOT certificate) applies only to a vehicle that is on a road, as opposed to private land. In 1968, a classic borderline case arose when a lorry was half on private land and half on a road at the time of an accident. It was held that the lorry was on a road and so insurance, tax and MOT certificate were all needed. A 'road' may also be a car park or some other place to which vehicles have access and which is not clearly kept as private.

CARS AS LITTER

An issue, which concerns many people, is the dumping of cars at the end of their useful life. Dumping vehicles is treated by the law as an environmental problem rather than a motoring issue, as responsibility for such matters rests with the local authority. The penalty for dumping a vehicle is a fine of up to £2,500 or three months' imprisonment or both. Local authorities have powers to remove abandoned vehicles and to charge the person responsible for dumping for the cost of proper disposal.

67

The Basic Requirements

Most drivers like to think that accidents happen to other people and not to them, but the statistics tell a different story. Even the most careful motorist is likely to be involved in an accident at some time and it is only sensible to be aware of what to do when an accident occurs. (For dos and don'ts when an accident happens *see* below.)

The lawyer's basic advice is, 'Say nothing – write down everything'. Remember that responsibility for the accident (and for the resulting losses, expenses and injuries) will depend upon who was to blame. What motorists say in the heat of the moment can be distorted and used against them in a court months or even years later. For instance, most people's natural inclination when speaking to a person injured by a collision with their car is to say, 'I'm sorry', but this can easily be misconstrued as meaning, 'I am sorry that I caused the accident', rather than, 'I'm sorry you have been injured'.

The motorist should take a note of the names and addresses of the other parties. Vehicle registration numbers and insurance details should also be recorded, if possible. The names and addresses of witnesses should also be obtained or, failing that, a note should be made of their car numbers so they can be traced through the DVLA (*see* page 553). All the details of the accident should be recorded. There should be a sketch plan showing the positions of all vehicles, road signs, road widths, obstructions to vision, position of witnesses, the location of any wreckage or debris, and so on. It is also useful to make a note of the road and weather conditions, the damage to other vehicles and the apparent extent of anybody's injuries.

Vehicles should not be moved until their positions have been recorded on a plan or marked on the road surface; evidence as to the point of impact is often crucial in working out how an accident occurred and whose fault it was.

Unless the accident is trivial, it is advisable to call the police, even though they are not obliged to attend and may refuse to do so if there are no injuries and if the damage is small. If the police do attend, it is advisable to make a note of the officers' numbers. The police will probably ask those involved to make short statements, but motorists should remember that what they say will be written down and a copy will eventually be supplied to the other motorist's insurers and lawyers. That being so, it is best to say nothing at this stage, beyond politely explaining to the police officer that you would rather not make a statement for the moment. However, the police can demand to be told the motorist's name and address (and that of the owner, if different), plus the vehicle, insurance and MOT particulars. This information should obviously be provided if requested.

If you are involved in a road accident

Don't
1 Assault or abuse the other driver.
2 Apologize, offer excuses or say anything that could later be used to suggest that you admitted responsibility for causing the accident – unless, of course, you clearly were to blame.
3 Move the vehicles until their positions have been recorded.
4 Make a statement to the police at this stage. Wait until you have calmed down. However, you are obliged to give your name, address and vehicle registration number, and to produce your driving licence, MOT certificate and (if anyone has been injured) your insurance certificate.

Do
1 Stop and remain at the scene for enough time to allow anyone else involved to speak to you.
2 Call the police and note the number of the police officer attending.
3 Note names and addresses of everyone involved. The other drivers must give you their names, addresses and vehicle registration numbers, and (if anyone has been injured) provide insurance details; similarly, you must provide them with this information on request.

4 Ask witnesses for their names and addresses. If these are not available, note their vehicle registration numbers if they are in cars, so that they can be traced at a later date.

5 Write down any comments or explanations made by any party to the accident or by a witness.

6 Note the apparent damage to any vehicles and the apparent extent of injuries suffered.

Afterwards

1 While the facts are still fresh in your mind, make a full description of exactly what happened. Note time, road conditions, road layout, signposts, damage to vehicles, any vision obstructions, other traffic, road markings, point of impact, etc. If you have a camera, take photos.

2 Report the accident to your insurance company.

3 Write to the motorist who is to blame, claiming damages for any loss, expenses and injury suffered.

4 If you have any injury see a doctor. The examination may provide vital evidence to be used at a later stage.

REPORTING THE ACCIDENT

To whom should the accident be reported? If the police attend there will be no need to notify them, but if they did not attend and particulars were not given to the other people involved, then the accident will have to be reported as soon as possible. (*See* pages 569–70 for the duty to stop after an accident to provide particulars to other people, and to report the accident to the police.)

It will also be necessary for motorists to report the accident to their insurers. Most policies require that the accident be reported within seven days, failing this the insurance will not cover that accident or future accidents. Further, if the policy is renewed with no mention of the accident having been made to the insurers, then the motorist will not have acted in 'perfectly good faith' and so the insurers will be able to declare that the policy is invalid. 'Reporting' an accident to insurers is, of course, different from 'claiming' under the policy and will not, itself, affect the motorist's no-claim bonus.

When filling in the insurer's accident report form, motorists should be perfectly honest and provide all the information that supports their version of how the accident happened. If the accident was not their fault, then they should say so clearly and unambiguously. The accident report form will contain questions similar to those asked when the proposal form was completed on the insurance being taken out. The insurers may well compare the two sets of answers to check that the motorist has not been in breach of the policy in any way (e.g. by using the car for unauthorized business travel) and that full and truthful answers were given when the insurance was first taken out. Any discrepancies may allow the insurers to 'repudiate liability' under the policy and so refuse to meet any claims.

68

Common Offences

FAILURE TO STOP AND GIVE PARTICULARS AFTER AN ACCIDENT

A motorist whose vehicle is involved in an accident must stop for long enough to allow the other people concerned to ascertain his name and address. Not only must he stop, but also he must exchange particulars with anyone reasonably requesting them. In addition, even if the motorist does stop, he may be obliged to report the accident to the police. If he fails to do so, this would be another charge that could be brought.

The sensible motorist will, of course, stop after any accident, however small, and exchange particulars with anyone else involved. Legally, though, the obligation to stop and to provide particulars exists only if the accident caused:

- injury to anybody or to an animal (which is restricted to horse, cattle, ass, mule, sheep, pig, goat or dog, but not a cat); or
- damage to any vehicle (except the motorist's own car) or to other property which is attached to the road or adjoining land (e.g. if a wall, fence, tree, building or street furniture is damaged).

So, to take an extreme example, a motorist who runs over a cat, and then collides with a piece of furniture left on the pavement, damaging both it and his own car, need not stop to provide particulars, nor indeed, need he report the accident to the police.

If the motorist is obliged to stop, he must give his name and address and that of the owner of the vehicle, plus the vehicle number to anyone who reasonably requests it – in practice, other motorists and those who have suffered injury or damage. The motorist should remain at the scene for a reasonable time to allow time for persons to approach him. He is not required to give particulars of his insurance or to produce his driving licence to the other motorist.

In practice, of course, sensible motorists will do so, if only because by producing their insurance certificate they will usually remove the need to report the accident to the police.

What is the position if the driver believes he has been recognized?

Scarll was involved in an accident, which required that he stop and exchange particulars. Believing that the other driver knew him and would be able to contact him should he wish to do so, Scarll did not stop as required. **Held: The driver was obliged to comply with the section even if he genuinely believed that a relevant party knew him.**

Scarll (1989)

The motorist might be fearful of reprisals if he or she gives her address; if this fear is soundly based it may be sufficient reason to give alternative contact details.

A motorist involved in an accident gave his own name and his solicitor's address as a contact address because he was concerned for his safety had he given his own address. The motorist was a bailiff often in possession of large sums of money. **Held: The use of the solicitor's address could fulfil the requirement as the motorist could be contacted for identification and post-accident negotiations.**

McCarthy (1998)

Both failure to stop and failure to provide particulars are endorsable offences, and an endorsement (plus 5–10 points) will be imposed unless there are special reasons (*see* page 587). If motorists can satisfy the court that they did not realize there had been an accident, they must be acquitted, but in practice that is a difficult defence to prove (*see* the penalty chart, pages 581–3).

FAILING TO REPORT AN ACCIDENT

An accident must be reported to the police if:

- someone was injured and at the time of the accident the motorist did not produce their insurance certificate to a police officer or someone reasonably entitled to ask for it (e.g. a traffic warden, someone injured); or

* they did not give their name and address at the time of the accident to someone reasonably entitled to ask for it.

If full particulars were exchanged at the time of the accident (including insurance details if someone was injured), motorists need not report the accident to the police. If there was no one present at the scene of the accident, and so there was nobody to ask for the particulars, motorists must report it to the police. If the accident has to be reported, a motorist should do so as soon as possible, and in no circumstances can they wait more than 24 hours. The accident must be reported in person; it is not good enough to phone the police station. If the motorist is found guilty of failing to report the accident, their licence will be endorsed (and he will receive 5–10 points) unless he can show special reasons for not endorsing. (For what to do when there is an accident *see* pages 567–8).

69

Paying for Damage

APPORTIONING BLAME

Motorists who have been involved in a road accident will recover compensation for their injuries, losses and other damage only if they have a comprehensive policy or can show that someone else was to blame for the accident (*see also* Chapter 75). If they have a comprehensive policy and a motorist claims on that policy, they will generally lose part of their no-claims bonus and will have to pay the excess – the first few pounds of the claim. If motorists have a third-party policy, it will cover them only for damages due to another person as a result of their own negligent driving; it will not compensate for their own losses, however caused.

If they can show that someone else was to blame for the accident, they will be able to claim from that person's insurers.

Unless motorists have a comprehensive policy they will have no automatic right to compensation. Generally, therefore, the right to compensation will be dependent upon showing that someone else was to blame for the accident. If that can be proved, then that person (and their insurers) will have to pay compensation.

Before dealing with the mechanics of making a claim against another motorist, one must first understand how the law apportions and fixes 'blame' for motoring accidents.

NEGLIGENCE

The law says that all motorists have a duty to take reasonable care to avoid injury, loss and damage to other road users. If they do not, they must compensate those other road users for the injury, loss and damage incurred. In short, they must pay them damages for their negligence.

Problems arise when one tries to apply that seemingly simple idea to practical events, for it is always a question of deciding whether or not the duty to take care has been broken. Clearly, if the 'reasonable' man or woman would not have acted as the motorist did, then there will have been a breach of the duty of care, and thus negligence, but the concept of this 'reasonable' individual is not as simple as it sounds. As a starting-point ask yourself, 'Who was to blame, bearing in mind that the "reasonable" motorist never disobeys the Highway Code and is always alert to the possibility of other motorists being less careful than they should be?' Usually, common sense will supply the answer.

Frequently, an accident will not be due to the 'negligence' of just one motorist; the other motorist(s) may have contributed to the accident by being less careful than they should have been, and so they are also to blame to some degree. In such cases, the law apportions the blame between the motorists and each will lose a corresponding proportion of their damages for the 'contributory negligence'.

A Ford pulls up and a Vauxhall runs into the back of it. Every motorist has a 'duty of care' to drive in such a way that he or she can pull up in an emergency without hitting the car in front. The Vauxhall's driver is in breach of this duty and thus negligent, and so liable to pay damages to the Ford's owner.

But suppose the accident occurred on the motorway and the Ford stopped in the carriageway without giving any signal. The Ford's driver would then have been in breach of his duty – first, not to stop on the motorway and, second, to signal his intentions, while the Vauxhall would have been in breach of the duty to keep a lookout for obstructions on the road and take avoiding action. Thus, a court might find both sides equally to blame and give them both only 50 per cent of their full damages.

However, suppose that the Ford had pulled up at a pedestrian crossing, and that the Vauxhall's driver had seen this and tried to brake but hit the Ford because of a brake failure. If the Vauxhall owner had no way of knowing that the brakes were faulty, and had the car serviced regularly, he could not be said to be to blame. The

Vauxhall driver had taken 'reasonable care to avoid injury, loss and damage to other road users' and this accident arose through an entirely unforeseeable failure of his brakes. Thus, the Vauxhall driver would not be negligent and the Ford driver could not recover damages from him. The only way the Ford driver would be able to recover any compensation is if he could:

- claim under his own comprehensive policy (but this would cost him his excess and no-claims bonus); or
- show that someone else, other than the Vauxhall driver, was negligent and that this negligence caused what was a reasonably foreseeable accident.

For example, if the Vauxhall was new, then the Ford driver might have a claim against the Vauxhall manufacturers because they were in breach of their duty to the general public to fit sound brakes to new cars. Alternatively, if the Vauxhall was not new, a garage that recently serviced its brakes might owe a duty to the Ford's driver (as a road user) to ensure that the Vauxhall's brakes were working correctly.

All road users, whether motorists or pedestrians, have a duty to take care. For instance, if a careless driver injures a careless pedestrian, then the pedestrian will forfeit some, if not all, of his or her damages.

A pedestrian decided to cross at traffic lights showing green in favour of approaching traffic. A motorist travelling too fast, and not keeping proper lookout for pedestrians, knocked the pedestrian down. Held: Responsibility for the accident should be shared evenly between the motorist and the pedestrian. The result was that the pedestrian was only able to recover half the damages. Fitzgerald v Lane (1988)

WHAT ABOUT LEARNERS?

The duty of care owed by a learner driver is the same as that owed by any other 'reasonable motorist'. Learners cannot escape liability by arguing that they were doing their incompetent best.

Mr Nettleship agreed to give Miss Weston driving lessons. She was a careful learner but on the third lesson she failed to straighten out after turning left; the car hit a lamp standard and Mr Nettleship's kneecap was broken. He sued Miss Weston for damages but she argued that she was not in breach of her duty to take care – she had taken all the care that she, as a learner, could take. Held: No, she was liable. As a motorist, she was required to drive to the standard of the 'reasonable motorist' not the 'reasonable learner motorist'. Nettleship (1971)

BREAKING THE HIGHWAY CODE

Generally, the fact that a motorist did not obey the Highway Code will be a good starting-point for fixing blame. But it does not always follow that the 'reasonable road user' would have observed the Highway Code and so negligence may not attach.

Miss Powell was struck by a car while walking along the left-hand side of the road at night. She had not been walking on the pavement because it was covered by snow, and she was not wearing light-coloured clothes. The car had been travelling quickly and without proper lights. The motorist argued that she was 25 per cent to blame for not observing the Highway Code. Held: No. While she was in breach of the Highway Code she had not been negligent, and so she recovered 100 per cent damages from the negligent motorist. Powell (1972)

MECHANICAL DEFECTS

The essence of attaching blame is that the defendant failed to take proper care. Generally, therefore, if an accident happens because of a latent mechanical defect that he or she could not have known about, they cannot be liable in negligence. However, it will be for the defendant to show that he took all necessary steps to stop the danger arising, for otherwise he will be liable.

A five-year-old lorry suffered a brake failure and killed George Henderson. His widow sued the owners of the lorry for negligence. They argued that they were not to blame since the accident had been caused by a latent defect in the brakes. They had visually inspected the brakes every week, but the failure occurred in a hidden pipe that could not be seen. Held: They were liable, since they had not conclusively shown that they had taken all steps to avoid the risk of brake failure. Henderson (1969)

On the other hand:

A van owned by the defendant collided with the rear of the claimant's stationary vehicle. The van's brakes had failed owing to a split pin becoming detached from the brake linkage. The defendant had had the van fully serviced by an engineer six weeks before the accident and produced an MOT certificate dated four weeks before the accident. Held: The defendant was not liable. Worsley v Hollins (1991)

WHEN BOTH MOTORISTS COULD HAVE BEEN TO BLAME

Often there is no clear proof of who was to blame – perhaps because there were no witnesses and the drivers cannot clearly recall what happened. When this happens, liability is often divided 50/50 between them and they both recover half their normal damages from each other. This is often applied when two vehicles meet head on in a narrow country road or collide at crossroads of equal status.

Two cars collided head-on at night. There were no witnesses; one driver was killed and the other was so seriously injured that he had no recollection of what happened. There was no evidence of what happened apart from marks on one side of the road. Held: It was no more probable that the accident had occurred on one side of the road than in the middle of the road and, accordingly, both drivers were equally to blame. Both insurance companies had to pay 50 per cent damages. Howard (1973)

FLASHING HEADLIGHTS

It is common for motorists to flash their headlights as a 'come on' sign. What happens if a driver obeys the signal only to find that it is not safe to do so and collides with another motorist? The answer is that the mere flashing of lights does not absolve motorists from their normal duty of care to other road users. In fact the motorist who is hit by the car will usually be able to sue the motorist who acted on the flashing lights and, occasionally, even the motorist who negligently flashed their lights when it was not safe. However, this presupposes (as always) that they were negligent and, exceptionally, this will not be so.

A car was in a side street waiting to cross a congested main road. A bus driver in the main road stopped and flashed his headlights at the car to indicate that he would let him cross. The car pulled out very slowly but collided with a motorcyclist who was overtaking the stationary bus. Could the motorcyclist sue the car driver and/or the bus driver? Held: No. On the particular facts of the case neither driver had been negligent. The car driver had come out with very great care and so did nothing wrong. The bus driver was also not negligent because the court held that the flashing of lights did not mean 'It is safe for you to cross' but merely 'Come on as far as I am concerned'. The motorcyclist did not receive any compensation. Clarke (1969)

A tanker driver indicated that a car driver could emerge from a side turning, whereupon it collided with a motorist travelling on the main road. No action was taken against the tanker driver. Worsfold v Howe (1980)

NOT WEARING SEAT BELTS

While all road users have a duty to take care not to harm other people, they also have a duty to look after themselves. An obvious way of reducing the severity of injuries received in a car accident is to wear a seat belt; a motorist who does not do so will probably be held not to have taken sufficient care to look after himself. Thus they too will have been negligent and so any damages they receive will be reduced proportionately to allow for their own negligence.

This assumes, of course, that there were seat belts fitted to the car, and also that wearing the seat belt would have minimized the injuries. If it can be shown that the seat belt would not have prevented injury, then the negligence in not wearing it will be ignored as being irrelevant. But such cases are rare and the general rule is that failure to wear a seat belt will result in a 25 per cent reduction in damages.

Mr Froom was injured in a car crash but he was not wearing the seat belt fitted to his car. He suffered head and chest injuries and also a broken finger. The medical evidence was that, apart from the broken finger, the injuries would probably have been prevented if he had been wearing the seat belt. In reply, Mr Froom argued that he did not like wearing a belt for fear of being trapped in the vehicle after a crash and besides, he did not drive at more than normal speed. Held: The reasonable motorist guards against the possibility of negligence by other road users by wearing a seat belt, since statistics show that the chance of injury increases fourfold when a seat belt is not worn. Where injuries would have been totally prevented by wearing a seat belt the damages should be reduced by 25 per cent. When the injuries would have been 'a good deal less severe', the damages should be reduced by 15 per cent. In Mr Froom's case a reduction of 20 per cent should be made. Froom (1975)

A passenger in a car involved in a head-on collision suffered severe facial and eye injuries. Held: Her damages were reduced by 20 per cent because she was not wearing a seat belt. She would have sustained significantly less-severe injuries if she had worn a seat belt. Salmon v Newland (1983)

Another case concerned a rear-seat passenger's failure to wear a seat belt. The case also makes the point about the relevance of the victim's negligence:

A rear-seat passenger who was seriously injured in a road accident succeeded in suing the driver. The court examined the effect of the fact that the passenger had not worn a seat belt. Held: The fact that no seat belt was worn could be taken into account and it could reduce the damages that the driver had to pay. However, the court went on to consider what would have happened if a seat belt had been worn: on the facts of the case the court found that injuries would have been the same, so the damages were due in full. The aim is not to penalize the victim because they have acted negligently; it is the effect of the negligence that matters. Biesheuvel (1998)

WHEN THE NEGLIGENT MOTORIST CANNOT BE TRACED

The victims of hit and run accidents may have no one to sue, since the negligent motorist will have disappeared. Similarly, if the motorist stopped but gave false particulars, the victim will be unable to sue him.

When this happens the Motor Insurers' Bureau (MIB) will compensate the victims. The MIB is funded by the insurance industry and it will nominate an insurance company to deal with the claim as though the untraced motorist was insured with them. However, as with claims against uninsured motorists, the claim must be restricted to the compensation for personal injury and damage to property in excess of £175.

Where the person responsible for the accident is uninsured it is not necessarily disastrous. Clearly the 'guilty' motorist could be sued, but a motorist without insurance is likely to be a motorist without funds. The MIB will assume responsibility for all save the first £175 of a claim against an uninsured driver. The address of the MIB is 152 Silbury Boulevard, Milton Keynes, MK9 1NG. (*See further* pages 608–9.)

THE 'NEGLIGENCE' BASIS OF COMPENSATION

Under our legal system victims of road accidents have no automatic right to compensation. Unless they can show that someone else was to blame for the accident, their only source of financial help is likely to be the DWP for benefits such as sickness benefit, and perhaps some compensation from their insurance company if they were motorists with a comprehensive insurance policy. If no one else can be blamed for the accident then the law will not entitle them to receive compensation.

A five-year-old boy ran out into the road from behind a parked car; he was running to an ice-cream van on the other side of the road. He was seriously injured by a passing car, even though the car was travelling at only 15 m.p.h. He sued (through his parents), arguing that the motorist had been negligent. Held: The motorist had not been negligent and so the little boy was not entitled to any compensation. The only way the motorist could have avoided hitting the boy would have been if he had been driving at 5 m.p.h. It was not reasonable to expect that, and so he was not liable. The five-year-old went without compensation. Kite (1983)

Even if the injured person can show that someone else was to blame, they may be held to have been negligent themselves and so forfeit some of their damages. For instance, motorists who do not wear their seat belts are likely to lose between 15 and 25 per cent of their damages (*see* page 573).

The present system of compensation is based on blame, and the law of negligence denies compensation to thousands of people every year. There are some 240,000 accidents and 3,700 fatalities on the road each year. The motor car is much safer than cycling, motor cycling or walking – that is, on an accident per mile travelled basis. What is clear is that a substantial number of victims do not claim compensation – a fact demonstrated by the growth of advertising by firms specializing in compensation claims.

CLAIMING COMPENSATION

If you intend to make a claim against another road user, then:

1 drive or tow the car home or to a garage and keep any repair or towing receipt;
2 report the accident to your own insurers. If you have a comprehensive policy, notify them that no claim is being made against them;
3 if the claim is substantial or involves anything other than very minor personal injury, consult a solicitor. If the claim is successful and it is for more than £5,000, the other side may have to pay most of your legal costs;
4 ask the garage for a written confirmation that the car is 'beyond economical repair' and their estimate of its pre-accident value;
5 write to the other motorist, claiming damages. A typical letter might read:

I refer to the accident on .... at .... involving motor car no. ....

This accident was caused by your negligent driving of a motor vehicle and accordingly damages are claimed for the personal injury, losses, expenses and inconvenience arising therefrom.

The wreckage is at present with Messrs .... at .... and can be inspected by you or your insurers on an appointment being made with Mr .... Please ensure that an inspection is made within the next fourteen days, failing which the necessary repairs will be put in hand (or the wreckage will be disposed of);

6 keep a full note of all losses and expenses arising out of the accident;
7 do not have the repairs carried out until you are fairly sure that the insurers will meet the cost or that your claim will be successful, as the garage bill will be your responsibility.

The insurers will be evasive and slow correspondents, but do not let them slow down the handling of the claim. If necessary, you should pester them with letters. If the repairs will involve replacing worn parts with new parts, the insurers will expect you to pay 'betterment' (i.e. a contribution to the cost) since the car will now be in a better condition than it was before the accident. They are entitled to insist on such a contribution, but always check that they are not charging too much.

Alternatively, if the vehicle is a write-off, try to agree a figure for its pre-accident value. Use local newspaper advertisements and garage estimates to support your valuation. Also check your insurance proposal form to see what valuation you placed on the car then. Do not be unrealistic about the valuation; insurance engineers can accurately assess the pre-accident condition of a vehicle from the wreckage and will detect untrue statements about the car's recorded mileage, interior condition, etc. Once the insurers agree that the vehicle is 'beyond commercial repair', then take steps to dispose of the wreckage, as the insurers will not be liable for storage charges from that date.

It may be that you cannot afford to buy a replacement vehicle until the insurance monies are received. But you probably cannot recover extra compensation for the increased period of inconvenience when you are without a car, nor for the cost of interest on money borrowed to buy the replacement car. As far as the law is concerned, your financial status (or lack of it) is irrelevant and the defendant should not have to pay higher damages just because you are hard up.

If the car has been repaired, you will generally be expected to pay the garage and to recover the amount afterwards from the insurers. Losses and expenses incurred in collecting the car will form part of the claim.

Formulate the amount of the claim. Include all losses and expenses reasonably incurred as a result of the accident, unless they are too unlikely. Items that can be legitimately claimed include the cost of travel home after the accident, travel to pick up the car, wages lost, stamps, telephone calls, private medical fees, prescriptions, new clothing to replace clothing damaged in the accident (but allow something for the fact that the damaged clothing was not new), cost of hiring a replacement vehicle (it must be of a suitable type; i.e. a Mini owner should not hire a Rover). Also losses and expenses incurred by members of your family, although strictly speaking they should be separate claims. If a vehicle isn't hired while the damaged car is being repaired, then claim the cost of bus, rail and taxi fares incurred, plus a small amount for inconvenience. However, allowance must be made for the money saved on not having to buy petrol, oil, etc. A figure of £30 per week for inconvenience and compensation for loss of use of the car is generally acceptable.

If possible, all these items of expense should be proved by receipts. Wage losses can be proved by a letter from the employer setting out the net (i.e. after tax) loss. If any DWP benefits were received (such as sickness benefit, invalidity benefit) as a result of the accident, then one-half of their total should be deducted from the wage loss;

unemployment and supplementary benefits are deducted in full when working out the wage loss.

Set out all these financial losses (called 'special damages' by lawyers) in list form and send them to the insurers. If there was any injury sustained in the accident try to negotiate a suitable figure for that as well, but it is important to remember that a solicitor should handle all but the most trivial personal injury claims. As a layperson, you may, unwittingly, settle your case for less than it is worth or you may not appreciate that what seems to be a trivial injury could have serious long-term consequences. Note that, except in a few limited cases, public funding is no longer available for personal injury claims.

The insurers will probably handle the claim very slowly. If you have a claim that is sound on liability (i.e. the other motorist was definitely to blame) you may well find it best to commence county court proceedings against the other motorist. This will almost certainly cause the insurance company to deal with the claim without any further delay. The steps to be taken to sue in the county court are set out in Chapter 97. (The specimen pleadings in the Appendix are from a claim arising out of a minor road accident.)

INSURANCE BROKERS

Sometimes a motorist's insurance broker will offer to negotiate the claim with the insurance company for him. The motorist should check in advance what the broker's fee will be.

These brokers do not have to belong to a professional body and accordingly motorists should try to ensure that their broker is competent and honest, or they may find that their claim has been under-settled. If the accident involved personal injury, it is advisable to use a solicitor rather than a broker.

If the broker cannot negotiate a proper settlement, he will not be able to act for you in court proceedings. Only a solicitor can sue on behalf of someone else. There is thus a temptation for brokers to under-settle claims and so recover commission, when a solicitor might have commenced proceedings and ended up with a larger amount of compensation for the client.

ON THE SPOT SETTLEMENTS

When an accident happens negligent motorists may offer innocent motorists an immediate cash settlement on a 'let's not bother the police' basis. If motorists are offered such a settlement, they should reject it. First, it may be an offence not to report the accident to the police (*see* page 569) and second, the claim may be worth much more than they are being offered. Only when a mechanic has inspected the car and a doctor has checked for any injuries should such a settlement be contemplated. Whether or not the offer is accepted, the accident will still need to be reported to the motorist's own insurers (*see* page 568).

An offer to settle may be phrased in these terms:

I refer to the motor accident at .... on .... As agreed, although I am not admitting any liability, I am prepared to pay you £ .... in full and final settlement of all your claims arising from that accident, and accordingly I enclose a cheque for that amount. Please acknowledge safe receipt by signing the attached copy of this letter and returning it to me.

This ensures that the other motorist cannot come back and claim more money at a future date.

70

Outline of Procedure

In the eyes of the law, motoring offences are no different from other offences. If the defendant is guilty, then he has committed a crime. Society, of course, generally takes a more lenient view and regards most motoring offences as being different from other criminal offences, presumably on the basis of 'There, but for the grace of God, go I'. This ambivalent attitude to motoring offences is reflected, for example, in the fact that Parliament has had to create a special offence of 'causing death by dangerous driving' because of the refusal of juries to convict motorists of manslaughter, even when there is clear evidence of gross negligence.

However, there is one legal difference between many motoring offences and most other offences, in that motoring offences are generally not concerned with the intention or knowledge of the accused. Most crimes involve, first, an illegal act and, second, some degree of intention to commit the illegal act. Most motoring offences need only the illegal act and not the intention to commit it. For instance, a motorist who drives at 40 m.p.h. in a 30 m.p.h. zone cannot expect to be acquitted because he did not know there was a 30 m.p.h. limit, or because his speedometer was working incorrectly (in itself an offence under the Construction and Use Regulations). The court would be concerned to know only: was there a 30 m.p.h. limit in force and was the accused exceeding 30 m.p.h? If so, then a conviction must result, although obviously the circumstances of the offence would be relevant when deciding on a suitable penalty.

Similarly, take the example of the motorist who does not know that his insurers have 'gone bust' and is, therefore, driving without insurance. He may be morally blameless but in the law's eyes will be guilty of driving without insurance and a conviction must result. The excuses will be relevant only after conviction, when the court is considering what penalty to impose.

However, this is not a universal rule, for there are a few motoring offences that require a form of guilty knowledge or intent on the part of the accused before they can be convicted. But such offences (e.g. dangerous driving, 'causing or permitting' charges) are the exception rather than the rule, whereas in non-motoring offences the reverse applies.

While, in legal theory, all motoring convictions are criminal convictions, a distinction is in fact made between the various categories of motoring offences, and this distinction is reflected in the way in which they are recorded.

Convictions usually regarded as 'criminal', mostly those for which imprisonment could be ordered, are recorded in national criminal records. Thus offences such as causing death by dangerous driving and taking a vehicle without consent would be recorded in the national criminal records.

Convictions resulting in an endorsement or in disqualification are recorded on the DVLA computer at Swansea. Every driver has a driver number, and the police or courts can apply for a computer print-out of his or her driving record. Some offences are recorded both in criminal records and at the DVLA.

Minor offences are not recorded in a central register.

Convictions do not remain on a driving licence (or in the DVLA computer) for ever. Most offences are removed when a licence is exchanged four or more years after a conviction. The main exceptions are drink-driving offences, which remain on a licence for 11 years.

When making job applications there will often be a question about offences; this will include motoring offences unless it says otherwise.

STARTING PROCEEDINGS

Because motoring offences are, in the eyes of the law, similar to other criminal offences, proceedings are begun in the same way (*see* pages 639–40 for ways in which criminal proceedings can be commenced). Most motoring offences begin by way of a summons.

Only in the more serious cases (such as dangerous driving or drink-driving offences) is the motorist likely to be arrested and taken to the police station. If motorists are arrested they are likely to be bailed to court rather than being brought to court in custody. Bail is the term used now to describe a legal duty to appear before a court or in some circumstances to appear at a police station for further inquiries. Failing to attend in answer to bail would be a serious separate offence. Apart from the question of prior notice, the points made below also apply to the charge sheet they will receive instead of the summons. For motorists who are arrested and detained, legal advice should be available at the police station from a duty solicitor or a private solicitor.

When served with a summons there are a few preliminary points that the motorist should consider before deciding whether to plead guilty or not guilty.

What exactly are the charges?

The charge will be set out in formal language, so motorists should read it carefully and, if necessary, seek legal advice. Often it will be important to check whether they are being prosecuted for 'using' the car, 'driving' the car, 'being in charge' of the car (e.g. when it is parked) or 'permitting' its use (e.g. when they allow someone else such as an employee to use it). It is worth checking that the correct wording is used for the facts of the particular case.

Should the police have notified a likely prosecution?

With certain offences, motorists must be warned that they might be prosecuted so that they can take steps to contact witnesses and collect evidence before too much time elapses. The warning can either be a verbal warning from the police at the time of the offence (typically: 'The facts will be reported with a view to consideration of the question of proceedings being taken against you') or a written notice of intended prosecution (or even a summons), served within 14 days of the offence. The notice is usually sent by post and will simply state that the police intend to prosecute. But just because a notice of intended prosecution is served, it does not necessarily mean that the police will prosecute, for the service of the notice simply allows the police to keep their options open while they decide whether or not to prosecute.

A warning of possible prosecution is needed only for the following offences:

- dangerous, careless or inconsiderate driving (or cycling);
- failure to comply with a traffic direction or sign;
- failure to comply with the directions of a police officer regulating traffic;
- leaving a vehicle in a dangerous position;
- speeding offences.

However, no notice is needed if an accident occurred at the time of the offence. So if, for instance, motorists are involved in a collision, however slight, they need not be warned that they might be prosecuted for careless driving. However, if they had not hit the other vehicle and there had been no accident, then they would have to be warned.

In practice, it is extremely unusual for a motorist to have a summons dismissed because no notice of intended prosecution was given. It is for the motorist to show that the notice was not given. Warnings at the roadside are now a routine part of police procedure and alternatively if the police can show that the notice was sent by post to their address, the court may find that it was served properly even if it was in fact returned by the post office.

Should the motorist defend the charge?

Once the motorist has checked these technicalities, he will have to decide whether to instruct a solicitor. In all but the most obvious cases it will be worthwhile taking legal advice, either from a solicitor, a law centre, a Citizens' Advice Bureau, or from the AA or RAC (if they are members). If the prosecution follows a serious accident, the motorist's insurance company may be prepared to instruct a solicitor to represent him since his liability to pay damages could be affected by the outcome of the criminal prosecution. The motorist should ask himself the following questions:

1 Is it worth paying legal fees to defend the charge? In a magistrates' court prosecution a motorist should recover all his legal costs if he is acquitted. Legal Aid (now called public funding) will be available only for the more serious motoring offence. The court is required to help the motorist with procedure in court.

2 What is the maximum possible penalty, and also what is the likely penalty? (*See* the penalty chart on pages 581–3.)

3 Does he have any previous motoring convictions that will affect the penalty? In particular, does he have any penalty points that could lead to disqualification under the penalty point rules (*see* page 588)?

4 If the offence is very trivial, is it worth incurring the inconvenience of defending it? For instance, with a parking summons it might be cheaper and more convenient to plead guilty rather than go to the inconvenience of attending court to defend the charge. However, a court should not accept a plea of guilty based upon convenience even for a trivial offence. If a motorist says, 'I plead guilty, but . . .' and then goes on

to give a defence, he will be asked to attend court to contest the case.

5 Does he have a defence to the charge? Although it is always for the prosecution to prove their case, there is no point in pleading not guilty when there is no hope of acquittal. Indeed, such a course of action usually rebounds; the court should give credit for a timely acceptance of guilt. There are also costs to consider: the court will order the defendant to pay the costs of the prosecution (which would probably have been lower had he pleaded guilty). This is especially true of breathalyser prosecutions, where many defendants plead not guilty when they clearly are guilty. A court, if appropriate, will see an early guilty plea as straightforwardness and a sign of regret; it should result in a more lenient penalty.

6 If the motorist is going to plead guilty, can he do so by post? It is possible to plead guilty by post to most motoring offences where the prosecutor allows this option, but it is important that defendants write to the court in good time and enclose their driving licence if required. Remember that it is not possible to plead 'not guilty' by post. A 'not guilty' plea means attendance at court by the defendant. (*See further* page 647.)

Fixed Penalties and Alternatives to Court

Fixed penalties can be given for a great many road traffic offences. Since 1982, endorsable offences, including speeding, are among the offences that can be dealt with in this way. There will be even more 'tickets' issued in the future. There is now a widespread and intensive use of cameras at traffic signals. Offences detected by camera will lead first to the vehicle keeper who will be asked to identify the driver at the time of the alleged offence.

What if a motorist is offered a fixed penalty? To accept a fixed penalty is to accept guilt for the offence in question. The considerations discussed on pages 578–9 apply but with the difference that the motorist knows, in advance, the penalty. If the fixed penalty is being offered for an endorsable offence, the effect of the penalty points will make these considerations all the more important. For most motorists who have offended, a fixed penalty represents a bargain offer and should be snapped up. It avoids costs and a fine, which would almost certainly be more than the fixed penalty.

A mistake made by many motorists is ignoring a fixed penalty. If a motorist is wrongly 'ticketed' it is up to the motorist to take action (as indicated on the ticket) and to seek a court hearing. If no action is taken proceedings will automatically go through to the point where bailiffs or police officers call for the penalty, which at that point will have been increased by at least 50 per cent and will be treated as a fine.

In some areas there may be alternatives to court quite apart from fixed penalties. Both driver and vehicle rectification schemes exist. With a vehicle rectification scheme the motorist is given a time period to repair a defect or scrap the vehicle. Provided that the police are satisfied that the motorist has complied, the matter ends there. With driver rectification the motorist undertakes a driver education course and on completion the offence is met with a caution. The motorist must opt for the scheme and whether or not a scheme is advantageous depends entirely on personal circumstances.

Guide to Penalties

The penalty chart (*see* below) sets out typical penalties for first-time offenders. It does not set out the maximum possible penalties, which may well be much greater. This is because the vast majority of motorists are not fined the maximum amount (e.g. some obstruction charges can carry a maximum penalty of up to £5,000 but, in practice, typical penalties are in the £50–£60 bracket). So maximum penalties are usually misleading.

Bear in mind that the typical penalties set out in the penalty chart are no more than very rough guidelines. It is not uncommon for a solicitor to have two clients with seemingly identical cases and find that one client, in one court, gets a sentence considered 'worth' twice that of the other client who seemingly had the good fortune to appear in a different court. In any event, the penalty imposed will depend on the specific facts of the incident, the court's impression of the motorist's ability to pay, any previous convictions and also that particular court's view of the seriousness of the offence in question. It is, therefore, only possible to set out 'typical penalties' as a rough and ready guide. The limitations of these figures should always be borne in mind.

If the offence is one for which a fixed penalty could have been imposed, the court will often wish to impose a penalty significantly above the fixed-penalty levels, which are currently £20 for a non-endorsable offence and £40 for an endorsable offence. If a fixed penalty was not offered because, for example, the officer did not have a pad of tickets, this needs to be pointed out to the court; if it is, the court may limit its penalty to the fixed-penalty level.

Apart from a fine or imprisonment, endorsement and disqualification are usually the major penalties that can be imposed on motoring offenders.

HOW TO USE THE PENALTY CHART

The penalty chart on the next few pages sets out the main motoring offences and gives rough guidelines for sentences for first offenders. It cannot be emphasized too strongly that these are no more than very approximate guidelines and under no circumstances should they be seen as definite recommendations. The aim of the penalty chart is simply to give an approximate indication of the author's informed guess of 'going rates' in 2000. Penalties shown are based upon private motor vehicles. Goods vehicles, large passenger vehicles or any commercial use may increase the level of penalty considerably.

Penalty Chart

Offence	Endorse?	Disqualify?	Maximum penalty	Likely penalty
Accidents				
Failing to stop	Must	May	£5,000	£240
Failing to report to police	Must	May	£5,000	£240
Alcohol				
Driving while unfit	Must	Must – 12 months	£5,000 6 months prison	£360 + prison and longer disqualification possible

Offence	Endorse?	Disqualify?	Maximum penalty	Likely penalty
Driving while over limit	Must	Must – 12 months	£5,000 6 months' prison	£360 + prison + longer disqualification for high levels
Failing to give specimen at roadside	Must	May	£1,000	£120
Failing to give specimen at police station	Must	Must – 12 months	£5,000 6 months' prison	£400 + prison + longer disqualification for high levels
In charge while unfit	Must	May	£2,500	£360
In charge while over limit	Must	May	£2,500 3 months' prison	£360
Defective parts				
Defective brakes	Must	May	£2,500	£100
Defective steering	Must	May	£2,500	£100
Defective tyres	Must	May	£2,500	£100
Defective (or no) lights	No	No	£2,500	£60
Other parts offences	No	No	£1,000	£50
Disqualified driver				
Driving while disqualified	Must	May	£5,000 6 months' prison	All options including prison
Documents				
Failing to produce licence or insurance or test certificate	No	No	£1,000	£60 each
No insurance	Must	May	£1,000	£360
Driving when not licensed	Must	May	£1,000	£150
No excise licence ('road tax')	No	No	£1,000 or 5 × duty lost	Relates to duty lost
No test certificate	No	No	£1,000	£90
Failing to notify ownership change	No	No	£1,000	£150
Double white lines				
Failing to comply	Must	May	£1,000	£100
Driving				
Dangerous driving	Must	Must*	£5,000 6 months' prison	All options including prison
Careless or inconsiderate driving	Must	May	£2,500	£180
Parking				
Parking in dangerous position	Must	May	£1,000	£100
Parking within pedestrian crossing	Must	May	£1,000	£100
Obstruction	No	No	£1,000	£60
Safety equipment				
No safety helmet	No	No	£500	£60
No seat belt	No	No	£500	£60
Speeding				
Excess speed	Must	May	£1,000	£150, disqualification for high speeds
Traffic signs				
Failing to obey traffic lights	Must	May	£1,000	£90

Offence	Endorse?	Disqualify?	Maximum penalty	Likely penalty
Other traffic signs	*	*	£1,000	£60
Motorways				
Driving in reverse	Must	May	£2,500	£240
Driving in wrong direction	Must	May	£2,500	£400, disqualification likely
Driving off carriageway	Must	May	£2,500	£120
Driving on slip-road in prohibited direction	Must	May	£2,500	£120
'U' turn on motorway	Must	May	£2,500	£350
Stopping on hard shoulder	No	No	£2,500	£100
Unlawful use of third lane	Must	May	£2,500	£300
Walking on motorway	No	No	£2,500	£60
Dishonesty				
Taking vehicle without consent	No	May	£5,000	All options
Aggravated vehicle taking	No	May	£5,000	All options

*Dependent on facts of the case.

73

Licence Endorsement and Penalty Points

An endorsement can be imposed for most motoring offences, the major exceptions being for parking, obstruction, no road fund licence, no MOT certificate and lighting offences.

For relevant offences an endorsement will be ordered unless the court decides that there are special reasons (*see* page 587) for not endorsing. The endorsement is entered on the motorist's driving licence and also on DVLA records, although the motorist can apply for it to be removed from the licence after four years (11 years if endorsement was for a drink-driving offence).

WHAT IS AN ENDORSEMENT?

An endorsement means that the conviction is 'endorsed' (i.e. written) on the motorist's driving licence. As such, an endorsement is not by itself much of a penalty, except for the fact that each endorsement has a number of penalty points that accompany it. Motorists will want to do all they can to avoid getting an endorsement as the penalty points can accumulate to the point where disqualification is normally ordered.

HOW CAN AN ENDORSEMENT BE AVOIDED?

The court has very little discretion to refuse to endorse if the law states that the offence carries endorsement. In the penalty chart (pages 581–3) there is a column headed 'Endorse?' and this shows the offences for which the court has to endorse. However, even in those cases, the court can refuse to endorse if it finds that there are 'special reasons' surrounding the way in which the offence was committed. So, if motorists can convince the court that there were special reasons, then the court may not endorse their licence, and – probably more importantly – the court cannot then impose any penalty points. In practice, very few motorists are able to argue legitimately that

there were special reasons (*see* page 587 for the rules on special reasons).

One other, very narrow, escape route from endorsement applies to offences of defective steering, brakes and tyres under the Construction and Use Regulations. In such a case, if motorists can prove that they did not know of the defect and had no cause to suspect it, they may avoid endorsement. However, the court will expect good vehicle maintenance to be established and the plea is effectively limited to sudden mechanical failure.

Penalty points

Before 1982, the rule used to be that motorists would lose their licence if they had three endorsements in three years. Now the rule is if they have 12 penalty points in three years they will lose their licence. Special rules apply to newly qualified drivers.

The more serious offences carry more penalty points. To see whether a particular offence carries points, refer to the penalty chart. If the offence is listed as having an endorsement, then points will normally have to be imposed.

Most offences carry a fixed number of penalty points (e.g. defective brakes carries three points). But some offences carry a range of penalty points and the court has discretion as to the number of points to impose within that range. The next table shows the penalty points for each endorsable offence and also the code that is used to endorse a licence.

Code	Offences	Penalty points
Offences in relation to accidents		
AC10	Failing to stop after an accident	5–10
AC20	Failing to give particulars or to report an accident within 24 hours	5–10
Offences of driving while disqualified		
BA10	Driving while disqualified by order of court	6
Careless driving offences		
CD10	Driving without due care and attention	3–9
CD20	Driving without reasonable consideration for other road users	3–9
CD40	Causing death by careless driving when unfit through drink	Disqualify
CD60	Causing death by careless driving with alcohol level above the limit	Disqualify
Construction and use offences (vehicles or parts dangerous)		
CU10	Using a vehicle with defective brakes	3
CU20	Causing or likely to cause danger by reason of use of unsuitable vehicle or using a vehicle with parts or accessories (excluding brakes, steering or tyres) in dangerous condition	3
CU30	Using a vehicle with defective tyres	3
CU40	Using a vehicle with defective steering	3
CU50	Causing or likely to cause danger by reason of load or passengers	3
Dangerous driving offences		
DD40	Dangerous driving	Disqualify
DD80	Causing death by dangerous driving	Disqualify
Drink or drugs offences		
DR10	Driving or attempting to drive with alcohol concentration above limit	Disqualify
DR20	Driving or attempting to drive when unfit through drink	Disqualify
DR30	Driving or attempting to drive, when refusing to provide a specimen for analysis	Disqualify
DR40	In charge of a vehicle with alcohol concentration above limit	10
DR50	In charge of vehicle when unfit through drink	10
DR60	Failure to provide a specimen for analysis in circumstances other than driving or attempting to drive	10
DR70	Failing to provide a specimen for breath test	4
DR80	Driving or attempting to drive when unfit through drugs	Disqualify
DR90	In charge of vehicle when unfit through drugs	10
Insurance offences		
IN10	Using a vehicle uninsured against third-party risks	6–8
Licence offences		
LC20	Driving otherwise than in accordance with a licence	3–6
Miscellaneous offences		
MS10	Leaving vehicle in a dangerous position	3
MS50	Motor racing on the highway	Disqualify
Motorway offences		
MW10	Contravention of motorway regulations (excluding speed limits)	3

Code	Offences	Penalty points
Pedestrian crossing offences		
PC20	Contravention of pedestrian crossing regulations with moving vehicle	3
PC30	Contravention of pedestrian crossing regulations with stationary vehicles	3
Speed limit offences		
SP20	Exceeding speed limit for type of vehicle (excluding goods/passenger vehicles)	3–6
SP30	Exceeding statutory speed limit on a public road	3–6
SP40	Exceeding passenger vehicle speed limit	3–6
SP50	Exceeding speed limit on a motorway	3–6
Traffic directions and signs offences		
TS10	Failing to comply with traffic light signals	3
TS20	Failing to comply with double white lines	3
TS30	Failing to comply with a 'stop' sign	3
TS40	Failing to comply with a direction of a constable or traffic warden	3
TS50	Failing to comply with a traffic sign (excluding stop signs, traffic lights or double white lines)	3

In cases where the table shows a range of points the court has discretion. It will obviously take into account the circumstances of the case, such as the seriousness of any accident, damage caused or the risk to others, and, in some courts, the previous driving record of the motorist. So, if motorists are being prosecuted for one of these offences, they would be unwise to plead guilty by post, in case the court imposes maximum penalty points. The motorist should appear in court to explain the mitigating circumstances and why a lower number of points should be imposed. To take the example of careless driving, the outcome for the motorist could be three points or nine points or anything in between; three points is one-quarter of the way towards a disqualification, nine points is three-quarters of the way towards a ban – a difference worth an appearance at court.

Where a disqualification is shown in the table but because of 'special reasons' it is not imposed, then an endorsement of penalty points should follow. However, if special reasons prevent disqualification, logically it should also prevent endorsement.

Convictions for more than one offence

Often a motorist will face more than one charge as a result of one incident. The question then arises of how many points should be imposed. The answer is that he will usually receive the points only for the most serious offence; he will not usually receive points for other offences committed on the same occasion.

A motorist is stopped on the motorway for speeding. When the police examine his car they discover that his brakes are not working. He is subsequently convicted of speeding (the decision is three points) and for a breach of the Construction and Use Regulations (which also carries three points). In fact, he will usually receive only three points (i.e. not six points).

A motorist is involved in a serious accident and subsequently prosecuted for dangerous driving (which carries 10 points) and for speeding (the decision is three points). She will usually receive 10 points (i.e. not 13 points).

This lumping of penalties together is usual if the offences are 'committed on the same occasion'. For instance, suppose a motorist drives from Bristol to London, and is seen driving carelessly in Bath and speeding near Heathrow. The offences were not committed on the same occasion and so he or she will incur points (between three and nine) for the careless driving and (between three and six) points for the speeding. On the other hand, if the two offences had happened at more or less the same time, then it would count as only one conviction for the purpose of points. The difficulty, of course, lies in deciding when offences are 'committed on the same occasion' and when they are different occasions. When there is a dispute on this point, the court has to decide.

Can points be avoided?

If the offence carries penalty points then the court must normally impose those points; it cannot decide that the offence was not serious enough to merit points. But points can be imposed only if the motorist's licence is also endorsed. So, if motorists can persuade the court not to endorse their licence (*see* page 584), then they will also avoid incurring points. However, an endorsement can be avoided only if motorists can persuade the court that there were 'special reasons' in their particular case. This is not as easy as it may seem because it is not the hardship to the individual motorist that matters (e.g. it may threaten his or her job) but the circumstances of the offence.

Special reasons

The fundamental rule on special reasons is that the circumstances must be connected with the offence and not with the offender. Thus, the mere fact that the offender will lose his job if his licence is endorsed cannot be a special reason, as it is a circumstance that relates to the offender, not the offence. On the other hand, the fact that the offence was committed after the motorist had consumed laced drinks could be a special reason, since it relates to the circumstances of the offence and not the offender's own personal circumstances.

Cases which have been held to be special reasons include:

- driving in an emergency situation where there is no alternative;
- driving under duress;
- driving without knowledge of having consumed alcohol;
- driving an exceptionally short distance.

Many motorists are convinced that there are special reasons why they should not have an endorsement, but only occasionally will they be correct. The best way to illustrate how strictly the rules on special reasons are applied is to consider examples of what have been held *not* to be special reasons:

- the motorist has been driving for many years without complaint or accident;
- he is a professional driver and will otherwise lose his job;
- he is disabled and relies on his car for transport, or he is disabled and only drove the car at the time of the offence because there was no public transport available;
- he will suffer financial hardship, or serious hardship will be caused to the defendant's family;
- he is a doctor and endorsement resulting in disqualification would cause medical services in his area to deteriorate;
- he is a soldier and must be able to drive on duty;
- domestic circumstances (such as a babysitter waiting at home) forced him to drive the car at the time of the offence;
- endorsement would result in disqualification and that would be too severe a penalty;
- the accident that occurred was not his fault;
- he was the person who actually summoned the police;
- the offence occurred late at night when there were few people about.

Special reasons are not just important when an endorsement is being considered. In the more serious motoring offences for which disqualification is mandatory (e.g. drink-driving) motorists can argue that there are special reasons why they should not be disqualified. Once again, the principle to be applied is that special reasons must be relevant to the offence, not to the offender (*see* page 556 for more examples of special reasons relevant to drink-driving).

74

Disqualification from Driving

TWELVE POINTS MEANS DISQUALIFICATION

The basic rule is that motorists who acquire 12 penalty points in a three-year period will lose their licence for at least six months. This is what is sometimes called 'totting up'. In fact, it is an oversimplification to say that 12 points in three years equals six months' disqualification: in many cases it will, but often the rules are complicated to apply.

THE THREE-YEAR PERIOD

In most cases, it is simply a matter of seeing whether the motorist has had points within the last three years. But special provisions have had to be built into the rules so as to prevent defendants gaining an advantage by postponing their court appearances (and so moving to a different three-year period). The basic rule is that offences committed within three years of the date of the latest offence – not the date when it comes to court – are taken into account. In fact, the rules can be difficult to apply, so anyone with a borderline case should take legal advice. Nevertheless, if the motorist has already been disqualified in the last three years, then that disqualification wipes the slate clean as regards points incurred before disqualification. So, if a motorist had 10 points one year ago, but was disqualified nine months ago, then only points imposed in the last nine months – since his or her disqualification – will be counted.

THE LENGTH OF DISQUALIFICATION

The normal rule is that 12 points in three years leads to a minimum of six months' disqualification. Note that this is the minimum period, although in practice if it is a first disqualification it is usually six months (not longer) that is imposed. But if the motorist has been disqualified before, within the last three years, and that earlier disqualification was for more than 56 days, then the minimum period is longer. The basic rule is:

- no disqualification in last three years – six months;
- one disqualification in last three years – one year minimum;
- more than one disqualification in last three years – two years minimum.

A penalty point disqualification has two consequences. First, it wipes the slate clean so that past penalty points no longer count. Second, it means that if there is another disqualification in the three-year period, then the court must impose a longer disqualification next time.

The minimum periods of disqualification apply in the vast majority of totting-up cases. The court does have a discretion, and it is allowed to impose a shorter period, or not to disqualify at all, if it can be persuaded that there are mitigating circumstances. This allows the court to take into account the personal circumstances of the motorist. It must be emphasized that the court will look for serious and exceptional hardship if that is to be sufficient reason for not disqualifying. It will not be impressed by vague talk of hardship and inconvenience; it will want clear evidence of exceptional hardship.

'Mitigating circumstances' for not disqualifying under the penalty points rules should not be confused with 'special reasons' for not endorsing a licence (*see* page 587). The important restriction on 'special reasons' is that they must be special to the circumstances of how the offence was committed (e.g. laced drinks) and not to the offender himself (e.g. he is a sales representative). With 'mitigating circumstances' for not disqualifying, it is different: the personal circumstances of the motorist are relevant and not the facts of the offence. Thus, nearly every example on page 587 of what was not a 'special reason' could be a valid example of a 'mitigating circumstance' for not disqualifying.

Anyone who is facing disqualification under the totting-up rules should consider instructing a solicitor to argue their case if they think they might be able to raise mitigating circumstances as to why they should not be disqualified.

Summary

The sequence of events is:

1 the motorist is convicted of an endorsable offence (*see* the penalty chart on pages 581–3 to check whether an offence is endorsable or not);

2 the magistrates will then endorse his licence, unless he can show there are special reasons for not doing so (*see* page 587 for what counts as a special reason);

3 if the licence is endorsed, the magistrates will then impose penalty points shown on pages 585–6. But if no endorsement was ordered, then no points can be imposed;

4 if points are imposed, the magistrates will then go on to see whether the motorist should also be disqualified under the totting-up rules (i.e. 12 points in three years). If so, he will normally be disqualified for at least six months, unless he can show that mitigating circumstances apply (*see* above for what this means);

5 special rules apply to new drivers who may be disqualified when they reach six penalty points; a motorist is a 'new driver' for his first two years with a full licence.

DISQUALIFICATION FROM DRIVING

There are three ways in which motorists can be disqualified from driving. First, they can be disqualified under the penalty points rules (i.e. because they have received 12 penalty points in the last three years; *see* above). Second, they may be disqualified for a single offence, if the court believes it is serious enough. Third, the law requires that for some offences the court must disqualify a motorist.

The second type of situation, where the court feels an offence is so serious that it should impose a discretionary disqualification, is difficult to describe, as courts may see offences differently. While any offence that is endorsable may be the subject of a discretionary disqualification, very few motorists need worry about this as a realistic outcome; disqualification cannot be imposed in a motorist's absence without specific warning, so a motorist will have an opportunity to seek advice should such a disqualification be indicated. Probably the most common examples of this type of disqualification are extremely high speeds (driving at more than 30 m.p.h. over a speed limit) and cases of deliberate uninsured driving where motorists may well find that they are required to attend court to say why they should keep their licence.

A glance at the penalty chart on pages 581–3 will show that the court, surprisingly often, has the power to disqualify, if it wants to. In practice, of course, the court will only occasionally disqualify for these offences and much will depend upon the circumstances of the particular case. But there is a growing school of thought that a short period of disqualification can be a far more effective penalty than a fine, and so it is becoming more frequent for courts to impose a short disqualification. The sort of offences that come within this category are: failing to stop after an accident; driving while disqualified; crossing double white lines; dangerous driving; deliberate no insurance; speeding more than 30 m.p.h. over the limit; traffic light offences; and taking a vehicle without consent. It may be reassuring to note that only about one per cent of speeding offenders and about one per cent of those convicted of careless driving are, in fact, disqualified.

The third route to disqualification is where offences are so serious that Parliament has said that they should normally result in automatic disqualification. Drink-driving is the best-known example. That offence, and certain others (e.g. death by dangerous driving and failing to provide a police station breath specimen), carry an automatic 12-month (minimum) ban. However, even with these serious offences the court can decide not to ban if there are 'special reasons' relating to the offence (e.g. laced drinks). (*See* page 587 for examples of what can be – and more importantly, what cannot be – special reasons.) There are more examples of special reasons in the section on drink-driving (*see* page 556).

THE EFFECT OF DISQUALIFICATION

If a court disqualifies, then the ban comes into effect immediately. Motorists cannot even drive from the courthouse garage in their car. If they defy the ban, and are caught, there is a fair chance of going to prison (about a 10 per cent chance). Even when the period of disqualification ends, they cannot simply get in their car and start driving again. A disqualification revokes a motorist's driving licence and he will have to get a new licence from the DVLA at Swansea. They may even have to take a driving test (if that was ordered by the court) or a medical (if the DVLA believe the motorist has a 'high risk' of alcohol abuse).

REMOVING THE DISQUALIFICATION

Motorists who have been disqualified can apply to the court for the ban to be lifted early. The application is made to the court that imposed the ban and it will be for offenders to convince the court that their character and recent conduct justify the return of their licence. The seriousness of the original offence and any pressing reason why they need their licence back will also be taken into account. The application cannot be made until at least two years have expired. Some serious offences attract very long periods of disqualification, for example a second drink-driving offence attracts a minimum three-year ban. The minimum periods to be served are:

- Disqualified for less than 4 years – can apply after 2 years
- Disqualified for 4–10 years – can apply when half the period has expired
- Disqualified for over 10 years – can apply after 5 years

When the court hears the application, the procedure is that the Crown prosecutor in court will outline the circumstances of the original offence (including any mitigating or aggravating circumstances). They will also say whether the applicant has been in trouble since his or her disqualification. Next, the applicant will be asked to state the grounds of their application and why they need to be able to drive. Usually, this will be because it will increase their chances of getting a job, in which case it is advisable to have strong supporting evidence from a prospective employer. Instead of removing the disqualification the magistrates may decide simply to reduce its length. Alternatively, of course, they may refuse to change the length of the ban (if so, the applicant cannot appeal, but can apply again in three months' time).

Public funding is not available for an application to remove a disqualification, although a motorist can choose to pay for a solicitor to attend.

Where a disqualification is for a drink-driving offence, the period may be reduced by attendance at a special alcohol education programme. This arrangement is only available if the motorist agrees at the time of sentence. Motorists should always accept this alternative, while fees are payable the early return of the licence is a major incentive and, in any event, a motorist can change his or her mind later without any penalty.

Personal Injury

Introduction

A wealth of law exists to provide compensation to people who have suffered injuries (both physical and psychological) from an accident. Although this body of law stretches back to the beginning of the last century, personal injury law and practice has changed dramatically over the past 10 years or so. This is partly due to changes in court rules that have affected all civil claims but there has also been a refining of the law, both in terms of different types of claim and the level of damages that are awarded. In addition, the funding of personal injury claims has changed with the withdrawal of public funding from the great majority of cases, and the substitution of the 'no win–no fee' agreement.

Where does all this leave the (injured) person in the street?

Overall, most of the changes have been for the better. The new court rules mean that cases proceed faster and should settle earlier and cost less. The use of 'no win–no fee' agreements means that a wider class of people can afford to bring claims. Also, the emphasis is now on individual rights and the level of damages awarded is slowly increasing. Solicitors dealing with personal injury claims tend to be specialists in this area of the law and this is good news for those seeking compensation for their injuries.

Bringing and winning a case

If you or a member of your family has been injured in an accident, how do you choose a solicitor? Can you bring a claim and win compensation? How will you afford your solicitor's fees? In this chapter we will examine first the *theory* and then the *practice* governing compensation claims for personal injury.

75

Liability

The law does not compensate people who are involved in 'pure' accidents, i.e. where in the true meaning of the word no one is to blame. For example, the fact that you were injured at work does not automatically mean that your employer will have to compensate you. How, then, do you 'establish liability' as solicitors put it? As will be explained more fully later, you must be able to show that someone else is at least in part to blame for the injuries you have sustained. In other words, he must have acted negligently.

In legal terms you will need to prove the essential ingredients of 'negligence' namely:

1 identify a defendant;
2 establish that the defendant owed you a 'duty of care';
3 prove that he breached that duty of care;
4 prove that the injuries and loss occurred as a result of the breach of duty of care.

Julie is walking around her local supermarket when she slips in a pool of water that has been left for several hours because the supermarket is short-staffed. She falls and fractures her ankle.

- *Identify a defendant* – the supermarket;
- *establish a duty of care* – it is accepted law that the owners/occupiers of shops owe a duty to shoppers;
- *prove a breach of duty* – this is where evidence will be needed to establish whether or not the supermarket took reasonable care to ensure that spillages were cleared up (on the facts detailed above, Julie would probably succeed in proving breach of duty);
- *prove that the breach of duty of care caused the injury* – a medical report will confirm the fall caused the fractured ankle.

A more detailed explanation of negligence follows.

IDENTIFY A DEFENDANT

The first step is to identify someone who may be to blame for your accident. In most cases this will be straightforward. For example, if you are hit by a car as you walk across the road, the driver of that car is the obvious defendant.

Normally, if the person or organization to blame is unknown this will preclude a claim. The notable exception is 'hit and run cases' (*see* MIB, page 609).

Sometimes, there is more than one person to blame. If proceedings are brought against several defendants, the court may decide that only one is to blame, or all of them or it may apportion blame among them all.

The claimant was injured in an accident involving a school bus whose brakes failed. The claimant brought proceedings against the driver, his employer, the bus company, the mechanics who serviced the bus and the manufacturers of the bus. Held: *Only the manufacturers were liable as it was a faulty brake design that caused the accident.*

McKee *v* Jones (1984)

ESTABLISH THAT THE DEFENDANT OWED A DUTY OF CARE

The extent of the legal duty of care owed by one person to another varies. In most cases the law simply says that we are obliged to act with reasonable care towards each other. The classic test is 'who are my actions (or more often omissions) likely to affect?' Continuing the road traffic example, it is well-established law (and common sense) that a driver of a car owes a duty of care to pedestrians as well as other road users. The list is endless and often obvious:

- teachers owe a duty to pupils;
- doctors to patients;
- employer to employee;
- host to guest;

● plumber to householder.

Some relationships, however, are less obvious; for example, does a policeman owe a duty of care to the victim of a crime? Does the man in the street owe a duty to come to the aid of someone who is injured? In both cases, the answer at present would probably be 'no'.

PROVE THAT THE DUTY OF CARE HAS BEEN BREACHED

The next step is to prove that the duty has been breached: what did the person do wrong? This aspect of negligence is often the most complicated to prove.

The test is whether the person injured was exposed to a foreseeable risk of injury that could reasonably have been avoided.

The court will examine all the circumstances of the accident:

● Did the motorist drive without due regard for other road users?
● Did the local authority have an appropriate system for pavement inspection and repair?
● Should the oil spillage at work have been spotted and cleared up sooner?

BREACH OF STATUTORY DUTY

In addition to the duties owed under the common law system, i.e. those established by judges deciding the issues in a court of law, duties are also imposed by statute law.

Various statutory regulations, for example, have imposed a duty on employers to safeguard the health and safety of their employees:

● the Provision and Use of Work Equipment Regulations 1992 impose a duty on employers to ensure that equipment provided at work is safe, suitable and in a good state of repair;
● the Workplace (Health, Safety and Welfare) Regulations 1992 impose a duty to maintain the workplace in an efficient state and in good repair;
● the Personal Protective Equipment at Work Regulations 1992 impose a duty to provide, where appropriate, suitable personal protective equipment;
● the Manual Handling Operations Regulations 1992 impose a duty on employers to take appropriate steps to reduce the risk of injury arising out of manual handling operations and provide appropriate training and not to require employees to lift weights which are so heavy as to be likely to cause injury.
See further Chapter 40.

Other statutory duty examples:

● the Occupiers' Liability Act 1957 sets out the duties of those who own or manage property to make sure the property is reasonably safe for visitors (*see further* Chapter 26);
● the Consumer Protection Act 1987 sets out manufacturers' liability for defective products (*see further* page 421);
● the Animals Act 1971 imposes liability on those who own dangerous animals (*see further* page 271).

CONTRIBUTORY NEGLIGENCE

A court may find that a defendant was responsible for an accident but that the claimant contributed to it by his own negligence. In that case the defendant will admit liability for the accident but allege contributory negligence and the court will need to determine the extent to which the claimant himself contributed to the accident (*see further* Chapter 69).

In a road accident involving two cars, A comes out from a side junction on to the major road into the path of B. A may accept most of the blame but allege that B contributed to the accident by driving so fast on the major road that he was unable to stop in time when A pulled out from the side road. If the case should come before a court the judge might decide that the principal cause of the accident was A's driving and hold him primarily liable, but that B by his negligence was 25 per cent responsible for his accident. B will therefore receive only 75 per cent of the total value of his claim for damages.

The claimant allowed the defendant to drive his car knowing that the defendant was unfit to drive through drink. The car was in a crash, the claimant suffered injury and sued. Held: the defendant had caused the claimant's injuries due to his negligent driving and was therefore liable. However, the claimant's damages should be reduced by 50 per cent for contributory negligence because he had allowed the defendant to drive knowing that the defendant had been drinking. Hall *v* Herbert (1993)

There are cases where, on the facts, the issue of contributory negligence does not arise; either the claimant will win outright or lose. Typically these are cases where there is no criticism of the claimant's actions; it is a matter of deciding whether or not the defendant was to blame.

VICARIOUS LIABILITY

This is where an individual or organization is held responsible for the actions of another, the most obvious example being where an employer is held responsible for the actions of an employee when the employee is acting in the course of his employment. If, for example, you broke your arm because the works engineer had wrongly installed a piece of machinery, you would look to claim from your employers and not from the works engineer, as your employer would be vicariously responsible for that employee's actions.

One of the main questions that can arise with vicarious liability is whether an employee was acting in the course of his employment when the accident occurred. If he was not acting in the course of his employment, the employer would not be held vicariously liable.

Employee A pushed an unsteady wash basin against employee B to frighten her. This injured employee B. Held: The employers were not vicariously liable. Employee A's act which caused the injury had nothing to do with anything employee A was employed to do and the act was therefore outside the scope of her employment.

Aldred *v* Nacanco (1987)

Is an employee 'acting in the course of employment' if the accident occurs while he is driving to and from work?

A and B were employed as power station laggers. Most of their work was based in the Midlands but, on this occasion, they were asked by their employer to work at a power station in Wales. It was agreed that they would be paid while travelling to and from the job. On the way back from Wales, while travelling in B's car, they had an accident. A (the passenger) was injured due to the negligence of B (the driver). Held: At the time of the accident they were 'on duty'

and therefore the employer was liable for B's negligence.

Smith *v* Stages (1989)

The distinction between being on and off duty is an important one. In most instances the drive to and from work will be outside the course of employment, i.e. off duty (*see further* page 396).

Independent contractors

An 'independent contractor' is someone employed by a person to work for him but without that person having any real direct control over the independent contractor. For example, a factory worker operating machinery will usually be an employee whereas a builder employed by a homeowner to build an extension to his property will usually be an independent contractor. If a person uses an independent contractor, he will not usually be liable for the independent contractor's negligence but there are exceptions to this general rule.

A person may be liable for the negligence of an independent contractor if, for example, that person has negligently selected an incompetent contractor or if he interferes with the work of the independent contractor to such an extent that he, in effect, has taken charge of the work which causes the accident.

76

Common Accident Scenarios

TRIPS AND SLIPS

These are a frequent source of personal injury claims. If you trip on the pavement and the obstruction is sufficiently large, you should succeed in a claim. Generally, the obstruction (e.g. raised paving stone) has to be at least one inch high, although this should not be taken as a definitive criterion, as each case will be decided on its merits. Other factors which may affect the success of a claim include the length of time the defect in the pavement has been present, the lighting in the area and how busy the pavement is. Also, the claimant's actions may be relevant, for example wearing high-heels which may have made the claimant more susceptible to tripping.

If you trip on the pavement and you intend to bring a claim for damages, you ought to photograph the scene as soon as possible. Include a ruler in the pictures positioned so as to clearly indicate the extent of the obstruction and sign and date the photographs on the back. If you slip in a supermarket you should report the accident to the manager and ensure the details are entered into an accident book.

The defect in a pavement was in the form of a triangular hole two inches across at its widest and one-and-a-quarter inches deep. In other respects, the pavement was in good condition. Held: This was not dangerous; to have held otherwise would have imposed an unreasonable burden upon local authorities.

Mills *v* Barnsley Metropolitan Borough Council (1992)

Similarly, if you slip on a grape in a supermarket, you may well have a claim but to succeed you will have to demonstrate that the slip occurred because the supermarket was not operating a suitable clean-up procedure. The mere fact that the grape was there will help in proving this, but will not necessarily be conclusive.

The claimant was injured when she slipped on some yoghurt that had been spilt on the floor. At the trial the defendant (the supermarket) gave evidence that spillages occurred about ten times a week and that staff had been instructed that if they saw any spillage on the floor they were to stay where the spill had taken place and call somebody to clear it up. Apart from general cleaning, the floor was brushed five or six times every day on which the supermarket was open. There was, however, no evidence before the court as to when the floor had last been cleaned before the claimant's accident. The claimant gave evidence that three weeks after the accident, when shopping in the same store, she had noticed that some orange squash had been spilt on the floor. She kept her eye on the spillage for about a quarter of an hour and during that time nobody came to clear it up. Since the claimant's accident was not one which would have happened if the floor had been kept clean and the spillages had been dealt with as soon as they occurred, it was for the defendant to explain that the accident had not arisen from any want of care on its part. Held: The accident had occurred because the defendant had failed to take reasonable care in keeping the floor clean and clear of spillages.

Ward *v* Tesco Stores Ltd (1975)

ROAD ACCIDENTS

Often, common sense will provide a good indication as to who is to blame in a road accident. If you run into the back of another car, you are very likely to blame. If another car comes out from a side road across give-way lines into the side of your car then that driver is very likely to blame.

How does the court decide who is to blame when a car hits a pedestrian? Because a driver is in charge of a vehicle capable of causing serious injury or death, the courts have decided that drivers ought to exercise greater care and control than pedestrians. So, to a certain extent, courts will excuse some lack of care and attention on the part of a pedestrian if he is hit by a car. This, of course, does not mean that a pedestrian can walk blindly out into the road and expect to be held blameless if he is hit by a car; it just means that in the balancing exercise undertaken by the court, lack of care by a motorist will be viewed more seriously than lack of care by the pedestrian. (*See further* Chapter 69.)

The highway

Sometimes, highway authorities can be held to blame for an accident. They are under a duty to maintain the highway under the Highways Act 1980 Section 41. The test is whether or not the local authority has had sufficient time to take whatever remedial measures were appropriate. Failure to do so within a reasonable timescale may amount to negligence.

Does 'maintaining' the road include clearing snow and ice?

The claimant was overtaking a lorry when he skidded on ice, hit a bridge and sustained severe injuries. Held: Under the Highways Act 1980, highway authorities are under a duty to keep the roads in reasonable repair so that they are safe for road-users but this does not include the removal of ice or snow. Goodes *v* East Sussex County Council (2000)

The duty to maintain the highway has been interpreted narrowly by the courts. A failure to erect a warning of a bend in the road is not a breach of the duty. Likewise, a failure to repaint or replace the 'slow' marking sign on the road is also not a breach of section 41.

ACCIDENTS AT WORK

Your employer owes you a duty to provide a safe working environment. If you are injured because machinery is unsafe and your employer knew, or ought to have known about it and could have done something which would have prevented the accident, you should succeed in a claim against your employer. Similarly, if you trip at work because of badly maintained carpeting, for example, your employer may be liable (*see further* Chapter 40).

Often, personal injury claims against employers relate to one-off incidents, for example an employee falling down stairs, catching his hand in machinery, or straining his back while lifting a heavy object. Sometimes a large group of people will all have a claim based on the same act or omission of their employer; cases such as the existence of asbestos in the workplace or repetitive strain injuries suffered by keyboard users.

The claimant was employed by the owner of a mine and worked underground. He was returning to the pit bottom when he was crushed by some haulage machinery. Held: The defendant was liable for breach of its duty to ensure a safe

system of work even though it may not have been responsible for the implementation or performance of that system.
Wilson and Clyde Coal Company Limited *v* English (1937)

A piece of machinery (called a manrider) carried employees from the coal face to the pit bottom. Employees were warned not to jump off while it was still moving. The claimant caught his foot under the moving manrider, was injured and brought a claim against his employer. Held: The employee had deliberately jumped off the manrider contrary to instructions and as it was his own act of disobedience which had caused the accident he was unable to recover damages. McMullen *v* National Coal Board (1982)

OCCUPIERS OF LAND

Those who 'occupy' land, i.e. those who have control over it, owe a duty of care to visitors, both lawful and unlawful. The duty is to take reasonable care for the safety of a visitor. Consequently, an ordinary householder is potentially liable to guests who come to his home.

The claimant fell down a flight of stairs while looking for the ladies' toilet in a public house. Held: The defendant was liable for not providing adequate lighting in the area where the fall took place. Smith *v* Sheppard (1955)

The duty of care imposed on occupiers of land by the law extends even to trespassers – but the standard of care owed to trespassers is lower than that which is owed to lawful visitors.

For example, in one case:

A child went through a hole in a fence and fell onto the conductor rail of a railway line. Held: The claim failed. Albeit that the claimant was a child, the standard of the duty of care owed to trespassers is less than the duty of care owed to lawful visitors.
Davies *v* British Railways Board (1984)

Over the years, however, the duty of care owed to trespassers has become stricter and stricter so that now the duty owed to a trespasser on land is only slightly lower than the duty owed to a lawful visitor.

HOLIDAY ACCIDENTS

This is a growing area of litigation.

Compensation for holiday injuries will be awarded if fault can be established. If the holiday was a package holiday, The Package Travel, Package Holidays and Package Tour Regulations 1992 apply. These regulations provide that package tour operators will be liable for the negligent acts and omissions of those that provide each part of the package holiday; for example, a tour operator would be responsible for the local operators in Spain running a boat trip as part of the holiday. This makes bringing a claim much easier because the claimant will be able to sue the English tour operator company in the English courts rather than a foreign company in a foreign court (*see further* page 427).

The holidaymaker dived into a hotel swimming pool while on a package holiday in Spain and sustained back injuries from hitting the bottom of the pool.

There could be a claim against the organizers of the package holiday. The success of the claim would depend on a number of factors, including the layout and the depth of the swimming pool and whether there were any warning signs.

The holidaymaker fell over the balcony of an Austrian hotel. It was not a package holiday.

There could be a claim against the owners of the hotel if, for example, the height of the balcony rail was dangerously low but the claim would have to be brought in Austria as the 1992 Regulations would not apply.

The holidaymaker was shot and robbed after straying into a dangerous area near to the hotel while on a package holiday in the USA.

There could be a claim against the tour operator if an appropriate warning to avoid this area had not been given. The holidaymaker might consider bringing proceedings in the USA, bearing in mind the much larger amount of damages awarded in that country.

The Package Travel, Package Holidays and Package Tour Regulations only apply to a prearranged combination of at least two of the following components when sold or offered for sale at an inclusive price: (a) transport; (b) accommodation; and (c) other tourist services.

Thus, the independent backpacker is not covered, nor is the person who rents a villa or books a discount flight that is not part of a package. It should also be noted that the Regulations only apply to items booked in advance. So they do not apply to excursions booked once the holiday has started. In one case, for example, the holidaymaker was injured during ski lessons booked through the holiday company, but after the start of the holiday. It was held that the Regulations did not apply.

What is the position if the Regulations do not apply?

The Package Travel, Package Holidays and Package Tour Regulations will often mean that an injured holidaymaker can sue the UK tour operator in the UK. But what of the independent traveller or other holidaymaker who is outside the scope of the Regulations? The answer is that the holidaymaker may be able to sue in the UK if the accident was caused by another UK national. For example, if an English person is injured in France by another English person, the victim can bring proceedings (sue)

in England – although those proceedings will be subject to French law. The law of England and Wales will be applied if it is considered more appropriate in the circumstances. The following case illustrates the point:

A father hired a car in Spain and was involved in an accident in which the mother and daughter were killed. The infant son sued the father. The applicable law was that of Spain, but it was successfully argued that it would be more appropriate for English law to apply.   Hamill (2000)

(*See further* pages 613 and 427.)

SPORTS ACCIDENTS

This is a new and developing area of law. The difficult aspect of claims arising out of contact sports is proving that someone should be held responsible for the injury.

The claimant was a professional footballer who was tackled and injured by an employee of the defendant club. Held: A simple error of judgement or a mistake on the part of the person tackling will not necessarily result in him being held liable. On the facts of this case, the person who had made the tackle had not intended to harm the claimant and the claimant was unsuccessful in his claim.

Elliot v Saunders and Liverpool FC (1994)

In a rugby match, it might be the referee's failure to control the scrums that caused the accident. In the case of a football match it might be one player's dangerous tackle on his opponent.

The claimant was a 17-year-old rugby player. There had been a number of collapsing scrums in the game, culminating in the one which seriously injured the claimant. There were special rules governing the control of scrums for players under the age of 19 years, which the judge decided the referee had failed to follow. Held: The referee was liable as he had allowed collapsing scrums to occur.   Nolan v Smolden (1996)

An amateur footballer's leg was broken as a result of a tackle in a local league match. On the facts it was clear that the defendant had behaved with reckless disregard for the claimant's safety. Held: The defendant was negligent because his tackle was below the reasonable and expected standards of a careful football player.   Condon v Basi (1995)

Spectators at sporting events

Claims can also be made by spectators. What is the legal position if a spectator at a Formula 1 motor racing event is injured following a crash? Much will depend on the facts. Was the cause of the crash bad course design? Were sufficient steps taken to ensure the safety of spectators?

Dangerous sports

Where the claimant has voluntarily participated in a potentially dangerous activity, for example horse riding, skiing, motorbike racing or bungee-jumping, another issue will affect the success of his claim: the extent to which the claimant can be said to have consented to or taken on the risk of injury. This is based on the legal principle that there can be no injury to the willing, i.e. a voluntary participant in an activity runs the risks that are normally associated with that activity.

Horse riding, for example, is an activity that involves a high risk of injury. It is arguable that you accept the possibility of being injured when you decide to participate in a riding activity. If you fall off your horse, you cannot necessarily then claim damages against the organizers of the event.

However, the participant only impliedly consents to the usual risks connected with the dangerous activity. For example, bungee-jumping is also a dangerous sport but if the bungee rope were to snap because the organizers had selected unsuitable rope they would almost certainly be liable. On these facts, the injury would not have been caused by the usual risks associated with bungee-jumping, but by the negligence of the organizers.

ANIMALS

Under the Animals Act 1971 owners of animals are liable to pay damages to those injured by the animal if:

- their animal is of a type commonly expected to be dangerous; or
- it has dangerous characteristics known to the owner.

The claimant employee of the defendant was loading the defendant's horse into a trailer in the course of his employment when the horse became suddenly violent and injured the claimant's arm. **Held:** *The claimant succeeded in his claim because the horse was unreliable and unpredictable, the defendant was aware of those characteristics and the claimant's injury was of a kind which a horse with these characteristics was likely to cause.* Wallace v Newton (1982)

In another case, a frisky horse caused the claimant driver to brake suddenly and collide with another vehicle. The claimant brought a claim for negligence against the rider of the horse. **Held:** *The rider was not negligent. The accident was due solely to the claimant's negligence in failing to slow down as he approached the horse. The horse's behaviour would not have surprised a sensible motorist. The rider was entitled to proper clearance and if the claimant did not have enough room to overtake the horse safely he should have stopped.* Carryfast Ltd v Hack (1981)

In the case of animals commonly domesticated in this country, strict liability is only imposed on an owner

where the animal's behaviour has been abnormal. For instance, during the particular time that a mare is in season, then the owner keeps that horse at his or her peril (because it is well known that, at that time, a horse will show abnormal characteristics). The courts have traditionally taken the approach that, for instance, if a horse causes damage as a result of being maliciously frightened by a third party (a stranger), the owner would not be held strictly liable (i.e. would not be to blame without any fault on the owner's part). This is because all other horses would do the same as that particular horse, if frightened, and so the owner will not be liable. However, the Court of Appeal has recently reinterpreted the Animals Act 1971 in finding that the owner of a horse was strictly liable for damage caused by the escape of the horse from a properly fenced field, when it panicked in fright. It follows from this that the owner of a horse will also be liable if the horse, while under proper control on a highway, is frightened by a group of malicious pedestrians and then causes damage. Even though that would be normal behaviour for a horse, the Court of Appeal has decided the Act imposes liability. (*See also* page 271.)

See further Chapter 25 and page 123.

SELF-HARM AND SUICIDE ATTEMPTS

When a person commits suicide or attempts to commit suicide, there may be liability on the part of those who were responsible for looking after him (e.g. the police or hospital authorities).

A clinically depressed person is owed a duty by those having custody of him to take reasonable steps to prevent him inflicting harm on himself, as the following two cases illustrate.

The police knew that the claimant had suicidal tendencies. They failed to inform the prison authorities of this when he was transferred to prison. He subsequently committed suicide. **Held:** *If the police had informed the prison authorities of the claimant's suicidal tendencies, his suicide could have been prevented. The police were therefore liable.* Kirkham v Chief Constable of Greater Manchester Police (1990)

In another case the claimant was a mental patient who was allowed to go to the toilet unattended. He climbed through a window and was injured. **Held:** *It was the duty of hospital staff to take reasonable care to avoid exposing a patient with mental problems to possible injury that a reasonable person ought to have foreseen might occur.* Kelly v Board of Governors of St Lawrence Hospital (1988)

To what extent may one be held responsible for the harm others inflict on themselves?

The claimant was drinking on a navy base and became so

drunk that he passed out into a coma and became asphyxi-
ated on his own vomit. There was evidence of widespread
laxity with regard to alcohol consumption at the base. **Held:**
The Ministry of Defence was not under a duty to take reason-
able care to prevent a member of its forces from drinking
himself to the point of unconsciousness at one of their duty-
free bars. However, once the deceased had collapsed and was
no longer capable of looking after himself, it was accepted by
the defendant that its supervision of him was inadequate. To
that extent, the defendant was in breach of a duty of care to
the claimant. However, the claimant in drinking himself into
a coma was held to be two-thirds liable for his own actions.
Barrett v Ministry of Defence (1995)

RESCUERS

When an individual negligently creates a dangerous situation, he may be liable to someone who is injured while
rescuing him from that situation.

The defendant attempted to board a moving train. The
guard (who was the claimant in the case) signalled to the
driver for him to stop but he gave an incorrect signal and
instead the train driver increased the speed. The claimant
tried to hold onto the defendant and both fell. **Held: The**
defendant owed a duty of care to the rescuer but in this case,
as the claimant's own action had contributed to his injury by
giving the wrong signal, his damages were reduced by 20 per
cent. Harrison v British Railways Board and others (1981)

A distinction is drawn between professional rescuers
(such as police and paramedics) and non-professional
rescuers (such as bystanders) who come to the rescue on
the spur of the moment. Professional rescuers accept that
they will be involved in dangerous and/or highly stressful
situations from time to time. Therefore, a claim for damages by a professional rescuer can be more difficult to
establish.

But is there any duty to attempt to rescue someone?
The answer is that there is no legal obligation on anyone
to attempt a rescue – but if they do, then a duty of care
will arise.

A climber became stranded 30 feet up the face of a rock-
climbing wall in an indoor centre. The centre staff
attempted a rescue which went wrong and the climber
suffered serious injuries. **Held: The staff had made an error**
of judgement but had not been negligent. On this basis,
they had acted reasonably and were not in breach of their
duty of care. Day v High Performance Sports (2003)

CHILDREN

The courts accept that children are sometimes mischievous and less able to appreciate risk. The consequence of

this is that courts will often require a higher standard of
care when children are involved. For example, school
buildings used by children will need to be of a higher
safety standard than office buildings.

The claimant, aged seven, ran out into the road from behind
a parked car and was hit by the defendant who was driving
his car too fast. **Held: The claimant was not at fault as he**
was behaving as a normal child, 'momentarily forgetful of
the perils of crossing the road'. Jones v Lawrence (1969)

However, this approach should be contrasted with the
decision in the unreported case of *Davies v Knowsley*
Metropolitan Council (1999) in which the judge commented, 'I take the view that children in general are more
competent and knowing than traditionally the law tends
to accept.'

The age of the child will usually be an important factor.
(*See further* Chapter 10.)

Bullying at school

A school can be liable to pupils (and ex-pupils) who have
suffered through bullying. In essence, a school is under a
duty to take reasonable care for the health and safety of
pupils in its charge. In deciding whether a school has
been in breach of its duty of care, the court will consider
what a reasonable body of professional opinion would
have done in the circumstances. If such a body of professional opinion would not have taken the steps alleged
to have been required, then a school will not be liable for
failing to take them either. This is a specialist area of law
and expert advice should be sought. It would seem that
a school that follows the proper guidelines for dealing
with bullying is unlikely to be found liable:

The school had a proper and well-documented bullying
reporting system in place, with a hierarchy in place to deal
with incidents and complaints of bullying. There was a
properly monitored school behaviour policy which had been
disseminated to staff, pupils and parents. On the facts, it
was held that the school was not liable for the bullying that
the claimants had suffered.
Faulkner v London Borough of Enfield (2002)

(*See also* page 122.)

PSYCHIATRIC INJURIES

If you suffer physical and psychiatric injuries arising from
the same accident, you will usually be able to recover
damages for both. What is the position if you suffer only
psychiatric injuries?

The law in this area has changed a great deal in recent
years. Claims for psychiatric injuries arising from stress
in the workplace are now commonplace. Other harmful

events embraced include those circumstances whereby a person suffers illness as a result of the shock of witnessing or being involved in an incident caused by the defendant's negligence. However, the courts have been cautious in extending the law in this area, and they do restrict the circumstances which could give rise to a claim.

Stress at work

Stress is a vague term that does not denote any particular clinical condition. A claimant must show that he is suffering from a clinically recognized prolonged duress stress disorder (PDSD) in order to recover damages; mere anxiety, distress or frustration will not be enough. Once an employer is put on notice that an employee is suffering from stress, then a duty of care arises.

The claimant was employed by the defendant for 17 years as a senior social worker. Pressure increased and requests for more staff were ignored. In 1986 the claimant suffered a nervous breakdown and did not return to work until March 1987. Upon his return an assistant social worker was appointed. The assistant lasted only one month, the heavy workload continued and further requests for help were ignored. The claimant suffered another nervous breakdown and his employment was terminated on grounds of ill-health in February 1988. Held: The defendant was liable on the basis that the first breakdown was not foreseeable but the second breakdown was foreseeable.

Walker *v* Northumberland County Council (1995)

All jobs have some degree of stress in them and an employer will not owe a duty of care unless and until he knows, or ought reasonably to have known, that a particular employee is suffering from stress because of the working environment. Most employees have an obligation to tell their employers if they are suffering from stress – since an employer will not, in most cases, ordinarily be assumed to know this.

The employee was a hard worker and an excellent performer. She left work for a few days after returning from holiday and did not return. She was diagnosed as suffering from depression and sued for stress at work. She claimed that she had complained of overwork and had warned her employer that her health might be adversely affected if nothing was done. However, the court decided that she was doing excessive overtime but had concealed this from her employer. In addition, she had taken two weeks' sick leave specifically asking the GP to state on the sick note that she was suffering from neuralgia. Accordingly, there was nothing to put the employer on notice that issues at work were putting her health at risk. The only time the employer had been warned that she was suffering from stress was shortly before she had left on her holiday. On the facts, the employer was not liable – there was a critical difference between the general knowledge that stress can cause illness,

and the specific knowledge needed that a real risk has arisen in relation to a particular employee.

Pratley *v* Surrey County Council (2002)

Potential claimants must inform their employers that they are suffering from stress and alert them to the problems as soon as possible. What they cannot do is assume that the employer knows that they are under stress.

Witnessing an accident

When dealing with claims resulting from the witnessing of events, the most important restriction is that of 'proximity'. This was demonstrated most graphically in the litigation arising out of the Hillsborough disaster where 95 football spectators were crushed to death at a football match due to the police's admitted negligent crowd control (*Alcock* v *Chief Constable of South Yorkshire* (1991)). The House of Lords established that in order for a claim for purely psychiatric injury to succeed, the person claiming damages must have a close link in both place and time with the event that occurred and have close ties with the 'primary victim' of the event. It was also established that the psychiatric injuries must result from seeing or hearing the event or its immediate aftermath.

The proximity test

In the Hillsborough case, relatives who had not witnessed the event but who had to identify the bodies of their relations in the mortuary nine or more hours later were not within the 'immediate aftermath' of the incident and they were not, therefore, sufficiently 'proximate'.

The case also established that witnessing the event on television was generally not sufficiently proximate. However, it was accepted that in some circumstances witnessing the event on television might give rise to a claim, if the victim could be clearly identified on an individual basis.

As far as determining who has sufficiently close ties with the victim to bring a claim, the House of Lords held that this covers parents and spouses and other relationships where it can be demonstrated that close ties existed which were as strong as those which normally exist between a parent and child or between spouses. This led to claims in respect of a brother and a brother-in-law succeeding as, on the facts, they each had very close relationships with the victim.

CLINICAL NEGLIGENCE

This is really a subject in itself, distinct from personal injury, but it is worth mentioning here. For a clinical negligence claim to succeed it is not sufficient just to prove that another doctor would have done things differently, but that no other reasonable body of medical opinion would agree with what the doctor did. This is known as the *Bolam* test.

Clinical negligence claims are dependent on expert medical opinion. Usually, it is clear that 'something has gone wrong' but it is far from obvious that the cause of the unexpected outcome might have been negligence on the part of a doctor. What is really required is the opinion of an independent expert on why the 'something has gone wrong'.

A goes into hospital for a straightforward back operation on a slipped disc. He is told that he will be in hospital for a few days and then may return home. After the operation, A wakes up and finds that he is paralysed from the waist down. The doctor is unable or unwilling to give him a satisfactory answer as to how or why his physical condition has happened. Does A have a claim?

This will depend, among other things, upon whether:
- the operation was negligently performed by the surgeon; and
- the paralysis was caused by that negligence.

Planned reform of compensation for medical negligence
In April 2000, the government established the NHS Litigation Authority to take over responsibility for all negligence cases. This had previously been done by individual NHS trusts. The chief medical officer for England, Sir Liam Donaldson, published a White Paper, entitled *Making Amends*, in July 2003 following a review of clinical negligence procedures. The proposals outlined in the White Paper include the following key changes:

- parents of babies born with severe neurological impairment, such as cerebral palsy, will be able to claim compensation up to £100,000 a year without having to prove a hospital's negligence;
- for smaller negligence claims, the new scheme would provide a package including an explanation and apology, remedial treatment, rehabilitation and care where needed, and financial compensation up to £30,000;
- the NHS Litigation Authority to be replaced by a new body to authorize pay-outs and administer the new scheme;
- claims to be investigated by experts. Payments will be made where there were serious shortcomings in the standards of care and the harm could have been avoided;
- patients will retain the right to sue in the courts if they prefer – but if they accept a settlement under the scheme they will lose the right to litigate;
- staff who report incidents should be exempt from disciplinary action.

Further information
AVMA (the Association for Victims of Medical Accidents) can offer advice on whether or not you have grounds for investigating a legal claim for negligence. They can also refer you to solicitors who have expertise in this complex field. AVMA's Helpline is 020 8686 8333; website: www.avma.org.uk

Damages

In English law, damages are awarded on the principle of restitution, meaning that, as far as possible, the law aims to put the claimant into the position in which he would have been if the accident had never happened. This is straightforward when you are compensating somebody for actual expenses, for example, loss of earnings. There is a fixed sum, and that sum together with interest will be the amount of the compensation claim. However, how do you compensate a claimant for his injuries under this principle?

In order to compensate claimants on a fair and consistent basis, the courts have developed a system for determining the amount of money to be awarded for each class of injury. This is done mainly by reference to previously decided cases. For example, if a solicitor wants to know what is the appropriate award for a broken leg he can look up previously decided cases concerning similar injuries to find out what the judges awarded in those cases. Also, reference may be made to the Judicial Studies Board Guidelines, which are referred to below.

WHAT CAN BE CLAIMED?

Damages fall into three main classifications:
- 'general' damages;
- 'special' damages;
- 'future' damages.

'General' damages are damages awarded for losses that cannot be quantified, namely damages for pain and suffering and loss of amenity.

'Special' damages are for actual losses up to the date of the trial, for example damages for loss of earnings.

'Future' damages reflect the losses that will arise in the future. They are usually the most complex to establish and often the largest element of a damages award.

GENERAL DAMAGES FOR PAIN, SUFFERING AND LOSS OF AMENITY

General damages for pain, suffering and loss of amenity (PSLA) are damages that are awarded for the injury itself.

Pain and suffering is self-explanatory. Loss of amenity encompasses all the activities of life which a claimant is prevented from doing or which he finds more difficult to do owing to the injury. For example, a keen gardener may have to give up gardening because of a back injury.

For assistance as to the types of awards for PSLA, the courts are likely to refer to guidelines produced by the Judicial Studies Board, which provides indicative awards for different types of injury (*see* below).

It is probably true to say that damages for PSLA in this country are regarded as low bearing in mind the awards that are routinely made in the USA for personal injury claims.

The difficulty is the value to be put on an injury. How much is a broken finger really 'worth'?

The Judicial Studies Board guidelines

These guidelines were prepared in an attempt to develop greater uniformity in the courts' approach to awards for pain, suffering and loss of amenity. They are not rigidly adhered to; they are intended to provide broad guidance as to the appropriate levels of compensation to be awarded for particular injuries and each type of injury is then graded according to its severity.

The following table lists a range of injuries, and the general damages that are likely to be awarded for each type, drawn from the Judicial Studies Board guidelines.

Injury	Lower end of scale £	Higher end of scale £
Quadriplegia (paralysis of all four limbs)	160,000	200,000
Severe brain damage	140,000	200,000
Paraplegia (paralysis of lower limbs)	110,000	140,000
Moderate brain damage	75,000	110,000
Total deafness	45,000	55,000
Severe post-traumatic stress	30,000	50,000
Severe facial scarring – female	24,000	48,000
Severe loss of function in wrist	24,000	30,000
Moderate whiplash to neck	7,000	12,500
Simple fracture of the forearm	3,250	9,500

How damages are assessed

Sometimes, because the claim has complicating features, the assessment of general damages for PSLA is not straightforward. For example, what happens if the claimant already has a medical history which 'overlaps' with the injury?

A diabetic suffered an injury to his leg that caused him pain when he walked faster than normal pace. Held: Previous ill health does not justify a reduction in the award. The damages would have been increased if the accident had adversely affected his ability to cope with the ill-health he suffered from prior to the accident. Mustard v Morris (1992)

What happens if there is a serious head injury with unusual behavioural consequences?

The claimant was a passenger who suffered brain damage in a car accident. Subsequently, he committed violent attacks on women. Held: He could recover damages for subsequent imprisonment even though he had underlying aggression. If it had not been for the accident the claimant would probably have been able to resist the inclination to carry out violent attacks. Meah v McCreamer (1985)

SPECIAL DAMAGES

These include:

- expenses incurred which would not have been incurred but for the accident;
- the cost of items damaged in an accident;
- loss of earnings (calculated net of tax and NI). This may also include loss of overtime and bonuses and loss of promotion prospects (*see* below);
- cost of care, i.e. caring services provided by paid carers or care provided free of charge by a friend or relative. In the latter case the value of the time spent by the

'carer' is based upon the charges that would have been payable to a professional carer, discounted by maybe one-quarter or one-third to take into account the fact that the services were provided out of 'mutual love and affection'. In practice, the assessment of the value of care provided by a family member or friend appears to have a ceiling of about £35,000 per year, with most awards being well below that amount. This contrasts with open-market commercial rates of £80,000 to £100,000 per year;

- cost of accommodation (e.g. the cost of adaptations to make a property wheelchair-friendly);
- cost of special aids and equipment (e.g. the cost of a wheelchair, or special orthopaedic mattress);
- travel costs (e.g. the travel expenses of relatives coming to visit the claimant in hospital);
- household costs (e.g. increased heating needed due to the effects of the injury, increased wear and tear on carpets due to wheelchair use);
- holidays (e.g. having to spend more on a hotel to ensure that it is wheelchair-friendly or, the cost of a holiday to get over the effects of an accident);
- medical costs (e.g. prescription fees, physiotherapy, acupuncture).

Damages for lost chance

The claim could include damages for 'lost opportunities' or 'lost chance', if the injury has an effect on the claimant's future job prospects, such as his ability to gain a promotion.

A bricklayer worked as a part-time professional kick-boxer. He was negligently injured and his claim included a lost-chance element, based on the chances of him doing well as a kick-boxer. His potential earnings were assessed on an 80 per cent chance of winning the British/European title; 66 per cent chance of moving to the USA; 40 per cent chance of winning the world championship; and 20 per cent chance of then retaining the world championship – with an overall discount of 20 per cent being applied to these chances. Langford (2001)

This case illustrates how the courts can consider a number of lost chances to the claimant. Thus, there is the opportunity to recover damages in a number of situations where one cannot prove the claim on a balance of probabilities, but can prove a 'significant chance' of a range of possibilities. A 20 per cent chance counts as a 'significant' chance.

What if the claimant has earnings that he has not previously declared?

The deceased had received monies from 'moonlighting' which he did not disclose to the DSS when claiming housing benefit and supplementary benefit. **Held:** *To allow the claim would be to countenance ongoing fraud and would be to treat the proceeds of illegally concealed earnings as providing a valid head of recovery by way of damages for loss or injury. The claim was dismissed.*   Hunter *v* Butler (1995)

Similarly, in another case the claimant was severely injured and claimed loss of full-time and part-time employment. Were the part-time earnings recoverable given that he had not disclosed these to the Inland Revenue? **Held:** *claimant could recover only the earnings not tainted by illegality, i.e. the full-time earnings.*

Duller *v* South East Lincs Engineers (1981)

FUTURE DAMAGES

These will often include the same elements of loss that are included in the category of special damages, the distinction being that they have yet to be incurred. Other elements of loss might include the loss of pension and cost of professional advice for the investment and management of the damages.

Calculation of future damages

If the court accepts that a claimant is going to incur losses or expenses in the future, an award will normally be made to compensate for those losses. Such an award is commonly made in those cases where the injuries are more severe and where, as a consequence, there are going to be continuing symptoms.

If the court accepts that a claimant will, as a result of his injuries, incur expenses of, say, £1,000 a year for medical costs owing to the injuries he received, and those expenses will continue for life, how is the award to be calculated?

First, the claimant's life expectancy has to be determined. If the injuries have not affected this, the calculation can be made quite simply by reference to the published government life-expectancy statistics. If the injuries have shortened the claimant's life expectancy, the opinion of a suitable medical expert will have to be produced on the claimant's actual life expectancy as a consequence of his injuries.

Second, how the lump-sum award for future loss should be calculated has to be decided. If the claimant has a life expectancy of a further 30 years, it would not be appropriate to award him 30 x £1,000 (i.e. £30,000) as this would ignore the benefit to the claimant of the return derived from the investment of his award. An appropriate lump sum must be calculated which, together with the return earned on the diminishing lump sum, would cover the yearly expense. Tables have been produced which are regularly referred to by the courts to help determine the appropriate figure to multiply by (called the multiplier) where there are future losses to be assessed. An appropriate multiplier for 30 years' worth of future losses might actually be 19, 20 or 21 (there are arguments for both sides as to exactly which tables are appropriate and how the calculations should be made). Therefore, still taking the example above, the actual award might be 20 x £1,000 = £20,000. The theory then is that the claimant can sensibly and cautiously invest that amount to cover the yearly expense.

There has been debate as to what represents 'sensible and cautious' investment. The defendant's representatives have argued that a little speculation to ensure higher returns is appropriate; the claimant's representatives have argued that only the very safest of investment strategies is appropriate when dealing with the investment of damages awarded for future losses in personal injury claims. The difference between those two views may amount to only one or two percentage points in terms of return, but it can have quite a dramatic effect when determining what lump sum is appropriate in the first place to cover future losses, especially if one is dealing with a young claimant.

EXEMPLARY AND AGGRAVATED DAMAGES

Exemplary and aggravated damages are rarely claimed or awarded. Exemplary damages are intended to punish a defendant whose conduct has been wholly inappropriate (by abusing or breaching their public responsibility) and aggravated damages are to compensate a claimant for aggravated harm not amounting to physical or mental injury such as injury to feelings.

INTEREST ON DAMAGES

Interest will normally be awarded on general damages for pain, suffering and loss of amenity at the rate of 2 per cent per year from the date proceedings were served. Interest on other items of past loss and expense will normally be allowed at the rate specified by the court from time to time from the date those expenses or losses were incurred.

Recoupment of benefits

Every claim for damages for personal injury has to be notified to the Compensation Recovery Unit (CRU). The CRU will then ensure that if the defendant pays an amount in respect of damages for the injury sustained, an amount equivalent to certain state benefits which the claimant has received is paid by the defendant's insurers to the CRU either out of the damages or separately.

It is also possible for other payments to be clawed back

from the damages, for example private medical costs, local authority care costs and certain hospital expenses.

PROVISIONAL DAMAGES

The court may award 'provisional damages' where there is a chance that the claimant will suffer some disease or deterioration at some time in the future linked to the injuries he has received, such as epilepsy following a head injury or lung cancer following exposure to asbestos.

In these cases, damages are awarded to the claimant on the assumption that he has not, and will not in the future, develop the disease or that his then condition will deteriorate, but this is subject to the proviso that he can apply to the court for further damages if this were to happen.

Usually, when the original judgment is given the judge will specify the disease or deterioration involved and period of time within which a further application can be made if the claimant's condition changes.

FATAL ACCIDENTS

If the negligence causes the claimant's death, it is possible for a claim to be brought for funeral and associated expenses and other heads of loss.

Dependency damages

This is the loss suffered by the dependants of the deceased. To be a 'dependant' you have to be within the prescribed categories and show that the loss has resulted from the termination of a relationship of financial dependency. A 'dependant' can include a spouse, former spouse, parents, grandparents, children, grandchildren, brothers, sisters, uncles, aunts and cohabitants.

Damages for bereavement

A fixed sum, currently £10,000, is payable to a surviving spouse or parent (if the deceased was a minor and the parents were married) or mother (if the deceased was a minor and the parents were unmarried).

Damages for pain and suffering

If the medical evidence shows that the deceased suffered pain for a period of time leading up to his death, damages may be awarded. However, the amount of such damages is likely to be small.

WHO WILL PAY?

Usually, when you are successful in your personal injury claim, there is no problem recovering the money that you have been awarded because the defendant will be insured against your claim.

For example, in:

● a road traffic accident – the defendant should be covered by car insurance;
● an accident at work – the defendant should be covered by employer's liability insurance;
● an accident at school – the defendant should be covered by the school's liability insurance;
● an accident at a supermarket – the defendant should be covered by the supermarket's public liability insurance.

However, not all defendants have insurance, and if insurance exists the sum covered may be insufficient – and not all types of claims may be covered.

A householder, for example, may not have insurance that covers your claim if you were to trip on a badly maintained carpet in his house. Similarly, if you were severely injured at a travelling funfair and have a claim against the organizers worth £2 million, it might be that the organizers only have public liability insurance for say the first £1 million. The insurers will cover the first £1 million, but if you get a judgment in excess of that amount, the excess would have to be paid personally by the organizers provided they had the means.

One of the first things a solicitor will check when dealing with a claim is the existence and adequacy of the insurance cover available to meet any judgment.

CRIMINAL INJURIES

The Criminal Injuries Compensation Authority (CICA) exists to compensate those who suffer injury as a result of being a victim of a crime of violence. It is a statutory authority based at Morley House, 26–30 Holborn Viaduct, London EC1A 2JQ. Tel: 020 7842 6800.

It is not necessary to have legal representation to bring a claim under the CICA scheme, but if the injuries are at all severe, it is sensible to consult a solicitor.

The following conditions must be satisfied in order to be eligible to bring a claim under the CICA scheme:

1 the applicant must have sustained physical or mental injury as a result of a crime of violence;
2 the crime must have been committed in England, Scotland or Wales;
3 the injury must be serious enough for the minimum award of £1,000 to apply;
4 the incident must have been reported to the police personally by the applicant (unless there are good reasons for failing to do so). The offender does not have to have been apprehended or prosecuted;

5 the application must be received by the CICA within two years of the incident. This time limit may be waived but only in special circumstances.

The application will be assessed by the CICA and, if accepted, an award will be made. The award will not be based upon what a court would award for personal injury claims; it is based upon a tariff published by the CICA. The maximum award which may be made under the scheme is £500,000. In practice, large awards are rare. The last annual report showed only 57 awards of over £25,000 and only five over £50,000 (out of a total of 76,000 applications that year). (*See* further on this topic in 'Civil liberties and human rights', Chapter 89.)

It should be noted that it may be possible to sue the assailant personally for damages but his means and lack of insurance will often make this inadvisable.

THE MOTOR INSURERS' BUREAU

If you are involved in an accident with a motorist, he will normally be insured for any claim for damages arising from the accident.

If the driver is uninsured, however, and you sue him, he may not have the money to pay any award for damages, or at least make it very difficult for you to recover the damages. If the driver's identity is unknown you will have nobody to sue. This is where a body known as the Motor Insurers' Bureau (MIB) will step in. The MIB will satisfy judgments against uninsured motorists – if the judgment remains unpaid after seven days – and will also deal with claims involving untraced motorists.

Uninsured motorists

Your solicitor will notify the claim to the motorist, and at the same time (or at a later stage when it becomes evident that the motorist has no insurance) notify the MIB of the claim. There are strict time limits within which the MIB has to be notified of stages in the legal proceedings, for example when proceedings are issued and when judgment is obtained. If the judgment is not paid within seven days, the MIB (or the insurers appointed to act as their agent) should pay the judgment and also deal with your solicitor's fees.

Untraced motorists

If the motorist is 'untraced', then it is not possible to issue proceedings, as a defendant has to be identified in court documents. The application will have to be made to the MIB under their 'untraced drivers agreement'. The MIB will, if it accepts the application, make an award in terms similar to those which would be made by a court. However, the MIB will make only a small payment towards solicitors' costs.

An applicant has to show that:

- the person who was responsible for the injury cannot be traced; and
- the injury must, on the balance of probability, have been caused by the untraced driver.

New rules came into force on 14 February 2003 covering all claims arising out of road traffic accidents caused by untraced drivers from that date onwards. The key changes are:

- it is now possible to recover compensation for property damage (subject to an excess of £300). But, if there is no associated personal injury then the MIB will not compensate for property damage if the vehicle is unidentified;
- the application form must be lodged with the MIB within nine months of the date of the accident if the claim is for property damage;
- no claim for property damage can be made if the applicant knew, or ought to have known, that the vehicle was uninsured;
- most claims for personal injury must be submitted within three years of the date of the accident;
- for personal injury claims, the claimant must report the accident to the police within 14 days (or as soon as reasonably possible);
- for property claims, the report to the police must be within five days (or as soon as reasonably possible), regardless of whether there is also an associated personal injury claim.

Time Limits

The law relating to time limits in personal injury cases would appear to be very simple but it is, in fact, a complex area of law. Basically, a claim for damages for personal injuries has to be commenced within three years from the date of the accident. 'Commenced' means that a claim form has to be lodged with the court within that period.

The law is different for persons under 18 years of age. They have until their twenty-first birthday (i.e. three years from becoming 18 years of age) to bring a claim. Persons classed as 'patients', i.e. those not capable of managing their own affairs, are not subject to the time limits.

Occasionally, time limits may be extended using the 'date of knowledge provisions'. These provisions are often relevant to clinical negligence cases where the claimant may not know that he has received negligent medical treatment until some time after that treatment.

Accidents on boats or aeroplanes may be subject to different time limits. Also, if your accident occurred abroad then the foreign country's time limits may be applicable. In a fatal accident the time limit is three years from the date of death. In a criminal injury claim directed to the Criminal Injuries Compensation Authority the time limit is two years from the date of the incident.

Ultimately, it is best to see a solicitor as soon as possible after an accident. It will be his responsibility to ensure that the time limits are not missed.

Practice

Theory is all well and good but what are the practical steps involved? What should you be doing? How much will it cost? How long will it take?

After an Accident – Important First Steps and Choosing a Personal Injury Solicitor

The action you should take will depend upon the type of accident and severity of the injuries you have sustained, but as a general rule you should:

- get witnesses' names and addresses;
- make notes;
- take photographs, if relevant, of any important details (scene of the accident, size of protruding paving stone, etc). If you are unable to do this yourself, you should get a friend or family member to do it for you as soon as possible;
- report the incident to someone in authority, for example foreman, policeman, shop manager;
- see a solicitor sooner rather than later while the evidence is still fresh in your mind if you are considering the possibility of making a claim.

Take care in choosing the solicitor. Do not just pick someone out of the *Yellow Pages* or go back to a firm you have used before simply because they had previously handled your house conveyance. Ideally, you should instruct a solicitor who is a member of the Law Society's Personal Injury Panel, as he or she will have experience in dealing with personal injury claims. Obtain recommendations from people who have used personal injury solicitors or contact support groups and other relevant organizations for their recommendations. For example:

The Law Society
113 Chancery Lane
London WC2A 1PL
Tel: 020 7242 1222
www.lawsociety.org.uk

Association of Personal Injury Lawyers
33 Pilcher Gate
Nottingham NG1 1QE
Tel: 0115 958 0585
www.apil.com

Spinal Injuries Association
76 St James's Lane
London N10 3DF
Tel: 0800 980 0501
www.spinal.co.uk

Headway
4 King Edward Court
King Edward Street
Nottingham NG1 1EW
Tel: 0115 947 1900
www.headway.org.uk

Richard Grand Society – the personal injury lawyers' alliance
63 Lincoln's Inn Fields
London WC2A 3LW
Tel: 020 7242 6462
www.richardgrandsociety.com

You should instruct someone with whom you feel comfortable. If you have a long and complex case which continues for a number of years you will need to build up a good relationship with your solicitor based upon trust and confidence. Having the right solicitor can make an enormous difference to how quickly and smoothly a claim proceeds, how confident you feel about the process and even what size award you eventually receive.

Do be honest and straightforward with your solicitor. Do co-operate with all requests for information. Your solicitor is there to help you and can only do his job properly if you give him the complete picture. For example, if you are claiming loss of earnings and your tax affairs are not in order, tell him. He will (or should) take full details and explain how this will affect the claim, and then advise accordingly (*see further* page 758).

Funding

PUBLIC FUNDING/THE LEGAL SERVICES COMMISSION

Since the end of April 2000, public funding (i.e. legal aid) has not been available for most personal injury claims. This has not affected existing claims which are legally aided but only a limited number of public funding certificates have since been granted for new personal injury claims.

However, it is still possible to get funding assistance from the Legal Services Commission for a personal injury claim in certain exceptional circumstances where, for example, the investigative costs may be very substantial or where the claim has some element of public interest. However, public funding is now very much a thing of the past for run-of-the-mill personal injury claims. (For further information on public funding *see* Chapter 100.)

CONDITIONAL FEE AGREEMENTS

The Conditional Fee Agreements (CFA) is the funding scheme which is commonly referred to as 'no win – no fee', a description which fails to convey the complicated nature of these agreements.

If you choose a CFA the money you will have to pay your solicitor depends upon whether you win or lose your case.

If you win you can receive from your opponent:

* damages;
* money to pay your solicitor's basic costs, VAT and disbursements;
* money to pay any success fee (excluding the finance element) you have agreed to pay your solicitor;
* the cost of litigation insurance taken out.

You will pay your solicitor's basic costs and expenses plus any success fee you have agreed to pay.

If you lose and you have taken out an appropriate policy of insurance, this will cover your liability for your opponent's legal costs and your own disbursements.

Insurance cover

At the outset of your case you will be advised to take out a policy of insurance to cover the risk of having to pay your opponent's costs and to pay the cost of your own disbursements. Solicitors are not insurance brokers and cannot give advice on all products which may be available. They are required, however, to recommend a suitable policy of insurance.

Payment of disbursements

As your claim proceeds your solicitor may ask you to pay for disbursements as they arise. These disbursements can amount to several hundreds of pounds in a simple claim and to several thousands of pounds in a more complicated claim. As many people cannot afford to pay such amounts loan schemes have been set up for the benefit of claimants. If you win your litigation the defendant will pay most if not all of the disbursements. If you lose, the insurance you have taken out will pay the disbursements.

Assume that the claim was successful, with damages awarded of £10,000. The basic cost of the claimant's solicitor was £3,000 and the agreed success fee was 50 per cent.

The defendant will pay:

damages	£10,000
basic costs	£ 3,000
success fee	£ 1,500
	£14,500

This example assumes that all your costs are recoverable from the defendant. In practice a small proportion of these costs will not be recoverable and will be paid out of damages.

On the other hand, if the claim is unsuccessful, no damages will be awarded and your solicitor will receive no costs. You will be ordered to pay the costs incurred by the defendants. The insurance policy you took out will pay your opponent's costs and your own disbursements.

LEGAL EXPENSES INSURANCE

Many everyday insurance policies have legal expenses cover. Common examples of policies which often have legal expenses cover include motor insurance, home contents insurance and holiday insurance. Such cover enables you to instruct a solicitor should you wish to pursue a personal injury claim (or other types of claims) and the solicitor's fees will be covered by the insurance. Often, the insurance policy will also cover you against having to pay the defendant's costs.

This type of insurance is potentially very worthwhile, but there are restrictions which should be noted.

1 you will have to demonstrate you have a claim which is worth pursuing;
2 the insurance cover may be limited to certain types of claims;
3 the amount of the legal costs covered may be insufficient;
4 you may not be able to choose your preferred solicitor

as insurers often insist that your claim is handled by solicitors appointed by them.

TRADE UNIONS

Trade unions normally operate schemes for assisting their members to bring a claim usually for accidents which occur in the workplace. The claims may be handled by the trade union's 'in-house' claims department or by their appointed solicitors. Most trade unions maintain 'panels' of personal injury firms to which their members will be referred.

EXPLANATION OF TERMS

Basic costs – refer to the normal charges of solicitors worked out on an hourly rate basis.

Success fee – is a percentage (up to a maximum of 100 per cent) of your solicitor's basic costs. A success fee is added to reflect the risk of the solicitor not being paid.

Disbursements – are expenses incurred on your case which may include court fees, experts' fees, inquiry agents' fees, etc.

81

Evidence and Experts

Evidence must be produced to prove a claim. For example, in a personal injury case where the claimant has lost earnings as a result of his injury he will have to prove that he has lost those earnings. It will not be sufficient for him to simply state to the court that he has lost a certain amount of wages. He will have to produce evidence of the loss. Payslips will have to be disclosed to prove the amount of the loss and a doctor's report must be produced to confirm that he was unfit for work for the relevant period.

Evidence takes many forms but the most common types include documents, written reports from experts, witness statements and photographs. Also, when a claim is being heard before a court, witnesses will be called to give oral evidence.

THE BURDEN AND STANDARD OF PROOF

When a claim for personal injury is brought, the claimant will be seeking to prove that the other party (the defendant) has committed a negligent act. Usually, the onus will be on the claimant to prove that the defendant did act negligently; in other words, the burden of proof will lie with the claimant.

In civil claims, including personal injury claims, the standard of proof is usually 'on the balance of probabilities'. So the claimant is required to prove that it was more likely than not that the defendant's negligence caused his injury. This contrasts with criminal cases, where the standard of proof necessary to secure a conviction is 'beyond reasonable doubt'.

TYPES OF EVIDENCE

The table below sets out examples of allegations that may have to be proved and the evidence that may be presented to court to prove them:

Allegation	Proof required
That injuries have been suffered	<ul><li>Photographs;</li><li>medical reports from doctors;</li><li>medical records</li></ul>
That expenses have been incurred	<ul><li>Receipts;</li><li>accounts</li></ul>
That there has been negligence on the part of the defendant	<ul><li>Witness statements;</li><li>expert evidence (e.g. accident reconstruction experts)</li></ul>
That the claimant will never be able to go back to work	<ul><li>Doctor's expert evidence;</li><li>the claimant's statement;</li><li>employment expert's evidence</li></ul>

EXPERTS

An 'expert' witness is an independent witness who can give evidence based upon his opinion in his area of expertise, for example a medical expert in orthopaedics. To be a valid expert witness, the person giving the evidence has to be able to demonstrate that they are an 'expert', e.g. by their qualifications and/or experience. They are then called by a party (or by both jointly) to give an opinion as to particular aspects of the claim.

There are strict rules restricting the number and type of experts who may be called upon to give evidence in court proceedings. The aim of the rules is to encourage the parties to appoint a 'joint expert'.

Experts commonly used in personal injury claims:

Type of expert	Details
Orthopaedic	In connection with injuries to the skeletal system
Neurologist	For head injuries
Psychiatrist	For stress, depression and other 'mental injuries'
Nurse	Where there are serious injuries resulting in a need for care
Architect	Where a house needs to be adapted to accommodate the claimant's physical injuries

Video evidence

It is very rare for video evidence (typically, showing a claimant seemingly in better physical condition than is pleaded) to be ruled inadmissible. Generally, the courts tend to allow this evidence to be shown at the trial. But what happens if the video evidence has been obtained by deception and also by trespass?

The claimant had a hand injury which she said left her significantly disabled. An investigator, posing as a market researcher, got access to the claimant's home and used a hidden camera to make video recordings. The question then arose as to whether those recordings could be used in evidence – with the defendants arguing that they showed that there was no disability. All parties agreed that the inquiry agent was guilty of trespass and would not have been admitted to the claimant's house if she had not misled the claimant as to her identity. **Held: *The video tape was admissible.*** Jones *v* University of Warwick (2003)

82

The Court System

The court system, under the new Civil Procedure Rules, is dealt with in more detail in Chapter 97. This chapter discusses aspects of the system which are particularly relevant to personal injury claims.

CLAIMS PROTOCOL

Prior to the commencement of proceedings solicitors must now follow a pre-action protocol in personal injury cases. The protocol requires the claimant to send the proposed defendant a letter of claim containing the following details:
- a clear summary of the facts;
- the nature of any injuries;
- any financial loss incurred;
- the name and address of the treating hospital and the hospital reference number (in road traffic accident cases).

The letter should also ask for details of the defendant's insurer and request that a copy of the letter is sent to the insurer. If the insurer is already known the letter can be sent directly to the insurer.

The defendant should reply within 21 days identifying the insurer (if any). If there has been no reply by the defendant within 21 days, the claimant is entitled to start court proceedings.

Where a response is received from insurers they are permitted three months to investigate the claim. At the end of the three-month period they are required to state whether liability is denied. If it is they must give reasons.

OFFERS TO SETTLE

The new rules actively encourage the parties to attempt to settle the case before they get to trial. The most important provision (contained in Part 36 of the Civil Procedure Rules) allows either side to make offers to settle which, if turned down by the other side and subsequently not 'beaten', will often carry costs and interests consequences.

C sues D for injuries suffered in a road accident. C makes a claim for damages for a whiplash injury. D admits liability. A medical report is produced showing that the injury was very minor.

During the proceedings, C makes a formal offer to settle his claim at £2,500 (Part 36 offer). D refuses the offer and fights on to trial. At trial C is awarded £3,000 damages. The judge is told about the previous offer to settle and consequently orders that D should pay extra interest and costs as he failed to 'beat' (i.e. get an award lower than) the offer to settle.

This can work the other way around, with payments into court (Part 36 payments). Continuing the above example, say D paid £3,250 into court, which C had turned down. C is subsequently awarded £3,000 at trial. The judge would most likely order C to pay D's costs from the time acceptance of the payment into court expired (21 days).

The whole point of these provisions is to encourage the parties to make sensible offers to get cases settled without incurring the expense and delay of a full trial.

INTERIM PAYMENTS

If you have a reasonably substantial claim for damages and the final assessment will take some time, it is possible to apply for an interim payment. This can be done either by agreement with the insurers or their solicitors, or by order of the court.

To succeed you will have to demonstrate that you have a substantial claim for damages which is very likely to succeed, and that it will be some time before the final assessment can take place. As a rule of thumb, you can generally expect to recover up to about one-third or one-half of the 'provable' value of your claim at the time of making the application. Of course, you will have to give credit for the interim payment when the final assessment takes place.

TRIAL

At the trial, the case will be heard by a judge, who will then decide the merits of the claim.

Trials can deal with liability (whether the defendant has been negligent) or quantum (how much compensation the claimant should be awarded), or both.

At the trial the claimant's solicitor will normally give an opening speech outlining the claim and the evidence that will be called. Evidence is then called by each side. Next, the defendant's solicitor will sum up and, lastly, the claimant's solicitor will do the same. The judge then makes his decision (called the 'judgment'), either there and then or after retiring to consider matters.

As soon as a judgment is available it should be scrutinized to consider the prospects of an appeal by either the claimant or the defendant. An appeal may be considered on the basis that the judge's findings of fact or law may have been incorrect. The appeal court will not, however, disturb the judge's findings of fact unless they are very obviously wrong (*see further* page 751).

MEDIATION/ALTERNATIVE DISPUTE RESOLUTION

Increasingly (and with the encouragement of the court rules), cases are decided by methods other than a conventional trial before a judge. Mediation usually takes the form of a meeting between the parties with an independent mediator who will try to facilitate a settlement agreeable to both parties. There are numerous organizations willing to undertake mediations but only a few provide a specialist service for personal injury and clinical negligence cases. Examples of those which have access to specialist mediators include:

WORKITOUT
63 Lincoln's Inn Fields
London WC2A 3LW
Tel: 020 7692 5502
www.workitout.co.uk

Centre for Dispute Resolution
Princes House
95 Gresham Street
London EC2V 7NA
Tel: 020 7600 0500
www.cedr.co.uk

83

Frequently Asked Questions

Q. *If I want to claim damages for my injuries, will I have to see a doctor?*

A. Yes. Usually, you will have to see a medical expert so that a report can be prepared verifying your injuries and providing a prognosis for the future if you have continuing symptoms.

Q. *Can the other side ask for copies of all my medical records?*

A. Very often, yes. They will argue that your medical records are necessary to help establish the injury you suffered, and determine what, if any, relevant past medical history you might have.

Q. *Will I pay tax on my damages?*

A. No, you will not be taxed when you receive the damages. You will be taxed in the usual way on interest the damages might earn, for example, in the building society.

Q. *Will I get an apology if I am proved right in my claim?*

A. Usually, no. A personal injury claim has one aim: to recover damages. However, an apology may be obtained if alternative dispute resolution procedures are used.

Q. *Are defendants allowed to undertake surveillance?*

A. This is sometimes used for the larger claims. Defendants may employ agents to undertake surveillance upon claimants, for example to prove that they are exaggerating their injuries. There is, however, likely to be some restriction placed upon surveillance as a result of the Human Rights Act 1998 especially in the home or on private property.

Q. *Why do personal injury claims take so long?*

A. In the past claims often took longer than necessary. Now, the situation is improving. The new Civil Procedure Rules have speeded up litigation, and many specialist solicitors are making genuine efforts to ensure that litigation progresses as quickly as is reasonably possible. However, cases can still take years to settle. This can be because of the severity of the injuries (e.g. a head injury followed by a slow recovery over many years, where the damages cannot properly be assessed until the recovery is complete). It is true to say that some cases still take longer than necessary, and if you are in doubt you should ask your solicitor for a full report as to progress to date.

Q. *Why do so many claims settle just before they are due to go to court for trial?*

A. This is still a common occurrence. The problem often is that the defendant's solicitors understandably want to settle at the lower end of the spectrum, and the claimant's solicitors will hold out for a higher figure. Against this background, the defendant's solicitors often want to avoid actually going to trial and will therefore increase their offer bit by bit until the case settles. This process tends to intensify in the run-up to a trial, sometimes resulting in the infamous 'steps of the court' settlement.

Civil Liberties and Human Rights

84

Introduction to the Human Rights Act 1998

The Human Rights Act 1998 came into force on 2 October 2000. This Act incorporates the European Convention on Human Rights into domestic law and is the most significant human rights reform for many years. For the first time positive rights, such as privacy and family life, freedom of expression and assembly, the right to a fair trial, freedom from arbitrary arrest, and freedom from discrimination, have been enshrined in domestic law. Those who claim that their fundamental human rights have been breached no longer necessarily have to endure the lengthy process of taking a case to the European Court of Human Rights in Strasbourg (though the right to take your case to Strasbourg remains an option for those who have been through the courts in this country).

However, the Convention is not a panacea for all human rights abuses. It is now over 50 years old and this is clearly discernible from the weakness of its equality provisions and its silence on increasingly important issues, such as the rights of children and standards in prisons. Also, the limitations it places on rights are very broad, and the anti-discrimination provisions are narrow. Nevertheless, the Human Rights Act will make a special difference to rights in this country, particularly in criminal proceedings.

WHO IS COVERED BY THE HUMAN RIGHTS ACT?

The Convention applies to all public authorities. It is unlawful for bodies like the police, government departments and local councils to violate the rights contained in the Convention. The Act does not impose duties directly on private individuals or companies unless they are performing public functions. A private security company, for instance, will be performing a public function when looking after prisoners for the police or the courts, but not when employed to guard private premises. Therefore, the Act (and the Convention) will bind them in respect of the former tasks but not the latter.

All courts and tribunals are public authorities for the purposes of the Act and are under a duty to respect Convention rights (particularly the right to a fair trial).

Any person who is a victim of a violation can use the Convention. A victim includes anyone directly affected by the actions (or inactions) of any public body. A victim might also include a person not necessarily directly affected by the action of a public body but could include someone indirectly affected. For example, a person who is likely to be subjected to surveillance by the police will be able to use the Act even though they have not (yet) had their privacy interfered with. However, a person who is no more affected than any other member of the public is unlikely to be able to use the Human Rights Act.

Whilst the Act is primarily intended to protect individual rights from interference by the state, there are certain circumstances in which the state is obliged to take positive steps to protect individuals from interference with their rights by other individuals or private bodies. Section 6 requires the public authorities – including the courts – to act in a manner that is compatible with Convention rights. The Court of Appeal has recognized that this could place the courts in a position where they have a positive obligation to protect individuals from interference with their Convention right to a respect for private life – even where the threat of interference emanated from a private media organization.

This approach seems to have been echoed in the stance of the court when dealing with the question of whether the murderers of James Bulger should be protected on release so that their whereabouts would not be published. Once again, the court took the view that it had a positive obligation to protect the claimants' right to life, to protect them from ill-treatment, and also to respect their private life, and those rights had to be protected against the media's freedom of expression. Thus an injunction was granted.

Another important development that has emerged

since the Human Rights Act has been in operation is that the Act is more far reaching than its title implies. Most people anticipated that it was going to be important in traditional areas of human rights (to protect private individuals or underdogs) but it has had a far more widespread impact than that in practice. Who, for example, could have predicted that one of the most important early decisions on the Act would be in the sphere of consumer credit?

A customer pawned his BMW car for £5,000. The fee for drawing up the pawn agreement was £250, which was added to the £5,000, making a total of £5,250. When the customer failed to keep up the monthly payments, proceedings were started against him. The customer then argued that the agreement was unenforceable on the basis that the lender had not complied with the strict terms of the Consumer Credit Act 1974 (because the £250 charge should have been separated out from the £5,000 in the consumer credit forms). A failure to comply with the 1974 Act renders the whole agreement unenforceable and not worth the paper it is written on. Held: The agreement was unenforceable. The end result was that the BMW was returned to the customer and he also recovered all the loan and interest moneys. But, of its own volition, the Court of Appeal intervened to suggest that the provision in the 1974 Act might be incompatible with Article 6(1) of the European Convention on Human Rights. Wilson v First County Trust (2000)

The Human Rights Act has also had a major impact on the planning system as the result of a court decision in December 2000 that the Secretary of State's ability to call in planning applications was incompatible with the European Convention on Human Rights (*Alconbury* v *Secretary of State* (2000)). This decision was subsequently reversed by the House of Lords but other aspects of the planning system remain vulnerable to challenge under the Act. One area in particular is the lack of third-party rights of appeal against planning decisions.

HOW CAN THE HUMAN RIGHTS ACT BE USED?

Public authorities have now had four years to change their policies and procedures to bring them into line with the rights in the Convention so most of what they do will comply. However, there will be a considerable number of unintentional violations of the Convention – public authorities will make mistakes and, in some cases, they will have good reasons not to want to go quite as far in respecting the rights in the Convention as they should.

Where there has been a breach of the Convention (or even where there is about to be) the victim can take proceedings in court. They may be able to take judicial review proceedings, obtain an injunction to stop the violation, force the public authority to take action or obtain damages and compensation.

The Act can also be used if you are subject to proceedings taken against you by a public authority, for instance if you are being sued or being prosecuted. You can use the Convention in tribunal proceedings, such as unfair dismissal proceedings.

INTERPRETING LAWS

The Human Rights Act may mean a new interpretation of old (and new) laws. The old judge-made law (the common law) will have to change if it does not respect the rights in the Convention. Nearly all secondary legislation (such as statutory instruments) is not valid if it does not comply with Convention rights. Even primary legislation (Parliamentary statutes) 'so far as it is possible to do so' has to be brought into line with Convention rights. However, if primary legislation cannot be read to comply with the Convention the higher courts can make what is called a 'declaration of incompatibility' which will allow the government to amend that law speedily.

WHICH RIGHTS?

Articles 2–12 and 14–18 of the Convention, plus Articles 1–3 of the First Protocol to the Convention, have been incorporated by the Human Rights Act (*see* below for the text of the Articles). Protocol 6 has also been incorporated (although this relates to the abolition of the death penalty which was abolished for all practical purposes in domestic law 35 years ago).

THE EUROPEAN CONVENTION ON HUMAN RIGHTS

The Convention was drafted over 50 years ago, and individuals from the UK have been able to take cases to the European Commission of Human Rights (which was abolished in November 1998) and the European Court of Human Rights since 1966. Over the last 30 years the Commission and Court in Strasbourg have interpreted the Convention in over 400 Court cases and over 1,000 Commission decisions.

The Court in Strasbourg has said that the Convention is designed to protect rights which are not just theoretical and illusory but practical and effective. The Court has also said that the Convention is a 'living instrument', that is the rights in the Convention are to be interpreted in line with current thinking.

This interpretation of the Convention is important because this is how our judges have been interpreting it since October 2000. The Convention often means more than the words in the Articles might suggest. For instance, the Court has decided that the right to a fair trial goes beyond merely what happens in the court itself – it can extend to what happens in the police station months before, if what happened there might have an effect on the fairness of the hearing (*Murray* v *UK* (1996)). In addition, the Court has said that the right to a fair trial includes a right of effective access to the court – there is no point having a right to a fair trial if a public body is preventing a person communicating with his or her lawyer or the court itself. (An example of this behaviour concerned a complaint about a prison which was blocking correspondence.)

There are now many textbooks on what the Convention means and, in most cases, it will be necessary to consult an expert for an authoritative answer.

Note: the Convention system has nothing to do with the 'Common Market', the EEC, the European Union or the separate European Courts of Justice.

THE RIGHTS THEMSELVES

There are three categories of rights in the Convention and they work in different ways:

1 the first set are *absolute* rights – these include Articles 2, 3, 4(1) and 7. They are not limited and they cannot be infringed no matter how necessary it might seem to be to do so;

2 the second set of rights are *limited* – good examples of such rights include Articles 4(2), 5, 6 and 12. In such articles the right is set out at the beginning and then there are specific limitations in the article itself. Limitations on the right that are not explicitly included in the article itself are not permissible and there is no general public interest limitation on rights;

3 the third set of rights are *qualified* – these include Articles 8, 9, 10, 11, 14 and Protocol 1, Article 1. Generally, in such articles the right is set out at the start and then is 'qualified'. Any infringement needs to be designed to promote a specific legitimate aim – 'in interests of national security, public safety, etc.' The infringement must be properly regulated by the law and must be 'necessary in a democratic society'. This latter concept means the interference with the right must be a proportionate response to the legitimate aim. If the aim can be achieved by a less intrusive method then that method must be used instead. Any interference with the right needs to be restricted as much as possible and should not use a sledgehammer to crack a nut.

The situations in which these rights may apply is detailed below (*see* the table on pages 626–8 for the full text of the rights).

Article 2

Article 2 is the right to life. It protects against the use of lethal force by public authorities unless its use is absolutely necessary (e.g. to protect the life of someone else). The right also has a more positive aspect. It imposes a duty on public bodies to go further than not causing unnecessary death themselves. There is also a duty to try to prevent death caused by private individuals. This duty extends to having in place adequate laws (against murder for instance) and an effective police force and court system to investigate deaths, etc. It will also even impose a duty on public bodies to take steps to prevent suicides (especially of those in institutions).

Article 3

Article 3 confers the right to be free from torture, inhuman or degrading treatment or punishment. The Court has decided that torture is deliberate, inhuman treatment causing very serious and cruel suffering. Inhuman treatment is treatment that causes intense physical and mental suffering. Degrading treatment is treatment that arouses in the victim a feeling of fear, anguish and inferiority capable of humiliating and debasing the victim, and possibly breaking his or her physical or moral resistance. As in Article 2 above, Article 3 also imposes a limited positive duty on public authorities to protect the rights of others even from infringement by other private parties. For instance, the Court has ruled that allowing a defence in criminal proceedings of 'reasonable chastisement' creates a real danger that children will be beaten by their parents (or step-parents in the case itself) and this may violate their rights under Article 3.

Article 5

Article 5 protects against arbitrary and unlawful detention. Note that only those exemptions listed 5(1)(a) to (e) can be used to justify detention. Any detention for other reasons will be a violation of Article 5. Any detention must be lawful. That means it must be sanctioned by the law specifically and any rules of procedure must be followed.

Article 6

Article 6 provides for a right to a fair trial and is, therefore, a very important right. Note that, in criminal proceedings, the right only applies to the defendant. In other proceedings the right only applies where there is a *civil right or obligation* at stake in the proceedings (it might not apply therefore, for instance, where the dispute was over, say, a discretionary social security benefit). Articles 6(2) and 6(3) only apply to criminal proceedings and are, in addition to the general right to a fair trial, provided by Article 6(1). However, despite the absence of a right to, for instance, public funding in civil proceedings in 6(1) itself, the European Court of Human Rights has imposed one. The Court has decided that, in some civil cases without such a right to legal aid, the person concerned could not have a fair trial. Note the importance of the right to 'open justice' and hearings in public in the Article.

Article 7

Article 7 is unlikely to be used in many circumstances because, generally, both the courts and Parliament are careful not to make retrospective criminal laws.

Article 8

Article 8 is the right to private and family life. Before October 2000 there was no right to privacy in ordinary law. This Article is, therefore, likely to be of use in combating new forms of technology that may interfere with our privacy (including privacy on the internet for instance). The right to private life includes our right to a private sexuality without interference from public authorities. The right to family life will also be of use to children, parents and others threatened with separation.

Article 9

Article 9 protects the right to freedom of religion and a positive right in this area was new for the UK. Nevertheless, there are few laws that prevent the practice of religion in this country. Some religions are better protected than others under our current law and this Article, in combination with Article 14, may help to redress this balance.

Article 10

Article 10 will be of particular use to journalists and the media. The right to freedom of expression also assists those people who wish to express their views by attending demonstrations and protests because these activities are protected as well. The Article does not include a right to freedom of information from public bodies, however – there is no specific 'right to know' in the Convention. It may, however, protect whistleblowers from dismissal or prosecution.

Article 11

Article 11 protects the right of freedom of assembly and may assist peaceful protesters, and the like, and separately protects the right to join (or not join) organizations such as trade unions and other groups. Note the specific restrictions that apply to the police and the armed forces.

Article 12

Article 12 does very little to promote rights. Note the 'right to marry' can be restricted by 'national laws' and does not, at least at present, give a right to those of the same sex to marry each other. The right to found a family may assist those who, for one reason or another, are restricted by the state from having children (e.g. prisoners who seek to have children using artificial insemination).

Article 14

Article 14 is a qualified right. Note first that the right to be free from discrimination only applies in relation to the other rights in the Convention. Therefore it would apply, for instance, to discriminatory searches by the police because the right of freedom from detention and the right to privacy were engaged. It would not apply to, say, the provision of services in shops or elsewhere, however, because no other Convention right was engaged (there is no 'right to shop' in the Convention). However, the 'other' right only has to be engaged. A person wishing to use Article 14 does not have to prove that the other Article was violated first.

Second, note that the expression 'or other status' in the list of protected groups is very wide.

In order to establish a violation it is necessary to show:

1 a difference of treatment in respect of another Convention right;
2 that that difference of treatment is not for a legitimate aim; or
3 that the difference of treatment is not a proportionate response to the aim for which it is designed.

Protocol 1, Article 1

Article 1 of Protocol 1 protects the peaceful possession of property. It is a qualified right. In most cases public authorities will be able to justify their actions in relation to the wider public interest (e.g. taxation). Nevertheless, in some cases the Article will require compensation to be paid for taking away a person's property (as in compulsory purchase, for instance). Recently, this Article, combined with the right to privacy in Article 8, has been used to claim rights of environmental protection for those living close to sources of pollution.

Protocol 1, Article 2

Article 2 of Protocol 1 protects the right to education, and the right to respect the philosophical or religious beliefs of parents. The right only protects primary and secondary education. The Article does not impose an obligation on the state to pay for education which respects philosophical and religious beliefs of parents, merely not to prevent it being available (but note it could be used in conjunction with the anti-discrimination provision in Article 14).

Protocol 1, Article 3

Article 3 of Protocol 1 does not give a right of election to bodies other than those which legislate (thus electing local councils is not protected, although elections to the European Parliament are). It also does not create a right to any specific system of election (either 'first past the post' or proportional representation will comply with the right). However, this Article might be of use in assisting those who find it difficult to register for the vote in ensuring they have a right to vote (the homeless, for instance).

The rights incorporated into the Human Rights Act 1998

This table details the rights contained in the European Convention on Human Rights that are incorporated into domestic law by the Human Rights Act 1998. Please note that Articles 15, 16 and 17 are not included here.

ARTICLE 2

1 Everyone's right to life shall be protected by law. No one shall be deprived of his life intentionally save in the execution of a sentence of a court following his conviction of a crime for which the penalty is provided by law.
2 Deprivation of life shall not be regarded as inflicted in contravention of this Article when it results from the use of force which is no more than absolutely necessary –
  (a) in defence of any person from unlawful violence;
  (b) in order to effect a lawful arrest or to prevent the escape of a person lawfully detained;
  (c) in action lawfully taken for the purpose of quelling a riot or insurrection.

ARTICLE 3

No one shall be subjected to torture or to inhuman or degrading treatment or punishment.

ARTICLE 4

1 No one shall be held in slavery or servitude.
2 No one shall be required to perform forced or compulsory labour.
3 For the purpose of this Article the term 'forced or compulsory labour' shall not include –
  (a) any work required to be done in the ordinary course of detention imposed in accordance with the provisions of Article 5 of this Convention or during conditional release from such detention;
  (b) any service of a military character or, in the case of conscientious objectors in countries where they are recognized, service exacted instead of compulsory military service;
  (c) any service exacted in case of an emergency or calamity threatening the life or well-being of the community;
  (d) any work or service which forms part of normal civic obligations.

ARTICLE 5

1 Everyone has the right to liberty and security of person. No one shall be deprived of his liberty save in the following cases and in accordance with a procedure prescribed by law –
  (a) the lawful detention of a person after conviction by a competent court;
  (b) the lawful arrest or detention of a person for non-compliance with the lawful order of a court or in order to secure the fulfilment of any obligation prescribed by law;
  (c) the lawful arrest or detention of a person effected for the purpose of bringing him before the competent legal authority on reasonable suspicion of having committed an offence or when it is reasonably considered necessary to prevent his committing an offence or fleeing after having done so;
  (d) the detention of a minor by lawful order for the purpose of educational supervision or his lawful detention for the purpose of bringing him before the competent legal authority;
  (e) the lawful detention of persons for the prevention of the spreading of infectious diseases, of persons of unsound mind, alcoholics and drug addicts or vagrants;
  (f) the lawful arrest or detention of a person to prevent his effecting an unauthorized entry into the country or of a person against whom action is being taken with a view to deportation or extradition.
2 Everyone who is arrested shall be informed promptly, in a language which he understands, of the reason for his arrest and of any charge against him.
3 Everyone arrested or detained in accordance with the provisions of paragraph 1(c) of this Article shall be brought promptly before a judge or other officer authorized by law to exercise judicial power and shall be entitled to trial within a reasonable time or to release pending trial. Release may be conditioned by guarantees to appear for trial.

4 Everyone who is deprived of his liberty by arrest or detention shall be entitled to take proceedings by which the lawfulness of his detention shall be decided speedily by a court and his release ordered if the detention is not lawful.

5 Everyone who has been the victim of arrest or detention in contravention of the provisions of this Article shall have an enforceable right to compensation.

ARTICLE 6

1 In the determination of his civil rights and obligations or of any criminal charge against him, everyone is entitled to a fair and public hearing within a reasonable time by an independent and impartial tribunal established by law. Judgment shall be pronounced publicly but the press and public may be excluded from all or part of the trial in the interests of morals, public order or national security in a democratic society, where the interests of juveniles or the protection of the private life of the parties so require, or to the extent strictly necessary in the opinion of the court in special circumstances where publicity would prejudice the interests of justice.

2 Everyone charged with a criminal offence shall be presumed innocent until proved guilty according to law.

3 Everyone charged with a criminal offence has the following minimum rights –
(**a**) to be informed promptly, in a language which he understands and in detail, of the nature and cause of the accusation against him;
(**b**) to have adequate time and facilities for the preparation of his defence;
(**c**) to defend himself in person or through legal assistance of his own choosing or, if he has not sufficient means to pay for legal assistance, to be given it free when the interests of justice so require;
(**d**) to examine or have examined witnesses against him and to obtain the attendance and examination of witnesses on his behalf under the same conditions as witnesses against him;
(**e**) to have the free assistance of an interpreter if he cannot understand or speak the language used in court.

ARTICLE 7

1 No one shall be held guilty of any criminal offence on account of any act or omission which did not constitute a criminal offence under national or international law at the time when it was committed. Nor shall a heavier penalty be imposed than the one that was applicable at the time the criminal offence was committed.

2 This Article shall not prejudice the trial and punishment of any person for any act or omission which, at the time it was committed, was criminal according to the general law recognized by civilized nations.

ARTICLE 8

1 Everyone has the right to his private and family life, his home and his correspondence.

2 There shall be no interference by a public authority with the exercise of this right except such as is in accordance with the law and is necessary in a democratic society in the interests of national security, public safety or the economic well-being of the country, for the prevention of disorder or crime, for the protection of health or morals, or for the protection of the rights and freedoms of others.

ARTICLE 9

1 Everyone has the right to freedom of thought, conscience and religion; this right includes freedom to change his religion or belief and freedom, either alone or in community with others and in public or private, to manifest his religion or belief, in worship, teaching, practice and observance.

2 Freedom to manifest one's religion or beliefs shall be subject only to such limitations as are prescribed by law and are necessary in a democratic society in the interests of public safety, for the protection of public order, health or morals, or for the protection of the rights and freedoms of others.

ARTICLE 10

1 Everyone has the right of freedom of expression. This right shall include freedom to hold opinions and to receive and impart information and ideas without interference by public authority and regardless of frontiers. This Article shall not prevent States from requiring the licensing of broadcasting, television or cinema enterprises.

2 The exercise of these freedoms, since it carries with it duties and responsibilities, may be subject to such formalities, conditions, restrictions or penalties as are prescribed by law and are necessary in a democratic society, in the interests of national security, territorial integrity or public safety, for the prevention of disorder or crime, for the protection of health or morals, for the protection of the reputation or rights of others, for preventing the disclosure of information received in confidence, or for maintaining the authority and impartiality of the judiciary.

ARTICLE 11

1 Everyone has the right to freedom of peaceful assembly and to freedom of association with others, including the right to form and to join trade unions for the protection of his interests.

2 No restrictions shall be placed on the exercise of these rights other than such as are prescribed by law and are necessary in a democratic society in the interests of national security or public safety, for the prevention of disorder or crime, for the protection of health or morals or for the protection of the rights and freedoms of others. This Article shall not prevent the imposition of lawful restrictions on the exercise of these rights by members of the armed forces, of the police or of the administration of the State.

ARTICLE 12

Men and women of marriageable age shall have the right to marry and to found a family, according to national laws governing the exercise of this right.

ARTICLE 14

The enjoyment of the rights and freedoms set forth in this convention shall be secured without discrimination on any ground such as sex, race, colour, language, religion, political or other opinion, national or social origin, association with a national minority, property, birth or other status.

PROTOCOL NO 1

ARTICLE 1

Every natural or legal person is entitled to the peaceful enjoyment of his possessions. No one shall be deprived of his possessions except in the public interest and subject to the conditions provided for by law and by the general principles of international law.

The preceding provisions shall not, however, in any way impair the right of the State to enforce such laws as it deems necessary to control the use of property in accordance with the general interest or to secure payment of taxes or other contributions or penalties.

ARTICLE 2

No person shall be denied a right to an education. In the exercise of any functions which it assumes in relation to education and to teaching, the State shall respect the right of parents to ensure such education and teaching in conformity with their own religious and philosophical convictions.

ARTICLE 3

The High Contracting Parties undertake to hold free elections at reasonable intervals by secret ballot, under conditions which will ensure the free expression of the opinion of the people in the choice of the legislature.

85

Police Powers and Individual Liberty

HELPING THE POLICE

The general rule is that no one is obliged to help the police with their inquiries. It may be a social or even moral duty to do so, but there is no law which says that you must. All the law requires is that you should not give false information to the police or waste police time. Most people, of course, do help the police. If everyone stood on their constitutional rights and refused to co-operate, the task of the police would become impossible.

When the police stop someone in the street and ask them to 'Come down to the station and help us with our inquiries', that request can be refused. The only way the police can make someone accompany them to the police station is to *arrest* them, and that can be done only in certain circumstances. The Police and Criminal Evidence Act 1984 changed the rules on the treatment of people who are 'helping the police with their inquiries'. But it still preserves the right of the suspect to refuse to help the police with their inquiries, and to leave the police station. The Home Office Code of Practice (issued under the Act) says:

Any person attending a police station voluntarily for the purpose of assisting with an investigation may leave at will unless placed under arrest. If it is decided that he should not be allowed to do so then he must be informed at once that he is under arrest . . . If he is not placed under arrest but is cautioned . . . the officer who gives the caution must at the same time inform him that he is not under arrest and that he is not obliged to remain at the police station but that if he remains at the police station he may obtain legal advice if he wishes.

The basic rule is that the police can keep someone in the police station only if arrested or if they voluntarily agree to being held by them (but *see* 'Searching someone', pages 635–6). Note that the police have considerably more powers in dealing with suspects accused of terrorist offences (*see* page 635).

A SUSPECT'S RIGHTS – ARREST

The police cannot arrest anyone unless they have lawful authority to do so, otherwise they run the risk of being sued for damages for false imprisonment and/or assault. With the more serious offences (generally those for which the maximum sentence could be five years or more in prison), a police officer automatically has power to arrest a suspect (*see* the list below). The police can also obtain an arrest warrant from a magistrate, although the powers of the police to arrest are now so wide that it is rarely necessary for them to do so. A warrant is obtained by 'laying an information': the police will hand in a written statement to the court and give evidence on oath. If the magistrate decides that there is a prima facie case against the accused, the warrant will be issued. The police can then serve the warrant on the accused and arrest the suspect.

Arrest without a warrant

The police can arrest someone without the need for a warrant if:
1 the person has committed, is in the act of committing, or is reasonably suspected to be committing, any 'arrestable' offence. An arrestable offence is an offence that could lead to five years', or more, imprisonment. Also included are:
   (a) armed assault;
   (b) arson;
   (c) actual bodily harm;
   (d) burglary;
   (e) death by reckless driving;
   (f) demanding money with menaces;
   (g) dishonest handling;
   (h) drug offences;
   (i) grievous bodily harm;
   (j) living off immoral earnings;
   (k) manslaughter;

(**l**) murder;

(**m**) some firearm offences;

(**n**) rape;

(**o**) indecent assault, and other serious sex offences;

(**p**) taking a motor vehicle without authority;

(**q**) theft (including shoplifting); and

(**r**) wounding.

(Note: this is not a complete list of all arrestable offences);

2 the person is guilty or is reasonably suspected of being guilty of an arrestable offence which has already taken place;

3 the person is reasonably suspected of being guilty of an arrestable offence which the police officer reasonably suspects has occurred;

4 the person is or is reasonably suspected of being about to commit an arrestable offence;

5 the person is seen breaching the peace or is acting so that a breach of the peace is likely to occur (this includes a situation where a person's conduct is likely to provoke others to commit a breach of the peace). A breach of the peace occurs 'whenever harm is actually done or is likely to be done to a person or in his presence to his property or a person is in fear of being so harmed through an assault, an affray, a riot or an unlawful assembly or other disturbance';

6 the person:

(**a**) is drunk and incapable of caring for him- or herself;

(**b**) refuses to take (or fails to take) a breath test;

(**c**) is soliciting; or

(**d**) refuses to give his or her name and address when legally obliged to (e.g. a motorist involved in an accident);

7 the person is suspected of driving while disqualified or under the influence of drink or drugs;

8 the person is suspected of committing:

(**a**) an offence relating to the control of alcohol at sporting events;

(**b**) an affray;

(**c**) disorderly behaviour or conduct; or

(**d**) failing to comply with lawful directions given by the police in respect of marches and demonstrations.

A variety of other obscure powers also give police officers and others powers of arrest.

A private individual can arrest someone without the need for a warrant (a 'citizen's arrest') if the offence comes within paragraphs 1, 2 or 5 above.

In addition, a police officer can arrest a person for any offence if the police officer has reasonable doubts either about a suspect's name or address or about whether the summons procedure can be used at the address given. A person can also be arrested by a police officer if there are reasonable grounds for believing that it will prevent:

* the person injuring him- or herself or others;
* the person suffering any other injury;
* harm to any vulnerable person;
* loss or damage to property;
* an offence against public decency; or
* the obstruction of the highway.

A person who is arrested must be informed of this fact, and of the grounds for the arrest, either at the time or as soon as practicable.

Rights on detention

As soon as a suspect is detained in the police station, he or she must be told why, and also that the following rights now apply:

* the right to see a solicitor (*see* pages 633–4);
* the right to have someone told of the detention (*see* page 634);
* the right to look at the codes of practice that the police should follow (in particular, to read the detailed detention code – *see* above).

In addition, the custody officer (i.e. the police officer responsible for all detained suspects – a different police officer from the one dealing with the suspect's case; usually a sergeant) must give the suspect a written note of these three legal rights. That written note will also include a caution (i.e. 'You do not have to say anything. But it may harm your defence if you do not mention when questioned something which you later rely on in court. Anything you do say may be given in evidence').

Police questioning

A suspect cannot be made to help the police. If they simply refuse to answer the police questions then there is nothing (in theory, anyway) that the police can do to force them to speak. First, there is a fundamental legal principle, which states that every suspect has the right to remain silent, although that silence can now be used against him, in certain circumstances, in any subsequent trial (*see* below). Second, the police should not use force or pressure to get answers to their questions. For instance, the code says:

No police officer may try to obtain answers to questions . . . by the use of oppression, or shall indicate, except in answer to a direct question, what action will be taken if . . . the person makes a statement or refuses . . .

If a person agrees to help the police (or if they are arrested), there are rules of conduct governing the manner in which they are to be questioned. The Police and Criminal Evidence Act 1984 sets out basic guidelines that have to be followed, and these are backed up by a detailed code of practice on the detention, treatment and questioning of detainees (generally called the detention code). The code sets out the rules that the police should follow, but these rules are not totally binding on the police (*see* 'Remedies: police complaints', page 633). So, if a police officer conducts an interview that does not follow the rules, it does not necessarily follow that the evidence obtained will be inadmissible – that is for the trial judge to decide. The judge will probably rule it out only if the interview was oppressive or where it would be unfair to include it.

There are other rules that the police have to observe, many of which are aimed at ensuring that unfair pressure is not put on suspects, for instance cells must be clean. There should be two light meals and one main meal each day. The suspect must be allowed at least eight hours' rest each day; interview rooms must be properly heated; suspects are not to be made to stand; there must be a break from interviewing at normal meal times and – as a general rule – there should be short refreshment breaks every two hours. The code sets out extremely detailed guidelines that should be followed. Another safeguard for the accused is that police must give a verbal 'caution'. The caution reminds the suspect of the fundamental legal right not to answer questions but now also contains the additional warning that their silence may be held against them – 'You do not have to say anything. But it may harm your defence if you do not mention when questioned something which you later rely on in court. Anything you do say may be given in evidence.' If the suspect has not been arrested but is merely 'helping the police with their inquiries' (i.e. voluntarily agreeing to be questioned – *see* above), then the caution must state the fundamental legal right: the right to leave the police station (and also to take legal advice).

This caution has to be repeated at various stages of the police investigation. In particular, it has to be given (and repeated):

- when a suspect is arrested;
- when a suspect is about to be interviewed;
- if there is a short break in the interview then he or she must usually be reminded that he or she is still under caution when the interview restarts.

The police sometimes ignore these rules. If the police should conduct their questioning in an improper manner, it is difficult for the suspect to prove afterwards that the rules were broken. And, of course, even if he or she can prove that the rules were not followed, the judge who hears the case may still allow the evidence to be heard. Generally speaking, if a suspect thinks that something that was said or done by an investigating officer prior to the start of the taped interview, which they suspect is improper or in breach of the rules then they should mention this in the interview and ask the officer to repeat it for the benefit of the tape. That way an objective record is maintained.

STATEMENTS AND ANSWERING QUESTIONS

As already stated, a suspect cannot be compelled to give a statement to the police or answer any of their questions. But there is no longer any absolute right to remain silent. A failure to mention some fact or explanation, either when arrested or when questioned by the police, which is later relied on at trial may be held against an accused if appropriate. This is what is known as the 'common sense' inference. If a defence advanced at trial is true then presumably it must have been known to the accused at the time of his arrest and interview. In which case why was it not mentioned first at that point and not many months later at trial?

There are therefore distinct disadvantages in refusing to answer questions in the police station. On the other hand there may be good reasons why an individual may not wish to answer questions. They may be upset, in shock, tired (interviews are often conducted in the early hours of the morning), they may be under the influence of alcohol or vulnerable due to a psychiatric condition or low intelligence. In other words, they may not do themselves justice if they are subjected to detailed questioning for reasons that have nothing to do with guilt or innocence. Always seek advice from a solicitor before answering questions. Their service is free for people detained and there will be someone on duty 24 hours a day. The following approach is recommended:

1 if the suspect has a straightforward explanation and feels comfortable answering questions then they should try and get their side of the story across to the police both on arrest and in interview;

2 if the suspect is in any doubt as to whether it is in their best interest to answer questions, they are strongly advised to wait until the solicitor can attend and advise them in person;

3 sometimes suspects will be reluctant to expose themselves to detailed questioning (for any number of reasons) but would still wish to make certain points so as to limit the negative effects of their silence at any future trial. One way of doing this is, with the help of a lawyer, to write out a short statement which can be read out at the start of the interview and then make no comment to all questions thereafter;

4 obviously, the police will urge the suspect to answer their questions but he or she should not be afraid to insist on his or her legal right to remain silent – even if it means that he or she remains in custody for a longer period. For instance, the police may refuse to grant 'police bail', which may mean a stay in custody overnight. Refusing bail for this reason would be unlawful but the police sometimes suggest that the

more co-operative the person is the quicker they will be released. Don't be bullied!

5 in virtually all cases the interview will take the form of a question and answer session which will be tape-recorded. The questions are likely to start with the details of the suspect's name and address and lead on to more important questions. It is not advisable to answer some questions and refuse to answer others. Apart from being difficult to do, if some questions are answered but not others this may have a very prejudicial effect at the trial, as it may give the impression of evasiveness. It is also difficult to remain completely silent in the face of questioning. Many lawyers advise their clients to answer 'no comment' to every question and many suspects find this more acceptable;

6 finally, suspects should not be tempted to 'make a deal' with the police whereby they make a statement admitting guilt in return for the police not bringing a more serious charge, unless legal advice has been taken.

As will be clear from the above, the whole question of whether to answer questions in the police station has now become quite complicated. A suspect is strongly advised to take legal advice before deciding on what course to take. A decision in the European Court of Human Rights has further emphasized the importance of the role of legal advice in any decision to refuse to answer questions.

Verbals

Following on from the problem of statements to the police is the vexed question of *verbals*. This is the word used to describe admissions, or incriminating statements, that the police falsely allege to have been made by the accused.

When the police question, arrest or charge a person, they keep a written record of the events and conversations. For example, the notebook might read, 'When charged, the accused said, "Fair enough, I did it,"' but the accused may later deny ever having said those words. Either he is lying or has been *verballed* by the police.

The end result has been that many criminal trials have revolved around whether the accused did make an admission or was 'verballed' by the police. In effect, there are mini-trials within the main trials, with police officers being accused of giving false evidence. Although tape-recording has cut down on the numbers of challenged 'verbals', there are increasing numbers of cases in which a statement was allegedly made by the suspect at the time of arrest, on the way to the police station or in the police cell. For obvious reasons, it is very important to say nothing at these times or at the very least to think carefully before doing so. The police should show the notes that they have made to the suspect and ask the suspect to sign

them. It is obviously important to sign them only if they are correct and to think very carefully before doing so. In many cases, it will be better to speak to a lawyer before signing anything.

BEING HELD BY THE POLICE BEFORE CHARGE

We have already seen that there are two fundamental and one limited right given to all suspects:

- you cannot be detained and held by the police unless you have been arrested (and unless you are prepared to help voluntarily by answering questions);
- you cannot be forced to answer any police questions;
- you can be detained only if there is not sufficient evidence to charge you and the police have reasonable grounds for believing that they need to detain you to obtain, or preserve, evidence or to obtain evidence by questioning you.

There is another basic right given to people held in detention against their will (i.e. arrested). This is the right not to be held for an unreasonably long time before being charged in writing for a specific offence. In general, a suspect cannot be held for more than 24 hours between being taken to the police station after arrest and being charged with a specific offence. At the end of that 24-hour period the police should either charge or release the suspect – unless they are being held for a 'serious' offence (*see* below), in which case the police may be able to hold the suspect for longer. In these 'serious' cases, a senior police officer can authorize detention for up to 36 (not 24) hours, and at the end of that time the police can ask a magistrates' court to agree to further detention without charging (up to 36 hours per application) up to a maximum of 96 hours (i.e. four days of detention and questioning without being charged). This court hearing is in private (i.e. relatives and friends cannot attend) but the suspect's lawyer can appear and argue why the detention should not be extended any further.

During detention the police must conduct regular reviews of the detention. These reviews are carried out by an inspector who is not involved in the case. The reviews are intended to consider whether the detention should continue and are held after the first six hours and then every nine hours thereafter. The suspect and his or her lawyer are entitled to make representations to the review officer. Unfortunately, such reviews seldom lead to release and are often irrelevant. Nevertheless, the suspect should use them to put pressure on the police to release them.

With the exception of terrorist suspects, very few suspects are held for longer than 24 hours. If someone is held for longer than is allowed under the legislation, then an application to the High Court for *habeas corpus* or judicial review should be made. Unfortunately, the practical difficulties of getting to court and obtaining an order mean that these protections are virtually worthless in practice.

Remedies

Suing for wrongful arrest (assault and/or false imprisonment)

If a person is wrongly arrested and detained by the police, then he or she may be able to sue for damages. However, this is possible only if the police acted unlawfully – in other words, if they did not have reasonable grounds for the arrest or to continue the detention. Just because a person is detained, and subsequently released, it does not follow that he or she is entitled to compensation from the police.

The number of successful cases against the police has dramatically increased over the last few years. Anyone who has been arrested and detained, particularly anyone who has been assaulted by the police, should consult a solicitor. In many cases public funding will be available. Damages awarded in such cases can sometimes be very high. When a person has been unlawfully detained they are entitled to a basic award of damages, which is calculated by reference to a sliding scale depending on the length of their detention (£500 for the first hour and an ever decreasing hourly rate until you reach the figure of £3,000 for the first 24 hours).

It is also possible to sue the police for 'malicious prosecution' if they charge and prosecute without reasonable and probable cause and are acting in pursuit of an improper or dishonest motive. A malicious prosecution in the magistrates' court coupled with a period of, say, 15 hours' false imprisonment would be likely to lead to a total damages figure of approximately £12,000–£16,000. These awards are made by juries and so they are notoriously difficult to predict.

Police complaints

If someone is treated badly by the police that person can make an official complaint about that officer's conduct. Complaints can be made for: unjustified assault, verbal abuse, racism, lying, releasing confidential information, corruption, oppressive behaviour, drunkenness and criminal conduct. Breaching the codes of practice is also a disciplinary offence. If a suspect wishes to make a complaint while they are in police custody then this must be recorded by the duty inspector as soon as reasonably practicable. If a suspect is considering raising any issue arising out of their treatment or detention it is a good idea to do so at this stage so there is a contemporaneous record of their complaint – but take legal advice first. Otherwise the procedure is to put the complaint in writing and send it to the Independent Police Complaints Commission. If the complaint is upheld, the officer will be disciplined. Police officers can also be prosecuted if the investigation reveals that criminal offences have occurred.

Legal advice should be sought before proceeding with a complaint, particularly if other court or criminal proceedings are going on at the same time. It is important to note that a malicious complaint could lead to action for libel (*see* page 696).

Suspect's rights

Apart from the right to refuse to answer questions (*see* above), all detainees are entitled to:
- see a solicitor;
- have someone told about the arrest;
- be released if not charged within 24 hours (*see* above).

However in the case of 'serious' offences, the suspect has fewer rights. The rights detailed above are not taken away – but they are reduced, largely because the police can postpone them. For instance, the police can delay the suspect's rights to see a solicitor, or have someone told of the detention. But this happens only if he or she is suspected of 'a serious arrestable offence'. Unfortunately, the law does not set out a neat, clear-cut definition of what is 'a serious arrestable offence'. Obviously, some particularly grave crimes are specifically mentioned (e.g. murder, rape, incest, death by dangerous driving); other crimes have to be looked at on their own merits to see whether they are 'serious'. The Police and Criminal Evidence Act 1984 gives only vague guidance – for instance, has the offence caused serious harm or financial loss to anyone? If so, then it will be a 'serious' offence, and so the police will be able to postpone some of the detainee's legal rights.

The right to see a solicitor

The detention code (made under the 1984 Act – *see* page 629) is quite clear about the right to see a solicitor: 'Any person may at any time consult and communicate privately, whether in person, writing or on the telephone, with a solicitor.' In fact, when the suspect arrives at the police station, the custody officer must give him or her a written notice setting out their legal rights, including the right to see a solicitor (*see* page 630). The suspect must be asked whether he or she wants to see a solicitor; if they say no, then they should sign so there is a written record of this. If they refuse to sign, then the police should assume that they do want to see a solicitor and they must make the necessary arrangements. In short, the general rule is that the suspect must specifically sign away the right to see a solicitor.

Unfortunately, research findings have shown that police

officers often have a tendency to discourage suspects from seeking legal advice. This is a breach of the code of practice and suspects should insist on their right to see a solicitor. However, as is usually the case, there is an exception to this basic rule. If it is a 'serious' offence then a superintendent can give authority for the suspect to be denied access to a solicitor (*see* 'Suspect's rights' above for what is a 'serious' offence). The officer can do this if he or she thinks that allowing access to a solicitor would:

- interfere with the evidence; or
- alert other (unarrested) suspects; or
- hinder the recovery of stolen property.

Although it was once frequently used by the police as a device to prevent suspects obtaining legal advice, a decision at the Court of Appeal has considerably reduced the police's ability to delay access to a solicitor. Research suggests that it is used in less than one per cent of cases and in order to justify its use the police would need to show that allowing a particular solicitor to have access would lead to any of the above consequences.

Perhaps more important, in any case (i.e. whether or not it is 'serious') a senior officer can decide that the interviewing of the suspect can go ahead, even though the solicitor has not yet arrived, if he or she thinks 'there is a considerable risk of harm to persons or serious loss of damage to property', or that 'awaiting the arrival of a solicitor would cause unreasonable delay to the processes of investigation'. If the police try to take advantage of this provision, the suspect should not answer any questions or make a statement until he or she has seen a solicitor. Faced with someone who will not speak until they have seen a solicitor, the police will usually wait for the solicitor. The incorporation of the European Convention on Human Rights into domestic law has re-emphasized the importance of the role of the lawyer in the police station and will render it unlawful for the police to prevent a suspect from receiving legal advice in all but the most exceptional situations.

If suspects want to see a solicitor then they can choose any solicitor they like. If they do not know the name or telephone number of a solicitor, or their chosen solicitor cannot be contacted or cannot attend, there is a duty solicitor on call 24 hours a day. The duty solicitor will be someone who specializes in criminal law and is in private practice in a local firm which takes part in a rota scheme to provide the service. Where there is to be an interview or some kind of identification procedure, or there is some suggestion of maltreatment by the police, the duty solicitor is obliged to come to the police station. Whether or not the suspect uses his or her own solicitor or the duty solicitor, the service can be provided free under the public funding scheme.

Obviously the competence of solicitors varies and in some cases the solicitor will send someone who is not a qualified solicitor to the police to advise the suspect. Some such clerks can provide a very expert service (even better than many solicitors), but many do not. Nevertheless, it is very important to obtain the legal advice because decisions made at this stage can have a fundamental influence on the outcome of the case.

The right to have someone told of the detention

The code explains that the suspect has 'the right not to be held incommunicado'. It goes on to say:

A detained person may on request have one person known to him or who is likely to take an interest in his welfare informed at public expense as soon as practicable of his whereabouts. If that person cannot be contacted the detained person may choose up to two alternatives.

However, as expected, there is an important exception. If it is a 'serious' offence that is being investigated (see above for what this means), then a senior police officer can decide that the right is not to apply; on the same basis that he or she can deny access to a solicitor (i.e. in order not to interfere with evidence; alert suspects; hinder recovery of property – *see* above). However, the senior officer cannot do this simply because they think it would cause 'unreasonable delay', although they can use this ground to deny access to a solicitor (*see* above).

The code also says that the suspect should be given writing materials to write letters or messages, if he or she asks for them; those letters are then to be sent (at the suspect's expense) as soon as is practicable, although the police can read them. Likewise, the code says that a suspect can speak on the phone to one person, although the police can listen in to the conversation. Once again, if it is a 'serious' offence, a senior officer can take away these rights (i.e. on the grounds given above). Similar rules apply when relatives or friends of a detainee inquire of the police if they are holding him or her; the basic rule is that they must be told (assuming the detainee agrees), but this need not happen if it is a 'serious' offence.

Bail

For the rules on granting bail, *see* pages 642–3.

Taking fingerprints, photographs and samples

The law now gives a wide right to take fingerprints. A senior police officer can authorize the taking of a suspect's fingerprints if he or she thinks the person has been involved in an offence, provided the taking of the fingerprints may tend to prove (or disprove) that guilt. Once a suspect has been charged, in writing, with a specific offence, the police have even greater powers. If the offence is of the sort that is recorded in police records (most non-trivial offences), then they can take fingerprints.

Previously, fingerprints and DNA samples taken from persons arrested would have to be destroyed in the event of the person being acquitted or if the charges were dropped or not pursued against the individual. The police now have powers to retain fingerprints and DNA samples lawfully taken from any person – regardless of whether or not they are subsequently convicted of an offence. These records will then be held on databases and used for subsequent detention of crime only.

Roughly similar rules apply to the taking of photos. If it is a recordable offence that he or she has been charged with, then the police can take photos. The power to take photographs of suspects and to retain those photographs has been extended by amendments to the Police and Criminal Evidence Act 1984 (PACE) brought about by the Anti-Terrorism, Crime and Security Act 2001. Under a new section 64A of PACE the police have wider powers to take photographs and to retain those photographs even where the suspect is subsequently released, not charged or acquitted of an offence. The person taking the photograph may require the removal of any item or substance worn on or over the whole or any part of the face, and if the request is not complied with, may remove the item in question. Although the police can use force to take a suspect's fingerprints there is no legal right for them to use force to take a photograph. So, if suspects refuse to co-operate (e.g. putting their hands in front of their faces), then in theory there is nothing the police can do, and if they use force the suspect would be able to sue for damages for assault.

An intimate sample (blood, semen, urine, pubic hair) may be taken by a doctor or a registered nurse if the superintendent authorizes it *and* the suspect consents. The authorization may be given only if the officer has reasonable grounds for believing the sample will confirm or disprove involvement in a serious arrestable offence.

If the suspect refuses to consent the court or jury may 'draw such inferences from the refusal as appear proper'. That is, the court is allowed to conclude that a refusal to give a sample is evidence of guilt. There are different rules for breath tests and blood or urine samples in cases of drink drivers. Non-intimate samples (hair other than pubic hair, sample from a nail or under a nail or a swab taken from part of a person's body other than an orifice) can be taken *without consent*. It can be authorized by a superintendent if the officer has reasonable grounds for believing the sample will confirm or disprove involvement in a serious arrestable offence.

Searching someone

The police do not have a general power to search members of the public. However, PACE does give them fairly extensive powers to stop and search suspected individuals.

Detailed guidelines are set out in a code on stop and search, but the basic effect is that a police officer can search someone if the police officer has reasonable grounds for thinking the person is carrying certain ('prohibited' is the word the Act uses) items. This covers offensive weapons (e.g. knife, razor, sharpened comb, etc.) or any item that could be used to commit an offence involving dishonesty, such as theft, stealing a car, burglary, etc. It follows that this could cover a screwdriver (it could be used to force a window), or a bundle of car keys. In practice, it is a vague criterion and gives the police a wide discretion in deciding whether to search.

The code says that the citizen must be told why he or she is being searched and why the constable is entitled to carry out the search; the constable must also identify himself. The search can extend to the suspect's car. In public the search is limited to removal of outer coat, jacket and gloves, but a more detailed search – as far as a complete strip search – can be carried out, in which case it must be by a police officer of the same sex and out of public view (e.g. in a police van or at the police station).

The code lays down detailed guidelines for the police to follow (but remember that the courts can still allow evidence to be given even though it was obtained by breaking one of the codes). It says:

It is important that powers of stop and search are used responsibly. An officer should bear in mind that he may be required to justify the use of the powers to a senior officer and in court, and also that abuse of the powers is likely to be harmful to the police effort in the long term. This can lead to mistrust of the police by the community. It is also particularly important to ensure that any person searched is treated courteously and considerately.

These words are obviously aimed at the over-use of police powers against young black people. In this connection it is necessary to remember that the police can stop and search only if they have 'reasonable grounds for suspicion'. If they do not have those grounds, then the search will be unlawful. What the code says is that:

Reasonable suspicion can never be supported on the basis of personal factors alone. For example, a person's colour, age, hairstyle or manner of dress, or the fact that he is known to have a previous conviction for possession of an unlawful article, cannot be used alone or in combination with each other as the sole basis on which to search that person. Nor may it be founded on the basis of stereotyped images of certain persons or groups as more likely to be committing offences.

The vital point is in deciding what are 'reasonable grounds' for suspicion, for the mere fact that the police officer does not find what he or she is looking for will not, of itself, mean that he or she did not have reasonable grounds for carrying out the search. The difficulty arises of how the citizen is to know whether the police officer has 'reasonable grounds'. For example, the police may have just received a report that someone looking like the citizen recently committed a theft in the vicinity. In those circumstances they might well be acting reasonably in searching him or her, but it puts the individual citizen in an impossible position.

Apart from this general power of stopping and searching, the police have additional powers that come into effect as soon as someone is arrested. A constable may search an arrested person on reasonable grounds that the person presents a danger to him- or herself or others or that the person may have concealed anything on him or her which might be used for escape or which might be evidence of an offence. Once at the police station, the police have further rights to search.

Following the implementation of the Anti-terrorism, Crime and Security Act 2001, persons detained in a police station may now be searched and examined to ascertain whether they have on them any mark that would tend to identify them as a person involved in the commission of an offence, or to facilitate the ascertainment of their identity. The police must have reasonable grounds for suspecting that the person is not who they claim to be.

Reasonable force can be used to search a person who has been arrested and is in the police station. It has to be by a person of the same sex and reasons must be given for the search. A strip search may occur only if the police consider that it is necessary. An intimate body search (of the anus, vagina, mouth, ear or nose) can occur only if authorized by a superintendent who has reasonable grounds that the suspect has concealed something which could cause injury or has concealed class A drugs (e.g. heroin or cocaine). Intimate searches must usually be carried out by a doctor or nurse.

TERRORISM ACT 2000

The Terrorism Act 2000 covers the whole of the UK and gives the police greater powers in terrorist cases. A police officer can arrest a person on suspicion that he or she is involved in the 'commission, preparation or instigation of acts of terrorism' connected with Northern Ireland, or any foreign country.

Once arrested the suspect can be detained for up to 48 hours and then for up to a further seven days with the consent of the Home Secretary. The police can take any 'reasonably necessary' steps to identify the suspect (e.g. photography, fingerprints and measurements). There is no absolute right to legal advice until after 48 hours and the right to have someone informed of your arrest can be delayed even beyond this period.

It is a criminal offence not to give the police specific information about people or events concerned with acts

of political violence, although this does not apply if the information would incriminate the suspect personally. This offence applies only to terrorism connected with Northern Ireland.

The Terrorism Act contains a broad definition of terrorism which includes a wide range of political or ideological crime. As a result this would cover road protesters or those intending to destroy genetically modified crops.

The Anti-terrorism, Crime and Security Act 2001, which was pushed through Parliament in the wake of the 11 September 2001 attacks on the United States, gives the Home Secretary the power to detain suspected terrorists without trial and indefinitely where their deportation is not possible.

Examination and detention at ports and airports

Under the Terrorism Act 2000, a person can be stopped, questioned and detained by examining officers (police, immigration or military) to find out whether they have any connection with, or information about, the use of violence in relation to Irish or international affairs. The examining officer can require the person to give their name, address, occupation, name of employer, purpose of their trip; search baggage and ask any reasonable questions. The officer can detain a person for up to 12 hours in the absence of any suspicion. As with Terrorism Act arrests elsewhere, reasonable suspicion allows detention for up to 48 hours and up to seven days with the authority of the Home Secretary.

The Terrorism Act also allows the Home Secretary to use an exclusion order to expel a person from either Great Britain or Northern Ireland, or from the whole of the UK.

ENTERING AND SEARCHING PROPERTY

The same basic rule applies as with the searching of a person, namely that the police have no general right of search. If they carry out an unauthorized search they will be trespassers, and so can be physically ejected and sued for damages.

But, as always, there are exceptions. The best-known exception is when the police obtain a search warrant. For a search warrant to be granted the police will have to show that the search is likely to uncover evidence which will be of substantial value in the investigation. The police will also have to explain why a warrant is necessary (e.g. the owner of the house cannot be contacted; the owner should not be given any advance warning, etc.). Unless the police can satisfy the court on all these points, then no search warrant should be granted. One point to note is that there must have been a 'serious' offence; the police cannot get a search warrant for a trivial offence.

Unfortunately, the police can now in many instances carry out a search without applying for a search warrant first, for instance to catch an escaped prisoner, to save life or prevent injury, to prevent serious property damage, to arrest a trespasser who has an offensive weapon, to prevent a breach of the peace (*see* page 630 for what this means).

Finally, the police also have a right to search the home (or other premises) of anyone who has committed an arrestable offence, to look for evidence. The police can also search the premises where the person was arrested or where the person was immediately before he or she was arrested, provided they have reasonable grounds for believing that they will find evidence relating to the offence. The search should not take place without written authorization from a police inspector, although there are exceptions to this rule.

Whenever the police carry out a search they should comply with the code of practice. For instance, this says:

Premises may be searched only to the extent necessary to achieve the object of the search . . . searches must be conducted with due consideration for the property and privacy of the occupier . . . and with no more disturbance than necessary . . . if the occupier wishes to ask a friend, neighbour or other person to witness the search then he must be allowed to do so, unless the officer in charge has reasonable grounds for believing that this would seriously hinder the investigation. A search need not be unreasonably delayed for this purpose.

This code, however, is not totally binding on the police. If they break it they cannot necessarily be sued, and – more important – the chances are that any evidence improperly obtained will still be usable against the suspect. Some evidence is subject to special safeguards and an order to search will be required from a crown court judge. This will include material subject to legal privilege – that is, generally, communications between lawyers and their clients, personal and confidential records held by third parties and confidential material held by journalists.

The police can use reasonable force to effect a lawful search. That means that if they are not invited in they can break in. Compensation will be available if the search was unlawful. The police must also, before leaving, be satisfied that the premises are secure either by arranging for the occupier to be present or by repairing any damage. A record must be made at the search and must include the statutory authority for the search, the names of the officers, a list of articles seized, whether force was used and a list of any damage caused. The Serious Fraud Office also has very wide powers to force individuals to provide information and documents for its investigations.

Police seizure of property

Generally, if the police carry out a lawful search (i.e. a search authorized by search warrant, written authority, etc.), then they can take anything they find which is material evidence or the fruit of a crime. This can be evidence of *any* crime, not just the crime for which the person has been arrested, or for which a search warrant was granted. The property can be kept for as long as is necessary for the police to complete their investigations. In practice, it seems that the police sometimes seize goods when they have no clear authority for doing so. When this happens the owner of the property can apply to the magistrates' court for an order to force the police to return the property. However, it is often better to take proceedings in the High Court or county court, particularly where the property is very valuable or the issues are complicated. Public funding may be available for proceedings in the High Court or county court but not for such applications in the magistrates' court.

IDENTIFICATION EVIDENCE

A suspect cannot be made to take part in an identification parade (ID parade). However, if he or she refuses the police may well arrange for him or her to be seen among a group of other people by the witness, in which case the witness may well make an identification. So it is generally advisable for a suspect to agree to an ID parade rather than allow an informal identification to take place. It is essential to take legal advice before agreeing to take part in an ID parade.

A suspect can insist upon an ID parade taking place in any case, unless it would be 'impracticable'. This means that if identification may be an issue at the trial, the defendant can insist on an ID parade.

A code of practice sets out the detailed rules on how an ID parade should be conducted. Perhaps its most important statement is that a 'suspect must be given a reasonable opportunity to have a solicitor or friends present'. The fundamental piece of advice for anyone asked to take part in an ID parade is to consult a solicitor as to whether they should agree, and also to arrange for the solicitor to be present.

The code also says that:
- the suspect should be given a leaflet setting out the suspect's rights;
- the witness should not be allowed a chance of seeing the suspect before the parade takes place;
- 'the parade shall consist of at least eight persons (in addition to the suspect) who so far as possible resemble the suspect in age, height, general appearance and position in life';
- one suspect only should be included in a parade unless

there are two suspects of roughly similar appearance, in which case they may be treated together with at least 12 other persons;

- 'the suspect may select his or her own position in the line';
- the line should be visited by only one witness at a time;
- the witness should be told that the suspect may, or may not, be in the line;
- if the witness asks to see members of the line moving, or to hear them talking, he or she should first be asked whether he or she can identify the suspect by appearance only; the witness should then be told that the members of the line were selected for their physical appearance only – not their similar voices;
- once the witness has left, the suspect should be told that he or she can change position in the line before the next witness inspects the line;
- at the end of the ID parade, the suspect can have his or her comments on the parade noted by the officer in charge.

If the guidelines are not followed, the trial judge may decide that the identification evidence obtained should be ignored. In effect, therefore, the position is the same as with a breach of any other code of practice.

In practice, it can often be difficult for a suspect to refuse to take part in an ID parade. The police will say that if he or she refuses, then they will confront the witness with him or her and ask the witness whether this is the correct person – which can be extremely risky from the suspect's point of view! Another practical problem can arise when, say, a young black person is held as a suspect, because the police might have great trouble in finding enough black youngsters to make up an ID parade. When this happens the suspect is often offered a 'group identification', as an alternative to an ID parade. For instance, the witness will wait beside the ticket barrier in a train station and the suspect will walk out of the station, mingling with other passengers. The code of practice sets out guidelines on how such group identifications are to be conducted, and any suspect who is offered one should seek the help of a solicitor, who can give practical help and ensure the procedures are followed correctly.

The code also lays down guidelines for when a witness is shown a selection of photographs:

- photo-identification should not be allowed if an ID parade can be arranged;
- the witness should be shown not less than 12 photos at a time;
- the photographs used should 'as far as possible all be a similar type' – for instance, a snapshot should not be included in a bundle of 'mug-style' criminal photographs;
- the witness should be told that the suspect's photo may or may not be included in the bundle;
- once a witness makes a firm identification by photo, he or she should then be asked to attend an ID parade and once one witness has made an identification, other witnesses should not be shown photographs but should take part in an identity parade instead.

Identification evidence in criminal trials

Identification evidence is notoriously unreliable. It has been shown on many occasions that people who positively identify a suspect are wrong because the suspect could not have been present at the time of the original sighting. The situation is made worse by the fact that the witness may be absolutely sure that they have identified the correct person.

There are therefore the following safeguards. Dock identifications can occur only in very rare cases and should always be resisted. This means that the witness cannot be asked if he or she sees in court the person he or she saw, unless they have previously picked out the suspect in an ID parade. Second, judges must remind jurors of the weaknesses and dangers of identification evidence. The judge should go through the identification evidence during the summing up, reminding the jury of any weaknesses in it.

86

The Criminal Law

Everyone knows what a 'crime' is. In the words of the *Oxford English Dictionary*, it is an 'act punishable by the law'. But people usually associate the word 'crime' with the more sensational or serious offences, such as murder, manslaughter and arson, and forget that such petty offences as careless driving, parking violations and leaving litter are also crimes. The only difference is in the severity of the punishment meted out to the offender.

The same principles of criminal justice apply to murderers as to shoplifters and others accused of comparatively trivial crimes. In the eyes of the law, a crime is a crime, however grave or trivial the offence may be.

PRINCIPLES OF CRIMINAL PROCEDURES

- The accused is presumed innocent until proved guilty;
- to prove guilt, the prosecution must show *beyond reasonable doubt* that he or she committed the offence. This means that if there is a reasonable doubt as to guilt, then there must be an acquittal (*cf.* the lighter standard of proof in civil cases, page 737);
- no one is under a duty to help the police with their inquiries, or to make a statement to them; further, this lack of co-operation cannot be held against them at the trial;
- a suspect can remain silent and it cannot be held against them (except in special circumstances);
- a defendant is tried on the facts of the case, not on the evidence of previous convictions; the court will not be told of any 'record', since that might create prejudice. Only if found guilty will 'form' be relevant, when it may influence the court's sentences; but the accused will forfeit the benefit of this rule if he or she falsely tells the court they are of good character, or if they attack the character of the prosecution witnesses;
- the trial is based on the oral evidence of witnesses; generally, written evidence is not allowed since there is no opportunity for its maker to be cross-examined.

It is allowed, however, when the contents of the written statement are not in dispute; also, the evidence of a witness must be of what he or she saw or heard and not hearsay (i.e. secondhand evidence). For instance, B cannot give evidence to say that A saw the defendant commit the crime. A has to come to court to give his or her own evidence;
- the accused is protected from trial by newspaper; the contempt of court rules prevent the papers from reporting anything other than the evidence given in the case; speculation by the press is prohibited;
- there are various protections that regulate the manner in which the police can detain and question a suspect (*see* page 630).

These safeguards are given to all people, whether they are murderers or litterbugs. The underlying principle is that it is better for some guilty people to go free than to take the risk of one innocent person being wrongly convicted. The principles are also designed to try to offset the inevitable imbalance of power between a prosecution taken by the state and the individual.

Criminal proceedings

There are two ways of bringing the suspect before the court: either by a summons or, alternatively, by arrest and charge (*see* the chart on page 641).

Issuing a summons

First, there is the *summons* to appear in court at a certain date and time. To obtain a summons, the police go before a magistrate and state where and when the accused committed the offence. This is called laying an information, and ordinarily must be done within six months of the offence. If the magistrate thinks there is a *prima facie* case (which is very likely because the suspect will never be present to contradict anything that the police might say), the summons will be issued commanding the accused to appear in court, usually at least one week afterwards. The police then serve the summons on the accused, usually by post.

Obviously, this procedure is used only in the less serious cases where there is no risk of the offender absconding. The accused person must attend the court on the dates given in the summons; if he or she does not, an arrest warrant can be issued. The only exception to the rule is when the summons states that the defendant can plead guilty by post, in which case there is no need to attend court in person (*see* page 647).

Arresting and charging

The second way of starting criminal proceedings is to arrest and charge the suspect. This is normally done in more serious cases, when a summons would be inappropriate. However, there are some occasions when an offence is not serious, but when a summons would not be suitable (e.g. the suspect's name and address may be false – in which case the police will want to be able to hold him or her while they check the details).

Unfortunately the police will often arrest and detain a person rather than using the summons procedure even though there is no real justification for this. However, the general rule remains that a summons is used for the less serious cases, whereas arrest and charging is used for the more serious cases. Arresting and charging are two different steps in the prosecution process. The suspect is arrested when the police take him or her into custody – in other words, by making it clear that the suspect has to go to the police station. The charging occurs in the police station: the custody officer reads out the formal description of the offence and hands the suspect a copy of the charge. It is thus a two-stage process – arresting, followed by charging at the police station (*see* page 629 for more on arrest powers).

TIME LIMITS ON CRIMINAL PROSECUTION

There are different rules for magistrates' court cases and for other cases.

Offences that can only be tried in the magistrates' court

These must generally be prosecuted within six months of the offence being committed. This means that the prosecutor must lay information before the magistrates and ask that a summons be issued within six months of the offence. However, there is no need for the summons to be served on the accused within the six-month period, or to be tried within that period. But, if the information is not laid within six months, the offender cannot be prosecuted for the offence.

However, with certain motoring offences the prosecution must be careful to give the accused notice of intended prosecution. This must be in the form of an oral warning at the time of the offence or a written warning (or summons) served within 14 days of the offence being committed (*see* page 578).

Note: The six-month rule in the magistrates' court is subject to a few minor exceptions, when statutes lay down longer or shorter periods.

Offences that can be tried in the magistrates' court or the crown court

These are not, generally, subject to any time limit. Thus a person can be charged with a serious offence that was committed many years ago, although often prosecutions will not be started if the time lag is substantial. However, there are a few offences that are subject to time periods.

Undue delay

In any case, if the delay before prosecution is considerable or caused by the prosecution, the court on the basis that it is an 'abuse of process' can stop the case. It will usually be necessary to show that the defendant has been prejudiced by the delay (i.e. the memory of witnesses has failed or an important witness has died).

Bringing a private prosecution

The vast majority of criminal prosecutions are brought by the Crown Prosecution Service (CPS) – in fact, about 99 per cent of the total. But the law allows private individuals to prosecute for most offences, for it has long been a principle of our laws that all citizens should have access to the criminal courts.

Most private prosecutions are started by the issuing of a summons in the magistrates' court (*see* page 645 for the procedure to be followed). Once a summons has been issued, the case will proceed in the normal manner for any magistrates' court case. The only difference would be that the private individual is prosecuting instead. Mischievous private prosecutions can be stopped in an indirect way. The Director of Public Prosecutions (DPP) has the power to take over the conduct of any criminal prosecution if he or she so chooses. Thus, if a private prosecution was thought to be against the public interest, the DPP might take over the case but then not present any prosecution evidence when it came to trial. The accused person, would, of course, have to be acquitted.

No one should embark on a private prosecution lightly. It is always preferable to get the CPS to prosecute. The private prosecutor should bear in mind that:

● if the case is lost he or she may have to pay the accused's legal costs;
● the prosecutor may be sued for damages if it can be

How Criminals are Taken to Court

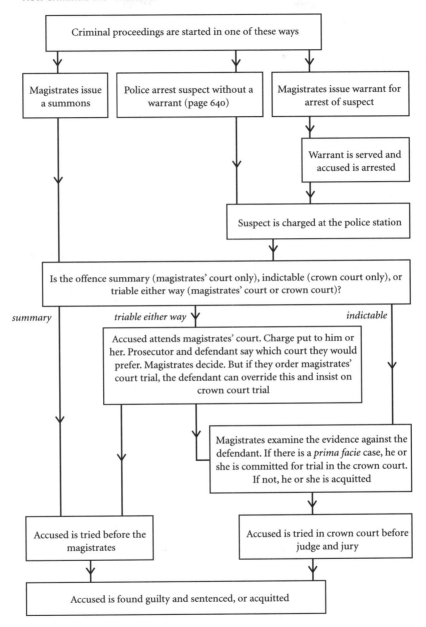

Criminal proceedings are started in one of these ways

Magistrates issue a summons

Police arrest suspect without a warrant (page 640)

Magistrates issue warrant for arrest of suspect

Warrant is served and accused is arrested

Suspect is charged at the police station

Is the offence summary (magistrates' court only), indictable (crown court only), or triable either way (magistrates' court or crown court)?

summary

triable either way

indictable

Accused attends magistrates' court. Charge put to him or her. Prosecutor and defendant say which court they would prefer. Magistrates decide. But if they order magistrates' court trial, the defendant can override this and insist on crown court trial

Magistrates examine the evidence against the defendant. If there is a *prima facie* case, he or she is committed for trial in the crown court. If not, he or she is acquitted

Accused is tried before the magistrates

Accused is tried in crown court before judge and jury

Accused is found guilty and sentenced, or acquitted

shown that he or she acted 'maliciously' in bringing the prosecution. In addition, if a citizen's arrest was made, a damages claim for false imprisonment could follow;

- even if the prosecutor wins, he or she is unlikely to recover all of the legal costs and expenses;
- often the accused will make counter-allegations against the prosecutor (e.g. in the typical dispute between two neighbours who are both making accusations against each other). When this happens, the magistrates frequently find it impossible to sort out who is in the right and who is in the wrong and it is common for the magistrates to bind over (*see* page 657) both the prosecutor and the accused;
- if the accused is able to opt for a crown court trial (*see* page 648) and does so, the private prosecutor will have to instruct a solicitor and barrister to act in the crown court. This could be very expensive.

Shoplifting

Shoplifting charges used to be brought by the individual shop owners (i.e. as private prosecutions) rather than by the authorities. However, these days most prosecutions are brought by the CPS. If, however, the shop owner is prosecuting, then the normal rules about private prosecutions will generally apply. That is, in the event of an unsuccessful prosecution, the shop could well face a damages claim for malicious prosecution and false imprisonment.

Bail

Once the accused has been arrested and charged, the question arises of whether he or she is to be released or held in custody – in legal terminology, *remanded on bail* or *remanded in custody*. If the prosecution was started by summons, the problem will not arise for the accused will not have been taken into custody; instead, they will simply have been told when they are to appear in court.

If the arrest was by warrant, the magistrate who issued it may have written on the back that the accused should have bail; if the warrant is 'backed for bail' in this way, the police have no choice but to release the accused after charge. If it is not backed for bail, then the police cannot release the accused on bail.

If the arrest was not by warrant it is for the police to take the initial decision whether to keep the person in custody until the next hearing of the court. Bail is granted entirely at their discretion and it is then called *police bail*. But if police bail is refused, the prisoner must be brought before a magistrate within 24 hours (48 hours at weekends and public holidays) and given a chance of asking the magistrate for bail. So when an accused person is arrested and charged, the power to hold them in custody is initially with the police.

Special rules apply to children and young people:

1. children under 14 years must be granted police bail unless charged with murder or manslaughter;
2. a young person between 14 and 17 years must be granted police bail unless a senior police officer believes that:
   (a) the young person should be detained in his or her own interest; or
   (b) the young person would not turn up in court if released; or
   (c) it would defeat the ends of justice to grant bail; or
   (d) the young person has committed murder, manslaughter or some other 'serious offence'.

Being detained in custody before charge

There are detailed rules on how long a suspect can be held in custody (*see* page 632).

Asking the magistrate for bail

Bail is very important. Keeping a person in custody before he or she has been convicted is a very serious step. It may result in the suspect losing his or her job and will have an inevitable effect on the accused's reputation.

Accordingly, the basic principle is that no one should be refused bail unnecessarily. Apart from the libertarian reasons for this, there are also practical (and financial) reasons for not putting remand prisoners into the already overcrowded prisons. The aim is that 'the number of persons remanded in custody should be kept to the minimum compatible with the interests of justice'. The Bail Act 1976 sets out the rules.

When deciding whether to grant bail, the magistrate will first look at the offence with which the accused is charged:

1. if the offence does not carry a possible prison sentence, bail should be refused only if the accused has previously been given bail and failed to turn up in court when required *and* the court now believes that it will happen again;
2. if the offence could carry a prison sentence, the magistrate need not grant bail if:
   (a) there are *substantial grounds* (i.e. more than mere suspicion) for believing he or she would abscond, commit an offence or obstruct the course of justice (e.g. 'get at' witnesses); or
   (b) there has been insufficient time since charging for the police to have collected information about his or her suitability for bail; or
   (c) he or she has previously jumped bail; or
   (d) if the case has been adjourned for a report to be prepared (such as a social, welfare, medical or probation report), then bail can be refused if it would be impracticable to make the inquiries or the report without the accused being kept in custody; or

(**e**) he or she should be kept in custody for his or her own protection.

In all other cases, the accused must be granted bail.

If bail is refused

The court must give its reasons for refusing bail, and a written note of these must be given to the defendant. The defendant will then go to prison but as a remand prisoner and will have special privileges not enjoyed by convicted prisoners (*see* page 663). The time spent as a remand prisoner will count as time served if he or she is subsequently convicted and sent to prison for the offence.

The remand in custody is normally for eight days at a time, and the prisoner will then come back before the magistrate. He or she will normally be remanded for a further eight days, and so on, until the case is ready for trial. However, the accused can opt to avoid these eight-day remands by agreeing to the remand being for a longer time: this will save the inconvenience of trips from prison to the court, and should not delay the trial in any way. The court can now also order remands every 28 days, provided the defendant is legally represented and at court when remanded for the longer period.

The court must consider the matter of bail on each occasion on which the defendant is remanded. However, a prisoner may only make two applications as of right. The first of those must be made on the defendant's first appearance at court. The second can be at any subsequent remand at which the defendant is present. Any further application must result from a change of circumstances.

A prisoner cannot make repeated applications for bail, unless there are new grounds. If there is a change of circumstances (e.g. someone who will stand surety; the defendant has fixed up a job) then a fresh application for bail can be made, but not otherwise. In practice, therefore, most prisoners see little point in insisting that they be re-remanded every eight days, and so they will often agree to being remanded for a longer time.

Appealing

If the magistrates refuse bail, then their decision can be appealed to the crown court. Legal aid (now referred to as public funding) will normally cover the legal costs.

A prisoner's friends and relatives will often urge the solicitor to appeal straight away, but this is not always wise. If the crown court judge upholds the magistrates' decision, it is unlikely that the magistrates will be persuaded to change their minds at a later date. So it might be much better to collect evidence that answers the magistrates' reasons for refusing bail and present this at the next hearing, rather than rush off and appeal to the crown court. It is also possible to appeal to a High Court judge but public funding is very rarely available. In cases punishable with a sentence of five years or more and taking a conveyance or aggravated vehicle taking the prosecution

have a right of appeal to the crown court. However this procedure can only be triggered if a notice is served on the person concerned within two hours of the bail hearing.

If bail is granted

The defendant will be given a written note of the court's decision and told when he or she should next appear in court. If the defendant does not turn up on that day but absconds, he or she will be guilty of an offence (maximum penalty three months' prison and/or £5,000 fine in a magistrates' court, 12 months' prison and an unlimited fine in the crown court). In addition, bail is unlikely to be granted again.

Often the bail will be granted subject to conditions. For instance, the defendant may have to surrender his or her passport, report to the police station once a day, agree to live in a certain place, agree not to go near a particular place, or deposit cash or valuables as security. The Bail Act states that 'no condition should be imposed unless it is necessary', but it seems clear that many magistrates impose conditions when they are not strictly necessary. When this happens, the accused should suggest to the magistrate that the conditions are unnecessary. The defendant can refuse to accept the conditions and, if remanded in custody, can apply to the crown court judge for bail to be granted free of conditions. Not surprisingly, few defendants are prepared to do this, and most simply accept the magistrate's conditions, however unreasonable they may be.

Often bail will be granted only if the defendant can find one or more sureties. A surety is a person who agrees to forfeit a fixed sum should the accused not turn up to court. The surety does not have to deposit any money with the police while the accused is on bail, for it is only if the accused fails to answer bail and the magistrates decide to enforce the surety's bond that he or she will have to produce the money. The amount at risk is called the 'recognizance'.

The surety will have to go either to the court or to the police station as the police will want to check that he or she is suitable. The Bail Act says that a surety's suitability will be based primarily on:

- financial resources (does he or she have the money to pay the recognizance if it should be enforced?);
- character and any criminal record;
- proximity (whether in terms of kinship, place of residence, or otherwise) to the person for whom he or she is to be surety.

The correct procedure is for the court to decide on the amount of recognizance required, bearing in mind the nature of the offence, the defendant's record and so on. The court should then consider the suitability of the sureties. The court should not decide that a large recognizance is needed simply because a particular surety is well off.

If the accused absconds and does not answer to bail, the surety may forfeit the sum due; this is called having the 'recognizance estreated'. The surety will have to appear before the magistrates and argue why the recognizance should not be forfeited. Forfeiture is not automatic, for the court will want to know the extent to which the surety was to blame for allowing the defendant to abscond.

Mrs Green stood surety for her husband, who was accused of importing cannabis. She told the court that her share of the family home was worth £3,000 and so she was accepted as surety for a recognizance of £3,000. Her husband later absconded. The magistrates ordered Mrs Green to forfeit the full £3,000, and she appealed against that decision. Held: The magistrates' decision would be overturned. They should have considered the extent to which Mrs Green was to blame for her husband defaulting. Moreover, magistrates should not accept a wife as a surety on the basis of matrimonial property. Since Mrs Green had done all she could to secure her husband's attendance, Lord Denning ordered that the recognizance should not be estreated. Green (1975)

However, that decision was very much a borderline case and subsequent decisions have made it clear that the 'blameworthiness' of the surety is not the only factor to be considered. Strictly speaking, if the surety has any doubts as to whether the accused will answer bail, he or she should take the accused to the police station and ask to be released from the surety. The police will then, of course, take the accused into custody until a suitable replacement surety can be found. In practice, magistrates are reluctant to allow sureties to be let off if the defendant absconds. Clearly, therefore, no one should stand surety unless they are sure that the accused will not abscond.

If the magistrates do insist that bail will be granted only subject to a surety, the defendant must be told why this is so, and then be given a written note of the reasons.

Young offenders

The law on bail for offenders under 17 years old has been through a series of changes. Most of those under 17 will continue to receive unconditional bail. But if conditions of bail are required, the court now has access to a wider range of possibilities. Apart from traditional conditions, electronic tagging is now available nationwide. For an electronic tag to be used:

- the young offender must be 12 or older;
- he must have been charged with, or convicted of, a violent or sexual offence, or an offence carrying 14 years or more in the case of an adult, or been charged with or convicted of an imprisonable offence which, together with other imprisonable offences, amounts to a recent history of repeatedly committing imprisonable offences while remanded on bail or to local authority accommodation;
- the youth offender team must have confirmed that the

physical arrangements can be made for that individual.

Bail with supervision and support, and bail with supervision and support and tagging are available. In 'street crime' areas, bail with intensive supervision and surveillance is available, including intensive supervision and surveillance with voice ID and tagging.

Legal aid

The vast majority of people who are prosecuted for the more serious criminal offences get legal aid – now referred to as public funding (*see* page 797 for the procedure). But public funding is not available for all criminal charges. Many magistrates take a fairly tough line and refuse to grant public funding unless the charge is serious. Anyone who is tried in the crown court can expect to receive public funding (assuming they pass the means test), and can also expect to receive public funding if up on a serious charge in the magistrates' court. If there is an element of dishonesty involved in the offence (e.g. theft, fraud, taking a car, etc.), then public funding will probably be granted. But someone charged with, say, drink-driving would not normally get public funding. If public funding is refused and the offence is one that could be tried in the crown court (*see* below), the refusal can be appealed to the Criminal Defence Service which has taken over the funding previously provided by the Legal Aid Board. For cases that can be heard only in the magistrates' court, there is no direct appeal, although a detailed letter from a solicitor about the case will sometimes result in public funding being granted. A refusal to grant public funding could be challenged by way of judicial review.

THE TRIAL OF THE CASE

Where will the case be tried?

What happens next will depend upon the type of offence, for this will determine whether the case is tried before the magistrates in a magistrates' court or before a judge and jury in the crown court. Magistrates hear the less serious cases – some 96 per cent of all criminal cases.

The offence will be:

- triable in the magistrates' court only (a *summary* offence); or
- triable in the crown court only (an *indictable* offence); or
- triable in the crown court or the magistrates' court (an offence *triable either way*).

All criminal cases start in the magistrates' court. If the offence is *summary*, then the trial will also take place in the magistrates' court. If it is *indictable*, the trial will take place in the crown court, but only after the magistrates have confirmed that there is the basis of a case against the accused and committed them for trial in the crown court.

With offences *triable either way*, the position is more complicated. The procedure now is for plea before venue, which in effect means that the accused is expected to indicate his plea. So that if he pleads guilty he can be dealt with more swiftly either in the magistrates' court or by way of committal for sentence in the crown court. If he indicates a not guilty plea he can then still proceed to elect trial in the crown court. Both the accused and the prosecutor can say which court they think should hear the case. The magistrates then say where they think the case should be tried. If that is in the magistrates' court, the next step is for the accused to be given the chance of overriding the magistrates' decision and insisting on the right to a jury trial in the crown court. With young offenders (i.e. under 17 years) different problems arise (*see* page 129 for youth court cases).

Opting for magistrates' court or crown court trial

If the defence is *triable either way* the defendant has to weigh up the pros and cons of trial in the magistrates' court and in the crown court. Note that at the time of writing, the government is currently considering proposals to restrict the defendant's choice as to mode of trial. If these proposals go ahead the decision as to where someone is tried will be made by the magistrates.

Advantages of trial in the magistrates' court

- *Speed* – if the plea is guilty then he or she can be sentenced more quickly. If the plea is not guilty, it can take just as long (or even longer) to get the case heard by magistrates as in the crown court. In all *either way* offences the accused is entitled to advance disclosure of the prosecution case and it is nearly always supplied on request in summary only, and in offence cases as well.
- *Cost* – it is cheaper to run a case in the magistrates' court. Many defendants obtain public funding and therefore cost is not a major factor, although if found guilty they are likely to pay a significantly larger contribution towards public funding costs in the crown court than in the magistrates' court.
- *Penalty* – generally, lighter penalties are imposed in the magistrates' court. But sometimes the magistrates commit the defendant to the crown court for sentencing in which case that advantage is lost.

Advantages of trial in the crown court

- *Acquittal* – the chances of being found not guilty are considerably higher in the crown court. Thus if the defendant has a lot to lose if convicted, he or she should always opt for crown court trial if it is available.
- *Evidence* – if evidence is to be challenged (i.e. the defendant challenges a confession alleged to have been made to the police), this can be dealt with properly only in the crown court. This is because the judge can decide on whether the jury should hear the evidence at all. In the magistrates' court, although it is possible to ask the magistrates to exclude evidence, they will have to hear it first before they do so and thus are very likely to be influenced even if they decide to exclude it. Also, in a crown court case the defence will be given all of the prosecution statements, not just a summary of the case, which may be all that is given if the case is tried in the magistrates' court.
- *Public funding* – there is much more chance of getting public funding if the case is to be tried in the crown court.

Trial in the magistrates' court

Whether the accused is being prosecuted by way of summons or by arrest and charge, the day will come when the case is listed for hearing in the court's daily case list – the list of cases to be tried on that day.

Generally the defendant must attend court on the date fixed for trial. The only exceptions are where he or she intends to plead *guilty* and:

- has been offered the choice to plead guilty by post and has done so (*see* page 647); or
- sends a solicitor or barrister to represent him or her in court and is going to plead guilty.

Otherwise, the court will usually issue an arrest warrant should the defendant not appear. Sometimes the case will simply be heard in the defendant's absence and he or she will be found guilty. However, this will normally be done only for a petty offence and when it is clear that the summons was properly served.

It may be that either the prosecution or the defence is not ready to proceed with the trial, perhaps because witnesses are not available or because the lawyers have not had sufficient time in which to investigate the case. If so, they may be able to persuade the magistrates to grant an adjournment and fix a new date for the trial.

The prosecution case will always be presented by a solicitor or barrister from the CPS. The police officer in charge of the case will have obtained full statements from all witnesses and will also have prepared a brief summary of the facts, setting out the main circumstances of the crime. This will have been served on the accused, usually with the summons. The CPS may not have given the defendant a copy of all the witness statements. Thus, he or she may not know all the evidence against them until it is revealed in the course of the trial as the prosecution witnesses give their evidence. This makes it extremely difficult for the defence to prepare its case in advance (cf. the position in the crown court, where the defence always

Trial in the Magistrates' Court

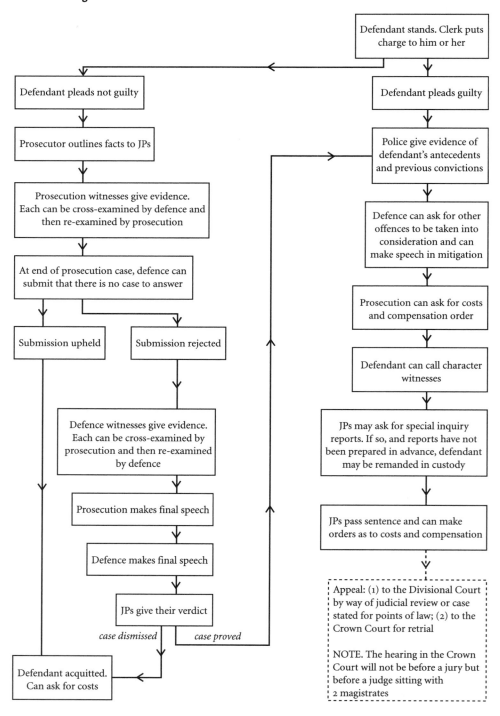

receives the prosecution statements before the trial begins). However, defendants facing *either way* offences are now given copies of the statements.

If the offence is at all serious, the accused will probably have taken legal advice, although he or she does not need to be represented by a lawyer and can act for themselves if they so wish.

The defendant may be tempted to plead 'guilty' just to 'get it all over and done with', but should avoid this temptation unless he or she really is guilty. Conversely, the case may be hopeless and the defendant may decide to plead 'not guilty' on the basis that he or she has nothing to lose. This is wrong, for there is something to lose. On conviction, the magistrates are unlikely to be sympathetic to a defendant who has wasted their time and that of the police and witnesses. In addition, the defendant may well be ordered to contribute to prosecution and witness costs – something that would probably have been avoided if he or she had pleaded guilty.

The procedure in the magistrates' court is fairly informal. In fact, the dictionary definition of 'summary' is a fair description of magistrates' court summary trials – 'brief, dispensing with needless details and formalities: done with dispatch'. Lawyers have long argued about the quality of trials in magistrates' courts, with many practitioners arguing that the magistrates are willing to accept police evidence, and that they are too overworked to be able to give each case the care and attention it deserves.

The case begins with the prosecution giving a brief explanation of the case to the magistrates. Prosecution witnesses are then called to give evidence, with the defence being able to cross-examine each of them. After all the prosecution witnesses have given their evidence, the defence can call its witnesses. They in turn can be cross-examined by the prosecution. At the completion of their evidence, the prosecution and the defence both make short speeches summarizing the reasons why the magistrates should return a verdict of guilty or not guilty.

The defendant does not have to call any witnesses and does not have to give evidence him- or herself. It is up to the prosecution to prove the case and therefore the defendant can sit back and let them try to do so. Obviously, in many cases it is important for the defendant to give evidence and to call witnesses who support his or her side of the case.

The magistrates then give their verdict. If they find the accused guilty, the CPS will read out any previous convictions recorded against the defendant. The defence can then make a speech in mitigation, arguing for a lighter sentence (*see* 'Sentencing offenders', page 653). It will probably be useful to produce evidence of the accused's employment prospects, earnings and family commitments; character witnesses can also be called. Before passing sentence, the magistrate may want a

medical or social inquiry report prepared; this is almost always true when the court is considering a custodial sentence for the first time or is dealing with a young offender. If so, the case will have to be adjourned for three or four weeks, if the report was not prepared in advance. Sentence will then be passed (*see* page 653). *See* the chart on page 646 for full details of the procedure.

Acquittal

If the verdict is not guilty, the defendant should ask for his or her legal costs to be paid. If the accused is publicly funded the defendant will never be entitled to a costs order as his or her costs will be paid by the Criminal Defence Service. A defendant's cost order should be made unless there are good reasons not to do so (e.g. the defendant's conduct). Unfortunately, this is rarely ordered unless the magistrates feel that the case against the defendant was so weak that it should never have been brought (*see* page 783). In no circumstances is the acquitted defendant entitled to any compensation for the strain of being accused of a criminal offence unless he or she can prove that the prosecution was malicious – to do so he or she will have to take separate proceedings.

Appeals

The prosecution cannot appeal if the accused is acquitted, unless the prosecution can argue that the magistrates got the law wrong. If the defendant is found guilty, an appeal against the conviction can occur only if the defendant pleaded 'not guilty' to the charge. The severity of the sentence can always be appealed, whether he or she pleaded guilty or not guilty. The appeal is to the crown court, and must be made within 21 days of the magistrates' decision. Special points of law may be appealed direct to the Divisional Court or the High Court (Queen's Bench Division) by either the prosecutor or the defendant.

Pleading guilty by post

The defendant may be given the opportunity to plead guilty by post if the charge against him or her is a summary offence that does not carry a maximum penalty of more than three months' imprisonment. Generally, the option of pleading guilty by post is offered only in the less serious motoring offences (e.g. careless driving). It is never possible to plead *not guilty* by post: to plead not guilty, you should appear in court in person. Also, it is not every defendant who can opt to plead guilty by post; it is for the prosecutor to decide whether to allow the defendant the choice to plead guilty by post. If this happens the sequence of events is:

1 the prosecutor serves on the accused:
   (a) a statement of facts, being a short summary of the facts of the case. This will form the basis of the evidence against the accused should he or she agree to plead guilty by post; and

(**b**) a notice explaining that the accused can plead guilty by post if he or she wants to but is not obliged to do so;

2 the defendant then decides whether he or she wishes to plead guilty by post. A letter must be sent to the court with the form attached to the notice of prosecution. In motoring cases, the driving licence will usually have to be sent. It is advisable for the defendant to reply well before the date fixed for the hearing, for otherwise he or she may have to pay the costs and expenses of witnesses who attend court unnecessarily. The defendant can withdraw the postal plea at any time before the trial of the case.

The defendant need not agree to plead guilty by post but instead can attend in person to plead either guilty or not guilty. It is not possible to plead not guilty by post;

3 if a postal plea is received, the court notifies the prosecutor;

4 when the case is tried, the clerk of the court will read to the magistrates the statement of facts and the defendant's plea in mitigation and details of his/her financial circumstances;

5 the magistrates then find the defendant guilty and consider the appropriate sentence. Usually the magistrates will pass sentence straight away, but sometimes they will adjourn the hearing so that the defendant can be present when sentenced. This will often be done if the magistrates feel they need more information, but it must be done if a severe sentence is to be imposed. The accused must be present in court if he or she is to be sentenced to:

(**a**) prison, detention centre or a suspended prison sentence; or

(**b**) disqualification. This is usually a disqualification from driving, but it also includes disqualification from owning an animal.

For instance, if the defendant pleads guilty by post to a charge of speeding, but already has 10 penalty points, the magistrates would then adjourn the hearing for up to four weeks so that a new date could be fixed when the defendant could attend court and argue why he or she should not lose their licence. If the accused does not appear at the new hearing date, a warrant may be issued.

Trial in the crown court

Nearly every case that is tried in the crown court must first pass through the magistrates' court. Cases involving violent or sexual offences against children will be dealt with slightly differently and the test of the sufficiency of evidence will be heard in the crown court at a pre-trial hearing. The magistrates will check that there is sufficient evidence against the accused to justify his or her being tried for the offence; if there is, they will commit him or her for trial in a crown court, but if there is not the case will be ended and the defendant discharged.

The committal proceedings

The committal proceedings are not a trial of the case by the magistrates. The magistrates' function is to see whether there is a *prima facie* case against the accused – in other words, to weed out the prosecutions that have no real chance of success. Thus, the purpose of the committal is to test the strength of the prosecution evidence and so, indirectly, to give the defendant a warning of the evidence that the prosecution will bring against him or her in the crown court trial. The defendant can waive their right to challenge the committal and accept that there is a *prima facie* case justifying committal. In many cases there will be sufficient evidence and the defendant will agree to the committal. The calling of live evidence at committal has been abolished.

When the defence agrees to the committal

The Criminal Justice Act 1967, clause 3, introduced a short form of committal for such cases. This allows the magistrates to commit the accused without having to consider the strength of the evidence. Thus the defendant voluntarily forgoes the examination of the evidence by the magistrates, but the court will let him or her do this only if all the defendants are legally represented at the committal hearing.

For the short form of committal to be available the prosecution must have previously served the defence with copies of all the statements made by relevant prosecution witnesses. The defence can then consider the strength of the prosecution evidence beforehand and so be able to decide whether there is the basis of a case against the accused. If there is, then they will almost certainly agree to a short-form committal. These days this is the usual form of committal, and it is called a 'Section 6(2)' since it derives from this section of the Magistrates' Courts Act 1980.

When the defence opposes the committal

If the defence does not believe that there is a *prima facie* case, a full committal can be held. This is done in the following way. The magistrates will consider only the written evidence (i.e. all of the prosecution statements previously taken from witnesses). This allows the magistrates to examine the prosecution evidence without the need for witnesses to attend court. This is called 'committal on the documents'.

Then the defence can submit that there is no case to answer. This is, of course, the sole issue before the magistrates. They are not considering whether the defendant is guilty or not, and if they commit for trial it will in no way be taken as an indication of guilt. Generally, it is for the defendant to decide on the type of committal

Committal Proceedings

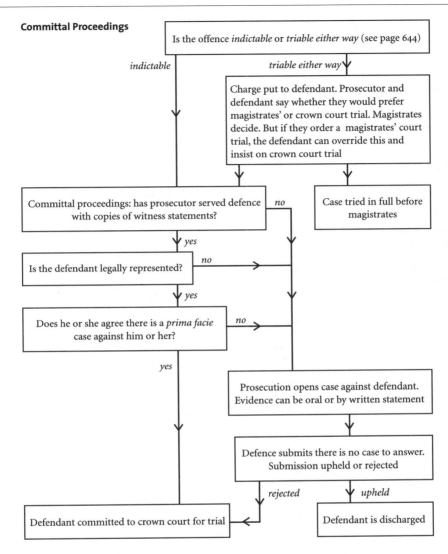

Is the offence *indictable* or *triable either way* (see page 644)

indictable

triable either way

Charge put to defendant. Prosecutor and defendant say whether they would prefer magistrates' or crown court trial. Magistrates decide. But if they order a magistrates' court trial, the defendant can override this and insist on crown court trial

Committal proceedings: has prosecutor served defence with copies of witness statements?   *no*

Case tried in full before magistrates

yes

Is the defendant legally represented?   *no*

yes

Does he or she agree there is a *prima facie* case against him or her?   *no*

yes

Prosecution opens case against defendant. Evidence can be oral or by written statement

Defence submits there is no case to answer. Submission upheld or rejected

rejected   *upheld*

Defendant committed to crown court for trial   Defendant is discharged

since the prosecution will only rarely demand a full, old-style committal.

Note also that to protect the defendant from adverse publicity which might affect the crown court trial, there are restrictions on what the press can report of the committal proceedings.

Bail after committal

After committal, if the magistrates refuse to grant the accused bail it is possible to appeal to the crown court (*see* page 643). Public funding is available for this appeal.

Delay in coming to trial

Unfortunately, there is often a considerable time-lag between the magistrates' court committal and the trial in the crown court. During this time the memories of the witnesses will start to fade, and the defendants will have the worry of the case hanging over them whether or not they are held in custody.

Preparing for trial

After the committal from the magistrates' court the accused will probably be granted public funding (virtually no applications are turned down), which will cover the greater part – if not all – of the legal costs (*see*

'Criminal legal aid', page 796). The solicitor will go through the prosecution statements and prepare the defence accordingly.

In all cases the prosecution have to prepare a bundle of unused material or a schedule stating what is unused which is called 'primary disclosure'. The defence (not in the magistrates' court) then have to prepare a defence case statement setting out the general nature of the defence and what aspects of the prosecution case are challenged or not accepted. Then the prosecution has to consider whether there is any secondary disclosure of material that they hold that is relevant to the defence case. Many criminal cases involve extensive evidence-gathering operations by the defence to get round what may be considered to be inadequate disclosure by the prosecution.

Note that the defence does not have to disclose any of its evidence to the prosecution unless there is an alibi defence or expert evidence is to be given. In the former case the prosecution must be given advance warning. This is supposedly to stop the defendant concocting a false alibi and then springing it on the prosecution during the crown court trial, when it would be too late for the police to obtain evidence to refute it. Accordingly, if the defendant intends to rely on an alibi he or she must give details of it to the prosecution within seven days of their committal by the magistrates (although this period can often be extended). Where the defence wishes to use expert evidence at the trial, the expert's report must be served in advance at the trial.

The accused's solicitor will instruct counsel (i.e. a barrister) to appear at the crown court hearing since, at present, only barristers or solicitors with higher audience rights are allowed to do the court work. If the case raises any difficult points the solicitor may well have a conference (i.e. a meeting) with counsel, probably with the accused also present.

There will normally be little warning before the case comes up for hearing; cases come on in turn and not by pre-arranged appointments. Thus the defendant and his or her lawyers may be told of the trial only a few days before it is due to start, and so have to arrange for all their witnesses to come to court at short notice. Frequently, the barrister instructed by the solicitor will be engaged in another case and so be unable to represent the accused at the trial: if so, the brief (i.e. the barrister's bundle of papers) will have to be passed on to another barrister, who will have no knowledge of the case and have only a short time in which to familiarize him- or herself with it.

Fraud cases

Serious fraud cases are dealt with slightly differently. The Criminal Justice Act of 1987 set up a Serious Fraud Office (SFO) to investigate offences. The SFO has considerable investigatory powers, including a requirement to force any person to attend and answer questions. The Fraud Investigation Group, part of the CPS, has a similar function and powers.

Where a fraud case is particularly serious or complex, the case will be transferred by the SFO from the magistrates' court to the crown court without the need for committal proceedings. The defendant will be served with the prosecution evidence in the normal way and can apply to the crown court to dismiss the case on the basis of insufficiency of evidence. If the defendant wishes to call oral evidence as a part of such an application, the consent of the judge will be necessary. These transfer proceedings, however, can be set aside if the defendant feels he or she has been treated unfairly.

THE TRIAL

To start the trial

When the day of the trial arrives the accused will be brought before the judge and the charge will be read out in the form of an indictment. It is possible that this will contain additional charges that have been added since committal, but the indictment should have been sent to the defence before the trial. Should the defendant be charged with any offences triable only in the magistrates' court but arising out of the same incident, they also may be included in the indictment so all the charges can be dealt with together.

The accused then pleads to the charge – either guilty or not guilty. If the plea is not guilty a jury will be sworn comprising 12 members. Once each juror has taken the oath, it is no longer possible to challenge the jury except where the defendant believes a particular juror is unlikely to try the case impartially (e.g. because he or she is a friend of the victim).

Prosecution case

The prosecution barrister opens the case by outlining the facts to the jury. Once he or she has done this, he or she then calls the prosecution witnesses. Each witness gives his or her evidence in the form of answers to questions put to them by the barrister. Once they have given their evidence they will usually be cross-examined by the defence. During examination, any evidence which is in dispute must be put to the witness so that they can give their own version of the facts and accept or refute any statements put to them. These days nearly all interviews with suspects take the form of tape-recorded interviews. Rather than play tapes of the interviews in court, it is often quicker to read through a transcript. The prosecuting barrister plays the part of the defendant and the interviewing police officer plays himself. Any points of law concerning the admissibility of evidence are usually dealt with as they arise and always in the absence of the jury. Once the jury has left the court, both barristers argue for/against the inclusion of the particular piece of evidence. The judge then rules on that point. Such a hearing is known as a *voir dire*, 'trial within a trial'. It is always preferable to avoid these when possible and, instead, the barristers can reach agreement between themselves before the trial starts.

Once the prosecution has concluded its evidence, the defence may wish to make a submission of 'no case to answer' on the basis that, after hearing all the prosecution evidence, no reasonable jury could go on to convict the defendant. The purpose of this is to prevent the jury from coming to a perverse decision at the end of the case and to save court time (currently valued at £2,600 per day). If the submission is successful, a formal verdict of not guilty is returned without the defence calling any evidence.

Defence case

If the 'no case' submission is unsuccessful or one is not made, then the defence will present its case. The defendant is under no obligation to give evidence but should he or she choose to do so, then they will be called first and any other witnesses follow the procedure of examination, cross-examination and re-examination – the same as for the prosecution witnesses. Note that with the abolition of the so-called right of silence the judge can invite the jury to draw an 'adverse inference' from the defendant's failure to give evidence if the jury think it appropriate.

It is worth mentioning that, as a general rule, the defence does not need to prove all parts of the alleged defence *beyond reasonable doubt*. Should the prosecution manage to do this, it would be very unwise for the defence not to call any evidence to refute the prosecution case. Any evidence the defence does call, however, needs only to create a reasonable doubt in the minds of the jurors. The defence does not have to prove anything beyond that. This principle should be explained to the jury several times during the course of the trial.

Speeches and the summing-up

Once all the evidence has been heard the barristers then go on to make their closing speeches. The defence always goes on to make its speech after the prosecution. However, in very short trials, the prosecution makes no speech at all.

The judge then sums up the case to the jury. First, he or she will summarize the evidence – any comments he or she may make at this stage are merely there to help and guide the jury, and can be adopted or dismissed as the jury wishes. The second part of the summing-up concerns the law and on this the jury must take the judge at his or her word. As far as they are concerned, he or she is the final arbiter on all legal matters.

The jury's verdict

After the judge has finished his or her summing-up, the jury retires to consider its verdict, preferably a unanimous one. If they have not all agreed on a verdict within two hours, the judge may – if he or she wishes – call them into court and tell them that he or she will accept a majority decision of the jury. The jury then retire again to see if they can now reach a verdict. But if they still cannot reach a verdict, they will have to sit on until the judge agrees that no decision can be reached. When that happens the hung jury is discharged and a new trial is ordered.

The verdict

If the defendant is acquitted, he or she will be freed and that will be the end of the case. The prosecution cannot appeal. Surprisingly though, the accused will not receive any compensation for the worry, strain, inconvenience and loss suffered, even if he or she has been kept in prison for several months. Only if it can be shown that the police acted 'maliciously' in prosecuting could the defendant sue them for damages – and usually the chances of proving 'malice' are difficult. However, the defendant will probably be awarded costs (i.e. legal expenses; *see* page 783).

If the defendant is convicted (i.e. found guilty), the judge will ask the police what is known about the prisoner. This is a request for details of the prisoner's criminal record. The prisoner's barrister will then make a speech in mitigation, asking for a lenient sentence. At this stage, the judge may well adjourn the case so that a medical or social inquiry report can be prepared on the prisoner. Often this will have been prepared in advance, but if not, the hearing will be adjourned, probably for two weeks or so. The defendant may be released on bail during this time but it is more usual to be remanded in custody since it will be 'administratively' more convenient to prepare the report if in prison.

The report will be of vital importance. The judge will pay great attention to it when deciding on sentence. It is, therefore, surprising that a copy of the report is usually not given to the defence before the trial, even when it is known that the accused intends to plead guilty. Moreover, it is usually the case that the social worker who wrote the report is not in court to be cross-examined on the conclusions, prior to sentencing.

Appealing

The defendant can appeal to the Court of Appeal, Criminal Division, against the severity of the sentence, the decision of the jury or on a point of law. The prosecution can appeal to the Court of Appeal if they believe that the sentence was 'unduly lenient'. The prosecution can also apply to the Court of Appeal to clarify a point of law that has arisen in the case, but this will not affect the acquittal of the defendant.

JURIES

Eligibility to serve

Anyone between the ages of 18 and 70 years and who is on the electoral register is liable to jury service. In addition, the person must have lived in the UK for a continuous period of five years since the age of 13 years; this condition is aimed at weeding out those people who do not have a proper understanding of the English language. But certain groups of people may be excused from serving, or may be unable to serve.

Ineligible people

Judges, JPs, solicitors, barristers, police officers, the clergy, legal executives, prison officers, prison governors, probation officers and members of boards of prison visitors are among those whose jobs make them ineligible for jury service. The person remains ineligible for 10 years after leaving the job, except for ex-judges and JPs, who remain ineligible for life.

Disqualified people

Anyone who has been sentenced to prison (or detention centre, youth custody, community service or a suspended sentence) within the last 10 years is disqualified from jury service. So, too, is anyone put on probation within the last five years. Also, a person sentenced to more than five years in prison is disqualified for life.

Excused people

Peers, MPs, members of the armed forces, doctors, dentists, nurses, midwives, chemists and vets can apply to be excused from jury service if they wish. So can a person who has sat on a jury (excluding a coroner's jury) within the last two years.

Being called for service

Usually about six weeks' notice is given. A person who is ineligible or disqualified should notify the court office. He or she must do this, for if they sit on the jury they will be committing a criminal offence. The summoning officer can excuse a person from jury service if there is 'good reason' for doing so. However, mere inconvenience will not be sufficient and the officer will want to be satisfied that severe inconvenience or great hardship would be caused. Good reasons would generally include holiday arrangements, exams, an illness in the family, pregnancy or a business that would otherwise have to close down. If the officer refuses to excuse the juror, application can be made to the High Court for the jury summons to be set aside. If the juror is excused service, it is likely to be only a temporary reprieve.

A person who fails to comply with a jury summons can be fined. The mere fact that an employer will not release a juror from work is not a defence; however, the employer might well be punished for contempt of court.

On the date stated in the jury summons, the juror should attend court. He or she will form part of the jury panel, i.e. all the prospective jurors. The jury for a case is selected by ballot, and once the twelve jurors needed for a jury have been selected, they take the juror's oath, in turn. Once the oath has been taken the juror cannot be challenged, but at any time before then either the defence or the prosecution can challenge the juror. Any challenges must be justified to the judge. The prosecution can also challenge jurors by asking them to 'stand by for the Crown', which means that the juror goes back to the jury panel and will have to serve only if there are insufficient people in the panel to make up a jury. Like the defence, the prosecution is also able to challenge 'for cause'.

Although a jury is normally composed of 12 jurors, it can be made up of fewer. At the start of the case there must be 12 jurors, but the trial can continue as long as there are nine jurors. So up to three jurors can fall ill or be released.

The judge has power to release a juror during the course of the trial if it would not interfere with the administration of justice to do so. This favour is only exercised occasionally; for instance, if a juror faces a domestic crisis or falls ill. However, it can also be exercised to allow a juror to go on holiday.

A juror was called for jury service on 16 July and was told that she would probably not be needed after 30 July. Her first case, on 16 July, was a theft offence, and the trial was expected to last only three or four days. But it had still not finished on 30 July. The juror told the judge that she had arranged to go on a camping holiday in Somerset with her family on the next day. She asked to be discharged and the judge agreed. The trial continued with 11 jurors. The defendant was convicted and appealed to the Court of Appeal, arguing that there had been an irregularity in the trial, i.e. the releasing of the juror. Held: No. 'Those summonsed to serve as jurors are entitled to such consideration as it is within the power of the courts to give them. If the administration of justice can be carried on without inconveniencing jurors unduly it should be. Discharging a juror whose holiday arrangements would be interfered with by having to stay on the jury after being sworn no longer hinders the administration of justice: trials can go on as long as there are nine jurors. Anyway, an aggrieved and inconvenienced juror is not likely to be a good one.'

Hambery (1977)

The finances of jury service

Compensation is fairly limited. It is made up of three different elements.

Daily travelling allowance

For car, motor-cycle and pedal cycle users, a specified rate per mile (but parking fees may not be recoverable) may be claimed by serving jurors. If you use the bus or train, you can claim the second-class return fare.

Subsistence allowance

In addition to the daily travelling allowance, jurors may also claim subsistence allowance.

If absent from home:
- for up to 5 hours   £2.22
- 5–10 hours   £4.51
- over 10 hours   £9.86
- overnight (Inner London within a five-mile radius of Charing Cross)   £72.58
- overnight (elsewhere)   £66.91

Financial loss allowance

The actual net loss (i.e. after tax, etc.) up to a maximum of £52.63 per day (or £26.32 if absent four hours or less). After 10 days, up to £105.28 can be paid (January 2003 figures).

The importance of jury service

As Lord Devlin said:

Each jury is a little Parliament. The jury sense is the parliamentary sense. I cannot see one dying and the other surviving. The first object of any tyrant in Whitehall would be to make Parliament utterly subservient to his will; and the next to overthrow or diminish trial by jury, for no tyrant could afford to leave a subject's freedom in the hands of his countrymen. So that trial by jury is more than one wheel of the constitution; it is the lamp that shows that freedom lives.

SENTENCING OFFENDERS

The punishment of offenders has four main aims:
1 to deter the offender and others from committing crimes;
2 to prevent further crimes (e.g. by taking away a person's driving licence);
3 to exact retribution for society;
4 to reform the offender via rehabilitation and training.

Making a speech in mitigation

Before a convicted person is sentenced he or she (or their lawyer) can make a speech in mitigation to the court. The purpose of mitigation is to persuade the court to impose a lighter sentence than it might otherwise have done. It is not an occasion for the defendant to repeat 'I didn't do it'; it is too late to argue about guilt, for the only matter to be decided is the sentence.

There are two elementary rules of mitigation:
1 do not say too much;
2 do not call too many character witnesses. Usually one will suffice. But make sure that the character witness is unrelated; for instance, the mother of the accused is hardly likely to be viewed by the court as an impartial observer.

Prison

Most offences have a fixed maximum prison sentence, but usually the offender will receive less than the maximum period.

Generally, a magistrates' court cannot impose a sentence of more than six months per offence, although the magistrates can sometimes get around this by committing the prisoner to the crown court for sentence in the hope that the judge will pass a longer sentence. If the accused is being sentenced for several offences, the maximum magistrates' court prison term is a total of 12 months.

If a prisoner is sentenced to prison for several offences at the same trial, the judge will say whether the sentences are to run *concurrently* or *consecutively*. This is best explained by an example: if a prisoner receives two sentences of one year each, he or she will serve only one year if the sentences run concurrently, but will serve two years if the sentences are to be consecutive. Most prison sentences are concurrent.

Prison should be seen as the last resort when sentencing an offender, partly because prison is not generally regarded as a reforming influence and also, of course, the cost of keeping someone in our crowded prisons is very high. Accordingly, there are many rules that limit the powers of the courts to send offenders to prison. Nevertheless, our prison population remains very high and our prisons are overcrowded.

First-time imprisonment

This cannot be imposed unless the accused is legally represented (unless he or she did not bother to apply for public funding or was rejected on financial grounds) and, in addition, the court feels that no other sentence would be appropriate. If the court feels that only prison would be appropriate, it must say why. Usually it will be because of the gravity of the offence or because of the defendant's previous record. Normally, first-time prison cannot be imposed.

An alternative to sending someone to prison is for the magistrates to have him or her held in the police cells (i.e. not in prison) for up to four days. It amounts to a short, sharp shock, and some magistrates have started to use this tactic as a weapon against drink-drivers who, apart from losing their licences, are given four days in the police cells.

Suspended sentence

Rather than send the offender to prison, the judge may sentence him or her to prison but say that the sentence will not come into effect if he or she behaves well for a fixed period of between one and two years. This option of suspending the prison sentence is only available if the sentence is for no more than two years. In order that the offender does not seem to go unpunished, a suspended sentence should usually go hand in hand with an order for compensation or a fine. If the offender commits another imprisonable offence during the fixed period, the court may bring the suspended sentence into effect and send him or her to prison.

If the prison sentence is for six months or less (as any magistrates' court prison sentence must be), the judge may suspend the sentence unless one of several exceptions applies. The most important exceptions cover crimes of violence and criminals who have previously received prison or borstal sentences; the net effect is that most first-time offenders in the magistrates' court do not go to prison.

Offenders under 21 years cannot receive a suspended sentence. The basic rule with any suspended sentence is that if the offender commits another imprisonable offence within the one-to-two-year period, he or she will go to prison for the original offence. However, this will not always be so, for the court:

- *cannot* activate the suspended sentence if he or she receives an absolute discharge, conditional discharge or probation for the subsequent offence;
- *need not* activate the suspended sentence if it would be 'unjust' to do so. Thus the court has a wide discretion, and often this will be exercised in the offender's favour if the subsequent offence is of a different type and nature from the first offence, or if the court does not

feel that the subsequent offence by itself justifies a term in prison.

Early release

Since October 1992 parole, for sentences of less than four years, and remission have been abolished but prisoners will continue to be entitled to early release. The new rules provide for a higher proportion of prisoners to be supervised on release and the rules attempt to restore meaning to the sentence imposed by the court. All offenders are now at risk of being recalled right up to the end of the sentence should they commit a further imprisonable offence. Rules vary according to the length of sentence and are as follows:

- *under 12 months* – automatic unconditional release. Generally, any time spent 'on remand' will still count in full towards a prisoner's early release date. The system is the same for young offenders, except that if they are under 22 years at the time of release they must be supervised for at least three months by the probation services. Prisoners are automatically released after serving half their sentence. They are not released on licence and do not need to be supervised, but they are liable to have the remaining part of their sentence reactivated if they re-offend before it expires (in addition to the sentence for the new offence);
- *more than 12 months and under four years* – automatic conditional release. These prisoners are released automatically on licence at the half-way point of their sentence. The release date can be delayed only by 'additional days' being imposed for breaches of prison discipline. The release is subject to licence conditions and will be supervised by the Probation Service up to the three-quarters point. The prisoner is liable to recall or fine if the conditions are breached. Any such breaches will be dealt with in the magistrates' court;
- *four years or more* – discretionary conditional release. Prisoners will become eligible for parole between the half-way and two-thirds points of the sentence. Should the prisoner be refused parole, he or she will be automatically released on licence at the two-thirds point of the sentence. They will be subject to licence conditions and supervised up to the three-quarters point, and liable to recall if the licence conditions are breached. The unexpired portion of the sentence can be reactivated if they re-offend between the three-quarters and full-term points.

There are separate rules which can apply to people convicted of sexual offences which can result in their having to serve the whole of their sentence if parole is not granted.

Generally, any time spent 'on remand' will still count

in full towards a prisoner's parole eligibility date. The system is the same for young offenders, except that if they are under 22 years at the time of release they must be supervised for at least three months by the probation services.

Life sentences

Different rules apply to prisoners who receive life sentences. Although life sentences are mandatory for murder, they can be given by a judge in other cases (e.g. rape, buggery, arson, attempted murder and manslaughter). A mandatory life-sentence prisoner – that is, one given a life sentence after a conviction for murder – has less-clearly defined rights than a discretionary life-sentence prisoner. For both kinds of life sentence, the judge will indicate the tariff – that is, the minimum number of years that the person should serve for the purposes of punishment. After that period has ended the person should be kept in custody only if they remain a danger to the public. In mandatory cases the decision to release them will be made by the Home Secretary following a recommendation by the Parole Board. The decision will be made in secret. However, in discretionary cases since October 1992, the review is carried out by a tribunal of the Parole Board, and the prisoner is entitled to see the reports written about him or her, attend the tribunal and be represented by lawyers with legal aid if necessary.

In May 2002, the Lord Chief Justice laid down minimum terms for life sentences. For less serious cases, a minimum term of 12 years must be served before referral to the Parole Board. In more serious cases, the minimum term before referral is 16 years. The presence of both aggravating and mitigating factors can vary these starting points both upwards and downwards.

Non-custodial sentences

These are now known as community sentences. Such a sentence will comprise one or more community orders, which are:
1 probation order;
2 community service order;
3 combination order;
4 curfew order;
5 supervision order;
6 attendance centre order.

These sentences are no longer treated as alternatives to custodial sentences but fall somewhere between custodial sentences and financial penalties. They form part of a structure of available sentences, so that each order or a combination of different ones can be used to make the punishment more appropriate to the offence and offender. Pre-sentence reports prepared by the probation services will usually be required before these sentences can be imposed and are sometimes mandatory.

Probation order

Probation can be for up to three years. But if the offender is over 16 years old, he or she cannot be put on probation unless he or she agrees. Sometimes conditions are imposed, such as residence in an approved hostel, or that the offender will keep in touch with the probation officer as required by the officer, or attend a probation centre, or undergo treatment for medical conditions, drug or alcohol dependency.

If the offender commits further offences while on probation, the court can impose a fresh punishment for the original offence. Similarly, if the offender does not comply with the terms of the probation order (e.g. does not attend appointments with the probation officer) he or she can be resentenced for the offence. Alternatively, the court might leave the probation order in force and impose a fine (up to £400).

Probation is a sentence in its own right. The qualifying age becomes 16 rather than 17 years.

Community service order (unpaid work to benefit the community)

This is no longer given instead of prison, but should be used in circumstances where restriction on a person's liberty is appropriate. The court will impose a sentence of between 40 and 240 hours, to be served within 12 months. The offender cannot insist on being able to do community service. It is available only when offered by the court, and after a pre-sentence report has recommended him/her for it. It is available only to offenders aged 16 years and over.

If the offender does not carry out the terms of the community service order, the court can impose a fresh sentence for the offence, including a fine or custody. Alternatively, they can order him or her to persevere with the order.

Combination order

This is essentially a mix of probation and community service. The purpose is both to punish the offender and to provide help and guidance to lessen the likelihood of re-offending. The probation part of the sentence must be for not less than 12 months, and not more than three years; and the community service part not less than 40 and not more than 100 hours. This order can also be combined with other community orders or with financial penalties.

Curfew order

Another sentence available to the court is the power to impose a curfew on offenders of 16 years or over. A pre-sentence report must be obtained and considered before such a sentence is passed. The maximum duration of an order is six months and the period of curfew is between two and 12 hours. These orders can be used in consultation with community orders and financial penalties. These orders may, when necessary, incorporate the use of electronic monitoring.

Supervision order

The order places a child under the supervision of a probation officer or social worker to advise, befriend and assess the child for an initial period of one year (which may be extended to three if appropriate). It can be imposed on those of 17 years and younger. Various requirements can be inserted into the order (e.g. residence, residential courses or merely to attend school regularly).

Attendance centre order

Its purpose is to impose a loss of leisure time on young offenders by ordering that they attend a centre for two or three hours on alternate Saturdays and, in that time, teach them the constructive use of leisure. Such an order can be imposed on anyone between 10 and 21 years with a maximum of 21 hours for anyone up to the age of 15 years, and 36 hours for those between 16 and 21 years.

Breach of community orders may result in:

- £1,000 fine;
- 60 hours (provided total does not exceed 240 hours);
- court may revoke order and deal with him or her for original offence;
- if offender is under 21 years, the court may impose an attendance centre order.

Financial penalties

In practice, this is by far the most important form of sentence, since 80 per cent of magistrates' court sentences are fines. The means of an offender will affect the amount of a fine but it should not influence the decision of whether or not to fine him/her.

Unit fine system

The power of the magistrates' court to impose fines is controlled by statute. Therefore, each offence punishable by the magistrates has a statutory maximum fine. The overall maximum is £5,000. The court must fix a fine which reflects the circumstances of the case but in so doing must take into account the offender's means, whether or not this has the effect of increasing or reducing the amount of the fine. Thus seriousness may be a combination of the elements of the offence (and any previous convictions and any mitigating circumstances) and the wealth of the offender. This formulation is a compromise between the traditional sentencing principles and the unit fine principle, which was largely abolished in 1995.

Maximum penalties

Each offence has a statutory maximum fine.

Level 1	Maximum £200
Level 2	Maximum £500
Level 3	Maximum £1,000
Level 4	Maximum £2,500
Level 5	Maximum £5,000

Offences triable either way (triable in both the magistrates' and crown court) are the more serious classes of offence and so are almost always Level 5, whereas less serious offences, such as street trading without a certificate, are Level 1.

The calculation of the offender's disposable income will be in accordance with rules made by the Lord Chancellor.

Enforcement

Usually if offenders are in a position of financial hardship, they will be given time to pay, generally in instalments. If the instalments are not kept up, the court is likely, on application, to allow further time in which to pay. Another alternative is to place offenders under the care of a probation officer who can encourage them to sort out their financial affairs.

A further alternative is an attachment of earnings order which can be made when the defaulter has steady long-term employment. Payments are deducted straight from the defaulter's income by the employer. The amount is set by the court. The court will also set a 'protected earnings rate' which ensures the defaulter's take-home pay never falls below a certain amount as a result of the fine (e.g. no payment towards the fine will be made if the person is sick and does not collect a full week's wages).

If all else fails, however, the defaulter who does not pay his or her fine can be, and often is, sent to prison. The sentence maxima are as follows:

Not more than 2 units – 7 days
More than 2 but not more than 5 units – 14 days
More than 5 but not more than 10 units – 28 days
More than 10 but not more than 25 units – 45 days
More than 25 but not more than 50 units – 3 months

Committal to custody for non-payment of fines will be imposed only when the court finds that there has been a wilful refusal to pay or culpable neglect.

The court can also impose a committal for a set number of days, and then suspend it on certain terms (e.g. on the payment of regular instalments). If the fine defaulter does not make regular payments, then he or she can be arrested and imprisoned without further notice. However, the defaulter is often brought back before the court to say why they should not be imprisoned. If the defaulter is having difficulty making payments, it is therefore very important that he or she apply to the court to vary the terms (e.g. the amount or frequency of payments) of the suspended committal.

For unpaid fixed-penalty fines (e.g. speeding, parking offences) and other small fines, the court may issue a distress warrant. This means that bailiffs will be sent to collect the money. This automatically increases the amount payable as the defaulter must pay both the fine and the bailiffs' costs.

Conditional discharge

If probation would be inappropriate, the offender may receive a conditional discharge instead. The conviction will stand but he or she will be released without punishment for a period of up to three years. If, during that time, he or she commits any other offences then they may be brought back and given a sentence for the original offence. This may or may not be prison.

Absolute discharge

Although the offender has been convicted of the crime, the court may feel that it would be wrong to punish him or her. If so, they may receive an absolute discharge. For example, the driver of a fire engine might pass through red lights on the way to an emergency call. Technically, he is guilty of an offence, for the law does not allow drivers of emergency vehicles to drive with any less care than ordinary road users (*see* page 571). But the court may feel that the police should have turned a 'blind eye' to the offence, or perhaps merely cautioned the driver, rather than prosecuted him. If so, the court might give the driver an absolute discharge.

Deferred sentence

The court may decide to postpone sentencing for up to six months. But this can be done only so that the court can take into account:

- conduct after conviction (e.g. making reparation for the offence); or
- any change in circumstances (e.g. more settled home life or a new job).

A sentence can be deferred only once and it cannot be deferred for successive periods of up to six months.

Binding over

Strictly speaking, an order that a person can be 'bound over to keep the peace' is not really a sentence at all. It is more in the way of preventive justice, for it allows the magistrates to warn citizens as to their future good conduct. If the person fails to keep the peace or to be of good behaviour during a stated period (up to twelve months) he or she may forfeit a sum of money. This sum is called a recognizance. Thus, a typical order would be to be 'bound over for nine months in the sum of £50'.

Before the binding-over order is made, the court must allow the person a chance of arguing against it. If the person does not agree to being bound over, he or she can be sent to prison for up to six months.

The important point to note is that one does not have to commit a criminal offence to be eligible for binding over. The court has wide powers to bind over, given by two different Acts:

- the Justices of the Peace Act 1361 allows an order to be made whenever the magistrates think there is likely to be a further breach of the peace;
- the Magistrates' Courts Act of 1980 allows an order to be made if the magistrates hear evidence that satisfies them that the original complaint against the person was justified.

These are, then, extensive powers. They are often used in neighbour disputes. The typical course of events is that Mr A issues a summons for assault against Mr B; but Mr B then replies with a summons for assault against Mr A. Both cases are heard together and the magistrate is faced with two families arguing out their private feud in the courtroom. Finding it impossible to decide who is in the wrong, the magistrate orders both Mr A and Mr B to be bound over. Naturally, both Mr A and Mr B are furious with the outcome, since they interpret the binding over order as a finding of guilt.

About 8,000 orders a year are made under the 1361 Act. Clearly, there is a danger that magistrates might misuse their wide powers. Demonstrators and protesters have been bound over for no good reason and, in effect, powers have been used to take away the right of free speech and protest.

Young offenders

There are various rules about the sentences that can be imposed on people aged under 21 years (*see* page 131).

CRIMINAL PENALTIES

Maximum penalties for criminal offences tried in the magistrates' courts:

Absconding	£5,000 and 3 months
Abusive words or behaviour	£5,000 and 6 months
Actual bodily harm	£5,000 and 6 months
Affray	£5,000 and 6 months
Air guns	£1,000, forfeiture

Airport security (breaches of)	£5,000
Ammunition	£5,000 and 6 months, forfeiture
Animals (cruelty to)	£5,000 and 6 months
Animals straying on highway	£1,000
Article with blade in public place	£5,000 and/or 6 months
Assault on police constable or person assisting police constable	£5,000 and 6 months
Bankrupt (undischarged obtaining credit)	£5,000 or 6 months
Begging	£1 or 14 days before one magistrate; £1,000 or 1 month if before two or more magistrates
Brothel keeping	£1,000 and 3 months; £2,500 and 6 months (previous conviction)
Builder's skip	
– depositing on highway	£1,000
– not complying with a condition	£1,000
– unlit on highway	£1,000
Burglary	£5,000 and 6 months
Children (cruelty to)	£5,000 and 6 months
Common assault	£5,000 or 6 months
– indictable common assault	£5,000 and 6 months
Computer misuse/unauthorized access	£5,000 and 6 months
– with intent to commit further offences	£5,000 and 6 months
unauthorized modification	£5,000 and 6 months
Criminal damage	
– value of property under £2,000	£2,500 and 3 months
– value of property over £2,000	£5,000 and 6 months
Crossbow (buying, hiring or possession by person under 17 years)	£1,000, forfeiture
Cruelty to animals	*see* Animals
Customs duty (avoiding)	three times value of goods or £5,000 and 6 months
Dangerous machinery	£5,000
Deception (obtaining by)	£5,000 and 6 months
Dishonestly handling	£5,000 and 6 months
Disorderly conduct	£1,000
Dogs	
– breeding or parting with fighting dogs	£5,000 and 6 months
– dog licence	£200
– dog worrying livestock	£1,000
– out of control in public place	£5,000 and 6 months
Drugs (possessions)	
– class A	£5,000 and 6 months
– class B	£2,500 and 3 months
Drunk	£200
– at or on the way to football match	£500
Drunk and disorderly	£1,000
Earnings of prostitution (living on)	£5,000 and 6 months
Enclosed premises (found on)	£1,000 or 3 months
Evasion of liability, obtaining by deception	£5,000 and 6 months
Excessive noise (nuisance order)	£5,000
Exposure (indecent)	£1,000 or 3 months
False alarm of fire	£2,500 and 3 months
False statement to obtain social security	£5,000 and 3 months
False weighing or measuring equipment	£5,000 (and 6 months if deliberate fraud)
Firearms (forfeiture for each of the following) in public place	£5,000 and 6 months
– purchasing, possessing, etc. without certificate	£5,000 and 6 months
– trespassing in a building	£5,000 and 6 months
– trespassing on land	£2,500 and 3 months
Food (selling food not of quality demanded)	£20,000 and 6 months
Football spectators	
– indecent or racialist chanting	£1,000
– throwing missiles	£1,000
Forgery	£5,000 and 6 months
Found on enclosed premises	£1,000 or 3 months
Game (trespassing on land in daytime in search of game)	£1,000; £5,000 if five or more trespassers
Glue (offering to supply to person under 18 for purpose of inhalation)	£5,000 and 6 months
Going equipped to steal	£5,000 and 6 months
Grievous bodily harm	£5,000 and 6 months
Handling stolen goods	£5,000 and 6 months
Harassing residential occupier	£5,000 and 6 months
Highway	
– builder's skip (depositing or leaving unlit)	£1,000
– straying animals on	£1,000
– wilful obstruction	£1,000
Indecency (gross between males)	£5,000 and 6 months
Indecency with child	£5,000 and 6 months
Indecent assault	£5,000 and 6 months
Indecent exposure	£1,000 or 3 months
Insulting words or behaviour	£5,000 and 6 months
Interference with vehicle	£2,500 and 3 months
Intoxicating liquor	
– possessing at or on way to a designated sporting event	£1,000 and three months

– selling outside permitted hours	£1,000
– selling to person under 18	£1,000 (and forfeiture of licence on second conviction)
– selling without a licence	£2,500 and 6 months (and forfeiture of liquor and containers)

Kerb crawling	£1,000

Landlord and tenant	
– unlawful eviction or harassment	£5,000 and 6 months
Liability, obtaining evasion of by deception	£5,000 and 6 months
Litter (including car dumping)	
– Environmental Protection Act 1990	£2,500
– Refuse Disposal (Amenity) Act 1978	£2,500 and 3 months
Loudspeakers	£5,000

Making off without payment	£5,000 and 6 months
Malicious communications	£2,500
Measuring equipment (false or unjust)	£5,000 plus 6 months if fraud (and forfeiture)

National Insurance	
– failing to pay contributions	£1,000 plus two years' arrears
– failing to return card	£1,000
Noise	£5,000

Obscenity – exposing person	£1,000 or 3 months
Obstructing a constable (or a person assisting a constable)	£1,000 and 1 month
Obstructing highway	£1,000
Obtaining evasion of liability by deception	£5,000 and 6 months
Obtaining pecuniary advantage	£5,000 and 6 months
Obtaining property by deception	£5,000 and 6 months
Obtaining services by deception	£5,000 and 6 months
Offensive letter	£2,500
Offensive weapon	£5,000 and 6 months' forfeiture

Payment, making off without	£5,000 and 6 months
Pecuniary advantage (obtaining by)	£5,000 and 6 months
Pedlar (trading without certificate)	£1,000 or 1 month before two or more magistrates
Poaching	£200, £1,000 if five or more trespassers (if violence used, £2,500 and 6 months)

Point, article with, in public place	£5,000 and 6 months
Possessing anything to damage or destroy property	£5,000 and 6 months
Prostitutes	
– living on earnings of	£5,000 and 6 months
– soliciting by prostitutes	£500/£1,000.
Public telephone (fraudulent use of)	£5,000 and 6 months
– indecent or false telephone calls	£5,000 and 6 months

Racially aggravated offences	
– actual bodily harm	£5,000 and 6 months
– common assault	£5,000 and 6 months
– criminal damage	£5,000 and 6 months
– disorderly behaviour	£2,500
– harassment	£5,000 and 6 months
– threatening behaviour	£5,000 and 6 months
– wounding	£5,000 and 6 months
Railway offences	
– avoiding fare	£1,000 or 3 months
– giving false name or address	£1,000 or 3 months
Resisting a constable or a person assisting a constable	£1,000 and 1 month

School attendance (parent not ensuring)	£1,000
Shotgun	
– loaded shotgun in a public place	£5,000 and 6 months, forfeiture
– purchasing or possessing without licence	£5,000 and 6 months, forfeiture
Skip	
– depositing on highway	£1,000
– not complying with a condition	£1,000
– unlit on highway	£1,000
Smuggling	three times value of goods or £5,000 and 6 months
Social Security	
– false statement to obtain	£5,000 and 6 months
– persistently refusing or neglecting to maintain oneself or a dependant	£2,500 and 3 months
Soliciting by prostitutes	£1,000
Statutory nuisance (noise)	£5,000
Stealing	£5,000 and 6 months
Straying animals on highway	£1,000

Taking motor vehicle or conveyance	£5,000 and 6 months, disqualification
Tattooing a minor	£1,000
Telephone	
– fraudulent use of public telephone	£5,000 and 6 months
– indecent or false calls	£1,000

Television licence evasion	£1,000
Theft	£5,000 and 6 months
Threatening to damage or destroy property	£5,000 and 6 months
Threatening words or behaviour	£5,000 and 6 months
Trade description	
– applying false trade description	£5,000
– supplying goods with false description	£5,000
Trespassing with a firearm	
– in a building	£5,000 and 6 months
– on land	£2,500 and 3 months
Trespassing on land during daytime in search of game, etc.	£200; £1,000 if five or more trespassers

Undischarged bankrupt obtaining credit	£5,000 and 6 months
Vehicle interference	£2,500 and 3 months
Violent disorder	£5,000 and 6 months
Wilful obstruction of highway	£1,000
Wilful obstruction of police constable (or person assisting police constable)	£1,000 and 1 month
Wounding	£5,000 and 6 months

87

Prisoners' Rights

Prisoners retain fundamental legal rights as citizens despite their imprisonment, apart from those taken away by a specific law or a necessary implication of the law. The Prison Act 1952 and Prison Rules (1999) both limit and confer rights. For instance, the Prison Rules give rights to food, clothing, exercise, a specified minimum number of visits and letters, and a fair hearing in disciplinary procedures.

Serious breaches of the above rights may be taken before the courts for judicial review. The courts will review decisions by the prison authorities which are unfair or legally wrong. Topics which have been taken to court include disciplinary adjudications, transfer, censorship and the separation of a woman from her baby. Unless there are exceptional circumstances, applications for judicial review should be lodged within three months of the date of the decision in question.

COMPLAINTS

Requests/complaints procedure

The prison authorities advise that requests or complaints should be dealt with by speaking to prison staff (i.e. the prisoner's wing, landing or personal officer and then a governor grade) in the first instance. If this does not resolve matters then a written request/complaint should be made on the forms available. Requests/complaints dealt with inside the prison should be answered within seven days. If the response is unsatisfactory then the next stage is to appeal to the area manager on a request/complaints appeal form. Request/complaints forms can be sent direct to the area manager if they are about 'reserved subjects' which cannot be dealt with inside the prison (i.e. parole), or under 'confidential access' (if you do not want to disclose the request/complaint to staff on your wing or landing). However, it should be noted that an area manager may disclose the contents to the prison if he or she feels it is appropriate.

Outside agencies

MPs in your home constituency or in the constituency where the prison is situated may take up a serious complaint with the Minister concerned. MPs can also ask the Parliamentary Commissioner for Administration (ombudsman) to investigate complaints of maladministration including breaches of the Prison Rules.

Solicitors may be consulted for advice and representation. The Commission for Racial Equality may be consulted where there are allegations of racial harassment or discrimination. The Queen or Parliament may be petitioned. Prison staff should have copies of the procedures involved. MEPs may also be petitioned. The Human Rights Act makes the European Convention on Human Rights part of UK law. The Convention guarantees certain fundamental rights, some of which are particularly relevant to prisoners. The Act means that if the prison authorities breach a prisoner's fundamental rights he can bring a claim under the Act. Such a claim must be brought within 12 months of the act violating the person's rights taking place. The working of the Human Rights Act is discussed in more detail in Chapter 84. A claim can still be made to the European Court of Human Rights once all domestic remedies have been exhausted, but all Convention arguments must be raised in those domestic proceedings before pursuing a case in Europe.

ACCESS TO LAWYERS

Prisoners have a right of access to a lawyer in criminal and civil proceedings. There is no need to air complaints internally before consulting with a solicitor/legal adviser. Prisoners who are party to legal proceedings will not have correspondence with their legal advisers read or stopped unless there is reason to suppose that the correspondence does not relate to the proceedings.

DISCIPLINE

The list of offences against prison discipline is set out in Rule 51 of the Prison Rules (Rule 50 of the Young Offender Institution Rules (YOI)). Prison governors deal with the less serious charges; more serious matters are referred to the police and Crown Prosecution Service (CPS) for prosecution in the outside criminal courts. In an intermediate category of offences, a prison governor may refer a prisoner to an adjudicator, who may sentence him to up to 42 additional days. Legal representation is permitted at such an adjudication.

Prisoners must be charged with any offence as soon as possible, and within 48 hours of the alleged offence being discovered (except in exceptional circumstances). A prisoner should be segregated only pending adjudication if it is justifiable under Rule 45, for the purpose of 'good order and discipline', and the reasons for segregation should be clearly recorded. Segregation for more than three days must be authorized by a member of the Board of Visitors or the Secretary of State.

Prisoners should be allowed to see statements or written material which will be used in evidence against them (except where the author of a medical report considers it should not be disclosed). Prisoners should be given sufficient time to prepare for the hearing, if necessary by asking for an adjournment. Prisoners may also apply for legal representation, or the assistance of a friend or adviser (a 'McKenzie Friend'), but this is not available as of right. If granted, a solicitor may be able to advise under the legal help scheme.

If the matter is referred to the police/CPS and a decision is made not to prosecute because the evidence is unsatisfactory, then the prisoner should not face a prison disciplinary charge. However, if criminal charges are dropped for other reasons, it will still be open to the governor to proceed with a disciplinary charge. But once evidence has been presented in court by the CPS, the prisoner will not be at risk of it being pursued against him as a disciplinary offence.

If found guilty of a disciplinary offence the prisoner may be punished by:

- caution;
- loss of privileges for a maximum of 42 days (21 days in YOI);
- stoppage of earnings for 82 days and of an amount not exceeding 42 days' earnings (42 days and an amount not exceeding 21 days in YOI);
- cellular confinement for a maximum of 14 days (seven days in YOI);
- exclusion from associated work for a maximum of 21 days.

In addition, those in a YOI may be removed from activities for a maximum of 14 days, be given up to two extra hours' work a day for up to 14 days, or removed from their wing or unit for up to 14 days.

A prisoner may appeal to the area manager against a finding of guilt on the basis that the procedure was unfair or contained an error, and/or appeal against the punishment imposed. Where the adjudication has been conducted unfairly or illegally, it may be possible to go to the High Court to review the decision.

Correspondence

All correspondence sent to or from prisoners in the dispersal system, category A prisoners, prisoners in units housing category A prisoners, and prisoners on the Escape List will normally be read (except where it is legally privileged). There is no routine reading of mail at category B (non-dispersal) prisons, category C prisons, open prisons and designated women's prisons and YOIs, and only a very small proportion of letters will be read in those establishments. In certain circumstances letters may be stopped (*see* Standing Order 5), and if this happens the prisoner will be told and may be allowed to rewrite the letter in question.

Categorization

On reception to prison prisoners are given a security categorization ranging from A (the highest) to D (the lowest). Category A prisoners have extra security restrictions, including the vetting and approval of their visitors by the police. Categorization is reviewed from time to time and prisoners can be moved to a higher or a lower security categorization.

Allocation

Prisoners have no right to choose the prison or the location in which they will be held. However, if a prisoner's allocation causes particularly severe problems (i.e. to family because of their age, illness or pregnancy) a prisoner can ask for a transfer. It is helpful if the prisoner can provide the relevant material to support his or her case (i.e. medical evidence) in such circumstances. If the prisoner is unsuccessful, he or she may wish to ask a solicitor, legal adviser, MP, etc. to intervene.

Transfers

Transfers may not be used as a form of punishment, but prisoners may be transferred in the interest of 'good order and discipline' under CI 28/93. In extreme cases allocation or transfer may be reviewed by the courts.

Segregation

Rule 45 of the Prison Rules (1999) (Rule 46 of the YOI Rules 1988) provides for the segregation of prisoners either 'in the interests of good order and discipline' or at their request for their 'own protection'. Segregation under this Rule should not be for more than three days without the authority of a member of the Board of Visitors or the Secretary of State.

Women prisoners

Women prisoners may be allowed to keep their babies with them until the age of nine months or 18 months, depending upon the prison where they are held. If the baby has reached these age limits before the mother has served her sentence, the mother may be forced to give up looking after her baby, either then or at an earlier stage. However, the Court of Appeal has held that this policy must not be applied rigidly and that each case must be looked at on its own merits. This means that there may be circumstances where it is appropriate for a child to remain with his/her mother beyond 18 months. Women and girls do not wear prison uniform but the prison will provide clothing if their own clothes are unsuitable or if they do not have enough clothes of their own. Women cannot be forced to have their hair cut unless the medical officer makes an order to that effect, and certain toiletries and sanitary protection will be provided by the prison.

Young Offender Institutions

Young Offender Institutions (YOIs) are governed by a separate set of rules (YOI Rules 1988) which are very similar to the Prison Rules. If a prisoner is under 17 years arrangements will be made for participation in education or training for at least 15 hours within the normal working week.

Race relations

The Prison Service has a public policy statement about race relations which should be displayed in every prison. This states that the Prison Service is committed to a policy of racial equality, and that all prisoners should be treated with humanity, respect and without discrimination. All prisoners have a right to practise their faith and should have equal access to facilities. It is a disciplinary offence for prison staff to use racially abusive language or conduct. All prisons have a race relations liaison officer and a race relations management team, who should meet regularly to check that the policy is being implemented.

Remand prisoners

Remand prisoners are those who are unconvicted, those awaiting extradition, deportation or removal from the UK as illegal entrants, and civil prisoners (i.e. in prison for not paying community charge, tax or maintenance). Those who are convicted but unsentenced are treated as convicted prisoners.

Although unconvicted, remand prisoners may still be disciplined under the procedure outlined above.

Clothes

Remand prisoners are allowed to wear their own clothes if they are suitable, clean and tidy. Clothes may be sent in from the outside or brought in by visitors and exchanged for ones which need washing. Male prisoners on remand may be issued with a prison uniform if they wish.

Visits

Remand prisoners are allowed as many visits as they wish subject to any limits or conditions imposed by the Home Secretary. These must be on at least three days each week and include the opportunity of a weekend visit at least once a fortnight. Visitors do not need a visiting order and up to three adults and the prisoner's children will be allowed at any one time.

Some prisons will allow visitors to hand in cigarettes, tobacco and toiletries, whereas in others they should be sent in by post. Money can also be sent into the prison and can be spent in the prison canteen.

Letters

Remand prisoners may send and receive as many letters as they like. Two second-class letters per week will be provided at public expense and any more will be paid for from prison earnings or private cash. Letters to legal advisers normally have to be paid for, but if a prisoner has no private cash the governor may allow letters essential to the defence to be sent at public expense. Letters are not usually read unless the prisoner is treated as a category A, or is on the escape list.

Work

Remand prisoners do not have to work unless they wish to do so. If they do work they will be paid a small amount of money, but in practice there is very little work available. If no work is available, remand prisoners will be paid a very small sum to cover basics. If they refuse work when offered, this money will be stopped and the prison is not obliged to offer any further work.

Medical treatment

Remand prisoners can apply to be treated by the doctor or dentist of their choice at their own expense although they can use the Prison Medical Service.

Convicted prisoners

Visits

Rule 35 sets out the minimum number of visits (and letters) allowed – two in a four-week period, but this can be reduced to once a month by the Home Secretary. Additional visits can be awarded as a privilege (Rule 8) or where it is considered necessary for the prisoner's or his family's welfare. A visiting order must be sent out to your visitors and they should bring this with them when they visit. Special visits may be allowed in the following circumstances:

- where there are personal or business difficulties which need to be sorted out after conviction;
- if they are necessary to the conduct of legal proceedings or the welfare of you and your family; or
- on the advice of a medical officer where a prisoner is seriously ill.

If the prison where a prisoner is held is a long way from his friends and family, the prisoner may save up his visits and apply for a temporary transfer to a local prison in order that visits can take place there. Category A prisoners are subject to special procedures. Visits may not be stopped as part of a punishment, but may be deferred if the punishment includes a period of cellular confinement.

Letters

Prisoners can send and receive a letter on reception to prison and at least one a week thereafter. The total number of letters allowed will vary from prison to prison and 'special letters' (i.e. extra letters at public expense) may be available in certain circumstances.

Work

Convicted prisoners are required to work for up to 10 hours a day unless a medical officer excuses them. It is a disciplinary offence for a prisoner to fail to work properly on purpose, or to refuse to work. However, the prison is under no obligation to provide prisoners with work.

Medical treatment

The Prison Medical Service is not part of the NHS, although prison doctors and medical officers can refer prisoners to NHS hospitals, or ask specialists to see a prisoner if they feel that a second opinion is appropriate, or are unable to deal with a prisoner's medical problems. Treatment by opticians and dentists is also available. All treatment in prisons must be with a prisoner's consent.

The Access to Health Records Act 1990 has given prisoners the right to see – and have copies made on request of – their medical records since 1 November 1991. Disclosure can be refused on the basis that it would cause serious harm to the physical or mental health of the patient or any other individual.

88

Criminal Records

DISCLOSURE AND USE OF PAST CONVICTIONS

The Rehabilitation of Offenders Act 1974 was an attempt to counter, at least in part, the prejudice that 'a leopard never changes its spots'. It was considered unfair that people who, at some time in the past, had acquired a conviction should have to carry it 'around their necks' for the rest of their lives. However, while the 1974 Act provides an opportunity for offenders to wipe the slate clean for certain purposes, it is very detailed and contains numerous exceptions to this basic principle.

How a sentence becomes 'spent'

The Rehabilitation of Offenders Act applies to all types of sentences, whether custodial, a fine, probation, absolute or conditional discharges, findings in a juvenile court that an offence has been committed, and convictions for certain offences relating to the armed forces. (Separate rules apply to findings in care proceedings.)

The rehabilitation period depends on the sentence and runs from the date of conviction. When the period has expired, the sentence becomes 'spent' and need not be revealed in the future – for example when applying for most jobs, completing an insurance proposal form, applying for credit facilities or for the tenancy of a property. However, there are *many* exceptions to this rule, for example where a person applies for a job which involves substantial access to children or applies to become a member of certain professions.

The table below details the rehabilitation periods which are set according to the sentence imposed. Certain periods are reduced by half where the offender was a juvenile (i.e. under the age of 18 years at the date of the conviction). The Act applies not only to convictions in this country, but also to convictions before courts outside the UK. The foreign sentence is treated as equivalent to the sentence which most nearly corresponds with it under UK law. However, the Act does not apply outside the UK, for example to an application for a job or a visa in a foreign country.

Sentence	Rehabilitation period
A sentence of imprisonment for more than 30 months	Never
A sentence of imprisonment or youth custody of more than 6 months but not more than 30 months	10 years for an adult, 5 for a young offender (i.e. under 18 years)
A sentence of imprisonment or youth custody of 6 months or less	7 years for an adult, 5 for a young offender
An order of detention in a detention centre	3 years
A fine	5 years for an adult, 2½ for a young offender
A community service order	5 years for an adult
Probation, bind-over to keep the peace or to be of good behaviour, conditional discharge	The date the order or bind-over ceases or, 1 year, discharge whichever is the longer
Hospital orders under the Mental Health Act 1983	5 years from the date of conviction to 2 years after the order expires whichever is the longer
Absolute discharge	6 months
Disqualifications and other order imposing disability prohibition or other penalty	The date the order ceases to have effect
For the armed forces A sentence of imprisonment within the armed forces	Same period as for other prison sentences (*see* above)

Sentence	Rehabilitation period
A sentence of detention arising from disciplinary proceedings	5 years for an adult, 2½ for a young offender
A sentence of discharge with ignominy or a dismissal with disgrace	10 years for an adult, 5 years for a young offender
A sentence of dismissal from the service	7 years for an adult, 3–4 years for a young offender

The rehabilitation period applicable

Certain sentences can *never* become spent. They are as follows:
- a sentence of life imprisonment;
- a sentence of imprisonment, youth custody (or the former sentence of corrective training) for a term of more than 30 months;
- the former sentence of preventive detention;
- a sentence of detention during Her Majesty's Pleasure for life;
- a sentence of custody for life.

It should be noted that it is the *length of the sentence imposed by the court* that is relevant and not, for example, the length of imprisonment actually served.

If a person is given a sentence which can never become spent, this also prevents any earlier unspent conviction from becoming spent.

Under the law, a sentence counts in the same way irrespective of whether someone is sent to prison or the sentence is 'suspended'. The periods of rehabilitation for either are therefore the same as shown in the table.

Where a person receives two or more prison sentences in the course of the same court case, the rehabilitation period depends on whether the sentences are ordered to take effect 'concurrently' (i.e. at the same time) or 'consecutively' (i.e. one after another). For example, if two six-month prison sentences are ordered to take effect concurrently, the sentences are treated separately, giving each conviction a rehabilitation period of seven years. However, if the two sentences are ordered to take effect consecutively, the sentences are treated as a single term of 12 months, with a rehabilitation period of 10 years.

Committing further offences

The essence of rehabilitation is that the person who has been convicted does not offend again. Therefore any subsequent conviction *during the rehabilitation period* of a previous conviction *may* extend the rehabilitation period of the first conviction. Whether it does depends, for example, on the seriousness of the subsequent conviction and the sentence imposed.

The effect of rehabilitation

The general principle under the Act is that a person who has become rehabilitated (i.e. their conviction has become spent) shall be treated as a person who has not committed, or been charged with, prosecuted for, convicted of or sentenced for, the offence concerned. Again, there are many exceptions to this general rule, with spent convictions being treated in different ways in different circumstances.

Evidence in legal proceedings

In proceedings before the civil courts or before a tribunal, arbitration, voluntary association, disciplinary or similar hearing you cannot be asked questions concerning any spent conviction and you can refuse to answer such questions – unless the court, tribunal or hearing is satisfied that justice cannot be done except by hearing the evidence involving the spent conviction.

This general rule does not apply in:
- criminal proceedings (but the Lord Chief Justice has ruled that no one should refer in open court to a spent conviction without the authorization of the judge, which authority should not be given unless the interests of justice so require);
- proceedings relating to adoption, the marriage of any minor, exercise of the High Court's discretion with respect to minors or the provision by any person of accommodation care or schooling for children;
- armed forces' disciplinary proceedings.

Employment

Questions are often asked by potential employers with respect to a person's previous convictions. The general rule under the Act is that you can treat such questions as *not* relating to spent convictions. Therefore, if you decide not to disclose a spent conviction, you cannot be denied employment or subsequently dismissed on the grounds that you failed to disclose it. (Although in exceptional circumstances, you may be prosecuted for the criminal offence of 'obtaining a pecuniary advantage by deception'.) Likewise, failing to disclose a spent conviction will not be proper grounds for excluding you from any office or profession. Nor can a spent conviction be grounds for prejudicing you in the way you are treated in any occupation or employment.

If, therefore, you are excluded or dismissed from

employment on the grounds of a spent conviction, you may be able to take the matter to court for compensation or to an industrial tribunal as wrongful dismissal. If you wish to pursue such action, you should first seek the assistance of a solicitor.

However, many occupations and offices are specifically excluded from this general rule and these are dealt with below. You should read these carefully. Some employers are adopting the practice of asking prospective, or existing, employees to obtain a copy of their criminal record under the provisions of the Data Protection Act 1998, which allows people the right to see their own computerized files – a right which was extended to manual records as of 24 October 2001. This record lists all your convictions, including those that are spent. Although this practice – known as 'enforced subject access' – is not unlawful, it is a misuse of the data protection laws and could be highly prejudicial to yourself.

If you are concerned about agreeing to such a request, you should seek assistance from a union official or the Office of the Information Commissioner at Wycliffe House, Water Lane, Wilmslow, Cheshire SK9 5AF. Telephone 01625 545745 (www.dataprotection.gov.uk).

Note that the Information Commissioner could only intervene if an employer were to record the details of the response on a processing system (or in a manual record) and then use that information to the detriment of the individual at some point in the future. (*See further* page 405.)

Services

Some contracts, such as proposals for insurance, are governed by the legal principle that all relevant information will be disclosed by the person seeking insurance whether it is asked for or not; otherwise the contract could be treated as invalid. Clearly, the existence of a driving offence or an offence for dishonesty may well be relevant to an insurance company. However, the 1974 Act specifically states that although the existing law requires that all relevant information in this situation should be disclosed, this does *not* extend to disclosing spent convictions.

Going abroad

It is important to remember that the Act applies only to the UK and has no effect so far as the laws of other countries are concerned. This means, for example, that applicants for immigration, work permits and travel visas to the USA are still obliged to make full disclosure of their criminal record, including spent convictions. Some foreign countries have legislation similar to the Rehabilitation of Offenders Act, but to discover what safeguards apply it is necessary to consult the laws of the country concerned – for example by asking their embassy in this country.

Defamation proceedings

A reference to a spent conviction in a newspaper article, for example, can give rise to a claim for damages for defamation. However, in order to protect free speech, the Act states that a person who is sued in defamation proceedings for disclosing a spent conviction may rely on the defences of 'justification' (i.e. the statement is true) and/or 'fair comment' (i.e. the statement was a fair comment on a matter of public interest). In order to succeed when such a defence is raised, the plaintiff would have to prove that the statement was published with *malice* – that is, it was published with some irrelevant, spiteful or improper motive.

In addition, the reporting of certain events and the making of statements in certain circumstances can give rise to the defence of 'absolute' or 'qualified privilege'. For example, fair and accurate newspaper reports of judicial proceedings are absolutely 'privileged' (i.e. protected) against a defamation action.

As the law relating to defamation is complex, specialist legal advice should be sought. Public funding is not available for defamation actions.

EXCEPTIONS TO THE ACT

The Act is frequently criticized for the many and wide exceptions made to the general principle that a person can become rehabilitated. If a person falls within any of the exceptions, they will be treated as if the Act had never been passed and are not entitled to rehabilitation for the spent conviction. These exceptions are listed in the Orders made by a relevant government minister, and largely relate to matters of national security, the care of those who are considered to be vulnerable and the administration of justice.

Excepted professions, occupations and offices

A number of professions, occupations and offices have been excepted from the general rule that a person does not have to disclose a spent conviction (*see* above). The table below lists the professions, occupations and offices which are excepted.

Excepted professions, occupations and offices

Medical practitioners	Veterinary surgeons
Lawyers	Opticians
Accountants	Nurses and midwives
Dentists	Pharmaceutical chemists
Judicial appointments	Traffic wardens
Police constables	Teachers
Prison Board of Visitors	Probation officers
Prison officers	Firearms dealers
Dealer in securities	Directors, controllers, etc.,
Managers or trustees of unit	of insurance companies or
trusts	building societies

If you apply, therefore, to join one of the professions, occupations or offices listed you will normally be asked (and must be told why) to disclose all previous convictions, including spent convictions, in order that your suitability for the position may be assessed. Furthermore, a spent conviction may be considered grounds for excluding or dismissing you from any profession, occupation or office listed.

Other excepted occupations include:

- any office or employment where the question is asked for the purpose of safeguarding *national security* (e.g. a person employed by the UK Atomic Energy Authority, the Civil Aviation Authority or an officer of the Crown);
- certain types of work in *health and social services* where the work involves access to people over 65 years, to people suffering from serious illness or mental disorder, alcoholics or drug addicts, to the blind, deaf and dumb, or is concerned with the provision to persons under 18 years of care, leisure or recreational facilities (*see* below for further details);
- applications for certain certificates and licences (e.g. concerning firearms, explosives and gaming), require that spent convictions be disclosed and can be taken into account by the licensing authority. Failure to disclose a spent conviction in these circumstances could result in the refusal or loss of the licence, certificate, etc. or even in prosecution for non-disclosure.

Disclosure of criminal background of those with access to children

In March 2002, a new system of criminal record checks was established. This system, called disclosures, enables all health and social care agencies to run checks on existing staff and people offered employment working with vulnerable individuals. A government agency, the Criminal Records Bureau (CRB), was set up to administer the new disclosure arrangements. The old system of checks, which was administered by local police forces, was poor. Many agencies were not able to run police checks, while

recruitment policy and practice among those that did was inconsistent.

Under the new system, employers recruiting staff and volunteers to work with children and vulnerable adults are able to carry out checks and obtain standard and enhanced disclosure certificates. The standard disclosure check covers jobs excepted from the Rehabilitation of Offenders Act 1974. These jobs include work that involves regular contact with children and vulnerable adults. Standard disclosure certificates show both spent and unspent convictions and also cautions, reprimands and final warnings held on the Police National Computer. They say if there is no record. The disclosures are issued to individuals and copied to the employer or other body registered with the CRB to receive this information.

The enhanced disclosure includes positions involving regular care, training, supervising or being in sole charge of children. It shows the same details as a standard disclosure. It may also show non-conviction information from local police records, which a chief police officer thinks is relevant in connection with a particular employment. For example, if a local police force has on file allegations that someone has sexually assaulted a child and that person has applied for a childcare position, then the chief officer is likely to disclose this information.

When someone is applying for a childcare position, both disclosures also show whether or not they are banned from working with children (*see further* page 406). People will also be banned from working with children by virtue of their inclusion on the lists of those considered unsuitable to work with children maintained by the Department of Education and Skills and the Department of Health. These are *List 99* and the Protection of Children Act 1999 List respectively. A person may also be banned from working with children by a criminal court which is sentencing him or her for certain offences against a child.

The Protection of Children Act 1999 List contains details of individuals dismissed from childcare organizations on grounds of misconduct that harmed a child or placed one at risk.

Prospective employers may also use the Department of Health's Consultancy Service and the Department of Education's *List 99* as a further check on a person's suitability. These hold lists of people who, because of a previous conviction or incident, are considered unfit to work with children and young people. Those people who are listed should have been informed at the time by the department concerned that their name had come to their attention, and why. They should also have been given the opportunity to make representations about the incident which they wish to record.

For further information, *see* Home Office Circular No. 102/88, *Protection of Children: Disclosure of Criminal Background of those with Access to Children* (in the statutory sector), and Home Office Circular No. 58/1989 (in the voluntary sector). Copies of these circulars are obtainable free from F2 Division, the Home Office, Queen Anne's Gate, London SW1H 9AT.

Anyone banned from working with children will be committing an offence punishable by a custodial sentence simply by applying for such work; similarly, anyone who employs such a person, knowing them to be banned, will also be committing a criminal offence.

Under the Care Standards Act 2000 the standard disclosure also shows whether or not a person is banned from working with vulnerable adults by virtue of their inclusion on the Protection of Vulnerable Adults list maintained by the Department of Health. Care staff may be placed on the list if they have been dismissed, resigned, retired, made redundant, transferred or suspended on the grounds of misconduct, which harmed or put at risk of harm a vulnerable adult. 'Vulnerable people' include people in care homes with a disability or illness.

Basic disclosure

The third level of disclosure provided by the CRB is basic disclosure. The basic disclosure certificate shows details of convictions on the Police National Computer which are unspent under the Rehabilitation of Offenders Act. Some administrative and other posts within the health and social care field, which do not bring postholders into contact with vulnerable people, will be subject to a basic disclosure only. Applicants will be expected to obtain this as a condition of employment because the employers themselves will not be able to.

Code of practice

Those employers and others wanting to make standard and enhanced disclosure checks have to become 'registered bodies' with the CRB, or make checks through an umbrella organization, which has been registered. Registered bodies will have to sign up to a code of practice, which will require them to adopt fair recruitment policies and practices in relation to ex-offenders. Under the code, employers have to have a written policy on the recruitment of ex-offenders, which can be given to applicants. Application forms and accompanying material must contain statements to the effect that a criminal record will not necessarily be a bar to obtaining employment, in order to reassure applicants that disclosure information will be used fairly.

Every subject of a disclosure must be made aware of the existence of the code and given a copy on request. The CRB website is at www.crb.gov.uk; the CRB telephone information line is 0870 90 90 811.

Police reporting of convictions

The general rule is that police information (including information on convictions) should not be disclosed unless there are important considerations of *public interest*

to justify departure from the general rule of confidentiality. Exceptions to this rule are made where there is a need:

* to protect vulnerable members of society;
* to ensure good and honest administration of law;
* to protect national security.

The effect of this means that, under Home Office Circular No. 45/1986, *Police Reports of Convictions and Related Information*, the police may disclose, when it is requested, information on a person's past convictions, cases pending and other such background information as would be admissible in court in the circumstances listed in the table below.

Under the same circular, the police are asked to report convictions as they occur to the professional bodies of those groups listed in the table below, particularly where the offences involve violence, dishonesty, drink or drugs, as they may reflect on a person's suitability to continue in a profession or office.

Police Disclosure of Convictions is Proper in Respect of:

* Those to be appointed to positions with substantial access to children (*see* above).
* Persons involved in the care of (or member of the same household as) a child subject to a case conference on non-accidental injury to children.
* Parents (and their cohabitants) to whom a local authority proposes to return a child in care.
* Applicants for compensation for criminal injury.
* Applicants to join the police.
* Applicants for certain licences – for example, gaming, lottery, sex establishments and entertainment licences.
* Applicants for, and holders of, licences as Heavy Goods Vehicles and Passenger Service Vehicle Operators.
* Applicants for licences as dealers in securities.
* Applicants for consumer credit licences.
* Applicants for casual post office work.
* Potential jurors in cases including national security and terrorism.
* Social inquiry reports and other reports by probation officers.
* Welfare reports for courts determining care and custody of children.
* Those subject to national security vetting.

Reporting Convictions of Those in Certain Professions and Occupations:

* Teachers (including student teachers) and youth workers
* Social workers
* Probation officers
* Medical practitioners
* Staff of the UK Atomic Energy Authority and British Nuclear Fuels Limited

- Pharmaceutical chemists
- Post Office staff
- Midwives and nurses ancillary staff
- Dentists
- Lawyers
- Magistrates
- Civil servants
- Staff of the Civil Aviation Authority
- BT staff

Unauthorized disclosure of convictions

The Act makes it an offence if:

- an official in the course of their official duties, unlawfully discloses someone else's spent conviction – the penalty is a maximum fine of £2,500 (as from October 1992);
- any person obtains details of spent convictions from any official record by means of fraud, dishonesty or a bribe – the penalty is up to six months' imprisonment and/or a maximum fine of £5,000 (as from October 1992).

If someone wrongfully reveals that you have a past conviction, you can:

- report the matter to the police and ask that the incident be investigated with a view to the person being prosecuted;
- sue the person concerned for *defamation* (*see* above);
- make a formal police complaint.

If, for example, the police reveal a conviction to an employer who is not within the categories set out in the table, it may be possible to bring a claim for damages. Although this has yet to be tested in the courts, a solicitor should be consulted to see if it is possible.

Sharing information

Under section 115 of the Crime and Disorder Act 1998, a new principle of information sharing has been formalized. This section gives power to any person to disclose personal information to police authorities and chief constables, local authorities, probation committees, health authorities or persons acting on their behalf of personal information so long as such disclosure is necessary for the purposes of any provision of the Act. These purposes include local crime audits, anti-social behaviour orders, sex offender orders and local child curfew schemes. This power to share information is subject to other existing safeguards, such as defamation, data protection legislation and duties of confidentiality. The principle of information sharing ensures that all persons have the power to disclose material, but does not impose any duty to do so. The Home Office has issued guidance on this information-sharing power which can be found in Chapter 5 of the Home Office Circular 9/1999: *Guidance on statutory crime and disorder partnerships.*

Notification requirements for persons involved in sexual offences

The Sex Offenders Act 1997 imposes requirements on persons who have been convicted, cautioned or acquitted by reason of insanity or some other mental or physical disability, of a sexual offence to notify the police of their name and address, within a short period, usually 14 days from conviction, finding or release from sentence. If there is a change of name or address, the police are required to be notified within 14 days.

Failure, without reasonable excuse, to comply with these notification requirements, or the provision of false information, is a criminal offence, punishable summarily with a fine and up to six months' imprisonment.

These obligations upon the person are *not* dependent upon an order of the court, although in practice many judges seem to assume that it is for them to impose such an order. In fact, the judge is permitted merely to certify the conviction or finding.

The applicable periods of notification for a person over 18 years at the relevant date are:

A person sentenced to life or 30 months' imprisonment or more	Indefinite period
A person admitted to hospital subject to a restriction order	Indefinite period
A person sentenced to more than 6 months' but less than 30 months' imprisonment	10 years from the relevant date
A person sentenced to 6 months' imprisonment or less	7 years from the relevant date
A person admitted to hospital without a restriction order being imposed	7 years from the relevant date
A person of any other description	5 years from the relevant date

In respect of a person under 18 years on the relevant date, the relevant periods of 10, 7 and 5 years, respectively, are halved.

The obligation on a person convicted and sentenced, or made the subject of a finding or a caution prior to the commencement of the Act (on 1 September 1997) does not constitute a penalty within Article 7 of the European Convention on Human Rights.

It would appear unlikely that a successful challenge could be made to either the Rehabilitation of Offenders Act 1974 and its exceptions, or the Sex Offenders Act 1997.

89

Victims of Crime

VICTIMS' RIGHTS

Lawyers have traditionally colluded in treating victims and witnesses as optional extras in the criminal justice system. Their evidence was required by the state in order to secure a conviction against the offender. Few 'rights' were recognized. Some rape victims complained that they had been violated twice: by their attacker and then in the way they were treated by the criminal justice system. Julia Mason was humiliated and abused over a period of six days at the Old Bailey by a defendant who conducted his own defence, wearing the clothing which he wore as he raped her. She took her complaint to the European Court of Human Rights. This resulted in the Youth Justice and Criminal Evidence Act 1999, which seeks to prevent such blatant abuse of human rights in the future.

An earlier edition of this Guide focused on the issue of compensation. A wider agenda of victims' rights has now been established. In 1995, Victim Support published a policy paper *The Rights of Victims of Crime* which grouped rights under the following headings:

- *to be free of the burden of decision relating to the offender* – the responsibility for dealing with the offender lies with the state and should not be placed on the victim. Decisions regarding the offender should be in the hands of the police, Crown Prosecution Service (CPS), courts and the prison service. There is a lively debate as to the role of the victim in sentencing. The Crime and Disorder Act 1998 has now introduced restorative justice into the youth justice system;
- *to receive information and explanation about the progress of their case, and to have the opportunity to provide their own explanation about the case for use in the criminal justice system* – the Glidewell Review of the CPS (1998) recommended that this responsibility should rest with the CPS;
- *to be protected in any way necessary* – a Home Office report *Speaking up for Justice* (1998) has led to a number of recommendations to protect vulnerable and intimidated witnesses, some of which have been enacted in the Youth Justice and Criminal Evidence Act 1999;
- *to receive compensation* – the state compensation scheme for victims of crimes of violence has been established on a statutory basis in the Criminal Injuries Compensation Act 1995;
- *to receive respect, recognition and support* – the failure of the criminal justice system to secure justice for victims was highlighted in the Macpherson Report into the death of Stephen Lawrence (1999).

THE HUMAN RIGHTS ACT 1998

The Human Rights Act 1998 has created a new landscape in which the courts will be required to search for a fair balance: between the interests of the individual and those of society at large; and between the rights of the defendant and those of victims and witnesses. Both the government and the criminal justice agencies will have positive duties to ensure that Convention rights are not violated. Challenges can be anticipated in the following areas:

- the obligation on the state to ensure adequate laws to protect individuals;
- the obligation on the police and local authorities to do all that can reasonably be required to protect individuals at risk of violence or harm;
- the obligation on the police and CPS to carry out adequate investigations and bring offenders to justice. There have been recent successful applications for judicial review where the CPS have declined to prosecute;
- the obligation on the police to protect vulnerable victims and witnesses;
- the rights of the victim in the criminal process. Recent decisions from both the Court of Appeal and the European Court of Human Rights have stressed the need to balance the rights of victims and witnesses against those of the defendant. Victims and pressure groups

may seek to intervene when defendants seek to raise human rights issues on appeal.

REPORTING CRIME

All victims reporting crime to the police should be given a leaflet (*Victims of Crime* (1999)). They will normally be referred to their local Victim Support Scheme, which offers support and practical assistance. Victims may choose to contact their local scheme before deciding whether or not to report the offence to the police. Access can be obtained through the Victim Supportline (0845 303 0900).

The 'Victims' Charter' sets out the service standards which victims can expect from the police, CPS, courts, probation service, Victim Support and its Witness Service, and Criminal Injuries Compensation Authority. The latest edition was published by the last government in 1996 and is currently being revised (it is available at www.homeoffice.gov.uk). There is also a specific leaflet on domestic violence (*Break the Chain* (1999)) and an information pack *Information for Families of Homicide Victims* (1998).

Both the Macpherson Report into the murder of Stephen Lawrence (1999) and *Speaking up for Justice* (the Home Office, 1998) seek to encourage the reporting of crime by vulnerable victims. Particular measures are recommended for victims of race crime, domestic violence and rape. Protection and reassurance should be provided. Appropriate interview techniques should be used. The police and the CPS should liaise to ensure that the needs of the complainants are met during the investigation, at trial and, if necessary, thereafter. These reports provide useful guidance to good practice against which performance can be assessed in determining whether a professional service has been provided.

GIVING EVIDENCE

A Home Office leaflet *Witness in Court* (1997) explains the court procedures. It should be sent as a matter of course to all prosecution witnesses. Victim Support provides a Witness Service at all crown courts. The service is being extended into magistrates' courts. The service is available to both prosecution and defence witnesses, to children as well as adults. A visit can be arranged to the courtroom prior to the trial. Information is provided on court procedure. Emotional support is offered, including someone to accompany the witness into court.

A Courts Charter (1998) sets out the service standards which a witness can expect when he attends a crown court. Many magistrates' courts have their own local charters. The standards relate to secure waiting areas, waiting times (a recommended maximum of two hours

in crown courts and one hour in magistrates' courts), services for child witnesses (including Child Witness Officers) and expenses. A *Statement of National Standards of Witness Care in the Criminal Justice System* was published in July 1996. Forty-two local trials issues groups, which include representatives of Victim Support and its Witness Service, monitor these standards. It is now permissible for prosecution counsel to speak to witnesses (it had been thought that this might lead to the coaching of witnesses). Witnesses should not be required to disclose their address in open court unless it is necessary for evidential purposes.

The Court of Appeal has ruled that a trial judge has a duty not only to ensure that the defendant has a fair trial, but also to protect the interests of witnesses and minimize their trauma in giving evidence (*R v Milton Brown* [1998]). Although this decision was in the context of a defendant who had represented himself, the principles apply equally to cross-examination by defence counsel. In *Doorson v Netherlands* (1996), the European Court of Human Rights ruled that even though Article 6 of the Convention did not refer specifically to the interests of witnesses, 'their life, liberty or security of person may be at stake' which are protected by other substantive provisions of the Convention. Articles 3 and 8 may be of particular relevance. Victim Support is concerned that the disclosure of a witness's medical records or notes of a similar person in a position of professional confidence may infringe Convention rights.

The prosecution is under a duty to identify any vulnerable and intimidated witnesses. Measures introduced by the Youth Justice and Criminal Evidence Act 1999 which implement recommendations from *Speaking up for Justice* include:

- the use of screens and video links;
- evidence given in private;
- the removal of wigs and gowns;
- video-recorded evidence in chief, cross-examination or re-examination;
- examination through an intermediary;
- aids to communication.

Further changes relate to trials of sexual offences. A defendant is no longer permitted to cross-examine the complainant. If the defendant refuses to act through a barrister, the court may appoint a legal representative. A complainant may no longer be questioned about their sexual history, except in the extremely limited circumstances specified in section 41 of the 1999 Act.

SENTENCE

A victim has no direct involvement in the sentencing process. The prosecution cannot argue for any specific sentence. Their role is merely to put the relevant facts before the court. When the police first take a witness statement, the victim should be given the opportunity to describe the effect of the crime in their own words.

A report of a pilot on the use of Victim Statements (Morgan and Sanders) was published in 1999. Victim Statements were introduced nationally from 2001. The emerging approach of the courts is that such a statement may be relevant as to the impact of the offence on the victim but that the views of the victim as to sentence are irrelevant. There is concern that such statements may raise expectations for victims which cannot be realized.

The Bar Code of Conduct requires advance disclosure by the defence of any intention to cast aspersions on the victim in mitigation. The prosecutor is under a duty to challenge any such aspersion which he knows to be untrue. The Criminal Procedure and Investigations Act 1996 permits the judge to restrict reporting of derogatory assertions made by the defence in mitigation where there are substantial grounds for believing the assertion is derogatory to the victim's character and is false or irrelevant to the sentence.

AFTER TRIAL

The Victims' Charter provides that if there is an appeal against conviction, or sentence in cases of homicide, rape, or sexual assault, the police will keep the victim informed of the date of the hearing, whether bail is granted, and the result of the appeal. This was extended to other offences in May 2000.

To date, victims have had no right to intervene in criminal appeals. This has changed with the Human Rights Act 1998. In judicial review proceedings in the High Court, voluntary organizations have been permitted to intervene. A number of human rights organizations intervened in the *Pinochet* extradition case. The judges have been less willing to permit similar interventions in criminal appeals. However, there may be a change of approach. The Macpherson Report suggested that victims might be allowed to apply to become 'civil parties' in criminal proceedings as in certain European jurisdictions. In *Thompson and Venables* v *UK* (1999), the European Court of Human Rights permitted the parents of James Bulger both to intervene and make oral representations to the court.

Responsibilities have been placed on the probation service to notify victims about the release of offenders sentenced to imprisonment on conviction for a serious sexual or violent offence. Guidance about this work was issued in a joint Victim Support and Association of Chief Officers of Probation Joint Statement *The Release of Prisoners: Informing, Consulting and Supporting Victims* (1996). An HM Inspectorate of Probation Thematic Inspection Report on Victims (2000) highlighted good practice and recommended improvements.

PROTECTION

Witness intimidation is made a criminal offence by the Criminal Justice and Public Order Act 1994. The conviction must be quashed and a retrial ordered where there has been a subsequent conviction for intimidating witnesses in the original trial which led to the acquittal (the Criminal Procedure and Investigations Act 1996).

A number of recent measures provide additional protection from harassment:

- the Protection from Harassment Act 1997 creates a new criminal offence of harassment and permits a civil court to grant an injunction;
- the Family Law Act 1996 streamlines domestic violence provisions across all courts with jurisdiction in family matters which can make non-molestation and occupation orders. A power of arrest may be attached;
- the Crime and Disorder Act 1998 permits a magistrates' court to make an anti-social behaviour order on the application of the police or a local authority;
- Part V of the Housing Act 1996 permits a local authority to bring an injunction against an anti-social tenant. A power of arrest may be attached.

Under the Youth Justice and Criminal Evidence Act 1999, witnesses may be eligible for one or more of the Act's special measures if they are:

- under 17;
- have a learning disability, physical disability, or mental disorder that the court considers significant enough to affect the quality of their evidence;
- are likely, because of their own circumstances and the circumstances relating to their case, to suffer fear or distress in giving evidence which is expected to affect its quality.

A victim of a sexual offence will be eligible unless he or she tells the court they do not want to be eligible.

The special measures include:

- the use of screens round the witness box so that the witness and the defendant cannot see each other;
- being asked questions through an intermediary;
- using aids to communication;
- barristers and judges removing their wigs and gowns;
- giving evidence from a separate room via a live TV link;
- giving evidence through an interview recorded on video before the trial;
- having cross-examination recorded on video before the trial.

STATE COMPENSATION FOR VICTIMS OF VIOLENT CRIME

State compensation for victims of violent crime was first introduced in 1964 on a non-statutory basis and was administered by the Criminal Injuries Compensation Board (CICB). Damages were assessed on the same basis as for a civil action for personal injuries arising from a road traffic incident or an accident at work. The current scheme was established under the Criminal Injuries Compensation Act 1995 and is administered by the Criminal Injuries Compensation Authority (CICA).

The CICA scheme broke the link with common law damages. It moved away from payment based on individual assessment, and provides for payment to be made on the basis of a tariff (scale) of awards that group together injuries of comparable severity and allocates a financial value to them. Injuries are classified under some 300 descriptions against 25 bands ranging from £1,000 to £250,000. Compensation is also paid for loss of earnings if the victim is unable to work as a result of the injury for more than 28 weeks. In such circumstances, compensation may also be paid for certain special expenses. Families of homicide victims are entitled to claim a fixed fatal award (£5,000–£10,000), compensation for loss of dependency and funeral expenses.

The 1996 tariff scheme was introduced for two reasons. First, to reduce the spiralling cost of the old scheme. The scheme was claimed to be the most generous in Europe, and probably the world. In 1965/6, just £0.4 million was paid out to 1,164 victims. By 1980/1, £21 million was paid to 20,000 victims and by 1990/1, £109 million to 35,000 victims. The cost is now more predictable and awards do not automatically increase in line with inflation. Second, to simplify the scheme so that it would be easier for victims to understand and cheaper for the CICA to administer. In March 1999, the Home Office introduced a consultation paper *Possible Changes to the Criminal Injuries Compensation Scheme*. This led to the scheme being revised and all applications received since 1 April 2001 are assessed under the 2001 Criminal Injuries Compensation Scheme. The main changes to the 1996 scheme are an increase in the level of awards and extending eligibility for fatal awards to same-sex partners.

In 1998/9, 78,651 new claims were made. Of the 74,859 claims which were resolved under the new scheme, 40,164 (53.7 per cent) resulted in an award. The highest award was £0.5 million. Compensation payments totalled some £200 million.

In order to establish a 'criminal injury', a victim must have suffered a personal injury in Great Britain which was directly attributable to:

- a crime of violence (including arson, fire-raising or an act of poisoning); or

- an offence of trespass on a railway (to compensate train drivers who suffer psychological injury as a result of suicides on railway lines);

- the apprehension or attempted apprehension of an offender or a suspected offender, the prevention or attempted prevention of an offence, or the giving of help to any constable who is engaged in any such activity.

It is not necessary for an assailant to have been convicted of any criminal offence. Indeed, it is not necessary for a crime to have been committed, if the victim who was seeking to prevent an offence, reasonably believed that an offence was taking place (*R v CICB, ex p Ince* [1973]). Most road traffic offences are specifically excluded from the scheme as the victim will usually be able to claim from the offender's insurance company or through the Motor Insurers' Bureau.

The injury must be sufficiently serious to qualify for the minimum award of £1,000. This extends to a minor indecent assault, a chipped tooth, a disabling but temporary mental anxiety provided that this is medically verified, a fractured rib, or a range of injuries lasting 6 to 13 weeks (e.g. double vision, sprained wrist or partial deafness). Minor multiple injuries will suffice where the injuries have necessitated at least two visits to a medical practitioner. At least three separate injuries must have been sustained under the following categories, at least one of which had significant residual effects six weeks after the incident:

- grazing, cuts, lacerations;
- severe and widespread bruising;
- severe soft tissue injury;
- black eye;
- bloody nose;
- hair pulled from scalp;
- loss of fingernail.

Examples of the Tariff

	£
Sprained wrist disabling for more than 13 weeks	2,500
Displaced fracture of nasal bones	1,500
Dislocated jaw	2,000
Fractured or dislocated wrist – substantial recovery	3,300
Scarring causing serious disfigurement to upper limbs	5,500
Moderate burns to face	5,500
Fractured or dislocated wrist – continuing disability	6,600
Pattern of severe child sexual abuse over a period in excess of 3 years	8,200
Non-consensual vaginal and/or anal intercourse	11,000
Severe burns to upper limbs	11,000
Loss of ear	11,000
Loss of kidney	22,000
Paralysis of leg	27,000

Loss of one eye	27,000
Permanent and extreme serious brain damage (no effective control of functions)	250,000

Exclusions from the scheme

Compensation may be withheld or reduced if the victim fails to report the incident to the police 'without delay', or fails to co-operate with the police in bringing the offender to justice. The crime must be reported even if there is no chance that the offender will be apprehended. These rules tend to be applied strictly.

Compensation may also be refused or reduced to 'undeserving victims' having regard to:

- their conduct 'before, during or after the incident'; or
- their character as established by unspent criminal convictions or available evidence.

The Court of Appeal has held that there is no limit to the sort of conduct which the CICA may take into account (*see Ince*). This includes the victim who provoked a crime or was under the influence of drink or drugs. Under the old CICB scheme, a victim who initiated or agreed to a fight would seldom receive compensation even where the injuries were quite disproportionate to what the victim did or said. This practice is in stark contrast to a civil claim where the victim would succeed.

It had been an article of faith of those who administered the CICB scheme that compensation should be refused where a victim has serious convictions irrespective of any causal connection between the offences and the injury sustained. Such offenders are seen to put themselves beyond the pale of criminal injury compensation. Thousands of people remain eligible for state benefits notwithstanding their criminal convictions. An independent Working Party convened by Victim Support (1993) recommended that this rule should be abolished.

Specific rules relate to violence within the family. Compensation will be refused if there is a likelihood that the offender might benefit from the award. If the victim is aged under 18 years, the CICA must be satisfied that it would be appropriate for an award to be made.

MAKING A CLAIM

The CICA are based at Tay House, 300 Bath Street, Glasgow G2 4LN (Tel: 0800 358 3601), from whom details about the scheme and an application form can be obtained. Claims must normally be made within two years of the incident. It is for the victim to establish their claim. The Victims' Charter provides that the CICA should issue decisions in 12 months. In practice, 60 per cent were issued in eight months, but 15 per cent took more than a year.

The principal reasons for claims failing in 1998/9 were:

- injury did not merit the minimum award of £1,000–32.3 per cent;
- failure to report without delay and/or co-operate with police – 23.9 per cent;
- no crime of violence established – 12.4 per cent;
- conduct before, during or after incident – 11.2 per cent;
- applicant's criminal record – 7.6 per cent;
- other reasons – 12.6 per cent.

Of the 74,859 claims which were resolved under the new scheme, 45 per cent succeeded at the stage of the initial decision. A victim may request a review of that decision. This must be in writing and specify the reasons for requesting the review. It must normally be made within 90 days of the original decision. The review will be conducted by a claims officer more senior than the officer who made the original decision. Reasons must be given for the review decision. In 1989/9, 39.9 per cent of reviews resulted in a successful outcome for the victim.

A victim may appeal against an adverse decision of appeal to the Criminal Injuries Compensation Appeals Panel. The Panel is based at 11th Floor, Cardinal Tower, Farringdon Road, London EC1M 3HS (www.cicap.gov.uk). A *Guide for Applicants* is available. A written notice of appeal specifying the reasons for appealing must normally be sent within 90 days of the review decision. Some appeals must be dealt with on the papers. Others may lead to an oral hearing. Reasons must be given for any decision. In 1998/9, only 44 per cent of appeals were resolved within the target time of six months. In 1998/9, 3,059 appeals were resolved of which 36.8 per cent resulted in a successful outcome.

Legal help, but not representation, is available from the Community Legal Service (*see* page 785). Recent statistics suggest that the lack of legal representation did not have a significantly adverse effect upon the prospects of success.

There is no further appeal, but decisions may be challenged by an application for judicial review in the High Court. There are a number of issues of concern which may lead to successful challenges under the Human Rights Act 1998:

- the manner in which the CICA handle reports from the police and which are not disclosed to a victim;
- witness statements which may influence a CICA decision are only made available to a victim on the morning of an appeal hearing;
- the inability of the CICA to hold an oral hearing prior to making a decision. This has an adverse impact on rape victims where there is an issue of consent.

REDRESS AGAINST THE OFFENDER

Criminal compensation orders

The Powers of Criminal Courts (Sentencing) Act 2000 permits a criminal court that convicts an offender to make a compensation order against the offender in respect of 'any personal injury, loss or damage' arising from the offence or any other offence which is taken into consideration in imposing sentence. A magistrates' court is limited to £5,000 for any one offence of which the offender is convicted (Magistrates' Courts Act 1980 section 40). In principle, this might seem to be a convenient and rapid means of avoiding the expense of resorting to civil litigation. In practice, the section is not as useful as it would appear. A court is obliged to have regard to the means of an offender and few offenders are likely to have the means to pay. Inevitably awards tend to be much lower than those that would be awarded in either a civil claim or by the CICA.

In 1997, magistrates' courts made 90,700 compensation orders. Some 50 per cent of offenders convicted of criminal damage, robbery and violence against the person, and some 25 per cent of offenders convicted of burglary or sexual offences, were ordered to pay compensation. The average amount of compensation for an indictable offence was £196. In the same year, crown courts made 6,500 compensation orders, the average size of which was £998. Nineteen per cent of offenders convicted of violence against the person or criminal damage, were ordered to pay compensation. This fell to some five per cent of those convicted of burglary and robbery. The difference in figures reflects the greater use of imprisonment in the crown courts.

The power to award compensation is remarkably wide and does not cover only damage to property or personal injury. It is not even necessary for the loss to be actionable in a civil claim. Modest amounts have been awarded for emotional distress. £25 was awarded for the terror caused to a householder by a stone being thrown through the window of their house (*Bond* v *Chief Constable of Kent*). The courts are discouraged from making any order where there is a difficult or complex issue relating to liability.

The courts will not impose an order which is unrealistic or which is likely to encourage the offender to commit further offences to meet the requirements of the order. If the offender is imprisoned, it is unlikely that a compensation order will be made. If a defendant is unemployed, the weekly figure is unlikely to be more than £5 per week. Instalments should not extend over an excessive period. Two years is normally considered to be the maximum, although three years is permissible in an exceptional case. The Criminal Procedure and Investigations Act 1996 section 53 permits a court to make an attachment of earnings order, provided that the offender agrees.

Where a court is minded to impose both a fine and compensation, but the offender lacks the means to pay both, the court must give preference to compensation (section 35(4A)). A court must give reasons when it is able to make a compensation order, but decided not to do so. There has been a marked decline in the extent to which compensation orders have been made. Between 1992 and 1997 for indictable offences, there was a decline from 26 per cent to 18 per cent in magistrates' courts, and from 10 per cent to eight per cent in crown courts.

Before making a compensation order, there must either be evidence of the loss or it must be agreed. The police should ask the victim about any loss or damage when the crime is reported and any witness statement is taken. The prosecution is under a duty to bring any potential claim to the attention of the court. Defence counsel who argue that a compensation order is an appropriate sentence are under a duty to satisfy themselves that their client has the ability to pay.

The local magistrates' court has the responsibility for enforcing the order. It also has the power to discharge or reduce a compensation order if the position of the offender has changed. If the offender does not pay, the victim will not receive the compensation. Victims' organizations have argued that the state should pay the compensation ordered in full to the victim and then recover the sum from the offender.

Restitution order

A restitution order may be made pursuant to the Theft Act 1968 section 28 ordering stolen property to be restored to its owner. As with compensation orders, criminal courts seem reluctant to make such orders except in the plainest of cases, when there can be no doubt as to where the property is and to whom it belongs.

A restitution order can also be made when the property has come into the hands of the police pursuant to the Police (Property) Act 1897. In this case there is no need for the property to have been stolen. It might, for example, be an item that was taken by the police to use as evidence. An order can be made in favour of the accused, as well as the victim.

Restorative justice

The Crime and Disorder Act 1998 introduced reparation into the youth justice system through three measures: the Final Warning, Action Plan Order and Reparation Order. It is a pre-condition that the victim should desire reparation. Community/group conferences, which bring victims and offenders together, were also introduced in some areas and may be used as part of the Final Warning stage (which replaced the old system of cautions). The Youth Justice and Criminal Evidence Act 1999 also moved into restorative justice by introducing community-led Youth Offending Panels, in which victims may participate.

A civil claim

A victim of crime is likely to have a civil claim for damages which he could pursue in the county court or the High Court. In practice, civil claims by victims are rare because there is little point in suing an offender who does not have the resources to pay damages (and any legal costs incurred).

There have been a small number of civil claims in high-profile cases where the CPS have declined to prosecute for rape or murder. In such circumstances, the judges will look for cogent evidence before finding for the victim. Success in such a claim will compel the CPS to review its position. In the OJ Simpson case in California (1997), successful civil proceedings were brought after the defendant had been acquitted of homicide.

A civil claim for damages will always be worth pursuing if the offender is insured in respect of the damage. Civil claims for road traffic accidents are common. A scheme operated by the Motor Insurers' Bureau (152 Silbury Boulevard, Central Milton Keynes, MK9 1NG, Tel: 01908 830001) operates where the driver has no insurance. Where the offender has not been traced, compensation for personal injury only may be available.

A private prosecution

Any private individual has the right to institute a private prosecution. Indeed, some have resulted in convictions for serious crimes where the CPS has declined to prosecute. However, the DPP may intervene and take over the conduct of the proceedings (the Prosecution of Offences Act 1985 section 6). The right to institute a private prosecution does not confer a right of access to police statements or evidence. A private prosecutor has the same obligations to ensure a fair trial for the defendant as the public prosecuting authorities.

Public funding is not available, but a private prosecutor is entitled to apply for their costs of prosecuting any indictable offence from public funds (Prosecution of Offences Act 1985 section 17). Such an application is normally made at the conclusion of the proceedings and would normally be granted were the court to be satisfied that the proceedings had been properly brought.

REDRESS AGAINST CRIMINAL JUSTICE AGENCIES

Complaints

Complaints procedures are operated by all the criminal justice agencies to which reference is made in this chapter, particulars of which can be obtained from the relevant organization and are summarized in the Victims' Charter. Complaints can also be made about a court. If you wish to complain about the conduct or behaviour of a judge, write to the Lord Chancellor, House of Lords, London SW1A 0PW.

Judicial review

The remedy that should be considered where the CPS has refused to prosecute is an application for judicial review. The applicant would need to establish that the CPS had exercised its decision not to prosecute improperly. There have been a number of recent successful applications where the CPS has refused to prosecute in respect of deaths in police custody and for manslaughter.

In March 2000, Timothy Jones brought an application for judicial review in respect of the DPP's refusal to bring a manslaughter prosecution in respect of his brother's death at the Horsham Docks. The High Court held that the DPP had acted irrationally and had failed to adequately address the relevant law. Moses J suggested that the DPP's decision 'beggared belief'. The court ordered the DPP to reconsider his decision not to prosecute.

The Human Rights Act will reinforce the duty of the CPS to ensure that the police carry out adequate investigations.

Civil action against the police

Public confidence in the police complaints procedure is low. Any victim of police malpractice (assault, false imprisonment or malicious prosecution) should consider a claim in the civil courts, where a trial by a jury may be available (*see* Chapter 97).

CONTACTS

Useful contacts are:

Organization	Contact details
Cruse – Bereavement Care	0870 167 1677
Commission for Racial Equality	020 7939 0000
ChildLine	0800 11 11

Men's Advice Line and Enquiries	020 8644 9914	Victim Supportline	0845 30 30 900 (PO Box 11431, London sw9 6zh)
National Association of Bereavement Services	0207 709 9090	Victim Support	020 7735 9166 (Cranmer House, 39 Brixton Road, London sw9 6dz)
National Child Protection Helpline	0800 800 5000		
RoadPeace	020 8964 1021		
Samaritans	0345 90 90 90		
Support after Murder and Manslaughter (SAMM)	020 7735 3838	Women's Aid National Domestic Violence Helpline	0845 702 3468

90

Mental Health and the Law

Areas in which the law concerns issues of mental health include detention in hospital, treatment, community care and the administration of the property and affairs of patients. The main source of law in this field is the Mental Health Act 1983. The 1983 Act makes provision for the compulsory detention and treatment of patients in hospital in a variety of circumstances. These include a process of civil commitment and of criminal sentencing. In the former case, the guiding principle is that as much treatment as possible is to be on a voluntary basis with compulsory powers being used only when essential. Practice and procedure under the Act is amplified by a code of practice (most recently in 1998) which acts as guidance to statutory authorities, managers and professional staff. Other important provisions of the Act include guardianship and Mental Health Review Tribunals (MHRTs).

The 1983 Act deals with a broad category of mental disorder which encompasses four sub-categories:

- mental illness;
- psychopathic disorder;
- mental impairment; and
- severe mental impairment.

There is no definition of mental illness in the Act, and its usage is largely a matter for the judgement of doctors. More colloquially, the term is understood to represent schizophrenic or depressive-type illnesses and includes anorexia nervosa. Psychopathic disorder is a legal term which covers the gamut of personality disorders described in psychiatry. There is currently a debate as to whether personality disorder is appropriately dealt with within mainstream mental health services, which concerns the question of 'treatability' (see page 680) and also the difficulty of making that diagnosis. The government has proposed a separate system of detention in special institutions for those capable of being assessed as being dangerous and severely personality disordered. There is as yet no legislation. 'Severe mental impairment' and 'mental impairment' are associated with a mental handicap. A person does not come within any of these categories merely by reason of being sexually promiscuous, because of immoral or deviant behaviour, or because of a dependency on alcohol or drugs.

The criteria for detaining a person in hospital under the Act were influenced by a ruling of the European Court of Human Rights and can be abbreviated to:

- the 'appropriateness' test – is the person suffering from a mental disorder (illness) of a nature or degree which warrants detention in hospital?; and
- the 'safety' test – is detention in the interest of the health and safety of the person or for the protection of others?

'Community care' is a term which gained currency in the late 1980s when large mental institutions were gradually closed down and patients moved into the community. It gained statutory status with the passing of the National Health Service and Community Care Act 1990 (NHSCCA) which came into effect in 1993. This made wide provision for assessments of vulnerable people in the community, including the mentally disordered, under existing legislation such as the National Assistance Act 1948 and the Mental Health Act 1983. It imposes certain duties on local social services departments to arrange multi-agency assessments and make provision for, among other things, housing. Allied to this is Department of Health guidance on the 'Care Programme Approach' (CPA) which is intended to provide a system of support for all those discharged from the specialist mental health services and not only those detained under a section. These processes overlap with the provision of after-care within the 1983 Act.

ADMISSION TO HOSPITAL

Admission can be voluntary (informal) or compulsory (formal). The majority of admissions are voluntary and, in these cases, the patients are free to discharge themselves at any time – even against medical advice.

There are several ways in which compulsory admission

can be authorized. The main scheme of the Act involves assessment by an approved social worker (ASW) supported by two medical recommendations from doctors approved under the Act. Applications for admission can be made by a patient's nearest relative or an ASW. The importance of the particular section under which admission is carried out relates to the length of detention, arrangements for discharge, and the power to give compulsory treatment.

The types of compulsory admission

Admission for assessment: Section 2

To be detained under this section, a patient need only be suffering from a broadly defined mental disorder which requires assessment (followed by treatment) in hospital in order that a proper diagnosis can be reached. The application can be made by the nearest relative (*see* below) or an ASW with two supporting medical recommendations. Admission is for a period of 28 days, after which a patient must either be discharged or the section converted to a section 3 admission for treatment. There is a right to a hearing before an MHRT.

Discharge can be ordered by the patient's doctor, the hospital managers, the nearest relative (*see* below) or the MHRT (*see* below).

Admission for treatment: Section 3

For admission under this section it is necessary for there to be a diagnosis under one of the four sub-categories of mental disorder (*see* above). Applications can be made by a nearest relative or ASW, as with section 2, on the ground that admission for treatment in hospital is necessary. Admission is initially for a period of six months, which can be renewed for a further six months and thereafter for periods of one year at a time. During each of these periods of renewal there is a right to a hearing before an MHRT.

In addition to satisfying the 'appropriateness' and 'safety' tests (*see* above), there is what is known as the 'treatability' test, which applies to those suffering from psychopathic disorder or mental impairment. This stipulates that treatment in hospital is 'likely to alleviate or prevent a deterioration' of that condition. It is this provision which creates the controversy when applied to the difficult category of psychopathic disorder and admission to hospital cannot be authorized if this test is not satisfied. This has given rise to much media attention in relation to those who are assessed as being a danger within the community and not amenable to treatment and hospital admission.

'Medical treatment' under the 1983 Act is widely defined to include 'nursing, and also includes care, habilitation and rehabilitation under medical supervision'. This is in addition to the more recognizable forms of medical treatment which come in the form of tablets or injections, and the more serious types of treatment such as brain surgery or ECT (*see* below). The breadth of this definition applies to the 'treatability' test. Supervised care, which has the effect of preventing deterioration of the symptoms of the disorder, such as aggression, even if not the disorder itself, could, in an individual case, be sufficient to fulfil the test.

Many argue that this is too broad and no different from locking a person up in hospital when they are no longer responding to, or are refusing, treatment, for the protection of the public; and that hospitals are not prisons. Others state that the therapeutic environment alone may encourage the refusing patient to change his mind about participating in treatment. This applies particularly to personality disordered people for whom treatment is normally a form of talking therapy which cannot be forcibly administered.

Discharge can be ordered by the patient's doctor, the hospital managers, nearest relative (*see* below) or MHRT (*see* page 685).

There is a joint statutory duty on health authorities and social services departments to provide after-care for patients discharged under this section. The failure to provide such after-care can be challenged in the High Court and an authority may be forced to provide after-care. In fulfilling this requirement a care programme is devised with a nominated key worker responsible for supervising the person concerned in the community and ensuring that he complies with the programme.

Since 1 April 1996 it has been possible to provide after-care under statutory supervision. This is known as 'supervised discharge'. This is a form of guardianship which contains no power to detain and treat in the community and is aimed at those 'revolving door' patients with health needs in the community, especially those likely to stop taking medication leading to a deterioration in their condition.

Emergency admission: Section 4

In a case of urgent necessity an application for admission for assessment under section 2 can be made by the nearest relative or an approved social worker, and with one doctor's recommendation, where there would otherwise be undesirable delay in completing the formalities for such an admission. A patient can be detained under this provision for a period of 72 hours only, unless within that time a second medical recommendation is obtained. It is only to be used in real emergencies and it is not renewable. There is no power to administer compulsory treatment.

Compulsory detention of a patient already in hospital: Section 5

A hospital inpatient may be compulsorily detained for up to 72 hours if the doctor in charge thinks that it is necessary to make an application under sections 2 or 3 (*see* above) for admission. This power can be used by a senior nurse for a period of six hours in relation to a voluntary patient receiving psychiatric treatment when it is not practicable to get the immediate attendance of a doctor and the patient is threatening to leave the hospital.

It is improper for this power to be used in any way to coerce a patient into remaining in hospital against his will. Arrangements must be made swiftly for admission formalities to be completed.

Guardianship: Sections 7 and 8

Again, an application may be made by a nearest relative or a social worker. The criteria are that a person is suffering from one of the four sub-categories of mental disorder which make guardianship appropriate and it is in the interests of their welfare or the protection of others to do so. Two medical recommendations are required. The effect of an application is that the guardian (usually the local social services authority) can require the person to live at a particular place, to attend at places for medical treatment or work or education and that it allows access to the patient to any doctor or ASW or other person.

A person cannot be detained or treated forcibly under this section. The aim is to provide community supervision with as little constraint as possible and to enable a person to achieve an independent life. It is usually used for elderly mentally disordered people or those with a mental handicap, but should also be considered for other mentally disordered individuals.

Discharge can be ordered by the person's doctor, social services authority, nearest relative or MHRT during the first six months of the order and, thereafter, during each period of renewal, i.e. six months and then yearly.

Detention by police or social worker: Sections 135 and 136

An ASW can apply to a magistrate for the police to be allowed to enter premises and take someone to a 'place of safety' (i.e. hospital, police station or residential home) when the person is believed to be suffering from a mental disorder and has been neglected or ill-treated, or is unable to look after themselves (section 135). A police station is to be used as a last resort and detention is allowed for a period of 72 hours. The police may also obtain the sanction of a magistrate to take into custody a patient who has absconded from compulsory detention. In either situation the police may use reasonable force.

Section 136 provides a wide power for a constable to remove a person from a public place to a place of safety whom he believes to be suffering from a mental disorder and to be in need of care and control, if he thinks it is in their interests or for the protection of others. Importantly, this power enables the police to remove and detain someone who has not committed an offence. This action is not supported by any medical evidence and is based on the subjective impression of the individual police officer alone. Detention for 72 hours is permitted during which time an assessment by a doctor and an ASW should be carried out with a view to deciding on future care.

Criminal court powers: Sections 37 and 41

Any criminal court can make a hospital or guardianship order (section 37) in respect of a defendant charged with an offence punishable by imprisonment. The criteria are similar to those under section 3 and include the 'treatability' test. The written or oral evidence of two doctors, one of whom will be responsible for treating the person, is required. Once such an order is made the person passes out of the criminal justice system and into the hospital system and is treated almost exactly as any other patient admitted under a civil section. He may be detained for an initial period of six months and may be discharged by a doctor. If the order expires without renewal, the patient may leave. An order under this section is not a punishment.

A crown court may also make an order restricting the discharge of the offender from hospital if it considers that it is necessary for the protection of the public from serious harm (section 41). Such restrictions are more usually unlimited in time and have the effect of involving the Home Secretary in decisions concerning leave of absence and discharge. A doctor does not have the power to discharge such a patient. Discharge is only possible through an MHRT or the Home Secretary. The powers relating to discharge include a conditional discharge where a person is to remain liable to recall, or otherwise absolute discharge. Once a person is adjudged to be eligible for a conditional discharge the requirements for detention no longer exist and an undue delay in making suitable arrangements for discharge has been held to violate the European Convention on Human Rights.

There are also powers for transferring convicted and unconvicted prisoners between court, prison and hospital.

Nearest relative

Who is the nearest relative?

Who the nearest relative is will be judged in accordance with the following list and in the order set out: spouse, child, parent, brother or sister, grandparent, grandchild, uncle or aunt, nephew or niece. A person who has been living with the patient for six months as a spouse will be regarded as such if the real spouse is permanently living separately. This would also include same-sex partners.

Discharging the patient

When discharging a patient admitted for assessment and treatment (sections 2 and 3), the nearest relative must give at least 72 hours' notice in writing to the hospital managers. Discharge may be barred if the treating doctor issues a report within the 72 hours stating that in his opinion if the patient is discharged he is likely to act in a manner dangerous to himself or to others. If this happens the nearest relative's only remedy is to apply to an MHRT, but not if the patient is detained under section 2.

Replacing the nearest relative

There are also provisions under which a nearest relative may be replaced on application to the county court by any relative, or other person with whom the patient had been living, or the local social services authority. The most important grounds on which this can be done is where the nearest relative is said to have unreasonably objected to an application for admission for treatment or guardianship, or to have exercised his power to discharge without regard to the welfare of the patient, or the interests of the public. The replaced nearest relative can apply to an MHRT for the patient's case to be reviewed. This procedure is a distressing one for relatives and should be used sensitively and sparingly.

Informing the nearest relative

When a detained patient is discharged, a hospital is under a duty to inform their nearest relative, but a patient or their nearest relative can request that this information is not given. There is no way in which a patient can prevent a nearest relative being consulted by a social worker on admission to hospital. This may be difficult where, for example, the nearest relative has a difficult or abusive relationship with the patient and constitutes a breach of the European Convention that the government has undertaken to reform.

Proposals in the government's draft Mental Health Bill would allow the patient to choose his or her 'nominated person' but would remove the existing powers of the nearest relative almost entirely. If the Bill passes into law it is unlikely to come into force before 2006.

Children

There is no minimum age limit for admission to hospital under the 1983 Act, except that only a person who has reached the age of 16 years can be subject to guardianship or supervised discharge. Once a child has reached 16 years, and is capable of expressing his or her own wishes,

there is no need for parental consent for admission on an informal basis.

Treatment in hospital

The 1983 Act deals specifically with the circumstances in which treatment may be forced on a psychiatric in-patient. None of the provisions apply to patients admitted under an emergency power, a doctor's or nurse's holding power, or where a defendant is remanded to hospital for a court report or to a person under guardianship.

Subject to this, the Act does apply to all patients (voluntary or detained) where the most serious treatments (brain surgery or the surgical implantation of hormones for the purposes of reducing male sex drive), are concerned and there are safeguards regarding such treatment: the patient's consent and a second medical opinion are required.

The second opinion doctor is appointed by the Mental Health Act Commission (MHAC). He must endorse the likely efficacy of the treatment and, together with two independent people, also appointed by the MHAC, must certify that the patient is capable of understanding the nature and purpose of the proposed treatment and has been able to offer proper consent to it. In the years between 1983 and 1995, 304 referrals for second opinions were made and surgery was authorized in 242 of them.

Otherwise, in relation to detained patients, their consent or a second opinion is required for other serious treatments such as ECT and *after* a treating doctor has been administering medicine to them for a period of *three months*. The patient's ability to consent must be certified by a doctor. If a second opinion becomes necessary it must address the patient's capacity as well as the efficacy of the medication. The opinion must also be based on consultation with two others, not medically qualified, but who have been professionally involved with the patient's treatment, one of whom must be a nurse. All the safeguards provided for in the Act can be overridden if treatment is needed urgently and the Act defines what this means.

Importantly, therefore, for a period of three months a treating doctor may administer medication to a detained patient against their will, although this may be unrealistic and counter-therapeutic in practice.

In all other cases not dealt with by the Act, the patient's informed consent to treatment is required (as in any treatment for a disorder unconnected with a patient's mental disorder). This means real consent of a patient with sufficient understanding to consent to the proposed treatment, after an explanation at least in broad terms by a doctor as to its effects and any risks involved. Without this, staff may be open to an action for damages for assault. Such treatment may also be a crime. A doctor can only proceed without consent if the treatment is urgently needed and must be able to demonstrate that it complies with acceptable standards of treatment.

Where a patient does not have the ability to consent, the refusal and the decision to treat must be considered very carefully by the doctors involved. The doctor's duty is to exercise his clinical judgement in the best interests of the patient and to act in accordance with prevailing standards of treatment. In cases of doubt as to the effect of a refusal, and especially if there is a threat to life, it is possible to apply to the courts for a decision. Psychiatric treatment with unpleasant side-effects is unlikely to breach the European Convention on Human Rights.

PATIENTS' CIVIL RIGHTS

The basic position is that a patient detained under the 1983 Act retains all civil rights which have not been specifically removed. There are various restrictions on the civil liberties of in-patients in mental hospitals (detained or not) and many of these are dealt with by the code of practice. Policies must be created carefully and decisions limiting a patient's rights must only take into account relevant factors and not be irrational. Restrictions imposed on a patient are potentially open to challenge in the High Court and may, additionally, violate the European Convention on Human Rights. It is unlikely that the conditions of detention in the UK generally will breach the European Convention as being inhuman or degrading.

Right to vote

The Representation of the People Act 2000 removed the bar on the use of a psychiatric hospital address for registration purposes. So both voluntary and detained civil patients can register as an elector either at the place of their detention or at another address with which they have a local connection. However, under the Mental Health Act 1983, people detained in hospital via the criminal courts are banned from voting.

Visits

Patients have no statutory right to visits but the code of practice sets out the rights of detained patients. They are entitled to maintain contact with or receive visits from anyone they wish, subject to some limited exceptions. Visitors may be excluded for medical reasons connected with adverse effects on the therapeutic process or the mental health of the patient, or on security grounds, if the visitor's behaviour is disruptive. Exclusion should be a last resort.

There should be a policy on the visits of the children of patients written in consultation with social services. Visits should only happen following a decision that they are in the child's best interests. Consideration of the right to family life of the patient and the child under the European Convention on Human Rights should be given.

The Act allows medical visits for the purpose of advising a nearest relative and others, including the Secretary of State, on issues relating to discharge. It also allows visits by Mental Health Act Commissioners in the pursuance of their duties in relation to detained patients. There are also provisions dealing with visits by Lord Chancellor's Visitors. These are aimed at assisting the court with questions relating to capacity where the administration of property and affairs is concerned.

Control and restraint

The code of practice sets out situations in which a patient may become difficult to manage and recognizes that it may sometimes be necessary to use restraint or seclusion as a last resort or in an emergency. Restraint should only be performed by trained staff. Seclusion is confinement in a room and should be for the shortest time possible.

Correspondence and communication

A person to whom mail (including parcels) is being sent by a detained patient can ask for it to be withheld. Special Hospital managers (Broadmoor, Rampton or Ashworth) have wider powers and outgoing mail can be withheld if it is likely to cause distress to anyone or to cause danger, and incoming mail may be held back for the safety of the patient or the protection of others. Mail can be opened and inspected in order to decide whether to withhold it or not. The patient whose mail is opened or withheld must be notified of that fact in writing. Such a decision may be reviewed by the MHAC (*see* below).

Patients should have reasonable access to telephones, but their use of ward-based telephones may be controlled to prevent abuse, fraud and the introduction into the hospital of prohibited substances and articles.

Information

In accordance with the code of practice, a hospital must ensure that detained patients are given and understand specific information on admission including in relation to proposed treatment, reasons for detention, applications to an MHRT and the role of the MHAC.

Personal searches

The code of practice deals with searches and advises that there should be an operational policy in place. The courts have decided that a power to detain a person under the Act necessarily implies a power to search them or their property with or without cause. This power is to be used only where there is a 'self-evident and pressing need' and in doing so the effect of a search on the mental health of a patient is a relevant consideration.

Marriage and conjugal rights

Detained patients are able to get married in hospital and there are special provisions relating to the requirements of the marriage notice. Anyone who does not believe that the patient is capable of giving valid consent to the marriage may enter a caveat with the Superintendent Registrar before the ceremony. The Superintendent Registrar will then adjudicate upon the issue. There are no rights to conjugal visits from spouses or other partners (including homosexual partners). The European Convention on Human Rights is relevant here but remains untested in relation to detained patients on this subject.

Diplomatic immunity

Owing to diplomatic privileges, diplomats and their families should not be made subject to the 1983 Act.

Jury service

Mentally disordered people who are resident in a psychiatric hospital, or who regularly receive treatment from a GP, cannot serve on a jury.

Driving licences

Driving licence applications (including applications for renewal) must declare whether the applicant is receiving in-patient treatment for a mental disorder, or is suffering from a mental disorder that could lead to their being detained. In such a case the Secretary of State for the Environment will usually refuse to grant a licence.

Clothes

Detained and voluntary patients have the right to wear their own clothes and cannot be forced to wear bed clothes (or hospital-provided clothes) all the time.

Property

Patients' property cannot be interfered with unless they consent or someone is authorized to do so by the Court of Protection (a special branch of the High Court which deals with the administration of the property of people who are unable to manage their own affairs).

Access to courts

If a patient feels that he has been dealt with badly, or that there is no legal power to detain him, he can take legal action and in some cases compensation may be appropriate. In certain instances the permission of the High Court or the Director of Public Prosecutions is necessary. If a person is so mentally disordered that they are unable to manage their affairs, then a litigation friend is required to take proceedings on their behalf. The advice of a suitably experienced solicitor is essential and public funding may be available. For more information contact the hospital patients' advocate, MIND (the National Association for Mental Health) or a Citizens' Advice Bureau.

Access to medical records

Except for a limited number of cases, patients are entitled to see any of their medical notes made after the end of October 1991. They are also entitled to see their section papers.

Type of case	*Who can apply to MHRT?*
Assessment (s. 2)	Patient in first 14 days. Nearest relative cannot apply.
Treatment (s. 3)	Patient can apply in first 6 months and thereafter during each period of renewal, i.e. 6 months and, thereafter, yearly. Nearest relative cannot apply.
Guardianship (ss. 7 and 8)	As above.
Emergency or doctor/nurse	Neither patient nor nearest relative holding power (ss. 4 and 5) may apply.
Hospital order (s. 37)	Patient or nearest relative in the second 6 months and, thereafter, yearly.
Restricted patient (ss. 37/41)	Patient in second 6 months and, thereafter, yearly. Nearest relative cannot apply.

Type of case	Who can apply to MHRT?
Barring of relative's discharge	Patient cannot apply (except in first 14 days of assessment (*see* above)). Nearest relative can apply within 28 days.
Reclassification of mental disorder	Patient within 28 days. Nearest relative within 28 days.

THE MENTAL HEALTH REVIEW TRIBUNAL

The Mental Health Review Tribunals are independent of hospitals, are chaired by a lawyer and include a psychiatrist and a lay member (who is usually a person with a social services background). They can only consider whether, as at the date of a hearing, the criteria for discharge set out in the 1983 Act have been met. The burden of proof is on the patient, who is entitled to be legally represented at the hearing. (This so-called 'reverse burden of proof' has been successfully challenged under the Human Rights Act, and a declaration of incompatibility with the Convention has been made. The government has already indicated within its review of the 1983 Act that this is to be changed in any new legislation.) The Act sets out when and by whom an application to the MHRT can be made. The main occasions are outlined in the table above. The Secretary of State is also able to refer a case to the MHRT.

Tribunal's powers to discharge

In any case before it (unless there is a restriction order), a tribunal has a discretion to discharge a patient. A tribunal must discharge a patient detained for assessment (section 2) if it is satisfied of any one of the following:

- that he is not suffering from a mental disorder severe enough to justify further detention for assessment (or assessment followed by treatment); or
- that detention is not necessary for the patient's own health or safety or for the protection of others.

In any other case (admission for treatment (section 3), or a hospital order (section 37)) a detained patient must be discharged if:

- he is not suffering from the form of mental disorder for which he was admitted, which is severe enough to warrant further detention in hospital for treatment; or
- detention is not necessary for treatment in the interests of his own health or safety or the protection of others; or
- in the case of a patient in respect of whom a doctor has issued a certificate preventing a nearest relative

from discharging them (*see* above), that the patient is not likely to act in a dangerous manner to others or themselves.

In exercising its discretion to discharge a patient the tribunal must consider the 'treatability' test (*see* above). It may also recommend, among other things, leave of absence with a view to discharge on a future date. The 'treatability' test is also relevant when considering the discharge of a restricted patient; however, it has been widely defined (*see* above).

In a restricted case (section 41), the tribunal must additionally consider the need for the patient to be liable to be recalled to hospital. If he should be, then a conditional discharge will be appropriate. If not, then that patient may be absolutely discharged. There is no general discretion to discharge. There is a power to defer a conditional discharge pending arrangements for after-care being made; however, the European Court of Human Rights has said that the patient's discharge must not be unduly delayed.

The only appeal against a decision of a tribunal is on a point of law.

Tribunal procedure

The procedure is contained in the MHRT Rules. The hearings are normally held in private at the patient's hospital. The patient may ask for it to be held in public at the discretion of the tribunal. The proceedings are usually informal and conducted by the tribunal as it thinks best. A patient is entitled to have legal or other representation, and the patient and his doctor may hear each other's evidence, question each other and call witnesses. There are no strict rules of evidence.

The hospital authority must provide certain reports, including a medical report, for the hearing and these must be disclosed to the patient or representative. In a restricted case the Secretary of State must provide a statement.

A solicitor can arrange an independent psychiatric and/or social work report if necessary (public funding will generally cover at least one).

The tribunal has power to take evidence on oath, to order witnesses to attend and to produce any documents. The medical member examines the patient before the hearing date and inquires into all relevant aspects of his health and treatment.

Advice and representation

It is most important that a patient should receive advice and representation when appealing to a tribunal. This can be given by a solicitor under public funding. There is a panel of solicitors experienced in this field of work approved by the Law Society. Every hospital should have a list of local approved solicitors. Alternatively, details are obtainable from the Law Society or MIND (Mindinfo Line: 0845 766 0163; website: www.mind.org.uk).

Expenses may be paid to the nearest relative, representatives of the patient or their nearest relative (unless they are lawyers) and any witnesses whose evidence the MHRT feels has been helpful. Expenses are rail fares, subsistence and any loss of earnings agreed by the tribunal.

MENTAL HEALTH ACT COMMISSION

The MHAC has powers designed for the protection of detained patients. The Commissioners can visit and report on practices in hospitals under the 1983 Act, visit patients and investigate complaints made by them. It has no power to discharge detained patients.

Inquiries

The Secretary of State has a power under the 1983 Act to set up an inquiry into any case in which he thinks it advisable to do so. The first inquiry into events at Ashworth Special Hospital, which reported in 1992, was set up under this provision. There is non-statutory guidance issued by the NHS Executive which obliges a health authority to set up an independent inquiry following a homicide by a patient who has been within its mental health services (detained or not).

Human Rights Act 1998

The approach to mental health law and consequently the experiences of detained patients will be significantly affected by this Act. This is in spite of the fact that the European Convention makes only passing reference to 'persons of unsound mind' in the same breath as infectious diseases, alcoholics and vagrants. Mental health issues were not, therefore, at the forefront of the minds of its drafters.

The European Court has already reached some landmark decisions in this field. These deal with the criteria for admission, the need for objective medical evidence, the independence of tribunals, the time-scale for tribunal hearings and delays around discharge.

There are still areas in which the 1983 Act is potentially incompatible with the Convention; for example, there is no requirement for objective medical evidence when a conditionally discharged patient is recalled to hospital.

91

Immigration, Nationality and Asylum

The law relating to immigration, nationality and asylum is extremely complex. Entry clearance and immigration officers expect applicants to know the rules and provide them with all the relevant facts relating to their application. An application will fail if it is not on the correct form or if all the evidence needed to meet the requirements of what are now very strict immigration rules is not provided. As a result, it is important to consult a firm of solicitors or a law centre, which has been awarded a franchise to provide immigration advice within the Community Legal Service. This will mean that their abilities have been assessed and that they have been deemed to be competent. It will also mean that they will be able to provide applicants with free legal help, if they meet the financial criteria for such help, and free representation at any immigration appeal hearing, if the case has legal merit and the financial criteria for such representation are met.

Immigration law is constantly changing and the Home Secretary is permitted to use a great deal of discretion when making decisions. Applicants should not rely on casual advice from friends or acquaintances. Even though a friend of a friend in similar circumstances was allowed to stay, that does not mean that a different individual will also be permitted to remain in the country. There are at least six pieces of legislation which can affect an individual's immigration status. In particular, the Nationality, Immigration and Asylum Act 2002, which received Royal Assent on 7 November 2002, radically overhauled the asylum system (*see further* below). In addition, an application will have to meet more complex criteria contained in the Immigration Rules. The rights of immigrants and asylum-seekers are also constantly being considered and reconsidered in the Immigration Appeal Tribunal and the higher civil courts and there may be a recent decision which affects an individual application.

Alternatively, applicants may be able to rely on one of many non-statutory concessions and policies adopted by the Home Office to deal with particular situations. The Home Office has decided that it will, as a general rule, not remove a family from the UK if a child within that family has lived here for more than seven years. A competent adviser will be aware of all these different sources of law.

A RIGHT TO ENTER AND REMAIN

Broadly speaking, individuals can only enter the UK as of right, and remain here without any restrictions, if they are British citizens. However, it is often very difficult to ascertain who is entitled to British citizenship. As the UK withdrew from its colonies abroad and they gained independence, some people retained a right to full British citizenship. This usually arose from the fact that they had lived in the UK for a number of years, or had a British parent. Others were provided with forms of British passports, which gave them an apparent nationality, but did not permit them to enter the UK, as of right. People born in the UK before 1983 are also entitled to British citizenship. However, people born here after that date will not automatically be entitled to citizenship.

As nationality law is also very complex, it is always worth individuals checking whether they may be entitled to British citizenship, in addition to the nationality already held, due to rights accrued by parents or even grandparents.

The Nationality, Immigration and Asylum Act 2002 introduced a number of measures amending British nationality legislation which came into effect on 7 November 2002. The changes include:

- the requirement for applicants for British citizenship to pass an English-language test;
- a citizenship ceremony involving an oath of allegiance;
- the power to take British nationality away if a British citizen has done anything 'seriously prejudicial to the vital interests of the UK';
- the right for children to be registered as British citizens.

There is a common travel area between the UK and the Irish Republic and, therefore, Irish citizens do not need permission to enter. They can, however, be deported and would be committing a criminal offence if they re-entered while that deportation order was still in existence.

Nationals of other member states of the European Economic Area (EEA), can enter the United Kingdom when they are exercising rights of free movement for the purposes of employment or self-employment, study or retirement. When they do so they can bring their immediate family with them.

Most other EEA countries no longer operate border controls between their countries, and across Europe policies on family reunion and the rights of foreign workers are being harmonized. The UK has retained its own system of immigration control, but in practice its immigration policies are increasingly influenced by practices adopted in other EEA countries.

It is likely that the EEA will expand over the next few years and some Eastern European and Baltic states will be permitted to join. Meanwhile, in anticipation of such an expansion, the EEA has made a number of Association Agreements with countries in Eastern Europe and the Baltic states, and their nationals are now permitted to enter in order to set up in business or self-employment. There is also a separate Association Agreement with Turkey, which gives certain rights to Turkish workers who have obtained employment in EEA countries.

APPLYING FOR PERMISSION TO ENTER OR REMAIN IN THE UNITED KINGDOM

Nationals of any other country have to seek permission to come to the UK and, once here, will need permission to extend their stay. If a person from one of what are termed 'visa national' countries, they will also have to obtain entry clearance from an entry clearance officer in their local British High Commission or Embassy before they travel. It is possible to check whether a person is a visa national by referring to the list attached to the Immigration Rules, but note that countries are also added to the list, from time to time, by the Secretary of State for the Home Office.

In most cases, individuals are likely to be given permission to enter for a clearly defined and short period of time and will be expected to leave the country at the end of that period. If a person enters as a visitor, for example, the maximum time they will be permitted to stay on any one occasion is six months. Those coming as students will usually be given permission to stay for a year and then have to apply for an extension, if their course continues beyond that point. Even those coming to join their husbands or wives, who are already entitled to remain in the UK, will initially only be given permission to enter for two years. This will be treated as a trial period for the marriage and, if it can be shown that it is continuing at the end of that time, indefinite leave to remain here will be granted.

There are very few other ways in which individuals can obtain permission to remain in the UK on a permanent or indefinite basis. Marriage to a British citizen, while here for a temporary purpose, is one of them. If the applicant is a minor and their parent is permitted to remain here indefinitely, they can also apply to remain on the same basis. Work permit holders can also apply after four years and refugees are granted indefinite leave once their asylum applications are granted.

It is sometimes possible to extend limited or temporary permission to remain or to obtain permission to remain in some other temporary capacity. However, those who do not obtain further permission and remain in the UK are committing a criminal offence. Those who overstay their leave may risk administrative removal with no right of appeal unless they can assert that such removal would breach their rights under the European Convention on Human Rights (ECHR). Illegal immigrants have the same limited right of appeal against removal. It should be noted that it is also possible to be deemed to be an illegal entrant if an applicant gave false information or omitted to mention relevant facts in order to obtain permission to enter the UK.

ASYLUM-SEEKERS

Those who have left their country because of persecution may be permitted to remain in the UK and should make an application for asylum. The law relating to asylum is very complex and no statements should be made or forms completed before taking legal advice.

The UK will only provide individuals with protection and permanent or indefinite permission to remain if they can show that they are protected by the Convention Relating to the Status of Refugees. The Convention is an international agreement entered into by most countries in the world. Protection under this Convention is offered to those who have suffered persecution for certain limited reasons. To succeed, applicants will have to show that they were persecuted by their government or by a group within their country, from which their government could not protect them. Applicants will also have to show that they were persecuted because of their race, religion, nationality or political opinion or because they belonged to a particular social group within their country. It will also be necessary for applicants to show that they could not seek protection elsewhere in their own country and that they will be persecuted if returned to their country in the future.

These criteria are strictly applied and applicants may find that even though they fear persecution, they will not be found to be refugees. For instance, if an individual is fleeing from civil war, they will have to show that they have a particular personal fear of persecution, which distinguishes them from everyone else. This may be very difficult to do. Applicants may also fear persecution from criminals or members of their own family or tribe. This is unlikely to entitle them to protection under the Refugee Convention. However, if it can be shown that they will suffer torture or inhuman and degrading treatment if returned to their country of origin, it is likely that they will be granted exceptional leave to remain here.

Exceptional leave is used by the Secretary of State for the Home Department to meet responsibilities imposed on the UK by a wide range of international human rights treaties and conventions. It is also used when there are very compassionate circumstances, which indicate that it would be inhumane to send a person back to their country of origin. One example would be where an individual was suffering from AIDS and there was no suitable treatment for their condition in their country of origin. It is also given when a decision to remove a parent or child would break up a family.

DISPERSAL

While applicants are waiting for a decision on their application for asylum and have nowhere to live and no money, they are now only entitled to temporary accommodation and a very basic level of financial support. It is now government policy that applicants should be housed throughout the UK and people are likely to be dispersed to any one of a number of designated areas, even if they have no contacts in that area and there are no members of their community there. The designated areas have been chosen primarily on the basis of availability of accommodation and linguistic resources. The existence of ethnic minority communities in those areas has been a secondary consideration, as has the availability of competent legal advice and other support services.

However, some applicants may have a particular need to be in London. If, for instance, an individual needed counselling from the Medical Foundation for the Care of Victims of Torture, or treatment because they were HIV positive or suffered from AIDS, or had any other serious medical problem and believed that the treatment needed will only be available in London, they should state this at the first opportunity. If applicants do so, they should be placed there, so that their special needs can be met.

Applicants will also be provided with vouchers, which can be exchanged for essential items such as food, and small amounts of cash. The total value of this financial support is set at 70 per cent of the basic income support level.

The National Asylum Support Service (NASS) is responsible for providing applicants with accommodation and financial support. This responsibility continues until 14 days after a final decision on an application or 14 days after appeal rights have been exhausted. After that time, and even if applicants are still pursuing judicial review of any decisions relating to their applications, they will have to leave their accommodation and all support will cease.

However, if applicants have children, accommodation and support will be extended until the time they are removed from the UK. If applicants cannot be removed from the country because, for example, they have no travel documents, an application for financial help to a limited Hard Cases Fund administered by NASS can be made.

The Nationality, Immigration and Asylum Act 2002 introduced a new asylum system based on a network of induction, accommodation and reporting centres as well as existing NASS accommodation. The key changes are:

- the set up of a national network of induction centres to provide a comprehensive reception service to all asylum applicants entering the UK. Each centre is to be located near a port and will provide full-board accommodation for 200–400 asylum applicants. A pilot induction centre has been operational since the beginning of 2002, and further centres are currently being developed;
- Application Registration Cards (ARCs) have replaced the Standard Acknowledgement Letter as the identity document for asylum applicants in the UK. The ARC is a plastic smartcard which provides biometric data about the asylum applicant (personal details, photograph, and the individual's fingerprint). It also states whether the cardholder is entitled to work;
- reporting and residence requirements to be imposed on all asylum-seekers with discontinuance of NASS support to asylum-seekers who fail without reasonable cause to report as required. People may be required to report to a report centre or police station up to 25 miles away or within a 90-minute journey by public transport;
- the introduction of accommodation centres, to provide food, healthcare, education and other facilities. A proportion of new asylum-seekers who request, and are eligible for, support will be offered places in accommodation centres. Those who refuse the offer of a place, voluntarily cease to reside in a centre or breach their conditions of residence will not qualify for other forms of support. The government is still in the process of identifying accommodation centre sites, and there have been issues with planning permissions for sites already

earmarked. It is not expected that these centres will be in place by 2005.

From 8 January 2003 asylum applicants will only be eligible to apply for NASS support if:

- they can prove they have applied for asylum – this only happens once they have been through the asylum-screening procedures;
- they meet the criteria for destitution;
- they apply for asylum 'as soon as reasonably practicable' after arrival in the UK.

NASS support will be withheld for all those in-country asylum applicants who:

- are unable to provide a clear and coherent account of how they came to the UK;
- are unable to provide coherent and accurate information about their circumstances, such as how they have been living in the UK so far;
- do not co-operate with the authorities with further inquiries.

However, it may be that a person deprived of the means of subsistence under these provisions (work not being permitted) is forced into a state of destitution which would breach his or her right not to be treated in an inhuman or degrading manner (contrary to Article 3 of the ECHR). The courts have upheld this principle in recent cases and routinely made interim injunctions ordering NASS to continue with support. Any asylum-seeker in such a plight should seek urgent specialist legal advice.

PERMISSION TO WORK

Applicants who want to work in the UK and who are not British citizens or EEA nationals, or do not have indefinite leave to remain will usually have to obtain a work permit from the Work Permits (UK) before they will be permitted to do so. Work Permits (UK) is part of the Immigration and Nationality Directorate of the Home Office. It must be the employer, and not the applicant, who makes the application, and they will usually have to show that they have been unable to fill the post in the UK or Europe and they have a need for a person of the applicant's specific skills. Permits can sometimes be obtained without fulfilling the requirement for advertising for the post. However, this is only for very senior posts or where there is an acknowledged and acute skill shortage in a particular area.

Since 23 July 2002, asylum applicants are no longer able to work or undertake vocational training until they are given a positive decision on their asylum application, irrespective of how long they wait for a decision. This measure does not affect asylum applicants who were allowed to work before 23 July 2002, or those who applied for their work restrictions to be lifted before 23 July 2002.

There are currently a number of new proposals and pilot schemes to provide permission to work to non-EEA nationals in certain job sectors where there are skill shortages. Expert advice should be sought on this to discover how to apply. The Home Office launched the Highly Skilled Migrant Programme in January 2002 which allows individuals with exceptional skills and experience to come to the UK to seek and take up work.

There are also certain categories of employees, such as ministers of religion, or commonwealth citizens with a grandparent who was a British citizen, who can work without a work permit. In addition, if an applicant is a young person, they may be able to enter as a working holidaymaker or an au pair. Students are also permitted to do part-time work, if it does not interfere with their course work.

APPEAL RIGHTS

If individuals apply to enter or remain in the UK for a reason, which is provided for in the Immigration Rules, and their application is refused, they will usually be entitled to a right of appeal to an Adjudicator within the Immigration Appellate Authority. They may subsequently also be entitled to a further appeal to the Immigration Appeal Tribunal and/or the Court of Appeal. An appeal against any decision to refuse to grant asylum can be made and since 2 October 2000 applicants can appeal on the grounds that a decision has breached their rights under the European Convention on Human Rights, as incorporated by the Human Rights Act 1998.

However, since October 2000, these rights of appeal have been consolidated and applicants have what is termed a one-stop appeal. It is, therefore, very important to raise any issue, which individuals want dealt with by the appellate authority, at the earliest opportunity. If this is not done it may not be possible to raise it at a later stage. In addition, challenges to the manner in which any decision has been made in the High Court may be made by way of an application for judicial review.

Applicants will now be entitled to free representation, by way of Controlled Legal Representation, for any appeal to an adjudicator or the Immigration Appeal Tribunal and litigation assistance for any application to the High Court or appeal to the Court of Appeal. Entitlement will depend upon the legal merits of the case and the applicant's financial circumstances.

The Nationality, Immigration and Asylum Act 2002 introduced a number of significant changes to the appeals system. The key changes are:

- people may have their asylum application certified as 'clearly unfounded' and be removed to their country of origin prior to appeal. This means that the asylum applicant is denied an in-country right of appeal;

- people may be removed prior to appeal to a safe third country regardless of the merits of their claim;
- people refused leave to appeal to the Immigration Appeal Tribunal only have a statutory review rather than full judicial review. This will be to a single High Court judge and only relating to matters of law rather than questions of fact.

FURTHER HELP

For further general advice, you should contact:

Immigration Law Practitioners Association, Tel: 020 7251 8383

Joint Council for the Welfare of Immigrants, 115 Old Street, London EC1V 9RT, Tel: 020 7251 8706

The Law Society (for a list of solicitors, firms and not-for-profit organizations with immigration franchises), 113 Chancery Lane, London WC2A 1PL, Tel: 020 7242 1222.

The Refugee Council, Tel: 020 7346 6777.

92

Political Demonstration and Protest

THE PUBLIC RIGHT TO MEET AND DEMONSTRATE

In the past there has been no statutory or specific common law right to demonstrate recognized within our domestic system of law. However, Article 10 of the European Convention on Human Rights states that everyone has the right to freedom of expression, and Article 11 protects the right to peaceful assembly and association. Freedom of expression includes demonstrating without using words as well as the expression of objectionable and provocative views. The protections afforded by Article 11, however, only apply to lawful demonstrations. Demonstrations are legal only if they do not involve a breach of the law, however trivial that breach may be – for instance, obstructing the highway.

These rights became part of our law when the Convention was incorporated into our domestic law on 2 October 2000. The effect of this is that from that date onwards all existing legislation and case law that has attempted to limit or restrict the right to free expression and/or lawfully demonstrate and assemble will have to be re-interpreted in such a way as to allow for these fundamental rights. It should be stressed, however, that neither of these rights are what are called 'absolute rights', and therefore they may be restricted or otherwise interfered with to the extent that it can be shown that such interference is lawful and 'necessary in a democratic society' (the test of proportionality).

The Public Order Act 1986 creates a set of rules which must be followed before a public procession can take place and offences which are committed if those rules are not adhered to. Under section 13 of that Act, the police have the power to ban processions if the chief officer of police reasonably believes that any conditions he or she might impose are insufficient to prevent serious public disorder. Any decision by the police to ban a demonstration may be challenged by way of judicial review in the High Court. If the police have objective grounds for believing that a planned demonstration is likely to descend into violence and disorder, then it is likely that such a ban will not breach Articles 10 and 11 as it satisfies the test of proportionality referred to above.

Section 14 of the same Act gives the chief officer of police, in certain circumstances, the power to prohibit any specified assembly or demonstration for a period of up to four days. Anyone who knowingly breaches this prohibition commits a criminal offence. The ambit of this criminal offence has recently been severely curtailed by the House of Lords, who concluded that, in the light of Article 11, this could not apply to a peaceful and otherwise lawful demonstrator.

This chapter is concerned with the offences that demonstrators might commit. The hope is that awareness of the possible charges will enable demonstrators to minimize their chances of acting illegally. The main offences are:

- committing a breach of the peace;
- obstructing the highway;
- obstructing/assaulting the police;
- insulting words and/or behaviour;
- affray;
- riot;
- violent disorder;
- picketing offences (*see* page 694).

Meetings and processions

If the meeting is to be on private property, the permission of the owner of the land must be obtained first, for otherwise the people at the meeting will be trespassers (*see* page 254), in which case they can be thrown off the land and sued in the civil courts for any loss occurring.

The Public Order Act 1986 section 39 makes it an offence in certain circumstances to enter land as a trespasser and to fail to leave it after a request by the occupier and a directive by the police to do so. The maximum penalty is three months' imprisonment. The Criminal Justice and Public Order Act 1994 section 68(1), creates an offence of 'aggravated trespass' where someone trespasses on land (in the open air) and does an act which is intended to intimidate, obstruct or disrupt persons engaged in any lawful activity. Any trespasser who has been directed to leave the land by a police officer who fails to leave as soon as is practicable, or who returns within three months also commits an offence. The maximum penalty for either offence is three months' imprisonment or a fine not exceeding level 4. If the meeting is to be on public land there may be a local by-law or a local Act that requires the organizers to give the local authority and the police 36 hours' notice. Failure to do so will be a criminal offence (with a maximum penalty fine).

So far as processions and marches are concerned, the Public Order Act 1986 provides that organizers must give advance notice to the police. Conditions such as rerouting can be imposed if the police reasonably believe there will be serious public disorder, or serious damage to property, or serious disruption to the life of the community, or if the purpose of the organizers is the intimidation of others. The police can ban a proposed procession if the chief officer reasonably believes there will be serious public disorder and that conditions will not prevent it. The Public Order Act 1986 creates controls over public assemblies and gives police the right to impose conditions on those organizing or taking part in an assembly. A public assembly is a meeting of more than 20 persons in a public place wholly or partly open to the air.

In London further restrictions apply, mainly derived from nineteenth-century Acts:

- when Parliament is sitting, no open-air meeting of a 'political nature' with more than 50 participants can be held north of the Thames within one mile of the Houses of Parliament;
- any open-air meeting or procession that obstructs the free passage of MPs to the House, or which causes disorder or annoyance in the neighbourhood, is illegal;
- special Department of the Environment permits are required for meetings etc. in Hyde Park and Trafalgar Square.

Co-operating with the police

In the face of these extensive police powers, it is clearly wise for organizers to co-operate with the police and do more than merely notify them of the intention to hold a public meeting or procession. For, however well-intentioned the organizers may be, they cannot foresee how their supporters (and, indeed, their opponents) will behave. So it is only common sense to liaise with the police before the event.

Private meetings

If the meeting is on private premises, anyone present can be told to leave; if they refuse, the organizers can eject them as trespassers. If they have paid to enter the meeting then they might have a contractual right to stay; to avoid this, the organizers would be well advised to display a notice at the entrance reserving their right to refund money and to ask people to leave.

The police do not have the right to enter private property without a warrant unless it is necessary to do so (among other reasons) for the purpose of saving life or to prevent serious damage to property. There are other powers of entry – for example, to recapture a person unlawfully at large or to arrest for an arrestable offence – but these are not relevant to meetings. Police may also enter premises to deal with or prevent a breach of the peace. A Home Office circular in 1909 expressed what is still the police point of view; namely, a 'preference for the policy of non-interference in ordinary political meetings, although on exceptional occasions it may become necessary to station police inside a meeting for the purpose of maintaining order'.

Organizations

Stewards

Stewards can be appointed at both public and private meetings. In practice, stewards are a very important means of controlling a crowd. The organizers should liaise with the police as to the number and organization of the stewards. Obviously, the stewards have the same status as other private individuals and are not accorded any special legal powers. Thus they cannot use force to ensure compliance with their wishes.

Fly-posting

Sticking posters in public places is illegal under the Town and Country Planning Acts (i.e. because they are treated as adverts – and planning permission is needed for any advertising hoarding), and often under local by-laws as well. The placing of posters and stickers is potentially criminal damage. Exceptions are advertisements for non-commercial events, including political, educational, social and religious meetings, if the prior consent of the owner of the hoarding, window, etc. is obtained. There are usually other detailed requirements, the most important of which is that the poster should be no more than six square feet in size. The local authority will provide further details. Posting an advertisement on someone else's property (e.g. window, lamp post) without permission is punishable – under the planning permission laws – by a fine in the magistrates' court.

Spray-painting

Painting slogans is likely to be illegal under local by-laws. In addition, it is likely to be criminal damage. The cost of repairing the damage can be high; water-based paint soaks into brickwork.

Collecting signatures

A person organizing a petition should take care not to obstruct the highway (*see* below).

Selling pamphlets, etc.

This does not require a street-trading licence, but there is always the risk of obstructing the highway. In the Metropolitan Police area, a licence is needed for charitable (or other benevolent) collections, but not for selling political papers, etc.

Picketing

There is a right to picket, but the right to picket is restricted to industrial disputes involving those doing the picketing and, in particular, does not cover non-industrial pickets (e.g. consumer picket, political picket). *See* the Public Order Act 1986 section 14 with regard to the effect on pickets.

Offences arising from meetings, demonstrations, etc.

Committing a breach of the peace

There is a breach of the peace whenever harm is actually done or is likely to be done to a person or in their presence to their property, or a person is in fear of being so harmed through an assault, an affray, a riot or other disturbance.

Generally, though, there must have been some physical force used or at least some behaviour that would lead one to expect a disturbance involving force – but even with that qualification it is still a widely drawn offence. The offence ranges from minor assaults, threats or obstructions through to more serious offences such as riot and affray. In practice, of course, a person committing a more serious offence would be prosecuted for that offence rather than face the more minor charge of breaching the peace.

A person who is guilty of a breach of the peace will be bound over to keep the peace. If they refuse to be bound over they can be sent to prison. A person can also be lawfully arrested if their conduct is such that it is likely to provoke others to breach the peace. This is particularly relevant where the form of demonstration or protest in question is specifically aimed at disrupting the lawful activities of others (hunt saboteurs are sometimes arrested on this ground).

Obstructing the highway

In the eyes of the law, the highway (including the pavement) is to be used for 'passing and re-passing' – a quaint phrase which means that it is to be used only for travelling from one place to another. Thus it is not to be used for parking one's car, holding a meeting, talking to a neighbour or selling newspapers from a stand, since all of these activities do not involve the use of the highway for 'passing and re-passing'. All are thus obstructions of the highway. To make the offence even wider, the courts have held that it is not even necessary for anyone to have actually been obstructed by the unauthorized act.

It is thus an offence that is easily committed and one for which a person can be arrested by a police officer without a warrant. In practice, though, the court will consider whether the defendant was using the highway 'reasonably' and this will mean taking into account the amount of traffic present, the time of day and the size of the road. Thus a person washing a car in a suburban road on a Sunday morning may be technically obstructing the highway, but will generally be held to have been using the highway 'reasonably', and so would not be prosecuted by the police.

For demonstrators who may be peacefully taking part in a demonstration or lobby, the law has usually been less understanding. The very vagueness of the charge makes it difficult to defend, and if a police officer told the court that he or she thought the demonstrator was causing an obstruction, it was extremely difficult for the demonstrator to avoid conviction. As long as the demonstrator has been acting lawfully in other regards it is likely that, since the advent of the Human Rights Act in October 2000, it will be more difficult to secure a conviction on this basis as the court will now have to give due regard to the individual's right to peaceful assembly under Article 11.

A procession which keeps moving is less likely to be an obstruction of the highway, for the participants can then argue that they were indeed using the highway for 'passing and re-passing'. For this reason, a procession or march is usually a legally safer form of protest than a rally or a lobby. The maximum penalty for obstructing the highway is a fine of £1,000 (level 3).

Obstructing/assaulting a police officer in the execution of his or her duty

The important words here are 'in the execution of his or her duty'. If the police officer was not acting in accordance with his or her legal powers and duties, then the charge must fail. For example, the person who refuses to allow a police constable (PC) to search their bags will not be obstructing the officer in the execution of his or her duty, unless the PC has legal authority to search the bags.

Policemen saw two teenagers going from house to house, so one of the policemen challenged the boys and asked them what they were doing. The boys ran off thinking that the policemen were thugs. The policemen gave chase and caught the boys, who then hit them. When prosecuted for assaulting an officer in the course of his duty, the boys argued that the policemen were not acting in the course of their duty, since the police can use force only to arrest someone, not to detain them for questioning. Held: *This was correct and the boys were acquitted.*   Kenlin (1967)

A youngster was shouting and swearing on a bus. A plain-clothes policeman told him to get off. He began to do so but then the policeman tried to detain him; the youth hit the policeman. Was he guilty of assaulting a policeman in the execution of his duty? Held: *No. The policeman had not arrested the youth and had no legal right to detain him. The policeman was therefore acting illegally in trying to detain the youth – and so was not 'acting in the execution of his duty'.*   Ludlow (1983)

Note that the accused need not know that the PC was, in fact, a police officer for an offence to be committed. So if I hit someone who turns out to be a plain-clothes police officer on duty, I can be prosecuted for the offence; but if he or she is not on duty, I will only face prosecution for simple assault. Both offences can be tried only in the magistrates' court. It has often been suggested that the offences should be triable in the crown court, before a jury, since they are both of a serious nature. The maximum penalty for assaulting a police officer is six months' prison and £5,000 fine; the maximum for obstructing a police officer is one month's prison and £1,000 fine.

Insulting words and/or behaviour

The Public Order Act 1986 section 4 creates an offence of threatening behaviour. A person is guilty if they use towards another threatening, abusive or insulting words or behaviour or distribute or display to another person any writing, sign or other visible representation which is threatening, abusive or insulting and:

- they intend that person to believe that immediate unlawful violence will be used against him or her; or
- they intend to provoke the immediate use of unlawful violence by that person or anyone else; or
- whereby that person is likely to believe that such violence will be used; or
- whereby it is likely that such violence will be provoked.

This offence can be committed in private as well as in public places, but not in a dwelling house, unless the words or behaviour are directed outside (e.g. abuse from window). The maximum penalty for a section 4 offence is six months' imprisonment and/or a fine of £5,000.

The Public Order Act 1986 section 5 creates an offence of disorderly conduct. It penalizes threatening, abusive or insulting words or behaviour or disorderly behaviour within the hearing or sight of a person likely to be caused harassment, alarm or distress. The maximum sentence on conviction is a fine of £1,000. Conduct which is disorderly is not criminal within this section unless it tends to annoy or insult such persons as are faced with it sufficiently deeply or seriously to warrant the interference of the criminal law. A person is guilty of section 5 only if he or she intends their words or behaviour to be threatening, abusive or insulting or is aware that it may be threatening, abusive or insulting. The offence is not arrestable unless the person ignores a warning. It is a defence for the defendant to prove that their conduct was reasonable. Arguably the fact the defendant has the burden of proving this defence breaches the 'presumption of innocence' contained in Article 6(2) of the European Convention. If the behaviour was intentional then section 4(a) may apply – the maximum sentence for which is six months' imprisonment.

Affray

The Public Order Act 1986 section 3 creates an offence of affray. A person is guilty of affray who uses or threatens violence towards another so as to cause a person of reasonable firmness to fear for their personal safety. The offence is triable in either the magistrates' or the crown court and the maximum sentence which can be imposed in the latter is three years' imprisonment and in the former six months. There is no requirement of numbers, as with riot or violent disorder, but the person who is likely to be caused to fear for their personal safety (who may be theoretical) must be different to the person threatened.

Violent disorder

The Public Order Act 1986 section 2 creates an offence of violent disorder. This is intended to deal with serious outbreaks of public disorder. A person is guilty who uses or threatens violence where three or more persons present together use or threaten violence so as to cause a person of reasonable firmness to fear for their personal safety. The offence is triable in either the magistrates' or the crown court, and the maximum sentence is five years. This offence was introduced to deal with group violence.

Riot

The Public Order Act 1986 section 1 creates an offence of riot. A person is guilty of riot when he or she uses violence where 12 or more persons present together use or threaten violence for a common purpose so as to cause a person of reasonable firmness to fear for their personal safety. The offence is triable only in the crown court and the maximum penalty is 10 years' imprisonment. A person is guilty of riot only if he or she intends to use violence or is aware that their conduct may be violent.

93

Freedom of Expression

Historically there has been no right to freedom of speech in the UK. Parliament has always been free to limit free expression, and courts, while regularly affirming the importance of free speech, have often restricted it when it conflicts with other state or individual interests. The Human Rights Act 1998 now incorporates the right of free expression guaranteed by Article 10 of the European Convention, although this too is subject to a number of qualifications. It remains to be seen how far its application will differ from the approach of English common law.

Any balancing approach necessarily means that free speech is not absolute. This may work to the advantage of the state on occasion, but free expression may also conflict with other *individual* interests and rights – and there is, in particular, constant tension between this right and the interest of individuals to enjoy freedom from, say, racial abuse or unfair attacks on their reputation. When considering a free speech issue which does not simply pit an individual against the state, it is therefore always useful to consider whether someone's privacy rights are arguably being infringed. English law has historically not recognized a general right of privacy, but both Parliament and the courts have in various ways safeguarded specific aspects of such a right. The Human Rights Act means that English law must now also give effect to the privacy guarantees contained in Article 8 of the European Convention on Human Rights, and in practice a measure which restricts speech in order to protect privacy is very likely to be immune from challenge by virtue of Article 10(2) (which allows, among other things, for restrictions necessary to protect the rights of others).

EUROPEAN CONVENTION LAW

Article 10 'is applicable not only to "information" or "ideas" that are favourably received or regarded as inoffensive or as a matter of indifference, but also to those that offend, shock or disturb the state or any sector of the population. Such are the demands of that pluralism, tolerance and broadmindedness without which there is no "democratic society"': *Handyside* v *UK* (1979). The 'ideas' safeguarded are not restricted to demonstrable facts, but also include value judgements, artistic expression and commercial speech. The qualifications to the right contained in Article 10(2) 'must be narrowly interpreted and the necessity for any restrictions must be convincingly established'.

In practice, the European Court has been particularly concerned to safeguard free expression in the political context. It has stated that 'freedom of political debate is at the very core of the concept of a democratic society which prevails throughout the Convention', and restrictions on media coverage of current affairs are subject to particular scrutiny. Relatively few cases have arisen involving restrictions on artistic speech, but states have generally been granted greater leeway to restrict such material if it is clearly offensive to a significant number of people (for example, bans on films which offend religious sensibilities have been upheld).

DEFAMATION

Defamation describes a cause of action whereby a person can sue to protect his reputation in the face of a statement about him which is untrue and lowers his reputation in the eyes of a right-thinking person. As well as protecting reputational rights, it is one of the most important ways in which English law operates to prohibit freedom of speech.

Traditionally, the law divided defamatory statements into those spoken (slander) and written (libel), with libel being regarded as more serious because of its relative permanence. The classification has been eroded by the advent of modern forms of communication, but it is now well established that cinematic and televisual defamation is to be regarded as libel. The same is true of cable, video, satellite and e-mail transmissions.

The modern significance of the difference between libel and slander is limited, but certain distinctions remain practically important. With libel, a claimant need not prove loss or damage: it is enough to show that the words were published and untrue. By contrast, slanderous statements are actionable only if they can be proved to cause financial damage (e.g. a lost contract) except, for historical reasons, where the statement involves:

1 an allegation that the claimant has committed a criminal offence;
2 an allegation that the claimant has a sexually transmitted disease;
3 an allegation that the unmarried female claimant is not a virgin or that the married one has committed adultery;
4 disparaging remarks about the claimant's office, profession, trade or business.

Mere injury to feelings or embarrassment are not enough to support an action for slander.

Suing for defamation

Defamation cases are relatively rare, largely because public funding is unavailable to claimants in this field. (The absence of public funding has been held by the European Commission to be consistent with Article 6 of the Convention.) Since most cases are extremely expensive to pursue, this acts as a strong deterrent to all but the wealthiest of claimants: the costs of retaining lawyers are likely to be high, and even a very strong case may leave a claimant seriously out of pocket if he is eventually unable to enforce a costs order against a bankrupted defendant. For this reason, most complaints of defamation will be settled or abandoned at some point between a solicitor's letter and trial.

There have, however, been two changes which may make defamation actions more attractive to a broader range of claimants. The first is that since the Defamation Act 1996, damages of up to £10,000 (along with orders requiring apologies and preventing further publication) may now be obtained by way of a 'fast track procedure' whereby a claim is dealt with summarily by a judge alone. Second, solicitors and barristers may agree to take on a case on a 'no win, no fee' arrangement. In practice, this may still involve considerable initial outlay, in that a claimant will almost certainly have to pay an insurance premium to cover the risks of losing and being ordered to pay an opponent's costs. The size of this premium will depend on a number of factors, the most important being the likely amount of such costs and the strength of the claim.

If a defamation case goes to trial, either side usually has the right to request that a jury be sworn – one of the few instances of juries being used in civil cases. A claimant using the fast-track procedure introduced by the 1996 Act, however, can ensure that the case is dealt with by a judge alone. In addition, a jury can be dispensed with if 'the court is of the opinion that the trial requires any prolonged examination of documents or accounts or any scientific or local investigation which cannot conveniently be made with a jury' – a provision notoriously made use of by Jonathan Aitken, in his abortive 1998 libel action against the *Guardian*.

It is for the judge to rule whether the statement is capable of being defamatory, while the jury decides whether it was in fact defamatory – and if so, how much damages the claimant should receive. Historically, juries were given no guidance as to the appropriate figure for damages – a state of affairs which led the European Court in 1995 to rule that an award of £1.5 million against Nikolai Tolstoy (for allegations made over the wartime conduct of Lord Aldington) had breached Article 10 of the European Convention. However, since the award in that trial (1989), the Court of Appeal has been granted a statutory power to reduce excessive awards on appeal, and it acted to limit extravagant awards further by ruling in the *Elton John* case that juries should be invited to consider comparisons with payments in personal injury cases, when fixing damages (*John* v *MGN Ltd* [1996]). This probably meets the risk of any future challenge under Article 10, although the matter remains to be tested.

What needs to be proved?

A claimant must prove three things:

1 that the statement had a defamatory meaning;
2 that the statement referred to the claimant;
3 that the defendant was responsible for 'publishing' the words.

The statement is defamatory

A defamatory statement is one which discredits the claimant, in the sense of tending to lower his reputation. When an action is taken, the law presumes that the defamatory statement is also false, although if the defendant can prove otherwise he will be able to rely on the defence of justification (*see* below). Although some statements will be unequivocally defamatory, there is often argument about the precise meaning to be attached to a statement, and a claimant may argue that words, which are on their face neutral, are defamatory by implication – that they contain an innuendo.

In one famous case an amateur golfer named Tolley successfully sued a firm of chocolate manufacturers over an advertisement (produced without his knowledge or consent) which showed him carrying their product in his pocket, and stating that it was as good as his drive. Although the advertisement was not defamatory on its face, it was found to contain the libellous innuendo that Tolley had been paid to consent to its publication, and so he had prostituted his reputation as an amateur golfer.

The claimant is the subject of the statement

The claimant must also prove that he was identified as the subject of the statement. Where it refers expressly to the claimant, this will be sufficient – even if this was accidental, and the person being referred to was in fact someone else (although in such circumstances, a defendant may make an offer of amends, as discussed below). If the statement does not refer expressly to the claimant, it may still be actionable if it is sufficiently particular to identify him. If, however, only a very small number of people would have recognized it as referring to the claimant, this may well lessen the size of a damages award.

The defendant was responsible for publication

Publication in this context simply means that the statement was made or shown to a person who was not the defendant. The number of people shown the statement is theoretically irrelevant, although where a statement is circulated to an individual or a very small group, the defendant may be able to argue that little or no damages should be payable.

Defences to a defamation action

Anyone who is threatened with proceedings for defamation should take legal advice. If the complaint is soundly based, the safest response is to write an immediate letter of apology. If, however, a claimant wishes to defend the statement, there are five main defences (justification, fair comment, absolute privilege, qualified privilege and the making of an offer of amends), as well as a number of less common ones. A few more unusual defences exist, and a number of partial defences operate to lessen damages.

Justification

A defendant will not be liable if he can prove that the statement is true, whatever his motive for publication. However, where a statement alleges that a claimant has a criminal conviction, the position is complicated by the Rehabilitation of Offenders Act 1974. The Act provides that a person can still sue for defamation if a 'spent' conviction is revealed, but if a defendant raises the defence of justification, the claimant will only win the case if he can prove 'malice' – which in this context, means spite, ill will or improper motive. One effect of this is that it is likely to be very difficult to obtain an injunction to prevent previous convictions being revealed – especially

when a defendant can plausibly argue that there is a public interest in revealing the information.

Fair comment

It is a complete defence to prove that a defamatory statement concerned a matter of public interest, and was made in good faith (i.e. believing in its truth) and without actual malice towards the claimant. The logic behind this defence is that a person should be entitled to express genuinely held opinions of people if – but only if – they are on a matter of public concern. To succeed with this defence of fair comment, the defendant must show that the words were opinion rather than factual assertions; and furthermore, that the opinion was fairly based on specific facts contained within the actual publication complained of. It is not enough to show that there exist other facts, not mentioned in the defamatory statement, which would support the opinion. The defence will also fail if a claimant is able to show that the defendant acted with malice when making the statement.

Absolute privilege

A defamation claim will fail if a defendant can show that the statement was made:

1 in the House of Commons or the House of Lords;
2 in connection with judicial proceedings (e.g. by a witness in a court case);
3 as part of a fair, accurate and contemporaneous report of judicial proceedings by the broadcast and print media.

This defence operates even if the statements were entirely untrue, and their originators acted out of deliberate malice towards a claimant.

Qualified privilege

The law protects the makers of statements which are made in a number of confidential or official situations where the public interest requires frankness and/or open reporting by the media. In the important 1999 case of *Reynolds* v *Times Newspapers*, the House of Lords refused to extend this to protect all political discussion of public figures, but nevertheless extended the scope of the defence considerably. Qualified privilege is now potentially available to the media in any case involving matters of serious public concern. Its actual availability will depend on a number of factors, including the seriousness of the allegations, the steps taken to verify them, whether a claimant's side of the story has been put, the urgency of publication and the 'tone' of the article concerned.

How these various factors will be interpreted by future courts will be of crucial importance to the scope of the defence of qualified privilege. Hitherto, it has only been understood to apply to a number of specific situations, including reports of parliamentary proceedings, non-contemporaneous court reports and statutory reports, and situations where the maker and recipient of a statement had a publicly recognized duty or interest which supported the communication being made. Examples of the latter category include job references and official complaints of crime or police misconduct. However, where a claimant can show that a defendant acted out of malice, he will be able to defeat the defence: thus if a person was wrongly described in an employer's reference as a 'bad timekeeper', any defamation action would only succeed if the claimant could show that the employer had made the comment in order deliberately to hurt him or her.

Offer of amends

In cases where the defendant can show that the defamatory statement was published as a result of a genuine mistake resulting in the misuse of the claimant's name, it is open to him to make an offer of amends. The offer must include a suitable correction and apology, steps to notify recipients of the statement that it is defamatory, and an offer of compensation and costs. If relied upon as a defence, the defendant cannot rely on any other defence (e.g. claiming at the same time that the statement was fair comment), although he may rely on it in mitigation. If such an offer is properly made but refused, and was still available at trial, this will operate as a complete defence.

Other defences

It is a defence to prove that a defamed person consented to publication, or that he is dead. In some cases, defendants have also successfully relied on the defence of jest or vulgar abuse, which in essence means that the statement was an obvious joke. Defendants should be warned, however, that in the context of a defamation action, jokes can be very hard to prove.

Certain specific defences are available to the distributors of libellous material. 'Innocent dissemination' can be claimed by defendants who can prove that they did not know about the libel, that there was no reason to know the work concerned contained libellous material, and that they were not negligent in failing to have such knowledge at the time of distribution. A related defence, commonly known as the internet defence, has since the passage of the Defamation Act 1996 protected those who are neither authors, editors nor publishers, who take reasonable care, and who neither know nor have reason to know that they have caused or contributed to publication of the defamatory material. In a highly significant ruling in early 2000, the High Court recognized that the defence could potentially be claimed by an internet service provider, but ruled that where Demon Internet (the ISP in question) had notice of a defamatory posting but failed to remove it, the latter two conditions for the defence's availability were not met.

CRIMINAL LIBEL

It is a criminal offence to publish a 'seditious libel', although the offence is rarely prosecuted any more. 'Sedition' includes the raising of discontent to established authority, class hostility, or attempts by unlawful means to change church or state. Given the broad potential scope of the offence, it is hedged by procedural safeguards which operate to limit its practical effect. To bring a case, a prosecutor must obtain permission from a High Court judge, who must be persuaded that the evidence of a serious offence is clear 'beyond argument', and that prosecution is in the public interest. Even with these protections against abuse, it is by no means clear that the offence would survive challenge under Article 10 of the European Convention.

OBSCENITY AND INDECENCY

The law governing the possession, production and distribution of sexually explicit material relies on only two terms: 'obscene' and 'indecent'. Obscene material is that with a tendency to 'deprave and corrupt'. Indecency is defined in relation to a failure to meet 'recognized standards of propriety'. Such material may be the subject of criminal prosecution, but can additionally or alternatively be seized pursuant to a magistrate's warrant and – after a hearing to determine its legality – then be forfeited and destroyed.

The prohibitions in this field of law have been hammered together over the years, and inconsistencies abound. For example, although it is illegal to publish 'obscene' material or to possess it for the purpose of publishing it, simply possessing it is legal. 'Indecent' material can lawfully be published (unless it portrays children – in which case, even possession is illegal), but offences may be committed if exactly the same material is imported, displayed or sent through the post. These uncertainties are increased by the vagueness of the phrases 'deprave and corrupt' and 'recognized standards of propriety'. Neither constitutes a test in any solid sense, and in practice, magistrates or jury members can take a largely idiosyncratic view of any particular image or book, and their decisions set no precedent for future cases. As a result, assessing the illegality of a specific item can only be an informed guess as to what a jury or bench in a particular area might think.

The test of obscenity – 'deprave and corrupt'

This term requires more than an immoral suggestion or depiction: the material, taken as a whole, must constitute a serious menace. The effect of the material is to be measured against the likely reader, and where a defendant can show that the likely audience is already so inured to material similar to that in question (e.g. where hard core bondage magazines are sold only to committed subscribers) he could argue that the likely audience would not be any further corrupted by the material. This defence will, however, fail if the prosecution can show that a 'significant proportion' of likely readers would have their 'addiction' to the material fuelled by further exposure to it.

Drugs and violence

It is not necessary to a successful prosecution that the material concerns sex. Material advocating the taking of illegal drugs has on occasion been prosecuted or forfeited, while the explicit depiction of brutal violence can fall within the statutory definition of obscenity (and it might also be indecent). Graphically violent material of a sexual nature is in practice nowadays the material most likely to be subject to police action.

Defence of merit

The Obscene Publications Act 1959 permits a defence that publication (in the case of magazines and books) is in the interests of science, literature, art or learning, or of other objects of general concern. The use of this defence was demonstrated in the first major case under the Act, when the publishers of *Lady Chatterley's Lover* were acquitted at the Old Bailey. A similar, but slightly narrower, defence applies to plays and films, which can be justified as being in the interests of drama, opera, ballet or any other art, or of literature or learning.

Indecency offences

It is no crime, generally, to publish or distribute indecent articles (unlike obscene ones), but a number of specific offences incorporate the indecency test. Thus it is a crime to send indecent matter through the post, or to put it on public display unless entry is restricted to persons over 18 years and payment is required, or the display is in a special part of a shop with an appropriate warning notice. The indecency offences do *not* apply to television broadcasts (although both the BBC and independent television apply internal prohibitions on indecent matters), to exhibitions inside art galleries or museums, exhibitions arranged by or in premises occupied by the Crown or local authorities, to theatrical performances, and to films in licensed cinemas.

Local authorities also have regulatory powers over sex shops and cinemas, and their licences invariably prohibit the public display of indecent material. Similarly, the music and entertainment licences granted by local authorities will often be conditional on the licensee ensuring that no indecent display takes place.

There is also an ancient (and very vague) offence of acting to corrupt public morals and outrage public decency, or conspiring to do so. The offence must be committed in public. It can still operate to restrict free expression, as was shown in 1990 when the offence was successfully used against both a sculptor and art gallery owner, where the latter had displayed the former's design of a human head, to which had been attached an earring made from a freeze-dried human foetus.

Customs regulations prohibit the importation of indecent articles, although they have been somewhat undermined by EU provisions on free trade (which take precedence over domestic law). A cardinal principle of the EU is that one member state should not set up trade barriers to goods from another member state if there is a legitimate internal market in the same goods. In the case of the UK, there is a 'legitimate' market in indecent (but not obscene) articles as long as the traders observe the restrictions noted above. The consequence is that the UK cannot prevent importation of indecent goods from other EU countries.

Children

Several offences exist dealing with the possession, production and distribution of indecent photographs of children under 16 years. Simply downloading such material from the world wide web is a serious criminal offence, even if no one but the defendant views the material.

BLASPHEMY

Blasphemy remains a crime in English law, and the European Court of Human Rights has held that its continued existence is consistent with Article 10. The offence prohibits outrageous comment on, and immoderate or offensive treatment of, the Christian faith and, more specifically, the Anglican, Roman Catholic, Methodist and Baptist branches of that faith. It excludes other denominations, and does not protect any other religion: attempts to launch private prosecutions in respect of *The Satanic Verses* failed for this reason. A blasphemer's intentions are irrelevant, although the jury must consider the nature of his likely audience in order to assess whether the publication would produce the necessary outrage. For newspapers and periodicals, there exist the same procedural safeguards as apply to criminal libel (*see* above).

RACIAL HATRED

It is a criminal offence to use threatening, abusive or insulting words or behaviour or displays, with the intention of stirring up racial hatred (or even just in circumstances where racial hatred is likely to be stirred up, unless the defendant can show that he did not intend his acts to be threatening, abusive or insulting and was not aware that they might be). The offence is not committed if it occurs entirely within a dwelling, but it can arise where the acts are committed in the dwelling but are visible or audible from the outside.

Similar offences apply to the publication, distribution or public performance of racially inflammatory material, or the possession of such material with a view to such publication, etc. It is a defence in all cases to show that one had no intent to stir up racial hatred and neither knew nor had reason to suspect that the material was threatening, abusive or insulting. The police can obtain a search warrant for such material and magistrates can order its forfeiture.

CONTEMPT OF COURT

Contempt of court penalizes a whole range of acts which are regarded by the courts as a threat to the administration of justice. It is often used to prevent or punish the disclosure of information, and in this sense it is an important inroad into freedom of expression. The courts have invented a whole range of offences, penalizing, for example, the naming of blackmail victims, and the televised re-enactments of ongoing trials; while the unauthorized tape recording of court proceedings and the disclosure of a jury's deliberations are similarly prohibited by particular statutes.

The type of contempt which most frequently restricts what the press can say is that known as 'strict liability contempt'. While a case is 'active' (or, to use an older phrase, *sub judice*), the media are liable if they publish anything which would cause a substantial risk of serious prejudice to the proceedings, irrespective of the intention or even (in most cases) the degree of care which they exercised. Criminal proceedings are active from the time an arrest takes place, or a warrant or summons is issued. Civil proceedings only become active when a date is fixed for the hearing. The degree of restriction imposed depends on which court or tribunal will hear the case. Nothing should be written or broadcast which might prejudice a *jury* against the defendant; in particular, no past misdeeds should be referred to, and reports should take care not to assume guilt. At the other end of the spectrum, the publication of material in cases to be tried by judges alone could only in very rare circumstances give rise to a contempt, since judges are expected to be able to ignore prejudicial matter.

Defences

There are two important special defences to charges of strict liability contempt. A *discussion in good faith of public affairs or other matters of general public importance* will not be contempt if the risk of prejudice is merely incidental. A second important defence is that it is not generally contempt to publish a *fair, accurate, good faith and contemporaneous report of legal proceedings held in public*. However, legal reports are subject to the power of the court to make a postponement order, until the end of a trial or until the conclusion of other associated proceedings which are at risk of prejudice.

Protection of sources

A court might ordinarily want to know the name of a journalist's source wherever this was relevant to an issue in the case, but the law recognizes that journalists should have special protection in such cases. Accordingly, no order should be made and no contempt will arise unless the party seeking disclosure can establish that this is 'necessary in the interests of justice or national security or for the prevention of disorder or crime'. This still grants a broad discretion to the court to make disclosure orders, but a 1996 European ruling (*Goodwin* v *UK*) has narrowed further the circumstances in which such an order will be appropriate. Each case will still depend on its own facts, however.

Special cases

By statute, rape victims may not be named unless the court orders otherwise. The press (unlike the rest of the public) have a right to attend youth court hearings, but are prohibited from identifying defendants or witnesses, or from publishing their photographs. In other courts, young people's anonymity is protected only if the court makes a specific order.

OFFICIAL SECRECY

Secrecy, it is sometimes said, is the British disease. The scope of the law for preventing and punishing the disclosure of governmental secrets represents one of the most important restrictions on free speech. As well as using laws of confidentiality and copyright to restrict disclosures (*see* below), the state is able to prosecute under the Official Secrets Acts of 1911 and 1989. The first is now restricted mainly to espionage cases, but the second applies to all information relating to security and intelligence, defence, and international relations and criminal investigations.

Members and former members of the security and intelligence services may be prosecuted under the 1989 Act if they disclose any information relating to security or intelligence whatsoever. Other categories of information give rise to offences if their disclosure is 'damaging'. People such as journalists and friends, who have obtained restricted information indirectly, may also be guilty if they disclose the information, although in their case disclosure must both be damaging and they must know or have reasonable cause to believe that it is damaging. The term 'damaging' is broadly defined in various subsections of the Act.

Other secrecy offences

Apart from the Official Secrets Acts, there are dozens of specific statutory offences of disclosing information in the hands of the government. Frequently, they are imposed in circumstances where a government department has powers to acquire the information under compulsion.

BREACH OF CONFIDENTIALITY

English law recognizes an obligation of confidentiality in certain situations, and it allows a claimant either to prevent breaches of this obligation or to recover damages after the event. It is in this area of law that English judges have come closest to recognizing a right of privacy, but it has also been used by the government to suppress free speech, most memorably during the *Spycatcher* disclosures of Peter Wright.

In order to obtain an injunction or damages, a claimant must show first that the information concerned was of a confidential nature. Where it has already been widely disseminated, this requirement will not be met, and it was for this reason that the government failed in its action against Peter Wright. Second, it must be shown that it was communicated in circumstances giving rise to an obligation of confidence. This may arise out of an express contractual agreement, while it is almost invariably implied by some relationships, such as that between a doctor and patient. There are no hard and fast rules as to when it might otherwise arise. Third, a claimant must establish that the defendant has made, or would make, wrongful use of the information. He will be unable to do this if the defendant can show that maintaining confidentiality would not be in the public interest. This means that disclosure of illegality or other impropriety is sometimes non-actionable, although during the *Spycatcher* litigation it was suggested that this defence might not be available where there existed alternative procedures (such as an internal complaints tribunal) through which issues of misconduct could be pursued.

It may be that in an appropriate case the government can claim damages which will effectively deprive a former employee of any profits made out of an express undertaking not to publish confidential information.

Pre-trial injunctions

If a claimant has advance notice that publication of arguably confidential information is planned, he can seek an injunction to prevent publication before trial. In deciding whether to grant an injunction, the court will assess where the 'balance of convenience' lies – and, in practice, this test is weighted strongly in favour of a claimant who can arguably claim that irreparable harm would result from publication (as is almost invariably done by the government in 'official secrecy' type cases). The converse argument, that the time between injunction and trial is likely to render publication unnewsworthy, is rarely granted as much weight – which, in turn, means that the defence is often not pursued, and free speech is suppressed without a trial. However, since the Human Rights Act 1998 came into force in October 2000, the balance may shift towards the right to freedom of expression.

COPYRIGHT

Copyright, in brief, gives the creator of a work which is original in some way, various rights over that work, the most important of which is the right to stop others reproducing a substantial part of it without consent. Breach of copyright entitles the owner to sue, whether or not he has actually suffered loss as a result. It applies only to material which has been reduced to permanent form, such as song lyrics, books and computer programs, but does not operate to protect ideas or information as such (which might, however, be protected by the law relating to confidentiality, discussed above). Thus, a newspaper could prevent reproduction of its photographs or a substantial part of its text, but a leaked scoop is not theirs to control.

Copyright is not infringed by the use of reasonable extracts for research or private study, criticism or review, and news reporting. It is also a defence to an action for breach of copyright to show that publication is in the public interest, which may be based on either serious misconduct by the claimant, or – in certain circumstances – the desirability that the information contained in the copyright material be disclosed to the public.

A copyright action *may* potentially be used by the government to prevent former secret service employees from profiting from disclosures of information which they obtained while members of the service, for example by writing a book of their experiences. In order to succeed with such a claim the government must show at least that a duty of confidentiality (*see* above) was owed and breached by the defendant. The questions of whether the material was subject to copyright, whether this was breached and whether the public interest defence applies, will depend on the facts of the case.

CONTROLS ON BROADCASTING, FILMS, VIDEO AND CABLE

Independent broadcasting (including that by satellite and cable) is licensed by the Independent Television Commission (ITC) and Radio Authority (RA). Although not broadcasters themselves, both bodies are under a duty to do all that they can to ensure that nothing is broadcast which 'offends against decency or is likely to encourage or incite to crime or to lead to disorder or to be offensive to public feeling'; that 'due responsibility' is exercised in relation to potentially exploitative or abusive religious programmes; and that subliminal messages are not put out. When issuing licences, the ITC and RA must consider not just the interests of high-quality and diverse programming, but also the need to ensure effective competition. There are specific controls on cross-media ownership by the same individual or company.

The BBC has similar duties imposed by its charter, and by its formal agreement with the government. Both the BBC and the ITC are also required to ensure due accuracy and impartiality in their news services. Unlike newspapers, which can openly propagate their owners' views, independent broadcasters are not permitted to editorialize on matters (other than broadcasting) which are of political or industrial controversy or relate to current public policy.

Breach of licensing conditions may entitle the ITC and RA to withdraw a licence. Unlicensed broadcasting is a criminal offence, and pirate radio equipment can be confiscated. The government also retains a residual power to direct that certain matters not be broadcast. This power was used in 1988 to ban spoken comment by or in support of Sinn Fein, the UDA and other organizations proscribed under the anti-terrorism laws.

The Broadcasting Standards Commission

The Broadcasting Standards Commission (BSC) has since 1998 been responsible for drawing up and regularly reviewing codes relating to broadcasting standards, and fairness and invasions of privacy, in relation to both radio and television programmes. The former deals with the portrayal of sex and violence, and taste and decency more generally. It is under a duty to monitor programming output, to receive and adjudicate on complaints of code violations, and to make regular reports to the government. It can require the broadcaster to publish the terms and outcome of any complaint, but cannot directly impose any further sanction such as compensation.

The British Board of Film Classification

Regulation of cinema is achieved by a hybrid system. The British Board of Film Classification (BBFC), a private body set up with the co-operation of the film industry, issues certificates of suitability in relation to most films. These have no direct effect, but are given legal force in practice by the power of local councils to license cinemas. Most licences will have a condition attached that only films with a BBFC certificate will be shown.

In relation to video films, the BBFC is a censor in law as well as practice. It is a criminal offence to supply an unclassified video, to possess such a video with intent to supply it, to supply unlabelled or misleadingly labelled videos, or to supply the video to a category of person inappropriate to a BBFC stipulation (e.g. someone who is too young, or a general retailer when the video is approved only for sale to sex shops). Certain videos are exempt from classification requirements (those which are educational, concerned with sports, religion or music, or games), unless to any significant extent they show or are likely to encourage human sexual activity (or associated force or restraint); mutilation, torture or gross violence towards humans or animals; techniques likely to be useful in the commission of offences; or criminal activity which, to a considerable extent, is likely to stimulate or encourage the commission of offences. The BBFC has to consider whether videos are suitable for viewing in the home, and must pay particular regard to 'any harm that may be caused to potential viewers, or through their behaviour, to society by the manner in which the work deals with' criminal behaviour, illegal drugs, violent or horrific behaviour or incidents, and human sexual activity. BBFC decisions in relation to videos can be appealed, although this can be both expensive and time-consuming.

UNWANTED DISCLOSURES OF PRIVATE FACTS

Since there is no independent right of privacy protected by English law, a person cannot be prevented or penalized for revealing information simply on the basis that someone else would wish it to be kept secret. (An action for breach of confidentiality may, however, be available, if the conditions set out above are made out.) Article 8 of the European Convention on Human Rights protects privacy, but the Strasbourg bodies have also consistently rejected complaints that it might be violated by unwanted disclosures of private facts (although the Court's comments in a 1997 decision involving threatened disclosure of a person's HIV status suggests that in an extreme case there would be a breach of the Article).

There are, however, specific situations in which disclosure might give rise to penalties and remedies. For example, the unauthorized disclosure of data may give rise to a right to compensation and/or to criminal proceedings, under the Data Protection Act 1998. The Act defines 'data' broadly, and as well as computer records, it can include material stored in card indexes or in paper files. Unduly intrusive newspaper stories can be investigated by the Press Complaints Commission, a voluntary body set up by the press to regulate itself. Its powers are, however, limited to making an adjudication, which the newspaper concerned will generally print: it has no power to order compensation or, indeed, to order anything at all.

94

Homelessness

Since 1977, local authorities have been obliged to provide accommodation for specified categories of homeless people. It had been thought that the duty was to provide 'permanent' accommodation, namely a council tenancy or something equivalent. However, in 1995 the courts decided (*R v LB Brent, ex p Awua* [1996]) that a six-month assured shorthold tenancy could suffice if the authority was satisfied that this was suitable accommodation for the applicant.

The current legislation is the Housing Act 1996 Part VII. This imposes a duty on local authorities to provide accommodation for a minimum period of two years for those homeless applicants to whom a full duty is owed. This period may be extended. The sole route to a secure tenancy of a council flat or a nomination to a housing association flat is through the authority's 'Allocation Scheme' adopted pursuant to Part VI of that Act. However, an authority must add to their housing register any homeless applicant to whom a full housing duty is accepted.

The Labour government was elected in May 1997 with a manifesto commitment to reinstate the duty to provide permanent accommodation for homeless applicants. To date, the government has not found the legislative time to enact a bill to achieve this. It has introduced regulations to require local authorities to give homeless applicants a higher priority under their Allocation Schemes.

The Housing Act 1996 Part VII is subject to a series of Orders and Regulations. A code of guidance was issued by the Department of the Environment, Transport and the Regions (DETR) and sets out how the provisions should be applied. It was last revised on 5 January 1999. The office of the Deputy Prime Minister (created in May 2002) has taken over responsibility for government policy on homelessness. A number of recent cases have clarified the nature of the obligations imposed on local authorities. The law has become horribly complicated. If advice is sought, a housing specialist is essential. Advice and assistance under the legal aid scheme is available.

QUALIFYING FOR ACCOMMODATION UNDER THE HOMELESSNESS PROVISIONS

Councils must provide housing for those who are:
- homeless; and
- eligible for assistance; and
- in priority need; and
- not homeless intentionally.

The duty to provide accommodation for the minimum period of two years (the 'full housing duty') only applies if the four criteria are satisfied. If they are not all satisfied, there will be a more limited duty to provide advice and assistance and/or to secure temporary accommodation for a limited period. It is necessary to understand these concepts before considering how the legislation works.

It is open to an authority to transfer the full housing duty to another authority under the *local connection* provisions. These apply where an applicant has no local connection with the authority to which they have applied, but do have such a connection to another authority.

There is a duty to provide temporary accommodation while the application is investigated. This arises if the authority has reason to believe that an applicant *may* be homeless, eligible for assistance and in priority need.

HOMELESSNESS

An applicant is homeless if he or she has no accommodation in the UK or elsewhere. People may be treated as having no such accommodation, and therefore homeless, even if they have somewhere to live in the following situations:
- when those who might reasonably be expected to live with the applicant as members of their family cannot physically occupy the accommodation. Membership of the same family may arise not only through blood or marriage ties but also, for example, through cohabitation or fostering arrangements. It would also extend to same-sex couples; or

● when it is not reasonable for them to continue to occupy the accommodation, for instance because of domestic violence, bad disrepair, overcrowding or harassment.

The Act also refers to people who are threatened with homelessness. This applies if an applicant is likely to become homeless within the next 28 days. No accommodation will be provided until they are homeless.

ELIGIBILITY FOR ASSISTANCE

Dependent children who live with an adult, those suffering from mental disability to an extent that they cannot understand the nature of an application, and illegal immigrants, are not eligible for assistance in their own names.

Since April 2000, most asylum-seekers have been housed and supported through the National Asylum Support Service (*see further* page 689).

PRIORITY NEED

A person has a priority need if:

● dependent children live with, or might reasonably be expected to live with, the applicant. This covers, for example, younger brothers and sisters, as well as the applicant's own children. Children are dependent until the age of 16 years (or 19 years if they attend full-time school or training); or

● she (or one of the family with whom she lives or could reasonably be expected to live) is pregnant; or

● s/he (or a member of their household) is vulnerable as a result of old age (over 60 years), mental illness or handicap or physical disability or other special reason; or

● s/he became homeless because of an emergency such as a flood, fire or other disaster.

A single person is unlikely to qualify for housing unless they are pregnant or vulnerable. A person is vulnerable if they are less able to fend for themselves so that injury or detriment would result while a less vulnerable person would be able to cope without harmful effect.

INTENTIONAL HOMELESSNESS

A person is intentionally homeless if they left their last established accommodation through their deliberate actions or neglect. Their conduct will not be classed as deliberate if it stemmed from unforeseen problems or a genuine ignorance of relevant facts. Common examples of intentional homelessness are:

● eviction because of a wilful or persistent refusal to pay rent or mortgage repayments;

● leaving accommodation that it was reasonable to

Homelessness

Must the local authority rehouse?

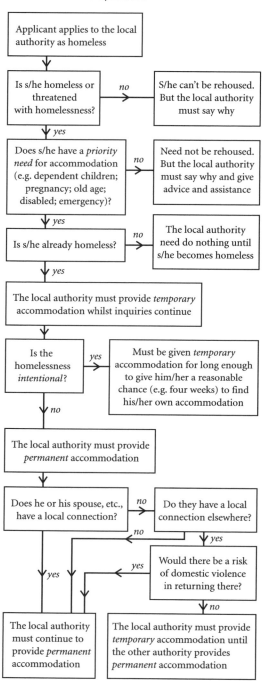

occupy in this country or abroad without making adequate alternative arrangements;

- eviction because of anti-social behaviour (such as unacceptable levels of noise, harassment, damage to the premises).

On the other hand, homelessness would not be intentional where:

- arrears problems arose through unforeseen difficulties such as job loss, illness or family breakdown;
- property was vacated in the genuine belief that there was other accommodation available.

In all circumstances, it must have been reasonable for the applicant to continue to occupy the accommodation. No finding of intentional homelessness could be made if the applicant was unable to afford the accommodation, there was harassment or domestic violence, or if there was severe overcrowding.

Occupiers should be careful not to give up accommodation too readily. Local authorities generally apply this provision very strictly in order to avoid full housing obligations. For example, many authorities require occupiers facing court possession proceedings to contest the claim fully. A failure to do so is treated as deliberate neglect and therefore intentional homelessness.

LOCAL CONNECTION

If the applicant has no local connection with the local authority to whom he applied, but does have such a connection with another authority, the full housing duty may be transferred to the second authority. This cannot occur if there is a risk of domestic violence. A dispute may arise between the two authorities as to whether the referral should be made. Regulations provide for how such a dispute should be resolved. The original authority must continue to provide accommodation until the duty has been placed on the second authority.

A local connection exists with a local authority area if an applicant, or a member of their household:

- was resident there (a working rule is six months in the previous 12 months, or three years in the previous five years);
- has a job there; or
- has family associations or other special connections with the area.

Since 6 December 1999, those asylum-seekers who are eligible for assistance (who claimed on arrival) can be referred more readily to another authority pursuant to the Homelessness (Asylum-seekers) (Interim Period) (England) Order 1999. Such a referral cannot be made if there is any risk of domestic violence.

APPLYING FOR HOUSING

A homeless applicant should apply to the housing department of the local housing authority. The application does not have to be in any particular form and need not be in writing. An authority is obliged to investigate an application, provided that it has *reason to believe* that the applicant *may* be homeless or threatened with homelessness. This is a low threshold to satisfy.

The interim duty

If an authority has reason to believe that the applicant may be homeless, eligible for assistance and in priority need, it must provide suitable temporary accommodation until it has completed its inquiries. (s. 188)

Although the Code of Guidance stresses that there is no obligation on an applicant to prove their entitlement to assistance, some authorities unlawfully turn applicants away. It may therefore be prudent to take papers confirming the applicant's immigration status and eligibility for accommodation.

Those applicants who are tenants of a council flat, but who seek to argue that they are homeless due to domestic violence or racial harassment are often wrongly referred to their local housing office to seek a transfer. A letter which sets out the nature of the application and the obligations imposed by the legislation on the authority is always useful.

THE HOUSING DUTIES

On completing their inquiries, an authority is obliged to notify the applicant of its decision. If any issue is decided against the interests of the applicant, reasons must be given. These are often inadequate. In such circumstances, the authority should be required to provide adequate reason before the applicant decides what further steps to take to challenge the decision.

The Housing Duties

Decision: the applicant is homeless, eligible for assistance, in priority need and did not become homeless intentionally.
The Full Housing Duty: to secure suitable accommodation for the minimum period of two years. It may be open to the authority to make a referral to another authority under the local connection provisions (s.193).

Decision: the applicant is *threatened with homelessness*, eligible for assistance, in priority need and is not threatened with homelessness intentionally.
Duty: to take reasonable steps to ensure that

accommodation does not cease to be available (s.195). The full housing duty will arise if applicant becomes homeless.

Decision: the applicant is homeless, eligible for assistance, in priority need, but became *homeless intentionally*.
Duty: to give advice and assistance and provide temporary accommodation for such period as will give them a reasonable opportunity to find their own accommodation (normally 28 days) (s.190).

Decision: the applicant is threatened with homelessness, eligible for assistance, in priority need, but is *threatened with homelessness intentionally*.
Duty: to give advice and assistance to prevent loss of accommodation (s.195(5)).

Decision: the applicant is *not* homeless, and/or is *not* eligible for assistance, and/or is *not* in priority need.
No housing duty. Duty to give advice (s.179).

THE FULL HOUSING DUTY

If an authority accepts the full housing duty to secure accommodation for two years, it is probable that the applicant will receive an offer of council or housing authority accommodation under the authority's Allocation Scheme within that period. This is a combination of two factors. First, the Allocation of Housing (Reasonable and Additional Preference) Regulations 1997 require an authority to give homeless applicants a reasonable priority under its Allocation Schemes. This was a device introduced by the new government to minimize the effects of the 1996 Act. Second, local authorities are equally unhappy with the 1996 Act and want to revert to the old law. The two-year rule creates an additional and burdensome bureaucracy for them, while creating unnecessary insecurity for homeless families.

The housing authority is not obliged to provide its own accommodation for the two-year minimum period. It may arrange for others, such as a housing association, to provide accommodation. In the short term, it may use bed and breakfast or private sector leased accommodation. Any accommodation must be *suitable* for the applicant.

The duty may cease if an applicant refuses an offer of suitable accommodation. It may also cease if the applicant refuses a suitable offer of a tenancy made under the authority's Allocation Scheme. The duty will cease if an applicant's immigration status changes and they cease to be eligible for assistance (e.g. an asylum application is refused).

At the end of the two-year period, if the applicant is still in temporary accommodation, the authority may extend accommodation if satisfied that the applicant still meets the statutory criteria. If it declines to do so, it is open to the applicant to make renewed application for accommodation.

SUITABLE ACCOMMODATION

Any accommodation offered by an authority must be suitable whether offered *before* or *after* a decision is reached. It is not sufficient for an authority merely to offer whatever accommodation is available at the time. It must make an assessment of the applicant's housing needs and arrange suitable accommodation to meet those needs. However, the courts have regard to the practical realities for inner city authorities, namely a housing stock limited in size and quality where demand far exceeds the available supply. In practice, most inner city authorities place homeless applicants in bed and breakfast, often outside their boundaries. The Code of Guidance discourages the use of such accommodation. The use of bed and breakfast may be an area of challenge under the Human Rights Act 1998 (Article 8).

If an applicant refuses an offer of accommodation, it is likely that the authority will argue that its duty to provide accommodation has ceased. The applicant should therefore think carefully before refusing an offer. Always visit the flat – note any disrepair or defects and report back to the housing officer. If there are any medical problems, obtain a letter from a GP. Accommodation will not be suitable if there is a real fear of domestic violence or racial harassment – take advice if intending to refuse. If a review is requested of the decision that the accommodation is suitable, check that the offer will be held open pending the review.

CHALLENGING AN ADVERSE DECISION

The following options should be considered:
- the 1996 Act now gives an applicant a right to request a review of the decision. Legal help is available under the Community Legal Service. The review must be requested within 21 days of notification of the decision. A more senior officer who was not involved with the original decision must conduct the review which should be completed within 56 days. The authority has discretion to extend any temporary accommodation pending this review;
- an applicant dissatisfied with a decision on review may appeal to the county court on a 'point of law'. The appeal must be issued within 21 days of the review decision. Some authorities do not complete the review within the statutory period of 56 days. Unless an extension of the timetable is agreed, the 21 days run from the date on which the review should have been completed. 'Point of law' extends to procedural irregularity or unfairness;
- certain decisions cannot be appealed to the county court, but an application for judicial review lies to the High Court. This is the appropriate remedy where an

authority refuses to investigate an application; refuses to provide temporary accommodation; provides unsuitable temporary accommodation; or refuses to extend the provision of temporary accommodation pending a review or an appeal to the county court;

- a further application can be made to a different local authority. The decision of the first authority does not bind the second authority (they are obliged only to take note of it). Authorities are increasingly reluctant to be seen as a soft option compared with their neighbours;

- where the refusal is on the ground of intentional homelessness, a fresh application for housing can be made in the name of another member of the household. If that person did not play a part in the deliberate act or neglect, a full duty to house may arise. Alternatively, a family with children could seek assistance from the social services authority under the Children Act 1989. Some social services departments may be able to recommend that accommodation be provided despite the adverse decision of the housing department. Other authorities may be able to assist with deposits or rent in advance for private rented accommodation.

THE FUTURE

In April 2000, the government published the *Housing Green Paper* which is available on www.detr.gov.uk. This restates the government's intention to restore the full housing duty. It also proposes the extension of the category of priority need to 16- and 17-year-olds, those with an institutional or care background and those fleeing harassment and domestic violence. Authorities could be given discretion to further extend the categories of priority need in areas where there is not an acute housing shortage.

PART ELEVEN

The English Legal System

95

Introduction to the English Legal System

So far this book has dealt with the law and the rights and obligations it gives and imposes. This chapter explains the system of justice: the institutions that make up the legal system, the fundamental principles underlying the system, sources of law and the role of Europe and European law.

WHY NOT THE UNITED KINGDOM LEGAL SYSTEM?

The United Kingdom comprises England, Wales, Scotland and Northern Ireland. This is the body recognized as 'the state' for international purposes. All four components of the UK have separate legal systems, except for Wales which shares the same court structure and body of law with England. Scotland and Northern Ireland have their own laws and court structure. There is no such thing as 'United Kingdom law'.

Great Britain	England, Wales and Scotland
The United Kingdom	Great Britain and Northern Ireland
The British Isles	The United Kingdom and the Isle of Man and the Channel Islands

AN UNWRITTEN CONSTITUTION

As every schoolboy and schoolgirl knows, this country has no written constitution. This, however, is a major over-simplification of the position. We have more than our fair share of constitutional documents, in the sense of something in writing dealing with the relationship between different institutions of government, or between the state and the individual's fundamental civil rights. For example:

- in the Magna Carta of 1215 the king promised to refrain from imposing any feudal tax save by the consent of the Common Council of the Realm;
- the Bill of Rights 1689 provided, amongst other things, that Parliamentary debates and election of MPs should be free from interference;
- the Act of Settlement 1701 stipulated who should become monarch on the death of the previous king or queen;
- the Parliament Acts of 1911 and 1949 dealt with the relative powers of the House of Commons and the House of Lords;
- the European Communities Act 1972 made the UK a part of the European Community ('the Common Market');
- judge-made (common) law is written down in law reports.

It is true to say, however, that there is no single, supreme document which sets out the first principles of the constitution and from which the government derives its power. The institutions of government derive their authority to act from a number of sources. This chapter describes the machinery of government (the institutions), the principles governing their actions and the sources of legal authority.

THE IMPACT OF THE HUMAN RIGHTS ACT 1998

The European Convention on Human Rights (*see* Chapter 84) sets out a number of fundamental political and civil rights, including the right to liberty, the right to a fair trial, respect for private and family life, freedom of thought, conscience and religion.

The UK government signed up to the European Convention on Human Rights over 50 years ago and, since 1966, has accepted the right of British citizens to petition the European Court of Human Rights in Strasbourg in respect of alleged breaches of the Convention. In October 2000, the Human Rights Act incorporated the European Convention on Human Rights into English law. What difference has this made and what is all the fuss about?

Under the Human Rights Act 1998:

- all legislation must be compatible with the Convention. When introducing legislation, government ministers have to make a statement about the compatibility of the bill with Convention rights;
- the courts must interpret legislation in accordance with the Convention. If a higher court decides that an Act of Parliament prevents someone from exercising their human rights, it is able to make a declaration of incompatibility, indirectly putting pressure on the government to change the law to bring it into line with the Convention;
- public authorities (including government departments, local authorities, the police, prisons, immigration officers, the courts and tribunals) must act in a way that is compatible with Convention rights;
- people can enforce their human rights under the Convention in the British courts, rather than incurring the time and expense of taking a case to Strasbourg. Taking a case to Strasbourg involves an average delay of five years and an average cost of £30,000.

You may still take a case to the European Court of Human Rights in Strasbourg, but that Court will need to be satisfied that you have exhausted all legal routes in the UK first. The European Court of Human Rights is discussed in Chapter 96.

In a nutshell, the Human Rights Act makes civil rights more accessible to people – in other words it is easier to litigate. It is not a bill of rights in the sense of a charter conferring powers on the institutions of government.

Enforcing your Convention rights

If you think that a public authority has breached your Convention rights, you can:

1 take the authority to court for breaching your rights. You must start the proceedings within one year of the breach. Proceedings can only be brought by people who believe that their Convention rights have been breached by a public authority (so you cannot take another individual to court for allegedly breaching your rights);

2 rely on the Convention rights in the course of any other proceedings involving a public authority, for example judicial review, criminal trial.

THE INSTITUTIONS

The institutions of government (i.e. the bodies wielding legal authority and power) are the legislature, the executive and the judiciary.

The Legislature	Makes laws
The Executive	Executes the laws
The Judiciary	Adjudicates when disputes occur

The monarch

The Queen is the head of state but the real rulers are 'Her Majesty's Ministers', i.e. the cabinet and ministers of government. It is often said that 'the Queen reigns, she does not rule'. In other words, the Queen plays an important role in the law-making process but she has no real power – for example, no Act of Parliament is valid unless it receives her approval (Royal Assent) but it is unthinkable that she would ever refuse to approve a bill.

The main functions of the monarch today are:

- to take part in formal and ceremonial events;
- to open and close Parliament;
- to dissolve and summon Parliament;
- to appoint a prime minister;
- to be the 'Fountain of Justice' (this means that justice is administered by Her Majesty's judges, and the monarch is technically present in the courts of law. Prosecutions are carried out in the name of the monarch and the monarch possesses the prerogative of mercy, in that convicted persons may be pardoned or reprieved by royal command, exercised through the Home Secretary);
- to be the 'Fountain of Honour' (this means that the monarch can grant peerages, knighthoods and other honours – most are conferred on the advice of the Prime Minister. Some honours remain within the personal gift of the monarch, for example the Order of Merit, the Royal Victorian Order, the Most Noble Order of the Garter, and the Most Noble and Ancient Order of the Thistle);
- to be the Head of the Commonwealth;
- to exercise the right of advice to Her Ministers.

The Queen's speech

At the beginning of each new session of Parliament, the Queen's speech outlines the laws which the government proposes to introduce in the coming session. This speech, while delivered by the Queen, is no longer written by her. It is a statement of the policies and proposals of the government in power. Parliament is not limited or restricted by the contents of the Queen's speech. This right to choose is symbolically preserved by the reading of a 'Bill for the Suppression of Clandestine Outlawries' *before* the reading of the Queen's speech to the House of Commons.

The executive

Her Majesty's government puts the laws into effect. The Queen is the nominal head of the government. The Prime Minister is the actual head of the government. The government is *not* Parliament. It is the combined activities of the cabinet, various government departments (both central – e.g. the Department of Works and Pensions – and local – e.g. the local authorities and public corporations) and the civil service. Together, they carry out the laws made by the legislature and perform the routine administration of the country. The executive is referred to as 'the Crown'. This term also encompasses the armed forces.

The government is not all-powerful. It must rule in accordance with the laws in force at the time. If it exceeds its powers or breaks the law, it is just as much subject to the law as any private individual. Furthermore, members of the government can be called to account by Parliament.

Parliament

Parliament is the legislature or law-making body. It consists of the House of Commons (the lower house) and the House of Lords (the upper house). Strictly speaking, the monarch is also an essential element of Parliament because no legislation can be created without the participation of the monarch.

The main functions of Parliament are:

- examining proposals for new laws and creating new law;
- scrutinizing government policy and administration. Parliamentary committees have the power to interview and question ministers;

- debating major issues – the public can ask their representative in Parliament to question government ministers;
- the House of Lords is also the highest court of appeal for England, Northern Ireland and, in civil cases only, for Scotland.

House of Commons

The House of Commons consists of 651 Members of Parliament (MPs) elected by universal adult suffrage. Candidates for election must pay a £500 deposit, which is forfeited if they fail to win at least one-twentieth of the total votes cast.

The Chairman of the House of Commons presides over debates and is known as the Speaker. He or she is elected by fellow MPs at the beginning of each Parliament.

House of Lords

The House of Lords consists of non-elected members. Membership of the House of Lords is comprised of the Lords Temporal and the Lords Spiritual.

The Lords Temporal

1 all hereditary peers and peeresses of the realm, except Irish peers;
2 all life peers created by the monarch;
3 the 12 Lords of Appeal in Ordinary ('Law Lords') (*see* Chapter 96).

Until 1999 (*see* 'House of Lords reform', below), there were over 1,200 peers who had the right to sit and vote in the House of Lords.

Who cannot sit in the House of Commons?

- Aliens
- Persons under the age of 21 years
- Certain persons suffering from mental illness
- Peers and peeresses in their own right, other than the holders of Irish peerages
- Clergy of the Church of England and the Church of Ireland, ministers of the Church of Scotland and priests of the Roman Catholic church
- Civil servants, police officers and members of the armed forces on the active list
- Sheriffs and returning officers as regards the constituencies of which they are returning officers
- People serving a term of imprisonment or detention for more than one year
- People convicted of treason
- Bankrupts
- Anyone guilty of corrupt or illegal practices at parliamentary elections
- Judges of the Supreme Court of Judicature, and the crown and county courts and stipendiary magistrates (*see* Chapter 96)
- Members of non-Commonwealth legislatures
- Holders of certain specified offices, usually offices of profit

The Lords Spiritual

These are the Archbishops of Canterbury and York, the Bishops of London, Durham and Winchester, and the 21 most senior other diocesan bishops of the Church of England.

The functions of the House of Lords are similar to those of the House of Commons in legislating, debating and questioning the executive. All bills (draft legislation) must go through both Houses before becoming Acts, and the Lords can amend all legislation.

Although the House of Lords can comment on a bill and recommend changes, it cannot actually stop it from being passed. The House of Commons can present a bill (except one to prolong the life of Parliament) for Royal Assent after one year, and in a new session, even if the Lords have not given their agreement.

House of Lords reform

In November 1999, the Labour government implemented its 1997 manifesto pledge to end the 700-year right of hereditary peers to sit and vote in the House of Lords. This was intended as the first phase in a process of reform to make the House of Lords more democratic and representative. The House of Lords Act, which received Royal Assent in November 1999, reduced the number of hereditary peers from around 900 to 92. It was agreed that 92 hereditary peers should be allowed to stay on until reform is complete.

The future for the House of Lords

Who will replace the hereditary peers and how will they be chosen? By February 2003, Parliament had failed to reach a consensus on the way forward for the Upper House. In September 2003, the government published a consultation paper outlining a limited number of profound changes:

- the government plans to introduce legislation to remove the right of the remaining 92 hereditary peers to sit and vote in the House of Lords;
- a statutory Appointments Commission is to be set up to select and oversee appointments to the House of Lords. The Commission will nominate independent (non-party) peers to sit in the House;
- the political parties will still be able to nominate their own political peers but the Commission will vet candidates for propriety;
- automatic peerages will continue to go to five prominent public figures on retirement: the Archbishop of Canterbury, the Archbishop of York, the Cabinet Secretary, the Queen's Principal Private Secretary and the Chief of the Defence Staff;
- retired members of the proposed Supreme Court (*see* page 722) will also be given peerages and seats in the Lords;

- peers will lose their seats if they are convicted of an offence and sentenced to more than 12 months in prison;
- the House of Commons will remain the dominant body in Parliament. The legislative powers of the House of Lords will not be altered.

The judiciary

Judges are an important part of the constitution. They are independent of government. Strictly speaking, the role of judges is to interpret the law laid down by Parliament and established legal principles, and make their decisions accordingly.

Yet, within the legal system, judges have power to make decisions against the government. Ministers of state can be ordered to attend in courts. Injunctions (court orders commanding or forbidding certain actions) can be made against individual ministers or government departments. In November 1991, the Home Secretary was held by the Court of Appeal to be personally in contempt of court after the Home Office had broken an undertaking not to deport a man who was seeking political asylum. The Home Secretary was ordered personally to pay the costs. The Master of the Rolls, Lord Donaldson, said: 'Ministers and civil servants are accountable to the law and to the courts for their personal actions.'

Chapter 96 deals in more detail with the courts and judges.

THE PRINCIPLES

The separation of powers: the executive, Parliament and the judges

The theory of the separation of powers is that no single element of power should be supreme. Each is subject to control by the others. The idea is to prevent the concentration of too much power in one of the agencies of the state, as this might lead to tyranny. The doctrine does not apply completely to the British constitution. For example, the Queen is head of the executive, head of the judiciary and an integral part of the legislature; until constitutional reform in June 2003, the Lord Chancellor was a member of the cabinet, the speaker of the House of Lords and the head of the judiciary under the Crown (*see further* page 722).

Independence of the judiciary

The principle that judges should be independent of pressure from government and other political groups is closely connected to the doctrine of the separation of powers. The rationale is that judges must be completely impartial when applying the law and should not allow any political bias to influence their judgment.

Examples of this principle in practice are:

- judges cannot sit as MPs;
- ministers of the Crown do not interfere with the discretion of a judge in any civil or criminal case;
- Parliament does not discuss matters under consideration by a judge at that moment.

The principle of judicial independence is reinforced by judges' protection from arbitrary removal and their immunity from civil suit. (*See further* Chapter 96.)

Parliamentary sovereignty

Parliament is supreme and sovereign in that only Parliament can change the law and there is no supreme law capable of overriding Acts of Parliament. There are no legal constraints on what the government can do, as long as its decisions are given legal backing by having a statute passed through Parliament. The courts must uphold parliamentary legislation and cannot rule that it is unlawful or invalid.

What is the impact of European law on parliamentary sovereignty?

European Community law overrides national law. So where Community law contradicts a provision of an Act of Parliament, Community law will prevail and would have to be followed by the British courts. Does this mean that the sovereignty of Parliament (i.e. the principle that Parliament is the supreme law-making body of the UK) has been eroded? The answer is both yes and no.

The UK entered the European Community and agreed to become subject to Community law by the European Communities Act 1972. In effect, Parliament limited its own sovereignty by the 1972 Act. However, in theory, the effect of the 1972 Act can always be reversed by a later Act of Parliament.

The doctrine of precedent

In a nutshell, this means that the lower courts are bound by the previous decisions of the higher courts. The decisions of the House of Lords (the highest court in the land) are binding on all the other courts trying similar cases; if no relevant House of Lords' decisions are on record, then the appropriate decision of the Court of Appeal would be binding, and so on, down through the hierarchy of courts (*see also* Chapter 96 for a guide to the courts). The decisions of the lower courts (i.e. the county courts and the magistrates' courts) are not binding.

The advantage of the system of precedent is that there is a consistency in the way the courts apply the law. The disadvantage is that it can lead to inflexibility, if a junior court is bound by an old House of Lords' decision that has not been reviewed for a long time. This potential for turgidity in the law was relieved slightly when the House of Lords decided, in 1966, that it was not bound by its old decisions and that it could reinterpret the law if it wished.

The Court of Appeal is, of course, bound by decisions of the House of Lords. Is it normally bound by its own previous decisions? The answer is yes, except where:

1 an earlier decision of the Court of Appeal was made in error; or
2 if there are two conflicting earlier decisions, the Court can choose one and override the other; or
3 where a decision conflicts with a later decision of the House of Lords.

SOURCES OF LAW

There are four sources of law in this country: common law, statute law, equity and European law.

Common law (or judge-made law)

The classic illustration of how the judges have made law is the history of the negligence claim. Basically, the law of negligence allows a victim to sue someone who has taken less care than he or she should have done. But this is a relatively recent concept. Until the nineteenth century there was no such action; there was merely a variety of situations in which negligence might give rise to liability. But the nineteenth century saw a drawing together of these actions under the overall category of the negligence claim. Slowly, standardized tests for determining liability were worked out.

It was not until 1932 that the House of Lords laid down a system of principles for the negligence claim and that was the real starting point of the law of negligence as we know it today. The House of Lords' decision in *Donoghue* v *Stevenson* (1932) created the modern law of negligence.

To lawyers, *Donoghue* v *Stevenson* is one of the best-known cases. It involved a young lady who became ill when she discovered a snail in the bottom of a bottle of ginger beer which she was drinking. She sued the manufacturer for damages. The case went all the way to the House of Lords, where it was decided that her claim should succeed.

As the years have gone by the principles in *Donoghue* v *Stevenson* have been extended. For instance, in 1932 the negligence action did not apply to negligent statements, but in 1964 the House of Lords held that it did cover such statements (*Hedley, Byrne* v *Heller*).

A solicitor was asked by a garage to give a reference for a client of his who was involved in buying an expensive car. The solicitor knew his client was on a fraud charge but as he did not believe it would affect his performance of the proposed contract, he did not mention it in the reference. The client defaulted and the solicitor had to pay £13,000 damages for giving an unreliable reference.

Edwards and others v Lee (1991)

As the law develops, so the scope of claims for negligence can be expanded:

A householder was burning off paint with a blowlamp. By mistake he set fire to his house. A fireman was injured in the efforts to put out the blaze. The fireman sued the householder for damages and the House of Lords decided that his claim should succeed. He was awarded £12,900.

Ogwo v Taylor (1987)

Common law decisions are not confined to the decisions of English courts. Decisions of other 'common law' countries (notably Australia, New Zealand and Canada) are often considered by English courts.

Common law is not paramount. Its principles can be cancelled, changed or extended by statute law. Nevertheless, it allows considerable opportunity for judges to alter and to make law. Judges can also create law in the way they interpret statutes (*see* below).

Statute law (Acts of Parliament)

Statute law overrides the common law; if the common law says one thing and an Act says something else, the judges must follow the Act.

How are Acts of Parliament made?

Bills are proposed Acts of Parliament. The bill must be 'read three times' in both Houses of Parliament and become law only when they receive the Royal Assent (the Queen's formal approval). After this the bill becomes part of the law and is known as an Act of Parliament.

Before bills are introduced into Parliament, the government may set out its proposals for changing the law in a White Paper. The government may invite interested groups (such as pressure groups, voluntary organizations or groups representing the interests of commerce and industry) to discuss and comment on its proposals. In that case, it will set out its proposals in a Green Paper.

Bills all have to go through a series of prescribed steps in their journey through both Houses of Parliament. The main steps are as follows:

1 *First reading* – the First reading is a formality. The title of the bill is formally presented.
2 *Second reading* – this is the first main occasion for debate on the general principles of the bill. The Second

reading usually takes place two weeks after the First reading.
3 *Committee stage* – generally once a bill has passed its Second reading (which it will do virtually automatically if it is a government bill) it goes to one of the standing committees of the House of Commons for detailed discussion – clause by clause. Individual provisions may be amended.
4 *Report stage* – the bill is then 'reported' to the House of Commons. At this stage further amendments may be made.
5 *Third reading* – the bill is reviewed in its final form, including any amendments made. Substantive amendments cannot be made at this stage to a bill in the House of Commons. A motion is put, 'that the bill be read a third time'. If it is carried, the bill is deemed to have passed the House of Commons. After passing its third reading in the Commons, the bill is sent to the House of Lords.
6 *Procedures in the House of Lords* – the procedure is similar. Financial legislation is not scrutinized in detail by the House of Lords. Bills can be further amended in the Lords. If the bill remains unopposed, it goes for the Royal Assent and then becomes law.

Private Members' bills

These are bills introduced by backbench MPs (i.e. a member of the House of Commons who is not a member of the government), rather than government bills. Few Private Members' bills reach the statute book, but they can generate publicity about a topic, which may put pressure on the government to introduce its own bill. Examples of Acts of Parliament which originated from Private Members' bills include the Matrimonial Causes Act 1937, the Murder (Abolition of Death Penalty) Act 1965 and the Local Government (Access to Information) Act 1985.

Who is to decide what these Acts of Parliament mean?

The answer is that the judges decide. Judges can therefore create law by the way they interpret statutes.

Legislation is written in precise and technical language by expert parliamentary draftsmen but the possibility remains that a situation may arise in practice which is not clearly covered by the wording of an Act, or that there may be some ambiguity as to the meaning or intention of a particular statutory provision. In those circumstances, the judges will decide how the Act should be interpreted, according to guidelines that they have developed over the years:

● *the context rule* – a statute cannot be asked to explain itself in the same way that a person can be asked what they mean. It is therefore necessary to look at a word or phrase in its setting. As Henry Fielding said: 'A word may be known by the company it keeps';

- *fringe meaning* – if a judge has difficulty in finding the meaning of a statute he or she may try to divine what Parliament intended when the Act was passed. An example of the sort of problem which gives rise to this difficulty is in the definition of a word like 'building'. Normally, that would present no problem if the structure were a bungalow or a school. But what about a shed, or a caravan with its wheels removed, or a converted railway carriage? In such circumstances it may be necessary to look further to try to find what was intended. Not all judges agree that this is a correct approach. According to Lord Simon in *Farrell* v *Alexander* (1977): 'The court is concerned to ascertain . . . not what [Parliament] meant to say, but the meaning of what they have said';

- *the mischief rule* – this rule was first developed in 1584 and is known as the 'Rule in Heydon's case'. What the judges have to do is to see what the law was before the Act was passed and ascertain the 'mischief' which resulted in the change in the law. They can look at Royal Commissions and departmental reports for details of the mischief at which the new law is aimed;

- *the literal rule* – this is an unpopular method of interpreting the law. It is the 'nothing added, nothing taken away' approach: stick to the law, however absurd the result may be. According to Glanville Williams in *Learning the Law*, 'The literal rule is a rule against using intelligence in understanding language. Anyone who in ordinary life interpreted rules literally, being indifferent to what the speaker or writer meant, would be regarded as a pedant, a mischief maker or an idiot';

- *the golden rule* – if, on the face of it, the words of an Act produce an absurd meaning, the courts are allowed to use an interpretation which avoids the absurdity. The sensible meaning has to be linguistically possible; the court cannot completely rewrite the Act so as to make it make sense. Lord Denning put it this way in *The Changing Law*: 'The judges are too often inclined to fold their hands and blame the legislature, when really they ought to set to work and give the words a reasonable meaning, even if this does involve a departure from the letter of them. By doing so they are more likely to find the truth';

- *Parliamentary statements* – until recently, the courts have refused to take account of anything said in Parliament during the passage of legislation as a subsequent aid to interpretation of the Act. However, in an important decision in 1993 (*Pepper* v *Hart*) the House of Lords decreed that parliamentary statements by ministers may be admissible in order to interpret an Act of Parliament when its meaning is ambiguous, obscure or may lead to an absurdity, and what was said in Parliament clearly discloses the mischief aimed at or the legislative intention behind the words.

Secondary legislation (statutory instruments)

These are regulations made by a government minister under powers delegated to that minister by a section in the parent Act of Parliament (known as the 'enabling provision'). Statutory instruments carry the force of law and usually deal with matters of detail or minor or routine changes to the law. They far outnumber Acts of Parliament and are often even more difficult to understand than the Acts themselves.

Statutory instruments (SIs) are drafted by lawyers in the government department concerned with the subject of the regulations. There may be a legal requirement in the parent Act to consult with people likely to be affected by the SI. They are laid before Parliament but are given much less rigorous scrutiny and most SIs are not debated at all, although they can be vetted by a committee of MPs and peers (the Joint Committee on Statutory Instruments). Unlike Acts of Parliament, SIs may be quashed by a court if the minister exceeded the ambit of the enabling provision in the Act or because of procedural irregularity.

Equity

Equity is a specific set of legal principles, distinct from the common law but supplementing it. Where the common law was defective or injustice resulted from too strict adherence to precedent, the system of equity developed as a corrective. The rules of equity can prevail over common law where there is a conflict between them.

Equity acts according to a number of principles, which are expressed as 'maxims'. These principles must be satisfied before the equitable rules can be applied. For example, one maxim is that 'He who comes to Equity must come with clean hands'. This means that claimants who are themselves in the wrong will not be granted an equitable remedy. Another maxim is that 'Delay defeats equities', meaning that, where the claimant takes an unreasonably long time to bring an action, the equitable remedies will not be available.

Whereas common law remedies are available as of right, most equitable remedies are discretionary – so the court does not have to award a remedy where it considers that the conduct of the party claiming the award is undeserving. Equitable remedies include injunctions (orders to do or refrain from a particular activity), rectification (putting right mistakes in legal documents) and rescission (cancellation of contracts).

Constitutional conventions

Conventions are not laws because they are not created by statute or judges and they are not recognized by courts of law. However, they are an important source of constitutional authority. Conventions may be described as binding rules of political behaviour which have gradually evolved and which are consistently observed. Examples include the convention that the Queen must assent to bills which have been passed through both Houses of Parliament or in accordance with the Parliament Act 1911, the convention that the Prime Minister will call regular meetings of the cabinet, and the convention that government ministers have to be members of one of the Houses of Parliament.

EUROPEAN LAW

Since the UK became a full member of the European Community, it has been subject to EC law. If there is a clash between national law (the law passed by Parliament) and Community law, the Community law takes priority. Community law gives rights to individuals to which member states must give effect. Community law has become increasingly important in the lives of the citizens of the UK.

The European Union

The European Union (EU) is made up of 25 countries ('Member States'), including 10 countries that joined the Union on 1 May 2004: Cyprus, Lithuania, Malta, Poland, the Czech Republic, Estonia, Hungary, Latvia, Slovakia and Slovenia. The enlarged EU of 25 countries and 454 million people will expand even further in 2007, when Bulgaria and Romania join.

The EU has a number of aims:

- economic development (the single market was established in 1993 and the single currency was launched in 1999);
- European unity (e.g. a common foreign and security policy and common positions within international organizations);
- European citizenship (confers a number of civil and political rights on European citizens, improving living and working conditions for citizens).

There are five main institutions involved in running the EU:

The Commission	Proposes Community law/ monitors compliance with the law	Initiates Community legislation, runs European common policies, implements the budget and monitors compliance with Community law. Refers alleged violations of Community law by Member States to the European Court of Justice. Based in Brussels. The executive organ of the EC.
The European Parliament	Advises on the law	The 626 members are elected by the citizens of the Member States. 87 MEPs are from the UK. The Council must take its views on proposed legislation into account. Limited ability to veto legislation.
The Council of Ministers	Decides on the law	Represents the governments of the Member States, whose heads of state meet twice a year to discuss policy. The EC's principal decision-making body: it is responsible for the final decision as to whether a Regulation should be made or a Directive should be issued.
The European Courts of Justice	Interprets the law	Ensures that Community law is complied with and applied uniformly by the national courts of the Member States. Sits in Luxembourg.
The Court of Auditors	Financial watchdog	Audits the accounts. Checks that the EC spends its money according to the budgetary rules and for proper purposes. Based in Luxembourg. Consists of 15 auditors from the Member States.

Petitioning the European Parliament

Any member of the public or group can petition the European Parliament with requests or grievances on matters within the EU's jurisdiction.

The European Ombudsman

The European Ombudsman appoints an ombudsman who is responsible for investigating disputes that may arise between citizens and administrative authorities of the Community institutions. Every European citizen has the right to apply to the European Ombudsman if they are the victim of maladministration at European level.

European Community law

European Community law is separate from, but superior to, national law. It applies uniformly in all the 15 Member States of the European Community. The European Communities Act 1972 gave the force of law in the UK to existing Community legislation, and provided for future Community law to have direct effect in the UK. In the case of any conflict between UK law and EC law, EC law will prevail.

Many laws of this country originated from Community law, particularly in the areas of employment law, environmental law, consumer protection, free movement of goods and free movement of services.

The sources of EC law are:

- *the Treaties* – the principal treaty is the Treaty of Rome which sets out the objectives of the European Community. For example, Article 119 of the Treaty of Rome provides that men and women should receive equal pay for equal work;
- *Regulations* – these are binding throughout the EC in exactly the terms in which they are made. They are, in theory, directly applicable in Member States. In practice, they may need to be supplemented by national legislation for their full implementation;
- *Directives* – these are binding in that the Member States must achieve the end result of the Directive. However, each Member State may decide upon the method and form of implementation. Directives generally require national legislation to implement them;
- *the decisions of the European Court of Justice* – (*see* Chapter 96).

In addition to issuing Regulations and Directives, the Council and the Commission can also make *decisions*, but these are only legally binding on the person (Member State or individual) to whom they are addressed.

USEFUL ADDRESSES

Information Unit
Commission of the European Communities
8 Storey's Gate
London SW1P 3AT
Tel: 020 7973 1992
Website: www.europa.eu.int/geninfo/icom-en.htm

Information Office
European Parliament
2 Queen Anne's Gate
London SW1H 9AA
Tel: 020 7227 4300
Website: www.europarl.org.uk

European Ombudsman
1 Avenue du Président Robert Schuman
B.P. 403 – F–67001 Strasbourg Cédex
Tel: 00 33 3 88 17 23 13
Website: www.euro-ombudsman.eu.int

House of Commons Information Office
House of Commons
Westminster
London SW1A 0AA
Tel: 020 7219 4272
Website: www.parliament.uk

European Court of Justice
Cour de Justice des Communautés européennes
L-2925 Luxembourg
Tel: (352) 4303.1
Website: www.curia.eu.int

Council of Europe
67075 Strasbourg Cédex
France
Tel: 00 33 3 88 41 20 33
Website: www.coe.fr

European Court of Human Rights
Council of Europe
F-67075 Strasbourg Cédex
France
Tel: 00 33 3 88 41 20 18
Website: www.echr.coe.int/

A Guide to the Courts

INTRODUCTION

This chapter provides a simple guide to the courts and judges. The courts in England and Wales are arranged into a hierarchy. The hierarchical structure reflects and supports the precedent doctrine described in the previous chapter. In other words, the courts lower down in the ranking order are bound by the decisions of the higher courts. The courts of Scotland and Northern Ireland are completely separate but follow the same system. The highest court in the land is the House of Lords. The decisions of judges in the House of Lords must be followed by all the other courts, including the courts of Scotland and Northern Ireland.

The Department for Constitutional Affairs is responsible for the administration of the court system and a number of tribunals through its main operational arm, the Court Service. The Court Service provides court staff, buildings and equipment for all the courts in the hierarchy, except magistrates' courts. Magistrates' courts are locally administered and financed by local authorities, which reclaim 80 per cent of their expenditure from the Department for Constitutional Affairs in the form of an annual grant.

The Department for Constitutional Affairs is also concerned with the appointment of judges, the provision of public funding and legal services and the promotion of reform and revision of English civil law.

The Lord Chancellor

In June 2003 the Department for Constitutional Affairs was created, incorporating most of the responsibilities of the former Lord Chancellor's Department. The three historic roles of the Lord Chancellor, as head of the judiciary, cabinet minister and Speaker of the House of Lords, were also dismantled, ending the anomalous position which meant a cabinet minister was in charge of appointing judges. The government intends to push ahead with plans for further constitutional reform, including abolishing the post of Lord Chancellor altogether. An independent Judicial Appointments Commission would take over the Lord Chancellor's responsibility for appointing judges. The Commission would draw up a shortlist of candidates for appointment as judges. Their recommendations would be passed to the constitutional affairs secretary, who would have the final say. An ombudsman will ensure that the process is fair.

The government also plans to create a supreme court, transferring the Law Lords who currently sit in the House of Lords to their own separate building, divorced from the legislature. The reform is designed to enhance the way the judiciary is kept separate from the state.

The Attorney General

The Attorney General (AG) and his deputy, the Solicitor General, are the government's chief legal advisers. The AG is the leader of the English Bar and has ministerial responsibility for the Crown Prosecution Service (CPS) (*see* below). The head of the CPS, the Director of Public Prosecutions, reports to him. The AG and Solicitor General represent the Crown in civil litigation in England and Wales, and may prosecute in England and Scotland in criminal cases of great importance or gravity, especially murder cases.

The Home Secretary

The Home Secretary is responsible for a wide range of matters connected with law and order, including the criminal law, the police, prison and probation services and penal policy.

CIVIL COURTS

Litigation in the civil courts may be begun by an individual, a company, or a public authority, whereas cases in the criminal courts are usually instigated by the CPS (*see* below). There are different rules about what evidence can be presented to the court in civil trials and the burden and standard of proof are different (see page 738). Juries are now very rare in civil trials and most cases are decided by a judge alone.

The following table summarizes the types of civil disputes that may be dealt with at the different courts in the civil court system.

Court	Judges who preside there	Examples of types of civil cases dealt with
Magistrates' court	Justices of the Peace Stipendiary magistrates	• Income tax, council tax and VAT arrears; • granting, renewing or removing licences from pubs and clubs; • adoption proceedings, local authority care and supervision orders, residence orders; • maintenance; • removing a spouse from the matrimonial home.
County court	Circuit judges and district judges	• Landlord and tenant disputes; • faulty goods and services; • traffic accidents, tripping and slipping cases, accidents at work (personal injuries); • some domestic violence cases; • some undefended divorce cases; • race and sex discrimination cases; • debt problems; • employment problems.
High Court: Family Division	The President of the Family Division and 16 High Court judges	• Complex defended divorce cases; • wardship; • adoption; • domestic violence. The divisional court deals with appeals.
High Court: Queen's Bench Division	Lord Chief Justice and 66 High Court judges	• Large and/or complex claims for compensation; • judicial review cases; • libel and slander cases. The divisional court deals with appeals.
High Court: Chancery Division	Lord Chancellor, Vice-Chancellor and 17 High Court judges	• Trusts; • contested wills; • winding up companies; • bankruptcy; • mortgages; • charities; • contested tax cases. The divisional court deals with appeals.
Court of Appeal: Civil Division	Lord Chief Justice, Master of the Rolls and the Lords Justices of Appeal	*Civil appeals* from the High Court, the county court, the Employment Appeal Tribunals and the Lands Tribunal.
House of Lords	Lords of Appeal in Ordinary	*Appeals* from the Court of Appeal or direct from the High Court.

Magistrates' courts

These are the lowest courts in the hierarchy of civil courts. They now deal with only a limited amount of civil litigation, such as non-payment of council tax arrears. The part of the magistrates' court that deals with family matters is called the Family Proceedings court. Magistrates also deal with the grant or refusal of applications for liquor and betting licences.

A case in the magistrates' court may be heard by two or three lay magistrates sitting together or one stipendiary magistrate sitting alone. (*See further* under 'Criminal courts', page 726.) In August 2000, all stipendiary magistrates became District Judges (magistrates' courts).

County courts

There are 250 county courts in England and Wales. The vast majority of cases which begin in the county court happen to be brought by litigants suing to recover a debt owed under the terms of a contract, for example, where a supplier of goods is not paid following delivery of the goods.

Since April 1999, cases are allocated to one of three tracks: the small claims track (for low-value disputes to be dealt with as quickly as possible under a simple procedure), the fast track (for larger and more complex claims), and the multi-track (for everything else). Each track involves different procedural steps to be taken by the parties. Straightforward cases up to the value of £50,000 in dispute are usually brought in a county court. All other civil cases are heard in the High Court.

District judges hear disputes that have been allocated to the small claims track. Circuit judges deal with larger-value cases (generally over £5,000).

The High Court

The High Court is based in London – with a few regional centres. The more substantial and complex cases are begun in the High Court.

There are three divisions of the High Court.

Chancery Division

The Chancery Division deals principally with disputes over land, wills and the administration of estates, bankruptcy and winding up of companies and intellectual property disputes. The Chancery Division is sub-divided into two specialist courts:

- the Companies court which handles company cases (mainly insolvency); and
- the Patents court (patents, registered designs, appeals

against the decision of the Comptroller General of Patents).

The Chancery Division hears appeals in tax matters from the Commissioners of Taxes. Bankruptcy appeals from the county courts and from the High Court Registrars under the Insolvency Act 1986 are heard by a single judge of the Chancery Division.

Queen's Bench Division

The Queen's Bench Division deals with other civil litigation. There is a right to trial by jury for fraud, libel, slander, malicious prosecution or false imprisonment cases. In all other cases the judge has a discretion to allow trial by jury but it is only used exceptionally. The Queen's Bench Division is split into the following specialist courts:

- the Crown Office List (actions against public authorities);
- the Admiralty court (shipping matters, especially collisions between ships and damage to cargo);
- the Commercial court (large and complex business disputes, such as international commercial contracts, international sale of goods, insurance, reinsurance and banking);
- the Technology and Construction court, formerly known as the Official Referees' court (disputes involving complicated technical matters such as building and engineering disputes and computer contract disputes).

The Queen's Bench Division also deals with appeals from magistrates' courts and crown courts, and can review the actions of individuals or organizations to ensure that they have acted legally and justly (this is called judicial review). It also hears appeals and applications under various statutory provisions, including those on planning matters under the Town and Country Planning Acts.

Family Division

The Family Division hears family disputes and also hears appeals from magistrates' and county courts in family matters.

From a county court or the High Court, there is an appeal to the Civil Division of the Court of Appeal. In exceptional cases involving matters of legal importance, there may be an appeal from the High Court direct to the House of Lords.

The Court of Appeal

The courtrooms and offices of the Court of Appeal are in the Royal Courts of Justice in The Strand in London. The Civil Division of the Court of Appeal hears appeals against decisions in the High Court, county courts and tribunals, such as the Employment Appeal Tribunal and the Lands Tribunal. The head of the Civil Division is the

Master of the Rolls, who will sit with two or three judges to hear an appeal.

From the Court of Appeal there can be an appeal to the House of Lords.

The House of Lords

This is the ultimate court of appeal in Great Britain and Northern Ireland, save that it has no jurisdiction to hear appeals in Scottish criminal cases. At least three of the Lords of Appeal must sit together to hear an appeal, but as many as seven can hear an appeal. Appeals are normally heard in a committee room, rather than in the legislative chamber and typically last two to three days.

The House of Lords is subject to decisions of the European Court of Justice on EU law matters.

Note that the government plans to create a new supreme court with the 12 existing Law Lords, who currently sit in the House of Lords, as members.

Appeals

If you are unhappy about a decision made by a judge in your case, you may be able to appeal against it. An important point to grasp is that an appeal is not an opportunity for the court to re-examine the facts of the case – the higher court will not retry the issues – it will examine whether the judge in the lower court exercised his discretion correctly, or interpreted the law correctly.

Grounds for appeal

There are two important points to note: you will in most cases need to obtain permission from the court to bring an appeal and you must have proper reasons (grounds) for appealing. You will need to show that the decision was either:

● wrong in law; or
● unjust because of a serious procedural or other irregularity in the proceedings.

There are strict time limits for bringing an appeal and you will have to pay a court fee, unless you are receiving certain state benefits. The court fee for an appeal to the Court of Appeal is £100 for an application and £200 for an appeal. Bear in mind that if you lose your appeal, you may be ordered to pay the other party's legal costs.

Virtually all appeals to the Court of Appeal now require permission – permission will be granted if there is an issue which ought to be considered by the Court of Appeal in the public interest, but will be refused if the appeal has no realistic prospect of success.

Staff in the Civil Appeals Office can give general advice about how to make an appeal – but cannot answer

The Civil Appeals System

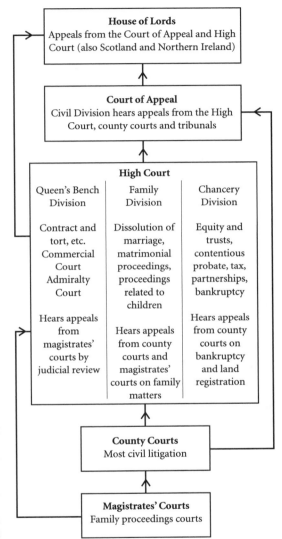

questions about whether or not an appeal should be made or whether the appeal is likely to succeed. The Civil Appeals Office is at Room E330, Royal Courts of Justice, The Strand, London WC2A 2LL, Tel: 020 7947 6000.

The diagram above illustrates the system of appeal in civil cases.

CRIMINAL COURTS

The Crown Prosecution Service

The Crown Prosecution Service (CPS) is the government department that prosecutes people in England and Wales who have been charged by the police with a criminal offence. The head of the CPS is called the Director of Public Prosecutions (DPP). The current DPP is David Calvert-Smith QC.

The CPS is independent of the police, although it works closely with the police and advises them on possible prosecutions. Once the police have investigated a crime and charged the suspect the CPS decides whether criminal proceedings should follow. In making this decision, the CPS is concerned with two issues:

1 is there a realistic prospect of conviction? If there is insufficient evidence the case cannot proceed;
2 is prosecution in the public interest? In serious cases, the public interest will rarely outweigh the case for prosecution.

If criminal proceedings are appropriate, CPS lawyers will prepare the case for court and prosecute the case (i.e. they will present the case against the defendant).

The majority of prosecutions are handled by the CPS but certain offences are still prosecuted by the police, while some are prosecuted by private organizations or government agencies such as the Inland Revenue.

Magistrates' courts

All criminal cases start in the magistrates' court and over 95 per cent of all criminal cases are dealt with there; there were 1,911,600 completed proceedings at magistrates' courts in 2000. In the same year, 95,300 defendants had proceedings completed.

Where will the case be tried?

This can depend on a number of factors, including the seriousness of the offence, whether the defendant wishes the case to be heard by a judge and jury and the appropriate sentence:

- *summary offences* (e.g. common assault). These offences are normally tried in the magistrates' court;
- *triable-either-way offences* (e.g. car crime, actual bodily harm and grievous bodily harm). The defendant may be tried in the magistrates' court unless he elects for a crown court trial or the magistrates feel that a crown court trial is more appropriate because their sentencing powers are insufficient;
- *indictable offences* (e.g. robbery, rape, murder, manslaughter and arson). The adult defendant must be tried in the crown court.

The decision as to where an either-way case should be heard is made at a hearing before the magistrates. If the defendant pleads guilty, the magistrates will convict him. If the defendant does not plead guilty, the magistrates will consider where the case should be tried. If they consider that it is more appropriate for the case to be tried in the magistrates' court, the defendant has the right to refuse to be tried there and to choose, or 'elect', to be tried at the crown court before a judge and jury instead. So, at the moment, a defendant can only be tried in the magistrates' court if he agrees. (*See* Chapter 86 for an explanation of how criminal proceedings are begun and how committal proceedings take place.)

Proposals for reform

The government has introduced proposals to remove the defendant's ability to elect for trial in the crown court. The Criminal Justice (Mode of Trial) (No 2) bill provides that the decision as to where either-way cases are heard should rest with magistrates.

Usually, three lay (i.e. not professional judges or lawyers) magistrates will sit together to hear the case. As most lay magistrates are not legally qualified, a qualified court clerk advises them on questions of law, legal procedure and practice. Magistrates are appointed by the Secretary of State for Constitutional Affairs and Lord Chancellor on the advice of local Advisory Committees, consisting of magistrates and other local people. The Secretary of State for Constitutional Affairs and Lord Chancellor will not generally appoint a person under 27 or over 65 years. Magistrates must retire at the age of 70 years.

In addition, the following will not be considered for appointment:

- anyone who is not of good character and personal standing;
- undischarged bankrupts;
- a serving member of Her Majesty's forces; a member of a police force or a traffic warden or any other occupation which might be seen to conflict with the role of a magistrate;
- a close relative of a person who is already a magistrate on the same bench.

Lay magistrates are unpaid but can claim allowances for travelling, subsistence and financial loss. Stipendiary magistrates are legally qualified, are usually solicitors and are paid. They tend to be appointed to sit in large, urban magistrates' courts. A stipendiary magistrate may sit alone to try a case and has the same powers as any two lay magistrates.

Crown court

As well as dealing with more serious cases, the crown court hears appeals against decisions of magistrates' courts and deals with cases sent for sentence from the magistrates' courts. Crown courts always sit with a jury when trying criminal cases. Trials are presided over by High Court judges, circuit judges or recorders, depending on the category of offence involved:

	Examples of offences in that class	Which judge will try the case?
Class 1	Murder, treason	Always a High Court judge
Class 2	Incitement to mutiny, piracy, manslaughter	A High Court judge or a circuit judge
Class 3	Criminal damage with intention to endanger life, indecent exposure, kidnapping	A High Court judge, circuit judge or recorder
Class 4	Obtaining property by deception, destroying or damaging property, abstracting electricity	Normally a circuit judge or a recorder. Can be tried by a High Court judge if the consent of the judge or presiding judge is given.

Defendants may appeal against conviction before a crown court to the Criminal Division of the Court of Appeal.

Jury service

People are randomly selected from the electoral register for jury service. Jurors are normally expected to serve a period of 10 working days and during that time could sit on more than one case. You can apply to be excused from jury service or to have jury service deferred until a later date if there is a good reason why you should not serve. According to a 1999 Home Office study of 50,000 people summonsed for jury service in June and July 1999 (Research Findings No. 102 *Jury Excusal and Deferral*), the most common reasons for granting excusal from jury service were medical, the care of young children or care of the elderly. Three-quarters of all deferrals were given for either work or holidays.

Court of Appeal

Applications to appeal, and for permission to appeal against decisions made by the crown court are dealt with by the Court of Appeal Criminal Division. The Criminal Division is presided over by the Lord Chief Justice, and appeals are heard by the Lord Chief Justice and Lords Justices, assisted by High Court judges as required.

House of Lords

The final court of appeal is the House of Lords. Note that the House of Lords has no power to hear a criminal appeal from Scotland.

OTHER COURTS

Privy Council

The Judicial Committee of the Privy Council is the ultimate court of appeal in both civil and criminal matters from the courts of the Isle of Man, the Channel Islands, the colonies and dependencies of the UK, and from the courts of some independent members of the Commonwealth which have retained the right of appeal. It also hears appeals from special tribunals, such as the General Medical Council and the General Dental Council.

The sort of work done by the Privy Council includes hearing appeals by convicted murderers who have been sentenced to death and deciding the lawfulness of the decisions of public authorities.

The European Court of Justice

The Court of Justice ensures that EC law is interpreted and applied consistently in each Member State. The Court sits in Luxembourg and comprises 15 judges – selected from each of the 15 Member States – and nine Advocates General. Note that the Advocates General are not prosecutors – their function is to deliver Opinions on cases brought before the Court, which is an important part of the procedure by which the Court reaches its final conclusions about a case. In fact, the Opinion of the Advocate General is usually a good indication of how the Court will decide.

The Court of Justice overrules all other courts (including the House of Lords) on matters of Community law and its decisions are binding on the courts of Member States.

What sorts of cases are dealt with by the European Court of Justice?

Interpretation or validity of Community law
A case before a national court may concern a question of Community law. Where the national court is in doubt about the correct interpretation or validity of Community law it can seek a ruling from the Court of Justice on the law. So, in this instance, the Court of Justice acts as a source of guidance to national courts, to enable them to apply Community law properly in the cases before them. Only a national court has the power to seek a ruling from the Court of Justice – an individual cannot apply direct to the Court of Justice for a ruling on the correct interpretation of Community law.

Mr Taylor complained that, as he was only 62 years old, under UK law he was not entitled to a Winter Fuel Payment. The relevant UK legislation stipulates that women of at least 60 years and men of at least 65 years are entitled to a payment. Mr Taylor asserted that the legislation discriminated against him as a man. The High Court asked the Court of Justice to deliver a ruling as to the compatibility of UK legislation with the rules of Community law concerning the equal treatment of men and women in matters of social security. In December 1999 the Court of Justice ruled that the UK legislation was not compatible with Community law. The Winter Fuel Payment should be made under the same conditions to men and women.

R *v* Secretary of State for Social Security ex parte Taylor (1999)

Examining the legality of Community acts
The Court of Justice can settle disputes between Community institutions, between Community institutions and Member States or between Member States. For example, the Commission or another Member State can bring an action against a Member State on the ground that it has failed to fulfil its obligations under Community law.

In November 1999 the Commission asked the Court of Justice to rule that France had failed to fulfil its obligations under a 1979 Community Directive relating to the protection of wild birds. The Court of Justice ruled that France had failed to comply with Community law.

The Court of Justice can impose a fine on any Member State that fails to comply with its judgment. The Court is not bound by its own previous decisions but it may cite earlier cases in its judgment and the Advocate General is likely to discuss earlier decisions in his opinion.

There are two important points to appreciate. First, the Court of Justice is not a court of appeal from decisions of national courts. This is because it is not the function of the Court of Justice to settle national disputes. It only provides interpretation or decides upon the validity of a Community act. It is for the national court (e.g. the House of Lords) to resolve the case on the basis of the Court of Justice's ruling.

The second point to note is that this court should not be confused with the European Court of Human Rights in Strasbourg, which hears cases where people think their human rights have been infringed (*see* below).

The judgments of the Court of Justice and the Opinions of the Advocates General are published in the *Reports of Cases before the Court of Justice and the Court of First Instance* in all the official languages of the Community. (*See* also the website at http://europa.eu.int.)

Court of First Instance

The Court of First Instance, based in Luxembourg, was created in 1989 to help the Court of Justice cope with a rapidly increasing caseload. It comprises 15 judges drawn from each of the 15 Member States of the Community. The Court of First Instance deals with actions brought by individuals or companies against decisions of the Community institutions which are addressed to them or which are of direct and individual concern to them. It also hears competition law cases and disputes between Community institutions and their employees. There is an appeal to the Court of Justice.

The new European Court of Human Rights

Since 1966, British citizens have been able to take a complaint of an alleged violation of their human rights under the European Convention on Human Rights of 1950 by one of the contracting states to the European Court of Human Rights (ECHR) in Strasbourg.

Until recently, the judicial institutions of the Convention system comprised a Court of Human Rights (set up in 1959) and a Commission (set up in 1954). The steady growth in the number of cases taken to Strasbourg (from 404 in 1981 to 12,000 in 1997) made it increasingly difficult to keep the length of proceedings within acceptable limits. In order to reduce delay and cost, a new simplified system with different procedural rules was devised. The old Court ceased to function in October 1998 and the Commission was abolished a year later. A single full-time court replaced them in November 1998.

What cases can the Court deal with?
- Applicants may be individuals, corporations, organizations or interest groups, subject to the proviso that the applicant must in all cases be a 'victim', so actions cannot be brought on behalf of others;
- you cannot bring a complaint against a private individual or a private organization. You can only complain about matters that are the responsibility of a public authority of one of the states that has signed up to the Convention;
- the application to the Court must be the final resort. You must have tried all the remedies in the state concerned and brought your case before the highest court which can deal with it. You have six months from the decision of the highest competent national court to apply to the Court.

Note that the Court is not a court of appeal from national courts and cannot change or quash their decisions.

How do I apply to the Court?

Send a letter to the Registrar of the Court at the following address:

The Registrar
European Court of Human Rights
Council of Europe
F-67075 Strasbourg Cédex
France

In your letter you should:

1 give a brief summary of your complaint;
2 indicate which of your Convention rights you think have been violated;
3 state what remedies you have already pursued;
4 list the official decisions in your case, giving the date of each decision, the court or authority which took it, and brief details of the decision itself.

Enclose with your letter a copy of the judgments, decisions and any other documents relevant to the complaint. You are not obliged to instruct a lawyer to represent you at this stage, but bear in mind that you will need a lawyer as the case progresses. You may be eligible for public funding to help with the legal fees.

The procedure

The 41 judges of the Court sit in their individual capacity and do not represent any state. The Court is divided into four sections. Committees of three judges within each section are responsible for much of the filtering of cases formerly carried out by the Commission. Each section also contains a chamber of seven judges. There is a Grand Chamber of 17 judges.

Briefly, the procedure is as follows:

1 *Is the application admissible?* – each individual application is assigned to a section. A Committee or a Chamber will decide whether the application is admissible or inadmissible. This stage of the procedure is usually in writing. There is no point, therefore, in coming yourself to the Court's offices.
2 *Examining the merits of the case* – if the application is admissible, the Chamber may invite the parties to submit further evidence and to attend a public hearing on the merits of the case. During this stage of the proceedings, the Registrar may attempt to secure a friendly settlement between the parties. These negotiations are confidential.
3 *Court gives its judgment* – the Chamber decides on the case by a majority vote. Within three months of the judgment of a Chamber, any party may request that the case be referred to the Grand Chamber if it raises a serious question of interpretation or application or a serious issue of general importance. The Grand Chamber decides by a majority vote and its judgments are final. All final judgments of the Court are binding on the respondent states concerned.

(*See* Chapters 84 and 95 for an explanation of the impact of the Human Rights Act 1998.)

Coroners' courts

Coroners are independent judicial officers (usually lawyers with at least five years' experience and sometimes medical doctors with a legal qualification) who will enquire into the causes of certain kinds of deaths:

1 deaths which are violent or unnatural (e.g. a homicide, a suicide, or a major disaster);
2 where the cause of death is unknown;
3 deaths which occur in prison.

The coroner may ask a pathologist to examine the body. If the death is not due to a natural cause the coroner will hold an inquest to ascertain who has died, how they died and when and where they died. An inquest is a public hearing in open court. An inquest is not a trial and the purpose is not to decide who is to blame for the death. The coroner takes a much more active part in the proceedings than a judge of an English court. The coroner decides when to hold the inquest, what evidence to call, who should be summonsed as witnesses and in what order the witnesses should give their evidence. Anyone who has a 'proper interest' may question a witness at the inquest. A 'properly interested' person can include a parent, a spouse or an insurer who has issued a life insurance policy on the deceased.

Most inquests are held without a jury but a jury will be called if:

- the death occurred in prison or in police custody; or
- the death resulted from an incident at work.

In these cases the jury, rather than the coroner, will make the final decision as to the cause of death.

Where a person is facing criminal charges in relation to the death, the inquest will be adjourned until the criminal proceedings have been concluded.

Coroners must be notified if a dead body is to be removed from England and Wales. They may also be asked for consent to removal of organs for transplant into other persons.

Treasure

If buried treasure is found, the coroner holds a treasure trove inquest. If the inquest finds that the treasure was accidentally lost, it is deemed to belong to the owner of the land. If, on the other hand, it is found to have been buried deliberately, the inquest will return a 'treasure trove' verdict and the treasure passes to the Crown (though compensation is usually paid to the finder).

The Treasure Act 1996 came into force in September 1997 in England, Wales and Northern Ireland, replacing the common law of treasure trove and widening the

Tribunal	What does it do?	Other points to note
Immigration Appeal Tribunal	Decides applications for leave to appeal and appeals against decisions made by the Immigration Adjudicator.	
Pensions Appeal Tribunal	Decides appeals against decisions of the Secretary of State for Works and Pensions in relation to war pensions.	No legal costs are awarded. Travelling and subsistence expenses may be reimbursed.
VAT and Duties Tribunals	Decides appeals against certain decisions of the Commissioners of Customs & Excise regarding VAT, Customs Duties, Excise Duties, Insurance Premium Tax and Landfill Tax.	Tribunal can award costs.
Special Commissioners of Income Tax	Decides appeals by taxpayers against direct taxes, other than Stamp Duty.	
Lands Tribunal	Decides questions relating to valuation of land on compulsory purchase, commercial rating appeals, leasehold valuation appeals, the discharge or modification of restrictive covenants and compensation for coal mining subsidence.	Tribunal can award costs. Public funding is available.
Transport Tribunal	Decides appeals against decisions of Traffic Commissioners concerning operators' licences for goods vehicles and public service vehicles.	Appeal lies to the Court of Appeal.
Agricultural Land Tribunals	Decides disputes between agricultural landlords and tenant farmers.	

definition of treasure which must be reported to the local coroner. Under the Act people must report all finds of treasure (which is defined in the Act) to the local coroner either within 14 days after the day they make the find or within 14 days after the day on which they realize that the find might be treasure. The obligation to report finds applies to everyone, including archaeologists.

Metal detectorists can obtain information about the new law (in a Code of Practice on the Treasure Act) free of charge from the Department of Culture, Media and Sport (Tel: 020 7211 6200).

Tribunals

Not all judicial business is carried out by judges in the ordinary courts. Much decision making is handled by specially constituted bodies of citizens in the tribunals.

Most tribunals are specialist bodies which decide disputes in a particular area of the law. Examples are the General Commissioners of Income Tax, the Lands Tribunal, Social Security Appeal Tribunals, Employment Tribunals and Mental Health Review Tribunals. The chairmen, and sometimes the members, are often selected by the appropriate minister from a panel of persons appointed by the Lord Chancellor. Usually the chairmen have legal training and hearings are held in public. Appeals on questions of law lie from most tribunals to the High Court. In some cases, such as the Lands Tribunal, appeal on a point of law lies to the Court of Appeal by way of case stated. The table below describes the work of a cross-section of tribunals.

Ombudsman scheme	Investigates complaints from members of the public against?	Contact details
Parliamentary Ombudsman	Government departments and other public sector bodies. Complaints must be referred by an MP. Also investigates complaints about refusal of access to information by those departments or bodies.	Millbank Tower, Millbank, London SW1P 4QP Tel: 020 7217 4163

Ombudsman scheme	Investigates complaints from members of the public against?	Contact details
Health Service Ombudsman	NHS Authorities and Trusts; family doctors and dentists, pharmacists, opticians, nurses and others providing NHS family health services; private hospitals or nursing homes if the complaint is about services provided for the NHS.	England: address as above Tel: 0845 0154033 Wales: 5th Floor, Capital Tower, Greyfriars Road, Cardiff CF1 3AG Tel: 0845 6010987
Local Government Ombudsman	Principal councils and certain other bodies.	There are three Local Government Ombudsmen in England, each dealing with complaints from different parts of the country. Advice line: 0845 602 1983
Independent Police Complaints Commission	Police officers in England and Wales.	68 Lombard Street London EC3V 9LJ Tel: 020 7868 1686
Legal Services Ombudsman	Solicitors, barristers, licensed conveyancers and legal executives in England and Wales (*see* Chapter 98).	3rd Floor, Sunlight House, Quay Street, Manchester M3 3JZ Tel: 0854 601 0794
Independent Housing Ombudsman	Certain landlords.	Norman House, 105–109 The Strand, London WC2R 0AA Tel: 020 7836 3630
Broadcasting Standards Commission	All television and radio (BBC, commercial broadcasters, text, cable, satellite and digital services).	7 The Sanctuary London SW1P 3JS Tel: 020 7808 1000
Estate Agents Ombudsman	Most of the large chains owned by banks, building societies and insurance companies, and offices under the management of members of the Incorporated Society of Valuers and Auctioneers, the National Association of Estate Agents and the Royal Institution of Chartered Surveyors. Does not deal with disputes over surveys or the letting of property. Complaint must be made within 12 months of the event.	Beckett House, 4 Bridge Street, Salisbury, Wiltshire SP1 2LX Tel: 01722 333306
Financial Ombudsman Service	The FOS replaced eight previous complaints bodies: the Office of the Banking Ombudsman (complaints against high street banks), the Building Societies Ombudsman (complaints against UK building societies and their connected undertakings), the Financial Services Authority Complaints Unit, the Insurance Ombudsman (complaints against general insurance companies), the Investment Ombudsman (disputes between members of IMRO and their customers), the Personal Insurance Arbitration Service, the Personal Investment Authority Ombudsman and the SFA Complaints Bureau.	South Quay Plaza 183 Marsh Wall, London E14 9SR Tel: 0845 080 1800
Funeral Ombudsman	Funeral directors and private crematoria who are members of the Ombudsman scheme.	26–28 Bedford Row London WC1R 4HE Tel: 020 7430 1112

Ombudsman scheme	Investigates complaints from members of the public against?	Contact details
Pensions Ombudsman	Trustees and managers of pension schemes set up by employers and personal pension schemes. Complaints about the sales and marketing of pensions schemes are dealt with by the Financial Ombudsman Service.	11 Belgrave Road, London SW1V 1RB Tel: 020 7834 9144
Prisons and Probation Ombudsman	Complaints from prisoners about their treatment in prison and people subject to probation supervision.	Ashley House, 2 Monck Street, London SW1P 2BQ Tel: 020 7035 2876
Waterways Ombudsman	British Waterways.	PO Box 406, Haywards Heath, West Sussex, RH17 5GF Tel: 01273 832 624

Ombudsmen

The first ombudsman was appointed in 1967 to check abuses of power by government departments (the Parliamentary Commissioner). They exist to deal with complaints from ordinary citizens about certain public bodies or private sector services. The service is provided free of charge. Each Ombudsman scheme varies in the type of complaint it handles, the powers it has and the procedures it uses.

Being a witness at court/the witness service

There are special facilities for child witnesses in many crown courts. Special arrangements include allowing child witnesses to give evidence from a private room via a TV link with the courtroom. Contact the Child Witness Officer at the crown court for more information.

It is a criminal offence to intimidate a witness, juror or anyone helping the police in an investigation. Many people find the experience of actually giving evidence in court quite frightening. The Witness Service, currently operating in all crown courts, was developed to help people cope with attending court and giving evidence. Since 2002, the service has been extended to all magistrates' courts nationwide. The Witness Service helps by offering:

1 a chance to look around a court room before you have to attend the trial;
2 a quiet place to wait during the trial;
3 information on court procedure and layout;
4 practical help, for example with expense forms;
5 an opportunity to talk about the experience of giving evidence following the trial.

The service is offered to both prosecution and defence witnesses.

The language of the courts

Using the courts system is a daunting and frustrating experience for many people, made worse by the legal system's retention of archaic and sometimes incomprehensible legal jargon. The Civil Procedure Rules 1998 (discussed further in Chapter 97) abolished the use of legal Latin and obscure terms and introduced more straightforward language (*see* Part 12 for a guide to legal terminology).

Old terminology	New terminology
Hearings in open court	Hearings in public
Hearings in chambers	Hearings in private
Ex parte hearings	Hearings without notice
Leave to appeal	Permission to appeal
Affidavit evidence	Written evidence

THE JUDGES

The hierarchy of judges

Senior judicial appointments are made by the Queen on the recommendation of the Prime Minister, who receives advice from the Lord Chancellor. Before making recommendations, the Lord Chancellor will consult senior members of the judiciary about the appointments (*see* below).

House of Lords

The Law Lords (or Lords of Appeal in Ordinary to give them their formal title) are the most senior judges in the country. They are appointed from among the experienced judges of the Court of Appeal in England and Wales, the Court of Session in Scotland, and the Court of Appeal in Northern Ireland. There are currently 12 Law Lords, headed by the Lord Chancellor.

Court of Appeal

There are 35 Lords Justices of Appeal, who are selected from the ranks of High Court judges. The head of the Court of Appeal is the Master of the Rolls.

High Court judges

A single judge will try civil cases which are heard in the High Court. High Court judges (or red judges) also try serious (Class 1) criminal offences in the crown court. For instance, they try murder and treason cases. They may also be requested to sit in the Court of Appeal or in other judicial bodies (e.g. the Employment Appeal Tribunal or the Restrictive Practices court).

Appointments may be made by promotions from another full-time office (usually the Circuit Bench) or from highly regarded barristers and (rarely) solicitors. Eligible barristers have usually been in practice for 20 or 30 years and hold the rank of Queen's Counsel (*see* page 815). In January 2000, only one of 101 High Court judges in total was a former solicitor.

Masters and Registrars

Masters and Registrars are responsible for dealing with most of the routine hearings in the High Court that are not handled by the judges.

Circuit judges

They are appointed by the Queen on the recommendation of the Lord Chancellor from barristers of at least 10 years' standing or from recorders who have held their posts for at least two years. Circuit judges try county court civil cases and the less serious criminal cases. Some can also hear public and/or private family law cases.

Recorders

Recorders sit in the crown court and county courts. They are part-time appointments from barristers or solicitors of at least 10 years' standing. They have the same jurisdiction as circuit judges but in the crown court they will hear the less complex or serious matters.

District judges

They are usually solicitors. They deal only with county court cases. They handle procedural matters and the smaller cases and most family law disputes.

What do I call the judge?

Different judges have different titles that come before their surnames, according to their rank. For example, a judge in the Court of Appeal might be called Lord Justice

Brown. The judge should also be addressed in the manner appropriate to his or her title.

Judge	Formal title	How should you address the judge?
District judge	Judge [name]	Sir or Madam
Circuit judge	Judge [name]	Your Honour
High Court judge	Mr Justice [name] or Mrs Justice [name]	My Lord or My Lady
Judges in the Court of Appeal	Lord Justice [name] or Lady Justice [name]	My Lord or My Lady
Law Lords	Lord [name] or Lady [name]	My Lord or My Lady

If you were writing to a judge in the Court of Appeal you should address the letter to 'The Right Honourable Lord Justice [name]'. A letter to a Law Lord should be addressed to 'The Right Honourable The Lord [name]'. A letter to a judge of the High Court should be addressed to 'The Honourable', etc.

Appointment

As the table below indicates, the ranks of the judiciary, particularly at the higher levels, remain swollen with white, Oxbridge-educated men. Women make up only 11 per cent of all judges in England and Wales and only 1.7 per cent of judges are from ethnic minority backgrounds. There has never been a female judge in the final court of appeal, nor has there been a black High Court judge. A 1999 study by the Labour Research Department revealed that 69 per cent of judges went to public school and 64 per cent went to Oxbridge.

[Correct as at 1 March 2003]	Women	Men
12 Lords of Appeal in Ordinary	0	12
5 Heads of Divisions	1	4
36 Lords Justices of Appeal	3	33
107 High Court judges	6	101
621 Circuit judges	60	561
1356 Recorders	171	1185
426 District judges	79	347
105 District judges (magistrates' courts)	22	83
150 Deputy District judges (magistrates' courts)	28	122

Much of the blame for this apparent under-representation of women and ethnic minorities is attributed to the heavy reliance on 'secret soundings', a key aspect of the process of selecting judges for office. The secret soundings system means that potential candidates for judicial office are selected on the basis of conversations between senior lawyers, judges and professional bodies behind closed doors. Critics of the system complain that the system supports an 'old boys' network' which promotes people on the basis of who they know, rather than drawing judges from the widest available pool of talent.

Following an inquiry into the judicial appointment process, chaired by Sir Leonard Peach and commissioned by the Lord Chancellor, a new, independent, Commissioner for Judicial Appointments was appointed at the beginning of 2001 by the Lord Chancellor, to oversee the selection process. The Commissioner can advise the Lord Chancellor, investigate appointments and attend interviews for judicial appointments. Critics of the current system, including the Law Society and the Commission for Racial Equality, insist that more radical reform is necessary and have urged the government to consider replacing the current role of the Lord Chancellor with that of an independent commission, which would take over responsibility for judicial appointments. In July 2003, the government published its plans to set up such a body (*see further* page 722).

Judicial salaries 2002–2003

The table below sets out judicial salaries per annum as from 1 April 2003.

Judges	£
Lord Chancellor	202,736
Lord Chief Justice of England and Wales	200,236
Master of the Rolls	181,176
Lords of Appeal in Ordinary ⎱ President of the Family Division ⎰	175,055
Lord Justices of Appeal	166,394
High Court Judges	147,198
Circuit Judges at the Central Criminal ⎫ Court in London (Old Bailey Judges) ⎬ Senior Circuit Judges ⎭	119,160
Circuit Judges	110,362
District Judges ⎫ District Judges (Magistrates' Courts) ⎬ Masters and Registrars of the Supreme Court ⎭	88,546 (outside London) 92,546 (London)

Removal

It is difficult to sack a judge once he or she has been appointed. Senior judges (those of the High Court and above) hold office 'during good behaviour' and may be removed from office only by the sovereign following a vote by both Houses of Parliament. This procedure has never been used to remove an English judge. It was used once in 1830 to remove Sir Jonah Barrington, a judge of the High Court of Admiralty in Ireland, after he was found guilty of misappropriating £922 for his own uses.

Circuit judges and recorders can be removed by the Lord Chancellor for 'misbehaviour' or incapacity. The only occasion on which the Lord Chancellor has ever removed a judge was in 1983 when he sacked Judge Bruce Campbell, a circuit judge, who was found guilty of smuggling cigarettes and alcohol into England in his yacht. A previous Lord Chancellor, Lord Mackay, made it clear in July 1994 that a conviction for drunk driving would probably amount to misbehaviour, as would any offence involving violence, dishonesty or moral turpitude or behaviour likely to cause offence, particularly on religious or racial grounds or behaviour that amounted to sexual harassment. In practice, serious misbehaviour is dealt with by the Lord Chancellor 'suggesting' to the judge in question that he or she should resign.

Retirement

All judges are required to retire at 70 years of age – although a judge may continue in office at the discretion of the Lord Chancellor. Judges must serve for 20 years before they qualify for full pension rights.

Suing a judge

Judges cannot be sued for things said or acts done in their judicial capacity in good faith.

A judge was hearing an appeal against deportation. The appellant was on bail but the judge ordered him to be kept in custody although he had no power to do so. The judge was sued for false imprisonment. Held: Although the judge had clearly acted wrongly, he could not be sued because he had been acting in a judicial capacity. Lord Denning said: 'Every judge of the courts of the land – from the highest to the lowest – should be protected to the same degree. If the reason underlying this immunity is to ensure "that they may be free in thought and independent in judgment", it applies to every judge, whatever his rank. Each should be protected from damages when he is acting judicially . . . So long as he does his work in the honest belief that it is within his jurisdiction, then he is not liable to an action. He may be mistaken in fact. He may be ignorant in law. What he does may be outside his jurisdiction – in fact or in law – but so long as he honestly believes it to be within his jurisdiction, he should not be liable.' Sirros (1974)

97

A Guide to Civil Proceedings

This chapter explains the basic procedure for bringing or defending a straightforward claim through the civil courts.

Court proceedings involve a serious commitment in terms of time and money. They can also, by their adversarial nature, permanently alter relationships between people. Litigation (or is it the lawyers?) tends to bring out the worst in people, so friends, neighbours, spouses and people in business relationships should consider whether it will be worth the price that is likely to be paid in terms of loss of goodwill.

Other basic issues that should be addressed by anyone contemplating starting court proceedings are:

- *What is the legal basis of the claim?* – one might have a sound moral argument, but does the law support the claim?
- *What can be achieved?* – what remedies will the court grant?
- *Can I prove it?* – the law requires a case to be proven to a certain standard of proof.
- *Is it too late?* – there are different time limits for bringing different types of claim. Once the time has passed, it will be too late to litigate.
- *Do I need a solicitor?* – the court procedure for claims for less than £5,000 is designed to suit people acting without a solicitor or barrister. Claims involving more money or complicated legal issues will need a solicitor.
- *Can I afford it?* – court fees, solicitors' fees and other expenses will need to be paid and there is always a risk of having to pay the other side's costs if the claim is unsuccessful.
- *Will the defendant be able to pay?* – there is no point in pursuing a claim for money (a debt or compensation) against a penniless person. The court cannot magically get blood out of a stone.
- *Can the defendant be located?*

WHAT IS THE LEGAL BASIS OF THE CLAIM?

In some cases, the law does not provide any protection, as the following examples illustrate.

Shane bought a secondhand lawnmower from his neighbour, Tom, at a car boot sale. Shane trusted his neighbour and assumed that the lawnmower would be in good working order. The lawnmower broke down within a week. Shane asked Tom for his money back, but Tom refused. Shane cannot sue Tom because the relevant law (the Sale of Goods Act 1979, as amended) does not apply to private sales. There is no legal basis for Shane's claim.

Mark is looking for a flat to rent. He sees a bedsit advertised in the local paper and, when he telephones to make an appointment to view the room, he is told that it is still available. The bedsit is in a house, the landlady tells him, where she also lives and he would have to share bathroom facilities with the other tenants. When Mark goes to see the bedsit later that day the landlady tells him that she has just let it to someone else. Mark strongly suspects that the landlady has turned him down because he is black. He wants to take her to court for discriminating against him but the Race Relations Act 1976 does not protect him in these circumstances. There is no legal basis for bringing the claim.

A solicitor will be able to advise as to whether there is a legal basis for bringing a claim. If there is a legally binding contract between the people in dispute, the claim can be based on the law of contract. For example, if A sold goods to B for a certain price and B does not pay the agreed sum when it is due, A can sue B for the debt. The law of contract, contained in Acts of Parliament (e.g. the Sale of Goods Act 1979) and previous cases decided by judges will be the legal basis of the claim. The law of contract governs whether there is a valid contract between A and B, what terms (e.g. as to when payment is due) are implied into the contract and what terms are valid or invalid.

Other examples of contract-based claims:

- A is sacked from his job without notice. He may be able to claim that he has been wrongfully dismissed because his employer has breached (or broken) the terms of his employment contract. (A may also be able to claim unfair dismissal at an employment tribunal. The unfair dismissal claim would be based on specific rights given to employees by unfair dismissal legislation.)

- A buys goods which later prove to be faulty. A sues the shop where he bought the goods. The claim is based on the Sale of Goods Act 1979, which implies certain conditions about the quality of goods into the contract between A and the shop. Breach of contract is the basis of most consumer claims.

- A is renting a house from B. In the lease, B agreed to carry out and pay for repairs to the structure of the house during the duration of the lease. The roof is damaged and starts leaking but B refuses to pay for the necessary repair work. A sues B for breach of contract.

- A books a holiday with travel agents. She specifically requests a hotel near to the beach. When she arrives at the hotel, she is disappointed to find that it is nowhere near the beach. A sues the travel agents.

Where injury, loss or damage is caused to a person or their property as the result of another person's failure to do what a reasonable person would do in the circumstances, the legal basis for the claim will be the law of negligence. For example, A is knocked down and injured while crossing the road by B in his car. B was talking on his mobile phone and not paying proper attention to the road. A can sue B; the claim will be based on B's negligence.

Other examples of negligence-based claims:

- A buys and eats a prawn sandwich in a café. The prawns have gone off and A is made ill by the food poisoning. A sues the café for negligence.

- A finds a lump in her right breast and goes to see her GP. The GP does not examine her properly and fails to diagnose breast cancer. A has to undergo intensive chemotherapy treatment that could have been avoided if a cancer diagnosis had been made earlier. A sues her GP for negligence.

- A hires a solicitor to help her with the legal aspects of buying a house. The solicitor does not study the title deeds properly and fails to notice that the owner of the neighbouring property has a right to walk across A's garden in order to gain access to his garage. After he has bought the house, A realizes that his neighbour has a right of way across his garden and sues the solicitor for negligence.

WHAT CAN BE ACHIEVED?

There are a range of remedies that may be awarded to a successful claimant at the conclusion of a case.

Damages

This is the most common element of any claim. The objective of damages is to put claimants in the same position as they would have been in if the wrong or breach had not been committed. Where the claim is for a specific sum of money that presents no difficulty, but in injury cases the exercise is necessarily artificial. (*See* Chapter 77 for an explanation of how damages are assessed in personal injury claims.)

Injunctions

An injunction is an order of the court requiring a party either to do a specific act (a mandatory injunction) or to refrain from doing a specific act (a prohibitory injunction). The general rule is that injunctions will not be made where monetary compensation will be a sufficient alternative. But in some cases, such as encroachment on land or domestic violence, injunctions are the only possibility.

Possession orders

Typically where the dispute involves land or property, the claimant may seek an order for possession of that land or property. For example, a building society may seek an order for possession against a defaulting borrower or a landlord may seek an order against a tenant in arrears with the rent. An order for possession may also be sought against squatters who have no right to be on the land.

Sequestration

Seizing assets and money. This is a temporary remedy, used to enforce compliance with a court order. It has often been used against trade unions who have defied orders in industrial disputes.

Bankruptcy/winding up/receivership

Under the insolvency laws and the Companies Acts, the courts may order individuals to become bankrupt, or companies to go into liquidation. (*See* further Part 6.)

Rectification/rescission

Mistakes do happen. Occasionally lawyers prepare documents which do not reflect what was agreed. There is an equitable jurisdiction within the courts to order that mistakes be put right, or that obligations wrongly entered into be cancelled.

CAN I PROVE IT?

There are two questions of proof which must be considered.

The burden of proof

The party asserting a fact must prove it to the court. If A is claiming that B breached their contract, the onus will be on A to prove that a contract existed between them, that B breached the contract and that A suffered loss as a result. If A is claiming that B was negligent, the obligation will be on A to prove all the elements of the claim, i.e. that a duty existed between A and B, that B breached the duty and that A suffered damage as a result. This is called the legal burden of proof.

A was a passenger in B's car. B crashed the car and A was injured. A sues B for negligence and B argues that A was partly to blame for the extent of his injuries because A did not wear a seatbelt. The onus will be on A to prove that B was negligent. The onus will be on B to prove that A did not wear a seatbelt.

The standard of proof

In civil cases, the claimant must show that his version of events is more likely to be true than the defendant's version. This is called the balance of probabilities. The standard of proof is much higher in criminal cases. The prosecution in criminal cases must prove every element of its case beyond a reasonable doubt.

The claimant should do his best to collect and preserve evidence which will help him to prove his claim in court at a later date.

IS IT TOO LATE?

Many people are unaware that there are strict time limits for bringing court proceedings. Once the relevant deadline (or 'limitation period') has passed, the claimant will lose the opportunity to pursue his claim through the courts.

- For claims based on contract, the claimant must start court proceedings within six years of the date of the breach of contract.
- For personal injury claims, the time period is three years. The three-year period runs from the date of the injury or death or the date the claimant first learnt about the injury.

If the claimant was under the age of 18 years when the accident happened, the three-year period only starts to run from his eighteenth birthday.

Sam is injured in a road traffic accident when he is 16 years old. The limitation period does not start running until he is 18 years old. Therefore, Sam has until his twenty-first birthday to commence the action, i.e. three years from his eighteenth birthday.

DO I NEED A SOLICITOR?

It would be naïve to suppose that the years of study, training and experience invested by solicitors in the practice of law could be supplanted by a browse through a couple of library books. The procedure for 'small' claims (i.e. under £5,000) is designed for people representing themselves but for higher-value claims, or disputes involving complex legal issues, a solicitor should be instructed. This issue is covered further in Chapter 98.

Can I afford it?

The cost of going to court includes solicitors' fees, court fees, witnesses' expenses (for travelling to court and attending the hearing), experts' reports (e.g. from a doctor, a mechanic or a surveyor), the cost of travelling to and from the court and taking time off work to attend the hearing. The expense of litigating should be weighed against the prospects of succeeding with the claim or defence.

Solicitors' costs are dealt with in Chapter 99 and sources of funding (including public funding) are covered in Chapter 100.

Will the defendant be able to pay?

If the claim is for money, the time, trouble and expense of court proceedings will be pointless if the defendant has not got the means to pay the debt or damages sought. Before starting court proceedings, it would be sensible to investigate whether the potential defendant is unemployed, bankrupt (or in compulsory liquidation if the defendant is a company), has other debts to pay, has stopped trading, or has no money or personal property of their own.

To find out whether a person is bankrupt, contact the Insolvency Service at Bankruptcy Public Search Room,

4th Floor, East Wing, 45–46 Stephenson Street, Birmingham B2 4UZ (Tel: 0121 698 4000). The claimant will need to tell them the full name of the person and their last address. Alternatively, you can search the register of bankruptcy orders and individual voluntary arrangements yourself at your local official receiver's office. Details of company liquidations, or company directors who have been disqualified, are available from: The Registrar of Companies, Companies House, Crown Way, Maindy, Cardiff CR4 3UX (Tel: 02920 388588). The disqualified directors register is also on the internet at www.companieshouse.gov.uk

If a person, firm or company has previously been taken to court and ordered to pay a claimant, any unpaid court orders (or 'judgments') will be recorded at the Register of County Court Judgments. Judgments remain on the register for six years or until the court order is paid. Anyone can search the register, either in person (for a fee of £4), or by writing (for a fee of £4.50) to the Register of County Court Judgments at 173–175 Cleveland Street, London W1P 5PE (Tel: 020 7380 0133). The applicant must be able to supply the defendant's full name and address.

A potential claimant should consider whether a person who has not paid previous court judgments is likely to bother paying the next one.

CAN THE DEFENDANT BE LOCATED?

When court proceedings are started, certain court documents must be sent to the person against whom the claim is made (the 'defendant'). It is therefore vital to have a current address for the defendant where he can receive the court documents. When a defendant appears to have disappeared, an enquiry agent may be able to help to trace his whereabouts.

Sending a letter before action

To reiterate, court proceedings are expensive, time-consuming and stressful and should be embarked upon as a last resort. Before resorting to litigation, always try complaining, negotiating and sending a letter before taking legal action.

Complaining

Make your complaint in an assertive, but not aggressive, manner, making it clear what the problem is and how the problem can be put right. Ask to speak to the person who has the authority to resolve your complaint. For example, if the problem concerns faulty goods, speak to the manager of the shop where you bought the item. Do not be fobbed off with excuses such as, 'It is our policy not to make refunds'. *See* Chapter 42 for more information.

Make a note of the person to whom you have spoken on each occasion and what was said or promised.

Negotiating

Bearing in mind the expense of court proceedings, it may be cost-effective to accept an offer for less than the full amount you are entitled to recover. If you owe someone money, it is always worthwhile making them an offer to settle the claim. In either case, you should put the offer in writing and head the letter with the words 'without prejudice'. The reason for this is that if your offer is rejected by the other side, he will not be able to use the offer against you in any subsequent court proceedings. If you owe someone money, ensure that any offer is accepted 'in full and final settlement' of the claim. Otherwise, your creditor may claim at a later date that the balance of the money is still owed.

Sending a letter before taking legal action

You should always write to the other party to the dispute before starting court proceedings. In the letter you should warn the other party that, if they fail to put the problem right then court proceedings will be commenced. This sort of letter can work particularly well in debt cases. For example, after outlining the relevant facts, the letter could be concluded with the words: 'Unless I receive your remittance for the sum of £x within the next seven days, proceedings will be commenced in the county court for recovery of the debt, together with interest and costs, without further notice'. It may even be worthwhile, depending on the amount that is owed, instructing a solicitor to write the letter for a small fee, as a letter from a solicitor carries a lot of weight.

THE CIVIL PROCEDURE RULES

The procedure for court cases started after 26 April 1999 is governed by the Civil Procedure Rules 1998 (CPR). The CPR changed the way that cases are run and also radically altered the underlying philosophy of litigating in the civil courts.

Under the old rules, the courts tended to turn a blind eye when the parties did not keep to the procedural timetable or deployed the rules purely to gain a tactical advantage, even if that meant increasing the legal costs and duration of the proceedings. Aggressive litigants could intensify the pressure to settle on their terms by driving up costs and dragging their feet on procedural steps. Winning was all that mattered. Under the CPR, how the game is played is important too. The balance of power in the management of litigation has shifted to the courts; the courts will set and enforce realistic timetables, determine what procedures are suitable for each case, and penalize the parties for unnecessary delay, expense or cynical tactical ploys.

The parties are expected to co-operate with each other, to share information and clarify the issues in dispute before proceedings have been started. The conduct of the parties in this respect is a factor that will heavily influence how costs are awarded by the courts. The courts use their power to award costs as a carrot to encourage good behaviour amongst the parties and a stick to punish them if they fail to co-operate.

The new approach recognizes the gritty reality that achieving justice in an adversarial system is intrinsically linked to the expense of running the case and the financial resources of the parties. The rules will be interpreted and exercised by the courts to give effect to the principal aims of reducing delay and expense. Achieving proportionality is an important aim, too. It means dealing with the case in ways which are proportionate to:

- the amount of money involved;
- the importance of the case;
- the complexity of the issues; and
- the financial position of each party.

These aims are encapsulated in what the rules refer to as 'the overriding objective': to deal with cases justly.

Do the Civil Procedure Rules apply?

Under the old system, there was one set of procedural rules for cases begun in the county courts (the County Court Rules 1981, commonly referred to as 'the green book') and a separate set of rules for cases begun in the High Court (the Rules of the Supreme Court 1965, also known as 'the white book'). Since 26 April 1999, nearly all proceedings in the county courts, the High Court and the Civil Division of the Court of Appeal are governed by one unified set of rules – the CPR, supplemented by practice directions.

TRANSITIONAL RULES

As for proceedings that were commenced prior to 26 April 1999 but are still in progress after that date, transitional rules dictate whether the old rules or the CPR will apply. Broadly speaking:

- the old rules will apply to undefended cases; but
- the CPR will apply to defended cases;
- the pre-action protocols will not apply but pre-action behaviour will be taken into account;
- there is a general presumption that the CPR will apply where proceedings come before a judge for the first time (at a hearing or on paper), subject to the judge's discretion to decide whether the CPR should apply.

OTHER RULES

One of the aims of the CPR was to introduce a single, simple procedural code for civil proceedings. It is still necessary, however, to refer to other statutes and statutory instruments. The jurisdiction of the High Court and the county courts remains regulated by the Supreme Court Act 1981, the County Courts Act 1984 and the High Court and County Courts Jurisdiction Order 1991 – as amended by the Civil Procedure (Modification of Enactments) Order 2001.

Substantial sections of the old Rules of the Supreme Court 1965 and the County Court Rules 1981 have also been retained under Schedule 1 and Schedule 2 of the CPR, respectively.

PROCEEDINGS NOT GOVERNED BY THE CIVIL PROCEDURE RULES

The CPR apply to all proceedings in the county courts, High Court and the Civil Division of the Court of Appeal except:

- insolvency proceedings;
- family proceedings;
- proceedings within the meaning of the Mental Health Act 1983;
- non-contentious probate proceedings;
- proceedings where the High Court acts as a Prize Court (e.g. Admiralty proceedings).

Terminology

One of the reasons why many people used to find the court process so daunting was the archaic and obscure legal language. The CPR confined much of the old legal jargon to the dustbin and introduced more terminology in plain English. The table on page 740 shows some of the old jargon together with its modern replacement under the CPR.

Preliminary steps

The CPR control not only what happens during the course of proceedings but also what steps must be taken before proceedings are commenced.

Gone are the days when aggressive or enthusiastic litigants could launch court proceedings with wild abandon. Under the old rules, there was no requirement on the parties to negotiate before litigating, parties tended not to share information and documentary evidence and a thorough investigation of the issues only took place when court proceedings were at an advanced stage.

Central to the underlying ethos of the CPR is the ideal

Old rules	CPR	What does it mean?
Plaintiff	Claimant	A person who makes a claim.
Defendant	Defendant	A person against whom a claim is made.
Pleadings	Statements of claim	The document in which each party sets out his case.
Writ/summons	Claim form	Form starting proceedings.
Discovery	Disclosure	Mutual disclosure of documents by the parties.
Minor/infant	Child	Person under 18 years of age.
In camera	In private	Public excluded from the proceedings.
Ex parte	Without notice	Application to court without notice to the other party.
Next friend/guardian ad litem	Litigation friend	Person representing a child.
Mareva injunction	Freezing injunction	To keep assets within the jurisdiction.
Anton Piller order	Search order	To compel search of the defendant's premises.

that court proceedings should be used as a last resort, and only after people have attempted to resolve their disputes out of court. If proceedings are subsequently started, the court will scrutinize the parties' pre-action behaviour, including whether they complied with the protocols or rejected a reasonable offer to settle, and may punish a lack of co-operation.

Pre-action protocols

Before starting proceedings, people should follow the procedural instructions set out in the pre-action protocols, if they apply. The protocols set a timetable for the parties in dispute to exchange information and documents.

The aims of this 'cards on the table' approach are to put the parties in a position where:

- they understand what issues are in dispute through better and earlier exchange of information and investigation;
- they can make a well-informed offer to settle the claim, rather than starting court proceedings; and
- if negotiations fail, they will be better equipped to keep to the court's strict procedural timetable, thereby reducing the delay and expense of the action.

The table sets out a summary of the steps required by the protocol for personal injury proceedings.

Personal Injury Protocol

Summary of steps to be taken

Claimant sends *letter* to the proposed defendant summarizing:

- the facts of the claim;
- the nature of his injuries;

- any financial loss suffered; and
- requesting details of the defendant's insurer.

Defendant should *reply within 21 days*, identifying the insurer.

If the defendant denies that he is to blame:

- he should send *documents* to the claimant which are material to the disputed issues;
- he will have a maximum of *3 months to investigate* the claim.

If the defendant alleges that the claimant is partly to blame, he should explain his reasons.

Note: The documents which should be disclosed include, for example, medical reports, repair and maintenance reports, and accident reports.

Experts' reports: There are also detailed instructions about selection of and access to experts. The aim is to instruct an expert who is acceptable to both the parties. If they cannot agree, the court will decide whether the costs of more than one expert's report should be recoverable.

There is a degree of flexibility about the deadlines set by the protocols but the court will expect an explanation as to why a protocol has not been followed or has been varied.

At the present time, protocols have been approved for personal injury and clinical negligence claims, defamation, professional negligence, judicial review, housing disrepair and construction and engineering disputes. However, the court will expect parties involved in any potential proceedings to act in accordance with the 'spirit' of the protocols, to act reasonably in the exchange of information and documents and generally in trying to avoid the necessity for the start of proceedings.

Penalties for non-compliance

There is considerable incentive for the parties to behave reasonably and in accordance with the protocols. Where proceedings are subsequently started, the court may reward a party for complying with the protocols and punish a party for non-compliance. Non-compliance might include failing to provide sufficient information or failing to respond to correspondence from the other party within a reasonable time.

The range of sanctions available to the court include ordering a party to pay a sum of money into court or ordering a party to pay all or part of the costs of the proceedings. The court may also order that there should be no interest payable on any compensation awarded to the claimant or award interest at a higher or lower rate.

Under the old rules, the level of investigation required by the protocols would have taken place much later in the course of proceedings, after the parties had exchanged pleadings. The new rules mean higher initial expenditure on solicitors' and experts' fees, but it is arguable that it is far more sensible for the parties to do the investigatory work at an early stage, before committing themselves to court proceedings.

Offers to settle

The ideal of avoiding litigation wherever possible is also promoted by new rules on offers to settle. The conduct of the parties in attempting to settle will be one of the considerations that the court will take into account when it decides which of the parties should pay the legal costs of the case and decides the amount of costs that should be awarded. Consequently, it will be in the interests of the parties to appear to have done everything they could to settle their differences out of court.

Defendants have always been able to make an offer to settle the whole or part of a dispute, with the incentive that some of their costs would be paid if the claimant recovers less than the amount of the offer at trial. Under the CPR, claimants will also be able to make offers to settle, before or after proceedings are commenced, with a special regime as to costs and higher rates of interest if not accepted.

STARTING PROCEEDINGS

Parties to actions

A person who makes a claim is usually called a claimant and a person against whom a claim is made is usually called a defendant. They are the 'parties' to the proceedings. In proceedings for divorce the parties are referred to as the petitioner and the respondent.

The table summarizes special rules about the capacity in which certain parties may sue or be sued.

Mrs Williams bought a steam iron from Morrison's Household Goods, a local shop in the village. The shop is owned by Jack Morrison, who is a sole trader (i.e. he is in business on his own, not in partnership with anyone else or as a limited company). The steam iron was faulty and Mrs Williams took it back to the shop and asked for her money back. Jack Morrison refused to refund her money or offer her a replacement. As Jack Morrison is in business as a sole trader, Mrs Williams can bring court proceedings against Morrison's Household Goods.

There are also rules about how different types of parties must be described in the court documents (*see* below).

Children and patients

Special rules apply where a party is a child or a patient. 'Children' are individuals under the age of 18 years. 'Patients' are individuals who, because of a mental disorder (within the meaning of the Mental Health Act 1983), are incapable of managing and administering their own affairs. Children and patients cannot sue or be sued on their own behalf. A 'litigation friend' must be appointed to act for them.

A child's litigation friend will normally be a parent, guardian or other relative. A patient's litigation friend is usually the person with whom the patient is living or who is caring for the patient. Alternatively, in either case the litigation friend can be the Official Solicitor.

Party	Where party is a claimant	Where party is a defendant
Child/patient	Must sue through litigation friend	Must be sued through litigation friend
Sole trader	Must use their own name	Can be sued in the name of the business
Partnership	Can sue in the name of the firm or the names of the individual partners	Can be sued in the name of the firm or individual partners may be sued
Limited company	Can sue in the company name	Can be sued in the company name

The main points to note are that:

- a litigation friend cannot be a person who has an interest in the claim which is opposed to that of the child or patient;
- where the litigation friend is representing a claimant, he or she is also liable to pay any costs which the claimant might be ordered to pay;
- the court has a discretion to allow a child to conduct proceedings without a litigation friend;
- when the child reaches 18 years, the appointment of his or her litigation friend ceases;
- when a patient recovers, the appointment of the litigation friend will continue until an application, supported by medical evidence, is made to the court by the patient, the litigation friend or any other party to the proceedings.

Limited companies

Companies are regarded as separate legal entities and can sue and be sued independently of their shareholders or directors. The old rule that a company or other corporation could not begin or carry on High Court proceedings except through a solicitor has been abolished. A company or other corporation may be represented at trial by an employee, if the employee has been authorized by the company or corporation to do so and the court gives permission.

Clubs and societies

The legal position depends on whether the club is a proprietor's club (i.e. the club is owned by a single individual or a company) or a members' club. With a proprietor's club, proceedings are brought by or against the owner in the usual way. With members' clubs the position is more complicated. The club itself has no separate legal status. If a club is sued it would be necessary to apply to the court to bring a 'representative action', naming individual members of the club (e.g. the committee), who are taken to represent the body of the club. It is very difficult for one club member to bring an action against the club – for, say, an injury at the club premises. Usually the committee owes no duty of care to individual members.

Trade unions

Trade unions have a legal entity which enables them to be sued in the courts for the wrongful acts or omissions of their officials.

Trustees

Trustees may sue and be sued, but their liability is generally limited to the assets of the trust which they are administering, unless they are guilty of improper behaviour, such as fraud.

The Crown

The Crown (i.e. the government) may sue and (with few exceptions) be sued in the same way as any private organization or individual.

Which court?

The claimant can start (or 'issue') proceedings in the High Court or in any one of the 230 county courts in England and Wales. There are detailed rules about the appropriate court for particular types of claim but, in general, claims that should be started in a county court include:

- money claims (a claim to recover a debt or damages) for less than £15,000;
- personal injury claims for less than £50,000;
- claims under the Consumer Credit Act 1974;
- claims for the recovery of land; and
- mortgage possession actions.

The claimant can start the proceedings in any county court. The court will transfer the case to another county court if necessary at a later stage in the proceedings (*see* below).

Claims that should be started in the High Court include:

- claims for libel or slander;
- applications concerning the decisions of local authority auditors;
- applications for judicial review; and
- applications for a writ of *habeas corpus*.

Additionally, a claim should be started in the High Court if the claimant believes that the claim ought to be dealt with by a High Court judge because of:

1 the financial value of the claim or the amount in dispute; and/or
2 the complexity of the facts, legal issues, remedies or procedures involved; and/or
3 the importance of the outcome of the claim to the public in general.

The claim can be issued in any of the district registries of the High Court, which are usually situated in the same building as the county court, or the Central Office of the High Court in London.

If proceedings are started in the High Court that should have been started in the county court, and vice versa, the claim will normally be transferred to the correct court. The claimant will be required to pay the costs of the transfer. A claimant who has mistakenly issued a claim in the High Court may also have an award of costs reduced by up to 25 per cent.

Issuing proceedings

Summary of Initial Steps

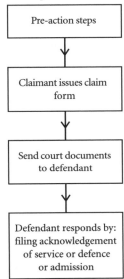

To start proceedings in the county court or High Court, the claimant must complete a claim form (usually form N1) and return it to the court together with:

- a copy for each defendant against whom the claim is made;
- the appropriate court fee.

The claim is issued on the date entered on the claim form by the court. The court will open a new file for the claim and assign a claim number to it.

Claim forms are available free from any county court and require the claimant to spell out the basic facts about the claim, including the name and address of the defendant, the value of the claim and what remedy is being sought. The claim form must be endorsed with a statement of truth (*see* below). The claimant should keep a copy of the claim form for his own use.

Statement of truth

A statement of truth is simply a statement that the party putting forward the document believes the facts stated in it are true. It must appear on every statement of case or witness statement presented by any party and should be signed by the party, or his solicitor, or his litigation friend.

The form of the statement of truth is as follows:

[I believe] [the (claimant or as may be) believes] that the facts stated in this [name document being verified] are true.

The court may strike out a statement of case which is not verified by a statement of truth.

A person who makes a false statement in a document verified by a statement of truth without an honest belief in its truth is liable for contempt of court (punishable by fines or imprisonment or both).

Particulars of claim

Full details about the claim may be set out in the claim form or separately in a document entitled Particulars of Claim. The separate particulars of claim can either be served with the claim form or within 14 days after the date on which the claim form was served and must be endorsed with a statement of truth.

Where particulars of claim are served separately from the claim form they must contain (usually at the top of the document):

- the name of the court in which the claim is proceeding;
- the claim number (this will be on the claim form);
- the title of the proceedings (the names of the parties);
- the claimant's address for service.

In any case, the particulars of claim must include:

- a concise statement of the facts relied on by the claimant;
- details of any interest claimed, including whether the interest is claimed under a contract, under a statute, or on some other basis;
- if the claimant is seeking aggravated damages, exemplary damages or provisional damages, a statement to that effect and the grounds for claiming them;
- a copy of the contract if the claim is based on a written agreement, or details of the words alleged to amount to a contract if the claim is based on an oral agreement;
- a statement of truth.

There are additional rules as to the contents of the particulars of claim for particular types of proceedings, including personal injury claims, fatal accident claims and claims for the recovery of land.

Statements of case

The formal documents setting out the parties' respective arguments in the case are called the statements of case. The claimant sets out details of his case against the defendant in the particulars of claim (either on the claim form or in a separate document).

The defendant presents his case in a defence, stating which of the allegations in the particulars of claim he denies and which, if any, he admits. The defendant should give reasons for denying an allegation and state his own version of events. It is important that the defendant answers each of the allegations made in the particulars of claim. He will be taken to have admitted any allegation which he fails to address. (*See* Appendix for an example of particulars of claim and defence.)

The claimant is not obliged to present a reply to the defence and there is no assumption that the claimant has admitted any matters raised by the defence if he stays silent. If he wished to respond to any issues raised by the defence he can do so in a reply.

Party	Statement of case presented in the proceedings	Contains details of
Claimant	Particulars of claim	The claim being made against the defendant
Defendant	Defence	The defendant's response to the particulars of claim
Claimant	Reply	Response to issues raised in the defence

Identifying the parties

The claimant must provide details of the defendant's name and address in the claim form. The form of words to be used in describing the parties in the claim form and other court documents will vary according to the capacity in which the party is suing or being sued:

Party	Description in court documents	Example
An individual	All known forenames and surname	Mr John Richard Brown
A child under 18 years	Child's name followed by ('a child by – his litigation friend')	Mary Jane Smith (a child by John Smith her litigation friend)
A child under 18 years conducting proceedings on his or her own behalf	Child's name followed by ('a child')	Mary Jane Smith (a child)
A patient within the meaning of the Mental Health Act 1983	Patient's name followed by ('by – his litigation friend')	Mary Jane Smith (by John Smith her litigation friend)
An individual who is trading under another name	The individual's name followed by 'trading as' and the trading name	Peter Brown, trading as Brown's Deliveries
An individual who is suing or being sued in a representative capacity	Say what the representative capacity is	Mr John Smith as the representative of Miss Sally Williams (deceased)
An individual who is suing or being sued in the name of a club or other unincorporated association	The individual's name followed by 'suing/sued on behalf of' and the name of the club or other unincorporated association	Mr John Smith, suing/sued on behalf of the Croydon Rangers Football Club
A firm	The name of the firm followed by 'a firm'	Williams & Co (a firm)
A company registered in England and Wales	The full name of the company	Morrison Electronics Limited
An overseas company	The full name of the company	McBurgers PLC

Adding or removing parties after issue

An existing party or a person who wishes to become a party can apply to the court to be added to or removed from the action.

Sally may bring proceedings against Justin for damages for negligence but, after issuing proceedings in the manner described above, she may discover that Hugh was also negligent. Sally may then want to add Hugh to the proceedings as a second defendant. Sally will need the court's permission to make the change and it is likely that she will be ordered to pay the costs of the application and any additional costs arising from the amendment.

In the case of adding a party, the amendment will only be possible if the limitation period has not expired and the person to be added has given his signed written consent.

Court fees

The claimant will have to pay a fee to the court for issuing the proceedings. The amount of the fee will depend on the value of the claim.

Where the claim is for money only (e.g. compensation or a debt), the current fees are set out in the table below.

Fees payable on issue of proceedings

Value of claim	County court fee
Up to £300	£30
Over £300, not over £500	£50
Over £500, not over £1,000	£80
Over £1,000, not over £5,000	£120
Over £5,000, not over £15,000	£250
Over £15,000, not over £50,000	£400
Over £50,000, not over £100,000	£600
Over £100,000, not over £150,000	£700
Over £150,000	£800

NB: *These are the figures from 1 April 2003*

The fees in the above table also apply where the defendant makes a claim against the claimant (a 'counterclaim'). The fee to be paid by the defendant depends on the amount of the counterclaim.

Where the claim is for something other than money, the fee is £130.

The table in the next column shows the court fees payable on commencement of proceedings in the High Court.

Fees payable on issue of proceedings

Value of claim	High Court fee
Up to £50,000	£400
Over £50,000, not over £100,000	£600
Over £100,000, not over £150,000	£700
Over £150,000	£800

Court fees are payable at other key stages in the progress of the case.

Court fees are also payable when either party applies for certain procedures, including:

- when a party makes an application (e.g. an application for judgment to be set aside or to vary a judgment);
- when a party requests a detailed assessment of costs, or appeals against a detailed assessment;
- when a party applies for an enforcement procedure (e.g. an application for a warrant of execution, an attachment of earnings order, a charging order or a garnishee order);
- when a party applies for a judgment summons.

Exemptions from court fees

People receiving one of the following means-tested state benefits may be exempted from paying court fees:

- income support; or
- your gross annual income is £14,213 or less and you receive:
  - Working Tax Credit and Child Tax Credit, or
  - Working Tax Credit which has a disability element, or severe disability element.
- income-based Jobseeker's Allowance.

People on low incomes can apply to the court for a reduction in the fee on the ground that payment would involve undue hardship owing to the exceptional circumstances of their case.

In either case, the claimant should complete the relevant court form applying for an exemption or reduction. A separate application must be made in relation to each fee that the person would otherwise have to pay.

Service

The claim form must be sent to (or 'served on') the defendant within four months of the date it was issued by the court. The time limit for service is six months where the defendant is out of the jurisdiction. Either the court or the claimant may carry out service on the defendant.

If requested to do so, the court will serve on the defendant:

- a copy of the claim form;

Court fees payable at later stages in the proceedings

How much?	When is fee payable?	Who pays?	Penalties for late payment
£80*	When the allocation questionnaire is filed	Claimant (or defendant if the case is proceeding on a counterclaim alone)	Statement of case can be struck out
Varies**	On filing of listing questionnaire	Claimant (or defendant if the case is proceeding on a counterclaim alone)	Statement of case can be struck out

*No fee is payable for claims for money of £1,000 or less.
**No fee payable at this stage for cases in the small claims track.

- the particulars of claim (if in a separate document); and
- a response pack;

usually by first-class post.

The response pack contains an admission form, a defence form and an acknowledgement of service form. Where particulars of claim are not served with the claim form, they must be served (together with the response pack) within 14 days of serving the claim form and within the four-month period.

Service by the claimant

Where the court has been unable to serve the documents, the responsibility falls on the claimant to effect service. The claimant may use any of the following methods to serve the documents on the defendant:

1 *Personal service* – this means physically giving the document to the defendant or leaving it with him. If the defendant will not accept delivery of the document, the service will be valid if the claimant tells him what it is and leaves it as nearly as possible in his possession or control. Personal service on a registered company or other corporation is carried out by leaving a document with a person holding a senior position (director, secretary, manager, chief executive) within the company. Personal service on a partnership is effected by leaving the document with any of the partners, or with a person having, at the time of service, management of the partnership business, at the firm's principal place of business.

2 First-class post.

3 Leaving the document at a valid address – the address for service of someone who is represented by a solicitor is the business address of the solicitor. The claim form may be served on the defendant's solicitor provided that the solicitor is authorized to accept service on the defendant's behalf and has notified the claimant that he or she is so authorized.

The following table shows the places where documents may be served, depending on the nature of the party to be served.

Nature of party to be served	Address for service
Individual	Usual or last known residence
Proprietor of a business	Usual or last known residence; or place of business or last known place of business
Individual who is suing or being sued in the name of a firm	Usual or last known address; or principal or last known place of business of the firm
Corporation incorporated in England and Wales (other than a company)	Principal office of the corporation; or any place where the corporation carries on activities and which has a real connection with the claim
Company registered in England and Wales	Principal office of the company; or registered office of the company; or any place of business of the company that has a real, or the most, connection with the claim (e.g. the shop where the goods were bought)
Any other company or corporation (e.g. an overseas company)	Any place of business of the company within the jurisdiction (e.g. a branch office in Great Britain); or any place within the jurisdiction where the corporation carries on its activities

4 Through a document exchange – service by DX is permitted where the party's address for service, or its headed notepaper, includes a DX address. It is not acceptable where the party has specifically stated that it would not accept service by DX.

5 By fax or e-mail – service by fax or e-mail is permitted only where the party, or its legal representative, has stated in writing that it will accept service of documents in this way.

If the claimant needs more time to serve the claim form and other documents because, for example, he is having difficulty in tracing the defendant, the application for an extension of time should be made before the four-month time limit expires.

Either party may use these methods of service to serve other documents in the proceedings.

What can the defendant do?

The defendant does not have to do anything until he receives the particulars of claim. Once he receives the particulars of claim (either with the claim form or separately), the defendant must act within 14 days.

The defendant may:

1 not respond to the claim form at all;
2 admit all of the claim;
3 admit part of the claim;
4 defend all of the claim.

Judgment in default

If the defendant does not respond to the claim form at all, or does not respond within the 14-day time limit, the claimant can ask the court to enter judgment against him (i.e. to rule that the defendant owes the amount claimed or an amount to be decided by the court) without a full trial of all the issues. This is called judgment in default.

The consequences are:

- the defendant will be ordered to pay the amount of the claim and costs;
- the court will send a copy of the order to the defendant;
- the defendant's name and address and details of the amount owed under the court order will be entered in the Register of County Court Judgments. Anyone, including banks and building societies, can inspect the Register to check a person's creditworthiness;
- the claimant can take steps to extract the money owed under the judgment from the defendant (this is called 'enforcement') or enforce the remedy granted by the court.

Defendant admits the claim

The defendant should complete the form of admission in the response pack and send it to the claimant's address for service, shown on the claim form, within 14 days. At this stage the defendant may ask the claimant for time to pay the money owed, ask to pay by instalments or he may offer a smaller sum to settle the claim.

The court's judgment is like a formal record of the outcome of the proceedings. If the defendant admits the claim but does not actually pay up, the court will not take any further step against him on its own initiative. The claimant will have to go back to court and start enforcement proceedings to extract the amount owed under the judgment against the defendant.

Defendant admits part of the claim

The defendant should complete forms N9A and N9B and return them to the court within 14 days after receiving the particulars of claim. The claimant has 14 days to respond to the defendant's offer. After 14 days have lapsed the proceedings will be 'stayed', which means that no further steps can be taken by either party. If the claimant accepts the partial admission, he should ask the court to record a judgment against the defendant. If he rejects the partial admission, the claim will continue as a defended claim.

Defending the claim

If he decides to defend the claim, the defendant must send to the court either an acknowledgement of service or a defence within 14 days of receiving the particulars of claim. Both of these forms are in the response pack. Filing an acknowledgement of service gives the defendant an extra 14 days (from service of the particulars) to file the defence at court.

The court will send a copy of the defence to the claimant.

Time limits for initial stages of a claim

Automatic transfer of case to defendant's county court

The claimant can start the court case in any county court but the court will automatically transfer the proceedings to the defendant's 'home court' when the defendant files a defence, where the claim is for a specified sum of money against a defendant who is an individual. The defendant's 'home court' will be the county court nearest to where the defendant works or lives or, if the defendant is represented by a solicitor, the county court nearest to the solicitor's business address.

If the claim is proceeding in the High Court, the defendant's home court will be the district registry for the district in which the defendant's address for service is situated, or, if there is no such district registry, the Royal Courts of Justice.

The parties will be notified if the court transfers the claim.

CASE MANAGEMENT BY THE COURT

Up until this stage in the proceedings, the court's role has been minimal and progress in the case has been achieved mainly through the exchange of various forms between the parties and the court. At this stage, the court will become actively involved in the progress of the case, with a view to minimizing expense and delay. The court will decide how the case will progress to trial, set a timetable for the case and ensure that the parties keep to it, and decide the length of the trial and what is to happen at the trial. This is called judicial case management.

The court has very wide management powers under the CPR, which it may exercise on an application by one of the parties or on its own initiative (in other words, it does not have to wait for a party to apply for help). For example, the court may extend or shorten the time limit applicable to any rule, decide to hold a hearing by telephone, stay the whole or part of the proceedings, or order a party to pay a sum of money into court if that party has, without good reason, failed to comply with a rule, practice direction or a relevant pre-action protocol.

Other aspects of active case management include identifying the issues, deciding which issues need investigation and trial and disposing of others, and considering whether the likely benefits of taking a particular step justify the cost of taking it.

The court will endeavour to ensure that the parties focus on the key issues in the case, rather than allowing themselves to be sidetracked by peripheral matters and applications which will create extra expense and unnecessary delay.

Power to strike out a statement of case

The ultimate sanction available to the court is to strike out a statement of case (i.e. claim, defence or counterclaim). If a statement of case is struck out then the court can enter judgment for the other party.

The court may strike out a statement of case or part of a statement of case if it appears to the court:

1 that the statement of case discloses no reasonable grounds for bringing or defending the claim (e.g. a defence which consists of only a bare denial or particulars of claim comprising the bald statement 'the defendant owes me £600');

2 that the statement of case is an abuse of the court's process or is otherwise likely to obstruct the just disposal of the proceedings; or

3 that there has been a failure to comply with a rule, practice direction or court order. This last point gives the court the teeth it needs to demand respect from the parties for its orders and directions.

Summary judgment

The court may order summary judgment against a claimant or a defendant where that party has no real prospect of succeeding on his claim or defence. Summary judgment means that the case is decided without a full trial of the issues. This is like the power to strike out in that it allows the court to dispense swiftly with issues that have no real prospect of success at trial.

The parties may also apply for summary judgment. The main points to note are:

- either party can apply if he can show that his opponent has a hopeless case;
- a claimant cannot apply for summary judgment until the defendant has filed an acknowledgement of service or a defence;
- if summary judgment is granted, the court will make a summary assessment of costs;
- if summary judgment is granted on a claim valued at less than £5,000 (which would otherwise normally be allocated to the small claims track), costs can be applied for in the usual way. The limited fixed costs regime will not apply;
- if there are any issues that are capable of investigation at trial then the court is likely to decide that there should be a full trial and no summary judgment.

Allocation

After the defence has been filed at court and served on the claimant, the court will send both parties an allocation questionnaire. The parties must complete the questionnaire and return it to the court together with an estimate of costs.

Allocation questionnaire

At the allocation stage, the court (a procedural judge in fact) will scrutinize the progress of the case and the behaviour of the parties so far. The allocation questionnaire is a key document in this process. For the first time, the parties will have to account for the way they have interacted with each other and handled the dispute prior to and since proceedings were commenced.

Issues covered by the questionnaire include:

- whether the parties wish there to be a one-month stay of proceedings to attempt to settle the case;
- whether the parties have complied with any relevant pre-action protocol and if not why not and the extent of non-compliance;
- whether the parties wish to apply for summary judgment; and
- what experts and witnesses will give evidence at the trial and the estimated length of the trial.

For claims over £5,000, the parties must also provide an estimate of costs incurred to date and the overall costs of the case.

The questionnaire must be completed by the parties and returned to the court within 14 days together with a fee of £80 (except for money claims for £1,000 or less). The 14 days runs from the date that the questionnaire is deemed to have been served on the party. The court will take a dim view of late payment of the fee or filing of the questionnaire and there are serious penalties, including having the statement of case of the guilty party struck out.

The tracks

Based on the information in the statements of case and the parties' responses in the allocation questionnaire, the court will allocate the claim to one of three tracks:

- the small claims track;
- the fast track;
- the multi-track.

Each track has a different way of handling claims. (*See also* page 724.) The main features of each track are summarized below:

Small claims track

1 For most claims up to £5,000 (e.g. consumer disputes, accident claims, disputes about ownership of goods, most disputes between landlord and tenant, other than possession disputes). This is, in effect, the old small claims arbitration system.
2 For personal injury claims where the amount claimed for pain, suffering and loss of amenity is not more than £1,000.
3 Simple procedure – the intention is that most people will be able to conduct their case in this track without a solicitor.
4 The court will give case management directions on allocation.
5 Informal trial, usually in public in a district judge's room. Strict rules of evidence will not apply. Affidavits will not be needed. Court will normally only allow one day for the hearing.
6 Only limited costs are recoverable. People may not want to instruct a solicitor for these claims for this reason.

Fast track

1 For claims between £5,000 and £15,000:
  (a) where the trial is not likely to last for more than one day (i.e. 5 hours); and
  (b) involving a limited amount of expert evidence.
2 For personal injury claims where the amount claimed for pain, suffering and loss of amenity does not exceed £50,000.
3 A fixed timetable of no more than 30 weeks from allocation to trial.
4 Standard directions are given.
5 Limited disclosure of documents.
6 There are fixed trial advocacy costs.
7 Recoverable costs are summarily assessed (i.e. decided on the spot in a rough-and-ready fashion) at the conclusion of the trial.

Multi-track

1 All other disputes ranging from straightforward cases just above the fast track limit to complex and weighty matters involving claims for millions of pounds and multi-party actions.
2 Most commercial cases will be dealt with on this track.
3 Claims where the hearing is likely to last for more than 1 day.
4 Directions will be tailored to fit the case. Court will hold a case management conference and a pre-trial conference.

When considering which is the most suitable track for a particular case, the court will consider several factors, including:

- the financial value of the claim;
- the type of remedy asked for;
- the complexity of the facts, law or evidence;
- the number of parties or likely parties;

- the value and complexity of any counterclaim;
- the amount of oral evidence that may be needed;
- the importance of the case to people not directly involved in it; and
- the views and circumstances of the parties to the dispute.

Stay of proceedings

A party may make a written request for the proceedings to be 'stayed' (or stopped) for one month before the case is allocated to one of the tracks while the parties attempt to settle the case by alternative dispute resolution (ADR) or other means. Alternatively, the court may, of its own initiative, direct that the proceedings be stayed for one month for the same reason. When deciding what costs to award, the court will take into account whether the parties have unreasonably refused to try ADR or behaved unreasonably in the course of ADR. The court will also encourage the use of ADR at case management conferences and pre-trial reviews.

This is a new rule and its existence underlines the court's power to interfere in the case for the purpose of encouraging co-operation and settlement between the parties. If a settlement is not reached the court will allocate the case and give directions in the usual way.

Value of the claim

The basic criterion for allocation to a particular track is the value of the claim. For this purpose, costs, interest and any element of contributory negligence claimed by the parties is ignored. If there is a counterclaim the court will look at the larger of the claims; for example, if the original claim was £10,000 but the defendant counterclaims for £20,000, the latter figure will be taken into account for allocation purposes.

Generally, claims will be allocated on their financial value but the court may also consider a number of other factors (*see* above).

Assessment of damages cases

Where the defendant has admitted liability or the claimant has obtained judgment in default but the amount of damages to be awarded to the claimant remains to be decided, a different procedure will apply. These cases will usually be scheduled for a hearing where the amount of damages will be decided.

Directions

Once the case has been allocated to the appropriate track, the court will give the parties instructions (or 'directions') on procedural steps to be taken and fix a timetable for the progress of the case to trial. The procedures after allocation and at the hearing (if the case gets that far)

vary according to the track to which the case is allocated. The rules about costs also vary (*see* Chapter 99).

The matters that will be dealt with by the court's directions include disclosure of documents, service of witness statements and expert evidence.

SUMMARY

Procedure in the small claims track

The small claims track is designed for people who will conduct their cases without the help of a solicitor or barrister. Consequently, the procedure after allocation is simpler and more straightforward than on the other tracks. The rest of this chapter focuses on the rules of procedure relevant to running a case in the small claims track.

In most small claims cases, the court will give standard directions and fix a date for the final hearing. The basic standard directions are:

1 each party must send to the court copies of any documents on which they intend to rely no later than 14 days before the hearing;
2 the original documents should be brought to the hearing;
3 the parties must notify the court immediately if the case is settled by agreement before the hearing date.

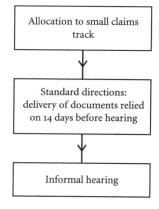

The standard directions vary depending on the type of case, so there are particular directions, for example, for holiday claims, building disputes and road accident claims. The court can also give special directions, usually where further clarification of the issues is needed. In that case, the court can order that further documents must be disclosed by the parties. If all the parties agree, the court can deal with a small claim without a hearing, basing its decision on the statements of case and documents.

Procedure in the fast track

Directions on the procedural steps to be taken up to trial are given at two stages in the fast track: when the case is allocated to the fast track and when the parties file listing questionnaires. Whenever possible, the directions will be given without the need for a hearing.

A typical timetable for preparation of a fast track case looks like this:

Disclosure	4 weeks
Exchange of witness statements	10 weeks
Exchange of experts' reports	14 weeks
Court sends listing questionnaires	20 weeks
Parties file listing questionnaires	22 weeks
Hearing	30 weeks

Time runs from when the parties are notified that the case has been allocated to the fast track. The court will fix a hearing date for not more than 30 weeks from allocation.

Procedure in the multi-track

Directions are given at two stages: at a case management conference and at a pre-trial conference.

At the case management conference, which is held by a procedural judge, the case will be reviewed and the parties, who will be expected to attend, will be encouraged to settle the dispute or consider ADR. Alternatively, the court may give directions and fix a timetable at the allocation stage.

At the pre-trial conference, the trial judge will review the parties' costs estimates, set a trial date and a timetable.

STEPS TO TRIAL

Disclosure

The parties must reveal to each other all the relevant documents (including audio tapes, video tapes, computer discs and photographs) in the case, even if they are not favourable to their arguments. The parties must each draw up and exchange a list of their documents and allow the other side to inspect all items on the list. The idea behind this procedure is that the parties should not be taken by surprise at the trial by issues or facts of which they were not previously aware. The disclosure of documents also allows the parties to evaluate the relative strengths of their case before trial.

In the small claims track, each party must exchange a copy of any document on which they intend to rely in court. If this direction is not complied with the documents may not be allowed as evidence at the hearing.

Expert evidence

Expert evidence, in the form of a report or presence of an expert at the hearing, is not allowed in small claims track cases unless the court gives permission. It is further discouraged for small claims by the fact that only limited costs can be claimed for expert evidence, with a limit of £200 for experts' fees. If a party is relying on an expert's report, this should be filed at court 14 days before the final hearing. (*See also* Chapter 81.)

Part 36 offers

These rules do not apply to cases in the small claims track. *See* page 616 for an explanation of how the rules work in relation to offers and the costs consequences of failing to beat an offer made by the other side.

Trial

In the small claims track, the final hearing will normally be before a district judge, in the judge's room (like an office) rather than a courtroom. The hearing will be much less formal than you might expect – the judge will not wear a wig or gown, the parties will sit around a table, the strict rules of evidence do not apply and, if the parties are not represented by lawyers, the district judge will help them by asking appropriate questions to draw out relevant information and explain any relevant matters of law. The district judge should be addressed as sir or madam.

AFTER THE HEARING

Rights of appeal

In the small claims track, a party may appeal against a decision of the district judge only on the grounds that:

- there was a serious irregularity affecting the proceedings; or
- the court made a mistake of law.

A circuit judge will decide whether the application for an appeal should be heard. If there is a hearing of the appeal, and the circuit judge allows the appeal, he will if possible dispose of the case at the same time without ordering the claim to be reheard.

Remedies

Any of the usual remedies may be granted in the small claims track – with the exception of freezing injunctions and search orders, which may only be obtained in the High Court.

Enforcement: getting your money

As already mentioned, obtaining a court judgment against someone who owes you money is not the end of the story. The court judgment is a piece of paper confirming that you are owed the money by the debtor. The court will not automatically take further steps against the debtor in order to extract payment. If the debtor does not pay up, you will need to go back to court and attempt to collect the judgment debt by one or more of the following methods. There will be a court fee to pay in each case.

You may find that the debtor deliberately makes himself scarce to avoid enforcement action. You will need to know where he is living or working in order to serve the necessary court papers on him. In that case, the first hurdle will be to locate the debtor. Enquiry agents can help with tracing debtors, but this is an expensive option and will not be cost-effective if you are chasing a small amount of money.

Bear in mind that it is a criminal offence to harass a debtor. The Administration of Justice Act 1970 section 40 provides that it is an offence to try to coerce a debtor into paying up by:

- making demands which 'are calculated to subject him, or members of his household to alarm, distress, or humiliation'. The frequency of the demands and the way they are made will be crucial. For instance, it would be harassment to call late at night with rough-looking men; it might be harassment to park a car marked 'debt collector' outside the debtor's house or to keep phoning up throughout the day;
- falsely suggesting that the debtor could be prosecuted for not paying. It is not a criminal offence to owe money, even if a court has entered judgment;
- falsely pretending to be acting in an official capacity or to have an official document in order to enforce payment. For instance, it would be harassment for the creditor to call at the debtor's home, claiming to be a court bailiff and producing what looked like a court order allowing them to seize the debtor's possessions.

Which court?

All of the following enforcement methods are available in the county courts and in the High Court. The advantage of enforcing in the High Court is that a higher rate of interest can be claimed on the judgment debt. Also, High Court sheriffs have a better reputation than county court bailiffs for successfully carrying out Warrants of Execution (*see* below).

- Where judgment has been obtained in the county court for £5,000 or more, it must be enforced in the High Court;

- where the judgment is for less than £600, it must be enforced in the county court;
- where the judgment is for between £600 and £5,000, the creditor can choose whether to enforce it in the county court or in the High Court.

The Oral Examination: finding out about the debtor's means

The judgment creditor (the person owed money under a court judgment) can ask the court to order the debtor to attend court to answer questions about his means (money in the bank, property he owns, his salary, etc.) and to produce relevant books and documents (bank statements, pay slips, etc.).

The creditor can use this information to decide which enforcement procedure is likely to be most effective. For example, if the debtor is self-employed then an Attachment of Earnings Order (*see* below) is not an option. If the Oral Examination reveals that the debtor owns a car, the creditor might consider a Warrant of Execution (sending the court bailiffs in to seize the car and sell it).

The court will arrange an Oral Examination hearing and the debtor will be sent a notice of the hearing together with a financial means questionnaire. At the hearing, an officer of the court will question the debtor as to his means. The creditor can also attend court and question the debtor. If the debtor does not turn up at the hearing, the court will set another date and the debtor will be warned that failure to attend the subsequent hearing could mean that he will be committed to prison for contempt of court.

In practice, this procedure is often useless. There is no way of compelling a crafty debtor to answer questions at the hearing and no way of checking that he is answering truthfully. It is easy for debtors to avoid giving information. The government is currently looking at ways of improving the system, to allow creditors access to better and more information about debtors' finances.

Warrant of Execution: sending the bailiff in

The creditor can apply to the court for an order instructing the court bailiff to seize and sell the debtor's personal property (e.g. his car, stereo, cooker, television, video). The goods are sold at auction and, after the bailiff's costs have been deducted, the proceeds are paid to the creditor up to the value of the judgment. (In the High Court the creditor should apply for a *Writ of Fieri Facias*, which will be enforced by High Court sheriffs, rather than bailiffs.)

This is the most popular choice of enforcement

methods, but is not necessarily the most effective. Research commissioned by the Lord Chancellor's Department (now replaced by the Department for Constitutional Affairs) revealed that in 1998 the county courts issued 694,000 warrants instructing bailiffs to seize goods or payments from debtors but only 242,000 produced payments of the debts.

The main reasons why the bailiffs may be unsuccessful are:

- some bailiffs give debtors seven days' notice of the execution of the warrant, giving debtors time to move items of any value to an unknown address;
- the bailiffs cannot forcibly enter the debtor's premises. Some debtors hide inside the house or refuse to open the door;
- debtors often claim that the property in question is owned by another person or is on hire purchase;
- debtors can apply to suspend the warrant at the last minute, giving themselves extra time to pay the debt;
- the seized goods are sold at auction for a fraction of their worth. Once the bailiffs' costs have been deducted, there is very little left for the debtor.

Garnishee Order: intercepting money owed to the debtor

This order allows a creditor to seize money owed by a third party to the debtor – it is most frequently used to obtain money held in a debtor's bank or building society account. The third party (called the garnishee) will be ordered to pay the money direct to the creditor, rather than to the debtor, up to the value of the judgment debt.

Shane (the judgment creditor) has obtained a judgment against Mark (the judgment debtor) in Croydon county court for the sum of £600. At the Oral Examination hearing, it transpires that Mark is owed £800 by Sharon. Shane obtains a Garnishee Order directing Sharon to pay £600 of the money she owes to Mark direct to Shane.

The debtor will not be given notice of the application for the Garnishee Order; he might otherwise withdraw the money from the bank or building society account, for example. The creditor will have to explain to the court the basis for his belief that the third party owes money to the debtor, for example, because that information was revealed at an Oral Examination or because the garnishee confirmed that information.

Where the intended garnishee is a bank or building society account, note that:

- the debtor will not be able to garnishee a joint account where one of the account holders is not one of the judgment debtors; for example, the creditor will not be able to garnishee a joint account held by a husband and wife where only the husband is the judgment debtor;
- the creditor will need to be able to provide the court with details of the name and branch of the bank or building society where the account is held and the account number;
- an order against a building society cannot require a payment which would reduce the balance in the account to a sum less than £1;
- before paying the creditor, the deposit-taking institution is entitled to deduct a prescribed sum (currently £50) in respect of administrative expenses.

If the garnishee fails to pay the debt to the creditor, the creditor can enforce the order against the garnishee in the same manner as for any other money judgment (i.e. by one or more of the methods described here).

Attachment of Earnings Order: the debtor's salary

This requires a debtor's employer to make regular deductions direct from pay. The court will decide the amount of the instalments on the basis of information received from the debtor and the debtor's employer. The employer will deduct the amount of each instalment and pay it into court on a regular basis. The order can apply to wages, commissions and bonuses.

The main points to note are:

- the order is available only where the amount remaining due under the judgment is at least £50;
- the order is not available in the High Court. If you obtained judgment in the High Court you will have to transfer proceedings to the county court in order to apply for this order;
- the order is not available if the debtor is unemployed or self-employed.

(*See also* page 326.)

Charging Order: putting a charge on the debtor's home

This order allows the creditor to secure the judgment debt against the debtor's property, such as a house, a long lease on a flat or shares. The debtor will not be able to sell the property without paying the creditor. The creditor can apply to the court to force a sale and so receive payment – note, though, that this will involve further legal proceedings, which may be expensive.

If the creditor knows where the debtor lives, then, provided that the land is registered, he can search the Land Registry to find out whether or not the debtor owns the property. The district judge has a discretion as to whether or not to grant the Charging Order and he or she may reject the application if the judgment debt is not for a large amount. The Charging Order should be registered at the Land Registry (if the land is registered) or on the Land Charges Register (if the land is unregistered). The procedure for obtaining a Charging Order is complex and legal advice should be sought.

Bankruptcy/insolvency proceedings

Threatening an individual or company with bankruptcy or winding up respectively can achieve a result – assuming, of course, that the debtor has the money. A creditor who is owed at least £750 can issue a statutory demand, which is a formal document threatening bankruptcy (or winding up) proceedings unless the debt is paid within 21 days. There is no court fee. (*See* Chapters 52 and 53 for a guide to commencing bankruptcy or winding up proceedings.)

Reform

An independent sample of over 100 cases in 1997 showed that only one-third of creditors were paid in full and on time and another third had received nothing. The government has recognized that the existing methods of enforcement are slow, costly and often ineffective. In January 2000 the Lord Chancellor, Lord Irvine, said: 'Taking someone to court is a daunting enough prospect in itself. But for too many people, getting a judgment in court is the easy part. Their problems begin after the hearing is over. Too often it is difficult for them even to find out whether the debtor has any assets, let alone to get paid what the court says they are entitled to have.' A Green Paper containing proposals to improve both civil and criminal enforcement procedures was published in July 2001 (and can be viewed at www.lcd.gov.uk). The proposals remain under consultation.

98

The Lawyers

The legal profession in England and Wales is populated with two types of lawyer: solicitors and barristers. A common misconception is that solicitors are generalists and barristers are specialists, in the same way that GPs may be considered generalists and medical consultants are specialists. This is no longer strictly true as far as the legal profession is concerned. The manner and method of work done by solicitors in the twenty-first century has undergone a dramatic change. The number of solicitors has increased from 22,233 in 1967 to 89,045 practising solicitors in 2002. (There were in fact 113,372 solicitors on the Roll in 2002 – the Law Society's record of solicitors qualified to practice.) At the present rate of growth, the practising profession will number 120,000 by 2010. With increasing numbers of solicitors and greater accessibility of legal information via the internet, solicitors are specializing in specific areas of the law, in order to compete more effectively with rival firms on the basis of their expertise and reputation.

Tighter regulation of this branch of the profession and more stringent standards of practice have also contributed to an increase in specialization. Furthermore, the government's legal aid reforms, brought about by the Access to Justice Act 1999, squeezed out a significant number of smaller firms relying on legal aid work for their bread and butter. Only firms that have met quality criteria will be awarded contracts to take on legal aid work.

The two branches of the profession are not as clearly defined as they once were. Solicitors now enjoy the same rights to represent their clients in the higher courts as barristers (i.e. not just the magistrates' courts and the county courts but also the crown court, the High Court, the Court of Appeal and the House of Lords). This is a relatively new development, however, and it remains to be seen how many solicitors will take advantage of their new privileges.

SOLICITORS

What do solicitors do?

There are 89,045 solicitors in England and Wales working in private practice, within companies or local and central government. The majority of solicitors work in private practice.

Solicitors' work falls into two broad types:

1 *Court work* – this is called 'contentious work' and, as that title suggests, it involves representing the client in court proceedings. Solicitors may appear as advocates (i.e. present the case in court themselves) in every court. Where court proceedings are subsequently begun, all prior work, such as advice, preparation and negotiations, will fall under the contentious work category.

2 *Non-court work* – this is called 'non-contentious' work and covers all other legal work where the solicitor's role is to act as a negotiator or mediator, rather than as an adversary. For example, conveyancing work, the preparation of wills, statements and contracts, the administration of estates, business and financial advice comes under this heading. Work done as a preliminary to proceedings is non-contentious provided that proceedings are not subsequently begun.

A firm of solicitors

Solicitors in private practice may work in partnership with other solicitors or set up in business on their own, in which case they are called sole practitioners. The solicitors who set up the partnership are called the partners. All other qualified solicitors working for the firm who are not partners are called assistant solicitors. Trainee solicitors are solicitors who have not qualified and been admitted as solicitors. In order to complete their education and training, all solicitors are required to serve a two-year 'apprenticeship', called the training contract, within a firm of solicitors. During the duration of the training contract they may deal with their own clients, but they should be supervised by an experienced solicitor.

Other personnel that may be encountered by a member of the public in their dealings with a typical high street solicitor's firm include legal executives and paralegal staff.

Legal executives

Many people who begin their work in a legal office at a junior level, for example as a legal secretary, accounts/office administrator, or outdoor clerk, go on to become legal executives by taking legal examinations set by the Institute of Legal Executives (ILEX) and becoming members of ILEX. Although they do not enjoy the same status as solicitors, in practice many legal executives do the same work as qualified solicitors, as well as more routine legal work.

Paralegal staff

The firm can charge the client for the work of paralegal staff (in other words, they are 'fee earners') but they do not usually have any professional legal qualifications. Typically, in addition to general administrative and secretarial work, they might, for example, conduct the first interview with the client or deal with some of the paperwork involved with a conveyancing transaction.

Claims assessors

There is no law preventing anyone from setting themselves up as a 'legal adviser' or 'claims assessor', even if they have no legal training. Claims assessors tend to offer their services in areas of the law involving accident claims and employment law disputes and typically offer a US style 'no win, no fee' contingency deal on fees, with clients having to pay between 30 and 45 per cent of their compensation, plus expenses at the conclusion of the case. Members of the public should be wary of unqualified and unregulated legal advisers, who are not required to carry insurance and are not governed by any code of ethics and conduct, unlike solicitors.

Licensed conveyancers

Licensed conveyancers are authorized to carry out property transactions on behalf of their clients, in exactly the same way as are solicitors. It is an offence under the Administration of Justice Act 1985 for anyone to describe himself as a licensed conveyancer, unless he holds a licence issued by the Council of Licensed Conveyancers. The Council of Licensed Conveyancers (16 Glebe Road, Chelmsford, Essex CM1 1QG, Tel: 01245 349 599) regulates the conduct of its members and has disciplinary machinery to deal with complaints.

Seeing a solicitor

A client is entitled to have his case or transaction handled by a qualified solicitor, if he expressly asks to see a solicitor.

Mr P asked for a solicitor to handle his domestic dispute. Unbeknown to Mr P, his case was in fact handled by a member of staff at the firm who, although experienced, was not qualified as a solicitor. The court decided that Mr P was entitled to refuse to pay the firm's bill because the firm had failed to correct the client's misconception that his case was being dealt with by a solicitor.

Pearless de Rougemont & Co (a Firm) *v* Pilbrow (1999)

The Law Society

The Law Society is the body that represents and regulates solicitors in England and Wales. Solicitors in Scotland and Northern Ireland are represented by the Law Societies of Scotland and Northern Ireland, respectively. The regulatory powers of the Law Society include stipulating education and training requirements and rules of professional conduct, and collecting contributions from its solicitor members to the Solicitors' Compensation Fund and, until recently, the Solicitors' Indemnity Fund (more about this later). Most solicitors are members of the Law Society. All solicitors are bound by the rules of conduct made by the Law Society.

The Law Society also has powers to 'intervene' in solicitors' firms and obtain possession of the solicitors' papers and have the client and office accounts frozen. The Law Society may make an 'intervention' where, for example, there has been a breach of the Solicitors' Accounts Rules, or where a solicitor is practising without a valid practising certificate. The Access to Justice Act 1999 extended the Law Society's powers to examine solicitors' files or demand details of bank accounts connected with the firm or any trust of which it was or is trustee.

Who may act as a solicitor?

No one may describe themselves as a solicitor or act in the capacity of a solicitor unless they have:

- completed their training and been 'admitted' as a solicitor; and
- their name appears on the Roll of Solicitors at the time; and
- they hold a current practising certificate issued by the Law Society.

It is a criminal offence to pretend or hold oneself out to be a solicitor.

The Roll of Solicitors is simply a list of solicitors who have been admitted. It is kept by the Law Society and any member of the public may inspect it, free of charge. The Law Society also keeps a record of the name of every solicitor holding a practising certificate, which may be inspected by the general public. This can be a useful way of tracing a solicitor. Contact the Law Society's public enquiry line on Tel: 0870 606 6575.

Acting without a practising certificate

The rule is that a person who is not qualified to act as a solicitor and who does not hold a practising certificate cannot recover their costs in respect of anything done by them or any other person in any action, suit or matter.

In most cases, if you win a court case, the other side in the litigation will be ordered by the court to pay your legal costs (i.e. your solicitor's fee for the work, and other expenses such as fees charged by a medical expert for giving evidence in a case). If the solicitor acting for you did not hold a practising certificate, you will not be able to recover any costs or expenses from the other side. However, the steps taken by the uncertificated solicitor on your behalf in the litigation will not be invalid – in other words, the outcome of the litigation itself will not be affected.

Mrs E brought a tripping claim against her local council (she had tripped over and injured herself in the street). She was represented in the court proceedings by a person who was admitted as a solicitor and was on the Roll of Solicitors but who did not hold a current practising certificate. The court decided that Mrs E's legal representative was not entitled to hold himself out as a solicitor in the litigation because he did not have a practising certificate. Consequently, he was not entitled to recover his fees for representing Mrs E in the court proceedings.

Edwards *v* St Helens Metropolitan Borough Council (2000)

Solicitors' privileges

A qualified solicitor with a current practising certificate is entitled to carry out the following functions.

Conduct litigation as a solicitor and appear as an advocate

'Conducting litigation' covers all the preparatory work involved in starting civil or criminal proceedings, including issuing the necessary documents. Solicitors are also entitled to represent their clients in court. Lay people may, however, represent themselves as 'litigants in person'. They may also ask a friend, who can be another layperson, to attend a trial or hearing in chambers with them. This person, called a 'McKenzie friend', may take notes, quietly make suggestions and give advice, but should not take part in the proceedings as an advocate.

Solicitors are entitled to appear as advocates in the lower courts (the magistrates' courts and the county courts). Solicitors who comply with additional training requirements laid down by the Law Society may represent clients in the higher courts (the High Court, the crown court, the Court of Appeal and the House of Lords).

Legal drafting

Draw up or prepare for fee, gain or reward certain legal documents for legal proceedings, contracts for sale of land, conveyance or transfer of real or personal estate.

Non-solicitors may not charge a fee for conveyancing or probate work.

Carry on investment business

Solicitors who carry on investment business must be authorized by the Law Society to do so. This involves obtaining an investment business certificate and paying a fee. When the Financial Services and Markets Act 2000 comes into force, solicitors' firms that want to provide 'mainstream investment business services' will have to opt into direct regulation by the Financial Services Authority. Firms limiting their activities to 'non-mainstream investment business' will be able to continue to do so automatically as members of the Law Society.

Found or oppose a grant of probate or letters of administration

As will be obvious from the proliferation of will-writing services on the high street, anyone may draft a will or power of attorney.

Administer oaths

It may be necessary to make a sworn written statement (called an *affidavit*) in order to comply with a particular legal requirement. In that case you will need to swear an oath before a solicitor that the contents of the statements are true. Only a practising solicitor may administer an oath for an affidavit, but he should not do so where he is personally interested or acting for one of the parties.

Instruct counsel

As a matter of convention, barristers will not accept instructions from anyone other than solicitors, accountants and patent agents. This means that members of the public cannot approach barristers directly and ask them to advise or represent them.

Rules of professional conduct

Solicitors are subject to rules that govern their professional behaviour and relations with clients. The rules derive from both statutory (Acts of Parliament) and non-statutory sources, including the Solicitors' Practice Rules. The Law Society can punish solicitors for breaching the rules.

Choosing a solicitor

When going through the process of choosing a solicitor, factors that are likely to be relevant include:

- does the solicitor specialize in the area of law connected with your problem?
- where is the firm located? It may be necessary to find someone who works close to home;
- is the firm prepared to work on legal aid?
- will the firm take on your case on a conditional fee basis (this is commonly known as a 'no win, no fee' arrangement)? (*See* page 612.)

The preferred option is to use someone who has acted for you in the past and whose service you were happy with. This assumes that the solicitor specializes in the area of law connected with your problem. If not, it is possible that another solicitor in the same firm is competent to take on the new matter. Failing that, the firm may be able to recommend a solicitor.

Other lines of enquiry include:

- ask around your circle of friends and acquaintances for a recommendation;
- if you belong to a professional organization, trade association or trade union, they may be able to suggest a suitable solicitor;
- the Law Society's public enquiry line (Tel: 0870 606 6575) will give you up to three names of solicitors' firms selected at random from the information provided by you;
- look in the *Yellow Pages*/local telephone directory/ specialist legal directory;
- if you have been injured in a road accident or in an accident at work or at home, you may need to see a specialist personal injury solicitor. The Law Society will give you details of a specialist personal injury solicitor near to your home or work who will be prepared to give you a free legal consultation. Call the Law Society's Accident Line freephone on 0500 192939.
- the internet – many firms now have a presence on the internet where they advertise their services. Some offer free initial consultations via e-mail. A good starting point for searching for a firm of solicitors on the internet is Delia Venables' website at www.venables. co.uk. Infolaw at www.infolaw.co.uk is also a useful site with links to firms.
- a Law Society website (at www.solicitors-online. com) allows people to search the Society's database of over 80,000 solicitors. You can search by the type of legal work you require or by entering the name of your town.

See also page 611.

The first meeting

The first appointment can be scheduled over the telephone or by calling in at the firm's office. You should explain the nature of your problem and check that the firm handles that sort of work. You might want to take a friend or family member along to the first meeting for moral support, in which case you might mention this. If a fee will be charged for the first meeting, it is quite all right to enquire about the charge.

The better prepared you are for the meeting, the easier it will be for the solicitor to grasp the facts of the matter and advise you more quickly (remember, time is money!). In preparation for the appointment, you should make a list of key points to take to the meeting, make a note of any questions that you want to ask, and collect together any relevant letters and documents (and do not forget to take them with you).

You should aim to present the facts as clearly as possible and avoid leaving anything out – the solicitor will decide which facts are pertinent. Do not be bashful about asking how much the case will cost and when you will be expected to pay – the solicitor is obliged to discuss this subject in any case (*see* Chapter 99). Nor should you hesitate to ask the solicitor to explain anything that you do not understand, especially any legal jargon the solicitor has used.

The solicitor should:

- analyse the nature of the problem or work to be done;
- advise, and if the firm is unable to deal with the matter, give details of a firm that can deal with it;
- discuss the likely cost of the matter;
- discuss how long the matter may take before it is resolved;
- explain the next step.

Following the first meeting, you are under no obligation to take the matter any further with that solicitor.

If you agree to retain the solicitor's services (i.e. you decide to 'instruct' the solicitor), the solicitor should send you a client care letter, containing information about legal costs. The following letter sets out the sort of information that you might expect to see in a typical client care letter. It is based on a specimen letter recommended by the Law Society.

A client care letter

Carrot, Turnip and Swede, Solicitors

21 March 2004

Dear Mr Pritchard

This letter explains the basis on which we will carry out all the work necessary in connection with your purchase of 8 Coronation Street, Warrington.

People responsible for your work

Mr Oliver Onion will carry out most of the work in this matter. He is an assistant solicitor specializing in residential conveyancing work. He is supervised by Mrs Carol Carrot, one of the senior partners at our firm, who is ultimately responsible for this matter.

If you need to telephone, please ask to speak to Mr Onion or myself. If we are unavailable, please leave a message with our secretary, Julie.

We will try to avoid changing the people who handle your work but if this cannot be avoided, we will inform you promptly who will be handling the matter (and why the change was necessary).

Charges and expenses

We will charge you a fixed fee of £800 for dealing with this conveyancing transaction on your behalf.

We will add VAT to our charge at the rate that applies when the work is done. At present, VAT is 17.5%.

In addition, there are other expenses for which you will have to pay.

VAT is payable on certain expenses.

We will discuss with you how you are to pay these charges.

If the work is not completed, we will charge you £70 per hour for each hour of work. We will charge for writing letters, and for making and taking telephone calls in units of 1/10th of an hour. Our charges for considering letters received will be in units of 1/20th of an hour.

We will inform you if any unforeseen extra work becomes necessary – for example, due to unexpected difficulties or if your requirements or the circumstances change significantly during the matter. We will also inform you in writing of the estimated cost of the extra work before incurring extra costs. We will attempt to agree an amended charge with you. If we cannot reach agreement, we will do no further work and charge you on an hourly basis for work to date, as set out earlier.

It is normal practice to ask clients to make payments on account from time to time. These payments help to meet our expected charges and expenses, and help to avoid delaying progress in the matter.

We will need £200 to enable us to pay expenses, before we start work on your matter. We will then pay expenses as they become due. These amounts will be shown as paid on your final bill.

Bills

We will send you a bill for our charges and expenses, usually when the work is completed. Payment of the bill is due to us within 28 days of our sending it to you. If you do not pay the bill within this time, we will charge interest on it at 15% per year on a daily basis, from the date on which payment of our bill is due.

If you have any query about the bill, you should contact me straight away.

Storage of papers and deeds

After completing the work, we are entitled to keep all your papers and documents while money is owing to us. We will keep our file of papers (except for any of your papers which you ask to be returned to you) for no more than 7 years and on the understanding that we have your authority to destroy the file 3 years after sending you our final bill. We will not destroy documents you ask us to deposit in safe custody.

We do not normally make a charge for retrieving stored papers or deeds in response to continuing or new instructions to act for you. However, we reserve the right to make a charge based on the time we spend on reading papers, writing letters or other work necessary to comply with the instructions.

Termination

You may terminate your instructions to us in writing at any time. For example, you may decide you cannot give us clear or proper instructions on how to proceed, or you may lose confidence in our work. We are entitled to keep all your papers and documents while money is owing to us.

We will decide to stop acting for you only with good reason and on giving you reasonable notice. If you or we decide that we will stop acting for you, you will pay our charges on an hourly basis and expenses as set out earlier.

Raising queries or concerns with us

We are confident that we will give you a high quality service in all respects. However, if you have any queries or concerns about our work for you, please take them up first with myself. If that does not resolve the problem to your satisfaction or you would prefer not to speak to me, then please take it up with this firm's client care partner who is Andrew Aubergine.

All firms of solicitors are obliged to attempt to resolve problems that clients may have with the service provided. It is therefore important that you immediately raise your concerns with us. We value you and would not wish to think you have any reason to be unhappy with us.

Conclusion

Your continuing instructions will amount to your acceptance of these terms of business, but please sign and date the enclosed copy of this letter and return it to us immediately. Then we can be confident that you understand the basis on which we will act for you.

We hope that by sending this letter to you we have addressed your immediate queries about the day-to-day handling of your work and our terms of business. However, if you have any queries, please do not hesitate to contact me.

This is an important document which we would urge you to keep in a safe place for future reference.

Yours faithfully

Mr Terence Turnip

The solicitor's responsibilities

A solicitor is generally free to decide whether or not to accept instructions from a particular client, but a solicitor may not turn down work on the basis of a client's race, sex, sexual orientation or disability.

There are some circumstances in which a solicitor must not accept instructions from a potential client, including where:

- the instructions would involve a breach of the law or of the principles of professional conduct, unless the client is prepared to change his instructions. An example of this would be where the client asks the solicitor to do something which would be a criminal offence;
- where the solicitor has insufficient time, experience or skill to deal with those instructions;
- where he suspects that the client is under untoward pressure from another person to pursue the matter. In that case, the solicitor should insist on seeing the client in private. This may be the case, for example, where the client is elderly and the solicitor suspects that he or she is being pressured by relatives.

Duty of care and skill

Once the solicitor has agreed to take the matter on, he is under a duty to carry out the work with reasonable care and skill. The duty of care and skill includes a duty to deal with the client's affairs promptly, for example, by dealing promptly with correspondence and responding to telephone calls received.

A complaint of undue delay can be made to the Office for the Supervision of Solicitors, the body that polices and punishes solicitors (*see* below). Furthermore, in cases of delay, the Law Society has the power to take possession of all papers and money relating to the matter and can deliver them to the client or to the client's new solicitor. Where the solicitor is guilty of avoidable delay in court proceedings, the court may impose a financial penalty on the solicitor. If the delay amounts to gross misconduct or gross negligence, the action may be struck out (i.e. not allowed to continue) and the solicitor may be ordered to pay costs and may be liable in damages.

Conflict of interests

The solicitor should not act where his own personal interests conflict with the client's, for example, where the solicitor plans to buy property from one of his own clients

or lend money to one of his own clients. Neither should a solicitor act where there is a conflict or a significant risk of a conflict between the interests of two or more clients. For example, a solicitor should not act for both husband and wife in a matrimonial matter.

Confidentiality

The solicitor and his staff must keep the client's business confidential at all times.

Information

The solicitor must keep the client properly informed about the progress of the work and the costs. There is also a requirement to inform the client of the firm's complaints procedures and of the name and status of the individual who is handling the client's affairs within the firm.

Authority

The solicitor should agree clearly with the client at the outset exactly what the parameters of the solicitor's authority are to be.

To summarize, the client is entitled to expect that the solicitor will:

- act with due care and skill, avoiding unnecessary delay;
- act in the client's best interests;
- keep him regularly informed about the progress of the case;
- keep him regularly informed about costs;
- ask him at each stage whether and how he wishes to proceed.

Changing solicitors

The client is free to change solicitors at any time but he should let the original solicitor know what he has decided. Where court proceedings have been started, formal notice of the change must be filed at court and sent to the opponent and the original solicitor before the change will be recognized by the court.

As a general rule, the solicitor can stop acting for the client if he has a good reason. The client must be given reasonable notice of the change. A good reason includes a situation where the solicitor cannot get clear instructions from the client, where the client has failed to give the solicitor a necessary cash advance to cover expenses (e.g. court fees, a fee for an expert's opinion, fees for registering documents at the Land Registry) or where the client is hindering the solicitor from conducting the case.

Client's papers and property

What happens to the client's papers and property when the client changes solicitors or the solicitor finishes his work for the client? The solicitor should account to the client for any money still held on behalf of the client and, at the client's request, return to the client all papers and property to which the client is entitled. The client is not entitled to all the documents in the solicitor's file. For example, the client is not entitled to receive a copy of letters written to him by the solicitor for which the solicitor has not charged any fee.

A solicitor is not entitled to charge for removing files from storage for collection by a former client, but a reasonable charge may be made for the cost of sending papers to the client or other solicitor. A solicitor may also charge for retrieving documents from the client's file at the request of the client.

The solicitor is entitled to keep the client's papers and property until the client pays his bill, but he cannot sell the client's property (*see* Chapter 99). If the solicitor loses the file or destroys it without the client's consent, the client could make a complaint to the Office for the Supervision of Solicitors (OSS) (*see* below).

Complaining about your solicitor

In 2002, there were 22,830 complaints against solicitors. The most common complaints were about delay, costs and failing to keep the client informed about the progress of the case.

The Law Society advises that a client with a complaint against his solicitor should try to sort it out informally with that solicitor first. The client should explain why he is unhappy and what he would like the solicitor to do to correct the problem.

The OSS (*see* below) produces a special form, the *Complaints Resolution Form*, which the client can use to set out the complaint to his solicitor. It is available from the OSS, solicitors or local Citizens' Advice Bureaux or on the internet at www.oss.lawsociety.org.uk. Allow the solicitor at least 14 days to reply.

Internal complaints procedure

If approaching the solicitor directly does not work, the client should refer the problem to the firm's own internal complaints procedure. Telephone and ask for the name of the person who handles complaints at the firm.

The Solicitors' Practice Rules require every principal in private practice to:

1 ensure the client is told the name of the person in the firm to contact about any problem with the service provided;

2 have a written complaints procedure and ensure that complaints are handled in accordance with it; and

3 ensure that the client is given a copy of the complaints procedure on request.

If the problem cannot be satisfactorily resolved by the solicitor in question or the firm's internal procedure, the next step is to contact the OSS.

The Office for the Supervision of Solicitors

The OSS was set up in September 1996 to replace the Solicitors' Complaints Bureau as the body responsible for regulating the solicitors' profession, guarding professional standards and investigating complaints about solicitors' service and conduct. It is, in practice, the body that polices and punishes solicitors. Although the arm of the OSS that handles complaints operates independently of the Law Society, it is financed by and derives its powers from the Law Society and the profession is effectively self-regulating.

The OSS will investigate complaints about poor service and misconduct. This includes complaints about delay, rudeness, dishonesty and a failure to return telephone calls or deal with letters. (*See* Chapter 99 for the procedure for complaining about legal costs.)

The OSS does not have the power to deal with complaints of professional negligence (which has a different legal meaning from misconduct or poor service) and cannot judge whether a solicitor was negligent – although it can advise on how to proceed with a claim for negligence and may refer the client to one of the solicitors on its negligence panel, offering one hour's free advice.

It should also be noted that the OSS cannot:

• require a solicitor to stop acting for a particular client;
• investigate a complaint about someone else's solicitor;
• deal with a complaint which is not about a solicitor or his staff;
• deal with complaints about barristers, licensed conveyancers, legal executives or solicitors in Scotland. These all have complaints bodies of their own;
• in some cases the OSS may not be able to investigate formally the handling of a matter which has not yet been completed as this may, for example, hamper court proceedings.

Complaints must be made to the OSS within three months of completion of the firm's internal complaints handling procedure or within six months of the matter complained of.

There is no time limit for bringing a complaint about serious misconduct, such as dishonesty or breaches of the Solicitors' Accounts Rules.

If the firm in question has not been given a chance to resolve the matter, the OSS will in some cases refer the complaint back to the solicitor in order to maximize his chances of settling the matter at this stage. Failing that, the OSS can carry out its own investigation and has the power, where appropriate, to:

• reduce a solicitor's bill in whole or in part;
• order the solicitor to pay compensation of up to £5,000;
• require a solicitor to correct a mistake at his own expense;
• discipline a solicitor for misconduct.

In the following illustration, based on an actual incident, the solicitors at fault added insult to injury by failing to respond adequately to the client's complaint of delay. The exasperated client eventually took his complaint to the OSS.

Mr Smith instructed AB & Co on a litigation matter. AB & Co was six weeks late in complying with a procedural step in the court case. At a later stage, Mr Smith asked AB & Co to supply him with a copy of a letter that had been sent to the barrister in the case. Mr Smith had to write two letters of request, and a copy of the letter was not sent until seven weeks after the initial request. When Mr Smith complained about the delay, the senior partner brushed the complaint aside, merely stating that he was satisfied with the way in which the matter had been dealt with. Mr Smith was understandably unhappy with this response but the firm then failed to reply to six of his telephone calls within the space of two weeks. Mr Smith's complaints of delay were upheld by the OSS. The solicitors' bill was reduced by about one-third and the firm was ordered to pay Mr Smith £250 compensation, an award that was enhanced by the firm's failure to consider and address the complaints properly.

Disciplinary sanctions

There are four sanctions available to the Compliance and Supervision Committee of the OSS where the complaint is upheld:

1 to find a breach, express regret but take no further action;
2 to express disapproval of conduct;
3 to reprimand;
4 to reprimand severely.

Minor cases of misconduct, such as breach of an undertaking where the undertaking was eventually complied with or conflict of interests where the solicitor ceased acting once the conflict was recognized, are usually dealt with by means of a reprimand. Reprimands are administered in private and the complainant will be told of the decision but asked not to seek publicity for the decision. The OSS keeps a permanent record of reprimands but it is not available for public inspection. Unfortunately, there is no way that new clients can check whether their solicitor has been disciplined by the OSS in the past.

Minor misconduct can also lead to conditions being imposed on solicitors' practising certificates, restricting the types of work they can undertake. These sanctions can affect solicitors' public funding franchising and eligibility for judicial appointments.

Serious offences, for example dishonesty or breach of the Solicitors' Accounts Rules, are referred to the Solicitors' Disciplinary Tribunal, in which case the OSS will act as 'prosecutor'.

The continued existence of the OSS hangs in the balance as it struggles to reduce a huge backlog of cases languishing in untouched files. The Lord Chancellor, Lord Irvine, has threatened to transfer control of

complaints to a new Legal Services Complaints Commissioner, unless the backlog is dramatically reduced and new cases are dealt with speedily. The Ombudsman's report for 2001 found that the number of outstanding files had been reduced from 17,000 in July 1999 to less than 6,000 by the end of 2000.

The OSS can be contacted at Victoria Court, 8 Dormer Place, Leamington Spa, Warwickshire CV32 5AE, Tel: 0870 606 6565. Website: www.oss.lawsociety.org.uk/

The Solicitors' Disciplinary Tribunal

As with the OSS, the Solicitors' Disciplinary Tribunal is largely funded by the Law Society but is constitutionally independent. Its members are solicitors and lay members. Allegations of misconduct are judged by a panel of two solicitors and one lay person (not a solicitor or a barrister) drawn from its members and are usually heard in public.

The Tribunal has much sharper teeth than the OSS. The ultimate weapon in its armoury of sanctions is the power to strike a solicitor's name off the Roll. A solicitor is not permitted to practise if his name does not appear on the Roll of Solicitors. He may not usually apply to have his name restored to the Roll for at least six years from the date of the Tribunal's decision.

The Tribunal can also:

● suspend the solicitor from practice, indefinitely or for a specified period;
● fine the solicitor up to £5,000 in respect of each proved allegation;
● in certain circumstances, prohibit a solicitor from taking on public funding work;
● order any party to pay costs.

Appeal from a decision of the Tribunal lies to the Queen's Bench Division of the High Court.

The Legal Services Ombudsman

A client who is unhappy with the way the OSS handled his complaint or the decision it reached has three months from the date of the final decision of the OSS to refer the matter on to the Legal Services Ombudsman.

The Ombudsman for England and Wales cannot be a qualified lawyer and is completely independent of the legal profession. The Ombudsman's services are free of charge. The position is currently held by Zahida Manzoor. The role of the Ombudsman is to investigate the way that the OSS has dealt with complaints against solicitors, where the client is dissatisfied with the outcome. She also supervises and investigates the way that complaints against barristers, licensed conveyancers and legal executives are handled.

If the Ombudsman is not satisfied that a complaint of professional misconduct (a breach of the Solicitors' Practice Rules) has been dealt with properly then she will refer the case back to be reconsidered by the OSS or other professional body concerned. Where the client's original complaint was about poor service (for example lack of communication), the Ombudsman will want to be satisfied that the client has received appropriate redress – such as an apology, or compensation, or a reduction in the lawyer's fees.

The strict three-month deadline for applying to the Ombudsman will not be extended unless there are 'special reasons'. 'Special reasons' are circumstances outside of the complainant's control that prevent him from referring the case to the Ombudsman in time, for example if the complainant or someone in his family was seriously ill. Even where there are special reasons, the Ombudsman will not normally investigate a complaint if the delay between receipt of the professional body's decision and referring the matter to the Ombudsman is more than 12 months.

Following an investigation the Ombudsman can:

- order the professional body (e.g. the OSS), the lawyer complained of, or both, to pay the complainant compensation for loss, distress or inconvenience. There is no maximum to the amount of compensation that can be awarded;
- recommend that the professional body reconsiders the original complaint or that it exercises its powers in relation to the lawyer complained of;
- formally criticize the professional body and/or the lawyer;
- take no further action. In previous years, this has happened in around two-thirds of cases.

There is no right of appeal against a decision of the Legal Services Ombudsman although her decisions are subject to judicial review (in which case the court will only look at the way in which she exercised her powers rather than the final decision arrived at).

Summary

To summarize, a client should:

1 ask his own solicitor to remedy the complaint;
2 use the firm's internal complaints handing service;
3 if still unhappy, contact the OSS;
4 apply to the Legal Services Ombudsman if dissatisfied with the way the OSS handled the complaint or its decision.

Suing a solicitor for negligence

In some circumstances, a solicitor's poor service or misconduct may also constitute negligence.

The majority of claims involve routine mistakes. For example, if a solicitor in drafting a will failed by mistake to include an important provision which the client would have wished to have included, he may be held to be negligent.

Negligence has a strict legal definition and not everything that goes wrong will amount to negligence by a solicitor. The solicitor must be shown to have fallen below the standard of competence and expertise demanded of a typical solicitor. Clients also have to show that their loss was caused by the negligence.

In this case the solicitors were instructed by a couple who were interested in buying a property that had been renovated. The sellers assured the solicitors that the necessary building regulation consent had been obtained for the renovations. The solicitors did not check the accuracy of this statement – in fact, there was no building regulation consent for the work. The buyers bought the house but it was just a matter of time before cracks developed and it transpired that the renovation works had not been properly carried out. When they discovered that building regulation consent had not been obtained, the buyers sued the solicitors for negligence. Held: The solicitors were negligent. They should have taken reasonable steps to inspect or otherwise check the existence of the building regulation consent.

Cottingham and Another *v* Attey Bower & Jones (a Firm) (2000)

The Negligence Panel Scheme

The OSS does not have the power to investigate allegations of negligence but it can refer a client to a solicitor who is a member of its Negligence Panel Scheme. That solicitor will give one hour's free advice on whether a solicitor was negligent in a particular case and, if so, what the client should do next.

Making a claim

It is advisable to use a solicitor to make a claim against another solicitor. Once the client's original solicitor has been notified of the negligence claim, the matter will be referred to his insurance company. The insurance company will assess the claim and may make an offer of money to settle the claim. If they decide not to settle the claim, the client may need to resolve the matter through the courts.

Insurance

All solicitors in private practice are required as a condition of practice to have professional indemnity insurance up to a maximum of £1 million per transaction. Since 1987 this compulsory insurance cover has been provided through a mutual fund, the Solicitors' Indemnity Fund Limited (SIF). In 1997/98, 45 per cent of all claims made against the SIF related to residential (36.47 per cent) and commercial (9.31 per cent) conveyancing – the largest category of all claims made.

Following two years of heated debate within the solicitors' profession, the Law Society decided that, as from 1 September 2000, solicitors should be given the option of obtaining cover on the open market, through a system of approved insurers or via a group scheme. The group scheme is run by a Managing General Agency that will administer insurance arrangements on behalf of a consortium of insurers.

Solicitors' Compensation Fund

The main function of the Solicitors' Compensation Fund is to pay back to clients any money which their solicitor has stolen from them. It will also replace money which a solicitor has taken from the client and failed to replace (this is called 'failing to account' for money). The Fund is maintained by the Law Society and made up of contributions collected annually from every solicitor in practice. No grant will be made from the Fund if there is another means by which the client can reclaim their money, such as through the solicitor, the solicitor's insurance company or a third party.

The applicant must be a person who has lost money through the actions of the solicitor within the course of a solicitor/client transaction of a kind which is part of the usual business of a solicitor. Subject to this, the applicant need not necessarily have been the solicitor's client.

A doctor was instructed to prepare a medical report for the purposes of a client's personal injury claim. The client gave his solicitor a cheque for £300 to pay the doctor for supplying the report. The solicitor pocketed the money and later went out of business. The Fund reimbursed the doctor.

One of the most common applications to the Fund concerns the following scenario:

On completion of his purchase of a property, the client transferred substantial funds to his solicitor to pay disbursements including stamp duty, the estate agent and the cost of registering the title to the property. The solicitor used the money for his own dishonest purposes and title to the property was not registered. Following an investigation, the Fund provided a sum to cover the disbursements.

The maximum amount that can be paid out to an applicant is £1,000,000 including interest and legal costs. Losses caused by a solicitor's professional negligence are not covered.

An application for a grant from the Fund must be made within a strict six-month time limit. Time starts to run from when an applicant became aware or ought to have become aware of the loss, or likelihood of loss, or failure to account. The application should be made on the Fund's application form, and supported by reasonable evidence to prove the claim, such as cash statements from the solicitor's file.

In practice, the Fund will not always demand evidence of the solicitor's dishonesty, in the form of a criminal conviction or a finding of dishonesty by the Solicitors' Disciplinary Tribunal. The Fund may be aware that a firm has been misappropriating or misusing client money because of its close links with the OSS (the body that 'polices' solicitors), in which case the firm may already have been investigated by the OSS and closed down.

Breach of contract

The agreement between the solicitor and the client is a contract for professional services. The solicitor may be liable to the client if he breaches an express or implied term of the contract.

Terms that are implied into every contract between solicitor and client include:

- the duty to protect the client's interests. For example, the solicitor must not act where there may be a conflict of interests, i.e. where he has a personal interest in the matter which might be opposed to that of the client;
- the duty to consult the client on all questions of doubt which do not fall within the express or implied discretion which is left to the solicitor;
- the duty to carry out the service with reasonable care and skill.

There is no implied term that the solicitor will win the case, and the solicitor cannot be held liable for losing provided that he exercised reasonable care and skill in dealing with the case. He should explain to the client the likely outcome of the litigation and the risks involved.

Becoming a solicitor

It takes a minimum of six years to train and qualify as a solicitor. All students must complete both the academic and vocational stages of training, as prescribed by the Law Society.

The academic stage of training is obtained by either:

1 a law degree plus the Legal Practice Course; or
2 a degree in any subject plus the Common Professional Examination or Post-graduate Diploma in Law or a Senior Status Law degree plus the Legal Practice Course; or
3 ILEX Part I and Part II Examinations plus Legal Practice Course.

The vocational stage of training is usually completed by:

1 serving a two-year full-time Training Contract; and
2 completing a Professional Skills Course (there are slightly different rules for non-graduates).

The process demands hard work and commitment and students should also be prepared to deal with financial hardship. Course fees for the Legal Practice Course (LPC) were between £3,500 and £9,000 in 2003 and ranged between £3,000 and £4,500 in 2003 for the Common Professional Examination (CPE). Discretionary grants for these courses are rarely available. It should also be borne in mind that competition for places on the LPC and CPE is fierce and there is no guarantee that, having completed the courses, students will be able to go on to secure a training contract position within a solicitor's practice.

There are three routes to qualification, as outlined below.

The law degree route

This is the quickest route and two-thirds of solicitors qualify this way. Three good passes (i.e. grade C or above) in GCE 'A' Levels will be needed to get a place on a law degree course. Science 'A' levels are as acceptable as arts subjects, and no one subject is a prerequisite for admission.

It is important that the law degree should cover the seven Foundations of Legal Knowledge, required by the Law Society to complete the academic stage of training. These are:

- law of contract;
- law of tort;
- criminal law;
- public law;
- property law;
- equity and trusts;
- law of the European Community.

If the degree does not cover all of the foundation subjects, candidates will be required to prepare for and pass the outstanding subjects in the CPE.

Applications for places on law degree courses are made through the University Admission Services (UCAS), PO Box 28, Cheltenham, Gloucestershire, GL50 3SA.

The non-law degree route

Students who obtain a degree in a subject other than law must take the CPE or Post-graduate Diploma in Law (PGDL). About 20 per cent of students qualify this way. The CPE tests students on each of the seven Foundation subjects (*see* above). Full-time students must complete the CPE within a maximum of three years and other than in exceptional circumstances, a candidate may not attempt any paper of the CPE on more than three occasions.

Places on full-time courses are allocated through the Central Applications Board and application forms for full-time courses are available from the Central Applications Board, PO Box 84, Guildford, Surrey GU3 1YX, www.lawcabs.ac.uk or Tel: 01483 451080. For part-time courses students should contact the academic institution direct.

The Diploma in Law course is approximately 36 weeks long and each institution has developed its own approach. A common clearing system operates for applications, administered by the Central Applications Board. Not all institutions are members of this system so it is best to check with the institutions before applying.

Alternatively, non-law graduates may take a two-year full-time or a three-year part-time Senior Status Law Degree, which includes the seven Foundation subjects. For admission to a course, students should apply direct to the University or College of Higher Education offering the course.

The Legal Practice Course

Everyone who qualifies, by whichever route, has to take the Legal Practice Course (LPC). The aim of the course is to equip candidates with the necessary knowledge and skills to function as a trainee solicitor during the Training Contract. Applications for full-time courses should be made through the Central Applications Board. For part-time courses candidates should contact the academic institution direct.

Before commencing the LPC the candidate must enrol as a student member of the Law Society and obtain from the Law Society a Certificate of Completion of the Academic Stage of Training. Candidates for student membership are required to satisfy the Law Society as to their character and suitability to become solicitors. Factors which will have a bearing on this include the candidate's bankruptcy, conviction of a criminal offence or liability to pay a penalty fare to a transport authority. None of these factors would be an automatic bar to student membership, however, and each case is considered on its merits.

The Certificate of Completion of the Academic Stage of Training confirms that the candidate has passed the seven Foundation subjects. A composite form for Student Enrolment and for a Certificate of Completion of the Academic Stage of Training may be obtained by ringing the Law Society Application Line on Tel: 0870 606 2555.

Obtaining a place on the LPC is no guarantee of a place in a Training Contract.

The non-graduate (ILEX) route

This is the longest route to qualification, usually taking about eight years, but it does allow candidates to earn as they train. To summarize, this method involves:

1 becoming a Member of the Institute of Legal Executives (MILEX); plus
2 becoming a Fellow of the Institute of Legal Executives (FILEX); plus
3 qualifying as a solicitor.

After completing stages 1 and 2, the candidate is qualified as a legal executive. At stage 3, most candidates are usually entitled to claim exemption from the CPE and the training contract requirement.

MILEX

The minimum educational requirement for training to be a legal executive is four GCSE/GCE 'O' Level passes. Mature students over 25 years of age may be considered without any formal qualifications. Candidates must complete ILEX Part I and then Part II examinations. Study is usually part-time at a local college or by taking a home study course and the exams are usually completed within four years. Candidates do not have to undertake any qualifying legal employment experience in order to achieve membership status.

FILEX

In order to qualify as a Fellow of the Institute of Legal Executives, candidates must:

* be 25 years of age; and
* be a Member of the Institute of Legal Executives; and
* have completed five years' qualifying legal experience, of which two years *must* have been completed after attaining membership status.

Stage 3

Legal Executives normally claim exemption from the PGDL or CPE by passing corresponding papers to the foundation subjects in the Institute's Part II exams plus one other substantive law subject.

Having completed the LPC (*see* page 765), the two-year Training Contract requirement is normally waived for FILEX, subject to qualifying conditions.

Those who are interested in following the Legal Executive route to becoming a solicitor should contact the governing body for Legal Executives, the Institute of Legal Executives, Kempston Manor, Bedford MK42 7AB, or Tel: 01234 841000. Their website is at www.ilex.org.uk.

Training contract

After completing the academic stage of training (degree, CPE/PGDL and LPC), the next hurdle is to secure and complete a two-year Training Contract in a firm of solicitors. Trainee solicitors are exposed to all aspects of working life as a solicitor, and are required by the Law Society to gain experience in at least three areas of law, with a mixture of contentious and non-contentious work. Trainees are also expected to gain practical experience of drafting documents, dealing with clients, attending court and tribunal hearings and researching legal queries. This is all done under the supervision of a 'principal', who is a senior solicitor in the office.

The quality of the experience gained during the training contract can vary enormously, largely due to the fact that the Law Society rarely checks that firms are complying with their training contract requirements and very few trainees are brave enough to complain about their employers. In 1999, only 256 firms were selected at random for monitoring by the Law Society. Some trainees spend their time labouring over menial and tedious tasks that other solicitors in the office would rather not do. It

is too early to tell whether a new monitoring scheme, introduced in July 2000, will improve matters for these trainees. The Law Society has targeted 400 firms for monitoring and trainees will be invited to telephone the Monitoring Unit anonymously.

The Law Society recommends a minimum wage of £15,300 for firms in Central London and £13,600 for firms elsewhere.

The number of people chasing training contracts is typically far in excess of the number of training places that are available and competition is fierce. It is usual to start applying for a training contract during the second year of undergraduate studies. The Law Society's website at www.lawsoc.org.uk provides a list of firms authorized to take trainee solicitors. Various publications publicize vacancies:

* the *Law Society Gazette* – this is also on the Law Society's website;
* *The Lawyer* magazine;
* National Press – *The Times* (Tuesday), *The Independent* (Wednesday).

Directories of solicitors' firms are also useful sources of information for applicants:

* *The Legal 500* – by John Pritchard, published by Legalease;
* *Chambers & Partners Directory* – published by Chambers & Partners Publishing;
* *Solicitors' & Barristers' National Directory* – published by the Law Society;
* Solicitors' Regional Directories – published by the Law Society.

The Training Contract can also be completed part time over a four-year period.

Professional Skills Course

All candidates must pass the Professional Skills Course (PSC), regardless of the route they take, before they can be admitted as a solicitor. The course is normally taken over the duration of the Training Contract.

Summary

To qualify as a solicitor, one must:

* have completed the academic stage of training;
* legal executives: have applied for exemption from the PGDL/CPE;
* be a student member of the Law Society;
* have completed the vocational stage of training.

For further information on a career as a solicitor, visit the Law Society's internet site at /www.lawsociety.org.uk or telephone their Automated Infoline on Tel: 01527 504455.

Crown Prosecution Service

For information about a training contract, contact the Crown Prosecution Service, The Staff Management Unit, 50 Ludgate Hill, London EC4M 7GG, Tel: 020 7273 8357.

Government

For details contact The Lawyers' Management Unit, Treasury Solicitor's Department, Queen Anne's Chambers, 28 Broadway, London SW1H 9JS, Tel: 020 7210 3000.

The Association of Magistrates' Courts

For more information regarding a career in the Magistrates' Court Service contact The Association of Magistrates' Courts, 79 New Cavendish Street, London W1M 7RB, Tel: 020 7436 8524.

BARRISTERS

There are over 9,000 barristers in independent practice in England and Wales. The majority of barristers work in London. About 3,000 practice outside London.

What work do barristers do?

Barristers' work falls into two categories:

1 *Court work* – barristers are specialist advocates. They represent the client at court and tribunal hearings. Until recently, barristers enjoyed a monopoly over appearing in the higher courts. Although there is no longer any restriction on solicitors representing their clients in the higher courts, in practice very few solicitors have taken up the higher court qualification and become solicitor advocates. Barristers continue to appear in most major cases in the English courts.

2 *Non-court work* – barristers give advice on obscure or difficult questions of law within their chosen fields of expertise. They also draft pleadings and other legal documents.

When appearing in court or advising clients, barristers are referred to as 'counsel'.

The General Council of the Bar

The General Council of the Bar, or the Bar Council, as it is known, is the governing body of barristers. It devises rules to govern the conduct of its members pertaining to:

- complaints and discipline;
- ethics and standards;
- education and training;
- equal opportunities;
- pupillage.

It represents the interests of its members, maintains records and provides a number of services for members.

The Inns of Court

Every practising barrister must belong to one of the four Inns of Court: Lincoln's Inn, Middle Temple, Inner Temple and Gray's Inn. The Inns of Court are voluntary unincorporated societies of equal standing. Although independent of each other, they tend to act together in their common interest through the Council of the Inns of Court.

The Inns of Court let accommodation to barristers, provide law libraries, common rooms and dining facilities to their members, award scholarships and bursaries to students and young barristers and organize moots and talks.

Circuits

For the purposes of the administration of justice, England and Wales are divided into six circuits: the Northern Circuit, the North Eastern Circuit, the Midland and Oxford Circuit, the South Eastern Circuit, the Western Circuit, and the Wales and Chester Circuit.

A barrister (other than a barrister whose only chambers are in London) is required to be a member of a circuit or of a specialist association. Each circuit has a 'mess', a society formed of barristers practising on the circuit. Each circuit mess lays down rules of professional etiquette for its circuit.

Organization

Unlike solicitors, barristers are not permitted to form themselves into partnerships with other barristers. They are obliged to work on a self-employed basis. It is normal for them to share staff and office facilities, however. Their offices are called 'chambers' and members of the same chambers pay a contribution towards the upkeep of the premises. The senior member of the chambers is normally the tenant of the premises. While the barristers share the expense of running the chambers, including the cost of employing administrative staff and a clerk, they do not normally share their income.

Barristers' clerk

The role of a barristers' clerk is a many and varied one. He will be the office administrator, accountant, business manager and agent for the barristers. The clerk allocates the work amongst the barristers in the chambers and negotiates the barristers' fees. For all this he is richly rewarded, usually receiving a commission of about 10 per cent of the barristers' fees.

Who may practise as a barrister?

A person may not practise as a barrister in England and Wales unless:

- they have been 'called to the bar'; and
- completed a pupillage; and
- obtained a practising certificate; and
- are a member of professional chambers.

Barristers are also obliged to be insured against claims for professional negligence with the Bar Mutual Indemnity Fund.

The 'cab rank' rule

The rule compares barristers to taxis in a rank: they must take the next passengers, whoever they are. Thus, all practising barristers must (irrespective of whether the client is privately paying or publicly funded):

- accept any brief to appear before a court in which they profess to practise;
- accept any instructions;
- act for any person on whose behalf they are briefed.

They must do so regardless of their own beliefs, the nature of the case or character of the person on whose behalf they are instructed.

There are so many exceptions to this rule that it is generally always possible for barristers legitimately to turn down cases. The rules forbid them to take on a case if in doing so they would be 'professionally embarrassed'. Professional embarrassment includes a lack of sufficient experience, inadequate time or opportunity to prepare the case, a risk of breach of confidences entrusted by another client and conflicts of interest. Barristers may also decline to accept a case if the fee offered is not a proper one to reflect the complexity of the case or the seniority of the barrister. In publicly funded cases, the fee paid is automatically considered to be a proper fee.

Complaints

In general, the most common causes of complaints concern rudeness, lateness and inability to understand arguments. Criminal clients tend to complain about their barristers' failure in court or poor advice on appeal. Complaints from clients involved in family disputes typically concern what they perceive as a poor settlement or poor representation in court.

Barristers, like solicitors, are essentially self-regulating and complaints are handled and judged by other barristers. Although lay representatives sit on the various panels that adjudicate complaints, barrister members of the panel can effectively veto any proposal to award compensation to a client on a finding of inadequate professional service. Conscious of the need to show that complaints are being handled fairly and impartially, the Bar Council created a new, non-lawyer, post of Complaints Commissioner in April 1997.

Complaints Commissioner

The Complaints Commissioner is the first link in the chain of complaints-handling bodies.

The Commissioner, who is appointed by the Bar Council, supervises the running of the complaints system and is the first port of call for clients with a complaint. He may suggest that the case should be sorted out informally between the barrister and the client or decide that a formal investigation is warranted.

The Bar Council produces a standard form for complainants to complete. The form requires straightforward details such as the name of the barrister and instructing solicitor and details of the complaint. Other information required at this stage will depend on the nature of the complaint; for example, if there is documentary evidence to support the client's claim then it would be helpful to enclose that with the form.

Where the matter requires investigation, the Bar Council writes to the barrister, the instructing solicitor and other relevant witnesses asking for their comments. The complainant is shown the barrister's comments and asked for his reaction. The Commissioner will then decide whether or not to take the matter any further.

The Complaints Department can be contacted at Northumberland House, 303–306 High Holborn, London WC1V 7JZ, Tel: 020 7440 4000.

The Professional Conduct and Complaints Committee of the Bar Council

Where a complaint is considered further, it will be passed to the Professional Conduct and Complaints Committee (PCC). This is comprised of barristers and some lay members. The PCC can decide:

- that the complaint should be dismissed; or
- that the barrister may be guilty of misconduct; and/or
- that the barrister may be guilty of professional misconduct.

In cases of misconduct, the barrister will be required to attend a hearing before a panel of between two and four barristers and a lay representative. The following disciplinary sanctions are available to the panel.

The barrister can be:

- advised about his behaviour;
- admonished;
- fined up to £5,000;
- suspended for up to three months (i.e. he will be unable to practise as a barrister for a given time);
- disbarred (i.e. he will cease to be a barrister).

In cases of serious misconduct, or where there is a serious dispute over the facts, the matter will be referred to the Disciplinary Tribunal of the Council of the Inns of Court, and the PCC will act as prosecutor. Serious misconduct generally involves some element of dishonesty (e.g. misleading the court, the client or another party), criminal conduct, or gross negligence of the sort that calls into question the individual's fitness to be a barrister or which has caused damage to the lay client.

Where there is a finding by the PCC of inadequate professional service, and this has caused the client inconvenience, loss or distress, the barrister can be required to:

- apologize;
- reduce or refund his fees;
- pay compensation up to a maximum of £5,000.

Compensation is only awarded for actual financial loss, for example wasted travelling expenses or the cost of putting a mistake right, and not for distress or inconvenience. Inadequate professional service is defined as conduct or provision of services that falls below what could reasonably be expected of a barrister in all the circumstances – generally it involves matters such as minor rudeness, bad clerking, delay, or minor negligence.

The Disciplinary Tribunal

Hearings of the Disciplinary Tribunal are open to the public and, where a disciplinary sanction is imposed, the complainant is informed of the Tribunal's decision. These are both relatively recent developments, forming part of the Bar Council's attempts to move away from the 'behind-closed-doors' impression of the system and introduce more transparency into the complaints-handling process. In the past, proceedings were held in private and the Tribunal's decisions were also kept private.

The Tribunal has the power to:

- disbar;
- suspend for any period;
- impose a fine up to a maximum of £5,000.

Barristers may appeal from a decision of the Tribunal to the Visitors of the Inns of Court.

Legal Services Ombudsman

A complainant may apply to the Legal Services Ombudsman if he is dissatisfied with the way that his complaint has been dealt with at any stage.

Suing for negligence

Until the year 2000, barristers (and solicitor advocates) were immune from being sued for negligence by their clients in respect of the entire conduct of the case in court. For example, if the barrister failed to argue a defence in court or failed to call an important witness at a hearing, it was not possible for the client to sue the barrister for negligence.

The immunity also extended to advice given before the court proceedings commenced, depending on the proximity of the advice and the court proceedings.

A woman tried to sue her barrister in respect of the advice the barrister had given her on the day of the hearing, before the hearing had begun. The advice had affected the amount that she had negotiated in a financial settlement with her ex-husband at the door of the court. The court decided that the barrister's advice, just before the hearing, was intimately connected with the conduct of the case in court. Therefore, the barrister could not be sued for negligence.
Kelley *v* Corston (1998)

What was the justification for affording barristers this privileged untouchable status? There were a number of arguments:

- that the possibility of being sued for negligence would inhibit the lawyer, consciously or unconsciously, from giving his duty to the court priority to his duty to his client;
- that the advocate might be exposed to vexatious claims by difficult clients;
- that it was contrary to the public interest for a court to retry a case which had been decided by another court.

This astonishing state of affairs existed until July 2000, when the House of Lords abolished the centuries-old immunity. The opportunity to re-examine the law arose in three appeals, which were heard together.

In one case, the client, Mr Simons, claimed that his solicitors had failed to prepare the case properly, resulting in an unsatisfactory settlement at the door of the court. Mr Simons refused to pay his bill. The solicitors sued Mr Simons and he counter-claimed for professional negligence. In defence, the solicitors claimed that advocates' immunity extended to preparatory work for a trial. The county court judge dismissed Mr Simons' counter-claim on the basis of immunity in October 1997. However, in December 1998, the Court of Appeal overturned the decision, along with claims of immunity by two other firms. The firms appealed and the House of Lords ruled unanimously that, in the light of modern conditions, it was no longer in the public interest in the administration of justice that advocates should have immunity from suit for negligence. Hall *v* Simons (2000)

Pro bono work

The Bar Pro Bono Unit, a charitable organization comprising some 920 barristers, will provide free legal advice and representation in any court or tribunal in deserving cases. Applicants must satisfy the Unit's criteria for acceptance:

- the case must have legal merit and deserve pro bono assistance;
- applicants must normally be financially ineligible for

Becoming a Barrister

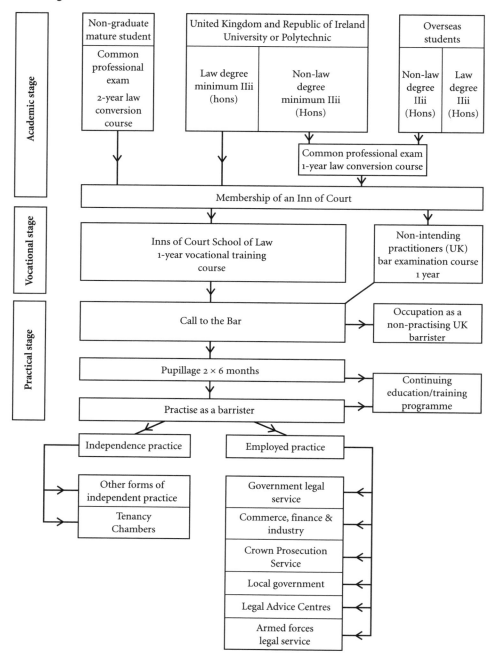

A barrister in independent practice must make his practice in England and Wales or in the Courts of the European Community his primary occupation and must hold himself out as being and must be willing at all times in return for payment of fees to render legal services to the public generally in England and Wales (Code of Conduct of the Bar, paragraph 208)

public funding and must demonstrate that they have no other means of financing their legal expenses (e.g. help from insurance or a trade union);

- the case must require the skills of an experienced barrister;
- preparation, advice and representation should normally be capable of completion within three working days. In exceptional cases, assistance can be given beyond that time limit;
- there should be no other source of help;
- where the applicant is a litigant in person, an assessment will be made as to whether a solicitor is also required to assist with the case.

Becoming a barrister

As with the solicitors' branch of the legal profession, most intending barristers are law graduates, although it is possible to become a barrister without a degree (*see* chart on page 770).

The graduate route

Both law and non-law graduates who have the minimum requirement of a lower-second-class honours degree may become members of one of the Inns of Court. Non-law graduates must first take the CPE and a one-year conversion course. They may then choose to be either 'non-intending' barristers (who will not practise) or 'intending' practitioners.

Each type of barrister will take his or her own one-year course (the equivalent to the solicitors' LPC). On successful completion of their courses, both will be 'called to the bar' (i.e. admitted as a barrister), but 'non-intending' barristers will not serve 'pupillage'. They will not be able to appear as counsel in any court and will have to describe themselves as 'non-practising'.

Barristers who intend to practise will serve for one year as a 'pupil' to a qualified practising barrister. On satisfactory completion of the first six months, pupils will be issued with a practising certificate and will then be able to take cases of their own (if they are sent any). It is likely to be two years or so before newly qualified barristers will have sufficient brief fees to maintain themselves. The Inns of Court, the Bar Council and the individual chambers in which barristers work all provide some funding, but these funds are limited and are given on a discretionary basis only.

The non-graduate route

Mature students can, if they pass the CPE, take a two-year conversion course and gain membership of an Inn of Court. They will then follow the same procedure as a graduate.

This training system is full of idiosyncrasies. For instance, to qualify students must:

- eat a certain number of 'dinners' (a meal at their Inn of Court); students are required to complete 12 qualifying units in order to be called to the Bar. This can be achieved through dinners (students are awarded one unit for each dinner), weekends in an Inn of Court or at a residential centre (counts as three units) or attending Education Days (counts as two units);
- buy a wig and gown;
- pay around £8,000 in course fees.

99

Legal Costs

Involvement in legal proceedings is always a gamble. When a dispute goes to court, there are financial risks involved. When the matter is non-contentious (for example drafting a contract or conveying a house), expenses will accrue that the client may not have anticipated. This chapter deals with how solicitors work out their fees, what the financial risks and 'hidden' expenses are and how a client can object to the solicitor's bill. Most of the chapter concerns costs in civil cases. Costs in criminal cases are dealt with at the end.

HOW MUCH WILL IT COST?

The issue of cost will be the first question on the lips of every prudent client. Clients should not feel embarrassed to make enquiries about costs as solicitors are obliged by their rules of professional conduct to discuss their fees, other expenses and financial risks at the outset of the case and as the matter progresses.

The 'costs' of a case are fees, VAT and expenses. In contentious cases (where court proceedings have begun), the client is potentially responsible for paying two sets of costs: his own solicitor's costs and his opponent's costs.

'Fees', or 'profit costs', are what the solicitor charges for doing the work (in other words, the charge for his time and skill). Solicitors usually base their fees on the amount of time they have spent dealing with a matter. There are no rules about what work a solicitor can charge for or how much they can charge but fees must be fair and reasonable. There are fixed fees for some court cases (*see* below).

Work that solicitors usually charge for includes:

Non-court work	Court work	Both
		Telephone calls to the client and the other side's solicitor
		Meetings with the client
		Writing letters
		Reading letters and other documents
	Preparing statements of case	
	Reading statements of case	
		Research
Drafting a contract		
		Completing forms
	Appearing at court	
	Discussing the case with a barrister	
	Meeting witnesses	

VAT (currently at 17.5 per cent) is charged on the sum total of fees and on those expenses which are subject to payment of VAT (e.g. a barrister's fee).

'Expenses' are also sometimes referred to as disbursements. For example, on a house purchase, the disbursements will include the fee that has to be paid to the Land Registry to register the property in the new owner's name, the cost of searches of the local land charges register to check that there are no adverse interests affecting the property and stamp duty on the purchase price. Where court proceedings are begun, disbursements may include court fees, the cost of commissioning an expert's report and barrister's fees.

COSTS INFORMATION

Solicitors are obliged by their rules of professional conduct to give their clients certain information about costs both at the outset and as a matter progresses (Rule 15 Solicitors' Practice (Costs Information and Client Care) (Amendment) Rule 1999 and the Solicitors' Cost Information and Client Care Code 1999). The information should be given clearly, with an explanation of unfamiliar words or legal jargon, and confirmed in writing to the client as soon as possible.

The Code provides that the solicitor should give the client the best information possible about the likely overall costs, including a breakdown between fees, VAT and disbursements. The solicitor should explain how the firm's fees are calculated and if charging rates may be increased.

Basis of firm's charges

The way that the solicitor's fees will be calculated should be established at the beginning of the case. How fees are calculated can vary from firm to firm, but the most common arrangements are:

- *a fixed fee* – it is agreed that a maximum fee will be paid, regardless of how much time the solicitor spends. This is the usual arrangement for conveyancing transactions;
- *an hourly rate* – this is the usual basis for charging. The longer it takes, the more it costs. Rates can vary from £100 an hour at a high street firm to £300 an hour at a big City firm;
- *a cost limit* – the solicitor works on the case until his fees reach an agreed figure. The client has the option to review the situation once the spending limit has been reached. The solicitor should not exceed the agreed limit without first obtaining the client's consent. If the client is involved in court action, however, it may not be possible to simply stop.

If time is a factor in the calculation of the fees, the solicitor should explain the time likely to be spent in dealing with a matter.

Estimates

Any estimate of likely costs should be realistic and the solicitor should make it clear at the outset if an estimate, quotation or other indication of cost is not intended to be fixed. The Law Society has issued guidance to solicitors about giving estimates for conveyancing transactions. The Law Society advises that the estimate should be inclusive of all charges, including VAT, stamp duty and disbursements. If not given in writing, the solicitor should confirm the estimate in writing as soon as the instructions are confirmed. The client should be warned that the estimate figure may have to be revised if the transaction proves more complex or time consuming than was expected.

Disbursements

The solicitor should explain what expenses a client may have to pay, either to the solicitor or to a third party, and at what stage in the matter those payments are likely to be needed.

Sources of funding

Other sources of funding for the case should also be discussed. The solicitor should discuss:

- whether the client is eligible for public funding (used to be called legal aid). The solicitor should also explain the nature of public funding – that the funding is a loan, rather than a gift, and that, if successful, the client may have to pay some or all of the loan back. It should also be made clear that the client may be obliged to pay a contribution to the cost of the case out of his own pocket, even if eligible for public funding (*see further* Chapter 100);
- whether the client's liability for his own costs may be covered by insurance;
- whether the client's liability for another party's costs may be covered by pre-purchased insurance and, if not, whether the client should consider obtaining after-the-event insurance cover. Insurance cover must be fully discussed where a conditional fee agreement is proposed;
- whether an employer or trade union or another person might be prepared to fund the client's case and be responsible for paying the other side's costs if the client is unsuccessful.

Risks

The financial risks involved in the case, including the risk of having to pay an opponent's costs, should be carefully considered and weighed against the likelihood of succeeding in the matter. In contentious matters, the solicitor should explain to a privately paying client that he will be responsible for paying the firm's bill in full, regardless of any order for costs made against the other side. The risks of having to pay an opponent's costs (i.e. the other side's solicitor's bill and other expenses) should also be fully explored.

Where the case is funded with public money, it should be made clear that the client may still be ordered by the court to contribute to the other side's costs if the case is lost. If the client wins, the other side may not be ordered to pay or be capable of paying the full amount of the client's costs.

Updating costs information

The Code also provides that the solicitor should keep the client properly informed about costs as a matter progresses. In particular, the solicitor should:

- tell the client, unless otherwise agreed, how much the costs are at regular intervals (at least every six months) and in appropriate cases deliver interim bills at agreed intervals;
- explain to the client (and confirm in writing) any changed circumstances which will or are likely to affect the amount of costs, the degree of risk involved, or the cost–benefit to the client of continuing with the matter;
- inform the client in writing as soon as it appears that a costs estimate or agreed upper limit may or will be exceeded; and
- consider the client's eligibility for legal aid if a material change in the client's means comes to the solicitor's attention.

The Office for the Supervision of Solicitors (the body that is responsible for disciplining solicitors) has the power to punish a solicitor for breaching the Code by disallowing all or part of the solicitor's costs and/or ordering a solicitor to pay compensation to the client (*see further* page 761).

Mrs A instructed XYZ & Co to help her in a case before the Employment Tribunal. The firm wrote to Mrs A setting out their hourly charges and an overall costs estimate. The letter said that 'if' Mrs A and the firm agreed that XYZ & Co would operate on a contingency fee basis (it explained what that meant), they would charge 10 per cent of the amount of any award in addition to the fees they had quoted. When Mrs A won her case the firm sent her a bill for the quoted fees plus a sum equivalent to 10 per cent of the amount awarded to Mrs A by the tribunal. Mrs A complained that the costs quotation she had been given had been exceeded. The Office for the Supervision of Solicitors (OSS) decided that the firm's letter had not made it clear that the firm considered that there was a contingency fee in existence. It was important to be careful when wording letters. Here the vital word in the letter was 'if', which gave the impression that the firm and Mrs A would agree a contingency fee basis for charging at a future date. The

OSS reduced XYZ & Co's bill to the amount that it would have been without the disputed 10 per cent contingency element. The firm was also ordered to pay £150 compensation for the anxiety caused to Mrs A.

Other information

The Law Society's guidelines on professional conduct advise that the client should be told the name and status of the person in the firm who will be dealing with the case on a day-to-day basis and the partner responsible for the overall supervision of the matter. There will be different charges for different personnel according to their status – partners will charge more than assistant solicitors, assistant solicitors may be more expensive than trainee solicitors and legal executives.

If the conduct or the overall supervision of the whole or part of the client's matter is transferred to another person in the firm, the client should be informed and the reasons for the change explained. The solicitor should also advise the client when it is appropriate to instruct counsel. When the client has to attend a hearing, he should be told the name of the solicitor or counsel who will be representing him.

Mr Pilbrow instructed P & Co solicitors to handle a dispute with his ex-wife. He telephoned the firm and asked for an appointment with a solicitor. Unbeknown to Mr Pilbrow, his case was actually handled by a clerk with no legal qualifications other than a law degree. When he subsequently discovered the mistake, Mr Pilbrow refused to pay the firm's bill. The court agreed that Mr Pilbrow was entitled to have his case dealt with by a solicitor, as he expected. The firm could not recover their charges from him.

Deposit

The solicitor may ask the client for a payment on account at the beginning of the matter to cover the expense of initial work done or to be done by the solicitor, or disbursements.

For non-contentious work the solicitors can only require the client to make a payment on account of disbursements. There is no right to require a payment on account of costs, unless the client agrees to this and the payment is made a condition of accepting instructions. In the absence of such an arrangement a solicitor cannot terminate the retainer if the client refuses to make the payment on account of costs.

In contentious matters the solicitor can require the client to make a payment on account of costs and disbursements. If the client fails to make the payment within a reasonable time the solicitor can terminate the retainer on reasonable notice.

The bill

The solicitor should deliver the bill to the client within a reasonable time of concluding the matter. There is no prescribed form of bill for non-contentious work but the bill should at least contain sufficient information to identify the matter and the period to which it relates. The Solicitors Act 1974 imposes additional requirements on solicitors:

- disbursements should be shown separately from solicitors' fees and it should be made clear whether disbursements are paid or unpaid, with credit given for payments received on account (section 67);
- the bill or any letter sent to the client with the bill must be signed by the solicitor or, if the costs are due to the firm, by one of the partners of the firm. Compliance with this rule is important. In the event that the client does not pay the bill, the solicitor will not be able to sue for his costs unless the signature provisions have been complied with. The firm's rubber stamp or a commonly used abbreviation of the firm's name will suffice. The signature of an assistant solicitor or legal executive will not, however, suffice.

For contentious work which is not the subject of a contentious business agreement, the bill may come in the form of a breakdown of charges into detailed items or simply state a gross sum payable by the client. If presented with a gross sum, the client is entitled to ask for a detailed bill within three months of delivery of the bill to him, provided the solicitor has not already started proceedings to sue for the bill. The solicitor must deliver a detailed bill to his client within a reasonable time.

Contentious and non-contentious work

All civil work done by a solicitor can be described as contentious or non-contentious. The distinction is important in this context because it affects the way that the client can complain about the bill.

Non-contentious (or non-court) work is any work that does not involve court proceedings in England and Wales or arbitration. It includes proceedings before all tribunals other than the Lands Tribunal and the Employment Appeals Tribunal. Examples of non-contentious work include the preparation of wills, the administration of estates and trusts out of court, conveyancing, drafting and negotiating contracts and planning and other public inquiries. Work done preliminary to proceedings (for example, advising a client) is non-contentious provided proceedings are not subsequently begun.

Contentious (or court) work is work where court proceedings are actually begun, including advice, preparation and negotiations where the proceedings are subsequently begun. Contentious work includes, for example, suing for a debt, defending a divorce, obtaining a divorce (where it is undefended) and applying for maintenance.

For non-court work, solicitors are constrained only by market forces in setting their charges. There are no fixed scales or rules about how much a solicitor can charge, subject to the proviso that fees must be fair and reasonable. What is a fair and reasonable fee will depend on all the circumstances of the case. The Solicitors' (Non-Contentious Business) Remuneration Order 1994 provides that the following factors are relevant:

- the complexity of the case;
- skill and specialist knowledge involved;
- time spent;
- number and importance of documents involved;
- place and circumstances in which the business is done;
- value of property or money involved;
- whether any land involved is registered (this applies to most land now);
- importance of the matter to the client;
- whether the solicitors' charges or the work done were approved.

Querying the bill

For non-court work only, the Law Society will check a solicitor's bill if the client thinks it is too high. The Law Society will issue a certificate, called a remuneration certificate, stating what it considers to be a fair and reasonable charge for the work. The remuneration certificate will either reduce or confirm the solicitor's bill – the charges will not be increased. The client will have to pay the amount stated in the remuneration certificate.

Obtaining a remuneration certificate

The solicitor should apply to the Law Society for a remuneration certificate at his client's request and deliver all relevant papers and documents to the Law Society to assist them in reviewing the bill. There is no charge by the Law Society and the solicitor cannot charge a fee for applying but the process is only available where:

- court proceedings have not been started;
- there has been no order for assessment of the bill through the courts (*see* below);
- the bill has not been paid;
- the bill is less than £50,000 (including VAT and disbursements).

There are strict time limits. The application must be made within one month of the solicitor notifying the client of his right to apply for a remuneration certificate or have the bill assessed by the court. The notice is usually printed on the bill in terms similar to the following.

Remuneration certificates

1 If you are not satisfied with the amount of our fee you have the right to ask us to obtain a remuneration certificate from the Law Society.
2 The certificate will either say that our fee is fair and reasonable, or it will substitute a lower fee.
3 If you wish us to obtain a certificate you must ask us to do so within a month of receiving this notice.
4 We may charge interest on unpaid bills and we will do so [at the rate payable on judgment debts, from one month after delivery of our bill].
5 If you ask us to obtain a remuneration certificate, then unless we already hold the money to cover these, you must first pay:
   ● half our fee shown in the bill;
   ● all the VAT shown in the bill;
   ● all the expenses we have incurred shown in the bill – sometimes called 'paid disbursements'.
   However, you may ask the Office for the Supervision of Solicitors at 8 Dormer Place, Leamington Spa, Warwickshire CV32 5AE to waive this requirement so that you do not have to pay anything for the time being. You would have to show that exceptional circumstances apply in your case.
6 Your rights are set out more fully in the Solicitors' (Non-Contentious Business) Remuneration Order 1994.

Detailed assessment

You may be entitled to have our charges reviewed by the court. (This is called a detailed assessment.) The procedure is different from the remuneration certificate procedure and it is set out in the Civil Procedure Rules.

If the solicitor has failed to notify the client of his right to ask for a remuneration certificate or apply for assessment, the time limit for applying is three months from the date of receipt of the bill by the client, where the solicitor has deducted his costs from money being held on account for the client.

Once the application has been made by the solicitor, the client can pay the bill in full without invalidating the application. It will be to the client's advantage to do this because:

● the solicitor is entitled to charge interest on the unpaid bill; and
● the solicitor can demand that the client pay 50 per cent of the charges plus VAT and disbursements anyway. The obligation to make this payment will only be waived by the Law Society in exceptional circumstances.

Interest will run from one month after the bill was delivered to the client. If the remuneration certificate is issued for less than the sum already paid, the client will be entitled to an immediate refund of the difference. Where the solicitor has applied for assessment by the court (*see* below), the right to a refund is suspended.

The client loses the right to require the solicitor to obtain a remuneration certificate:

● after the bill has been paid (other than by deduction from monies held by the solicitor on account);
● after one month has passed from the date when the bill has been delivered and the client has been notified of his rights;
● after the bill has been assessed by the court;
● where the client fails to make the required payment of 50 per cent of the costs plus VAT and disbursements or applied for a waiver of that requirement within one month of being notified of his rights;
● where the client fails to make the required payment within one month of written notification that he has been refused a waiver of that requirement.

Assessment by the court

This process, which used to go by the confusing title of 'taxation', applies to both non-contentious work and cases where court proceedings have started. A costs officer of the court will assess the bill and either approve it or reduce it. For non-contentious cases the client should apply to the High Court in London and, for contentious cases, the application should be made to the court that dealt with the case.

The application for assessment must be made within one month of receiving the bill. If the application is made later than that, the court is not obliged to assess the bill and if more than 12 months have passed it will be very unusual for a court to agree to assess the bill.

Unlike the remuneration certificate process, assessment is not free. If the bill is reduced by more than 20 per cent, the solicitor will normally have to pay the costs of assessment, but the client will still have to pay the reduced bill. If the bill is reduced by less than 20 per cent the client will have to pay the costs of assessment, as well as the reduced bill.

The right to a remuneration certificate and assessment by the court are not mutually exclusive. The client can seek an order for assessment after obtaining a remuneration certificate. However, once an assessment order has been made, any application for a remuneration certificate will be nullified.

Overcharging

If the costs officer reduces the bill for non-contentious work by more than 50 per cent the officer is under a duty to notify the Law Society. If the Law Society decides that the amount charged is unreasonable, it may take disciplinary action against the solicitor on the ground that the solicitor has taken unfair advantage of the client.

Paying someone else's costs

A client may be liable to pay the costs of another person's solicitor in non-contentious matters. For example, it is common for a lease to contain a clause requiring the lessee to pay the landlord's solicitor's costs relating to the grant of the lease.

It is also common for a lease to contain provisions requiring the tenant to obtain a licence (written permission) from his landlord before he can assign the lease, underlet, change the use of the premises or carry out alterations. The lease may oblige the tenant to pay the costs and disbursements of the landlord in relation to preparing the licence.

In these situations, the solicitor must put his client in the picture as to his potential liability. The solicitor will probably obtain an estimate of the potential costs at the outset and try to reduce the estimated bill during negotiations.

A client who has paid or is liable to pay another person's solicitor's bill (such as a tenant who must pay his landlord's legal costs) can apply for assessment of the bill by the court. Provided that the landlord gives his consent, the client will be entitled to seek a remuneration certificate.

Contentious work

Once court proceedings have been commenced the client exposes himself to the risk of paying not only his own solicitor's costs but also his opponent's costs. The solicitor should explain the risks of litigation at the outset of the case and at every stage during the progress of the case when costs will be relevant to the client's decision whether to continue or withdraw.

The main points to grasp are:
- the client will be responsible for paying the firm's bill in full regardless of any order for costs made against an opponent;
- the client may have to pay the opponent's costs as well as the client's own costs if the case is lost;
- even if the client wins, the opponent may not be ordered to pay or be capable of paying the full amount of the client's costs. Any shortfall must be met out of the client's pocket;
- if the opponent's case is publicly funded the client may not recover costs, even if successful.

Overview: what happens at the end of the case

At the end of the case, the court will decide:
- who should be liable for costs;
- the amount of costs that should be awarded;
- on what basis costs should be assessed.

The general rule is that the loser pays the winner's costs. The amount that the loser must pay towards the winner's costs is assessed by the court. There are two forms of assessment: summary assessment and detailed assessment. In some cases, the costs are fixed, so the loser will be ordered to pay a set amount towards the winner's solicitor's charges. The amount that is allowed depends on the value of the claim. In fast track cases, limits are placed on the sum recoverable in respect of costs at the trial.

Where the winner's case was publicly funded, the recoverable costs are fixed by the Legal Services Commission.

The client is ultimately responsible for ensuring that his own costs get paid. If there is any shortfall between what the loser is ordered to pay and the actual amount of the winner's solicitor's bill, the winner will have to make up the shortfall.

Conditional Fee Agreements

Whether he wins or loses the case, the client is ultimately responsible for making sure that his own legal costs get paid. The position under a conditional fee (or 'no win, no fee') agreement is slightly different. Under a Conditional Fee Agreement the client will not have to pay his own solicitor's fees if he loses (hence the title 'no win, no fee') but he will be responsible for his own disbursements as well as paying the winner's success fee and insurance premium. The client should take out after-the-event insurance to cover this risk (*see further* pages 798–9).

WHO SHOULD BE LIABLE FOR COSTS?

The court will decide liability for costs. The general rule is that the unsuccessful party will be ordered to pay the costs of the successful party, but the court has a wide discretion to make whatever order as to costs it thinks fit. For example, the court might decide to order a party to pay only a proportion of another party's costs or costs incurred from a certain date only or each party to pay their own costs.

In deciding what order to make about costs, the court will take into account all the circumstances. The conduct of the parties is an important factor. Behaving well and in line with the underlying ethos of the Civil Procedure Rules (CPR) will influence the court's decision on costs (*see further* Chapter 97). Behaving well means:

- co-operating with the opposing party;
- disclosing and exchanging information at an early stage;
- identifying the real issues in dispute and resolving other issues out of court;
- only using litigation as a last resort;
- keeping the expense of bringing or defending a claim in proportion to the issues at stake.

The court will also look at any payment into court or admissible offer to settle made by a party.

Payment of costs on account

Where the court has ordered a party to pay costs, it may order an amount to be paid on account before the costs are assessed. This is in line with the principle that a party who has been awarded costs by the court should be immediately compensated for all or part of his or her outgoings in relation to the proceedings. The payment should generally be made within 14 days of the order.

Interim costs orders

The court can make an order about costs at any stage in the case, and in particular it may make interim costs orders when it deals with interim applications. This means that the court may look at the costs of the interim application in isolation from the other costs of the case. Where the interim hearing is likely to last less than one day, the court may decide which party is entitled to the costs of the application there and then.

Under the old rules, parties would use interim applications as a tactical weapon to delay the progress of the case through the system and to increase financial pressure on their opponents by increasing the costs of the case. The CPR seek to address these problems by introducing a 'pay as you go' system for immediate assessment of interim costs. The idea is that parties will think twice before using interim applications to drive up the expense of the proceedings or as a stalling tactic and the number of frivolous applications will be reduced.

Offers to settle and payments into court under Part 36

The CPR encourage parties to settle their disputes by offering financial incentives for accepting reasonable offers rather than blithely pushing the case forward to trial. Under the CPR both the claimant and the defendant can make offers to settle, before proceedings have started and once proceedings have commenced, at any stage up to trial. The requirement to comply with pre-action protocols should put the parties in a position to make a well-informed decision about any offer before proceedings are commenced. The part of the CPR governing offers to settle and payments into court (Part 36) does

not apply to cases on the small claims track, that is, claims for less than £5,000.

There are costs consequences of unreasonably rejecting an offer to settle or payment into court or failing to do better than an offer to settle or payment into court at trial. The main points to note are:

- offers and payments-in under Part 36 must remain open for acceptance for 21 days;
- if an offer or payment-in is accepted, the claimant will be entitled to costs up to the date of serving notice of acceptance;
- if at trial the claimant fails to beat a Part 36 payment or a defendant's Part 36 offer, the claimant will be liable for costs after the period for which the offer or payment-in was open for acceptance;
- if the claimant does better than a Part 36 offer, he may be awarded additional costs and interest;
- where the claimant makes a Part 36 offer, if at trial the claimant does better than the offer, the court may penalize the defendant by ordering him to pay the claimant's costs on the indemnity basis (*see* page 780) and interest on those costs at up to 10 per cent above base rate. The court may also order interest on the whole or part of the money awarded to the claimant at up to 10 per cent above base rate for some or all of the period starting with the latest date at which the defendant could have accepted the offer without needing the permission of the court.

Wasted costs orders against solicitors

The court can order that a party's legal representative should be personally liable for 'wasted' costs (Rule 48.7 CPR). 'Wasted costs' means any cost incurred by a party as a result of any improper, unreasonable or negligent act or omission on the part of any legal or other representative or any employee of such a representative. It also covers the situation where costs are incurred by a party which, in the light of any such act or omission occurring after they were incurred, the court considers it unreasonable to expect that party to pay.

The court can order that a legal representative should either pay wasted costs or order that the costs of the legal representative should be disallowed in whole or in part. The court must give the legal representative a chance to attend a hearing to argue why the order should not be made.

An order for wasted costs will be made if the court considers that:

- the legal representative has acted improperly, unreasonably or negligently;
- his conduct has caused a party to incur unnecessary costs; and
- it is just in the circumstances to order him to compensate that party for the whole or part of those costs.

All of these points must be proved to the satisfaction

of the court. A party to the proceedings can apply for a wasted costs order against a legal representative or the court can make the order on its own initiative.

Misconduct

The court can also make a legal representative personally liable for costs under Rule 44.14 CPR where it considers that the legal representative's conduct before or during proceedings was unreasonable or improper. This costs order can also be made against a party. Again, this rule impresses on all participants in the litigation the consequences of failing to behave well and in keeping with the principles underlying the new procedural regime.

The court may disallow all or part of the costs which are being assessed or order the party at fault or his legal representative to pay costs which he has caused any other party to incur.

PROCEDURE FOR ASSESSING THE AMOUNT OF COSTS

The amount of costs to be awarded will be assessed by the court. There are two alternative procedures for deciding the amount of costs to be paid: by summary assessment or by detailed assessment. The court will decide which method is suitable, but the summary procedure will be the rule rather than the exception.

Summary assessment

Under the summary assessment procedure, the court decides the amount of costs to be paid there and then, usually on a rough-and-ready basis. The method is used for interim applications, where the hearing has lasted less than one day. The court will deal with the costs of the interim application on a pay as you go basis. It is also the procedure for assessing costs at the conclusion of trials in the fast track, when the court will deal with the costs of the entire claim.

The party claiming entitlement to costs must provide the court and the paying party with a written statement of costs at least 24 hours before the relevant hearing. Failure to meet this deadline will be taken into account by the court in deciding what order to make about the costs of the claim, hearing or application. The court will assess costs and specify a global sum, inclusive of VAT, which is payable within 14 days of the order, unless the court extends the time for payment.

Detailed assessment

Under the detailed assessment procedure, costs are assessed by a costs officer at the conclusion of proceedings. This procedure is used for multi-track cases and interim applications lasting more than one day. Costs payable by a child or patient to his solicitor should also be assessed on this basis.

The receiving party should commence detailed assessment proceedings within three months of termination of proceedings by serving a notice of commencement and a copy of the bill of costs on the paying party and any other parties. Following assessment a final costs certificate will be issued and costs are payable within 14 days of the date of the certificate.

A client may apply to have his own solicitor's costs assessed in this way if he wishes to challenge the bill (*see* above under 'Assessment by the court').

Summary of Differences

Summary assessment	Detailed assessment
Costs assessed by the court there and then	Costs assessed by a costs officer at the conclusion of proceedings
Suitable for: • fast track trials; • short interim applications; • where paying party is a child or patient; • where paying party is an assisted person under Legal Aid Act 1988.	Suitable for: • multi-track claims; • interim applications lasting more than one day; • where receiving party is a child or patient; • where receiving party is an assisted person under Legal Aid Act 1988.

NB: *The* paying party *is the party liable to pay costs. The* receiving party *is the party entitled to be paid costs.*

THE BASIS OF QUANTIFICATION

Costs will be assessed either on the standard basis or on the indemnity basis. In either case, the court will not allow costs that have been unreasonably incurred or are unreasonable in amount.

The standard basis

The usual rule in contentious litigation is that costs are payable on the standard basis. Where the amount of costs is to be assessed on the standard basis the court will allow costs that are proportionate to the matters in issue. Any doubt which the court may have as to whether costs were reasonably incurred or were reasonable and proportionate in amount will be resolved in favour of the paying party.

The indemnity basis

Where the amount of costs is to be assessed on the indemnity basis, the court will resolve any doubt which it may have as to whether costs were reasonably incurred or were reasonable in amount in favour of the receiving party. This is a more generous basis of assessment than the standard basis.

Assessments between solicitor and own client are dealt with on the indemnity basis. So where a client challenges his solicitor's bill, the bill will be assessed under the detailed assessment procedure on the indemnity basis. However, the court will apply the following presumptions as to the reasonableness of the costs:

1. that costs were reasonably incurred if they were incurred with the express or implied approval of the client;
2. that costs were reasonable in amount if the amount was expressly or impliedly approved by the client; and
3. that costs were unreasonably incurred if they are unusual in nature or amount and the solicitor did not tell the client that for that reason they might not be recoverable from the other side.

Standard basis	Indemnity basis
Benefit of the doubt as to reasonableness of costs given to:	
the party liable to pay costs	the party entitled to be paid costs

Factors which the court must take into account in deciding whether costs were reasonable or unreasonable:

- the conduct of the parties, including in particular – conduct before as well as during the proceedings and the efforts made, if any, before and during the proceedings in order to try and resolve the dispute;
- the amount or value of any money or property involved;
- the importance of the matter to all the parties;
- the particular complexity of the matter or the difficulty or novelty of the questions raised;
- the skill, effort, specialized knowledge and responsibility involved;
- the time spent on the case; and
- the place where and the circumstances in which the work or any part of it was done.

Small claims

The only costs that are recoverable in small claims (that is, most cases where the financial value of the claim does not exceed £5,000 and personal injury claims where damages are not more than £1,000) are:

- the court fees that have been paid by the successful party; and
- a fixed sum to cover the claimant's solicitor's costs of issuing the proceedings; and
- limited witness expenses and experts' fees.

Fixed costs

Under the Civil Procedure Rules, certain legal costs that can be claimed from the losing party are limited or 'fixed'. The fixed costs that can be claimed on issue of the claim, on entry of judgment and on enforcement depend on the value of claim.

For fast track cases (that is, straightforward cases where the value of the claim is between £5,000 and £15,000), the costs of a solicitor advocate or barrister preparing for and appearing at the trial are fixed. The amount that will be awarded to the successful party by the court is linked to the value of the claim.

Fast-track trial costs

Value of claim	Costs recoverable from losing party
Not exceeding £3,000	£350
Between £3,001 and £10,000	£500
Exceeding £10,000	£750

These are the costs that *must* be awarded to the successful party in respect of the trial, unless the court decides to award nothing or:

- it was also necessary for the successful party's solicitor to attend the trial, in which case the court can award an additional £250; or
- the court considers it necessary to direct a separate trial of an issue, in which case it may award an additional amount not exceeding two-thirds of the amount payable for the claim, subject to a minimum of £350; or
- the court decides to reduce the award because the successful party has behaved unreasonably or improperly during the trial; or
- the court decides to increase the award because the party due to pay costs has behaved improperly during the trial.

Litigants in person (people who represent themselves in court) will be entitled to two-thirds of the amount in the table above if they can prove financial loss; otherwise they are entitled to £9.25 per hour reasonably spent doing the work.

Where fixed costs are awarded, there is likely to be a shortfall between the actual amount of the solicitor's bill and the amount that can be claimed under the fixed costs regime from the losing party. The receiving party will be responsible for making up the shortfall in his own solicitor's bill.

Note: The CPR apply to proceedings commenced after 26 April 1999. Where proceedings were issued before 26 April 1999, the CPR will apply to defended cases 'so far as practicable' (according to the Practice Direction to Part 51 of the CPR). Undefended cases will proceed to trial under the old procedural rules (those in force prior to 26 April 1999). In terms of costs, any assessment of costs which takes place after 26 April 1999 will be in accordance with the CPR. However, the cost of work undertaken before 26 April 1999 will not be disallowed if the cost would have been allowed on a taxation (the equivalent of assessment under the old rules) before 26 April.

Costs under the CPR – the new landscape

The problem of costs is the most serious problem besetting our litigation system.

So said Lord Woolf in June 1995. Lord Woolf was commissioned by the then Lord Chancellor, Lord Mackay of Clashfern, to review the rules and procedures of the civil courts of England and Wales. The fruits of the review were Lord Woolf's Interim Report in 1995, and then his Final Report into the civil justice system, published in July 1996. The reports identified the fundamental flaws in the old system: it was too expensive in that costs often exceeded the value of the claim; too slow in bringing cases to a conclusion and too unequal between the powerful, wealthy litigant and the under-resourced litigant; too uncertain in that it was difficult to forecast what litigation would cost and how long it would last and too incomprehensible to many litigants. Furthermore, the system was too fragmented in the way it was organized and too adversarial: cases were run by the parties, not by the courts, and the rules of court, all too often, were ignored by the parties and not enforced by the court.

In a nutshell, the system was too expensive and too slow. Lord Woolf recognized that procedural changes aimed at reducing costs and delay would be ineffectual until the culture of litigation – the attitudes of the parties, their legal advisers and the judges – also fundamentally altered. The new system, he proposed, should be based on principles of co-operation and openness between the parties, the use of litigation as a last resort, the emphasis on alternative dispute resolution and the use of pre-litigation protocols to encourage early exchange of information. The courts would ensure that parties adhered to the new ethos, with costs penalties for failure to comply.

The main recommendations of the report were adopted in the Civil Procedure Rules 1998 (CPR), which came into effect on 26 April 1999, and supplementary practice directions. Under the new system the court controls the timetable of cases and the costs. Under the old system, judges were back-seat drivers. The parties and their legal advisers controlled the pace and expense of cases. Now judges steer cases through the system under strict timetables. They will not let cases drag on and on, incurring unnecessary costs. Failure of the parties to meet a procedural deadline, failure to exchange information and generally cooperate before proceedings are commenced and failure to conduct the case in the spirit of the new rules will carry costs consequences.

Under the old system, there was very little communication between the parties before court proceedings commenced. That meant that it was difficult to identify the real issues in dispute and the parties tended not to investigate claims properly before proceedings were started. Under the new regime, parties cannot afford the luxury of issuing proceedings gratuitously. Pre-action protocols specify what is to be done before beginning proceedings and insist upon better and earlier exchange of information between the parties.

Suing on the bill

If a client does not pay the solicitor's bill for contentious or non-contentious work, the solicitor can start court proceedings to recover the debt. Generally speaking, the solicitor has to wait one month from delivery of the bill before bringing an action. The solicitor can seek the court's permission to issue proceedings within the month if the client is about to go bankrupt or leave the country.

There are also important rules about signing the bill that may affect whether the solicitor can sue on the bill (*see* page 775).

For non-contentious work where the bill is not more than £50,000, the solicitor must not sue or threaten to sue until he has given the client written notice of his right to require the solicitor to apply for a remuneration certificate from the Law Society and of the statutory provisions relating to assessment of the bill by the court. A statutory demand (a document threatening bankruptcy proceedings if the debt is not paid within a specified period) can be served prior to service of the notice on the client – but the solicitor will not be able to issue a bankruptcy petition without leave.

If the client makes an application to the court for the bill to be assessed within one month of delivery of the bill or obtains an order for the bill to be assessed, the solicitor cannot sue on the bill or proceed with an action until the assessment is complete.

For contentious work, there is no duty on the solicitor to inform the client of his right to apply for an assessment. The Solicitors Act 1974 section 61 provides that a solicitor may not bring an action on a contentious business agreement without the leave of the court. However, the Law Society has advised that there is no need to obtain the court's leave under section 61 before suing on a bill calculated in accordance with agreed rates.

Interest on unpaid bills

For non-contentious work, the solicitor can charge interest on the whole or any outstanding part of the unpaid bill, provided that the client has been given written notice of his rights to challenge the bill. Interest will run from one month after delivery of the bill. The interest rate will be either that rate agreed between the parties in their terms of business or the rate under Article 14 of the Solicitors' (Non-contentious Business) Remuneration Order 1994, i.e. the same rate as that payable on judgment debts.

For contentious work, the solicitor can charge interest if:

- the right to charge interest was expressly reserved in the original retainer agreement;
- the client later agreed to pay interest for a contractual consideration; or
- the solicitor has sued the client and claimed interest at the rate specified by the court rules.

The solicitor's lien

Once the solicitor has submitted his bill, he is entitled to a 'lien' over the client's property with regard to any unpaid costs, until payment has been made in full. In other words the solicitor can confiscate the client's property and hold it until the client pays the bill.

There are three ways in which the lien can be enforced against the client:

1 withhold the client's file or other property in the solicitor's possession – this is the most common form of lien;
2 where the solicitor has recovered property for the client in an action to which the bill relates, he can apply to the court for an order that the property can be retained as security for the solicitor's costs;
3 apply to the court for a charging order over the client's property as security for the solicitor's assessment costs.

Some types of property cannot be confiscated. For example, the solicitor cannot exercise the lien over the client's will, original court documents or property held by the solicitor as a trustee or mortgagee. A lien may not be exercised over property which comes into the possession of a firm, which then dissolves, and then comes into the possession of the new firm.

The solicitor cannot sell or otherwise dispose of the client's property and would be liable to the client for damages for its loss. The solicitor is not obliged to give the client copies of any documents subject to the lien, unless the court orders him to allow the client to inspect them.

The most common scenario where a solicitor may exercise a lien over the client's property is where the retainer between solicitor and client has been discharged in the middle of court proceedings and the client instructs new solicitors to act for him. Here the solicitor will have the upper hand because, if the client does not pay his fees, he can hold on to the client's file. The client will need the papers in the file in order to continue with his case. In this situation, can the client insist that the solicitor hand over the papers to the new solicitors? The answer depends on who discharged the retainer.

Where the client discharged the retainer, whether he had a good reason for doing so or not, the solicitor is under no obligation to hand over the papers. He can keep the papers until his costs are paid in full, subject to the client's right to have the costs assessed. Where the solicitor terminated the retainer, the solicitor should pass the papers to the client's new solicitors on the understanding that the new solicitors will hand them back to the first solicitor on the conclusion of the case or the termination of the new solicitor's retainer. If the client does not appoint new solicitors, but is representing himself in the proceedings, the court may order the documents to be deposited with the court.

Foreign lawyers' fees

The issue of who is responsible for paying a foreign lawyer's fees is the subject of various codes and agreements. The Council of the Law Society has approved the International Bar Association's International Code of Ethics, and the Council of Bars and Law Societies of the European Community Code of Conduct. There is a consensus between the codes that where a solicitor or barrister instructs a foreign lawyer to advise on a case or to cooperate in handling it, he is responsible for payment of the foreign lawyer's charges, except where there is express agreement between them to the contrary. When a solicitor or barrister recommends or introduces a client to a foreign colleague, he will not be responsible for the payment of the latter's charges, but neither will he be entitled to a share of the fee of the foreign colleague. The 1975 guidelines agreed by the Conference of Presidents of European Bar Associations also support this view. It cannot be assumed that this principle will be supported in all jurisdictions, however; in particular, it is not generally recognized in the United States.

When instructing a foreign lawyer it is important to clarify from the outset:

- whether the solicitor personally or the client will be responsible for the foreign lawyer's fees;
- how these fees will be calculated; and
- whether or not they are payable for abortive transactions or for instalments of work completed.

Complaints about fees should be referred to the foreign lawyer's own professional body (the foreign equivalent of the Law Society or Bar Council). Sources of advice on the cost of local professional services may be obtained from the British High Commission or Embassy.

When instructing English solicitors practising abroad, the Law Society will not be able to certify the fees in the event of a dispute unless the retainer is governed by English law.

Costs in criminal cases

In civil cases the general rule is that the loser pays the winner's costs. In criminal cases this rule cannot be applied rigidly. Often the convicted defendant will not be able to pay because he or she has no money or is going to prison.

The costs of the acquitted defendant

If the accused is acquitted the court can:

- award him/her no costs, so that they have to pay their own costs (unless they are publicly funded);
- order the prosecutor to pay their costs. If the prosecution is brought by the CPS, they will have to pay the costs; otherwise the body prosecuting (such as the Department of Works and Pensions, the local authority, Customs & Excise, etc) will have to pay;
- order that costs be paid from central funds (i.e. by the government).

The court has a considerable discretion in deciding which order to make. Magistrates' courts have tended to be reluctant to make costs orders. However, with legal aid becoming more difficult to obtain, there has been a shift of emphasis in favour of paying costs to an acquitted

defendant. Crown courts have always been more willing to award costs.

Whenever there has been an acquittal, the defendant should automatically ask his/her solicitor to apply for costs; the court will never award them unless asked to do so!

If a court orders a prosecutor to pay costs, it is sometimes taken as a sign of disapproval of the conduct of the prosecution. In the crown court the basic rule is that an acquitted defendant should receive his/her costs, from central funds. The court might make a different order if:

- the prosecution acted spitefully or brought the prosecution without reasonable cause. Then the costs would almost certainly be paid by the prosecutor and not out of central funds;
- the defendant brought suspicion on him or herself by their own conduct, misleading the prosecution into thinking it had a stronger case against him/her than it really did. Here it would be normal for a defendant to pay his/her own costs;
- the defendant was acquitted on a technicality, even though there was ample evidence to convict him/her. Again, the defendant would normally have to pay his/her own costs.

If defendants have public funding, they can still have their costs paid by the prosecution or out of central funds, but the amount of costs will be no more than could be obtained from public funding. The amount of the costs recoverable can also include work done from the time of arrest, witness expenses and the accused's own expenses, but loss of wages cannot be claimed.

The costs of the successful prosecutor

If the defendant is convicted then the court can order, in respect of the prosecution's costs:

- that no order is made – the prosecution bears its own cost; or
- that the costs are paid by the defendant: except in substantial trials (with rich defendants!) this will generally mean the defendant paying a fixed contribution towards the prosecution costs; or
- that costs be paid out of central funds.

100

Public Funding and Help with Legal Costs

Obtaining legal advice and representation from a solicitor is an expensive business. Fees will vary with the type of work involved, the size of the firm and the seniority of the solicitor instructed within a particular firm. Solicitors tend to charge for their work by the hour and charges can range from about £100 an hour at a typical high street firm to as much as £500 an hour for a top partner in the City. This chapter explores the range of available options for help with legal costs.

There is a system of public funding of cases, mainly for people on a low income with few savings. However, there is, as they say, no such thing as a free lunch. Even if he qualifies for a level of public funding under the means test that is applied, the client may still be required to make a contribution to costs out of his own pocket throughout the progress of the case. Also, the funding is a loan, not a gift. What should be made clear from the start, by the solicitor advising the client under this sort of arrangement, is that if he wins the case, he may have to pay back the public funding out of his winnings. More about this 'sting in the tail' later.

PUBLIC FUNDING

People on a low or modest income, with little or no capital, may apply to have their solicitor's bill (or 'costs') paid for them from the public purse. The worthy principle supporting this provision of public money is that people who cannot afford to pay a solicitor to help them with a legitimate legal grievance should not be denied professional legal advice and representation.

Public funding used to be called legal aid. The old legal aid system was swept away by the Access to Justice Act 1999 and replaced with a scheme based on new structures and priorities.

The main changes under the new system are:
- a new Legal Services Commission – a non-departmental public body – administers the Community

Legal Service, the Community Legal Service Fund and the Criminal Defence Service;
- the Community Legal Service – a major reorganization of legal advice providers into local networks via which the public can gain easier access to quality-assured legal advice and information;
- the Community Legal Service Fund funds civil cases and replaces civil legal aid;
- the Criminal Defence Service funds criminal cases and replaces criminal legal aid;
- since April 2001, only solicitors' firms who have been awarded a contract by the Legal Services Commission may deliver publicly funded legal services for civil and family cases;
- the removal of public funding for most personal injury cases. To fill the gap left by the withdrawal of funding for these cases, the government has heavily promoted the use of conditional fee ('no win, no fee') agreements (*see* below);
- the old merits test has been replaced with a new Funding Code. The Funding Code sets out the criteria for deciding whether cases should receive public funding.

The old system	The new system
The Legal Aid Board	The Legal Services Commission
Uncoordinated CABs, law centres, solicitors and other advice providers	The Community Legal Service
Civil and family legal aid	The Community Legal Service Fund
Criminal legal aid	The Criminal Defence Service
Advice and assistance (the Green Form scheme)	Legal help
Civil legal aid and ABWOR (assistance by way of representation)	Legal representation

THE LEGAL SERVICES COMMISSION

The Legal Services Commission (LSC) is a non-departmental public body, with a wider remit than the old Legal Aid Board that it replaced on 1 April 2000. It is responsible for establishing and maintaining the Community Legal Service, which provides the framework for local networks of legal and advice services, supported by local partnerships of funders and service providers. The Commission manages the Community Legal Service Fund and the Criminal Defence Service and contracts with solicitors who meet certain standards of service to provide publicly funded legal services under those schemes.

Under the old civil legal aid scheme, any solicitor could do publicly funded work for a client. The new contracting arrangements have reduced the number of solicitors who may handle publicly funded work from some 11,000 to 5,500. Since April 2001, only solicitors who have contracts with the Commission are able to do publicly funded work under the civil scheme. You should look for the CLS logo.

THE COMMUNITY LEGAL SERVICE

The aim of the Community Legal Service (CLS), the jewel in the crown of the government's reforms, is to make it easier for people to find good quality legal help and advice.

To improve the accessibility of legal information and advice at grassroots level, legal advice providers, such as solicitors, law centres and citizens' advice bureaux, have been reorganized into local networks. To assure the public of the quality of the service, advice providers who meet the standards of service set by the LSC have been awarded a Quality Mark.

At the heart of the local networks, Community Legal Service Partnerships bring together funders of legal services (including the LSC, local authorities and charities) and advice providers. The Partnerships will assess the local need for legal services, target funding at the areas of greatest need and set up local referral networks to ensure that people are referred to a quality-marked provider who can offer them the service they need. The government aims to have Partnerships operating in 90 per cent of areas by April 2002.

The CLS is backed up by a directory and website. The directory lists advice providers in each local area to enable people to find places where they can get relevant help and information. The directory can be accessed by telephoning 0845 608 1122 or 0845 609 6677 for the hearing impaired. The CLS website, at www.justask.org.uk, includes an electronic version of the CLS directory and a search engine which allows people to key in their legal problem and search 400 sites for relevant information. It

The old 'picnic' logo is now defunct.

Community Legal Service

This is the new logo for civil cases.

Criminal Defence Service

This is the Criminal Defence Service logo.

features information in six community languages (Bengali, Cantonese, Gujarati, Hindi, Punjabi and Urdu).

Some CLS members offer some or all of their services free but other groups will continue to charge for their work. Public money from the CLS Fund may be available depending on the kind of case and the financial position of the applicant.

THE COMMUNITY LEGAL SERVICE FUND

Public funding for civil cases is available from the Community Legal Service Fund, which replaces civil legal aid. 'Civil' cases concern matters not dealt with under the criminal law, such as divorce, debt, welfare benefits or eviction. Since April 2001, only solicitors who have contracted with the LSC are able to take on CLS-funded cases.

The Community Legal Service funding has been withdrawn from most personal injury claims. Instead, accident victims who cannot afford to pay privately for legal help will have to find a solicitor who is able to take their case under a conditional fee agreement (*see* below). CLS Funding is still available for clinical negligence claims – where, for example, a patient's condition has been misdiagnosed by a doctor or an operation has gone badly wrong.

The table below sets out the categories of case where

funding will generally be made available. Funding will not be made available for certain categories of cases, such as conveyancing, the making of wills and matters of trust law, because they are not considered to have sufficient priority to justify funding.

Type of problem	Is CLS funding available?
Personal injury caused by negligence – e.g. person injured in car crash, at work, in slipping or tripping accident	No – except for exceptionally expensive claims and those with a significant wider public interest
Clinical negligence	Yes – must instruct specialist solicitor under contract with the LSC
Conveyancing	No – unless related to other court proceedings where an order was made
Housing – e.g. rent or mortgage arrears, repairs, eviction	Yes
Matters of company or partnership law or matters connected with running a business	No – unless related to a family dispute or family proceedings
Cases brought or defended by sole traders in the course of their business or after the business has ceased to trade	No – except for cases brought by or against sole traders in a non-business capacity, e.g. personal insolvency proceedings
Matters of trust law	No – unless related to a family dispute or family proceedings
Making of wills	No – except for people aged 70 years or over, disabled persons, or a parent of a disabled person who wishes to provide for that person in a will, or a parent of a minor who wishes to appoint a guardian for that minor in a will
Defamation or malicious falsehood	No
Employment	Yes – the preparation of a case before the Employment Tribunal but not representation at the Employment Tribunal itself
Family and children	Yes
Divorce	Yes
Mental health	Yes
Credit, debt, buying goods	Yes
Welfare benefits	Yes
Immigration, nationality or asylum	Yes
Challenging decisions of public bodies like the Benefits Agency or the Home Office	Yes
Care in the community provided by a social services or health care authority	Yes
Actions against the police	Yes

Only individuals may apply for CLS funding. Firms, partnerships, companies and other corporate bodies are not eligible. Unlike the Legal Aid Act 1988, the Access to Justice Act 1999 contains no provision for funding to be granted to companies on the grounds that they are acting in a representative, official or fiduciary capacity. If the proposed client is a company, funding will be refused.

A one-man company has a contract dispute with another person and wishes to bring proceedings alleging breach of contract. No funding will be provided. The primary test is who will be a party to the proceedings, not who will benefit from the outcome of the proceedings. In this case the cause of action would belong to the company, not the owner, even though the case would be as important to the owner of the company as if the proceedings had been brought in his own name.

There are different levels of help for which CLS funding is provided in civil matters and each level has its own legal definition, criteria and procedures:

Level of service	Type of help
Legal help	Initial advice and assistance with any legal problem
Help at court	Allows a solicitor or adviser to speak on the client's behalf at certain court hearings, without formally acting for them in the whole proceedings

Level of service	Type of help
Legal representation	Representation by a solicitor or other adviser in legal proceedings. Available in two forms: investigative help (funding is limited to investigation of the strength of a claim) or full representation (funding is provided to represent a client in legal proceedings)
Emergency legal representation	Legal representation provided on an emergency basis
Support funding	Partial funding of very expensive cases which are otherwise funded privately, under a conditional fee agreement
Family mediation	Mediation for a family dispute
Approved family help	Advice and assistance in relation to a family dispute. Available in two forms: help with mediation (legal advice and assistance for clients attending family mediation) or general family help (legal advice and assistance on family matters where the client is not attending family mediation)

At all levels, whether an application for funding will be accepted depends on:

1 whether the applicant's *income and capital* are below certain thresholds; and

2 whether the case satisfies certain *criteria*.

The merits test for civil cases under the old legal aid scheme has been replaced with rigorous new criteria designed to target taxpayers' money on the strongest cases and priority areas. Broadly speaking, the criteria to be taken into account in most cases are the chances of the case succeeding at trial, the likely damages and the likely costs. Different criteria apply to different cases.

Where a case has been deemed to be of high priority, for example where a roof over someone's head is at stake, or the welfare of a child, there will be less stringent success criteria.

High-priority cases

- Child protection;
- where the client is at risk of loss of life or liberty;
- domestic violence;
- welfare of children;
- allegations of serious wrongdoing or breaches of human rights by public bodies;
- housing proceedings;
- advice about employment rights, social security entitlements and debt.

PAYING BACK THE LSC

If the publicly funded ('assisted') client loses his case, the LSC will pay his solicitor's bill. The court will not order an assisted client to pay his opponent's costs (the other side's solicitor's bill) unless the opponent can show that the client can afford to pay. The assisted client may also have to pay compensation or transfer property to his opponent, if that was at stake in the dispute.

If you lose

You may have to pay:

- the other side's solicitor's bill, to the limit of your means; plus
- compensation/property to the other side.

If you win

If the assisted client wins the case, the court may order his opponent to pay the client's costs. If the opponent is also assisted (i.e. financed his case with public funding), the court will only order him to pay what he can afford. This will leave the client's solicitor with a shortfall. Equally, if the opponent is ordered to pay all of the client's costs, but fails to pay in full, the client's solicitor is left with a shortfall. For example, the loser may fail to pay because he goes bankrupt or disappears. In these circumstances, any money or property recovered by the client in the proceedings, or as a result of a settlement or compromise of the dispute, will be put towards paying the shortfall in the solicitor's bill. This deduction is called the statutory charge.

The statutory charge

You may have to pay any shortfall in your solicitor's bill from money or property you recovered in the proceedings.

The amount of the statutory charge will be:

- the amount of money the LSC has spent on *funding* services at all levels in connection with the dispute;
- less any *costs* recovered by the client in the proceedings or dispute;
- less any *contribution* the client has been required to make towards costs out of his own pocket during the progress of the case.

Once the solicitor's charges have been fully satisfied, the client will receive the remainder of the money or property awarded in the proceedings. The client's solicitor, or other legal service provider, should explain from the start of the case how the statutory charge works and whether it may apply.

When is money or property recovered or preserved?

The statutory charge applies to money or property 'recovered or preserved' by the assisted person in any proceedings in connection with which the services were funded by the LSC. It also applies where the dispute was settled or compromised by the parties. A claimant or applicant 'recovers' property or money if it is the subject of a successful claim. Money or property is 'preserved' by a defendant or respondent if a claim fails.

The statutory charge can also attach to money or property awarded to a dependent child or a creditor of the assisted person, where the award is for the benefit of the client.

Mrs Williams brings divorce proceedings against her husband. She receives funding from the LSC for legal representation. The court orders that the family home should be transferred to the couple's children. Mrs Williams will continue to live with the children in the family home. The statutory charge will apply to the family home because Mrs Williams will benefit from the transfer to the children.

If the client is seeking public funding for a dispute involving a small amount of money or property of low value, it may not be worthwhile pursuing the claim when the operation of the statutory charge is taken into account.

Mrs Jones's solicitor recovers £550 for her under the legal help scheme. At the end of the case, the solicitor's bill is £500. The operation of the statutory charge means that Mrs Jones will receive only £50. £500 of the money she gained as a result of the proceedings is applied by the LSC to paying the solicitor's bill.

The following table summarizes under which levels of service the statutory charge may arise.

Level of service	Does the statutory charge arise?
Legal help	Yes – only in family, personal injury and clinical negligence cases
Help at court	Yes – only in family, personal injury and clinical negligence cases
Family mediation	No
Approved family help: help with mediation	No
Approved family help: general family help	Yes
Legal representation	Yes
Support funding	Yes

The purpose of the statutory charge is threefold: to ensure that people pay towards the cost of their cases as far as they are able, to encourage people to act reasonably and not to incur excessive legal costs and to put the person whose legal costs are publicly funded in a similar position to a privately paying client.

Essentially, the statutory charge represents public money that must be recouped. Solicitors and other suppliers of legal services are responsible for ensuring that the system works properly. The solicitor is under a duty to report to the regional office of the LSC straight away when the client recovers or preserves property. Any money or property recovered in the dispute or proceedings for which the client had publicly funded services must be paid direct to the client's solicitor, not to the client. Where the client is no longer instructing a solicitor, the money or property must be paid directly to the LSC. Exempt money (*see* below) can be passed on to the client.

Certain items are exempt from the statutory charge. The statutory charge does not apply if the money or property recovered or gained consists of:

- maintenance payments; or
- payments up to £3,000 in a matrimonial property settlement; or
- most state benefits; or
- 50 per cent of any redundancy payment; or
- any money received as a result of an order made by an Employment Appeal Tribunal.

Mrs Smith and her two children have been abandoned by her husband. Her solicitor advises her under the legal help scheme and as a result she successfully claims income support and obtains a maintenance order against her husband from the magistrates' court. Her total income as a result is £150 per week. The solicitor's fee is £100. The fee will not come out of her income support or her maintenance as both are exempt from the statutory charge. The solicitor's fee is paid in full by the LSC.

Waiving the charge

In family, personal injury or clinical negligence cases where legal help or help at court was provided, the statutory charge can be waived in part or full if enforcement:

- would cause *grave hardship* or *distress*; or
- would be *unreasonably difficult* because of the nature of the property.

If the property recovered or preserved is an essential item, such as a cooker, refrigerator or furniture, the LSC will waive the operation of the charge. If the property is a luxury item, such as jewellery, a video or television, it is unlikely that the LSC will consider that depriving the client of that item would cause grave hardship. If the client is on a low income, or income support, the LSC will usually give authority to waive the charge if the client has suffered a financial loss and the compensation recovered is to remedy that loss, but not if the compensation has an element of profit.

If the item is of genuine sentimental value, for example a wedding ring, the LSC is likely to waive the operation of the charge on the grounds of grave distress. The LSC will waive the charge where there is a real difficulty in enforcement, as opposed to inconvenience or delay, for example where the property is outside the jurisdiction.

There is also a very limited exception, where the charge may be waived, in legal representation cases (*see* page 790).

Postponing the charge

In some circumstances the charge does not have to be paid immediately. The LSC will postpone enforcement of the charge if the property subject to the charge is the home of the client or their family or, in a family case, money to be used to buy a home for the client or their family. (*See also* page 61.) The LSC will register the charge at the Land Registry (like a mortgage) or, if the home has not yet been bought, they will register the charge after the property has been bought. The LSC will only allow this if it is satisfied that the home will provide appropriate security for the charge. The charge will not be enforced until the home is sold.

The LSC will charge interest until the house is sold and they recover their money. From 1 April 2002, the rate of interest has been 5 per cent. It may go up or down each April. Unlike under the old legal aid regulations, the client's liability to pay interest does not depend on them having signed a form agreeing to do so. Interest will start to run from when the charge is registered on the lesser of either:

1 the amount owed under the charge; or
2 the value of the property at the time of recovery.

If a flat or house with low or negative equity is recovered or preserved, the client will not be charged interest on the full value of the charge. Instead, interest will accrue on 'such lower sum as the Commission considers equitable in the circumstances', under the Community Legal Service (Financial) Regulations 2000. If and when the property recovers in value, the LSC will be able to get back the value of the charge (i.e. the full amount owed), not just the value of the property at any previous point in time.

Solicitors and other suppliers of legal services need to prepare their clients for this by explaining not only that:

- the charge will arise on property they win or keep in the case; but
- they may well come out of the proceedings with a registered charge on their home; and
- that charge will attract interest.

LEGAL HELP

Legal help allows people to get free initial legal advice and assistance from a solicitor or other organization. This level of service was previously carried out under the Green Form scheme.

The scheme covers two hours' worth of work by a solicitor (three hours in cases of divorce or judicial separation), up to a financial limit of £500. Once the solicitor's charges reach a total of £500, the solicitor must apply to the LSC for an extension of time to finish the work under the scheme. The sort of help that tends to fall within the scheme includes general advice on any legal problems, writing letters, negotiating, getting a barrister's opinion and preparing a written case for a court or tribunal. The costs of mediation may be covered.

It does not cover:

- formally starting or conducting court proceedings;
- being represented by a solicitor in court or at a tribunal.

Where a child under the age of 16 years requires legal help, a parent or guardian should apply on his behalf. The parents' or guardian's means will usually be taken into account in assessing the financial eligibility of the child.

In order to succeed in an application for legal help, the applicant must be able to show that their capital and income are within the financial limits and that the case satisfies certain criteria.

The financial conditions

The applicant will be eligible for legal help under the financial conditions of the scheme provided that his 'disposable capital' is not more than £3,000 and his 'disposable income' is not more than £621 per month.

If the applicant is married or living with someone else as a couple, the partner's capital and income will usually be taken into account for the purposes of the financial assessment. This will not be the case where the couple live apart because the relationship is over or the legal matter concerns a 'conflict of interest' with the partner or spouse (for instance where the applicant wants legal advice about a divorce).

DISPOSABLE CAPITAL

A person will be eligible for legal help if his capital does not exceed £3,000.

In making the calculation, all savings (e.g. cash, investments, money in a bank or the National Savings Bank) and anything of substantial value (such as jewellery or antiques) are included.

The following are not included:
- the house the client lives in (but any value over £100,000, after allowing a maximum of £100,000 for any mortgage, must be included);
- all household furniture and effects, clothing and tools of the trade;
- the object on which advice is being sought. For instance, if the applicant is in dispute about who owns an antique ornament, the value of the ornament is not included;
- back to work bonus under the Jobseekers Act 1995 section 26;
- payments under the Community Care (Direct Payments) Act 1996.

The disposable capital is the sum that is left after making all the allowable deductions. If the sum exceeds £3,000 the applicant will be above the limit and funding for legal help will not be made available.

DISPOSABLE INCOME

If the actual gross income in the past month of you and your partner exceeds £2,288 you will not be eligible. A higher limit applies if you have more than four dependent children in your family for whom you receive child benefit. If your gross income is £2,288 or less, your solicitor will then calculate your disposable income. If disposable income is more than £621 per month, the applicant will not qualify for legal help.

Applicants in receipt of income support or income-based Jobseeker's Allowance will be automatically eligible for legal help, provided that their disposable capital is less than £3,000.

The calculation of disposable income is based on the applicant's actual income plus their partner's income less:
- income tax and national insurance contributions;
- £45 for client and/or partner in receipt of salary or wage;
- child care expenses incurred because of employment;

- housing costs;
- £135.14 per month for a dependent adult relative;
- allowances for dependent children: £167.29 per month;
  The following payments do not count as income:
- Disability Living Allowance;
- Attendance Allowance;
- Constant Attendance Allowance;
- Council Tax Benefit;
- Housing Benefit;
- payments made under the Earnings Top-up scheme;
- payments made under the Community Care Direct Payment scheme.

The applicant will not be required to pay any contribution to the cost of the case out of his income or capital.

Criteria for legal help

In addition to the income and capital tests, the applicant's case must satisfy the criteria for legal help. Help will only be provided where there is sufficient benefit to the client to justify work or further work being carried out and it is reasonable for the matter to be funded.

HELP AT COURT

Like legal help, help at court does not cover the issue and conduct of court proceedings. Only informal advocacy can be provided, provided that advocacy is appropriate and will be of real benefit to the client and it is not more appropriate for help to be provided through legal representation. The income and capital limits are identical to those for legal help.

LEGAL HELP AND HELP AT COURT: WHEN THE CASE IS OVER

In family, clinical negligence and personal injury cases where legal help or help at court has been provided, the client may have to pay back the cost of funding to the LSC. This deduction is called the statutory charge (discussed above). The statutory charge may be waived in part or in full if enforcement would cause grave hardship or distress or would be unreasonably difficult because of the nature of the property.

LEGAL REPRESENTATION

This is the same level of service previously provided by ABWOR and civil legal aid. It covers all the work leading up to and including representation by a solicitor or barrister in civil court proceedings and some tribunal proceedings.

Legal representation is available for cases in all civil courts, from the county court to the House of Lords and the family proceedings courts, but not the coroners court.

Funding is also provided for certain tribunal proceedings, including in the Employment Appeal Tribunal, the Mental Health Review Tribunal, Immigration Adjudicator and Immigration Appeal Tribunal.

Mr Brown has been dismissed from his job and wished to claim unfair dismissal in the Employment Tribunal. As his case qualifies for funding under the legal help scheme, a solicitor will do all the necessary work involved in preparing the case for the Employment Tribunal hearing. The funding will not cover the solicitor representing Mr Brown at the Employment Tribunal itself. Mr Brown will need to apply for legal representation to cover this.

Funding at this level is only available for actual or contemplated proceedings before the courts or tribunals. Where funding is sought by a defendant or other party to proceedings, the proceedings must actually have started.

Legal representation does not include the provision of mediation or arbitration. However, help may be given at this level in relation to mediation or arbitration, and the payment of a mediator's or arbitrator's fees may be covered as an allowable expense.

There are two forms of legal representation.

Investigative help

Investigative help enables the applicant's solicitor to investigate the strength of a claim where the prospects of success are unclear. Only a minority of cases will go through the investigative help stage. Investigative help includes the issue and the conduct of proceedings only so far as necessary to obtain disclosure of relevant information or to protect the client's position in relation to any urgent hearing or time limit for the issue of proceedings.

Full representation

Full representation enables the applicant's solicitor to do all the work needed to take legal proceedings to trial and beyond.

Investigative help is not available for family cases. There is a separate level of service for this type of work in family cases, called general family help (*see* page 795).

For personal injury, clinical negligence, immigration, family and mental health review tribunal matters, legal representation is only available from solicitors who have contracted with the LSC to undertake work in those specific categories. Applicants should look for the Community Legal Service logo. For other cases, any solicitor with a contract to carry out CLS work may take up the case.

To qualify for legal representation applicants must qualify financially and the case must meet the criteria applicable to the type of case and the level of service.

Financial tests

There are different financial qualifications for different cases.

Type of case	Financial test
Immigration adjudication matter	Same test as for legal help
Immigration appeal tribunal matter	Same test as for legal help
Mental health review tribunal matter	No financial test
Certain family cases in the magistrates' court	Same test as for family mediation (and may have to pay contribution from income)
Other cases	*See* below

For all other cases, financial eligibility is based on an assessment of the applicant's disposable income and disposable capital. Applicants in receipt of income support or income-based Jobseeker's Allowance will qualify for funding automatically without having to pay a contribution.

If your gross monthly income exceeds £2,288, you will not be eligible for funding. A higher limit applies if there are more than four children in your family for whom you receive child benefit. If your gross monthly income is £2,288 or less, your solicitor will then assess your disposable income. If disposable income is £707 or less, you will qualify on income.

CONTRIBUTION FROM INCOME

In some cases, applicants will be required to pay a contribution towards the cost of their case, even if their disposable income is within acceptable limits.

If you are eligible for legal representation before the immigration adjudicator or immigration appeal tribunal, no contributions are payable from either income or capital.

For all other types of legal representation, if your disposable income is £267 per month or less you will pay no contribution. If it is between £268 and £707 per month inclusive, you will have to pay towards the cost of your case from income.

Contributions from income are paid on an ongoing basis. The monthly contribution will be assessed in accordance with the following table:

Band	Monthly disposable income	Monthly contribution
A	£268–£393	¼ of income in excess of £267
B	£394–£522	£32.50 plus ⅓ of income in excess of £393
C	£523–£707	£75.50 plus ½ of income in excess of £522

So, for example, if disposable income is £303 per month, the contribution will be in Band A. The excess income is £40 and therefore the monthly contribution will be £10 per month.

The first contribution must be paid when you accept your offer of funding, with further contributions every month after that for as long as your case is being funded by the LSC. Contributions may be waived where the contributions already paid are more than the likely total costs of the proceedings.

DISPOSABLE CAPITAL

Applicants must show that their 'disposable capital' is within financial limits in order to qualify for legal representation. Your disposable capital will be assessed in the same way as for legal help (*see* page 789). To qualify for legal representation before the immigration adjudicator or immigration appeal tribunal, you must not have more than £3,000 in capital. If disposable capital is £8,000 or less, you will qualify for all other types of legal representation.

With the exception of legal representation before the immigration adjudicator or immigration appeal tribunal, if your disposable capital is more than these limits you may still be offered funding if your case is likely to be expensive.

CONTRIBUTION FROM CAPITAL

In some cases, even if the applicant is eligible for funding, he will be required to pay a contribution towards the cost of the case from capital.

There are different rules for different types of case.

Type of case	Is a contribution from capital payable?
Immigration adjudication or immigration appeal tribunal matter	No
Some family cases in the magistrates' court	No
Other types of case	*See* below

For all other cases, the applicant will not be required to contribute towards the cost of the case if the disposable capital is £3,000 or less.

The applicant will not be required to make a contribution if he is in receipt of income support or income-based Jobseeker's Allowance.

If the disposable capital is over £3,000, the applicant will be asked to pay all his disposable capital over £3,000.

Retired people

Special provisions apply to men and women over 60 years if their disposable income is less than £267 per month (excluding net income earned from capital). For them certain savings are disregarded, even though their total savings may be over the normal capital limit.

Monthly disposable income (excluding net income derived from capital) £	Amount of capital disregarded £
Up to 25	100,000
26–50	90,000
51–75	80,000
76–100	70,000
101–125	60,000
126–150	50,000
151–175	40,000
176–200	30,000
201–225	20,000
226–250	10,000

(These capital disregards for pensioners do not apply to legal representation before the immigration adjudicator or Immigration Appeal Tribunal and to legal representation for a limited range of family cases in the magistrates' court.)

Standard criteria

All applications for legal representation and support funding must satisfy certain standard criteria. Under the standard criteria an application may be refused if:

1 alternative funding is available to the client (through insurance or otherwise) or if there are other persons or bodies who can reasonably be expected to bring or fund the case. Alternative funding does not include funding by means of a conditional fee agreement;

2 there are complaint systems, ombudsman schemes or forms of alternative dispute resolution which should be tried before litigation is pursued;

3 the case has been or is likely to be allocated to the small claims track (where the value of the claim is under £5,000);

4 it appears premature or if it appears more appropriate for the client to be assisted by some other level of service, such as legal help or help at court;

5 it appears unreasonable to fund representation.

Criteria for full representation

For full representation, the case must also pass three further tests: the prospects of success, the cost–benefit test and CFAs.

The prospects of success

The prospects of success (i.e. the likelihood of the case succeeding before a judge or other tribunal) must generally be more than 50 per cent. Where the claim is primarily for damages (i.e. money), a successful outcome for a claimant would be obtaining judgment (a court order) for substantive damages or obtaining judgment for an amount greater than a payment into court. Where the applicant is a defendant to proceedings, a successful outcome would be the dismissal of the case or a substantial reduction in the size of the claim.

Where the prospects of success are poor (less than 50 per cent) or unclear (where further investigation is needed) the claim for funding is likely to fail. Where the prospects of success are borderline (where, because there are difficult disputes of fact, law or expert evidence, it is not possible to say the prospects of success are better than 50 per cent), funding will be refused unless the case has a significant wider public interest or is of overwhelming importance to the client.

The cost–benefit test

The cost–benefit test is whether what is to be gained from the proceedings justifies the likely costs (what it will cost to fund the case). There are different forms of cost–benefit test for different types of claims.

If the claim is primarily for damages (i.e. money) by the client and does not have a significant wider public interest, the cost–benefit test is:

- if the prospects of success are very good (80 per cent or more), likely damages must exceed likely costs;
- if the prospects of success are good (60–80 per cent), likely damages must exceed likely costs by a ratio of 2:1 (i.e. expected damages of at least two times the likely costs); however, for clinical negligence cases a ratio of only 1.5:1 is required;
- if the prospects of success are moderate (50–60 per cent), likely damages must exceed likely costs by a ratio of 4:1 (2:1 in clinical negligence cases).

If the claim is not primarily for damages (including any application by a defendant or a case which has overwhelming importance to the client) but does not have a significant wider public interest, the cost–benefit test is: would a reasonable privately paying client be prepared to litigate, having regard to the prospects of success and all other circumstances?

If the claim has a significant wider public interest, the test is a general one that the likely benefits of the proceedings must justify the likely costs. An example of a claim with a wider public interest is a test case which could establish liability for harm done by a dangerous product.

Conditional Fee Agreements

Full representation will be refused if the nature of the case is suitable for a CFA and the client is likely to avail himself of a CFA. (*See further page 798.*)

THE STATUTORY CHARGE

Any money or property that the client is awarded with the help of public funding will be used first to repay some or all of his legal costs to the LSC. This deduction is called the statutory charge (discussed in full above) and it applies where the other side in the dispute fails to pay the client's costs (i.e. his solicitor's bill) in full. The shortfall is met from any money or property recovered or preserved by the client.

In legal representation cases, the LSC can only waive the charge where:

- the proceedings have a significant wider public interest; and
- the LSC considered it cost-effective to fund legal representation for certain claimants, but not for others who might have benefited.

This very limited exception will only be relevant in cases where the LSC has funded a case on grounds of public interest. These cases are likely to be the ones where the client has agreed not to settle without the LSC's permission. The LSC will not be able to waive the charge if the case did not start out on this very specialized basis.

The statutory charge can also be postponed, i.e. not

collected immediately, where the money or property recovered or preserved is going to be used to buy a family home (*see* above). In that case, the money owed to the LSC will be registered as a charge (like a mortgage) on the client's home and will be subject to payment of simple interest.

EMERGENCY LEGAL REPRESENTATION

In some circumstances, both investigative help and full representation may be granted on an emergency basis where the matter is urgent.

SUPPORT FUNDING

Support funding is available for personal injury claims where the case has high investigative costs (disbursements over £1,000 or profit costs (i.e. your own solicitor's charges) over £3,000) or high overall costs (disbursements over £5,000 or profit costs over £15,000). Funding may be provided to pay the excess above those thresholds, even though the case is primarily proceeding privately under or with a view to a CFA.

FAMILY MEDIATION

Funding is also provided specifically for different levels of help in family cases. Family mediation provides free mediation for couples in dispute about children, money or property. Mediation is not a substitute for legal advice. It is an alternative method of resolving disputes in a neutral environment with the help of a mediator, rather than entirely through legal proceedings.

Family mediation is provided through mediators under contract with the LSC, whose services are paid for by the LSC. Applicants in receipt of income support or income-based Jobseeker's Allowance are automatically entitled to family mediation. For others, eligibility is dependent on a means test. If your gross income exceeds £2,288 per month, you will not be eligible. A higher limit applies if you have more than four dependent children in your family for whom you receive child benefit. If your gross monthly income is £2,288 or less, your mediator will assess your disposable income. You qualify if your disposable income is £707 per month or less and your disposable capital is £8,000 or less. Disposable income and disposable capital are calculated on the same basis as the means test for legal help (*see* above).

The applicant's partner's income and capital will be taken into account in assessing disposable income and disposable capital unless:

- the couple live apart because the relationship is over; or

- there is a conflict of interest between the couple in the matter for which they are seeking mediation.

If the applicant is living with a new partner then the new partner's income and capital will be included.

If the applicant is eligible for publicly funded mediation he will not be required to make any contribution to the cost out of his own funds. The statutory charge does not apply to any property recovered or preserved under family mediation.

In some cases, mediation is obligatory before legal representation will be granted in family proceedings. Those eligible for family mediation can obtain free legal advice through legal help or help with mediation.

APPROVED FAMILY HELP

There are two forms of approved family help: help with mediation and general family help.

Help with mediation

This is legal advice for people who are attending family mediation. Apart from legal advice, it can also cover help in drawing up an agreement reached in mediation, help in obtaining a court order to confirm such an agreement and related conveyancing work. Applicants who are eligible for family mediation will automatically qualify for help with mediation. Otherwise, the means test is the same as for family mediation. Only solicitors who are under contract with the LSC may provide this service. Eligible applicants will not be required to make any contribution to the cost of the legal advice out of their own resources and the statutory charge does not apply.

How much help the applicant is entitled to will depend on the subject of the mediation.

If the mediation is about	Client is entitled to legal help until the solicitor's charges reach
Children issues only	£150
Financial issues only	£250
Children and financial issues	£350

The solicitor can apply to the LSC regional office for an extension of this limit if necessary.

General family help

This is available where no mediation is in progress. It is often used to obtain disclosure of information from the other party to enable negotiations to take place. Eligibility is based on the same means test as that for legal representation and contributions to the cost of the case may be payable on the same basis as under legal representation.

The statutory charge may apply to any property recovered or preserved.

The application for either form of approved family help is assessed by the LSC regional office. If the application is refused on merits, there is a right of review by the LSC's regional director and, ultimately, by the LSC's funding review committee.

Summary: Financial Eligibility Limits

Level of service	Income limit	Capital limit
• Legal help • Help at court • Legal representation before immigration adjudicators and the Immigation Appeal Tribunal	Gross income not to exceed £2,288** per month Disposable income not to exceed £621 per month Automatically eligible on income if in receipt of income support or income-based JSA	£3,000 Capital must be assessed in all cases
• Family mediation • Help with mediation • General family help* • Support funding*	Gross income not to exceed £2,288** per month Disposable income not to exceed £707 per month	£8,000 Automatically eligible on capital if in receipt of income support or income-based JSA
• Other legal representation*	Automatically eligible on income if in receipt of income support or income-based JSA	

* May be subject to contribution from income and/or capital.
** A higher gross income limit applies if you have more than four dependent children – see table below.

Number of children in family	Gross monthly income not to exceed
0–4	£2,288
5	£2,433
6	£2,578
7	£2,723
8 or more	Add £145 to above figure for each additional child

MAKING THE APPLICATION

As illustrated by the table below, for some levels of service the solicitor or other advice provider is authorized to decide whether the case deserves CLS funding. In other cases, an application has to be made to the LSC.

In most cases the application for legal representation funding should be made to one of the regional offices of the LSC. The client's solicitor would usually make the application on his behalf. The regional office can either grant or refuse the application. If an application is refused because the client does not qualify financially, there is no right to have the decision reviewed.

If the application is refused because it does not meet any other criteria applied to that type of case there is a right to have that decision reviewed by the regional director. If the refusal of funding is confirmed by him or her, there is a further right to review by the funding review committee.

Level of service	*How is the application made?*
Legal help	The solicitor/advice provider decides whether the case should be funded
Help at court	The solicitor/advice provider decides whether the case should be funded
Legal representation before immigration adjudication, immigration appeal tribunal or mental health review tribunal	The solicitor/advice provider decides whether the case should be funded
Legal representation other than above	Application is made to the LSC
Approved family help	Application is made to the LSC
Family mediation	The mediator decides whether the case is suitable for mediation

CRIMINAL LEGAL AID

Public money is also made available to help people accused of a criminal offence or needing legal advice about a criminal matter. In certain cases, whether or not financial help will be provided depends on the individual's means (how much income and savings they have got) and whether the case is considered deserving of funding. Everyone is entitled to free advice from a solicitor if they are questioned by the police and free representation by a solicitor in the magistrates' court. Legal aid is not available for people seeking to pursue a private prosecution against another person – i.e. to take court proceedings against someone they believe has committed a crime.

The LSC replaced the Legal Aid Board as administrator of the criminal legal aid scheme. The new criminal legal aid scheme is called the Criminal Defence Service. The main change effected by the reforms in this area is the introduction of contracting. Under the old criminal legal aid scheme, any solicitor could carry out legally aided work. From April 2001, only solicitors who hold a contract with the LSC are able to deliver criminal legal aid services in the police station and the magistrates' court. Since 2003, crown court work is also delivered under contract. Solicitors must meet the LSC's quality standards in order to be awarded a contract.

Public funding for criminal cases is made available at the following levels of service.

Level of service	*Type of help*
1 Advice and assistance	Solicitor provides 2 hours' advice (excluding advocacy)
2 Advocacy Assistance	Representation at court for certain types of cases
3 Representation	Preparing the defence and representation at court
4 The duty solicitor schemes	Free advice for all at the police station or free representation at the magistrates' court

ADVICE AND ASSISTANCE

At this level, a solicitor will generally provide up to £300 worth of work including general advice, writing letters, negotiating, getting a barrister's opinion and preparing a written case. The scheme does not cover representation at court. The solicitor can apply for a financial extension to do more work.

Children under the age of 16 years are eligible for Advice and Assistance, but a parent or guardian may make the application on the child's behalf.

In order to qualify for help under the scheme, the applicant must be able to show that his disposable *capital* (savings and valuable possessions) and disposable *income* (weekly wage less tax and other allowances) are within the current financial limits. Capital and income of a spouse or partner will be taken into account in making the assessment, unless the couple live apart or there is a conflict of interest between them.

The applicant will qualify for Advice and Assistance if his disposable income is £91 per week or less and his disposable capital is £1,000 or less. If the applicant does qualify, he will not have to pay any contribution from his own money towards the cost of case.

Applicants whose disposable capital exceeds £1,000 will not be eligible. People in receipt of Income Support, income-based Jobseeker's Allowance, Working Tax

Credit, Child Tax Credit* or Working Tax Credit with disability element* will be eligible, provided that their disposable capital is not more than £1,000.

The solicitor will fill in the application form and work out whether the applicant qualifies for help.

ADVOCACY ASSISTANCE

Advocacy Assistance covers the cost of a solicitor preparing the case and representing the applicant in certain proceedings, including:

- prisoners facing disciplinary charges before the prison governor/controller;
- certain life prisoners and detainees at HM prisons who appear before a parole board;
- individuals who have failed to pay a fine or obey a court order of the magistrates' court and risk imprisonment.
- individuals facing certain proceedings under the Crime and Disorder Act 1998, e.g. anti-social behaviour orders;
- individuals appearing at early hearings in the magistrates' court;

To qualify for this help, the applicant must show that the case satisfies a *merits* test, which is based on reasonableness. There is no financial test, except in prison law cases where the applicant must show that his disposable *capital* and disposable *income* are below a certain level.

The applicant will qualify financially if weekly disposable income is £192 or less. The capital limit is £3,000 with allowances of £335 for one dependant, £535 for two dependants plus £100 for each additional dependant. If you receive either income support or income-based JSA you will automatically qualify on capital.

There are no contributions for either of these levels of service.

Making the application

If the solicitor holds a contract with the LSC to do this kind of work then he will be able to assess whether the applicant is eligible.

REPRESENTATION

Representation covers all types of criminal proceedings and may cover the cost of:

- preparation of the defence by a solicitor;
- representation by a solicitor or barrister in court;
- legal advice about appealing against a verdict or sentence of the magistrates' court or the crown court or a decision of the Court of Appeal;
- preparation of the notice of appeal;

* Only if gross annual income does not exceed £14,213.

- bail applications.

The applicant for representation should complete the forms. The advice and assistance scheme may cover the cost of a solicitor helping with this. The court will decide whether the applicant should receive representation, based on the information in the forms.

The decision to grant representation depends on whether it is in the *interests of justice* to grant representation.

The interests of justice

The court will consider the following factors (contained in Schedule 3 to the Access to Justice Act 1999) in deciding whether it is in the interests of justice to grant public funding:

(**a**) if the defendant is convicted he is likely to go to prison or lose his job; or

(**b**) where the case involves complex legal issues; or

(**c**) where the defendant cannot understand the proceedings and state his own case because of language problems, or mental or physical disability;

(**d**) where the nature of the defence involves tracing and interviewing witnesses or expert cross-examination of a witness for the prosecution; or

(**e**) where legal representation of the accused is desirable in the interests of someone other than the accused (e.g. where it is undesirable that the accused should cross-examine a young child in a sexual offence case).

For serious cases, such as where the defendant has been accused of murder or rape, it will always be in the interests of justice to grant representation. Minor offences, such as minor motoring offences, are not usually eligible.

Since the introduction of the Criminal Defence Service in April 2001, the means test has been abolished for cases where representation is sought.

THE DUTY SOLICITOR SCHEMES

There are two duty solicitor schemes, for which everyone is eligible, regardless of how wealthy they are. Under the 24-hour scheme, people being questioned by the police are entitled to free legal advice and assistance. Under the Magistrates' Court scheme, individuals appearing for the first time in the magistrates' court are entitled to representation by a solicitor.

The 24-hour scheme

Everyone who is questioned by the police, at the police station or elsewhere, is entitled to free legal advice, whether they have been arrested or not and regardless of their income and capital or savings.

People can ask the police to contact the duty solicitor, ask for a list of local solicitors or ask the police to contact their own solicitor. Duty solicitors are 'on call' 24 hours a day. They are independent and are not employed by the police.

The duty solicitor will advise about:

- bail;
- if necessary, asking for your case to be put off until another day;
- whether you should plead guilty or not guilty;
- getting your own solicitor and applying for representation;
- the type of sentence you might get;
- representing you when you first go before the magistrates (under the Magistrates' Court scheme);
- fines or other court orders where there is risk of imprisonment.

On 1 January 2000, 1,267 requests to see a duty solicitor were received from police stations, the highest demand for one day that there has ever been.

The Magistrates' Court scheme

Under this scheme, solicitors are made available to help people on their first court appearance at the magistrates' court. Except for some minor cases, everyone is entitled to free advice from the duty solicitor on the first occasion that they have to appear in court for any particular offence. Again, there is no means test and no contribution is payable under the scheme.

Abolition of means test

The government has abolished the means test for representation. Instead, if a case satisfies the 'interests of justice' merits test (i.e. that the case is more than trivial) then funding will automatically be provided by the courts. For crown court defendants who are convicted and are able to pay a contribution, the court may make an order at the end of the trial so that they contribute. Defendants who may have the means to contribute will be investigated and their assets could be frozen pending the outcome of the trial. There is no recovery of costs against defendants tried in the magistrates' court.

LEGAL FUNDING ABROAD

Many foreign countries have public funding schemes, but most do not cover as much as ours. England and Wales have an agreement with some European countries that they can pass on, through the LSC, applications from people seeking public funding for civil proceedings in those countries.

Although the foreign country decides the application on its own rules, you can make your application through the LSC.

The LSC will transmit the application on your behalf to the relevant authority in the foreign country. You can, if you qualify financially, get legal help from your solicitor to help you with the application, including obtaining any necessary translations.

The countries covered by this agreement are: Austria, Azerbaijan, Belgium, Bulgaria, Czech Republic, Denmark, Eire, Estonia, Finland, France, Greece, Italy, Lithuania, Luxembourg, Netherlands, Norway, Poland, Portugal, Spain, Sweden, Switzerland and Turkey.

If you need public funding outside these countries you should approach the United Kingdom representative (embassy/consulate) of the country concerned for information.

OTHER WAYS OF PAYING

Conditional Fee Agreements

These agreements are also referred to as 'no win, no fee' agreements, confusingly and incorrectly suggesting that you will pay nothing to your solicitor if you lose your case. This is not the case. In a conditional fee agreement (CFA), the solicitor agrees that he will not receive his fee if the case is lost. In exchange, the solicitor receives an increased fee if the case is won: the amount of the increase (the 'success fee') is agreed at the start of the case and will depend on the probability of winning the case. The riskier the case, the higher the success fee will be, subject to a maximum that may be charged of 100 per cent.

Although the solicitor's fees will not be payable if the case is lost, the client will still have to pay for expenses incurred in investigating and pursuing the case. These expenses are called 'disbursements' and may include court fees, experts' fees, accident report fees, official search fees, travelling expenses and barrister's fees. The client can insure against the risk of having to pay the disbursements by taking out legal expenses insurance. Premiums range between £95 for road traffic cases and £8,000 for medical negligence cases. The losing client will also have to pay the winning party's success fee and insurance premium.

Conditional fee agreements can apply to all civil cases, including personal injury cases, human rights cases in the European Court of Human Rights, and insolvency cases – but not matrimonial proceedings.

Remember:

1 to shop around for the best deal being offered. Compare the success fees that different firms will want if you win the case. Also ask about insurance cover that may be available;
2 to agree the success fee with your prospective solicitor before he takes up the case.

Legal expenses insurance

Check your household and motoring insurance policies. You may already have cover for your legal costs.

After the event (ATE) legal expenses insurance policies cover legal expenses when the disputed event has already happened, but the expenses of the resulting court case have not yet been incurred. Where the policy is sold in conjunction with a CFA ('no win, no fee') agreement, it will cover the court fees, expert witnesses' fees and other expenses, which the client might otherwise have to pay for even if he loses the case.

Where there is no CFA agreement in place, an ATE policy can cover the fees of the client's own solicitor, which will not be increased if the case is won.

Organizations offering free legal advice

Action for Victims of Medical Accidents is a charity working for the fair treatment of victims of medical accidents.

Bank Chambers
1 London Road
Forest Hill
London SE23 3TP
Tel: 020 8291 2793
Fax: 020 8699 0632

The Bar Pro Bono Unit provides up to three days' free legal advice and representation for cases where public funding is not available and the applicant cannot afford to pay for their case and a barrister is needed:

7 Gray's Inn Square
Gray's Inn
London WC1R 5AZ
Tel: 020 7831 9711
Fax: 020 7831 9733

The Children's Legal Centre is an independent national organization concerned with law and policy affecting children and young people in England and Wales. An Education Advocacy Unit represents children excluded from school and with special educational needs:

The University of Essex
Wivenhoe Park
Colchester CO4 3SQ
Tel (advice): 01206 873821
Fax: 01206 874026

Look for details of your local Citizens' Advice Bureau in the phone book or on the web at www.nacab.org.uk

Alternatively, contact:
NACAB (National Association of Citizens' Advice Bureaux)

Myddleton House
115/123 Pentonville Road
London N1 9LZ
Tel: 020 7833 2181
Fax: 020 7833 4371

The Disability Discrimination Act Representation and Advice Project has been set up to bring together people seeking to take cases under the Disability Discrimination Act (*see* Chapter 38 in the Employment section) and solicitors and barristers who have volunteered their services. Applications will only be considered where they are referred by agencies accepted by the project. These include disability charities and law centres.

11 Broadway House
Jackman Street
London E8 4QY
Tel: 020 7254 8434

The Disability Law Service is a free service offering legal information and representation and advice on disability for people with mental, physical and sensory disabilities and their families or enablers:

Disability Law Service
Network for the Handicapped Ltd
Room 241
2nd Floor
49–51 Bedford Row
London WC1R 4LR
Tel: 020 7831 8031
Fax: 020 7831 5582

The Free Representation Unit can only appear at tribunals when public funding is not available. Cases are referred to the FRU by Citizens' Advice Bureaux, other advice centres and solicitors:

49–51 Bedford Row
London WC1R 4LR
Tel: 020 7831 0692

Law centres provide free legal advice and representation on social welfare issues, such as housing, immigration, employment or welfare benefits, to people who live or work within their catchment areas. Look for your local law centre on the web at www.lawcentres.org.uk or contact the Law Centres Federation, the co-ordinating body for law centres:

Duchess House
18/19 Warren Street
London W1P 5DB
Tel: 020 7387 8570
Fax: 020 7387 8368

See also page 384 for a list of organizations offering advice and assistance for employment law related matters.

PART TWELVE

Legal Jargon

An A–Z Guide

abate – To reduce or make less (e.g. general *legacies* are abated – reduced proportionately when the deceased's estate is insufficient to pay all the general legacies in full; a nuisance is abated when it is reduced).

abstract of title – A summary of the legal title to *unregistered land*. The abstract shows the history and validity of the title; cf. an epitome of title, which lists all the documents going back to the *root of title*.

abuse of process – An act that has no real merit and is designed to slow down or interfere with the proper administration of justice. So, an action begun after a similar action has already been heard and dismissed may be an abuse of process and may be struck out.

ACAS – See *Advisory, Conciliation and Arbitration Service*.

accord and satisfaction – When a creditor accepts an agreement suggested by the debtor, which satisfies the debt and so prevents the creditor from suing the debtor.

acknowledgement of service – A form which may be completed by a defendant or his solicitor within a specified period confirming that the particulars of claim (or in some circumstances the claim form) beginning a legal action, have been delivered. If neither the acknowledgement of service nor defence is completed in time, *judgment in default* may be obtained against the defendant.

action – Civil proceedings in a court of law.

act of God – 'An extraordinary circumstance which could not be foreseen, and which could not be guarded against' (Pandorf 1886). Insurance policies do not usually cover acts of God.

actus reus – The guilty act; cf. *mens rea*.

address for service – The address given on a claim form, acknowledgement of service or defence stating where the party may be sent (or served with) documents. The law requires that an address for service within England and Wales be provided.

adjournment – The postponement of a hearing or part of a hearing to another day.

adjudication – A method of reducing the length and complexity of disputes found in construction contracts. The process is less formal than an arbitration or court hearing. The original contract specifies the type of dispute that may be resolved by adjudication, sets out the procedure and states whether the adjudicator's decision is final or may be reviewed in a subsequent arbitration.

administration, administration order – An insolvency practitioner may be appointed to run a company for a limited period to give it an opportunity to rearrange its financial affairs and avoid (hopefully) liquidation. During administration the company may not be sued. If the company successfully reorganizes itself it will come out of administration and continue as normal. If it does not, it will usually be wound up.

administrator, administratrix – The personal representative appointed by the court to administer the estate of someone who has died intestate (i.e. without a will) or who left a will which did not appoint executors.

admiralty – Part of the High Court that deals with disputes relating to shipping, especially collisions between ships.

ADR – See *Alternative dispute resolution*.

ad valorem – According to the value, for example, stamp duty on sale of land is charged according to the price paid.

Advisory, Conciliation and Arbitration Service (ACAS) – A statutory body set up to resolve disputes between employers and employees. It has a duty to try to help parties in an Employment Tribunal reach agreement without going to a full hearing.

affidavit – A written statement to be used as evidence in court proceedings. The deponent swears (or affirms) as to its truth before a commissioner for oaths, a solicitor or a court official, who then witnesses the deponent's signature.

affirmation – A written statement which the maker solemnly declares to be true. Similar to an affidavit but no *oath* is taken.

aggravated damages – The damages awarded to a claimant in libel actions by a jury to compensate for the suffering caused by the defendant's high-handed or insulting conduct following the libel.

allocation – The procedure by which the court assigns a case to a particular procedural track. The parties must complete an allocation questionnaire giving details about the case to enable the court to allocate it.

Alternative dispute resolution (ADR) – An informal process to settle a dispute with the help of an independent third party or mediator. Each side makes a short presentation and has separate discussions with the mediator who then encourages the parties to reach a compromise. The compromise is not binding until a contract formally settling the dispute is signed. The process may be evaluative – that is, when the mediator expresses his view on the merits, or facilitative – where the mediator simply encourages discussion.

amendment – The formal alteration of documents used in legal proceedings. The consent of the opposing party or of the court is usually required for such changes.

amicus curiae – A friend of the court. A barrister appointed in certain cases to assist the court who can bring matters that have been overlooked to the court's attention.

ancient lights – Windows which have had an uninterrupted access of light for at least 20 years. Buildings cannot be erected which interfere with this right of light.

annul – When court proceedings, or their outcome, are declared no longer to have effect.

antenuptial – Before marriage.

Anton Piller order – See *search order*.

appellant – A party who, having been unsuccessful, applies to a higher court for the alteration or reversal of the lower court's decision.

application – A request to a court for an order, usually by the issue of an application notice. The court may require an oral hearing but may deal with the matter on the telephone or simply on the papers.

application notice – A form which has to be completed by a party who wishes to ask the court to make an order. The form has to state the grounds on which the order is sought and either has to contain a statement of truth or be accompanied by a witness statement. The application notice has replaced the summons and notice of motion.

arbitration – The hearing of a dispute by an independent third party (an arbitrator) rather than a court. The parties will usually have agreed in a contract that any dispute should be submitted to arbitration and will have set out the form of arbitration. Many professional bodies run arbitration schemes.

arraign – To bring an accused person to the bar of the court so that the indictment can be read to him or her.

arrestable offence – A criminal offence carrying a maximum penalty of five years' or more imprisonment. All arrestable offences allow the offender to be arrested without a warrant.

assault – Strictly speaking, merely attempting to strike another person is an assault. If touching takes place, then it is *battery*. In practice, the word 'assault' is always taken to include the battery.

assessment of costs – The procedure by which a court official, known as a costs judge, decides how much of the winning party's legal expenses should be paid by the losing party. A long and expensive process unless a summary assessment is made.

assessment of damages – The process of calculating how much a winning party should be paid by a losing party, when it has not been calculated at the trial. The court will have decided that the defendant is liable to pay compensation but not the amount.

attestation – The signature of a witness to the signing of a document by another person.

attorney – Since the Judicature Act 1875, attorneys have been officially called solicitors.

Attorney-General – The chief law officer of the Crown and head of the barristers' profession.

automatism – An involuntary act done by a person who is not aware of what he or she is doing or who is unable to control his or her muscles.

autrefois – A person cannot be tried for the same offence twice.

award – The decision of an arbitrator. It is the arbitration equivalent of a judgment.

bailiff – An officer of the court who assists in the service of its documents and the enforcement of its orders, for example by seizing goods to ensure payment of a judgment.

bailment – When goods are left by one person (the 'bailor') with another (the 'bailee') to hold in accordance with instructions, for example leaving luggage at railway luggage offices.

bank holidays – In England and Wales, these are laid down in the Banking and Financial Dealings Act 1971 as Easter Monday, the first and last Mondays in May, the last Monday in August, 26 December and, if either 25 or 26 December is a Sunday, then also 27 December.

bankruptcy – When a court takes over a debtor's assets on behalf of his or her creditors. *See* Chapter 52.

Bar – The barristers of England and Wales.

battery – Using force on another person, whether or not harm results.

Beddoes order – Permission given to trustees by a court to bring an action on behalf of beneficiaries of the trust. Without it, trustees may have to pay the costs of the action personally and be unable to reimburse themselves from the trust's assets.

bench – The term used to describe the magistrates and judges in a court.

beneficiary – A person who is entitled to property which is held for him or her by trustees. Also, someone who receives a gift under a will.

bequeath – To leave *personal* (cf. *real*) property under a will. The gift is called a *legacy*.

bill of costs – A very detailed analysis of all the expenses incurred in a case. The document is laborious to produce and is usually prepared by a specialist in drafting such documents, called a costs draftsman. A bill of costs has to be drawn up where a successful party to litigation is seeking costs from the losing party on an assessment.

bona vacantia – Goods that do not have an owner. Generally, they go to the finder except in cases of shipwreck and treasure trove, when they go to the Crown.

brewster sessions – Annual meeting of licensing justices to consider applications (and renewals) for licences to sell alcoholic liquor.

bridle-way – A public right of way to pass on horseback.

brief – Formal instructions to a barrister to appear at a trial or other court hearing.

brief fee – The payment which becomes due to a barrister when the brief is delivered to him. It may be a substantial sum and will probably have to be paid even if the case does not go ahead, for example because the parties reach a compromise.

burden of proof – The obligation of proving the case.

by-law – Rules laid down by a local authority or other body in accordance with powers given to them by an Act of Parliament. These local rules have the full force of law.

Calderbank letter – A written offer of settlement which will not be shown to the court unless the person to whom the offer is made obtains an order which is less favourable than the offer. In that case the writer of the letter will ask the court to make the other party pay the costs of the action from the date of receipt of the letter. See also *Part 36 offer*.

capital punishment – Death by hanging is now restricted to high treason and piracy with violence.

case management – The power of judges given by the CPR to ensure that cases proceed through the courts in the most appropriate way. The judges can be proactive in ordering parties to take certain steps. The parties and the courts have an overriding obligation to ensure that cases are dealt with justly.

case management conference – An important procedural stage, early in a case, where the court considers the case and gives directions as to its future conduct.

case stated – When a case is submitted by a court to a higher court for its opinion, the lower court will summarize the facts of the case and the relevant points of law. Most commonly arises when a magistrates' court decision is appealed to the Divisional Court of the Queen's Bench Division.

cause of action – A legal right of someone who has suffered loss or other injury to obtain compensation from the wrongdoer. A number of ingredients have to be present to allow the injured party to get compensation.

caveat emptor – Let the buyer beware.

certiorari – An order of the High Court to review and quash the decision of the lower court which was based on an irregular procedure.

champerty – Financing another's legal action in return for a share of the profits. Such a contract is unenforceable, but is not a criminal offence.

Chancery Division – Part of the High Court which deals particularly with matters relating to land, trusts, insolvency and companies.

charge on land – A *mortgage*.

charity – A body that has legally charitable objectives. Only bodies which are for the relief of poverty, the advancement of education, the advancement of religion, or for other purposes beneficial to the community, can qualify as charities.

chattels – All property other than *freehold* real estate.

Chattels can be 'chattels real' (leaseholds) or 'chattels personal' (all other property – also called pure personalty).

c.i.f – Cost, insurance, freight. The cost of the goods includes these items.

civil law – The law administered by the civil courts (i.e. non-criminal law).

Civil Procedure Rules (CPR) – The rules which govern the procedure of the High Court and county courts, introduced on 26 April 1999. They replaced the old Rules of the Supreme Court and County Court Rules and were intended to simplify procedure. The brainchild of Lord Woolf.

claimant – The person who brings legal proceedings. Formerly known as plaintiff.

claim form – The document by which an action is commenced. Formerly known as a writ.

Class F – A spouse whose name is not on the title deeds of the matrimonial home can register a Class F charge which warns all purchasers that she claims the right to live in the home, even if it is sold by the other spouse. *See* Chapter 5.

codification – The bringing together into one Act of Parliament of all the law on one topic without altering the law.

come off the record – An application to the court by a solicitor for permission to stop acting for someone, usually because the solicitor has not been paid or because he is not receiving proper instructions from his client.

Commercial Court – Part of the Queen's Bench Division of the High Court that deals principally with international commercial contracts, international sale of goods, insurance, reinsurance and banking.

common law – Principles of law derived from decisions of the court, rather than from a code or statute.

commorientes – When people die together at the same time, their deaths are presumed to have occurred in order of seniority by age.

Companies Court – Part of the Chancery Division of the High Court that deals with the affairs of companies, especially insolvency.

company voluntary arrangements – An arrangement between a company and its creditors usually to allow a company to avoid insolvent liquidation and its creditors to recover at least part of their debt more quickly. It requires the consent of the creditors but not the court.

complaint – The initial step in beginning civil proceedings in the magistrates' court.

compromise agreement – A settlement between an employee and employer of a dispute between them. Provided certain conditions have been complied with, including that the employee was represented by a lawyer when reaching the agreement, the employee cannot subsequently bring a case in an employment tribunal.

condonation – When one spouse forgives the other's matrimonial misconduct. It is no longer a bar to divorce.

conference (with counsel) – A meeting between the barrister, solicitor and sometimes client and expert in a case to discuss its progress and prospects. When the meeting is with leading counsel it is called a consultation.

consideration – If a person promises to do something for another (e.g. pay money) that promise can be enforced only if the other person gave, or promised, something of value in return; that is said to be the consideration for the promise. Thus every contract requires consideration. The only exception is when the promise is in a *deed*.

conversion – A tort which arises when someone's title to his or her chattels is denied or if a bailee negligently allows his or her bailor's goods to be damaged.

conveyance – A written document transferring ownership of *land* from one person to another.

coroner – A solicitor, barrister or medical practitioner appointed to inquire into the death of anyone who is killed or who dies in suspicious circumstances or in prison. The inquiry is called an inquest.

corporeal hereditaments – Visible, tangible property (e.g. house, car, books).

costs – The expenses relating to legal services. It includes fees paid to solicitors, barristers, experts and the court. *See* Chapter 99.

COT3 – A form used to record agreements between an employer and employee (or ex-employee) which have been reached with the assistance of ACAS.

counsel – Another term for barrister.

counterclaim – When defendants are sued they can include in their defence any claim that they may have against the plaintiff, even if it arises from a different matter.

county court – Courts which deal with civil litigation where claims are low in amount or where the claim is very straightforward.

Court of Appeal – The court which determines applications to reverse or vary orders made by the High Court.

coverture – Legal status of a married woman.

crime – Defined in Halsbury's *Laws of England* as an

unlawful act or default which is an offence against the public and which renders the person guilty of the act liable to legal punishment.

cross-examination – The questioning of a witness in court on behalf of a party other than that which asked him to give evidence.

crown court – The court which deals with more serious criminal matters. Cases are decided by a jury.

cur. adv. vult. (***curia advisari vult***) – A phrase often seen in law reports meaning that the court retired to consider its judgment rather than giving it at the end of the hearing. Literally 'the court advised itself'.

curtesy – An ancient right whereby a widower had a life estate in the land of his late wife. Very rare nowadays.

curtilage – The garden, field, yard, etc., surrounding a house and which belongs to the house.

custom – An unwritten law dating back to time immemorial.

damage feasant – Damage by animals of A on the land of B. If B seizes the animals (distress damage feasant) he or she cannot sue for damages.

damages – Money which the court orders paid to compensate for a wrong or injury done. Special damages compensate for financial loss which has occurred before the trial and general damages are an estimate of future loss.

declaration – An order in which the court sets out the legal position between parties without ordering either to take any action, such as paying damages. For example, the court might declare that if A does a certain act it would be a breach of contract with B.

declaratory judgment – When the court makes a declaration as to the law, or rights between parties, without making an order to enforce those rights.

deed – A written document that has been signed, sealed and delivered by its maker. The signature is witnessed. These days, makers only sign, for there is rarely any need for them formally to *seal* or deliver the deed.

default – A failure to comply with a court order or the rules of court, especially those requiring action within a specified time. Where a defendant fails to file an acknowledgement of service or defence in time the claimant may obtain judgment in default by showing that the proceedings were properly served and not acknowledged.

defence – A document in which a defendant sets out the answer to the claims made. A defence is a type of statement of case and follows the particulars of claim.

defendant – A person who is sued or prosecuted, or who has any court proceedings brought against him or her.

demise – The grant of a lease in land.

deponent – A person who swears an affidavit or makes an affirmation.

deposition – A statement made on oath by a witness.

detinue – An action formerly brought to recover chattels wrongly detained, but abolished by the Torts (Interference with Goods) Act 1977.

devise – A gift of *land* in a will (if not land, it is a bequest).

directions – A court order setting out a timetable for future procedural steps.

Director of Public Prosecutions (DPP) – The DPP is a solicitor or barrister of at least 10 years' standing who works under the Lord Chancellor. Only the DPP can prosecute for certain serious crimes.

disbursements – A solicitor's expenses on behalf of his client, for example photocopying charges, travel expenses and fees paid to experts and barristers.

disclosure – In many civil actions the parties disclose all their relevant documents to each other, even if the disclosed documents injure their case.

discontinuance and withdrawal – A situation where a claimant abandons proceedings. A consequence of this is an obligation to pay the defendant's costs.

dismissal – A refusal by a court to grant an order or application, or an order by the court that the action itself should be struck out.

distrain – To levy *distress*.

distress – Seizing a personal chattel from a debtor or wrongdoer in satisfaction of the debt, etc.

Divisional Court – An appeal court of at least two High Court judges. It deals with matters such as judicial review and some appeals from county courts, magistrates' courts and tribunals.

dock brief – A prisoner being tried on indictment (i.e. in the crown court) can request any robed barrister in court to represent him or her for a nominal fee. The practice has become rare since the introduction of public funding.

domicile – Where a person has their permanent home.

dominant tenement – Land which has the benefit of rights over another piece of land; for example, if plot A has a right of light over plot B, plot A is the dominant tenement and plot B is the *servient tenement*.

duty solicitor – Many magistrates' courts have rotas of

solicitors who attend the court and give advice and help to unrepresented defendants.

easement – The right which an owner of land (called the *dominant tenement*) has over the land of another person, called the *servient tenement* (e.g. right of way, light, support).

employment tribunal – A body which decides disputes arising in respect of employment including complaints of unfair dismissal and disability, sex and race discrimination. Formerly known as industrial tribunals.

enactment – An Act of Parliament, or part of an Act.

encumbrance – A liability affecting property (e.g. a lease, *mortgage, restrictive covenant*).

enforcement – Various procedures to compel someone to comply with a court order or judgment. See also *execution*.

engross – When a draft document has been approved by everyone concerned, it is then retyped in its final form. That is the engrossment.

equity – Body of doctrines and maxims which developed alongside the common law, and which aimed to mould the rigid and inflexible common law principles into a more just and equitable legal system.

equity of redemption – The right of a mortgagor (i.e. borrower) to redeem his or her *mortgage* after the date stated in his or her mortgage deed.

estate – An interest in *land* (e.g. a lease).

estoppel – A rule which prevents a person denying the truth of a statement or the existence of facts which they have led another to believe; for example, if X spends money on Y's property because Y says he will give it to X, then Y may not be able to change his mind and refuse to give the property to X.

eurodefence – A defence based on EC law, especially that dealing with anti-competitive practices.

European Court of Human Rights – Hears applications from the European Human Rights Commission in Strasbourg for enforcement of the European Convention on Human Rights. If a complaint is upheld, a government must change the law.

European Court of Justice – The court of the EC which decides questions of European law. It sits in Luxembourg.

execution – Enforcing a court's judgment by compelling the defendant to comply with it; for example, a bailiff who seizes goods by *distress* is executing the judgment. The word also describes the formal signing of a document such as a deed or will.

executor (executrix) – A personal representative appointed by will.

exhibit – An attachment to an affidavit, affirmation or witness statement, usually a copy of a document referred to in it.

ex parte – See *without notice*.

expert witness – An expert witness can give his or her opinion on a subject. This is an exception to the general rule that witnesses must not tell the court their opinions: for example, a witness cannot say, 'I thought he was driving dangerously.'

extinguishment – When a right or obligation ends: for example, a debt is repaid and so the right to sue for recovery of the debt is extinguished.

Family Division – Part of the High Court that deals with matters relating to children (such as custody, adoption, financial support), divorce and financial arrangements following divorce.

fast track – The procedural pathway which a case is likely to follow if the value claimed is greater than can be brought in the small claims court but is not more than £15,000. A trial of a fast track case should last no more than one day and the case should come to trial speedily.

fatal accident – When a man is killed by the negligence of another, his or her dependants can sue for their financial loss arising from his death. Only the spouse, parent, grandparent, child, grandchild, nephew, niece or cousin can sue; a cohabitant cannot sue (Fatal Accidents Act 1976).

fee simple – The absolute ownership of land. Basically the same as a freehold.

fee tail – An interest in land which descends to the direct issue (i.e. children) of the owner and which he or she cannot give to anyone else.

feme covert – A married woman.

feme sole – An unmarried woman (i.e. spinster, widow, divorced woman).

fieri facias – A court order to sheriffs requiring them to seize a debtor's goods to pay off a creditor's judgment.

filing – Delivering a document by post or otherwise, to the court.

foreclosure – When a mortgagee (e.g. a building society) forecloses on a *mortgage*, the mortgagor (the borrower) forfeits his or her *equity of redemption*. The court therefore allows the mortgagee to take possession of the property, sell it and deduct the amount it is owed from the proceeds of sale. Any balance goes to the mortgagor.

forum conveniens – The appropriate court for a particular dispute. The test in England and Wales is whether the interests of justice are best served by proceedings here or abroad.

forum non conveniens – A court that is inappropriate for any particular dispute.

freehold – cf. *leasehold*, under which property is held for a specified period of time.

freezing order – An order forbidding a defendant from disposing of assets before trial and in particular from removing them from England and Wales. It is sometimes possible to obtain a so-called worldwide freezing order, restraining a defendant from dealing with assets anywhere in the world. Formerly known as a *Mareva injunction*.

frustration – A contract is frustrated if it becomes impossible to perform because of a reason that is beyond the control of the parties (e.g. war). The contract is cancelled.

full and final settlement – An agreement between parties that the proceedings should end and that neither party should sue the other in the future in connection with the dispute.

further information – More extensive or precise details of a party's case. Usually provided in response to a request for further information. Formerly known as further and better particulars and interrogatories.

garnishee order – When a creditor commences proceedings against someone who owes his or her debtor money, so as to intercept the repayment before it reaches the debtor; for example, A is owed money by B, but B is owed money by C; A can obtain a garnishee order against C.

good faith – Honestly.

goodwill – 'The whole advantage, wherever it may be, of the reputation and connection of the firm' (Trego (1896)).

ground rent – The rent paid by a person with a long lease (commonly 99 years) to the freeholder.

group action – Legal proceedings where the court allows a number of persons to act together because of the similarity of their cases. Often known as class actions.

guarantor – A person who guarantees another's debts; also called a *surety*.

guardian *ad litem* – See *litigation friend*.

habeas corpus – (Latin for 'that you have the body'.) A court order which requires that a named individual be produced before the court; applied for when a person is illegally detained.

half-blood – The relationship between people who have one common ancestor, for example between A and B who have the same father but different mothers.

headnote – A summary at the beginning of a law report which sets out the main points of the case.

hearing – The presentation of a case in court. The main hearing is usually called the trial, but there may be preliminary hearings before masters or judges in chambers or in open court.

hearsay – Statements, written or oral, which are given by someone other than the witness giving evidence in court and which are relied on as being true. They are generally not allowed although there are wide exceptions in civil litigation. A classic example of hearsay is 'he told me that . . .'

heirloom – 'Any piece of household stuff which, by custom of some countries, having belonged to a house for certain descents, goes with the house after the death of the owner, unto the heir and not to the executors.' (Termes de la Ley)

High Court – The civil court to which the most serious cases are brought. Part of the Supreme Court set up by the Judicature Acts 1873–75, its full name is the High Court of Justice.

high seas – The seas more than 5 kilometres from the coast.

holding charge – A minor charge used as a device for holding a suspect while a more serious offence is investigated.

holograph – A document written in the maker's own handwriting, for example a holograph will.

hostile witness – A court can declare a witness to be hostile if it believes that he or she is hostile to the party calling him or her and that he or she is unwilling to tell the truth. This then allows the witness to be cross-examined by the party who called him or her. (Parties cannot usually cross-examine their own witnesses.)

ignorance of the law is no excuse – 'Every man must be taken to be cognizant of the law, otherwise there is no knowing of the extent to which the excuse of ignorance might be carried. It would be urged in almost every case' (Bailey (1800)).

illegal – An act is illegal when it involves breaking the criminal law; cf. an *unlawful* act.

immovables – *Land* and the property attached to it.

in camera – When evidence is not heard in open court – for instance, because it relates to a person's sexual capacity or to official secrets. Proceedings cannot be reported.

in chambers – A hearing which takes place in rooms attached to the High Court. Under the CPR all hearings, including hearings in chambers, are open to the public although in practice, because of constraints of space, only the parties and their lawyers are likely to attend. The offices of counsel are also called chambers.

indemnity – The reimbursement by an insurer of a financial loss, or full compensation for someone who has suffered loss, ordered by the court.

indictable offence – An offence which could be tried on indictment in the crown court.

indictment – The written accusation, prepared by the Crown, charging a crown-court defendant. It is read out at the beginning of the trial.

infant – A person under 18 years. Also called a minor.

information – Strictly speaking, an information is any proceeding brought by the Crown other than by *indictment*. In practice, the word is now mainly used to describe a statement placed before a magistrate which informs him or her of the commission of an offence for which a summons or warrant must be issued by the magistrate. This is called 'laying an information'.

inherent jurisdiction – The power of the court to regulate its own procedure derived from traditional and successive use, rather than from any statutory authority.

injunction – A court order requiring someone to do, or to refrain from doing, something.

inquest – An inquiry into a suspicious death. See *coroner*.

insolvency practitioner – A person, usually a lawyer or accountant, licensed by the president of the Board of Trade and Industry, and the Secretary of State for Trade and Industry to act as a liquidator or administrator.

instructions (to counsel) – A formal document prepared by a solicitor setting out the facts of a matter and seeking a barrister's advice on specific legal points. It is often accompanied by documents. Instructions are also given by a solicitor seeking an expert's independent opinion.

interim – In the meantime. An 'interim order' in an action is made prior to the full hearing of the case, when a 'final order' will be made. The hearing of the application for an interim order will be an *interlocutory* proceeding.

interim payment – A sum which the court may order a defendant to pay to a claimant 'on account' before the final judgment. Typically, such a payment is ordered where it is likely that the claimant will win the case but is in financial difficulties.

interlocutory – An interim stage in the course of the action (e.g. interlocutory injunction). 'Interlocutory

proceedings' usually describe the events in a civil case between its commencement (by issuing a *writ* or summons) and its ending (by judgment being given).

inter partes – A court hearing with all parties to the proceedings present. Contrast without notice. Follows an application made with notice.

interpleader summons – When a person holds property to which they have no claim, but two or more people claim it from him or her, he or she can issue an interpleader summons asking the court to decide who has the best claim to the property.

interrogatories – See *further information*.

intervener – A person who intervenes in an action to which he or she is not a party. Generally applies to a woman accused of adultery in another's divorce and who wishes to intervene to deny that allegation.

inter vivos – Made between people who are alive (e.g. a gift *inter vivos*); cf. a testamentary gift.

intestate – Dying without leaving a will (*see* page 162).

invitation to treat – An offer to receive an offer: for example, a shopkeeper's display of goods in a window is an invitation to treat – he or she is offering the customer an opportunity to offer to buy those goods, whereupon he or she might accept that offer.

issue – Offspring (i.e. children, grandchildren, etc.).

jactitation of marriage – If A wrongly claims to be married to B, then B can ask the court to confirm that they are not married.

jointly and severally – If A and B are jointly and severally liable to C, then C has three possible courses of action: he can sue A or B, or A and B.

joint tenancy – When two or more people hold property as joint tenants, they own it between them, and if one dies the other(s) take his or her share: for example, A, B and C own a house; if C dies his share passes to A and B, who now have half each, instead of one-third each. The alternative to having a joint tenancy is to have a *tenancy in common*.

joint tortfeasors – Two or more people who are responsible for a *tort*. For example, A negligently drives his car into B. But A was acting in the course of employment for C, her employer, who therefore has a *vicarious liability* for A's negligence. Thus, as far as B is concerned, A and C are joint tortfeasors. They are *jointly and severally* liable.

judgment – A court's decision. A judgment usually imposes some action on a losing party such as paying compensation. The judgment may be interim (i.e. during the pre-trial phase) or final. The word also describes the document in which the judge explains the decision.

judgment creditor – A person who has obtained a judgment ordering the opposing party to pay them money.

judgment debtor – A debtor who has had a court judgment for the debt made against him or her, but who has not yet paid off the debt.

judgment in default – A claimant can enter judgment in default against a defendant who fails to carry out a procedural step in time: for example, fails to file a defence to the claim.

judicial review – A High Court procedure for challenging decisions of public or administrative bodies, tribunals and inferior courts, usually on the basis of abuse of power or failure to act in accordance with the rules. The remedies available include *certiorari, mandamus, prohibition, declaration* and *injunction*.

judicial separation – Similar to divorce in that it makes both husband and wife single persons again for all legal purposes. However, unlike a divorce, it does not allow either party to remarry.

junior counsel – A barrister who has not been appointed Queen's Counsel. Many barristers remain juniors throughout their careers and the description does not necessarily mean that the barrister is young or inexperienced.

jurat – The sentence at the end of an affidavit or statutory declaration which shows when, where and before whom it was made.

juries – Twelve men and women summoned to decide questions of fact in criminal and certain civil cases. In criminal cases, trial by jury is restricted to the crown court. Civil cases are decided by a judge unless the court orders a jury trial, typically in libel actions.

jurisdiction – The limitations of a court's power. These may be territorial or financial and the court may have no power to make certain types of order. Our courts have jurisdiction over England, Wales, Berwick on Tweed, territorial waters and British boats and ships on the *high seas*.

kin – Blood relatives.

knock for knock – Agreement between insurance companies to pay claims made by their own insured and so avoid the expense of claiming from each other (*see* Chapter 69).

laches – Unreasonable delay in pursuing a legal right. See *limitation*.

land – 'Land in the legal signification comprehendeth any ground, soil or earth whatsoever, as meadows, pastures, woods, moors, waters, marshes, furzes and heath . . . It legally includeth also all castles, houses and other buildings' (Coke).

Land Charges Register – A register of all adverse rights and interests affecting *unregistered land* (e.g. *mortgages, restrictive covenants, easements, Class F*, etc.). Unless the right or interest is registered it will not bind an innocent purchaser of the property.

laying an information – Starting magistrates' court criminal proceedings (see *information*).

leader or leading counsel – A barrister who has been appointed Queen's Counsel (see also *junior counsel*).

leading question – One which suggests the answer or which allows only a 'yes' or 'no' answer, for example 'Were you scared?' Allowed only in cross-examination.

leasehold – An estate in land that is less than a *freehold*. Generally used to describe an interest for a fixed term (e.g. for 99 years).

leave of the court – See *permission of the court.*

legacy – A gift of *personal property* by will (cf. *devise*).

legal professional privilege – A right to keep certain documents confidential so they do not have to be produced to the other side on disclosure. They include communications between a client and his solicitor, and the solicitor's or barrister's working papers (see *privilege*).

legal separation – The same as *judicial separation.*

legitimation – Legitimization of a child born out of wedlock by the subsequent marriage of the parents.

lessee – Person who takes a lease (i.e. the tenant).

lessor – Person who grants a lease (i.e. the landlord).

letter before action – The letter which it is usual to write to the opposing party or his solicitors giving him a last chance to settle a dispute before court action is taken.

liability – The issue of whether a case has been made against a party, in other words whether they are responsible. It could be described as whether someone has to pay, rather than how much someone has to pay, which is a question of *quantum*.

lien – A creditor has a lien over property of the debtor until the debt is paid off: for example, if a solicitor holds title deeds to a house for a client who has not paid the solicitor's bill, the solicitor need not release the title deeds until the bill has been paid.

limitation – Court proceedings must be begun within

the limitation period. There are different periods for different types of claims (*see* page 737).

liquidated sum – A specific sum, or a sum that can be worked out as a matter of arithmetic; cf. *unliquidated damages*, when the amount is not easily ascertainable.

liquidation – The procedure under which a company is dissolved. It may be voluntary, that is decided upon by the shareholders, or compulsory, that is ordered by a court. If a company dissolved by its shareholders is solvent the liquidation is called 'members voluntary'. If it is insolvent the process is called 'creditors voluntary'.

liquidator – Person who winds up a company.

lis alibi pendens – Proceedings in a court which are similar, related to or the same as an action in a second court, and which may be reason to prevent the second set of proceedings from going ahead, so avoiding duplication.

listing questionnaire – A document which has to be completed by the parties shortly before trial so that the court can be satisfied that the case is ready for trial and so that the court can set a timetable for trial.

litigant in person – A party to legal proceedings who does not employ a solicitor or barrister, but acts on his own behalf and presents his own case to the court.

litigation friend – A person appointed to act on behalf of a minor or a mentally disabled person in bringing or defending legal proceedings. Formerly *guardian ad litem* or *next friend*.

litigation privilege – One of the grounds on which documents do not have to be produced to the opposing party on disclosure. To qualify, the document must have been created for the sole or main purpose of litigation.

London Gazette – Government journal for publication of official notices (e.g. proclamations; winding up; receivership orders).

long vacation – Generally, the whole of August. The Supreme Court transacts only urgent business during this time.

Lord Chancellor – Senior government minister. Responsible for the administration of justice. Sits also as a judge in the House of Lords.

McKenzie friend – A person who helps a *litigant in person*, often not legally trained. They will attend court and be the advocate for the litigant in person.

McNaghten Rules – Three rules for use when deciding whether an accused person can plead insanity as a defence.

maintenance pending suit – In divorce, nullity or separation proceedings the court can order maintenance to be paid before the full hearing of the petition.

mandamus – A command from the Divisional Court of the High Court that a lower court does something, for example hears a claim which it denied having jurisdiction to hear.

Mareva injunction – See *freezing order*.

Mary Bell order – An exception to the normal court presumption of freedom to publish details relating to a ward of court if the details are unconnected with court proceedings. Where the court is convinced direct and exceptional damage to a ward will be caused by publicity, it can order restrictions on any reporting affecting the child.

master – An official of the High Court, junior in status to a judge, who deals with procedural matters and disputes before a trial.

Master of the Rolls – Most senior judge in the Court of Appeal.

mens rea – The 'criminal intention' to commit a crime. The *mens rea* and the *actus reus* together make the crime.

mesne profits – Damages payable by trespassers who have stayed in possession after their right to occupy the land has ended, for example a tenant who stays on after the end of his tenancy. Generally, the mesne profits will equal the rent for the premises.

messuage – A dwelling-house with its *curtilage*.

minor interest – An interest in *registered land* (e.g. *mortgage*) which binds purchasers only if it is registered on the title register.

misdemeanour – Criminal offences used to be either misdemeanours or (more serious) felonies. The classification was abolished in 1967.

misfeasance – The improper or negligent carrying out of a legal act (e.g. a company director who misapplies the company's money).

moiety – One half.

mortgage – A loan of money on the security of a property. The lender is the mortgagee and the borrower is the mortgagor.

multi-track – The procedural path which a case will follow when it is not appropriate for it to be on the small claims or fast track. Most High Court cases are multi-track.

naturalization – Whereby an alien becomes a citizen and subject of his or her adopted country.

negotiable instrument – A transferable security (e.g. cheque, promissory note, bill of exchange).

nemo dat quod non habet – No one can give what does not belong to him. So a thief cannot pass ownership of property to a person who buys it from him: it still belongs to the person from whom it was stolen.

next friend – See *litigation friend*.

nolle prosequi – The claimant discontinues his action. More usually in a criminal case when the *Attorney-General* stays a prosecution; he has power to do this in any indictable prosecution.

non-cohabitation order – Magistrates' court order releasing a spouse from the obligation to live with the other spouse.

non-contentious business – Non-court legal work (e.g. conveyancing, probate). *See* page 755.

Norwich Pharmacal. – A procedure to obtain documents from a person who is not a party to an action but is alleged to have been involved in wrongdoing.

notice – A formal warning of an intended step in an action. Notice is said to be given or served. Either way, the formal rules of service apply.

notice of appearance – The employer's formal response when an employee or ex-employee goes to an employment tribunal. The employer uses the form IT3.

notice to admit – An invitation by one party to the other to agree certain facts or documents and so remove the obligation to prove them at trial. A notice is usually served in relation to matters which are not contentious but which would otherwise have to be proved by evidence. If the opposing party does not admit facts or documents that are subsequently proved at trial they will be ordered to pay the costs incurred.

nuncupative will – An oral will. Valid only if made while on active service.

oath – A religious form of words either spoken by a witness in the witness box prior to giving evidence to announce the intention to speak the truth, or spoken by a deponent on an affidavit on swearing the truth of its contents and the contents of any exhibits to the affidavit. See *affirmation*.

obiter dicta – Those parts of a judgment which are not crucial to the court's decision but which are useful indications of the court's views on aspects of the law. cf. *ratio decidendi*, which is the critical part of the case.

official referee – Layperson appointed by the High Court to try complex matters in which he or she is a specialist (e.g. accountancy disputes).

official solicitor – Acts in High Court cases as a *litigation friend* for those who have no one to assist them – mainly represents minors, mentally disabled persons and individuals in contempt cases.

Old Bailey – The Central Criminal Court. One of the crown courts.

open court – A court hearing to which the public has access – in contrast to a hearing *in camera*.

opinion – The written views of counsel.

option – A right to buy something.

oral examination – Procedure by which a judgment debtor can be brought before the court by a judgment creditor to be asked about their assets to enable the judgment creditor to decide how best to enforce their judgment.

order – An interim or final decision of the court normally set out in a formal court document.

originating summons – See *Part 8 claim*.

overriding objective – The obligation of parties, lawyers and judges to apply the CPR to deal with cases justly; that includes ensuring the parties are on an equal footing, saving expense, dealing with the case proportionately, expeditiously and fairly.

parol – An informally made contract. Previously used to describe any contract not under *seal* but now generally taken to mean an oral contract.

Part 8 claim – Legal proceedings brought to decide legal issues or the interpretation of documents. A special claim form has to be used. Formerly known as 'originating summons' procedure.

Part 36 offer – An offer to settle the case made under the provisions of part 36 of the CPR which may be made either by the claimant or defendant. If an offer is not accepted and the party to whom the offer was made does less well at trial than the terms of the offer there may be severe costs and interest sanctions.

particulars – See *further information*.

particulars of claim – Details of a claimant's case which must be set out either in the claim form or served 14 days after. (Formerly *statement of claim*.)

passing off – A *tort* whereby A passes off his goods or business as being that of B (e.g. by using a similar name or label). B can apply for an *injunction* and *damages*.

payment into court – Literally a payment into the court's bank account. It is usually made to comply with a court order, for example as a condition of being allowed to defend an action, or as an offer of settlement, in which case the money can be withdrawn by the party accepting the offer. As an offer of settlement, it can protect a defendant from having to pay costs if the damages awarded at trial are less than the sum paid into court. See also *Part 36 offer.*

peppercorn rent – A nominal rent which it is not intended that the landlord will collect (e.g. a red rose on Midsummer Day). But it preserves the landlord's legal title.

per incuriam – A mistaken decision by a court; other courts need not follow it.

periodic tenancy – A tenancy which is not for a fixed term. The tenant pays rent periodically (e.g. weekly, monthly) and the tenancy continues until notice is given by either party. *See* Chapter 20.

perjury – An assertion made on oath, which the maker knows is not true or which he is not qualified to make.

permission of the court – The court's agreement to a party taking a particular step. For example, typically the court's permission is necessary for a party to appeal a judgment. Formerly known as *leave.*

personal property – All property except *land*. Also called personalty.

petition – An application for certain types of order, especially in relation to insolvency and divorce. For example, an application to wind up a company is made by petition.

plaintiff – Former term for a person who sues (i.e. brings a civil action). Now called a *claimant.*

plc – A public limited company. Most used to have 'Ltd' after their names, but changed this to 'plc' when UK company law was brought into line with EC law in 1981.

pleadings – Formal written documents in a civil action. The plaintiff submits a statement of claim, the defendant a defence. The new term under the CPR is *statement of case.*

polygamy – Legally having more than one spouse.

portion – Parental gift to establish a child in life.

possessory title – Title acquired by a squatter, through adverse possession.

practice direction – A written instruction issued by a court or by the Lord Chancellor setting out new procedures, clarifying existing procedures or indicating the court's policy on a particular matter. Most of the Civil Procedure Rules are accompanied by practice directions which give more detailed instructions than the Rules themselves.

pre-action protocol – Rules, usually introduced by a practice direction, which govern how parties must behave before issuing proceedings. For example, a protocol might require a possible defendant to give specified types of information to a possible claimant.

pre-emption – A right of first refusal if a property is sold.

preliminary issue – An issue, usually of law, which is decided by a court before the trial itself. In order for the court to agree to hear such an issue it has to be shown that the court's decision will have a great effect on the case and is likely to save costs. A frequent example is where the defendant claims that the action has been brought too late and the limitation period has expired.

premium – In a tenancy, the premium is the price paid other than in rent; for example, a flat is sold on a 99-year lease at an annual rent of £50, for £15,000 – the £15,000 is the premium.

prescription – Method of acquiring rights over another's land by usage over a period of time.

presumption of death – 'If a person has not been heard of for seven years, there is a presumption of law that he is dead' (Lal Chand (1925)).

pre-trial checklist – A form which has to be completed in many High Court actions setting out how a party intends to conduct the action.

pre-trial review – Preliminary meeting of parties in county court actions to consider administrative matters and what agreement can be reached prior to the trial.

privacy – There is no *tort* of interfering with another's privacy, although the European Convention on Human Rights states that 'everyone has the right to respect for his private and family life, his home and his correspondence'.

privilege – Documents or other communications which do not have to be produced to the opposing side on *disclosure*. The main grounds of privilege are *legal professional privilege* and *litigation privilege*.

profit a prendre – The right to take something off someone else's *land* (e.g. collect firewood).

prohibition – An order of a Divisional Court of the High Court preventing an inferior court from doing something (e.g. hearing a case that is outside its jurisdiction).

proof of evidence – A statement given by a witness to a solicitor which will form the basis of the witness's evidence at trial. A proof is confidential, unlike a *witness statement*, and is not shown to the other side.

provisional damages – A preliminary award of compensation to a claimant in a personal injuries claim where it is likely that the claimant will, at some time in the future, suffer serious disease or physical or mental deterioration, the effects of which cannot be predicted at the time of the trial.

public interest immunity certificate – A certificate signed by an appropriate minister, which asserts that the material which it identifies is subject to public interest immunity, and not to be disclosed. The judge at trial must balance the interest in maintaining secrecy against the interest in the disclosure of relevant evidence.

public policy – Acts which are against public policy are illegal (e.g. gambling debts cannot be sued for; nor can a prostitute sue for her payment).

purchaser – Generally taken to mean one who buys property, but, strictly speaking, it covers any person who acquires the *fee simple* in land other than by descent (for instance, a person who receives the land as an *inter vivos* gift).

putative father – The man who is alleged to be the father of an illegitimate child.

quantum – The amount of compensation which a losing party has to pay to the winning party. Quantum should be contrasted with *liability* which is the issue of whether someone has to pay compensation at all.

quantum meruit – As much as he or she has earned.

Queen's Bench Division (QBD) – Part of the High Court which deals with most types of general actions.

Queen's Counsel (QC) – An appointment by the Crown denoting a senior barrister. QCs are also called *leading counsel* or silks, because they wear silk gowns in court. They are called King's Counsel when the sovereign is a king. A QC normally works with a *junior counsel* and does not normally draft *statements of case*.

Queen's Proctor – A solicitor representing the Crown who can intervene in divorce cases (for instance, if the divorce was obtained on the basis of false evidence) before the decree is made absolute.

rack rent – 'A rent that represents the full annual value of the holding' (Newman (1975)).

ratio decidendi – The reason for a judicial decision. Only these principal reasons are binding on lower courts. Other comments in a judgment which are not directly relevant to the decision are called *obiter dicta*, and only have persuasive authority.

real property – Freehold estates in *land*; it is often used to describe any interest in land.

reciprocal enforcement – A method, endorsed by statute, by which a judgment of a court in one *jurisdiction* is

recognized by a court in another jurisdiction and *enforced* as if it were a judgment of that jurisdiction.

recognizance – Sum of money that will be forfeited by an accused person who fails to answer to his or her bail.

re-examination – The further questioning of a party's own witness to restore credibility or explain answers given in *cross-examination*.

refresher – A barrister's daily fee for attendance at trial if the trial lasts longer than one day. The first day, plus preparation for trial, is covered by a *brief fee*.

registered land – Land that is registered under the Land Registration Act 1925. *See* page 178.

registrar – An official of the county court who acts as a judge.

relator – A private individual on whose suggestion the *Attorney-General* brings an action for the public good – a relator action.

remainder – When a person has an interest in land that will come into their possession when someone else's interest ends, they have an interest in remainder, for example, A gives land to B for life, the remainder to C. (See *reversion*.)

rentcharge – A rental payment on freehold land. Largely abolished in 1977 except when used to enforce covenants between freeholders.

replevin – Recovering goods seized by the sheriff or bailiff, after paying off the *judgment debtor*.

reply – A *statement of case*. The *claimant's* response to the *defence*.

representative action – Legal proceedings brought by a few individuals on behalf of a larger number, where all have a broadly similar complaint.

request for further and better particulars – See *further information*.

requisition – An inquiry by a purchaser of *land* concerning the vendor's title to that land.

res ipsa loquitur – The matter speaks for itself. Normally a plaintiff must prove his or her case, but in accident claims in which the circumstances raise a prima facie indication of negligence, the defendant has to prove he or she was not negligent. The circumstances indicate negligence – it speaks for itself.

respondent – The party defending an appeal against a judgment of a lower court. See *appellant*. A respondent is also the defendant in matrimonial and judicial review proceedings, the employer against whom a case is brought in an employment tribunal, and the defendant to an insolvency petition.

restitutio in integrum – Restoring the status quo.

restrictive covenant – A covenant that allows one land-owner to control the use of another's land. *See* page 172.

retrospective legislation – An Act that applies to a period before the Act was passed.

reversion – If an owner of land disposes of it for a period, after which it will revert back to him or her, he or she is said to hold the reversion. For example, a landlord grants a lease for 20 years; he will acquire the freehold in 20 years' time. See also *remainder*.

right of re-entry – Right of landlord to take possession if tenant breaks the terms of the tenancy.

riparian – Connected with the bank of a river or stream.

root of title – Title deed which forms the basis of the vendor's title to the *land*. Must be at least 15 years old.

Rules of the Supreme Court – See *Civil Procedure Rules*.

salvage – The right of a person who saves a ship or its cargo from shipwreck to receive compensation. Usually assessed by the court.

seal – Used to be the impression of a piece of wax on to a document. Now a small red sticky label is used instead, although the absence of the seal will not invalidate the document, since 'to constitute a sealing neither wax nor wafer nor a piece of paper, not even an impression is necessary' (Sandilands (1871)).

search order – A very powerful court order allowing a party to search an opponent's premises and seize evidence which it fears may be destroyed. It is sometimes called a civil search warrant. It used to be known as an *Anton Piller order*, after the case in which the order was first made.

section 6(2) committal – Short form of committal by magistrates.

security for costs – Money which a claimant has to pay into court as a condition of bringing or continuing an action. The defendant must show that the claimant may not be able to meet any costs order or that the defendant will not be able to enforce any costs order because the claimant is not in England, Wales or another EU country.

service – Formal delivery of a *statement of case, claim form*, notice or other document. For the purposes of litigation, service may be personal, by literally handing the document to the relevant person. More often, one uses an address for service. Service outside the *jurisdiction* requires *permission of the court*.

servient tenement – See *dominant tenement*.

set aside – The cancellation of a judgment or order.

set off – A defence which comprises a claim by a defendant that the claimant owes him money.

settlement – Tying *land* up for the future by leaving it to trustees to hold for successive limited owners.

sheriff – Landowner appointed in each county with responsibility for parliamentary elections and the enforcement of court orders.

sine die – Indefinitely.

skeleton argument – A summary of its arguments which each party has to lodge with the court before a hearing.

slip rule – A means of correcting clerical errors or omissions in judgments or orders. It involves an application to court.

small claims track – An informal arbitration procedure in the county court for the resolution of minor disputes, often brought by consumers complaining about goods or services.

solicitor-advocate – A solicitor authorized to conduct cases in court. The authorization may extend to all courts or may be limited to some only, for example to civil courts. Until recently only barristers could conduct cases in open court.

Solicitor General – A qualified lawyer and serving Member of Parliament appointed by the government as deputy to the *Attorney-General*.

solus agreement – When a retailer agrees to buy all their goods from one supplier. Common in the petrol-supply business.

special damage – Financial loss that can be proved (e.g. wage loss).

specialty contract – A contract under seal.

specific performance – When a party to a contract is ordered to carry out their part of the bargain (e.g. to sell a house). Ordered only if damages (money) would be an inadequate remedy.

split trial – A trial where the issue of *liability*, or fault, is heard first. If the claimant is successful, the trial will then consider the amount of compensation known as the *quantum* of damages.

stakeholder – One who holds money as an impartial observer. He or she will part with it only if both parties agree or if ordered by the court.

stare decisis – To stand by decided matters. Alternative name for the doctrine of precedent.

statement in open court – A statement agreed by both parties to a libel action as a settlement which is read in open court and reported by the press.

statement of case – Collectively, the formal documents in which parties set out details of their case. A *defence* is an example of a statement of case. Statements of case have to contain a *statement of truth*.

statement of claim – See *particulars of claim*.

statement of truth – The statement 'I believe that the facts stated in [this document] are true.' It must be contained in all witness statements and statements of case. Proceedings for contempt of court may be brought against a person if he makes or causes to be made a statement in a document verified by a statement of truth without an honest belief in its truth.

statement of value – A description, which must be included in a *claim form*, of how much money a *claimant* is seeking to recover.

statute – An Act of Parliament.

statute-barred – When there has been so much delay before commencing proceedings that the *limitation* period has expired.

statutory instrument – Subordinate legislation made by the Queen in Council or a minister, in exercise of a power granted by *statute*.

stay of execution – An order suspending enforcement of a judgment or order.

stay of proceedings – When a court action is stopped by the court.

striking out – An order that an action, specific allegations or defences be abandoned. Among the grounds for such an order are excessive delay by the person concerned, and that an action has no chance of success.

structured settlement – A method of settling actions involving severe personal injuries where damages are paid by instalments, often throughout the injured person's life.

subpoena – See *witness summons*.

subrogated claim – Where a right to sue is passed to a third party, the third party's claim is known as a subrogated claim. For example, if an insurer pays a claim they may recover the money by action in the name of the policyholder.

substituted service – When a document cannot be served on the defendant or their solicitor, the court may allow substituted service by, for example, its being sent to the last known address, or advertised in newspapers.

sue – To bring legal proceedings.

summary assessment of costs – A procedure enabling a successful party to interim procedures to be awarded a lump sum for costs to be paid immediately, without the need for a long and expensive assessment.

summary judgment – Procedure whereby a party to an action can show that the other party has no reasonable prospect of successfully defending or succeeding on the claim. Usually adopted near the start of a case, it provides the parties with the means of obtaining a judgment quickly at a single hearing where the parties will rely on witness statements.

summons – See *application notice*.

surety – A *guarantor*.

taxation of costs – Examination and approval by the court of legal fees. See *assessment*.

Technology and Construction Court – A part of the High Court which deals with disputes involving technical matters such as construction and computer contract disputes. Formerly known as Official Referees' Court.

tenancy in common – When two or more people hold land as tenants in common, they each have equal shares in it. If one dies his share does not pass to the other (cf. *joint tenancy*). For example, A, B and C own a house. If C dies, his share will pass under his will to his family, etc. A and B will still own one-third each of the house; the other third will be owned by the person who inherited C's share. Joint owners are presumed to be joint tenants, not tenants in common.

term of years – A lease for a fixed period of duration.

testate – Dying having left a will.

testator – The person who makes a will.

third party – Literally, not the claimant or the defendant, but a third party to an action.

third-party proceedings – When a party to an action sues someone else. For example, A sues B for damages after B drove his car into A. But B's negligent driving was partly caused by C, a pedestrian, who was jay-walking. B starts third-party proceedings against C, and if the court orders B to pay damages to A, it can also order C to pay damages to B.

Tomlin order – An order disposing of an action on agreed terms which are set out in a schedule to the order. The schedule is usually confidential and the order, while bringing the action to an end, gives either party the right to go back to court if the agreed terms are not complied with.

tort – A civil wrong (other than breach of contract) giving rise to the right to bring an action in the civil courts (e.g. nuisance, negligence, trespass, defamation).

track – The procedural pathway which the court decides it is appropriate for a case to follow. May be small claims, fast or multi.

transcript – A verbatim report of a court's proceedings. This must be prepared by an approved person (usually, in London, a member of the Association of Official Shorthand Writers Ltd). In some cases, the transcript is now prepared on computer and is available virtually instantaneously.

Treasury counsel – Barristers who receive briefs from the *Director of Public Prosecutions* for *Old Bailey* prosecutions. They are nominated by the *Lord Chancellor.*

trial – A hearing before a court, normally involving witnesses giving evidence, at which all issues of fact and law are tried and the court gives its decision. It is usually held in open court. See *in camera, split trial.*

trial bundle – An agreed selection of documents obtained on disclosure. The files are paginated for use by all the parties and the judge at trial.

ultra vires – Outside the powers (e.g. of a company).

undertaking – A promise by a party or their solicitor or barrister made in the course of legal proceedings. A breach of undertaking is treated in the same way as a breach of an injunction, i.e. the person may be in contempt.

unenforceable – A contract or other right that cannot be enforced because of a technical defect (e.g. *statute-barred*).

unlawful – An act is unlawful when it involves a breach of the law and so allows civil proceedings to be brought. It does not involve a breach of the criminal law (cf. *illegal*).

unless order – A court order where the court imposes a severe penalty for failure to comply with its terms. For example, unless a defendant complies with its disclosure obligations the defence will be struck out and judgment given in favour of the claimants.

unliquidated damages – Damages which cannot be arithmetically calculated in advance and are dependent upon the opinion (and generosity) of the court (e.g. for the loss of a limb). (See *liquidated sum*.)

unregistered land – *Land* that is not *registered land.*

unsound mind – As defined in the Mental Health Act 1983. *See* Chapter 90.

vexatious litigant – A person who cannot bring any action without the permission of the court, because he or she has previously brought vexatious or frivolous proceedings.

vicarious liability – When one person is responsible for the actions of another because of their relationship: for example, an employer is liable for the actions of his or her employee. The claimant can sue either or both of them.

void – Of no legal effect. If a marriage is void it is as though it had never taken place (cf. *voidable*).

voidable – Capable of being set aside. A voidable marriage will end when it is annulled (i.e. avoided) but it will be recognized as having existed until that time (cf. *void*).

volenti non fit injuria – A person cannot sue over an injury to which he or she has consented. 'Knowledge of the risk of injury is not enough. Nor is a willingness to take the risk of injury. Nothing will suffice short of an agreement to waive any claim for negligence' (Nettleship (1971)).

volunteer – A person who is given, or who inherits, property without giving any *consideration.*

wager – A bet. A betting or gambling debt is *unenforceable* as being contrary to *public policy.*

want of prosecution – Serious delay on the part of a claimant in pursuing a claim. The defendant may use this as a reason for an order striking out the action.

warned list – A list of the cases about to come to trial.

waste – Causing lasting damage to land (e.g. by a tenant).

winding up – The dissolution of a company by a court.

with costs – If judgment is entered 'with costs', it means that the winner's *costs* will be paid by the loser. *See* Chapter 99.

without notice – An application made to the court without informing and in the absence of the opposing party. Such applications should only be made in cases of great urgency. Formerly known as *ex parte* applications.

without prejudice – Communications between parties to negotiate a settlement which cannot be referred to if the matter is not settled and goes to trial.

witness – A person giving evidence either in a statement or orally.

witness statement – A signed statement setting out the evidence a witness will give at trial. Witness statements are exchanged prior to trial. A witness statement is nearly always used instead of an examination in chief, with the witness appearing only for cross-examination and re-examination. A witness statement has to contain a *statement of truth.*

witness summons – An order requiring a witness to attend court to give evidence or to produce documents. The reasonable expenses of the witness have to be paid by the person issuing the summons. A summonsed witness who fails to appear may be fined or imprisoned for contempt of court.

writ – See *claim form*.

writ *ne exeat regno* – A High Court order restraining a person from leaving England and Wales without the consent of the Crown or permission of the court.

Appendix

1. Example of particulars of claim in the county court

IN THE CASTLE ACRE COUNTY COURT   Case No. 9203422

BETWEEN

EDWARD PRICE-JONES   Claimant

AND

SUSAN TRACEY FYFIELD   Defendant

PARTICULARS OF CLAIM

1. On 10th February 2000 the Claimant was driving his car along the Littlepoe road in Mudford, heading out of the town, when he was in collision with a car driven by the Defendant.

2. The said collision was caused by the negligence of the Defendant.

PARTICULARS OF NEGLIGENCE

1. Overtaking two cars when it was not safe to do so into the path of the Claimant's car and colliding with the Claimant;

2. Driving too fast;

3. Failing to give any proper warning of her approach

4. Failing to keep any or any proper look out or to observe or heed the presence or approach of the Claimant;

5. Failing to apply her brakes in time or at all or so to steer slow down control or otherwise manage her vehicle as to avoid the said collision;

6. Failing to observe or obey traffic signs;

7. Failing to take sufficient or any account of the road conditions.

3. The Claimant will in addition to the matters pleaded in paragraphs 1 to 2 inclusive rely upon the fact that on 15th April 2000 the Defendant was convicted by the

Example of particulars of claim in the county court (continued)

Mudford Magistrates' Court of the offence of having driven without due care and attention on 10th February 2000. She was fined £500 and had 5 penalty points imposed. The facts upon which the conviction was based were the facts as alleged in paragraphs 1 to 2 herein which caused the injuries loss and damages to the Claimant. The said conviction is relevant to the issue of negligence.

4. By reason of the matters aforesaid the Claimant has suffered loss and damage.

PARTICULARS OF SPECIAL DAMAGE

1976 Mini Clubman Saloon, damages beyond repair. Value -   £850.00

Accessories and contents of Mini Clubman:

i.	Toolbox and tools	£68.00
ii.	5 cassettes smashed in crash @ £6.99 each	£34.95
iii.	Petrol can with gallon of petrol	£10.70
iv.	2 large sponge dice lost in wreckage	£5.25

Fares and travel expenses   £11.25

Loss of earnings   £53.92

Total   £1034.05

AND THE CLAIMANT CLAIMS:
1) Under paragraph 4 above £1034.05
2) Interest pursuant to Section 69 of the County Courts Act 1984.
3) Costs

STATEMENT OF TRUTH

The Claimant believes that the facts stated in these particulars of claim are true.

DATED this   day of   2000.

Signed.....................

Edward Price-Jones, Claimant whose address for service is 17 Council Houses, Canal Lane, West Acre Norfolk

To the Court Manager and to the Defendant

Example of particulars of claim in the county court (continued)

IN THE CASTLE ACRE COUNTY COURT　　Case No. 9203422

BETWEEN

EDWARD PRICE-JONES　　Claimant

AND

SUSAN TRACEY FYFIELD　　Defendant

DEFENCE

1. The Defendant admits that on 10th February 2000 a collision occurred along the Littlepoe Road out of Mudford, between the Claimant's Mini Clubman saloon and the Defendant's Ford Cortina.

2. The Defendant denies that this collision was caused by her negligence as alleged in paragraph 2 of the Particulars of Claim or at all.

3. The Defendant admits that on 15th April 2000 she was convicted of the offence of driving without due care and attention. She denies that this has any relevance to the Claimant's claim.

4. The collision was caused solely by the negligence of the Claimant.

PARTICULARS OF NEGLIGENCE

The Claimant was negligent in that he:

a) Drove too fast;

b) Failed to keep a proper look out;

c) Drove on the wrong side of the road;

d) Drove on to and across the white line on the road;

e) Ran in to the front of the Defendant's Ford Cortina;

Example of particulars of claim in the county court (continued)

f) Failed to maintain the engine of his car in such condition so that it did not emit clouds of smoke, thereby making it impossible for the defendant to see the approach of the claimant in his vehicle;

g) Failed to slow down, stop, swerve, or take such other action as was necessary to avoid the collision.

5. If, which is denied, there was any negligence on the part of the Defendant, the said collision was nevertheless caused or substantially contributed to by the Claimant. The defendant repeats the allegations set out in paragraph 4 above.

6. The defendant does not admit that the Claimant suffered loss and damage as alleged in the Particulars of Claim. She puts the Claimant to full proof of the alleged losses.

7. Save as aforesaid the Defendant denies each and every allegation in the Statement of case as if the same were here set forth and traversed seriatim.

Dated the   day of   2000.

STATEMENT OF TRUTH

The Defendant believes that the facts stated in the defence are true.

Signed..................

Served the   day of   2000
by Toft & Tweed, solicitors, of Manour House, Church Road, Little Snoring, Norfolk, BW44 1PG solicitors for the Defendant.

To:

The Court Manager and the Claimant

2. Divorce petition

Before completing this form, read carefully the enclosed NOTES FOR GUIDANCE

In the KING'S LYNN County Court*

No.

~~In the Principal Registry*~~

*Delete as
appropriate

(1) On the 10th day of February 2000
Elizabeth Constantine Dereham was lawfully married to
Eustace Ross Charles Dereham (hereinafter called "the the petitioner
respondent") at The Register Office in the District of Ganymede in the County of
Rutland.

(2) The petitioner and respondent last lived together as husband and wife at "The Haven", 34
Manea Road, Ganymede, Rutland.

(3) The petitioner is domiciled in England and Wales, and is by occupation a
Fashion Designer and resides at "The Haven", 34 Manea Road, Ganymede,
Rutland and the respondent
is by occupation a Financial Consultant
and resides at "The Haven", 34 Manea Road, Ganymede,
Rutland.

(4) There are no children of the family now living *except*

Lucinda Rian Dereham (D.O.B. 17/06/90)

(5) No other child, now living, has been born to the petitioner/respondent during the marriage
(so far as is known to the petitioner) *except*

Divorce petition (continued)

(6) There are or have been no other proceedings in any court in England and Wales or elsewhere with
reference to the marriage (or to any child of the family) or between the petitioner and respondent with
reference to any property of either or both of them *except*

(7) There are no proceedings continuing in any country outside England or Wales which are in respect of
the marriage or are capable of affecting its validity or subsistence *except*

(8) (This paragraph should be completed only if the petition is based on five years' separation.) No
agreement or arrangement has been made or is proposed to be made between the parties for the support
of the petitioner/respondent (and any child of the family) *except*

(9) The said marriage has broken down irretrievably.

(10) The Respondent has behaved in such a way that the Petitioner cannot reasonably
be expected to live with the Respondent.

Divorce petition (continued)

(11) Particulars

1. From the commencement of the marriage the Respondent has failed to accept the responsibilities of married life and has continued to enjoy the existence of a bachelor leaving the Petitioner to care for their young child and to run the home.

2. The Respondent goes out every evening and weekend, and frequently stays away from the former matrimonial home over night, without advising the Petitioner of his intentions. The Petitioner remains at home worried as to the Respondent's whereabouts and not knowing whether or not he is to return.

3. The Respondent has just completed a 2 week holiday from work, in which time he spent no time whatsoever at the matrimonial home nor with the Petitioner and the child.

4. The Respondent leaves the running of the home entirely up to the Petitioner including the payment of all bills and offers the Petitioner no moral support whatsoever. There is a total lack of communication between the Petitioner and the Respondent, and the Respondent shows the Petitioner no love nor affection.

5. The Respondent is constantly criticising the Petitioner causing the Petitioner to feel "useless" depressed and lonely.

6. The Petitioner has attempted on numerous occasions to talk to the Respondent about her feelings of loneliness and rejection and to persuade the Respondent to change his ways, but the Respondent has refused to take note and considers that he is behaving within the marriage reasonably and properly. Following the Respondent's absence from the matrimonial home during his 2 week holiday the Petitioner has finally concluded that the marriage has irretrievably broken down.

Divorce petition (continued)

Prayer

The petitioner therefore prays

(1) **The suit**

That the said marriage be dissolved

(2) **Costs**

That the   may be ordered to pay costs of this suit

(3) **Ancillary relief**

That the petitioner may be granted the following ancillary relief:

(a) an order for maintenance pending suit

   a periodical payments order

   a secured provision order

   a lump sum order

   a property adjustment order

(b) **For the children**

   a periodical payments order

   a secured provision order

   a lump sum order

(4) **Children**

The names and addresses of the persons to be served with this petition are:-

Respondent:— c/o Fipps, Chish & Kelchupp, 40 Market Square, Ganymede, Rutland

Co-Respondent (adultery case only):—

The Petitioner's address for service is:— c/o Peek & Nashe, 29 Market Square, Ganymede, Rutland

Dated this   day of   20

Address all communications for the court to: The Chief Clerk, County Court.

The Court office at

is open from 10 a.m. to 4 p.m. (4.30 p.m. at the Principal Registry) on Mondays to Fridays only.

Signed

3. Draft transfer of registered land

HM Land Registry
Specimen Form

TR1

Transfer of whole of registered title(s)

(If you need more room than is provided for in a panel, use continuation sheet CS and staple to this form)

1. Stamp Duty

Place "X" in the box that applies and complete the box in the appropriate certificate.

□ in the Schedule to the Stamp Duty (Exempt Instruments) Regulations 1987.

□ I/We hereby certify that this instrument falls within category

□ It is certified that the transaction effected does not form part of a larger transaction or of a series of transactions in respect of which the amount or value or the aggregate of the consideration exceeds the sum of

2. Title Number(s) of the Property *(leave blank if not registered)*   SH 123456

3. Property   Tyrley Grange, Turnberry, Shropshire, TU2 2UT

If this transfer is made under section 37 of the Land Registration Act 1925 following a not-yet-registered dealing with part only of the land in a title, or is made under rule 72 of the Land Registration Rules 1925, include a reference to the last preceding document of title containing a description of the property.

4. Date

5. Transferor *(give full names and Company's Registered Number if any)*

Robin Twemlow

6. Transferee for entry on the register *(Give full names and Company's Registered Number if any. For Scottish Co. Reg. Nos., use an SC prefix. For foreign companies give territory in which incorporated.*

Unless otherwise arranged with Land Registry headquarters, a certified copy of the transferee's constitution (in English or Welsh) will be required if it is a body corporate but is not a company registered in England and Wales or Scotland under the Companies Acts.

Roger Redmond and Belinda Blue

7. Transferee's intended address(es) for service in the U.K. *(including postcode)* for entry on the register

Tyrley Grange, Turnberry, Shropshire, TU2 2UT

8. The Transferor transfers the property to the Transferee.

9. Consideration *(Place "X" in the box that applies. State clearly the currency unit if other than sterling. If none of the boxes applies, insert an appropriate memorandum in the additional provisions panel.)*

□ The Transferor has received from the Transferee for the property the sum of *(in words and figures)*

□ One hundred and forty thousand pounds (£140,000)
(insert other receipt as appropriate)

□ The Transfer is not for money or anything which has a monetary value

P.T.O

Draft transfer of registered land (continued)

10. The Transferor transfers with *(place "X" in the box which applies and add any modifications)*

□ full title guarantee   □ limited title guarantee

11. Declaration of trust   *Where there is more than one transferee, place "X" in the appropriate box.*

□ The transferees are to hold the property on trust for themselves as joint tenants.

□ The transferees are to hold the property on trust for themselves as tenants in common in equal shares.

□ The transferees are to hold the property on trust *(complete as necessary)* on trust for themselves as to 40% for Belinda Blue and as to 60% for Roger Redmond

12. **Additional Provision(s)** *Insert here any required or permitted statement, certificate or application and any agreed covenants, declarations, etc.*

The Transferees jointly and severally covenant with the Transferor from now on (a) to perform the covenants referred to in entry No 1 on the Charges Register so far as they relate to the property and are capable of being enforced, and (b) to indemnify the Transferor against liability for any future breach of these covenants.

13. **The Transferors and all other necessary parties should execute this transfer as a deed using the space below.** *Forms of execution are given in Schedule 3 to the Land Registration Rules 1925. If the transfer contains transferees' covenants or declarations or contains an application for a restriction, it must also be executed by the Transferees.*

Signed as a deed by
Robin Twemlow in
the presence of

Signature of witness

Name

Address

Signed as a deed by
Roger Redmond in
the presence of   Sign here

Signature of witness

Name

Address

Signed as a deed by
Belinda Blue in
the presence of   Sign here

Signature of witness

Name

Address

SPECIMEN FORM

Index of Cases

Index of Legislative Material

General Index